FIXED INCOME SECURITIES

Valuation, Risk, and Risk Management

Pietro Veronesi
University of Chicago

WILEY

JOHN WILEY & SONS, INC.

VP & PUBLISHER: George Hoffman
ASSOCIATE PUBLISHER: Judith Joseph
ASSOCIATE EDITOR: Jennifer Manias
EDITORIAL ASSISTANT: Emily McGee
ASSOCIATE DIRECTOR OF MARKETING: Amy Scholz
ASSISTANT MARKETING MANAGER: Diane Mars
MARKETING ASSISTANT: Laura Finley
MEDIA EDITOR: Greg Chaput
PRODUCTION MANAGER: Micheline Frederick
SENIOR PRODUCTION EDITOR: Richard DeLorenzo
COVER DESIGNER: Madelyn Lesure
COVER PHOTO: © Ed Freeman/Riser/Getty Images

For general information on our other products and services please contact our Customer Care Department with the U.S. at 877-762-2974, outside the U.S. at 317-572-3993 or fax 317-572-4002.

Wiley also publishes its books in a variety of electronic formats. Some content that appears in print, however, may not be available in electronic format.

Library of Congress Cataloging-in-Publication Data:

Veronesi, Pietro.
    Fixed income securities :valuation, risk, and risk management / Pietro Veronesi.
        p. cm.
    Includes bibliographical references and index.
    ISBN 978-0-470-10910-6 (cloth)
  1. Fixed-income securities. 2. Risk management. I. Title.
    HG4650.V47 2010
    658.15′5–dc22

                                                            2009043712

10 9 8 7 6 5 4 3 2 1

To Tommaso
Gabriele,
Sofia,
and Micaela

CONTENTS

PART II   TERM STRUCTURE MODELS: TREES

PREFACE

It is now the middle of 2009 and finally this book is completed. It has been very exciting to write a text on the risk and return of fixed income securities, and their derivatives, in the middle of what many consider the biggest financial crisis since the Great Depression. In these three years of work the world of finance changed, as many key players in fixed income markets either collapsed (e.g., the investment banks Bears Stearns and Lehman Brothers), have been acquired by the U.S. government (e.g., the two mortgage giant agencies Freddie Mac and Fannie Mae), or have been acquired by other banks (e.g., the investment bank Merrill Lynch). In this turmoil, the U.S. government has taken the center stage: On the one hand, the Federal Reserve decreased its reference short-term interest rate, the Federal Funds target rate, to almost zero, and acted swiftly to set up lending facilities to provide liquidity to the financial system. On the other hand, the U.S. Treasury used Congress-approved funds to bail out a number of financial institutions, while the Federal Deposit Insurance Corporation (FDIC) extended guarantees on the short-term debt of banks in risk of default.

What will this financial turmoil do to fixed income markets around the world?

While it is still hard to forecast how long the recession will last, a certain fact for now is that fixed income markets will get bigger. And this for several reasons: First, governments' debt will expand in the future, as governments across the globe increase their spending to stimulate demand and jump start their economies.[1] To do so, governments will need to borrow even more than in the past, thereby increasing government debt and thus affecting

---

[1]There is much disagreement on whether such fiscal stimulus will in fact work. However, there is little doubt that it will increase government debt.

the size of available fixed income securities. For instance, the U.S. government debt in marketable securities stood at about $6 trillion at the end of 2008, around 40% of the U.S. Gross Domestic Product (GDP), and the congressional budget office (CBO) predicted an additional $1.8 trillion U.S. deficit for 2009. A March 2009 analysis of the CBO about the President's budget proposal even predicted an increase in U.S. debt held by the public to 56.8% of GDP by 2009 and up to 80% of GDP by 2019.[2]

Second, in 2008 the U.S. government took upon its shoulders the two mortgage giants Freddie Mac and Fannie Mae, and therefore their trillion dollars' worth of debt can now be considered as safe (or as risky) as U.S. government securities, further expanding the effective size of U.S. government debt. The debt securities issued by these mortgage giants are not as simple as U.S. Treasury securities, as they have a number of additional features, such as embedded options of various kinds, that make their valuation and risk assessment difficult. The two agencies need to issue these types of securities to hedge against the variation in the value of the mortgage backed securities (MBS) that they hold in their assets, a variation that is mainly due to interest rate fluctuations. Indeed, the three agencies Fannie Mae, Freddie Mac, and Ginnie Mae hold or guarantee about half of the roughly $9 trillion U.S. mortgage market. This implies that about four to five trillion dollars worth of mortgage backed securities are now guaranteed by the U.S. government. It is only because of this guarantee, in fact, that the three agencies have been able to issue mortgage backed securities since the last quarter of 2008, whereas the private market completely dried up. Given the sheer size of the MBS market, it is as important as ever to understand the pricing and hedging of such complex fixed income securities.

More generically, a deep understanding of the forces that affect the valuation, risk, and return of fixed income securities and their derivatives has never been so important. Not only will fixed income markets be expanding in the future, as mentioned above, but in the past two years investors across the world dumped risky securities and purchased safe U.S. government securities, which pushed their prices up and their yields down. Understanding the forces that move the term structure of interest rates is important to determining what will happen to these prices once the crisis is over. For instance, how safe is an investment in long-term U.S. Treasuries? While the U.S. is (still) very unlikely to default, default risk is but one of the risks that affect the value of Treasury bonds, and an understanding of the possible losses from an investment in "safe" Treasury bonds is key, especially in an environment of low interest rates such as the current one. Indeed, the large expansionary monetary policy of the Federal Reserve, which was necessary to keep the banking sector from collapsing due to lack of liquidity, may spur a bout of inflation in the future. Inflation will affect the rate of return on nominal long-term bonds, and therefore the prices of fixed income securities will adjust. Is an investment in long-term U.S. Treasury bonds really safe? What about agency mortgage backed securities, which are guaranteed by the U.S. government as well? Is such an investment riskier than an investment in Treasury securities? How can derivatives help hedge risks?

---

[2]See *A Preliminary Analysis of the President's Budget and an Update of CBO's Budget and Economic Outlook*, Congressional Budget Office, March 2009.

About this Book

This book covers "fixed" income securities, their valuation, their risks, and the practice of risk management. I put quotation marks around the term "fixed" because nowadays most of the so-called fixed income securities have streams of income payments that are all but fixed. And it is exactly this fact, that most "fixed" income securities in modern financial markets actually do not have a "fixed income," that makes the analysis of these debt instruments difficult. Let's put some numbers down to see this more precisely. Consider once again the U.S. market: As of the end of 2008, the U.S. debt stood at about $6 trillion, approximately 90% of which is in Treasury securities that indeed have a fixed income, namely, with constant coupons that are paid over time. However, about 10% of the U.S. debt is in Treasury Inflation Protected Securities (TIPS), that pay a coupon that is not fixed at all, but fluctuates together with the realized U.S. inflation rate. These fluctuations make their valuation harder. On top of the $6 trillion Treasury debt, there is a $9 trillion mortgage backed securities market, whose securities (e.g., pass throughs, collateralized debt obligations, and so on) have streams of payments that are not fixed, but depend on various factors, including interest rates' fluctuations. In addition, we should add the large swap market, now the main reference market for fixed income security dealers, which had a global market value of about $8 trillion in 2008. Once again, swaps do not have fixed income. And finally, the whole fixed income derivatives market, which includes forwards, futures, and options, adds a few more trillion dollars.

What keeps these markets together?

The concept that I use throughout this text is that of no arbitrage and the law of one price, that is, the fact that two securities that have the same cash flows should have the same price. In well-functioning markets, there shouldn't be (large) arbitrage profits that are left on the table, as arbitrageurs would step in and trade them away. It is important to start from the no arbitrage principle to link all of these markets together. Then, after we have understood the concept of no arbitrage, we can look back and try to understand why sometimes apparent arbitrage opportunities seem to appear in the market, in the form of spreads between securities that look similar. Typically, the answer is risk, that is, it may be risky to set up an arbitrage strategy and carry it out. The 2007 - 2009 crisis provides in fact an important example of market disruptions, and this book contains several examples and case studies discussing the risk and return of setting up and carrying out what appear to be arbitrage strategies.

Why this Book?

The world of fixed income markets is becoming increasingly more complex, with debt securities that have the most varied payoff structures, and fixed income derivatives that are growing in sheer size and complexity. Indeed, in many instances it is no longer clear what a real "derivative" security is. Typically, we think of a derivative security as a security whose value can be derived from the value of another, more primitive security from the rules of no arbitrage. However, when the size of a derivative market becomes larger than the one of the primitive securities, which price depends on which is not clear at all. The swap market, for instance, which we still call a derivative market and whose size at the beginning of the

1990s was negligible, now has a global market value of over $8 trillion, and a notional of over $350 trillion. While we can think of swaps as derivatives, in the more generic sense as hedging devices or non-funded financial instruments, their valuation does not derive from anything in particular, but only from the demand and supply of investors who use them for their needs to hedge or speculate in interest rates.

As the world of fixed income securities becomes more complex, I believe that anyone who studies fixed income securities must be exposed more directly to this complexity. This book provides a thorough discussion of these complex securities, the forces affecting their prices, their risks, and of the appropriate risk management practices. The idea here, however, is to provide a methodology, and not a shopping list. I do not go over all of the possible fixed income securities, structured products, and derivative securities that have ever been invented. I provide instead examples and methodologies that can be applied quite universally, once the basic concepts are understood. For this reason, the book is filled with real-world examples and case studies, as discussed below. End-of-chapter exercises using real-world data and real-world securities cement the important concepts.

In addition, in modern financial markets, countries' central banks, such as the Federal Reserve in the United States, actively intervene in fixed income markets to affect interest rates in the attempt to spur real growth and keep inflation low. A fixed income book cannot sidestep the central banks' influence on fixed income securities. I devote a chapter to discussing the Federal Reserve system, and the relation among interest rates, the real economy, and inflation. A large recent advance in academic literature links no arbitrage models with the activities of central banks, and this is important. Similarly, the academic literature has uncovered numerous stylized facts about the time variation of yields, which I also briefly summarize in a chapter. For instance, the old idea that an increasing yield curve predicts higher future interest rates has been proven false in the data time and again, and we should teach our students the implications of this empirical evidence. In particular, an increasing yield curve does not predict future higher rates, but future higher bond returns (i.e., if anything, lower future rates). That is, the literature has uncovered facts about the time variation of risk premia, which we should talk about in fixed income books. Without comprehending why yields move, students cannot have a complete understanding of fixed income markets.

The book also highlights the fact that most of the analysis of fixed income securities must rely on some models of the term structure, that is, some particular assumptions about the movement of yields through time. We use such models to link different types of instruments by no arbitrage and therefore establish the price of one, perhaps complex, security by using the price of a more primitive security. Such models are used by market participants both to design arbitrage strategies in proprietary trading desks, or to value portfolios of derivatives for trading or accounting purposes, or to determine hedge ratios for risk management reasons. However, this book aims at clarifying two important issues: First, models have parameters and parameters need data to be estimated. Thus, the use of data and computers to determine models' parameters, and therefore to value fixed income securities, is just part of the fixed income game. We cannot propose to teach students even the basics of fixed income markets without a long and careful look at the data, and without knowing how to use data to fit models.

Second, the book clarifies that models are "just models," and they are always an incomplete description of a much more complex real world. We will see that different models may yield different answers about the value of the same derivative security even when using the same data to estimate their parameters. There isn't one right model. Each model has pros and cons and there is always a tradeoff between using one or another model. For instance, some models generate simple pricing formulas for relatively complex securities, and this simplicity is useful if a trader needs to compute the prices of a large portfolio of derivatives quickly. However, such models may be too simplistic to design an arbitrage strategy. More complex models take into account more features of the data, but they are also harder to implement. Finally, some models may work well in some type of interest rate environments, while others do not because of assumptions that must be made. In this book, we cover several models, and we go over their properties, the approximations of reality they make, and their possible drawbacks. The use of examples and case studies, as well as end-of-chapter exercises enables readers to grasp these differences and understand why one or another model may be useful in one or another circumstance.

Finally, my aim in writing this book was also to endow anybody who is interested in fixed income markets, even readers without a strong analytical background, to understand the complexities, the risks, and the risk management methodologies of real-world fixed income markets. With this desire in mind, I wrote the book in a way to cover all of the important concepts in each part of the book, as each part may require a different level of mathematical sophistication. Parts I and II of the book are accessible to students familiar with basic calculus, while Part III requires a more analytical background. Still, as discussed below, Parts I and II are sufficient to cover a complete course in fixed income, and they do cover all of the deep concepts that I believe anyone who studies fixed income and plays any role in these markets should possess. The world of fixed income securities has become more complex, and students who aim at working in this environment must now be able to recognise and work with this complexity.

I now describe the three parts of the book in more detail.

Part I: Basics

Part I of the book, Chapters 1 to 8, covers the basics of fixed income pricing, risk, and risk management. After introducing the main fixed income markets in Chapter 1, Chapter 2 contains the building blocks of fixed income relations, namely, the notion of discounts, interest rates, and the term structure of interest rates. The chapter also discusses the basic bond pricing formula, as well as some important methodologies for extracting discounts from observable bond prices. A case study at the end of the chapter further illustrates these concepts within the pricing of inverse floaters, which are popular fixed income securities yielding higher-than-market returns if interest rates decline.

Chapter 3 contains the basics of risk management: The chapter introduces the concept of duration, and its use to design effective hedging strategies, as in asset-liability management. The chapter also introduces the popular risk measures of Value-at-Risk and expected shortfall. The chapter illustrates these concepts with a discussion of the (likely) risks embedded in the portfolio of Orange County, which lost $1.6 billion and declared bankruptcy in 1994. Chapter 4 contains some refinements in the risk management techniques introduced in Chapter 3: In particular, the chapter illustrates the notion of bond convexity, and its implication for risk and risk management, as well as the concepts of yield curve's slope and curvature dynamics. This chapter shows that the notion of duration is an incomplete measure of risk, and relatively simple modifications to the model allow for much better hedging performances, especially through the notion of factor neutrality.

Chapter 5 introduces basic interest rate derivatives, such as forwards and swaps. Besides describing their properties and their pricing methodology, several examples throughout the chapter also illustrate the use of such derivative contracts for an effective risk management strategy. The chapter ends with a case study discussing the risks embedded in a popular trade, a swap spread trade, a case that also provides further understanding of the swap market itself. Chapter 6 is the second introductory chapter on derivative securities, covering futures and options. In particular, the chapter illustrates the notion of options as financial insurance contracts, which pay only if some particular event takes place. After the description of futures and options contracts, several examples discuss the usefulness of these contracts for risk management. In addition, the chapter contains a discussion of the pros and cons of using forwards, futures, and options for hedging purposes.

A book on fixed income securities must mention the impact that monetary policy has on interest rates. Chapter 7 discusses the Federal Reserve policy rules, and covers in particular the Federal Funds rate. A case study at the conclusion of the chapter illustrates the activities of the Federal Reserve by using the financial crisis of 2007 - 2008 as an example. The chapter also introduces the Federal funds futures, and the information contained in such derivative contracts to predict future movements in the Federal funds rate. This chapter also connects the movement of interest rates over time to real economic growth and inflation rate, as the Federal Reserve acts to keep the economy growing and the inflation rate low. As the focus is on inflation, this chapter also covers the Treasury Inflation Protected Securities (TIPS), Treasury securities that pay coupons and principal that are linked to the realized inflation rate. Finally, this chapter contains the academic evidence about the variation over time of interest rates, and the fact that risk premia to hold bonds are time varying. In particular, this chapter answers the question of why the term structure of interest rates, on average, slopes upward.

The final chapter of Part I is Chapter 8, which contains a discussion of the mortgage backed securities (MBS) market, its main players, and the securitization process. Given that the financial market turmoil of 2007 - 2008 started in the mortgage backed securities markets, the chapter also describes some of the events during this period of time. This introductory chapter to mortgage backed securities also contains a discussion of the main measures of prepayment speed, as well as their impact on the pricing and risk exposure of several MBS, such as simple pass throughs, collateralized mortgage obligations, and principal only and interest only strips. The concept of negative convexity is thoroughly discussed, and illustrated by using data from the main trading market of agency pass throughs, the To-Be-Announced (TBA) market. A case study at the end of the chapter also demonstrates how we can measure the duration and convexity of MBSs (and other securities) by using data instead of pricing formulas.

Part II: Binomial Trees

The second part of the book introduces readers to the concept of term structure modeling and no arbitrage strategies. Chapter 9 illustrates these important concepts in the simple framework of one-step binomial trees. I use this chapter to discuss both the relative pricing of different fixed income instruments, the notion of risk premium of a fixed income security, as well as the popular pricing methodology called risk neutral pricing. The chapter does not use any more mathematics than Part I does, but it is the first step into a bigger world, the world of no arbitrage term structure models. Chapter 10 extends the analysis to multi-step trees. Students will learn the concepts of dynamic replication and hedging. These are strategies that allow a trader to hedge a contingent payoff in the future by using a portfolio of other fixed income securities, and understanding them is at the heart of no arbitrage pricing. The chapter also discusses a simple methodology to build long-term trees from the prediction of future short-term interest rates, as well as the concept of risk adjusted probabilities and risk premia. Real-world examples including the pricing of long-term structured derivatives illustrate how the methodology can be readily applied to price relatively complex securities. Finally, the chapter introduces the concept of spot rate duration, which is a concept of duration analogous to the one introduced in Chapter 3, but for securities defined on binomial trees.

Chapter 11 applies the concepts described in the previous two chapters to illustrate the no arbitrage pricing of numerous derivative securities. The chapter uses two popular models, the Ho-Lee model and Black, Derman, and Toy model, to show the differences in pricing between different models, even when the inputs are the same. These differences allow me to describe the various properties of the models. We use these models also to price standard derivatives, such as caps, floors, swaps and swaptions. In addition, the chapter introduces the notion of implied volatility, that is, the volatility of interest rates that is implied by the value of options. Building on these multi-step binomial tree models, Chapter 12 investigates the pricing of American options, that is, options that can be exercised any time before maturity. Several securities have embedded American options, including callable bonds and mortgage backed securities. This chapter illustrates the concepts of American options, and the methodology to price them, by going through several examples, such as Treasury callable securities, American swaptions, and mortgage backed securities. This chapter also shows the negative convexity that is generated by the American option feature embedded in such securities.

Finally, Chapter 13 illustrates a new methodology, Monte Carlo simulations, to price very complex securities on binomial trees. There are securities that cannot be easily priced on binomial trees because their payoff at maturity may depend on a particular path of interest rates. However, we can use computers to simulate interest paths *on the tree* itself, and therefore obtain the prices and hedge ratios of these securities by simulation. The chapter applies the methodology to relatively complicated real-world securities, such as amortizing swaps and mortgage backed securities.

Part III: Continuous Time Models

Part III covers more advanced term structure models that rely on continuous time mathematics. While this part is self contained, as it contains all of the important mathematical concepts, readers should be ready to see a substantial step up in the analytical requirement compared to the previous two parts of the book, which, as mentioned, instead only require a background in basic calculus.

Chapter 14 introduces the notions of Brownian motion, differential equations and Ito's lemma. I introduce the concept of a Brownian motion by relying on the intuition developed on binomial trees, namely, as a limiting behavior of rates as the time-step in the binomial tree converges to zero. Differential equations are introduced only through examples, as my aim here is to provide students with the notion of differential equations, and not the methodology to solve for them. I also illustrate the concept of Ito's lemma by relying on the convexity concepts discussed earlier in Chapter 4. I apply the concepts of Brownian motions and Ito's lemma in Chapter 15 to illustrate the notion of no arbitrage, and obtain the fundamental pricing equation, an equation that we can use to compute the price of any fixed income derivative. I focus on the Vasicek model, a model that is relatively simple but also realistic, and provide several examples on the pricing of real-world securities. In this chapter I tackle the issue of how to estimate the model's parameters, and show the potential shortcomings of the model. The chapter also illustrates the use of this model for the pricing of options.

Chapter 16 takes the model one step further, and discusses the issue of dynamic re-balancing and relative value trades. Essentially, all fixed income securities are linked to each other by the variation of interest rates, and therefore they move in a highly correlated fashion. An interest rate model allows us to compute the price of one security by using a portfolio of other securities, so long as the latter is properly rebalanced over time as interest rates change. The methodology is illustrated through various real-world examples, as well as a case study at the end of the chapter which features real data, and demonstrates the methodology in action. The chapter also illustrates some drawbacks of using simple models.

Chapter 17 introduces the second important result of continuous time finance, namely, the Feynman Kac formula, which provides the solution to the fundamental pricing equation obtained in Chapter 16. This formula is at the basis of the risk neutral pricing methodology widely used by market participants to price fixed income securities. In addition, this formula also justifies the use of some type of Monte Carlo simulations to price fixed income securities. The chapter provides numerous real-world examples, as well as a case study discussing the fair valuation of the leveraged swap between Bankers Trust and Procter & Gamble, which was at the center of a famous court case in 1994. Indeed, Chapter 18 covers the topics of risk measurement and risk management within continuous time models: In particular, I illustrate the notion of market price of risk, the fair compensation that a fixed income investor should expect to realize when he or she purchases a fixed income security, as well as Monte Carlo simulations for risk assessment. I illustrate the use of Monte Carlo simulations for risk assessment both in examples, as well as in a case study at the end of the chapter. The chapter also includes an economic model of the term structure, which links the continuous time models illustrated in earlier chapters to the variation in expected inflation, and the compensation for risk that investors require to hold nominal securities when there is inflation.

Chapter 19 discusses no arbitrage models, which are models similar to the ones intro-duced in Chapter 11 on binomial trees, but in continuous time. The inputs of these models are the bond prices, and the outputs are the prices of derivative securities. The chapter offers several applications, and further highlights the pros and cons of different types of models. I carry on this discussion in Chapter 20, which illustrates the Black's formula to price standard derivatives, such as caps, floors, and swaptions. This chapter also links back to Chapter 11 in what concerns the notion of implied volatility. The chapter also discusses the important concepts of flat and forward volatility, as well as the dynamics of the term structure of volatility over time. These concepts are so important in modern financial mar-kets that I decided to present this material in isolation from the previous chapters in Part III, so that the material in this chapter stands alone, and can also be used as a concluding chapter after Chapter 11.

Chapter 21 introduces a more recent pricing methodology, the forward risk neutral pricing methodology, as well as the more recent Heath, Jarrow, and Morton (HJM) model, and the Brace, Gatarek, and Musiela (BGM) model. Several applications show the usefulness of these new models to obtaining the price of even more complicated securities, although often by relying on Monte Carlo simulations.

I conclude this third part of the book, and the book itself, with Chapter 22, which extends the concepts developed in the previous chapters to the case in which the yield curve is driven by multiple factors. Luckily, the main concepts developed earlier readily extend to multifactor models. I show the additional flexibility offered by these multifactor models to price interesting additional structured notes and derivative securities, such as those that depend on multiple points of the term structure.

Pedagogical Strategy

This book employs a hands-on strategy to highlight the valuation, the risks, and the risk management of fixed income securities. The text is filled with real-world examples and case studies, which I use to show step by step the fair valuation of most securities, the return an investor should expect from an investment, and the riskiness of such an investment. I always use data to set up an example or to illustrate a concept, not only because it makes the lesson more relevant, but because it shows that we can actually tackle real-world valuation problems by studying the concepts illustrated in each chapter.

Examples

Each chapter contains many numerical examples illustrating the concepts introduced in the chapter. Sometimes I use examples to motivate new important concepts. As mentioned, such examples are always based on real data and therefore on real situations. Even so, examples are stripped down versions of much more complex problems, and I use such examples to illustrate one issue at a time.

Case Studies

The book contains several end-of-chapter case studies. These case studies apply the concepts developed in the chapter to more complex real-world situations. Such situations may involve the pricing of some structured derivatives, or their risk assessment using some measures of risk, or describe an arbitrage trading situation and the risk involved in carrying it out. Unlike the examples, which are tightly focused on the particular issue just being discussed in the chapter, a case study describes a situation and then carries out the whole analysis, although of course still within the topic discussed in the chapter. I use case studies also to show that we must often make many approximations when we apply relatively simple formulas or models to real-world data. That is, the world is much more complicated than the simple models or formulas would imply.

Not all chapters have case studies, as it depends on the topic of each chapter. If a chapter is too simple, for instance, because it is only introductory, then it is hard to apply the concept to a real-world situation, which tends to be complicated.

Data

The book relies heavily on real-world securities data. I use data to illustrate the examples in the body of the textbook as well as to discuss the case studies at the end of chapters. In addition, most of the exercises require some data analysis. These data are collected in spreadsheets, which are available with the textbook. The decision to rely foremost on the use of data as a pedagogical device springs from my beliefs that only by *doing* the analysis with real-world numbers can a student really understand not only the concepts illustrated in the particular chapter, but also the complexity of applying models to the real world. From the very beginning we will see that it is actually hard to apply the simple formulas of fixed income models, even the most elementary ones such as a present value formula, to real-world data. It is important for students to realize this fact early on, and it is this challenge that makes the study of fixed income markets so fascinating.

Exercises

Each chapter contains several exercises that cover the topics discussed, and highlight additional features of real-world fixed-income securities or trading methodologies. A solutions manual is available to instructors. The exercises are an integral part of the learning strategy: Most exercises are data driven and require the use of computers, either spreadsheets (for Parts I and II) or a programming software (for Part III). In modern financial markets computers are just a necessary part of the analysis toolbox. For instance, in Part I exercises require spreadsheets to compute the prices of complicated securities from simpler ones, or their duration and convexity. In Part II, the exercises require spreadsheet programs to build binomial trees that fit real-world fixed income securities, such as bonds, swaps and options. Moreover, in some chapters, the exercises require students to carry out Monte Carlo simulations, on the binomial trees, to value real-world fixed income securities with embedded options, such as the Bermudan callable bonds of Freddie Mac.

In Part III, the exercises again rely on real-world data to fit more complex models of the term structure, and ask students to price relatively complex securities. In addition, exercises often require students to carry out a risk analysis, by computing hedge ratios or risk measures. The hands-on approach will make clear why practitioners use one model or another in the various circumstances: Students will experience firsthand the difficulties of dealing with data even when using relatively simple models.

Software

There are numerous examples in the book which use real-world data to illustrate the concepts discussed in each chapter. Together with the data sets in such examples, I also include all of the spreadsheets (for Part I and II) or computer codes (for Part III) that generate the results of the analysis in the numerical examples. These spreadsheets and computer codes should be used as a guide not only to better understand the examples themselves, but also to carry out a similar analysis in the end-of-chapter exercises.

For Instructors

The material in this book can be taught at two different levels: An introductory level and an advanced (but not very advanced) level.

Course I: Introduction to Fixed Income Securities

Parts I and II introduce basic analytical tools, and students familiar with basic calculus should be able to follow them relatively easily. This material covers a full semester fixed income course for both MBA or undergraduate students. Yet, notwithstanding the relative simplicity of these two parts of the book, the hands-on strategy, the real-world examples, the case studies, and the focus on real-world securities provide a strong foundation for the important concepts in fixed income asset pricing, from no arbitrage to risk premia, from duration to positive and negative convexity, from risk measurement to risk neutral pricing. Students at the end of the course will have the tools to tackle the proper analysis of real-world securities, assess their risk, and perform Monte Carlo simulations (on binomial trees) to value complex securities. These tools are very important to uncover the often hidden risks in some structured interest rate securities.

Pedagogically, the chapters' order already offers guidance on how to progress with the material. Each chapter's content often contains the seeds of concepts described in future chapters. For instance, in Chapter 1 I describe the repurchase agreement (repo) market, because in Chapter 2, which covers the present value formulas and the use of the law of one price, I can leverage on the repo market to describe how financial institutions actually carry out long-short strategies. Similarly, in Chapter 2 I describe floating rate notes, not only because I can then use this concept to illustrate the pricing of inverse floaters (a case study at the end of the same chapter), but also because in Chapter 5 I use the same concept to describe the pricing of swaps, which is the largest fixed income market by notional amount (about $350 trillion at the end of 2008). The chapters are highly interrelated and cross-reference each other, and therefore I believe it is pedagogically important to move forward chapter by chapter.

There is one final remark I want to make in regard to an introductory course in fixed income. Part II of the book, and especially Chapter 11, discusses the pricing and hedging of plain vanilla derivatives, such as caps, floors, swaps, and swaptions. This chapter also dicusses the concepts of implied volatility, flat volatility and forward volatility in the context of two specific models, the Ho-Lee model and the Black, Derman, and Toy model. This part should therefore be useful to link this material to the notion of implied volatility from the Black formula, the standard market formula used to *quote* standard derivatives. With this link in mind, I wrote Chapter 20 in Part III in a way that does not need any of the more advanced material in the earlier chapters of Part III. I just introduce the Black formula, and discuss the dynamics of implied volatilities over time, and the concept of flat and forward volatility. The formula is as difficult as the Black and Scholes formula for options on stocks, so depending on how advanced the students are, they may or may not find the material challenging.

Course II: An Advanced Course in Fixed Income Securities

The advanced course would make full use of Part II and Part III of the book. This is the course I regularly teach to the second year MBA students at the University of Chicago Booth School of Business, and it is also appropriate for students enrolled in master in finance programs. The prerequisites for my course include an investment course and a basic options course, although I often allow students with a solid mathematical background to take the course without the prerequisites. I cover briefly the concepts in Chapters 1 to 6, which serve mainly to set the notation for the course. I then teach both binomial trees (Part II) and continuous time models (Part III), more or less in the progression described in the book. Indeed, Chapter 14 refers to Chapter 11 to introduce the notion of a Brownian motion as the limit of a binomial tree, as the step size becomes infinitesimally small. The key concepts that are explored in Part II are then also repeated in Part III, but by using continuous time methodologies. Students find it very useful to see the same concepts introduced in binomial trees repeated in a continuous time framework, as their intuition becomes solidified, especially through the plentiful examples. However, the greater flexibility offered by the continuous time model enables me to discuss many more models which are not covered in binomial trees, even with many stochastic factors (in Chapter 22). Students tend to enjoy the comparison across models, and why some models work in some interest rate environments and not in some others. To this end, I give my students challenging, data-oriented homeworks to make them aware not only of the vast possibilities offered by fixed income term structure models, and their usefulness to price, hedge or implement a risk analysis of a given security, but also to have students realize the limitations of such fixed income models, and the fact that models need data for their effective application to the real world. My homework is always based on real-world securities that need to be priced, hedged, or, more generically, analyzed, and I wrote most of the end-of-chapter exercises in this book with this aim in mind, namely, to have students analyze real-world securities by using the models discussed in each chapter. Sometimes the analysis require students to gather data from other sources available on public Web sites, such as the LIBOR fixes available at the British Bankers' Association Web site, or the swap rates, available at the Federal Reserve Web site. The data analysis is an integral part of the book and the learning experience. In term of material, finally, my students also find it useful to connect the economic model discussed in Chapter 18 to the Vasicek model, discussed earlier, as well as to the evidence on expected return in Chapter 7, as they see the connections between risk, risk aversion, return, market price of risk, and, ultimately, pricing.

Conclusion

To conclude this introduction to the book, let me mention that I truly hope that this book will encourage readers and students to analyze fixed income markets in a very systematic way, always looking for the reason why some events occur, some trades seem possible, or some models may or may not work. I hope that my decision to have two full parts of the book requiring only a minimal analytical background will push readers to try to correctly assess the riskiness of complex fixed income securities, to see better what they are buying, and whether there is any reason why a security may appear to yield a higher-than-market return. Similarly, regulators may use the same tools to assess the fair valuation of complex securities, at least to first order, without needing a Ph.D. in mathematics or physics. In the same way, nowadays it is much harder to understand how the engine of a car works, compared to the past, and mechanics need to have a better knowledge about these new engines, participants in fixed income markets, whether traders, risk managers, regulators and so on, cannot hope to use old tools to understand modern markets, as their complexity has just increased through time, and new tools are necessary. I hope this book will provide the tools, even to the less mathematically oriented reader, to understand the complexities of fixed income modern markets.

PIETRO VERONESI

Chicago
June, 2009

ACKNOWLEDGMENTS

First of all, I want to thank my students at the University of Chicago Booth School of Business, whose enthusiasm for fixed income securities convinced me to write this book. Their feedback on earlier versions of the manuscript was invaluable. I also thank John Heaton (The University of Chicago Booth School of Business), Jakub Jurek (Princeton University), Nick Roussanov (The Wharton School, University of Pennsylvania), and Richard Stanton (The Haas School of Business, University of California at Berkeley) for being so brave to adopt an early draft of this book in their MBA or Master courses, so that I could collect very valuable feedback from them and their students. I also would like to thank Monika Piazzesi (Stanford University) and Jefferson Duarte (Rice University) for their early feedback, as well as Senay Agca (George Washington University), David T. Brown (University of Florida), Robert Jennings (University of Indiana), Robert Kieschnick (University of Texas at Dallas), David P. Simon (Bentley College), Donald J. Smith (Boston University), Michael Stutzer (University of Colorado), Manuel Tarrazo (University of San Francisco), and Russ Wermers (University of Maryland) for their comments. Francisco Javier Madrid and Nina Boyarchenko provided precious help with some exercises and case studies, and I thank them for this. I also thank Chetan Dandavate and Camilo Echeverri for pointing out some important typos in the manuscript. I am also indebted to the development editor, Peggy Monahan-Pashall, who went through the 800 pages of the manuscript, and not only corrected all my English mistakes, but provided valuable constructive feedback on the write up itself. I also thank Jennifer Manias, the Associate Editor, for helping with the logistics of the publication process. Finally, this book exists also because my editor, Judith Joseph of Wiley, pushed me to write it. Maybe I should have not listened, but it is too late now.

P. V.

PART I

FIXED INCOME MARKETS

CHAPTER 1

AN INTRODUCTION TO FIXED INCOME MARKETS

1.1 INTRODUCTION

In the past two decades, fixed income markets have experienced an impressive growth, both in market value and in complexity. In the old days, until the end of the 1980s, fixed income markets were dominated by government debt securities, such as United States government Treasury bills, notes, and bonds. These securities were also relatively simple, as the U.S. government mainly issued bonds paying a fixed amount of money semi-annually. Although other governments, such as those of the United Kingdom and Italy, also experimented with other types of debt securities whose semi-annual payments were not fixed, but rather linked to a floating index, for instance, the inflation rate, such markets were relatively small. Thus, the U.S. government debt market was the main reference for global fixed income markets.

Today, however, the U.S. government debt is no longer the dominant fixed income market, not so much because the U.S. debt shrank over the past two decades, but rather because other fixed income markets rose substantially relative to U.S. debt and became the main reference for fixed income pricing. Table 1.1 provides a snapshot of the sizes of fixed income markets as of December 2008. The first block of markets comprises the traditional fixed income markets, including U.S. government debt securities, municipal bonds, federal agency securities and the money market. The total size of these debt markets is around $15 trillion. The next block shows the size of the mortgage backed securities and asset-backed securities markets. In particular, the mortgage backed securities market stands as a $8.9 trillion market, a good $3 trillion larger than U.S. debt.

3

Table 1.1   The Size of Fixed Income Markets: December 2008

Market	Market Value (billion of dollars)	Notional (billion of dollars)
U.S. Treasury Debt	5,912.2	
U.S. Municipal Debt	2,690.1	
U.S. Federal Agency Securities	3,247.4	
U.S. Money Market	3,791.1	
Mortgage Backed Securities	8,897.3	
Asset-Backed Securities	2,671.8	
OTC Interest Rate Swaps	16,572.85	328,114.49
OTC Interest Rate Forwards	153.19	39,262.24
OTC Interest Rate Options	1,694.22	51,301.37
Exchange Traded Futures		19,271.05
Exchange Traded Options		35,161.34
U.S. Corporate Debt	6,280.6	
Credit Derivatives	5,651	41,868

Source: Securities Industry and Financial Market Association (SIFMA) and Bank for International Settlements (BIS).

Similarly, the next block of markets in Table 1.1 shows the interest rate derivatives markets. Interest rate swaps, in particular, have a market value of $16 trillion, and a notional value of $328 trillion. Although neither figure can be compared directly to the U.S. debt market, for a number of reasons discussed in Chapter 5, the sizes of these markets once again demonstrate that the U.S. debt market has been eclipsed by other types of securities. In particular, although in the 1980s and 1990s we would think of swaps as derivative securities, which "derive" their price from the value of primary securities, such as Treasuries, it is hard to believe that this is still the case now due to its sheer size. To any extent, we should consider the swap market a primary market whose value is driven by investors', speculators' and end users' fluctuating demands. Finally, corporate debt has increased dramatically in the past few years, with a debt value of about $6.2 trillion. Note too that the growing market of credit derivatives has reached a market value of $5.6 trillion, and a notional value of $42 trillion.

The changes in these markets are evident also in Figures 1.1 and 1.2. Considering first the Treasury debt market, we see that from 1986 to 1996 it grew steadily. The economic expansion that started in 1991, which would end in 2001, also generated a government surplus between 1996 and 1999, which led the U.S. government to initiate a policy of debt buyback. This is evident in the decrease in the face value of government debt during this period. The U.S. debt started growing again in 2001, to reach about $5.9 trillion in December 2008. The interesting fact about Figure 1.1, though, is the rise of another market, which has become a dominant market in the U.S., namely, the market of mortgage backed securities. From its value of only $372 billion in 1985 it increased steadily over time, to become larger than the U.S. debt market in 1999, and to become $3 trillion larger than the U.S. debt market by December 2008. The growth in this market is due to the growth of the U.S. real estate market, which boomed in the 2000s to reach its peak in 2006, as well as the steady increase in leverage of U.S. households, who had been taking larger

Figure 1.1   The Growth in Market Size

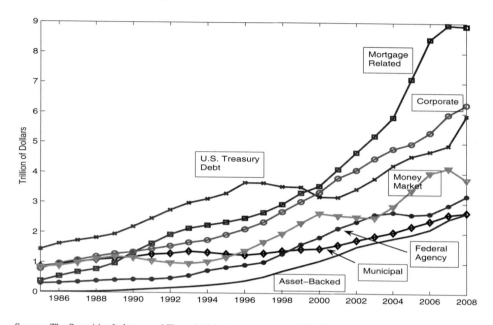

Source: The Securities Industry and Financial Markets Association (SIFMA)

and larger mortgages and home equity loans to finance consumption. The slight decrease in this market size visible at the end of the sample, in 2008, is indeed a reflection of the decline in the housing market and the U.S. recession that started in January 2007. Finally, a similar growth occurred in corporate debt, which next to U.S. debt was comparatively small in 1985, but grew steadily over the years, to reach $6.2 trillion by December 2008.

Figure 1.2 plots the stunning growth in interest rate derivatives markets. The interest rate swaps market, which was negligible at the beginning of the 1980s, experienced an exponential growth, reaching $328 trillion (notional) by December 2008. The figure also plots the combinations of over-the-counter (OTC) and exchange-traded interest rate options, which also grew considerably during this time frame, to reach about $100 trillion notional by December 2007, although it declined to $86 trillion by December 2008, in the midst of the 2007 - 2009 financial crisis. Similarly, forward rate agreements and futures contracts also grew over time, although at a much slower rate.

The bottom line of this discussion is that fixed income markets are very large and still growing. Moreover, there is not a dominant market: What we called a derivative market in the past is now larger in sheer size than the primary market. The big question is what is keeping the prices of the interest rate instruments tied to each other. That is, all of these instruments are highly correlated. For instance, if the Federal Reserve drops the Fed funds rate, then we may expect all of the short-term interest rates to fall. How do these rates move together? The answer is no arbitrage, that is, the possibility does not exist for arbitrageurs to take large positions in different securities whenever the prices across markets do not line up. The concept of "line up" will become clear in future chapters. For now, we turn to describing individual markets in more detail.

Figure 1.2   The Growth in Derivatives Markets: Notional

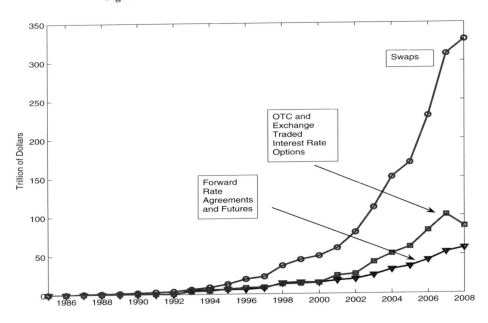

Source: SIFMA and Bank for International Settlement

1.1.1   The Complexity of Fixed Income Markets

The previous section illustrates the growth in size of fixed income markets. The complexity of fixed income markets is also extraordinary. Table 1.2 reports a snapshot of rates in the U.S. fixed income markets on September 18, 2007. The table corresponds to screen BTMM from Bloomberg terminals, and it is widely used by traders to quickly grasp the relative positions of bond prices and interest rates across markets. The number of securities described in this table is daunting. Starting from the top left corner, we have:

1. Federal funds rate quotes;

2. U.S. Treasury bill prices and yields at various maturities;

3. Eurodollar deposit rates at various maturities;

4. Repo and reverse repo rates;

5. U.S. Treasury bond yields and prices with various maturities;

6. Commercial paper quotes;

7. 90-day Eurodollar futures for various maturities;

8. Federal funds futures for various maturities;

9. LIBOR fixes;

10. Foreign exchange rates;

11. 30-years mortgage backed securities;

12. 10-year Treasury note futures;

13. Swap rates for various maturities;

14. Other key rates, such as the prime.

How do all these market rates move together?

The notion is that these quantities are all highly correlated with the same events. For instance, if there are worries of an increase in future inflation, we can expect the Federal Reserve to increase the target Fed Funds rate (see Chapter 7). In turn, this expectation as well as the rules of no arbitrage, discussed below, have an impact on other short-term borrowing rates, such as the short-term LIBOR, the short-term Eurodollar rates and so on. In this chapter we define only the terms appearing in Table 1.2. In the following chapters, we describe the relations between these markets and many others that do not appear in Table 1.2. The key concept is the concept of no arbitrage, which is helpful to introduce right away.

1.1.2   No Arbitrage and the Law of One Price

At the source of the ripple-through effect from one market to the next is the notion of no arbitrage. In its *pure form*, an arbitrage opportunity is defined as follows:

Definition 1.1 *An* **arbitrage opportunity** *is a feasible trading strategy involving two or more securities with either of the following characteristics:*

1. *It does not cost anything at initiation, and it generates a sure positive profit by a certain date in the future;*

2. *It generates a positive profit at initiation, and it has a sure nonnegative payoff by a certain date in the future.*

The **no arbitrage** *condition requires that no arbitrage opportunities exist.*

A pure arbitrage trade consists in taking positions that generate, magically to some extent, always nonnegative cash flows, and with certainty, some positive cash flow. There are three key elements in Definition 1.1: The trade (1) costs nothing; (2) yields positive profits with certainty; and (3) the profits arrive within a known time. For instance, if an arbitrageur finds two securities that pay exactly $100 in six months, but one trades at $P_1 = \$97$ and the other at $P_2 = \$98$, then an arbitrageur can apply the trader's motto "buy low and sell high," and purchase 1 million units of Security 1 at $97 and sell 1 million units of Security 2 at $98, realizing an inflow of $1 million. In six months, the two securities generate exactly the same cash flow and therefore the trader is hedged: Whatever he or she receives from Security 1 is then given to the holder of Security 2.

Of course, these types of pure arbitrage opportunities are hard to find in financial markets. Because of transaction costs and the lack of perfect co-movement among variables, some risks do in fact exist, and arbitrageurs must take them into account while they trade. The rules of no arbitrage, however, are still key to defining some relationships that must exist

Table 1.2   A Snapshot of U.S. Treasury and Money Market Rates

FED FUNDS

BID/ASK	5 1/8	5 1/36
LST/OPEN	5 1/8	5 1/8
HIGH/LOW	5 1/8	5 1/8
DJIA	13479.91	+76.49

US T-BILL YIELD/PRICE

4W	3.88	0.12	3.82	3M	3.81
3M	4.16	0.02	4.07	6M	4.17
6M	4.31	0.02	4.17	1Y	4.15
S&P 500 FUT	1947	+7.20			

EURO $ DEP

3M	5.5000	5.6000
6M	5.3300	5.4300
1Y	5.0300	5.1300
CCMP	2592.02	+10.36

REVERSE

O/N	5.15
1W	4.95
2W	4.85
1M	4.70

REPO

	5.05
	4.85
	4.75
	4.60

LIBOR FIX

1W	5.25875
1M	5.49625
2M	5.55375
3M	5.58750
4M	5.53625
5M	5.48313
6M	5.42000
1Y	5.11250

US BONDS YLD/BID/ASK/CHG

	YLD	BID	ASK	CHG
4 08/31/09	4.117	99-25	99-24+	-03
4 1/2 05/15/10	4.128	100-29	100-29+	-04
4 1/8 08/31/12	4.241	99-15	99-15+	-05+
4 3/4 08/15/17	4.493	102-00	102-01	-07
5 05/15/37	4.735	104-05	104-06	-19+
CRB	324.31			-.56

DEALER CP

15D	5.060
30D	5.350
60D	5.400
90D	5.410
120D	5.380
180D	5.240

90D EUR $ FUT

DEC	95.07
MAR	95.38
JUN	95.51
SEP	95.56
DEC	95.56
MAR	95.51

FUNDS FUT

SEP	95.01
OCT	95.11
NOV	95.30
DEC	95.39
JAN	95.44
FEB	95.56

SWAP RATES

3Y	4.809
5Y	4.918
10Y	5.174

Key Rates

Prime	8.25
BLR	7.00
FDTR	5.25
Discount	5.75

SPOT FOREX

JPY	115.8000
EUR	1.3875
GBP	1.9983
CHF	1.1876
MXN	11.1030
CAD	1.0233

30Y MBS

GNMN 6.0	100-24	100-25	-02
GOLD 6.0	100-09	100-10	00
FNMA 6.0	100-07	100-08	-01

10yr Note Fut

CBT	109 - 20	-04+

CRUDE OIL

NYM WTI	80.80	+.23

Source: Bloomberg. Screen BTMM. Date: September 18, 2007.

across assets prices, which in turn determine the relative prices of fixed income instruments. In this book we will see how these rules of no arbitrage allow us to both compute the fair value of fixed income instruments and to investigate their relative prices. Just as important, we will focus on the impact that no arbitrage has on the *risk* of fixed income instruments and therefore their *risk management.* At the basis of much of the analysis is the law of one price, discussed next:

Fact 1.1 *The* **law of one price** *establishes that securities with identical payoffs should have the same price.*

If the law of one price does not hold for some securities, then an arbitrage opportunity exists. Indeed, the logic is the same as the one of the previous example: if two securities have the same cash flows in the future but trade at different prices today, then an arbitrageur could buy the underpriced security and sell the overpriced one, realizing a profit today. Since the cash flows are the same in the future, the arbitrageur is perfectly hedged.

Before we investigate how no arbitrage and the law of one price allow us to study the valuation, risk, and risk management practices of fixed income instruments, let's take a closer look at the fixed income markets, using the entries in Table 1.2 as a guide. We begin with government debt, appearing under the heading of U.S. T-Bills and U.S. Bonds in Table 1.2.

1.2 THE GOVERNMENT DEBT MARKETS

Essentially all countries issue debt to finance their operations. U.S. government debt has always occupied a special place in fixed income markets, mainly because it is perceived to have an extremely low probability of default. That is, investing in U.S. Treasury securities is considered "safe," as the government *will* repay its debt to investor. The quotation marks around the word "safe" underly an important caveat, though, which is what makes the analysis of fixed income securities so interesting. A U.S. Treasury bond can be considered a "safe" investment in terms of its risk of default: As noted, the issuer will in all likelihood repay its debt to its creditors (investors). The rationale behind its default safety is that these bonds are backed by the ability of the U.S. government to levy taxes on its citizens in the future to pay the debt back.

However, an investment in a U.S. Treasury bond may *not* be safe in terms of its return on investment over a short period of time. To provide an example, Figure 1.3 plots the life cycle of a 20-year bond, from its issuance in February 1986 to its maturity on February 2006.[1] The variation over time of the price of the bond is quite stunning, with run ups of over 30 percent within two years (e.g., between 1991 and 1993), and run downs at even higher speed (e.g., 1994). An investor buying this bond in 1993 would have suffered severe capital losses within the next year or so.

In addition to the potential capital losses in the bond price during a shorter period of time than the bond's maturity, an investment in U.S. Treasury securities entails additional sources of risk. The first is that most of the Treasury securities are nominal securities, that is, they pay coupons and principal in dollars. Therefore, if between the purchase of

---

[1]Data excerpted from CRSP (Daily Treasuries) ¤2009 Center for Research in Security Prices (CRSP), The University of Chicago Booth School of Business.

Figure 1.3   The February 2006, 9.375%, 20-Year Bond Price Path

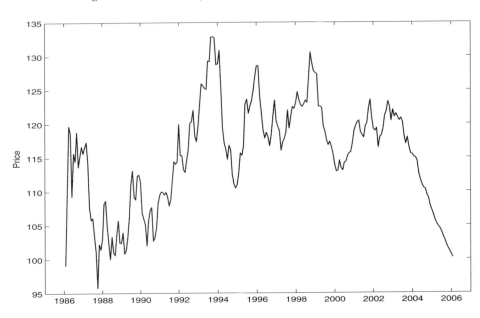

Source: Center for Research in Security Prices

the bond and its maturity (e.g., 30 years) the U.S. enters a period of sustained inflation, the effective value of coupons and principal decreases, as investors cannot purchase as many consumption goods. This inflation risk must be taken into account in the analysis of Treasury securities. A related risk concerns the fact that the coupon and principal payments are in U.S. dollars, which may entail a currency risk for an overseas investor. For instance, European investors who purchased safe U.S. Treasury notes in 2005 have been hurt by the devaluation of the dollar with respect to the euro between 2006 and 2008.

The U.S. government issues various types of securities. Table 1.3 lists the types of securities. Treasury bills (T-bills) are short-term debt instruments, with maturity up to one year.[2] They do not pay any cash flow over time, only the principal at maturity. Treasury bills are issued very frequently, typically every week for bills up to six months, and every four weeks for one-year bills.

Treasury notes (T-notes) are medium-long term debt instruments, with maturity up to 10 years. These notes carry a fixed coupon that is paid semi-annually up to the maturity of the note. They are issued every month, except the ten-year note, that is issued less frequently. Treasury bonds (T-bonds) are longer-term debt instruments with maturity of 30 years at issuance. As with Treasury notes, bonds also carry a semi-annual coupon. The Treasury issues these long-term bonds every six months.

In 1997 the U.S. government started issuing TIPS – Treasury Inflation Protected Securities – that is, securities that are indexed to inflation. Investors in T-notes and T-bonds are subject to inflation risk: Because the payment of coupons and final principal is in nominal

[2]The Treasury suspended the issuance of one year Treasury bills from August 2001 to June 2008.

Table 1.3   U.S. Treasury Debt Securities

Name	Maturity	Coupon Rate	Principal
Treasury Bills	4, 13, 26, and 52 weeks	None	Fixed
Treasury Notes	2, 5, and 10 years	Fixed, semi-annual	Fixed
Treasury Bonds	30 years	Fixed, semi-annual	Fixed
TIPS	5, 10, and 20 years	Fixed, semi-annual	Adjusted for inflation

terms (i.e., simply U.S. dollars), if inflation increases substantially during the life of the debt instruments, these sums of money will be able to buy less of consumer goods. The TIPS offer protection to investors against this possibility: Because the principal is adjusted for inflation, higher inflation translates into both a higher final payoff at maturity of the bond, and higher coupons as well, since the coupon is defined as a fixed percentage of *current* principal (which increases with inflation). TIPS are issued with maturities of 5, 10 and 20 years.

The issuance calendar of the U.S. Treasury is very dense. Table 1.4 provides a snapshop of the issuing activity of the U.S. Treasury as of July 15, 2009. Market participants refer to the most recently issued Treasury securities as **on-the-run** securities, while all the others are called **off-the-run**. On-the-run Treasury securities tend to trade at a premium compared to similar off-the-run Treasury securities, which tend to be less liquid than the on-the-run securities.

1.2.1   Zero Coupon Bonds

Zero coupon bonds are securities that pay only the principal at maturity. A simple example is the Treasury bill described in Table 1.3. Other zero coupon bonds are available in the U.S. market through the STRIPS program. STRIPS (Separate Trading of Registered Interest and Principal Securities) are zero coupon bonds created from available U.S. Treasury notes and bonds by splitting the principal and each of the coupons from the bond. The U.S. Treasury does not issue these securities directly to investors, but investors can purchase them and hold them through financial institutions and government securities brokers and dealers. As an example of the available STRIPS on a particular date, Table 1.5 reports the stripped coupons available on September 25, 2008. The stripped coupon are the zero coupon bonds that are created only from the coupon interest payments of Treasury notes and bonds. In addition, a similar table is available for the stripped principals. The availability of these zero coupon bond securities with maturity up to 30 years enables investors to be more effective in their investment strategies and in their risk management practices, as we will discuss in later chapters.

1.2.2   Floating Rate Coupon Bonds

The bonds issued by the U.S. government have a fixed coupon rate. A floating rate coupon bond is like a standard coupon bond, but its coupon is indexed to some other short-term interest rate, which changes over time. While the U.S. government does not issue floating rate bonds, other governments do. For instance, Italy issues the CCT bond, which is an Italian Treasury debt security whose coupon rate is indexed to the six month rate of Italian 6-

Table 1.4   Issuance Acitivity of Bonds, Notes, and TIPS: January 15, 2009 to July 15, 2009

Security	Term	Type	Issue Date	Maturity Date	Interest Rate %	Yield %	Price per $100	CUSIP
3-YEAR		NOTE	7/15/2009	7/15/2012	1.5	1.519	99.944485	912828LB4
9-YEAR	10-MONTH	NOTE	7/15/2009	5/15/2019	3.125	3.365	97.998772	912828KQ2
10-YEAR		TIPS	7/15/2009	7/15/2019	1.875	1.92	99.592335	912828LA6
29-YEAR	10-MONTH	BOND	7/15/2009	5/15/2039	4.25	4.303	99.104142	912810QB7
2-YEAR		NOTE	6/30/2009	6/30/2011	1.125	1.151	99.94874	912828LF5
5-YEAR		NOTE	6/30/2009	6/30/2014	2.625	2.7	99.651404	912828KY5
7-YEAR		NOTE	6/30/2009	6/30/2016	3.25	3.329	99.510316	912828KZ2
3-YEAR		NOTE	6/15/2009	6/15/2012	1.875	1.96	99.753523	912828KX7
9-YEAR	11-MONTH	NOTE	6/15/2009	5/15/2019	3.125	3.99	92.968581	912828KQ2
29-YEAR	11-MONTH	BOND	6/15/2009	5/15/2039	4.25	4.72	92.50169	912810QB7
2-YEAR		NOTE	6/1/2009	5/31/2011	0.875	0.94	99.871675	912828KU3
5-YEAR		NOTE	6/1/2009	5/31/2014	2.25	2.31	99.718283	912828KV1
7-YEAR		NOTE	6/1/2009	5/31/2016	3.25	3.3	99.689717	912828KW9
3-YEAR		NOTE	5/15/2009	5/15/2012	1.375	1.473	99.713432	912828KP4
10-YEAR		NOTE	5/15/2009	5/15/2019	3.125	3.19	99.44721	912828KQ2
30-YEAR		BOND	5/15/2009	5/15/2039	4.25	4.288	99.36198	912810QB7
2-YEAR		NOTE	4/30/2009	4/30/2011	0.875	0.949	99.853739	912828KL3
5-YEAR		TIPS	4/30/2009	4/15/2014	1.25	1.278	100.113235	912828KM1
5-YEAR		NOTE	4/30/2009	4/30/2014	1.875	1.94	99.691687	912828KN9
7-YEAR		NOTE	4/30/2009	4/30/2016	2.625	2.63	99.968223	912828KR0
3-YEAR		NOTE	4/15/2009	4/15/2012	1.375	1.385	99.970714	912828KK5
9-YEAR	9-MONTH	TIPS	4/15/2009	1/15/2019	2.125	1.589	103.325496	912828JX9
9-YEAR	10-MONTH	NOTE	4/15/2009	2/15/2019	2.75	2.95	98.298568	912828KD1
2-YEAR		NOTE	3/31/2009	3/31/2011	0.875	0.949	99.853739	912828KH2
5-YEAR		NOTE	3/31/2009	3/31/2014	1.75	1.849	99.529266	912828KJ8
7-YEAR		NOTE	3/31/2009	3/31/2016	2.375	2.384	99.942292	912828KT6
3-YEAR		NOTE	3/16/2009	3/15/2012	1.375	1.489	99.667005	912828KG4
9-YEAR	11-MONTH	NOTE	3/16/2009	2/15/2019	2.75	3.043	97.504473	912828KD1
29-YEAR	11-MONTH	BOND	3/16/2009	2/15/2039	3.5	3.64	97.456658	912810QA9
2-YEAR		NOTE	3/2/2009	2/28/2011	0.875	0.961	99.830481	912828KE9
5-YEAR		NOTE	3/2/2009	2/28/2014	1.875	1.985	99.479306	912828KF6
7-YEAR		NOTE	3/2/2009	2/29/2016	2.625	2.748	99.22194	912828KS8
3-YEAR		NOTE	2/17/2009	2/15/2012	1.375	1.419	99.871395	912828KC3
10-YEAR		NOTE	2/17/2009	2/15/2019	2.75	2.818	99.411068	912828KD1
30-YEAR		BOND	2/17/2009	2/15/2039	3.5	3.54	99.264139	912810QA9
2-YEAR		NOTE	2/2/2009	1/31/2011	0.875	0.925	99.901394	912828JY7
5-YEAR		NOTE	2/2/2009	1/31/2014	1.75	1.82	99.667162	912828JZ4
20-YEAR		TIPS	1/30/2009	1/15/2029	2.5	2.5	99.063837	912810PZ5
3-YEAR		NOTE	1/15/2009	1/15/2012	1.125	1.2	99.77965	912828KB5
9-YEAR	10-MONTH	NOTE	1/15/2009	11/15/2018	3.75	2.419	111.579767	912828JR2

Source: U.S.Treasury Web Site http://www.treasurydirect.gov/RI/OFNtebnd accessed on July 16, 2009.

Table 1.5 Stripped Coupon Interest on September 25, 2008

Year	Maturity Month	Day	Bid	Ask	Chg	Asked Yield	Year	Maturity Month	Day	Bid	Ask	Chg	Asked Yield
2008	11	15	99.898	99.918	0.001	0.6	2023	8	15	50.039	50.059	-0.487	4.7
2009	2	15	99.478	99.498	-0.068	1.31	2023	11	15	49.424	49.444	-0.489	4.71
2009	5	15	98.979	98.999	-0.056	1.59	2024	2	15	48.815	48.835	-0.529	4.71
2009	8	15	98.473	98.493	-0.146	1.72	2024	5	15	48.286	48.306	-0.532	4.71
2009	11	15	97.982	98.002	-0.194	1.78	2024	8	15	47.746	47.766	-0.553	4.7
2010	2	15	97.487	97.507	-0.236	1.83	2024	11	15	47.194	47.214	-0.555	4.7
2010	5	15	96.879	96.899	-0.277	1.93	2025	2	15	46.797	46.817	-0.408	4.69
2010	8	15	96.294	96.314	-0.318	2	2025	5	15	46.221	46.241	-0.371	4.69
2010	11	15	95.722	95.742	-0.359	2.05	2025	8	15	45.537	45.557	-0.372	4.71
2011	2	15	94.83	94.85	-0.413	2.23	2025	11	15	44.972	44.992	-0.297	4.72
2011	5	15	94.304	94.324	-0.442	2.23	2026	2	15	44.357	44.377	-0.297	4.73
2011	8	15	93.274	93.294	-0.539	2.42	2026	5	15	43.879	43.899	-0.298	4.72
2011	11	15	92.957	92.977	-0.481	2.34	2026	8	15	43.332	43.352	-0.298	4.73
2012	2	15	91.072	91.092	-0.48	2.78	2026	11	15	42.828	42.848	-0.299	4.73
2012	5	15	90.705	90.725	-0.515	2.69	2027	2	15	42.445	42.465	-0.262	4.71
2012	8	15	89.274	89.294	-0.566	2.94	2027	5	15	41.934	41.954	-0.263	4.72
2012	11	15	88.498	88.518	-0.589	2.97	2027	8	15	41.467	41.487	-0.263	4.71
2013	2	15	87.478	87.498	-0.607	3.07	2027	11	15	41.025	41.045	-0.206	4.71
2013	5	15	86.684	86.704	-0.647	3.1	2028	2	15	40.685	40.705	-0.11	4.69
2013	8	15	85.988	86.008	-0.666	3.11	2028	5	15	40.216	40.236	-0.11	4.69
2013	11	15	85.014	85.034	-0.725	3.18	2028	8	15	39.694	39.714	-0.111	4.7
2014	2	15	83.999	84.019	-0.763	3.26	2028	11	15	39.178	39.198	-0.111	4.71
2014	5	15	83.172	83.192	-0.814	3.29	2029	2	15	38.686	38.706	-0.092	4.71
2014	8	15	82.185	82.205	-0.828	3.36	2029	5	15	38.277	38.297	-0.033	4.71
2014	11	15	81.257	81.277	-0.903	3.41	2029	8	15	37.815	37.835	-0.033	4.71
2015	2	15	79.706	79.726	-0.462	3.58	2029	11	15	37.493	37.513	-0.015	4.69
2015	5	15	78.898	78.918	-0.489	3.6	2030	2	15	37.138	37.158	-0.015	4.68
2015	8	15	77.972	77.992	-0.502	3.64	2030	5	15	36.749	36.769	-0.015	4.68
2015	11	15	76.772	76.792	-0.525	3.73	2030	8	15	36.463	36.483	0.063	4.66
2016	2	15	75.885	75.905	-0.538	3.77	2030	11	15	36.084	36.104	0.063	4.66
2016	5	15	74.437	74.457	-0.573	3.9	2031	2	15	35.691	35.711	0.063	4.65
2016	8	15	73.593	73.613	-0.599	3.92	2031	5	15	35.282	35.302	-0.074	4.65
2016	11	15	72.086	72.106	-0.707	4.06	2031	8	15	34.957	34.977	-0.074	4.64
2017	2	15	71.16	71.18	-0.483	4.09	2031	11	15	34.656	34.676	-0.074	4.63
2017	5	15	70.144	70.164	-0.491	4.14	2032	2	15	34.438	34.458	-0.074	4.61
2017	8	15	69.036	69.056	-0.482	4.21	2032	5	15	34.264	34.284	-0.075	4.58
2017	11	15	68.213	68.233	-0.505	4.23	2032	8	15	33.918	33.938	-0.075	4.58
2018	2	15	67.643	67.663	-0.468	4.21	2032	11	15	33.556	33.576	-0.075	4.57
2018	5	15	66.816	66.836	-0.474	4.23	2033	2	15	33.337	33.357	-0.076	4.55
2018	8	15	65.674	65.694	-0.559	4.3	2033	5	15	32.984	33.004	-0.075	4.55
2018	11	15	64.851	64.871	-0.565	4.32	2033	8	15	32.674	32.694	-0.076	4.54
2019	2	15	63.626	63.646	-0.601	4.4	2033	11	15	32.329	32.349	-0.076	4.54
2019	5	15	62.904	62.924	-0.609	4.4	2034	2	15	32.008	32.028	-0.075	4.54
2019	8	15	61.826	61.846	-0.596	4.46	2034	5	15	31.651	31.671	-0.075	4.54
2019	11	15	61.081	61.101	-0.602	4.47	2034	8	15	31.357	31.377	-0.076	4.53
2020	2	15	60.194	60.214	-0.312	4.51	2034	11	15	31.008	31.028	-0.075	4.53
2020	5	15	59.29	59.31	-0.314	4.54	2035	2	15	30.662	30.682	-0.076	4.53
2020	8	15	58.475	58.495	-0.316	4.56	2035	5	15	30.321	30.341	-0.075	4.53
2020	11	15	57.716	57.736	-0.319	4.58	2035	8	15	29.983	30.003	-0.075	4.53
2021	2	15	56.876	56.896	-0.373	4.61	2035	11	15	29.649	29.669	-0.075	4.53
2021	5	15	56.128	56.148	-0.393	4.62	2036	2	15	29.339	29.359	-0.075	4.53
2021	8	15	55.368	55.388	-0.396	4.64	2036	5	15	29.268	29.288	0.161	4.49
2021	11	15	54.649	54.669	-0.416	4.65	2036	8	15	28.865	28.885	0.389	4.5
2022	2	15	53.989	54.009	-0.454	4.66	2036	11	15	28.664	28.684	0.161	4.49
2022	5	15	53.282	53.302	-0.475	4.67	2037	2	15	28.249	28.269	0.384	4.5
2022	8	15	52.599	52.619	-0.477	4.68	2037	5	15	28.212	28.232	0.161	4.47
2022	11	15	51.869	51.889	-0.479	4.7	2037	8	15	27.901	27.921	0.386	4.47
2023	2	15	51.144	51.164	-0.481	4.71	2038	2	15	27.331	27.351	0.23	4.46
2023	5	15	50.606	50.626	-0.484	4.7							

Source: *The Wall Street Journal.*

month T-bills (BOT). In addition, interest rate floaters are issued by financial institutions and corporations, as well as government agencies, such as the government mortgage companies Ginnie Mae, Freddie Mac, and Fannie Mae, within their collateralized mortgage obligations programs.

1.2.3   The Municipal Debt Market

The U.S. federal government issues debt to finance federal government expenses, such as health care and military expenses. Individual municipalities also issue debt independently to finance local projects. For instance, the City of Chicago issued bonds for $983,310,000 in 2003 to pay for an expansion project of its O'Hare International Airport.

The most interesting feature of "muni" bonds is that the interest income from their coupons is tax-exempt. As a consequence, the yield is lower than other regular Treasury notes and bonds, as the latter pay an income that is taxable according to investors' income tax rates.

1.3   THE MONEY MARKET

When we speak of the money market, we refer to the market for short-term borrowing and lending. Banks and financial institutions have various means of borrowing and lending at any point in time. The entries in Table 1.2 summarize these channels.

1.3.1   Federal Funds Rate

Banks and other financial institutions must keep some amount of capital within the Federal Reserve. Balances at the Federal Reserve yield a small rate of return, which was in fact zero until September 2008. It is in the interest of banks to maintain their reserves as close to the limit as possible. Banks with a reserve surplus may then lend some of their reserves to banks with a reserve deficit. The effective Federal funds rate is the size-weighted average rate of interest that banks charge to each other to lend or borrow reserves at the Federal Reserve. Chapter 7 describes this market in more detail.

1.3.2   Eurodollar Rate

The Eurodollar rate is the rate of interest on a dollar deposit in a European-based bank. These are short-term deposits, ranging from 3 months to one year. In particular, the 90-day Eurodollar rate has become a standard reference to gauge the conditions of the interbank market. For instance, the market for Eurodollar futures and options, financial derivatives traded at the Chicago Mercantile Exchange that allow financial institutions to bet on or hedge against the future evolution of the Eurodollar rate (see Chapter 6), is among the largest and most liquid derivative markets in the world.

1.3.3   LIBOR

LIBOR stands for London Interbank Offer Rate. The British Bankers Association publishes daily the LIBOR rates. These rates correspond to the average interest rate that banks charge to each other for short-term uncollateralized borrowing in the London market. The rates available are very similar to the Eurodollar rates (see Table 1.2). LIBOR is however one of the most important benchmark rates, used often as the reference index in the large over-the-counter derivatives market. As explained in Chapter 5, interest rate swaps, the single largest derivatives market (see Table 1.1), use LIBOR rates as the reference rates to determine the size of cash flows implied by a contract.

1.4 THE REPO MARKET

The last entry in the top row of Table 1.2 reports the repo and reverse repo rates. The repo market plays an important role in the fixed income industry, as it is used by traders to borrow and lend cash on a collateralized basis. Because borrowing is collateralized, it is considered a safer way to lend cash, and this contributed to its growth over the years, making the repo market one of the most important sources of financing for traders. First of all, the formal definition:

Definition 1.2 *A* ***repurchase agreement (repo)*** *is an agreement to sell some securities to another party and buy them back at a fixed date and for a fixed amount. The price at which the security is bought back is greater than the selling price and the difference implies an interest rate called the* repo rate.

A ***reverse repo*** *is the opposite transaction, namely, it is the purchase of the security for cash with the agreement to sell it back to the original owner at a predetermined price, determined, once again, by the repo rate.*

The best way to understand a repo transaction is to consider it as collateralized borrowing. A trader entering into a repo transaction with a repo dealer is borrowing cash (the sale price) in exchange for the security, which is held hostage by the repo dealer. If at the end of the repo term the trader were to default, the repo dealer could sell the security and be made whole. The following example illustrates the trade:

■ EXAMPLE 1.1

Suppose that a trader on September 18, 2007 (time t) wants to take a long position until a later time T on a given U.S. security, such as the 30-year Treasury bond. Let P_t denote the (invoice) price of the bond at time t. Figure 1.4 provides a schematic representation of the repo transaction: At time t, the trader buys the bond at market price P_t and enters a repurchase agreement with the repo dealer. Hence, the trader delivers the bond as collateral to the repo dealer and receives the cash to purchase the bond. In fact, the repo dealer typically gives something less than the market price of the bond, the difference being called a *haircut*. At time t the trader and the repo dealer agree that the trader will return back the amount borrowed, $(P_t - haircut)$, plus the repo rate.

What happens then at time T? At time T, the trader gets back the bond from the repo dealer, sells the bond in the market to get P_T and pays $(P_t - haircut)$ plus the repo interest to the dealer. The repo interest is computed as the repo rate agreed at time t times the time between t and T. For instance, if n days pass between the two

Figure 1.4   Schematic Repo Transaction

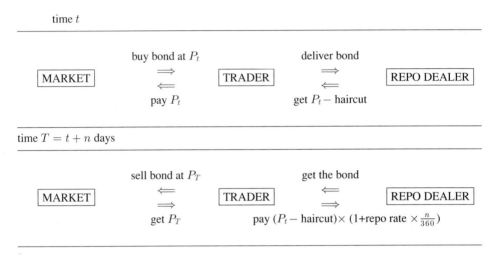

dates, we have

$$\text{Repo interest} = \frac{n}{360} \times \text{Repo rate} \times (P_t - \text{haircut}) \qquad (1.1)$$

where the denumerator "360" stems from the day count convention in the repo market.

The profit to the trader is then $P_T - P_t$–Repo interest. In percentage terms, the trader only put up the haircut (the margin) as own capital. Hence, the return on capital is

$$\text{Return on capital for trader} = \frac{P_T - P_t - \text{Repo interest}}{\text{Haircut}}$$

The position is highly leveraged and entails quite large risks. The case study in Section 3.7 of Chapter 3 discusses the risk and return of such leveraged transactions.

The term T of the repo transaction is decided at initiation, i.e., time t. In particular, most repurchase agreements are for a very short term, mainly overnight. However, as shown in Table 1.2, longer-term agreements reach 30 days or even more. Recall also that the repo rate is decided at time t.

Between t and T the trader (who is long the bond) earns the interest that accrues on the bond. Because the trader has to pay the repo rate during this period, setting up the repo transaction tends to generate a positive or negative stream of payments, depending on whether the interest earned on the bond is above or below the repo interest. We say that the trade implies a *positive carry* if the interest on the bond is above the repo rate and *negative carry* if the interest on the bond is below the repo rate.

1.4.1 General Collateral Rate and Special Repos

Other important definitions and characteristics of repo markets are as follows:

1. **General Collateral Rate (GCR)**: This is the repo rate on most Treasury securities, such as the off-the-run Treasuries. Because most Treasury securities have similar

characteristics in terms of liquidity, market participants require the same interest rate for collateralized borrowing.

2. **Special Repo Rate:** At times, one particular Treasury security is in high demand and hence the repo rate on that security falls to a level substantially below the GCR. As an example, on-the-run Treasury securities typically are "on special," in the sense that the repo rate charged for collateralized borrowing is smaller than the GCR.

Why does a security that is in high demand entail a lower (special) repo rate? To understand the logic, consider the next example, which entails a reverse repo, whose rates are also quoted in Table 1.2.

■ **EXAMPLE 1.2**

Consider a trader who thinks a particular bond, such as the on-the-run 30-year Treasury bond, is overpriced and wants to take a bet that its price will decline in the future. If the trader does not have the bond to sell outright, then he or she can enter into a reverse repo with a repo dealer to obtain the bond to sell. More specifically, in a reverse repo, the trader essentially (A) borrows the security from the dealer; (B) sells it in the market; and (C) posts cash collateral with the dealer. Figure 1.5 shows a schematic representation of the trade.

The trader is now *lending* money to the repo dealer against the bond. Therefore, the trader is now entitled to receive the repo rate. However, the trader, who wants to speculate on the decrease in the bond price, is happy to forgo part or all of the repo rate in order to get hold of the bond. If many traders want to undertake the same strategy of shorting that particular bond, then that bond is in high demand, and the repo rate for *that* bond declines below the general collateral rate. That bond is said to be "on speacial." The profit from the reverse repo transaction is then

$$\text{Profit} = (P_t - P_T) + \text{Repo interest}$$

where the repo interest is computed as in Equation 1.1, namely, the amount deposited with the repo dealer (P_t) times the repo rate times $n/360$, where n is the number of days between the two trading dates t and T.

As mentioned, the repo market has grown steadily over the years. Table 1.6 shows the average *daily* amount outstanding in these contracts.[3] Since borrowing is collateralized by the value of the asset, the repo rate is lower than other borrowing rates available to banks, such as LIBOR. Figure 1.6 plots the time series of the one month and the three month T-Bill, Repo and LIBOR rates from May 1991 to April 2008. As it can be seen, for both maturities, the safe T-bill rate is the smallest and the LIBOR is the highest of the three rates, as borrowing and lending at the LIBOR rate are riskier as the loans are uncollateralized.

We cover additional details regarding the repo market and its uses by market participants in a number of case studies. For instance, in Chapters 3 and 4 we discuss the use of repurchase agreements to increase portfolio leverage, in Chapter 5 we illustrate the use of the repo market to carry out a swap spread arbitrage trade, and in Chapter 16 we use

---

[3] The amount outstanding of repurchase agreements need not equal the amount outstanding of reverse repurchase agreements, as each column reflects the size of collateralized borrowing or lending of security dealers only, and not the whole universe of repo counterparties.

Figure 1.5   Reverse Repo Transaction

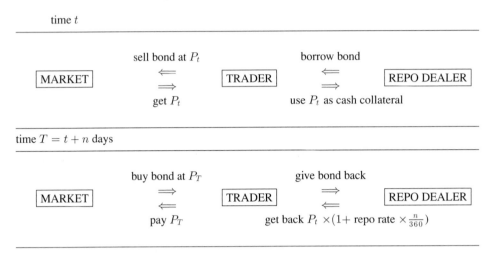

repo transactions to implement a relative value arbitrage trade on the yield curve through a dynamic long/short strategy.

1.4.2   What if the T-bond Is Not Delivered?

Consider the reverse repurchase agreement displayed in Figure 1.5. At maturity of the repo contract (time T), the trader must return the bond to the repo dealer in exchange for the cash amount $P_t \times (1 + \frac{n}{360} \times$ repo rate$)$. What happens if the trader does not return the security? Such an occurrence is called a **fail**, and up to May, 2009 such a failure to deliver would have simply implied that the repo dealer in this example would have kept the cash received, P_t, plus the repo interest. The cost for failing to deliver for the trader was simply to forgo the repo interest. The financial crisis of 2007 - 2009 led the Federal Reserve to lower the reference Fed funds rate to close to zero, and repo rates also fell to essentially zero. When the repo rate is zero, however, the cost for a trader to fail to deliver the bond is very small, as the trader may keep the bond itself if this bond is particularly valuable. The financial crisis of 2007 - 2009 generated a 'flight-to-quality,' meaning that investors dumped all risky securities and strongly demanded safe U.S. Treasuries, as the demand for safe collateral increased. This increase in demand for U.S. Treasuries made it difficult or costly for traders who have short positions to find the bonds to return to their counterparties in the reverse repo transactions. Given the small cost of failing to deliver, the number of fails spiked in the last quarter of 2008. Figure 1.7 reports the cumulative weekly failures of delivering Treasury securities, in millions of dollars, by primary dealers, and the 2008 spike is clearly visible. The figure however also shows that sustained periods of delivery fails occurred in the past as well, such as in 2001 and in 2003. We should mention that a spike in delivery fails can also be due to a snowball effect, as the failure to deliver from a security dealer implies that another security dealer who was counting on the delivery to

Table 1.6   Financing by U.S. Government Securities Dealers

| | Reverse Repurchase and Repurchase Agreements (1) Average Daily Amount Outstanding 1981 - 2006 ($ Billions) | | |
	Reverse Repurchase	Repurchase	Total
1981	46.7	65.4	112.1
1982	75.1	95.2	170.3
1983	81.7	102.4	184.1
1984	112.4	132.6	245
1985	147.9	172.9	320.8
1986	207.7	244.5	452.2
1987	275	292	567
1988	313.6	309.7	623.3
1989	383.2	398.2	781.4
1990	377.1	413.5	790.5
1991	417	496.6	913.6
1992	511.1	628.2	1,139.3
1993	594.1	765.6	1,359.7
1994	651.2	825.9	1,477.1
1995	618.8	821.5	1,440.3
1996	718.1	973.7	1,691.8
1997	883	1,159.0	2,042.0
1998	1,111.4	1,414.0	2,525.5
1999	1,070.1	1,361.0	2,431.1
2000	1,093.3	1,439.6	2,532.9
2001	1,311.3	1,786.5	3,097.7
2002	1,615.7	2,172.4	3,788.1
2003	1,685.4	2,355.7	4,041.1
2004	2,078.5	2,868.2	4,946.7
2005	2,355.2	3,288.4	5,643.6
2006	2,225.2	3,388.3	5,613.5

(1) Figures cover financing involving U.S. government, federal
agency, and federal agency MBS securities.

Source: Federal Reserve Bank of New York
obtained from SIFMA web site: *http://www.sifma.net/story.asp?id=1176*

Figure 1.6   Short-Term Rates: 1991 - 2008

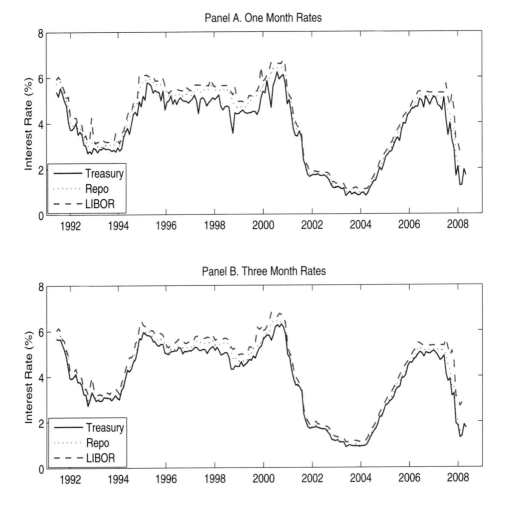

Source: Federal Reserve Board, British Bankers Association, Bloomberg.

Figure 1.7   Primary Dealers Fails to Deliver: 1990 to 2009

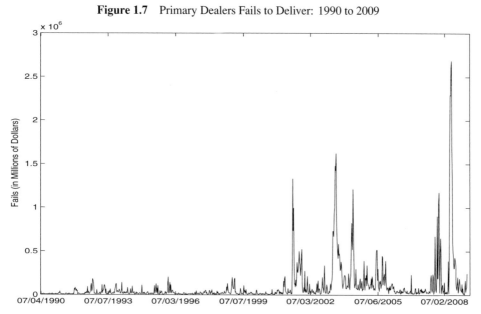

Source: Federal Reserve Bank of New York.

settle his or her own obligation may be unable to deliver as well, and so on, generating a domino effect.[4]

Starting May 1, 2009, the Federal Reserve imposed a penalty charge of 3% over its Fed funds rate for failing to deliver the bonds in the repo transactions the Federal Reserve conducts daily in its open market operations (see Chapter 7 for details on the Fed conduct of monetary policy). In addition, the Federal Reserve has been encouraging market participants to adopt a similar charge as part of best practices in repo market transactions. An interesting outcome of such a penalty on a failure to deliver is that on May 1, 2009, the repo rate for some Treasury securities that were on special became negative.[5] How is it possible that an interest rate is negative? The reason is that a trader who has to deliver a given Treasury security to a conterparty is willing to pay to get hold of the security rather than incurring the penalty. In particular, the trader can enter into a reverse repo with another repo dealer at a negative repo rate to obtain the Treasury security to deliver to the original counterparty.

1.5 THE MORTGAGE BACKED SECURITIES MARKET AND ASSET-BACKED SECURITIES MARKET

One of the interesting patterns evident in Figure 1.1 is the dramatic growth experienced by the mortgage backed securities market, which hit the $8.9 trillion mark by the end of 2008. Chapter 8 describes this market in detail as well as the type of securities that are exchanged

---

[4]See the "Guide to FR2004 Settlement Fails Data," Federal Reserve of New York. See also the article by Michael J. Fleming and Kenneth D. Garbade, "When the Back Office Moved to the Front Burner: Settlement Fails in the Treasury Market after 9/11," *Federal Reserve Bank of New York Economic Policy Review*, November 2002.
[5]See Bloomberg.com Web site http://www.bloomberg.com/apps/news?pid=20601009&sid=a85sg4IKcjCM.

in it. However, as a brief introduction, the source of the mortgage-backed securities market is relatively simple: homeowners across the U.S. finance their homes through mortgages, issued by local savings & loans, thrifts, and other banks. When a bank issues a mortgage to a homeowner, the mortgage rests on the asset side of the bank's balance sheet. The mortgage is a fixed income instrument: It is a promise from the homeowner to make certain cash payments in the future. These cash payments are affected by numerous events, discussed further in Chapter 8, which make them risky for the bank. In particular, if a local bank provides mortgages to a local community only, it is subject to the risk that these homeowners may all default at the same time because of local geographical factors. For instance, if the local community is highly specialized in a particular industrial sector, and the latter goes into an economic crisis, one could expect large layoffs in that community, which in turn would increase the probability that homeowners will default on their mortgage payment obligations. Similarly, if the house prices of that particular community decline, the collateral in the mortgage contract declines, and the local bank is then in a more risky position than before.

Mortgage backed securities allow a bank to diversify this risk. The idea is to resell its mortgages, now on the asset side of the bank, for cash. In order to improve the liquidity and to mitigate credit risk, the market evolved into one in which *many* similar mortgages are pooled together to form a large collateral of assets. These assets, which have better characteristics in terms of diversification of risk, make up the collateral on debt securities issued to individual investors, called mortgage backed securities. In summary, an investor in a mortgage backed security obtains a legal claim to the cash flows (coupons) that are paid by the original homeowner.

The mortgage backed securities trade in the market. For instance, in Table 1.2, the heading "30 Y MBS" reports the prices of popular mortgage-backed securities, those issued by Ginnie Mae (GNMN 6.0), Freddie Mac (GOLD 6.0) and Fannie Mae (FNMA 6), the three largest players in the mortgage-backed securities market. From an investment perspective, a large part of the mortgage-backed securities market is considered default free, because these three big players – Ginnie, Freddie and Fannie – have an implicit or explicit backing of the full faith of the U.S. government. Indeed, while Ginnie Mae has always been a government entity, Fannie and Freddie entered conservatorship in September 2008, which implies that their own debt securities but especially their mortgage-backed securities are default free. Still, compared to Treasury debt securities mortgage-backed securities have many peculiarities regarding the timing of promised cash flows, which may vary unexpectedly due to changes in interest rates, or changes in housing prices, or a severe recession. These unexpected variations in cash flows make mortgage-backed securities risky and, for this reasons, such securities typically offer an additional return on investment, compared to Treasury securities. Chapter 8 discusses this market in more detail.

Similarly to the mortgage backed securities market, the asset backed securities market involves the issuance of debt instruments to investors, collateralized by various types of loans, such as auto loans, credit cards, and the like. The market is smaller in size, as shown in Table 1.1.

Table 1.7   Borrowing rates for firm A and B

	Firm A	Firm B
Fixed Rate	15%	12%
Floating Rate	LIBOR + 3%	LIBOR + 2%

1.6   THE DERIVATIVES MARKET

Table 1.2 also reports quotes of several derivative securities. As show in Table 1.1, the interest rate derivatives market is huge and it has been growing steadily for the past three decades, as illustrated in Figure 1.2. Chapters 5 and 6 explore these markets in more detail, and provide some early examples of uses of derivative contracts for corporations and traders. Additional examples discussing the fair valuation and the risk of derivative securities are offered throughout the book, as we explore the modeling devices applied by financial institutions to price and hedge these securities.

The swap contract is the largest market of all. While future chapters discuss the pricing, hedging and the risk involved in swaps, it is informative at this point to see the economic need that led to the creation of this market at the beginning of the 1980s.

1.6.1   Swaps

Interest rate swap contracts were introduced in the early 1980s to take advantage of some apparent arbitrage opportunity that was surfacing in the corporate bond market. The following is a stylized example of common situations occurring at that time.

■ **EXAMPLE 1.3**

Consider the following situation. There are two firms, Firm A and Firm B. Firm A wants to raise $M = \$10$ million using fixed rate coupon bonds, while Firm B wants to raise $M = \$10$ million using floating rate coupon bonds. Let the market rates available to the two firms be the ones in Table 1.7. That is, Firm A can either borrow at a fixed coupon rate of 15% or at a floating rate with coupon linked to the six-month LIBOR rate plus 3%. Firm B, instead, can borrow fixed at 12% or floating at LIBOR + 2%. Note that the rates available to B are always lower than the ones available to A, reflecting a difference in credit risk.

An investment bank observing the rates in Table 1.7 may offer the following deal to the two firms.

First, Firm A issues a floating rate bond at LIBOR + 3%, while Firm B issues a fixed rate bond at 12%. Second, the two firms swap coupon payments. In particular, they could consider the following swap deal:

- Firm A pays B a fixed rate payment at 11% per year; and

- Firm B pays A a floating rate payment at LIBOR.

Figure 1.8   A Swap Deal

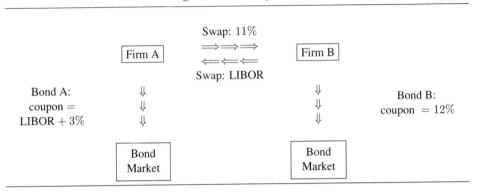

Consider now the net cash flow from each of these firms when we take together the bond issuance and the swap deal. For every future coupon date, we have:

$$\text{Firm A Pays}: \quad \underbrace{(\text{LIBOR} + 3\%)}_{\text{to market}} + \underbrace{11\% - \text{LIBOR}}_{\text{swap deal}} = 14\%$$

$$\text{Firm B Pays}: \quad \underbrace{12\%} \quad \underbrace{-11\% + \text{LIBOR}} = \text{LIBOR} + 1\%$$

Figure 1.8 shows the cash flows in every period. Overall, we observe that Firm A pays 14% instead of 15%, which was its fixed coupon market rate. Similarly, Firm B pays LIBOR +1% instead of LIBOR +2%, which was its market rate. Both firms then gain from entering this deal.

The early swaps managed to arbitrage some relative price discrepancy that existed between floating rates and fixed rates. The notion was that if a spread exists because of the risk of default, it should be the same across floating and fixed coupon bonds. The difference in spreads between the two firms across asset classes, floating and fixed coupon bonds, generates the possibility of a trade. How can we compute the gains from a swap trade? The size of the pie that the two firms can divide through a swap is given by the difference in comparative advantage implicit in Table 1.7. In other words, the spread on the fixed coupon is 3%(= 15% − 12%) while the spread on floating coupon is only 1%(= (LIBOR +3%) − (LIBOR +1%)). The difference in spreads provide the total gains that can be split between the two firms:

$$\text{Gains from trade} = \text{Fixed spread} - \text{Floating spread} = 3\% - 1\% = 2\% \qquad (1.2)$$

In the example we divided the gains from trade equally between the two firms. In reality, the exact split depends on the relative contractual strength of each firm: Firms with higher creditworthiness would tend to get a higher coupon.

In addition, some part of the gain would also accrue to the investment bank that brokers the deal.

The initial spur to swap trading was due to exploit arbitrage opportunities. At that time, investment banks would also reap substantial profits from relatively large spreads. However, as we will discuss in more detail in Chapter 5 and elsewhere, the growth in the swap market came about because of the extreme usefulness of swaps as a convenient means for cash management and risk management. Financial institutions, corporations, and even governments use swaps (a) to change the sensitivity of their cash flows to fluctuations in interest rates; (b) to alter the timing of their payments and revenues; (c) or even simply for investment purposes within complex trading strategies.

1.6.2 Futures and Forwards

Table 1.2 also reports the quotes of futures contracts, for instance, the "90 Day Eurodollar Futures,"Eurodollar,futures the "Fed Funds Futures," and the "10-year Treasury Note Futures." Futures contracts, discussed in detail in Chapter 6, are contracts according to which two counterparties decide to exchange a security, or cash, or a commodity, at a prespecified time in the future for a price agreed upon today. The quote represents the price at which delivery will take place in the future. For interest rate futures, such as Eurodollar or Fed funds, the quoted "price" is given by "100− futures rate." For instance, the 90-day Eurodollar futures contract with maturity "December," quoted at 95.07 in Table 1.2, establishes the rate today, $4.93\% = 100 - 95.07$, at which the party long the futures could deposit dollars in the Eurodollar market in December for the following 90 days.[6] The futures market thus provides a convenient way for market participants to lock-in a future interest rate: For instance, a corporation that has a large receivable due in December can exploit the futures market to lock in the rate (4.93%) at which it can park the sum of money for the following 90 days. In addition, the futures market is often used by market participants to gauge the market expectation about future movement in interest rates. Important in futures contracts is the fact that either counterparty may be called to make payments in the future.

Table 1.2 does not report quotes of forward contracts, although we see from Table 1.1 that forward contracts make up a sizable share of the fixed income market. Forward contracts are similar to futures contracts, in that two counterparties agree today that they will exchange a security (or cash) in the future at a price that is decided today. Just like futures contracts, forward contracts allow institutions to lock in interest rates for the future. Unlike futures, forward contracts are not traded on regulated exchanges but only on the over-the-counter market. Chapters 5 and 6 describe these contracts and delve into the differences between futures and forwards.

1.6.3 Options

Table 1.2 does not provide any quotes for interest rate options, as we obtained this table from the BTTM screen from a Bloomberg terminal, which only reports U.S. Treasury and money market rates. But options contracts are a vital part of the fixed income market. Table 1.1 shows that indeed the options' market is quite larger than the futures and forward markets. In addition, options are implicitly embedded in several other securities, such as callable bonds, mortgage backed securities, and other types of structured notes. But first of all:

What is an option?

---

[6]In fact, this futures is cash settled, so the deposit does not actually need to take place. See Chapter 6.

Intuitively, an option is the financial equivalent of an insurance contract: It is a contract according to which the option buyer, who purchases the insurance, receives a payment from the option's seller, who sold the insurance, only if some interest rate scenario occurs in the future. For instance, a corporation that issues a floating rate bond – a bond whose coupon is tied to the level of a short-term floating rate – may be worried about an interest rate hike in the future, a scenario that may drain too much financial resources from the coporation. The corporation may purchase insurance against such scenarios, by purchasing a financial option, called a cap, that pays only if the floating reference interest rate increases above some cutoff point, called the strike rate. This contract would be a good hedge for the firm against interest rate hikes, because, if the interest rate does increase above the strike rate, then the option's seller must pay the corporation a contractually agreed-upon cash flow, which the corporation can use to pay its own liability to its bond holders.

Many options are implicit in many securities. A homeowner who financed the purchase of his or her home using a adjustable rate mortgage (ARM), for instance, most likely also bought (probably unknowingly) an option against an increase in interest rates. The reason is that standard adjustable rate mortgages contain a provision stating that the maximum rate the homeowner will have to pay over the life of the mortgage is capped at some level. Therefore, the loan contract is equivalent to a standard floating rate loan contract plus an option that pays if interest rates become too high, just like in the example of the corporation above. Similarly, a homeowner who financed the purchase of his or her home using a fixed rate mortgage also bought an option to pay back the mortgage whenever he or she likes. In particular, homeowners pay back loans when the interest rate declines. The bank making the mortgage implicitly sold the option to the homeowner, and the option premium is embedded in the mortgage rate. Considering that the mortgage backed securities market has become the dominant fixed income market in the U.S. (its value as of December 2008 is about $9 trillion, compared to only $6 trillion of the U.S. debt), the understanding of the impact of options on fixed income instruments has never been more important.

1.7   ROADMAP OF FUTURE CHAPTERS

In this chapter we described some of the major fixed income markets. Starting with the next chapter, we begin to analyze each market in much more detail. In Chapter 2 we cover the basics of fixed income instruments, that is, the notion of a discount, of an interest rate, and how we compute the fair valuation of Treasury bills, notes, and bonds. At the end of the chapter we also show how we can use this information to obtain the price of some simple structured securities, such as inverse floaters, which are popular securities if an investor wishes to bet on a decrease in interest rates. Fixed income securities present many risks for investors, even if they are issued or guaranteed by the U.S. government and therefore they are default free. Indeed, long-term bonds, for instance, may suffer strong capital losses in response to a generalized increase in interest rates. Chapters 3 and 4 discuss the types of risk embedded in fixed income securities, the issue of risk measurement, as well as the practice of risk management, such as asset-liability management and immunization strategies. Chapters 5 and 6 cover popular fixed income derivatives, such as forward rates, swaps, futures, and options, and their uses by market participants. Chapter 7 links the fixed income market to the real economy. In particular, we talk about monetary policy, economic growth, and inflation. In this context, we also discuss the market for TIPS, the inflation-protected debt securities. Finally, Chapter 8 discusses the residential mortgage backed securities market, in terms of the types of securities as well as their riskiness from an investment perspective. This chapter concludes the first part of the book, which aims at providing some basic notions of fixed income securities.

Chapter 9 begins the second part of the book, which concerns the fair valuation of derivative securities by no arbitrage. In particular, we begin with simple, one-period binomial trees to explain the relations that have to exist between any pair of fixed income securities. In this chapter we also introduce a popular pricing methodology called risk neutral pricing. Chapter 10 expands the concepts of one-period binomial trees to multiple periods, and discusses the issue of dinamic hedging, the standard methodology of hedging a risk exposure by rebalancing the portfolio over time as the interest rate changes. Chapter 11 applies the methodology illustrated in the two earlier chapters to real-world securities. In particular, it covers some popular models for the pricing of fixed income instruments, as well as their estimation using real data. These concepts are further developed in Chapter 12, which details the pricing and hedging of an important class of derivatives, called American options. Such options are implicitly embedded in numerous debt securities, from callable bonds to mortgage backed securities. Chapter 13 illustrates a powerful methodology for valuing and hedging complicated securities, namely, the Monte Carlo simulations methodology. This methodology involves using computers to simulate interest rate paths and price paths and then using those simulated quantities to compute current prices and hedge ratios. We apply this methodology to real world securities, such as corridor notes, ammortizing index swaps, mortgage backed securities, and collateralized debt obbligations. This chapter concludes the second part of the book.

The third part of the book is mathematically more advanced, and some familiarity with advanced calculus is required. In particular, Chapter 14 introduces continuous time methodologies, the notion of a Brownian motion, and Ito's lemma. We apply these continuous time methodologies and the rules of no arbitrage in Chapter 15 to compute the fair valuation of Treasury notes and bonds, as well as derivative securities, such as options. Compared to the second part of the book, which also accomplishes similar goals, the concepts discussed in this part of the text are more realistic, and moreover provide analytical formulas for the pricing and hedging of numerous securities, a very convenient property for traders who are pressed for time. Chapter 16 discusses the notion of dynamic hedging, that is, the practice by market participants of frequently rebalancing their portfolios to hedge their risk exposure. Chapter 17 introduces the notion of risk neutral pricing in continuous time models. In addition, we develop for this class of models the Monte Carlo simulation approach to pricing and hedging securities, a methodology widely used by market participants. In well-functioning markets, any risk embedded in fixed income securities should be compensated for by a risk premium on its rate of return, either through a high coupon or a low purchasing price. The link between risk and return of fixed income securities is the object of Chapter 18. In particular, we discuss the fact that if a security is providing an above-market coupon or rate of return, then most likely this security is exposed to some risk, which perhaps is not made completely explicit. To make this point clearer, we discuss a famous case involving a special swap between Procter & Gamble and the investment bank Bankers Trust. Finally, Chapters 19 to 22 cover more advanced models for fixed income security pricing. These chapters discuss several examples in which models are applied to real world securities, and draw some distinctions among them.

1.8   SUMMARY

In this chapter we covered the following topics:

1. Arbitrage strategies: These are strategies that cost nothing to enter into, and provide sure money within a certain time. In well-functioning markets we should not expect arbitrage strategies to persist for a long time. Indeed, pure arbitrage strategies are rare in the market. The rules of no arbitrage determine the relative pricing across fixed income securities and explain their high correlation.

2. U.S. Treasury market: The U.S. issues four types of securities: short-maturity T-bills, medium-maturity T-notes, long-maturity T-bonds, and TIPS, the inflation-protected securities. The size of the U.S. debt market is no longer dominant in fixed income markets, as other markets became even larger, notably the mortgage backed securities market and the derivatives market.

3. Money markets and money markets rates: This market is the source of short-term borrowing by financial and non financial institutions. The main money market rates are the commercial paper rate, LIBOR, and the Federal funds rate. The LIBOR rate, the rate at which banks in London borrow from each other on an uncollateralized basis, is the main reference rate in numerous derivative securities.

4. Repurchase agreements and the repo rate: In collateralized borrowing between two counterparties, the repo rate is the borrowing or lending rate within a repurcahse agreement. Because the borrowing is collateralized, the rate is lower than the LIBOR rate, for instance.

5. Mortgage backed securities market: This is the largest debt market in United States. Mortgage backed securities are collateralized by pools of residential and non residential mortgages and sold to investors who then receive claims to the mortgages coupons. These securities present numerous additional risks for investors compared to Treasury securities.

6. Swaps market: A swap is a contract according to which two counterparties agree to exchange cash flows in the future. This market is very large in size, and although considered a derivative market, its sheer size makes it equivalent to a primary market, in the sense that the prices of swaps are really not derived from those of other securities, but rather they depend on the relative size of demand and supply of these contracts by market participants.

CHAPTER 2

BASICS OF FIXED INCOME SECURITIES

2.1 DISCOUNT FACTORS

Receiving a dollar today is not the same as receiving it in a month or in a year. There are numerous reasons why people would like to have money today rather than in the future. For one, money today can be put in a safe place (a bank or under the mattress) until tomorrow, while the opposite is not easily doable. That is, money in hands gives its holder the option to use it however he or she desires, including transferring it to the future through a deposit or an investment. This option has a value on its own. If we agree that households and investors value $1 today more than $1 in the future the question is then how much $1 in the future is worth in today's money. The value of what $1 in the future would be in today's money is called the discount factor. The notion of discount factors is at the heart of fixed income securities.

It is easiest to introduce the concept by looking at a concrete example. The U.S. government, as with most governments, needs to borrow money from investors to finance its expenses. As discussed in Chapter 1, the government issues a number of securities, such as Treasury bills, notes, and bonds, to investors, receiving money today in exchange for money in the future. The U.S. Treasury is extremely unlikely to default on its obligations, and thus the relation between purchase price and payoff of U.S. Treasury securities reveals the market time value of money, that is, the exchange rate between money today and money in the future. Example 2.1 illustrates this point.

■ **EXAMPLE 2.1**

On August 10, 2006 the Treasury issued 182-day Treasury bills. The issuance market price was $97.477 for $100 of face value.[1] That is, on August 10, 2006, investors were willing to buy for $97.477 a government security that would pay $100 on February 8, 2007. This Treasury bill would not make any other payment between the two dates. Thus, the ratio between purchase price and the payoff, $0.97477 = \$97.477/\$100$, can be considered the market-wide discount factor between the two dates August 10, 2006 and February 8, 2007. That is, market participants were willing to exchange 0.97477 dollars on the first date for 1 dollar six months later.

Definition 2.1 *The* **discount factor** *between two dates, t and T, provides the term of exchange between a given amount of money at t versus a (certain) amount of money at a later date T. We denote the discount factor between these two dates by $Z(t, T)$.*

In the above example, the two dates are $t = $ August 10, 2006 and $T = $ February 08, 2007. The discount factor is $Z(t, T) = 0.97477$.

In short, the discount factor $Z(t, T)$ records the time value of money between t and T. Since it is a value (what is the value today of $1 in the future), it is essentially a price, describing how much money somebody is willing to pay today in order to have $1 in the future. In this sense, the notion of a discount factor is un-ambiguous. In contrast, as we shall see below, the related notion of an interest rate is not un-ambiguous, as it depends on compounding frequency, for instance. Exactly because discount factors unambiguously represent a price – an exchange rate between money today versus money tomorrow – they are at the heart of fixed income securities analysis. In the following sections we describe their characteristics in more detail.

2.1.1 Discount Factors across Maturities

Definition 2.1 and Example 2.1 highlight that the discount factor at some date t (e.g., August 10, 2006) depends on its maturity T (e.g., February 8, 2007). If we vary the maturity T, making it longer or shorter, the discount factor varies as well. In fact, for the same reason that investors value $1 today more than $1 in six months, they also value $1 in three months more than $1 in six months. This can be seen, once again, from the prices of U.S. Treasury securities.

■ **EXAMPLE 2.2**

On August 10, 2006 the U.S. government also issued 91-day bills with a maturity date of November 9, 2006. The price was $98.739 for $100 of face value. Thus, denoting again $t = $ August 10, 2006, now $T_1 = $ November 9, 2006, and $T_2 = $ February 8, 2007, we find that the discount factor $Z(t, T_1) = 0.98739$, which is higher than $Z(t, T_2) = 0.97477$.

---

[1] These data are obtained from the Web site http://www.treasurydirect.gov/RI/OFBills, accessed on August 22, 2006.

This example highlights an important property of discount factors. Because it is always the case that market participants prefer \$1 today to \$1 in the future, the following is true:

Fact 2.1 *At any given time t, the discount factor is lower, the longer the maturity T. That is, given two dates T_1 and T_2 with $T_1 < T_2$, it is always the case that*

$$Z(t, T_1) \geq Z(t, T_2) \tag{2.1}$$

The opposite relation $Z(t, T_1) < Z(t, T_2)$ would in fact imply a somewhat curious behavior on the part of investors. For instance, in the example above in which $T_1 =$ November 9, 2006 and $T_2 =$ February 8, 2007, if $Z(t, T_1)$ was lower than $Z(t, T_2) = 0.97477$, it would imply that investors would be willing to give up \$97.477 today in order to receive \$100 in six months, but *not* in order to receive the same amount three months earlier. In other words, it implies that investors prefer to have \$100 in six months rather than in three months, violating the principle that agents prefer to have a sum of money earlier rather than later. Moreover, a violation of Relation 2.1 also generates an arbitrage opportunity, which we would not expect to last for long in well functioning financial markets (see Exercise 1). In Chapter 5 we elaborate on this topic, showing also that a violation of Relation 2.1 amounts to the assumption that future nominal interest rates be negative.

2.1.2   Discount Factors over Time

A second important characteristic of discount factors is that they are not constant over time, even while keeping constant the time-to-maturity $T - t$, that is, the interval of time between the two dates t and T in the discount factor $Z(t, T)$. As time goes by, the time value of money changes. For instance, the U.S. Treasury issued a 182-day bill on $t_1 =$ August 26, 2004, with maturity $T_2 =$ February 24, 2005, for a price of \$99.115. This price implies a discount factor on that date equal to $Z(t_1, T_1) = 0.99115$. This value is much higher than the discount factor with the same time to maturity (six months) two years later, on August 10, 2006, which we found equal to 0.97477.

Figure 2.1 plots three discounts factors over time, from January 1953 to June 2008.[2] The top solid line is the 3-month discount factor, the middle dotted line is the 1-year discount factor, and bottom dashed line is the 3-year discount factor. First, note that indeed on each date in the sample, the discount factor with shorter time to maturity is always higher than the discount factor with longer time to maturity. Second, the variation of discount factors over time is rather substantial. For instance, the 3-year discount factor is as low as 0.6267 in August 1981, and as high as 0.95 in June 1954 and in June 2003.

Why do discount factors vary over time? Although this is a topic of a later chapter, it is useful to provide here the most obvious, and intuitive, reason. Figure 2.2 plots the time series of expected inflation from 1953 to 2008.[3] Comparing the discount factor series

---

[2]Data excerpted from CRSP (Fama Bliss discount bonds) ¤2009 Center for Research in Security Prices (CRSP), The University of Chicago Booth School of Business. We discuss methodologies to estimate discount factors from bond data in Section 2.4.2 and in the Appendix.

[3]The expected inflation series is computed as the predicted annual inflation rate resulting from a rolling regression of inflation on its 12 lags. We present more details in Chapter 7.

Figure 2.1 Discount Factors

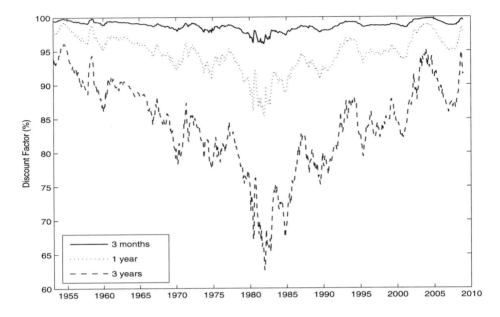

Source: Center for Research in Security Prices (CRSP)

plotted in Figure 2.1 with the expected annual inflation series in Figure 2.2 it appears that expected inflation is an important determinant of discount factors. The intuition is also quite straightforward: Inflation is exactly what determines the time value of money, as it determines how much goods money can buy. The higher the expected inflation, the less appealing it is to receive money in the future compared to today, as this money will be able to buy a lesser amount of goods.

Although expected inflation is the most obvious culprit in explaining the variation over time of discount factors, it is not the only one. In Chapter 7 we look at various explanations that economists put forward to account for the behavior of discount factors and interest rates. These explanations are related to the behavior of the U.S. economy, its budget deficit, and the actions of the Federal Reserve, as well as investors' appetite for risk (or lack thereof). These macro economic conditions affect the relative supply and demand of Treasury securities and thus their prices.

2.2 INTEREST RATES

Grasping the concept of a rate of interest is both easier and more complicated than absorbing the concept of a discount factor. It is easier because the idea of interest is closer to our everyday notion of a return on an investment, or the cost of a loan. For instance, if we invest $100 for one year at the rate of interest of 5%, we receive in one year $105, that is, the original capital invested plus the interest on the investment. The same investment strategy could be described in terms of a discount factor as well: The discount factor here is the

Figure 2.2 Expected Inflation

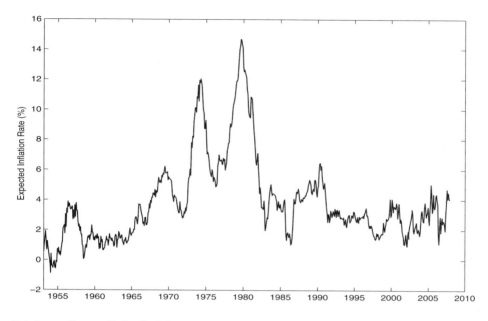

Data Source: Bureau of Labor Statistics.

exchange rate between having $105 in one year or $100 today, that is $0.9524 = \$100/\$105$. This latter number, which is equivalent to the 5% rate of interest, perhaps less intuitively describes the return on an investment.

The concept of an interest rate, however, is also more complicated, because it depends on the compounding frequency of the interest paid on the initial investment. The compounding frequency is defined as follows:

Definition 2.2 *The* **compounding frequency of interest accruals** *refers to the annual number of times in which interest is paid and reinvested on the invested capital.*

Indeed, to some extent, mentioning only an interest rate level is an incomplete description of the rate of return of an investment, or the cost of a loan or mortgage. The compounding frequency is a crucial element that must be attached to the interest rate figure.

For instance, in the above example, we implicitly assumed that the 5% rate of interest is applied to the original capital only once (and hence the $105 result). However, if interest accrues, say, every 6 months, then the correct amount at maturity would be

$$(\$100) \times \left(1 + \frac{5\%}{2}\right) \times \left(1 + \frac{5\%}{2}\right) = \$105.0625,$$

which is higher than $105. If interest accrues every month, then the correct amount at maturity would be

$$(\$100) \times \left(1 + \frac{5\%}{12}\right) \times \dots [\,12 \text{ times }]\dots \times \left(1 + \frac{5\%}{12}\right) = \$105.11,$$

which is higher still. This example shows the following:

Fact 2.2 *For a given interest rate figure (e.g. 5%), more frequent accrual of interest yields a higher final payoff.*

Looking at interest rates from a different perspective, consider an investment in a security that costs $100 today and that pays $105 in one year, as in our earlier example. What is the rate of interest on this security? The intuitive answer is 5%, because we invest $100 and obtain $105, and thus the return equals $5\% = (\$105 - \$100)/\$100$. However, once again, the correct answer really depends on the frequency with which interest accrues on the security. If the interest accrues once a year, then 5% is the correct answer. However, if the interest accrues every half a year, for instance, the correct answer is given by $r = 4.939\%$. In fact, $(\$100) \times (1 + 4.939\%/2) \times (1 + 4.939\%/2) = \$105$, which is indeed the payoff from the investment of $100. Similarly, if the interest accrues every month, then the correct answer to the same question is given by $r = 4.89\%$, as $(\$100) \times (1 + 4.89\%/12) \times \ldots [\, 12 \text{ times} \,] \ldots \times (1 + 4.89\%/12) = \$105$.

Fact 2.3 *For a given final payoff, more frequent accrual of interest implies a lower interest rate figure.*

This discussion emphasizes also the crucial difference between a *rate of return* on an investment, and an *interest rate*, which are related, but different, concepts. The rate of return is indeed the difference between payoff and initial investment, divided by the latter. In the example, $5\% = (\$105 - \$100)/\$100$ is the rate of return on the investment. The rate of interest corresponds instead to the (annualized) rate of return on the investment *within the compounding period*, but it differs from it otherwise. For instance, if the rate of interest is 5% and it accrues semi-annually, then within a six-month period the rate of return on the investment is 2.5%, that is, from $100 we have in six months $102.5. If we annualize this semi-annual return we obtain 5%, which corresponds to the rate of interest. Note, however, the rate of interest and the rate of return differ for a one-year horizon. In one year, the original investment will pay $105.0625, as we obtained earlier, and thus the rate of return is 5.0625%>5%. When the horizon is longer, the discrepancy between the annualized interest rate figure and the annualized rate of return on the investment is larger.

2.2.1 Discount Factors, Interest Rates, and Compounding Frequencies

The examples above illustrate that discount factors and interest rates are intimately related, once we make explicit the compounding frequency. Given an interest rate and its compounding frequency, we can define a discount factor. Vice versa, given a discount factor, we can define an interest rate together with its compounding frequency. In this section we make the relation explicit.

Two compounding frequencies are particularly important: semi-annual compounding and continuous compounding. The semi-annual compounding frequency is the standard benchmark, as it matches the frequency of coupon payments of U.S. Treasury notes and bonds. The continuous compounding, defined below, is also important, mainly for its analytical convenience. As we shall see, formulas and derivations are much simpler under the assumption that the interest on an investment accrues infinitely frequently. This is of course an abstraction, but a useful one.

2.2.1.1 *Semi-annual Compounding*   Let's begin with an example:

■ **EXAMPLE 2.3**

Let $t =$ August 10, 2006, and let $T =$ August 10, 2007 (one year later). Consider an investment of \$100 at t at the semi-annually compounded interest $r = 5\%$, for one year. As mentioned earlier, this terminology means that after six months the investment grows to $\$102.5 = \$100 \times (1 + 5\%/2)$, which is then reinvested at the same rate for another six months, yielding at T the payoff:

$$\text{Payoff at } T = \$105.0625 = (\$100) \times (1 + r/2) \times (1 + r/2) = (\$100) \times (1 + r/2)^2$$

Given that the initial investment is \$100, there are no cash flows to the investor during the period, and the payoff at T is risk free, the relation between money at t (\$100) and money at T ($= \$105.0625 =$ payoff at T) establishes a discount factor between the two dates, given by

$$Z(t, T) = \frac{\$100}{\text{payoff at } T} = \frac{1}{(1 + r/2)^2}$$

This example underlies the following more general statement:

Fact 2.4 *Let $r_2(t, T)$ denote the (annualized) semi-annually compounded interest rate between t and T. Then $r_2(t, T)$ defines a discount factor as*

$$Z(t, T) = \frac{1}{\left(1 + \frac{r_2(t,T)}{2}\right)^{2 \times (T-t)}} \tag{2.2}$$

The logic of this fact lies in the example above. The semi-annually compounded interest rate $r_2(t, T)$ defines a payoff at maturity T given by

$$\text{Payoff at } T = \text{ Investment at } t \ \times \left(1 + \frac{r_2(t, T)}{2}\right)^{2 \times (T-t)}.$$

Since the payoff at T is known at t, the relation between investment today at t and the payoff at T defines the time value of money, and $Z(t, T)$ given in Equation 2.2 defines the rate of exchange between money at T and money at t.

Similarly, given a discount factor $Z(t, T)$, we can obtain the semiannually compounded interest rate. The following example illustrates the point.

■ **EXAMPLE 2.4**

On March 1, 2001 (time t) the Treasury issued a 52-week Treasury bill, with maturity date $T =$ February 28, 2002. The price of the Treasury bill was \$95.713. As we have learned, this price defines a discount factor between the two dates of $Z(t, T) = 0.95713$. At the same time, it also defines a semi-annually compounded interest rate equal to $r_2(t, T) = 4.43\%$. In fact, $\$95.713 \times (1 + 4.43\%/2)^2 = \$100$. The semi-annually compounded interest rate can be computed from $Z(t,T) = 0.95713$ by solving for $r_2(t,T)$ in Equation 2.2:

$$r_2(t,T) = 2 \times \left(\frac{1}{Z(t,T)^{\frac{1}{2}}} - 1 \right) = 2 \times \left(\frac{1}{0.95713^{\frac{1}{2}}} - 1 \right) = 4.43\% \qquad (2.3)$$

Fact 2.5 *Let $Z(t,T)$ be the discount factor between dates t and T. Then the semi-annually compounded interest rate $r_2(t,T)$ can be computed from the formula*

$$r_2(t,T) = 2 \times \left(\frac{1}{Z(t,T)^{\frac{1}{2 \times (T-t)}}} - 1 \right) \qquad (2.4)$$

2.2.1.2 More Frequent Compounding Market participants' time value of money – the discount factor $Z(0,T)$ – can be exploited to determine the interest rates with any compounding frequency, as well as the relation that must exist between any two interest rates which differ in compounding frequency. More precisely, if we let n denote the number of compounding periods per year (e.g., $n = 2$ corresponds to semi-annual compounding), we obtain the following:

Fact 2.6 *Let the discount factor $Z(t,T)$ be given, and let $r_n(t,T)$ denote the (annualized) n-times compounded interest rate. Then $r_n(t,T)$ is defined by the equation*

$$Z(t,T) = \frac{1}{\left(1 + \frac{r_n(t,T)}{n} \right)^{n \times (T-t)}} \qquad (2.5)$$

Solving for $r_n(t,T)$, we obtain

$$r_n(t,T) = n \times \left(\frac{1}{Z(t,T)^{\frac{1}{n \times (T-t)}}} - 1 \right) \qquad (2.6)$$

For instance, a \$100 investment at the monthly compounded interest rate $r_{12}(0,1) = 5\%$ yields by definition

$$\text{Payoff at } T = \$100 \times \left(1 + \frac{r_{12}(0,1)}{12} \right) \times \cdots [\, 12 \text{ times} \,] \cdots \times \left(1 + \frac{r_{12}(0,1)}{12} \right) = \$105.1162$$

Thus, the monthly compounded interest rate $r_{12}(0,1) = 5\%$ corresponds to the discount factor $Z(0,1) = \$100/\$105.1162 = 0.95133$, and vice versa.

2.2.1.3 Continuous Compounding. The continuously compounded interest rate is obtained by increasing the compounding frequency n to infinity. For all practical purposes, however, daily compounding – the standard for bank accounts – closely matches the continuous compounding, as we see in the next example.

Table 2.1 Interest Rate and Compounding Frequency

Compounding Frequency	n	$r_n(t, t+1)$
Annual	1	5.000%
Semi-annual	2	4.939%
Monthly	12	4.889%
Bi-monthly	24	4.883%
Weekely	52	4.881%
Bi-weekly	104	4.880%
Daily	365	4.879%
Bi-daily	730	4.879%
Hourly	8760	4.879%
Continuous	∞	4.879%

■ **EXAMPLE 2.5**

Consider the earlier example in which at t we invest $100 to receive $105 one year later. Recall that the annually compounded interest rate is $r_1(t, t+1) = 5\%$, the semi-annually compounded interest rate is $r_2(t, t+1) = 4.939\%$, and the monthly compounded interest rate is $r_{12}(t, t+1) = 4.889\%$. Table 2.1 reports the $n-$times compounded interest rate also for more frequent compounding. As it can be seen, if we keep increasing n, the $n-$ times compounded interest rate $r_n(t, t+1)$ keeps decreasing, but at an increasingly lower rate. Eventually, it converges to a number, namely, 4.879%. This is the continously compounded interest rate. Note that in this example, there is no difference between the daily compounded interest rate ($n = 252$) and the one obtained with higher frequency ($n > 252$). That is, we can mentally think of continuous compounding as the daily compounding frequency.

Mathematically, we can express the limit of $r_n(t, T)$ in Equation 2.6 as n increases to infinity in terms of the exponential function:

Fact 2.7 *The* **continuously compounded** *interest rate* $r(t, T)$, *obtained from* $r_n(t, T)$ *for* n *that increases to infinity, is given by the formula*

$$Z(t, T) = e^{-r(t,T)(T-t)} \tag{2.7}$$

Solving for $r(t, T)$, *we obtain*

$$r(t, T) = -\frac{\ln(Z(t, T))}{T - t} \tag{2.8}$$

where "$\ln(.)$" *denotes the natural logarithm.*

Returning to Example 2.5, we can verify Equation 2.8 by taking the natural logarithm of $Z(t, T) = \$100/\$105 = .952381$ and thus obtaining

$$r(t, T) = -\frac{\ln(Z(t, t+1))}{1} = 4.879\%$$

2.2.2   The Relation between Discounts Factors and Interest Rates

The previous formulas show that given a discount factor between t and T, $Z(t, T)$, we can define interest rates of *any* compounding frequency by using Equation 2.2, 2.5, or 2.7. This fact implies that we can move from one compounding frequency to another by using the equalities implicit in these equations. For instance, for given interest rate $r_n(t, T)$ with n compounding frequency, we can determine the continuously compounded interest rate $r(t, T)$ by solving the equation

$$e^{-r(t,T)(T-t)} = Z(t, T) = \frac{1}{\left(1 + \frac{r_n(t,T)}{n}\right)^{n \times (T-t)}} \tag{2.9}$$

Because of its analytical convenience, in this text we mostly use the continuously compounded interest rate in the description of discount factors, and for other quantities. Translating such a number into another compounding frequency is immediate from Equation 2.9, which, more explicitly, implies

$$r(t, T) = n \times \ln\left(1 + \frac{r_n(t,T)}{n}\right) \tag{2.10}$$

$$r_n(t, T) = n \times \left(e^{\frac{r(t,T)}{n}} - 1\right) \tag{2.11}$$

To conclude, then, this section shows that the time value of money can be expressed equivalently through a discount factor, or in terms of an interest rate with its appropriate compounding frequency. At times, it will be convenient to focus on discount factors and at other times on interest rates, depending on the exercise. We should always keep in mind that the two quantities are equivalent.

2.3   THE TERM STRUCTURE OF INTEREST RATES

In the previous sections we noted that the primitive of our analysis is the discount factor, from which we define interest rates of various compounding frequencies. Interest rates, though, have a big advantage over discount factors when we analyze the time value of money: their units can be made uniform across maturities by annualizing them. The following example illustrates the point.

■ **EXAMPLE 2.6**

On June 5, 2008, the Treasury issued 13-week, 26-week and 52-week bills at prices $99.5399, $99.0142, and $97.8716, respectively. Denoting t = June 5, 2008, and T_1, T_2, and T_3 the three maturity dates, the implied discount factors are $Z(t, T_1) = 0.995399$, $Z(t, T_2) = 0.990142$, and $Z(t, T_3) = 0.978716$. The discount factor of longer maturities is lower than the one of shorter maturities, as Fact 2.1 would imply. The question is then: How much lower is $Z(t, T_3)$, say, compared to $Z(t, T_2)$ or $Z(t, T_1)$? Translating the discount factors into annualized interest rates provides a better sense of the relative value of money across maturities. In this case, the continuously compounded interest rates are

$$r(t, T_1) = -\frac{\ln(0.995399)}{0.25} = 1.8444\%;$$

$$r(t, T_2) = -\frac{\ln(0.990142)}{0.5} = 1.9814\%;$$

$$r(t, T_3) = -\frac{\ln(0.978716)}{1} = 2.1514\%.$$

The time value of money rises with maturity: The compensation that the Treasury has to provide investors to make them part with money today to receive money in the future, i.e., hold Treasury securities, increases the longer the investment period.

The term structure of interest rates is defined as follows:

Definition 2.3 *The* **term structure of interest rates**, *or* **spot rate curve**, *or* **yield curve**, *at a certain time* t *defines the relation between the level of interest rates and their time to maturity* $T - t$. *The* **discount curve** *at a certain time* t *defines instead the relation between the discount factors* $Z(t, T)$ *and their time to maturity* $T - t$.

Figure 2.3 provides examples of spot curves $r(t, T)$ at four different dates.[4] These dates have been chosen also because the spot curves had different "shapes." Traders refer to these different shapes with particular names, which we now describe.[5]

Panel A of Figure 2.3 plots the term structure of interest rates on October 30, 1992. On the horizontal axis we have time to maturity $m = T - t$ for m that ranges from 3 months ($m = 0.25$) to 10 years ($m = 10$) (the letter "m" stands for "maturity"). The vertical axis represents the interest rate level $r(t, t + m)$ that corresponds to the various maturities. As can be seen, the term structure of interest rates on October 30, 1992 was increasing, which is a typical pattern in the United States. The difference between the 10-year interest rate and the short-term interest rate is about 4%. This difference is called the term spread, or slope, of the term structure of interest rates.

Definition 2.4 *The* **term spread**, *or* **slope**, *is the difference between long-term interest rates (e.g. 10-year rate) and the short-term interest rates (e.g. 3-month rate).*

Typically, in the U.S. the term spread is positive. How is the term spread determined? Like discount factors, the term spread depends on numerous variables, such as expected future inflation, expected future growth of the economy, agents' attitudes toward risk, and so on. It is worth mentioning that although the expectation of future higher interest rates may determine today's term structure of interest rates, this is not the only channel. We will discuss more precisely the determinants of the term structure of interest rates in later chapters.

The shape of the term structure of interest rates is not always increasing. Panels B - D of Figure 2.3 plot the shape of the term structure on other occasions. In particular, Panel B illustrates a *decreasing* term structure of interest rates, as occurred on November 30, 2000. Panel C plots a term structure that is first rising and then decreasing. This shape is called *hump* and, in the example, took place on March 31, 2000. Finally, Panel D plots a term

---

[4]We calculated the spot curves using the extended Nelson Siegel model (see Section 2.9.3 in the appendix at the end of the chapter) based on data from CRSP (Monthly Treasuries) ¤2009 Center for Research in Security Prices (CRSP), The University of Chicago Booth School of Business.

[5]We are using the continuously compounded interest rate $r(t, T)$ to describe the curve. This is arbitrary. We could use any other compounding frequency, but as mentioned earlier, the continuously compounded frequency has some analytical advantages, as we shall see.

Figure 2.3   The Shapes of the Term Structure

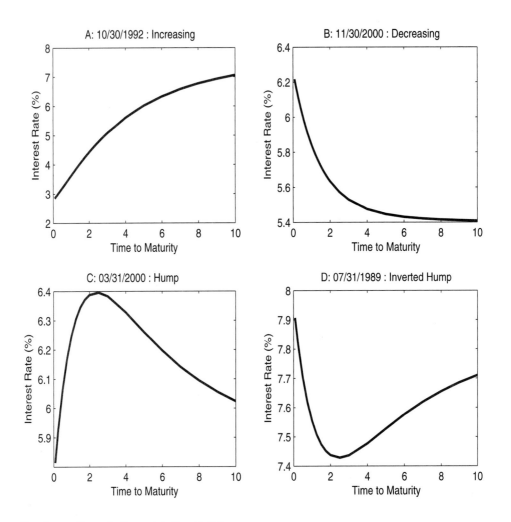

Data Source: Center for Research in Security Prices

structure that is first decreasing and then increasing. This shape is called an *inverted hump*. The example in the Panel D is for July 31, 1989.

2.3.1   The Term Structure of Interest Rates over Time

As for discount factors, the term structure of interest rates depends on the date t at which it is computed. This is evident in Figure 2.3, as on three different dates we have three different shapes of the term structure. In particular, the dates corresponding to Panel C and Panel B of Figure 2.3 are only eight months apart, and yet the term structures are quite different in shape. In addition, besides the change in shape, the term structure also moves up and down as a whole.

Different dates correspond to different term structure of interest rates. For instance, Figure 2.4 plots the term structure of interest rates on three different dates, at six-months intervals, namely, from January 31, 1994 to January 31, 1995. In all three cases, the term structure of interest rates is increasing, but it is clear that it is lower and steeper for the first date, while it is higher and flatter for the third date. The increase in the term structure is rather substantial: The short-term rate passed from 2.9% to 5.5%, while the long rate passed from 5.7% to 7.5%. This large change in the term structure of interest rates may have a devastating effect on the value of portfolios heavily invested in fixed income instruments. As we discuss in this and Chapter 3, it was is exactly in 1994 that Orange County, a rich county in California, lost $1.6 billion and went bankrupt. The unexpected hike in interest rates together with an aggressive leveraged investment portfolio were the main causes of the debacle.

Figure 2.4   The Term Structure of Interest Rates on Three dates

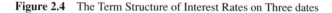
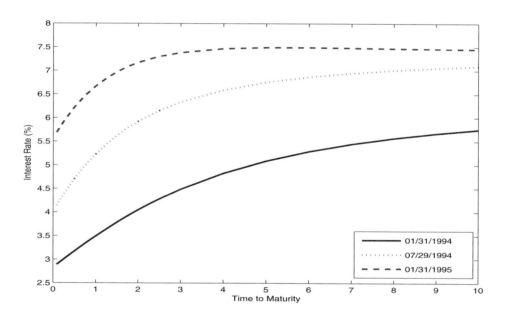

Data Source: Center for Research in Security Prices

As we did for discount factors, we can plot various points of the term structure of interest rates over time. Figure 2.5 graphs the term structure with maturities 3 months, 1 year, and 5 years from 1965 to 2008.[6] The first pattern that we see in Figure 2.5 is that interest rates move up and down substantially. The second clear pattern is that all of the interest rates move together: They go up and down at roughly the same time. However, it is also clear that they do not move up and down by the same amounts. To see this, let us consider the dotted line at the bottom of the plot, and the dashed line at the top. They correspond to the 3-month and 5-year interest rates, respectively. As can be seen, they both go up and down

[6]Data excerpted from CRSP (Fama Bliss Discount Bonds and Fama Risk Free Rate) ¤2009 Center for Research in Security Prices (CRSP), The University of Chicago Booth School of Business.

at roughly the same time. We can also see that the term spread, the distance between the two rates, changes over time as well. For instance, focusing on the last part of the period, 2000 - 2006, we see that while the 3-month rate moved from over 6% down to 1%, then went back up to 5%, the 5-year rate moved from 6% down to 3%, and then back up to 5%. That is, the spread was zero both at the beginning and at the end of this sample, but it was large in the middle.

Figure 2.5 The Term Structure over Time

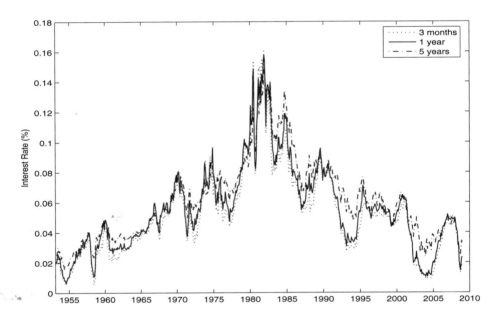

Source: Center for Research in Security Prices

Why does the term spread change over time? Once again, there are numerous reasons that contribute to the variation of both interest rates and term spreads, such as fluctuations in expected inflation, expected economic growth, and risk attitude of investors. We will review some recent theories in Chapter 7

2.4 COUPON BONDS

U.S. government Treasury bills involve only one payment from the Treasury to the investor at maturity. That is, their coupon rate is zero. They are thus an example of zero coupon bonds, bonds with no intermediate cash flows between issue date and maturity. The knowledge of the prices of zero coupon bonds allows us to determine the discount factor $Z(t, T)$, as described in the previous sections. More specifically, a government zero coupon bond at time t with maturity T has a price equal to

$$P_z(t, T) = 100 \times Z(t, T) \tag{2.12}$$

The subscript "z" is a mnemonic term for "zero" in zero coupon bond.

The Treasury issues zero coupon bonds with maturities up to only 52 weeks. For longer maturities, the Treasury issues securities that carry a coupon, that is, they also pay a sequence of cash flows (the coupons) between issue date and maturity, in addition to the final principal. In particular, the U.S. government issues Treasury notes, which are fixed income securities with maturity up to 10 years; Treasury bonds, which have maturities up to 30 years; and TIPS (Treasury Inflation Protected Securities), which have coupons that are not constant, but rather are linked to a recent inflation rate figure. We will talk about TIPS more exhaustively in Chapter 7. For now, we only consider Treasury notes and bonds. For convenience, we refer to both types as coupon bonds.

2.4.1 From Zero Coupon Bonds to Coupon Bonds

In this section we establish a relation between the prices of zero coupon bonds and coupon bonds. This relation forms the basis of much of the analysis that follows in later chapters, and so it is particularly important.

First, note that a coupon bond can be represented by the sequence of its cash payments. For instance, the 4.375% Treasury note issued on January 3, 2006 and with maturity of December 31, 2007, pays a cash flow of $2.1875 on June 30, 2006, December 31, 2006, and June 30, 2007, while it pays $102.1875 on December 31, 2007. Given the sequence of cash flows, which are certain in the sense that the U.S. Government is extremely unlikely to default, we could compute the value of the bond itself if we knew the discount factors $Z(t, T)$ to apply to each of the four dates. In fact, we can discount each future cash flow using its own discount factor, and sum the results.

Fact 2.8 *Consider a coupon bond at time t with coupon rate c, maturity T and payment dates $T_1, T_2,...,T_n = T$. Let there be discount factors $Z(t, T_i)$ for each date T_i. Then the value of the coupon bond can be computed as*

$$
\begin{aligned}
P_c(t, T_n) &= \frac{c \times 100}{2} \times Z(t, T_1) + \frac{c \times 100}{2} \times Z(t, T_2) + ... \\
&\quad ... + \left(\frac{c \times 100}{2} + 100 \right) \times Z(t, T_n) \\
&= \frac{c \times 100}{2} \times \sum_{i=1}^{n} Z(t, T_i) + 100 \times Z(t, T_n) \qquad (2.13) \\
&= \frac{c}{2} \times \sum_{i=1}^{n} P_z(t, T_i) + P_z(t, T_n) \qquad (2.14)
\end{aligned}
$$

The subscript "c" is a mnemonic device for "coupon" in coupon bond. Formula 2.14 shows that the coupon bond can be considered as a portfolio of zero coupon bonds.

■ **EXAMPLE 2.7**

Consider the 2-year note issued on $t =$ January 3, 2006 discussed earlier. On this date, the 6-month, 1-year, 1.5-years, and 2-year discounts were $Z(t, t + 0.5) = 0.97862$, $Z(t, t + 1) = 0.95718$, $Z(t, t + 1.5) = 0.936826$ and $Z(t, t + 2) = 0.91707$.

Therefore, the price of the note on that date was

$$P_c(t, T_n) = \$2.1875 \times \sum_{i=1}^{4} Z(t, t + 0.5 \times i) + \$100 \times 0.91707 = \$99.997,$$

which was indeed the issue price at t.

We can also represent the value of the coupon bond by using the semi-annual interest rate $r_2(t, T_i)$, where T_i, $i = 1, ..., n$, are the coupon payment dates. This representation is derived from the basic one above, but it can be useful nonetheless to report it:

$$P_c(t, T_n) \;=\; \sum_{i=1}^{n} \frac{c/2 \times 100}{\left(1 + r_2(t, T_i)/2\right)^{2 \times (T_i - t)}} + \frac{100}{\left(1 + r_2(t, T_n)/2\right)^{2 \times (T_n - t)}} \quad (2.15)$$

A useful fact is the following:

Fact 2.9 *Let the semi-annual discount rate be constant across maturities, $r_2(t, T_i) = r_2$ for every T_i. At issue date $t = 0$, the price of a coupon bond with coupon rate equal to the constant semi-annual rate $c = r_2$ is equal to par.*

$$P_c(0, T_n) \;=\; \sum_{i=1}^{n-1} \frac{c/2 \times 100}{\left(1 + r_2/2\right)^{2 \times T_i}} + \frac{100 \times (1 + c/2)}{\left(1 + r_2/2\right)^{2 \times T_n}} = 100 \quad (2.16)$$

To understand the above fact, consider a 1-year note. Then, we can write

$$P_c(0, T_2) \;=\; \frac{c/2 \times 100}{1 + r_2/2} + \frac{100 \times (1 + c/2)}{(1 + r_2/2)^2} \quad (2.17)$$

$$=\; \frac{c/2 \times 100}{1 + r_2/2} + \left(\frac{100}{1 + r_2/2}\right) \times \left(\frac{1 + c/2}{1 + r_2/2}\right) \quad (2.18)$$

$$=\; \frac{c/2 \times 100}{1 + r_2/2} + \left(\frac{100}{1 + r_2/2}\right) \times 1 \quad (2.19)$$

$$=\; \frac{100 \times (1 + c/2)}{1 + r_2/2} \quad (2.20)$$

$$=\; 100 \quad (2.21)$$

This argument can be extended to many periods. The intuition is that any additional periods increase the cash flow by $c/2$ while they also increase the discount rate by the same amount $r_2/2$. The two forces move in opposite directions (more cash flows imply higher prices, while the additional discount implies lower price).

2.4.1.1 *A No Arbitrage Argument*   We can establish Equation 2.13 also by appealing to a no arbitrage argument. In well-functioning markets in which both the coupon bond $P_c(t, T_n)$ and the zero coupon bonds $P_z(t, T_i)$ are traded in the market, if Equation 2.13 did not hold, an arbitrageur could make large risk-free profits. For instance, if

$$P_c(t, T_n) < \frac{c}{2} \times P_z(t, T_1) + \frac{c}{2} \times P_z(t, T_2) + ... + \left(1 + \frac{c}{2}\right) \times P_z(t, T_n) \quad (2.22)$$

then the arbitrageur can buy the coupon bond for $P_c(t, T_n)$ and sell immediately $c/2$ units of zero coupon bonds with maturities $T_1, T_2,..,T_{n-1}$ and $(1 + c/2)$ of the zero coupon bond with maturity T_n. This strategy yields an inflow of money to the arbitrageur that is equal to the difference between the right-hand side and the left-hand side of Equation 2.22. At every other maturity T_i the arbitrageur has a zero net position, as he receives the coupon from the Treasury and turns it around to the investors to whom the arbitrageur sold the individual zero coupon bonds. We note that this reasoning is the one that stands behind the law of one price, introduced in Fact 1.1 in Chapter 1, the fact that securities with identical cash flows should have the same price. The following example further illustrates the concept.

■ **EXAMPLE 2.8**

In Example 2.7, suppose that the 2-year note was trading at \$98. An arbitrageur could purchase, say, \$98 million of the 2-year note, and sell \$2.1875 million of the 6-month, 1-year and 1.5-year zero coupons, and \$102.1875 million of the 2-year zero coupon bond. The total value of the zeros the arbitrageur sells is \$99.997 million, realizing approximately \$2 million. The strategy is risk free, because at each coupon date in the future, the arbitrageur receives \$2.1875 million from the Treasury, which he simply turns over to the investors who bought the zero coupon bonds. Similarly, at maturity, the arbitrageur receives \$102.1875 million from the Treasury, and again turns it around to the investors of the last coupon.

In well-functioning markets such arbitrage opportunities cannot last for long. Thus, Equation 2.13 should hold "most of the time." It may happen that due to lack of liquidity or trading, some arbitrage opportunities may be detectable in the relative pricing of zero coupon bonds, such as STRIPS, and coupon bonds. However, these arbitrage opportunities are seldom exploitable: As soon as an arbitrageur tries to set up an arbitrage like the one described above, prices move instantly and the profit vanishes. Because expert arbitrageurs know this fact, some apparent mispricing may persist in the market place. We will regard such situations as "noise," that is, a little imprecision in market prices due to liquidity or external factors that sometimes impede the smooth functioning of capital markets.

2.4.2 From Coupon Bonds to Zero Coupon Bonds

We can also go the other way around: If we have enough coupon bonds, we can compute the implicit value of zero coupon bonds from the prices of coupon bonds. Equation 2.13 can be used to *estimate* the discount factors $Z(t, T)$ for every maturity. The following example illustrates the reasoning:

■ **EXAMPLE 2.9**

On $t =$ June 30, 2005, the 6-month Treasury bill, expiring on $T_1 =$ December 29, 2005, was trading at \$98.3607. On the same date, the 1 year to maturity, 2.75% Treasury note, was trading at \$99.2343. The maturity of the latter Treasury note is $T_2 =$ June 30, 2006. Given Equation 2.13, we can write the value of the two securities as:[7]

$$P_{bill}(t, T_1) = \$98.3607 \quad = \quad \$100 \times Z(t, T_1) \tag{2.23}$$

$$P_{note}(t, T_2) = \$99.2343 \quad = \quad \$1.375 \times Z(t, T_1) + \$101.375 \times Z(t, T_2) \tag{2.24}$$

We have two equations in two unknowns [the discount factors $Z(t, T_1)$ and $Z(t, T_2)$]. As in Section 2.1, from the first equation we obtain the discount factor $Z(t, T_1) = \$98.3607/\$100 = 0.983607$. We can substitute this value into the second equation, and solve for $Z(t, T_2)$ to obtain:

$$Z(t, T_2) = \frac{\$99.2343 - \$1.375 \times Z(t, T_1)}{\$101.375} = \frac{\$99.2343 - \$1.375 \times 0.983607}{\$101.375} = 0.965542$$

The prices of coupon bonds, then, implicitly contain the information about the market time value of money. This procedure can be iterated forward to obtain additional terms.

■ **EXAMPLE 2.10**

On the same date, $t =$ June 30, 2005, the December 31, 2006 Treasury note, with coupon of 3%, was trading at \$99.1093. Denoting by $T_3 =$ December 31, 2006, the price of this note can be written as

$$P_{note}(t, T_3) = \$99.1093 \quad = \quad \$1.5 \times Z(t, T_1) + \$1.5 \times Z(t, T_2) + \$101.5 \times Z(t, T_3) \tag{2.25}$$

We already determined $Z(t, T_1) = 0.983607$ and $Z(t, T_2) = 0.965542$ in Example 2.9. In Equation 2.25 the only unknown element is $Z(t, T_3)$. This is one equation in one unknown, and so we can solve for the $Z(t, T_3)$ to obtain

$$
\begin{aligned}
Z(t, T_3) \quad &= \quad \frac{\$99.1093 - \$1.5 \times (Z(t, T_1) + Z(t, T_2))}{\$101.5} \\
&= \quad \frac{\$99.1093 - \$1.5 \times (0.983607 + 0.965542)}{\$101.5} \\
&= \quad 0.947641
\end{aligned}
$$

If we have a sufficient amount of data, we can proceed in this fashion for every maturity, and obtain all of the discount factors $Z(t, T)$. This methodology is called the bootstrap methodology.

Definition 2.5 *Let t be a given date. Let there be n coupon bonds, with coupons c_i, maturities T_i and prices denoted by $P(t, T_i)$. Assume that maturities are at regular intervals of six months, that is, $T_1 = t + 0.5$ and $T_i = T_{i-1} + 0.5$. Then, the **bootstrap methodology** to estimate discount factors $Z(t, T_i)$ for every $i = 1, ..., n$ is as follows:*

1. The first discount factor $Z(t, T_1)$ is given by

$$Z(t, T_1) = \frac{P_c(t, T_1)}{100 \times (1 + c_1/2)} \tag{2.26}$$

---

[7]Notice a little approximation in this computation: The T-note would pay its coupon on December 31, 2005, rather than December 29. We assume that both dates correspond, approximately, to T_1.

2. *Any other discount factor $Z(t, T_i)$ for $i = 2, ..., n$ is given by*

$$Z(t, T_i) = \frac{P_c(t, T_i) - c_i/2 \times 100 \times \left(\sum_{j=1}^{i-1} Z(t, T_j) \right)}{100 \times (1 + c_i/2)} \qquad (2.27)$$

This procedure is relatively simple to implement, as the example above shows. One of the issues, though, is that bond data at six-month intervals are not always available. Unfortunately, this procedure requires all of the bonds, because otherwise the iterative procedure stops and there is no way to keep going. The appendix at the end of this chapter reviews some other methodologies that are widely used to estimate the discount factors $Z(0, T)$ from coupon bonds.

2.4.3   Expected Return and the Yield to Maturity

How can we measure the expected return on an investment in Treasury securities? Assuming the investor will hold the bond until maturity, computing the expected return on an investment in a zero coupon bond is relatively straightforward, as the final payoff is known and there are no intermediate cash flows. Thus, quite immediately, we have

$$\text{Return on zero coupon bond} = \frac{1}{Z(t, T)} - 1 \qquad (2.28)$$

This is the return between t and T. It is customary to annualize this amount, so that

$$\text{Annualized return on zero coupon bond} = \left(\frac{1}{Z(t, T)} \right)^{\frac{1}{T-t}} - 1 \qquad (2.29)$$

This, of course, corresponds to the annually compounded yield on the zero coupon, as in Equation 2.6 for $n = 1$.

For coupon bonds it is more complicated. A popular measure of return on investment for coupon bonds is called yield to maturity, which is defined as follows:

Definition 2.6 *Let $P_c(t, T)$ be the price at time t of a Treasury bond with coupon c and maturity T. Let T_i denote the coupon payments times, for $i = 1, ..., n$. The semi-annually compounded* **yield to maturity***, or* **internal rate of return***, is defined as the constant rate y that makes the discounted present value of the bond future cash flows equal to its price. That is, y is defined by the equation*

$$P_c(t, T) = \sum_{i=1}^{n} \frac{c/2 \times 100}{(1 + y/2)^{2 \times (T_i - t)}} + \frac{100}{(1 + y/2)^{2 \times (T_n - t)}} \qquad (2.30)$$

Before moving to interpret this measure of return on investment, it is important to recognize a major distinction between the formula in Equation 2.30 and the one that we obtained earlier in terms of discount factors, namely Equation 2.15. Although they appear the same, it is crucial to note that the yield to maturity y is defined as the particular *constant* rate that makes the right-hand side of Equation 2.30 equal to the price of the bond. Instead,

Equation 2.15 is the one defining the price of the bond from the discount factors $Z(t,T)$. Unless the term structure of interest rates is exactly flat, the yields at various maturities are different, and will not coincide with the yield to maturity y. Indeed, to some extent, the yield to maturity y can be considered an average of the semi-annually compounded spot rates $r_2(0,T)$, which define the discount $Z(0,T)$. However, it is important to note that this "average" depends on the coupon level c. In fact:

Fact 2.10 *Two different bonds that have the same maturity but different coupon rates c have different yield to maturities y.*

This fact is easily illustrated with an example:

■ **EXAMPLE 2.11**

Columns 1 to 6 of Table 2.2 display coupon rates, maturities, and quotes of the latest issued Treasury notes on February 15, 2008.[8] Column 7 shows the discount curve $Z(0,T)$ obtained from the bootstrap procedure discussed in Section 2.4.2, and Column 8 reports the continuously compounded spot rate curve $r(0,T)$.

On February 15, 2008, traders could buy or sell two Treasury securities with the same maturity $T = 9.5$ years, but with very different coupon rates. In particular, a T-note with coupon $c = 4.750\%$ and a T-bond with coupon $c = 8.875\%$ were available. Using the discount factors $Z(0,T)$ in Table 2.2 and the formula in Equation 2.15 we can determine the fair prices of the two securities. In particular, we have[9]

$$\text{Price T-note}_{c=4.750} = \frac{4.750}{2} \times \left(\sum_{T=0.5}^{9.5} Z(0,T) \right) + 100 \times Z(0,9.5)$$
$$= 107.8906 \tag{2.31}$$
$$\text{Price T-bond}_{c=8.875} = \frac{8.875}{2} \times \left(\sum_{T=0.5}^{9.5} Z(0,T) \right) + 100 \times Z(0,9.5)$$
$$= 141.5267 \tag{2.32}$$

What are the yield to maturity of these two securities? Solving Equation 2.30 for the two bonds, the yield to maturity of the $c = 4.75$ T-note and $c = 8.875$ T-bond are, respectively

$$y_{c=4.750} = 3.7548\%. \tag{2.33}$$
$$y_{c=8.875} = 3.6603\% \tag{2.34}$$

As it can be seen from Equations 2.33 and 2.34, the bond with the higher coupon has lower yield to maturity y.

[8]Data excerpted from CRSP (Daily Treasuries) ¤2009 Center for Research in Security Prices (CRSP), The University of Chicago Booth School of Business.
[9]We use fair prices, i.e., prices obtained from the same discount curve $Z(0,T)$, to better illustrate the concept of yield to maturity and its relation to a bond coupon rate. It turns out however that on February 15, 2008, the 5-year T-bond with $c = 8.875$ was actually trading at 140.0781, about 1% less than its fair price computed in ation 2.32. This lower price is due to the lack of liquidity of bonds that have been issued long in the past ared to the latest issued T-notes used to compute the discount curve $Z(0,T)$.

Table 2.2   Term Structure on February 15, 2008

Coupon Rate (%)	Maturity Date	Time to Maturity	Bid	Ask	Mid	Bootstrap Discount	Spot Curve	Discount with $y = 3.7548\%$	Discount with $y = 3.6603\%$
4.125	8/15/2008	0.5	100.9844	101.0156	101.0000	98.9590	2.0930	98.1572	98.2027
4.500	2/15/2009	1.0	102.6094	102.6406	102.6250	98.1892	1.8274	96.3484	96.4378
4.875	8/15/2009	1.5	104.4766	104.5078	104.4922	97.3147	1.8147	94.5729	94.7045
4.750	2/15/2010	2.0	105.5078	105.5391	105.5234	96.2441	1.9141	92.8301	93.0024
4.125	8/15/2010	2.5	105.0859	105.1172	105.1016	95.0822	2.0172	91.1194	91.3309
5.000	2/15/2011	3.0	108.2344	108.2656	108.2500	93.7612	2.1473	89.4403	89.6895
5.000	8/15/2011	3.5	109.0000	109.0313	109.0156	92.2213	2.3137	87.7920	88.0775
4.875	2/15/2012	4.0	109.1719	109.2031	109.1875	90.6046	2.4666	86.1742	86.4945
4.375	8/15/2012	4.5	107.3281	107.3594	107.3438	88.7259	2.6582	84.5862	84.9400
3.875	2/15/2013	5.0	105.1406	105.1719	105.1563	86.9809	2.7896	83.0274	83.4134
4.250	8/15/2013	5.5	106.8125	106.8438	106.8281	85.0858	2.9365	81.4974	81.9142
4.000	2/15/2014	6.0	105.2344	105.2656	105.2500	83.1241	3.0806	79.9956	80.4420
4.250	8/15/2014	6.5	106.3281	106.3594	106.3438	81.1114	3.2207	78.5214	78.9962
4.000	2/15/2015	7.0	104.3750	104.4063	104.3906	79.0613	3.3564	77.0744	77.5765
4.250	8/15/2015	7.5	105.4063	105.4375	105.4219	76.8759	3.5064	75.6541	76.1822
4.500	2/15/2016	8.0	106.7188	106.7500	106.7344	74.8256	3.6251	74.2600	74.8130
4.875	8/15/2016	8.5	109.0000	109.0313	109.0156	72.6763	3.7548	72.8915	73.4684
4.625	2/15/2017	9.0	106.9375	106.9688	106.9531	70.8392	3.8306	71.5483	72.1480
4.750	8/15/2017	9.5	107.8750	107.9063	107.8906	69.1582	3.8818	70.2298	70.8513
3.500	2/15/2018	10.0	97.8750	97.9063	97.8906	68.1581	3.8334	68.9356	69.5779

Data excerpted from CRSP (Daily Treasuries) ¤2009 Center for Research in Security Prices (CRSP), The University of Chicago Booth School of Business.

To verify the yield to maturity computed are indeed correct, Table 2.2 also reports the discount factors $Z^y(0, T) = (1 + y/2)^{-2 \times T}$ implied by Equations 2.33 and 2.34. Using these two discounts $Z^y(0, T)$ instead of $Z(0, T)$ in Equations 2.31 and 2.32, respectively, we indeed obtain the correct prices:

$$\text{Price T-note }_{c=4.750} = \sum_{T=0.5}^{9.5} \frac{4.750/2}{\left(1 + \frac{3.7548\%}{2}\right)^{2 \times T}} + \frac{100}{\left(1 + \frac{3.7548\%}{2}\right)^{2 \times 9.5}} = 107.8906$$

$$\text{Price T-bond }_{c=8.875} = \sum_{T=0.5}^{9.5} \frac{8.875/2}{\left(1 + \frac{3.6603\%}{2}\right)^{2 \times T}} + \frac{100}{\left(1 + \frac{3.6603\%}{2}\right)^{2 \times 9.5}} = 141.5267$$

This example shows that there is something curious in the definition of yield to maturity. Why does the coupon rate affect the yield to maturity? To understand the intuition, we need to note that y correctly measures the expected return on an investment only under the strict condition that *the investor can reinvest all of the coupons at the rate y over the life of the bond.*

To see this, let us compute the total payoff at maturity T assuming that the investor can reinvest all of the coupons paid at dates $T_1, T_2, ..., T_{n-1}$ at the constant rate y for the remaining periods $T - T_1, T - T_2, ..., T - T_{n-1}$. This is given by the following:

$$\text{Total payoff at } T = \frac{c \times 100}{2} \times (1 + y/2)^{2 \times (T - T_1)}$$

$$+\frac{c \times 100}{2} \times (1 + y/2)^{2 \times (T - T_2)}$$

$$\dots$$

$$+\frac{c \times 100}{2} \times (1 + y/2)^{2 \times (T - T_{n-1})}$$

$$+\frac{c \times 100}{2} + 100$$

$$= \frac{c \times 100}{2} \times \left(\sum_{i=1}^{n} (1 + y/2)^{2 \times (T - T_i)} \right) + 100$$

We can now compute the present value of the total payoff at T, using y as the constant semi-annual yield and thus $Z^y(t, T) = (1 + y/2)^{-2(T-t)}$ as the discount factor. This gives

$$
\begin{aligned}
\text{Present value of} &= Z^y(t, T) \times \left[\frac{c \times 100}{2} \times \left(\sum_{i=1}^{n} (1 + y/2)^{2 \times (T - T_i)} \right) + 100 \right] \\
\text{total payoff at } T & \\
&= \frac{c \times 100}{2} \times \left(\sum_{i=1}^{n} \frac{(1 + y/2)^{2 \times (T - T_i)}}{(1 + y/2)^{2 \times (T - t)}} \right) + \frac{100}{(1 + y/2)^{2 \times (T - t)}} \\
&= \frac{c \times 100}{2} \times \left(\sum_{i=1}^{n} \frac{1}{(1 + y/2)^{2 \times (T_i - t)}} \right) + \frac{100}{(1 + y/2)^{2 \times (T - t)}} \\
&= P(t, T)
\end{aligned}
$$

We find then that the price of the bond is (by definition) equal to the present value of the total payoff at T, discounted at the yield to maturity y, under the assumption that all of the coupons can be reinvested at same rate y over the life of the bond.

Given that it is practically impossible for an investor to reinvest all of the coupons at the constant yield to maturity y, this latter measure is in fact a poor measure of expected return. Indeed, the definition of a return on an investment cannot be given without a precise definition of the time interval during which the security is held. For instance, a 10-year STRIP provides the *certain* annualized return in Equation 2.29 *if* the security is held until maturity. However, if the investor sells the bond after one year, the return may be higher or lower than the promised yield (Equation 2.29) depending on what happens to interest rates. A substantial increase in interest rates, for instance, will tend to lower prices of long-term bonds, and thus the investor can end up with a capital loss. In later chapters we use modern financial concepts to precisely define the *expected* return on an investment during a given period, as well as the no arbitrage restrictions that must exist across bonds.

Why then do traders use the notion of yield to maturity y in their every day trading? Given a coupon rate c, Equation 2.30 shows that there is a one-to-one relation between the price P_c of the bond and the yield to maturity y. Thus, a trader can quote the same bond by using P_c or y. To some extent, then, the yield to maturity is just a convenient way of quoting a bond price to other traders.

2.4.4 Quoting Conventions

We end this section on Treasury bonds with a few remarks on the market quoting convention for Treasury bills and Treasury bonds.

2.4.4.1 Treasury Bills. Treasury bills are quoted on a discount basis. That is, rather than quoting a price $P_{bill}(t, T)$ for a Treasury bill, Treasury dealers quote the following quantity

$$d = \frac{100 - P_{bill}(t, T)}{100} \times \frac{360}{n} \qquad (2.35)$$

where n is the number of calendar days between t and T. For instance, on August 10, 2006 the Treasury issued a 182-day bill at a price of \$97.477 for \$100 of face value. Treasury dealers quoted this price as

$$d = \frac{100 - 97.477}{100} \times \frac{360}{182} = 4.99\%$$

where d is an annualized discount rate on the face value of the Treasury bill.

Given a quote d from a Treasury dealer, we can compute the price of the Treasury bill by solving for $P_{bill}(t, T)$ in Equation 2.35:

$$P_{bill}(t, T) = 100 \times \left[1 - \frac{n}{360} \times d\right] \qquad (2.36)$$

2.4.4.2 Treasury Coupon Notes and Bonds. Coupon notes and bonds present an additional complication. Between coupon dates, interest accrues on the bond. If a bond is purchased between coupon dates, the buyer is only entitled to the portion of the coupon that accrues between the purchase date and the next coupon date. The seller of the bond is entitled to the portion of the coupon that accrued between the last coupon and the purchase date. It is market convention to quote Treasury notes and bonds without any inclusion of accrued interests. However, the buyer agrees to pay the seller any accrued interest between the last coupon date and purchase price. That is, we have the formula

$$\text{Invoice price} = \text{Quoted price} + \text{Accrued interest} \qquad (2.37)$$

The quoted price is sometimes referred to as the **clean price** while the invoice price is sometimes also called **dirty price**.

The accrued interest is computed using the following intuitive formula:

$$\text{Accrued interest} \quad = \quad \text{Interest due in the full period} \times$$

$$\times \frac{\text{Number of days since last coupon date}}{\text{Number of days between coupon payments}}$$

Market conventions also determine the methodology to count days. There are three main ways:

1. Actual/Actual: Simply count the number of calendar days between coupons;

2. 30/360: Assume there are 30 days in a month and 360 in a year;

3. Actual/360: Each month has the right number of days according to the calendar, but there are only 360 days in a year.

Which convention is used depends on the security considered. For instance, Treasury bills use actual/360 while Treasury notes and bonds use the actual/actual counting convention.

2.5 FLOATING RATE BONDS

Floating rate bonds are coupon bonds whose coupons are tied to some reference interest rate. The U.S. Treasury does not issue floating rate bonds, but governments of other countries as well as individual corporations do. We present an example of floating rate bond in Example 2.12. It is important to spend some time on the pricing of floating rate bonds as a similar methodology applies to numerous other interest rate securities, such as floaters and inverse floaters (see Case Study in Section 2.8) as well as derivative instruments, such as interest rate swaps (see Chapter 5).[10]

■ **EXAMPLE 2.12**

The Italian Treasury regularly issues CCT (Certificati di Credito del Tesoro), which are floating rate bonds with 7 years to maturity. The CCT semi-annual coupon is equal to the most recent rate on the six-month BOT (the Italian Treasury bill), plus a spread (fixed at 0.15%). There is a six-month temporal lag between the determination of the coupon and its actual payment.

Unless otherwise specified, we therefore define a floating rate bond as follows:

Definition 2.7 *A semi-annual* **floating rate bond** *with maturity T is a bond whose coupon payments at dates $t = 0.5, 1, ..., T$ are determined by the formula*

$$\text{Coupon payment at } t = c(t) = 100 \times (r_2\,(t - 0.5) + s) \tag{2.38}$$

where $r_2(t)$ is the 6-month Treasury rate at t, and s is a spread.[11] Each coupon date is also called **reset date** *as it is the time when the new coupon is reset (according to the formula).*

2.5.1 The Pricing of Floating Rate Bonds

The pricing of floating rate bonds is simple, although the logic may appear a little complicated at first. Consider the case in which the spread $s = 0$. In this case, the following is true

Fact 2.11 *If the spread $s = 0$, the ex-coupon price of a floating rate bond on any coupon date is equal to the bond par value.[12]*

To understand the logic, consider first the following simple example

---

[10] In this chapter we only review the pricing of floating rate bonds for the case in which the coupon rate is linked to the same interest rate that is also used for discounting purposes, which grealy simplifies the analysis and provides the formulas needed for future applications.

[11] For notational simplicity, in this section the six month rate is denoted by $r_2(t)$ instead of $r_2(t, t + 0.5)$.

[12] Ex-coupon means that the price does not incorporate the coupon that is paid on that particular day. Par value is the bond's principal amount.

■ **EXAMPLE 2.13**

Consider a one year, semi-annual floating rate bond. The coupon at time $t = 0.5$ depends on *today*'s interest rate $r_2(0)$, which is known. If today $r_2(0) = 2\%$, then $c(0.5) = 100 \times 2\%/2 = 1$. What about the coupon $c(1)$ at maturity $T = 1$? This coupon will depend on the 6-month rate at time $t = 0.5$, which we do not know today. This implies that we do not know the value of the final cash flow at time $T = 1$, which is equal to $100 + c(1)$. Computing the present value of this uncertain cash flow initially seems hard. And yet, with a moment's reflection, it is actually simple. Consider an investor who is evaluating this bond. This investor can project himself to time $t = 0.5$, six months before maturity. Can the investor at time $t = 0.5$ guess what the cash flow will be at time $T = 1$? Yes, because at time $t = 0.5$ the investor will know the interest rate. So, he can compute what the value is at time $t = 0.5$. Suppose that at time $t = 0.5$ the interest rate is $r_2(0.5) = 3\%$, then the coupon at time $T = 1$ is $c(1) = 100 \times r_2(0.5)/2 = 1.5$. This implies that the value of the bond at time $t = 0.5$ is equal to

$$\text{Value bond at } 0.5 = \text{Present value of } (100 + c(1)) = \frac{100 + 1.5}{1 + 0.03/2} = 100,$$

which is a round number, equal to par. What if the interest rate at time $t = 0.5$ was $r_2(0.5) = 6\%$? In this case, the coupon rate at time $T = 1$ is $c(1) = 100 \times r_2(0.5)/2 = 103$, and the value of the bond at $t = 0.5$ is

$$\text{Value bond at } 0.5 = \text{Present value of } (100 + c(1)) = \frac{100 + 3}{1 + 0.06/2} = 100$$

Still the same round number, equal to par. Indeed, *independently* of the level of the interest rate $r_2(T_1)$, we find that the value of the bond at $t = 0.5$ is always equal to 100:

$$
\begin{aligned}
\text{Value bond at } 0.5 &= \text{Present value of } (100 + c(1)) = \frac{100 + 100 \times r_2(0.5)/2}{1 + r_2(0.5)/2} \\
&= \frac{100 \times (1 + r_2(0.5)/2)}{1 + r_2(0.5)/2} \\
&= 100.
\end{aligned}
$$

Even if the investor does not know the cash flow at time $T = 1$, because it depends on the future floating rate $r_2(0.5)$, the investor *does* know that at time $t = 0.5$ the ex-coupon value of the floating rate bond *will be* 100, independently of what the interest rate does then. But then, he can compute the value of the bond at time $t = 0$, because the coupon at time $T_1 = 0.5$ is known at time $t = 0$ as it is given by $c(0.5) = 100 \times r_2(0)/2 = 101$. Thus, the value at time $t = 0$ is

$$\text{Value bond at } 0 = \text{Present value of } (100 + c(0.5)) = \frac{100 + 1}{1 + .02/2} = 100$$

The result that at time $t = 0.5$ the ex-coupon bond price of this floating rate bond is always equal to 100 may appear puzzling, but it is actually intuitive. When the interest rate moves from $r_2(0) = 2\%$ to $r_2(0.5)$ it has two effects:

1. It changes the future cash flow $c(1) = 100 \times r_2(0.5)$.

- If the interest rate $r_2(0.5)$ rises, the future cash flow increases.

- If the interest rate $r_2(0.5)$ declines, the future cash flow declines.

2. It changes the discount rate to apply to the future cash flows.

- If the interest rate $r_2(0,5)$ rises, the discount rate increases.

- If the interest rate $r_2(0,5)$ declines, the discount rate declines.

The two effects, called "cash flow effect" and "discount effect," work in opposite directions. If the interest rate increases, the future cash flow increases, but it is discounted by a higher rate.

The institutional feature of lagging the coupon payment by six months allows for this cash flow and discount effect to exactly cancel each other out, leaving the value of the bond at 100 at any reset date.

What if there are additional dates? The reasoning is the same, and we work backwards. Table 2.3 contains the description of computations for the valuation of a 2-year floating rate bond. Briefly, starting from the top of the table, the ex-coupon value at $T = 2$ is simply the principal 100. The cum-coupon value is principal times the semi-annual interest rate $r_2(1.5)/2$ determined six months earlier, at $t = 1.5$. We can compute the present value as of $t = 1.5$ of the total cash flow at time $T = 2$, resulting in the ex-coupon price still equal to 100. The logic is the same as in Example 2.13. The cum-coupon price at $t = 1.5$ is then 100 plus the coupon, which equals 100 times the semi-annual rate determined at $t = 1$. Thus, the present value as of $t = 1$ of the total cash flow at time $t = 1.5$ (i.e., coupon plus value of bond at $t = 1.5$) is equal to 100, again. And so on until $t = 0$.

2.5.2 Complications

We must discuss two simplifying assumptions made above: First, the spread s on the floating rate is zero. Second, the time 0 of the valuation is a reset date. Fortunately, the generalization to the more realistic case is simple.

First, if the spread s is nonzero we can decompose the total cash flow per period in two parts, the floating part and the fixed part. This decomposition results in the equality

Floating coupon with spread s = Floating coupon with zero spread + Fixed coupon s

We can then value independently each component on the right-hand side, as we already know how to value a floating coupon bond with zero spread (see previous section) and a sequence of fixed coupon payments equal to s. Indeed, the present value of the fixed sequence of payments equal to s is $\sum_{t=0.5}^{T} s \times Z(0,t)$. Therefore, we have the equality:

$$\text{Price floating rate bond with spread } s = \text{Price floating rate bond with zero spread}$$
$$+ s \times \sum_{t=0.5}^{n} Z(0,t)$$

Table 2.3   The Valuation of a 2-year Floating Rate Bond

Time	Rate	Coupon	Ex-Coupon Price	Cum-Coupon Price
2	$r_2(2)$	$c(2) = 100 \times \frac{r_2(1.5)}{2}$	$P_{FR}(2) = 100$	$P_{FR}^C(2) = 100 + c(2)$ $= 100 \times \left(1 + \frac{r_2(1.5)}{2}\right)$
1.5	$r_2(1.5)$	$c(1.5) = 100 \times \frac{r_2(1)}{2}$	$P_{FR}(1.5) = \dfrac{P_{FR}^C(2)}{1 + \frac{r_2(1.5)}{2}}$ $= \dfrac{100 \times \left(1 + \frac{r_2(1.5)}{2}\right)}{1 + \frac{r_2(1.5)}{2}}$ $= 100$	$P_{FR}^C(1.5) = P_{FR}(1.5) + c(1.5)$ $= 100 \times \left(1 + \frac{r_2(1)}{2}\right)$
1	$r_2(1)$	$c(1) = 100 \times \frac{r_2(0.5)}{2}$	$P_{FR}(1) = \dfrac{P_{FR}^C(1.5)}{1 + \frac{r_2(1)}{2}}$ $= \dfrac{100 \times \left(1 + \frac{r_2(1)}{2}\right)}{1 + \frac{r_2(1)}{2}}$ $= 100$	$P_{FR}^C(1) = P_{FR}(1) + c(1)$ $= 100 \times \left(1 + \frac{r_2(0.5)}{2}\right)$
0.5	$r_2(0.5)$	$c(0.5) = 100 \times \frac{r_2(0)}{2}$	$P_{FR}(0.5) = \dfrac{P_{FR}^C(1)}{1 + \frac{r_2(0.5)}{2}}$ $= \dfrac{100 \times \left(1 + \frac{r_2(0.5)}{2}\right)}{1 + \frac{r_2(0.5)}{2}}$ $= 100$	$P_{FR}^C(0.5) = P_{FR}(0.5) + c(0.5)$ $= 100 \times \left(1 + \frac{r_2(0)}{2}\right)$
0	$r_2(0)$	-	$P_{FR}(0) = \dfrac{P_{FR}^C(0.5)}{1 + \frac{r_2(0)}{2}}$ $= \dfrac{100 \times \left(1 + \frac{r_2(0)}{2}\right)}{1 + \frac{r_2(0)}{2}}$ $= 100$	

At reset dates the price of the floating rate bond with zero spread is just par (=100), so that[13]

$$\text{Price floating rate bond with spread } s \quad = \quad 100 + s \times \sum_{t=0.5}^{T} Z(0,t) \qquad (2.39)$$

The second complication is that the valuation may be outside reset dates. Consider first Example 2.13. If today is not $t = 0$, but $t = 0.25$, how do we value the floating rate bond? The backward induction argument up to $t = 0.5$ still holds: At time $t = 0.5$ the ex-coupon bond price will be worth 100 and the cum-coupon bond price will be worth $\$101 = \$100 + \$100 \times 2\%/2$. The only difference from before is that we now have to discount the amount 101 not back to $t = 0$ at the rate $r_2(0) = 2\%$, but back to $t = 0.25$ at the current 3-month rate. For instance, if the quarterly compounded 3-months rate is also 2%, that is $r_4(0.25, 0.5) = 2\%$, then

$$\text{Value bond at } 0.25 = \text{Present value of } \$101 = \frac{\$101}{(1 + 0.02/4)} = \$100.4975$$

In this case, the value of the bond depends on the current interest rate. If for instance $r_4(0.25, 0.5) = 1\%$, the value of the bond at 0.25 is $\$100.7481$.

The same reasoning applies more generally. Let us denote by 0 the last reset date, and by t the current trading day. Then, we know that at the next reset date, time 0.5, the ex-coupon value of the floating rate bond will be $\$100$. Thus, the cum-coupon value of the floating rate bond at the next reset date is

$$P_{FR}^C(0.5, T) = 100 + c(0.5) = 100 + 100 \times r_2(0)/2$$

Therefore, the value at time $0 < t < 0.5$ of this cash flow is

$$P_{FR}(t, T) = \text{Present value of } P_{FR}^C(0.5, T) = Z(t, 0.5) \times 100 \times [1 + r_2(0)/2]$$

We summarize these results in the following:

Fact 2.12 *Let T_1, T_2, ... T_n be the floating rate reset dates and let the current date t be between time T_i and T_{i+1}: $T_i < t < T_{i+1}$. The general formula for a semi-annual floating rate bond with zero spread s is*

$$P_{FR}(t, T) = Z(t, T_{i+1}) \times 100 \times [1 + r_2(T_i)/2] \qquad (2.40)$$

where $Z(t, T_{i+1})$ is the discount factor from t to T_{i+1}. At reset dates, $Z(T_i, T_{i+1}) = 1/(1 + r_2(T_i)/2)$, which implies

$$P_{FR}(T_i, T) = 100 \qquad (2.41)$$

It may be useful to note that although between coupon dates the value of a floating rate bond depends on the interest rates, its sensitivity to variation in interest rate is very small, as we shall see more fully in later chapters.

---

[13]The spread s often reflects a lower credit quality than the reference rate used. The appropriate discount factors should then be used to discount future cash flows. For instance, if the reference rate is the LIBOR, then the LIBOR curve should be used, as discussed in Chapter 5.

2.6 SUMMARY

In this chapter, we covered the following topics:

1. Discount factors: The discount factor is the value today of one dollar in the future. Discount factors decrease with the time horizon and also vary over time.

2. Interest rates: The promised rate of return of an investment, an interest rate needs a compounding frequency to be well defined. They are quoted on an annualized basis.

3. Compounding frequency: This is the frequency with which interest on an investment is accrues over time. Continuous compounding refers to the limit in which payments accrue every instant. Practically, daily compounding is very close to continuous compounding.

4. Term structure of interest rates: The term structure of interest rate is the relation between the interest rates and maturity. Investment horizons affect the interest rate to be received on an investment or paid on a loan.

5. Zero coupon bonds: These are securities that pay only one given amount (par) at maturity. Examples are Treasury bills or STRIPS.

6. Coupon notes and bonds. These are securities that pay a sequence of coupons and the principal back at maturity. Examples are Treasury notes and bonds, which pay a coupon semi-annually. T-notes have maturity up to ten years, while bonds have up to thirty years.

7. Bootstrap: This procedure is for computing discount factors at various maturities from data on coupon notes and bonds. It requires the availability of notes and bonds at semi-annual intervals.

2.7 EXERCISES

1. Figure 2.3 shows that the term structure of interest rates can be declining, with short-term spot rates higher than long-term spot rates. How steep can the decline in spot rates be? Consider two STRIPS: One has 3-years to maturity and yields a continuously compounded rate $r(0, 3) = 10\%$, while the second has 5 years to maturity and yields a continuously compounded rate $r(0, 5) = 5\%$. Discuss whether this scenario is possible, and, if not, what arbitrage strategy could be set up to gain from the mispricing.

2. Compute the price, the yield and the continuously compounded yield for the following Treasury bills. For the 1-year Treasury bill also compute the semi-annually compounded yield.

    (a) 4-week with 3.48% discount (December 12, 2005)

    (b) 4-week with 0.13% discount (November 6, 2008)

    (c) 3-month with 4.93% discount (July 10, 2006)

    (d) 3-month with 4.76% discount (May 8, 2007)

(e) 3-month with 0.48% discount (November 4, 2008)

(f) 6-month with 4.72% discount (April 21, 2006)

(g) 6-month with 4.75% discount (June 6, 2007)

(h) 6-month with 0.89% discount (November 11, 2008)

(i) 1-year with 1.73% discount (September 30, 2008)

(j) 1-year with 1.19% discount (November 5, 2008)

3. You are given the following data on different rates with the same maturity (1.5 years), but quoted on a different basis and different compounding frequencies:

- Continuously compounded rate: 2.00% annualized rate

- Continuously compounded return on maturity: 3.00%

- Annually compounded rate: 2.10% annualized rate

- Semi-annually compounded rate: 2.01% annualized rate

You want to find an arbitrage opportunity among these rates. Is there any one that seems to be mispriced?

4. Using the semi-annually compounded yield curve in Table 2.4, price the following securities:

(a) 5-year zero coupon bond

(b) 7-year coupon bond paying 15% semiannually

(c) 4-year coupon bond paying 7% quarterly

(d) 3 1/4-year coupon bond paying 9% semiannually

(e) 4-year floating rate bond with zero spread and semiannual payments

(f) 2 1/2-year floating rate bond with zero spread and annual payments

(g) 5 1/2-year floating rate bond with 35 basis point spread with quarterly payments

(h) 7 1/4-year floating rate bond with 40 basis point spread with semiannual payments

5. Consider a 10-year coupon bond paying 6% coupon rate.

(a) What is its price if its yield to maturity is 6%? What if it is 5% or 7%?

(b) Compute the price of the coupon bond for yields ranging between 1% and 15%. Plot the resulting bond price versus the yield to maturity. What does the plot look like?

6. Consider the data in Table 2.4. Consider two bonds, both with 7 years to maturity, but with different coupon rates. Let the two coupon rates be 15% and 3%.

(a) Compute the prices and the yields to maturity of these coupon bonds.

(b) How do the yields to maturity compare to each other? If they are different, why are they different? Would the difference in yields imply that one is a better "buy" than the other?

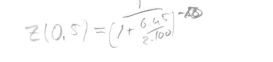

$$Z(0,5) = \left(1 + \frac{6.45}{2.100}\right)^{-10}$$

Table 2.4   Yield Curve on March 15, 2000

Maturity	Yield	Maturity	Yield	Maturity	Yield
0.25	6.33%	2.75	6.86%	5.25	6.39%
0.50	6.49%	3.00	6.83%	5.50	6.31%
0.75	6.62%	3.25	6.80%	5.75	6.24%
1.00	6.71%	3.50	6.76%	6.00	6.15%
1.25	6.79%	3.75	6.72%	6.25	6.05%
1.50	6.84%	4.00	6.67%	6.50	5.94%
1.75	6.87%	4.25	6.62%	6.75	5.81%
2.00	6.88%	4.50	6.57%	7.00	5.67%
2.25	6.89%	4.75	6.51%	7.25	5.50%
2.50	6.88%	5.00	6.45%	7.50	5.31%

Yields calculated based on data from CRSP (Daily Treasuries).

7. Today is May 15, 2000.

   (a) Compute the discount curve $Z(0, T)$ for $T =$ 6 month, 1 year, 1.5 years, and 2 years from the following data:

   - A 6-month zero coupon bond priced at $96.80 (issued 5/15/2000)
   - A 1-year note with 5.75% coupon priced at $99.56 (issued 5/15/1998)
   - A 1.5-year note with 7.5% coupon priced at $100.86 (issued 11/15/1991)
   - A 2-year note with 7.5% coupon priced at $101.22 (issued 5/15/1992)

   (b) Once you get the discount curve $Z(0, T)$ you take another look at the data and you find the following 1-year bonds:

   i. A 1-year note with 8.00% coupon priced at $101.13 (issued 5/15/1991)

   ii. A 1-year bond with 13.13% coupon priced at $106.00 (issued 4/2/1981)

   Compute the prices for these bonds with the discounts you found. Are the prices the same as what the market says? Is there an arbitrage opportunity? Why?

8. On May 15, 2000 you obtain the data on Treasuries in Table 2.5. Compute the semiannual yield curve, spanning over 9 years, from the data using the bootstrap procedure.

9. The Orange County case study at the end of the chapter discusses the pricing of inverse floaters, and provides a decomposition of inverse floaters in terms of a coupon bond, a floating rate bond, and a zero coupon bond (see Equation 2.43). Find an alternative decomposition of the same security, and compute the price. Do you obtain the same price? Discuss your findings in light of the law of one price discussed in Chapter 1.

Table 2.5   Bonds and Notes on May 15, 2000

Cusip	Issue Date	Maturity Date	Name	Coupon	Bid	Ask
912827ZE	8/15/1990	8/15/2000	NOTE	8.750%	100.5742	100.6055
912827ZN	11/15/1990	11/15/2000	NOTE	8.500%	100.8906	100.9219
912810CT	1/12/1981	2/15/2001	BOND	11.750%	103.8047	103.8359
912810CU	4/2/1981	5/15/2001	BOND	13.125%	105.9805	106.0117
912810CW	7/2/1981	8/15/2001	BOND	13.375%	107.6406	107.6719
912810CX	10/7/1981	11/15/2001	BOND	15.750%	112.3945	112.4258
912810CZ	1/6/1982	2/15/2002	BOND	14.250%	111.9297	111.9609
912827F4	5/15/1992	5/15/2002	NOTE	7.500%	101.2031	101.2344
912827G5	8/15/1992	8/15/2002	NOTE	6.375%	99.0469	99.0781
912810DA	9/29/1982	11/15/2002	BOND	11.625%	110.6680	110.6992
912810DC	1/4/1983	2/15/2003	BOND	10.750%	109.5117	109.5430
912810DD	4/4/1983	5/15/2003	BOND	10.750%	110.3281	110.3594
912810DE	7/5/1983	8/15/2003	BOND	11.125%	112.1523	112.1836
912810DG	10/5/1983	11/15/2003	BOND	11.875%	115.3086	115.3398
912827N8	2/15/1994	2/15/2004	NOTE	5.875%	97.1172	97.1484
912810DH	4/5/1984	5/15/2004	BOND	12.375%	118.8984	118.9297
912810DK	7/10/1984	8/15/2004	BOND	13.750%	124.9375	124.9688
912810DM	10/30/1984	11/15/2004	BOND	11.625%	118.2969	118.3281
912827S8	2/15/1995	2/15/2005	NOTE	7.500%	102.8633	102.8945
912810DQ	4/2/1985	5/15/2005	BOND	12.000%	121.6133	121.6445
912810DR	7/2/1985	8/15/2005	BOND	10.750%	117.0664	117.0977
912827V8	11/15/1995	11/15/2005	NOTE	5.875%	95.9844	96.0156
912810DU	1/15/1986	2/15/2006	BOND	9.375%	112.0352	112.0664
912827X8	5/15/1996	5/15/2006	NOTE	6.875%	100.6055	100.6367
912827Y5	7/15/1996	8/15/2006	NOTE	7.000%	101.2031	101.2344
912827Z6	10/15/1996	11/15/2006	NOTE	6.500%	98.7500	98.7813
9128272J	2/15/1997	2/15/2007	NOTE	6.250%	97.4883	97.5195
9128272U	5/15/1997	5/15/2007	NOTE	6.625%	99.5625	99.5938
9128273E	8/15/1997	8/15/2007	NOTE	6.125%	96.7578	96.7891
9128273X	2/15/1998	11/15/2007	NOTE	5.500%	93.1328	93.1641
9128274F	5/15/1998	5/15/2008	NOTE	5.625%	93.7852	93.8164
9128274V	11/16/1998	11/15/2008	NOTE	4.750%	87.9766	88.0078
9128275G	5/17/1999	5/15/2009	NOTE	5.500%	92.8242	92.8555

Data excerpted from CRSP (Daily Treasuries) ¤2009 Center for Research in Security Prices (CRSP),
The University of Chicago Booth School of Business.

2.8   CASE STUDY: ORANGE COUNTY INVERSE FLOATERS

With the tools we have developed in this chapter we can price all sorts of securities.[14] An interesting security to price is an inverse floater. These securities became very popular during the Orange County bankruptcy at the end of 1994, since it is estimated that a significant fraction of the county's portfolio comprised these securities. The bankruptcy of Orange County is a classic example of the risk that is inherent in interest rate securities, and we will discuss this case study more thoroughly in Chapters 3 and 4 after we introduce some tools to measure interest rate risk. In this section we pave the way for the discussion of risk in the next chapters by investigating the methodology to value inverse floaters. Because we are interested in understanding the dynamics behind Orange County's financial problems, we assume that we are beginning our analysis on December 31, 1993 (a year before the county declared bankruptcy).

2.8.1   Decomposing Inverse Floaters into a Portfolio of Basic Securities

An inverse floater is a security that pays a lower coupon as interest rates go up (hence the name inverse floater). For this to work, we need to establish a fixed reference rate from which to subtract the floating rate. To keep things simple, we assume that the inverse floater promises to pay 15% minus the short-term interest rate on an annual basis with 3 years maturity. That is, the coupon on the bond is:

$$c(t) = 15\% - r_1(t-1) \qquad (2.42)$$

where $r_1(t-1)$ denotes the annually compounded rate at time $t-1$, and we adopt the usual convention according to which the cash flow at time t, $c(t)$, depends on the interest rate one period earlier, namely $t-1$ in our case as payments are annual. The assumption of the annual payment frequency for the inverse floater is made for simplicity, so that the calculations are easier to follow. Notice also that Equation 2.42 contains a further simplification, namely, the fact that the coupon is always positive, which would be violated if the short rate were ever larger than 15%. In reality, if this situation occurs, the bond does not pay any coupon [i.e., $c(t) = 0$ if $r(t-1) > 15\%$]. To take this case into account we need to develop further tools, as we will do in Parts II and III of this book. For the time being assume that we know with certainty that the short rate is always below 15%.

An interesting fact arises by looking at the formula in Equation 2.42: Coupon payments are a combination of a fixed rate and a floating rate bond. So, for the coupon payments, this is the same as having a long position in a fixed rate bond and a short position in a floating rate bond, as such positions would entail receiving a fixed coupon and paying a floating coupon.[15] If we follow this strategy, however, we find that at maturity $T = 3$ the principal we receive from the fixed rate bond has to be used to pay for the principal of the floating rate bond. That is, only a long position in the fixed rate and short position in the floating rate bond does not exactly mimic an inverse floater. We can solve this problem by

---

[14]Thanks to Francisco Javier Madrid for his help in putting this case together. Descriptive material is from the case study ERISK: Orange County, downloaded from http://www.erisk.com/Learning/CaseStudies/OrangeCounty.asp.
[15]An investor has a long position in a bond if he holds the bond in the portfolio. In contrast, a short position means that the investor sold the bond without actually having it in the portfolio. The short position is accomplished by first borrowing the bond from a broker, typically in the repo market, and then selling it to the market. It is the responsibility of the investor who sold the bond short to make the regular coupon payments to the counterparty.

adding to the portfolio a 3-year zero coupon bond. From the law of one price (see Fact 1.1 in Chapter 1) the price of an inverse floater is then:

$$\text{Price inverse floater} = P_z(0,3) + P_c(0,3) - P_{FR}(0,3) \qquad (2.43)$$

where we recall that $P_z(0,3)$, $P_c(0,3)$, and $P_{FR}(0,3)$ denote the prices of a zero coupon bond, a coupon bond, and a floating rate bond with three years to maturity.

2.8.2 Calculating the Term Structure of Interest Rates from Coupon Bonds

The next challenge is to determine the term structure of the interest rates so as to obtain the discount rates for the bonds. A first idea might be to find zero coupon bonds for all these periods. The problem is that we might not necessarily find all the data we want. An alternative is to look at all bonds that are being quoted in the market today (December 31, 1993) and use this data to plot the yield curve. The reasoning is that every day, quotes are available on bonds maturing at different dates. As we saw in this chapter, in absence of arbitrage opportunities, any bond with coupon c that matures in three years (even if it was issued, for example, seven years ago), must have the same price as a 3-year bond, issued today, with coupon c. Additionally, through Equations 2.26 and 2.27 we can convert coupon paying bonds into zero coupon bonds. This exercise, however, may prove more challenging than it sounds. Look at Table 2.6, which reports all the bond price quotes available on December 31, 1993. There are 224 bonds quoted. To perform the bootstrap analysis, we need many fewer bonds. How do we pick the bonds to bootstrap out the term structure of interest rates?

After some careful (and time consuming) analysis of the data in Table 2.6, we resolve to use the subsample of data, contained in Table 2.7, which are nicely spaced at 6-month intervals. The last two columns of the table provide the discount factors $Z(0,T)$ computed from either bid prices or ask prices.[16]

2.8.3 Calculating the Price of the Inverse Floater

Recall that the value of the inverse floater can be computed from the value of a zero coupon bond, a coupon bond with coupon rate equal to 15%, and a floating rate bond, all of them with maturity equal to three years. Given the discount factors in Table 2.7, we can obtain values for these standard bonds. For simplicity, we use the average discount $Z(0,T) = 0.5 \times Z_A(0,T) + 0.5 \times Z_B(0,T)$ for the following calculations.

1. **Three-year zero coupon bond**. Three years from December 31, 1993 corresponds to the maturity date December 31, 1996. The discount factor $Z(0,3) = 0.8745$. Thus, $P_z(0,3) = 100 \times 0.8745 = \$87.45$.

2. **Three-year, 15% fixed coupon bond**. Given the discount factors $Z(0,T)$ for $T = 1, 2, 3$, we can compute the price of a coupon bond by applying the bond pricing formula in Equation 2.13, with the only caveat that in this exercise coupons are annually paid, and thus we do not have to divide them by 2 (as instead we do in Equation 2.13). More precisely, Table 2.8 carries out the calculation, and obtains the price of the fixed coupon bond $P_c(0,T) = \$128.83$.

---

[16]Recall that the bid and ask prices are the quotes at which security dealers are ready to buy or sell the securities. Because they make a profit from the spread between them, the ask price is higher than the bid price.

Table 2.6   Bond Quotes on December 31, 1993

Maturity	Coupon	Bid	Ask	Maturity	Coupon	Bid	Ask	Maturity	Coupon	Bid	Ask
19940106	0.000	99.960	99.961	19950415	8.375	105.500	105.563	19980531	5.375	101.125	101.188
19940113	0.000	99.904	99.908	19950430	3.875	99.938	100.000	19980630	5.125	100.063	100.125
19940115	7.000	100.094	100.156	19950515	10.375	108.500	108.563	19980715	8.250	112.500	112.563
19940120	0.000	99.841	99.846	19950515	12.625	111.563	111.688	19980731	5.250	100.469	100.531
19940127	0.000	99.788	99.795	19950515	5.875	102.531	102.594	19980815	9.250	116.750	116.813
19940131	4.875	100.125	100.188	19950515	8.500	106.000	106.063	19980831	4.750	98.375	98.438
19940203	0.000	99.724	99.728	19950515	11.250	109.656	109.719	19980831	4.750	98.375	98.438
19940210	0.000	99.666	99.671	19950531	4.125	100.250	100.313	19980930	4.750	98.375	98.438
19940215	9.000	100.688	100.750	19950630	4.125	100.188	100.250	19981015	7.125	108.188	108.250
19940215	6.875	100.406	100.469	19950715	8.875	107.125	107.188	19981031	4.750	98.188	98.250
19940215	8.875	100.656	100.719	19950731	4.250	100.281	100.344	19981115	3.500	98.969	99.969
19940217	0.000	99.612	99.617	19950815	4.625	100.875	100.938	19981115	8.875	115.750	115.813
19940224	0.000	99.551	99.557	19950815	8.500	106.875	106.938	19981130	5.125	99.625	99.688
19940228	5.375	100.344	100.406	19950815	10.500	110.031	110.094	19981231	5.125	99.625	99.688
19940303	0.000	99.489	99.492	19950831	3.875	99.688	99.750	19990115	6.375	105.031	105.094
19940310	0.000	99.423	99.427	19950930	3.875	99.594	99.656	19990215	8.875	116.156	116.219
19940317	0.000	99.367	99.371	19951015	8.625	107.625	107.688	19990415	7.000	107.844	107.906
19940324	0.000	99.306	99.311	19951031	3.875	99.531	99.594	19990515	9.125	117.875	117.938
19940331	5.750	100.625	100.688	19951115	11.500	113.063	113.188	19990715	6.375	105.000	105.063
19940331	8.500	101.250	101.313	19951115	5.125	101.688	101.750	19990815	8.000	112.938	113.000
19940331	0.000	99.248	99.253	19951115	8.500	107.688	107.750	19991015	6.000	103.219	103.281
19940407	0.000	99.173	99.178	19951115	9.500	109.531	109.594	19991115	7.875	112.625	112.688
19940414	0.000	99.113	99.119	19951130	4.250	100.063	100.125	20000115	6.375	105.063	105.125
19940415	7.000	101.031	101.094	19951231	4.250	100.000	100.063	20000215	8.500	116.125	116.188
19940421	0.000	99.047	99.053	19960115	9.250	109.625	109.688	20000415	5.500	100.844	100.906
19940428	0.000	98.990	98.997	19960131	7.500	106.344	106.406	20000515	8.875	118.375	118.438
19940430	5.375	100.656	100.719	19960215	4.625	100.688	100.750	20000815	8.750	118.000	118.063
19940505	0.000	98.920	98.927	19960215	7.875	107.125	107.188	20001115	8.500	116.844	116.906
19940512	0.000	98.849	98.856	19960215	8.875	109.156	109.219	20010215	11.750	136.219	136.344
19940515	7.000	101.313	101.375	19960229	7.500	106.500	106.563	20010215	7.750	113.719	113.781
19940515	9.500	102.219	102.281	19960331	7.750	107.188	107.250	20010515	13.125	145.313	145.438
19940515	13.125	103.563	103.625	19960415	9.375	110.750	110.813	20010515	8.000	114.344	114.406
19940519	0.000	98.780	98.788	19960430	7.625	107.094	107.156	20010815	13.375	147.875	148.000
19940526	0.000	98.714	98.723	19960515	4.250	99.719	99.781	20010815	7.875	113.813	113.875
19940531	5.125	100.719	100.781	19960515	7.375	106.625	106.688	20011115	15.750	164.031	164.156
19940602	0.000	98.653	98.661	19960531	7.625	107.375	107.438	20011115	7.500	111.563	111.625
19940609	0.000	98.582	98.591	19960630	7.875	108.688	108.750	20020215	14.250	155.656	155.781
19940616	0.000	98.516	98.525	19960715	8.125	108.188	108.188	20020515	7.500	111.844	111.906
19940623	0.000	98.439	98.449	19960731	7.875	108.219	108.281	20020815	6.375	104.250	104.313
19940630	5.000	100.813	100.875	19960815	4.375	99.844	99.906	20021115	11.625	140.344	140.469
19940630	8.500	102.500	102.563	19960831	7.250	106.813	106.875	20030215	10.750	134.813	134.938
19940630	0.000	98.391	98.401	19960930	7.000	106.594	106.656	20030215	6.250	103.250	103.313
19940715	8.000	102.406	102.469	19961015	8.000	108.938	109.000	20030515	10.750	135.313	135.438
19940728	0.000	98.113	98.125	19961031	6.875	106.125	106.188	20030815	11.125	138.656	138.781
19940731	4.250	100.469	100.531	19961115	4.375	99.563	99.625	20030815	5.750	99.625	99.688
19940815	8.750	103.188	103.250	19961115	7.250	107.156	107.219	20031115	11.875	144.750	144.875
19940815	6.875	102.063	102.125	19961130	6.500	105.250	105.313	20040515	12.375	149.969	150.094
19940815	8.625	103.125	103.188	19961231	6.125	104.531	104.594	20040815	13.750	161.406	161.531
19940815	12.625	105.531	105.594	19970115	8.000	109.469	109.531	20041115	11.625	145.219	145.344
19940825	0.000	97.841	97.854	19970131	6.250	104.594	104.656	20050515	12.000	149.375	149.500
19940831	4.250	100.469	100.531	19970228	6.750	106.063	106.125	20050815	10.750	139.531	139.656
19940922	0.000	97.563	97.578	19970331	6.875	106.531	106.594	20060215	9.375	128.906	129.031
19940930	4.000	100.313	100.375	19970415	8.500	111.375	111.438	20150215	11.250	154.250	154.313
19940930	8.500	103.594	103.656	19970430	6.875	106.563	106.625	20150815	10.625	147.375	147.438
19941015	9.500	104.438	104.500	19970515	8.500	111.531	111.594	20151115	9.875	138.750	138.813
19941020	0.000	97.249	97.265	19970531	6.750	106.219	106.281	20160215	9.250	131.531	131.594
19941031	4.250	100.531	100.594	19970630	6.375	105.156	105.219	20160515	7.250	108.188	108.250
19941115	10.125	105.438	105.500	19970715	8.500	111.875	111.938	20161115	7.500	111.031	111.094
19941115	6.000	101.969	102.031	19970731	5.500	102.344	102.406	20170515	8.750	125.938	126.000
19941115	8.250	103.875	103.938	19970815	8.625	112.469	112.531	20170815	8.875	127.594	127.656
19941115	11.625	106.750	106.813	19970831	5.625	102.563	102.625	20180515	9.125	130.969	131.031
19941117	0.000	96.924	96.942	19970930	5.500	102.188	102.250	20181115	9.000	129.625	129.688
19941130	4.625	100.875	100.938	19971015	8.750	113.125	113.188	20190215	8.875	128.219	128.281
19941215	0.000	96.646	96.665	19971031	5.750	102.969	103.031	20190815	8.125	119.094	119.156
19941231	4.625	100.906	100.969	19971115	8.875	113.781	113.844	20200215	8.500	123.906	123.969
19941231	7.625	103.813	103.875	19971130	6.000	103.781	103.844	20200515	8.750	127.219	127.281
19950115	8.625	104.875	104.938	19971231	6.000	103.781	103.844	20200815	8.750	127.281	127.344
19950115	4.250	100.531	100.594	19980115	7.875	110.438	110.500	20210215	7.875	116.438	116.500
19950215	3.000	100.250	101.250	19980131	5.625	102.281	102.344	20210515	8.125	119.719	119.781
19950215	10.500	107.344	107.406	19980215	8.125	111.500	111.563	20210815	8.125	119.719	119.781
19950215	5.500	101.844	101.906	19980228	5.125	100.438	100.500	20211115	8.000	118.406	118.469
19950215	7.750	104.281	104.344	19980331	5.125	100.344	100.406	20220815	7.250	109.094	109.156
19950215	11.250	108.125	108.188	19980415	7.875	110.719	110.781	20221115	7.625	114.156	114.219
19950228	3.875	100.063	100.125	19980430	5.125	100.250	100.313	20230215	7.125	108.156	108.219
19950331	3.875	100.031	100.094	19980515	9.000	115.250	115.313	20230815	6.250	98.656	98.719

Table 2.7   Discount Factors $Z(0, T)$ on December 31, 1993

Maturity	Coupon	Bid	Ask	$Z_B(0, T)$	$Z_A(0, T)$
19940630	0.000	98.3911	98.4012	0.9839	0.9840
19941231	7.625	103.8125	103.8750	0.9639	0.9645
19950630	4.125	100.1875	100.2500	0.9423	0.9429
19951231	4.250	100.0000	100.0625	0.9191	0.9196
19960630	7.875	108.6875	108.7500	0.9014	0.9019
19961231	6.125	104.5313	104.5938	0.8743	0.8748
19970630	6.375	105.1563	105.2188	0.8466	0.8471
19971231	6.000	103.7813	103.8438	0.8203	0.8208
19980630	5.125	100.0625	100.1250	0.7944	0.7950
19981231	5.125	99.6250	99.6875	0.7703	0.7708

Data Source: CRSP.

Table 2.8   The Price of a 15% Fixed Coupon Bond

Date	Cash Flow	Discount $Z(0, T)$	Discounted Cash Flow
19931231			
19941231	0.15	0.9642	0.1446
19951231	0.15	0.9193	0.1379
19961231	1.15	0.8745	1.0057
		Sum	1.2883
		Price ($\times 100$)	128.83

3. **Three-year floating rate bond**. From Section 2.5, we recall that the value of a floating rate bond is always equal to par at reset dates. Thus, we have $P_{FR}(3) = \$100$.

In conclusion, the value of the inverse floater is given by

$$\text{Price inverse floater} = P_z(0, 3) + P_c(0, 3) - P_{FR}(0, 3) \qquad (2.44)$$
$$= \$87.45 + \$128.83 - \$100 \qquad (2.45)$$
$$= \$116.28 \qquad (2.46)$$

2.8.4   Leveraged Inverse Floaters

Within Orange County's portfolio there were many different types of inverse floaters (e.g. different maturities and maximum interest rates). In addition, the portfolio contained some leveraged inverse floaters.[17] The main difference between these and the plain vanilla inverse

---

[17] See Mark Grinblatt and Sheridan Titman, Financial Markets and Corporate Strategy (2nd Edition), McGraw-Hill Primis, 2006, Chapter 23.

floaters discussed earlier is that the parity of floating rate to fixed rate is greater than one. For example, consider a 3-year leveraged inverse floater that pays a coupon of 25% minus two times the short-term interest rate. To price this security, we need to revise the steps we took to price inverse floaters.[18] The coupon is given by

$$c(t) = 25\% - 2 \times r_1(t-1) \tag{2.47}$$

What is a portfolio of bonds that pays this cash flow? A portfolio that is long a 25% fixed coupon bond and short *two* floating rate bonds achieves the coupon described in Equation 2.47. However, such a position at maturity entails that we receive \$100 from the long position and we must pay \$200 from the short position. In order to receive \$100 overall, we must also be long two zero coupon bonds. Thus, overall, we have

$$\text{Price leveraged inverse floater} = 2 \times P_z(0,3) + P_c(0,3) - 2 \times P_{FR}(0,3) \tag{2.48}$$

We already know from the previous section the prices $P_z(0,3) = \$87.45$ and $P_{FR}(0,3) = \$100$. The computation of the price of fixed-coupon bond with coupon rate equal to 25% yields a price of $P_c(0,3) = \$156.41$. Thus, we immediately find

$$\begin{aligned}
\text{Price leveraged inverse floater} &= 2 \times \$87.45 + \$156.41 - 2 \times \$100 \tag{2.49}\\
&= \$131.32 \tag{2.50}
\end{aligned}$$

This case study illustrates that we can readily apply the tools covered in this chapter to value more complex securities, such as inverse floaters and leveraged inverse floaters. In the next chapter we will follow up with this analysis and study the risk embedded in these securities. Finally, we note that dealing with real data and real markets often poses additional problems in the valuation and risk analysis of fixed income instruments: For instance, the computation of the discount curve $Z(0,t)$ requires the analysis of the data in Table 2.6, which is not straightforward. The next section illustrates additional methodologies used in practice to deal with such large quantities of data.

2.9 APPENDIX: EXTRACTING THE DISCOUNT FACTORS $Z(0,T)$ FROM COUPON BONDS

The Orange County case study in the previous section makes it apparent that the bootstrap methodology discussed in Section 2.4.2 has limited applicability, and this for two reasons. First, for short-term maturities, there are too many bonds that mature on the same day to choose from. To perform the bootstrap methodology, we then must cherry pick the bonds that we deem have the highest liquidity (e.g., notes over bonds). Second, for longer maturities not all of the bonds may be available. In this case, some approximation is necessary. Sometimes it is possible to use the bonds that expire a few days earlier or later than the ones in the six-month cycle needed for the bootstrap. But often the gap across maturities may span longer periods, in which case the bootstrap methodology does not work well.

---

[18]We maintain the assumption that the coupon is always positive, that is that rates are always below 25%/2

2.9.1 Bootstrap Again

The iterative procedure described in the text is simple, but cumbersome. An easier way to obtain the same result is to use the matrix notation. Let $t = 0$, for convenience, so that T denotes both maturity date and time to maturity. Every coupon bond i is characterized by a series of cash flows and a maturity T^i. We can denote the total cash flow paid at time T_j as $c^i(T_j)$. In particular, denoting c^i the coupon rate of bond i, we have $c^i(T_j) = 100 \times c^i/2$ for $T_j < T^i$ and $c^i(T^i) = 100 \times (1 + c^i/2)$ and finally $c^i(T_j) = 0$ for $T_j > T^i$. We can put these cash flows in a row vector as follows:

$$\mathbf{C}^i = \left(c^i(T_1), c^i(T_2), ..., c^i(T_n) \right)$$

We can denote by $\mathbf{Z}(0)$ the vector of discount factors for various maturities T_i, that is

$$\mathbf{Z}(0) = \begin{pmatrix} Z(0, T_1) \\ Z(0, T_2) \\ \vdots \\ Z(0, T_n) \end{pmatrix}$$

The price of a coupon bond can be written using vector multiplication as:

$$P_c^i(0, T) = \mathbf{C}^i \times \mathbf{Z}(0)$$

We can denote the column vector of bond prices available at time 0 as

$$\mathbf{P}(0) = \begin{pmatrix} P_c(0, T_1) \\ P_c(0, T_2) \\ \vdots \\ P_c(0, T_n) \end{pmatrix}$$

We then obtain a system of n equations with n unknowns [the unknowns are the values of $Z(0, T_1), ..., Z(0, T_n)$]

$$\mathbf{P}(0) = \mathbf{C} \times \mathbf{Z}(0)$$

where $\mathbf{C}$ is the cash flow matrix:

$$\mathbf{C} = \begin{pmatrix} c^1(T_1) & c^1(T_2) & ... & c^1(T_n) \\ c^2(T_1) & c^2(T_2) & ... & c^2(T_n) \\ \vdots & & \ddots & \vdots \\ c^n(T_1) & c^n(T_2) & ... & c^n(T_n) \end{pmatrix}$$

Essentially, each row i of $\mathbf{C}$ corresponds to the cash flows of bond i for all the maturities $T_1,...,T_n$. In contrast, each column j describes all the cash flows that occur on that particular maturity T_j from the n bonds. The discount factors can then be obtained by inverting the cash flow matrix:

$$\mathbf{Z}(0) = \mathbf{C}^{-1} \times \mathbf{P}(0)$$

2.9.2 Regressions

As mentioned, we rarely have such nicely spaced data. Sometimes we in fact have too many maturities and sometimes we do not have enough maturities available to carry out the bootstrap procedure. The regression methodology deals with the case in which there are too many bonds compared to the number of maturities. This is typically the case when we consider maturities up to five years. For instance, in Table 2.6 there are 164 bonds with maturity of less than five years, but there are only 60 months in five years, implying that many months have multiple bonds maturing in them.

When we compute the cash flow matrix:

$$
\mathbf{C} = \begin{pmatrix}
c^1(T_1) & c^1(T_2) & \ldots & c^1(T_n) \\
c^2(T_1) & c^2(T_2) & \ldots & c^2(T_n) \\
\vdots & & \ddots & \vdots \\
c^N(T_1) & c^n(T_2) & \ldots & c^n(T_n)
\end{pmatrix}
$$

we end up with N rows (N = number of bonds) and $n < N$ columns (n = number of maturities). Since the solution to bootstrap involves inverting the matrix $\mathbf{C}$, we have a problem, as the matrix $\mathbf{C}$ must have an equal number of rows and columns to be inverted.

We can slightly change the bootstrap methodology to deal with this problem. For every bond $i = 1, ..., N$ let

$$
P_c^i(0, T^i) = \mathbf{C}^i \times \mathbf{Z}(0) + \varepsilon^i \tag{2.51}
$$

where ε^i is a random error term that captures any factor that generates the "mispricing." These factors include data staleness, lack of trading or liquidity. If we look at Equation 2.51, we see a regression equation of the type

$$
y^i = \alpha + \sum_{j=1}^{n} \beta^j x^{ij} + \varepsilon^j
$$

where the data are $y^i = P_c^i(0, T^i)$ and $x^{ij} = C_{ij}$, and the regressors are $\beta^j = Z(0, T_j)$. From basic Ordinary Least Squares (OLS) formulas, we then find

$$
\mathbf{Z}(0) = (\mathbf{C}' \times \mathbf{C})^{-1} \mathbf{C}' \times \mathbf{P}(0)
$$

For this procedure to work, however, we must have more bonds than maturities, which does not occur for longer maturities. Curve fitting treats this latter problem.

2.9.3 Curve Fitting

Let's consider approaching the problem from a completely different angle. In particular, we can postulate a parametric functional form for the discount factor $Z(0, T)$ as a function of maturity T and use the current bond prices to *estimate* the parameters of this functional form. One popular model is the following:

2.9.3.1 The Nelson Siegel Model
The Nelson Siegel model is perhaps the most famous model. The discount factor is posited to be given by

$$
Z(0, T) = e^{-r(0,T)T} \tag{2.52}
$$

where the continously compounded yield with maturity T is given by

$$r(0,T) = \theta_0 + (\theta_1 + \theta_2)\frac{1 - e^{-\frac{T}{\lambda}}}{\frac{T}{\lambda}} - \theta_2 e^{-\frac{T}{\lambda}} \tag{2.53}$$

where θ_0, θ_1, θ_2 and λ are parameters to be estimated from the current bond data.

The estimation proceeds as follows. For given parameter values $(\theta_0, \theta_1, \theta_2, \lambda)$, it is possible to compute the value of bond prices implied by the Nelson Siegel model. For each bond $i = 1, .., N$ with coupon c^i and cash flow payment dates maturity T_j^i, for $j = 1, .., n^i$, the Nelson Siegel model implies that the bond price should be

$$P_c^{i,\ NS\ model} = 100 \times \left(\frac{c^i}{2}\sum_{j=1}^{n_i} Z(0, T_j^i) + Z(0, T^i)\right) \tag{2.54}$$

For the same bond, we have the price quoted in the market, $P_c^{i,\ data}$ (note that this has to be the *invoice* price and not the *quoted* price). For each given set of parameters $(\theta_0, \theta_1, \theta_2, \lambda)$ we can compute the difference between model prices and data. Namely, we can compute

$$J(\theta_0, \theta_1, \theta_2, \lambda) = \sum_{i=1}^{N} \left(P_c^{i,\ NS\ model} - P_c^{i,\ data}\right)^2 \tag{2.55}$$

The Nelson Siegel model works perfectly if the model prices equal the data, i.e., if for every $i = 1, ..., N$ we have $P_c^{i,\ NS\ model} = P_c^{i,\ data}$. In this case, $J(\theta_0, \theta_1, \theta_2, \lambda) = 0$. The set of parameters $(\theta_0, \theta_1, \theta_2, \lambda)$ that achieves this objective would be the one to use to determine the discount factors $Z(0, T)$.

In general, however, it will not be possible to find parameter values that price all of the bonds exactly, because of staleness in the data, lack of liquidity, or lack of degrees of freedom in the Nelson Siegel model (we only have four parameters, after all). Therefore, the procedure is instead to find parameters $(\theta_0, \theta_1, \theta_2, \lambda)$ that *minimize* the quantity $J(\theta_0, \theta_1, \theta_2, \lambda)$ in Equation 2.55.

Figure 2.6 compares three methodologies of computing the term structure of interest rates: The bootstrap, the Nelson Siegel model, and the Extended Nelson Siegel model, further discussed below. The data are those contained in Table 2.6. The results of the bootstrap methodology are already contained in Table 2.7 in the form of discount function $Z(0, T)$. As it can be seen, the bootstrap method generates a yield curve that has a dip at maturity $T = 2.5$. It is not clear from the data why the dip in yield is present at that point: It could be a liquidity issue, or staleness, or simply an error in the database. The problem with bootstrap is that correcting for these sources of imprecision is hard.

The solid line in Figure 2.6 plots the fitted yield curve according to the Nelson Siegel model. The parameter estimates are $\theta_0 = 0.0754$, $\theta_1 = -0.0453$, $\theta_2 = -7.3182 \times 10^{-009}$ and $\lambda = 3.2286$. The Nelson Siegel curve cuts through the bootstrapped curve smoothly. If the dip of the 2.5 year yield was a data error, it gets corrected in the minimization of errors. Indeed, note that we did not use only the ten bonds in Table 2.7 to fit the Nelson Siegel model, but the whole of 161 bonds with maturity less than five years in Table 2.6.

Can the Nelson Siegel model fit all of these data reasonably well? Figure 2.7 plots both the bond prices (stars) and the model prices (diamonds) for the various maturities: The model works well if the stars are close to the diamonds. The figure shows that indeed for most bonds this is the case, indicating that the model is doing quite well. The figure also shows that indeed at $T = 2.5$ there is a star that differs substantially from the diamond. This is in fact the bond that makes the bootstrap methodology fail at that maturity: The price seems too high compared to what the Nelson Siegel model – and in fact all of the other bonds around it – would imply. This fact suggests that either there is a trading opportunity available, or that that data point is an aberration and should be corrected. Unfortunately, such a correction is not easy if we use the bootstrap methodology.

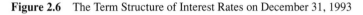

Figure 2.6   The Term Structure of Interest Rates on December 31, 1993

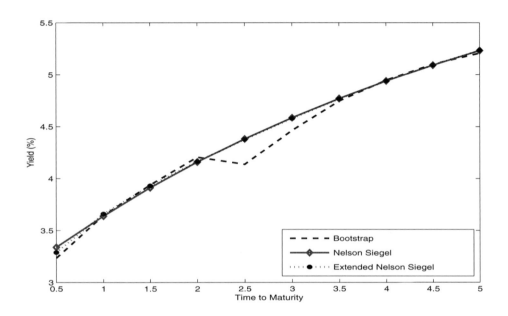

Source: Center for Research in Security Prices.

2.9.3.2   *The Extended Nelson Siegel Model*   The Nelson Siegel model works well, but it lacks the flexibility to match term structures that are highly nonlinear. The economist Lars Svensson proposed an extension to the model, which is the one most widely adopted. In particular, we assume:

$$r(0,T) \;=\; \theta_0 + (\theta_1 + \theta_2)\, \frac{1 - e^{-\frac{T}{\lambda_1}}}{\frac{T}{\lambda_1}} - \theta_2 e^{-\frac{T}{\lambda_1}} + \theta_3 \left(\frac{1 - e^{-\frac{T}{\lambda_2}}}{\frac{T}{\lambda_2}} - e^{-\frac{T}{\lambda_2}} \right) \quad (2.56)$$

where the parameters to estimate are 6: θ_i, $i = 0, .., 3$ and λ_1 and λ_2. The procedure is otherwise the same as in the case of the Nelson Siegel model. Figure 2.6 shows the results of applying the extended Nelson Siegel model to the data in Table 2.6. The parameter estimates are $\theta_0 = 0.0687$, $\theta_1 = -0.0422$, $\theta_2 = -0.2399$, $\theta_3 = 0.2116$, $\lambda_1 = 0.9652$, and $\lambda_2 = 0.8825$. The outcome of the two procedures is almost the same. Indeed, the extended Nelson Siegel model has been put forward to capture severe non-linearities in the shape of the term structure of interest rates, a situation that did not occur in 1993.

Figure 2.7 The Fit of the Nelson Siegel Model

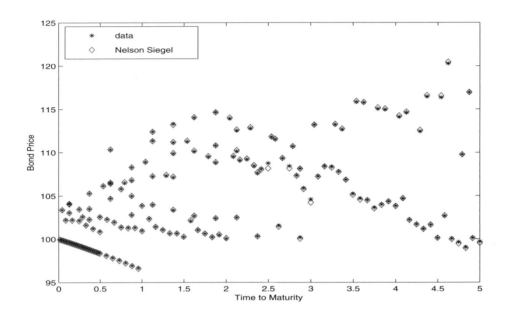

2.9.4 Curve Fitting with Splines

This is an extension of the curve fitting methodology described in Section 2.9.3, with a different specification of the discount factor $Z(t,T)$ as a function of maturity T. In essence, the idea is to assume that the discount function $Z(t,T)$ is given by a weighted average of basis functions $f_\ell(T)$, where the weights are chosen to best match the bond prices.

Specifically, the discount function is given by

$$Z(t,T) = 1 + \sum_{\ell=1}^{L} a_\ell f_\ell(T) \tag{2.57}$$

What are the functions $f_\ell(T)$? Many alternatives have been proposed.

1. **Simple polynomials:**
$$f_\ell(T) = T^\ell$$

This is the simplest case, where the discount function is the Lth-order polynomial

$$Z(t,T) = 1 + \sum_{\ell=1}^{L} a_\ell T^\ell$$

and the coefficients a_ℓ have to be estimated to minimize the distance between observed prices in the data $P_c^i(0,T_i)$ and the theoretical prices $\widehat{P}^i(0,T_i) = \sum_{j=1}^{n_i} c(T_j^i) \times Z(0,T_j^i)$, where T_j^i is the jth-s cash-flow date of bond i. The problem with polynomial functions is that they do not allow for a sufficient number of shapes, without going into a very high order polynomial. In this case, however, the discount function lacks the necessary stiffness to avoid being contaminated by small errors in data.

2. **Piecewise polynomial functions, or, spline**: Intuitively, a polynomial spline can be thought of as a number of separate polynomial functions, joined smoothly at a number of so called "joints", "breaks," or "knot" points. Using this method, each polynomial can be of low order and hence retain some stiffness, that is, a more stable curve. Cubic splines are the most used functions (so, third order), as they generate smooth forward curves. Of course, inside the family of splines there are many specifications, such as (to give some names):

   (a) Exponential cubic splines; and

   (b) B-splines.

However, a number of other problems arise with these functions, the most important being the decision of *how many* knot points to include and, in addition, *where* to position them. We do not delve any more into this issue, as it is beyond the scope of this chapter, but relevant readings are available in the references to this chapter at the end of the book.

CHAPTER 3

BASICS OF INTEREST RATE RISK MANAGEMENT

Interest rates change substantially over time, and their variation poses large risks to financial institutions, portfolio managers, corporations, governments, and, in fact, households. Anyone who directly or indirectly invests in fixed income securities or borrows money is subject to interest rate risks. This chapter discusses the basics of interest rate risk management. In particular, we discuss first how to measure risk for fixed income instruments, by introducing the notion of duration, value-at-risk and expected shortfall. Then, we also cover the basic techniques to mitigate financial risk, such as immunization and asset liability management.

3.1 THE VARIATION IN INTEREST RATES

Interest rates change substantially over time. Panel A of Figure 3.1 plots the time series of yields from 1965 to 2005.[1] The various lines, all very close to each other, are the continuously compounded yields of zero coupon bonds for maturities from 1 month to 10 years. The most immediate fact that springs out from Panel A of this figure is that all yields move up and down roughly together. For instance, they were all relatively low in the 1960s,

---

[1] The spot rate curves are calculated by fitting the extended Nelson Siegel model to coupon bond data from CRSP (Monthly Treasuries) ¤2009 Center for Research in Security Prices (CRSP), The University of Chicago Booth School of Business.

they were all relatively high in the late 1970s and early 1980s, and they were all relatively low in the late 1990s.

Figure 3.1   Zero Coupon Bond Yields and the Level of Interest Rates: 1965 - 2005

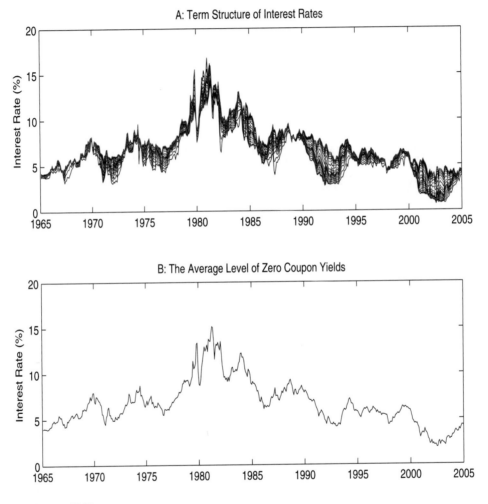

Data Source: CRSP.

Panel B of Figure 3.1 plots the simple average of yields graphed in Panel A. We may refer to this average generically as the level of interest rates.

Definition 3.1 *The* **level of interest rates** *is the average yield across maturities.*

As the level of interest rates changes over time, banks, bond portfolio managers and corporations worry about the impact that the swings in interest rates have on the value of their assets and liabilities. Two famous examples come to mind, namely, the savings and loan crisis in the 1980s and the bankruptcy of Orange County, California, in 1994.

3.1.1   The Savings and Loan Debacle

The savings and loan debacle in the 1980s is a standard example of what can go wrong when interest rates shift. A savings and loan earns a large part of its revenues from the difference between the long-term mortgages it provides to home owners and the short-term deposit rate it offers to depositors. When interest rates increased at the end of the 1970s, savings and loans were receiving their fixed coupons from mortgages contracted in the past, when rates were low, but suddenly they had to pay interest on deposits at the new higher deposit rates. Because depositors could choose where to put their money, banks were forced to offer high deposit rates, otherwise depositors would withdraw their deposits and invest in other securities, such as Treasuries. A withdrawal of funds is the worst nightmare for a bank, as depositors' money is not in the bank any longer: It has been loaned to others. The spread between the rate earned on assets and the (higher) rate paid on liabilities quickly put many savings and loans out of business.

3.1.2   The Bankruptcy of Orange County

In 1994 Orange County, California, lost $1.6 billion when the interest rate unexpectedly increased from 3% to 5.7% over the course of the year.[2] The substantial loss from the total asset pool of $7.5 billion forced Orange County to declare bankruptcy. Through the use of a mix of structure notes and leverage, Orange County's portfolio stood to make subtantial above market returns were the interest rate not to increase in the near future. But interest rates did increase, and the fund went down. This famous case highlights yet another example of the large losses that interest rate movements may bring about in portfolios that are "too sensitive" to interest rates.

3.2   DURATION

The examples above calls for (a) a systematic methodology to assess the riskiness of a bond portfolio to movements in interest rates; and (b) a methodology to effectively manage such risk. We tackle the former problem in this section, and the latter in the next.

Definition 3.2 *The **duration** of a security with price P is the (negative of the) percent sensitivity of the price P to a small* parallel *shift in the level of interest rates. That is, let $r(t, T)$ be the continuously compounded term structure of interest rates at time t. Consider a uniform shift of size dr across rates that brings rates to $\overline{r}(t, T)$, given by*

$$r(t, T) \longrightarrow \overline{r}(t, T) = r(t, T) + dr$$

Let the price of the security move by dP as a consequence of the shift:

$$P \longrightarrow \overline{P} = P + dP$$

---

[2] See the case study ERISK: Orange County, downloaded from the web site
http://www.erisk.com/Learning/CaseStudies/OrangeCounty.asp.

The duration of the asset is then defined as[3]

$$\text{Duration} = D_P = -\frac{1}{P}\frac{dP}{dr} \tag{3.1}$$

The shift dr is a small uniform change across maturities, such as, for instance, 1 basis point: $dr = .01\%$. The notion of duration then measures the impact that such a uniform change on the yield curve has on the price of the security P. This can be seen by reorganizing Equation 3.1 as follows:

Fact 3.1 *Given a duration D_P of a security with price P, a uniform change in the level of interest rates brings about a change in the value of*

$$\text{Change in portfolio value} = dP = -D_P \times P \times dr \tag{3.2}$$

■ **EXAMPLE 3.1**

A \$100 million bond portfolio has a duration equal 10, $D_P = 10$. This implies that one basis point increase in the level of interest rates $dr = .01\%$ generates a swing in portfolio value of

$$\begin{aligned}
\text{Change in portfolio value} = dP &= -10 \times \$100 \text{ million} \times .01/100 \\
&= -\$100,000
\end{aligned}$$

That is, the portfolio manager stands to lose \$100,000 for every basis point increase in the term structure.

How can we compute the duration of a security? Before we can answer this important question, however, we need to recall the following two concepts from calculus. To simplify our analysis, we will only consider continuously compounded interest rates, as in the definition above. Below, we also review the more traditional notion of duration that uses semi-annually compounded yield to maturity in its definition.

Definition 3.3 *Let A and a be two constants and x be a variable. Let $F(x) = A \times e^{ax}$ be a function of x. Then, the first **derivative** of F with respect to x, denoted by dF/dx, is given by*

$$\text{Derivative of } F(x) \text{ with respect to } x = \frac{dF}{dx} = A \times a \times e^{ax} = a \times F(x) \tag{3.3}$$

An example of the function $F(x)$ is the zero coupon bond formula studied in Chapter 2

$$P_z(t,T) = 100 \times Z(t,T) = 100 \times e^{-r(T-t)}.$$

---

[3]The duration definition in Equation 3.1 is often referred to as the "modified duration," to differentiate it from the Macaulay definition of duration, discussed below. In this book, we will rarely use the Macaulay duration, and therefore we reserve the term duration for modified duration.

In this case the constant A is the notional 100, the constant a equals the time to maturity $T - t$, and the variable x equals the continuously compounded interest rate r. The notion of the first derivative of $P_z(t, T)$ with respect to r then gives the sensitivity of the zero coupon bond to the interest rate r.

Fact 3.2 *Let $P_z(r, t, T)$ be the price of a zero coupon bond at time t with maturity T and continuously compounded interest rate r. The first derivative of $P_z(r, t, T)$ with respect to r is*

$$
\begin{aligned}
\frac{d\,P_z}{d\,r} &= 100 \times \left[\frac{d\left(e^{-r(T-t)}\right)}{dr}\right] \\
&= 100 \times \left[-(T - t) \times e^{-r(T-t)}\right] \\
&= -(T - t) \times P_z(r, t, T)
\end{aligned}
\tag{3.4}
$$

To emphasize that the zero coupon bond price depends on the current interest rate r, in this section we denote it by $P_z(r, t, T)$, that is, we add r as one of the arguments in $P_z(t, T)$. Visually, the first derivative represents the *slope* of the curve $P_z(r, t, T)$, plotted against r, at the current interest rate level. More specifically, Figure 3.2 plots the price of a 20-year zero coupon bond for various values of r, ranging from 0 to 15%. In the plot $T - t = 20$, as the zero coupon bond has 20 years to maturity. Suppose today the interest rate is $r = 6\%$. The straight dotted line in the Figure is the *tangent* to the curve $P_z(r, t, T)$ at the point $r = 6\%$. The slope of this tangent is the first derivative of $P_z(r, t, T)$ with respect to r, dP_z/dr.

3.2.1 Duration of a Zero Coupon Bond

We are now in the position of computing the duration of a zero coupon bond. The only thing we have to remember is Definition 3.2, and the rule of the first derivative in Definition 3.3 when applied to a zero coupon bond (Equation 3.4). It is instructive to go through the steps to compute the duration of a zero coupon bond, $D_{z,T}$, where the notation "z" reminds us that this calculation is done for a zero coupon bond.

$$
\begin{aligned}
D_{z,T} &= -\frac{1}{P_z(r, t, T)}\left[\frac{dP_z(r, t, T)}{dr}\right] \tag{3.5} \\
&= -\frac{1}{P_z(r, t, T)} \times [-(T - t) \times P_z(r, t, T)] \\
&= T - t \tag{3.6}
\end{aligned}
$$

The duration of a zero coupon bond is given by its time to maturity $T - t$. This makes it very simple to compute, indeed.

■ **EXAMPLE 3.2**

A portfolio manager has $100 million invested in 5-year STRIPS. The duration of this portfolio is then 5, implying that a one basis point increase in interest rates decreases

Figure 3.2 First Derivative of a Zero Coupon Bond with Respect to Interest Rate r

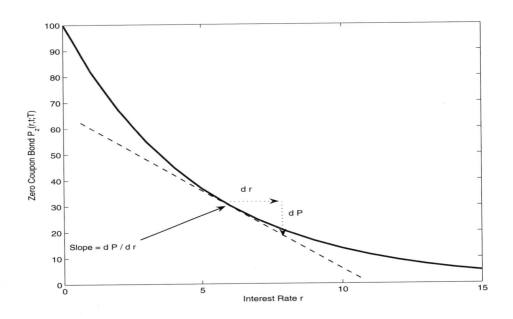

the value of the portfolio approximately by

$$dP \approx -D_P \times P \times dr = -5 \times \$100 \text{ million} \times .01\% = -\$50,000$$

3.2.2 Duration of a Portfolio

What is the duration of a portfolio of securities? Consider a portfolio made up of N_1 units of security 1, and N_2 units of security 2. Let P_1 and P_2 be the prices of these two securities, respectively. The value of the portfolio is then

$$W = N_1 \times P_1 + N_2 \times P_2$$

Let D_1 and D_2 be the duration of security 1 and security 2, respectively. By definition,

$$D_i = -\frac{1}{P_i}\frac{d\,P_i}{d\,r}$$

How can we determine the duration of the portfolio? We can apply the definition of duration in Definition 3.2 and reorganize the expressions:

$$
\begin{aligned}
\text{Duration of portfolio} \quad = \quad D_W &= -\frac{1}{W}\frac{d\,W}{d\,r} \\
&= -\frac{1}{W}\frac{d(N_1 \times P_1 + N_2 \times P_2)}{d\,r} \\
&= -\frac{1}{W}\left[N_1 \times \frac{dP_1}{d\,r} + N_2 \times \frac{dP_2}{d\,r}\right]
\end{aligned}
\tag{3.7}
$$

$$= \frac{1}{W}\left[N_1 \times P_1 \times \left(-\frac{1}{P_1}\frac{dP_1}{dr}\right) + N_2 \times P_2 \times \left(-\frac{1}{P_2}\frac{dP_2}{dr}\right)\right]$$

$$= \frac{N_1 \times P_1}{W}D_1 + \frac{N_2 \times P_2}{W}D_2$$

$$= w_1 D_1 + w_2 D_2 \tag{3.8}$$

where

$$w_1 = \frac{N_1 \times P_1}{W} \quad \text{and} \quad w_2 = \frac{N_2 \times P_2}{W} \tag{3.9}$$

The expression in Equation 3.8 shows that the duration of a portfolio is a weighted average of the durations of the assets, where the weights correspond to the percentage of the portfolio invested in the given security.

■ **EXAMPLE 3.3**

A bond portfolio manager has $100 million invested in 5-year STRIPS and $200 million invested in 10-year STRIPS. What is the impact of a one basis point parallel shift of the term structure on the value of the portfolio?

We can answer this question by computing the duration of the portfolio: The 5-year and 10-year strips have duration of 5 and 10, respectively. The total portfolio value is $300 million. Thus, the duration of the portfolio is

$$\text{Duration of portfolio} = \frac{100}{300} \times 5 + \frac{200}{300} \times 10 = 8.3$$

Therefore, a one basis point increase in interest rates generates a portfolio loss of

$$\text{Loss in portfolio value} = \$300 \text{ million} \times 8.3 \times 0.01\% = \$249,000$$

Generalizing the formula in Equation 3.8 to n securities, we obtain:

Fact 3.3 *The duration of portfolio of n securities is given by*

$$D_W = \sum_{i=1}^{n} w_i D_i \tag{3.10}$$

where w_i is the fraction of the portfolio invested in security i, and D_i is the duration of security i.

3.2.3 Duration of a Coupon Bond

We can apply the result in Fact 3.3 to compute the duration of a coupon bond. As discussed in Section 2.4, a coupon bond with coupon rate c and n future coupon payments can be considered a portfolio of zero coupon bonds, in which $c/2$ is invested in the first $n-1$ zeros, and $1 + c/2$ in the n-th zero:

$$P_c(0, T_n) = \sum_{i=1}^{n-1} \frac{c}{2} \times P_z(0, T_i) + \left(1 + \frac{c}{2}\right)P_z(0, T_n) \tag{3.11}$$

The duration of a coupon bond can then be computed by using Equation 3.10. Define the weights

$$w_i = \frac{c/2 \times P_z(0, T_i)}{P_c(0, T_n)} \quad \text{for } i = 1, .., n-1$$

$$w_n = \frac{(1 + c/2) \times P_z(0, T_n)}{P_c(0, T_n)}$$

Then, the duration of the coupon bond is

$$D_c = \sum_{i=1}^{n} w_i D_{z, T_i} \tag{3.12}$$

$$= \sum_{i=1}^{n} w_i T_i \tag{3.13}$$

That is, the duration of a coupon bond is a weighted average of coupon payment times T_i.

■ **EXAMPLE 3.4**

Consider a 10-year, 6% coupon bond. Given a discount curve $Z(0, T)$, we can compute its duration by following the calculations in Table 3.1. In this table, the second and third columns present the payment times and the payment amounts. The discount factor curve $Z(0, T)$ is in the fourth column. In the fifth column we compute the discounted cash flows, the sum of which gives the price $P_c(0, T) = \$107.795$ at the bottom of the table. The weights in column 6 equal the discount cash flows in column 5 divided by the price. Finally, the last column reports the weighted payment times: $\omega_i \times T_i$. The duration is given by the sum of these weighted payment times, reported at the bottom of the table: $D_c = 7.762$. Different from zero coupon bonds, the duration of the coupon bond is shorter than its maturity.

3.2.4 Duration and Average Time of Cash Flow Payments

While we have derived the formula for duration in Equation 3.13 from the definition of duration as the percentage sensitivity of a security to changes in interest rates (see Definition 3.2), some confusion sometimes arises about the notion of duration because sometimes people *define* duration as the average time of payments, as in Equation 3.13 (see also Section 3.2.6). These two interpretations are equivalent for fixed rate bonds, that is, bonds that pay fixed coupons: A zero coupon bond with maturity of 5 years has duration equal to 5. This is both the average time of payments (there is only one), and also the percentage loss in value from an increase in interest rates. A similar situation exists for coupon bonds. However, for many securities that do not have fixed payments, the equivalence is broken. The following provides a simple example:

Table 3.1 Duration of Coupon Bond, Coupon = 6%

Period i	Payment Time T_i	Cash Flow CF	Discount $Z(0, T_i)$	Discounted Cash Flow $\text{CF} \times Z(0, T_0)$	Weight w_i	Weight $\times T_i$ $w_i \times T_i$
1	0.5	3	0.976	2.927	0.027	0.014
2	1.0	3	0.952	2.855	0.026	0.026
3	1.5	3	0.929	2.786	0.026	0.039
4	2.0	3	0.906	2.718	0.025	0.050
5	2.5	3	0.884	2.652	0.025	0.061
6	3.0	3	0.862	2.587	0.024	0.072
7	3.5	3	0.841	2.524	0.023	0.082
8	4.0	3	0.821	2.462	0.023	0.091
9	4.5	3	0.801	2.402	0.022	0.100
10	5.0	3	0.781	2.344	0.022	0.109
11	5.5	3	0.762	2.286	0.021	0.117
12	6.0	3	0.744	2.231	0.021	0.124
13	6.5	3	0.725	2.176	0.020	0.131
14	7.0	3	0.708	2.123	0.020	0.138
15	7.5	3	0.690	2.071	0.019	0.144
16	8.0	3	0.674	2.021	0.019	0.150
17	8.5	3	0.657	1.972	0.018	0.155
18	9.0	3	0.641	1.923	0.018	0.161
19	9.5	3	0.626	1.877	0.017	0.165
20	10.0	103	0.610	62.858	0.583	5.831
			Price	107.795	Duration	7.762

■ **EXAMPLE 3.5**

Recall that in Section 2.5 of Chapter 2 we considered the price of a floating rate bond. In particular, Fact 2.12 shows that if T_i denotes the last reset date, T_{i+1} denotes the next reset date, t is the current time, with $T_i < t < T_{i+1}$, then the price of a floating rate bond with maturity T and semi-annual payments is given by (see Equation 2.40)

$$P_{FR}(t,T) = Z(t,T_{i+1}) \times 100 \times [1 + r_2(T_i)/2] \qquad (3.14)$$

where $r_2(T_i)$ is the reference rate that is determined at the last reset date. The duration of the floating rate bond is then

Duration of floating rate bond at t

$$= D_{FR} = -\frac{1}{P_{FR}(t,T)} \frac{d\,P_{FR}}{d\,r} \qquad (3.15)$$

$$= -\frac{1}{P_{FR}(t,T)} \left[\frac{d\,Z(t,T_{i+1})}{d\,r}\right] \times 100 \times \left[1 + \frac{r_2(T_i)}{2}\right]$$

$$= -\frac{1}{P_{FR}(t,T)} \left[-(T_{i+1} - t)\right] \times Z(t,T_{i+1}) \times 100 \times \left[1 + \frac{r_2(T_i)}{2}\right]$$

$$= T_i - t \qquad (3.16)$$

where the last equality stems from using again Equation 3.14. Equation 3.16 shows that the duration of a floating rate bond is simply equal to the time left to the *next* coupon payment date $T_{i+1} - t$. In particular, if today is coupon date (but the coupon has not been paid yet), the duration is zero.

This example shows that even if the average time of future cash flows can be relatively long – a floating coupon bond with 10 years to maturity, for instance, has an average time of future payments of several years – the duration could be very small. Conversely, we will see securities for which the duration is actually longer than their maturity, or securities for which the duration is negative. Given that in modern times the notion of duration is mainly used for risk management purposes, and in particular to compute the sensitivity of a security to parallel shifts in the term structure, we must be careful in interpreting duration as an average time of future payments, as this interpretation *only* holds for securities with *fixed* cash flows.

3.2.5 Properties of Duration

It is important to realize that the duration of a coupon bond depends crucially on the level of the coupon rate. As the coupon rate increases, the duration is lower. The first three columns of Table 3.2 show this effect for the case in Example 3.4. What is the intuition? There are two ways to see this result intuitively:

1. *Lower Average Time of Cash Flow Payments:* The higher the coupon, the larger are the intermediate coupons relative to the last one (in 10 years). Thus, the average time of coupon payments gets closer to today.

2. *Lower Sensitivity to Interest Rates:* The higher the coupon rate, the larger are cash flows in the near future compared to the long-term future. Cash flows that arrive sooner rather than later are less sensitive to changes in interest rates (for instance, a

Table 3.2   Duration versus Coupon Rate and Interest Rate

Coupon c	Price P_c	Duration D	Interest Rate r_2	Price P_c	Duration D
0	61.03	10.00	1%	147.47	8.13
2%	76.62	8.95	3%	125.75	7.95
4%	92.21	8.26	5%	107.79	7.76
6%	107.79	7.76	7%	92.89	7.56
8%	123.38	7.39	9%	80.49	7.35
10%	138.97	7.11	11%	70.12	7.12
12%	154.56	6.88	13%	61.44	6.90

cash flow arriving tomorrow has no sensitivity to interest rates). Thus, an increase in coupon rate implies an overall lower sensitivity to changes in discount rates.

For the same reason, the duration of a coupon bond decreases with the general level of interest rates, as we see for the last three columns of Table 3.2. In this case, the coupon rate is kept at 6%, but the semi-annual interest rate r_2 – constant across maturities – increases from 1% to 13%. Note that the duration drops from 8.13 to 6.90. Once again, a higher interest rate (across maturities) implies that short-term cash flows have a relatively higher weight in the value of the bond, and thus a lower sensitivity to changes in interest rates.

3.2.6   Traditional Definitions of Duration

We defined the duration as

$$D = -\frac{1}{P}\frac{dP}{dr} \tag{3.17}$$

where r is the continuously compounded interest rate. This definition of duration is simple to apply in order to compute the duration of interest rate securities, from zero coupon bonds to portfolios of securities. For instance, Equation 3.17 shows that the duration of a *fixed* coupon bond equals the average time of payment times, which is a relatively simple formula to determine the sensitivity of a coupon bond to parallel shifts in the yield curve.

Traditionally, however, the duration is not defined against the continuously compounded interest rate but rather against the semi-annually compounded yield to maturity. In this case, the definition of the modified duration as the (negative of the) sensitivity of prices to changes in interest rates (Equation 3.17) does not correspond exactly to the simple formulas derived earlier, and a small adjustment is needed. In particular, consider a security with yield to maturity y (see Section 2.4.3 in Chapter 2). Recall that by definition of yield to maturity, the price of the coupon bond on a coupon date can be written as

$$P_c(0,T) = \sum_{j=1}^{n} \frac{c/2 \times 100}{\left(1 + \frac{y}{2}\right)^{2 \times T_j}} + \frac{100}{\left(1 + \frac{y}{2}\right)^{2 \times T_n}} \tag{3.18}$$

A little algebra shows that the modified duration (MD) of this coupon bond, when defined against the yield to maturity y, is given by

$$MD = -\frac{1}{P}\frac{dP}{dy} = \frac{1}{\left(1 + \frac{y}{2}\right)} \sum_{j=1}^{n} w_j \times T_j \tag{3.19}$$

where

$$w_j = \frac{1}{P_c(0,T)} \left(\frac{c/2 \times 100}{\left(1 + \frac{y}{2}\right)^{2 \times T_j}} \right), \, w_n = \frac{1}{P_c(0,T)} \left(\frac{100 \times (c/2 + 1)}{\left(1 + \frac{y}{2}\right)^{2 \times T_n}} \right)$$

In other words, when we use the semi-annual compounded yield to maturity y to define the modified duration, then the modified duration of a fixed rate bond can be computed as the weighted average of cash flow maturities times an adjustment given by $(1/(1 + \frac{y}{2})$. The weighted average of cash flow maturities in Equation 3.19 is called the **Macaulay duration**

$$D^{Mc} = \sum_{j=1}^{n} w_j \times T_j \tag{3.20}$$

We will rarely use the variation in the semi-annually compounded yield to maturity for risk management purposes, and rather use the variation in the continuously compounded spot curve. Not only does this choice allow for simpler formulas, as we showed in the previous sections, but it also implies that the durations of different assets are defined against the variation of the same interest rates, namely, the spot rates. Instead, a definition in terms of yield to maturity hinges on the notion of yield to maturity itself, which, as discussed in Chapter 2 (Section 2.4.3) has some issues, such as the fact that it is bond specific, it depends on the coupon rate, and so on. In addition, for several fixed income securities the notion of yield to maturity is not well defined, because they may have floating rate coupons or embedded options. The notion of a parallel shift in the spot curve is always well defined for any interest rate security, and whenever an analytical formula is not available, we can always rely on computers to obtain an approximate quantity, called effective duration. We apply such a strategy for instance in Chapter 8 in the context of mortgage backed securities.

3.2.7   The Duration of Zero Investment Portfolios: Dollar Duration

The definition of duration in Equation 3.1 implicitly implies that the security, or the portfolio, has nonzero value. However, in many interesting cases involving no arbitrage strategies, the security or the portfolio may have a value of exactly zero. In this case, we resort to the dollar duration:

Definition 3.4 *The **dollar duration** $D^\$$ of a security P is defined by*

$$Dollar\ duration = D_P^\$ = -\frac{dP}{dr} \tag{3.21}$$

That is, the dollar duration corresponds to the (negative of the) sensitivity of the price P to changes in the level of interest rate r. Since dP is the change in the price of the security, in dollars, the name dollar duration follows. Combining Equations 3.1 and 3.21 we obtain:

Fact 3.4 *For a nonzero valued security or portfolio with price P, the relation between duration and dollar duration is*

$$-\frac{dP}{dr} = D_P^\$ = P \times D_P \tag{3.22}$$

$$\Rightarrow D_P = -\frac{1}{P}\frac{dP}{dr}$$

In this case, the relation between the dollar duration of the portfolio and the dollar duration of its individual components is given by the sum of the dollar durations:

Fact 3.5 *The dollar duration of portfolio of n securities, denoted by $D_W^\$$ is given by*

$$D_W^\$ = \sum_{i=1}^{n} N_i D_i^\$ \tag{3.23}$$

where N_i is the number of units of security i in the portfolio, and $D_i^\$$ is the dollar duration of security i.

■ **EXAMPLE 3.6**

Dollar Duration of a Long-Short Strategy

Let the term structure of interest rates be flat at 4% (semi-annually compounded). Consider an arbitrageur who is contemplating going long a 4% coupon bond by borrowing at the current floating rate. To keep the analysis simple, suppose the arbitrageur can enter into term repos with maturity of six months and that the haircut is zero. Because the term structure of interest rate is flat, a 4% coupon bond would be valued at par ($100), which is the amount the arbitrageur needs to borrow. The portfolio has value of zero at time $t = 0$ when the trade is set up. However, the trade is risky, because if interest rates move up, then the arbitrageur will suffer a decrease in value in the long position that is not paralleled by an equivalent decrease in value in the short (borrowing) position.

More specifically, borrowing at the 6-month term repo is essentially equivalent to shorting a 6-month floating rate bond. Thus, the long-short portfolio can be written as
$$W = P_c(0, T) - P_{FR}(0, T) = 0$$
Let the duration of the fixed rate bond be 8.34. The duration of the floating rate bond is 6 months, as discussed in Example 3.5. Thus, using Equation 3.22, we find

$$
\begin{aligned}
\text{Dollar duration of } P_c(0, T) &= \$100 \times \text{Duration of fixed rate bond} \\
&= \$100 \times 8.34 = \$834 \\
\text{Dollar duration of } P_{FR}(0, T) &= \$100 \times \text{Duration of floating rate bond} \\
&= \$100 \times 0.5 = \$50
\end{aligned}
$$

Thus, the dollar duration of the long-short portfolio is

$$\text{Dollar duration of long-short portfolio} = \$834 - \$50 = \$784 \tag{3.24}$$

Again using Equation 3.21, we have that one basis point increase in interest rate dr generates change in the long-short portfolio:

$$\text{Change in portfolio value} = dW = -D_W^\$ \times dr = -\$784 \times .01/100 = -.0784 \tag{3.25}$$

That is, the long-short portfolio with trade size of $1 million, for instance, stands to lose $78,400 for every basis point increase in the level of interest rates.

The dollar losses due to a basis point increase in the level of interest rates, as computed in Equation 3.25 is a common measure of interest rate risk. Traders refer to it as the "price value of a basis point," or PVBP, or PV01:

Definition 3.5 *The **price value of a basis point** PV01 of a security with price P is defined as*

$$Price \; value \; of \; a \; basis \; point = PV01(or PVBP) = -D_P^\$ \times d\,r \qquad (3.26)$$

3.2.8 Duration and Value-at-Risk

Value-at-Risk (VaR) is a risk measure that attempts to quantify the amount of risk in a portfolio. In brief, VaR answers the following question: With 95% probability, what is the maximum portfolio loss that we can expect within a given horizon, such as a day, a week or a month? Methodologies for the computation of VaR are many and range from highly complex to fairly simple. In this section we discuss two methodologies that are based on the concept of duration: The historical distribution approach and the normal distribution approach.

Definition 3.6

*Let α be a percentile (e.g. 5%) and T a given horizon. The $(100-\alpha)\%$ T **Value-at-Risk** of a portfolio P is the maximum loss the portfolio can suffer over the horizon T with $\alpha\%$ probability. In formulas, let $L_T = -(P_T - P_0)$ denote the loss of a portfolio over the horizon T (a profit if negative). The VaR is that number such that:*

$$Prob\,(L_T > VaR) = \alpha\% \qquad (3.27)$$

For instance, a $100 million bond portfolio may have a 95%, 1-month VaR of $3 million. This VaR measure implies that there is only 5% probability that the portfolio losses will be higher than $3 million over the next month.

The VaR measure is based on the volatility of the underlying assets in the portfolio. For bond portfolios, the volatility is determined by movements in the interest rates. In fact, through duration, we can estimate the sensitivity of a portfolio to fluctuations in the interest rate. Recall Equation 3.2:

$$dP = -D_P \times P \times dr \qquad (3.28)$$

Given the value of the portfolio P and its duration D_P, we can transform the probability distribution of interest rate changes dr into the probability distribution of portfolio changes dP, and from the latter, we can compute the portfolio potential losses. The 95% VaR corresponds to the 5% worst case of distribution of dP. A simple example is given by the case in which dr has a normal distribution:

Fact 3.6 *Let dr have a normal distribution with mean μ and standard deviation σ. Then Equation 3.28 implies that dP has a normal distribution with mean and standard deviation given by:*

$$\mu_P = -D_P \times P \times \mu \quad and \quad \sigma_P = D_P \times P \times \sigma. \qquad (3.29)$$

That is:

$$dr \sim N(\mu, \sigma^2) \quad \Longrightarrow \quad dP \sim N(\mu_P, \sigma_P^2) \tag{3.30}$$

The 95% VaR is then given by

$$95\% \ VaR = -(\mu_P - 1.645 \times \sigma_P) \tag{3.31}$$

where -1.645 *corresponds to the 5-th percentile of the standard normal distribution, that is, if* $x \sim \mathcal{N}(0, 1)$ *then* $Prob(x < -1.645) = 5\%$. *The 99% VaR is computed as in Equation 3.31 except that the number "1.645" is substituted by "2.326."*

This result of course relies on Equation 3.28, which is only an approximation. If dr is not normal, Equation 3.31 does not hold. The next example illustrates one popular approach to dealing with this latter case.

■ **EXAMPLE 3.7**

A portfolio manager has $100 million invested in a bond portfolio with duration $D_P = 5$. What is the 95% one-month Value-at-Risk of the portfolio?

1. **Historical Distribution Approach.** We can use the past changes in the level of interest rates dr as a basis to evaluate the potential changes in a portfolio value dP. Panel B of Figure 3.1 shows the historical observations of the level of interest rates up to 2005. Panel A of Figure 3.3 shows the monthly changes in the level of interest rates, while Panel B makes a histogram of these variations. As we can see large increases and decreases are not very likely, but they do occur occasionally. We can now multiply each of these changes dr observed in the plot by $-D_P \times P = -5 \times 100$ million to obtain the variation in dP. Panel C of Figure 3.3 plots the histogram of the changes in the portfolio i.e., the portfolio profits and losses (P&L).[4] Given this distribution, we can compute the maximum loss that can occur with 95% probability. We can start from the left-hand side of the distribution, and move rightward until we count 5% of the observations. That number is the 95% monthly VaR computed using the historical distribution approach. In this case, we find it equal to $3 million. That is, there is only 5% probability that the portfolio losses will be higher than $3 million.

2. **Normal Distribution Approach.** From Fact 3.6, a normal distribution assumptin on dr translates into a normal distribution on dP. Using the data plotted in Panel A of Figure 3.3, we find that the monthly change in interest rate has mean $\mu = 6.5197 \times 10 - 006$ and stadard deviation $\sigma = .4153\%$. Therefore, $\mu_P = -5 \times 100 \times \mu = -.0033$ and $\sigma_P = 5 \times 100 \times \sigma = 2.0767$. The standard normal distribution is plotted along with the (renormalized) histogram in Panel C of Figure 3.3. The 95% VaR is then equal to 95% VaR $= -(\mu_P - 1.645 \times \sigma_P) = \$3.4194$ million.

---

[4]We renormalized the histogram to make it comparable with the normal distribution case, discussed in the next point.

Figure 3.3 Changes in the Level of Interest Rates: 1965 - 2005

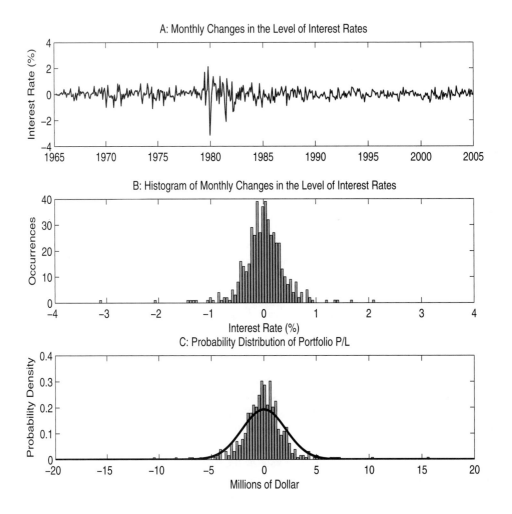

Data Source: CRSP.

3.2.8.1 *Warnings* It is worth emphasizing immediately a few problems with the Value-at-Risk measure of risk, as well as some potential pitfalls:

1. VaR is a statistical measure of risk, and as with any other statistical measure, it depends on distributional assumptions and the sample used for the calculation. The difference can be large. For instance, in Example 3.7 the VaR varies depending on whether we use the normal distribution approach or the historical distribution approach.

2. The duration approximation in Equation 3.28 is appropriate for *small* parallel changes in the level of interest rates. However, by definition, VaR is concerned with *large* changes. Therefore, the duration approximation method is internally inconsistent.

The problem turns out to be especially severe for portfolios that include derivative securities, either implicitly or explicitly. We will return to this issue in later chapters.

3. The VaR measures the maximum loss with 95% probability. However, it does not say anything about how large the losses could be if they do occur. The tails of the probability distribution matter for risk. For instance, in Example 3.7 the 99% VaR using the historical distribution approach is $5.52 million, while this figure is only $4.83 million using the normal distribution assumption. The tails of the normal distribution are thin, in the sense that they give an extremely low probability to large events, which instead in reality occur with some frequency.

4. The VaR formula used in Equation 3.31 includes the *expected* change in the portfolio $\mu_P = -D_P \times P \times E[dr]$. The computation on the expected change $E[dr]$ is typically very imprecise, and standard errors are large. Such errors can generate a large error in the VaR computation. For this reason, it is often more accurate to consider only the *unexpected VaR*, that is, consider only the 95% loss compared to the expected P&L μ_P. Practically, we simply need to set $\mu_P = 0$ in Equation 3.31.

3.2.9 Duration and Expected Shortfall

Some of the problems with VaR can be solved by using a different measure of risk, called the expected shortfall. This measure of risk answers the following question: How large can we expect the loss of a portfolio to be when it is higher than VaR? As mentioned in point 3 in the above Subsection 3.2.8.1, the VaR measure does not say anything about the tails of the statistical distribution. This is an especially important problem when the underlying risk factor has a fat-tailed distribution, as shown in Figure 3.3, or when the portfolio contains highly nonlinear derivative securities, as we will see in later chapters.

Definition 3.7 *The* **expected shortfall** *is the expected loss on a portfolio P over the horizon T conditional on the loss being larger than the $(100 - \alpha)\%$, T VaR:*

$$Expected\ shortfall = E[L_T | L_T > VaR] \tag{3.32}$$

For instance, a $100 million portfolio may have a 95%, 1-month expected shortfall of $4.28 million, meaning that when a bad event hits (losses higher than VaR), the portfolio stands to lose $4.28 million in average.

The calculation of expected shortfall is only slightly more involved than the one of VaR. For instance, for normally distributed variables, we have the following result:

Fact 3.7 *Consider Fact 3.6. Under these assumptions:*

$$95\%\ Expected\ shortfall = -\left(\mu_P - \sigma_P \times \frac{f(-1.645)}{\mathcal{N}(-1.645)}\right) \tag{3.33}$$

$$= -(\mu_P - \sigma_P \times 2.0628) \tag{3.34}$$

where $f(x)$ denotes the standard normal density and $\mathcal{N}(x)$ is the standard normal cumulative density,[5] *The 99% expected shortfall is obtained as in Equation 3.34 except with the number "2.6649" in place of "2.0628."*

A quick comparison of Equations 3.34 and 3.31 shows that for the normal distribution case, the expected shortfall contains the same information as the Value-at-Risk, as the only difference is the coefficient that multiplies σ_P. But this is in fact exactly the reason for a new measure of risk: The expected shortfall is very useful precisely for those situations in which the portfolio losses are not expected to be normally distributed.

■ **EXAMPLE 3.8**

Consider again Example 3.7. The 95%, 1-month expected shortfall is easily computed in the case of a normal distribution, as we must simply change the coefficient "1.645" that multiplies σ_P with the coefficient "2.0628" (and similarly for the 99% expected shortfall). Given $\mu_P = -.0033$ and $\sigma_P = 2.0767$, we obtain

$$\text{(Normal disttribution approach):}\quad 95\%\ ES\ =\ \$4.2871\ \text{mil};\quad 99\%\ ES = \$5.5374\ \text{mil} \tag{3.35}$$

The numbers are quite different for the case in which the historical distribution approach is used. How do we compute the expected shortfall in this case? The methodology is just a slight modification of the VaR computation. In the VaR case, we first rank all of the portfolio P&L realizations under the various interest rate scenarios from the worst to the best, and then pick the 5% worst case. For the expected shortfall, we take the average of all of the realizations below the 5% worst case. A similar precedure is used for the 1% expected shortfall calculation. In this case, we obtain:

$$\text{(Historical distribution approach):}\quad 95\%\ ES\ =\ \$5.0709\ \text{mil};\quad 99\%\ ES = \$9.3344\ \text{mil} \tag{3.36}$$

We note in particular that the 99% expected shortfall is substantially larger under the historical distribution approach than under the normal distribution approach. This finding is a reflection of the fat-tailed distribution that characterizes the interest rate changes, and thus of the P&L dP, as shown in the bottom panel in Figure 3.3. In particular, extreme portfolio realizations occur more frequently than according to the normal distribution. It is worth pointing out that in contrast the VaR measure does not capture well the risk embedded in the tails of the distribution. For instance, in Example 3.7 the 99% VaR is $5.52 million, which is higher than the figure obtained under the normal distribution approach ($4.83 million), but not much higher. The expected shortfall is much better able to capture the risk from tail events.

3.3   INTEREST RATE RISK MANAGEMENT

Interest rate risk management is a key activity for banks, bond portfolio managers, corporations, governments, and, in fact, households. To understand the risks in interest rate fluctuations, consider the following example.

---

[5]That is, $f(x) = 1/\sqrt{2\pi} \times e^{-x^2/2}$ and $\mathcal{N}(x) = \int_{-\infty}^{x} f(y)dy$.

■ **EXAMPLE 3.9**

Ms. Caselli retired at the age of 60, with $1,000,000 in her retirement account. She now has to decide where to invest this amount of money for the next, say, 30 years. Treasury bonds are the only type of security she would consider, given her age. Should she invest in long-term bonds or short-term bonds? Consider the two extremes:

1. Invest all of $1,000,000 in 6-months T-bills.

2. Invest all of $1,000,000 in 30-year T-bonds.

What is the difference between these two strategies? If Ms. Caselli is going to consume only the interest on her investment, strategy 1 is more risky than strategy 2. Indeed, under strategy 1, fluctuations in interest rates imply fluctuations in the amount of money available for consumption. For instance, an interest rate change from 4% to 1% decreases Ms. Caselli's annual interest income from $40,000 to $10,000, a rather dramatic change. Instead, assuming that the 30-year bond sells at par and that the coupon rate is 4%, strategy 2 provides a certain $40,000 per year for all 30 years.

Most likely, Ms. Caselli is interested in using up some of her capital for consumption purposes. Indeed, cashing nothing but interest income may not produce enough funds on which to survive. If cash flow comes from the amount of capital available, the sensitivity of capital itself to interest rates becomes a big issue. For instance, look again at strategy 2. Assume that the zero coupon yield curve is flat at 4% (semi-annually compounded), so that a 30-year T-bond with 4% coupon trades at par. Such coupon bond has a duration of 17.72. Consider now an interest rate increase of 3% from 4% to 7% (as happened, for instance, in 1994). The capital losses on the investment would be approximately

$$\text{Capital losses} \approx 17.72 \times \$1 \text{ million} \times .03 = \$531,000$$

That is, a 3 percent increase in the interest rate may more than halve the savings of Ms. Caselli. If Ms. Caselli is not planning to consume out of her capital, this capital loss is of no consequence: She still possesses the same bond as before, which will keep paying the same $40,000 per year. But if she is planning to use up some of the capital for consumption, this strategy is clearly risky.

This example illustrates how the type of interest rate risk management that an institution or a person may want to engage in depends on the goals of the institution or individual.

3.3.1 Cash Flow Matching and Immunization

Ms. Caselli, in Example 3.9, can purchase an annuity from a financial institution. For instance, the financial institution may agree to pay $28,767 every six months for 30 years in exchange for the $1,000,000 deposit. Where is this number coming from? Assuming a flat term structure at a semi-annually compounded interest rate of 4%, the present value of this stream of cash flows is about $1,000,000:

$$\$1,000,000 = \$28,767 \times \sum_{i=1}^{60} \frac{1}{\left(1 + \frac{4\%}{2}\right)^i} \tag{3.37}$$

where 60 is the number of payments.

How can the financial institution now hedge this commitment to pay exactly $28,767 twice a year for 30 years? What risks does it take?

1. **Cash Flow Matching.** The financial institution can purchase a set of securities that pays exactly $28,767 every six months. For instance, it can purchase 60 zero coupon bonds, each with a $28,767 face value, and with maturities of 6 months, 1 year, 1.5 years, and so on up to 30 years. The value of these securities is, by construction, equal to $1,000,000, as the present value in Equation 3.37 applies to this case. One drawback of this strategy, though, is that the financial institution should find exactly the type of securities that are required for the cash flow matching, such as the sequence of zero coupon bonds with $28,500 face value at 6-month intervals. Such an endeavor may be problematic, and costly, as many securities are nonliquid.

2. **Immunization.** The financial institution can engage in a dynamic immunization strategy. Such a strategy involves the choice of a portfolio of securities with the *same present value and duration of the cash flow commitments to pay*. Immunization is preferred over cash flow matching as it allows the institution to choose bonds that have favorable properties in terms of liquidity and transaction costs. If executed properly, this method generates the desired stream of cash flows.

While the cash flow matching is relatively straightforward, it is instructive to work through an example illustrating the immunization strategy. We continue with Example 3.9.

■ **EXAMPLE 3.10**

The financial institution that took up the commitment to pay $28,767 every six months can ensure the ability to pay by engaging in the following dynamic strategy. Let $x_t\%$ denote the fraction of the total capital – $1,000,000 at initiation – invested in the 4%, 30-year bond, as described in Example 3.9. Assume that the remaining $(1 - x_t)\%$ is kept as cash in a deposit account, thereby yielding the overnight deposit rate. The duration of the annuity promised to Ms. Caselli is about 12.35. The 30-year coupon bond has a duration of 17.72, while the overnight deposit has zero duration, as the deposit rate resets daily. Because the immunization strategy calls for equating the duration of the portfolio with the one of the annuity, it then requires that at time 0:

$$x_0\% \times 17.72 + (1 - x_0\%) \times 0 = 12.34 \implies x_0 = 71\%$$

Assume that the financial institution rebalances every six months. Then, at any time $t = .5, 1, 1.5, ..., 30$ the financial institution:

- collects the $\frac{4\%}{2}$ coupon from the 30-year bond;

- collects the interest cumulated over the six months on the cash deposit;

- pays the annuity cash flow of $28,767 to Ms. Caselli; and

- reinvests the remaining balance in long-term bonds and overnight deposit according to the rule:

$$\text{Percentage investment in long-term bond} = x_t = \frac{\text{Duration of annuity}}{\text{Duration of long-term bond.}}$$

$$(3.38)$$

Table 3.3 illustrates the strategy. Column (1) reports the time at which coupon payments are made, and rebalancing takes place. For convenience, assume that annuity payments and the long-term bond coupon payments occur on the same date. Column (2) reports a possible path of interest rates, from 4% to 11% and down again to 8% in the course of 30 years. These interest rates have been simulated. Column (3) computes the balance of the financial institution. It starts out with $1 million, and then the balance declines as the financial institution makes coupon payments to Ms. Caselli. We are more explicit about the information in this column below. Column (4) reports the present value of the annuity, assuming that the term structure is flat and equal to the interest rate in Column (2). Column (5) indicates the duration of the annuity. Note that both the present value and the duration of the annuity tend to decline over time. Columns (6) and (7) report the present value and duration, respectively, of the 4%, 30-year T-bond that is used in the immunization strategy. Column (8) reports the fraction of capital x_t invested in the 30-year bond, obtained from using Equation 3.38. Column (9) shows the total cash obtained at the end of each six-month period t, from the investment in overnight deposits at the beginning of the period. That is,

$$\text{Interest payment [column (9)]} = W_t \times (1 - x_t) \times r_t/2 \qquad (3.39)$$

Similarly, Column (10) represents the total coupon received from the 30-year bond investment

$$\text{Coupon payment [column (10)]} = \frac{W_t \times x_t}{\text{Price T-bond in Column (6)}} \times 4\%/2 \qquad (3.40)$$

Finally, returning to Column (3), the total amount of capital at the institution is updated by taking into account inflows and outflows. That is

$$
\begin{aligned}
W_{t+1} \;=\;& W_t \times (1 - x_t) + W_t \times x_t \times \text{Capital gain on T-bond} & (3.41)\\
& + \text{Interest in (9) at } t + \text{coupon in (10)} & (3.42)\\
& - \text{Annuity coupon (\$28,767)} & (3.43)
\end{aligned}
$$

Notice from the last row in Table 3.3 that the strategy still leaves $69,375 at maturity. If the interest rate was constant for the overall period and equal to 4%, then the final amount of wealth W_T would be exactly zero. There is a reason why the final wealth came up positive – due to the convexity of bond prices with respect to interest rates – that we discuss in Chapter 4.

Was this luck? That is, if we consider a different path of interest rates, would we still get a positive number? Or are there instances in which the final wealth was negative? To convince ourselves that this dynamic immunization strategy works, we can repeat the above exercise many times, for many interest rate scenarios, and plot the histogram of the final value W_T. This is done in Figure 3.4. As it can be seen, the strategy works well, as the final wealth is always positive.

3.3.2 Immunization versus Simpler Investment Strategies

How does the immunization strategy compare to other simpler strategies, such as investing fixed proportions in the long-term T-bond and cash? The panels in Figure

Table 3.3 Example of Immunization Strategy

(1)	(2)	(3)	(4) PV Annuity	(5) D Annuity	(6) PV T-bond	(7) D T-bond	(8)	(9) Interest Payment	(10) Coupon T-bond
t	r_2	W_t					x_t		
0.5	4.00%	1,000,000.00	1,000,000.00	12.35	1.00	17.73	0.70	6,069.48	13,930.52
1.0	4.53%	931,694.92	931,527.35	11.84	0.91	17.00	0.70	6,394.58	14,198.57
1.5	5.46%	834,369.76	833,021.75	11.12	0.79	15.88	0.70	6,818.28	14,817.53
2.0	5.80%	798,630.50	797,418.94	10.79	0.75	15.42	0.70	6,949.54	14,901.35
2.5	5.07%	858,995.30	855,333.53	11.08	0.84	16.03	0.69	6,727.23	14,125.61
3.0	5.70%	798,169.63	794,486.32	10.59	0.77	15.31	0.69	6,997.57	14,430.69
3.5	5.97%	770,555.63	767,029.58	10.32	0.74	14.94	0.69	7,111.90	14,430.83
4.0	5.51%	802,061.06	797,212.37	10.43	0.79	15.24	0.68	6,975.91	13,867.73
4.5	5.75%	775,789.15	771,099.47	10.17	0.76	14.90	0.68	7,094.48	13,838.82
5.0	5.62%	780,072.25	774,970.46	10.10	0.78	14.89	0.68	7,054.71	13,518.96
5.5	5.41%	789,534.15	783,823.66	10.05	0.81	14.92	0.67	6,967.50	13,154.64
6.0	4.44%	863,655.83	853,748.21	10.34	0.93	15.51	0.67	6,387.38	12,332.29
6.5	3.84%	909,537.36	896,984.46	10.45	1.03	15.76	0.66	5,880.42	11,770.13
7.0	4.37%	851,902.96	839,884.97	10.04	0.95	15.19	0.66	6,309.03	11,906.61
7.5	4.85%	803,888.62	792,339.74	9.68	0.88	14.69	0.66	6,648.02	11,997.12
8.0	5.22%	767,558.29	756,355.88	9.37	0.84	14.28	0.66	6,882.78	12,008.02
8.5	5.80%	720,606.80	709,848.70	9.00	0.78	13.75	0.65	7,219.58	12,133.76
9.0	6.21%	688,142.41	677,682.96	8.71	0.74	13.35	0.65	7,429.60	12,138.47
9.5	7.10%	633,131.27	623,058.85	8.27	0.66	12.70	0.65	7,834.29	12,422.01
10.0	7.90%	589,160.97	579,458.13	7.90	0.61	12.14	0.65	8,132.71	12,628.90
10.5	8.77%	547,447.66	538,080.12	7.52	0.55	11.57	0.65	8,401.06	12,856.82
11.0	8.00%	574,852.24	563,207.45	7.61	0.61	11.84	0.64	8,227.02	12,148.50
11.5	8.34%	555,509.40	543,902.64	7.39	0.59	11.56	0.64	8,354.68	12,038.36
12.0	7.91%	567,397.43	554,342.75	7.36	0.62	11.62	0.63	8,215.15	11,532.52
12.5	7.96%	559,108.10	545,629.81	7.21	0.62	11.45	0.63	8,233.98	11,269.64
13.0	8.59%	529,197.45	516,057.51	6.93	0.59	11.05	0.63	8,481.00	11,279.49
13.5	9.55%	491,704.85	479,048.80	6.59	0.54	10.55	0.62	8,813.42	11,424.64
14.0	9.27%	495,447.31	481,641.25	6.52	0.56	10.52	0.62	8,733.50	10,977.17
14.5	10.09%	465,514.05	452,081.69	6.23	0.52	10.11	0.62	9,009.18	11,013.67
15.0	10.49%	449,693.51	436,142.65	6.04	0.51	9.86	0.61	9,135.49	10,837.50
15.5	10.19%	452,268.71	437,477.20	5.95	0.53	9.80	0.61	9,046.62	10,380.01
16.0	10.10%	448,755.10	433,060.02	5.83	0.54	9.67	0.60	9,002.83	10,010.52
16.5	10.84%	425,079.56	409,594.85	5.59	0.51	9.33	0.60	9,243.38	9,931.53
17.0	11.34%	408,561.98	392,937.71	5.39	0.50	9.06	0.59	9,387.23	9,743.14
17.5	12.08%	388,211.13	372,656.40	5.16	0.48	8.74	0.59	9,600.17	9,615.89
18.0	11.95%	385,320.32	368,625.65	5.04	0.49	8.60	0.59	9,532.93	9,203.05
18.5	11.58%	386,506.22	368,186.27	4.94	0.52	8.49	0.58	9,356.17	8,733.27
19.0	11.45%	382,431.96	362,838.04	4.81	0.53	8.32	0.58	9,237.02	8,340.71
19.5	11.63%	372,563.61	352,126.89	4.64	0.53	8.08	0.57	9,218.34	8,024.12
20.0	11.94%	360,381.56	339,248.28	4.46	0.53	7.82	0.57	9,242.82	7,733.61
20.5	11.82%	354,983.36	332,387.26	4.32	0.55	7.60	0.57	9,072.49	7,350.17
21.0	11.69%	349,068.99	324,921.21	4.16	0.57	7.37	0.57	8,874.41	6,973.10
21.5	11.35%	345,393.43	319,247.45	4.02	0.59	7.13	0.56	8,556.37	6,571.90
22.0	11.48%	334,579.86	307,161.34	3.84	0.60	6.84	0.56	8,426.27	6,249.34
22.5	11.35%	326,472.31	297,276.29	3.67	0.62	6.56	0.56	8,158.47	5,895.98
23.0	10.98%	320,443.04	288,950.85	3.51	0.65	6.26	0.56	7,745.83	5,523.33
23.5	10.15%	318,131.85	283,432.61	3.35	0.70	5.97	0.56	7,078.31	5,123.72
24.0	10.30%	303,990.10	267,790.08	3.15	0.71	5.62	0.56	6,876.17	4,825.62
24.5	10.72%	287,314.17	249,904.43	2.94	0.71	5.25	0.56	6,770.09	4,545.18
25.0	10.32%	276,993.67	236,955.12	2.75	0.74	4.89	0.56	6,252.49	4,213.72
25.5	9.51%	268,191.16	224,811.75	2.56	0.78	4.51	0.57	5,521.92	3,875.08
26.0	9.97%	249,375.96	204,603.79	2.34	0.79	4.11	0.57	5,359.27	3,603.08
26.5	10.15%	232,116.30	185,357.01	2.12	0.80	3.70	0.57	5,027.23	3,320.09
27.0	9.54%	217,795.73	167,873.19	1.91	0.84	3.28	0.58	4,343.35	3,021.95
27.5	10.38%	196,476.08	145,132.50	1.68	0.84	2.84	0.59	4,180.27	2,763.55
28.0	10.79%	176,812.76	123,208.88	1.45	0.85	2.39	0.60	3,771.06	2,501.20
28.5	10.12%	158,948.97	101,873.37	1.22	0.89	1.94	0.63	2,981.69	2,242.73
29.0	9.64%	138,908.31	78,608.20	0.98	0.92	1.47	0.67	2,210.22	2,016.28
29.5	8.99%	117,422.88	53,876.71	0.74	0.95	0.99	0.75	1,308.69	1,852.74
30.0	8.30%	94,234.40	27,622.23	0.50	0.98	0.50	1.00	0.00	1,924.37
		69,375.15			1.00				

Figure 3.4   Performance Immunization Strategy in Simulations

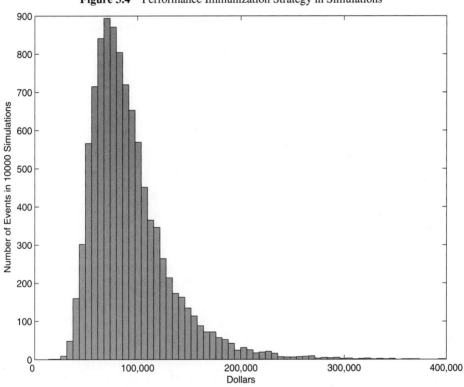

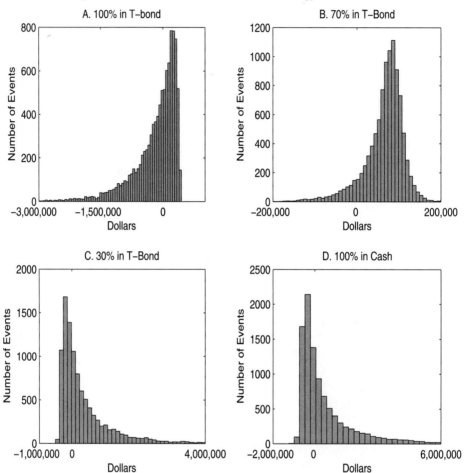

Figure 3.5   Performance Fixed Investment Strategy in Simulations

3.5 plot the results of an analysis similar to the immunization strategy in Figure 3.4, but in which the investment in long-term T-bond x_t is kept fixed at 100% (Panel A), 70% (Panel B), 30% (Panel C), 0% (Panel D). The figure clearly shows that in these cases, the bank stands to lose money with some probability. For instance, if the financial institution was to keep 100% invested in the long term T-bond, it would stand to lose money about 50% of the time. Instead, the constant strategy of 70% and 30% in the long term bond stands to lose money about 10% and 40% of the time, respectively. On the other hand, a 100% investment in cash only (Panel D) also is not appropriate, as the strategy loses money again about 50% of the time.

3.3.3   Why Does the Immunization Strategy Work?

What is the intuition behind immunization strategies? Why do they work? Think again about the two extremes: 100% investment in long-term bonds loses money when interest

Table 3.4 The Duration Mismatch

	Assets	Liabilities
Commercial Banks	Long-term loans (High D)	Deposits (Low D)
Insurance Companies	Short-Term T-Bonds (Low D)	Long-Term Commitments (High D)
Pension Plans	Medium-Term T-Bonds (Low D)	Long-Term Commitments (High D)
Corporations	Long-Term Receivables (High D)	Floating Rate Bonds (Low D)

rates go up, because bond prices decline when interest rates increase. Similarly, a 100% investment in cash loses money when interest rates go down. If the interest rate goes to zero, for instance, then there is not enough capital to make up the annuity coupon. Clearly, the safer strategy is in the middle. Indeed, the immunization strategy effectively ensures that the losses on the cash investment due to declining interest rates are compensated by the capital gains on the long-term bond. The duration enters the picture here, as it measures the sensitivity of bond prices to interest rate changes.

3.4 ASSET-LIABILITY MANAGEMENT

Asset liability management is the most classic example of interest rate risk management. Many financial institutions have a duration mismatch between their assets and their liabilities, as illustrated in Table 3.4. For instance, a commercial bank collects deposits – a short-term liability whose interest rate changes daily – to make medium- and long-term loans to other business or households. If the medium- and long-term loans have fixed coupons, as in fixed rate mortgages for instance, then the duration of the assets is relatively long, for instance 5 years or more. On the other hand, deposits have a duration close to zero, as the short term interest rate needs to be adjusted frequently as market conditions change.

What happens if there is a hike in interest rates?

The analysis in previous sections shows that the value of the assets drop, while the value of the liabilities does not change. In flow terms, the bank now has to pay a high rate on the deposits, but still receives a low coupon from its assets. In essence, the bank is in trouble.

The duration analysis in the previous sections can be applied more generally to analyze the relative potential duration mismatch between assets and liabilities. One important problem is that financial institutions have very complex asset composition. However, quite independent of the types of assets, it is possible to compute the duration of the overall portfolio of assets. Indeed, we can consider the total assets of the firm as a portfolio of securities (e.g. individual loans, receivables, and so on) and thus use the earlier formula in Equation 3.8 to compute the duration of assets as a weighted average of the durations of its components. For instance, if a firm has n individual loans, whose values are A_1, A_2,...,A_n and their durations are $D_{A,1}$, $D_{A,2}$,..., $D_{A,n}$, then we can compute the duration of assets as

$$\text{Duration of assets } D_A = \sum_{i=1}^{n} w_{A,i} D_{A,i}$$

where

$$w_{A,i} = \frac{A_i}{\sum_{i=1}^{n} A_i}$$

Similarly, financial institutions also have very complex liabilities, as they do not finance their loans only with deposits, but also with longer-term vehicles (e.g., certificates of deposit), long-term bonds, and, of course, equity. In the same fashion as with assets, the financial institution can consider its liabilities as a portfolio and compute the duration of liabilities. Denoting L_1, L_2,...,L_m the current value of each of its m liabilities (excluding equity), and $D_{L,1}$, $D_{L,2}$,...,$D_{L,m}$ their durations, we obtain

$$\text{Duration of liabilities } D_L = \sum_{i=1}^{n} w_{L,i} D_{L,i}$$

where

$$w_{L,i} = \frac{L_i}{\sum_{i=1}^{n} L_i}$$

The aim of asset - liability management is often taken to minimize the impact that the variation in the level of interest rates has on the value of equity. Since equity E is given by total assets (A) minus total liability (L),

$$E = A - L$$

we have that duration mismatch occurs whenever $D_E \neq 0$. Treating equity as a portfolio, we obtain

$$D_E = \frac{A}{A - L} \times D_A - \frac{L}{A - L} \times D_L \tag{3.44}$$

Therefore, $D_A^\$ = A D_A \neq L D_L = D_L^\$$ results in a duration mismatch problem, and variation of interest rates affect the value of equity.

■ **EXAMPLE 3.11**

Consider a hypothetical financial institution mainly engaged in making long-term loans. The balance sheet of such financial institution may look like the one in Table 3.5. Total assets are around $2.4 billion, with a dollar duration of $19.74 billion. Total liabilities are $1.8 billion with a dollar duration of only $5 billion. As a consequence, the market value of equity is $600 million, but with a dollar duration of $14.740 billion. The implication of this mismatch is that a parallel upward shift in interest rates of 1% generates a decline in assets far greater than in liabilities, implying an equity decline of $147.4 million. In percentage, this corresponds to a 24%decline in market value of equity.

To reduce or eliminate this maturity mismatch, the financial firm may alter the composition of its portfolio. One possibility is to issue long-term debt to increase the duration of liabilities. Intuitively, if interest rates increase the financial institution gains from making coupon payments on its long term debt that are below the current rate. Another far more common possibility is to use derivative securities, such as swaps, to alter the duration of assets. We explore further this methodology in Chapter 5, after we cover the properties of swaps and other derivative securities.

3.5   SUMMARY

In this chapter we covered the following topics:

Table 3.5 Asset and Liabilities of a Financial Institution

	Assets				Liabilities		
Item	Amount	Duration	Dollar Duration	Item	Amount	Duration	Dollar Duration
Cash	100	0	0	Deposits	600	0	0
S.T. Loans	300	0.8	240	S.T. Debt	400	0.5	200
M.T. Loans	500	3	1500	M.T. Debt	400	4	1600
L.T. Loans	1500	12	18000	L.T. Debt	400	8	3200
Total	2400		19740	Total	1800		5000
				Equity	600		14740

1. Duration: The (negative of the) percentage sensitivity of a security to parallel shift in the term structure of interest rates is known as duration. As an example, the duration of zero coupon bonds is just their time to maturity.

2. Duration of a portfolio of securities: This can be computed as the weighted average of durations of the individual securities in the portfolio, where the weights equal the percentage holdings of the securities.

3. Dollar duration: Unlike duration, the dollar duration measures the (negative of the) dollar changes in prices due to a parallel shift in the term structure of interest rates. This can be used for securities or strategies that require a zero investment.

4. Value-at-Risk: VaR is a risk measure that computes the maximum losses a portfolio can sustain, within a given horizon, with a given probability. For instance, a 95%, one month VaR provides the maximum loss a portfolio sustains with 95% probability.

5. Expected Shortfall: A risk measure that computes the expected losses on a portfolio, conditional on these losses being larger than VaR, expected shortfall is a measure that is better able to deal with tail events than VaR.

6. Immunization: Immunization is a strategy to make a portfolio insensitive to changes in interest rate.

7. Asset-Liability Management: This is a strategy of choosing the (dollar) duration of liabilities to match the (dollar) duration of assets. It helps reduce the sensisitivy of equity to changes in interest rates, and ensures that cash flows received from assets are sufficient to pay the cash flows from liabilities.

3.6 EXERCISES

1. Today is May 15, 2000, and the current, semi-annually compounded yield curve is in Table 3.6. Compute the duration for the following securities:

   (a) 3-year zero coupon bond

   (b) 3 1/4-year coupon bond paying 6% semiannually

   (c) 1-year coupon bond paying 4% quarterly

Table 3.6   Yield Curve on May 15, 2000

Maturity	Yield	Maturity	Yield	Maturity	Yield
0.25	6.33%	2.75	6.86%	5.25	6.39%
0.50	6.49%	3.00	6.83%	5.50	6.31%
0.75	6.62%	3.25	6.80%	5.75	6.24%
1.00	6.71%	3.50	6.76%	6.00	6.15%
1.25	6.79%	3.75	6.72%	6.25	6.05%
1.50	6.84%	4.00	6.67%	6.50	5.94%
1.75	6.87%	4.25	6.62%	6.75	5.81%
2.00	6.88%	4.50	6.57%	7.00	5.67%
2.25	6.89%	4.75	6.51%	7.25	5.50%
2.50	6.88%	5.00	6.45%	7.50	5.31%

Notes: Yields are calculated based on data from CRSP (Daily Treasuries).

(d) 6-year floating rate bond with a zero spread, paying semiannually

(e) 3-year floating rate bond with a 35 basis point spread, paid semiannually

(f) 4 1/4 year floating rate bond with 50 basis point spread, paid semiannually

2. An investor is planning a $100 million short-term investment and is going to choose among two different portfolios. This investor is seriously worried about interest rate volatility in the market. Compute the duration of the portfolios. Which one is more adequate for the investor's objective? Assume today is May 15, 2000, which means you may use the yield curve presented in Table 3.6

Portfolio A

- 40% invested in 4 1/4-year bonds paying 5% semiannually
- 25% invested in 7-year bonds paying 2.5% semiannually
- 20% invested in 1 3/4-year floating rate bonds with a 30 basis point spread, paying semiannually
- 10% invested in 1-year zero coupon bonds
- 5% invested in 2-year bonds paying 3% quarterly

Portfolio B

- 40% invested in 7-year bonds paying 10% semiannually
- 25% invested in 4 1/4-year bonds paying 3% quarterly
- 20% invested in 90-day zero coupon bonds
- 10% invested in 2-year floating rate bonds with zero spread, paying semi-annually
- 5% invested in 1 1/2 -year bonds paying 6% semiannually

3. Compute the Macaulay and modified duration for the same securities as in Exercise 1.

4. Using the yield curve in Table 3.6, compute the dollar duration for the following securities:

(a) Long a 5-year coupon bond paying 4% semiannually

(b) Short a 7-year zero coupon bond

(c) Long a 3 1/2-year coupon bond paying 7% quarterly

(d) Long a 2-year zero spread floating rate bond paid semiannually

(e) Short a 2 1/4-year zero spread floating rate bond paid semiannually

(f) Short a 5 1/4-year floating rate bond with a 25 basis point spread paid semiannually

5. The investor in Exercise 2 is still worried about interest rate volatility. Instead of a duration measure, the investor wants now to know the following:

(a) What is the dollar duration of each portfolio?

(b) What is PV01 for each portfolio?

(c) Does the conclusion arrived at in Exercise 2 stand?

6. Due to a series of unfortunate events, the investor in Exercise 2 just found out that he must raise $50 million. The investor decides to short the long-term bonds in each portfolio to raise the $50 million. In other words, for portfolio A the investor would spend the same on all securities except for the 7-year coupon bonds (paying 2.5% semiannually) from which the investor will short enough to get to $50 million. For portfolio B the investor would spend the same on all other securities except for the 7-year coupon bonds (paying 10% semiannually) from which the investor will short enough to get to $50 million.

(a) How many bonds of each kind does the investor have to short?

(b) What is the new dollar duration of each portfolio?

(c) Does the conclusion arrived at in Exercise 2 stand?

Exercises 7 to 12 use the two yield curves at two moments in time in Table 3.7, and the following portfolio:

- Long $20 million of a 6-year inverse floaters with the following quarterly coupon:

$$\text{Coupon at } t = 20\% - r_4(t - 0.25)$$

where $r_4(t)$ denotes the quarterly compounded, 3-month rate.

- Long $20 million of 4-year floating rate bonds with a 45 basis point spread paying semiannually.

- Short $30 million of a 5-year zero coupon bond.

7. You are standing on February 15, 1994:

(a) What is the total value of the portfolio?

(b) Compute the dollar duration of the portfolio.

8. You are worried about interest rate volatility. You decide to hedge your portfolio with a 3-year coupon bond paying 4% on a semiannual basis.

Table 3.7   Two Term Structures of Interest Rates

Maturity	02/15/94 Yield (c.c.)	02/15/94 $Z(t,T)$	05/13/94 Yield (c.c.)	05/13/94 $Z(t,T)$
0.25	3.53%	0.9912	4.13%	0.9897
0.50	3.56%	0.9824	4.74%	0.9766
0.75	3.77%	0.9721	5.07%	0.9627
1.00	3.82%	0.9625	5.19%	0.9495
1.25	3.97%	0.9516	5.49%	0.9337
1.50	4.14%	0.9398	5.64%	0.9189
1.75	4.23%	0.9287	5.89%	0.9020
2.00	4.43%	0.9151	6.04%	0.8862
2.25	4.53%	0.9031	6.13%	0.8712
2.50	4.57%	0.8921	6.23%	0.8558
2.75	4.71%	0.8786	6.31%	0.8406
3.00	4.76%	0.8670	6.39%	0.8255
3.25	4.89%	0.8531	6.42%	0.8117
3.50	4.98%	0.8400	6.52%	0.7959
3.75	5.07%	0.8268	6.61%	0.7805
4.00	5.13%	0.8145	6.66%	0.7663
4.25	5.18%	0.8023	6.71%	0.7519
4.50	5.26%	0.7893	6.73%	0.7387
4.75	5.31%	0.7770	6.77%	0.7251
5.00	5.38%	0.7641	6.83%	0.7106
5.25	5.42%	0.7525	6.86%	0.6977
5.50	5.43%	0.7418	6.89%	0.6846
5.75	5.49%	0.7293	6.93%	0.6713
6.00	5.53%	0.7176	6.88%	0.6619

Notes: Yields are calculated based on data from CRSP (Daily Treasuries).

   (a) How much should you go short/long on this bond in order to make it immune to interest rate changes?

   (b) What is the total value of the portfolio now?

9. Assume that it is now May 13, 1994 and that the yield curve has changed accordingly (see Table 3.7).

   (a) What is the value of the unhedged portfolio now?

   (b) What is the value of the hedged portfolio?

   (c) Is the value the same? Did the immunization strategy work? How do you know that changes in value are not a product of coupon payments made over the period?

10. Instead of assuming that the change took place 6 months later, assume that the change in the yield curve occurred an instant after February 15, 1994.

   (a) What is the value of the unhedged portfolio?

   (b) What is the value of the hedged portfolio?

11. Now use the February 15, 1994 yield curve to price the stream of cash flows on May 13, 1994.

   (a) What is the value of the unhedged portfolio?

   (b) What is the value of the hedged portfolio?

12. From the answers to the Exercises 7 - 11, answer the following:

   (a) What is the change in value in the portfolio due to the change in time only, without change in interest rates?

   (b) Is this difference a loss?

   (c) Once we have adjusted for paid coupons, what is the change in value of the portfolio due to interest rate movements?

3.7 CASE STUDY: THE 1994 BANKRUPTCY OF ORANGE COUNTY

As discussed in Section 3.1.2, in 1994 Orange County lost $1.6 billion out of a portfolio of $7.5 billion in assets as a result of an unexpected increase in interest rates, from 3% to 5.7%.[6] Figure 3.6 shows the sudden steep increase in the level of interest rates in 1994.

   The lessons learned in this chapter will help us understand what type of exposure Orange County had in its portfolio that could lead to a loss of this magnitude.

---

[6]This section and the next are based on publicly available information and they are only meant to illustrate the concepts introduced in this chapter. No claim of wrongdoing by any party is made here. Descriptive material is from the case study ERISK: Orange County, downloaded from http://www.erisk.com/Learning/CaseStudies/OrangeCounty.asp.

Figure 3.6   The Level of Interest Rates, 1992 - 1994

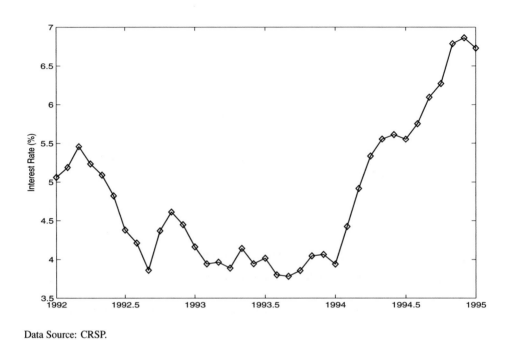

Data Source: CRSP.

3.7.1   Benchmark: What if Orange County was Invested in Zero Coupon Bonds Only?

A useful starting point is to suppose that the Orange County portfolio was invested only in zero coupon bonds and then find the maturity of these bonds necessary to bring a loss of $1.6 billion. We can do this by using the concept of duration introduced in Section 3.2. Recall that duration is defined as the (negative of the) sensitivity of a security, or a portfolio, to parallel shifts in the term structure of interest rates. More specifically, Equation 3.1 defines duration as

$$\text{Duration} = D_P = -\frac{1}{P}\frac{dP}{dr} \tag{3.45}$$

We know that the portfolio value before the hike in interest rates was approximately $7.5 billion, and thus $P = 7.5$. In addition, the change in the level of interest rates was $dr = 6.7\% - 4\% = 0.027$. Finally, the loss was $dP = -1.6$. Substituting into Equation 3.45 we find

$$\text{Duration} = -\frac{1}{7.5}\frac{-1.6}{.027} = 7.90 \tag{3.46}$$

That is, if Orange County's portfolio was invested only in Treasury securities, given the ex-post losses, we would gather that the duration of this portfolio should have been around 7.90. From Equations 3.5 and 3.6, the duration of a zero coupon bond is equal to its time to maturity. Thus, Orange County would have been hit by the same type of losses as if all of its portfolio was invested in zero coupon bonds with 7.9 years to maturity.

3.7.2   The Risk in Leverage

Orange County's portfolio, however, was not only invested in Treasury securities. By using the repo market, Orange County effectively levered up the portfolio position to $20.5 billion (see Chapter 1 to review the repurchase agreements contract.) Essentially, the Treasurer of Orange County could pledge the portfolio's highly liquid Treasury securities as collateral in a repo transaction so as to obtain other funds to invest further in Treasuries or other securities.

For now, we only consider the effect of leverage. First, the duration of the levered portfolio now has to be computed using the assets and liability formula in Equation 3.44, that is

$$\text{Duration leveraged portfolio} = w_A \times D_A + w_L \times D_L \tag{3.47}$$

where $w_A = A/(A - L) = 20.5/7.5$ and $w_L = -L/(A - L)$. The liability is given by the repo transactions, which are financed at the overnight rate. The duration of liabilities, thus, is approximately zero. That is, $D_L \approx 0$. The duration of assets, in contrast, is given by

$$D_A = -\frac{1}{20.5}\frac{-1.6}{.027} = 2.89 \tag{3.48}$$

Of course, $w_A \times D_A = 7.90$ as before. The point of this calculation, however, is that the portfolio of Orange County may well have been invested only in short-term zero coupon bonds with maturity 2.89. Although such an investment per se appears very safe, the presence of the large leveraged position generates a much higher duration of the leveraged portfolio itself, which could lead to the $1.6 billion losses when the interest rates moved by 2.7%, as they did in 1994.

3.7.3   The Risk in Inverse Floaters

Although the main reason for having a record-breaking loss in the Orange County portfolio was leverage, the trigger was the change in interest rates and its effect on inverse floaters. Recall from Chapter 2 that inverse floaters have a coupon that moves inversely to short-term floating rates. This implies that when interest rates go up, the price of inverse floaters receive a negative shock from two channels:

1. The discount channel: If interest rates go up, prices of zero coupon bonds fall as future cash flows are worth less in today's money.

2. The cash flow channel: If interest rates go up, the actual cash flow is reduced because coupon payments move inversely to interest rates.

The sensitivity of inverse floaters to interest rates can be calculated through the concept of duration. How can we compute the duration of an inverse floater? Here, we must remember that an inverse floater is given by a portfolio of more basic securities, of which we can compute the duration easily.

In particular, recall from Chapter 2, Equation 2.43, that we can write the price of a (plain vanilla) inverse floater with maturity T with annual payments and coupon $c(t) = \bar{c} - r_1(t - 1)$ as

$$\text{Price inverse floater } P_{IF}(0, T) = P_z(0, T) + P_c(0, T) - P_{FR}(0, T) \tag{3.49}$$

Table 3.8 The Duration of the 15% Fixed Rate Bond

Date	Cash Flow	Discounted Cash Flow	Weight w	T	$w * T$
12/31/1994	0.15	0.1446	0.1123	1	0.1123
12/31/1995	0.15	0.1379	0.1070	2	0.2141
12/31/1996	1.15	1.0057	0.7807	3	2.3421
	Total Value	1.2884		Duration:	2.6685

where $P_z(0, T)$ is the price of a zero coupon bond, $P_c(0, T)$ is the price of a $\bar{c}$ coupon bond, and $P_{FR}(0, T)$ is the price of a floating rate bond, all of them with maturity T. Thus, we can compute the duration of the inverse floater by applying the formula for the duration of a portfolio, namely, Equation 3.10.

We consider here the simple case discussed in Chapter 2, $\bar{c} = 15\%$, $T = 3$ and coupon payments are annual. In this case, we obtained $P_{IF}(0, 3) = \$116.28$, $P_z(0, 3) = 87.45$, $P_c(0, 3) = 128.83$, and $P_{FR}(0, 3) = 100$. The duration of the inverse floater can be computed then as

$$D_{Inverse} = w_{Zero} \times D_{zero} + w_{Fixed} \times D_{Fixed} + w_{Floating} \times D_{Floating} \qquad (3.50)$$

where $w_{Zero} = P_z(0, 3)/P_{IF}(0, 3) = 0.7521$, $w_{Fixed} = P_c(0, 3)/P_{IF}(0, 3) = 1.1079$, and $w_{Floating} = -P_{FR}(0, 3)/P_{IF}(0, 3) - .8600$ are the weights. The duration of a zero coupon bond equals its time to maturity, thus $D_{zero} = 3$. The duration of a floating rate bond with annual coupons is equal to the time of the first coupon at reset dates. Thus, $D_{Floating} = 1$. The only term left to calculate is the duration of the fixed rate bond D_{Fixed}. Table 3.8 performs the computation, obtaining $D_{Fixed} = 2.6684$.

We can substitute everything into Equation 3.50, to find

$$\begin{aligned}
D_{Inverse} &= w_{Zero} \times D_{zero} + w_{Fixed} \times D_{Fixed} + w_{Floating} \times D_{Floating} \\
&= 0.7521 \times 3 + 1.1079 \times 2.6685 - .8600 \times 1 \\
&= 4.35
\end{aligned}$$

The duration of the 3-year inverse floater is 4.35. It is important to note that the duration is higher than the inverse floater maturity (3 years). In this sense, the notion of "duration" as a temporal average of cash flows plays no role here, as we are interpreting the duration as the sensitivity of the security's price to changes in interest rates. Depending on how cash flows move with interest rates, this sensitivity can be larger or smaller than the maturity of the security itself.

3.7.4 The Risk in Leveraged Inverse Floaters

Recall that a leveraged inverse floater has a coupon that moves (inversely) to interest rates by more than one-to-one. For instance, the leveraged inverse floater discussed in Section 2.8.4 of Chapter 2 has a coupon

$$c(t) = 25\% - 2 \times r_1(t - 1) \qquad (3.51)$$

Table 3.9 The Duration of the Leverage Inverse Floater

Security	Value	Weight w	Duration D	$D * w$
$2 \times P_z(3)$	174.91	1.3320	3.00	3.9959
$P_c(3)$	156.41	1.1911	2.5448	3.0311
$-2 \times P_{FR}(3)$	-200.00	-1.5231	1.00	-1.5231
Total Value:	103.78		Duration:	5.5040

Recall also from Chapter 2 that the price of the leveraged inverse floater can be computed as:[7]

$$\text{Price leveraged inverse floater} P_{LIF}(0, T) = 2 \times P_z(0, T) + P_c(0, T) - 2 \times P_{FR}(0, T) \tag{3.52}$$

To compute the duration of the leveraged inverse floater we need to compute the duration of the fixed-coupon bond. Using the same steps as in Table 3.8 but with coupon rate $c = 25\%$ we find that the duration of the coupon bond in this case is $D_c = 2.5448$. Given this information, we can now compute the duration of the leveraged inverse floater. Table 3.9 contains the calculations. The 3-year leveraged inverse floater has a duration of 5.5040, almost twice its maturity. This security is very sensitive to changes in interest rates, indeed.

3.7.5 What Can We Infer about the Orange County Portfolio?

With these data we can get a sense of the composition of the Orange County portfolio. It appears that the portfolio had about $2.8 billion in "inverse floaters [...], index amortizing notes, and collateralized mortgage obbligations."[8] For simplicity, we assume that $2.8 billion was invested only in leveraged inverse floaters. Assuming the remaining part of the portfolio was invested in safe Treasury securities, what should have the duration of this additional investment been?

Let $x = 2.8/20.5 = 0.1366$ be the fraction of total assets invested in leveraged inverse floaters. Then, we know that

$$\text{Duration of assets} = x \times \text{Duration of leveraged inverse floater} + (1-x) \times \text{Duration of T-bills} \tag{3.53}$$

From $x = 0.1366$, the duration of leveraged inverse floaters $(= 5.5040)$ and the duration of assets $(= 2.89)$

$$\text{Duration of T-bills} = \frac{2.89 - 0.1366 \times 5.5040}{1 - 0.1366} = 2.4764 \tag{3.54}$$

That is, the $20.5 billion Orange County portfolio could well have been mainly invested in short-term Treasury bonds (with duration of only 2.4764). Yet, the large leverage and the very high duration of leveraged inverse floaters may still have produced large losses as the interest rate increased.

---

[7]We are still making the simplifying assumption that we know that $c(t) > 0$ for sure, i.e. that $r_1(t) < 25\%/2$.
[8]See ERisk Case, Orange County (2001), page 2.

3.7.6   Conclusion

In conclusion, this case illustrates the risk embedded in fixed income securities, and, in particular, in leveraged positions. Structured securities, such us leveraged inverse floaters, contain additional risks that the risk manager must be aware of. In particular, this case emphasizes that even if the average maturity of the instruments may be very low, the risk of such securities or portfolio may be very high. In this sense, the interpretation of duration as the weighted average of cash flow payments is strongly misleading. As illustrated in the case, the Orange County portfolio could well have been mainly invested in short-term Treasuries and leveraged inverse floaters. Yet, this portfolio still has a large sensitivity to interest rates, and therefore it is very risky.

3.8   CASE ANALYSIS: THE EX-ANTE RISK IN ORANGE COUNTY'S PORTFOLIO

In hindsight it seems that Orange County's investment strategy paved the way for its own disaster, but any reasonable assessment must be made using *ex ante* information. In particular, was there anything that ex ante could have warned Orange County's Treasurer and its creditors regarding the potential risk that the portfolio was bearing? We can answer this question by using the concepts of Value-at-Risk and expected shortfall introduced in Sections 3.2.8 and 3.2.9, respectively. We compute these risk measures under both the historical distribution and normal distribution approach by making use of all the information available up to January 1994.[9]

1. **Historical Distribution Approach.** We can use the past changes in the level of interest rates dr as a basis to evaluate the potential changes in a portfolio value dP. Panel A of Figure 3.7 shows the historical changes in the average level of interest rates at the monthly frequency. Panel B makes a histogram of these changes, that is, describes the frequency of each possible change. As can be seen, large increases and decreases are not very likely, but they do occur occasionally. We can now multiply each of these changes dr observed in the plot by $-D_P \times P$ to obtain the variation in dP. Figure 3.8 plots the histogram of the changes in the portfolio (i.e. the portfolio profit and loss, or P&L). Given this distribution, we can compute the maximum loss that can occur with 99% probability. We can start from the left-hand side of the distribution, and move right until we count 1% of the observations. That number is the 99% monthly VaR computed using the historical distribution approach. In this case, we find it equal to $715 million. That is, there is only 1% probability that Orange County portfolio could lose more than $715 million in one month. The corresponding expected shortfall, obtained by averaging all of the portfolio losses that are lower than $715 million, turns out to be $990 million. That is, the expected monthly loss of the Orange County portfolio in case of an extreme event is $990 million.

2. **Normal Distribution Approach.** We can also use some assumption about the distribution of interest rates. For instance, if dr is normally distributed, so is dP.

---

[9]It should be mentioned that by this date Value-at-Risk and expected shortfall were not yet been introduced as risk measures, and therefore Orange County's Treasurer could have not done the following calculations.

From the data in the top panel of Figure 3.7 we can compute the historical mean and standard deviation of dr, and thus obtain the mean and standard deviation of dP. In particular, we find

$$\text{Mean}(dr) = \widehat{\mu}_{dr} = 4.71E^{-05}; \quad \text{Std}(dr) = \widehat{\sigma}_{dr} = 0.00432;$$

which implies

$$\text{Mean}(dP) = -D_P \times P \times \widehat{\mu}_{dr} = -0.0028; \quad \text{Std}(dP) = D_P \times P \times \widehat{\sigma}_{dr} = 0.2563$$

Figure 3.8 also reports the normal density with mean $\mu_P = -.0028$ and standard deviation $\sigma_{dP} = 0.2563$. In this case, the 99% maximum loss can be computed from the properties of the normal distribution, resulting in VaR $= -(\mu_P - 2.326 \times \sigma_{dP}) = $ $598 million. This number is smaller than the one obtained under the historical distribution approach, because of the fat-tailed distribution of the portfolio P&L, as shown in Figure 3.8: Extreme realizations are more likely under the historical distribution than under the normal distribution. Indeed, from Fact 3.7 the 99% expected shortfall in the case of the normal distribution is only $680 million, which is much smaller than the $990 million expected shortfall obtained under the historical distribution approach.

The VaR numbers computed above are relatively small compared to the ex-post $1.6 billion loss. It is important to realize, though, that the VaR so computed is a *monthly* figure, while Orange County losses accrued over a six-month period. How can we compute a 6-month VaR? Using the normal distribution approach and assuming that monthly changes in interest rates are independent and identically distributed – a strong assumption as there is some predictability in yields, as discussed in Chapter 7 – the annualization can be performed by multiplying the mean μ_P by 6 and the monthly standard deviation σ_P by $\sqrt{6}$. In this case we obtain a 99% 6-month VaR equal to $1.48 billion, close to the actual loss suffered by Orange County.

3.8.1 The Importance of the Sampling Period

The VaR calculation is very sensitive to the sample used in the calculation. In fact, the top panel of Figure 3.7 shows that the volatility of the level of interest rates had been relatively low in the decade before 1994. The large estimate of the monthly standard deviation of interest rates $\sigma_{dr} = 0.00432$ is mainly due to the large volatility in the 1970s and beginning of the 1980s. If we restrict the sample to compute the standard deviation of interest rate changes dr to the more recent period, such as five years, we find the much smaller standard deviation $\sigma_{dr} = 0.0028$. The 6-month, 99% VaR in this case is $668 million, a large number, but much smaller than the actual ex-post losses.

What sample period is more relevant? The large shift up in the interest rate was probably unexpected. However, it is a common mistake to confuse a low volatility period as a safe period. History shows time and again that low volatility periods are followed by high volatility periods. Thus, reliance on the recent past would miss the probability that in fact volatility *will* go up, and with it, the risk of large losses. The use of a longer sample that takes into account such facts is therefore more conservative for the risk manager.

Figure 3.7   The Monthly Changes in the Average Level of Interest Rates

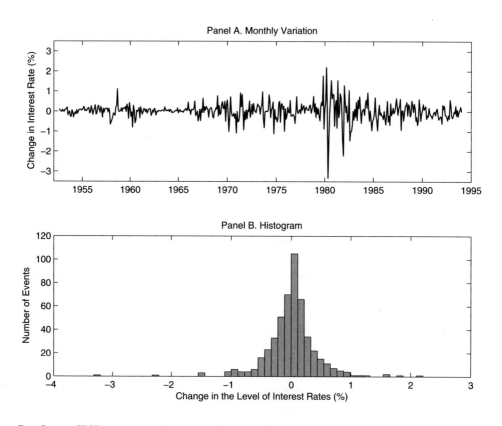

Data Source: CRSP.

3.8.2   Conclusion

The ex-ante measurement of risk is difficult and full of potential pitfalls. In the previous section, we computed several numbers in the attempt to measure the risk embedded in the Orange County portfolio. The numbers we computed vary greatly depending on (a) the type of model (e.g., normal versus historical); (b) the horizon (one month versus six months); (c) the sample used (last five years versus longer sample); (d) the type of risk measure (VaR versus Expected Shortfall).

The natural question is then the following: Which one of these measures is best? Unfortunately, this is hard to tell. While it sounds intuitive that we should always use the most conservative measure of risk, i.e. the one implying the largest possible losses, there are good reasons also to not be too conservative, as a portfolio manager who is overly conservative may miss important profit opportunities. The main goal of this case is to show that the measurement itself of risk is difficult, and so the portfolio manager should always be suspicious of any risk measure, and always ask *how* such a measure was calculated. The major risk for a portfolio manager is in fact to rely too much on these measures of risk,

Figure 3.8 The Distribution of the Monthly P&L of the Orange County Portfolio

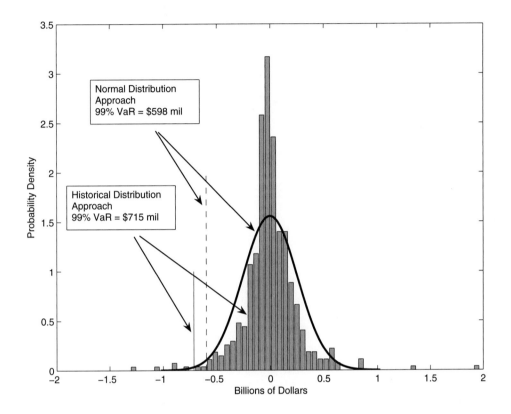

forgetting that they are fragile, in the sense that they greatly depend on the way they are computed.

3.9 APPENDIX: EXPECTED SHORTFALL UNDER THE NORMAL DISTRIBUTION

In this appendix we derive the formula in Equation 3.34 for the expected shortfall under the normal distribution case. Let dP denote the P&L of the portfolio, so that the loss is $L_T = -dP$. Clearly, $L_T > VaR$ when $dP < -VaR$. Let z be the "quantile" corresponding to the VaR. For instance, $z = 1.645$ for the 95% VaR, and recall from Equation 3.30, $dP \sim N(\mu_P, \sigma_P)$. We then have

$$
\begin{aligned}
E\left[L_T | L_T > VaR\right] &= -E\left[dP | dP < -VaR\right] = -E\left[dP | dP < (\mu_P - \sigma_P \times z)\right] \\
&= -\left\{\mu_P + \sigma_P \times E\left[\left(\frac{dP - \mu_P}{\sigma_P}\right) \middle| \left(\frac{dP - \mu_P}{\sigma_P}\right) < -z\right]\right\}
\end{aligned}
$$

$$(3.55)$$

The quantity $X = \left(\frac{dP - \mu_P}{\sigma_P} \right)$ is a standardized normal distribution. Since

$$E[X|X < -z] = \frac{\int_{\infty}^{-z} x f(x) dx}{\int_{\infty}^{-z} f(x) dx} = \frac{-f(-z)}{\mathcal{N}(-z)}$$

the formula in Equation 3.34 follows from substituting this latter expression into Equation 3.55.

CHAPTER 4

BASIC REFINEMENTS IN INTEREST RATE RISK MANAGEMENT

In this chapter we review some basic refinements in interest rate risk management. The concept of duration discussed in Chapter 3 is a good first approximation to measure the risk embedded in fixed income instruments. However, it is possible to improve upon it, and this is accomplished in two ways: First, we realize that the relation between a bond price and the interest rate is not linear, which is the implicit assumption in the duration approximation. Second, we also realize that the term structure of interest rates does not move in a parallel fashion, which is a second important assumption of the duration concept. By generalizing the risk model along these two dimensions we are able to obtain more precise measures of risk, as well as improve upon risk management practices.

4.1 CONVEXITY

The relation between bond prices and interest rates is not linear. Assume for instance a flat term structure of interest rates at rates $r = .01$, $r = .02$,...,$r = .15$. Figure 4.1 plots the values of 5-, 10-, 20- and 30-year zero coupon bonds against these interest rates. We see that as the interest rate r increases, the zero coupon bonds decrease, and they become flatter and flatter as the interest rate becomes higher and higher. This pattern is especially true for long-dated zero coupon bonds.

This observation has an impact on the practice of interest rate risk management. In Chapter 3 we explored the notion of duration, that is, the (negative of the) percentage change in a security price due to a small parallel shift in the term structure of interest rates.

Figure 4.1   Zero Coupon Bond Prices versus Interest Rates

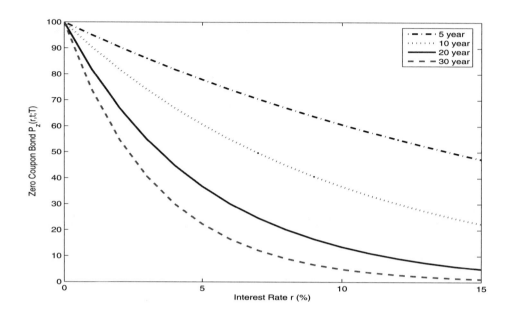

As Figure 4.2 shows, though, if the change in interest rates is substantial, the approximation that uses the notion of duration is not very good. In the figure, the approximation of the change in the bond price implemented through the concept of duration follows the straight line. Instead, the true bond price follows the curved line. Clearly, for small changes in interest rate, the straight line and the curved line are very close to each other. However, for large changes, the approximation is relatively poor. For instance, for this 20-year zero coupon bond, a change of interest rate from 5% to 2.5% implies an increase in the bond price from \$36.79 to \$60.65. In contrast, because the duration of a zero coupon bond equals its maturity $D = 20$, the duration approximation implies an increase to $\$36.79 - D \times P \times dr = \$36.79 + 20 \times \$36.79 \times 2.5\% = \$55.18$, a much smaller value.

To obtain a more accurate measure of the impact that a change in the term structure has on bond prices, we must take into account the convexity of the bond with respect to the interest rate. The convexity can be measured by referring to the notion of second derivative. In a nutshell, while the first derivative measures the slope of a function (see Definition 3.3 in Chapter 3), the second derivative measures the curvature of a function.

Definition 4.1 *The **second derivative** of a function $F(x)$, denoted by $\frac{d^2\ F(x)}{d\ r^2}$, is the first derivative of the first derivative*

$$\frac{d^2\ F(x)}{d\ r^2} = \frac{d\left(\frac{d\ F(x)}{d\ r}\right)}{d\ r}$$

In particular, let $F(x) = A \times e^{ax}$ be a function of x. From Definition 3.3, the first derivative of $F(x)$ is $\frac{dF}{dx} = aF(x)$, still a function of x. Then, the second derivative of $F(x)$ with

Figure 4.2   Bond Price Approximation with Duration

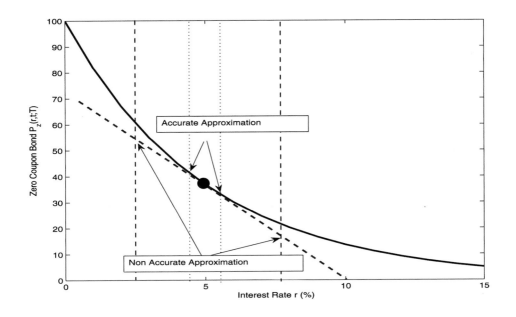

respect to x, is given by

$$Second\ derivative\ of\ F(x)\ with\ respect\ to\ x = \frac{d^2 F}{dx^2} = A \times a^2 \times e^{ax} = a^2 \times F(x)$$

What does the second derivative of a function $F(x)$ measure? While the first derivative of a function $F(x)$ measures the slope of the function at a point x, the second derivative measures the curvature of the function in the same point x. The curvature of the function is effectively measured by the change in slope, as illustrated in Figure 4.3. If the change in slope is zero, then the function $F(x)$ is a straight line, and thus there is no curvature. In this case, the second derivative is in fact zero.

Putting together the notion of second derivative in Figure 4.3 with the problem of duration illustrated in Figure 4.2, we see that knowledge of the second derivative of the bond price function can help to increase the precision of the approximation of bond price changes due to changes in the interest rate.

Definition 4.2 *The **convexity** of a security with price P measures the percentage change in the price of the security due to the curvature of the price with respect to the interest rate r. Formally*

$$Convexity = C = \frac{1}{P} \frac{d^2 P}{d r^2} \qquad (4.1)$$

Figure 4.3   Second Derivative

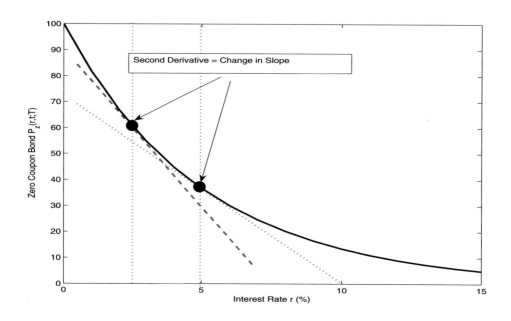

Once we compute the convexity (Equation 4.1) of a security, we can compute a better approximation of the impact of changes of interest rates on bond prices. In fact, putting together duration and convexity, we find the following:

Fact 4.1 *An approximation of the percentage impact of interest rates on the price of a security is given by*

$$\frac{dP}{P} = -D \times dr + \frac{1}{2} \times C \times dr^2 \tag{4.2}$$

In other words, the convexity term C *augments* the precision of the approximation made by the duration term, but it does not substitute for it. We provide some examples below.[1] Figure 4.4 depicts the benefits from using both duration and convexity to approximate the impact of (large) interest rate changes on bond prices. While the straight, dotted line represents the approximation using only duration, also shown in Figure 4.2, the dashed line represents the approximation using duration *and* convexity.

4.1.1   The Convexity of Zero Coupon Bonds

As in the case of duration, convexity can be computed from first principles for coupon bearing bonds. We start from zero coupon bonds, recalling that the price of a zero coupon

---

[1]Equation 4.2 stems directly from the application of a second-order Taylor expansion to the price of the security, a result that also shows the need to multiply by 1/2 the convexity term C.

Figure 4.4   Duration plus Convexity Approximation

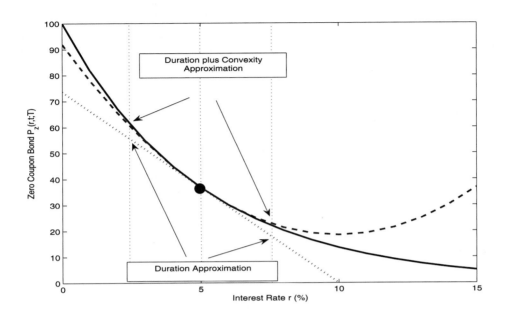

bond is given by

$$P_z(r, t; T) = 100 \times e^{-r \times (T-t)}$$

The first derivative of the bond with respect to r is $dP_z/dr = -(T-t) \times P_z(r, t; T)$. Thus, the convexity of the zero coupon bond is

$$
\begin{aligned}
C_z &= \frac{1}{P_z} \times \frac{d^2 P_z}{d r^2} & (4.3) \\
&= \frac{1}{P_z} \times \{(T-t)^2 \times P_z(r, t; T)\} & (4.4) \\
&= (T-t)^2. & (4.5)
\end{aligned}
$$

■ **EXAMPLE 4.1**

In Figure 4.2 we consider the impact that a 2.5% decline in the interest rate has on a 20-year zero coupon bond. We discovered that the price changes from \$36.79 to \$60.65, while the duration approximation only yields a change to \$55.18, a much smaller value. Convexity helps close the gap. In fact, we have $C_z = 20^2 = 400$. Thus, the percentage change in price due to a 2.5% decline in interest rate is

$$\frac{dP}{P} = 20 \times 0.025 + \frac{1}{2} \times 400 \times (0.025)^2 = 0.6250$$

The approximate price of the bond after the decline is then $P_z(r, t; T) + dP = \$36.76 + 0.625 \times \$36.76 = \$59.78$, much closer to the actual value of \$60.65. Figure 4.4 plots this case, in fact.

4.1.2   The Convexity of a Portfolio of Securities

Like duration, the convexity of a portfolio of securities is equal to the weighted average of the convexities of the individual securities, where the weights correspond to the relative value of each asset in the portfolio. The derivation of this formula is identical to the one for the duration of a portfolio in Section 3.2.2, and we therefore omit it here. The final result is the following:

Fact 4.2 *Let N_i, $i = 1, ..., n$ be the units of securities 1,..,n in a portfolio, and let P_i be their prices. The value of the portfolio is $W = \sum_{i=1}^{n} N_i P_i$. Let C_i be the convexity of security i. Then*

$$\text{Convexity of portfolio} \quad = \quad C_W = \sum_{i=1}^{n} w_i C_i \tag{4.6}$$

where

$$w_i = \frac{N_i \times P_i}{W} \tag{4.7}$$

4.1.3   The Convexity of a Coupon Bond

As an application of the convexity formula in Equation 4.6, we derive the convexity of a coupon bond. Recalling that a coupon bond can be considered as a portfolio of zero coupon bonds, we obtain:

Fact 4.3 *The **convexity** of a **coupon bond** with maturity T, coupon c, price $P_c(t, T)$ and n payment times $T_1, ... , T_n = T$ is given by*

$$C = \sum_{i=1}^{n} w_i \times C_{z,i} \tag{4.8}$$

where $C_{z,i} = (T_i - t)^2$ and

$$w_i = \frac{c/2 \times P_z(t, T_i)}{P_c(t, T)} \quad \text{for } i = 1, .., n-1, \tag{4.9}$$

$$w_n = \frac{(1 + c/2) \times P_z(t, T_n)}{P_c(t, T)}. \tag{4.10}$$

Substituting, we obtain the convexity formula

$$C = \frac{1}{P_c(t, T)} \times \left[\sum_{i=1}^{n-1} \frac{c}{2} \times P_z(t, T_i) \times (T_i - t)^2 + \left(1 + \frac{c}{2}\right) \times P_z(t, T_n) \times (T_n - t)^2 \right]$$

Table 4.1 Duration and Convexity Computation for 10-year, 5% Coupon Bond

Period i	Time T_i	Cash Flow CF	Discount $Z(0, T_i)$	Discounted Cash Flow $CF \times Z(0, T0)$	Weight w_i	Weight$\times T_i$ $w_i \times T_i$	Weight$\times T_i^2$ $w_i \times T_i^2$
1	0.5	2.5	0.9778	2.44	0.024	0.0118	0.0059
2	1.0	2.5	0.9560	2.39	0.023	0.0231	0.0231
3	1.5	2.5	0.9347	2.34	0.023	0.0338	0.0508
4	2.0	2.5	0.9139	2.28	0.022	0.0441	0.0882
5	2.5	2.5	0.8936	2.23	0.022	0.0539	0.1348
6	3.0	2.5	0.8737	2.18	0.021	0.0633	0.1898
7	3.5	2.5	0.8543	2.14	0.021	0.0722	0.2526
8	4.0	2.5	0.8353	2.09	0.020	0.0806	0.3226
9	4.5	2.5	0.8167	2.04	0.020	0.0887	0.3992
10	5.0	2.5	0.7985	2.00	0.019	0.0964	0.4818
11	5.5	2.5	0.7808	1.95	0.019	0.1036	0.5701
12	6.0	2.5	0.7634	1.91	0.018	0.1106	0.6633
13	6.5	2.5	0.7464	1.87	0.018	0.1171	0.7612
14	7.0	2.5	0.7298	1.82	0.018	0.1233	0.8631
15	7.5	2.5	0.7136	1.78	0.017	0.1292	0.9688
16	8.0	2.5	0.6977	1.74	0.017	0.1347	1.0778
17	8.5	2.5	0.6822	1.71	0.016	0.1400	1.1896
18	9.0	2.5	0.6670	1.67	0.016	0.1449	1.3040
19	9.5	2.5	0.6521	1.63	0.016	0.1495	1.4206
20	10.0	102.5	0.6376	65.36	0.631	6.3101	63.1010
				$P = 103.58$		$D = 8.0309$	$C = 73.8682$

■ **EXAMPLE 4.2**

A corporation buys $100 million (par value) of a 10-year coupon bond that pays a 5% semi-annual coupon. Assume that the term structure of the interest rates is flat at the continuously compounded rate of 4.5%. Table 4.1 shows that the price of the bond is $103.58, implying a position in the bond of $103.50 million and a duration of 8.03. This duration value implies that an increase of the yield by 1%, from 4.5% to 5.5%, entails an approximate loss of 8%, as

$$\frac{dP}{P} \approx -D \times 0.01 = -0.0803 = -8\%$$

Table 4.1 shows that the convexity of the position is 73.87. Adding convexity instead entails an approximate loss of 7.66%, computed as follows:

$$\frac{dP}{P} \approx -D \times 0.01 + \frac{1}{2} \times C \times (0.01)^2 = -0.07662 = -7.66\%$$

We can verify that the latter approximate variation is closer to the real change by simply recomputing the price of the bond when the term structure is flat at 5.5%. A computation analogous to the one in Table 4.1 shows that the price declines to $95.63 from $103.58, implying a loss equal to

$$\frac{dP}{P} = \frac{\$95.63 - \$103.58}{\$103.58} = -7.67\%$$

This is indeed very close to the calculation made using the convexity adjustment.

4.1.4 Positive Convexity: Good News for Average Returns

Predicting the short-run changes in the level of interest rates is extremely hard. When the level of interest rates is low, we can expect it to increase in the long term future, and likewise when the level of interest rates is very high we can expect it to decrease. But predicting the change in the level of interest rates day by day is extremely difficult. Suppose we have invested $100 million in a 20-year zero coupon bond. Given a change in the level of interest rates equal to dr, the duration computation allows us to compute the expected return, by using the formula

$$\frac{dP}{P} = -D \times dr = -20 \times dr \tag{4.11}$$

Thus, if the level of interest increases by one basis point ($dr = .01\%$) we stand to lose $0.2\% = 20 \times .01\%$ of our investment, that is $200,000. Similarly, if the level of interest rate decreases by one basis point ($dr = -.01\%$), we stand to gain $200,000. Can we forecast how much money we can make between today and tomorrow? The answer is that if we cannot forecast the change in interest rate dr we cannot forecast the return itself. We will use the notation $E[dr]$ to indicate the expected change in the level of interest rate, and $E[dP/P]$ to represent the expected return from the investment. Since we just said that $E[dr] = 0$, Equation 4.11 implies

$$E\left[\frac{dP}{P}\right] = -20 \times E[dr] = 0$$

What if we consider the convexity term? Using Equation 4.2 and recalling that for a 20-year zero coupon bond the convexity is $C = 400$, we find

$$E\left[\frac{dP}{P}\right] = -20 \times E[dr] + \frac{1}{2} \times 400 \times E[dr^2] \tag{4.12}$$

What is $E[dr^2]$? In statistics, when $E[dr] = 0$ this quantity corresponds to the variance of the change in level of interest rates. That is, it measures the size of the daily fluctuations in interest rates. The key insight is that although we do not know the direction in which the interest rate will move between today and tomorrow, it is extremely likely it *will move*. That is, the variance of interest rates is positive, $E[dr^2] > 0$. Figure 4.5 plots the daily changes in the level of interest rates over the past three decades: It appears clear that every day the level of interest rates moves.[2]

---

[2]We computed daily spot curves using the extended Nelson Siegel model based on data from CRSP (Daily Treasuries) ¤2009 Center for Research in Security Prices (CRSP), The University of Chicago Booth School of Business.

Figure 4.5   Daily Changes in the Level of Interest Rates

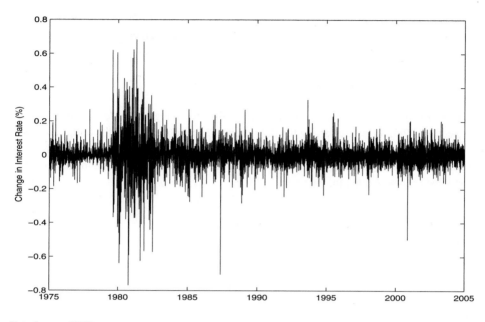

Data Source: CRSP.

Why is this significant to the return on the investment in the 20-year bond? The reason is that given the variance of interest rates of about $E[dr^2] = 5.5351 \times 10^{-007}$ we find

$$E\left[\frac{dP}{P}\right] = -20 \times 0 + \frac{1}{2} \times 400 \times E[dr^2] = 1.11 \times 10^{-04} > 0 \qquad (4.13)$$

Although this number seems extremely small, it is a daily expected return. To better gauge the magnitude, we can annualize the expected return by multiplying this number by 252, the number of trading days in a typical year. In this case, we find

$$\text{Annualized expected return from convexity} = 1.11 \times 10^{-04} \times 252 = 2.79\%$$

Similarly, considering the $100 million investment, convexity yields a daily dollar return of $11,070 = 1.11 \times 10^{-04} \times 100$ million.

Is this positive average return stemming from the fluctuation of the level of interest rates a "free lunch"? No: As we shall see more formally in later chapters, this positive average return on the investment is counterbalanced by a lower yield to maturity of the bond, everything else equal. Indeed, no arbitrage conditions entail that a precise relation must exist between the convexity of the bond and its yield to maturity.

4.1.5   A Common Pitfall

A common pitfall is to think of "convexity" as the "change in duration." As the definition above shows, it is not. As a simple example, the duration of a zero coupon bond is constant independent of the interest rate, as it is equal to its time to maturity. Yet, as shown earlier, the convexity of a zero coupon bond is most definitely not zero.[3]

The correct statement is instead that the curvature of a function, represented by its second derivative, is indeed equal to the change in slope of the function, given by the first derivative. Adopting the terminology used in Chapter 3, we can call **dollar convexity** the quantity

$$\text{Dollar convexity} = C^\$ = \frac{d^2 P}{d r^2} \tag{4.14}$$

In this case, indeed, the *dollar* convexity is related to the change in *dollar* duration, defined in Section 3.2.7. In particular, by the definition of second derivative, the dollar convexity equals the change of the negative of the dollar duration. Note that the dollar convexity of a zero coupon bond is not constant, as it equals $(T - t) \times P_z(r, t; T)$ and the zero coupon bond does depend on the interest rate.

4.1.6 Convexity and Risk Management

Taking into account convexity improves the performance of interest rate risk management practices, especially in an environment with substantial shifts in the yield curve. To motivate the convexity hedging strategy, consider again Example 4.2.

■ **EXAMPLE 4.3**

Suppose that the corporation in Example 4.2 is worried about the losses that its portfolio may suffer from an upward shift in the term structure of interest rates. Let us consider first a duration hedging strategy. For simplicity, let us assume that the corporation decides to enter into a position of k 10-year zero coupon bond $P_z(0, T)$ to hedge away the interest rate risk. From Table 4.1, the value of this zero coupon bond is $P_z(0, T) = 100 \times Z(0, T) = \$63.76$. Its duration, of course, is $D_z = 10$. Denoting again by P the value of the bond ($P = \$103.58$ from Table 4.1), what is the position k in the zero coupon bond such that the portfolio $V = P + k \times P_z(0, T)$ is insensitive to a parallel shift in the yield curve? From Chapter 3, we must have $dV = 0$, which implies

$$k = -\frac{D \times P}{D_z \times P_z(0, T)} = \frac{8.03 \times 103.58}{10 \times 63.76} = -1.3045 \tag{4.15}$$

That is, to hedge against a parallel shift in the term structure, the corporation must short 1.3045 units of a 10-year zero coupon bond. We assume that the corporation achieves this short position through the repo market (see Chapter 1), that is, it borrows the zero coupon bond from a repo dealer, sells it to the market for $1.3045 \times P_z(0, T) =$

---

[3]I cannot resist mentioning the anecdote that made me write this subsection: In my years at Chicago Booth, several times my students were asked the following questions during job interviews: "What is the duration of a 20-year zero coupon bond?" My students would reply "20". The interviewer would then ask: "What is the convexity of the 20-year zero coupon bond?" My students (always well prepared) would answer "400" ($= 20^2$). The interviewer would then say "Ah! I caught you! You see, the duration of the zero coupon bond is independent of interest rates, *therefore* the convexity of the zero coupon bond is zero". Unfortunately, the interviewer was plainly wrong, as the discussion in this section demonstrates.

$83.18, and deposits the cash amount with the repo dealer. This assumption implies that the short position is achieved at zero cost for the corporation.[4]

Consider now a parallel shift in the yield curve. Let's explore three scenarios: A small parallel shift with a change of $dr = 10$ basis point, a medium-large parallel shift with $dr = 1\%$, and a very large parallel shift with a change of $dr = 2\%$. How does the duration hedge perform under these three scenarios? To answer this question, we need to recompute the values of the bonds P and $P_z(0, T)$ for the new interest rate scenarios, compute the new value of the portfolio $V = P + k \times P_z(0, T)$, and then take the difference from the original portfolio value. This exercise is illustrated in Panel A of Table 4.2. Column 1 reports the size of the change in interest rate. Columns 2 and 3 report the values of the bond P and the zero coupon bond $P_z(0, T)$, respectively, for each interest rate scenario, while Column 4 shows the position in the zero coupon bond, which does not change across scenarios. Column 5 finally reports the change in portfolio value dV. As can be seen, the change in portfolio value is extremely small when the parallel shift is small, $dr = 10$ basis points. However, a larger increase in the yield curve still produces a loss, which increases with the increase in interest rates. In addition, note that the hedged portfolio loses money both when interest rates increase and when interest rates decrease.

Example 4.3 shows that the hedged portfolio loses money both when interest rates increase and when interest rates decrease if the size of these shifts is large. This behavior of the hedged portfolio is due to the fact that the hedged portfolio is not convexity hedged. Indeed, we can write the change in the hedged porfolio as follows:[5].

$$d\,V = d\,P + k \times d\,P_z$$

Substituting for both $d\,P$ and $d\,P_z$ the approximation in Equation 4.2 we find

$$
\begin{aligned}
d\,V \quad = \quad & -D \times P \times dr + \frac{1}{2} \times P \times C \times dr^2 && \text{(Change } d\,P) \\
& +k \times \left(-D_z \times P_z \times dr + \frac{1}{2} \times P_z \times C \times dr^2 \right) && \text{(Change } k \times d\,P_z)
\end{aligned}
$$

Pulling together the terms in dr and dr^2 we obtain

$$d\,V \quad = \quad -(D \times P + k \times D_z \times P_z) \times dr + \frac{1}{2} \times (P \times C + k \times P_z \times C) \times dr^2$$

$$(4.16)$$

Duration hedging (Equation 4.15) eliminates the first parenthesis in Equation 4.16. However, the second parenthesis in the equation is generally not zero. If the parenthesis is negative, then the duration hedging strategy tends to generate a loss irrespective of a positive or negative change in interest rate dr because $dr^2 > 0$. Vice versa, if the parenthesis is instead positive, then the duration hedging strategy tends to generate a gain.

One strategy to hedge against both small *and* large variations in interest rates is to choose both k and the maturity T of the zero coupon bond to make both parentheses in Equation

---

[4]Alternatively, the corporation can use forward contracts or futures contracts, which also have zero cost, as discussed in Chapters 5 and 6.
[5]For notational simplicity, we denote here the zero coupon bond by P_z rather than the more cumbersome $P_z(0, T)$.

Table 4.2   Duration Hedging versus Duration and Convexity Hedging

Panel A: Duration Hedging

Spot Curve Shift	P	$P_z(0,T)$	Position	Change in Portfolio Value
Initial Values	103.58	63.76	-1.3045	
$dr = 0.1\%$	102.75	63.13	-1.3045	-0.0003
$dr = 1.0\%$	95.63	57.69	-1.3045	-0.0318
$dr = 2.0\%$	88.38	52.20	-1.3045	-0.1210
$dr = -0.1\%$	104.41	64.40	-1.3045	-0.0003
$dr = -1.0\%$	112.29	70.47	-1.3045	-0.0350
$dr = -2.0\%$	121.84	77.88	-1.3045	-0.1474

Panel B: Duration and Convexity Hedging

Spot Curve Shift	P	$P_z(0,T_1)$	$P_z(0,T_2)$	Postion k_1	Position k_2	Change in Portfolio Value
Initial Value	103.58	91.39	63.76	-0.4562	-1.1737	
$dr = 0.1\%$	102.75	91.21	63.13	-0.4562	-1.1737	0.0000
$dr = 1.0\%$	95.63	89.58	57.69	-0.4562	-1.1737	0.0003
$dr = 2.0\%$	88.38	87.81	52.20	-0.4562	-1.1737	0.0023
$dr = -0.1\%$	104.41	91.58	64.40	-0.4562	-1.1737	0.0000
$dr = -1.0\%$	112.29	93.24	70.47	-0.4562	-1.1737	-0.0003
$dr = -2.0\%$	121.84	95.12	77.88	-0.4562	-1.1737	-0.0027

4.16 equal to zero. Alternatively, we can use two securities to hedge both duration and convexity simultaneously. The latter strategy is simpler to implement because we can then choose freely from all possible available securities, including derivative instruments such as forwards or futures, discussed in Chapters 5 and 6.

ore specifically, let P_1 and P_2 be the prices of two securities, such as a short-term and a long-term zero coupon bond, with D_1, D_2, C_1, and C_2 their durations and convexities, respectively. Let k_1 and k_2 be the position in these two bonds. The value of the hedged portfolio is then given by

$$V = P + k_1 \times P_1 + k_2 \times P_2$$

The portfolio is hedged if a change in interest rate dr does not affect its value, that is, if $dV = 0$. Taking into account also the convexity effect in Equation 4.2, we obtain:

$$
\begin{aligned}
dV &= dP + k_1 \times dP_1 + k_2 \times dP_2 \\
&= -D \times P \times dr + \frac{1}{2} \times C \times P \times dr^2 && \text{(Change } dP \text{ in original bond)} \\
&\quad -k_1 \times D_1 \times P_1 \times dr + \frac{1}{2} \times k_1 \times C_1 \times P_1 \times dr^2 && \text{(Change } dP_1 \text{ in bond 1)} \\
&\quad -k_2 \times D_2 \times P_2 \times dr + \frac{1}{2} \times k_2 \times C_2 \times P_2 \times dr^2 && \text{(Change } dP_2 \text{ in bond 2)}
\end{aligned}
$$

We can pull together the terms in dr and dr^2:

$$
\begin{aligned}
dV &= -(D \times P + k_1 \times D_1 \times P_1 + k_2 \times D_2 \times P_2) \times dr \\
&\quad + \frac{1}{2} \times (C \times P + k_1 \times C_1 \times P_1 + k_2 \times C_2 \times P_2) \times dr^2
\end{aligned}
$$

Thus, in order for the portfolio to be immune to changes in interest rates, we must have $dV = 0$ for both small changes in interest rates (small dr) and large changes in interest rates (large dr which implies large dr^2). This is achieved by choosing k_1 and k_2 such that:

$$
\begin{aligned}
k_1 \times D_1 \times P_1 + k_2 \times D_2 \times P_2 &= -D \times P && \text{(Delta Hedging)} \\
k_1 \times C_1 \times P_1 + k_2 \times C_2 \times P_2 &= -C \times P && \text{(Convexity Hedging)}
\end{aligned}
$$

The solution of this system of two equations in two unknowns is

$$
k_1 = -\frac{P}{P_1} \times \left(\frac{D \times C_2 - C \times D_2}{D_1 \times C_2 - C_1 \times D_2} \right) \tag{4.17}
$$

$$
k_2 = -\frac{P}{P_2} \times \left(\frac{D \times C_1 - C \times D_1}{D_2 \times C_1 - C_2 \times D_1} \right) \tag{4.18}
$$

We now return to Example 4.3 and see the improvement in hedging performance.

■ **EXAMPLE 4.4**

Consider again Example 4.3, but assume that in addition to the zero coupon bond with maturity $T_2 = 10$, the corporation also uses a zero coupon bond with short maturity $T_1 = 2$. From Table 4.1 the price of the 2-year zero coupon bond is $P_z(0, T_1) = \$91.39$. From the same table, the convexity of the bond we want to hedge is $C = 73.87$. Denoting by $D_1 = 2$, $D_2 = 10$, $C_1 = 4$, and $C_2 = 100$ the durations and convexities of the two zero coupon bonds, respectively, applying the formulas in Equations 4.17 and 4.18 we obtain

$$k_1 = -0.4562 \quad \text{and} \quad k_2 = -1.1737.$$

That is, to hedge the portfolio against both small and large changes in interest rates, the corporation must short 0.4562 units of the 2-year zero coupon bond, and 1.1737 units of the 10-year zero coupon bond.

Does the hedging strategy work any better than the simpler duration hedging strategy? Panel B of Table 4.2 illustrates the performance of the hedging strategy under the three scenarios of a small, medium-large, and very large shift in the yield curve. In particular, Column 1 displays the interest rate scenarios, Columns 2 to 4 contain the values of the original bond, the 2-year zero coupon bond, and the 10-year zero coupon bond, respectively. Columns 5 and 6 show the positions in the short-term and long-term bond, respectively. Finally, Column 7 contains the change in value of the hedged portfolio. As we would expect, the changes of the hedged portfolio are much smaller than under duration hedging in Panel A, even for a relatively large variation in the term structure of interest rates.

4.1.7 Convexity Trading and the Passage of Time

Example 4.3 and the discussion following it highlight a seemingly profitable trading strategy. If we go long bonds with high convexity, such as long-term bonds, and duration hedge the interest rate risk using bonds with low convexity, such as short-term bonds, we gain positive returns from convexity. That is, in Equation 4.16 the first parenthesis is always zero, because of hedging, while the second parenthesis is always positive, entailing a positive flow of money. For instance, a standard convexity trading strategy is the barbell-bullet portfolio strategy: A barbell bond position consists of a portfolio that is long both high duration and low duration assets, while a bullet bond position is a position long a medium duration asset. The strategy then consists in going long a barbell position, and hedging it with a bullet position, with the same duration. Such a strategy results in a positive convexity strategy.

The question is then whether the convexity trading strategy represents an arbitrage opportunity. The answer is no. The reason is that the duration hedging argument leaves out an important dimension of bond return, and this is time. That is, a zero coupon bond, for instance, gains value over time simply because time passes, even if interest rates do not move. This predictable part in the variation of bond prices is not taken into account in the duration/convexity hedging strategies discussed above, but it must be taken into account if we want to consider a dynamic investment strategy. Unfortunately, trading strategies that also take into account the price variation due to the passage of time require the development of more complex models, such as those discussed in Part II and Part III of this book. From these models we discover that the convexity trading strategy has an important drawback, and this is the fact that the gain in value from higher convexity is offset by a lower gain due to the passage of time, a relation that is known as the Theta-Gamma relation (see Section 16.5 in Chapter 16). In other words, there is really one more term in Equation 4.16 showing the changes in value in the bond P and in the zero coupon bond P_z due to time, and these changes exactly offset the convexity gain.

4.2 SLOPE AND CURVATURE

In Chapter 3 we looked at the level of interest rates over time, and discussed the fact that all interest rates tend to go up and down together. That is, the general level of interest rates is the first quantity to watch out for when we either invest in fixed income securities or engage in risk management practices. Panel A of Figure 4.6 plots the time series of the term structure of interest rates in the United States, from 1965 to 2005.

Figure 4.6   Slope and Curvature of the Term Structure of Interest Rates: 1965 - 2005

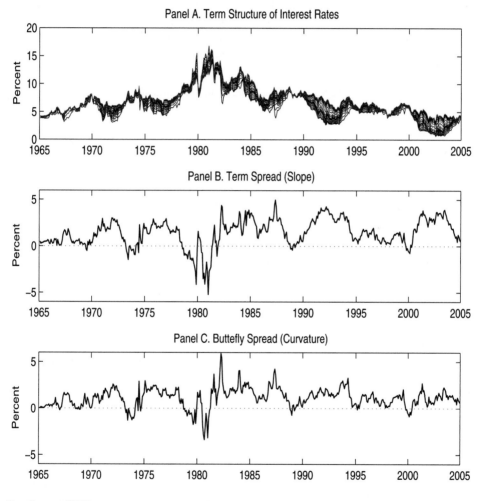

Data Source: CRPS.

A look at Panel A of Figure 4.6, however, also reveals that the term structure of interest rates is not moving up and down in a parallel fashion. If it was moving in a parallel fashion, we should see lines at equal distances over time. Instead, what we see in Panel A of Figure 4.6 is that the interest rates sometimes are further apart from each other, as they were around 1993 and 2003, while other times they are very close to each other, as in 1989, 1995 and 2005. Indeed, Panel B of the figure plots the *term spread* of the term structure of interest rates over time. Recall that the term spread was introduced in Chapter 2, Definition 2.4, and it is given by the difference between a long-term interest rate (in the figure, the 10-year rate) and a short-term interest rates (in the figure, the 1-month interest rate). Clearly, the term spread greatly fluctuates over time, moving between -5% to 5%. This movement may or may not be accompanied by changes in the level of interest rates. For instance, comparing Panel B of Figure 4.6 with Panel B of Figure 3.1, we see that in 1993 and 1998, the level (average) of interest rates was about 5%. However, in 1993, the term spread (slope) was around 4% while in 1998, it was around 0%.

A second quantity that is also time varying but not fully accounted for by the level and the slope of the term structure is the curvature of the term structure of interest rates, that is, the relative pricing of short-, medium- and long-term bonds. Figure 4.7 provides an example of two term structures of interest rates, with approximately the same level of interest rates and the same slope (term premium), but two different curvatures.

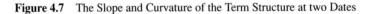

Figure 4.7   The Slope and Curvature of the Term Structure at two Dates

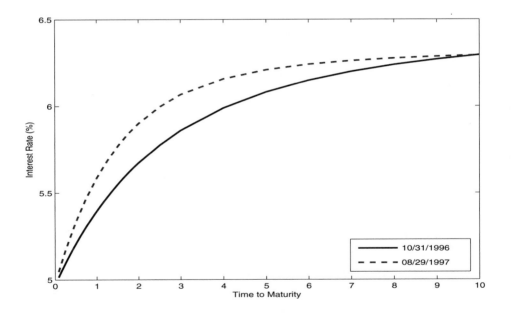

Data Source: CRPS.

ore explicitly, the term structure at the end of August 1997 appears more curved than the one at the end of October 1996. One way to measure the curvature of the term structure of interest rates is to consider the relative pricing of short-, medium- and long-term bonds. A popular measure of the curvature of the term structure is called the butterfly spread, defined as follows:

Definition 4.3 *A* **butterfly spread** *is given by the following quantity*

$$Curvature = -Short\text{-}term\ yield + 2 \times Medium\text{-}term\ yield - Long\text{-}term\ yield$$

Table 4.3 The Slope and Curvature of the Term Structure at Two Dates

Date	1-month Yield	5-year Yield	10-year Yield	Slope	Curvature
10/31/1996	5.01 %	6.08 %	6.30%	1.29 %	0.85%
08/29/1997	5.05 %	6.21%	6.29 %	1.24 %	1.08 %

Notes: Yields are calculated based on data from CRSP.

To understand this measure of curvature, consider again Figure 4.7: Table 4.3 reports the actual yields on the two dates, the slope and curvature measures. We see that while the slope is almost identical, the curvature computed from the butterfly spread is much higher.

4.2.1 Implications for Risk Management

Why is all this important for risk management? In Chapter 3 we considered the duration based risk management practice of hedging against *parallel* shifts of the term structure of interest rates. That is, hedging only against changes in the average level of interest rates. However, interest rates do not move in a parallel fashion. This is important: A bond portfolio that could be duration hedged may still suffer large losses if the slope or the curvature of the term structure changes. The next example demonstrates the problem.

■ **EXAMPLE 4.5**

Suppose that on April 1, 2004 a fixed income fund has $100 million (par amount) invested in a 3.875 coupon bond expiring on February 15, 2013. The price of this bond on that day is $101.50 (per $100 of face value). The term structure of interest rates on that day is displayed in Table 4.4. With these data, the duration of the bond is equal to

$$D = 7.491 \tag{4.19}$$

An effective duration hedge can be achieved by using, for instance, the zero coupon bond maturing on February 15, 2005. The duration of the zero coupon bond is $D_S = 0.87$. Duration hedging is then achieved by taking a position k_S in the short-term zero coupon bond equal to

$$k_S = -\frac{D \times P}{D_S \times P_S} = \frac{7.491 \times 101.5}{0.87 \times 99.0019} = -8.83$$

That is, the fund must short 8.83 short-term bonds for each unit of long-term bond held. Assume that the short position k_S in short-term bonds is taken through the repo market, so that any cash inflow is deposited with the repo dealer and the net position of the fund is simply equal to $V = \$101.5$.

What happened between April 1, 2004 and April 15, 2004? The term structure of interest rates indeed shifted up by about 0.5%, on average, across all maturities.

The two term structures on the two dates are plotted in Figure 4.8, and also reported in Columns 3 and 6 of Table 4.4, respectively. An effective duration hedging should have largely hedged the potential losses due to the shift in interest rates. This can be seen by direct computation: In fact, we can add 0.50% to each of the interest rates in the second column of Table 4.4 and recompute the value of the hedged portfolio. We find that such a parallel shift in the term structure of interest rates would change the value of the hedged portfolio from $101.50 to $101.57, implying a small (0.07%) increase in value.

In sharp contrast, the new term structure of interest rates implies a large negative drop in price of the portfolio. In fact, the value of the hedged portfolio using the new term structure interest rates contained in Column 5 of Table 4.4 is

$$V_{4/15/2004} = \$98.20,$$

a decline of 3.30%. In other words, the hedging strategy did not work as expected. It did work partially, as the unhedged portfolio would have dropped instead to

$$V_{4/15/2004}^{\text{no hedge}} = \$97.42,$$

a decrease of 4.01%. But the fact that the allegedly hedged portfolio also dropped substantially in value is quite bad for the duration hedging strategy.

The previous example highlights that the hedging of interest rate risk cannot be fully accomplished by using the notion of duration. More specifically, from Figure 4.8, the reason why the duration hedged portfolio in Example 4.5 dropped in value is that between April 1 and April 15 the slope of the term structure changed as well. Since the long end increased by more than the short end, the price of the security used to hedge (i.e., the short-term bond) did not increase sufficiently compared to the drop of the long-term bond. Therefore, we must extend our risk management methodology to take into account changes in the slope and curvature of the term structure.

4.2.2 Factor Models and Factor Neutrality

How can we expand the duration methodology to take into account that slope and curvature can change over time? Let's begin by considering level, slope and curvature as factors that drive the term structure of interest rates.

Definition 4.4 *Consider T_1, T_2,...,T_n to be n points on the current term structure of interest rates, and let $r_i = r(t, T_i)$ be the corresponding zero coupon rate. A **factor model** for the dynamics of the term structure of interest rates assumes that the instantaneous change of the various points on the curve, dr_i, is due to a set of common factors ϕ_1, ϕ_2,...,ϕ_m*

$$dr_1 = \beta_{11}d\phi_1 + \beta_{12}d\phi_2 + ...\beta_{1m}d\phi_m \tag{4.20}$$
$$dr_2 = \beta_{21}d\phi_1 + \beta_{22}d\phi_2 + ...\beta_{2m}d\phi_m \tag{4.21}$$
$$\vdots \quad \vdots \qquad \vdots \quad \vdots$$
$$dr_n = \beta_{n1}d\phi_1 + \beta_{n2}d\phi_2 + ...\beta_{nm}d\phi_m \tag{4.22}$$

where β_{ij} determines the impact that the variation in each of the factors $d\phi_j$, $j = 1,..,m$ has on each individual interest rate r_i, $i = 1,...,n$.

Table 4.4 Interest Rates in April, 2004

aturity Date T	1 April 2004			15 April 2004		
	Time to Maturity T	Yield r(0,T)	Discount $Z(0,T)(\times 100)$	Time to Maturity $T-t$	Yield $r(t,T)$	Discount $Z(0,T)(\times 100)$
20040815	0.37	1.00%	99.6293	0.33	1.12%	99.6283
20050215	0.87	1.15%	99.0019	0.83	1.31%	98.9140
20050815	1.37	1.32%	98.2068	1.33	1.67%	97.7961
20060215	1.87	1.55%	97.1458	1.83	1.98%	96.4300
20060815	2.37	1.79%	95.8461	2.33	2.28%	94.8167
20070215	2.87	2.01%	94.3856	2.83	2.55%	93.0378
20070815	3.37	2.22%	92.7813	3.33	2.77%	91.1796
20080215	3.87	2.44%	90.9886	3.83	2.99%	89.1559
20080815	4.37	2.66%	89.0279	4.33	3.22%	86.9737
20090215	4.87	2.83%	87.1094	4.83	3.40%	84.8449
20090815	5.37	3.02%	85.0175	5.33	3.62%	82.4343
20100215	5.87	3.19%	82.9229	5.83	3.79%	80.1709
20100815	6.37	3.32%	80.9208	6.33	3.90%	78.0958
20110215	6.87	3.44%	78.9194	6.83	4.03%	75.9416
20110815	7.37	3.59%	76.7659	7.33	4.16%	73.6930
20120215	7.87	3.69%	74.8008	7.83	4.25%	71.6587
20120815	8.37	3.77%	72.9193	8.33	4.33%	69.6940
20130215	8.83	3.86%	71.1246	8.79	4.43%	67.7355

Notes: Yields and discounts are calculated based on data from CRSP.

Figure 4.8 The Shift Up in the Term Structure in April, 2004

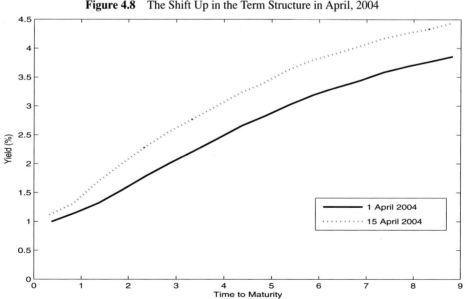

Table 4.5 The Sensitivity of Interest Rates to Level, Slope, and Curvature

Factor	3 month	6 month	1 year	Maturity 2 year	4 year	6 year	8 year	10 year
β_{i1} (Level)	1.0967	1.1686	1.1154	0.9940	0.9333	0.9264	0.9267	0.9279
β_{i2} (Slope)	-0.1794	-0.1506	-0.2540	-0.3010	0.0080	0.3158	0.5297	0.6737
β_{i3} (Curv.)	-0.3184	-0.1131	0.1761	0.3723	0.1790	-0.1076	-0.3224	-0.4708
R^2	97.56%	92.45 %	96.16%	99.99%	97.98%	96.90%	96.57%	96.56%

To clarify Definition 4.4, in the case of duration-based risk management we considered only parallel shifts. That is, we considered only one factor ($m = 1$ above), called parallel shift, and all of the $\beta_{i1} = 1$. In this case, an increase in the "factor ϕ_1" generates an increase in the overall term structure of interest rates at all points $T_1,...,T_n$. Definition 4.4 generalizes this case to multiple factors, in which ϕ_2 could be slope and ϕ_3 could be curvature, as plotted in Figure 4.6.[6]

How do we use a model such as that supplied by Equations 4.20 through 4.22? Suppose that we have available the β_{ij} coefficients. Then, we can neutralize the impact of changes in factors, such as level, slope and curvature, much in the same way as we did for duration. To be concrete, consider the case in which $\phi_1 = $ level, $\phi_2 = $ slope and $\phi_3 = $ curvature. Table 4.5 contains estimates of the sensitivities β_{ij} for various maturities $T_1 = $ 3-months, $T_2 = $ 6-months, ... , $T_n = $ 10-years. We will discuss later how to obtain these coefficients. For now, assume we have them. The question is how do we use this information to quantify risk and set up an effective risk management strategy.

4.2.3 Factor Duration

uch in the same way as in Chapter 3 when we computed the sensitivity of bond prices to parallel shifts in the yield curve (duration analysis), we can compute the sensitivity of a bond price to each of the factors (level, slope, and curvature). The methodology is very similar. Consider first the notion of factor duration, which is analogous to parallel shifts but defined on the factors themselves:

Definition 4.5 *The **factor duration** of an asset with price P with respect to factor j (e.g., slope) is defined as*

$$D_j = -\frac{1}{P}\frac{d\,P}{d\,\phi_j} \tag{4.23}$$

where $\frac{d\,P}{d\,\phi_j}$ represents the sensitivity of the asset price to changes in factor j.

---

[6]An important caveat is the following: As it is true in the notion of duration, there is no time dimension in the factor model in Equations 4.20 to 4.22. The interpretation of the model is to gauge the impact that factors ϕ_j, $j = 1, .., m$ would have on the value of a portfolio if suddenly they moved up or down. This notion is important to understanding the connection with no arbitrage models described in Part III of the book.

The factor duration measures the (negative of the) percentage impact of factor j on the price P. For instance, if the factor is the level, the factor duration is essentially equivalent to the conventional duration we talked about in Chapter 3. Note that the definition can also be given also for slope and curvature.[7]

As we did for the case of duration, we begin by analyzing a zero coupon bond with price $P_z(t, T_i)$ and time to maturity $(T_i - t)$. In particular, if factor j (e.g. slope) moves from ϕ_j to $\overline{\phi}_j = \phi_j + d\phi_j$, what is the impact on the price of the zero coupon $P_z(t, T_i)$? The methodology is as follows: The variation in factor j, $d\phi_j$, has an impact on the yield r_i that corresponds to the maturity of the zero coupon bond we are analyzing. The size of this impact of ϕ_j on r_i is given by the coefficient β_{ij} in Equations 4.20 - 4.22, and provided in Table 4.5. That is, assuming that only factor j moves, $dr_i = \beta_{ij} d\phi_j$. Since dr_i has an impact on the zero coupon bond price given by its first derivative with respect to the yield to maturity, we can compute the total sensitivity of the bond price to changes in the factor. More specifically, this chain rule, or domino effect (the factor has an impact on interest rate that has an impact on price) can be expressed mathematically as follows:

$$\frac{dP_z(t, T_i)}{d\phi_j} = \frac{dP_z(t, T_i)}{dr_i} \times \frac{dr_i}{d\phi_j} = \frac{dP_z(t, T_i)}{dr_i} \times \beta_{ij} \tag{4.24}$$

Recalling that $\frac{dP_z(t, T_i)}{dr_i} = -(T_i - t) \times P_z(t, T_i)$ we obtain the factor duration of the zero coupon i with respect to factor j:

$$
\begin{aligned}
D_{j,z} &= -\frac{1}{P_z(t, T_i)} \frac{dP_z(t, T_i)}{d\phi_j} \\
&= -\frac{1}{P_z(t, T_i)} \left(-(T_i - t) \times P_z(t, T_i) \times \beta_{ij} \right) \\
&= (T_i - t) \times \beta_{ij} \tag{4.25}
\end{aligned}
$$

The formula is the same as for the duration, with the additional twist that β_{ij} enters into the picture. Note that given the parameters in Table 4.5 we have $\beta_{i1} \approx 1$ for the level factor, thereby obtaining the standard definition of duration for the first factor.

Since the equation for the duration of a zero coupon bond is similar to the one for the standard duration (with the addition of β_{ij}) it is intuitive that all of the other results we obtained in Chapter 3 also hold. In particular:

Fact 4.4 *The **factor duration of a portfolio** is the weighted average of the factor duration of the individual assets, where the weights equal the relative value of each asset with respect to the total value of the portfolio.*

For instance, as an application of this fact, we obtain:

Fact 4.5 *Consider a coupon bond with price $P_c(t, T)$, maturity T, coupon c, and payment dates $T_1, T_2, ..., T_n$. The **factor duration** of a **coupon bond** with respect to factor j is given by*

$$D_j = \sum_{i=1}^{n} w_i \times (T_i - t) \times \beta_{ij} \tag{4.26}$$

---

[7]The negative sign in front of the expression in Equation 4.23is for symmetry with respect to the definition of duration in Chapter 3.

where $w_i = c/2 \times P_z(t, T_i)/P_c(t, T)$ *for* $i = 1, .., n - 1$ *and* $w_n = (1 + c/2) \times P_z(t, T_n)/P_c(t, T)$

The notion of factor duration allows us to compute the percentage variation of bond prices due not only to changes in level of interest rates (as in standard duration), but also due to changes in the slope and curvature. In particular, we have the following fact:

Fact 4.6 *Consider an asset with price P and factor durations D_1, D_2, and D_3 with respect to the three factors ϕ_1, ϕ_2, and ϕ_3. Then, the percentage change in price is approximately equal to*

$$\frac{dP}{P} = -D_1 \times d\phi_1 - D_2 \times d\phi_2 - D_3 \times d\phi_3 \tag{4.27}$$

■ **EXAMPLE 4.6**

As in Example 4.5, on April 1, 2004, consider the 3.875% bond maturing on February 15, 2013. Given the term structure of interest rates on that date in Table 4.4, the data in Table 4.5, Equation 4.26 yields the following factor durations:

$$D_1 = 6.9624; \quad D_2 = 4.0797; \quad D_3 = -2.5741 \tag{4.28}$$

These numbers can be interpreted as follows: First, D_1 has the same meaning as duration (and in fact, the value is very similar to the one obtained in Equation 4.19), namely, an increase in the average level of interest rates by one basis point, $d\phi_1 = 0.01\%$, will decrease the bond price by 0.069624%. Similarly, D_2 implies that an increase in slope by $d\phi_2 = 0.01\%$ will decrease the bond price by 0.040797%. Finally, D_3 implies that an increase in curvature by $d\phi_3 = 0.01\%$ will increase the bond price by 0.025741%.[8]

4.2.4 Factor Neutrality

Consider now a portfolio P with factor durations D_1 and D_2 with respect to level and slope factors ϕ_1 and ϕ_2, respectively.[9] To implement factor neutrality, we need to select *two* other securities, one for each factor we want to neutralize, in appropriate proportions. For instance, we could use short- and a long-dated zero coupon bonds, denoted by P_z^S and P_z^L. For each of these two bonds we can compute the factor durations. Let's denote by $D_{z,1}^S$ and $D_{z,2}^S$ the factor durations of the short-dated zero coupon bond, and by $D_{z,1}^L$ and $D_{z,2}^L$ those of the long-dated zero coupon bond. In order to immunize the portfolio against changes in level and slope, we must choose a number of short-term and long-term zero coupon bonds, k_S and k_L, such that the variation of the portfolio plus the two bonds is approximately zero.

---

[8]One drawback of defining level, slope and curvature as average interest rate, term spread, and butterfly spread, respectively, is that changes in level, slope and curvature are not independent from each other. For instance, when the term structure is strongly upward sloping, a decline in slope is also accompanied by a decline in curvature, as the term structure flattens out. The appendix at the end of this chapter provides a more advanced methodology to obtain independent factors with the same interpretation.

[9]For convenience, we only illustrate the case with two factors. The methodology with three factors is identical.

That is, such that the change in $V = P + k_S \times P_z^S + k_L \times P_z^L$ satisfies

$$dV = dP + k_F \times dP_z^S + k_L \times dP_z^L = 0$$

We can substitute into dP, dP_z^S and dP_z^L the equivalent of expressions in Equations 4.27 with only two factors, obtaining the following equation:

$$
\begin{aligned}
0 = & -D_1 \times P \times d\phi_1 - D_2 \times P \times d\phi_2 \\
& + k_S \times (-D_{z1}^S \times P_z^S \times d\phi_1 - D_{z2}^S \times P_z^S \times d\phi_2) \\
& + k_L \times (-D_{z1}^L \times P_z^L \times d\phi_1 - D_{z2}^L \times P_z^L \times d\phi_2)
\end{aligned}
$$

Pool together all the elements containing $d\phi_1$ and $d\phi_2$

$$
\begin{aligned}
0 = & -(D_1 \times P + k_S \times D_{z1}^S \times P_z^S + k_L \times D_{z1}^L \times P_z^L) \times d\phi_1 \\
& -(D_2 \times P + k_S \times D_{z2}^S \times P_z^S + k_L \times D_{z2}^L \times P_z^L) \times d\phi_2
\end{aligned}
$$

In order for the equation to be zero for all possible values of $d\phi_1$ and $d\phi_2$, each parenthesis on the right-hand side must be zero. We therefore obtain a system of two equations in two unknowns:

$$
\begin{aligned}
k_S \times D_{z1}^S \times P_z^S + k_L \times D_{z1}^L \times P_z^L &= -D_1 \times P \\
k_S \times D_{z2}^S \times P_z^S + k_L \times D_{z2}^L \times P_z^L &= -D_2 \times P
\end{aligned}
$$

The solution of this system is:

$$k_S = -\frac{P}{P_z^S} \left(\frac{D_1 \times D_{z2}^L - D_2 \times D_{z1}^L}{D_{z1}^S \times D_{z2}^L - D_{z2}^S \times D_{z1}^L} \right) \tag{4.29}$$

$$k_L = -\frac{P}{P_z^L} \left(\frac{D_1 \times D_{z2}^S - D_2 \times D_{z1}^S}{D_{z1}^L \times D_{z2}^S - D_{z2}^L \times D_{z1}^S} \right) \tag{4.30}$$

Example 4.5 shows the shortcomings of duration hedging. We now follow up with that example to highlight the better hedging performance achieved by factor neutrality.

■ EXAMPLE 4.7

As discussed, the reason of the underperformance of the duration hedged portfolio in Example 4.5 is the change in shape of the term structure between April 1 and April 15, 2004. In particular, the shift was *not* parallel, as long-term yields shifted up by more than short-term yields. Since hedging was performed using a short-term bond, the change in the shape of the term structure generated the losses.

Hedging against changes in slope mitigates the problem. In particular, we now apply the hedging strategy in Equations 4.29 and 4.30 using the zero coupon bonds maturing on February 15, 2005 and on February 15, 2013. Because we are using zero coupon bonds, we can directly apply Equation 4.25 for the computation of factor durations. Given the data in Tables 4.4 and 4.5, we obtain

$$D_1^S = 0.9729; \quad D_2^S = -0.2215 \tag{4.31}$$

$$D_1^L = 8.1912; \quad D_2^L = 5.3150 \tag{4.32}$$

Using Equations 4.29 and 4.30 we obtain that the positions k_S and k_L in the short-term and long-term zero coupon bonds are

$$k_S = -0.5266; \quad k_L = -1.1259$$

As in Example 4.5, assume that the short positions in these short- and long-term zero coupon bonds occur through the repo market. The question is then whether this hedged portfolio was better able to weather the increase in the interest rates in the first two weeks of April 2004. The answer is yes. Using the data on the right-hand side of Table 4.4, we obtain a value of the hedged portfolio

$$V_{4/15/2004}^{Hedged} = 100.9076,$$

implying a drop in value of only 0.58%. We must compare this number with the drop in value of the duration hedged portfolio, which was about 3.30%.

4.2.5   Estimation of the Factor Model

Where do the β_{ij} in Table 4.5 come from? They can be *estimated* by using historical data on yields and the factors. In particular, we can proceed as follows: Let $\tau_1, \tau_2,..., \tau_n$ be n given *times to maturity*, which we keep fixed. For instance, $\tau_1 = $ one month, $\tau_2 = 2$ months, ... ,$\tau_n = 10$ years. We are interested in finding out how much a change in each of the factors ϕ_j affects the rates at these maturities. Let h be the time interval corresponding to our historical data. For instance, if we have daily data, $h = 1/252$, while if we have monthly data, then $h = 1/12$. For each time to maturity τ_i, consider the change in the zero coupon bond yield $r(t, t + \tau_i)$ between t and $t + h$,

$$\Delta r_i(t) = r(t + h, t + h + \tau_i) - r(t, t + \tau_i)$$

So, if $\tau_i = 1$ year, then $\Delta r_i(t)$ is the change of the 1-year yield during the time interval h. Similarly, denote by $\phi_j(t)$ factor j. As in the previous section, we think of $\phi_1(t) = $ level, $\phi_2(t) = $ slope and $\phi_3(t) = $ curvature, whose time series are plotted in Panel B of Figure 3.1 in Chapter 3 and Panels B and C in Figure 4.6. Using these data, we approximate the factor model (Equations 4.20 through 4.22) as follows:

$$\Delta r_1(t) \quad = \quad \alpha_1 + \beta_{11}\Delta\phi_1(t) + \beta_{12}\Delta\phi_2(t) + \beta_{13}\Delta\phi_3(t) + \varepsilon_1(t)$$

$$\Delta r_2(t) \quad = \quad \alpha_2 + \beta_{21}\Delta\phi_1(t) + \beta_{22}\Delta\phi_2(t) + \beta_{23}\Delta\phi_3(t) + \varepsilon_2(t)$$

$$\vdots \quad = \quad \vdots \tag{4.33}$$

$$\Delta r_n(t) \quad = \quad \alpha_n + \beta_{n1}\Delta\phi_1(t) + \beta_{n2}\Delta\phi_2(t) + \beta_{n3}\Delta\phi_3(t) + \varepsilon_n(t)$$

where $\varepsilon_1(t),...$,$\varepsilon_n(t)$, are random errors denoting the fact that our factor model is unlikely to be a perfect model of the variation of interest rates, and $\alpha_1,...,\alpha_n$ represent the average change in interest rates that is not due to the assumed factors (these numbers are small).

Given data on yields $r_i(t)$ and factors $\phi_j(t)$, we can *estimate* the coefficient β_{ij} by using a *regression* analysis. As we might anticipate, Table 4.5 contains the results of this regression analysis. It is worth mentioning a few interesting features of the coefficients β_{ij}: The first row contains β_{i1}, the sensitivity of yields to the first factor, the level factor. Since all of the yields move up and down in tandem, we would expect the coefficient to be relatively constant across maturities, and close to one. And indeed, this is the case.

The second row contains the estimates of β_{i2}, the sensitivities of yields to the second factor, the slope factor. The coefficients are negative for low maturities and positive for high maturities. The interpretation is that if this factor kicks in it lowers the short-term yields and increases the long-term yields. That is, the slope increases. Finally, the third row contains the estimates of β_{i3}, the sensitivities of yields to the curvature factors. The coefficients are negative for short- and long-term bonds, and positive for medium-term bonds. Again, when the curvature factor increases it decreases the short- and long-yields, but it increases the medium-term ones. In other words, this factor bends the term structure of interest rates.

The key insight for risk management from this exercise is in fact contained in the fourth row of Table 4.5, which reports the R^2 from the regression. The R^2 quantifies the power of the three factors to explain the movements of the various points of the term structure over time. For instance, $R^2 = 99.99\%$ for the 4-year interest rate means that the changes in the 4-year yield are essentially entirely explained by the three factors level, slope and curvature discussed earlier. A glance to the R^2's shows that these three factors explain most of the variations of all of the yields. This fact has an important implication for risk management: An effective risk management strategy can be attained by using only three securities in proportions chosen to hedge the three factors. For instance, a financial institution that holds bonds with many different maturities can achieve an effective risk management of its assets' variation in prices by using only three other securities, such as zero coupon bonds or interest rate derivatives.

4.3 SUMMARY

In this chapter we covered the following topics:

1. Convexity: The rate of decrease in bond prices due to a parallel shift in the term structure declines as we increase interest rates is called converxity. That is, if the level of interest rates rises, bond prices decline by less than their predicted decline from duration. Vice versa, if the level of interest rates declines, bond prices increase by more than their predicted increase from duration. Convexity measures this difference. The convexity of a zero coupon bond is its time to maturity squared.

2. Convexity of a portfolio: As with duration, the convexity of a portfolio can be computed as the weighted average of the convexities of the securities in the portfolio, where the weights are the percentage position of the securities in the portfolio.

3. Term Structure Slope: The term structure of interest rates not only changes level over time, but also shape. In particular, the spread between long-term and short-term yields, the slope of the term structure, changes over time.

4. Term Structure Curvature: The term structure has curvature whenever the short-, medium-, and long-term rates do not lie on a straight line. A hump-shaped term structure has positive curvature. The curvature of the term structure, the relative

Table 4.6   Yield Curve on May 15, 2000

aturity	Yield	Maturity	Yield	Maturity	Yield
0.25	6.33%	2.75	6.86%	5.25	6.39%
0.50	6.49%	3.00	6.83%	5.50	6.31%
0.75	6.62%	3.25	6.80%	5.75	6.24%
1.00	6.71%	3.50	6.76%	6.00	6.15%
1.25	6.79%	3.75	6.72%	6.25	6.05%
1.50	6.84%	4.00	6.67%	6.50	5.94%
1.75	6.87%	4.25	6.62%	6.75	5.81%
2.00	6.88%	4.50	6.57%	7.00	5.67%
2.25	6.89%	4.75	6.51%	7.25	5.50%
2.50	6.88%	5.00	6.45%	7.50	5.31%

Notes: Yields are calculated based on data from CRSP.

yield of medium coupon bonds with respect to the long term and the short term, changes over time.

5. Factor duration: This is the (negative of the) sensitivity of a security price to changes in a factor (level, slope and curvature), in percentage.

6. Factor neutrality: Duration hedging is only with respect to the level of interest rates. Factor neutrality is the active hedging of slope and curvature in addition to the level of interest rates. It helps in particular for portfolios that are tilted toward the short term or the very long term.

7. Principal Component Analysis: This advanced methodology, discussed in the appendix to the chapter, extracts independent factors (level, slope, and curvature) from the term structure of interest rates. It helps to obtain more effective hedge ratios.

4.4   EXERCISES

1. On May 15, 2000 the semi-annually compounded yield curve was as in Table 4.6. Calculate the convexity for the following securities:

    (a) 4-year zero coupon bond

    (b) 2 1/4-year coupon bond paying 5% semiannually

    (c) 2-year coupon bond paying 3% quarterly

    (d) 3 1/2-year floating rate bond with 20 basis point spread, paid semiannually

    (e) 4 1/4-year floating rate bond with 35 basis point spread, paid semiannually

2. It is May 15, 2000 and an investor is planning to invest $100 million in one of the two portfolios below. The investor's main concern is the change in interest rates that might affect the short-term value of the portfolio. Compute the change in price of the security stemming from duration and convexity. Which portfolio is less sensitive to changes in interest rates? The portfolios are the following:

Portfolio A

- 30% invested in 5-year coupon bonds paying 4% quarterly
- 25% invested in 4 1/4-year coupon bonds paying 6% semiannually
- 20% invested in 90-day zero coupon bonds
- 15% invested in 2 1/2-year floating rate bonds with zero spread paid quarterly
- 10% invested in 6-year zero coupon bonds

Portfolio B

- 40% invested in 7-year coupon bonds paying 2% semiannually
- 30% invested in 3 1/4-year floating rate bonds with 50 basis point spread paid semiannually
- 20% invested in 4-year coupon bonds paying 3.5% semiannually
- 10% invested in 90-day zero coupon bonds

3. Consider Exercise 2. You are told that the mean of daily change in interest rates is zero and that the variance of the daily change of interest rates is $3.451 \times 10 - 7$. What is the annualized expected return taking into account convexity?

4. Rework Example 4.3 but using a 2-year zero coupon bond for hedging, instead of the 10-year zero coupon bond. How do the results in Table 4.2 change?

5. Consider the trade of purchasing a 10-year coupon bond and hedge the interest rate risk using a 2-year zero coupon bond. Assume the term structure of interest rates is flat at the 4.5% continuously compounded interest rate. Compute the profits/losses from the strategy under various scenarios of interest rate variation, such as a positive or negative shift of 10 basis points, 1%, or 2% (see e.g., Example 4.3). Perform this exercise assuming (a) The trade is performed over one day; (b) The trade is performed over one week; (c) The trade is performed over one month. How do the results change under these various scenarios? Discuss your results.

6. Compute the level factor and the butterfly spread for each term structure in Table 4.7.

   (a) Which period had the highest slope?

   (b) Which period had the highest curvature?

   (c) Can you recognize the periods with higher slope or curvature on a graph?

   (d) Which interval saw the greatest change in slope?

   (e) Which interval saw the greatest change in curvature?

7. Using Tables 4.8 and 4.9, compute the factor duration of level, slope, and curvature, for each of the following securities on February 15, 1994:

   (a) 4-year zero coupon bond

   (b) 2 1/2-year coupon bond paying 3% semiannually

   (c) 3 1/4-year floating rate bond with zero spread paid semiannually

   (d) 4 1/4-year floating rate bond with 35 basis point spread paid semiannually

Table 4.7   Term Structures

DATE	1 month	3 month	6 month	1 year	2 year	3 year	5 year	7 year	10 year
9/26/2008	0.21%	0.87%	1.54%	1.81%	2.11%	2.38%	3.05%	3.41%	3.85%
9/10/2008	1.58%	1.65%	1.87%	2.06%	2.22%	2.42%	2.91%	3.23%	3.65%
8/25/2008	1.66%	1.74%	1.96%	2.12%	2.33%	2.62%	3.04%	3.36%	3.79%
8/11/2008	1.77%	1.87%	2.05%	2.27%	2.56%	2.84%	3.27%	3.57%	3.99%
7/25/2008	1.72%	1.75%	1.95%	2.35%	2.70%	3.01%	3.45%	3.73%	4.13%
7/10/2008	1.48%	1.67%	2.01%	2.20%	2.44%	2.72%	3.10%	3.40%	3.83%
6/25/2008	1.49%	1.81%	2.22%	2.48%	2.82%	3.11%	3.54%	3.78%	4.12%
6/10/2008	2.00%	2.02%	2.24%	2.53%	2.91%	3.20%	3.54%	3.77%	4.11%

Notes: Yields are calculated based on data from CRSP.

Table 4.8   Level, Slope and Curvature

	3 month	6 month	1 year	2 year	3 year	5 year	7 year	10 year
β (Level)	1.0180	0.9509	0.9196	1.0344	1.0299	1.0180	1.0111	1.0180
β (Slope)	-0.2568	-0.3252	-0.4317	-0.3507	-0.1424	0.2432	0.5205	0.7432
β (Curvature)	-0.3284	-0.1404	0.0847	0.3228	0.3240	0.1716	-0.1058	-0.3284
R^2	99.65%	99.69%	98.88%	99.61%	99.77%	99.90%	99.73%	99.90%

8. In this exercise you need to describe an immunization strategy for a portfolio, given the factors in Table 4.8. The term structures of interest rates at two dates are in Table 4.9.

(a) You are standing at February 15, 1994 (see table) and you hold the following portfolio:

- Long $30 million of a 6-year inverse floater with coupon paid quarterly
- Long $30 million of a 4-year floating rate bond with a 45 basis point spread paid semiannually
- Short $20 million of a 3-year coupon bond paying 4% semiannually

   i. What is the total value of the portfolio?
   ii. Compute the dollar duration of the portfolio.

(b) You are worried about interest rate volatility. You decided to hedge your portfolio with the following bonds:

- A 3-month zero coupon bond
- A 6-year zero coupon bond

   i. How much should you go short/long on these bonds in order to make the portfolio immune to interest rate changes?
   ii. What is the total value of the portfolio now?

(c) Assume that it is now May 13, 1994 and that the yield curve has changed accordingly.

Table 4.9 Two Term Structures of Interest Rates

aturity	02/15/94 Yield (c.c.)	02/15/94 $Z(t,T)$	05/13/94 Yield (c.c.)	05/13/94 $Z(t,T)$
0.25	3.53%	0.9912	4.13%	0.9897
0.50	3.56%	0.9824	4.74%	0.9766
0.75	3.77%	0.9721	5.07%	0.9627
1.00	3.82%	0.9625	5.19%	0.9495
1.25	3.97%	0.9516	5.49%	0.9337
1.50	4.14%	0.9398	5.64%	0.9189
1.75	4.23%	0.9287	5.89%	0.9020
2.00	4.43%	0.9151	6.04%	0.8862
2.25	4.53%	0.9031	6.13%	0.8712
2.50	4.57%	0.8921	6.23%	0.8558
2.75	4.71%	0.8786	6.31%	0.8406
3.00	4.76%	0.8670	6.39%	0.8255
3.25	4.89%	0.8531	6.42%	0.8117
3.50	4.98%	0.8400	6.52%	0.7959
3.75	5.07%	0.8268	6.61%	0.7805
4.00	5.13%	0.8145	6.66%	0.7663
4.25	5.18%	0.8023	6.71%	0.7519
4.50	5.26%	0.7893	6.73%	0.7387
4.75	5.31%	0.7770	6.77%	0.7251
5.00	5.38%	0.7641	6.83%	0.7106
5.25	5.42%	0.7525	6.86%	0.6977
5.50	5.43%	0.7418	6.89%	0.6846
5.75	5.49%	0.7293	6.93%	0.6713
6.00	5.53%	0.7176	6.88%	0.6619

Notes: Yields and discounts are calculated based on data from CRSP.

Table 4.10   Factor Sensitivity (1952 - 1993)

			Maturity			
	3 m	1 y	2 y	3 y	4 y	5 y
Parallel: $\beta_{i,1}$	0.4617	0.4893	0.4215	0.3780	0.3507	0.3222
R^2	0.76	0.94	0.95	0.92	0.86	0.84
Slope: $\beta_{i,2}$	-0.7868	-0.1080	0.1581	0.2655	0.3787	0.3610
R^2	0.99	0.95	0.96	0.97	0.96	0.95
Curvature: $\beta_{i,3}$	0.4047	-0.7976	-0.1040	0.1481	0.3483	0.2144
R^2	0.99	0.99	0.96	0.97	0.97	0.96

    i. What is the value of the unhedged portfolio now?

    ii. What is the value of the hedged portfolio?

    iii. Is the value the same? Did the immunization strategy work? How do you know that changes in value are not a product of coupon payments made over the period?

(d) Instead of assuming that the change took place 3 months later, assume that the change in the yield curve occurred an instant after February 15, 1994.

    i. What is the value of the unhedged portfolio?

    ii. What is the value of the hedged portfolio?

4.5   CASE STUDY: FACTOR STRUCTURE IN ORANGE COUNTY'S PORTFOLIO

In Chapter 3 we performed a duration analysis of inverse floaters and the portfolio of Orange County. In this section, we repeat the exercise, but this time to gauge the sensitivity of the portfolio to the level, slope, and curvature factors described in previous sections. We will conclude with an application of the factor model to compute the Value-at-Risk of the portfolio.

4.5.1   Factor Estimation

We use principal component analysis, explained in the Appendix at the end of this chapter, to compute the sensitivities of interest rates to three factors, using data from 1952 to 1994. The results are contained in Table 4.10.

4.5.2   Factor Duration of the Orange County Portfolio

We now assume that the Orange County portfolio has $2.8 billion invested in inverse floaters (see Section 3.8 of Chapter 3), and the remaining part in 3-year zero coupon bonds, for

Table 4.11   Factor Durations of a 3-year Zero Coupon Bond

Factor j	Maturity $T_i = 3$	β_{ij}	$D_{z,j}(3)$
1	3	0.3780	1.1340
2	3	0.2655	0.7965
3	3	0.1481	0.4443

simplicity.[10] We must compute the factor durations of the portfolio, that is, the sensitivity of the portfolio to each of the factors. Let $D_{P,1}$, $D_{P,2}$, and $D_{P,3}$ be the three factor durations of the portfolio to level (factor ϕ_1), slope (factor ϕ_2) and curvature (factor ϕ_3). We will use them to compute the variation in the portfolio changes dP, according to Equation 4.27, that is

$$dP = P \times (-D_{P,1} \times d\phi_1 - D_{P,2} \times d\phi_2 - D_{P,3} \times d\phi_3) \qquad (4.34)$$

We first need to compute the factor duration of the zero coupon bond and the inverse floater. Table 4.11 shows the computations of the factor durations for the 3-year zero coupon bond. From Table 4.10 we select the column corresponding to the 3-year maturity (Column 4) and multiply the corresponding sensitivities β_{ij} by the maturity of the zero, i.e., $T_i = 3$.

We now turn to the factor duration of the inverse floater. In this case, we need to use the same methodology as for the duration of a portfolio. Recall that the inverse floater can be replicated by a long position in a 3-year fixed rate coupon and a 3-year zero coupon, and a short position in floating rate bond. The factor duration satisfies the same formula used for the standard duration (see Equation 3.50 in Chapter 3):

$$D_{IF,j} = w_{zero} \times D_{z,j}(3) + w_{fixed} \times D_{c,j} + w_{floating} \times D_{Fl,j}$$

where $w_{zero} = 0.7521$, $w_{fixed} = 1.1079$, and $w_{floating} = -0.8600$ are the weights computed in Chapter 3 for the same exercise, and $D_{c,j}$ and $D_{Fl,j}$ denote the factor durations of the fixed and floating rate bond, respectively. We already have the factor durations $D_{z,j}(3)$ for the 3-year zero coupon bond in Table 4.11. We now need to compute the factor durations of the fixed rate bond and the floating rate bond. Recalling that a fixed rate bond is simply a portfolio of zero coupon bonds, Table 4.12 computes the factor durations for the fixed rate bond.

Finally, we need the factor duration of the floating rate bond. However, as with the standard duration, this coincides with the factor duration of a zero coupon bond with maturity equal to the first reset date. In this example, the coupon payments are annual, and thus the factor duration of the floating rate bond coincides with the factor duration of a 1-year bond, which is contained in the second column in Table 4.12. Table 4.13 finally obtains the factor durations of the 3-year inverse floater. It is interesting to compare the factor durations of the inverse floater to those of a 3-year coupon bond. We see that while the 3-year coupon bond is strongly affected by parallel shifts (the first factor) but only

---

[10]This approximation slightly increases the duration of the Orange County portfolio compared to Section 3.8 of Chapter 3, but it simplifies our calculations, as we only have factor sensitivities at maturity $T = 2$ and $T = 3$. To compute the sensitivity at other maturities we would need an additional interpolation step.

Table 4.12 Factor Durations of a 3-year Zero Coupon Bond

Factor j	$D_{z,j}(1)$	$D_{z,j}(2)$	$D_{z,j}(3)$	$\Longrightarrow$	$D_{c,j}$
1	0.4893	0.8430	1.1340	$\Longrightarrow$	1.0305
2	-0.1081	0.3162	0.7965	$\Longrightarrow$	0.6435
3	-0.7976	-0.2081	0.4444	$\Longrightarrow$	0.2352
		Weights			
	0.1123	0.1070	0.7807		

Table 4.13 Factor Durations of Inverse Floater

Factor j	$D_{z,j}(3)$	$D_{c,j}$	$D_{Fl,j}$	$\Longrightarrow$	$D_{IF,j}$
1	1.1340	1.0305	0.4893	$\Longrightarrow$	1.5738
2	0.7965	0.6435	-0.1081	$\Longrightarrow$	1.4049
3	0.4444	0.2352	-0.7976	$\Longrightarrow$	1.2807
		Weights			
	0.7521	1.1079	-0.8600		

mildly affected by curvature (the third factor), the inverse floater shows a strong sensitivity across all factors. This means that any change in *any* of the factors has a large impact on the inverse floater, compared to the fixed rate bond of the same maturity.

Finally, we can compute the factor duration of the portfolio itself, obtaining

$$
D_{P,j} = \frac{2.8}{20.5} \times D_{IF,j} + \frac{20.5 - 2.8}{20.5} \times D_{z,j}(3) = \left\{ \begin{array}{l} 1.1941 \\ 0.8796 \\ 0.5587 \end{array} \right. \tag{4.35}
$$

4.5.3 The Value-at-Risk of the Orange County Portfolio with Multiple Factors

We can now apply the same methodology as in Section 3.8 of Chapter 3 and compute the Value-at-Risk when we decompose the variation in interest rates in multiple factors. For simplicity, we use only the normal distribution approach. That is, we assume that the three factors $d\phi_1, d\phi_2$, and $d\phi_3$ are distributed according to a jointly normal distribution. The construction of these factors from principal component analysis implies that they are also independent (see the appendix at the end of the chapter). From Equation 4.34, then, dP also has a normal distribution, with mean and standard deviation given by

$$
\begin{aligned}
\text{Mean}(dP) = \mu_P &= P \times [-D_{P,1} \times \text{mean}(d\phi_1) - D_{P,2} \times \text{mean}(d\phi_2) \\
&\quad - D_{P,3} \times \text{mean}(d\phi_3)] \\
\text{Std}(dP) = \sigma_P &= P \times [D_{P,1} \times \text{std}(d\phi_1) + D_{P,2} \times \text{std}(d\phi_2) + D_{P,3} \times \text{std}(d\phi_3)]
\end{aligned}
$$

Table 4.14 Statistical Properties of the Level of Interest Rate and the Three Factors

	dr	$d\phi_1$	$d\phi_2$	$d\phi_3$
mean	$4.71E - 05$	1.0986e-004	0	0
st.dev	0.00432	0.0107	0.0034	0.0015

From the time series of factors, we can compute the mean and standard deviations of the factors $d\phi^j$, which are in Table 4.14. Using this information, we obtain $\mu_P = -0.00269$ and $\sigma_P = 0.34031$. Thus, the 99% monthly VaR is

$$99\% \text{ monthly VaR} = -\mu_P + 1.634 \times \sigma_P = \$794 \text{ million}$$

Using only the standard duration as in Section 3.8 of Chapter 3 we obtain instead VaR = \$660 million, which is smaller.[11] The reason why using only the traditional duration we obtain a smaller VaR is that in this calculation we use the volatility of the average level of interest rates for our computations, which is relatively small. The decomposition into factors allows us to take into full consideration not only the parallel shifts, but also other additional factors, which push up the VaR number.

4.6 APPENDIX: PRINCIPAL COMPONENT ANALYSIS

The factors we used in the previous sections were, to some extent, *ad hoc*. We chose to define the level factor as the average yield across maturities, the slope factor as the difference in yields between the 10-year and 1-month bond, and finally, the curvature factor as the butterfly spread. Of course, given that we defined these factors somewhat arbitrarily, there is always the possibility that a better choice of factors exists. In particular, these factors should satisfy some conditions in order to structure an effective risk management strategy:

1. First, the factors ought to "explain" a very large proportion of the variation of the yields of bonds at various horizons.

2. Second, the factors should be independent of each other.

The first condition is intuitive: If the factors do not explain the variation of interest rates, they won't be of very much use to a risk manager. The second condition is also intuitive: If the level of interest rates moves inversely to its slope, for instance, then our hedging strategy must take this joint movement into account. Instead, the factor neutrality discussed in the previous section does not.

Principal component analysis (PCA) is a statistical technique that identifies the best factors from historical yields, where the term best is in the sense of the two conditions mentioned above. We now cover the basics of PCA, with a warning that this material is more advanced than the material in previous sections, and it can be skipped by the less mathematically sophisticated reader.

---

[11]The portfolio here is slightly different from the one in Section 3.8 of Chapter 3, as discussed earlier.

First, note that all the factors defined earlier are linear combinations of the underlying yields $r_i(t)$. For instance, the level of interest rate was defined as the average of yields across maturities, which implies it is given by $\phi_1 = \sum_{i=1}^{n} 1/nr_1(t)$, where n is the number of maturities. We will still impose this restriction, that is, for $i = 1, 2, 3$ we are going to define factors as follows

$$\phi_i^{PCA}(t) = a_{i1} \times r_1(t) + ... + a_{in} \times r_n(t)$$

Denote the covariance between $\Delta r_k(t)$ and $\Delta r_\ell(t)$ by

$$\sigma_{k\ell} = Cov\left(\Delta r_k(t), \Delta r_\ell(t)\right)$$

Principal component analysis determines the factors one at a time as follows. Consider the first factor $\phi_1^{PCA}(t)$. The objective is to find coefficients $a_{11}, ..., a_{1n}$ to maximize the variance of $\Delta \phi_1^{PCA}(t)$:

$$\max_{a_{11},...,a_{1n}} Var\left(\Delta \phi_i^{PCA}\right) = \sum_{k=1}^{n}\sum_{\ell=1}^{n} a_{1k} a_{1\ell} \sigma_{k\ell} \tag{4.36}$$

under the restriction

$$\sum_{j=1}^{n} a_{1j}^2 = 1. \tag{4.37}$$

Since $\Delta \phi_1^{PCA}(t)$ is a linear combination of all the yields and it is obtained by maximizing its variability, it is intuitive that it will covary substantially with all the yields $\Delta r_1(t), ..., \Delta r_n(t)$. In a sense, it is as if we are maximizing some weighted average of the R^2 of the multiple regressions

$$\Delta r_1(t) = \alpha_1 + \beta_{11}\Delta \phi_1^{PCA}(t) + \varepsilon_1(t)$$

$$\Delta r_2(t) = \alpha_2 + \beta_{21}\Delta \phi_1^{PCA}(t) + \varepsilon_2(t)$$

$$\vdots = \vdots \tag{4.38}$$

$$\Delta r_n(t) = \alpha_n + \beta_{n1}\Delta \phi_1^{PCA}(t) + \varepsilon_n(t)$$

Once we solve the maximization in Equation 4.36 and therefore estimate the first component, we can compute the residual of the regressions in Equations 4.38: For all $i = 1, .., n$ we compute

$$\widehat{\varepsilon}_i(t) = \Delta r_i(t) - \alpha_i - \beta_{i1}\Delta \phi^{PCA}(t)$$

The residuals $\widehat{\varepsilon}_i(t)$ provide the amount of variation in the various rates that the first factor $\phi_1^{PCA}(t)$ is not able to explain. Hence, we can compute the change in the second factor $\Delta \phi_2^{PCA}(t)$ as

$$\Delta \phi_2^{PCA}(t) = a_{21} \times \widehat{\varepsilon}_1(t) + ... + a_{2n} \times \widehat{\varepsilon}_n(t)$$

We find again the $a_{21}, ..., a_{2n}$ that maximize

$$\max_{a_{21},...,a_{2n}} \quad Var\left(\Delta\phi_2^{PCA}(t)\right) \tag{4.39}$$

conditional again on $\sum_{j=1}^n a_{2j}^2 = 1$. And so on.

The outcome of this methodology is to obtain factors that explain a large variation of the cross-section of yields. Moreover, because at every step we are using the residuals of the yields, the factors so constructed are independent of each other. That is, PCA generates factors that satisfy conditions 1 and 2 above. The actual implementation of PCA is not as difficult as it may appear from the methodology described above, and it is further described in the next subsection. Here, instead, we focus on the outcome.

Figure 4.9   Coefficients on Level, Slope and Curvature from PCA

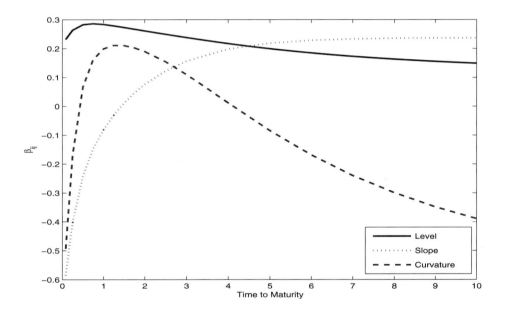

Figure 4.9 shows the coefficients β_{ij}^{PCA} estimates from the PCA across maturity. The solid line denotes the coefficients β_{i1}^{PCA} that multiply the first factor coming from the first maximization in Equation 4.36. The plot shows that all of these coefficients are approximately equal to each other across maturities. Because all of the β_{i1}^{PCA} are similar to each other, the first factor computed from the PCA analysis has been called the level factor: When this first factor $\phi_1(t)$ increases, all of the yields increase by about the same amount. The level of β_{ij}^{PCA} is smaller than the one in Table 4.5 because in PCA we constrain the squared coefficients to sum to one. This is simply a renormalization, as the factor $\phi_1(t)$ becomes automatically scaled up to take this into account. One important difference between this methodology and the one developed in the previous sections is the fact that the level factor computed from PCA according to Equation 4.36 is a *result* of the statistical methodology, and not an assumption as we made in Section 4.2. Panel A of Figure 4.10 plots the level factor from PCA.

Figure 4.10 Level, Slope and Curvature Factors from PCA

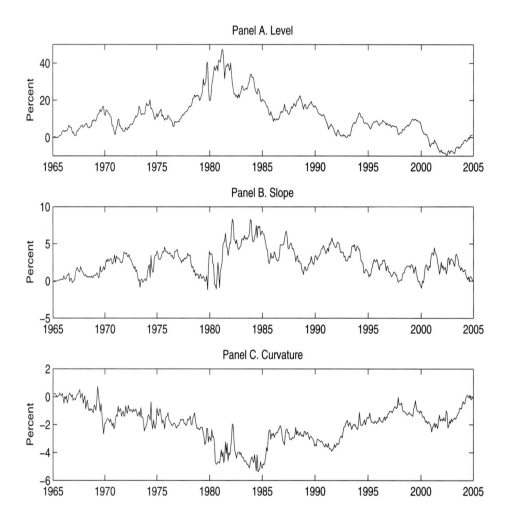

The dotted line in Figure 4.9 shows the coefficients β_{i2} multiplying the second factor $\phi_2(t)$. The second factor that comes out of the methodology described above is called a slope factor exactly because the coefficients β_{i2} are negative for short-term maturities and positive for long-term maturities. That is, when the second factor $\phi_2(t)$ increases, the short-term yields decline and the long-term yields increase: i.e., the term structure becomes steeper. The historical time series of the second factor obtained from PCA is plotted in Panel B of Figure 4.10. Finally, the dashed line in Figure 4.9 shows the coefficients β_{i3}^{PCA} multiplying the third factor $\phi_3(t)$: The coefficients are negative for short- and long-term yields, and positive for medium-term yields. That is, when the third factor increases, the yield curve becomes more curved. For this reason, the third factor from PCA is called curvature. The historical time series of the curvature factors is plotted in Panel C of Figure 4.10.

Table 4.15 The Sensitivity of Interest Rates to PCA Level, Slope, and Curvature

Factor	3 months	6 months	1 year	2 year	4 year	6 year	8 year	10 year
				Maturity				
				Panel A: Level				
β_{i1}^{PCA}	0.2637	0.2827	0.2835	0.2612	0.2172	0.1848	0.1633	0.1490
R^2	75.50 %	88.23%	96.32%	95.89%	89.12%	81.13%	70.73%	61.12%
				Panel B: Slope				
β_{i2}^{PCA}	−0.4017	−0.2410	−0.0807	0.0757	0.1983	0.2286	0.2355	0.2369
R^2	98.26%	96.56%	97.33%	96.94%	98.77%	97.26%	89.84%	81.20%
				Panel C: Curvature				
β_{i3}^{PCA}	−0.1679	0.0672	0.1994	0.1899	0.0117	−0.1690	−0.2996	−0.3890
R^2	99.49%	96.76%	99.25%	98.98%	98.78%	99.98%	99.40%	97.94%

The R^2 in Panels A, B, and C refer to the total R^2 from including Factor 1, Factors 1 and 2, and all three factors, respectively.

4.6.1 Benefits from PCA

As mentioned before, and worth emphasizing, PCA has additional benefits over the more intuitive methodology described earlier, namely, of defining the level, slope, and curvature factors straight as yield average, term spread, and butterfly spread, respectively. These additional benefits are the following:

1. The first additional benefit is that PCA explains an even greater fraction of the variation of yields. This is shown in Table 4.15. This table contains additional information compared to Figure 4.9. In particular, it shows the ability of each of the factors to explain the variation in the interest rates, through the measure R^2. For instance, the first PCA factor (level) explains 75% of the variation in the 3-month yield, 95.89% of the variation of the 2-year rate, and 61.12% of the variation of the 10-year rate. The first and second factors together explain the largest part of the variation in the term structure: The R^2 of the rates up to 6 years are all above 96%. The three factors together explain almost all of the variation, with R^2 typically above the 99%. It is important to note that these R^2s are always above the ones obtained using the ad hoc factors in Table 4.5, showing that the factors obtained from PCA are better at explaining the variation of yields, which is what a risk manager wants.

2. The second additional benefit is that the PCA factors are in fact *independent* from each other. This implies that risk management practices can be more easily performed using PCA factors than the ad hoc factors discussed earlier. We demonstrate this in the next example.

■ **EXAMPLE 4.8**

In this example we perform the same exercise as in Example 4.7, but we use the PCA factors to hedge against level and slope. The only difference from before is that we must use now the parameters in Table 4.15 to compute both the factor durations of the 3.875% bond (expiring on February 15, 2013) and the position in the short-term and long-term bonds k_S and k_L. Note that the hedging formulas in Equations 4.29 and 4.30 are still valid even under the new methodology to compute the factors. In particular, using again the zero coupon bonds maturing on February 15, 2005 and on February 15, 2013, we find the following:

$$
\begin{aligned}
\text{Long-term coupon bond} \quad &: \quad D_1 = 1.2162; \quad D_2 = 1.7240; \\
\text{Short-term zero} \quad &: \quad D_1^S = 0.2473; \quad D_2^S = -0.0704; \\
\text{Long-term zero} \quad &: \quad D_1^L = 1.3793; \quad D_2^L = 2.0864.
\end{aligned}
$$

Using Equations 4.29 and 4.30 we obtain that the position k_S and k_L in the short-term and long-term zero coupon bonds are

$$
k_S = -0.2669; \quad k_L = -1.1917
$$

In this case, on April 15 2007 the hedged portfolio is worth $V_{4/15/2004}^{Hedge} = \$101.29$, i.e. a drop of only 0.20%, against the 0.50% using the ad hoc factors, and the 3.30% using only duration.

4.6.2 The Implementation of PCA

In practice, the implementation of PCA is not as cumbersome as it seems, but it requires the use of advanced computer packages. Start from the variance-covariance matrix of $\Delta r_i(t)$'s, which we denote by $\mathbf{M} = Cov(\Delta r_i(t))$. This is a $n \times n$ matrix. The properties of this matrix are such that there are numbers λ_i and associated vectors

$$
\mathbf{v}_i = \begin{pmatrix} v_{i1} \\ \vdots \\ v_{in} \end{pmatrix}
$$

such that the following relation holds

$$
\mathbf{M}\mathbf{v}_i = \lambda_i \mathbf{v}_i \tag{4.40}
$$

The numbers λ_i are called *eigenvalues* and the associated vector $\mathbf{v}_t$ is called *eigenvector*. These eigenvalues and eigenvectors can be efficiently computed numerically through the use of computers. Commercial packages are available for their computation.

Consider the maximization problem in Equations 4.36 and 4.39. Using vector notation $\mathbf{a}_1 = (a_{11}, ..., a_{1n})$, we can form the Lagrangean as $\mathcal{L}(\mathbf{a}_1) = \mathbf{a}_1' \mathbf{M} \mathbf{a}_1 - \lambda(\mathbf{a}_1' \mathbf{a}_1 - 1)$. The first order condition is

$$
\frac{\partial \mathcal{L}(\mathbf{a}_1)}{\partial \mathbf{a}_1} = \mathbf{M}\mathbf{a}_1 - \lambda \mathbf{a}_1 = 0 \tag{4.41}
$$

which we recognize is satisfied by the eigenvalues λ_i and eigenvectors $\mathbf{v}_i$ in Equation 4.40. This result implies that, assuming we have available a computer package to compute the eigenvalues and the eigenvectors of M, the procedure is then the following:

1. Compute the eigenvalues of $\mathbf{M}$, denote them by $\lambda_1 > \lambda_2 > ... > \lambda_n$ and let $\mathbf{v}_1, \mathbf{v}_2, ..., \mathbf{v}_n$ be their (normalized) eigenvectors.

2. From Equation 4.41 $\mathbf{v}_1$ is the solution to the first maximization in Equation 4.36, that is $\mathbf{v}_1 = (a_{11}, ..., a_{1n})$

3. Accordingly, we set

$$\Delta \phi_1^{PCA}(t) = \sum_{k=1}^{n} v_{1k} \Delta r_k(t)$$

4. We then run the regression in Equation 4.38 and compute the residuals $\widehat{\varepsilon}_1(t), .., \widehat{\varepsilon}_n(t)$

5. A similar argument as above shows that $\mathbf{v}_2$ is the solution to the second maximization in Equation 4.39. Accordingly, we set the second factor

$$\Delta \phi_2^{PCA}(t) = \sum_{k=1}^{n} v_{2k} \widehat{\varepsilon}_k(t)$$

6. We run the regression in Equation 4.33 with two factors. And so on

The result of this procedure are contained in Table 4.15 and Figures 4.9 and 4.10.

CHAPTER 5

INTEREST RATE DERIVATIVES: FORWARDS AND SWAPS

Interest rate "derivatives" play a central role in modern financial markets. The quotation marks around the word "derivatives" is almost mandatory nowadays. Traditionally, we think of a derivative security as a security whose value depends on the value of some other more basic security. That is, the value of the derivative security "derives" from the one of a primitive security. That's the traditional view, which was fine at the time in which basic derivative securities, such as forwards, futures, and swaps, were introduced in the 1970s and 1980s. Nowadays, however, the market size of interest rate derivatives is much larger than the market of the primary securities. For instance, in this chapter we learn how to compute the value of swap contracts from discount factors, possibly obtained from the prices of Treasury securities, as discussed in Chapter 2. However, as we do so, we must keep in mind that while as of December 2008 the market size of U.S. Treasury securities was around $5.9 trillion, the global market value of swaps was about $16 trillion. The obvious question is then whether the value of swaps depends on the value of Treasuries, or vice versa. Here we are in a "chicken-and-egg" situation, because we cannot be sure anymore which one is the primary market and which are the "derivative markets." In this chapter we learn that some relations – no arbitrage relations – must exist between the values of the securities. If the *relative values* between Treasuries and derivatives get out of line, then speculators will step in and correct the market imbalance. We should think of all of these markets as moving in sync, and when one moves because of its own forces, the others – whether derivatives or primary – should adjust accordingly.

Figure 5.1   A Forward Investment Need

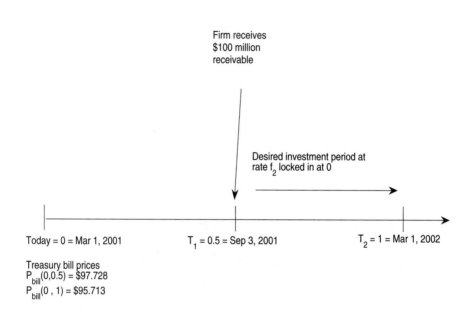

5.1   FORWARD RATES AND FORWARD DISCOUNT FACTORS

It is convenient to introduce the concept of forward rate through an example:

■ **EXAMPLE 5.1**

Let today be March 1, 2001.[1] Suppose a firm sold a piece of equipment to a client for $100 million. The client will pay in six months, i.e. on T_1 = September 4, 2001 (the first business day in September 2001). Suppose the firm does not need that cash immediately, but it will need it six months later, at T_2 = March 1, 2002, to fund some capital investment. Today, the firm would like to fix the interest rate to be applied on the receivable of $100 million for the six month period from T_1 to T_2. Figure 5.1 illustrates the investment need. The firm calls up its bank to ask for a quote, and the bank quotes the (semi-annually compounded) annualized rate of f_2 = 4.21%.[2] That is, the bank is ready to commit *today* to receive in six months (at T_1) $100 million from the firm, and return six months later (at T_2) the amount $102.105 = $100 \times (1 + f_2/2)$ million. The rate, f_2, which the bank commits to today is called *forward rate*.

---

[1]The date 2001 may seem peculiar. This choice was driven by the fact that in March, 2001 the U.S. Treasury still issued 1-year Treasury bills, a practice that it discontinued shortly thereafter until recently. The presence of 1-year Treasury bills makes the example easier to follow, although the same argument can be repeated using Treasury STRIPS, or synthetically produced zero coupon bonds.
[2]The subscript "2" in f_2 denotes semi-annually compounding, as the notation used for interest rates. See Equation 5.3 below for details.

Table 5.1   Trading Strategy to Compute Forward Rate

Today (Time 0)	T_1	T_2
Sell short $97.728 m of T-bills maturing at T_1	(a) Receive $100 m from firm (b) Close short position	
Buy $M = 1.02105 = \frac{\$97.728}{\$95.713}$ of T-bills maturing at T_2		(a) Receive $1.02105 \times \$100$ m (b) Give total to firm
Total Net Cash Flow = 0	Total Net Cash Flow = 0	Total Net Cash Flow = 0

The question is: How does the bank determine the forward rate f_2?

By no arbitrage. In fact, on March 1, 2001 (today), the value of 6-months Treasury bills is $97.728 and the value of 1-year Treasury bills is $95.713. In order to guarantee the rate f_2 to the client, the bank can perform the following strategy (see Table 5.1): First, today the bank borrows T-bills with maturity $T_1 = 6$ months and sells them for $97.728 million. This amount of cash is then invested in 1-year T-bills expiring in T_2. Given the price of the latter of $95.713 the bank can now purchase $M = 1.02105 = \$97.728/\$95.713$ million of 1-year T-bills (for $100 of face value). Today, the net cash flow remaining to the bank is zero, as all the cash obtained from the sale of the T_1 T-bill has been used to purchase T_2 T-bills.

Second, at time T_1 the bank must pay back $100 million to the counterparty it borrowed the T_1 T-bills from. However, this is also the time in which the firm will give the bank $100 million. So, also at T_1 the net cash flow is zero, as the bank receives $100 million from the firm and uses it to close the short position. Finally, at time T_2 the $M = 1.02105$ T-bills mature, and the bank receives $M \times \$100 = \$102.105$ million. This is exactly the cash flow that the bank promised the firm in return on the investment of $100 million at T_1.

Indeed, the return for the firm from T_1 to T_2 is $2.105\% = (\$102.105 - \$100)/\$100$, which implies the annualized interest rate of $f_2 = 2.105\% \times 2 = 4.21\%$.

This example shows that the term structure of interest rates, or equivalently, the discount factors $Z(0, T)$, contain all the information needed to establish the time value of money *in the future*. In the example, the current 1-year discount is $Z(0, 1) = 0.95713$, while the 6-month discount is $Z(0, 0.5) = 0.97728$. That is, $1 in one year is worth 95.71 cents in today's money, while $1 in six months is worth 97.73 cents in today's money. Implicitly, these two exchange rates (of money in the future for money today) imply an exchange rate of money in six months versus money in one year, given by the ratio of the two discounts

$$F(0, 0.5, 1) = \frac{Z(0, 1)}{Z(0, 0.5)} = 0.97938 \tag{5.1}$$

That is, given the information today (time 0), $1 in one year is equivalent to 97.93 cents in six months. Given the two values of $Z(0, 0.5)$ and $Z(0, 1)$, it cannot be otherwise without generating an arbitrage opportunity. Indeed, the reasoning behind the computation of the time value of money between future dates implied by the current term structure of interest rates is the same that applies to foreign exchange rates: If 1 U.S. dollar is worth 1.25 euros and 1 dollar is worth 1.6 British pounds, the exchange rate between euros and British pounds must be 0.78=1.25/1.6.

One way to interpret $F(0, 0.5, 1)$ determined in Equation 5.1 is as the current market projection of the future discount factor $Z(0.5, 1)$, which is not known today. For this reason, we call F the forward discount factor.

Definition 5.1 *The **forward discount factor** at time t defines the time value of money between two future dates, T_1 and $T_2 > T_1$. Given the discount factors $Z(t, T_1)$ and $Z(t, T_2)$, the forward discount factor is given by*

$$F(t, T_1, T_2) = \frac{Z(t, T_2)}{Z(t, T_1)} \tag{5.2}$$

From its definition in Equation 5.2, $F(t, T_1, T_2)$ has the standard properties of a discount factor, as discussed next.

Fact 5.1 *The forward discount factor has the following properties:*

  1. $F(t, T_1, T_2) = 1$ for $T_2 = T_1$;

  2. $F(t, T_1, T_2)$ is decreasing in T_2.

The second property stems from Equation 5.2: As we increase T_2, only the numerator in the formula changes, and this is decreasing with T_2. Thus, $F(t, T_1, T_2)$ decreases with T_2.

Going back to the previous example, because $F(0, 0.5, 1)$ is a discount factor between times $T_1 = 0.5$ and $T_2 = 1$, we can also compute its implied semi-annually compounded interest rate by using the same formula as in Equation 2.4 in Chapter 2, in which $Z(t, T)$ is substituted for $F(0, 0.5, 1)$:

$$f_2(0, 0.5, 1) = 2 \times \left(\frac{1}{F(0, 0.5, 1)^{\frac{1}{2 \times 0.5}}} - 1 \right) = 4.21\%,$$

which is what we found earlier in Example 5.1. Indeed, we have the following definition:

Definition 5.2 *The **forward rate** at time t for a risk free investment from T_1 to T_2, and with compounding frequency n, is the interest rate determined by the forward discount factor in Equation 5.2,*

$$f_n(t, T_1, T_2) = n \times \left(\frac{1}{F(t, T_1, T_2)^{\frac{1}{n \times (T_2 - T_1)}}} - 1 \right) \tag{5.3}$$

The continuously compounded forward rate is obtained for n that grows to infinity:

$$f(t, T_1, T_2) = -\frac{\ln(F(t, T_1, T_2))}{T_2 - T_1} \tag{5.4}$$

As it is true with spot rate and discount factors, there is an equivalence between forward rates and forward discount factors: Given a forward discount factor, we can determine a forward rate from Equations 5.3 or 5.4. Conversely, given a forward rate with its compounding frequency, we can determine the forward discount factor as follows:

Fact 5.2 *Given a n-times compounded forward rate* $f_n(t, T_1, T_2)$, *the forward discount factor is*

$$F(t, T_1, T_2) = \frac{1}{\left(1 + \frac{f_n(t, T_1, T_2)}{n}\right)^{n \times (T_2 - T_1)}} \tag{5.5}$$

Given a continously compounded forward rate $f(t, T_1, T_2)$, *the forward discount factor is*

$$F(t, T_1, T_2) = e^{-f(t, T_1, T_2)(T_2 - T_1)} \tag{5.6}$$

To conclude this section, note that if for any two dates T_1 and $T_2 > T_1$ the discount factor $Z(t, T)$ is increasing, i.e. $Z(t, T_1) < Z(t, T_2)$, then from Equation 5.2 the forward discount factor $F(t, T_1, T_2) > 1$, which in turn implies that both $f_n(t, T_1, T_2) < 0$ and $f(t, T_1, T_2) < 0$. That is:

Fact 5.3 *If the discount factor* $Z(t, T)$ *is increasing between two dates* T_1 *and* $T_2 > T_1$, *that is,* $Z(t, T_1) < Z(t, T_2)$, *then the forward rate at t for an investment between* T_1 *and* T_2 *is negative.*

In the context of Example 5.1, a situation in which $Z(0, T_1) < Z(0, T_2)$ would imply that the bank would be willing to quote a *negative* interest rate f_2 to the firm for the future investment between T_1 and T_2, which is not reasonable. The discount factors $Z(t, T)$ must therefore be decreasing with maturity T, as we already noticed in Section 2.1.1 in Chapter 2.

5.1.1 Forward Rates by No Arbitrage

The argument used in Example 5.1 to establish the forward rate f_2 that the bank will apply to the firm's investment at time T_1, as agreed upon today, is a no arbitrage argument. It may prove useful to view it again, more generally, as follows. Suppose that at time t we need to invest some amount of money \$$W$ until a future date T_2. Consider any intermediate date T_1, and assume that risk free zero coupon bonds are available for an investment from t to T_1 and for an investment from t to T_2. As we know, the prices of these zero coupon bonds are $P_z(t, T_1) = 100 \times Z(t, T_1)$ and $P_z(t, T_2) = 100 \times Z(t, T_2)$.[3] The following two possible strategies are available to us:

---

[3] As discussed in Chapter 1 zero coupon bonds for long maturities are available for purchase in U.S. through the STRIPS program.

Strategy 1. Invest $\$W$ in T_2 zero coupon bonds. Since we can purchase $\$W/P_z(t, T_2)$ zero coupon bonds and the zero coupon bonds pay $\$100$ at T_2, the payoff at T_2 is

$$\text{Payoff at } T_2 \text{ of strategy } 1 = \left(\frac{\$W}{P_z(t, T_2)}\right) \times \$100 \qquad (5.7)$$

Strategy 2. Invest $\$W$ in T_1 zero coupon bonds, and agree with a bank on a semi-annually compounded forward rate f_2 to be applied for an investment from T_1 to T_2. Since we can purchase $\$W/P_z(t, T_1)$ zero coupon bonds and the zero coupon bonds pay $\$100$ at T_1, the payoff at T_2 is

$$\text{Payoff at } T_2 \text{ of strategy } 2 = \left[\left(\frac{\$W}{P_z(t, T_1)}\right) \times \$100\right] \times (1 + f_2/2)^{2 \times (T_2 - T_1)} \quad (5.8)$$

Because under either strategy the investor obtains an amount of money at time T_2 that is *known today*, and thus without any risk, the two strategies must yield the same payoff, otherwise an arbitrage opportunity arises. For instance, if strategy 2 yielded a higher payoff than strategy 1, then anybody holding T_2 bonds would sell them to purchase T_1 bonds and would at the same time enter into agreements with banks for a forward investment at the rate f_2. This strategy would push down the price of T_2 bonds and rise the price of T_1 bonds, as well as forward rates f_2, reequilibrating financial markets.

In order for markets to be in equilibrium, we must have

$$\text{Payoff at } T_2 \text{ of strategy } 2 = \text{Payoff at } T_2 \text{ of strategy } 1 \qquad (5.9)$$

or, substituting for the expressions in Equations 5.7 and 5.8:

$$\left[\left(\frac{\$W}{P_z(t, T_1)}\right) \times \$100\right] \times (1 + f_2/2)^{2 \times (T_2 - T_1)} = \left(\frac{\$W}{P_z(t, T_2)}\right) \times \$100 \qquad (5.10)$$

From this equation, we can substitute for the prices of zero coupon bonds $P_z(t, T_1) = 100 \times Z(t, T_1)$ and $P_z(t, T_2) = 100 \times Z(t, T_2)$, and then simplify from both sides $\$W$ and $\$100$. As an intermediate step, we can write

$$(1 + f_2/2)^{2 \times (T_2 - T_1)} = \frac{Z(t, T_1)}{Z(t, T_2)} \qquad (5.11)$$

Comparing with Equation 5.2, the right hand side of this last equation is the reciprocal of the forward discount factor $Z(t, T_1)/Z(t, T_2) = 1/F(t, T_1, T_2)$. Solving for f_2, we indeed obtain Equation 5.3 for $n = 2$

$$f_2 = f_2(t, T_1, T_2) = 2 \times \left(\frac{1}{F(t, T_1, T_2)^{\frac{1}{2 \times (T_2 - T_1)}}} - 1\right) \qquad (5.12)$$

5.1.2   The Forward Curve

In the case of forward rates and forward discount factors, we have three time indices: t, which is the time when we decide we want to lock in the future interest rate, and then the two future dates T_1 and T_2 during which the investment will take place. In this section, it is convenient to set $t = 0$, and denote the first of the two future dates by T. Finally, assume that the future investment (at T) will be for a period of length Δ. In addition, and again for convenience, we focus in this section on the continuously compounded forward rate, which can then be denoted by

$$f(0, T, T + \Delta) = -\frac{\ln(F(0, T, T + \Delta))}{\Delta} \tag{5.13}$$

Keeping fixed Δ, we can plot the forward rate $f(0, T, T + \Delta)$ with respect T. The resulting curve is called forward curve.

Definition 5.3 *The* **forward curve** *gives the relation between the forward rate $f(0, T, T + \Delta)$ and the time of the investment T.*

For example, Figure 5.2 plots the forward curve $f(0, T, T + 0.25)$ for T that varies from three months to ten years.[4] The figure also plots the underlying spot curve $r(0, T)$ for the same period. The forward curve and spot curve seem to move in tandem: Roughly, they go up and down at the same time. In fact, there is a precise relation between forward curves and spot curves, as, remember, the forward curve is derived from the same discount factors that determine the spot curve.

Figure 5.2   The Spot Curve and the Forward Curve

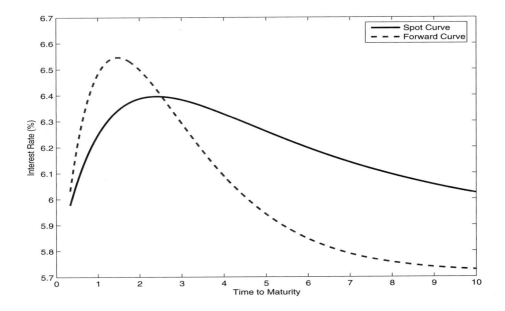

Data Source: CRSP.

[4]Both the yield curve and the forward curve are calculated based on data from CRSP (insert database name) © 2009 Center for Research in Security Prices (CRSP), The University of Chicago Booth School of Business.

Indeed, by definition of the forward discount factor, we find:

$$
\begin{aligned}
F(0,T,T+\Delta) &= \frac{Z(0,T+\Delta)}{Z(0,T)} \\
&= \frac{e^{-r(0,T+\Delta)(T+\Delta)}}{e^{-r(0,T)T}} \\
&= e^{-r(0,T+\Delta)(T+\Delta)+r(0,T)T} \\
&= e^{-r(0,T)\Delta-(r(0,T+\Delta)-r(0,T))(T+\Delta)}
\end{aligned}
$$

Substituting now into Equation 5.13 we obtain

$$
f(0,T,T+\Delta) = r(0,T) + (T+\Delta) \times \frac{r(0,T+\Delta)-r(0,T)}{\Delta} \tag{5.14}
$$

This equation shows the key relation between forward rates and spot rates. For any maturity T, the forward rate between T and $T+\Delta$ equals the spot rate with maturity T plus a term that is positive if the spot curve is rising, and it is negative if the spot curve is declining at T. To see this last point, note that the numerator of the last term in Equation 5.14 is the difference in the spot curve between the two maturities T and $T+\Delta$. If this difference is positive and Δ is sufficiently small, then the term structure is increasing at T. If that difference is instead negative, the spot curve is decreasing at T. This formula implies the following:

Fact 5.4 *When the spot curve is increasing, the forward curve is above the spot curve. When the spot curve is decreasing, the forward curve is below the spot curve. When the spot curve is flat, the forward curve equals the spot curve.*

The pattern described in Fact 5.4 is apparent in Figure 5.2.

To better understand the relation that exists between forward rates $f(0,T,T+\Delta)$ and the underlying spot curve $r(0,T)$, consider now a set of dates, $T_1, T_2,..., T_n$, with $T_{i+1} = T_i + \Delta$. Let also $T_1 = \Delta$. For each pair of dates, we can rewrite the forward discount (Equation 5.2) as

$$
Z(0,T_{i+1}) = Z(0,T_i) \times F(t,T_i,T_{i+1}) \tag{5.15}
$$

Using also Equation 5.4, the following relations hold

$$
\begin{aligned}
Z(0,T_1) &= e^{-r(0,T_1)\times\Delta} & (5.16) \\
Z(0,T_2) &= Z(0,T_1) \times e^{-f(0,T_1,T_2)\times\Delta} \\
\vdots &= \vdots \\
Z(0,T_i) &= Z(0,T_{i-1}) \times e^{-f(0,T_{i-1},T_i)\times\Delta} & (5.17) \\
\vdots &= \vdots \\
Z(0,T_n) &= Z(0,T_{n-1}) \times e^{-f(0,T_{n-1},T_n)\times\Delta} & (5.18)
\end{aligned}
$$

By substituting $Z(0,T_1)$ from the first equation into the second, and $Z(0,T_2)$ from the second into the third, and so on up to T_n, we find that an alternative expression of $Z(0,T_n)$ is

$$Z(0, T_n) = e^{-(r(0,T_1) \times \Delta + f(0,T_1,T_2) \times \Delta + ... + f(0,T_{n-1},T_n) \times \Delta)} \tag{5.19}$$

By definition of the continuously compounded yield $r(0, T_n)$, $Z(0, T_n) = e^{-r(0,T_n) \times T_n}$, we must have

$$r(0, T_n) \times T_n = (r(0, T_1) \times \Delta + f(0, T_1, T_2) \times \Delta + ... + f(0, T_{n-1}, T_n) \times \Delta) \tag{5.20}$$

This last relation yields the following:

Fact 5.5 *The continuously compounded spot rate $r(0, T_n)$ is equal to the average of forward rates up to T_n*

$$r(0, T_n) = \frac{1}{T_n} \sum_{i=1}^{n} f(0, T_{i-1}, T_i) \times \Delta \tag{5.21}$$

where for convenience, we denote $T_0 = 0$ and $f(0, 0, T_1) = r(0, T_1)$.

Since the spot rate with maturity T is an average of forward rates, it becomes quite intuitive that if the forward rate is above the spot rate, then the spot rate must be increasing for the next step, as the incremental rate added to the average is above the average, pushing the average up. Similarly, if the forward rate is below the spot rate with the same maturity, the spot rate curve must decline in the next step, as the new additional element in the average is below the average.

5.1.3 Extracting the Spot Rate Curve from Forward Rates

Sometimes we do not have available zero coupon bond prices to compute the discount factors $Z(0, T)$. However, we may have data of forward rates $f(0, T_i, T_{i+1})$, for a set of maturities T_i, $i = 1, ..., n$ with $T_{i+1} = T_i + \Delta$, where Δ is an interval of time. Because from these forward rates we can compute the forward discount factors $F(0, T_i, T_{i+1})$ (see Equation 5.6), we can then use Equation 5.15 to extract the zero coupon yield curve. Essentially, this methodology amounts to using Equations 5.16 - 5.18 in reverse, from forwards to discount factors $Z(0, T_i)$. The next example illustrates this bootstrap methodology.

■ **EXAMPLE 5.2**

Let today be May 5, 2008. The third column in Table 5.2 contains continuously compounded forward rates at the quarterly frequency ($\Delta = 0.25$).[5] Note that the first forward rate corresponds to the spot rate itself $f(0, 0, 0.25) = r(0, 0.25)$. The first entry in the third column determines the first discount

$$Z(0, 0.25) = e^{-f(0,0,0.25) \times 0.25} = e^{-2.7605\% \times 0.25} = 0.993123$$

which is reported in Column 4. Next, we compute the discount for the maturity $T_2 = 0.5$. Using Equations 5.6 and 5.15 we obtain:

$$\begin{aligned} Z(0, 0.5) &= Z(0, 0.25) \times e^{-f(0,0.25,0.5) \times 0.25} \\ &= 0.993123 \times e^{-2.9460\% \times 0.25} \\ &= 0.986521 \end{aligned}$$

---

[5] Section 6.5 in Chapter 6 describes the source of these data.

Table 5.2   Forward Rates and Spot Curve on May 5, 2008

Step i	Maturity T_i	(c.c.) Forward Rate $f(0, T_{i-1}, T_i)$ (%)	Discount $Z(0, T_i)$ ($\times 100$)	(c.c.) Spot Rate $r(0, T_i)$ (%)
1	0.2500	2.7605	99.3123	2.7605
2	0.5000	2.6677	98.6521	2.7141
3	0.7500	2.8132	97.9607	2.7471
4	1.0000	3.0088	97.2267	2.8125
5	1.2500	3.1917	96.4539	2.8884
6	1.5000	3.3664	95.6456	2.9680
7	1.7500	3.5501	94.8005	3.0512
8	2.0000	3.7118	93.9248	3.1338
9	2.2500	3.8440	93.0265	3.2127
10	2.5000	3.9700	92.1078	3.2884
11	2.7500	4.0899	91.1708	3.3613
12	3.0000	4.1800	90.2230	3.4295
13	3.2500	4.2474	89.2701	3.4924
14	3.5000	4.3150	88.3123	3.5512
15	3.7500	4.3884	87.3487	3.6070
16	4.0000	4.4466	86.3830	3.6595
17	4.2500	4.4913	85.4186	3.7084
18	4.5000	4.5395	84.4546	3.7546
19	4.7500	4.5953	83.4900	3.7988

Original Data Source: Bloomberg

again reported in Column 4. We can proceed for every $i = 2, ..., 19$ and use the formula

$$Z(0, T_i) = Z(0, T_{i-1}) \times e^{-f(0, T_{i-1}, T_i) \times 0.25}$$

Column 4 contains the resulting discount factors $Z(0, T_i)$ for every maturity. Column 5 uses these discount factors to obtain the continuously compounded spot rate

$$r(0, T_i) = -\frac{\ln(Z(0, T_i))}{T_i}$$

5.2   FORWARD RATE AGREEMENTS

Definition 5.4 *A* **Forward Rate Agreement (FRA)** *is a contract between two counterparties, according to which one counterparty agrees to pay the forward rate* $f_n(0, T_1, T_2)$ *on a given notional amount N during a given future period of time from* T_1 *to* $T_2 = T_1 + \Delta$, *while the other counterparty agrees to pay according to future market floating rate* $r_n(T_1, T_2)$. *The net payment between the two counterparties at the maturity* T_2 *of the contract is then given by*

$$\text{Net payment at } T_2 = N \times \Delta \times [r_n(T_1, T_2) - f_n(0, T_1, T_2)] \qquad (5.22)$$

Above, $\Delta = T_2 - T_1$, *typically a quarter or six months, while the subscript* $n = 1/\Delta$ *denotes the corresponding compounding frequency, e.g.,* $n = 4$ *or* $n = 2$ *for quarterly or semi-annual compounding.*

To understand the logic of FRAs, it is useful to go back to Example 5.1.

■ **EXAMPLE 5.3**

Recall from Example 5.1 that today $(t = 0)$ is March 1, 2001, that a firm has a receivable of $100 million in six months $(T_1 = 0.5)$, and the firm wishes to invest this amount for an additional six months (until $T_2 = 1$). An alternative strategy to the one described in Example 5.1 is for the firm to enter into a six-month FRA with a bank for the period T_1 to T_2, and notional $N = \$100$ million. That is, today the bank agrees to pay in one year $(T_2 = 1)$ the amount $N \times f_2(0, 0.5, 1)$, where $f_2(0, 0.5, 1)$ is the current semi-annually compounded forward rate for the period T_1 to T_2, while the firm agrees to pay on the same day the amount $N \times r_2(0.5, 1)$, where $r_2(0.5, 1)$ is the semi-annually compounded spot interest rate at time $T_1 = 0.5$. That is, they exchange the payment at $T_2 = 1$

$$\text{Net payment of the firm at } T_2 = \frac{N}{2} \times [f_2(0, 0.5, 1) - r_2(0.5, 1)] \qquad (5.23)$$

where we must divide by two because the interest is only over six months. Recall $f_2(0, 0.5, 1) = 4.21\%$. We now see that the firm reaches exactly the same outcome as in Example 5.1.

Indeed, at $T_1 = 0.5$ when the firm receives its $100 million receivable, the firm can simply invest this amount at the market interest rate $r_2(0.5, 1)$. How much money will the firm have at time $T_2 = 1$? At this time, the firm receives the payoff from the investment, plus the net payment given in equation (5.23). In total

$$
\begin{aligned}
\text{Total amount} \atop \text{at } T_2 \quad &= \quad \left\{ \$100 \text{ million} \times \left[1 + \frac{r_2(0.5, 1)}{2} \right] \right\} \qquad \text{(Return on investment)} \\[2mm]
&\quad + \left\{ \frac{N}{2} \times [f_2(0, .5, 1) - r_2(0.5, 1)] \right\} \qquad \text{(FRA payment)} \\[2mm]
&= \quad \$100 \text{ million} \times \left[1 + \frac{f_2(0, .5, 1)}{2} \right] \\[2mm]
&= \quad \$102.105 \text{ million}
\end{aligned}
$$

The firm is in exactly the same position as in Example 5.1.

What about the bank? In particular, the bank now is exposed to interest rate risk, as the FRA yields a negative payoff if $f_2(0, 0.5, 1) > r_2(0.5, 1)$. However, a little modification to the strategy in Table 5.1 ensures the bank is hedged as well. The new modified strategy is shown in Table 5.3. At time 0, the bank strategy is the same: The bank shorts T_1 T-bills and purchases $M = 1.02105\, T_2$ T-bills. At time T_1 the bank must come up with $100 million to pay the short position. The bank can borrow this amount of money, at the current rate $r_2(0.5, 1)$. At time T_2, the bank total cash flows are as follows

$$
\text{Total CF} \atop \text{of bank at } T_2 \quad = \quad \left\{ -\$100 \text{ m} \times \left[1 + \frac{r_2(0.5, 1)}{2} \right] \right\} \qquad \text{(Pay back loan)}
$$

Table 5.3   Trading Strategy to Compute Forward Rate

Today (Time 0)	T_1	T_2
Sell short $97.728 m of T-bills maturing at T_1	(a) Borrow $100 m at rate $r_2(0.5, 1)$ (b) Close short position	Pay $100 m $\times \left(1 + \frac{r_2(0.5,1)}{2}\right)$
Buy $M = 1.02105 = \frac{\$97.728}{\$95.713}$ of T-bills maturing at T_2		Receive $1.02105 \times \$100$ m
Enter FRA with Firm		Pay $\frac{100\ m}{2} \times [f_2(0, 0.5, 1) - r_2(0.5, 1)]$
Total Net Cash Flow = 0	Total Net Cash Flow = 0	Total Net Cash Flow = 0

$$+ \{1.02105 \times \$100 \text{ m }\} \qquad (T_2 \text{ T-bills mature})$$
$$+ \left\{ \frac{\$100 \text{ m}}{2} \times [r_2(0.5, 1) - f_2(0, 0.5, 1)] \right\} \qquad (\text{FRA payment})$$
$$= \quad 0$$

A *perfect hedge.*

5.2.1   The Value of a Forward Rate Agreement

When two counterparties enter into a FRA, there is no exchange of money at the time of the contract inception (time 0). In other words, the *value* of the forward rate agreement is zero at inception. However, as time passes and forward rates change, the value of the forward rate agreement changes as well. The following example demonstrates the issue.

■ **EXAMPLE 5.4**

Consider again Example 5.3 and suppose that three months after the initiation of the contract, on June 1, 2001, the firm decides to close its FRA with the bank. So far, the two counterparties have not exchanged any money, so it may appear that the firm could simply call the bank and ask to close the contract. But as interest rates changed between March 1 and June 1, so did the *value* of the forward rate agreement. To see this, from Table 5.3 we note that at initiation (today = 0) the bank sold one T-bill maturing at T_1 and bought $M = 1.02105$ T-bills maturing at T_2. This portfolio (long T_2 T-bills and short T_1 T-bills) exactly hedges the bank commitment to the FRA, as discussed in Example 5.3. Since it produces exactly the cash flow that the firm will receive, the value of this portfolio must reflect the value of the FRA for the firm. Thus, for every $t \le T_1$, we have

$$\text{Value of FRA to the firm at } t = V^{FRA}(t) = M \times P_{bill}(t, T_2) - P_{bill}(t, T_1) \qquad (5.24)$$

where, recall $M = P_{bill}(0, T_1)/P_{bill}(0, T_2)$. For instance, at initiation we have

$$V^{FRA}(0) \quad = \quad M \times P_{bill}(0, T_2) - P_{bill}(0, T_1)$$

$$= \frac{P_{bill}(0, T_1)}{P_{bill}(0, T_2)} \times P_{bill}(0, T_2) - P_{bill}(0, T_1)$$

$$= 0$$

showing that there is no exchange of money at initiation.

On June 1, 2001 ($= t$), the T_1 T-bill price was $P_{bill}(t, T_1) = \$99.10$ and the T_2 T-bill price was $P_{bill}(t, T_2) = \$97.37$. Therefore

$$V^{FRA}(t) = 1.02105 \times P_{bill}(t, T_2) - P_{bill}(t, T_1) = 1.02105 \times \$97.37 - \$99.1$$

$$= \$0.319638 \text{ million}$$

On June 1, 2001, the value of the forward rate agreement initiated 3 months earlier was worth \$319,638 to the firm. Simply calling up the bank and exiting from the FRA would be a mistake, as the firm would lose this amount of money. Of course, knowing this, the bank would pay this sum of money to the firm in case it wanted to exit from the contract, minus some transaction costs.

More generally, we can compute the value of the FRA by considering separately the payments of the two counterparties. In particular, let's first decompose the payment of the FRA as follows

$$\text{Net payment at } T_2 = N \times \Delta \times [f_n(0, T_1, T_2) - r_n(T_1, T_2)]$$

$$= N \times [1 + f_n(0, T_1, T_2)\Delta] - N \times [1 + r_n(T_1, T_2)\Delta]$$

$$= \text{Fixed leg payment} - \text{Floating leg payment}$$

We can then value the two legs separately. The fixed leg is the simplest, as this corresponds to a fixed payment at time T_2 and thus we can discount it, as if it was a zero coupon bond:

$$\begin{array}{l} \text{Value of fixed leg at } t \\ V^{fixed}(t) \end{array} = \text{Present value of } N \times [1 + f_n(0, T_1, T_2)\Delta]$$

$$= Z(t, T_2) \times N \times [1 + f_n(0, T_1, T_2)\Delta]$$

The value of the floating leg requires a little trick, as we do not know today (t) what the payment will be at time T_2. First, we compute the value of the floating leg at T_1:

$$\begin{array}{l} \text{Value of floating leg at} T_1 \\ V^{floating}(T_1) \end{array} = \text{Present value of } N \times [1 + r_n(T_1, T_2)\Delta]$$

$$= Z(T_1, T_2) \times N \times [1 + r_n(T_1, T_2)\Delta]$$

$$= \frac{1}{[1 + r_n(T_1, T_2)\Delta]} \times N \times [1 + r_n(T_1, T_2)\Delta]$$

$$= N$$

Because the floating leg at T_1 is always equal to N *independently* of the floating rate $r_n(T_1, T_2)$, we then find

$$\begin{array}{l} \text{Value of floating leg at } t \\ V^{floating}(t) \end{array} = \text{Present value of } V^{floating}(T_1)$$

$$= Z(t, T_1) \times N$$

Combining the value of the floating leg with the value of the fixed leg, we obtain

Fact 5.6 *The* **value** *at time t of a forward rate agreement in which counterparties exchange at T_2 the cash flow*

$$\text{Net payment at } T_2 = N \times \Delta \times [f_n(0, T_1, T_2) - r_n(T_1, T_2)]$$

is given by

$$
\begin{aligned}
\text{Value of FRA at } t = V^{FRA}(t) &= V^{fixed}(t) - V^{floating}(t) \\
&= N \times [M \times Z(t, T_2) - Z(t, T_1)] \quad (5.25)
\end{aligned}
$$

where

$$M = 1 + f_n(0, T_1, T_2)\Delta = \frac{Z(0, T_1)}{Z(0, T_2)}$$

The definition of M ensures that indeed the value of the FRA is zero at initiation

$$V^{FRA}(0) = N \times [M \times Z(0, T_2) - Z(0, T_1)] = 0$$

We can rewrite the value of the FRA in Equation 5.25 in a more intuitive way: Factor out $Z(t, T_2)$ and obtain the following:

Fact 5.7 *The* **value** *of a FRA can be expressed equivalently as follows:*

$$
\begin{aligned}
V^{FRA}(t) &= N \times Z(t, T_2) \times \left[M - \frac{Z(t, T_1)}{Z(t, T_2)} \right] \\
&= N \times Z(t, T_2) \times \Delta \times [f_n(0, T_1, T_2) - f_n(t, T_1, T_2)] \quad (5.26)
\end{aligned}
$$

as we recall that by definition of a forward rate we have $1 + f_n(t, T_1, T_2)\Delta = Z(t, T_1)/Z(t, T_2)$.

Equation 5.26 is intuitive, and its logic is better explained by going back to Example 5.4.

■ **EXAMPLE 5.5**

In Example 5.4 the firm would like to exit the FRA 3 months after inception, call it time t. Instead of calling up the counterparty and asking to close the contract, the firm can achieve the same result by entering into a *new* FRA at time t with the reversed payoff, that is

$$\text{Payoff of reverse FRA at } T_2 = \frac{N}{2} \times [r_2(T_1, T_2) - f_2(t, T_1, T_2)] \quad (5.27)$$

Clearly, the payoff of the FRA at time t depends on the current forward rate $f_2(t, T_1, T_2)$ instead of the old one $f(0, T_1, T_2)$. The total payoff for the firm at T_2 is then

$$
\begin{aligned}
\text{Total payoff at } T_2 \text{ of old FRA} \\
\text{+ new FRA}
\end{aligned}
= \left\{ \frac{N}{2} \times [f_2(0, T_1, T_2) - r_2(T_1, T_2)] \right\}
$$

$$+ \left\{ \frac{N}{2} \times [r_2(T_1, T_2) - f_2(t, T_1, T_2)] \right\}$$

$$= \frac{N}{2} [f_2(0, T_1, T_2) - f_2(t, T_1, T_2)]$$

That is, at the time of the decision to close the original FRA contract, the firm will end up with a positive payoff if the current forward rate declined since inception, and vice versa. Since $P_{bill}(t, T_1) = \$99.10$ and $P_{bill}(t, T_2) = \$97.37$, the current forward is $f_2(t, T_1, T_2) = 2 \times (.991/.9737 - 1) = 3.55\% < f(0, T_1, T_2) = 4.21\%$. The time T_2 payoff is then $N/2 [f_2(0, T_1, T_2) - f_2(t, T_1, T_2)] = \$328, 272$, which is known at the earlier time t. Therefore, the present value is

$$
\begin{aligned}
V^{FRA}(t) &= Z(t, T_2) \times \frac{N}{2} \times [f_2(0, T_1, T_2) - f_2(t, T_1, T_2)] \\
&= 0.9737 \times \$328, 272 = \$319, 638
\end{aligned}
$$

as we obtained earlier.

5.3 FORWARD CONTRACTS

In a forward rate agreement, two counterparties agree to exchange cash flows according to the difference between the forward rate (known at initiation of the contract) and the future spot rate. An equivalent strategy for an investor to lock in a given rate of return in the future is to agree to purchase a given Treasury security in the future, at a price determined today. Consider again Example 5.1.

■ **EXAMPLE 5.6**

On March 1, 2001 (today = time 0), the firm may enter into a forward contract with a bank to purchase six months later ($T_1 = 0.5$) \$100 million-worth of 6-months Treasury bills for a price P^{fwd}, for \$100 par value, specified today.

What purchase price would the bank quote to the firm for the 6-month T-bills?

The answer is simply the forward discount factor $F(0, .5, 1)$ computed in Equation 5.1, multiplied by 100. That is

$$\text{Forward price} = P^{fwd} = 100 \times F(0, .5, 1) = \$97.938 \tag{5.28}$$

To see why, go back to Table 5.1, and consider the bank's trading strategy at time 0. Recall that from the (short) sale of T_1 T-bills, the bank purchases $M = 1.02105$ million of T_2 T-bills. Recall also that the net cash flow to the bank at time 0 is zero. At time T_1 the bank has to cover the short position, and uses the \$100 million from the firm, as in Table 5.1. Note that at this point the bank holds an amount $M = 1.02105$ million of T_2 T-bills, which now have maturity $T_2 - T_1 = $ six months. Therefore, the bank can use these M 6-month T-bills to honor the terms of the forward contract. That is, at T_1 the bank simply delivers its own holdings M of 6-month T-bills to the firm. This number M of T_2 T-bills is exactly the number of 6-month T-bills that are needed to ensure the firm gets $100 million-worth of 6-month T-bills, as the firm requested. In fact, given the forward price P^{fwd} in Equation 5.28, we have

$$\frac{\$100 \text{ million}}{P^{fwd}} = 1.02105 \text{ million} = M$$

This example leads to the following definition:

Definition 5.5 *A **forward contract** is a contract between two counterparties in which one counterparty agrees to purchase and the other agrees to sell a given security at a given future time, and at a given price, called the **forward price**. Denoting by $P^{fwd}(0, T, T^*)$ the forward price at time 0 for delivery at time T of a security expiring at T^*, whose value at T we denote by $P(T, T^*)$, the payoff at T of the forward contract is*

$$\text{Payoff from long forward contract} = P(T, T^*) - P^{fwd}(0, T, T^*) \tag{5.29}$$

The payoff from being short the forward contract is the negative of Equation 5.29.

In Example 5.6 the underlying security was a 6-month Treasury Bill: The forward contract yields the payoff in Equation 5.29 at time T because the firm receives a security worth $P(T, T^*)$ but it pays $P^{fwd}(0, T, T^*)$.

The next example illustrates that hedging with the forward contract yields the same return on investment as the hedging strategy performed with forward rate agreements.

■ **EXAMPLE 5.7**

Consider again Example 5.6, and let $P^{fwd}(0, 0.5, 1) = 100 \times F(0, 0.5, 1) = \$97.938$ be the forward price quoted at time 0 for the investment between $T_1 = 0.5$ to $T_2 = 1$, as determined in the example. Let the firm enter into a forward contract to purchase $M = 1.02105$ million of 6-month T-bills on $T_1 = 0.5$ (with $100 principal). The payoff from the forward contract at time $T_1 = 0.5$ is then given by

$$\text{Payoff forward contract at } T_1 = M \times (P_{bill}(T_1, T_2) - \$97.938)$$

Ex post, the fear of the firm that the interest rate would decline is in fact realized, and the price of the 6-month T-bill at T_1 turns out to be $P_{bill}(T_1, T_2) = \$98.89 > \$97.938$. Thus, the payoff from the forward contract is:

Payoff forward contract at $T_1 = 1.02105$ million $\times$ ($98.89 - $97.938) = $972,043.54$

The firm at T_1 can then invest this additional amount, $972,043.54, together with the receivable $100,000,000 into the new T-bill. In particular, it will be purchasing an amount of T-bills equal to

$$\text{Investment in T-bills at } T_1 = \frac{(\$100,000,000 + \$972,043.54)}{\$98.89} = 1,021,054.136$$

where the T-bills have $100 principal. At maturity T_2 the total amount realized is then $102,105,413.6, which implies a realized annualized rate of return equal to

$$\text{Annualized rate of return} = \frac{1}{T_2 - T_1} \times \left(\frac{\text{Payoff at } T_2}{\text{Investment at } T_1} - 1 \right)$$

$$= 2 \times \left(\frac{1{,}021{,}054.136}{100{,}000{,}000} - 1 \right)$$
$$= 4.21\% \qquad (5.30)$$

This is exactly equal to the forward rate determined in Example 5.1 and is in fact independent of the realized Treasury bill $T_1 = 0.5$, $P_{bill}(T_1, T_2)$. The higher the value of the T-bill at maturity, the higher is the payoff from the forward contract. But more it becomes more expensive to purchase T-bills for an investment between T_1 and T_2. These two effects exactly cancel each other out, and the firm is guaranteed the forward rate.

It is convenient for later reference to establish the result in the following:

Fact 5.8 *Consider a forward contract in which one counterparty agrees to buy at a future date T a zero coupon bond $P_z(T, T^*)$. The forward price is given by the forward discount factor (multiplied by the notional).*

$$P_z^{fwd}(0, T, T^*) = F(0, T, T^*) \times 100 \qquad (5.31)$$

5.3.1 A No Arbitrage Argument

It is useful to look at the arbitrage argument that makes Equation 5.31 true. Assume $P_z^{fwd}(0, T, T^*) > F(0, T, T^*) \times 100$. Recalling that

$$F(0, T, T^*) = \frac{Z(0, T*)}{Z(0, T)} = \frac{P_z(0, T^*)}{P_z(0, T)},$$

an arbitrageur can:

1. Sell forward the zero coupon $P_z(T, T^*)$ at forward price $P_z^{fwd}(0, T, T^*)$.

2. Short exactly $F(0, T, T^*)$ zero coupon bonds with maturity T for the amount $F(0, T, T^*) \times P_z(0, T) = P_z(0, T^*)$, the price of a zero coupon with maturity T^*.

3. Use the proceeds from step 2 to purchase one zero coupon with maturity T^*.

At time 0 there is no net cash flow for the arbitrageur. At time T the arbitrageur:

1. Delivers the zero coupon $P_z(T, T^*)$, which he or she owns, and receives $P_z^{fwd}(0, T, T^*)$, thereby closing the forward contract.

2. Covers the short position by paying $F(0, T, T^*) \times 100$.

The net cash flow at time T is then $P_z^{fwd}(0, T, T^*) - F(0, T, T^*) \times 100 > 0$. There is no uncertainty or risk in this strategy, and thus it is an arbitrage. If $P_z^{fwd}(0, T, T^*) < F(0, T, T^*) \times 100$, the reverse strategy also leads to an arbitrage, thus Equation 5.31 must hold.

5.3.2   Forward Contracts on Treasury Bonds

Forward contracts can be written on any type of security. Of special interest are forward contracts on Treasury notes and bonds.

Fact 5.9 *Consider a forward contract in which one counterparty agrees to purchase at a future date T a Treasury bond with coupon rate c and with maturity $T^* > T$. Let T_1, T_2, ..., $T_n = T^*$ be the coupon dates* after T, *the maturity of the forward contract. Then, the* **forward price** *is given by*

$$
\begin{aligned}
P_c^{fwd}(0,T,T^*) \ &= \ \frac{c \times 100}{2} \times F(0,T,T_1) + \frac{c \times 100}{2} \times F(0,T,T_2) \quad (5.32) \\
&\quad + ... + \left(\frac{c \times 100}{2} + 100 \right) \times F(0,T,T_n) \\
&= \ \frac{c \times 100}{2} \times \sum_{i=1}^{n} F(0,T,T_i) + 100 \times F(0,T,T_n) \quad (5.33) \\
&= \ \frac{c}{2} \times \sum_{i=1}^{n} P_z^{fwd}(0,T,T_i) + P_z^{fwd}(0,T,T_n) \quad (5.34)
\end{aligned}
$$

Comparing the forward price $P_c^{fwd}(0,T,T^*)$ in Equation 5.33 with the bond pricing formula in Equation 2.13 in Chapter 2, the similarity is evident. Essentially, as discussed in Definition 5.1 and shown in Equation 5.2, the forward discount factor $F(0,T,T_i)$ is used in lieu of the current discount $Z(0,T_i)$ as the aim is to convert money at time T_i into money at time T and not 0. Given our previous discussion about the forward discount factor, Equation 5.33 should come to no surprise. However, it is beneficial to review a no arbitrage argument that establishes Equation 5.33. In equation (5.33) suppose that

$$
P_c^{fwd}(0,T,T^*) > \frac{c}{2} \times \sum_{i=1}^{n} P_z^{fwd}(0,T,T_i) + P_z^{fwd}(0,T,T_n) \quad (5.35)
$$

An arbitrageur can:

1. Sell the underlying bond forward at the forward price $P_c^{fwd}(0,T,T^*)$.

2. Short $N = \left(\frac{c}{2} \times \sum_{i=1}^{n} F(0,T,T_i) + F(0,T,T_n) \right)$ zero coupon bonds maturing on T.

3. Use the proceeds to purchase $c/2$ zero coupon bonds with maturities T_1 to T_{n-1}, and $1 + c/2$ zero coupon bond with maturity $T_n = T^*$.

At time 0, there is no net cash flow for the arbitrageur. At time T, the arbitrageur must:

1. Sell all of zeros he holds and purchase the coupon bond $P_c(T,T^*)$. The law of one price ensures that the price of this bond at T is the same as the value of sum of zeros. The arbitrageur can then deliver the coupon bond in exchange of $P_c^{fwd}(0,T,T^*)$.

2. Cover the short position in N zeros established in Step 2 by paying $\$100 \times N$.

The net cash flow is $P_c^{fwd}(0,T,T^*) > \$100 \times N$, which from Relation 5.35 is positive yielding an arbitrage.

5.3.3 The Value of a Forward Contract

What is the value of a forward contract after initiation? Once again, the answer relies on the cost (or profit) of closing the position. Just as an illustration, consider the forward contract already discussed in Fact 5.9. We then have the following result:

Fact 5.10 *Consider a forward contract in which one counterparty agrees to purchase at a future date T a Treasury bond with coupon rate c and with maturity $T^* > T$. Let T_1, T_2, ..., $T_n = T^*$ be the coupon dates after T. The value of the forward contract for every $t < T$ is*

$$V^{fwd}(t) = Z(t,T) \times \left[P_c^{fwd}(t,T,T^*) - K \right] \tag{5.36}$$

where $K = P_c^{fwd}(0,T,T^*)$ is the delivery price agreed upon at initiation.

To see why Equation 5.36 holds, consider the investor who is long the forward contract, meaning that she committed to purchasing the coupon bond for a price $K = P_c^{fwd}(0,T,T^*)$. In order to close it before T, say at $t < T$, the investor can enter *short* the contract to receive the same bond at the *current* forward price $P_c^{fwd}(t,T,T^*)$. Putting the two trades together, at T the investor will pay $P_c^{fwd}(0,T,T^*)$ from the old contract in exchange for the bond, which she will deliver to the counterparty of the new (time t) contract for a price of $P_c^{fwd}(t,T,T^*)$. Overall, at T the investor will make $\left[P_c^{fwd}(t,T,T^*) - P_c^{fwd}(0,T,T^*) \right]$. This amount is known today (t), and thus its present value represents the value of the forward contract, yielding (5.36).

5.3.3.1 *The Forward Price and the Value of a Forward Contract*
It is easy to get confused between the forward price and the value of a forward contract. The forward price is *not* the price at which one trader can buy a forward contract. In fact, at initiation, it does not cost anything to enter into a forward contract, as there is no money exchange between the counterparties at time $t = 0$. The reason is that a forward contract is an agreement *today* to exchange money *in the future* (and not today). The forward price is the price at which we agree today to buy or sell the security in the future. Once the contract has been initiated and the forward price has been set, though, then the value of the now old forward contract changes over time with the variation of interest rates or the underlying security. Thus, if a trader wants to enter into a forward contract at an *old* forward price [e.g., $P_c^{fwd}(0,T,T^*)$ in Equation 5.36], he may need to pay or receive money depending on whether in the meantime current market conditions increased or decreased the forward price.

5.4 INTEREST RATE SWAPS

Interest rate swaps have become the dominant interest rate over-the-counter (OTC) derivative security of modern financial markets. According to the Bank for International Settlements, as of December 2008 the interest rate swap market had a total market value of $8 trillion ($357 trillion notional), against $87 billion of forward rate agreements ($39 trillion notional) and $1.1 trillion of OTC options ($62 trillion notional). These numbers may be compared against the U.S. Treasury debt at that time, which was around $5.9 trillion. In this section we look at the pricing of plain vanilla interest rate swaps, and the implications for financial markets.

Definition 5.6 *A plain vanilla* **fixed-for-floating interest rate swap** *contract is an agreement between two counterparties in which one counterparty agrees to make n fixed payments per year at an (annualized) rate c on a notional N up to a maturity date T, while at the same time the other counterparty commits to make payments linked to a floating rate index* $r_n(t)$.[6] *Denote by* $T_1, T_2,..., T_n = T$ *the payment dates, with* $T_i = T_{i-1} + \Delta$ *and* $\Delta = 1/n$, *the net payment between the two counterparties at each of these dates is*

$$\text{Net payment at } T_i = N \times \Delta \times [r_n(T_{i-1}) - c] \tag{5.37}$$

The constant c is called **swap rate**.

The following example illustrates the cash flows involved in an interest rate swap with semi-annual payments.

■ **EXAMPLE 5.8**

A firm and bank decide to enter into a fixed for floating, semi-annual, five-year swap with swap rate $c = 5.46\%$ and notional amount $N = \$200$ million. The reference floating rate is the six months LIBOR. In this swap contract, the firm agrees to pay to the bank every six months ($T_i = 0.5, 1, 1.5, ..., 5$) the amount

Cash flow from firm to bank at $T_i = \$200$ m $\times 0.5 \times 5.46\% = \$4.56$ million

In exchange, the bank pays the firm at every T_i an amount that depends on the 6-month LIBOR $r_2(T_{i-1})$. It is crucial to note that the reference rate for the payment at time T_i is *not* the LIBOR at T_i, but the one determined six months before, at $T_{i-1} = T_i - 0.5$. This timing convention is important, as we shall see, to obtain simple formulas to value swap contracts.

Cash flow from bank to firm at $T_i = \$200$ m $\times 0.5 \times r_2(T_{i-1})\%$

Table 5.4 illustrates the cash flows from the bank to the firm and vice versa. The noteworthy point is that the cash flows from the bank to the firm in Column 3 vary over time, and in particular they have a six months lag from the time the LIBOR, in Column 2, is realized. In this particular instance, the firm would receive a negative net cash flow, as the reference floating rate declined from 4.951% at initiation to a much lower number.

It is important to reiterate that in a swap contract the two counterparties agree to exchange cash flows in the *future*, not *today*. Therefore, there is a zero net cash flow at initiation of the contract. As in forward contracts and in forward rate agreements, nobody buys or sells a swap, in that no exchange of money occurs at initiation.

Before studying the fair pricing of swaps, it is useful to examine one more example in which a firm uses a swap to hedge against interest rate risk.

---

[6]Recall that the subscript n on the interest rate $r_n(t)$ denotes the compounding frequency. For notational convenience, I also drop the maturity index in the reference rate, that is, $r_n(t) = r_n(t, t + \Delta)$ when $\Delta = 1/n$.

Table 5.4 Example Cash Flows in Fixed-for-Floating Swap

Time	LIBOR	Flow from Bank to Firm	Flow from Firm to Bank	Net Cash Flow to Firm
0.0	4.951 %			
0.5	3.460 %	$ 4.951 m	$ 5.460 m	$ -0.509 m
1.0	2.040 %	$ 3.460 m	$ 5.460 m	$ -2.000 m
1.5	1.800 %	$ 2.040 m	$ 5.460 m	$ -3.420 m
2.0	1.339 %	$ 1.800 m	$ 5.460 m	$ -3.660 m
2.5	1.201 %	$ 1.339 m	$ 5.460 m	$ -4.121 m
3.0	1.170 %	$ 1.201 m	$ 5.460 m	$ -4.259 m
3.5	1.980 %	$ 1.170 m	$ 5.460 m	$ -4.290 m
4.0	3.190 %	$ 1.980 m	$ 5.460 m	$ -3.480 m
4.5	3.996 %	$ 3.190 m	$ 5.460 m	$ -2.270 m
5.0	4.976 %	$ 3.996 m	$ 5.460 m	$ -1.464 m

■ **EXAMPLE 5.9**

Today is $t = 0 =$ March 1, 2001. Consider a firm that sold a piece of equipment to a highly rated corporation, and it is then due to receive payments in 10 equal installments of $5.5 million each over 5 years. The firm would like to use these $5.5 million semi-annual cash flows to hedge against the coupon payments the firm must make to service a $200 million, floating rate bond that it issued some time in the past, and also expiring in 5 years. Suppose that the floating rate on the corporate bond is tied to the LIBOR, at LIBOR + 4 bps. The 6-month LIBOR on March 1, 2001 is currently at 4.95% and so the next interest rate payment the firm must make is $(4.95 + 0.04)\%/2 \times 200$ million $= \$4.9$ million. So, the next floating rate coupon payment is covered. However, if the LIBOR were to increase by more than 0.51% in the next 5 years, the cash flows from the installments would not be sufficient to service the debt.

A solution is to enter into a fixed-for-floating swap with an investment bank, in which the firm pays the fixed semi-annual swap rate c, over a notional of $200 million, and the bank pays the 6-month LIBOR to the firm. On March 1, 2001, the swap rate for a 5-year fixed-for-floating swap was quoted at $c = 5.46\%$. So, in this case, the *net* cash flow to the firm from the swap contract is

$$\text{Net cash flow to the firm at } T_i = \$200 \text{ million} \times \frac{1}{2} \times [r_2(T_{i-1}) - 5.46\%]$$

where $r_2(t)$ is the six month LIBOR at time t.

Why does this swap resolve the problem?

Consider the net position of the firm (see Figure 5.3): at every T_i the firm

1. receives 5.5 million;

2. pays $(r_2(T_i - 0.5) + 4bps)/2 \times 200$ million on its outstanding floating rate debt;

3. receives $r_2(T_i - 0.5)/2 \times 200$ million from the bank as part of the swap; and

Figure 5.3   Hedging with Swaps

time T_i

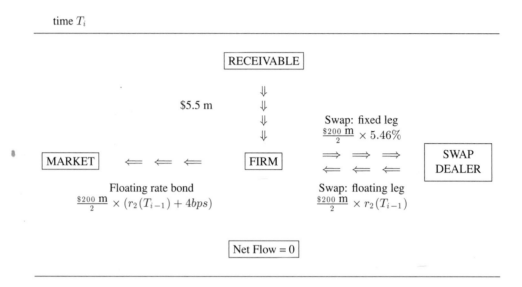

4. pays $5.46\% \times 0.5 \times 200$ million to the bank as part of the swap.

Summing up, the firm's net cash flow position from the receivable, debt, and swap is

$$
\begin{aligned}
\text{Total cash flow at } T_i \; &= \; 5.5 \text{ million} && \text{(Receivable)} \\
&\quad -(r_2(T_i - 0.5) + 4bps)/2 \times 200 \text{ million} && \text{(Debt)} \\
&\quad +0.5 \times [r_2(T_i - 0.5) - 5.46\%] \times 200 \text{ million} && \text{(Swap)} \\
&= \; 5.5 - 0.04\% \times 100 - 5.46\% \times 100 \\
&= \; 0
\end{aligned}
$$

That is, the firm is perfectly hedged: The risk in the fluctuations of the LIBOR stemming from its liabilities has been eliminated by the swap (the firm receives the LIBOR from the bank, and pays the LIBOR + .04% to bond holders). The remaining fixed components sum up to zero. Figure 5.3 illustrates the flow of cash at every T_i.

The swap contract allows the firm to use a sequence of fixed cash flows (the receivables) to hedge a sequence of floating cash flows (the LIBOR-based coupons). Using the terminology developed in Chapter 3, the firm is facing a duration mismatch, as its assets (the receivables) have long duration, while its liabilities (the floating rate bond) have low duration. The swap contract eliminates the duration mismatch. Indeed, this flexibility to change the nature of future cash flows without any payment at initiation has made the swap an excellent instrument for corporations and governments to implement effective cash flow management strategies. Section 5.5 further explores these applications.

5.4.1 The Value of a Swap

How do we value a swap? Consider the swap counterparty who makes the fixed payments at (annualized) rate c every six months at dates T_1, T_2, ..., T_M, and receives at the same times floating rate payments linked to a floating rate $r_2(T_i - 0.5)$. The sequence of net cash flows for this counterparty is the same as the one for a portfolio that is long a floating rate bond, and short a fixed rate bond with coupon c. The value of the swap is then readily available. In fact, recall that in Chapter 2 we have already obtained the value of coupon bonds (Section 2.4) and of floating rate bonds (Section 2.5). A direct application of those results yields the value of the swap. More specifically, from the equivalence

$$\text{Value of swap} = \text{Value of floating rate bond} - \text{Value of fixed rate bond} \qquad (5.38)$$

we obtain

$$V^{swap}(t; c, T) = P_{FR}(t, T) - P_c(t, T) \qquad (5.39)$$

where $V^{swap}(t; c, T)$ is the value of a swap at time t, with swap rate c and maturity T, $P_{FR}(t, T)$ is the value of a floating rate bond as in Equation 2.40 in Chapter 2, and $P_c(t, T)$ is the value of fixed coupon bond, with coupon rate c, given in Equation 2.13 in the same chapter.

At payment dates T_i, the value of the floating rate bond is $P_{FR}(T_i, T) = 100$. Also, using the price of the bond $P_c(T_i, T)$ in Equation 2.13 we then obtain

$$V^{swap}(T_i; c, T) = 100 - \left(\frac{c}{2} \times 100 \times \sum_{j=i+1}^{M} Z(T_i, T_j) + Z(T_i, T_M) \times 100 \right) \qquad (5.40)$$

■ **EXAMPLE 5.10**

Let's revisit Example 5.9. The discount factors $Z(0, T)$ on March 1, 2001 are in the second column of Table 5.5. We can apply formula in Equation 5.40, obtaining

$$V^{swap}(0; c, T) = 100 - \left(\frac{0.0546}{2} \times 100 \times 8.69 + 0.7628 \times 100 \right) \approx 0 \qquad (5.41)$$

The value of the swap in Example 5.9 is (almost) zero, reflecting the fact that it does not cost anything to enter a swap contract at initiation.

5.4.2 The Swap Rate

How is the swap rate c determined? The contract specification implies that there is no exchange of money at inception of the swap contract. This implies that at inception, the value of the contract is zero. If the swap contract must have zero value at initiation of the contract, Equation 5.39 immediately provides a rule to determine the value of the swap rate c.

Fact 5.11 *The swap rate c is given by that number that makes $V^{swap}(0; c, T)$ in Equation 5.39 equal to zero. Rewriting the equation generically for any payment frequency n and*

Table 5.5   LIBOR Discounts and Swap Curve on March 1, 2001

Maturity T	$Z(0,T)$	Swap Curve
0.5	0.9758	4.951
1.0	0.9527	4.910
1.5	0.9289	4.980
2.0	0.9050	5.050
2.5	0.8808	5.135
3.0	0.8565	5.220
3.5	0.8327	5.285
4.0	0.8090	5.350
4.5	0.7858	5.405
5.0	0.7628	5.460

Data Source: Federal Reserve.

payment dates $T_1, \ldots T_M$, we have

$$V^{swap}(0; c, T) = 100 - \left(\frac{c}{n} \times 100 \times \sum_{j=1}^{M} Z(0, T_j) + Z(0, T_M) \times 100 \right) \quad (5.42)$$

Solving this equation for c we find

$$c = n \times \left(\frac{1 - Z(0, T_M)}{\sum_{j=1}^{M} Z(0, T_j)} \right) \quad (5.43)$$

As it can be seen, Equation 5.43 provides a relatively simple rule to compute the swap rate, given a discount curve $Z(0, T_j)$ for the payment dates T_j.

■ **EXAMPLE 5.11**

In Example 5.10, given the discount factors in the second column of Table 5.5, the swap rate 5.46% makes the swap value equal to zero. Thus, $c = 5.46\%$ is exactly the proper swap rate, as it would be quoted by the bank in Example 5.9.

5.4.3   The Swap Curve

What are the appropriate discount factors $Z(t, T)$ to price swaps? Over the years, the swap market grew so much that market forces determine the swap rate for every possible future maturity. For instance, if corporations fear an increase in short-term rates and decide to move to fixed rate financing, they may increase the demand for fixed-for-floating swaps, in which they pay a fixed rate. This is equivalent to them selling fixed rate bonds, with the implication that the price of fixed rate bonds decreases. That is, to keep the value of swaps at par, the implicit coupon, the swap rates c, must increase. This increase in swap rates in turn affects the time value of money, and thus the discount factors $Z(t, T_j)$ that are implicit in swaps.

Definition 5.7 *The* **swap curve** *at time t is the set of swap rates (at time t) for all maturities T_1, T_2, ..., T_M. We denote the swap curve at time t by $c(t, T_i)$ for $i = 1, ..., M$;*

Swap rates are quoted daily by swap dealers for swap contracts up to thirty years to maturity.[7] Given the size of the swap market, the swap curve $c(t, T)$ has become in fact a reference point to determine the time value of money for financial institutions. Indeed, given the set of swap rates $c(t, T_i)$, we can compute the implicit discount factors $Z(t, T_i)$, by applying a bootstrap methodology, similar to the one discussed in Chapter 2, Section 2.4.2 for Treasury bonds, and in Section 5.1.3 for forward rates. Specifically, we can invert Equation 5.43 and find that for $i = 1$

$$Z(t, T_1) = \frac{1}{1 + \frac{c(t, T_1)}{n}} \tag{5.44}$$

while for $i = 2, ..., M$

$$Z(t, T_i) = \frac{1 - \frac{c(t, T_i)}{n} \times \sum_{j=1}^{i-1} Z(t, T_j)}{1 + \frac{c(t, T_i)}{n}} \tag{5.45}$$

■ **EXAMPLE 5.12**

The last column of Table 5.5 contains the swap curve data as of March 1, 2001. What is the zero curve that is implicit in the swap curve? Starting with Equation 5.44, we find

$$Z(0, 0.5) = \frac{1}{1 + \frac{0.04951}{2}} = 0.9758$$

Moving to Equation 5.45 for $i = 2$, we have

$$\begin{aligned} Z(0, 1) &= \frac{1 - \frac{0.0491}{2} \times Z(0, 0.5)}{1 + \frac{0.0491}{2}} \\ &= \frac{1 - 0.02455 \times 0.9758}{1 + 0.02455} \\ &= 0.9527 \end{aligned}$$

Similarly, for $i = 3$, we have

$$\begin{aligned} Z(0, 1.5) &= \frac{1 - \frac{0.0498}{2} \times (Z(0, 0.5) + Z(0, 1))}{1 + \frac{0.0498}{2}} \\ &= \frac{1 - 0.0249 \times (0.9758 + 0.9527)}{1 + 0.0249} \\ &= 0.9289 \end{aligned}$$

and so on. The result is the set of discount factors $Z(0, T)$ in the second column of Table 5.5

---

[7]Daily data are available, for instance, at the Federal Reserve Board Web site: http://www.federalreserve. gov/Releases/h15/data.htm .

5.4.4 The LIBOR Yield Curve and the Swap Spread

The previous section showed the computation of the discount factors $Z(t,T)$ that are implicit in the market swap rates $c(t,T)$. In Chapter 2, Section 2.4.2, we obtained the discount factors $Z(t,T)$ from Treasury bonds. It is a good question to wonder what is the relation between the two. To differentiate between the two types of discount factors, let us denote the discount factors obtained from swap rates as $Z^L(t,T)$, where the superscript "L" stands for "LIBOR": It is customary to refer to the swap-rate implied discount factors as the LIBOR discount, and its term structure as the LIBOR curve. The reason is that the underlying floating rate is the LIBOR.

Panel A of Figure 5.4 shows the Treasury and LIBOR discount factors on January 4, 2005. Panel B plots the continuously compounded zero coupon yields that are implied by the two discount curves in Panel A. Clearly, the LIBOR yield curve is higher than the Treasury yield curve. One of the reasons for this difference is that the LIBOR curves also contain a spread due to the probability of default of swap dealers. This spread is typically very small, but it can become substantial during turbulent periods, such as the credit crisis of 2007 - 2008. The case study at the end of this chapter further illustrates the variation in the swap spread over time, with a particular emphasis to the events in 2007 - 2008.

Figure 5.4   Treasury and Swap Discount and Yield on January 4, 2005

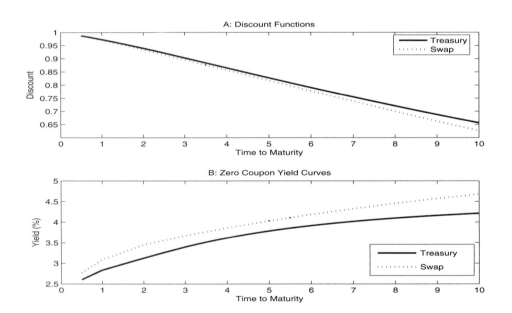

Data Source: Federal Reserve and CRSP.

Panel A of Figure 5.5 plots the 5-year zero coupon yield implied by the swap curve and from the Treasury curve, from 1986 to 2005. Panel B plots the time series of the 5 year swap spread, that is, the difference between the two zero coupon yields. As we can see from both panels, the swap spread varies substantially over time. This variation prompted proprietory trading desks and hedge funds to speculate on the fact that the swap spread is unlikely to become negative, and unlikely to move to infinity. When the swap spread is large, for instance, speculators may bet on the fact that the spread will shrink in the future by taking a short position on the Treasury bonds, and enter in a fixed-for-floating swap, as a fixed rate receiver. We study a swap spread trade in the case analysis at the end of this chapter (see Section 5.8).

Figure 5.5 The 5-year Zero Coupon Treasury and Swap Yield

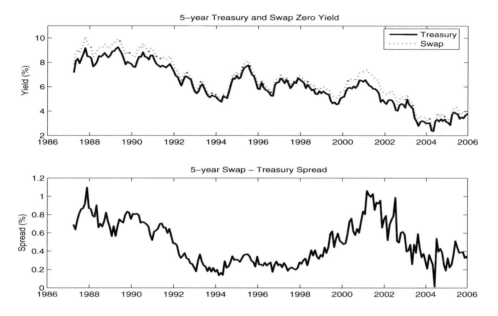

Data Source: Bloomberg and CRSP.

5.4.5 The Forward Swap Contract and the Forward Swap Rate

The same way it is possible to lock in a future interest rate today by entering into a forward rate agreement, it is also possible to lock in a future swap rate by entering into a forward swap contract.

Definition 5.8 *The* **forward swap contract** *is a contract in which two counterparties agree to enter into a swap contract at a predetermined future date and for a predetermined swap rate f^s, called the* **forward swap rate***.*

The next example illustrates the forward swap contract.

■ **EXAMPLE 5.13**

Consider Example 5.9, but assume now that on March 1, 2001, the firm signed a contract to deliver one year later (on March 1, 2002) a large piece of equipment. The payment will be made in 8 equal installments of $5.5 million each over the next 4 years, starting on September 1, 2003. Assume the firm plans to use these cash inflows to meet the payments of a floating rate bond issued some time in the past. As explained in Example 5.9, the firm can enter into a fixed-for-floating swap in which it pays fixed and receives floating. The problem is that the firm will start receiving payments much further in the future, and therefore it will need to enter into such a fixed-for-floating swap one year from now, on March 1, 2002. The firm is worried however that the 4-year swap rate may increase between now and March 1, 2002, an event that may unduly increase its cash outflows from the hedging program. Therefore, the firm decides to enter into a forward contract with a bank, in which the bank and the firm agree *today* that the 4-year swap rate in the future will be $f_2^s = 5.616\%$, to be paid semi-annually in exchange of the 6-month LIBOR.[8]

The question then is the usual: How can the bank commit today to enter into a swap contract in the future at a given swap rate f_2^s? To answer this question, we may recall that the value of a fixed-for-floating swap in which a counterparty receives the fixed rate c can be regarded as a portfolio that is long a coupon bond, with coupon rate c, and short a floating rate bond, that has value of 100 at reset dates. The payoff from entering a forward swap contract is then the same as entering into a forward contract to purchase a fixed rate bond with coupon rate c for par value 100. That is, the payoff from a forward swap is

$$\text{Payoff forward swap} = P_c(T, T^*) - 100 \tag{5.46}$$

where

$$P_c(T, T^*) = \frac{c \times 100}{2} \times \sum_{j=1}^{m} Z(T, T_j) + 100 \times Z(T, T^*)$$

and $T_1, T_2, ..., T_m$ are the swap's reset dates, with $T_m = T^*$.

What is the value today of the payoff in Equation 5.46?

Notice that this payoff is the same as the payoff of a forward contract to receive a coupon bond at T for a delivery price $K = 100$. We discussed the valuation of such a forward contract in Section 5.3.3. Specifically, the value of such forward contract is provided in Equation 5.36 in which the delivery price happens to be equal to par, $K = 100$. The value of the forward swap contract today is then

$$V(0, T) = Z(0, T) \left[P_c^{fwd}(0, T, T^*) - 100 \right] \tag{5.47}$$

where from Equation 5.33

$$P_c^{fwd}(0, T, T^*) = \frac{c \times 100}{2} \times \sum_{j=1}^{m} F(0, T, T^*) + 100 \times F(0, T, T_m) \tag{5.48}$$

While in a standard forward contract the delivery price is chosen to make the value of the forward contract equal to zero at initiation, in a forward swap contract it is the swap rate c that is chosen to make the value of the forward contract equal to zero. Thus, we must look for c such that $V(0, T) = 0$ in Equation 5.47. This condition implies

$$\frac{c \times 100}{2} \times \sum_{j=1}^{m} F(0, T, T_j) + 100 \times F(0, T, T^*) = 100 \tag{5.49}$$

---

[8] As usual, the subscript "2" denotes the semi-annual compounding frequency.

Solving for c, and denoting the result as the forward swap rate $f_2^s(0, T, T^*)$, we obtain

$$f_2^s(0, T, T^*) = 2 \times \frac{1 - F(0, T, T^*)}{\sum_{j=1}^m F(0, T, T_j)} \tag{5.50}$$

Comparing Equation 5.50 with Equation 5.43 (for $n = 2$), we see that the forward swap rate is the swap rate that is implicit in the forward curve. That is, in the same way we obtain the current swap rate from the discount curve $Z(0, T_j)$, we can compute the the forward swap rate from the forward discount curve $F(0, T, T_j)$. We summarize this result next for future reference:

Fact 5.12 *The* **forward swap rate** *of a forward swap contract to enter into a swap at time T, with maturity T^*, payment frequency n, and payment dates T_1, T_2,...,T_m (with $T_m = T^*$) is given by*

$$f_n^s(0, T, T^*) = n \times \frac{1 - F(0, T, T)}{\sum_{j=1}^m F(0, T, T_j)} \tag{5.51}$$

■ **EXAMPLE 5.14**

Returning to Example 5.13, we can use the LIBOR discount data in Table 5.5, reported also in the Column 2 of Table 5.6, to compute the forward swap rate to enter on March 1, 2002 (one year from now) into a 4-year swap. For every $T_j = 1.5, 2, ...,$ 5, we can compute the forward discount factor

$$F(0, 1, T_j) = \frac{Z(0, T_j)}{Z(0, 1)}$$

This calculation is in Column 3 of Table 5.6. Applying the formula in Equation 5.50 we obtain

$$f_2^s(0, 1, 5) = 5.616\%$$

5.4.6 Payment Frequency and Day Count Conventions

In the previous sections we considered the case in which the two counterparties make payments at the same time, for instance, every six months. Many swap contracts, however, have payment dates at different frequency. For instance, a commonly used fixed-for-floating contract specifies that the floating rate is tied to the 3-month LIBOR and pays at a quarterly frequency, while the fixed rate counterparty pays at a semi-annual frequency. Different frequencies in payments pose no particular problems in the valuation of swaps, because the value of a swap is given by the difference in value between the floating leg and the fixed leg, and we are able to value them independently. The case study in Section 5.8 at the end of this chapter further discusses this issue.

One more issue to explore concerns the day count conventions used in the computation of cash flows. In the previous section we implicitly assumed an actual/actual convention, for simplicity. To be precise, the floating leg uses the actual/360 day count convention,

Table 5.6 LIBOR Discounts and Forward Discounts on March 1, 2001

Maturity T	$Z(0,T)$	$F(0,1,T)$
0.5	0.9758	-
1.0	0.9527	-
1.5	0.9289	0.9750
2.0	0.9050	0.9499
2.5	0.8808	0.9245
3.0	0.8565	0.8990
3.5	0.8327	0.8740
4.0	0.8090	0.8492
4.5	0.7858	0.8248
5.0	0.7628	0.8007

Data Source: Federal Reserve.

while the fixed leg uses the 30/360 day count convention. Therefore, a little adjustment to the payoffs has to be made. Although day count conventions are important in order to compute the exact values of fixed income securities and for day-to-day trading, we will often abstract from these institutional details in our calculations. The reason is that they distract the attention from more fundamental concepts in fixed income, such as no arbitrage and the relative values of fixed income instruments. The understanding of the risk and return of fixed income instruments and the forces that keep their prices close to each other is far more important than delving into the day count conventions, or other minor institutional details, which computers compute automatically anyway. To put it differently, it is unlikely that financial institutions may be at risk of losing billion of dollars because of the misunderstanding of day count conventions, but it is likely they may face these risks if they do not understand the rules of arbitrage and the fundamental variations of fixed income instruments.

5.5 INTEREST RATE RISK MANAGEMENT USING DERIVATIVE SECURITIES

Derivatives such as interest rate forwards and swaps are particularly useful in performing an effective interest rate risk management. We already illustrated the use of these securities in risk management in Examples 5.1 to 5.9. In this section we extend the concepts discussed in Chapter 3 to illustrate some of the uses of derivatives for asset-liability management or duration matching. Indeed, we now show that by carefully choosing the characteristics of the derivative security, the duration of a portfolio that contains the derivative security can be tailored with a great deal of accuracy to the needs of a corporation.

Section 3.4 in Chapter 3 introduces the issue of asset-liability duration mismatch. We can use derivatives, such as forwards and swaps, to effectively perform duration matching strategies. In fact, Example 5.9 illustrates exactly such a duration mismatch: The firm in that example is paying a floating rate on its bonds, but it is receiving a fixed coupon from the receivables. That is, it effectively has a duration mismatch, featuring assets with long duration and liabilities with short duration. As the example illustrates, a carefully crafted fixed-for-floating swap is able to completely eliminate the duration mismatch, as the firm's total net cash flows are exactly zero.

As discussed in Section 3.4 in Chapter 3, corporations and financial institutions have very complex assets and liabilities. In this case, an immunization strategy is better suited to deal with a potential duration mismatch. In particular, a financial institution may then use derivative securities to close the duration gap. For instance, a fixed-for-floating swap does not cost anything to enter into, but it can dramatically change the duration of a portfolio.

More specifically, since a swap can be considered a long-short portfolio (long a floating rate bond and short a fixed rate bond), as discussed in Chapter 3, Example 3.6, the dollar duration of the swap can be computed as

$$D_{swap}^{\$} = D_{floating}^{\$} - D_{fixed}^{\$}$$

where $D_{fixed}^{\$}$ and $D_{floating}^{\$}$ are the dollar durations of the fixed and floating bonds that are underlying the swap. Denoting N the notional on the swap, we may choose the notional amount so that the duration of equity is zero, that is, such that a parallel shift in the term structure has no impact on the equity value. This objective is accomplished if the following equation holds:

$$D_{E}^{\$} = D_{A}^{\$} + N D_{swap}^{\$} - D_{L}^{\$} = 0 \qquad (5.52)$$

We now illustrate the use of swaps for asset-liability management in the next example.

■ **EXAMPLE 5.15**

Consider Example 3.11 in Chapter 3. That example, recall, involves a hypothetical financial institution with a total asset size of around \$2.4 billion and assets' dollar duration of \$19.74 billion. The firm has also total liabilities at \$1.8 billion with a liabilities' dollar duration of only \$5 billion. The market value of equity is \$600 million, but with a dollar duration is \$14.740 billion. The implications of this mismatch between the assets and liabilities dollar durations is that a parallel upward shift in interest rates of 1% generates a decline in assets far greater than in liabilities, implying an equity decline of \$147.4 million. In percentage, this corresponds to a 24% decline in market value of equity.

How can derivatives, and in particular swaps, help stabilize the value of equity?

Assume that the term structure of interest rates is flat at 4% (semi-annually compounded). In this case, the current swap rate is also 4%. By using the same steps as in Example 3.6 in Chapter 3, the dollar duration of a fixed-for-floating swap (receiving fixed) can be found to be \$784 for \$100 of notional.[9] Clearly, the financial institution has a duration of assets that is higher than the one of its liabilities, and therefore would like to enter into a swap in which it *pays* fixed and receives floating, which has the opposite duration of −\$784 (per \$100 notional). From Equation 5.52, we can choose the notional N to make the dollar duration of equity $D_{E}^{\$} = 0$. The notional that solves the equation is \$1.889 billion.

[9]The long-short portfolio strategy in Example 3.6 in Chapter 3 exactly represents a fixed-for-floating swap.

5.6 SUMMARY

In this chapter, we covered the following topics:

1. Forward discount factors: This is the discount factor implicit in the current yield curve to discount dollars in the far future to the nearer future, but not today. It provides the "exchange rate" between dollars at T_2 for dollars at $T_1 < T_2$.

2. Forward rate: The forward rate is an interest rate implicit in the current term structure of interest rates determining the fair rate of interest for an investment (or a loan) at a future date T_1 with payment at a later date T_2. It is determined by the forward discount factor.

3. Forward rate agreement (FRA): A FRA is a contract between two counterparties to exchange one cash flow in the future, namely, the forward rate in exchange of the future spot rate. Forward rate agreements are widely used to hedge againsts variations in interest rates.

4. Forward contract: This is a contract between two counterparties in which they agree that at some predetermined date, they will exchange a security, such as a Treasury note, for a cash price that is also predetermined at initiation of the contract. Forward contracts are equivalent to forward rate agrements.

5. Swap: A swap is a contract between two counterparties to exchange cash flows in the future. In a fixed-for-floating swap a counterparty pays a fixed coupon while the other pays a rate linked to a floating rate, typically the LIBOR rate. The fixed rate is called the swap rate, and it is set at initiation of the contract so that the value of the swap is zero.

6. Swap curve: The relation between swap rates and the maturity of the underlying swap is called the swap curve.

7. LIBOR curve: The discount curve implicit in LIBOR based instruments, such as swaps, differs from the Treasury curve as it embeds the risk of default of swap counterparties.

8. Forward swap contract: A contract between two counterparties in which they agree to enter into a given swap contract in the future, with a predetermined swap rate, called the forward swap rate, and has a predetermined maturity.

5.7 EXERCISES

1. On May 15, 2000 the term structure of interest rates is as shown in Table 5.7. Compute the discount factors $Z(0, T)$, the forward discount factors $F(0, T - \Delta, T)$, and the forward rates $f(0, T - \Delta, T)$, where $\Delta = 0.25$.

2. Table 5.8 contains the continuously compounded forward rates $f(0, T - \Delta, T)$, where $\Delta = 0.25$. The first entry is the current spot rate, as for $T = 0.25$ we have $f(0, 0, 0.25) = r(0, 0.25)$. Compute the forward discount factors $F(0, T - \Delta, T)$, the current discount factors $Z(0, T)$, and the current term structure of interest rates.

Table 5.7   The Term Structure of Interest Rates on May 15, 2000

Maturity	Yield (c.c.)	Maturity	Yield (c.c.)	Maturity	Yield (c.c.)
0.25	6.17%	2.75	6.78%	5.25	6.71%
0.50	6.52%	3.00	6.76%	5.50	6.63%
0.75	6.32%	3.25	6.77%	5.75	6.69%
1.00	6.71%	3.50	6.76%	6.00	6.62%
1.25	6.76%	3.75	6.63%	6.25	6.63%
1.50	6.79%	4.00	6.77%	6.50	6.61%
1.75	6.77%	4.25	6.77%	6.75	6.58%
2.00	6.72%	4.50	6.71%	7.00	6.57%
2.25	6.72%	4.75	6.66%		
2.50	6.79%	5.00	6.70%		

Notes: Yields calculated based on data from CRSP.

Table 5.8   A Term Structure of Forward Rates

Maturity	Forward Rate	Maturity	Forward Rate	Maturity	Forward Rate
0.25	3.53%	2.75	6.09%	5.25	6.12%
0.50	3.58%	3.00	5.29%	5.50	5.70%
0.75	4.19%	3.25	6.48%	5.75	6.81%
1.00	3.99%	3.50	6.20%	6.00	6.50%
1.25	4.54%	3.75	6.34%	6.25	6.59%
1.50	5.00%	4.00	6.00%	6.50	7.06%
1.75	4.76%	4.25	5.99%	6.75	6.87%
2.00	5.88%	4.50	6.58%	7.00	6.37%
2.25	5.30%	4.75	6.26%		
2.50	4.92%	5.00	6.69%		

Table 5.9 Two Discount Curves

August 15, 2000		November 15, 2000	
Maturity	$Z(0,T)$	Maturity	$Z(0,T)$
0.25	0.9844	0.25	0.9848
0.50	0.9690	0.50	0.9692
0.75	0.9531	0.75	0.9545
1.00	0.9386	1.00	0.9402

Source: Bloomberg.

3. Today is May 15, 2000 and the continuously compounded term structure of interest rate is shown in Table 5.7. You are faced with the two investment strategies below. Is there an arbitrage opportunity?

- Invest $100 million in 2.5-year zero coupon bonds.

- Invest $100 million in a 1-year zero coupon bond and agree with the bank to invest the proceeds for the following 1.5 years at the quoted forward rate, which is: $f_2(0, 1, 2.5) = 7.56\%$.

4. On May 15, 2000 you enter into a 1-year forward rate agreement (FRA) with a bank for the period starting November 15, 2000 to May 15, 2001. You know that currently the price of the 6-month zero coupon is $96.79 and the price of the 1-year zero coupon is $93.51.

   (a) What is the agreed-upon forward rate in the transaction?

   (b) What is the value of the forward at inception?

5. Consider Exercise 4 again. Three months later (August 15, 2000) you have second thoughts and consider that maybe you should get out of the transaction. You receive the data in the first two columns of Table 5.9.

   (a) What is the value of the FRA on August 15, 2000?

   (b) Consider now November 15, 2000.

      i. What is the value of the FRA now?

      ii. What is the 6-month semi-annual rate?

      iii. What will the balance to be paid be at the end of the FRA?

6. On May 15, 2000, a company is interested in purchasing $50 million worth of 1 1/2-year zero coupon Treasuries with the proceeds of a sale of equipment to take place in 6 months. The company is interested in locking in the price of the Treasuries today through a forward contract. Use the data in Table 5.10 to answer the following:

   - What would the forward price be of the Treasuries?

   - How many bonds will the company purchase?

Table 5.10   Two Discount Curves

May 15, 2000		November 15, 2000	
Maturity	$Z(t,T)$	Maturity	$Z(t,T)$
0.25	0.9847	0.25	0.9848
0.50	0.9679	0.50	0.9692
0.75	0.9537	0.75	0.9545
1.00	0.9351	1.00	0.9402
1.25	0.9189	1.25	0.9269
1.50	0.9031	1.50	0.9147
1.75	0.8882	1.75	0.9023
2.00	0.8742	2.00	0.8897

Data Source: CRSP.

7. Consider Exercise 6. Six months have now passed so that today is November 15, 2000. You want to calculate the payoff from being long the forward contract. Using the data in Table 5.10 answer the following

   (a) What is the amount of the payoff if you are long the forward contract?

   (b) Do you make money or lose money?

8. Consider the following transaction:

   (a) On June 30, 2008 a financial institution purchases $100 million worth of a 2-year Treasury note paying a 2.88% coupon priced at $100.50. At the same time the financial institution enters into a forward contract with the seller of the Treasury note in which it will sell the same T-note three months later (no accrued interest payments will be made). Use the (continuously compounded) yield curve on June 30, 2008 in Table 5.11 to answer the following:

      i. How many bonds does the financial institution purchase?

      ii. What is the quoted price for the Treasuries in three months?

   (b) Recall the definition of a repo agreement (Chapter 1). In this transaction the buyer agrees to acquire a security and to resell it to the seller at a specified time. This is similar to the outright purchase of a Treasury plus the forward contract.

      i. Calculate the implied repo rate for this security.

      ii. The actual 3-month repo rate for June 30, 2008 was 2.05%. Is this the same as the implied repo rate you calculated? Explain.

      iii. Assuming that this is a pure arbitrage opportunity, what steps would the financial institution have to follow to take advantage of it?

      iv. Is the implied repo rate the same as the return on investing in a 3-month bond?

   (c) Consider the following: The repo agreement simply uses the security as collateral and does not depend on the maturity of the bond, yet the transaction we described depends on the maturity, since it affects both the spot price on the bond and the forward price. Additionally, there are coupon payments in this

Table 5.11   The Yield Curve on June 30, 2008

Maturity	0.25	0.5	0.75	1	1.25	1.5	1.75	2
Yield (c.c.)	1.71%	2.09%	2.29%	2.37%	2.32%	2.38%	2.48%	2.61%

Source: Bloomberg.

Table 5.12   The Yield Curve on May 5, 2008

Maturity	0.25	0.5	0.75	1	1.25	1.5	1.75	2
Yield (c.c.)	2.70%	2.76%	2.86%	2.95%	3.09%	2.98%	3.07%	3.20%

Source: Bloomberg.

bond which also affect the value of the spot price and the forward price. It seems paradoxical that while the repo rate depends only on the length of the loan, the equivalent transaction takes into account maturity of the collateral (Treasury) and its coupon payments.

   i. Compute the implied 3-month repo rate using a 2-year zero coupon bond (obtain the spot and forward prices from the discounts you obtain from the yields).

   ii. Compute the implied 3-month repo rate using all zero coupon securities with maturities from 3 months up to 1-3/4 years.

   iii. Does the implied repo rate change? Why or why not?

9. Today is May 5, 2008, and the (continuously compounded) yield curve is given in Table 5.12. Calculate the semi-annual swap rate for all maturities between 6 months and 2 years (every six months).

10. Today is January 2, 2008. The LIBOR curve is shown in the first column of Table 5.13. You decide to enter into a 1-year fixed-for-floating swap agreement with quarterly payments and $100 million notional.

   (a) What is the 1-year swap rate for a quarterly fixed-for-floating swap?

   (b) What is the value of the agreement at inception?

   (c) Calculate the value of the swap for each one of the subsequent dates in Table 5.13.

11. As of December 2, 2008, the 30-year swap spread had been negative for a whole month. In particular, on that day, the 3-month repo rate was 0.5%, the LIBOR rate was 2.21%, the 30-year swap rate was 2.85%, and the semi-annually compounded yield-to-maturity of the 4.5% Treasury bond maturing on May 15, 2038 was 3.18%.

   (a) Is there an arbitrage? Discuss the swap spread trade that you would set up to take advantage of these rates.

Table 5.13   The LIBOR Curve: January, 2008 – October, 2008

Months	2-Jan	1-Feb	3-Mar	1-Apr	1-May	2-Jun	1-Jul	1-Aug	1-Sep	1-Oct
1	4.57%	3.14%	3.09%	2.70%	2.72%	2.46%	2.46%	2.46%	2.49%	4.00%
2	4.64%	3.11%	3.04%	2.69%	2.76%	2.57%	2.65%	2.66%	2.68%	4.05%
3	4.68%	3.10%	3.01%	2.68%	2.78%	2.68%	2.79%	2.79%	2.81%	4.15%
4	4.65%	3.07%	2.97%	2.66%	2.82%	2.75%	2.89%	2.89%	2.94%	4.09%
5	4.61%	3.05%	2.91%	2.64%	2.85%	2.83%	3.01%	3.00%	3.02%	4.07%
6	4.57%	3.02%	2.86%	2.62%	2.88%	2.90%	3.12%	3.08%	3.11%	4.04%
7	4.50%	2.97%	2.81%	2.58%	2.90%	2.94%	3.15%	3.10%	3.12%	4.04%
8	4.42%	2.92%	2.76%	2.54%	2.92%	2.98%	3.19%	3.12%	3.14%	4.04%
9	4.35%	2.88%	2.71%	2.51%	2.93%	3.02%	3.22%	3.14%	3.15%	4.04%
10	4.29%	2.85%	2.68%	2.50%	2.95%	3.06%	3.25%	3.17%	3.16%	4.04%
11	4.24%	2.83%	2.65%	2.48%	2.97%	3.10%	3.29%	3.20%	3.18%	4.04%
12	4.19%	2.82%	2.63%	2.47%	2.98%	3.14%	3.32%	3.22%	3.20%	4.04%

Source: Bloomberg.

(b) Assuming that the U.S. government is less likely to default than swap dealers, how can you rationalize these rates? What risks would setting up this trade involve? Discuss. (Recall that there was an ongoing credit crisis).

5.8   CASE STUDY: PIVE CAPITAL SWAP SPREAD TRADES

On June 30, 2006 PiVe Capital[10] û- a small hedge fund û- was looking to make a profit on the swap spread. The swap spread is the difference in coupon from a swap and a Treasury, and it is present because of the higher probability of default of a swap counterparty than that of the government. Although it varies significantly over time, as Figure 5.5 shows, whenever it is positive it implies that receiving fixed from the swap and shorting the Treasury would generate a positive cash flow over time. Clearly, this is only one side (the fixed side). The second part has to do with floating rates. To receive fixed coupons in the swap, the fund has to pay LIBOR over time, which must be taken into account in the trade. However, partly offsetting this cash outflow, PiVe Capital can short the Treasury note through the repo market in a reverse repo transaction,[11] thereby obtaining the repo rate from a repo dealer as an inflow of cash.

More specifically, on June 30, 2006 the market presented the following data:[12]

- 3-month LIBOR: 5.5081%.

- 3-month repo rate: 5.27%.

- 5-year swap rate: 5.69%.

- 5-year T-note with a 5.125% coupon priced at $100.1172.

[10]This is a fictituous name. Any reference to existing companies is purely coincidental.

[11]See Chapter 1 and the Orange County case in Chapter 3.

[12]LIBOR, Repo and Swap rate data are from Bloomberg. Treasury securities data are excerpted from CRSP (Daily Treasuries) © 2009 Center for Research in Security Prices (CRSP), The University of Chicago Booth School of Business.

Table 5.14   3-month LIBOR - Repo Spread Distribution: January, 2000 - June, 20006

					Percentiles					
Mean	St.Dev.	1%	5%	10%	25%	50%	75%	90%	95%	99%
0.21%	.07%	0.05%	0.13%	0.14%	0.17%	0.20%	0.25%	0.29%	0.31%	0.37%

Data Source: Bloomberg.

The swap spread is typically computed by comparing the yield to maturity of the Treasury note with the swap rate of the same maturity. The yield to maturity of the 5-year T-note can be computed using the formula in Equation 2.30 in Chapter 2, that is, by solving for y in the formula

$$100.1172 = 100 \times \left[\frac{c}{2} \times \sum_{j=1}^{10} \frac{1}{(1+y/2)^j} + \frac{1}{(1+y/2)^{10}} \right]$$

We obtain $y = 5.10\%$, implying that the spread is

$$SS = 5.69\% - 5.10\% = 0.59\%$$

or 59 basis points. That is, receiving the fixed rate from the swap and paying the yield in short T-notes would return 59 basis points per year.

To secure this return of 59 basis points, PiVe Capital has to pay the LIBOR rate, as part of the swap, and receives the repo rate, as part of the reverse repo transaction. The spread between LIBOR and repo (LRS) is

$$LRS = 5.5081\% - 5.27\% = 0.2381\%$$

The net spread is $SS - LRS = 35.19$ bps. This spread is not as large as it had been in the past, but the LIBOR-repo spread has been historically relatively stable at around 21 bps and so this net spread ($SS - LRS$) still appears a relatively safe trade. Indeed, using daily data from January 2000 to June 2006, the distribution of the LIBOR-repo spread is shown in Table 5.14. According to historical data, then, the mean LRS was 21 bps, and the median (50% percentile) was 20 bps. In addition, the 95 and 99 percentiles were still only 31 bps and 37 bps, respectively. That is, there is only 1% probability that the LRS would be above 37 basis points. Even in these extreme circumstances, the net spread would be at least $0.59\% - 0.37\% = 22$ bps, still a relatively good spread. Moreover, there are solid chances that the LRS would decline, as its 10% percentile is only 14 bps.

PiVe Capital finally decided that, given historical trends, the net spread was high enough. To recap, in order to reap these benefits PiVe must enter into the following transactions:

1. Short the 5-year bond through a reverse repo transaction. In cash flow terms, the fund would receive the repo rate and pay the coupon.

2. Enter into a fixed-for-floating swap, in which PiVe would receive fixed and pay LIBOR.

5.8.1 Setting Up the Trade

5.8.1.1 *Reverse Repo*   PiVe Capital wants to set up a $100 million trade. Because the T-note trades at $100.1172, it will need to sell

$$N = \frac{\$100\text{million}}{100.1172} = 998,829 \text{ Treasury notes (for \$100 par value)} \qquad (5.53)$$

Assuming zero haircut for simplicity, PiVe Capital then borrows $N = 998,829$ 5-year T-notes from the repo dealer, sells them in the cash market for $100 million, and gives this cash to the repo dealer. Assume PiVe enters into a term reverse repo with 3-months maturity. After three months, then, the repo dealer will have to pay PiVe Capital $100 million × Repo rate, where the repo rate $= 5.27\%$, as above. At this time, if PiVe Capital wants to keep the short position in the T-note, it must roll over the reverse repo position with the repo dealer. Since in the meantime the price of the T-note will have changed, likely the amount of cash with the repo dealer would have changed as well. Assume for simplicity that the two counterparties simply roll over the $100 million loan for an additional three months, irrespective of the price of the T-note. This simplifying assumption allows us to better compare the reverse repo transaction to the fixed-for-floating swap, described below.

Because the repo dealer keeps the $100 million at every reset date (i.e., every three months), the total cash flow to PiVe Capital every quarter is

$$\text{Reverse repo CF}(t) = \begin{cases} \frac{\$100 \text{ mm}}{4} \times r(t-0.25) - N \times 100 \times \frac{5.125\%}{2} & \text{if } t \text{ is a coupon} \\ \frac{\$100 \text{ mm}}{4} \times r(t-0.25) & \text{date otherwise} \end{cases}$$

where N is the number of 5-year T-notes, 5.125% is the T-note coupon rate, and $r(t)$ denotes the 3-month repo rate. Note that to keep things simple, we approximate the quarter by "1/4" for the computation of repo cash flows, and the semester by "1/2" for the computation of the T-note cash flows. In reality, the day count convention for repo rates is Actual/360, and the day count convention for T-notes is Actual/Actual, and so some adjustments to the cash flows would be necessary.

5.8.1.2 *Fixed-for-Floating Swap*   PiVe Capital has to enter into a 5-year, fixed-for-floating swap in which it pays the 3-month LIBOR rate and receives the 5-year fixed swap rate. In a plain vanilla fixed-for-floating swap, the floating payments occur at quarterly frequency, while the fixed payments occur at semi-annual frequency, therefore exactly matching the payment frequency of the reverse repo transaction discussed earlier. The swap cash flows are then given by

$$\text{Swap CF}(t) = \begin{cases} \$100 \text{ mm} \times \frac{5.69\%}{2} - \frac{\$100 \text{ mm}}{4} \times \ell(t-0.25) & \text{if } t \text{ is fixed payment date} \\ -\frac{\$100 \text{ mm}}{4} \times \ell(t-0.25) & \text{otherwise} \end{cases}$$

where $\ell(t)$ is the 3-month LIBOR rate at time t. Again we approximate the quarter by "1/4," instead of Actual/360 for LIBOR. The fixed component of swaps is on 30/360 basis, and so "1/2" is the correct value in this case.

5.8.2   The Quarterly Cash Flow

What is the quarterly cash flow of the trade? It is useful to decompose the quarterly cash flow in two components, the swap spread (SS) component and the LIBOR-repo spread (LRS) component. We know that every six months, the swap spread component of the cash flow is

$$
\begin{aligned}
\text{SS CF every six months} \quad &= \quad \$100 \text{ mm} \times \frac{5.69\%}{2} - N \times 100 \times \frac{5.125\%}{2} \\
&= \quad \$285,499.73
\end{aligned}
$$

where N is the number of T-notes that PiVe Capital shorted. This cash flow is fixed and accrues every six months. It does not depend on extant interest rates, and it will keep flowing to PiVe Capital until maturity.

The second component is the LIBOR-repo spread, which every quarter is given by

$$
\text{LRS CF every three months} \quad = \quad \frac{\$100 \text{ mm}}{4} \times (r(t - 0.25) - \ell(t - 0.25))
$$

where we recall that $r(t)$ denotes the repo rate at t and $\ell(t)$ the LIBOR rate at t. As mentioned, on June 30 the $r(0) = 5.27\%$ while $\ell(0) = 5.5081\%$, implying an initial cash flow In September 30, 2006 equal to

$$
\text{LRS CF on September 30, 2006} = -\$59,525.00 \tag{5.54}
$$

Since the LIBOR-repo spread is relatively stable, PiVe Capital expected to receive approximately

$$
\begin{aligned}
\text{Total expected net cash flow per year} \quad &= \quad 2 \times \$230,499.43 - 4 \times \$59,525.00 \\
&= \quad \$699,098.85
\end{aligned}
$$

Indeed, for the first year, things seem to play out well. Figure 5.6 shows the net cash flows per quarter (the vertical bars) as well as the cumulative cash flows from the start of the trade (the solid line).

The first shock however was in December 2007, when the total net cash flow, albeit positive, was much smaller than before. On March 2008 the net cash flow, which was only given by the LIBOR-repo spread component, was substantially negative, eating up most of the cumulative cash flows made so far by PiVe Capital. On June 30, 2008 matters did not improve, as the total inflow from the swap spread coupons was almost entirely paid in the LIBOR-repo spread. In September 30, 2008 the last cash flow was extremely negative, dragging to negative the entire cumulative sums.

What happened? Figure 5.7 plots the daily swap spread[13] and LIBOR-repo spread from July, 2000 to June, 2008 at the daily frequency. The first dashed vertical line corresponds to June 30, 2006, the beginning of the trade. As mentioned, the LIBOR-repo spread had been relatively stable before June, 2006, and (almost) always below 50 bps for the entire sample. The swap spread on June 30, 2006 was at the peak of recent years, although still lower than its peak in 2000. Recall though that the movement of the swap spread itself is

---

[13]The swap spread in this figure is computed as the difference between the 5-year constant maturity rate from the Federal Reserve Board and the 5-year swap rate. Data are from the Federal Reserve.

Figure 5.6 Net Cash Flows from Swap Spread Trade

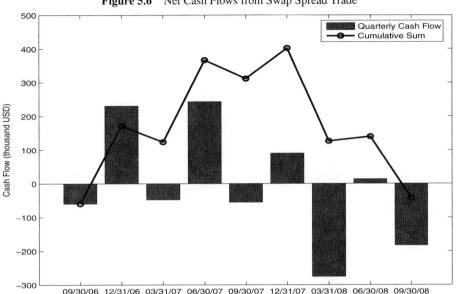

not affecting the cash flows after the initiation of the trade, because both the swap rate and the coupon are then fixed. The horizontal line in the figure indeed denotes the 59 basis points that PiVe Capital would make annually from the difference between the fixed swap rate and the fixed coupon.

The problem was that the credit crisis that started in August of 2007 unexpectedly pushed up the LIBOR-repo spread to an unprecedented 1.2%. Because borrowing and lending in the LIBOR market is on an uncollateralized basis, fear of counterparty default and the ensuing credit crunch made the LIBOR rate diverge substantially from the repo rate. The latter is in fact perceived as a "safer" rate, as it is collateralized. Unfortunately, PiVe Capital had to pay LIBOR and receive repo, and the large spread generated a significant outflow of money over time. Note that the LIBOR rate in fact decreased in August and September, as a result of the Federal Reserve cut of its reference interest rates. Yet, the spread is what matters for PiVe, and not the level of the LIBOR per se.

5.8.3 Unwinding the Position?

Given the large quarterly payments due to the increase in the LIBOR-repo spread, the principals of PiVe Capital started thinking about whether they should unwind their position. The first question, of course, would be whether such an unwind of the reverse repo and the swap would generate a net inflow or outflow of cash. We now compute the value of the reverse repo and of the swap to calculate the total value of the trade. The latter determines whether unwinding the position would generate a net inflow (i.e. a capital gain) or an outflow (i.e. a capital loss).

5.8.3.1 The Value of the Reverse Repo Given our assumptions, computing the value of the reverse repo position at every quarter t is relatively straightforward: Because we assume that PiVe Capital and the repo dealer simply roll over the $100 million loan

Figure 5.7   The Swap Spread and LIBOR-Repo Spread

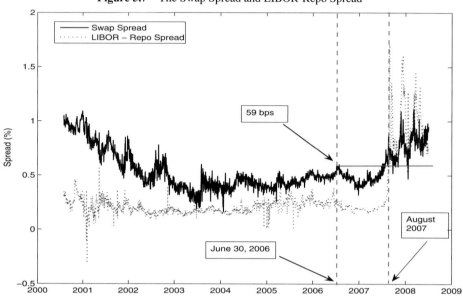

Source: Federal Reserve and Bloomberg.

every quarter, the "value" of the repo position on rollover quarter t after the payment of interest and coupon (if any) is

$$\text{Value reverse repo at } t = \$100\text{mm} - N \times P_{note}(t, T)$$

where $P_{note}(t, T)$ is the value of the T-note at time t. This is given by the quoted value plus accrued interest. Between rollover quarters, a little adjustment has to be made to the value of the $100 million loan, as by closing the position PiVe Capital would receive any accrued interest on the repo position, which depends on the repo rate determined on the last rollover date.

The dotted line in Panel A of Figure 5.8 shows the value of the reverse repo. After June, 2006 the T-note increased in value quite substantially, pushing the value of the reverse repo down into negative territory. As mentioned, under these circumstances the repo dealer would likely request PiVe Capital to post additional collateral. The dotted line can then be interpreted simply as the additional collateral that PiVe Capital has to post over time.

5.8.3.2   *The Value of the Fixed-for-Floating Swap*   The value of the swap at initiation is zero, as the swap rate $c = 5.69\%$ is the rate that makes the swap value zero. However, as time passes and interest rates fluctuate, the value of the swap changes as well, as discussed in Section 5.4.1. In particular, from Equation 5.39 we have that the value of the swap at any time t is given by

$$\text{Value swap at } t = P_{FR}(t, T) - P_c(t, T)$$

where $P_{FR}(t, T)$ is the value of a quarterly floating rate bond at time t with maturity date T, and quarterly coupons equal to the 3-month LIBOR. $P_c(t, T)$ is the value of a fixed rate coupon bond with maturity T and semi-annual coupons equal to the swap rate, namely $c = 5.69\%$.

In Section 2.5 in Chapter 2 we discuss how to price floating rate bonds. In particular, recall that at reset dates $P_{FR}(t,T) = \$100$, while between reset dates we must also consider the present value of the next coupon, now fixed at the LIBOR determined on the past reset date. The fixed coupon bond can be computed using the usual formula

$$P_c(t,T) = \frac{100 \times 5.69\%}{2} \times \sum_{i=1}^{n_t} Z(t,T_i) + 100 \times Z(t,T_{n_t})$$

where n_t is the number of payments remaining at time t, T_i are the payment dates, and $Z(t,T_i)$ is the discount curve. The last issue is what discount curve $Z(t,T_i)$ should we use? Because we are pricing a swap, using the swap curve appears the most reasonable methodology. To do so, every t we can recompute the discount curve $Z(t,T_i)$ from the quoted swap rates. In particular, we use the bootstrap procedure in Equations 5.44 and 5.45. More specifically, we use data on LIBOR rates for maturities up to 6 months, and then, given $Z(t, t+0.5)$, we can apply Equation 5.45 to obtain the curve from quoted swap rates. Figure 5.9 plots the term structure of interest rates from June 30, 2006 to June 30, 2008. As can be seen, the LIBOR curve was essentially flat on June 30, 2006, but it dropped dramatically in August 2007 and especially in January 2008.

The solid line in Panel A of Figure 5.8 plots the value of the swap over time. Because PiVe Capital is long the coupon bond implicit in the swap, the value of the swap increases over time, as the (average) yield curve decreases. If at any point PiVe Capital decides to close the swap position, the solid line represents the inflow of money that it would receive at that time.

5.8.3.3 *Aggregate Value*

As mentioned in the previous section, in December 2007, PiVe Capital would suffer the first big cash flow decrease. This cash flow is still positive, as the semi-annual coupon spread remains higher than the *quarterly* LIBOR-repo spread, but it is much smaller than in the past. Note that the cash flow realized in December 2007 depends on quantities determined in September 2007. Thus, PiVe Capital could forecast this shortfall three months in advance. If it wanted to get out of the position, it would have to close the swap and close the repo transaction. Panel B of Figure 5.8 shows the sum of the swap value and the reverse repo value, which corresponds to the total amount Pive Capital would receive or pay if it wanted to close the position. In September 2007, this amount is close to zero. If PiVe Capital were to close the position then, the trade would still yield a total positive cumulative cash flow of about \$311,000 (see the solid line in Figure 5.6).

Unfortunately, the principals of PiVe Capital decided that the credit crisis was going to be short lived, and the aggressive response of the Federal Reserve would push the LIBOR-repo spread back in line soon enough to keep the positive cash flows going forward. And if they needed to, they could always unwind the position later.

As we know from the previous section, the LIBOR-repo spread failed to converge back to reasonable numbers, and PiVe Capital started paying large amount of money every quarter. It is now March 2008, and the principals decide that it is better to unwind the swap spread trade positions. The cumulative cash flows still show a positive amount, so not all is lost.

5.8.3.4 *The Surprise*

As PiVe Capital started unwinding the position, the principals found the good news that the value of the swap was now \$10.21 million. Indeed, the LIBOR yield curve now ranges between 2.7% at 1 month, and 3.3% at 5 years, which pushes up the value of the fixed part of the swap to $110.21 million. Because the floating part is always equal to $100 million at reset dates, by closing the position PiVe Capital would obtain an inflow of $10.21 million.

However, as PiVe Capital closes the swap, it has also to close the reverse repo. The bad news is that now the T-note that PiVe is shorting is trading at $110.23. Given the accrued interest of $1.28, the total losses from the short position amount to $100 million $-N \times \$111.51 = -\$11.38$ million.

In sum, to close the position on March, 2008 PiVe Capital receives $10.21 million from the swap, but it has to pay $11.38 million on the reverse repo, for a total loss of $1.16 million. This number far outweights the cumulative cash flows so far received from PiVe Capital.

Panel B of Figure 5.8 shows the total value of the trade over time, and indeed, starting at November 2007, the value has been consistently negative. Why is the value of the swap spread trade negative? To understand what happened, we have to look again at Figure 5.7. As can be seen from the solid line, the swap spread increased substantially around November 2007. This implies that the yield of Treasuries decreased compared to the swap rates. This change is not surprising, as during crisis periods investors purchase safe U.S. Treasury securities, pushing their yields down. The relative decrease of the yield increased the value of the Treasury note *by more* than the increase in the fixed rate bond implicit in a swap. Because in this swap spread trade PiVe Capital was long the bond implicit in the swap and short the Treasury note, an increase in the swap spread implies a decrease in the value of the position, that is, a capital loss. Indeed, note that initially, from June 2006 to June 2007, the swap spread actually decreased over time. Accordingly, Panel B in Figure 5.8 shows that the *value* of the swap spread position increased in the first year of the trade. Had PiVe Capital unwound the position around December 2006, it would have made $170,974 total from the cash flow side, and about $756,341.33 as a capital gain from closing the positions, for a total of $927,315.76 within the six months from inception of the trade. Unfortunately, PiVe Capital didn't close the position, and suffered a capital loss instead.

5.8.4 Conclusion

This case study illustrates the risks embedded in fixed income, relative value trades. There are two types of risk in such trades: The first source of risk is the variation in the cost-of-carry, which is the cash-flow per period that a trade is expected to generate. In the case of a swap spread trade, it is the difference between the swap spread and the LIBOR-repo rate. Typically this difference is positive, implying that setting up the trade generates a positive cash flow. However, floating rates can move, and thus we have to take into account the fact that the cash flow can turn negative at times, as it did in 2007 - 2008. The second source of risk is given by the potential capital losses due to the variation in the underlying spread. Indeed, in a relative value trade speculators bet on the convergence of the underlying spread to an average level. In the case study, the swap spread was high in 2006, although not very high, and PiVe Capital bet that the spread would narrow. If the swap spread narrowed, then the hedge fund would make substantial capital gain profits. However, even for those trades in which a hedge fund can reasonably expect that sooner or later the spread will narrow, the hedge fund manager must keep in mind that it is possible that a spread may widen further

Figure 5.8   The Swap Spread Trade Value

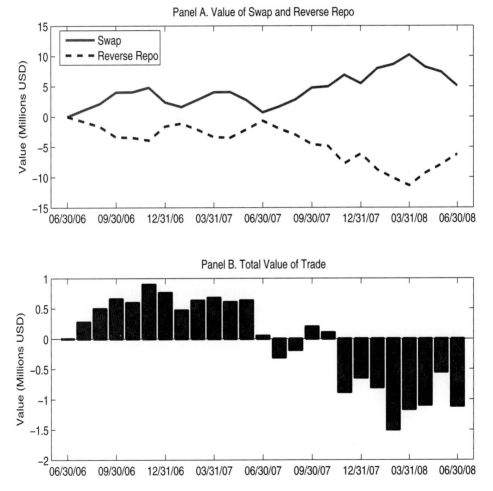

Panel A. Value of Swap and Reverse Repo

Panel B. Total Value of Trade

Figure 5.9   The LIBOR Curve: June 2006 – June 2008

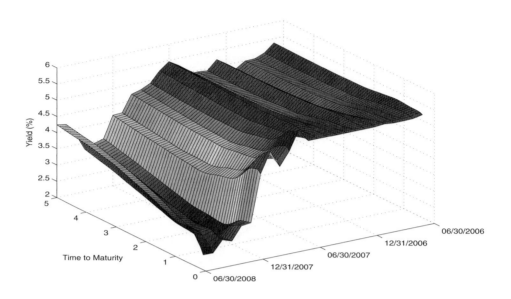

before it narrows. If the spread widens, then the hedge fund would sustain potentially large capital losses. It is then key for the hedge fund's survival that it has sufficient capital in cash or a large borrowing capacity that makes it able to withstand the capital loss. During periods of crisis, all risk-based spreads – the spreads between a risky securities and Treasury securities – tend to widen, as investors dump risky securities and purchase safe U.S. Treasuries. This flight-to-quality indeed took place during the credit crisis of 2007 - 2008, as spreads across a wide spectrum of abitrage strategies widened substantially.

CHAPTER 6

INTEREST RATE DERIVATIVES: FUTURES AND OPTIONS

6.1 INTEREST RATE FUTURES

Futures contracts are quite similar to forward contracts (see Chapter 5), as they also are contractual agreements between two counterparties to deliver a certain security (or cash) at a predetermined time in the future and for a predetermined price, called the **futures price**. However, futures contracts differ from forward contracts in a few key respects:

1. The futures contract is traded on a regulated exchange, such as the Chicago Board of Trade (CBOT) or the Chicago Mercantile Exchange (CME). The exchange defines the characteristics of the contract and it acts as a counterparty to investors who want to go long or short the contract. In addition, it also guarantees that payments will be honored at maturity, through the exchange clearinghouse.

2. The security underlying the futures contract is standardized, in the sense that the futures contract clearly specifies the type of security that is eligible for delivery, as well as the time and the method of delivery of the security. That is, there is no room for customized requests from clients.

3. The profits and losses are marked-to-market daily, meaning that they accrue over time to short and long traders with daily frequency.

Table 6.1   Some Futures Contracts

Futures Contract	Exchange
30-year U.S. Treasury bond futures	CBOT
2-, 5-, and 10-year U.S. Treasury note futures	CBOT
5-, 10-, and 30-year interest rate swap futures	CBOT
30 day Federal Funds	CBOT
Eurodollar	CME
LIBOR	CME
2-, 5-, 10-year interest rate swap futures	CME
13-week T-bill	CME
Euribor	Euronext
Eurobund	Eurex

Interest rate futures are available on numerous exchanges and on numerous instruments. Table 6.1 provides a partial list of interest rate futures, and the exchanges on which they trade.

6.1.1   Standardization

The 10-year, U.S. Treasury note futures, whose contract characteristics are contained in Table 6.2, provide a clear example of standardization. This futures contract trades on the Chicago Board of Trade, and it is among the most traded and liquid futures contract in the world. The standardization is clearly shown in the items "deliverable grade" and "contract months." The deliverable grade item specifies in detail the type of Treasury note that is eligible for delivery. To enhance liquidity and trading in the futures contract, the exchange specifies a large range of possible Treasury notes that are eligible for delivery, specifically, all those Treasury notes that have at least 6 1/2 years to maturity, but no more than 10. The short side of the futures contract, i.e. the counterparty who commits to delivering the security, can then choose any of these securities to deliver to the long side, i.e. the counterparty who commits to purchasing the security. To make these securities comparable with one another, the futures price at maturity will be multiplied by a conversion factor that (almost) eliminates the differences in bond prices due to differences in coupon rates.[1]

Similarly, the contract months item defines the possible maturities of the futures contract. By establishing only four expiration months, and even a specific period in the month, the exchange (CBOT) can enhance market liquidity. Indeed, if many more maturities were available, the number of contracts traded per maturity would be smaller, and market liquidity would suffer. As explained below, however, substantially decreasing the number of available maturities has an important drawback as it increases the maturity mismatch between the available contract maturities and the hedging needs of end users of the futures contracts. If the maturity mismatch becomes too large, then corporations may opt out

---

[1] If the futures contract was defined on a specific Treasury note, such as the one that is closest to 8 years to maturity at delivery time, then some investors might "squeeze" the short side by buying a large amount of available 8 years notes. Because the short side must deliver at maturity, it will be willing to pay a large premium to just get hold of the note to deliver. This possibility would break the futures market itself, as expecting this behavior, investors would not enter into the short side of a futures contract to start with.

Table 6.2   10-Year U.S. Treasury Note Futures (Chicago Board of Trade)

Contract Size
One U.S. Treasury bond having a face value at maturity of $100,000 or multiple thereof.

Deliverable Grades
U.S. Treasury notes maturing at least 6 1/2 years, but not more than 10 years, from the first day of the delivery month. The invoice price equals the futures settlement price times a conversion factor plus accrued interest. The conversion factor is the price of the delivered note ($1 par value) to yield 6 percent.

Tick Size
Minimum price fluctuations shall be in multiples of one-half of one thirty-second (1/32) point per 100 points ($15.625 rounded up to the nearest cent per contract).

Price Quote
Points ($1,000) and one half of 1/32 of a point; i.e., 84-16 equals 84 16/32, 84-165 equals 84 16.5/32.

Contract Months
Mar, Jun, Sep, Dec

Last Trading Day
Seventh business day preceding the last business day of the delivery month. Trading in expiring contracts closes at noon, Chicago time, on the last trading day.

Last Delivery Day
Last business day of the delivery month.

Delivery Method
Federal Reserve book-entry wire-transfer system.

Trading Hours
Open Auction: 7:20 am - 2:00 pm, Central Time, Monday - Friday
Electronic: 6:00 pm - 4:00 pm, Central Time, Sunday - Friday

Ticker Symbols
Open Auction: TY
Electronic: ZN

Daily Price Limit
None

Margin Information
Initial Margin: $1,890 (per contract)
Maintenance Margin: $ 1,400 (per contract)

Source: CBOT Web site, http://www.cbot.com/cbot/pub/cont_detail/1,3206,1520+14433,00.html, accessed on June 11, 2008.

from the futures market in favor of less liquid, but highly customized over-the-counter forward contracts. The exchange must then weigh the need of corporations to have many maturities per year available for hedging purposes against the decrease in liquidity if too many maturities were in fact available.

The 10-year U.S. Treasury note futures and the 30 year U.S. Treasury bond futures have numerous peculiarities which we will study in more detail in Chapter 11.

6.1.2 Margins and Mark-to-Market

One essential feature of futures contracts is marking-to-market, that is, the profits and losses from the futures contract trading activity accrue to traders with daily frequency. To understand the logic, it is useful to think about forward contracts, described in Chapter 5. Consider a forward contract to buy at time T a given coupon bond with maturity $T^* > T$ (see Fact 5.9 in Chapter 5). As we know, the value of entering into a forward contract is zero at initiation $t = 0$. Now, let one day pass by. As interest rates move, so does the forward price, and from Equation 5.36 the value of the forward contract at $t = dt = 1/252 = 1$ day, is

$$V^{fwd}(dt) = Z(dt, T) \times \left[P_c^{fwd}(dt, T, T^*) - P_c^{fwd}(0, T, T^*) \right] \tag{6.1}$$

Because it did not cost anything to enter into the forward contract, the amount $V^{fwd}(dt)$ is the daily profit or loss: For instance, if the forward price increases, then the forward contract gains in value, and vice versa. In a typical forward contract, there is no exchange of money between the two counterparties as $V^{fwd}(t)$ changes from one day to the next. However, in principle, the two counterparties can decide to *mark-to-market* the forward contract, meaning that every day the party with negative $V^{fwd}(dt)$ pays this amount to the other one, thereby resetting the value of the forward contract to zero. The profits and losses from the forward position accrue over time to the counterparties. This practice is very popular across dealers and investment banks as it limits the credit risk exposure from derivative transactions. Indeed, from the discussion following Equation 5.36 daily mark-to-market is equivalent to the strategy calling for the daily closing of the old forward contract [with forward price $P_c^{fwd}(t - dt, T, T^*)$] and opening a new one [with forward price $P_c^{fwd}(t, T, T^*)$]. Thus, the profit / loss at any time t is given by

$$\text{Profit / Loss at } t = V^{fwd}(t) = Z(t, T) \times \left[P_c^{fwd}(t, T, T^*) - P_c^{fwd}(t - dt, T, T^*) \right] \tag{6.2}$$

We now see that receiving the sequence of payments $V^{fwd}(t)$ at daily frequencies, that is, times $t = dt, 2 \times dt, 3 \times dt, \dots T$, is equivalent to the original payoff from the forward contract, namely, Equation 5.29. The important point to notice is that the sequence of cash flows $V^{fwd}(t)$ occur at time t, while the final payoff is at maturity T. Thus, we have to take the *future* value of each of these cash flows from t to T. To do so we must multiply each of the cash flows at time t in Equation 6.2 by $1/Z(t, T)$. We then obtain

$$\text{Total profits / losses at } T \quad = \quad \frac{V^{fwd}(dt)}{Z(dt, T)} + \frac{V^{fwd}(2 \times dt)}{Z(2 \times dt, T)} + \dots + V^{fwd}(T) \tag{6.3}$$

From Equation 6.2, we see that for every t,

$$\frac{V^{fwd}(t)}{Z(t, T)} = \left[P_c^{fwd}(t, T, T^*) - P_c^{fwd}(t - dt, T, T^*) \right],$$

which implies

$$\text{Total profits / losses at } T \quad = \quad \left[P_c^{fwd}(dt, T, T^*) - P_c^{fwd}(0, T, T^*) \right]$$
$$+ \left[P_c^{fwd}(2 \times dt, T, T^*) - P_c^{fwd}(dt, T, T^*) \right]$$

$$\vdots$$
$$+ \left[P_c^{fwd}(T, T, T^*) - P_c^{fwd}(T - dt, T, T^*) \right]$$
$$= \left[P_c(T, T^*) - P_c^{fwd}(0, T, T^*) \right]$$

where the last equality stems from eliminating all of the common terms [e.g., "$P_c^{fwd}(dt, T, T^*)$" in the first row cancels with "$-P_c^{fwd}(dt, T, T^*)$" in the second row, and so forth], and the fact that at maturity, the forward price equals the price of the bond $P_c^{fwd}(T, T, T^*) = P_c(T, T^*)$. We have established the following:

Fact 6.1 *In a forward contract, marking-to-market does not change the final payoff to either counterparty.*

Futures markets work exactly in this fashion: Every day the futures price, $P^{fut}(t, T)$, moves and thus profits and losses are credited or debited to the traders' accounts with the exchange. In particular, if one trader is long k futures contracts at t, the profit or loss at the end of trading day t is

$$\text{P\&L from futures at } t = k \times \text{Contract size} \times \left[P^{fut}(t, T) - P^{fut}(t - dt, T) \right] \quad (6.4)$$

To enter into a futures position, a trader must post an initial amount of money in a specific account with the exchange, called the *initial margin*. For instance, Table 6.2 shows that the initial margin for the 10-year, U.S. Treasury note futures is $1,890 per contract. As the futures price moves, the margin account is debited or credited, depending on the movement. If the total amount in the account declines below the *maintenance margin*, the exchange issues a *margin call* and the trader must replenish the trading account back to the initial margin. If the trader fails to do so, the futures contract is closed.

Marking-to-market and the requirement for traders to keep a minimum amount of money as a collateral to the trade limits the credit risk that the exchange takes from each trader.

6.1.3 The Convergence Property of Futures Prices

Interest rate futures prices are harder to analyze than forward prices, so we will discuss them in more detail after we introduce some modeling devices in Chapter 11. However, one property that futures prices have in common with forward prices is the fact that they must converge to the value of the underlying security (or cash amount, if cash settled) by maturity date. That is, futures prices $P^{fut}(t, T)$ on a security with value $P(t)$ at time t have the property that at maturity $P^{fut}(T, T) = P(T)$. This fact makes it almost equivalent to using forward contracts or futures contracts for some hedging purposes, at least in principle. The next example illustrates the similarities, and the differences, between futures and forward contracts for hedging purposes.

■ **EXAMPLE 6.1**

Consider again Example 5.3 in Chapter 5. On March 1, 2001 (today = time 0), a firm is worried that the interest rate may decline in the next six months, when it will receive the payment from the sale of a piece of equipment. In particular, the firm will receive on September 4, 2001 a $100 million receivable that needs to be invested for another six months. Instead of entering into a forward rate agreement (FRA) as in Example

5.3, the firm may decide to use futures contracts to hedge against a decline in interest rates. For instance, the firm may go long k Eurodollar futures contracts. Table 6.3 contains the details of the Eurodollar futures contract. In particular, although the variable underlying the futures is a rate (the 3-month LIBOR), the quote is in prices given by $P^{Fut}(t, T) = 100 - f_4^{Fut}(t, T)$, where $f_4^{Fut}(t, T)$ is the 3-month futures LIBOR rate at T, expressed as a percentage. For instance, the quote $P^{Fut}(t, T) = 95.365$ implies a rate $f_4^{Fut}(t, T) = (100 - 95.365)/100 = 4.635\%$. In particular, at maturity, the futures price will be equal to $P^{Fut}(T, T) = 100 - r_4^{LIBOR}(T)$. This quoting convention implies that a long position in the Eurodollar futures hedges against a decline in interest rates. Given the contract size of $1 million, the daily profits and losses from the futures contract are then given by

$$\text{Daily P\&L} = \$1,000,000 \times 0.25 \times \frac{\left(P^{Fut}(t + dt, T) - P^{Fut}(t, T)\right)}{100} \quad (6.5)$$

$$= \$1,000,000 \times 0.25 \times \left(f_4^{Fut}(t, T) - f_4^{Fut}(t + dt, T)\right) \quad (6.6)$$

where 0.25 reflects the fact that the Eurodollar futures is a 90-day interest rate, and $dt = 1/252 = 1$ day.

On March 1, 2001, the September, 2001 futures contract was quoted at $f_4^{Fut}(0, T_1) = 4.635\%$, where $T_1 =$ September 17, 2001 is the futures maturity. To hedge the $100 million position, the firm must go long 100 Eurodollar futures contracts. The futures rate on September 4, 2001 ($= t$) was $f_4^{Fut}(t, T_1) = 3.520\%.$[2] The total P/L from the futures contract between March 1 and September 4, 2001, is then:[3]

$$
\begin{aligned}
\text{Total} & \\
\text{profit/losses} &= 100 \times \$1,000,000 \times 0.25 \times \left(4.635\% - f_4^{Fut}(dt, T_1)\right) \\
\text{from futures} & \\
&\quad + 100 \times \$1,000,000 \times 0.25 \times \left(f_4^{Fut}(dt, T_1) - f_4^{Fut}(2dt, T_1)\right) \\
&\qquad \vdots \qquad\qquad \vdots \\
&\quad + 100 \times \$1,000,000 \times 0.25 \times \left(f_4^{Fut}(t - dt, T_1) - 3.520\%\right) \\
&= 100 \times \$1,000,000 \times 0.25 \times (4.635\% - 3.520\%) = \$278,750
\end{aligned}
$$

Table 6.4 also reports the daily P/L for a selected period of time.

On September 4, 2001 (first business day of the month) the firm receives the $100 million receivable, which it can now invest at the current interest rate for the next six months. Because the firm is hedging with a LIBOR-based contract, let's assume it can invest for six months using a 6-month LIBOR. The six month LIBOR on September 4, 2001 is $r_2(t, t + 0.5) = 3.55\%$. Thus, the firm's total payoff at time $T_2 =$ March 1, 2002 is

$$\text{Total amount at } T_2 = (\$100 \text{ mil} + \$278,750) \times \left(1 + \frac{3.55\%}{2}\right) = \$102.059 \text{ million}$$

---

[2]Note that the firm will unravel the position at $t =$ September 4, 2001, which is a little earlier than the maturity of the futures contract $T_1 =$ September 17, 2001.

[3]We are ignoring for now the impact of the timing of cash flows on the final payoff. See discussion in Section 6.1.4 below.

Table 6.3 CME Eurodollar Futures

Underlying Instrument
3-month LIBOR: London Interbank Offered Rate on 3-month U.S. dollar deposits.

Contract Size
$1,000,000

Tick Size
Trading can occur in .0025 increments ($6.25/contract) in the expiring front-month contract;
in .005 increments ($12.50/contract) in the four serial and all forty quarterly expirations.

Price Quote
$P^{Fut}(t) = 100 - f_4^{Fut}(t)$, where f_4^{Fut} is the 3-month "expected" LIBOR rate.

Contract Months
Mar, Jun, Sep, Dec, extending out 10 years (total of 40 contracts) plus the four nearest serial
expirations (months that are not in the March quarterly cycle).

Last Trading Day
Seventh business day preceding the last business day of the delivery month. Trading in expiring
contracts closes at noon, Chicago time, on the last trading day.

Final Settlement
Cash settlement to the British Bankers Association survey of 3- month LIBOR.

Trading Hours
Open Outcry: 7:20 a.m. û 2:00 p.m.
CME Globex Electronic Markets: 5:00 p.m. û 4:00 p.m. the following day;
on Sunday, trading begins at 5:00 p.m.

Source: CME Interest Rate Product Guide and Calendar, 2007.

This number is not too dissimilar from the one obtained using the forward contract, or the forward rate agreement, namely, 102.105 million.

Figure 6.1 plots the September, 2001 Eurodollar futures and the 3-month LIBOR. The convergence property is apparent.

6.1.4 Futures versus Forwards

In this subsection we discuss the relation between futures and forwards, as well as the pros and cons in using them for hedging purposes.

First of all, what is the relation between futures prices and forward prices? They are very closely related. In particular, consider a forward contract to receive at time T_1 a zero coupon bond $P_z(T_1, T_2)$ for the delivery price (or forward price) $P_z^{fwd}(0, T_1, T_2)$. The payoff at maturity T_1 of this security is

$$\begin{aligned}
\text{Forward contract payoff at } T_1 &= \text{Value of zero coupon bond} - \text{Delivery price} \\
&= P_z(T_1, T_2) - P_z^{Fwd}(0, T_1, T_2)
\end{aligned}$$

Consider now a futures contract that is otherwise analog to the forward contract above. Because of mark-to-market, every trading day t the daily P/L from a *short* position in

Table 6.4 Profits and Losses from Futures Position

Date	Quote	Rate	Daily P/L	Cumulative P/L
1-Mar-01	95.3650	4.635%		
2-Mar-01	95.3200	4.680%	-112.50	-112.50
5-Mar-01	95.3200	4.680%	0.00	-112.50
6-Mar-01	95.3500	4.650%	75.00	-37.50
7-Mar-01	95.3900	4.610%	100.00	62.50
8-Mar-01	95.4050	4.595%	37.50	100.00
9-Mar-01	95.3400	4.660%	-162.50	-62.50
12-Mar-01	95.3650	4.635%	62.50	0.00
13-Mar-01	95.3650	4.635%	0.00	0.00
14-Mar-01	95.5250	4.475%	400.00	400.00
15-Mar-01	95.6250	4.375%	250.00	650.00
16-Mar-01	95.6000	4.400%	-62.50	587.50
19-Mar-01	95.5550	4.445%	-112.50	475.00
20-Mar-01	95.6350	4.365%	200.00	675.00
21-Mar-01	95.7000	4.300%	162.50	837.50
22-Mar-01	95.7650	4.235%	162.50	1,000.00
23-Mar-01	95.6700	4.330%	-237.50	762.50
26-Mar-01	95.6700	4.330%	0.00	762.50
27-Mar-01	95.5200	4.480%	-375.00	387.50
28-Mar-01	95.5700	4.430%	125.00	512.50
29-Mar-01	95.6200	4.380%	125.00	637.50
30-Mar-01	95.6900	4.310%	175.00	812.50
⋮	⋮	⋮	⋮	⋮
1-Aug-01	96.4650	3.535%	0.00	2,750.00
2-Aug-01	96.4300	3.570%	-87.50	2,662.50
3-Aug-01	96.4300	3.570%	0.00	2,662.50
6-Aug-01	96.4300	3.570%	0.00	2,662.50
7-Aug-01	96.4300	3.570%	0.00	2,662.50
8-Aug-01	96.4850	3.515%	137.50	2,800.00
9-Aug-01	96.5050	3.495%	50.00	2,850.00
10-Aug-01	96.5350	3.465%	75.00	2,925.00
13-Aug-01	96.5475	3.453%	31.25	2,956.25
14-Aug-01	96.5325	3.468%	-37.50	2,918.75
15-Aug-01	96.5000	3.500%	-81.25	2,837.50
16-Aug-01	96.5375	3.463%	93.75	2,931.25
17-Aug-01	96.5650	3.435%	68.75	3,000.00
20-Aug-01	96.5450	3.455%	-50.00	2,950.00
21-Aug-01	96.5650	3.435%	50.00	3,000.00
22-Aug-01	96.5475	3.453%	-43.75	2,956.25
23-Aug-01	96.5475	3.453%	0.00	2,956.25
24-Aug-01	96.5250	3.475%	-56.25	2,900.00
27-Aug-01	96.5200	3.480%	-12.50	2,887.50
28-Aug-01	96.5525	3.448%	81.25	2,968.75
29-Aug-01	96.5575	3.443%	12.50	2,981.25
30-Aug-01	96.5900	3.410%	81.25	3,062.50
31-Aug-01	96.5700	3.430%	-50.00	3,012.50
4-Sep-01	96.4800	3.520%	-225.00	2,787.50

Data Source: Bloomberg.

Figure 6.1 Eurodollar Futures and the three month LIBOR

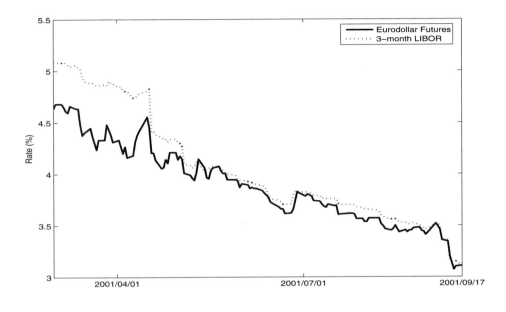

Source: Bloomberg.

futures is given by (see Equation 6.4)

Daily P&L from short futures $= (P/L)_t = \left[P_z^{fut}(t, T_1, T_2) - P_z^{fut}(t - dt, T_1, T_2) \right]$

(6.7)

Ignoring for now the time value of money, the total payoff at time T_1 of a short position is given by the sum of the daily profits and losses:

$$
\begin{aligned}
\text{Total P/L of short futures at } T_1 &= (P/L)_{dt} + (P/L)_{2dt} + \dots + (P/L)_T \qquad (6.8) \\
&= \left[P_z^{fut}(0, T_1, T_2) - P_z^{fut}(dt, T_1, T_2) \right] \\
&\quad + \left[P_z^{fut}(dt, T_1, T_2) - P_z^{fut}(2 \times dt, T_1, T_2) \right] \\
&\quad \vdots \\
&\quad + \left[P_z^{fut}(T_1 - dt \times dt, T_1, T) - P_z^{fut}(T_1, T_1, T_2) \right] \\
&= \left[P_z^{fut}(0, T_1, T_2) - P_z(T_1, T_2) \right]
\end{aligned}
$$

It follows that if we enter into a forward contract at time 0 and hedge it with a futures position, we obtain that the total payoff is given by the difference between futures and forward prices:

$$
\begin{aligned}
\text{Long forward + Short futures payoff} &= \left[P_z(T_1, T_2) - P_z^{Fwd}(0, T_1, T_2) \right] \\
&\quad + \left[P_z^{fut}(0, T_1, T_2) - P_z(T_1, T_2) \right] \\
&= P_z^{fut}(0, T_1, T_2) - P_z^{Fwd}(0, T_1, T_2)
\end{aligned}
$$

Given that both the futures price and the forward price are known at time 0 and the fact that it costs nothing to enter into either a forward or a futures, we must have the no arbitrage condition

$$\text{No arbitrage} \Longrightarrow P_z^{fut}(0, T_1, T_2) - P_z^{Fwd}(0, T_1, T_2) = 0$$

We therefore obtain the following:

Fact 6.2 *Under the following two assumptions:*

1. *we ignore the difference in timing of cash flows between a forward or a futures contract; and*

2. *the futures and forward contract payoff occur on the same date (T_1);*

then the futures price must equal the forward price:

$$P_z^{fut}(0, T_1, T_2) = P_z^{Fwd}(0, T_1, T_2) \tag{6.9}$$

Equation 6.9 is obtained under assumptions 1 and 2 in Fact 6.2. Both assumptions are violated in practice: First, futures do in fact generate cash flows over time, a fact that makes Equation 6.8 incorrect. Instead, the correct expression is one that includes the future value of each daily P/L. Second, there is often a mismatch between forward and futures payoff timing: For instance, while a plain vanilla Forward Rate Agreement on the three month LIBOR would pay the amount $N \times \Delta \times [f_4(0, T_1, T_2) - r_4(T_1, T_2)]$ at $T_2 = T_1 + \Delta$, the Eurodollar futures contract pays the same payoff at T_1.

These differences slightly change the relation between futures prices and forward prices. However, the difference between forward prices and futures prices is small, and thus Equation 6.9 is a good approximation, especially if the maturity T is not large and the volatility of interest rates is also small. We explore the exact relation between futures and forwards in Chapter 21. Section 6.5 below provides additional insights on the relation between futures and forward prices.

6.1.5 Hedging with Futures or Forwards?

Example 6.1 highlights two possible shortcomings of futures versus forward:

1. **Basis Risk.** The available maturity of the bond, or the particular instrument may not be the exact instrument to hedge all of the risk. Using a forward rate agreement, a firm could perfectly hedge the risk. Using futures, the firm would retain some residual risk, as the available instruments (the Eurodollar futures, based on the 3-month LIBOR) is not perfectly correlated with the interest rate to hedge (which is a 6-month rate). Moreover, there is a (mild) maturity mismatch between the needs of the firm and the available maturities, as the Eurodollar futures expire in the middle of September, while the receivable arrives at the beginning of September.

2. **Tailing of the Hedge.** The cash flows arising from the futures position accrue over time, which implies the need of the firm to take into account the time value of money between the time at which the cash flow is realized and the maturity of the hedge

position (maturity T in the example). This will call for a reduction in the position in futures, compared to the description in the example. We follow up on this notion in Exercise 9.

On the other hand, futures also have numerous advantages compared to forwards, which may more than compensate for the two problems above.

1. **Liquidity**. Because of their standardization, futures are more liquid than forward contracts, meaning that it is easy to get in and out of the position.[4] For the highly traded futures contracts, such as the 10-year U.S. Treasury note futures or the Eurodollar futures, bid/ask spreads are relatively low and going in and out of positions is relatively inexpensive. This is not true for forward contracts, because as they are traded only over-the-counter, closing a position may be expensive.

2. **Credit Risk**. The existence of a clearinghouse guarantees performance on futures contracts, while the same may not be true for forward contracts. The clearing house hedges itself through the mark-to-market provision: As soon as one trader's account falls below the margin requirements, a margin call is issued and, if the account is not replenished, the position is closed. This mechanism guarantees to some extent that no large credit exposure is mounted for any single trader.

6.2 OPTIONS

All of the derivative contracts discussed so far, namely forward rate agreements, forward contracts, swaps and futures, share two common features:

1. It costs nothing to enter in such derivative contracts;

2. Either counterparty may be called to make a payment at maturity.

For instance, a forward rate agreement costs nothing at inception, but the payoff at maturity T_2 of the FRA is

$$\text{Payoff of FRA at } T_2 = N \times \Delta \times [r_n(T_1, T_2) - f_n(0, T_1, T_2)]$$

where $r_n(T_1, T_2)$ is the reference floating rate at T_1, $f_n(0, T_1, T_2)$ is the corresponding forward rate at 0, and $\Delta = T_2 - T_1 = 1/n$ is the compounding interval. The payoff to either party at maturity can be both positive or negative.

Options are different in both respects. First, there *is* an exchange of money when the two counterparties enter into an option contract: One counterparty, the option buyer, pays an amount of money, the option premium, to the other counterparty, the option seller. Second, at maturity, the option buyer never makes a positive net payment, while the option seller may suffer a net outflow under some circumstances that depend on the underlying variable.

The variety of interest rate options is very large, and in the next few subsections we describe the most popular. First, it may be useful to describe a few generic characteristics that are common across the various types of options. The next definition introduces some of the terminology, and the effective option's payoff.

---

[4]The level of liquidity really depends on the futures contract, as some are in fact quite illiquid, with large bid/ask spreads.

Definition 6.1 *A* **call option** *defined on the variable* $F(t)$, *with maturity* T *and strike price* K, *is a contract between two counterparties, the option buyer and the option seller, according to which:*

(A) *Any time* t *prior to maturity, the option buyer has the right to ask the option seller for the payment of the following effective payoff:*

$$\text{Call option payoff} = \max(F(t) - K, 0) \qquad (6.10)$$

(B) *The option seller has the obligation to pay this amount to the option buyer at* t.

(C) *In return for the right to obtain the payment in Equation 6.10, the option buyer pays an* **option premium** *to the option seller at time 0.*

The act of requesting the payment in Equation 6.10 is called **exercising** the option. If the option can be exercised only at maturity T, then the option is termed **European**. If the option can be exercised any time before maturity, it is called **American**.[5]

Finally, a **put option** is the same as above, except that its payoff is

$$\text{Put Option Payoff} = \max(K - F(t), 0) \qquad (6.11)$$

Definition 6.1 is generic, and it describes the *effective* payoff from an option contract. This payoff may arise in different ways, depending of the nature of the option.

1. **Bond Options**. The underlying variable in a bond option is a fixed coupon instrument, such as a U.S. Treasury note. In this case, the underlying variable in Definition 6.1 is the coupon bond price $F(t) = P_c(t, T_B)$, where T_B is the maturity of the coupon bond, with $T_B > T$. A *call option* contract then specifies that the option's buyer has the right, but not the obligation, to *purchase* the underlying security any time before or at maturity T for a price K set at initiation. Because the option buyer will never exercise the option if $P_c(t, T_B) < K$ – it is better to purchase the coupon bond in the cash market in this case – effectively the option buyer is entitled to the payoff described in Equation 6.10. The option seller in turn must effectively make the payment in Equation 6.10, as he or she must deliver a coupon bond valued $P_c(t, T_B)$ but only receives the strike price $K < P_c(t, T)$.

   The inverse argument holds for *put options*: In this case, the option buyer has the right, but not the obligation, to *sell* the coupon bond at $P_c(t, T_B)$ for a price K. Because again the option buyer will not exercise the option unless $K > P_c(t, T_B)$, the option buyer is effectively entitled to the payoff in Equation 6.11. The option seller has the obligation to purchase the coupon bond at a higher price (K) than the market price, and therefore suffers a loss.

2. **Interest Rate Options**. The underlying variable is an interest rate, such as the 13-week Treasury discount rate, or the 3-month LIBOR. In this case, $F(t)$ in Definition 6.1 is an interest rate, such as $F(t) = r_4(t)$, and the strike price K is in fact a strike

---

[5]The terms "American" and "European" have nothing to do with the location where the options are traded.

"rate." These options are cash settled. Table 6.5 shows the contract details, for instance, of the IRX option on the 13-week discount rate listed at the CBOE.

A class of popular interest rate options that are traded in the over-the-counter market is caps and floors. A quarterly *cap* with maturity T and strike rate K is a security that pays at times $T_1, T_2, \dots T_n$, with $T_i = T_{i-1} + 0.25$ the sequence of cash flows

$$\text{Payoff of a cap at } T_i = N \times 0.25 \times \max(r_4(T_{i-1}) - K, 0)$$

where the reference rate $r_4(t)$ is the 3-month LIBOR rate. A floor, instead pays the amount $N \times 0.25 \times \max(K - r_4(T_{i-1}), 0)$. A cap, therefore, is given by a portfolio of n interest rate options.

3. **Futures Options.** The underlying is the futures price of another contract, such as the 10 year, U.S. T-note futures. In this case, the variable in Definition 6.1 is a futures price $F(t) = F^{fut}(t, T_F)$, where T_F is the maturity of the futures. A *call option* contract then specifies that the option's buyer has the right, but not the obligation, to enter into a long futures position any time before or at maturity T for a futures price K set at initiation. Exchanges that list futures contracts typically also list options on their own futures contracts, as we can see from Table 6.6. Tables 6.7 and 6.8 show the terms of the contracts for the 10-year, U.S. T-note futures option, and the Eurodollar futures option, respectively. The description of the futures contracts themselves are in Tables 6.2 and 6.3.

4. **Swaptions**. The underlying is a swap. In this case, the underlying variable in Definition 6.1 is the current swap rate $F(t) = c(t, T)$, where T is the maturity of the swap, and the strike price K is a strike "swap rate." A call option contract, or *payer swaption*, then specifies that the option buyer has the right, but not the obligation, to enter into a swap and pay only the strike rate K, instead of the market rate, for the life of the swap. Clearly, an option buyer would exercise the option only if the current swap rate is higher than the strike price, $c(t, T) > K$, otherwise it is better to let the option expire and enter into a swap as a fixed payer at the market rate. As we shall see, the payoff for this option is as in Equation 6.10. A put option contract, or a *receiver swaption*, instead specifies that the option buyer has the right to enter into a swap and receive the strike price K instead of the market rate. Again, in this case an option buyer would exercise the option only if the strike rate K is above the market rate, that is, if $K > c(t, T)$, leading to a payoff of the form in Equation 6.11.

The next subsections provide some examples. Before we turn to these examples, it is useful to introduce additional terminology.

Definition 6.2 *An option is said to be* **in-the-money (ITM)** *when it is profitable for the option's buyer to exercise it. In particular, a call option is in-the-money if $F(t) > K$ while a put option is in-the-money if $F(t) < K$.*

An option is said to be **out-of-the-money (OTM)** *when it is not profitable to exercise it. In particular, a call option is out-of-the-money if $F(t) < K$ while a put option is out-of-the-money if $F(t) > K$.*

An option is said to be **at-the-money (ATM)** *when $F(t)$ is (approximately) equal to the strike price K.*

Table 6.5   CBOE 13-week Treasury Bill Option (IRX)

Underlying Variable
10 × the discount rate of the most recently auctioned 13-week U.S. Treasury bill. The new T-bill is substituted weekly on the trading day following its auction, usually a Monday.

Multiplier
100

Strike Price Intervals
2 1/2 points. A 1-point interval represents 10 basis points.

Premium Quotation
Stated in decimals. One point equals $100. The minimum tick for options trading below 3.00 is 0.05 ($5.00) and for all other series, 0.10 ($10.00).

Expiration Date
Saturday immediately following the third Friday of the expiration month.

Expiration Months
Three near-term months plus two additional months from the March quarterly cycle (March, June, September and December).

Exercise Style
European

Settlement of Option Exercise
Annualized discount rate on the most recently issued T-bill on the last trading day as reported by the Federal Reserve Bank of New York at 2:30 p.m. Central Time.
Exercise will result in delivery of cash on the business day following the expiration date.
The exercise-settlement amount is equal to the difference between the exercise-settlement value and the exercise price of the option, multiplied by $100.

Last Trading Day
Trading in interest rate options will ordinarily cease on the business day (usually a Friday) preceding the expiration date.

Trading Hours
7:20 a.m. û 2:00 p.m. (Central Time)

Source: CBOE Web Site.

Table 6.6 Some Exchange Traded Options Contracts

Options Contract	Exchange	Underlying	Exercise
30-year US T-bond	CBOT	30-year US T-bond futures	American
10-year US T-note	CBOT	10-year US T-note futures	American
5-year US T- note	CBOT	5-year US T-note futures	American
Eurodollar	CME	Eurodollar futures	American
LIBOR option	CME	LIBOR futures	American
30 day Federal Fund	CME	Federal Funds futures	American
13-week T-bill	CME	Federal Funds futures	American
Euroyen TIBOR option	CME	Euroyen futures	American
13-week Treasury bill	CBOE	13-week T-bill discount rate	European
5-year Treasury note	CBOE	Yield on the 5-year T-note	European
10-year Treasury note	CBOE	Yield on the 10-year T-note	European
30-year Treasury note	CBOE	Yield on the 30-year T-bond	European
Euribor	Euronext	Euribor futures	American
Eurobund	Eurex	Eurobund futures	American

Figure 6.2 illustrates the payoff diagrams for options on bonds. The payoff for calls and puts in this case are

$$\max(P(T, T_B) - K, 0) \quad \text{and} \quad \max(K - P(T, T_B), 0), \qquad (6.12)$$

respectively, where T is the exercise time, K is the strike price, and $P(T, T_B)$ is a reference bond. Panel A of Figure 6.2 plots the payoff for a call option buyer: If the price of the bond increases above the strike price (the dotted line), the option buyer gets a positive payoff, otherwise he or she receives nothing. The diagram also reports the areas commonly referred to as in-the-money (ITM), out-of-the-money (OTM), and at-the-money (ATM). The payoff to the call option seller is depicted in Panel B. The payoff diagram is the mirror image of the call option buyer. Panels C and D show the payoff diagrams for a put option buyer and a put option seller, respectively.

Because an option buyer pays a premium to the option seller, the payoff is not a profit. To compute the profit for the option buyer, we must decrease the total payoff by the premium paid.[6] Similarly, to compute the profit to the option seller, we must increase the payoff by the option premium. Figure 6.3 shows the payoffs (solid line) and the profits (dashed line) for option buyers and option sellers. Notice that, in particular, an option seller's profit is at most the premium obtained for selling the option.

6.2.1 Options as Insurance Contracts

The best way to understand options contracts is to consider them as insurance contracts. As in any insurance contract, there is a premium to pay up front, and a payment at maturity that occurs if some adverse event happens. For instance, if you purchase an annual theft insurance for your car, you pay a premium up front to the insurance company. If your car

---

[6]In fact, we have to take the future value of the option premium to take into account the time value of money: the premium is paid at 0 while the payoff at T.

Table 6.7   10-Year U.S. Treasury Note Option (Chicago Board of Trade)

Contract Size

One CBOT 10-year U.S. Treasury note futures contract (of a specified delivery month) having a face value at maturity of $100,000 or multiple thereof.

Expiration

Unexercised 10-year Treasury note futures options shall expire at 7:00 p.m. Central Time on the last day of trading.

Tick Size

1/64 of a point ($15.625/contract) rounded up to the nearest cent/contract.

Contract Months

The first three consecutive contract months (two serial expirations and one quarterly expiration) plus the next four months in the quarterly cycle (Mar, Jun, Sep, Dec). There will always be seven months available for trading. Serials will exercise into the first nearby quarterly futures contract. Quarterlies will exercise into futures contracts of the same delivery period.

Last Trading Day

Options cease trading at the same time as the underlying futures contract on the last Friday preceding by at least two business days the last business day of the month preceding the option contract month. Options cease trading at the close of the regular daytime open auction trading session for the corresponding 10-year Treasury note futures contract.

Last Delivery Day

Last business day of the delivery month.

Trading Hours

Open Auction: 7:20 am - 2:00 pm, Chicago time, Monday - Friday
Electronic: 5:30 pm - 4:00 pm, Chicago time, Sunday - Friday

Ticker Symbols

Open Auction: TC for calls, TP for puts
Electronic: OZN for calls, OZNP for puts

Strike Price Intervals

Strike prices will be listed in integral multiples of one-half of one point ($500 per contract) to bracket the settlement price of the underlying 10-year U.S. Treasury note futures contract. Strike prices will included the at-the-money strike price plus the next 50 consecutive higher and the next 50 consecutive lower strike prices.

Exercise

The buyer of a futures option may exercise the option on any business day prior to expiration by giving notice to the Board of Trade clearing service provider by 6:00 pm, Central Time. Options that expire in-the-money are automatically exercised into a position, unless specific instructions are given to the Board of Trade clearing service provider.

Source: CBOT web site, http://www.cbot.com/cbot/pub/cont_detail/0,3206,1520+14438,00.html, accessed on August 27, 2008.

Figure 6.2 Interest Rate Options Payoff Profiles

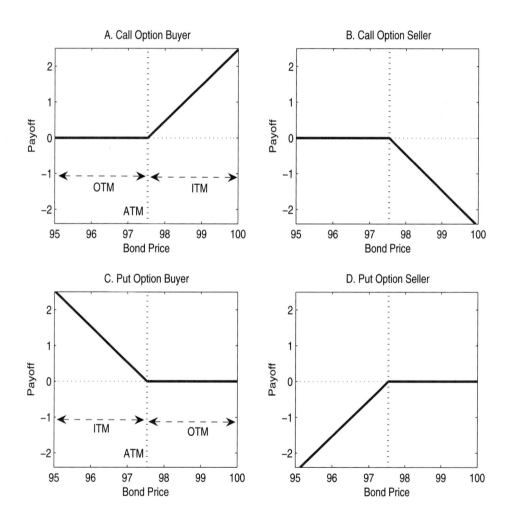

Figure 6.3 Option Payoff versus Option Profit

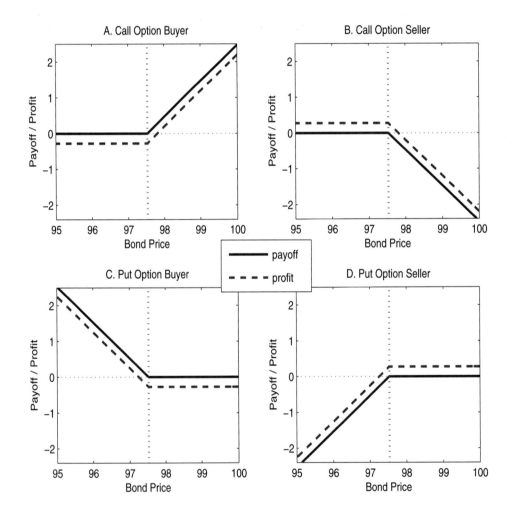

Table 6.8   CME Eurodollar (Quarterly) Options

Underlying Instrument
The CME Eurodollar futures contract expiring in the same month, and on the same day,
of the option.

Contract Months
The first eight months in the March quarterly cycle (Mar, Jun, Sep, Dec).

Exercise (Strike) Prices
25-basis-point increments, e.g., 95.25, 95.50, 95.75, etc. The two nearest
contract months are eligible for 12.5 basis point increments.

Expiration/Settlement
Cash settle at the same time and on the same day as the underlying futures contract.

Exercise
The option is American style, and it can be exercise any day before maturity up to 7:00 pm
(Chicago time). All in-the-money options are automatically exercised at maturity.

Minimum Price Fluctuation (Tick)
.0025 = $6.25/contract for the nearest expiring option (if underlying futures eligible);

Trading Hours
Open Outcry: 7:20 a.m. û 2:00 p.m.
CME Globex Electronic Markets: 5:00 p.m. û 4:00 p.m. the following day;
on Sunday, trading begins at 5:00 p.m.

Source: CME Interest Rate Product Guide and Calendar, 2007.

gets stolen, the insurance company pays some amount that depends on the car value, but
if the car does not get stolen, you receive nothing. Similarly, if you purchase an interest
rate option to cover yourself against an increase in future interest rates, you pay an up
front option premium. If the interest rate indeed increases, you receive a cash amount that
depends on the level of the reference interest rate, but if the interest rate does not increase,
you receive nothing. It is important to remember that you do not receive anything in the
good event: If the insurance company does not pay you it is because nobody stole your car,
which is good. If you bought insurance against an interest rate hike and the insurance did
not pay, this is good, as it means that the bad event did not occur.[7]

In a theft insurance policy, the amount of coverage and deductibles affect the level of
the insurance premium. Similarly, in financial options the amount of coverage depends on
the strike price: If you purchase an interest rate option to cover yourself against an increase
in interest rates, the higher the strike price and the lower is the payment if the interest rate
increases. This corresponds to lower insurance coverage, ex ante, and indeed it generates
a lower option premium that you have to pay up front. Finally, in a theft insurance policy,
the premium is higher when the risk that the car will be stolen is higher. Similarly, as we

---

[7]Ex post, of course, you wish you did not buy the insurance in this case, as you "wasted" the insurance (option)
premium. But this is an ex-post reasoning, while the hedging program has to be set up ex-ante, before knowing
what would happen.

are going to see, the interest rate option premium also depends on some type of interest rate risk, its volatility.[8]

It is convenient to illustrate the idea of insurance in the hedging example discussed in Examples 5.6 and 5.7 in Chapter 5.

■ **EXAMPLE 6.2**

Recall that today is March 1, 2001, and a firm is worried that the 6-month interest rate could decline in the next six months, when it will receive a $100 million receivable. The firm intends to invest this cash at $T_1 = 0.5$ for the next six months by purchasing safe Treasury bills. Let $P_{bill}(T_1, T_2)$ denote the six month T-bill at $T_1 = 0.5$ with maturity $T_2 = 1$. In Example 5.6 in Chapter 5 the firm hedged by entering into a forward contract with a bank. This forward contract, an OTC instrument, allowed the firm to purchase six months later ($T_1 = 0.5$) $100 million-worth of 6-month Treasury bills for a price $P^{fwd} = \$97.938$, for $100 par value, specified today. The payoff of the forward contract is then

$$\text{Payoff of forward contract} = P_{bill}(T_1, T_2) - P^{fwd}$$

That is, if the price of T-bills increases, which is what the firm worries about, then the forward contract pays a positive amount.

Of course, if instead the interest rate increases, the forward contract generates a negative cash flow, as the price of the T-bill $P_{bill}(T_1, T_2)$ would fall below the forward price P^{fwd}. A hedger may prefer to hedge only against the decrease in the interest rate, but not against an increase. That is, she would prefer to purchase an insurance against an interest rate decline. With this insurance, the firm can eliminate the bad event (a lower interest rate) but keep the upside potential, that is, the fact that if the interest rate instead increases, the firm can invest the $100 million receivable to purchase T-bills at a lower price than P^{fwd}.

A call option on the 6-month T-bill allows a firm to achieve exactly this latter outcome. The call option enables the firm to purchase T-bills at maturity T_1 for *at most* the predetermined strike price, such as $K = \$97.938$. This implies the payoff at T_1 is

$$\text{Payoff of call option contract} = \max\left(P_{bill}(T_1, T_2) - K, 0\right)$$

Of course, this payoff does not come for free and the firm has to pay the option premium, which can be relatively expensive.

Assume that the bank asks the firm an option premium equal to[9]

$$Call(K) = \$0.2701 \text{ (for \$100 principal of T-bills)},$$

for an option with maturity $T_1 = 0.5$ and strike price $K = \$97.938$.

---

[8]There are also many elements that are different between financial options and regular theft insurance. For instance, deductibles are used in insurance market to attenuate the moral hazard problem, according to which full coverage tend to induce a riskier behavior of the insured. An important difference between financial insurance and theft insurance concern the calculation of the insurance (option) premium, as it is discussed in later chapters.
[9]This premium is computed using the Ho-Lee model option pricing formula, developed in Chapter 17.

How many options does the firm have to buy?

The total premium to be paid can be computed as follows: If the option will be exercised, the firm wants to purchase $100 million-worth of T-bills at T_1 at the strike price $K = \$97.938$. Therefore, the firm needs to purchase $M = \$100m/\$97.938 = 1.02105$ million of T-bills (with $100 principal). Assuming each option is defined on a T-bill with $100 principal, then the firm needs to purchase M options. The total cost of the option position is then

$$\text{Total option premium} = M \times Call(K) = \$275,762.5 \tag{6.13}$$

To summarize, by paying $275,762.5, the firm can insure against a decrease in the interest rate. If the interest rate does not fall and perhaps in fact rises, then the $P_{bill}(T_1, T_2)$ decreases, and it is better for the firm to purchase the 6-month T-bill in the market, rather than exercise the option. If instead the interest rate does in fact decrease, the firm can exercise the option and purchase the T-bill at $K = \$97.938$ instead of at its higher market price, thereby hedging the bad outcome.

The previous example illustrates the calculation of the option's premium to hedge against a decline in interest rates. The next example follows up with the ex-post outcome and the performance of the hedging strategy.

■ **EXAMPLE 6.3**

Consider Example 6.2. What happened next? The 6-month interest rate did in fact decline, and the 6-month T-bill price on September 4, 2001, was $P_{bill}(T_1, T_2) = \$98.89 > \$97.938 = K$. In this case, the firm would exercise the option, and obtain the payoff

$$
\begin{aligned}
\text{Option payoff on September 4, 2001} &= M \times (\$98.89 - \$97.938) \\
&= \$972,043.54
\end{aligned}
$$

This amount has to be invested by the firm together with the receivable of $100 million. The return on the additional amount makes up for the lower interest rate, that is, for the higher price of the T-bill $P_{bill}(T_1, T_2) = \$98.89$. In fact, the total investment in T-bills is given by

$$
\begin{aligned}
\text{Investment in T-bills (with \$100 principal)} &= \frac{\$100,000,000 + \$972,043.54}{\$98.89} \\
&= 1,021,054.136
\end{aligned}
$$

Because each T-bill yields $100 at T_2, the investment's final payoff at T_2 is $102,105,413.6. In turn, this final payoff entails:

$$
\begin{aligned}
\text{Gross annualized return on investment} &= \frac{1}{T_2 - T_1}\left(\frac{\text{Final payoff at } T_2}{\text{Investment at } T_1} - 1\right) \\
&= 2 \times \left(\frac{102,105,413.6}{100,000,000} - 1\right) \\
&= 4.21\% \tag{6.14}
\end{aligned}
$$

This is the same rate of interest that the firm would have received with a regular forward contract, as discussed in Example 5.7 in Chapter 5.

Gross versus Net Return. The calculation in Equation 6.14 is misleading about the real rate of return realized by the option strategy. In fact, we haven't taken into account the option premium paid by the firm at time 0. To compute the fair return on the option strategy and compare it to a forward contract, we *must* subtract the option premium paid at time 0, given in Equation 6.13, from the final option payoff (Equation 6.14). To take into account the time value of money from 0 to T_1, we can use the discount factor implied by the 6-month T-bill at time 0, $P_{bill}(0, T_1) = \$97.728$, i.e. $Z(0, T_1) = 0.97728$. We then obtain that the net option payoff on September 4, 2001 is

$$
\begin{aligned}
\text{Net option payoff on September 4, 2001} &= \$972,043.54 - \frac{\$275,762.5}{0.97728} \\
&= \$689,870.06
\end{aligned}
$$

Using the net option payoff instead of the gross payoff in Equation 6.14, we find that the investment in T-bills is given by

$$
\begin{aligned}
\text{Investment in T-bills (with \$100 principal)} &= \frac{\$100,000,000 + \$689,870.06}{\$98.89} \\
&= 1,018,200.729
\end{aligned}
$$

Given the implied final payoff at T_2 is then equal to $\$101,820,072.9$, the annualized return on the $100 million receivable is

$$
\begin{aligned}
\text{Net annualized return on investment} &= 2 \times \left(\frac{101,820,872.9}{100,000,000} - 1 \right) \\
&= 3.64\% \quad\quad (6.15)
\end{aligned}
$$

The lower rate obtained under the option contract is due to the premium paid to keep the upside potential of a higher interest rate, a fact that that did not happen ex-post.

6.2.2 Option Strategies

Call and put options are the building blocks of more complex strategies. We can follow up on Example 6.2 to illustrate some of the most common strategies.

6.2.2.1 Deductibles

The firm in Example 6.2 may be interested in insuring only against *substantial* declines in the 6-month interest rate, while keeping the risk for smaller declines. In this case, it can purchase T-bill options with a higher strike price, which pay only if the T-bill price increases substantially. This strategy would be cheaper, as the firm retains some of the interest rate risk. For instance, setting a strike price $K = \$98.28$ the total cost of the option would be $\$137,994.5$, but the option would start paying off only if the 6-month rate declines to $r_K = 2 \times (1/K - 1) = 3.5\%$. Ex post, given that the T-bill rate indeed moved to $P_{bill}(T_1, T_2) = \$98.89 > 98.28$, this strategy would have generated an implied net rate of 3.215%, less than the rate computed under full coverage in Equation 6.15, as it is to be expected: The firm wanted to keep some risk so as to pay less insurance, and when the bad outcome materializes it obtained a lower overall payoff.

6.2.2.2 Collars Alternatively, the firm may decide to give up some of the return stemming from an increase in interest rates in order to help pay for the premium to cover against lower interest rates. In this case, it can sell some put option on T-bills, whose premium can be used to offset the cost of the purchase of the call option described above. This strategy is called a **collar strategy**. An especially popular collar strategy is one for which the premium received from the put sold exactly offsets the premium for the call purchased. That is, there is no ex-ante cash outflow from the collar strategy.

For instance, the firm in Example 6.2 could purchase call options with strike price $K_C = \$98.28$ and sell put options with strike price $K_P = \$97.596$. Given the $100 million receivable, the firm needs to purchase exactly $M_C = \$100 \, \text{m}/K_C = 1,017,501$ options with strike price K_C and sell $M_P = 1,024,633$ options with strike price K_P.[10] Using an option pricing formula that we develop in later chapters, the total cost of purchasing the option equals the total gain from selling put. That is, the following relation holds

$$M_C \times Call(K_C) = M_P \times Call(K_P)$$

If at T_1 the interest rate declines, so that the T-bill price $P_{bill}(T_1, T_2) > K_C = \$98.28$, then the firm receives additional funding to compensate for the higher price of T-bills. This is the same situation as in Example 6.2. In contrast, if the interest rate increases, so that the T-bill price $P_{bill}(T_1, T_2) < K_P = \$97.596$, then the firm will have to pay the put payoff to the counterparty. This drain in cash will decrease the amount of investment that the firm can make for the following six months. However, the drain is exactly compensated for by the lower price of the T-bills (or higher interest rate), which the firm needs to purchase for the next six months. Panel A of Figure 6.4 shows the *profit* from the collar strategy for various values of the T-bill price at T_1. The collar pays when the T-bill price is high, thereby hedging the lower interest rates, and requires a payment when the T-bill price is low, compensated for though by the now higher rate.

Panel B of Figure 6.4 plots the implied rate of return from T_1 to T_2 that is obtained from the hedging strategy for various scenarios at T_1. For easier reference, the $x-$axis now plots the 6-month interest rate that is equivalent to the T-bill price on the $x-$axis in Panel A. For this reason, the interest rate runs from a high number (low T-bill price in Panel A) to a low number (high T-bill price in Panel A). The $y-$axis reports instead the implied interest rate, computed exactly as in Equation 6.15, but for the collar strategy. We see that when the interest rate declines (right-hand side of the plot), the effective rate realized by the collar strategy also declines, but only down to 3.5%. If the interest rate declines further, the firm is hedged. Similarly, if the interest rate increases (left-hand side of the plot), then the rate of return for the firm increases, and the upside potential is realized. If the interest rate increase above $4.93\% (= 2 \times (100/K_P - 1))$, however, then the realized return flattens out at that level. Any further increase in the interest rate would not generate any additional return for the firm.

For comparison with the collar strategy, Figure 6.4 also plots the forward rate that the firm would obtain by simply entering into a forward contract on the T-bill with a forward price $P^{fwd} = \$97.938$, as already discussed in Example 5.7 in Chapter 5. The zero cost collar strategy and the forward contract indeed share a common feature: They do not cost anything at initiation. Therefore, the comparison of the effective rate at time T_1 in Figure

---

[10]These numbers of options guarantee that the firm invests exactly $100 million-worth of T-bills at K_C and at K_P.

Figure 6.4   Zero Cost Collar Strategy

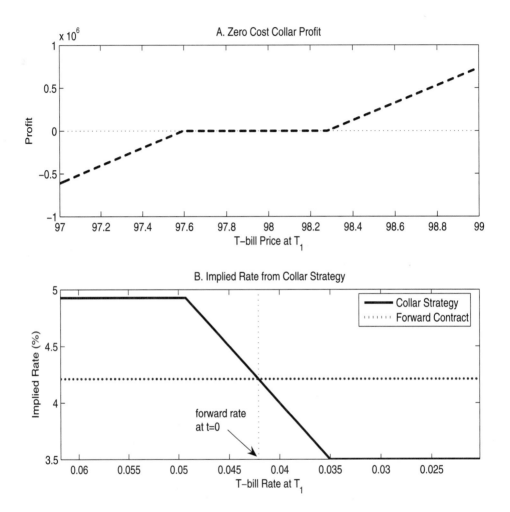

6.4 provides an intuition of the tradeoff implied by collar strategy: By entering a long call option and a short put option in a way to make the strategy zero cost, the firm is trading off some upside (left-hand side of the figure) for some downside (right-hand side of the figure). By choosing different strike prices the firm can tailor how much upside it wants to trade for a better coverage on the downside.

6.2.2.3 Yield-Enhancing Strategies   One popular set of strategies among investors and investment banks goes under the name of yield enhancing strategies. The idea is the following. Consider a coupon bond sold at par. The coupon rate equals, by definition, its yield to maturity. To make the coupon higher, however, it is common to augment the bond with a short option position. For instance, one could issue a bond that pays a fixed coupon so long as a reference rate is below a given cutoff level, but such that the coupon would decline if the interest rate rises above the cutoff. For instance, a possible strategy is to have

a coupon defined as follows

$$\text{Coupon at } T_i = c - \max(r(T_{i-1}) - r_K, 0)$$

In other words, so long as the reference rate is below the strike rate r_K, the coupon is fixed at c. However, if the reference rate increases above r_K, then the coupon is reduced. As we have seen for inverse floaters, this type of security yields a higher coupon than market so long as the rate $r(T_{i-1}) < r_K$, but it would fall in price very quickly if the interest rate increases above r_K. Why is the coupon rate higher than with regular bonds? The reason is that the investor who buys a bond with this coupon is effectively purchasing a straight fixed rate bond with coupon c and selling an option (in fact, a cap). The premium from the short cap position is embedded in the coupon rate, so that the bond still prices at par. We investigate the risk and return of some of these structures in later chapters.

6.2.3 Put-Call Parity

Consider a collar strategy (see Subsection 6.2.2.2) long one call with strike price K_C and short one put with strike price K_P with maturity T_1. Let these options be European, meaning that they can be exercised only at maturity T_1. Consider now the special case in which the strike prices are the same, that is, $K_C = K_P = K$. In this case, the payoff from the collar strategy is

$$\begin{aligned} \text{Payoff long call / Short put} \ &= \ max(P(T_1, T_2) - K, 0) - max(K - P(T_1, T_2), 0) \\ &= \ P(T_1, T_2) - K \end{aligned}$$

This is the same payoff of a long forward contract, establishing the fact that

$$\text{Call} - \text{Put} = \text{Long forward} \tag{6.16}$$

This relation is called **put-call parity**. In particular, the value of a forward contract on a bond $P(T_1, T_2)$ for given delivery price K is given by

$$V^{fwd}(0) = Z(0, T_1) \times \left(P^{fwd}(0, T_1, T_2) - K \right)$$

where $P^{fwd}(0, T_1, T_2)$ is the forward price of the underlying bond $P(T_1, T_2)$. From the put-call parity, we then have

$$Call(K) = Put(K) + Z(0, T_1) \times \left(P^{fwd}(0, T_1, T_2) - K \right)$$

If we have put prices available, then we can compute call prices, and vice versa.

6.2.4 Hedging with Futures or with Options?

Once we consider options as insurance contracts, it is easier to think about the pros and cons of options versus futures to hedge interest rate risk. The main trade off is costs versus upside potential: Linear contracts such as futures, forwards, and swaps have no costs, but also no upside. Options, on the other hand, cost money, and eliminate only the adverse events.

One issue to take into account in the choice of futures (or forwards, or swaps) and options is the hedger's anticipated reaction to the good events. In other words, while futures pay when the adverse event occurs, they also generate an outflow of cash from the firm when the "good" event occurs. This means that corporate earnings, for instance, may be depressed if the hedge loses money, notwithstanding the good outcome.[11] Is the hedger willing to accept the possibility of large cash outflows during good times? Would the CEO of the company understand that the hedge is supposed to require money when the adverse event is not occurring? When the trader in charge of the hedging program asks the CEO for the cash amount in order to cover the futures' margin calls, what would be the reaction of the CEO? Would the trader be tagged as a rogue trader?

For instance, in Chapter 5, Example 5.9, a firm is engaged in a complicated hedging strategy in order to match the cash flows of its liabilities, linked to a floating rate, to the cash flows of its assets, which is a fixed rate receivable. The concern of the firm is that if the LIBOR rate increases in the future, the cash outflows to pay for the debt may be larger than the cash inflows from the receivables, generating a cash shortfall. The fixed-for-floating swap discussed in Example 5.9 exactly matches the cash inflows with outflows, and the firm is *perfectly hedged* going forward. After initiation of the contract, in March 2001, the 6-month LIBOR *did* decrease substantially, and the sequence of realized LIBOR is reported in Table 5.4. The last column of this table shows that the firm must make substantial payments to honor the swap contract, even at the rate of many millions of dollars every six months. Taken in isolation, and with the benefit of hindsight, the hedge with swaps was not a good deal, as it looked like a bet on a future increase in interest rates, a bet gone bad. It is very important, in these cases, to keep the focus on the overall strategy, that is, the fact that because of the swap position, now the total net cash flow of the firm is in fact zero, independent of the movement of interest rates. This was the objective of the hedging strategy. Yet, if it is possible to forecast ex ante that large cash outflows generated by the swap itself may generate internal problems between the trader and the CEO, for instance, or the possibility of loss in competitiveness – other competing firms may have lower borrowing rates if the interest rate declines – then an insurance contract may be preferable. Indeed, the insurance contract can be tailored to eliminate only the really bad outcomes, that may hamper the firm from functioning.

■ **EXAMPLE 6.4**

Consider again Example 5.9 in Chapter 5. An insurance strategy may be as follows: At the moment, the 6-month LIBOR rate $r_2(0) = 4.95\%$ is sufficiently low, to ensure that the semi-annual receivable of $5.5 million covers the floating coupon due $c(0.5) = (r_2(0) + 4bps) \times 0.5 \times 200$ m $= 4.99$ million. However, were the LIBOR rate to increase above 5.46%, then the receivable of $5.5 million would not be sufficient to pay for the floating rate coupon. An insurance is to purchase a sequence of interest rate options that pay anytime the 6-month LIBOR is above $r_K = 5.46\%$. This option is called a cap. In particular, a five year, semi-annual cap pays a cash flow at every T_i equal to

$$\text{Cap cash flow at } T_i = N \times \Delta \times \max\left(r_2(T_{i-1}) - r_K, 0\right)$$

---

[11]This problem is partly mitigated by hedge accounting, which allows a firm to match these negative cash flows against the (positive) value of the primary risk exposure being hedged. However, hedge accounting not always is feasible.

where $\Delta = T_i - T_{i-1}$ is the time between payments, N is the notional amount, and $r_2(t)$ is the 6-month LIBOR rate at t. Like the floating rate bond issued by the firm, the cap pays at time T_i an amount linked to the LIBOR defined at the *previous* reset date, T_{i-1}.

Given a notional amount $N = 200$ million, the premium for such a cap is

$$5\text{-year cap premium} = \$5,998,733$$

By paying this amount, the firm covers itself from hikes in the interest rate for the next five years, but it would not have to make any payment in case the interest rate declines. That is, it insured itself against increases in interest rates.

As we know from Table 5.4 in Chapter 5, the 6-month LIBOR indeed declined during the following five years. In this case, the option would expire worthless, as it would make no payment. Although there is a temptation to think that the firm lost money on the option, as the firm paid almost $6 million for it, we must recall that the decline in interest rates is a good outcome for the firm, as now the firm has to make lower payments from the liabilities, but still obtain a fixed $5.5 million receivable. The cap was an insurance policy.

As mentioned earlier, the option premium can be decreased by following some other strategies. For instance, if the firm is willing to bear some more interest rate risk (a deductible in the insurance terminology), it could insure itself only for interest rate increases above $r_K = 6.5\%$ instead of $r_K = 5.46\%$. In this case, the option premium would drop to approximately $3.4 million. Similarly, the firm may decide to keep the upside potential only within a given interval of interest rates, and therefore buy a collar, meaning that it can buy the cap to protect against interest rates, but also sell a floor so as to partially pay for it.

6.3 SUMMARY

In this chapter we covered the following topics:

1. Futures: A futures contract is similar to a forward contract, in which the counterparty short the contract agrees to sell a prespecified security on a prespecified date and at a prespecified price to the counterparty long the contract. The latter agrees to buy the security and to pay the prespecified price. Some futures contracts are cash settled, meaning that no exchange of security actually takes place. Characteristics of futures contracts are that they are:

   - Traded in regulated exchanges.
   - Standardized: The maturity of the contracts as well as the delivery securities are decided by the exchange.
   - Marked-to-market: Profits and losses accrue to the counterparties on a daily basis.

2. Convergence property: This is when the futures price converges at maturity to the price of the unlderlying contract.

3. Options: Options are contracts in which the counterparty long the contract has the right, but not the obligation, to purchase (for a call) or sell (for a put) the security underlying the contract, at a prespecified price and within a prespecified time. The counterparty short the contract is obliged to sell (if a call) or purchase (if a put) the security at the prespecified price.

4. European and American Options: European options are options that can be exercised only at maturity. American options are options that can be exercised anytime before maturity.

5. Put-Call parity: For European options, a put minus a call with the same strike price equals a forward contract. Therefore, a put equals a call minus a forward contract.

6. Collar Strategies: An options' portfolio that is long a call and short a put option.

6.4 EXERCISES

1. This exercise uses the data in Table 6.9. Suppose that on February 15, 1994 a firm wants to enter into a forward contract to purchase 5-year Treasuries, with coupon rate 6%, in two years:

   (a) Compute the forward price.

   (b) What is the value of the forward contract at initiation?

   (c) Compute the value of the forward contract on each of the next five days.

   (d) Assume the firm and the counterparty mark to market the forward contract; describe the cash flows between the counterparties over time.

   (e) Panel B contains overnight rates. Compute the total profit / loss on the contract after two, three, four, and five days.

2. On March 21, 2007 a firm enters into 100 90-day Eurodollar futures contracts (contract size is $1,000,000). The quoted futures price on this day is: $93.695. Over the life of the contracts, prices move as in Table 6.10.

   (a) What will the daily P&L from futures for the quoted dates be?

   (b) What will the cumulative P&L for the quoted dates be?

   (c) You find out that 90-day Eurodollar futures are subjected to the following requirements: Initial Margin: $1,485 (per contract); Maintenance Margin: $1,110 (per contract).

      i. What will the cash flow of the contract be, assuming that the firm never takes money from the margin account?

      ii. What will the cash flow of the contract be if the firm decides to take every profit from the contract instead of leaving it in the margin account?

3. Consider the data in Table 6.11, where $P^{fut}(t, T_1)$ is the price of a 90-day Eurodollar futures contract expiring on April 14, 2008; $f(t, T_1, T_2)$ is the time t forward rate

Table 6.9   Semi-annually Compounded Yield Curves

	Panel A: Yeld Curves					
Date	2/15/1994	2/16/1994	2/17/1994	2/18/1994	2/22/1994	2/23/1994
5/15/1994	3.57%	3.69%	3.81%	4.32%	3.15%	3.15%
8/15/1994	3.59%	3.59%	3.71%	3.55%	3.49%	3.54%
11/15/1994	3.80%	3.84%	3.70%	3.72%	3.66%	3.71%
2/15/1995	3.86%	3.89%	3.92%	4.08%	4.07%	4.19%
5/15/1995	4.01%	4.03%	4.05%	4.12%	4.21%	4.36%
8/15/1995	4.18%	4.18%	4.24%	4.32%	4.34%	4.44%
11/15/1995	4.27%	4.29%	4.36%	4.43%	4.46%	4.59%
2/15/1996	4.48%	4.48%	4.56%	4.55%	4.65%	4.75%
5/15/1996	4.58%	4.58%	4.65%	4.71%	4.73%	4.83%
8/15/1996	4.62%	4.62%	4.70%	4.75%	4.73%	4.81%
11/15/1996	4.76%	4.77%	4.86%	4.90%	4.90%	5.00%
2/15/1997	4.81%	4.81%	4.89%	4.94%	4.92%	5.01%
5/15/1997	4.95%	4.96%	5.04%	5.11%	5.09%	5.18%
8/15/1997	5.04%	5.04%	5.13%	5.19%	5.19%	5.27%
11/15/1997	5.14%	5.13%	5.22%	5.29%	5.29%	5.38%
2/15/1998	5.20%	5.19%	5.30%	5.37%	5.36%	5.41%
5/15/1998	5.25%	5.25%	5.36%	5.43%	5.41%	5.50%
8/15/1998	5.33%	5.34%	5.45%	5.53%	5.50%	5.58%
11/15/1998	5.38%	5.38%	5.50%	5.56%	5.54%	5.62%
2/15/1999	5.45%	5.45%	5.57%	5.63%	5.61%	5.70%
5/15/1999	5.49%	5.50%	5.61%	5.68%	5.66%	5.74%
8/15/1999	5.50%	5.50%	5.62%	5.68%	5.66%	5.75%
11/15/1999	5.57%	5.56%	5.68%	5.76%	5.73%	5.82%
2/15/2000	5.61%	5.61%	5.71%	5.80%	5.80%	5.87%
5/15/2000	5.65%	5.66%	5.76%	5.85%	5.84%	5.91%
8/15/2000	5.71%	5.72%	5.82%	5.91%	5.90%	5.93%
11/15/2000	5.76%	5.77%	5.87%	6.01%	5.94%	6.03%
2/15/2001	5.78%	5.81%	5.92%	5.99%	5.96%	6.04%
5/15/2001	5.83%	5.84%	5.95%	6.03%	6.03%	6.11%
8/15/2001	5.85%	5.88%	5.96%	6.07%	6.08%	6.15%
11/15/2001	5.92%	5.94%	6.03%	6.13%	6.13%	6.21%

	Panel B: Overnight Rates				
	2/16/1994	2/17/1994	2/18/1994	2/22/1994	2/23/1994
	3.54%	3.78%	3.90%	4.44%	2.88%

Notes: Yields calculated based on data from CRSP (Daily Treasuries) © 2009 Center for Research
in Security Prices (CRSP), The University of Chicago Booth School of Business.

Table 6.10   Eurdollar Futures

Date	Price	Date	Price	Date	Price	Date	Price
21-Mar-07	93.635	7-May-07	93.185	21-Jun-07	93.095	7-Aug-07	93.150
22-Mar-07	93.685	8-May-07	93.175	22-Jun-07	93.210	8-Aug-07	93.260
23-Mar-07	93.570	9-May-07	93.245	25-Jun-07	93.190	9-Aug-07	93.205
26-Mar-07	93.500	10-May-07	93.095	26-Jun-07	93.080	10-Aug-07	93.250
27-Mar-07	93.320	11-May-07	92.825	27-Jun-07	93.090	13-Aug-07	93.340
28-Mar-07	93.330	14-May-07	92.935	28-Jun-07	93.015	14-Aug-07	93.335
29-Mar-07	93.330	15-May-07	92.870	29-Jun-07	92.945	15-Aug-07	93.335
30-Mar-07	93.375	16-May-07	92.895	2-Jul-07	92.965	16-Aug-07	93.370
2-Apr-07	93.340	17-May-07	93.010	3-Jul-07	92.975	17-Aug-07	93.445
3-Apr-07	93.355	18-May-07	93.090	5-Jul-07	92.930	20-Aug-07	93.380
4-Apr-07	93.380	21-May-07	93.120	6-Jul-07	92.950	21-Aug-07	93.415
5-Apr-07	93.340	22-May-07	93.120	9-Jul-07	92.995	22-Aug-07	93.405
6-Apr-07	93.455	23-May-07	93.050	10-Jul-07	93.035	23-Aug-07	93.440
9-Apr-07	93.395	24-May-07	92.925	11-Jul-07	93.025	24-Aug-07	93.390
10-Apr-07	93.245	25-May-07	92.915	12-Jul-07	93.065	27-Aug-07	93.385
11-Apr-07	93.240	29-May-07	92.895	13-Jul-07	93.120	28-Aug-07	93.480
12-Apr-07	93.175	30-May-07	92.865	16-Jul-07	93.185	29-Aug-07	93.620
16-Apr-07	93.060	31-May-07	93.010	17-Jul-07	93.185	30-Aug-07	93.565
17-Apr-07	93.170	1-Jun-07	93.060	18-Jul-07	93.265	31-Aug-07	93.510
18-Apr-07	93.265	4-Jun-07	93.120	19-Jul-07	93.265	4-Sep-07	93.345
19-Apr-07	93.080	5-Jun-07	93.195	20-Jul-07	93.260	5-Sep-07	93.370
20-Apr-07	93.060	6-Jun-07	93.225	23-Jul-07	93.295	6-Sep-07	93.510
23-Apr-07	93.115	7-Jun-07	93.140	24-Jul-07	93.290	7-Sep-07	93.515
24-Apr-07	93.100	8-Jun-07	93.065	25-Jul-07	93.190	10-Sep-07	93.450
25-Apr-07	93.020	11-Jun-07	93.140	26-Jul-07	93.170	11-Sep-07	93.505
26-Apr-07	93.135	12-Jun-07	93.185	27-Jul-07	93.235	13-Sep-07	93.490
27-Apr-07	93.015	13-Jun-07	93.150	30-Jul-07	93.230	14-Sep-07	93.620
30-Apr-07	93.025	14-Jun-07	93.145	31-Jul-07	93.310	17-Sep-07	93.540
1-May-07	93.085	15-Jun-07	93.020	1-Aug-07	93.265	18-Sep-07	93.420
2-May-07	93.135	18-Jun-07	92.995	2-Aug-07	93.190	19-Sep-07	93.485
3-May-07	93.250	19-Jun-07	93.010	3-Aug-07	93.140	20-Sep-07	93.495
4-May-07	93.250	20-Jun-07	93.060	6-Aug-07	93.160	21-Sep-07	93.590

Source: Bloomberg.

Table 6.11 Futures and Forward Rates

Date	$P^{fut}(t,T_1)$	$f(t,T_1,T_2)$	$Z(t,T_1)$	$Z(t,t+dt)$	Date	$P^{fut}(t,T_1)$	$f(t,T_1,T_2)$	$Z(t,T_1)$	$Z(t,t+dt)$
16-Oct-07	95.3900	4.9377%	0.9751	0.9998	15-Jan-08	96.5900	3.6628%	0.9902	0.9998
17-Oct-07	95.5150	4.8740%	0.9753	0.9998	16-Jan-08	96.5700	3.6452%	0.9904	0.9998
18-Oct-07	95.5700	4.7691%	0.9756	0.9998	17-Jan-08	96.6250	3.7057%	0.9906	0.9998
19-Oct-07	95.6850	4.6475%	0.9761	0.9998	18-Jan-08	96.7150	3.6295%	0.9908	0.9998
22-Oct-07	95.6700	4.5410%	0.9768	0.9998	22-Jan-08	97.1500	3.3133%	0.9916	0.9998
23-Oct-07	95.6700	4.6208%	0.9769	0.9998	23-Jan-08	97.2450	3.0388%	0.9926	0.9999
24-Oct-07	95.7750	4.5184%	0.9772	0.9998	24-Jan-08	97.0350	3.0847%	0.9928	0.9999
25-Oct-07	95.7750	4.4484%	0.9776	0.9998	25-Jan-08	97.0650	3.2957%	0.9928	0.9999
26-Oct-07	95.7350	4.4708%	0.9777	0.9998	28-Jan-08	97.1250	3.1394%	0.9932	0.9999
29-Oct-07	95.7000	4.4837%	0.9781	0.9998	29-Jan-08	97.1050	3.1414%	0.9933	0.9999
30-Oct-07	95.6800	4.5514%	0.9784	0.9998	30-Jan-08	97.1850	3.1548%	0.9934	0.9999
31-Oct-07	95.5500	4.5478%	0.9784	0.9998	31-Jan-08	97.2400	3.0024%	0.9936	0.9999
1-Nov-07	95.6700	4.6967%	0.9784	0.9998	1-Feb-08	97.1700	2.9729%	0.9938	0.9999
2-Nov-07	95.7950	4.5323%	0.9787	0.9998	4-Feb-08	97.1450	3.0675%	0.9939	0.9999
5-Nov-07	95.7250	4.5183%	0.9790	0.9998	5-Feb-08	97.2400	3.0789%	0.9940	0.9999
6-Nov-07	95.7050	4.5836%	0.9790	0.9998	6-Feb-08	97.2700	2.9475%	0.9941	0.9999
7-Nov-07	95.7550	4.5498%	0.9792	0.9998	7-Feb-08	97.2650	2.9297%	0.9942	0.9999
8-Nov-07	95.8950	4.5025%	0.9794	0.9998	8-Feb-08	97.2900	2.9512%	0.9943	0.9999
9-Nov-07	95.9300	4.4121%	0.9797	0.9998	11-Feb-08	97.2950	2.9227%	0.9946	0.9999
12-Nov-07	95.9300	4.3647%	0.9801	0.9998	12-Feb-08	97.2900	2.9167%	0.9947	0.9999
13-Nov-07	95.8000	4.3561%	0.9803	0.9998	13-Feb-08	97.2800	2.9124%	0.9948	0.9999
14-Nov-07	95.7900	4.4676%	0.9803	0.9998	14-Feb-08	97.2650	2.9325%	0.9949	0.9999
15-Nov-07	95.9450	4.4416%	0.9803	0.9998	15-Feb-08	97.2600	2.9446%	0.9950	0.9999
16-Nov-07	95.9450	4.3667%	0.9804	0.9998	19-Feb-08	97.1900	2.9701%	0.9953	0.9999
19-Nov-07	95.8350	4.4307%	0.9806	0.9998	20-Feb-08	97.1550	3.0113%	0.9954	0.9999
20-Nov-07	95.8300	4.4359%	0.9807	0.9998	21-Feb-08	97.2000	3.0612%	0.9955	0.9999
21-Nov-07	95.9500	4.4164%	0.9808	0.9998	22-Feb-08	97.1500	3.0026%	0.9956	0.9999
23-Nov-07	95.9500	4.3945%	0.9810	0.9998	25-Feb-08	97.1200	3.0499%	0.9958	0.9999
26-Nov-07	96.0950	4.4663%	0.9813	0.9998	26-Feb-08	97.1450	3.0541%	0.9959	0.9999
27-Nov-07	95.9700	4.3768%	0.9815	0.9998	27-Feb-08	97.1900	3.0192%	0.9960	0.9999
28-Nov-07	95.8900	4.4886%	0.9815	0.9998	28-Feb-08	97.2500	2.9751%	0.9961	0.9999
29-Nov-07	95.9850	4.4769%	0.9816	0.9998	29-Feb-08	97.3800	2.9505%	0.9963	0.9999
30-Nov-07	96.0000	4.4795%	0.9817	0.9998	3-Mar-08	97.3550	2.8894%	0.9965	0.9999
3-Dec-07	95.9700	4.4383%	0.9821	0.9998	4-Mar-08	97.3400	2.8963%	0.9966	0.9999
4-Dec-07	95.9650	4.4606%	0.9822	0.9998	5-Mar-08	97.3000	2.8999%	0.9967	0.9999
5-Dec-07	95.9650	4.4754%	0.9823	0.9998	6-Mar-08	97.3350	2.9099%	0.9968	0.9999
6-Dec-07	95.8750	4.4785%	0.9825	0.9998	7-Mar-08	97.4800	2.8230%	0.9969	0.9999
7-Dec-07	95.7400	4.5479%	0.9826	0.9998	10-Mar-08	97.4850	2.8266%	0.9972	0.9999
10-Dec-07	95.7250	4.6552%	0.9829	0.9998	11-Mar-08	97.4000	2.7963%	0.9974	0.9999
11-Dec-07	95.7050	4.6395%	0.9831	0.9998	12-Mar-08	97.4450	2.8098%	0.9975	0.9999
12-Dec-07	95.8100	4.6333%	0.9833	0.9998	13-Mar-08	97.4900	2.7437%	0.9976	0.9999
13-Dec-07	95.7350	4.5007%	0.9836	0.9998	14-Mar-08	97.6350	2.7150%	0.9977	0.9999
14-Dec-07	95.6400	4.5878%	0.9838	0.9998	17-Mar-08	97.7700	2.4805%	0.9981	0.9998
17-Dec-07	95.7000	4.6172%	0.9842	0.9998	18-Mar-08	97.5500	2.4785%	0.9982	0.9999
18-Dec-07	95.7850	4.5908%	0.9844	0.9998	19-Mar-08	97.5600	2.5706%	0.9982	0.9999
19-Dec-07	95.8450	4.5211%	0.9846	0.9998	20-Mar-08	97.5275	2.5822%	0.9983	0.9999
20-Dec-07	95.8700	4.4680%	0.9849	0.9998	25-Mar-08	97.4350	2.6602%	0.9986	0.9999
21-Dec-07	95.8250	4.4625%	0.9851	0.9998	26-Mar-08	97.4250	2.6671%	0.9987	0.9999
24-Dec-07	95.8050	4.4741%	0.9855	0.9998	27-Mar-08	97.4275	2.6716%	0.9987	0.9999
27-Dec-07	95.8050	4.5054%	0.9859	0.9998	28-Mar-08	97.4250	2.6844%	0.9988	0.9999
28-Dec-07	95.8850	4.4921%	0.9863	0.9998	31-Mar-08	97.4400	2.6704%	0.9990	0.9999
31-Dec-07	95.9350	4.4191%	0.9866	0.9998	1-Apr-08	97.3800	2.6633%	0.9990	0.9999
2-Jan-08	96.0600	4.3892%	0.9869	0.9998	2-Apr-08	97.3200	2.6937%	0.9991	0.9999
3-Jan-08	96.0850	4.2369%	0.9872	0.9998	3-Apr-08	97.3075	2.7304%	0.9992	0.9999
4-Jan-08	96.1950	4.2555%	0.9874	0.9998	4-Apr-08	97.3600	2.7352%	0.9993	0.9999
7-Jan-08	96.2200	4.1396%	0.9879	0.9998	7-Apr-08	97.3150	2.7120%	0.9995	0.9999
8-Jan-08	96.2300	4.1183%	0.9882	0.9998	8-Apr-08	97.2550	2.7066%	0.9995	0.9999
9-Jan-08	96.3300	4.0523%	0.9884	0.9998	9-Apr-08	97.2800	2.7082%	0.9996	0.9999
10-Jan-08	96.4000	3.9889%	0.9887	0.9998	10-Apr-08	97.2800	2.6974%	0.9997	0.9999
11-Jan-08	96.5800	3.8858%	0.9891	0.9998	11-Apr-08	97.2850	2.6974%	0.9997	0.9999
14-Jan-08	96.6300	3.6526%	0.9900	0.9998	14-Apr-08	97.2912	2.7088%	1.0000	0.9999

Source: Bloomberg.

for 90-day LIBOR at April 14, 2008; $Z(t, T_1)$ is the LIBOR discount from t to April 14, 2008; and $Z(t, t + dt)$ is the overnight LIBOR discount (where $dt = 1$ day).

   (a) On April 14, 2008 the 90-day LIBOR was 2.7088%. Did the rates converge?

   (b) What was the total profit / loss on April 14, 2008 of a futures contract entered on October 16, 2007?

   (c) What would be the total profit / loss on April 14, 2008 of a forward contract entered on October 16, 2007?

   (d) Calculate the total profit / loss at each date for the futures contract.

   (e) Calculate the total profit / loss at each date for the forward contract.

   (f) How close are profits / losses over time? Plot the values.

4. Suppose that on October 16, 2007 a firm loses a lawsuit and has to pay $100 million within 9 months. Currently it has no money to pay, so it decides to sell a piece of equipment. Although the equipment could go for up to $150 million, the firm is desperate and is willing to take much less so as to make the lawsuit payment. A buyer comes up, who offers to buy the equipment at a significant discount and will pay for it in six months. The firm's CFO thinks that the deal might work if they enter into a futures contract or a forward contract.

   (a) Using only the information available on October 16, 2007 in Table 6.11, what is the least that the firm should accept, if it decides to enter into a futures contract?

   (b) Using only the information available on October 16, 2007 what is the least that the firm should accept, if it decides to enter into a forward contract?

5. Following up on Exercise 4, let it now be April 16, 2008. The 90-day LIBOR rate is 2.7088%. Using the information in Exercise 4:

   (a) What is the total amount available to invest in the 90-day LIBOR from the futures contract?

   (b) What is the total amount available to invest in the 90-day LIBOR from the forward contract?

   (c) After 90 days, does the firm receive enough money from the futures contract? Is it exactly the amount that is needed?

   (d) After 90 days, does the firm receive enough money from the forward contract? Is it exactly the amount that is needed?

6. Consider again Exercise 4. Imagine that back on October 16, 2007, the firm decided to sell the equipment for $98.78 million receiving the cash in 6 months. The CFO looks at the 3-month LIBOR at the time and sees that it is at 5.2088%. If the rate holds for only 6 months he could invest the proceeds from the sale and make a $67,000 gain because the return will be $100.067 million at the time of the lawsuit payment. So, he decides to forgo any type of hedging.

   (a) Given past data on the 3-month LIBOR, compute the statistical distribution of possible cash flows in nine months. Specifically, proceed as follows:

   i. Using past data, compute the change in the 3-month LIBOR over six-month periods. Use these changes as possible scenarios about the fluctuations in the 3-month LIBOR over the *next* six months, and compute the distribution of the total amount available in nine months. How frequently would the firm have enough cash to pay for the lawsuit?

   ii. Altenatively, use past data to run the regression

$$r_{t+1} = \alpha + \beta r_t + \epsilon_{t+1}$$

where r_t is the LIBOR rate at time t, and $\epsilon_{t+1} \sim \mathcal{N}(0, \sigma^2)$. Use the estimated parameters α, β and σ together with the current LIBOR rate $r_{today} = 5.2088\%$ to *simulate* LIBOR rates at $t = today+$ six months. According to this calculation, how frequently would the firm have enough cash to pay for the lawsuit?

  (b) On an ex post basis, will the firm have enough cash to pay the lawsuit? How much will the surplus / deficit be?

7. On October 16, 2007, the firm from Exercise 4 decides to enter into a Eurodollar futures contract with expiration on April 14, 2008, so it buys 100 contracts (each is worth $1,000,000). The firm decides that it will create a separate account in which it will simply store the daily P/L of the futures contracts until expiration.

  (a) Using the information in Table 6.11, how much money will the firm receive in six months?

  (b) Suppose that futures prices moved instead according to Table 6.12. How much money will the firm receive in six months?

8. In the previous exercises we assumed that the firm just sat on the profits / losses from the futures contract. This is quite unrealistic because the firm would either invest the profits or borrow to cover the losses from the contract. Assume that the firm decides to do so by investing / borrowing from the time of the profit / loss until the expiration of the contract. In this case we know from Table 6.11 the present value of a dollar on T_1 [see the column for $Z(t, T_1)$], if we want to know the value of receiving a dollar now (t) at a future date T_1, all we have to do is divide the dollar by $Z(t, T_1)$.

  (a) Compute the profit / loss of the firm for the futures prices presented in Exercise 3.

  (b) What is the total return for the firm after investing the money?

  (c) Assuming that the discounts $Z(t, T_1)$ in Table 6.11 also apply for the alternative scenario for futures in Table 6.12, compute for this latter case the profit / loss of the firm from the futures position.

  (d) In the latter case, what is the total return for the firm after investing the money?

9. Comparing the results from Exercises 7 and 8 we can see that whether the firm invests/borrows the proceeds from the hedging activity yields quite a different final amount at maturity T_1. In particular, it appears that the firm is buying too many futures contracts. The adjustment to this excess is called *tailing the hedge*. To do

Table 6.12 Alternative Futures Price Movement

Date	Price	Date	Price	Date	Price	Date	Price
16-Oct-07	95.390	29-Nov-07	94.795	16-Jan-08	94.210	29-Feb-08	93.4000
17-Oct-07	95.265	30-Nov-07	94.780	17-Jan-08	94.155	3-Mar-08	93.4250
18-Oct-07	95.210	3-Dec-07	94.810	18-Jan-08	94.065	4-Mar-08	93.4400
19-Oct-07	95.095	4-Dec-07	94.815	22-Jan-08	93.630	5-Mar-08	93.4800
22-Oct-07	95.110	5-Dec-07	94.815	23-Jan-08	93.535	6-Mar-08	93.4450
23-Oct-07	95.110	6-Dec-07	94.905	24-Jan-08	93.745	7-Mar-08	93.3000
24-Oct-07	95.005	7-Dec-07	95.040	25-Jan-08	93.715	10-Mar-08	93.2950
25-Oct-07	95.005	10-Dec-07	95.055	28-Jan-08	93.655	11-Mar-08	93.3800
26-Oct-07	95.045	11-Dec-07	95.075	29-Jan-08	93.675	12-Mar-08	93.3350
29-Oct-07	95.080	12-Dec-07	94.970	30-Jan-08	93.595	13-Mar-08	93.2900
30-Oct-07	95.100	13-Dec-07	95.045	31-Jan-08	93.540	14-Mar-08	93.1450
31-Oct-07	95.230	14-Dec-07	95.140	1-Feb-08	93.610	17-Mar-08	93.0100
1-Nov-07	95.110	17-Dec-07	95.080	4-Feb-08	93.635	18-Mar-08	93.2300
2-Nov-07	94.985	18-Dec-07	94.995	5-Feb-08	93.540	19-Mar-08	93.2200
5-Nov-07	95.055	19-Dec-07	94.935	6-Feb-08	93.510	20-Mar-08	93.2525
6-Nov-07	95.075	20-Dec-07	94.910	7-Feb-08	93.515	25-Mar-08	93.3450
7-Nov-07	95.025	21-Dec-07	94.955	8-Feb-08	93.490	26-Mar-08	93.3550
8-Nov-07	94.885	24-Dec-07	94.975	11-Feb-08	93.485	27-Mar-08	93.3525
9-Nov-07	94.850	27-Dec-07	94.975	12-Feb-08	93.490	28-Mar-08	93.3550
12-Nov-07	94.850	28-Dec-07	94.895	13-Feb-08	93.500	31-Mar-08	93.3400
13-Nov-07	94.980	31-Dec-07	94.845	14-Feb-08	93.515	1-Apr-08	93.4000
14-Nov-07	94.990	2-Jan-08	94.720	15-Feb-08	93.520	2-Apr-08	93.4600
15-Nov-07	94.835	3-Jan-08	94.695	19-Feb-08	93.590	3-Apr-08	93.4725
16-Nov-07	94.835	4-Jan-08	94.585	20-Feb-08	93.625	4-Apr-08	93.4200
19-Nov-07	94.945	7-Jan-08	94.560	21-Feb-08	93.580	7-Apr-08	93.4650
20-Nov-07	94.950	8-Jan-08	94.550	22-Feb-08	93.630	8-Apr-08	93.5250
21-Nov-07	94.830	9-Jan-08	94.450	25-Feb-08	93.660	9-Apr-08	93.5000
23-Nov-07	94.830	10-Jan-08	94.380	26-Feb-08	93.635	10-Apr-08	93.5000
26-Nov-07	94.685	11-Jan-08	94.200	27-Feb-08	93.590	11-Apr-08	93.4950
27-Nov-07	94.810	14-Jan-08	94.150	28-Feb-08	93.530	14-Apr-08	93.4888
28-Nov-07	94.890	15-Jan-08	94.190				

this we must find a 'tailing factor' through which we adjust the number of futures contracts in order to return to the desired levels (the ones obtained from Exercise 7):

$$\text{Tailed hedge} = \text{Untailed hedge} \times \text{Tailing factor}$$

Looking at the work done to calculate the future value of investing/borrowing the profits/losses from the futures contract we see that the key difference is when we divide by $Z(t, T_1)$. To undo this we need to multiply again by $Z(t, T_1)$. For our specific case we have that in the untailed hedge we bought 100 contracts which means that:

$$\text{Tailed hedge} = 100 \times Z(t, T_1)$$

Note that the match is not exact because we compute the tailing factor at one period, multiplying by $Z(t, T_1)$, and invest in the next, dividing by $Z(t + 1, T_1)$.

(a) After 'tailing the hedge', how much money does the firm receive in six months if futures prices move according to Table 6.11? Is it different than the original computation?

(b) After 'tailing the hedge', how much money does the firm receive in six months if futures prices move according to Table 6.12? Is it different than the original computation?

10. Today is $t = 0$. You are given the following data:

- The 6-month zero coupon bond is priced at $98.24
- The 9-month zero coupon bond is priced at $97.21
- Call option (European) on the 13 week Treasury bill with maturity in 6-months and strike price of $99.12 is priced at $0.2934
- Put option (European) on the 13 week Treasury bill with maturity in 6-months and strike price of $99.12 is priced at $0.1044

(a) Are the securities priced correctly?

(b) Assume that someone tells you that she is 100% sure that the call option is priced correctly. Can you design a strategy to take advantage of the arbitrage opportunity, if there is one?

6.5 APPENDIX: LIQUIDITY AND THE LIBOR CURVE

In this section we discuss in more detail some issues related to the construction of the LIBOR curve, introduced in Section 5.4.3 in Chapter 5. The LIBOR curve is the reference discount curve that traders use to discount LIBOR-based cash flows. One important complication in the computation of the LIBOR curve is the fact that swaps, which are over-the-counter securities, are not very liquid instruments. Therefore the LIBOR curve extracted from swaps may not accurately reflect the true time value of money, but it contains a premium for liquidity. Whenever possible, using liquid exchange-traded securities is preferable. For the LIBOR curve, in particular, the use of Eurodollar futures is preferable to swaps, as Eurodollar futures, described in Table 6.3, are among the most traded, and liquid, futures

Table 6.13   Interest Rate Data on May 5, 2008

LIBOR Rates			EURODOLLAR FUTURES					
Maturity				Futures	Time to	Quote	Futures	Implied (c.c.) Forward
Month	Years	Rates (%)	Contract	Maturity	Maturity	(Mid)	Rate (%)	Rate (%)
1	0.0833	2.6975	EDM8	Jun08	0.112	97.350	2.650	2.641
2	0.1667	2.7375	EDU8	Sep08	0.364	97.300	2.700	2.690
3	0.2500	2.7700	EDZ8	Dec08	0.614	97.070	2.930	2.917
4	0.3333	2.8044	EDH9	Mar09	0.860	96.900	3.100	3.083
5	0.4167	2.8400	EDM9	Jun09	1.112	96.700	3.300	3.279
6	0.5000	2.8737	EDU9	Sep09	1.364	96.535	3.465	3.439
12	1.0000	2.9938	EDZ9	Dec09	1.614	96.325	3.675	3.643
			EDH0	Mar10	1.860	96.195	3.805	3.767
Swap Rates			EDM0	Jun10	2.112	96.050	3.950	3.906
Maturity			EDU0	Sep10	2.364	95.925	4.075	4.023
(Year)	Bid	Ask	EDZ0	Dec10	2.614	95.795	4.205	4.146
1	2.857	2.865	EDH1	Mar11	2.860	95.725	4.275	4.208
2	3.191	3.194	EDM1	Jun11	3.112	95.645	4.355	4.279
3	3.484	3.49	EDU1	Sep11	3.364	95.570	4.430	4.345
4	3.718	3.721	EDZ1	Dec11	3.614	95.480	4.520	4.425
5	3.891	3.896	EDH2	Mar12	3.863	95.430	4.570	4.465
7	4.174	4.177	EDM2	Jun12	4.115	95.370	4.630	4.514
10	4.448	4.453	EDH2	Sep12	4.367	95.310	4.690	4.562
			EDZ2	Dec12	4.616	95.235	4.765	4.625

Source: Bloomberg.

in the world. Indeed, traders typically compute the LIBOR curve from three sources of information: (1) LIBOR fixes for overnight or very short maturities, (2) Eurodollar futures for maturities up to three years – liquidity is low for longer maturities – and, (3) swaps for longer maturities.

Table 6.13 provides the data for this exercise, obtained on May 5, 2008. First, the LIBOR rates in Column 3 provide the discounts for short maturities. For simplicity, we extract the LIBOR curve at a quarterly frequency. Denoting by $r_4(t)$ the 3-month LIBOR rate at t, the first discount is then given by

$$Z(0, 0.25) = \frac{1}{1 + r_4(0) \times 0.25} = \frac{1}{1 + .0277 \times 0.25} = 99.3123\%$$

Columns 4 to 7 report Eurodollar futures prices $P^{fut}(0, T_i, T_{i+1})$ where $T_{i+1} = T_i + 0.25$. From the definition of the Eurodollar futures convention, we can convert these futures prices into futures *rates* as $f_4^{fut}(0, T_i, T_{i+1}) = 100 - P(0, T_i, T_{i+1})$, where the subscript "4" denotes the quarterly compounding. Column "futures rates" in Table 6.13 reports the outcome of this calculation.

The next question is how to use futures rates to obtain the discount curve. If these were *forward* rates instead of futures rates, we could use the methodology illustrated in Section 5.1.3 in Chapter 5 to obtain the discount factors $Z(0, T)$. Luckily, we have seen in Section 6.1.4 that futures and forwards prices (and rates) are related to each other. Specifically, Fact 6.2 shows that under two particular assumptions, they are in fact the same. As discussed right afterward, these assumptions are both violated, especially for Eurodollar futures. However, as we shall see in Chapter 21, there is a simple correction that can be made to convert futures rates into forward rates.

Fact 6.3 *The continuously compounded forward rate $f(0, T_i, T_{i+1})$ and futures rate $f^{fut}(0, T_i, T_{i+1})$ are related by*

$$f(0, T_i, T_{i+1}) = f^{fut}(0, T_i, T_{i+1}) - \frac{1}{2}\sigma^2 T_i T_{i+1} \tag{6.17}$$

where σ is the annualized volatility of the underlying LIBOR rate.[12]

The volatility σ can be computed from the history of interest rate movements.[13] Specifically, from historical data we can compute the annualized standard deviation of changes in the 1-month LIBOR rate, which gives us $\sigma = 0.01$. The last column of Table 6.13 contains the continously compounded forward rates obtained from Equation 6.17. Note that to apply this correction, we must first convert the quarterly compounded futures rates into continuously compounded ones, using the formula $f^{fut}(0, T, T + 0.25) = 4 \times \ln[1 + f_4^{fut}(0, T, T+0.25)/4]$. Given the forward rates, we can compute the discount using the same procedure as in Section 5.1.3 in Chapter 5. One intermediate step, however, is necessary to compute discounts at a quarterly frequency. In particular, we interpolate the semi-annual forward rates from Table 6.13 to obtain quarterly forwards, reported now in the second column in Table 6.14. To avoid misunderstandings, it is important to recall that the "Maturity" in Table 6.13 refers to the maturity of the futures contract. This implies that a maturity T in Table 6.13 then corresponds to the forward rate from T to $T + 0.25$ in the last column. In contrast, in Table 6.14 the column "Maturity" refers to the time at which the forward delivery actually takes place. The first entry, for instance, is simply the continuously compounded LIBOR rate, which matures at $T = 0.25$. The entry corresponding to $T = 0.5$ is instead the interpolated value of the two first forward rates, 2.641% and 2.690%, in the last column of Table 6.13, and so on. Given the forward rates, we can finally compute the discounts up to $T = 3$ using Equation 5.15, as illustrated in Example 5.2 in Chapter 5.

For maturities longer than 3 years, we use swap rates to extract the LIBOR discount curve. The original quotes are in Table 6.13. Column 3 of Table 6.14 reports linearly interpolated swap rates for intermediate maturities at a semi-annual frequency, which is the frequency of payments for the fixed rate payer in a plain vanilla swap. These swap rates are converted into a discount factor $Z(0, T)$ starting with maturity $T = 3.5$ according to Equation 5.45 in Chapter 5, for $\Delta = 0.5$. The starting discount for the procedure is $Z(0, 3) = 90.223\%$ obtained from the first part of the procedure. Since this procedure only provides the discounts at semi-annual frequency, the remaining discounts at the other quarterly dates are obtained by linear interpolation of the adjacent discounts. For instance, $Z(0, 4.25) = 0.5 \times Z(0, 4) + 0.5 \times Z(0, 4.5)$, where the latter two are instead computed from the semi-annual swap rates. Column 4 in Table 6.14 reports the method or data used to compute each of the discounts in column 5. Column 6 reports the implied spot rates.

The last three columns in Table 6.14 show the computation of the discount factors $Z(0, T)$ and spot rates $r(0, T)$ for the case in which swap rates are used starting at $T = 1$ instead of $T = 3.5$, that is, for the shortest maturity swap data are available. As can be seen, the spot rates obtained from swaps are always higher than those obtained from

---

[12]The adjustment in Equation 6.17 holds under a specific model, called the Ho-Lee model, which is developed in Chapter 17.
[13]The volatility σ can also be computed from options, as in Chapter 17.

Figure 6.5 LIBOR Forward Curve when Using Futures and Swaps

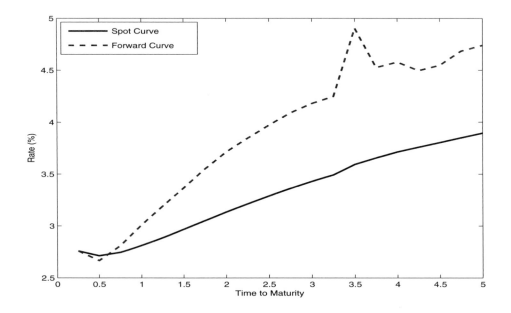

Eurodollar futures. The difference is attributed to a liquidity premium that characterizes the over-the-counter swap contracts.

One issue with the methodology of computing the yield curve using securities with different liquidity is that the forward curve may display an unusual behavior. For instance, Figure 6.5 plots the spot curve (the solid line) and the forward curve (the dashed line) obtained from the procedure in Table 6.14. Because of the sudden increase in the spot rate at maturity $T = 3.5$, which is due to the change from the use of futures to swaps, the forward curve displays a sudden bump, which is clearly an artifact of the change in liquidity of the instrument. A methodology to resolve the problem is to smooth out the bump in the forward curve, and obtain the yield out of the smoothed forward curve.

Table 6.14 LIBOR CURVE on May 5, 2008

Maturity	Interpolated Forward	Interpolated Swap Rates	Method	Discount	Spot Rate	Method	Swap-Based Discount	Swap-Based Spot Rate
0.250	2.760		LIBOR	99.312	2.760	LIBOR	99.312	2.760
0.500	2.668		FUT	98.652	2.714	FUT	98.652	2.714
0.750	2.813		FUT	97.961	2.747	FUT	97.961	2.747
1.000	3.009	2.861	FUT	97.227	2.813	SWAP	97.198	2.842
1.250	3.192		FUT	96.454	2.888	INTERP	96.394	2.938
1.500	3.366	3.027	FUT	95.646	2.968	SWAP	95.589	3.007
1.750	3.550		FUT	94.800	3.051	INTERP	94.720	3.100
2.000	3.712	3.193	FUT	93.925	3.134	SWAP	93.850	3.174
2.250	3.844		FUT	93.027	3.213	INTERP	92.940	3.254
2.500	3.970	3.340	FUT	92.108	3.288	SWAP	92.029	3.322
2.750	4.090		FUT	91.171	3.361	INTERP	91.068	3.402
3.000	4.180	3.487	FUT	90.223	3.430	SWAP	90.107	3.472
3.250	4.247		FUT	89.270	3.492	INTERP	89.148	3.535
3.500	4.315	3.603	SWAP	88.182	3.593	SWAP	88.188	3.591
3.750	4.388		INTERP	87.190	3.656	INTERP	87.196	3.654
4.000	4.447	3.720	SWAP	86.198	3.713	SWAP	86.204	3.711
4.250	4.491		INTERP	85.234	3.759	INTERP	85.241	3.757
4.500	4.539	3.807	SWAP	84.271	3.803	SWAP	84.277	3.801
4.750	4.595		INTERP	83.290	3.849	INTERP	83.296	3.848
5.000		3.894	SWAP	82.309	3.894	SWAP	82.316	3.892

CHAPTER 7

INFLATION, MONETARY POLICY, AND THE FEDERAL FUNDS RATE

A treatment of interest rate determination and bond pricing has to take into account the impact of monetary policy on interest rates. In this chapter we briefly review the Federal Reserve System (the Fed) and the tools of monetary policy. In particular, we discuss the way the Federal Reserve sets its main instrument of monetary policy, namely, the Federal funds rate. The importance of the Federal funds rate, which is an overnight rate, in affecting other short-term interest rates is apparent in Panel A of Figure 7.1, which plots the Fed funds rate along with other short term interest rates, such as the three month T-bill rate and the three month Eurodollar rate.[1]

7.1 THE FEDERAL RESERVE

The Federal Reserve is in charge of conducting U.S. monetary policy. The goals of the monetary policy are spelled out in the Federal Reserve Act (Section 2a), which states that the Federal Reserve should seek *"to promote effectively the goals of maximum employment, stable prices, and moderate long-term interest rates."* The Federal Reserve has only limited power in affecting prices, employment, and interest rates, and the mechanism by which it can do so is far from perfect. Indeed, although nowadays most economists agree that the Federal Reserve is able to affect prices and real economic activity, there is still a large

---

[1] Clearly, the plot per se does not entail a causal relation between Fed funds rate and the other short-term rates, but there is a large agreement that short-term rates react to monetary policy. See e.g., Cochrane and Piazzesi (2002).

Figure 7.1   Federal Funds Rate and other Interest Rates

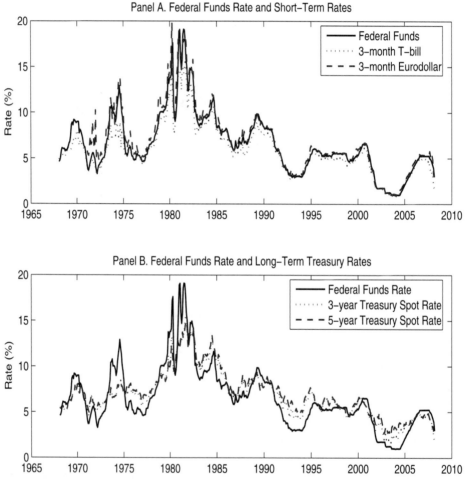

Source: Federal Reserve.

disagreement on the exact economic mechanism at work, as well as the size of the impact of the Federal Reserve's intervention in the market. One simple way to think about the issue is to consider the Federal Reserve as trying to pilot a little sailboat in the middle of major storm: By skillfully steering the boat's wheel right and left, it is possible to give some directions to the sailboat and perhaps avoid large underwater rocks. However, waves, winds and currents of various sorts may eventually determine the ultimate course of the boat. Indeed, as some sailors know, sometimes "too much" steering and wrong moves may even cause the sailboat topple over and sink, whereas less proactive piloting might save the boat, if not its direction. Piloting the economy safely through the waves of economic booms and recessions is most definitely a difficult, and sometimes impossible, task for the Federal Reserve, especially given the limited tool set at its disposal. We now turn to discuss the tools of monetary policy, and their impact on interest rates.

7.1.1   Monetary Policy, Economic Growth, and Inflation

The Federal Reserve controls the money supply, that is, the total amount of money available in the economy. The total money supply not only depends on the total amount of physical currency available in the economy – i.e., the total amount of dollar bills and coins – but also on the additional money that is created through the banking system. To grasp the idea, suppose you win $1 million at the lottery, and the Federal Reserve prints out this amount of money to pay you the prize. Most likely, you will not keep the $1 million at home, but you will deposit it in a bank. The bank itself may keep about 10% of it in reserves at the Federal Reserve bank, and lend the remaining $900,000 to a homeowner, for instance, who may use it to purchase a home. The home seller receives the $900,000 and likely will deposit this amount in another bank, which will retain another 10% of this deposit as reserves, and lend the rest to other borrowers. And so on. That is, the initial $1 million of physical currency printed out by the Federal Reserve generates far more currency that can be used for transactions. The total money supply is then a multiple of the available physical currency, a multiple that is generated by the banking system through the lending/borrowing channel. How large is this multiple? If each bank keeps the same fraction of deposits as reserves, e.g., 10% in the previous example, and if all of the loans end up going into other deposits, then the answer is actually surprisingly simple: It is simply the ratio of deposits over reserves, that is, 10 in the previous example.[2] In other words, if banks keep 10% of deposits in reserves, the total money supply is ten times the total amount of currency printed by the Federal Reserve. This multiple is called the **money multiplier**.

It follows from the above discussion that the Federal Reserve affects the total money supply through both the amount of currency that it actually prints and the reserve requirements, which in turn affects the money multiplier. However, note that if you did not deposit the $1 million in a bank to start with, but decided to keep it at home in your own safe, then the channel is broken. Similarly, if the bank decided to keep a larger fraction of deposits in reserves, the multiplier is smaller. Therefore, the relation between the amount of currency printed by the Federal Reserve and the actual money supply depends crucially on the desire of people to keep currency in their pockets compared to depositing it in a bank, and the amount of reserves that banks decide to keep in addition to any regulatory requirement.

---

[2]To see this, let f be the fraction of deposits kept in reserves. Then, the total amount of money created by an additional dollar is $\$1 + \$1 \times (1-f) + [\$1 \times (1-f)] \times (1-f) + ... = \$1 \times \sum_{j=0}^{\infty} (1-f)^j = \frac{\$1}{f}$.

That is, the Federal Reserve does not have full control of the money supply, but it can only affect it through its monetary policies decisions, as further discussed in the next section.

How does money supply affect real output? In the short run, an unexpected increase in money supply tends to lower interest rates, as there is a temporary excess of funds available for lending. A lower interest rate in turn stimulates aggregate demand, as individuals may decide to borrow more money to spend it for consumption (e.g., purchase a new car or a new home), while firms find it cheaper to borrow money for investment purposes, thereby increasing the demand for intermediate goods or machinery. This stimulus to the aggregate demand increases real output, and decreases unemployment, as firms need to hire new workers to produce more to meet the increased aggregate demand. Vice versa, a tightening of the money supply increases interest rates, which induce individuals to save more and thus consume less, and firms to decrease investments as it costs more to borrow. As aggregate demand declines, so does real output.

Why doesn't the Federal Reserve then keep expanding the money supply to foster growth and employment? Unfortunately, while an increase in money supply stimulates the economy in the short run, it also increases inflation, which instead has a detrimental effect on economic growth in the long run. Indeed, while at the short horizon there is a tradeoff between low unemployment and high inflation,[3] it turns out that at the long horizon an increase in money supply growth only generates higher inflation, with not much gain in real economic growth. Thus, the Federal Reserve tends to conduct its monetary policy on a temporary basis, increasing money supply during recessionary periods to stimulate the economy, but tightening the money supply when the economy expands too quickly to keep inflation under control. Indeed, a long expansionary monetary policy tends to increase investors' expectation of future inflation, which in turn increases long-term nominal rates and decreases economic activity. Section 7.2 below further discusses the relation between inflation, employment growth, and monetary policy, while Section 7.4 investigates the relation between inflation and nominal rates. We now turn in the meantime to describe the tools of monetary policy.

7.1.2   The Tools of Monetary Policy

The Federal Reserve has three main tools of monetary policy:

1. **Open market operations**, which are interventions in the market to buy or sell Treasury securities.

2. **Reserve requirements**, which are the amount of reserves that depository institutions (banks) are required to have at the Federal Reserve Bank.

3. **The Federal discount rate**, which is the rate at which the Federal Reserve lends to FDIC-approved depository institutions.

By far the main tool of active monetary policy is the first one, open market operations, which are decided by the **Federal Open Market Committee** (FOMC). The reserve requirement is the responsability of the **Board of Governors** of the Federal Reserve, and the

---

[3]The short-run negative relation between unemployment and inflation is typically referred to as the Phillips curve, after the economist A. W. Phillips who first showed this relation in British data in 1958.

Federal discount rate is set by the boards of directors of the Federal Reserve banks, subject to review and determination by the Board of Governors.

7.1.3   The Federal Funds Rate

The Federal Open Market Committee meets about eight times a year, according to a predetermined calendar, to discuss its monetary policy actions. The main instrument the Federal Reserve uses to have an impact on the economy is altering the **Federal funds rate**. The Federal funds rate is the rate at which depository institutions can borrow or lend overnight reserves at the Federal Reserve Bank. Each depository institution is required to keep reserves with the Federal Reserve – about 10% of the amount of its deposits. Because of its daily operations a depository institution may run a deficit of reserves, and rather than simply replenish them, it may be cheaper to borrow such funds from another depository institution that may be running a surplus. The Federal funds rate is the rate at which these borrowing and lending transactions occur.[4] The incentive to keep reserves at the Federal Reserve Bank close to the limit stems from the fact that these reserves pay an interest that is lower than the rate of available alternative investments, and therefore it is costly to hold large reserves. Indeed, up until October 2008 such reserves actually paid zero interest.

The Federal funds rate itself then is not *decided* by the Federal Reserve, but it is an equilibrium level resulting from lending and borrowing of reserves at the Federal Reserve Bank. However, open market operations have a large impact on this equilibrium rate, as they affect the total amount of reserves available to depository institutions. For instance, if the Fed buys Treasury securities in an open market operation from one of the depository institutions, it pays for them by crediting the depository institution's account at the Federal Reserve. Because the depository institution can then lend these cash balances to other banks at the Fed funds rate, the open market operation effectively increases the total supply of cash balances available for lending, which in turn tends to decrease the equilibrium market clearing Fed funds rate. Vice versa, if the Fed sells Treasury securities to a depository institution, it effectively drains the total available cash balances of the depository institutions available for lending at the Fed funds rate. In this case, the equilibrium Fed funds rate tends to increase.

At FOMC meetings, the Federal Reserve decides a *target* Federal funds rate, and then changes the size of open market operations or their direction to keep the effective equilibrium Federal funds rate close to the target Federal funds rate. If the Federal Reserve wants to have a permanent impact on the Fed funds rate, then it carries out open market operations by an outright purchase or sale of Treasury securities, which will permanently affect the total amount of reserve balances available to depository institutions. However, more often the Federal Reserve only wishes to counterbalance temporary or seasonal variations in the total supply of reserves. In this case, the Federal Reserve carries out open market operations through repurchase and reverse repurchase agreements, that is, contractual agreements in which the Federal Reserve sells (or buys) Treasury securities to (or from) primary dealers with the agreement to buy them back (or sell them back) at an

---

[4]The Federal funds rate is *not* the rate at which banks can borrow from the Federal Reserve. That one is called the discount rate. Also, depository institutions differ in terms of credit rating, and so the rate at which these transactions occur differs across institutions. The reported rate is the one pertaining to the depository institutions with the highest creditworthiness.

agreed upon future date, such as the following day (overnight repo) or a couple of weeks (long-term repo). For more details about repo transactions, see the discusion in Chapter 1. Section 7.7 below further discusses the workings of U.S. monetary policy in the context of the subprime credit crisis of 2007 - 2008. This financial crisis, the largest in U.S. history since the Great Depression, saw the Federal Reserve at the center stage, as it used all of the monetary policy tools at its disposal – as well as new ones – in its attempt to prevent the U.S. economy from entering into a long and deep recession.

It should be mentioned that because the Federal funds rate is a borrowing rate among depository institutions, it is higher than the short-term Treasury bill rate, as it incorporates a little premium for default. For the same reason, it is also higher than the repo rate, the rate for collateralized borrowing. Indeed, the Fed funds rate is closer to the LIBOR, which as we know from Chapter 1 is the interbank uncollataralized borrowing rate.

7.2 PREDICTING THE FUTURE FED FUNDS RATE

The prediction of future interest rate movements is a hard task. Indeed, in the short run, say daily or weekly, the change in interest rate is almost unpredictable, and the best guess of the interest rate tomorrow is the interest rate today. For the medium-to-long horizon, in contrast, interest rate movements up and down are predictable to some extent. For instance, from Figure 7.1 we see that in 2003 the Federal funds rate hit its lowest level in past history, at less than 1%.[5] Simple reasoning that such a scenario was very unusual for the Federal funds rate led many market participants to believe that the interest rate would soon increase again (as in fact it did). Many observers, however, were worried that the Federal Reserve could get stuck in a Japan-style zero interest rates' environment. That is, the fact that the Fed funds rate had been higher in the past was no guarantee that it would increase again in the future.

Let's look at the relation between the Federal funds rate and some important macroeconomic variables, such as inflation and employment.

7.2.1 Fed Funds Rate, Inflation and Employment Growth

According to its mandate, the Federal Reserve must promote employment, stable inflation and low long-term interest rates. It is then useful to see whether there is any relation between these variables and the main tool of Federal Reserve intervention, the Federal funds rate. Starting with medium-to-long term Treasury rates, Panel B of Figure 7.1 plots the Fed funds rate and the 3-year and 5-year zero coupon Treasury spot rates. Indeed, the variation of these medium-to-long term yields is correlated with the variation of the overnight Federal funds rate, although this correlation is much less pronounced than the one of short-term rates, as depicted in Panel A.

Figure 7.2 shows the relation between the Federal funds rate, the annual inflation level (Panel A) and employment growth (Panel B), as proxied by Nonfarm payroll growth rate. We use this variable over the many other employment related variables, as it appears the most correlated with the variation of the Fed funds rate. Panel A shows that indeed as inflation increased and decreased in the 1960s and 1970s, the Federal funds rate followed

---

[5]In December 2008, however, the Federal funds rate hit essentially zero, beating the record low level of 2003.

Figure 7.2   Federal Funds Rate, Inflation and Employment

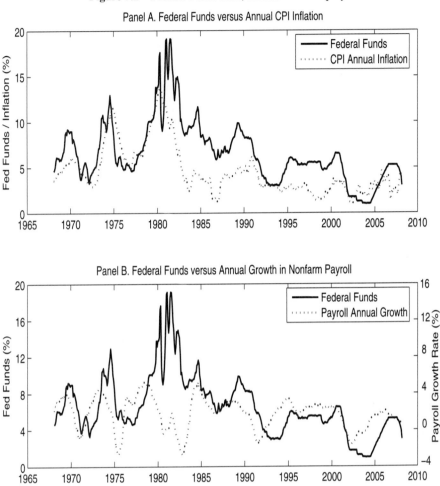

Panel A. Federal Funds versus Annual CPI Inflation

Panel B. Federal Funds versus Annual Growth in Nonfarm Payroll

Source: Federal Reserve and Bureau of Labor Statistics.

it quite closely. In the 1980s, in particular, the Federal funds rate remained high for a substantial amount of time while inflation was not under control. The connection between inflation and the Federal funds rate is attenuated in the 1990s, as the low inflation appears to be considered under control. Indeed, Panel B shows that in the 1990s and 2000s, the Fed funds rate is moving in sync with the annual growth rate in Nonfarm payroll.

Of course this analysis is only suggestive as the conduct of monetary policy is very complex: In particular, every month the Federal Reserve observes hundreds of indicators about the economy and it must filter the information that these indicators provide so as to decide the best course of action in terms of monetary policy and interest rate determination. The sheer amount of data is daunting: they include economic growth indicators, price indices of various sorts, employment indicators, a whole host of financial variables, and the health of the banking system. In addition, the Fed avails itself of sophisticated econometric techniques that have been put forward by economists and statistician to squeeze the most important information out of these many variables.

We can illustrate the relation between the Fed funds rate, inflation and employment by looking at the variables in Figure 7.2. Let us start from the easiest possible way of predicting future Fed funds rates. As it is clear from Figure 7.2, the Fed funds rate, as does any other rate, goes up and down, and it hovers around 6.57%, which is its average during the period. Thus, if we see that the Fed funds rate extremely low, such as 1% as in 2003, we can reasonably expect that it will go back up, as soon as economic conditions improve, or inflation starts moving up again. Similarly, if the interest rate is very high, we could reasonably expect it will sooner or later decline again, as soon as inflation is under control. Therefore, the simplest way to predict the Fed funds rate is to try to forecast it using its current level. Namely, we can run the following regression:

$$r^{FF}(t+1) = \alpha + \beta_1 \times r^{FF}(t) + \epsilon(t+1) \tag{7.1}$$

The coefficient β_1 tells us the relation between the Fed funds rate at time $t+1$ given its value at t. Using the data in Figure 7.2 Panel A of Table 7.1 shows the regression results, where the horizon column is the predicting horizon. For instance, the first row shows the predictability of the Fed funds rate one month ahead. The second row shows the predictability of the Fed funds rate three months ahead. And so on. The columns headed "α" and "β" show the numerical values estimated from the regression in Equation 7.1, while the following two columns report the estimates' standard errors (se).[6] Finally, the last column reports the regression R^2, which is a number between 0 and 1 describing how good the right-hand side variable in Equation 7.1 is in predicting the left-hand side variable. For instance, the table shows that it is much easier to accurately predict the interest rate in one month ($R^2 = 96.66\%$) than in one year ($R^2 = 57.59\%$).

As discussed, the Fed funds rate reacts also to the labor market conditions and the inflation rate. It appears sensible then to try to forecast the future Fed funds rate by using information also from the business cycle. In particular, Panel B of Table 7.1 reports the results of the following regression:

$$r^{FF}(t+1) = \alpha + \beta_2 \times X^{Pay}(t) + \beta_3 \times X^{Inf}(t) + \epsilon(t+1) \tag{7.2}$$

where $X^{Pay}(t)$ is the annual growth in nonfarm payrolls, and $X^{Inf}(t)$ is the annual growth in the CPI index. Both these series are plotted in Figure 7.2. The regression makes it apparent that the Federal Reserve reacts to labor market conditions and inflation. Both coefficients β_2 and β_3 are positive, showing that a decrease in the growth of rate in nonfarm payroll tends to generate a decrease in the Fed funds rate, while an increase in the inflation tend to increase the Fed funds rate, as intuition would have it.

Inflation and nonfarm payroll growth explain a good deal of the variation in the Fed funds rate, about 50% or so, but not all of it. In particular, the R^2 is lower than in Panel A, in which the only regressor was the Fed funds rate itself. There are two reasons for this: First, the Federal Reserve does not only react to payroll growth and inflation, but it considers a whole host of macroeconomic variables, as discussed earlier. Second, the regression analysis above has at its core assumption that the parameters β_2 and β_3 remain constant for the whole sample used in the analysis, in this case the 40 year sample period from 1968 - 2008. The Federal Reserve monetary policy has likely changed over the years,

---

[6]In this and the following tables, the standard errors are computed using the Newey-West adjustment for autocorrelation and heteroskedasticity in the errors. For robustness, only nonoverlapping data are used in the estimation. For instance, for the annual forecasting regression we only use data at the annual frequency.

and therefore forcing the parameters to remain constant decreases the ability of the model to predict future interest rates. Sophisticated econometric techniques that take into account the variations in these parameters have been develped, but we will not explore them here, as they are beyond the scope of this chapter.

Instead, we can check whether the past Fed funds rate $r^{FF}(t)$ is a sufficient predicting variable of future Fed funds rates, or whether adding information from the macroeconomy helps. We therefore run the regression including both the past Fed funds rate and the macroeconomic variables discussed earlier:

$$r^{FF}(t+1) = \alpha + \beta_1 \times r^{FF}(t) + \beta_2 \times X^{Pay}(t) + \beta_3 \times X^{Inf}(t) + \epsilon(t+1) \quad (7.3)$$

Panel C of Table 7.1 reports the results. The results indeed show that adding macroeconomic information helps increase the predictive power of the regression. The last column in Panel C reports the "adjusted R^2," which like the R^2 measures the ability of the right-hand side variables in Equation 7.3 to predict the left-hand side variable, but it also corrects for the number of regressors used. For instance, if we add a regressor on the right-hand side variable that is not helping at all to forecast the Fed funds rate, the adjusted R^2 declines. As can be seen, this last number is substantially higher than the R^2's in both Panel A and B.

Which variable is more important to predict future Fed funds rate, payroll growth or inflation? Once we account for lagged Fed Funds rate in the regression, we find that the coefficient on the inflation variable β_3 is not significant. This means that its standard errors [Column "$se(\beta_3)$"] are so large that the coefficient β_3 cannot statistically be considered any different from zero. That is, the fact that it is different from zero may be due just to chance, to the particular sample used. This does not mean that the Federal Reserve does not react to inflation. Indeed, recall that β_3 was instead different from zero in Equation 7.3. The lack of significance implies that lagged Fed funds rate contains all of the information about future Fed funds rates that is also included in the inflation rate itself. That is, the current inflation rate does not add anything to the prediction of future Fed funds rates above and beyond the current level of Fed funds itself. Instead, payroll growth does add information to forecast future Fed funds rates.

7.2.2 Long-Term Fed Funds Rate Forecasts

How can we use the information in Table 7.1 to forecast future interest rates? Suppose it is February 2008. The current level of the Fed funds rate is $r^{FF}_{Feb08} = 2.98\%$. According to the model in Equation 7.1, the forecasted rate one month ahead would be

$$\widehat{r}^{FF}_{Mar08} = \alpha + \beta \times r^{FF}_{Feb08} = 0.1019 + 0.9840 \times 2.98\% = 3.0342\%$$

where we set $\epsilon(t+1) = 0$ in our forecast, because its expected value is in fact zero. To compute the two-months-ahead value, we need to insert the predicted one-month-ahead into Equation 7.1 again:

$$\widehat{r}^{FF}_{Apr08} = \alpha + \beta \times r^{FF}_{Mar08} = 0.1019 + 0.9840 \times 3.0342\% = 3.0876\%$$

and so on. By repeating this procedure, we obtain the solid line in the top panel of Figure 7.3. This shows that the model predicts an increase in the future Fed funds rate. The reason

Table 7.1   Predicting the Fed Funds Rate: 1968 - 2008

Panel A: Fed Funds Rate on Past Fed Funds Rate

Horizon	α	β_1	$se(\alpha)$	$se(\beta)$	R^2 (%)
1m	0.1019	**0.9840**	0.1191	0.0220	96.66
3m	**0.5312**	**0.9190**	0.2891	0.0516	84.31
6m	**1.1433**	**0.8255**	0.3946	0.0676	67.93
1y	**1.5285**	**0.7611**	0.7784	0.1420	57.59

Panel B: Fed Funds Rate on Past Payroll Growth and Inflation

Horizon	α	β_2	β_3	$se(\alpha)$	$se(\beta_2)$	$se(\beta_3)$	R^2 (%)
1m	**1.9946**	0.3386	**0.8675**	0.4711	0.1558	0.1020	53.14
3m	**1.7750**	0.4323	**0.8829**	0.6879	0.2266	0.1537	54.97
6m	**1.7134**	0.5499	**0.8468**	0.8213	0.2777	0.2064	52.72
1y	1.1656	**0.8634**	**0.8095**	0.9722	0.2855	0.2784	58.75

Panel C: Fed Funds Rate on Past Fed Funds Rate, Payroll Growth, and Inflation

Horizon	α	β_1	β_2	β_3	$se(\alpha)$	$se(\beta_1)$	$se(\beta_2)$	$se(\beta_3)$	R^2 (%)	$\overline{R}^2$ (%)
1m	-0.0196	**0.9594**	**0.0731**	0.0326	0.097	0.017	0.0203	0.0271	96.82	96.81
3m	0.1259	**0.8170**	**0.2122**	0.1506	0.1768	0.0576	0.0521	0.0918	85.91	85.74
6m	0.4162	**0.6411**	**0.3528**	0.2833	0.3313	0.0895	0.1338	0.1879	72.70	71.99
1y	0.2175	**0.5300**	**0.7309**	0.319	0.7138	0.0988	0.202	0.2524	71.08	69.52

Notes: Coefficients in bold are statistically significant at 1% confidence level.

is that the current Fed funds rate is below its historical average, and therefore the model forecasts that in the long run it will revert back to its long term average.

The other lines in Figure 7.3 report the outcome of the same forecasting exercise, but we use the α and β obtained from the regression that uses quarterly data (the second row in Panel A of Table 7.1), semi-annual data (the third row in Panel A) or annual data (the fourth row in Panel A). These forecasts are similar to the ones obtained from the monthly frequency: We should not expect to obtain exactly the same forecast, as different sampling frequencies capture different dynamic aspects of the behavior of the interest rate.

7.2.2.1 Adding Macro Variables

The long-term forecasts of the Fed funds rates performed above only use information about the past Fed funds rate. As we have shown in Panel C of Table 7.1 adding macroeconomic information helps to forecast future interest rates. Therefore, it may be advisable to also use information from macroeconomic variables to formulate long term forecasts. We can perform exactly the same exercise as in the previous section, but now also include macroeconomic variables. In particular, given the current value of Fed funds rate ($r^{FF}_{Feb\ 08} = 2.98\%$), payroll growth ($X^{Pay}_{Feb\ 08} = 0.6250\%$) and inflation ($X^{Inf}_{Feb\ 08} = 4.0380\%$), we can insert them into Equation 7.3 and obtain the prediction of the Fed funds rate for March 2008 as

$$
\begin{aligned}
r^{FF}_{Mar\ 08} &= \alpha + \beta_1 \times r^{FF}_{Feb\ 08} + \beta_2 \times X^{Pay}_{Feb\ 08} + \beta_3 \times X^{Inf}_{Feb\ 08} \\
&= -0.0196 + 0.9594 \times 2.98 + 0.0731 \times 0.6250 + 0.0326 \times 4.0380 \\
&= 3.0167\%
\end{aligned}
$$

Figure 7.3   Long-Term Federal Funds Rate Forecasts

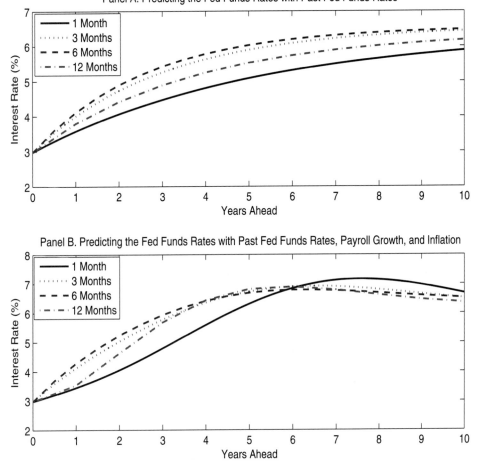

Panel A. Predicting the Fed Funds Rates with Past Fed Funds Rates

Panel B. Predicting the Fed Funds Rates with Past Fed Funds Rates, Payroll Growth, and Inflation

Unlike when we use use the past Fed funds rate to predict future Fed funds rates, we now find a roadblock. In particular, we cannot proceed because in order to use the same equation to predict $r^{FF}_{Apr\ 08}$, we need to have a forecast not only of $r^{FF}_{Mar\ 08}$, which we have, but also of $X^{Pay}_{Mar\ 08}$ and $X^{Inf}_{Mar\ 08}$, which we do not have.

How do we move forward then? The solution is to use the same three variables $r^{FF}(t)$, $X^{Pay}(t)$, and $X^{Inf}(t)$ to also forecast future payroll growth and future inflation. In other words, we can run the following two additional regressions:

$$X^{Pay}(t+1) = \alpha^{Pay} + \beta^{Pay}_1 \ r^{FF}(t) + \beta^{Pay}_2 \ X^{Pay}(t) + \beta^{Pay}_3 \ X^{Inf}(t) + \epsilon^{Pay}(t+1)$$
$$X^{Inf}(t+1) = \alpha^{Inf} + \beta^{Inf}_1 \ r^{FF}(t) + \beta^{Inf}_2 \ X^{Pay}(t) + \beta^{Inf}_3 \ X^{Inf}(t) + \epsilon^{Inf}(t+1)$$

Given the parameter estimates (not reported), we can then proceed exactly as in the previous section: Given the three values of the right-hand side variables at any time t, $r^{FF}(t)$, $X^{Pay}(t)$, and $X^{Inf}(t)$, we can use the regressions to compute their values at $t+1$. Given the value at $t+1$, we can compute the value at $t+2$, and so on.

Panel B of Figure 7.3 reports the results for the Fed Funds rate forecast. Consider the solid line, which uses estimates obtained from monthly frequency. The forecast is similar to the one obtained in Panel A using only the Fed funds rate, but it now presents a difference in terms of dynamics. In particular, the Fed Funds rate is predicted to increase slowly at first, to pick up its rate of increase up to the maximum of about 7%, and then decline back to its long-term average of 6.5%. Eye balling the historical variation in the Fed funds rate in Figure 7.2, and especially the last few decades, we see that indeed its dynamics over time are characterized by periods in which it is stable at some value, and then suddenly increases or decreases for a few consecutive months. This pattern is partly captured by the joint dynamics of Fed funds rate, payroll growth, and inflation.

7.2.3 Fed Funds Rate Predictions Using Fed Funds Futures

Fed funds futures have been trading on the CBOT since 1988.[7] The description of the contract is in Table 7.2. As discussed in Chapter 6, if a trader enters into the Fed funds futures at a futures rate $f^{Fut}(t;T)$, the payoff is approximately[8]

$$\text{Payoff at } T = \$5 \text{ million} \times \left(r^{FF}(T) - f^{Fut}(t;T) \right) \tag{7.4}$$

Intuitively, if some traders think that the Federal Reserve will increase the Fed funds target rate at the next meeting (or earlier), then they would expect a positive payoff from Equation 7.4. If many traders have these beliefs, then they would bid up the Fed funds futures $f^{Fut}(t;T)$. We should then expect that a high Fed funds futures would be correlated with a high future Fed funds rate. Panel A in Table 7.3 contains the results of the regression:

$$r^{FF}(t+h) = \alpha + \beta \times f^{Fut}(t, t+h) + \epsilon(t+h) \tag{7.5}$$

where h is the Fed funds futures horizon at initiation.[9]

---

[7]The Chicago Board of Trade (CBOT) is now part of the Chicago Mercantile Exchange (CME) group.
[8]As in any futures contract, profits and losses accrue during the life of the futures, and therefore we must take into account the time value of money. Such calculations are neglected in Equation 7.4.
[9]These results are obtained from using the "Generic" Federal funds futures data from Bloomberg, Inc, for various maturities $h = 1, 2, .., 6$. The "Generic" futures contract with maturity h is the contract that is closest to the

Table 7.2   30-Day Fed Funds Futures (Chicago Board of Trade)

Contract Size
$5 million

Tick Size
$20.835 per 1/2 of one basis point (1/2 of 1/100 of one percent of $5 million on a 30-day basis rounded up to the nearest cent).

Price Quote
100 minus the average daily Fed funds overnight rate for the delivery month (e.g. a 7.25 percent rate equals 92.75).

Contract Months
First 24 calendar months

Last Trading Day
Last business day of the delivery month. Trading in expiring contracts closes at 2:00 pm, Chicago time on the last trading day.

Settlement
The contract is cash settled against the average daily Fed funds overnight rate, rounded to the nearest one-tenth of one basis point, for the delivery month. The daily Fed funds overnight rate is calculated and reported by the Federal Reserve Bank of New York.

Trading Hours
Open Auction: 7:20 am - 2:00 pm, Central Time, Monday - Friday
Electronic: 5:30 pm - 4:00 pm, Central Time, Sunday - Friday

Ticker Symbols
Open Auction: FF
Electronic: ZQ

Daily Price Limit
N/A

Source: CBOT Web site, http://www.cbot.com/cbot/pub/cont_detail/0,3206,1525+14446,00.html, accessed on September 10, 2008.

The results in Panel A of Table 7.3 show that indeed there is a good deal of predictability of the future Fed funds rates from Fed funds futures. The R^2 are relatively high across maturities, even for the one-year ahead forecast horizon. Since the sample is different, we cannot compare the results in this table with those in Table 7.1. It is illustrative to report the same results discussed earlier, but for the shorter sample 1989 - 2008. Panel B reports the result of the regression in Equation 7.1. Comparing with the longer period (Panel A in Table 7.1) we see that during the past two decades the Fed funds rate has become more persistent (i.e. less variable), and thus easier to predict. The R^2s are uniformly higher in the shorter sample than in the longer sample. Comparing now Panels A and B of Table 7.3 we see that the Federal funds futures indeed improves upon the past Fed funds rate in predicting the future Fed funds rate, especially for the longer forecasting horizon. Market expectations about monetary policy are reflected in current prices – especially the Fed funds futures – which in turn help predict the future movement in interest rates.

Interestingly, Panel C of Table 7.3 shows that the level of predictability obtained using the Fed funds futures alone (Panel A) is similar to the one we obtained using the past Fed funds rate, payroll growth and inflation. Indeed, to see whether the Fed funds futures provides any *additional* information compared to the other three variables, we can include it in the predicting regression as well. Panel D of Table 7.3 performs this exercise, and shows that indeed nonfarm payroll growth is still a significant predictor of Fed funds rates, even after considering the information from the Fed funds futures itself. Although a topic of subsequent chapters, one way to interpret this result is to realize that it is not exactly accurate to consider the Fed funds futures as an unbiased forecast of future interest rates. Indeed, the Fed funds futures contains a mix of market forecast of the Fed funds rate as well as market participants' risk attitude towards speculation in the futures market. This risk attitude is also reflected in the futures, thereby biasing the forecast (see Example 7.2 below for a similar argument in the case of forward rates). If this bias depends on market conditions, such as the business cycle, then we would conclude that adding back a business cycle related variable, such as payroll growth, may add forecasting power to the Fed funds futures itself.[10]

In Table 7.3 we have four ways of forecasting future Fed Funds rates: (a) using only the past Fed funds rate; (b) adding to it macroeconomic information; (c) using Fed funds futures; and (d) all of the above. Are these forecasts any different, or do they look alike, as we saw in Figure 7.3? Figure 7.4 plots the forecasts of future Fed funds rates as of February, 2008 for these four cases up to a one-year horizon. As can be seen, when we use only past information, the forecasting model tends to generate an upward forecast [case (a) and (b)]. In contrast, when we also consider the information from the Fed funds futures [case (c) and (d)], the market is forecasting an additional decrease in the Fed funds rate (as it indeed happened). In retrospect, part of the reason for the different forecasts stems from the particular circumstances surrounding the economy at the beginning of 2008. As discussed in Section 7.7 below, the U.S. economy was undergoing a major *credit* crisis, and the Federal Reserve was worried about the impact that failing banks might have on the

desired maturity. The futures price is rolled over from the previous month. Because the regression uses monthly data, the fact that Fed funds futures has monthly maturities does not generate any bias in the estimates. The only caveat is for the annual regression $h = 12$: Because the Fed funds futures appears to lack liquidity for such a long horizon, we used the 6-month futures $h = 6$ in the regression instead.

[10]See Piazzesi and Swanson (2008) for a related discussion.

Table 7.3   Predicting the Fed Funds Rate: 1989 - 2008

Panel A: Fed Funds Rate on Fed Funds Futures

Horizon (Months)	α	β	$se(\alpha)$	$se(\beta)$	R^2
1	-0.0032	**0.9943**	0.0148	0.0038	99.72
3	-0.0510	**0.9895**	0.0794	0.0171	98.20
6	-0.0101	**0.9530**	0.2291	0.0384	91.12
12	0.9549	**0.7214**	0.5013	0.0723	65.79

Panel B: Fed Funds Rate on Past Fed Funds Rate

Horizon (Months)	α	β	$se(\alpha)$	$se(\beta)$	R^2
1	0.0352	**0.9866**	0.0443	0.0086	99.09
3	0.1876	**0.9450**	0.1607	0.0263	94.87
6	0.5181	**0.8597**	0.3435	0.0504	83.68
12	**1.4685**	**0.6245**	0.5069	0.08	51.19

Panel C: Fed Funds Rate on Past Fed Funds Rate, Payroll Growth, and Inflation

Horizon (Months)	α	β_1	β_2	β_3	$se(\alpha)$	$se(\beta_1)$	$se(\beta_2)$	$se(\beta_3)$	$\overline{R}^2$
1	0.0024	**0.9546**	**0.0958**	0.0062	0.0541	0.01	0.0173	0.0224	99.35
3	0.0464	**0.8437**	**0.2840**	0.0212	0.1254	0.0278	0.0454	0.0553	97.10
6	0.2203	**0.6431**	**0.5511**	0.1113	0.2367	0.0483	0.0672	0.1084	92.35
12	**1.2677**	**0.2895**	**0.8719**	0.1603	0.3900	0.1183	0.1117	0.1635	73.34

Panel D: Fed Funds Rate on Past Fed Funds Rate, Payroll Growth, Inflation, and Futures

Horizon (Months)	α	β_1	β_2	β_3	β_4	$se(\alpha)$	$se(\beta_1)$	$se(\beta_2)$	$se(\beta_3)$	$se(\beta_4)$	$\overline{R}^2$
1	-0.0112	**0.1395**	**0.0242**	0.0062	**0.8454**	0.0289	0.0586	0.0089	0.0112	0.0603	99.73
3	-0.0525	0.0948	**0.1246**	0.0212	**0.8445**	0.1074	0.1350	0.0386	0.0376	0.1426	98.46
6	-0.0295	0.0419	**0.3885**	0.1113	**0.7298**	0.2259	0.2941	0.0814	0.0951	0.3405	94.33
12	**0.9981**	-0.7180	**0.5711**	0.0925	1.1813	0.3871	0.7106	0.1211	0.1122	0.7864	79.65

Notes: Coefficients in bold are statistically significant at 1% confidence level.

Figure 7.4   Federal Funds Rate Forecasts

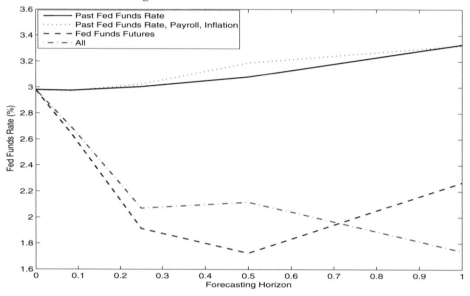

long-term growth of the economy. Credit conditions are not part of the macro-economic variables used in the regression analysis, while such "soft" information is embedded in the Fed funds futures.

7.3   UNDERSTANDING THE TERM STRUCTURE OF INTEREST RATES

Why does the term structure of interest rates tend to slope upwards? What is the risk involved in investing in Treasury securities? Can we predict medium-to-long term yields? What about returns? In this section we look at some generic relations that have to hold across yields, and the empirical evidence about their behavior over time. We begin with one example.

■ EXAMPLE 7.1

Suppose today the continuously compounded 1-year spot rate is 3%. Assume that we have perfect foresight and we know that next year the 1-year spot rate will be 5%. What then should today's 2-year yield be? To answer this question, we begin in the future and work backward. If we know for sure that next year the 1-year yield will be 5%, we also know that the price of a zero coupon bond next year will be

$$P_z(1,2) = e^{-r(1,2)\times 1} \times 100 = e^{-5\%} \times 100 = 95.1229$$

Discounting this price to today, we have that the price today of a 2-year zero coupon bond is

$$P_z(0,2) \quad = \quad e^{-r(0,1)\times 1} \times P_z(1,2) = 0.970445 \times 95.1229 = 92.3116$$

Today's 2-year yield is then $r(0,2) = -\ln(.923116)/2 = 4\%$, the average between today 1-year rate, 3% and next year 1-year rate, 5%. Is this surprising?

Note that we can rewrite

$$
\begin{aligned}
P_z\,(0,2) &= e^{-r(0,1)\times 1} \times P_z\,(1,2) = e^{-r(0,1)\times 1} \times e^{-r(1,2)\times 1} \times 100 \\
&= e^{-r(0,1)-r(1,2)} \times 100
\end{aligned}
$$

Because from the definition of the 2-year yield

$$
P_z\,(0,2) = e^{-r(0,2)\times 2} \times 100
$$

equating the right-hand sides of the last two equations implies that under perfect foresight

$$
r\,(0,2) \times 2 = r\,(0,1) + r\,(1,2)
$$

or

$$
r\,(0,2) = \frac{1}{2}r\,(0,1) + \frac{1}{2}r\,(1,2) \tag{7.6}
$$

The long-term yield is a weighted average of the current short-term yield and the short-term yield next period.

This example shows that if market participants are perfectly certain about the next year's 1-year rate, then the 2-year yield is a weighted average of today's and next year's 1-year rates. In other words, if market participants are certain that next year rates will be higher than today's, then the today's yield curve will reflect this information by sloping upward. Similarly, if market participants are certain that next year rates will be lower than today's, then today's yield curve slopes downward.

This positive relation between market participants' expectations about future rates and the current shape of the yield curve goes under the name of *expectation hypothesis*. Note, though, that market participants' expectations of future rates are not the only determinants of the current shape of the term structure of interest rates. We now introduce a simple model illustrating other factors that affect the term structure of interest rates.

7.3.1 Why Does the Term Structure Slope up in Average?

In this section we highlight the importance of investors' risk aversion in determining the shape of the term structure of interest rates. The intuition is related to the risk of investing in long-term bonds versus short-term bonds, a tradeoff already illustrated in Chapter 3 (see Section 3.3). In a nutshell, on average investors in the bond market are averse to risk. As discussed in Chapter 3, longer-term bonds have a higher duration than short-term bonds, and thus they are riskier. As a consequence, investors demand a higher yield to hold long-term bonds over short-term bonds, thereby making the term structure of the interest rate slope upward, on average. We now formalize this intuition within a formal model.

Let $r(t,T)$ be the continuously compounded yield between time t and time T. Let today be t and as in Example 7.1 consider one-year-ahead predictions of future yields. Let $r(t+1,T)$ be the yield next year for the bond maturing at time T. This future yield is obviously unknown to market participants at t. Assume that $r(t+1,T)$ has a normal distribution with mean $E_t(r(t+1,T))$ and variance $V_t(r(t+1,T))$, where the subscript t denotes that this expectation depends on the information up to t:

$$
r(t+1,T) \sim \mathcal{N}\left(E_t(r(t+1,T)), V_t(r(t+1,T))\right) \tag{7.7}
$$

For given yield $r(t + 1, T)$, the value of a zero coupon bond at time $t + 1$ with maturity T will be

$$P_z(t + 1, T) = e^{-r(t+1,T) \times (\tau - 1)} \times 100 \qquad (7.8)$$

where $\tau = T - t$ is time to maturity of the bond at t. What is the value today of the zero coupon bond maturing at time T? Since $P_z(t + 1, T)$ is not known today, we have

$$P_z(t, T) = e^{-(r(t,t+1)+\lambda)} \times E_t[P_z(t + 1, T)] \qquad (7.9)$$

where λ denotes a *risk premium* for investing in long-term bonds for a one-year horizon compared to safe 1-year zero coupon bonds. We discuss this premium further below. From the properties of the log-normal distribution,[11] we have

$$P_z(t, T) = e^{-(r(t,t+1)+\lambda)} \times e^{-E_t(r(t+1,T)) \times (\tau - 1) + \frac{(\tau - 1)^2}{2} V_t(r(t+1,T))} \times 100 \qquad (7.10)$$

Substituting also $P_z(t, T) = e^{-r(t,T) \times \tau} \times 100$ we finally obtain the following decomposition for the long-term yield:

$$
\begin{aligned}
r(t, T) &= \left[\frac{1}{\tau} \times r(t, t + 1) + \frac{(\tau - 1)}{\tau} \times E_t(r(t + 1, T)) \right] && \text{(Expected future yield)} \\
&+ \frac{\lambda}{\tau} && \text{(Risk premium)} \\
&- \frac{(\tau - 1)^2}{2\tau} V_t(r(t + 1, T)) && \text{(Convexity)}
\end{aligned}
$$

$$(7.11)$$

Equation 7.11 shows the factors that affect the current long-term rate $r(t, T)$. The first term in brackets on the right-hand side is the weighted average between the current short-term rate, and the expected long-term yield next year. This is the same term appearing on the right hand side of Equation 7.6 in Example 7.1, and simply says that if market participants expect *future* long-term yields to be high, then the *current* yield is high as well.

The second term, λ, is a risk premium that market participants require to hold long-term zero coupon bonds with maturity T over safe short-term bonds with maturity $t + 1$. To understand the role of this term, note that we can rewrite Equation 7.9 equivalently as:

$$E_t \left[\frac{P_z(t + 1, T)}{P_z(t, T)} \right] = \left[\frac{100}{P_z(t, t + 1)} \right] \times e^{\lambda} \qquad (7.12)$$

The left-hand side is the expected gross return between t and $t+1$ from investing in the zero coupon bond maturing at time T, while the term in square parenthesis on the right-hand side is the return during the same period from investing in a zero coupon with maturity $t + 1$. This latter return is known at time t and thus is riskless. Because $e^{\lambda} > 1$ if and only if $\lambda > 0$, Equation 7.12 says that the expected return during t and $t + 1$ on the long-term bond is higher than the safe one-year return on a Treasury bill if and only if $\lambda > 0$. Higher λ implies the long-term bond has a higher expected return compared to a riskless one-year T-Bill return.

---

[11] Given $x \sim \mathcal{N}(\mu_x, \sigma_x^2)$ and a constant A, we have $E\left[e^{Ax}\right] = e^{A\mu_x + \frac{A^2}{2}\sigma_x^2}$.

Why does a higher risk premium λ imply a higher yield to maturity? Because the long-term bond pays no coupons, the only way a higher expected return can be achieved between t and $t+1$ is if the bond has a lower price at t. As we know, a lower price of the bond today implies a higher yield, and the term λ in Equation 7.11 follows.

The last term in Equation 7.11 is related to the variance of the long-term yield $r(t+1, T)$, and it is called convexity term. The source of this term is the nonlinear relation that exists between the yield $r(t+1, T)$ and the price $P_z(t+1, T) = e^{-r(t+1,T) \times (\tau - 1)} \times 100$. Higher volatility of the future yield implies a higher price, due to Jensen's inequality, everything else equal.[12] Thus, a higher future yield volatility tends to decrease today's yield. Although it appears counterintuitive that higher volatility of future yields – which is related to risk – decreases the current yield, we should recall the discussion in Section 4.1.4 in Chapter 4, according to which the same convexity implies that higher volatility of future yields increases average returns, everything else equal. The lower yield counterbalances the positive convexity effect on return.

The expression for the long-term yield in Equation 7.11 has some interesting implications, which are best described within the context of a simple example.

■ **EXAMPLE 7.2**

Consider again Example 7.1, but let $r(0, 1) = 5\%$, and let market participants' expectation of next year 1-year rate also be 5%: $E[r(1, 2)] = 5\%$. Under perfect foresight, $r(0, 2) = 5\%$. However, if $r(1, 2)$ is random and thus not known today, this result only holds when the risk premium term equals the convexity term, $\lambda = \frac{1}{2} V(r(1, 2))$, as can be seen from equation (7.11).

However, if the risk premium term is higher than the convexity term, $\lambda > \frac{1}{2} V(r(1, 2))$, then $r(0, 2) > 5\% = r(0, 1)$. That is, the term structure of interest rates is rising even if market participants do *not* expect the 1-year rate to increase between this year and next year. Vice versa, a rising term structure of interest rates does not necessarily imply an expectation of higher future rates. Indeed, one interesting implication of this fact is that the forward rate is also higher than 5%, $f(0, 1, 2) > 5\% = E[r(1, 2)]$. That is, the forward rate is higher than the future rate that is expected by market participants. It follows that observing a high market forward rate need not imply that market participants are expecting higher rates in the future. It may well be that they require a high risk premium to hold long-term bonds.

7.3.2 The Expectation Hypothesis

As mentioned in Section 7.3, the expectation hypothesis refers to the theory that the slope of the term strucure of interest rates only reflects market participants' expectation of future interest rates. This hypothesis has been at the center of much research in the past two decades, and, notwithstanding its intuitive appeal, it has not received much empirical support. In this section, we link the expectation hypothesis to the model illustrated in the previous section, and discuss its empirical support.

---

[12] Jensen's inequality states that given any random variable x, for any convex function $f(x)$, $E[f(x)] > f(E[x])$.

In particular, if

$$\lambda = \frac{(\tau - 1)^2}{2} V_t \left(r \left(t + 1, T \right) \right), \tag{7.13}$$

then Equation 7.11 implies that the term structure only depends on expected future yields. Indeed, after substituting in Equation 7.11 the condition in Equation 7.13, setting $T = \tau - t$, and subtracting on both sides $r \left(t, t + \tau \right) \times \left(\tau - 1 \right) / \tau$, a little algebra yields the equivalent expression

$$E_t \left[r \left(t + 1, t + \tau \right) - r \left(t, t + \tau \right) \right] = \frac{1}{(\tau - 1)} \left[r \left(t, t + \tau \right) - r \left(t, t + 1 \right) \right] \tag{7.14}$$

That is, the slope of the term structure (on the right-hand side) is related to the expected change in the yield $r \left(t, t + \tau \right)$ between t and $t + 1$ (on the left-hand side), as postulated by the expectation hypothesis.

It is important to establish whether the relation in Equation 7.14 is true or not if we want to understand the forces shaping the yield curve. This understanding is in turn important for investors to make informed investment decisions, and for monetary authorities to take correct policy actions. Campbell and Shiller (1991) test this relation by running the regression

$$\left[r \left(t + 1, t + \tau \right) - r \left(t, t + \tau \right) \right] = \alpha + \beta \frac{1}{(\tau - 1)} \left[r \left(t, t + \tau \right) - r \left(t, t + 1 \right) \right] + \varepsilon \left(t + 1 \right) \tag{7.15}$$

where $\varepsilon \left(t + 1 \right)$ are error terms that are independent of the slope of the term structure. Collecting time series data on yields, we can compute the time series of the left-hand side and the right-hand side, and then test the hypothesis that $\alpha = 0$ and $\beta = 1$. Using zero coupon yield data from 1964 to 2006,[13] Panel A of Table 7.4 shows the regression results for maturities $\tau = 2, .5$. In particular, β is not only drammatically different from 1 for every maturity, but it is *negative,* and significantly so.

It is important to understand the meaning of the result in Panel A of Table 7.4. The negative β implies that a positively sloped term structure predicts a *decrease* of future yields, and vice versa. This is the opposite of the expectation hypothesis, and runs against the basic intuition about the meaning of the yield curve. In the data, a positively sloped term structure does not predict future higher rates.

This result is important, because not only does it imply that the expectation hypothesis (7.14) is violated – a high long-term yield spread does *not* predict higher future rates on average – but also that the remaining term in Equation 7.11, namely

$$LRP_t(\tau) = \lambda - \frac{(\tau - 1)^2}{2} V_t \left(r \left(t + 1, T \right) \right), \tag{7.16}$$

must depend on the slope of the term structure. In Equation 7.16, $LRP_t(\tau)$ stands for "Log Risk Premium" from holding a bond with time to maturity $\tau = T - t$, as further discussed below. Indeed, if Equation 7.13 does not hold, then we can rewrite Equation 7.11 as

$$E_t \left[r \left(t + 1, t + \tau \right) - r \left(t, t + \tau \right) \right] = \frac{1}{(\tau - 1)} \left[r \left(t, t + \tau \right) - r \left(t, t + 1 \right) \right] - LRP_t(\tau) \tag{7.17}$$

---

[13] Specifically, we used the Fama Bliss discount bond data obtained from CRSP.

Because in Table 7.4 we find that on average, changes in long-term yields are inversely related to the slope of the term structure, it follows that $LRP_t(\tau)$ must be positively related to the slope of the term structure.

What is the implication of these results? If we observe a strongly sloped term structure, we should not hastily conclude that the market expects higher future rates. Quite the opposite, a strongly sloped term structure implies that market participants require a high risk premium to hold long-term bonds. This high risk premium in turn implies that on average, we should expect a high capital gain in long-term zero coupon bond in the next year. A capital gain in zero coupon bonds can only occur through a strong price increase, which in turn can only occur if its bond yield decreases compared to today. The implication is then that a strongly sloped term structure predicts *lower* future yields, on average, as documented empirically in Table 7.4.

7.3.3 Predicting Excess Returns

The relation between a premium on long-term bonds and the slope of the term structure can also be seen by examining the return on investments in long-term bonds versus short-term bonds. In fact, the return in Equation 7.9 can also be rewritten as (see Appendix):

$$E_t\left[\log\left(\frac{P_z(t+1,T)}{P_z(t,T)}\right) - \log\left(\frac{100}{P_z(t,t+1)}\right)\right] = LRP_t(\tau) \qquad (7.18)$$

where $LRP_t(\tau)$ is the Log Risk Premium defined in Equation 7.16. From this equation and Equation 7.13, it follows that the expectation hypothesis implies $LRP_t(\tau) = 0$. Fama and Bliss (1987) show that the log risk premium is not zero, but it is related to the forward spread, the difference between the forward rate and the short term spot rate. Denote by

$$LER_t(\tau) = \left[\log\left(\frac{P_z(t+1,t+\tau)}{P_z(t,t+\tau)}\right) - \log\left(\frac{100}{P_z(t,t+1)}\right)\right] \qquad (7.19)$$

the log excess return from holding the long-term zero coupon bond with time to maturity τ over the short-term one year zero coupon bond. Note that log excess return $LER_t(\tau)$ defined in Equation 7.19 is the ex-post realized empirical counterpart to the log risk premium $LRP_t(\tau)$ in Equation 7.18: $LRP_t(\tau) = E_t[LER_t(\tau)]$. Fama and Bliss (1987) then run the following regression:

$$LER_t(\tau) = \alpha + \beta\left[f(t,t+\tau-1,t+\tau) - r(t,t+1)\right] + \varepsilon(t) \qquad (7.20)$$

The expectation hypothesis has $LRP_t(\tau) = 0$, and therefore $\alpha = \beta = 0$. Panel B of Table 7.4 shows that instead β is significantly different from zero, and indeed positive. This finding, again, shows that the excess log return is in fact predictable: When the forward spread is strongly positive, that is, the term structure is positively sloped, on average investments in long-term bonds generate a higher return compared to short term bonds.

More recently, Cochrane and Piazzesi (2005) have shown that a specific combination of forward rates successfully predicts excess log returns. The predicting factor is defined by

$$x_t = \gamma_0 + \gamma_1 r(t,t+1) + \gamma_3 f(t,t+2,t+3) + \gamma_5 f(t,t+4,t+5)$$

Table 7.4   Predictability

Panel A: Yield Change Prediction from Slope					
Maturity τ	α	$se(\alpha)$	β	$se(\beta)$	R^2
2	-0.01	0.27	-0.83	0.52	0.03
3	0.09	0.24	-1.23	0.62	0.05
4	0.16	0.21	-1.59	0.70	0.07
5	0.17	0.21	-1.56	0.76	0.06
Panel B: Log Excess Return Prediction from Forward Slope					
Maturity τ	α	$se(\alpha)$	β	$se(\beta)$	R^2
2	-0.01	0.27	0.92	0.26	0.14
3	-0.19	0.49	1.22	0.34	0.15
4	-0.43	0.69	1.43	0.44	0.16
5	-0.16	0.93	1.11	0.51	0.07
Panel C: Log Excess Return Prediction from Cochrane Piazzesi Factor					
Maturity τ			β	$se(\beta)$	R^2
2			0.47	0.07	0.30
3			0.88	0.13	0.33
4			1.22	0.19	0.35
5			1.43	0.24	0.32

Notes: Regression results based on Fama Bliss discount bond data from CRSP.
Sample: 1964 – 2006.

where γ_i, $i = 0, 1, 3, 5$ are estimated from average log excess returns across maturities.[14] Cochrane and Piazzesi (2005) run the regression

$$LER_t(\tau) = \beta \times x_t + \varepsilon(t) \tag{7.21}$$

Panel C of Table 7.4 gives the results in the 1964 – 2006 sample. The coefficients are strongly positive, and the R^2 higher than in Panel B, showing that including information on the whole term structure helps predict bond excess returns.

7.3.4 Conclusion

The expectation hypothesis, the assumption that a positively sloped term structure of interest rates implies that market participants expect higher future yields, has been largely rejected by the data. In fact, quite the opposite implication is true: A positively sloped term structure predicts lower future yields, because it is related to a risk premium that market participants require to hold long-term bonds. This result is also consistent with the fact that the forward spread – the difference between the forward rate and the current short term spot rate – predicts well monthly and annual returns on long term bonds. In short, returns on zero coupon bonds are predictable by using some predicting factors and this is due to a variation in risk premia, rather than variation in expectation of future yields.

These empirical findings have an important implication for bond investors. For instance, if a bond investor interprets a positively sloped term structure as an indication of a future increase in yields, then he may be led to sell bonds today to avoid capital losses when interest rates increase. Because the empirical literature has established that in average, a positively sloped term structure is correlated with lower future yields, the investors should rather increase the position in bonds.

One important warning, however, is the following: a positively sloped term structure is associated with a higher risk premium (and this is why it predicts higher future returns). However, if there is a risk premium, there must be somewhere some risk that induces the risk premium. That is, holding long-term bonds on the premise that they will yield a higher return on average does not mean that this return is riskless. In fact, if a long-term bond has a risk premium, it is quite possible that the market anticipates the possibility of large capital losses in this long-term bond, and that's why it is underpriced (or, the yield is high).

What is the risk that a bond holder is facing when he purchases long-term bonds? There are many. For instance, for the given expectation of future inflation, a higher uncertainty about the actual level of future inflation increases risk, because if it turns out that inflation suddenly increases, the Fed will be led to increase the Fed funds rate, pushing down the price of long term bonds. Such losses can be substantial, as the Orange County case study discussed in Section 3.7 in Chapter 3 shows.

7.4 COPING WITH INFLATION RISK: TREASURY INFLATION-PROTECTED SECURITIES

Treasury coupon bonds are in nominal terms, as they pay a sequence of coupons and the final principal in dollars. Clearly, how much of a good one can buy with the dollar coupons

---

[14]The parameters γ are estimated in a first stage regression, in which $\overline{LER}_t = 0.25 \times \sum_{\tau=2}^{5}$ is regressed on a constant and $(r(t, t+1), f(t, t+2, t+3),$ and $f(t, t+4, t+5))$. The resulting estimates are $\gamma_0 = -3.26$, $\gamma_1 = -1.87, \gamma_3 = 3.94,$ and $\gamma_5 = -1.64$.

and final principal depends on the inflation between the purchase of the bond and the coupons or principal payments. Over long periods, the difference in purchasing power can be quite significant. The CPI index, computed monthly by the Bureau of Labor Statistics (BLS), provides a weighted average of the value of a basket of representative goods that U.S. consumers purchase.[15] The change in the CPI over time measures the realized inflation during the period.

Consider a household with a monthly income of $10,000$ and let the CPI represent the price of the basket itself. The amount of the consumption basket that the household can buy at a given time t_1 is $Q(t_1) = \$10,000/CPI(t_1)$. For instance, if $CPI(t_1) = 10$, then the household can purchase 1000 units of the basket underlying the CPI index. If the basket was only made up of $10-hamburgers, the household could purchase $Q(t_1) = 1000$ hamburgers in month t_1. Consider now a later time t_2 and assume that the household monthly income did not change. Because of inflation, however, assume the $CPI(t_2) = 20$. Then, the household could only purchase $Q(t_2) = \$10,000/CPI(t_2) = 500$ hamburgers, a big loss in consumption, even if the nominal income did not change between the two periods.

The ratio between the quantities the households could purchase, $Q(t_2)/Q(t_1)$, measures the loss in purchasing power of the dollar between the two dates. This ratio is given by $Q(t_2)/Q(t_1) = CPI(t_1)/CPI(t_2)$. For instance, in the previous example $CPI(t_1)/CPI(t_2) = 0.5$, which means that at t_2 the household can purchase only one half of the goods it could purchase at t_1 with the same amount of dollars.

How does the purchasing power change over time? The solid line in Panel A of Figure 7.5 plots the loss in purchasing power over a five year period from 1968 - 2005, that is, the ratio $CPI(t)/CPI(t+5)$. For instance, in January 1968 (the first observation), the ratio was 0.8. This implies that the loss in the value of the dollar between January 1968 and January 1973 (five years later) meant that in January 1973 consumers could purchase only 80% of what they could purchase in January 1968. Similarly, in 1976 the index was about 0.61, which implies that one dollar in 1981 (five years after 1976) could only purchase 60% of what it could purchase in 1976.

The dotted line in Panel A shows the *ex-ante* time value of one dollar five years in the future, that is, the discount factor $Z(t, t+5)$. Most often the ex-ante market value of one dollar in the future $Z(t, t+5)$ is below the realized loss in value, $Z(t, t+5) < CPI(t)/CPI(t+5)$. This implies that a zero coupon bond at time t is sufficiently cheap to make up for the ex-post loss in purchasing power of the dollar. However, it also happens that $Z(t, t+5) > CPI(t)/CPI(t+5)$, which has the opposite implication: The ex-post loss in purchasing power is above the ex-ante value of one dollar in the future. That is, the price of a zero coupon bond is too high compared to the realized loss in value of the payoff from the investment. This is called *inflation risk*.

Indeed, Panel B of Figure 7.5 presents inflation risk from the opposite perspective. This figure plots the realized inflation between t and $t+5$ (the solid line) and the return on a 5-year zero coupon bond made at time t (the dotted line). If the return on a zero coupon bond is above inflation, then an investment in the zero coupon bond is sufficient to cover the increase in consumption good prices. However, as it can be seen, in multiple occasions in the 1970s the return on the zero coupon bond was not sufficient to cover the inflation rate.

---

[15] In fact, there are several measures of the CPI, which differ in location and type of goods. The one we refer to here is non-seasonally-adjusted CPI-U, which is the average of the consumption goods in urban cities, which is the index used for TIPS.

Figure 7.5   Ex-Post and Ex-Ante Time Value of Money on a Five Year Horizon

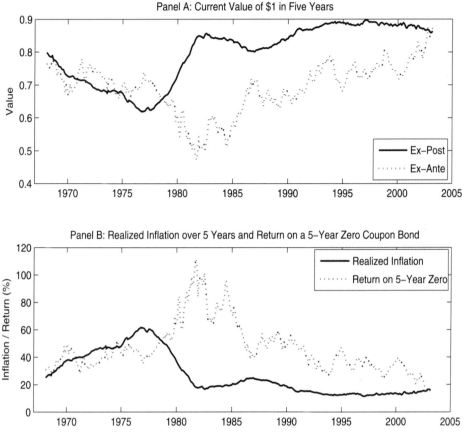

Data Source: Bureau of Labor Statistics and CRSP.

The ex-post inflation was too high compared to the anticipated value. Investors anticipating a high inflation rate would require a higher return on a zero coupon bond to cover the loss in value of the dollar.

Definition 7.1 Inflation risk *refers to the loss of purchasing power of the dollar. All assets that pay fixed amount of dollars in the future are subject to inflation risk.*

To cover themselves from inflation risk, investors may require a risk premium on securities that pay in dollars. This can be seen in Figure 7.5: From Panel A the price of a zero coupon bond sank in the 1980s, as investors were wary of the high future inflation, which did not materialize ex post. The zero coupon bond price remained very low until the end of the 1990s, in fact, even as inflation had decreased substantially. Panel B makes the same point from a return perspective: The required return on a zero coupon bond over a 5 year period was over 100% in the 1980s to compensate for the fear of high inflation.

In 1997, the U.S. Treasury introduced Treasury Inflation Protected Securities (TIPS) to provide investors an investment vehicle that covers against inflation risk. This in turn could benefit the Treasury itself, as investors in TIPS would not require an additional risk premium to hold nominal bonds.[16] A decade later, about 10% of the total government debt is in fact in TIPS.

7.4.1 TIPS Mechanics

TIPS are coupon bonds issued with maturities of 5, 10, and 20 years. The coupon rate of TIPS is a constant fraction of the principal. The principal, however, is not fixed, but it changes over time in response to inflation. If the CPI increases, then the principal amount increases proportionally. This implies that the coupon per period increases also with the CPI, as does the final principal amount. The Treasury publishes index ratios, which are simply given by the change in the CPI index between the issuance of the TIPS and the reference CPI reading. The reference CPI reading is not the current CPI, however, but the average of the CPI value at the beginning of the month of the coupon payment and the CPI value at the beginning of the previous month. Table 7.5 contains quotes from Treasury nominal coupon notes and bonds and TIPS on November 26, 2007. In particular, the last three columns of Panel C report the reference CPI of each of the TIPS, and the "current" CPI, out of which the index ratio is computed. Given the index ratio, it is possible to compute the next coupon payment, as it is given by

$$\text{Coupon payment} = \frac{\text{Coupon rate}}{2} \times 100 \times \text{Index ratio}$$

The quote in Table 7.5 is for November 26, 2007. The CPI used to compute the index ratio is not, as noted above, the November CPI (released typically during the third week of each month by the BLS). Instead, it is the average between the August and September, 2007 CPI reading, which were in fact 207.917 and 208.490, respectively.[17] It follows that an investor in TIPS is subject to a small inflation risk, the inflation that occurs during the two months between the CPI measure and the actual payment.

7.4.2 Real Bonds and the Real Term Structure of Interest Rates

To understand the valuation of inflation linked securities, it is useful to describe the concept of "real bonds." In Chapter 2 we examined the borrowing and lending problem of the Treasury in terms of dollars. The Treasury borrows some amount of dollars at time t to return some more in the future T. Although it is intuitive to use dollars as a unit of account to describe borrowing and lending, as well as the concept of interest rates, this is by no means unique. Borrowing and lending can occur in any unit, as we know from day-to-day life. You can borrow a car from a friend and return it filled up with gas. There is no dollar exchange here, and the implicit "interest rate" depends on the price of gas. Similarly, and more relevant for finance, gold mine companies often use gold bullion loans to finance

---

[16]On the other hand, the TIPS program also prevents the government from gaming the investors and cover its nominal government debt by an inflationary monetary policy.

[17]The first day of the month is always equal to the CPI of three months before, in this case the CPI used on November 1, 2007 = 207.917 = August reading. Because November 26 is 25 days after the first of November, the calculation is $25/30 \times 208.490 + 5/30 \times 207.917 = 208.3945$.

Table 7.5 Treasury Securities on November 26, 2007

Panel A: Treasury Bills

Coupon	Maturity	BID	ASK
	12/20/2007	3.54	3.5
	2/21/2008	3.05	3
	5/22/2008	3.24	3.23

Panel B: Nominal Treasury Notes and Bonds

Coupon	Maturity	BID	ASK
3 5/8	10/31/2009	101.25	101.25
4 1/2	5/15/2010	103.75	103.7813
3 7/8	10/31/2012	102.7188	102.7188
4 1/4	11/15/2017	103.1563	103.1563
5	5/15/2037	111.7813	111.8438

Panel C: TIPS

Coupon	Maturity	BID	ASK	Issue Date	Issue Price	First Coupon	Reference CPI	CPI	Index Ratio
2	4/15/2012	104.2188	104.2813	4/30/2007	102.667	10/15/2007	202.9214	208.3945	1.02697
2 5/8	7/15/2017	110.125	110.2188	7/16/2007	102.722	1/15/2008	207.2564	208.3945	1.00549
2 3/8	1/15/2027	109.5313	109.7188	1/31/2007	99.57	7/15/2007	201.6645	208.3945	1.03337
3 3/8	4/15/2032	133.4063	133.625	10/15/2001	98.314	4/15/2002	177.5	208.3945	1.17405

Data Source: Bloomberg, Inc.

exploration and mine development: In a gold bullion loan a mining company borrows some amount of gold at time t with the agreement of returning some more amount of gold at a later time T, plus possibly gold coupons delivered over time. Once again, there is no explicit reference to dollars in the transaction, and the effective "dollar" interest rate depends on the realized price of gold.

Real bonds are bonds that are denominated in units of a good, such as gold, instead of dollars. Relevant to inflation linked securities are bonds that are denominated in units of the consumption basket that underlies the CPI index calculation.

Exactly as we did in Chapter 2 when we discussed the discount factor $Z(t; T)$, we can now consider the *real* discount factor $Z^{real}(t; T)$.

Definition 7.2 *The* **real discount factor** $Z^{real}(t; T)$ *defines the exchange rate between consumption goods at t versus consumption goods at a later date T.*

The quantity $Z^{real}(t; T)$ measures the units of the consumption basket that a consumer is willing to give up at time t in order to receive one unit of consumption good at time T. The reasonable behavioral assumption is that to induce somebody to give up some consumption good today (t), he or she must receive more of it at the later date T. That is, $Z^{real}(t; T) < 1$.[18]

The definition of a real discount factor allows us to then define anything else in terms of it, exactly as we did in Chapter 2. In fact, all of the concepts described there for the *nominal* discount factor $Z(t; T)$ can be equally defined in terms of the *real* discount factor $Z^{real}(t; T)$.

For instance, given a real discount factor, we can compute the real interest rate in the usual fashion. In the next definition we only consider the continuously compounded real interest rate. The definition of the real rate at any other compounding frequency can be obtained as in Chapter 2.

Definition 7.3 *The continuously compounded* **real interest rate** *can be obtained from the real discount factor as the solution to the equation*

$$Z^{real}(t; T) = e^{-r_{real}(t;T)(T-t)} \times 1 \tag{7.22}$$

In particular,

$$r_{real}(t; T) = -\frac{\ln\left(Z^{real}(t; T)\right)}{T - t} \tag{7.23}$$

The **real term structure of interest rates** *at time t is given by $r_{real}(t; T)$ for various maturities T.*

Similarly, the value (in consumption goods) of a real coupon bond, with maturity T and coupon rate c is given by

$$P_c^{real}(t; T) = \frac{c \times 100}{2} \sum_{i=1}^{n} Z^{real}(t; T_i) + 100 \times Z^{real}(t; T)$$

---

[18]For instance, if somebody borrows your car and gives it back to you after five years, perhaps you are not too happy, even if it is in the same conditions as it was when you lent it. Likely, you want something else in addition to the original car, as compensation for the fact that you could not use it for all that time.

7.4.3 Real Bonds and TIPS

We can finally see the connection between real bonds and TIPS, and therefore obtain a pricing formula. It is convenient to start from zero coupon bonds. Suppose an investment bank purchases a TIPS and strips the coupons from principal, generating a series of zero coupon bonds. These zero coupon bonds pay an amount that is tied to the CPI. Denoting by $Idx(T)$ the CPI adjustment for maturity T (recall, it depends on the CPI two months earlier), the payoff of a zero coupon TIPS is as follows:

$$\text{Zero coupon TIPS payoff at } T = 100 \times \frac{Idx(T)}{Idx(0)} \qquad (7.24)$$

Note that the ratio $Idx(T)/Idx(0)$ represents the increase in the price of the consumption good between 0 and T (minus two months). Let for simplicity $Idx(T)$ represent in fact the *cost* of purchasing exactly one unit of the consumption basket underlying the CPI. It follows that $100 \times Idx(T)$ is the price at T of 100 units of the consumption basket. Given the *real* discount factor $Z^{real}(t;T)$ introduced in the previous section, it follows that the value today (at t) of this payoff is simply

$$\text{Present value of } 100 \times Idx(T) = Z^{real}(t;T) \times 100$$

This present value though is expressed in terms of units of the consumption basket. We can convert this value to dollars by multiplying it by the *current* price of the consumption basket $Idx(t)$. We then obtain

$$\text{Dollar present value of } 100 \times Idx(T) = Z^{real}(t;T) \times Idx(t) \times 100$$

Finally, the left-hand side is not exactly equal to the payoff of the zero coupon TIPS. We must also divide it by the value of the index at time 0, $Idx(0)$, obtaining the pricing formula

$$\text{Dollar value of a zero coupon TIPS} = P_z^{TIPS}(t;T) = Z^{real}(t;T) \times \frac{Idx(t)}{Idx(0)} \times 100 \qquad (7.25)$$

In the above computation we are implicitly making the assumption that the time lag between the final payment T and the index determination does not matter. This assumption simplifies the computation significantly.

Given the value of zero coupon TIPS, we can compute the value of any coupon bearing TIPS. For instance, a TIPS value at t, with maturity T, and coupon rate c is given by

$$P_c^{TIPS}(t;T) = \frac{Idx(t)}{Idx(0)} \times \left[\frac{c \times 100}{2} \sum_{i=1}^{n} Z^{real}(t;T_i) + Z^{real}(t;T) \right] \qquad (7.26)$$

7.4.4 Fitting the Real Yield Curve

If we had the value of the real discounts $Z^{real}(t;T)$ we could then price all the TIPS directly from Equation 7.26. Unfortunately, $Z^{real}(t;T_i)$ are not observable, but they are embedded in the prices of TIPS. This is also true for the Treasury nominal discount curve $Z(t;T)$. However, as explained in Chapter 2 for nominal bonds, we can use the price of

TIPS to "back out" the discount factors $Z^{real}(t; T_i)$ itself. One limitation compared to the case of Treasuries is that we do not have available as many bond prices, and therefore the bootstrapping strategy discussed in Section 2.4.2 is not applicable. However, in the Appendix of Chapter 2 we reviewed the curve fitting method using a flexible function for the discount factor, such as the Nelson Siegel model. In this subsection we use the data in Table 7.5 to illustrate the computation of the real curve.

■ EXAMPLE 7.3

Recall the curve fitting methodology we employed in Chapter 2, Section 2.9.3.2. Indeed, from the pricing formula in Equation 7.26, for each TIPS we can compute the adjusted TIPS price, given by

$$\widehat{P}_c^{TIPS}(t; T) = \frac{P_c^{TIPS}(t; T)}{Idx(t)/Idx(0)} = \frac{c \times 100}{2} \sum_{i=1}^{n} Z^{real}(t; T_i) + Z^{real}(t; T) \quad (7.27)$$

The right-hand side of Equation 7.27 is exactly the same formula used in nominal bonds in Chapter 2. We can then now use the same steps as in other fitting exercises. In particular, we compute the adjusted invoice prices, by calculating the accrued interest to be paid to the seller of the TIPS. Next, we posit a model for the discount curve $Z^{real}(0; T)$. Here, we use the extended Nelson Siegel model, which states that the continuously compounded (real) interest rate is given by

$$r_{real}(0, T) = \theta_0 + (\theta_1 + \theta_2) \frac{1 - e^{-\frac{T}{\kappa_1}}}{\frac{T}{\kappa_1}} - \theta_2 e^{-\frac{T}{\kappa_1}} + \theta_3 \left(\frac{1 - e^{-\frac{T}{\kappa_2}}}{\frac{T}{\kappa_2}} - e^{-\frac{T}{\kappa_2}} \right) \quad (7.28)$$

There are six parameters to estimate from the quoted prices.[19] The solid line in Panel A of Figure 7.6 plots the term structure of real rates $r_{real}(0; T)$ across maturity. The real rate is between 1.5% at the low end of the term structure to over 2% at the high end.

7.4.5   The Relation between Nominal and Real Rates

To conclude this chapter, we could reasonably ask what is the relation between nominal bonds and inflation indexed bonds? Clearly, the values of these securities cannot be completely independent of each other. For instance, if the real discount $Z^{real}(t; T)$ decreases, this means that households value future consumption less, and thus want a higher compensation to hold real (or inflation linked) bonds. A nominal bond provides a fixed amount of dollars in order to purchase the consumption good: However, if such consumption good is not as valuable in today's "consumption value," it is intuitive that the nominal bonds will have a lower price as well. This discussion can be formalized as follows.

Consider a nominal zero coupon bond at time 0 with maturity T. Its nominal (dollar) price is

$$P_z(0, T) = e^{-r(0,T) \times T} \times \$100 \quad (7.29)$$

---

[19] From Table 7.5 there are only four quoted prices, but we search for six parameters. If these were linear equations, there would be infinite solutions. However, the high non-linearity of the problem makes the problem well defined, and a unique solution (estimate) can be found. The estimated parameters are $\theta_0 = 6277.748$, $\theta_1 = -6277.734$, $\theta_2 = -6288.682$, $\theta_3 = 0.029$, $\kappa_1 = 3641.997$ and $\kappa_2 = 4.688$.

Figure 7.6   Real and Nominal Rates on November 26, 2007

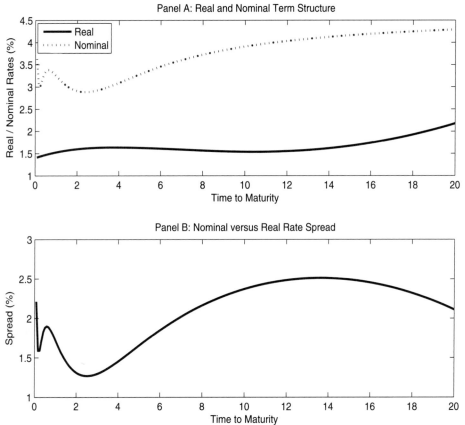

Data Source: Bloomberg.

Having $100 at T will allow us to purchase a quantity $\$100/Idx(T)$ of the consumption bundle. We consider first the case in which investors have perfect foresight of future inflation.

7.4.5.1 Nominal and Real Rates under Perfect Foresight

Suppose that we have perfect foresight, so that we know exactly what the CPI index ($Idx(T)$) is at T. It follows that the present value of this amount of consumption good can be obtained by discounting it using the *real* rate:

$$\text{Present value of } \frac{\$100}{Idx(T)} = e^{-r_{real}(0,T) \times T} \times \frac{\$100}{Idx(T)}$$

This present value is expressed in terms of consumption good, while we want a dollar price. We obtain the conversion to dollars by multiplying the present value by the current CPI index $Idx(0)$:

$$\text{Dollar present value of } \frac{\$100}{Idx(T)} = \left(e^{-r_{real}(0,T) \times T} \times \frac{Idx(0)}{Idx(T)} \right) \times \$100 \qquad (7.30)$$

Comparing this equation with Equation 7.29 we see that in either case we are discounting $100 to today. Since we are assuming perfect foresight regarding inflation, it follows that the two discounts are identical to each other, obtaining the relation

$$e^{-r(0,T) \times T} = e^{-r_{real}(0,T) \times T} \times \frac{Idx(0)}{Idx(T)} \qquad (7.31)$$

Let π be the constant continuously compounded, annualized inflation rate between 0 and T, that is, π is defined by

$$Idx(T) = Idx(0) \times e^{\pi \times T} \qquad (7.32)$$

We then obtain from Equation 7.31

$$r(0,T) = r_{real}(0,T) + \pi$$

Under perfect foresight, the nominal rate equals the real rate plus the (annualized) inflation rate.

7.4.5.2 Nominal and Real Rates under Uncertain Inflation

Because we do not know the inflation rate between 0 and T (if we did, we would not need TIPS), we need to modify the analysis in two ways: First, we need to introduce some randomness in future inflation. Second, we have to take into account the fact that investors in nominal bonds want to be compensated with a risk premium.

Assume for instance that π in Equation 7.32 has a normal distribution with mean $\bar{\pi}$ and variance σ_π^2:

$$\pi \sim \mathcal{N}(\bar{\pi}, \sigma_\pi^2)$$

This implies that the expected loss in purchasing power is

$$E\left[\frac{Idx(T)}{Idx(0)} \right] = e^{-\bar{\pi} \times T + \frac{T^2}{2} \sigma_\pi^2}$$

Second, assume that investors require an (annualized) inflation risk premium κ to hold a security that pays in dollars, instead of being indexed to inflation. The present value expression analogous to Equation 7.30 but that takes into account the randomness of inflation and the inflation risk premium is then given by

$$\text{Dollar present value of } expected\, \frac{\$100}{Idx(T)} \;=\; E\left[e^{-(r_{real}(0,T)+\kappa)\times T}\frac{Idx(0)}{Idx(T)}\right] \times \$100$$

$$= e^{-(r_{real}(0,T)+\kappa)\times T} \times e^{-\bar{\pi}\times T + \frac{T^2}{2}\sigma_\pi^2} \times \$100$$

Since this expression must equal to Equation 7.29, it then follows that

$$r(t,T) = r_{real}(t,T) + \bar{\pi} + \kappa - \frac{T}{2}\sigma_\pi^2 \tag{7.33}$$

That is, the nominal rate equals the real rate, plus the expected inflation and an inflation risk premium. In addition, there is a (negative) convexity term that appears in the equation, which is due to the convex relation between the CPI index $(Idx(T))$ and its growth rate π. Variation of the real rate then affects the nominal rate, even if the expected inflation and risk premium are constant. Vice versa, even if the real rate is constant, the nominal rate may increase or decrease because of variation in expected inflation or the inflation risk premium κ.

■ **EXAMPLE 7.4**

To illustrate the relation between nominal and real rate, consider again Example 7.3. Fitting the extended Nelson Siegel model to the T-bill, T-notes, and T-bond prices in Table 7.5 we obtain the nominal spot rate curve $r(0; T)$ depicted as the dotted line in Panel A of Figure 7.6. The difference between the two curves provides an estimate of the combined level of expected inflation $\bar{\pi}$, risk premium κ, and convexity $-(T/2)\sigma_\pi^2$. This quantity is plotted in Panel B of Figure 7.6.

7.5 SUMMARY

In this section we covered the following topics:

1. Basics of monetary policy and the Federal Reserve's role in the economy: The Fed has the dual mandate to keep low inflation (stable prices) and low unemployment. The Fed affects interest rates and thus the return on fixed income instruments through the determination of its target Federal funds rate and discount rate.

2. Fed funds rate and macro variables: The Federal funds rate moves over time in relation to inflation and payroll growth. These macro variables help predict future Fed funds rates.

3. Fed funds futures. Fed funds futures help predict future Fed funds rates. Macro variables add explanatory power.

4. Expectation hypothesis: The expectation hypothesis states that long-term yields depend only on market participants' expectation of future yields. It is strongly rejected in the data, implying that risk premia and, in fact, time varying risk premia are a fundamental source of variation in bond yields.

Table 7.6   Parameter Estimates of Model 1 and Model 2

	α	β_1	β_2	β_3	β_4
Model 1	-0.000196	0.9594	0.0731	0.0326	
Model 2	-0.000112	0.1395	0.0242	0.0062	0.8454

5. Risk premium: A risk premium is the higher average return on an investment over a given horizon, such as one year, that market participants require to hold long-term bonds over safe short-term bonds, whose return over the investment horizon is known. The evidence shows that the risk premium is correlated with the slope of the term structure of interest rates.

6. Treasury Inflation Protected Securities (TIPS): TIPS are Treasury securities whose principal is indexed to inflation, specifically, the consumer price index (CPI). These securities offer protection against an increase in inflation.

7. Real rate: The real rate is the rate of interest of an investment net of inflation.

8. Real term structure of interest rates: The relation between yields of real zero coupon bonds and maturity is known as the real term structure of interest rates. It can be estimated from TIPS.

7.6 EXERCISES

1. In this chapter we estimated two models to predict the Fed funds rate

$$r^{FF}(t) = \alpha + \beta_1\, r^{FF}(t-1) + \beta_2\, X^{Pay}(t-1) + \beta_3\, X^{Inf}(t-1)$$
$$r^{FF}(t) = \alpha + \beta_1\, r^{FF}(t-1) + \beta_2\, X^{Pay}(t-1) + \beta_3\, X^{Inf}(t-1) + \beta_4\, f^{Fut}(t, t+1)$$

Table 7.6 summarizes the estimates in Tables 7.1 and 7.3.

(a) Use the estimates in Table 7.6 to perform a one-month-ahead prediction of the Fed funds target rate using the data in Table 7.7. That is, for instance, using the entries on Dec-06, compute the predicted Fed funds rate on Jan-07. Similarly, using the data on Jan-07 to predict the Fed Funds rate on Feb-07. And so on. Perform the exercise using both models.

(b) The first column in Table 7.7 provides the actual ex-post Fed Funds target rate. Plot both models predictions of the Fed funds rate and the actual values. How close are the estimates?

(c) Compute the sum of squared errors for both models. Based on this calculation, which model seems to be more accurate?

2. Today is December 12, 2008 and TIPS prices are in Table 7.8.

(a) Use the extended Nelson Siegel model in Equation 7.28 to calculate the real discount curve and real yield curve.

Table 7.7 Fed Funds Target Prediction

Date	Fed Funds Target	Payroll Growth	Annual Inflation	Fed Funds Futures
Dec-06	5.25%	0.08%	2.08%	5.24%
Jan-07	5.25%	0.07%	2.44%	5.25%
Feb-07	5.25%	0.13%	2.75%	5.25%
Mar-07	5.25%	0.06%	2.57%	5.25%
Apr-07	5.25%	0.11%	2.68%	5.25%
May-07	5.25%	0.10%	2.65%	5.25%
Jun-07	5.25%	0.07%	2.37%	5.25%
Jul-07	5.25%	0.00%	1.94%	5.25%
Aug-07	5.25%	0.08%	2.76%	5.25%
Sep-07	4.75%	0.12%	3.54%	4.66%
Oct-07	4.75%	0.07%	4.37%	4.63%
Nov-07	4.50%	0.01%	4.12%	4.22%
Dec-07	4.25%	-0.01%	4.40%	4.16%
Jan-08	3.50%	-0.05%	4.12%	2.96%
Feb-08	3.00%	-0.06%	4.00%	2.67%
Mar-08	2.25%	-0.01%	3.88%	2.17%
Apr-08	2.25%	-0.04%	4.08%	2.00%
May-08	2.00%	-0.05%	4.90%	2.01%
Jun-08	2.00%	-0.04%	5.52%	2.01%
Jul-08	2.00%	-0.06%	5.36%	2.02%
Aug-08	2.00%	-0.12%	4.94%	2.02%
Sep-08	2.00%			

Data Source: Federal Reserve and Bureau of Labor Statistics.

Table 7.8   TIPS Data on December 12, 2008

Security	Maturity	Price	Coupon	IndexRatio
1	1/15/2014	91 7/32	2	1.18406
2	1/15/2016	91	2	1.10231
3	7/15/2014	90 1/2	2	1.16067
4	1/15/2026	85 25/32	2	1.10231

Source: Bloomberg.

(b) Your estimates for the extended Nelson Siegel model's parameters should be close to $\theta_0 = 6278.3013$, $\theta_1 = -6278.227$, $\theta_2 = -6289.189$, $\theta_3 = -0.18763$, $\kappa_1 = 27056.491$, and $\kappa_2 = 32.190532$. Given Equation 7.28, which describes the application of the extended Nelson Siegel model to real interest rates, can you see what the short-term interest rate $r(0)$ [i.e., $r(0, T)$ when $T \longrightarrow 0$] is by looking only at the parameters?

(c) Using the real term structure, price the a 2% Coupon TIPS with maturity 4/14/2012 and index ratio 1.07817.

(d) On December 12, 2008, the TIPS priced in Part (c) was actually trading at 95 15/16. Is your price close to trading price?

3. Consider the TIPS data in Table 7.8. Assume that you decide to make a portfolio from Securities 1 and 3 in the table. Specifically, you decide to strip the coupons from the TIPS. You decide to short the next five coupon payments of Security 1 and go long the next five coupon payments of Security 3.

(a) Because you are essentially short and long 2% in real terms, is the price of the total position zero? Explain.

(b) What is the nominal price of this position? Assuming today is December 12, 2008, use the estimates for the extended Nelson Siegel model (Equation 7.28) given in the previous exercise, i.e., $\theta_0 = 6278.3013$, $\theta_1 = -6278.227$, $\theta_2 = -6289.189$, $\theta_3 = -0.18763$, $\kappa_1 = 27056.491$ and $\kappa_2 = 32.190532$. Do you have to pay or do you receive money?

(c) The next coupon payment occurs on January 15, 2009, and you are given the index ratios for these two securities on that date. They are 1.16196 for Security 1 and 1.08173 for Security 3. What will the actual cash flow be at that date? Do you receive money or do you pay money?

(d) Is this portfolio similar to holding inflation risk or is it more like holding insurance against inflation risk?

4. Consider the TIPS data in Table 7.8. Assume that you decide to make a *costless* portfolio from Securities 1 and 3 in the table. Specifically you decide to strip the coupons from the TIPS. You decide to short the next five coupon payments of Security 1 and go long the next five coupon payments of Security 3.

    (a) In order to be costless, what will be the ratio of Security 3 to Security 1 that you will have to purchase?

    (b) What will the next coupon payment be in nominal terms?

    (c) What will the coupon payments of this position be in real terms?

    (d) What will the price of this position be in real terms? Can you back out the nominal price from the real price?

5. An important feature of TIPS is that the principal amount cannot go below 100. In other words, if the index ratio goes under one this parameter is automatically set to one. This is important in cases when there is deflation (negative inflation), because in this scenario the value of the principal decreases. Yet given the previously stated rule, the fall in the reference CPI cannot go below its original value at inception. Usually there is little or no deflation so index ratios on TIPS tend to accumulate high values: Even in the event of deflation the value is too high to send it below one. Yet this isn't the case for recently issued on-the-run TIPS. Suppose today is January 16, 2002 and you have the TIPS data in Panel A of Table 7.9.

    (a) Use the data in Panel A to estimate the extended Nelson Siegel model (see Equation 7.28) and compute the term structure of real interest rates. The parameter values you get for the extended Nelson Siegel model should be similar to the following: $\theta_0 = 6278.3013$, $\theta_1 = -6278.271$, $\theta_2 = -6289.657$, $\theta_3 = 0.0573662$, $\kappa_1 = 27056.491$, and $\kappa_2 = 24.225094$.

    (b) Consider now the TIPS in Panel B of Table 7.9. You notice that the index ratio is very close to one: This means that the security has not accumulated much inflation since it was issued (October 15, 2001). This makes it very easy for it to go below one if there is a little deflation in the next period. What happens to this bond if there is deflation? Is the cash from the coupon higher, lower, or the same as if there wasn't any inflation?

    (c) Is this bond more or less valuable than any of the others in Panel A?

    (d) Consider the real term structure of interest rates computed above. Given those parameters, what is the price of this security?

    (e) What is the squared pricing error of this security? Is it very different from the ones for the other securities in Panel A?

    (f) What is the difference in terms of the clean prices?

    (g) Does this analysis reflect you answer in Part (c) above?

7.7 CASE STUDY: MONETARY POLICY DURING THE SUBPRIME CRISIS OF 2007 - 2008

The subprime crisis in 2007 to 2008 offers the occasion to observe the Federal Reserve in action, as the Fed made use of all of the existing monetary policy tools, and introduced new ones, in its attempt to avoid allowing the U.S. to enter into a long recession. Table 7.10 lists the key events taking place.[20]

---

[20]Thanks to Javier Madrid who put together this case study.

Table 7.9 TIPS Data on January 16, 2002

Security	Maturity	Price	Coupon	IndexRatio
		Panel A: TIPS		
1	1/15/2011	100.66	3.50	1.02017
2	1/15/2010	105.81	4.25	1.05533
3	4/15/2029	107.13	3.88	1.08006
4	4/15/2028	102.56	3.63	1.09778
		Panel B: On-the-run TIPS		
5	4/15/2032	99.88	3.38	1.00031

Source: Bloomberg.

7.7.1 Problems on the Horizon

In mid-2007 the economy seemed to be in good shape, but reports of higher than expected default rates on loans, specifically in mortgage backed securities (MBS) linked to the subprime mortgage market were starting to surface. On June 12, 2007, Bear Stearns - an investment bank - reported a 23% loss on one of its hedge funds (at one time worth $642 million). The High-Grade Structured Credit Strategies Enhanced Leverage Funds were part of the whole wide range of asset management strategies based on collateralized debt obligations (CDOs) that Bear Stearns had developed in the past few years. Bear Stearns was the No. 2 underwriter of mortgage bonds after Lehman Brothers, another investment bank. Bear Stearns looked to liquidate the fund but found little demand for it. But the Bear Stearns news was not so noteworthy in an otherwise sound economy, and at its FOMC meeting on June 28, 2007, the Federal Reserve decided to keep the rates unchanged, as inflation had been rising and payroll growth was still strong.

In July 2008 some additional bad news hit the market. First, reports came out that in May, defaults increased 87% when compared to the previous year, especially in the area of loans in the subprime market. On July 19, 2007, Fed Chairman Ben J. Bernanke testified to the Senate that losses on securities tied to subprime mortgages could range as high as $100 billion. On July 24, 2007, Countrywide, one of the nation's largest independent mortgage lenders, announced that it was forced to take impairment charges due to the rising number of delinquencies and mortgage defaults. Since 2006, Countrywide was the U.S. top financier of mortgages, with 20% share of the market. Still, at its scheduled FOMC meeting on August 7, the Federal Reserve decided to keep rates unchanged because of concerns about inflation.

Just two days after the Fed decision to maintain rates unchanged, a sequence of events effectively heralded what many have termed the worst financial crisis since the Great Depression. First, Countrywide mentioned in an SEC filing that the market problems were unprecedented disruptions. By this time Countrywide had lost a third of its value (equivalent to $8.8 billion in market capitalization). Other financials such as Washington Mutual, the largest U.S. savings and loan, and MGIC Investment, the No. 1 mortgage insurer, faced similar woes. But the main concern for the Federal Reserve was an unexpected disruption in the credit market: On August 9, 2007 something unusual happened. Both the overnight LIBOR and the Fed funds rate had risen sharply over the Fed funds target (see Figure

Table 7.10   The Events of the Subprime Crisis: 2007 – 2008

Date	Event
Friday, June 15, 2007	Bear Sterns tries to liquidate holdings of one hedge fund (MBS).
Thursday, June 28, 2007	FOMC meeting. No rate change.
Friday, July 6, 2007	NFP go up by 132,000; unemployment is at 4.5% and inflation is at 2.65% (June).
Tuesday, July 17, 2007	Fed announces investigation on subprime mortgages, due to increase in defaults 87% year to year.
Tuesday, July 24, 2007	Countrywide reports losses due to high defaults.
Friday, August 3, 2007	NFP go up by 92,000; unemployment is at 4.6% and inflation is at 2.37% (July).
Tuesday, August 7, 2007	FOMC meeting. No rate change.
Thursday, August 9, 2007	Fed injects $24 billion through open market operations.
Friday, August 10, 2007	FOMC unscheduled meeting. Fed injects $35 billion through open market operations. Fed announces it will take $19 billion in MBS through 3-day repo agreements at Fed funds rate. Secondary market for mortgages evaporates, pushing Countrywide and Washington Mutual into deeper trouble.
Thursday, August 16, 2007	FOMC unscheduled meeting. Countrywide takes $11.5 billion credit.
Friday, August 17, 2007	Fed cuts discount rate to 5.75% (down by 50 bps). Additionally, primary credit loans can now be taken for terms up to 30 days, instead of overnight.
Wednesday, August 22, 2007	Countrywide raises $2 billion by selling 16% stake to Bank of America.
Friday, September 7, 2007	NFP go down by 4,000; unemployment is at 4.6% and inflation is at 1.94% (August).
Tuesday, September 18, 2007	FOMC meeting. Fed cuts Fed funds target rate and discount rate by 50 bps to 4.75% and 5.25%, respectively.
Friday, October 5, 2007	NFP go up by 110,000 and unemployment is at 4.7% and inflation is at 2.76% (September); Aug revised to + 89,000.
Wednesday, October 31, 2007	FOMC meeting. Fed cuts Fed funds target and discount rate by 25 bps to 4.50% and 5.00%, respectively.
Friday, November 2, 2007	NFP go up by 166,000; unemployment is at 4.7% and inflation is at 3.54%. (October)
Thursday, December 6, 2007	FOMC unscheduled conference call to set up Term Auction Facility and foreign exchange swap agreement with ECB.
Friday, December 7, 2007	NFP go up by 94,000; unemployment is at 4.7% and inflation is at 4.37% (November)
Monday, December 10, 2007	FOMC meeting. Fed cuts Fed funds target and discount rate by 25 bps to 4.25%, and 4.75%, respectively.
Wednesday, December 12, 2007	Fed starts Term Auction Facility (TAF) designed to provide liquidity to banks. Fed lends money to banks accepting a wide range of collateral.
Thursday, December 20, 2007	Change in reserve requirements.
Friday, January 4, 2008	NFP go up by 18,000; unemployment rate is at 5.0% and inflation is at 4.12% (December).
Wednesday, January 9, 2008	FOMC unscheduled conference call discussing possible risks of inflation, and necesity of cutting interest rates further and its timing.
Friday, January 11, 2008	Countrywide acquired by Bank of America for $4.1 billion.
Tuesday, January 22, 2008	Fed cuts Fed funds target rate and discount rate by 75 bps to 3.50%, and 4.00%, respectively.
Tuesday, January 29, 2008	FOMC meeting. Fed cuts Fed funds target rate and discount rate by 50 bps to 3.00% and 3.50%, respectively.
Friday, February 1, 2008	NFP go down by 17,000; unemployment is at 4.9% and inflation is at 4.40% (January).

Wednesday, February 27, 2008	Fed Chairman proposes a core inflation target between 1.5% and 2% in a report to Congress
Friday, March 7, 2008	NFP go down by 63,000; unemployment is at 4.8% and inflation is at 4.12% (February).
Friday, March 7, 2008	Fed boosts size of TAF to $100 billion.
Tuesday, March 11, 2008	Fed expands securities lending program, under the Term Securities Lending Facility (TSLF) which lends up to $200 billion of Treasury securities to primary dealers for up to 28 days (instead of overnight) by pledge of other securities including MBS.
Sunday, March 16, 2008	Bear Stearns collapses. JP Morgan Chase agrees to acquire it for $2/share.
Sunday, March 16, 2008	Fed cuts discount rate to 3.25%. (down by 25 bps)
Sunday, March 16, 2008	Fed starts the Primary Dealer Lending Facility (PDLF), providing funding to primary dealers in exchange for a specified range of collateral
Monday, March 17, 2008	FOMC meeting. Fed cuts Fed funds target rate and discount rate by 75 bps to 2.25% and 2.50%, respectively
Friday, April 4, 2008	NFP go down by 80,000; unemployment is at 5.1% and inflation is at 4.00% (March).
Wednesday, April 30, 2008	FOMC meeting. Fed cuts Fed funds target rate and discount rate by 25 bps to 2.00% and 2.25%, respectively.
Friday, May 2, 2008	NFP go down by 20,000; unemployment is at 5.0% and inflation is at 3.88% (April).
Friday, June 6, 2008	NFP go down by 49,000; unemployment is at 5.5% and inflation is at 4.08% (May).
Wednesday, June 25, 2008	FOMC meeting, no rate change due to concerns on inflation.
Thursday, July 3, 2008	NFP go down by 62,000; unemployment is at 5.5% and inflation is at 4.90% (June).
Thursday, July 24, 2008	FOMC unscheduled conference call in which TSLF is extended to 01/30/09 and allows options to be offered (up to $50 billion).
Friday, August 1, 2008	NFP go down by 51,000; unemployment is at 5.7% and inflation is at 5.52% (July).
Tuesday, August 5, 2008	FOMC meeting, no rate change due to concerns on inflation.
Friday, September 5, 2008	NFP go down by 84,000; unemployment is at 6.1% and inflation is at 5.36% (August).
Sunday, September 7, 2008	Fannie Mae and Freddie Mac placed under government 'conservatorship'.
Sunday, September 14, 2008	Merrill Lynch merges into Bank of America.
Monday, September 15, 2008	Lehman Brothers defaults on its commercial paper as it goes bankrupt ($613 billion debt).
Tuesday, September 16, 2008	FOMC meeting, no rate change due to concerns on inflation.
Tuesday, September 16, 2008	Government bails out American International Group (AIG) with a $85 billion package.
Wednesday, September 17, 2008	Lehman Brothers bought separetly by Barclays and Nomura Bank.
Friday, September 19, 2008	Fed starts Asset-Backed Commercial Paper Money Market Mutual Funds Liquidity Facility which provides liquidity to banks holding asset backed securities.
Friday, September 26, 2008	Washington Mutual is acquired by JP Morgan Chase.
Wednesday, October 1, 2008	Federal Reserve starts to pay Interest on Required Reserve Balances and Excess Balances.
Friday, October 3, 2008	NFP go down by 159,000; unemployment is at 6.1% and inflation is at 4.94%(September)
Friday, October 3, 2008	Wachovia merges into Wells Fargo Bank.
Tuesday, October 7, 2008	Fed announces creation of the Commercial Paper Funding Facility (CPFF)
Wednesday, October 8, 2008	FOMC unscheduled meeting. Fed cuts Fed funds target rate and discount rate by 50 bps to 1.50% and 1.75%, respectively.
Tuesday, October 21, 2008	Fed announces creation of the Money Market Investor Funding Facility (MMIFF)
Wednesday, October 22, 2008	Adjustment of formula for interest on required reserve balances

Sources: *The Wall Street Journal*, Financial Times, Bureau of Labor Statistics.

Figure 7.7 Borrowing Rates during the Subprime Crisis

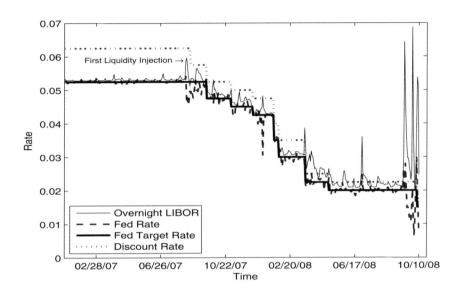

7.7),with the increase in the LIBOR being particularly dramatic. This prompted the Fed to intervene to return rates to the target.

7.7.1.1 *Open Market Operations*
The Fed faced the problem that rates were going beyond the target, which meant that demand for funds was exceeding their supply. The Fed decided to inject $24 billion on Thursday, August 9 and another $35 billion on August 10, 2007 through open market operations. The specific transaction used to inject this liquidity was repurchase agreements (see Chapter 1), and was performed, as usual, through designated institutions called primary dealers. In particular, on August 9, 2007 the Federal Reserve Bank of New York received $34.7 billion in bids submitted for 14-day repos on Treasuries. Of these $4 billion were accepted with a 5.18% rate (weighted average). So for every $100 of Treasuries the seller would have to pay $0.39 in interest after 14 days.

7.7.1.2 *Open Market Operations with Mortgage Backed Securities*
Also, in addition to the $35 billion in funds made available by the Fed in August 10, $19 billion was made available through a 3-day MBS repo agreement which meant that instead of Treasuries the Fed was willing to take MBS as collateral for the repo agreement. The MBS given had to be high-investment grade (minimum default risk). This allowed primary dealers that were heavy in MBS (such as Lehman Brothers and Bear Stearns) to obtain extra financing. On August 9, 2007 the Federal Reserve Bank of New York received $36.5 billion in bids submitted for 14-day repos on Treasuries. Of these $5.93 billion were accepted with a 5.33% rate (weighted average). Interest payment per $100 of MBS to the seller would be $0.40 to be paid in 14 days.

7.7.2 August 17, 2007: Fed Lowers the Discount Rate

August 16, 2007 was another bad day. Markets were shaken on news that Countrywide took a $11.5 billion line of credit to maintain liquidity, which further wore on the subprime market and increased the actual size of the crisis. Both the Dow Jones Industrial and the NASDAQ fell sharply. As a response to these events, and worries of a widespread credit crisis, the Federal Reserve lowered the rate offered as the discount rate. The discount rate is the rate at which depository institutions can borrow funds from the Fed. Originally thought to be a measure of last resort in case a bank couldn't fulfill its reserve requirements in a day, the Fed decided to lower the discount rate in an effort to increase liquidity in the market. The rate was lowered from 6.25% to 5.75%. Historically, the discount rate was usually moved in unison with the Fed funds target rate, always maintaining the same spread. Up to this date the spread was one percentage point. Yet by lowering the discount rate unilaterally by 50 basis points the spread was halved.

In addition, the Federal Reserve increased the type of collateral accepted for loans within the discount window facility, and the lending terms for primary credit (i.e. to sound institutions) extended from overnight to up to thirty days. One important point to note is that only FDIC approved depository institutions have access to the discount window, but not all primary dealers are in fact depositary institutions. We return to this point below.

7.7.2.1 *The SOMA Securities Lending Program*
An additional policy tool that the Federal Reserve has is the System Open Market Account (SOMA) Securities Lending Program, in which a bank can bid for Treasury securities from the SOMA portfolio to be held overnight. Each day, at noon, the New York Fed holds an auction in which primary dealers bid, with the fee to be paid, for the securities. Loans are given on a bond-versus-bond lending scheme, in which the primary dealer must offer Treasury bills, notes, bonds and inflation-indexed securities (instead of cash) as collateral. Because Treasuries are used in repo agreements, there is an incentive to take advantage of this program to trade on specials. To limit these trades, the New York Fed normally imposes a minimum bid on the lending fee. On August 21, the minimum lending fee was reduced to 50 basis points.

7.7.3 September - December 2007: The Fed Decreases Rates and Starts TAF

As the credit crisis worsened, the Federal Reserve decreased the Fed funds target rate and the discount rate at its FOMC meetings on September 18, October 31, and December 12 (see Figure 7.7), to 4.25% and 4.75%, respectively. At the December FOMC meeting, the Federal Reserve started a new policy, TAF, discussed next.

7.7.3.1 *Term Auction Facility (TAF)*
Under this policy eligible depository institutions can bid for a given amount of funds auctioned by the Fed. The loans are collateralized. Requirements for entering the auction are the same as those for primary credit loans through the discount window. The auction works in the following way. Suppose a bank having primary credit status decides to participate in the program. On December 17, 2007, the day of the first auction, it enters the auction with an amount and a bid in terms of interest rate. The amount of the bid cannot be more than 10% of the funds offered and the interest rate on the bid is subject to a prespecified lower limit. In this case the minimum rate to be offered was 4.17% and the funds offered were $20 billion in a 28-day loan. Because the

funds have a 28-day maturity, they follow the same collateralization requirements as for the discount window. So the bank could pledge its $10 million in T-bills for $9.8 million for 4.7%, for instance. Once the bids close, the Fed awards the first set of funds to the highest bidder and then goes down the list awarding the funds to those with the next highest bids. The rate at which the last participant is awarded funds is called the stop-out rate (or lowest successful bid). On this date the stop-out rate was 4.65%, which means that the bank in our example got the loan.

7.7.4   January 2008: The Fed Cuts the Fed Funds Target and Discount Rates

In January, 2008 the Federal Reserve slashed both its reference interest rates. Worried about a worsening economic outlook, the Federal Reserve dropped both the Fed funds target rate and discount rate by 75 basis points on January 22 at an unscheduled meeting, and then again by an additional 50 basis points just a few days later, at its scheduled FOMC meeting. By January 29, the Fed funds target rate and discount rate dropped to 3.00% and 3.50%, respectively.

7.7.5   March 2008: Bearn Stearns Collapses and the Fed Bolsters Liquidity Support to Primary Dealers

On March 11, 2008, the Fed announced that the SOMA Securities Lending Program would be expanded both in length to 28 days and in the range of collateral allowed, including investment grade corporate securities, municipal securities, mortgage-backed securities, and asset-backed securities. Essentially, under the expanded program, primary dealers could swap riskier securities, such as MBS, for safer securities, such as Treasuries.

On Sunday, March 16, Bearn Stearns collapsed. JP Morgan Chase agreed to acquire Bearn Stearns for $2/share. On the same date, the Fed further closed the gap between the discount rate and the Fed funds target rate, as the discount rate was lowered by 25 basis points to 3.25%. This narrowed the gap to only 25 basis points. Subsequently, the Fed funds target rate and discount rate were decreased again on March 17 (by 75 basis points) and on April 30 (by 25 basis points) to reach 2% and 2.25%, respectively. These would be the last interest rate cuts for a while because of concerns about inflation picking up. The Fed did however announce additional programs instead.

7.7.5.1   *Primary Dealer Credit Facility (PDCF)*   On March 16, right after the Bearn Stearns collapse, the Fed started the Primary Dealer Credit Facility. This program allowed primary dealers to obtain overnight loans from the Federal Reserve Bank of New York. Institutions could borrow up to whatever their margin-adjusted collateral would allow. The rate charged for the overnight loan was the same as the one for primary credit institutions in the discount window. In fact, in terms of the collateral allowed, the rates charged and the limits on borrowing, this program is identical to the discount window. The key difference is that primary dealers, which do not have access to the discount window, are allowed to participate in this program instead. Nonetheless, the Federal Reserve established an additional fee for primary institutions that access this facility on more than 30 business days out of 120 business days.

7.7.6 September – October 2008: Fannie Mae, Freddie Mac, Lehman Brothers, and AIG Collapse

During September, 2008 a number of major events took place: First, on September 7, Fannie Mae and Freddie Mac, the two giant government-sposored agencies and key players in the mortgage backed securities market, were placed under conservatorship, as they were finding it difficult to meet their financial obbligations. Second, on September 15, Lehman Brothers declared bankruptcy. Right afterward, the government bailed out American International Group (AIG) with an $85 billion package. As the interbanking market reacted badly to the news (see Figure 7.7), the Federal Reserve started yet another program to support liquidity, discussed next.

7.7.6.1 *Asset-Backed Commercial Paper (ABCP) Money Market Mutual Funds (MMMF) Liquidity Facility (AMLF)* This program allows U.S. depository institutions and bank holding companies to finance their purchases of high-quality asset-backed commercial paper (ABCP) from money market mutual funds (MMMF). The AMLF is administered by the Federal Reserve Bank of Boston, and allows loans at the primary credit discount rate subject that these funds are used to meet responsibilities.

7.7.6.2 *Interest on Required Reserve Balances and Excess Balances* In 2006, Congress passed the Financial Services Regulatory Relief Act, which authorized the Fed to pay interest on balances held by or on behalf of depository institutions at Federal Reserve banks effective October 1, 2011. This effective date was advanced to October 1, 2008 by the Emergency Economic Stabilization Act of 2008. As pointed out earlier, holding reserves, either required or excess, at a Federal Reserve bank implies an opportunity cost (effectively a tax) on these funds, as they could be gaining interest.

Interest payments on required reserves are obtained by averaging the Fed funds target rate over the maintenance period (usually calculated weekly) minus a spread. Interest on excess reserves is computed by taking the minimum Fed funds target rate over the maintenance period minus a spread. An example is given in Table 7.11

7.8 APPENDIX: DERIVATION OF EXPECTED RETURN RELATION

Take logs on both sides of Equation 7.12 to find

$$\log\left[E_t\left[P_z\left(t+1,T\right)\right]\right] - \log\left[P_z\left(t,T\right)\right] = \log\left(100\right) - \log\left[P_z\left(t,t+1\right)\right] + \kappa \quad (7.34)$$

From the assumption about normally distributed yield

$$\log\left[E_t\left[P_z\left(t+1,T\right)\right]\right] = -E_t\left[r\left(t+1,T\right)\right] \times \left(\tau - 1\right) + \frac{\left(\tau - 1\right)^2}{2}V\left[r\left(t+1,T\right)\right]$$

Note now that

$$
\begin{aligned}
E_t\left[\log\left(P_z\left(t+1,T\right)\right)\right] &= E_t\left[\log\left(e^{-r(t+1,T)(\tau-1)}\right)\right] \\
&= -E_t\left[r\left(t+1,T\right)\right] \times \left(\tau - 1\right) \\
&= \log\left[E_t\left[P_z\left(t+1,T\right)\right]\right] - \frac{\left(\tau - 1\right)^2}{2}V_t\left[r\left(t+1,T\right)\right]
\end{aligned}
$$

Table 7.11 Example of Interest Paid on Reserves at the Federal Reserve Bank

Panel A: Interest Paid on Required Reserve Balances

Maintenance Period (Ending On)	Rate	Average Target Fed Funds Rate During Maintentance Period	Spread
October 29, 2008	1.33%	1.43%	0.10%
October 22, 2008	1.40%	1.50%	0.10%
October 15, 2008	1.40%	1.50%	0.10%

Panel B: Interest Paid on Excess Reserve Balances

Maintenance Period (Ending On)	Rate	Minimum Target Fed Funds Rate During Maintenance Period	Spread
October 29, 2008	0.65%	1.00%	0.35%
October 22, 2008	0.75%	1.50%	0.75%
October 15, 2008	0.75%	1.50%	0.75%

Substitute, to find that Equation 7.34 can be rewritten as

$$E_t \left[\log \left(P_z \left(t+1, T\right)\right)\right] - \log \left[P_z \left(t, T\right)\right] + \frac{\left(\tau - 1\right)^2}{2} V_t \left[r \left(t+1, T\right)\right] = \log \left(100\right) - \log \left[P_z \left(t, t+1\right)\right] + \kappa$$

or

$$E_t \left[\log \left(\frac{P_z \left(t+1, T\right)}{P_z \left(t, T\right)}\right) - \log \left(\frac{100}{P_z \left(t, t+1\right)}\right)\right] = \kappa - \frac{\left(\tau - 1\right)^2}{2} V_t \left[r \left(t+1, T\right)\right]$$

CHAPTER 8

BASICS OF RESIDENTIAL MORTGAGE BACKED SECURITIES

The residential mortgage backed securities market reached a market size of about $8.9 trillion by the end of 2008. This is almost $3 trillion larger than the marketable U.S. Treasury debt at the same time. Clearly related to the real estate market, it is no surprise that the size of this market has been growing steadily over the years. The market for mortgage backed securities serves the important role of transferring risks from those who have it, the small banks, savings and loans, and so forth, to those who are better able to bear it, namely, investors. The latter are more diversified and thus potentially in a better position to bear the risks of lending money to individuals. The process through which mortgages to individuals are sold to others is called securitization. While we expand our discussion on residential mortgage backed securities, a very similar procedure is followed to securitize almost any type of security, from credit cards, to car loans, from commercial loans to corporate bonds.

8.1 SECURITIZATION

Before we delve into a discussion of the market for residential mortgage backed securities, let's take a closer look at the concept of securitization. The essential idea is in fact simple: Some institutions hold in their assets investments that are too risky for them, and they would like to sell them to investors who are better able to bear their risk. Since the assets per se are too concentrated and not sufficiently diversified, it is hard for a financial institution to sell individual ones to anyone for a reasonable price. A solution is the following: Several

Figure 8.1 The Securitization Process

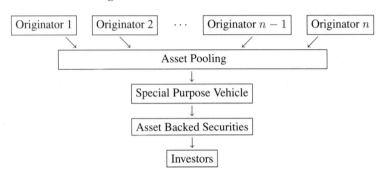

Table 8.1 Examples of Securitized Products

Security's Name	Collateral Assets
Residential Mortgage Backed Securities (RMBS):	Residential mortgages with similar characteristics
Commercial Mortgage Backed Securities (CMBS):	Commercial mortgages with similar characteristics
Assets Backed Securities (ABS):	Receivables, such as auto loans, credit cards and so on
Collateralized Debt Obligations (CDO):	Investment and high yield corporate bonds, other structured products, credit default swaps
Collateralized Loan Obligations (CLO):	Corporate loans

institutions may get together, pool similar assets in a portfolio to diversify away the risk embedded in each asset, and then sell the portfolio to investors. In order to pool the assets, individual financial institutions can create a standalone firm, called a special purpose vehicle (SPV), which formally buys the assets by raising the necessary capital from investors. In the case in which these assets are mortgages, the securities issued by the SPV to investors are called residential mortgage backed securities (RMBS).

Figure 8.1 describes the securitization process. In this figure, the originator is the financial institution that wants to pool some assets to sell separately. The issuer is the party that purchases the assets from the originators. As mentioned, the originator often creates a SPV to make the pool bankruptcy remote. The idea here is to separate the SPV assets – the collateral backing the securities – from the balance sheet of the issuer. Trustees are typically also appointed to ensure that the SPV in fact delivers on its contractual obligations. There are other third parties involved as well, that are not represented in Figure 8.1. For instance, there are mortgage servicers who are responsible for collecting the payments from the homeowners and sending them to the investors, and other third parties who provide additional credit guarantee to investors.

Securitization occurs in the residential mortgage market, in which individual savings and loans, thrifts, and other banks pool the mortgage loans on their assets, and sell them to SPVs in exchange for cash. Originators may also sell their mortgage loans to other issuers, such as Freddie Mac or Fannie Mae, in exchange for residential mortgage backed securities (instead of cash), which can then be sold in the secondary market or kept on the banks' assets. Not only residential mortgages are securitized, but also a large spectrum of other assets, as indicated in Table 8.1

8.1.1   The Main Players in the RMBS Market

There are two types of RMBS: Agency MBS and non-agency MBS. Agency MBS are those ones in which government agencies are involved. The major players involved in residential mortgage backed securities are:

1. Ginnie Mae: Government National Mortgage Association (GNMA). Formed by the U.S. Congress in 1968, Ginnie Mae is a wholly-owned government corporation within the U.S. Department of Housing and Urban Development. In 1970, Ginnie Mae developed and guaranteed the first mortgage backed security. Ginnie Mae's main function is to guarantee the timely payments of RMBS backed by loans made through the Federal Housing Administration (FHA) program, the Office of Public and Indian Housing (PIH) program, and the Department of Veteran Affairs (VA) Home Loan program. Ginnie Mae does not make or purchase loans, nor does it buy, sell, or issue securities. Instead, it only guarantees MBS that are issued by approved private lending institutions, which pool loans and issue RMBS.[1]

2. Fannie Mae: Federal National Mortgage Association (FNMA). Initially created in 1938 as a government agency, it changed in 1968 into a shareholder-owned company, although with a Federal charter, until the credit crisis of 2007–2009 forced the U.S. Government to place Fannie Mae in conservatorship (that is, an effective nationalization). As does Ginnie Mae, Fannie Mae provides credit guarantees on mortgage loans that are securitized through Fannie Mae. As opposed to Ginnie Mae, Fannie Mae also mantains a large mortgage portfolio and issues debt to finance its portfolio. By directly operating in the secondary market, Fannie Mae provides liquidity in the mortgage market, which in turn allows banks to grant mortgages to individual homeowners at more convenient rates than otherwise possible. Fannie Mae issued its first mortgage backed security in 1981. Since then, Fannie Mae has become one of the largest agency issuers of MBS.[2]

3. Freddie Mac: Federal Home Loan Mortgage Corporation (FHLMC). Also a stockholder-owned institution until the credit crisis of 2007 – 2008, Freddie Mac was chartered by the government in 1970 in order to stabilize U.S. residential mortgage markets and expand opportunities for homeownership and affordable rental housing. Freddie Mac follows the same business model as Fannie Mae.[3]

Mortgage backed securities guaranteed by Ginnie Mae are default free securities, as they have the explicit backing of the U.S. government. Mortgage backed securities issued or guaranteed by Fannie Mae and Freddie Mac have also been considered quite safe investments, in terms of default, as there has been a general market perception that in case of financial trouble, the U.S. government would step in and rescue the two agencies. In retrospect, such a belief was actually accurate, as the U.S. governement did in fact rescue the two agencies when they faced financial troubles during the credit crisis of 2007 – 2008. These two institutions are very large: As of December, 2007 Fannie Mae had about $882 billion of assets, while Freddie Mac had about $794 billion. Together, these two agencies

[1] Source: Ginnie Mae Annual Report, 2006.
[2] Source: An Introduction to Fannie Mae, 2007.
[3] Source: Freddie Mac Annual Report, 2006.

guarantee around $5 trillion of mortgages, which is slightly more than half of the market of residential mortgage backed securities.

8.1.2   Private Labels and the 2007 - 2009 Credit Crisis

In addition to the three government institutions, residential mortgage backed securities are also issued by other institutions. Table 8.2 shows the issuance of mortgage backed securities between 1996 and 2008. Although the largest share of RMBS is issued by government-sponsored agencies, nonagency mortgage backed securities issuance share increased over time up to 2007. This large increase in the private label market parallels the acceleration in U.S. house prices that occurred from 2000 to 2006, as shown in Figure 8.2. Part of the reason for the increase in the private label markets is that government-sponsored agencies have restrictions on the type of mortgages they can take on. For instance, they can only securitize so-called conventional mortgages, that is, with principal amount below a given cutoff ($417,000 in 2008), with a loan-to-value ratio of at most 80%. The increase in house prices increased the demand for jumbo mortgages, i.e., those whose principal amount is above the cutoff discussed earlier, providing an incentive for other private players to enter the securitization business. In addition, more and more households requested mortgages with a loan-to-value ratio higher than 80%, which cannot be securitized through the government sponsored agencies. The private label market filled the gap, assuming some risks, of course, as the value of the collateral (the house price) was providing a lower cushion against the probability of default.

The downturn in house prices in 2007 and 2008, and the subsequent financial crisis (see the discussion in Section 7.7 of Chapter 7), made investors wary of purchasing mortgage backed securities that are not backed by the full faith of the U.S. government. Because of the lack of investors willing to purchase nonagency MBS, in 2008 nonagency MBS issuance dropped dramatically, as shown in Table 8.2. In fact, a month-by-month breakdown shows that starting in September of 2008, the issuance of MBS by institutions other than the three U.S. agencies has been essentially zero. This lack of demand for nonagency MBS directly affects the market for nonconventional mortgage loans, that is, those with large principal (jumbo loans) or with a high loan-to-value ratios.

The securitization market is a vital part of the U.S. credit system. As the mortgage backed securities market grew to an almost $9 trillion market, banks became accustomed to a new business model according to which they would originate mortgage loans with the explicit intention to sell them in the securitized market. If the securitization market were to collapse – in the sense that there would no longer be private investors willing to purchase the pools of mortgages – so would the mortgage lending market itself, as banks would not want to keep the mortgage risks in their portfolio. The U.S. Treasury and the Federal Reserve are very much aware of this problem, as some of their policies in 2008 were directed to boost the securitization market. For instance, on November 25, 2008 the Federal Reserve announced "a program to purchase the direct obligations of housing-related government-sponsored enterprises (GSEs)– Fannie Mae, Freddie Mac, and the Federal Home Loan Banks – and mortgage backed securities (MBS) backed by Fannie Mae, Freddie Mac, and Ginnie Mae" (see Federal Reserve Board Press Release, November 25, 2008). Why only agency debt and MBS? Under its mandate, the Federal Reserve cannot directly purchase risky debt. In order to do so, the U.S. Treasury has to be involved. Indeed, in the fall of 2008, the U.S. Treasury announced the Trouble Asset Relief Program (TARP), a $700 billion

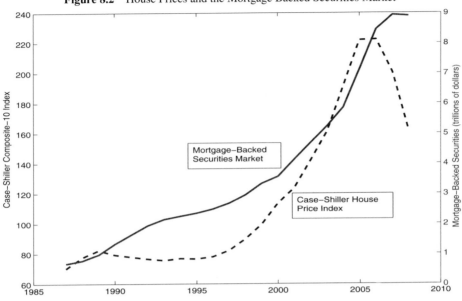

Figure 8.2   House Prices and the Mortgage Backed Securities Market

Source: SIFMA and Standard & Poor / Case-Shiller.

program aimed at purchasing, directly or indirectly, mortgage backed securities and other securitized products from banks. A number of additional initiatives aimed at helping the ailing securitization market have since been announced.

8.1.3   Default Risk and Prepayment in Agency RMBSs

The credit crisis of 2007 – 2009 is characterized by an unusually large number of homeowners' defaults, meaning that homeowners stopped paying the monthly mortgage coupons. Because of defaults, a large number of houses went into forclosure, forcing banks to sell them at fire-sale prices. The Case Shiller index in Figure 8.2 includes foreclosed home prices, which are partly responsible for the substantial decrease in housing prices in 2008.

To understand the pricing of residential mortgage backed securities, however, we have to understand the type of risk that an investor in RMBS is facing, and here we need to distinguish between agency RMBS (the vast majority of the market) and nonagency RMBS. An investor who purchased agency RMBS is *not* exposed directly to the credit risk of the mortgages in the RMBS pool. The reason is that the agencies insure investors against the default of individual mortgages: In case of default, the agency steps in and repays the face value of the mortgage to the investors. The risk for RMBS investors is then to receive the money invested sooner than they expected. For instance, investors who in 2006 invested in 30-year RMBS would have an horizon of several years, as the underlying pool is expected to make payments for many years. A wave of defaults, however, would imply a large cash flow back to the investors, as the agencies step in to repay the mortgages. Prepayments – receiving cash flows too early compared to the expected life of the mortgage – are the most interesting characteristics of RMBS. The remaining part of this chapter is devoted to studying this phenomenon, and its pricing and risk implications.

Table 8.2   Mortgage Related Issuance

Year	Agency	Nonagency	Total	Agency Share	Nonagency Share
1996	440.7	51.9	492.6	89.46%	10.54%
1997	535.0	69.4	604.4	88.52%	11.48%
1998	952.0	191.9	1,143.9	83.22%	16.78%
1999	884.9	140.5	1,025.4	86.30%	13.70%
2000	582.3	101.7	684.0	85.13%	14.87%
2001	1,454.8	218.8	1,673.6	86.92%	13.08%
2002	1,985.3	288.5	2,273.8	87.31%	12.69%
2003	2,725.8	440.6	3,166.4	86.09%	13.91%
2004	1,375.2	532.7	1,907.9	72.08%	27.92%
2005	1,321.0	901.2	2,222.2	59.45%	40.55%
2006	1,214.7	917.4	2,132.1	56.97%	43.03%
2007	1,372.2	773.9	2,146.1	63.94%	36.06%
2008	1,299.2	40.5	1,339.7	96.98%	3.02%

Notes: Agency issuance includes GNMA, FNMA, and FHLMC mortgage backed
securities and CMOs. Nonagency issuance includes both
private-label MBS and CMOs. Quantities are $ billions.
Souce: SIFMA. Government-Sponsored Enterprises, Thomson Financial, Bloomberg

8.2   MORTGAGES AND THE PREPAYMENT OPTION

Before further discussing the mortgage backed securities market, it is important to review some basic facts about standard fixed rate mortgages. Consider for instance a 30-year fixed-rate mortgage, with mortgage rate of $\bar{r}^m_{12}$. The subscript denotes the frequency of compounding: Because mortgage coupons are paid at the monthly frequency, the compounding frequency is $n = 12$. The superscript m denotes that it is a mortgage rate, which is different from the Treasury rate, as detailed below. Suppose that L is the amount of the mortgage lent from the bank to the homeowner. According to the standard present value relation, the periodic coupon must then satisfy

$$L = \sum_{i=1}^{30 \times 12} \frac{C}{\left(1 + \frac{\bar{r}^m_{12}}{12}\right)^i} \tag{8.1}$$

It is convenient to define the following constant

$$A = \frac{1}{1 + \frac{\bar{r}^m_{12}}{12}} \tag{8.2}$$

Because we can then rewrite $L = \sum_{i=1}^{30 \times 12} C \times A^i$, we obtain that the coupon in Equation 8.1 is given by

$$C = \frac{L}{\sum_{i=1}^{30 \times 12} A^i} \tag{8.3}$$

It is important to note an important distinction between a mortgage and a regular bond: In a regular bond the periodic coupon comprises only the interest on the bond's principal, while the principal itself is repaid only at maturity. In a mortgage, instead, the principal is repaid during the life of the mortgage together with the interest. Indeed, the coupon C contains two components: One component is the interest payments and the other component is the principal repayment. The fractions of the total coupon C that is related to interest payment and principal repayment vary over time. The reason is that the interest amount paid is determined by the amount of outstanding principal, which declines over time as principal payments occurs. The larger the outstanding principal, the larger the amount of interest that has to be paid, and thus the larger is the fraction of interest payment in the coupon. More specifically, the interest and the principal paid at any time t are given by:

$$\text{Interest paid at } t = \quad I_t \quad = \quad \frac{\overline{r}_{12}^m}{12} \times L_t \tag{8.4}$$

$$\text{Principal paid at } t = L_t^{paid} \quad = \quad C - I_t \tag{8.5}$$

The amount of principal declines over time, as the principal remaining next month equals the amount of principal this month minus what is paid during this month:

$$L_{t+1} = L_t - L_t^{paid} \tag{8.6}$$

Panel A of Figure 8.3 plots the scheduled principal outstanding L_t over time, for a 30-year, 6%, $300,000 mortgage. Panel B plots the interest rate and the principal paid component of the monthly coupon, which is about $C = \$1797.7$.

Given the coupon payments C's to be made over the life of the mortgage, the mortgage itself can be considered as any other bond. Indeed, the mortgage rate $\overline{r}_{12}^m$ is simply the internal rate of return of the bond (see Section 2.4.3). In fact, the updating formula in Equation 8.6 implies the following:

Fact 8.1 *Let the outstanding principal be determined by Equation 8.6 and let n be the number of mortgage payments at time t. Then, the outstanding principal is*

$$L_t \quad = \quad \sum_{i=1}^{n} \frac{C}{(1 + \frac{\overline{r}_{12}^m}{12})^i} \tag{8.7}$$

$$= \quad C \times A \times \frac{1 - A^n}{1 - A} \tag{8.8}$$

where A is given in Equation 8.2.[4]

It is convenient to think about a mortgage as a special bond with only regular coupons, and no final lump sum principal payment. As with any bond, as interest rates move, the bond (mortgage) changes in value. In particular, the homeowner may compute the *value* of his debt to the bank by using the standard pricing formula

$$\text{Value of mortgage debt} = P(t) = \sum_{i=1}^{n} \frac{C}{(1 + r_{12}^m(t, T_i)/12)^i}$$

[4]The step from Equation 8.7 to Equation 8.8 is justified by the fact that for $A < 1$, $\sum_{i=1}^{n} A^i = A \times (1 - A^n)/(1 - A)$.

Figure 8.3   Scheduled Principal Balance, Scheduled Interest, and Principal Payments

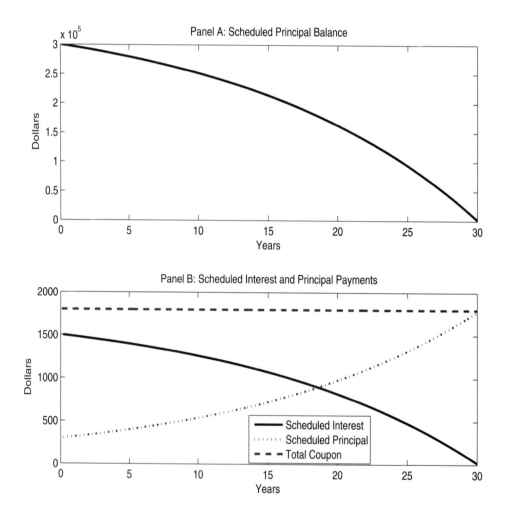

where n is the number of payments left at time t and $r_{12}^m(t, T_i)$ are appropriate spot rates, related to the current term structure of mortgage rates. It is important to note the distinction between the fixed mortgage rate $\bar{r}_{12}^m$, which is fixed during the life of the mortgage, and the term structure of spot rates $r_{12}^m(t, T_i)$ which should be used to discount future cash flows. This term structure of interest rates used to discount future cash flows is not the same as, but it is related to the Treasury curve. Chapters 12 and 13 discuss further the pricing of mortgages and mortgage backed securities in formal term structure models. In this chapter, we instead look at simple models to value mortgage backed securities, and their risk.

Consider now a homeowner: At every t the homeowner can compare the amount of principal left to pay, L_t, with the market value of his liability to the bank $P(t)$. As in any bond, $P(t)$ increases in value whenever interest rates decline. Thus, when interest rates decline, the market value of the mortgage owner's liability $P(t)$ increases to a higher level than the principal remaining L_t, and it becomes in the homeowner's interest to *refinance* the mortgage. That is, the homeowner can simply extinguish the old liability and open a new mortgage with $P^{new}(t) = L_t$. This latter mortgage will have a lower monthly payment C, as the mortgage rate is lower than before.

■ **EXAMPLE 8.1**

The years 2001 to 2003 saw record refinancing levels: When the Federal Reserve acted to prevent a recession by lowering the Federal funds rate from 6% to less than 1%, it set in motion a chain reaction in which banks were able to lower mortgage rates as well, as their own funding cost decreased substantially. The fixed 30-year mortgage rate decreased during this period from 8.6% to 5.83%. The one-year adjustable rate dropped even more, from about 7% in 2000 to 3.76% in 2003. Homeowners had then the choice between keeping the old higher mortgage rate or refinancing at lower rates. The lower level of mortgage rates generated a large wave of refinancing, as shown in Figure 8.4. This figure reports the Mortgage Bankers' Association (MBA) refinancing index from early 1990 to late 2007.[5] The MBA refinancing index is based on the number of applications for refinancing, and it is computed from a weekly survey. The large spike in 2002 - 2003 clarifies the relation between the level of interest rates (low) and the decision of homeowners to refinance their mortgages.

8.2.1 The Risk in the Prepayment Option

Why is the prepayment such a big issue? The mortgage rate that the bank receives from the mortgage owner is the return on capital on the bank's investment. The bank would like to receive this rate of return for as long as possible after the mortgage is made. However, if the mortgage owner has the choice of closing the mortgage (prepaying), the bank will miss this lucrative rate of interest. In particular, because the prepayment will occur mainly when interest rates decline, the bank that receives the capital back won't be able to reinvest it at the same rate of return. In other words, it will lose the mortgage rate. Of course,

---

[5]The historic time series of the MBA refinancing index is from Bloomberg.

Figure 8.4   Refinancing and the Federal Funds Rate

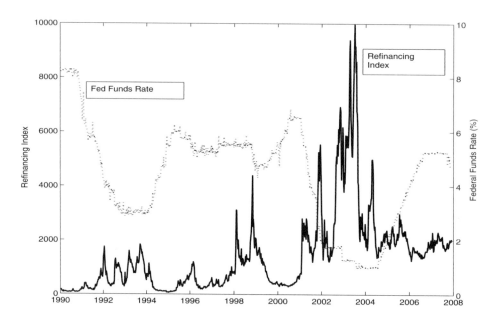

Source: Federal Reserve and Bloomberg.

anticipating the prepayment, the bank will increase the mortgage rate to start with, so that it obtains partial compensation for the risk of prepayment.[6]

Note that prepayment risk is fundamentally different from default risk. While in the case of default on a security the bank does not receive its money back, in the case of prepayment the bank actual *does* receive its money back, although perhaps at a time in which investment opportunities are not optimal. Interestingly, homehowners' defaults actually have an impact on the timing of prepayments in the case of agency RMBS, because if a homeowner defaults on his or her mortgage payment, the agency must step in and pay back the mortgage amount to the RMBS investors, thereby triggering prepayment.

8.2.2   Mortgage Prepayment

The general level of interest rates is an important factor of prepayment. However, it is not the only one. There are numerous reasons why homeowners pay mortgages early. What other factors determine prepayment?

1. Seasonality: Summers are characterized by large prepayments, as this is the period in which people move from one place to another for various reasons. Typically, these prepayments show up in payments to investors by the end of summer or early fall, as there are some processing delays.

---

[6]See Chapter 12 for a discussion of the way a mortgage rate should be increased to take into account the prepayment risk that the bank bears.

2. Age of mortgage pool: As shown in Figure 8.3, young mortgages are characterized by large interest rate payments and low principal. By paying early (whenever possible) homeowners can save the interest rate payments. Because refinancing is costly, however, homeowners tend not to refinance new or recently refinanced mortgages right away, implying a slow prepayment rate in the first few years.

3. Family circumstances: Defaults, disasters, or sale of the house.

4. Housing prices: If the property value of a house declines, it is more difficult to refinance, and thus prepayments tend to decline. Vice versa, if the property value of a house increases, the homeowner sometimes takes equity out by refinancing the loan, inducing a prepayment. The availability of home equity lines, however, reduces homeowners' incentives to refinance and thus prepayments.

5. Burnout effect: Mortgage pools heavily refinanced in the past tend to be insensitive to interest rates. The reason behind the burnout effect is subtle, and it runs as follows: If a mortgage pool has been heavily refinanced in the past, it must be the case that most or all of the homeowners that could take advantage of refinancing opportunities already did so in the past, and thus they are no longer in the pool. The only homeowners left in such a mortgage pool are those who could not take advantage from past refinancing possibilities, which makes them less likely to take advantage of new refinancing opportunities as well, such as a further decline in interest rates.[7] The mortgage pool then becomes less sensitive to changes in interest rates when heavy refinancing activity already occurred in the past.

8.3 MORTGAGE BACKED SECURITIES

Mortgage backed securities derive their characteristics from the features of the mortgages underlying the pool. Three quantities are particularly important in determining the value of a mortgage backed security:

1. The Weighted Average Maturity of the mortgages in the pool (WAM).

2. The Weighted Average Coupon of the mortgages in the pool (WAC).

3. The speed of prepayments.

The average maturity and average coupon of a mortgage backed security pool are relatively simple concepts: For each mortgage in the pool we can compute the time to maturity and the coupon, and then WAM and WAC are simply the weighted averages of time and coupon, where the weights are the relative size of each mortgage.

The speed of prepayment is the only concept that is a little elusive. The industry practice is to refer to some average prepayment rates to describe the speed of prepayment. In fact, because as we shall see the value of a mortgage backed security depends on the speed of prepayment, it has been customary to describe the value of a MBS in terms of its speed of prepayment. We now introduce standard measures of prepayment, which are useful to then determine the speed of prepayment.

---

[7]There are numerous reasons why homeowners may not take advantage of refinancing opportunities, ranging from impaired credit scores and low property value to simple inattention to current market mortgage rates.

8.3.1 Measures of Prepayment Speed

There are many measures of prepayment speed. The industry practice is to use relatively simple measures of prepayment mainly to describe, perhaps with a single number, the expected profile of future cash flows. For instance, if we expect no prepayments for a while, then we can expect cash flow far in the future. If instead we believe that the current market is characterized by a high speed of prepayments, then we should expect the MBS cash flows in the near future and less in the future, as when the mortgage is paid back, no further coupons will be paid. In this chapter we examine only the most common measures of prepayment.

8.3.1.1 *Constant Maturity Mortality*

This measure of prepayment is quite basic in nature: It assumes there is constant probability that the mortgage will be prepaid after the next coupon. If p is this probability, we have

$$\Pr\left(\text{Prepayment at time } t = 1\right) = p$$
$$\Pr\left(\text{Prepayment at time } t = 2\right) = (1-p)\,p$$
$$\Pr\left(\text{Prepayment at time } t = 3\right) = (1-p)^2\,p$$

The measure p is monthly, as coupon payments are made monthly. Generally, the industry uses an annualized rate, called the **conditional prepayment rate** (CPR), obtained from p as follows:

$$\Pr\left(\text{Survival up to time } t = 12\right) = (1-p)^{12} = (1-CPR)$$

Thus, the CPR is computed from p as

$$CPR = 1 - (1-p)^{12}$$

and vice versa

$$p = 1 - (1-CPR)^{\frac{1}{12}}$$

This measures the speed at which prepayment occurs.

8.3.1.2 *PSA Experience*

An industry benchmark in the description of prepayment speed is provided by the 100% PSA. The 100% PSA, established by the Public Securities Association (PSA), makes the following assumptions:

1. CPR = 0.2% of the principal is paid in the first month;

2. CPR increases by 0.2% in each of the following 30 months; and

3. CPR then levels off at 6% until maturity.

This measure is simple, as it makes the amount of prepayment depend only on the age of the mortgage pool. It is an industry benchmark, or convention, to express the current belief about the speed of prepayments. By scaling up or down the CPR in the PSA description, we obtain faster or slower speeds of prepayments. For instance, Figure 8.5 plots the 100% PSA line, together with the 150% and 200% PSA. In the next section we provide examples of the use of PSA for MBS pricing.

Figure 8.5 PSA Prepayment Convention

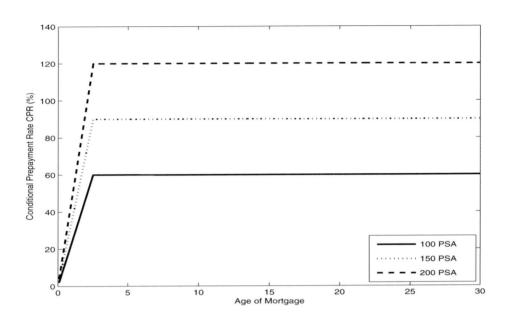

8.3.2 Pass-Through Securities

A pass-through security is the simplest mortgage backed security: It represents a claim to a fraction of the total cash flow that is flowing from the homeowners to the pool of mortgages. This simple structure implies that all investors in pass-through securities are exposed to the prepayment risk.

■ **EXAMPLE 8.2**

Consider a MBS pass through with principal $600 million. The original mortgage pool has a WAM = 360 months (30 years), and WAC = 6.5%. The pass-through security pays a coupon equal to $r_{12}^{PT} = 6\%$, lower that the average coupon rate of the mortgage pool, both to ensure there is enough cash available for coupon payments, and also to provide a compensation for the MBS issuer (e.g., Fannie Mae or Freddie Mac).

How do we compute the value of the pass through? We can use the PSA level to determine the speed of prepayment, and therefore the timing and size of future cash flows. In particular, given a PSA level, for instance 200% PSA, we obtain the CPR_t for each month t and thus the corresponding monthly prepayment rate p_t:

$$p_t = 1 - (1 - CPR_t)^{1/12} \tag{8.9}$$

Given that the PSA level determines exactly the amount of principal that is paid back, we can compute the value of the pass-through security by first computing the sequence of cash flows, and then, treating these as certain cash flows from a highly rated company, we discount them to today using the appropriate discount rate. Note that Agency MBS are essentially default risk free, implying that the coupons will be paid to the investors.

To compute the sequence of cash flows, consider a given time t during the life of the mortgage pool in which L_t is the outstanding principal at the beginning of the period. From this value, we can compute the following quantities for time t:

$$\text{Mortgage interest payment:} \quad I_t = \frac{r_{12}^m}{12} \times L_t \quad (8.10)$$

$$\text{Scheduled principal:} \quad Pay_t^{scheduled} = C_t - I_t \quad (8.11)$$

$$\text{Principal prepayment:} \quad Pay_t^{prepaid} = p_t \times L_t \quad (8.12)$$

Given the scheduled principal payments and prepayments, we can finally update both the outstanding principal and the total coupon flow at the beginning of the following month $t + 1$:

$$\text{Outstanding principal:} \quad L_{t+1} = L_t - Pay_t^{scheduled} - Pay_t^{prepaid} \quad (8.13)$$

$$\text{Update of scheduled coupon:} \quad C_{t+1} = (1 - p_t) \times C_t \quad (8.14)$$

The first Equation 8.13 implies that the new total principal is equal to the previous month principal minus scheduled and unscheduled principal payments. The prepayment of mortgage also decreases the total flow from coupon, as shown in Equation 8.14. In particular, the new total flow from the pool coupons equals the previous month coupon flow adjusted for the fraction of prepaid mortgages. For instance, if 100% of homeowners prepay their mortgages at time t, then $p_t = 1$, and the coupon at time $t+1$ is zero, as we would expect. Conversely, if nobody repays the mortgages, then $p_t = 0$, and $C_{t+1} = C_t$, that is, the total coupon flow is constant.

These calculations are shown in Table 8.3 for the first 36 months. In Table 8.3, the first column reports the month and the second column shows the constant prepayment rate (CPR) implied by a 200% PSA. The third column displays the monthly prepayment rate, as from Equation 8.9. Using these values, Column 4 computes the coupon C_t as in Equation 8.14, except for its first entry (first row), which instead uses the coupon implied by the weighted average coupon (WAC), the weighted average maturity (WAM) and the initial principal balance, according to the formula in Equation 8.3.[8] Column 5 reports the mortgage interest payment, computed using Equation 8.10. The principal scheduled and the principal prepaid are computed next, using Equations 8.11 and 8.12, respectively. The total cash flow of the pass-through security does not depend though on the mortgage interest rate, but on the pass-through interest rate r^{PT}. Thus, Column 8 reports the pass-through interest payment, computed as:

$$\text{Pass-through interest payment:} \quad I_t^{PT} = \frac{r_{12}^{PT}}{12} \times L_t \quad (8.15)$$

The pass-through interest rate, scheduled mortgage principal, and mortgage prepayment sum up to form the total cash flow of the pass-through security at the given month

$$\text{Total cash flow:} \quad CF_t = I_t + Pay_t^{scheduled} + Pay_t^{prepaid} \quad (8.16)$$

---

[8]More specifically, $C = L/(\sum_{i=1}^{WAM} A^i)$ where $A = 1/(1 + WAC/12)$.

Table 8.3 Computations: Cash Flows of Pass-Through Security

Month i (1)	CPR (2)	p (3)	Coupon (4)	Mortgage Interest (5)	Principal Scheduled (6)	Principal Prepaid (7)	Pass-Through Interest (8)	Total Cash Flow (9)	Principal L_t (10)	Discount $Z(0,T)$ (11)
1	0.20%	0.03%	3.79	3.25	0.54	0.20	3.00	3.74	599.26	0.9979
2	0.40%	0.07%	3.79	3.25	0.55	0.40	3.00	3.94	598.31	0.9958
3	0.60%	0.10%	3.79	3.24	0.55	0.60	2.99	4.14	597.16	0.9938
4	0.80%	0.13%	3.78	3.23	0.55	0.80	2.99	4.34	595.81	0.9917
5	1.00%	0.17%	3.78	3.23	0.55	1.00	2.98	4.53	594.25	0.9896
6	1.20%	0.20%	3.77	3.22	0.55	1.20	2.97	4.73	592.50	0.9876
7	1.40%	0.24%	3.77	3.21	0.56	1.40	2.96	4.92	590.54	0.9855
8	1.60%	0.27%	3.76	3.20	0.56	1.60	2.95	5.11	588.39	0.9835
9	1.80%	0.31%	3.75	3.19	0.56	1.79	2.94	5.30	586.03	0.9814
10	2.00%	0.34%	3.74	3.17	0.56	1.99	2.93	5.48	583.48	0.9794
11	2.20%	0.37%	3.72	3.16	0.56	2.18	2.92	5.66	580.73	0.9773
12	2.40%	0.41%	3.71	3.15	0.56	2.38	2.90	5.84	577.80	0.9753
13	2.60%	0.44%	3.69	3.13	0.56	2.57	2.89	6.02	574.67	0.9733
14	2.80%	0.48%	3.68	3.11	0.56	2.75	2.87	6.19	571.35	0.9713
15	3.00%	0.51%	3.66	3.09	0.56	2.94	2.86	6.36	567.85	0.9692
16	3.20%	0.55%	3.64	3.08	0.56	3.12	2.84	6.53	564.16	0.9672
17	3.40%	0.59%	3.62	3.06	0.56	3.30	2.82	6.69	560.29	0.9652
18	3.60%	0.62%	3.60	3.03	0.56	3.48	2.80	6.84	556.25	0.9632
19	3.80%	0.66%	3.58	3.01	0.56	3.65	2.78	7.00	552.04	0.9612
20	4.00%	0.69%	3.55	2.99	0.56	3.82	2.76	7.15	547.65	0.9592
21	4.20%	0.73%	3.53	2.97	0.56	3.99	2.74	7.29	543.10	0.9572
22	4.40%	0.76%	3.50	2.94	0.56	4.15	2.72	7.43	538.38	0.9552
23	4.60%	0.80%	3.48	2.92	0.56	4.31	2.69	7.56	533.51	0.9532
24	4.80%	0.84%	3.45	2.89	0.56	4.47	2.67	7.69	528.48	0.9512
25	5.00%	0.87%	3.42	2.86	0.56	4.62	2.64	7.82	523.31	0.9492
26	5.20%	0.91%	3.39	2.83	0.56	4.77	2.62	7.94	517.98	0.9473
27	5.40%	0.95%	3.36	2.81	0.55	4.91	2.59	8.05	512.52	0.9453
28	5.60%	0.98%	3.33	2.78	0.55	5.05	2.56	8.16	506.92	0.9433
29	5.80%	1.02%	3.29	2.75	0.55	5.18	2.53	8.27	501.19	0.9414
30	6.00%	1.06%	3.26	2.71	0.55	5.31	2.51	8.36	495.33	0.9394
31	6.00%	1.06%	3.23	2.68	0.54	5.25	2.48	8.27	489.54	0.9375
32	6.00%	1.06%	3.19	2.65	0.54	5.19	2.45	8.18	483.81	0.9355
33	6.00%	1.06%	3.16	2.62	0.54	5.13	2.42	8.08	478.15	0.9336
34	6.00%	1.06%	3.12	2.59	0.53	5.07	2.39	7.99	472.55	0.9316
35	6.00%	1.06%	3.09	2.56	0.53	5.01	2.36	7.90	467.01	0.9297
36	6.00%	1.06%	3.06	2.53	0.53	4.95	2.34	7.81	461.53	0.9277

The total cash flow is provided in Column 9 of Table 8.3. Finally, the last column updates the new amount of principal remaining, according to Equation 8.13.

The value of the pass-through security is then obtained by treating the cash flows in Column 9 as known amounts of dollars in the future, without any uncertainty. Thus, they are simply discounted by using a discount function appropriate for this credit rating. Some of these pass-through securities are default free: For instance, Ginnie Mae originated pass-through securities are guaranteed against default by the full faith of the U.S. Government, and thus investors in these securities are not subject to default. Similarly, over the years market participants believed also that the securities issued by Fannie Mae and Freddie Mac had small default risk, as it was believed that the U.S. governmnet would bail these agencies out in case of financial troubles.[9] If we think of these securities having zero or small default risk, then we can use the Treasury discount curve to discount these cash flows. Assume for instance a flat term structure with constant (continuously compounded) 5% yield. The corresponding discount $Z(0, T)$ is reported in the last column. For this exercise, the value of the pass-through security is $635 million, above its par value of $600 million.

8.3.3   The Effective Duration of Pass-Through Securities

Pass-through MBS have some peculiarities in terms of their sensitivity to interest rate movements. The reason is that as interest rates decline, homeowners may decide to refinance their mortgages. This refinancing activity increases the conditional prepayment rate. That is, it increases the PSA, which could easily move from 200%, for instance, to 300%. This change has an impact on the sensitivity of the pass-through security to interest rates. The next example illustrates the issue.

■ **EXAMPLE 8.3**

Consider the pass-through MBS discussed in Example 8.2. In that example, we assume that the current PSA level is PSA = 200%. Consider now the calculation of its duration assuming first that the PSA level is unaffected by the change in interest rate. In this case, because the pass-through MBS has a constant coupon, we can compute its duration as in Chapter 3, Section 3.2.3, and obtain a duration value of $D = 5.83$.

Consider now the case in which if the interest rate moves down from 5% to 4.50%, the PSA increases from 200% to 250%, while if the interest rate moves up from 5% to 5.50%, the PSA decreases from 200% to 150%. How can we compute the duration of the pass-through security in this case? We can apply the definition of duration in Definition 3.2 in Chapter 3, namely

$$D = -\frac{1}{P}\frac{d\,P}{d\,r}$$

---

[9]This belief proved correct ex post, as both Fannie Mae and Freddie Mac went into conservatorship in September, 2008 as a consequence of the mortgage backed security market turmoil of 2007 and 2008.

Given this definition, we can approximate the duration of the pass-through security while taking into account the impact of interest rate changes on PSA levels as follows:

$$D \approx -\frac{1}{P} \frac{P(+50bps) - P(-50bps)}{2 \times 50bps} \tag{8.17}$$

where $P = \$634.76$ is the current value of the pass-through security, obtained in Example 8.2, and $P(+50bps)$ and $P(-50bps)$ are the values of the same pass-through security when we increase and decrease the interest rate by 50 basis points, respectively, and the PSA levels accordingly. By carrying out exactly the same computations as in Example 8.2 but for the two cases in which the interest rate is either 5.5% or 4.5%, and the PSA level is 150% or 250%, respectively, we find

$$P(+50bps) = \$619.13$$
$$P(-50bps) = \$647.45$$

Substituting these values into Equation 8.17 we obtain

$$D \approx -\frac{1}{\$634.76} \frac{\$619.13 - \$647.45}{2 \times 50bps} = 4.46$$

This duration is much smaller than the duration that we obtained when we neglected the impact on the change in PSA due to changes in interest rates, which was 5.83. Missing the impact of interest rate variation on the speed of prepayment may grossly overstate the sensitivity of the pass-through security to changes in interest rates, and thus the performance of any duration-based hedging activity.

This example highlights a potential pitfall in the risk assessment of mortgage backed securities, namely, the necessity to take into account the variation in prepayment speed due to the change in interest rates. Because of this variation in prepayment speed, analytical formulas for the computation of duration are not available, and thus we must rely on approximations, as illustrated in Example 8.3. This approximation is called effective duration:

Definition 8.1 *The* **effective duration** *of a mortgage backed security is given by the formula*

$$D \approx -\frac{1}{P} \frac{P(+x\ bps) - P(-x\ bps)}{2 \times x\ bps} \tag{8.18}$$

where P is the current price of the MBS, and $P(+x\ bps)$ and $P(-x\ bps)$ are the prices of the same security after we shift upward or downward the yield curve by x basis points, respectively. In this computation, the price of the MBS takes into account the variation in the prepayment speed induced by the variation in interest rates.

To compute the effective duration of a MBS we need the predicted variation of the pool prepayment speed that is induced by a parallel shift in the term structure of interest rates. Market participants use sophisticated models to predict such variation. The case study in Section 8.7 futher illustrates the computation of the effective duration of a pass-through security by relying on market participants' forecasts of the change in prepayment speed. In addition, the case study also illustrates the use of historical market data on MBS prices and interest rates to estimate the effective duration of a pass-through security.

8.3.4 The Negative Effective Convexity of Pass-Through Securities

A second feature of prepayments is to induce a negative convexity of the MBS price with respect to interest rates. Typically, fixed income securities increase substantially in price as interest rates decline (see Chapter 4). However, if the interest rate decline makes the rate of prepayment increase, then the price of the security does not increase as much, generating a negative convexity.

■ **EXAMPLE 8.4**

Consider Table 8.4. The first two columns show the impact of interest rates on the price of the pass through in Example 8.2, when the speed of prepayment is kept constant at 200% PSA. The price of the pass through increases substantially as rates decline, as we know is typical of any interest rate security. Suppose now that as the interest rate declines, the speed of prepayments increases. As an example, the second three columns of Table 8.4 show the case in which as the interest rate declines from 6% to 2% (Column 4) the PSA increases from 100% to 500%. Similarly, if the interest rate increases, the PSA declines. The higher prepayment rate moves the price of the pass through closer to its principal value, which is $600 million. Indeed, if everybody prepayed at the same time, the value of the pass through would be exactly equal to $600 million, as it would equal its principal amount. In reality, even with dramatic decreases in interest rates, many households do not prepay their mortgages. Still, even if the PSA increases only to 500%, the value of the pass-through security goes up only to $688 million, compared to $765 million in the case of constant PSA.

Figure 8.6 plots the value of the pass-through security in Table 8.4 with respect to the interest rate for the two cases in which the PSA is constant at 200% (the dotted line) and the case in which the PSA increases as interest rates decline (the solid line). As is clear from the picture, the slope of the solid line is smaller when interest rates are low than when they are high. This implies that the pass-through security with changes in PSA is less sensitive to interest rate variation when interest rates are low, while it is more sensitive when interest rates are high, as shown in Table 8.4. In other words, the pass-through security in Figure 8.6 displays negative convexity.

The negative convexity of pass-through securities illustrated in the previous example, and further documented in Section 8.3.5 below, is a source of risk for investors. Mechanically, the source of the negative convexity is the higher prepayment that is induced by lower interest rates, which pushes the pass-through price toward its outstanding principal amount. Economically, the investor in a pass-through security has implicitly written American call options to the homeowners of the mortgages in the pool (see Chapter 6): When interest rates decline and thus the value of the loan increases above the outstanding principal, homeowners exercise the option and repay their mortgages to investors (by refinancing them). As we know from Figure 6.2 in Chapter 6, the payoff profile of a short call option is negatively convex. Thus, adding these short call options to the long position in the pool of mortgages generates the negative covexity of the pass-through security.

Indeed, pass-through securities have a higher yield than equivalent Treasury securities, even if they have no default risk when issued by Ginnie Mae, for instance. We can see this from Table 8.5. This table reports a sample of Ginnie Mae (GNMA) pass-through prices at selected dates at which they were trading close to par-value (100). Because the

Table 8.4 Pass-Through Security Value versus Interest Rate and PSA

Constant PSA = 200%		Increasing PSA with Lower Interest Rate		
Interest Rate	Value	Interest Rate	PSA	Value
2.00%	764.57	2.00%	500	687.80
2.50%	740.00	2.50%	450	681.64
3.00%	716.72	3.00%	400	674.76
3.50%	694.63	3.50%	350	666.97
4.00%	673.66	4.00%	300	658.00
4.50%	653.73	4.50%	250	647.45
5.00%	634.76	5.00%	200	634.76
5.50%	616.71	5.50%	150	619.13
6.00%	599.50	6.00%	100	599.33
6.50%	583.08	6.50%	90	576.96
7.00%	567.41	7.00%	80	554.53
7.50%	552.44	7.50%	70	532.06
8.00%	538.12	8.00%	60	509.54
8.50%	524.42	8.50%	50	487.01
9.00%	511.30	9.00%	40	464.45

Figure 8.6   The Value of a Pass-Through MBS with Respect to the Interest Rate

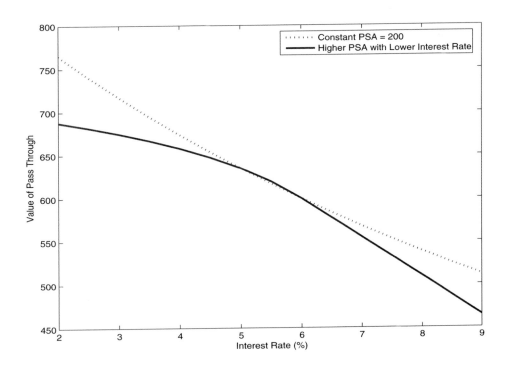

Table 8.5   A Sample of Par Value Ginnie Mae Pass-Through Prices and Treasury Yields

	Ginnie Mae Pass-Through					Treasury Constant Maturity Rates		
Date	Bid	Ask	Coupon	WAC	WAM	10-Year	20-Year	30-Year
09/26/1997	100.0313	100.0000	7.0	7.5	315	6.08	6.43	6.37
06/12/1998	100.0313	100.0000	6.5	7.0	324	5.43	5.75	5.66
08/07/1998	100.0000	99.96875	6.5	7.0	327	5.40	5.72	5.63
05/05/2006	100.1250	100.0938	6.0	6.5	315	5.12	5.35	5.20
07/28/2006	99.96875	99.9375	6.0	6.5	318	5.00	5.17	5.07
08/17/2007	100.0938	100.0625	6.0	6.5	320	4.68	5.06	5.00

Source: Bloomberg and Federal Reserve Board.

pass-through security is trading around par value, we can compare directly its coupon rate, in Column 4, to the yields of similar "close to par value" Treasury securities, given by the Treasury constant maturity rates in Columns 7 to 9.[10]. Column 6 of the table reports the weighted average maturity of the underlying pool, providing an idea of the maximum maturity of the pass-through security. Comparing the coupon rates of the pass-through securities in Column 4 to the constant maturity rates in Columns 7 to 9, it is clear that the pass-through securities have a higher coupon rate, even if they trade at the same price (par value). We can interpret this spread over Treasuries as the option premium implicitly received by pass-through MBS investors from the sale of call options.[11]

Why is negative convexity such a big issue? To answer this question, we should recall the discussion in Section 4.1.4 of Chapter 4. In that section, we argued that the positive convexity of bonds is good news for bond investors. The reason, recall, was that because interest rates keep moving day-by-day in an unpredictable manner, the positive convexity of a bond generates positive capital gain returns, on average. Negative convexity generates instead negative capital gain returns, on average, as interest rates move randomly through time. Because of this average negative capital gain return, investors in pass-through securities require a higher coupon rate on the pass-through securities compared to equivalent Treasuries. Thus, an equivalent way to interpret the higher yield of pass-through securities with respect to Treasuries is as compensation for the average capital loss due to negative convexity.

How can we measure the negative convexity of pass-through securities? Because of the changes in prepayment speed there are no analytical formulas available. Therefore we must rely on an approximation, similar to the effective duration in Definition 8.1. In particular,

---

[10]According to the U.S. Treasury Web site, the U.S. Treasury computes the constant maturity rates by interpolating yields only of recently issued (on-the-run) Treasury securities, as they tend to trade around par value. See http://www.ustreas.gov/offices/domestic-finance/debt-management/interest-rate/yieldmethod.html (accessed on April 29, 2009).

[11]We should mention that part of the spread may be due to other reasons, such as the difference in liquidity between GNMA pools and Treasury securities.

recalling the definition of convexity in Definition 4.2 in Chapter 4, namely

$$C = \frac{1}{P}\frac{d^2 P}{dr^2}$$

we obtain the approximating formula outlined in the following definition.

Definition 8.2 *The* **effective convexity** *of a mortgage backed security is given by the formula*

$$C \approx \frac{1}{P}\frac{P(+x\ bps) + P(-x\ bps) - 2 \times P}{(x\ bps)^2} \tag{8.19}$$

where P is the current price of the MBS, and $P(+x\ bps)$ and $P(-x\ bps)$ are the prices of the same security after we shift upward or downward the yield curve by x basis points, respectively. In this computation, the price of the MBS takes into account the variation in the prepayment speed induced by the variation in interest rates.

As an illustration of the formula in Equation 8.19, consider again Example 8.4.

■ **EXAMPLE 8.5**

Consider again Example 8.4. We want to compute the convexity of the pass-through security when the current interest rate is $r = 5\%$. Referring to Table 8.4, we can apply the formula in Equation 8.19 with $x = 50$. In this case, we have

$$
\begin{aligned}
C &\approx \frac{1}{P}\frac{P(+50\ bps) + P(-50\ bps) - 2 \times P}{(50\ bps)^2} \\
&= \frac{1}{634.76}\frac{619.13 + 647.45 - 2 \times 634.76}{(50\ bps)^2} \\
&= -184.89
\end{aligned}
$$

As expected from Figure 8.6 and the previous discussion, the effective convexity of the MBS is negative.

We further illustrate the characteristics of pass-through securities and look at the data in the next section.

8.3.5 The TBA Market

The secondary market for pass-through securities is quite active. In particular, Ginnie Mae, Fannie Mae, and Freddie Mac regularly issue new pass-through securities, whose prices become the market reference. Most of the MBS trading is on a "To-Be-Announced" (TBA) basis, which means that traders do not know the exact composition of the pool underlying the trade when they bid for the security. These pools are quite homogenous, however, and differences are small. Essentially, the TBA market can be thought of as a forward market, in which two counterparties agree today that they will exchange in the future cash for a pass-through pool. However, at the time of the trade the mortgage pool has not been set up by the originators. Yet, since the pool has been sold already for a given price, banks are able to offer lock-in mortgage rates to homeowners, as they know they would be able to later sell the mortgage to the given pool in the secondary market.[12] Liquidity in the TBA market has then important benefits for the borrowers themselves, as they would receive a better mortgage rate if the bank knows that it will not have to bear the risk of default of the new borrower. Only Ginnie Mae, Fannie Mae, and Freddie Mac pass-through securities are allowed to trade in the TBA market.

Panel A of Figure 8.7 plots quotes on GNMA 7 from January, 1995 to November, 2008. The GNMA 7 prices are for a generic pass through issued by Ginnie Mae with a 7% coupon. Note that these quotes are for the latest issued GNMA with 7% coupon, and so the prices reported in the figure are not for the same pass through over time. In particular, the maturity is not decreasing over time, as it should if the underlying pool of mortgages remained the same. Still, because of the TBA market and the relatively uniformity of underlying pools, trades occur at these prices even if the underlying security changes slightly from one time to the other. Panel A also reports the 30-year mortgage rate, which moves opposite to the price of GNMA pass through. The interesting pattern to notice is that while in the first part of the sample, when the average mortgage rate was around 7.5%, large variations in the mortgage rate resulted in large variation in GNMA prices, this behavior is less evident in the second part of the sample, when mortgage rates averaged less than 6%. That is, the two lines still move in opposite directions, but the increase in prices due to a decrease in the mortgage rate is smaller when the mortgage rate is low. This behavior is due to the negative convexity of GNMA pass throughs induced by the prepayment option, as discussed earlier in Section 8.3.4. That is, as mortgage rates decrease, homeowners refinance their mortgages and thus prepay the old mortgages. The prepayment makes the mortgage pool value get closer to the principal value, generating a negative convexity.

The negative convexity of GNMA price with respect to the mortgage rate is shown in Panel B of Figure 8.7, which reports the scatterplot of the GNMA prices versus the mortgage rates. More specifically, each star ("+") in the scatterplot represents a realized combination of GNMA price and mortgage rate, as they appear in Panel A of the same figure. For example, the data point in the far right of the plot has a price / rate combination of $(89.5625, 0.0922)$, which is the first observation in the data sample, appearing at the beginning of the time series plot in Panel A (i.e., January 1995). As Panel B shows, when the mortgage rate declines, the price of GNMA rises, but at an increasingly lower rate. Indeed, the figure also displays a solid line that is fitted through the data to best characterize the relation between prices and mortgage rates. This solid line clearly shows the negative convex relation between GNMA prices and mortgage rates in the data.[13] Figure 8.8 plots the PSA measure of the GNMA 7 pool and the mortgage rate. As can be seen, a lower mortgage rate corresponds in average to a higher prepayment speed, which in turn explains the negative convexity of MBS prices.

8.4   COLLATERALIZED MORTGAGE OBLIGATIONS

Collateralized mortgage obligations (CMOs) are securities with structures that are more complex than pass through securities.[14] The main idea behind this type of security is that

---

[12]See e.g., "General Description of the TBA Market," by the Security Industry and Financial Market Association (SIFMA), available on the Web site http://www.sifma.org/capital_markets/TBA-MBS.shtml, or "Enhancing Disclosure in the Mortgage Backed Securities Market," January 2003, SEC Staff Report.

[13]More specifically, we compute the solid line in Panel B of Figure 8.7 through a polynomial regression. We first regress $P_t = \alpha_0 + \sum_{i=1}^{4} \beta_i (r_t^m)^i + \epsilon_t$ and then plot the fitted value of the regression.

[14]CMOs are also called REMICs for Real Estate Mortgage Investment Conduit.

Figure 8.7   GNMA 7 Prices and Mortgage Rates

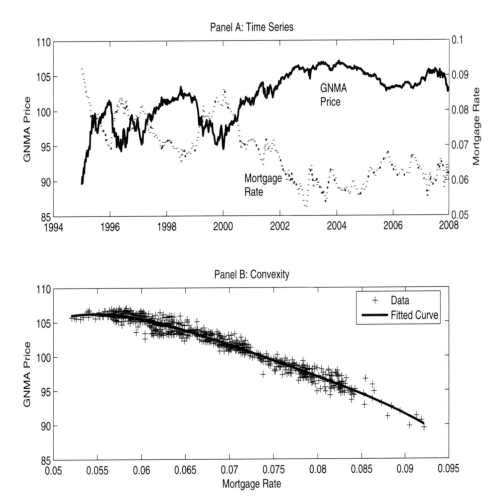

Data source: Bloomberg and Federal Reserve Board.

Figure 8.8   GNMA 7 PSA and Mortgage Rates

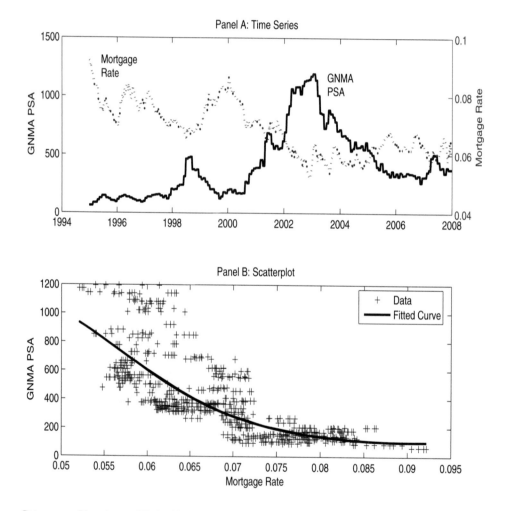

Data source: Bloomberg and Federal Reserve Board.

it offers different levels of exposure to prepayment risk. This in turn affects its risk and return characteristics, including its duration and sensitivity to interest rate variation. The advantage of structuring CMOs with different risk return characteristics is to appeal to different investors' clienteles, which may increase the liquidity of these securities. Indeed, CMOs must satisfy a number of requirements in order to also receive a high credit rating, a property that makes them suitable for investment from a larger set of potential investors and thus increases liquidity. While agency CMOs are perceived default free, non-agency CMOs must instead be over-collateralized to obtain a high credit rating, meaning that the total value of securities issued is much lower than the value of the assets in the pool. In addition, many CMOs pay quarterly coupons, instead of monthly ones, making them more in line with other investment vehicles.

In the remainder of this chapter we go over the most common types of structures.

8.4.1 CMO Sequential Structure

The first step in a sequential structure CMO is to divide the total principal into smaller groups, which are called "Tranche A," "Tranche B," "Tranche C" and so on. These tranches then receive the following cash flow: (i) a fixed coupon rate payment, in percentage of the tranche principal; (ii) sequentially, all of the principal payments, scheduled or prepaid, up to the point at which the whole principal of the tranche is paid out. At that point, the investor buying that particular tranche has received all of his or her money back, and thus the tranche is fully retired. The principal payments, scheduled and unscheduled, then start flowing to the next tranche in the sequence (from which we get the name sequential structure).

Sometimes, a "Tranche Z" is also added. This tranche receives no cash flows (the letter "Z" stands for zero, as zero coupon bond), but the coupon is accrued over time to its principal. Once all the other classes have been retired, then principal payments go to the class Z. The tranche Z allows the issuers to lessen the impact of prepayments on the early tranches by shifting cash flows between tranches, with the Z getting whatever is left over when the others are paid off. The following example illustrates the methodology.

■ **EXAMPLE 8.6**

Let's consider Example 8.2 again. This time, however, we subdivide all of the cash flows generated by the pass-through security (Column 9 in Table 8.3) into smaller cash flows into four classes, A, B, C, and D. For instance, suppose that Tranche A has $250 million principal, Tranche B $150 million, Tranche C $125 million and Tranche D $75 million. Let each tranche have a coupon of 6%, as the original pass through does. Table 8.6 illustrates the procedure. The first column is the month, the second column is the total cash flow of the pass-through security, as seen in Column 9 of Table 8.3. This cash flow is now divided across the four tranches. Initially, tranche A receives both principal payments and interest. The interest component is computed as the coupon rate (6%) times the remaining balance in Column 3. The principal payment is given by the total of scheduled and prepaid principal from the original pool. For instance, the first principal payment is $0.74 = $0.54 + $0.20, where $0.54 is the scheduled principal, and $0.20 is the prepaid principal, as shown in Columns 6 and 7 in Table 8.3. Similarly, in month 2, Tranche A investors receive a total of principal equal to $0.95 = $0.55 + $0.40, where $0.55 and $0.40 are the scheduled and prepaid principal. And so on.

Tranche B to D in these first months are paid the interest only, but no principal at all. For instance, Tranche B receives an interest of $0.75 = $\frac{6\%}{12} \times 150$, which determines all of its cash flow. In the illustration in Table 8.6, Tranche B begins receiving principal payments in month 60, when all of the principal of Tranche A ($250 million) has been paid back to investors. The procedure to define principal payments to Tranche B is the same as the one we discussed for Tranche A. For instance, in month 61 Tranche B receives $4.14 of principal, of which $0.46 is a scheduled payment and $3.68 is a prepayment. In this illustration, Tranche B is paid back in month 105, and thus principal payments are made to Tranche C. This latter tranche is paid back in month 180, and principal payments begin to be made to Tranche D.

Once the cash flows are determined, we can compute the value of each tranche by using the standard present value formula. In this case, we obtain that Tranche A is valued at $256.42 million, Tranche B at $158.42 million, Tranche C at $135.71 million, and Tranche D at $84.21 million. Of course, because the tranche cash flows sum to the original pass- through cash flows, the sum of the values of tranches is the same as the value of the pass-through MBS, that is, $634.76 million.

It is important to note that the different allocation of principal payments drastically changes the sensitivity of the MBS to interest rate movements. For instance, the effective duration of Tranche A is 1.96, of Tranche B is 3.99, of Tranche C is 6.27 and of Tranche D is 10.04. Since the pass-through security is a portfolio of tranches, the duration of the pass through equals the weighted average of durations (see Chapter 3), that is, 4.46, as discussed earlier.

The speed of prepayments affects the time at which the various tranches are paid back. The illustration in Table 8.6 assumes 200% PSA. If for instance we considered 100% PSA, then Tranche A is retired in month 96 (instead of 60), Tranche B in month 171 (instead of 105), Tranche C in month 267 (instead of 180). The duration of individual tranches changes accordingly, in this case, up to 3.70 for Tranche A, 8.15 for Tranche B, 11.39 for Tranche C, and 13.96 for Tranche D.

8.4.2 CMO Planned Amortization Class (PAC)

The PAC securities are also in tranches: A, B, C and Companion. Tranches A, B, C and so on receive prepayments according to a prespecified schedule, which is related to PSA levels chosen ex ante by the MBS issuer. This benchmark PSA-related principal payments is kept fixed for the duration of the contract. However, since this predefined PSA schedule may imply prepayments that are higher or lower than the actual prepayments from homeowners, the difference is absorbed by a Companion Tranche. The implication is that Tranches A, B, C etc. have deterministic future cash flows and thus they can be priced as any coupon bond. In contrast, the Companion Tranche absorbs all of the prepayment risk, and thus its price is highly affected by prepayments.

To make this methodology operational, an upper and lower PSA level is defined first. Given the principal amount of the tranche, these two PSA levels determine two profiles of

Table 8.6   Collateralized Mortgage Obligation – Sequential Structure

Month	Total CF	Tranche A Balance	Pri.	Int.	CF	Tranche B Balance	Pri.	Int.	CF	Tranche C Balance	Pri.	Int.	CF	Tranche D Balance	Pri.	Int.	CF
1	3.74	250.00	0.74	1.25	1.99	150.00		0.75	0.75	125.00		0.63	0.63	75.00		0.38	0.38
2	3.94	249.26	0.95	1.25	2.19	150.00		0.75	0.75	125.00		0.63	0.63	75.00		0.38	0.38
3	4.14	248.31	1.15	1.24	2.39	150.00		0.75	0.75	125.00		0.63	0.63	75.00		0.38	0.38
4	4.34	247.16	1.35	1.24	2.59	150.00		0.75	0.75	125.00		0.63	0.63	75.00		0.38	0.38
5	4.53	245.81	1.55	1.23	2.78	150.00		0.75	0.75	125.00		0.63	0.63	75.00		0.38	0.38
6	4.73	244.25	1.76	1.22	2.98	150.00		0.75	0.75	125.00		0.63	0.63	75.00		0.38	0.38
7	4.92	242.50	1.96	1.21	3.17	150.00		0.75	0.75	125.00		0.63	0.63	75.00		0.38	0.38
8	5.11	240.54	2.16	1.20	3.36	150.00		0.75	0.75	125.00		0.63	0.63	75.00		0.38	0.38
9	5.30	238.39	2.35	1.19	3.55	150.00		0.75	0.75	125.00		0.63	0.63	75.00		0.38	0.38
10	5.48	236.03	2.55	1.18	3.73	150.00		0.75	0.75	125.00		0.63	0.63	75.00		0.38	0.38
11	5.66	233.48	2.75	1.17	3.91	150.00		0.75	0.75	125.00		0.63	0.63	75.00		0.38	0.38
12	5.84	230.73	2.94	1.15	4.09	150.00		0.75	0.75	125.00		0.63	0.63	75.00		0.38	0.38
55	6.29	22.72	4.43	0.11	4.54	150.00		0.75	0.75	125.00		0.63	0.63	75.00		0.38	0.38
56	6.22	18.29	4.38	0.09	4.47	150.00		0.75	0.75	125.00		0.63	0.63	75.00		0.38	0.38
57	6.15	13.91	4.33	0.07	4.40	150.00		0.75	0.75	125.00		0.63	0.63	75.00		0.38	0.38
58	6.08	9.58	4.28	0.05	4.33	150.00		0.75	0.75	125.00		0.63	0.63	75.00		0.38	0.38
59	6.01	5.30	4.23	0.03	4.26	150.00		0.75	0.75	125.00		0.63	0.63	75.00		0.38	0.38
60	5.94	1.06	1.06	0.01	1.07	150.00	3.13	0.75	3.88	125.00		0.63	0.63	75.00		0.38	0.38
61	5.87					146.87	4.14	0.73	4.87	125.00		0.63	0.63	75.00		0.38	0.38
62	5.81					142.73	4.09	0.71	4.81	125.00		0.63	0.63	75.00		0.38	0.38
63	5.74					138.64	4.05	0.69	4.74	125.00		0.63	0.63	75.00		0.38	0.38
64	5.68					134.59	4.00	0.67	4.68	125.00		0.63	0.63	75.00		0.38	0.38
65	5.61					130.59	3.96	0.65	4.61	125.00		0.63	0.63	75.00		0.38	0.38
66	5.55					126.63	3.91	0.63	4.55	125.00		0.63	0.63	75.00		0.38	0.38
67	5.48					122.72	3.87	0.61	4.48	125.00		0.63	0.63	75.00		0.38	0.38
100	3.74					15.51	2.66	0.08	2.74	125.00		0.63	0.63	75.00		0.38	0.38
101	3.70					12.85	2.63	0.06	2.70	125.00		0.63	0.63	75.00		0.38	0.38
102	3.65					10.22	2.60	0.05	2.65	125.00		0.63	0.63	75.00		0.38	0.38
103	3.61					7.61	2.57	0.04	2.61	125.00		0.63	0.63	75.00		0.38	0.38
104	3.57					5.04	2.54	0.03	2.57	125.00		0.63	0.63	75.00		0.38	0.38
105	3.53					2.50	2.50	0.01	2.51	125.00	0.02	0.63	0.65	75.00		0.38	0.38
106	3.49									124.98	2.49	0.62	3.11	75.00		0.38	0.38
107	3.45									122.49	2.46	0.61	3.07	75.00		0.38	0.38
108	3.41									120.03	2.43	0.60	3.03	75.00		0.38	0.38
109	3.37									117.60	2.40	0.59	2.99	75.00		0.38	0.38
110	3.33									115.20	2.38	0.58	2.95	75.00		0.38	0.38
111	3.29									112.82	2.35	0.56	2.91	75.00		0.38	0.38
112	3.25									110.48	2.32	0.55	2.87	75.00		0.38	0.38
175	1.52									5.99	1.12	0.03	1.15	75.00		0.38	0.38
176	1.50									4.87	1.10	0.02	1.13	75.00		0.38	0.38
177	1.48									3.77	1.09	0.02	1.11	75.00		0.38	0.38
178	1.46									2.68	1.08	0.01	1.09	75.00		0.38	0.38
179	1.45									1.61	1.06	0.01	1.07	75.00		0.38	0.38
180	1.43									0.54	0.54	0.00	0.55	75.00	0.51	0.38	0.88
181	1.41													74.49	1.04	0.37	1.41
182	1.39													73.45	1.03	0.37	1.39
183	1.38													72.43	1.01	0.36	1.38
184	1.36													71.41	1.00	0.36	1.36
185	1.34													70.41	0.99	0.35	1.34
186	1.33													69.42	0.98	0.35	1.33
187	1.31													68.44	0.97	0.34	1.31

total principal (scheduled and prepaid) for the tranche, which are determined by using the same methodology as in Equations 8.10 through 8.16. Denote these total principals

$$Pay_t^{hi,total} = Pay_t^{hi,scheduled} + Pay_t^{hi,prepaid}$$
$$Pay_t^{lo,total} = Pay_t^{lo,scheduled} + Pay_t^{lo,prepaid}$$

as they correspond to the high PSA and low PSA. Unlike what we may think at first, it is *not* the case that $Pay_t^{hi,total} > Pay_t^{lo,total}$ all the time. In fact, initially, $Pay_t^{hi,total}$ is higher than $Pay_t^{lo,total}$, as the higher assumed prepayment rate implies a higher cash flow. However, the higher initial cash flows imply that the principal is depleted more quickly, and thus, sooner or later, $Pay_t^{hi,total} < Pay_t^{lo,total}$. Because of this behavior of planned cash flows for a given PSA level, we must be careful to determine the promised cash flow to Tranches A, B, and so forth, so that with high probability, the total amount of prepayments from homeowners is sufficient to pay for the scheduled PSA-related prepayment. PAC cash flows are determined by the formula

$$\text{Promised CF } C_t^{pac} = I_t + \min\left(Pay_t^{hi,total}, Pay_t^{lo,total}\right) \tag{8.20}$$

This choice ensures that as long as homeowners' prepayment speed is within the prespecified *hi* and *lo* PSA levels, there will be enough cash flows coming from homeowners to pay for the promised cash flow of the tranche. The companion tranche then absorbs any difference between the total cash flows from the pass through and the one promised to the PAC Tranche investors. That is

$$\text{Companion Tranche CF } C_t^{Com} = C_t^{PT} - C_t^{pac} \tag{8.21}$$

where C_t^{PT} denotes the total cash flow in the original pass-through security. The PAC profile of total principal payments (scheduled and unscheduled) is then given by

$$Pay_t^{pac} = \min\left(Pay_t^{hi,total}, Pay_t^{lo,total}\right)$$

Since these amounts provide a firm schedule, the amount of PAC principal must equal the sum of Pay_t^{pac} from 0 to maturity. That is, we set

$$L_0^{pac} = \sum_{t=1}^{360} Pay_t^{pac} \tag{8.22}$$

The Companion Tranche principal is set as a residual, so that $L_0^{Com} = L_0 - L_0^{pac}$. Let's look at an example to see this methodology in practice.

■ **EXAMPLE 8.7**

Consider Example 8.2 again. Once more, we divide all of the cash flows generated by this pass through (Column 9 in Table 8.3) into two smaller cash flows, going to Tranche A and its Companion Tranche. Let's assume that the PSA range is $\text{PSA}^{hi} = 300\%$ and $\text{PSA}^{lo} = 80\%$. The calculations above imply that the PAC Tranche has principal equal to \$356.69 million, and the Companion Tranche has principal equal to \$243.31 million.

Figure 8.9 shows the two cash flow profiles, with the high PSA spiking up initially, and then declining below to the cash flow profile of the low PSA. The PAC scheduled cash flow, then, is computed as the minimum between these two cash flows, to make sure that changes in the speed of prepayments of the original pool do not generate too small of a cash flow or too large of a cash flow that cannot be absorbed by the Companion Tranche.

How does the PAC scheduled cash flow depend then on a realized (true) PSA? That is, the scheduled cash flow is determined by using the issuer's best guess of what future real prepayments will be. However, in reality, prepayments depend on market conditions, interest rates, housing prices and so on. These other factors will have an impact on the speed of prepayment. Figure 8.10 shows four panels with the cash flow to the PAC Tranche and the Companion Tranche, under four different assumptions about the realized (true) PSA. For instance, suppose that the true PSA is 100%. Panel A of Figure 8.10 shows the profile of the PAC Tranche cash flow, which equals in fact the one in Figure 8.9. The Companion Tranche has to absorb any difference between the true cash flow from the pass through (the solid line) and the one promised to the PAC Tranche holders (the dashed line). The resulting cash flow of the Companion Tranche is shown as the dotted line.

Consider now the case in which prepayments accelerate, perhaps because the Federal Reserve decreased the Fed funds rate and mortgage rates declined. Panel B shows the cash flow profile when the PSA goes up to 200%. This change makes the total cash flow from the pass through (the solid line) increase substantially. However, this increase in prepayments does not affect the PAC Tranche cash flow, as its profile (the dashed line) does not change at all. The impact is instead on the Companion Tranche, whose cash flow increases substantially. Panel C displays the same plot but under a realized 300% PSA. In this case for a while the Companion Tranche can absorb the difference in prepayment between the promised cash flows and the true cash flows. However, as the Companion Tranche receives principal prepayments, its principal declines and at some point it is fully retired. This is for the same reason that tranches A, B and so on are retired in the sequential structure discussed earlier. As soon as the capital of the Companion Tranche is depleted, the cash flow of the PAC Tranche equals the one of the pass through. Effectively, with the Companion Tranche retired, the PAC Tranche reverts back to the original pass through, and thus prepayment risk is back fully in force.

What happens if the realized (true) PSA is actually above the highest forecasted PSA? As shown in Panel D of Figure 8.10, in this case, the Companion Tranche's principal is repaid very quickly, and thus the cash flow of the PAC Tranche has to jump suddenly to the one of the pass through. Once again, in this case, the PAC Tranche cash flows are no longer determined by the original promised schedule, rather they revert back to the ones of a standard pass-through security, with all the (prepayment) risk that it embeds.

What is the price impact of changes in PSA to the PAC Tranche and Companion Tranche? By construction, so long as the PSA level is within the boundaries and the Companion Tranche is not retired, the PAC Tranche cash flow is given by its scheduled cash flow. As such, the price does not change at all. For instance, the price of the PAC Tranche corresponding to Panels A, B, and C in Figure 8.10 is $377.16 million. That is, moving the PSA between 100% and 300% does not change

Figure 8.9   PAC Scheduled Cash Flow

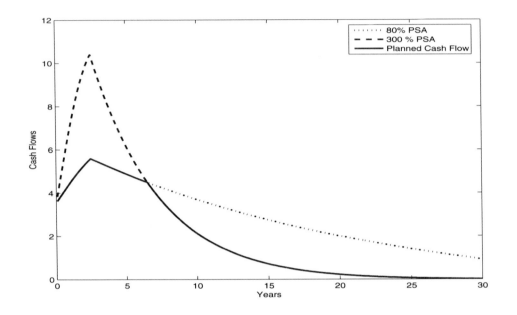

the value at all. In this sense, this tranche is not subject to prepayment risk. Since the pass through security *is* affected by changes in PSA, it must be the case that the Companion Tranche value changes substantially with PSA. Indeed, the value of the Companion Tranche in the three panels is $269.77, $257.62, and $250.54 million, respectively. This variation induces a strong negative convexity effect. This negative relation between interest rates and the Companion Tranche is evident in Panel A of Figure 8.11. This figure reports the result of the same exercise carried out in Table 8.4 and Figure 8.6. Namely, as the interest rate declines, the PSA is increased accordingly to capture the increase in prepayment that lower interest rates would trigger. The PAC Tranche displays essentially a linear relation with interest rates, except for low interest rates. From Table 8.4 we assume that PSA reaches all the way to 500%, which is much larger than the upper PSA amount of 300%. We know that in this case, the PAC reverts back to a pass through, and hence the negative convexity. The Companion Tranche displays a much stronger negative convexity than the original Pass Through, with its valuation becoming almost constant as interest rates decline.

8.4.3   Interest Only and Principal Only Strips.

Interest only and principal only strips constitute perhaps the simplest way to cut up the cash flow from the original pass-through security.

- *Interest-Only* (IO) strips receive all of the interest payment from the underlying collateral and none from the principal. So, for instance, if interest rates decline and

Figure 8.10   PAC Scheduled Cash Flow and True PSA

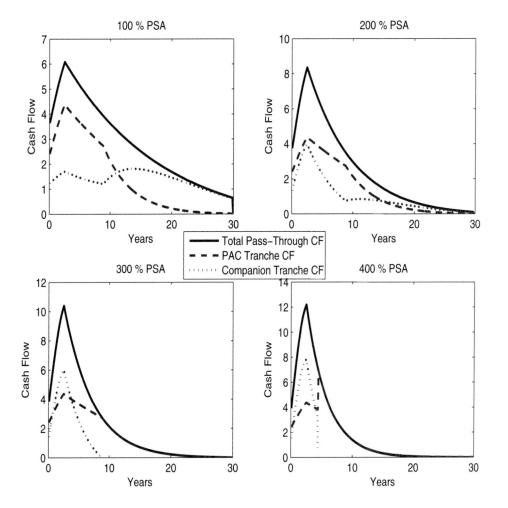

Figure 8.11   PAC and Companion Tranche Value

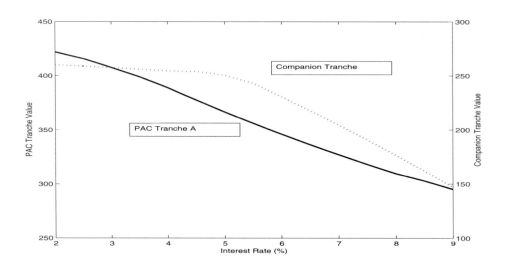

many homeowners prepay their debt, lower interest payments will occur in the future as now less principal is available to compute the interest. As a consequence, an investor who is long the IO will receive lower future cash payments (and the IO loses value).

- *Principal-Only* (PO) strips receive all of the principal payments, both scheduled and unscheduled, from the underlying principal, and no interest. So, for instance, if homeowners prepay their debt because interest rates decline, all of the prepayment goes to the PO strips. As a consequence, an investor who is long the PO will receive a higher cash flow in the immediate future. A decline in interest rates therefore has a large impact on the price of the PO.

IOs and POs have some additional peculiarities that are worth illuminating in the next example.

■ **EXAMPLE 8.8**

Consider once again the pass through in Example 8.2 and the computations in Table 8.3. The payments to the IO strip simply correspond to the interest payments for the pass through, contained in Column 8 of Table 8.3. The payments to the PO strip correspond to the sum of Columns 6 and 7 of the same table. The interesting part about IOs and POs is their behavior as the speed of prepayment changes. Table 8.7 shows the impact that lower interest rates and higher PSA have on the value of the strips. The most interesting effect is the fact that IO value decreases substantially as interest rates decline and PSA increases. In contrast, to counterbalance, the PO strip must increase dramatically to ensure a higher total value, as shown earlier in Table 8.3 for the pass-through security. This behavior greatly affects the effective

Table 8.7   Value and Duration of IO and PO Strips

Interest Rate	PSA	IO Value	PO Value
2.00%	500	131.75	556.05
2.50%	450	140.05	541.58
3.00%	400	149.71	525.05
3.50%	350	161.06	505.91
4.00%	300	174.57	483.42
4.50%	250	190.86	456.59
5.00%	200	210.78	423.98
5.50%	150	235.52	383.61
6.00%	100	266.75	332.58
6.50%	90	267.07	309.89
7.00%	80	267.35	287.18
7.50%	70	267.59	264.47
8.00%	60	267.79	241.76
8.50%	50	267.95	219.06
9.00%	40	268.07	196.38

duration of IO and PO strips. Indeed, consider again the case in which the current rate is $r = 5\%$, and PSA = 200%. By applying the formula in Equation 8.18 we can compute the effective duration of IO and PO strips as follows:

$$D^{IO} \approx -\frac{1}{P^{IO}} \frac{P^{IO}(+50\ bps) - P^{IO}(-50\ bps)}{2 \times (50\ bps)} = -\frac{1}{210.78} \frac{235.52 - 190.86}{2 \times (50\ bps)}$$
$$= -21.19$$
$$D^{PO} \approx -\frac{1}{P^{PO}} \frac{P^{PO}(+50\ bps) - P^{PO}(-50\ bps)}{2 \times (50\ bps)} = -\frac{1}{423.98} \frac{383.61 - 456.59}{2 \times (50\ bps)}$$
$$= 17.21$$

The effective duration of the IO strips is negative, and substantial, consistently with the previous discussion. In contrast, the effective duration of the PO strips is strongly positive. This is not surprising, as the weighted average of the effective durations of the IO and PO strips must add up to the effective duration of the original pass-through security, which we found to be 4.46 in Example 8.3. Thus, if the IO strips have a large negative duration, it must be the case that PO strips have a large positive duration.

8.5 SUMMARY

In this chapter we covered the following topics:

1. Securitization: Securitization is the process through which financial institutions pool similar assets in a portfolio and sell the portfolio to investors. Investors purchasing the portfolio of assets receive claims on the cash flows generated by the assets in the portfolio. Such assets are the collateral of the portfolio. If such assets are residential

mortgages, then the claims the investors obtain are called residential mortgage backed securities. These assets can also be commercial mortgages, credit card receivables, auto loans, and so on.

2. Fixed Rate Mortgages: In a fixed rate mortgage, the monthly mortgage payment contains two components: Principal payment and interest rate payment. The interest rate payment depends on the outstanding balance, and thus it is initially high and declines over time.

3. Prepayment option: Homeowners have the right to prepay their mortgages, which they tend to do when interest rates decline. Prepaying the mortgage implies that banks receive their money earlier than expected, and can only reinvest at now lower interest rates.

4. CPR and PSA: These are measures of prepayment speed. CPR assumes a constant prepayment rate over the life of the mortgage backed security, while PSA assumes lower prepayment for young pools of mortgages.

5. Pass-Through Mortgage Backed Securities: This securities are collateralized by pools of mortgages, which are claim to the cash flows originating from the pool of mortgages. In particular, they offer no protection against prepayments.

6. Negative Convexity: Although like any other bond, the value of a mortgage and thus of pools of mortgages increases when interest rates decline, the value increases at a declining rate, as homeowners repay their mortgages.

7. Collateralized Mortgage Obligations (CMOs): CMOs are structured securities that offer various cash flow profiles to investors in MBS. Collateralized by an underlying pass through security, CMOs typically allocate principal payments to various classes according to specific formulas. For instance, Sequential Tranches receive principal payments sequentially over time. Similarly, PAC Tranches receive principal payments according to a specific formula, while any discrepancy from the formula is channeled to a Support tranche.

8.6 EXERCISES

1. Mortgage backed securities make coupon payments on a monthly basis. This means that the yield curve should be estimated in this frequency. Unfortunately, Treasuries traded on a given day are not enough in order to use the standard bootstrap techniques to obtain the monthly yield curve, as the maturity usually spans for up to 30 years. Other techniques such as the Extended Nelson Siegel model discussed in Chapter 2 should be used instead to obtain the yield curve. Given the data on bonds in Table 8.8 traded on December 1, 2000, compute the monthly yield curve and the discounts for the next 30 years.

2. Consider the following MBS pass through with principal $300 million. The original mortgage pool has a WAM = 360 months (30 years) and a WAC = 7.00%. The pass through security pays a coupon equal to 6.5%. Instead of the yield curve, you are given the following parameters from the extended Nelson Siegel model (see

Table 8.8 Treasury Securities on December 1, 2000

Coupon	Maturity	Mid	Coupon	Maturity	Mid	Coupon	Maturity	Mid
0.000	12/7/2000	99.898	5.875	11/30/2001	99.801	5.500	2/15/2008	99.676
0.000	12/14/2000	99.784	6.125	12/31/2001	100.066	5.625	5/15/2008	100.457
0.000	12/15/2000	99.748	6.250	1/31/2002	100.250	4.750	11/15/2008	94.941
0.000	12/18/2000	99.699	14.250	2/15/2002	109.434	5.500	5/15/2009	99.586
0.000	12/21/2000	99.646	6.250	2/28/2002	100.316	6.000	8/15/2009	102.883
0.000	12/28/2000	99.567	6.500	3/31/2002	100.707	6.500	2/15/2010	106.598
4.625	12/31/2000	99.832	6.375	4/30/2002	100.684	5.750	8/15/2010	101.734
0.000	1/4/2001	99.438	7.500	5/15/2002	102.277	11.250	2/15/2015	152.938
0.000	1/11/2001	99.316	6.500	5/31/2002	100.941	10.625	8/15/2015	147.813
0.000	1/18/2001	99.200	6.250	6/30/2002	100.664	9.875	11/15/2015	140.813
0.000	1/25/2001	99.081	6.000	7/31/2002	100.402	9.250	2/15/2016	134.875
4.500	1/31/2001	99.707	6.375	8/15/2002	101.008	7.250	5/15/2016	114.938
0.000	2/8/2001	98.843	6.125	8/31/2002	100.625	7.500	11/15/2016	117.719
0.000	2/15/2001	98.726	5.875	9/30/2002	100.301	8.750	5/15/2017	131.156
0.000	2/22/2001	98.608	5.750	10/31/2002	100.148	8.875	8/15/2017	132.688
5.000	2/28/2001	99.703	11.625	11/15/2002	110.707	9.125	5/15/2018	136.250
0.000	3/1/2001	98.490	5.625	11/30/2002	100.031	9.000	11/15/2018	135.438
0.000	3/8/2001	98.381	5.625	12/31/2002	99.992	8.875	2/15/2019	134.281
0.000	3/15/2001	98.265	5.500	1/31/2003	99.727	8.125	8/15/2019	126.281
0.000	3/22/2001	98.151	6.250	2/15/2003	101.207	8.500	2/15/2020	130.973
0.000	3/29/2001	98.035	5.500	2/28/2003	99.742	8.750	5/15/2020	134.039
4.875	3/31/2001	99.535	5.500	3/31/2003	99.723	8.750	8/15/2020	134.281
0.000	4/5/2001	97.911	5.750	4/30/2003	100.273	7.875	2/15/2021	124.375
0.000	4/12/2001	97.804	10.750	5/15/2003	111.461	8.125	5/15/2021	127.500
0.000	4/19/2001	97.686	5.500	5/31/2003	99.742	8.125	8/15/2021	127.656
0.000	4/26/2001	97.569	5.375	6/30/2003	99.461	8.000	11/15/2021	126.391
5.000	4/30/2001	99.520	5.250	8/15/2003	99.148	7.250	8/15/2022	117.688
0.000	5/3/2001	97.471	4.250	11/15/2003	96.355	7.625	11/15/2022	122.406
0.000	5/10/2001	97.359	4.750	2/15/2004	97.527	7.125	2/15/2023	116.313
5.625	5/15/2001	99.750	5.250	5/15/2004	98.969	6.250	8/15/2023	105.531
0.000	5/17/2001	97.245	6.000	8/15/2004	101.434	7.500	11/15/2024	121.844
0.000	5/24/2001	97.142	5.875	11/15/2004	101.086	7.625	2/15/2025	123.594
0.000	5/31/2001	97.032	7.500	2/15/2005	107.125	6.875	8/15/2025	114.063
0.000	6/7/2001	96.922	6.500	5/15/2005	103.867	6.000	2/15/2026	102.719
5.750	6/30/2001	99.723	6.500	8/15/2005	103.930	6.750	8/15/2026	112.750
5.500	7/31/2001	99.555	5.750	11/15/2005	101.344	6.500	11/15/2026	109.531
7.875	8/15/2001	101.133	5.625	2/15/2006	100.324	6.625	2/15/2027	111.281
0.000	8/30/2001	95.663	6.875	5/15/2006	106.098	6.375	8/15/2027	108.094
5.500	8/31/2001	99.504	7.000	7/15/2006	106.750	6.125	11/15/2027	104.785
5.625	9/30/2001	99.563	6.500	10/15/2006	104.563	5.500	8/15/2028	96.574
5.875	10/31/2001	99.789	6.250	2/15/2007	103.555	5.250	11/15/2028	93.250
7.500	11/15/2001	101.262	6.625	5/15/2007	105.723	5.250	2/15/2029	93.402
0.000	11/29/2001	94.368	6.125	8/15/2007	103.180	6.125	8/15/2029	105.969

Source: Data excerpted from CRSP (Daily Treasuries) © 2009 Center for Research in Security Prices (CRSP), The University of Chicago Booth School of Business.

Table 8.9   Tranches of a 6.5% Pass-Through Security

Tranche	Principal	Interest
Tranche A	175	6.50%
Tranche B	75	6.50%
Tranche C	30	6.50%
Tranche D	20	6.50%

Chapter 2): $\theta_0 = 6,278.30$, $\theta_1 = -6,278.25$, $\theta_2 = -6,292.47$, $\theta_3 = 0.04387$, $\lambda_1 = 27,056.49$, and $\lambda_2 = 30.48$. That is, to compute the continuously compounded zero coupon yield with maturity T, the formula is

$$r(0,T) \quad = \quad \theta_0 + (\theta_1 + \theta_2)\frac{1 - e^{-\frac{T}{\lambda_1}}}{\frac{T}{\lambda_1}} - \theta_2 e^{-\frac{T}{\lambda_1}} + \theta_3 \left(\frac{1 - e^{-\frac{T}{\lambda_2}}}{\frac{T}{\lambda_2}} - e^{-\frac{T}{\lambda_2}} \right)$$

(8.23)

The discount with maturity T is then $Z(0,T) = e^{-r(0,T) \times T}$.

(a) What is the price of the pass through? Assume a constant PSA = 150%.

(b) Compute the duration of this security assuming that the PSA remains constant at 150%.

(c) Compute the effective duration of this security assuming that the PSA increases to 200% if the term structure shifts down by 50 basis points, while it decreases to 120% if the term structure shifts up by 50 basis points. Comment on any difference compared to your result in part (b).

(d) Compute the effective convexity of this security under the same PSA assumptions as in part (c). Interpret your results.

3. Consider the following MBS pass through with principal $300 million. The original mortgage pool has a WAM = 360 months (30 years) and a WAC = 7.00%. The pass-through security pays a coupon equal to 6.5%. Use the same spot rate $r(0,T)$ as computed in Exercise 2 for your calculations. This security is divided into four tranches (A,B,C, and D), each with the principal in Table 8.9:

(a) What is the price of each tranche? Assume a constant PSA = 150%.

(b) Compute the effective duration of the various tranches assuming that the PSA increases to 200% if the term structure shifts down by 50 basis points, while it decreases to 120% if the term structure shifts up by 50 basis points. Which tranche is more sensitive to interest rate movements? Which tranche is less sensitive?

(c) Compute the effective convexity of the various tranches under the same PSA assumptions as in part (b). Interpret your results.

(d) If you decide to buy all the tranches, is this the same as holding the MBS pass through in Exercise 2? (e.g., Does it have the same price? Same duration?)

Table 8.10   Tranches of a 6.5% Pass-Through Security

Tranche	Principal	Interest
Tranche A	175	6.50%
Tranche B	75	6.50%
Tranche C	30	6.50%
Tranche Z	20	6.50% (accrual)

4. Consider the following MBS pass through with principal $300 million. The original mortgage pool has a WAM = 360 months (30 years) and a WAC = 7.00%. The pass-through security pays a coupon equal to 6.5%. Use the same spot rate $r(0, T)$ as computed in Exercise 2 for your calculations. This security is divided into four tranches (A,B,C, and Z), each with the principal in Table 8.10. Tranche Z is an *accrual* tranche that does not receive payments until all other tranches are paid off. This means that interest payments are accrued (nominally added to the principal of the tranche) until the other tranches' principal is fully paid.

   (a) What is the price of each tranche? Assume a constant PSA = 150%.

   (b) Compute the effective duration of the various tranches assuming that the PSA increases to 200% if the term structure shifts down by 50 basis points, while it decreases to 120% if the term structure shifts up by 50 basis points. Which tranche is more sensitive to interest rate movements? Which tranche is less sensitive?

   (c) Is Tranche Z more sensitive to interest rate changes than Tranche D from Exercise 4? What about tranches A, B, and C? Are they more sensitive to interest rate changes if they are supported by Tranche D or by Tranche Z?

   (d) Compute the effective convexity of the various tranches under the same PSA assumptions as in part (b). Interpret your results.

   (e) If you decide to buy all the tranches, is this the same as holding the MBS pass through from Exercise 2 (e.g. Does it have the same price? Same duration?).

5. Consider the following MBS pass through with principal $300 million. The original mortgage pool has a WAM = 360 months (30 years) and a WAC = 7.00%. The pass through security pays a coupon equal to 6.5%. Use the same spot rate $r(0, T)$ as computed in Exercise 2 for your calculations. The security is divided into a Plan Amortization Class (PAC) and a support tranche according to Table 8.11.

   The PAC has an upper collar of 300% PSA and a lower collar of 85% PSA.

   (a) What is the price of each tranche? Assume a constant PSA = 150%.

   (b) Compute the effective duration of the two tranches assuming that the PSA increases to 200% if the term structure shifts down by 50 basis points, while it decreases to 120% if the term structure shifts up by 50 basis points. Which tranche is more sensitive to interest rate movements? Which tranche is less sensitive?

Table 8.11   Tranches of 6.5% Pass Through Security

Tranche	Principal	Interest
PAC	181.34	6.50%
Support	118.66	6.50%

(c) Compute the effective convexity of the various tranches under the same PSA assumptions as in part (b). Interpret your results.

(d) If you decide to buy all the tranches, is this the same as holding the MBS pass through from Exercise 3 (e.g., Does it have the same price? Same duration?).

6. Consider the following MBS pass through with principal $300 million. The original mortgage pool has a WAM = 360 months (30 years) and a WAC = 7.00%. The pass-through security pays a coupon equal to 6.5%. Use the same spot rate $r(0, T)$ as computed in Exercise 2 for your calculations. The pass through is divided into a Principal Only tranche and an Interest Only tranche.

   (a) What is the price of each tranche? Assume a constant PSA = 150%.

   (b) Compute the effective duration of the IO and PO tranches assuming that the PSA increases to 200% if the term structure shifts down by 50 basis points, while it decreases to 120% if the term structure shifts up by 50 basis points. Which tranche is more sensitive to interest rate movements? Which tranche is less sensitive?

   (c) Compute the effective convexity of the IO and PO tranches under the same PSA assumptions as in part (b). Interpret your results.

   (d) If you decide to buy all the tranches, is this the same as holding the MBS pass through from Exercise 2 (e.g., Does it have the same price? Same duration?).

7. The following exercise is based on a series of investments made in 1993 by City Colleges of Chicago (CCC), a system of community colleges. Its treasurer decided to invest up to 70% of its portfolio in the lower tranches of a Fannie Mae MBS: FNMA 1993-237.[15] All payments within this trust were Principal-Only (PO); this particular type of security was called a Stripped Mortgage Backed Security (SMBS). The FNMA 1993-237 had a principal balance of $425 million with a WAM = 348 and WAC = 8.27%. Because all tranches were PO, the coupon rate of the underlying pass through is not needed. The security was divided in the tranches and types reported in Table 8.12, where PAC stands for Planned Amortization Class, TAC stands for Targeted Amortization Class, and SUP stands for Support Class.

   In Table 8.12, UC and LC stand for the upper collar and the lower collar for the PACs. TAC are similar to PAC but, instead of using a range of PSA, use only a single value

---

[15] Information for this case was obtained from documents rendered by the United States Court of Appeals for the Fifth Circuit: Westcap Corp. vs. City Colleges of Chicago (CCC) available in Lexis (25502). CCC also invested in another similar security: FNMA 1993-205, which we omitted to simplify the exercise.

EXERCISES **323**

Table 8.12 Tranches in FNMA, 1993-237

Tranche	Principal	Type	UC	LC
A	127.50	PAC	550%	135%
B	51.00	PAC	550%	135%
C	25.50	PAC	550%	135%
E	68.00	TAC	300%	
G	59.50	TAC	450%	
H	93.50	SUP		
Total	425.00			

of PSA to create a schedule of payments. The prospectus for the security pointed out the following principal distribution plan:

> Principal will be distributed monthly on the Certificates in an amount (the "Principal Distribution Amount") equal to the aggregate distributions of principal concurrently made on the SMBS. On each Distribution Date, the Principal Distribution Amount will be distributed as principal of the Classes in the following order of priority:
>
> (a) sequentially, to the A, B and C Classes [Planned Amortization Class (PAC)], in that order, until the principal balances thereof are reduced to their respective Planned Balances for such Distribution Date;
>
> (b) sequentially, to the E and G Classes [Targeted Amortization Class (TAC)], in that order, until the principal balances thereof are reduced to their respective Targeted Balances for such Distribution Date;
>
> (c) to the H Class [Support Class], until the principal balance thereof is reduced to zero;
>
> (d) to the G and E Classes, in that order, without regard to their Targeted Balances and until the principal balances thereof are reduced to zero;
>
> (e) to the A Class, without regard to its Planned Balance and until the principal balance thereof is reduced to zero; and
>
> (f) concurrently, to the B and C Classes, in proportion to their then current principal balances, without regard to the Planned Balances and until the principal balances thereof are reduced to zero.

On October 1, 1993 the market faced the yield curve summarized by the following Extended Nelson Siegel model parameters (see Chapter 2 and Equation 8.23 above): $\theta_0 = 6,278.30$, $\theta_1 = -6,278.30$, $\theta_2 = -6,291.28$, $\theta_3 = 0.70906$, $\lambda_1 = 27,056.50$, and $\lambda_2 = 20.2312$.

(a) According to industry experts you find out that the PSA is currently at 450%.

  i. Assuming a constant PSA rate, value the tranches of FNMA 1993-237.

  ii. What is the duration of each of the tranches? Are G and H the tranches with the highest duration?

(b) CCC decides to invest \$100 million, divided equally into tranches G and H. After 6 months you receive new data to compute the yield curve (it is now April

4, 1994) according to the Extended Nelson Siegel model: $\theta_0 = 6,278.30$, $\theta_1 = -6,278.30$, $\theta_2 = -6,291.28$, $\theta_3 = 0.97584$, $\lambda_1 = 27,056.50$, and $\lambda_2 = 20.2249$.

  i. Have interest rates risen? Stayed the same? Or fallen?

  ii. What will the value of the portfolio be on April 4, 1994 assuming that the PSA stays the same?

(c) You find out that on April 4, 1994 the PSA is actually 200%.

  i. Is the change in the PSA a reflection of what happens to the yield curve? Why or why not?

  ii. Will this change offset the P/L in the portfolio's value from the change in interest rates?

  iii. Compute the price of each tranche at April 4, 1994. Do the changes reflect what you expected from the duration calculation?

  iv. What is the gain / loss of the portfolio at this time?

8.7 CASE STUDY: PiVe INVESTMENT GROUP AND THE HEDGING OF PASS-THROUGH SECURITIES

It is June 8, 2007, and the principals of PiVe Investment Group are considering how to best hedge their recent investment of $300 million in pass through securities. In particular, they just invested in the Ginnie Mae I pass through security, GNSF 6, in the TBA market, which was trading at a discount. The underlying pool of this pass-through security has a WAC of 6.5% – very close to the current mortgage rate for new 30-year fixed-rate mortgages of 6.59% – and a WAM of 320 months. The pass through security has a coupon of 6%, and it is now quoted in the TBA market at bid/ask prices = [99.4375 / 99.40625].

The underlying decision to purchase this pass-through security was based on its substantial spread over Treasuries compared to the security PSA level. The principals of PiVe Investment Group noticed that the median "street" forecast of the long-term PSA level from SIFMA (Securities Industry and Financial Markets Association) was only a 225% PSA, and forecasts ranged between 172 and 304 (see Table 8.13).[16] The current term structure of interest rates was almost flat around the 5% rate, as the short-term rates were around 5% while the long-term rates were around 5.4%. Given the term structure of interest rates, the principals obtained a value of the GNSF 6 of $P = 104.05$ at the median 225% PSA, much higher than the traded price. Other PSA scenarios also generated higher prices than the traded price. In particular, they obtained $P = 104.63$ at 172% PSA and $P = 103.38$ at 304% PSA. PiVe Investment Group used to gauge the attractiveness of their investments by computing the implied spread over Treasuries that justified the traded price. In this case, a uniform continuously compounded spread of 1.015% over all maturities gave a price of $P = 99.43$, which is within the bid/ask prices.

PiVe principals were very aware of the source of the price discount: The negative convexity induced by prepayment risk. Since the WAC was close to the current mortgage rate, a further decline in interest rates might spur a large refinincing wave, such as the one

---

[16]Information about SIFMA prepayment tables is available at the SIFMA Web site *www.sifma.org/research/ statistics/mbs_prepayment.html*.

experienced in 2001 - 2002, implying that the price would flatten out at around 100 instead of increasing in value, as other Treasury securities would. Moreover, this negative convexity tends to generate trading losses in average, which conterbalance the higher yield.[17] Still, the 1% spread over Treasuries seemed to be a large compensation for such prepayment risk, and this judgment spurred the purchase of this particular security. The principals are now deciding how to hedge away interest rate risk.

8.7.1 Three Measures of Duration and Convexity

The principals of PiVe Investment Group are looking at three different measures of duration, which are not exactly identical to each other, and they must consider which one to use to set up an effective hedging strategy against the movement of interest rates.

8.7.1.1 *Simple Duration*   Given the current median market forecast of the PSA level of 240%, the principals of PiVe computed first a benchmark value of duration. Keeping the PSA constant, they can compute the duration in the usual way as for Treasuries. In particular, it is simple to see that from the definition of duration, we obtain

$$D = -\frac{1}{P}\frac{dP}{dr} = \sum_{i=1}^{320} w_i \times T_i$$

$$C = \frac{1}{P}\frac{d^2P}{dr^2} = \sum_{i=1}^{320} w_i \times T_i^2$$

where T_i are the monthly payment times, and the weights are

$$w_i = \frac{CF_i \times \widehat{Z}(0, T_i)}{P}$$

In this formula, the CF_i are computed from the projected PSA level, and $\widehat{Z}(0, T_i)$ represents the discount obtained by adding the 1.03% spread over Treasuries that is needed to match the price from the constant PSA to the traded price. This calculation implies a duration equal to $D = 4.39$ and $C = 36.1590$.

The principals of PiVe capitals were skeptical about this computation, though. While the duration figure appears reasonable, the convexity figure appears wrong, as it implies a positive convexity instead of a negative one. This doubt prompted PiVe principals to search for alternative methodologies.

8.7.2 PSA-Adjusted Effective Duration and Convexity

PiVe principals recognized an important shortcoming of the earlier computations, and this was the fact that the PSA is not allowed to change with the interest rate. The second methodology corrects the shortcoming as it takes into account changes in the PSA that are induced by variations in interest rates. In particular, the first step in computing the PSA-adjusted duration and convexity is to estimate the change in the PSA level that is induced by a change in interest rates. Luckily, SIFMA projection tables contain the median

---

[17]See discussion in Chapter 4.

"street" forecast of PSA under various scenarios about the change in interest rates. These projections are contained in Table 8.13. For instance, according to these projections, a decrease in the yield curve of 50 basis points would result in an increase in the PSA from 225% to 312%, while an increase in the yield curve by the same amount would decrease the PSA from 225% to 179%. The principals of PiVe reasoned that they could compute the value of the security under the two scenarios of an increase and decrease in interest rates while taking into account the predicted change in the PSA, and thus obtain a better measure of duration and convexity. These are given by the effective duration and convexity formulas in Equations 8.18 and 8.19, respectively:

$$D \approx -\frac{1}{P}\frac{P(+50bps) - P(-50bps)}{2 \times 50bps}$$

$$C \approx \frac{1}{P}\frac{P(+50bps) + P(-50bps) - 2 \times P}{(50bps)^2}$$

where P is the current traded price, and $P(+50bps)$ and $P(-50bps)$ are the pass-through security prices under the two scenarios of an increase and decrease in the yield by 50 basis points, respectively. PiVe obtained $P(-50bps) = 101.43$, where the calculation also used the market forecast $PSA = 312$, and $P(+50bps) = 96.79$, where the calculation also used $PSA = 179$. Substituting these numbers in the formulas above, PiVe principals obtained a duration equal to $D \approx 4.68$ and a convexity $C \approx -251.08$. While the duration is only a slightly higher value than the benchmark duration – probably due to the large decrease in the PSA if the interest rate increases – the convexity measure is completely different from the benchmark value, and it now conforms to intuition about prepayment risk.

To check their computations, PiVe principals also computed the approximate duration and convexity implied by a large change of interest rates, of 100 bps:

$$D \approx -\frac{1}{P}\frac{P(+100bps) - P(-100bps)}{2 \times 100bps} = -\frac{1}{99.43}\frac{94.00 - 102.24}{2 \times 100bps}$$

$$= 4.14$$

$$C \approx \frac{1}{P}\frac{P(+100bps) + P(-100bps) - 2 \times P}{(100bps)^2} = \frac{1}{99.43}\frac{94.00 + 102.24 - 2 \times 99.43}{(100bps)^2}$$

$$= -262.63$$

In this case, the duration approximation is slightly smaller than the benchmark computation, but again the convexity number is negative, and similar to the one they obtained previously.

8.7.3 Empirical Estimate of Duration and Convexity

As the principals of PiVe Investment Group were discussing these issues and reading the research literature on hedging interest rate risk, they were struck by a figure they saw in a recent academic paper, soon to be published in the *Review of Financial Studies*. In this article, written by Professors Jefferson Duarte, Francis Longstaff and Fan Yu,[18] Figure 3 plots the price of the 30-year Ginnie Mae I against the five year swap rate. It appears from the figure that there is a strong relation between these two variables. The principals

---

[18] See Duarte, Longstaff, and Yu (2007). This section presents a much simplified version of their more rigorous approach. See the paper for details.

Table 8.13 Mortgage Prepayment Projection

GNMA I 30 Y									
Participating dealers: BS CITI CTW GC GS JPM LB ML MS UBS									
Yield Curve Scenarios									
Avg -300	Avg -200	Avg -100	Avg -50	Avg Base	Avg +50	Avg +100	Avg +200	Avg +300	Low - High
983	854	508	312	225	179	156	130	116	172–304

Source: SIFMA.

of PiVe immediately gathered some data, and found that indeed there is a strong relation: The results of their analysis is in Figure 8.12. Panel A reports the time series of both the the quoted TBA price of GNSF 6 and the 5-year swap rate from June, 1995 to May, 2007. The two series are almost the mirror image of each other, although it appears that when the swap rate declines the price of GNSF 6 does not increase as much as it declines when the swap rate increases. This asymmetry is due to the negative convexity of GNSF 6 with respect to interest rate. Panel B highlights this negative convexity, as the figure contains a scatter plot of the two series in Panel A. Panel B also plots the fitted value of the simple fourth order polynomial regression:

$$P_t = \alpha + \sum_{i=1}^{4} \beta_i \times c_t(5)^i + \epsilon_t$$

where P_t is the GNSF price and $c_t(5)$ the 5-year swap rate at time t. The fitted value is presented as the bold line in the figure. The R^2 of this regression is 94.3%.[19]

This empirical estimate of the relation between GNSF 6 prices and the swap rate also allows the PiVe principals to compute its duration and convexity. In particular, given the fitted value of the regression, they can compute the first and second derivative of GNSF 6 price P with respect to the 5-year swap rate:[20]

$$\frac{d\,P}{d\,c(5)} = \beta_1 + 2 \times \beta_2 \times c(5) + 3 \times \beta_3 \times c(5)^2 + 4 \times \beta_4 \times c(5)^3 \qquad (8.24)$$

$$\frac{d^2\,P}{d\,c(5)^2} = 2 \times \beta_2 + 6 \times \beta_3 \times c(5) + 12 \times \beta_4 \times c(5)^2 \qquad (8.25)$$

Given the current swap rate of $c(5) = 5.61\%$, these formulas imply $\frac{d\,P}{d\,c(5)} = -444.66$ and $\frac{d^2\,P}{d\,c(5)^2} = -14731.4$. Because a parallel shift in the term structure induces an equal

[19]The estimated coefficients are $\alpha = 116.8853$, $\beta_1 = -1.2070e + 003$, $\beta_2 = 4.5123e + 004$, $\beta_3 = -7.4270e + 005$, and $\beta_4 = 3.8397e + 006$. They are significant with simple standard errors. However, given the persistence of the two time series, a Newey West correction of standad errors shows that parameters are not significant. The high R^2, the flip/flow sign of the regression coefficients and their lack of statistical significance is evidence of multicollinearity, typical in polynomial regressions. See Duarte, Longstaff and Yu (2007) for a more advanced estimation methodology that does not suffer from these problems.

[20]The result follows from the rules of the first and second derivative of a function $F(x) = x^i$ with respect to x. These are $F'(x) = i \times x^{i-1}$ and $F''(x) = i \times (i-1) \times x^{i-2}$.

increase in the swap rate,[21] we obtain the following estimates of the duration and convexity

$$\text{Empirical Duration} \quad = \quad -\frac{1}{P}\frac{d\,P}{d\,c(5)} = \frac{444.66}{99.4219} = 4.4725 \qquad (8.26)$$

$$\text{Empirical Convexity} \quad = \quad \frac{1}{P}\frac{d^2\,P}{d\,c(5)^2} = \frac{-14731.4}{99.4219} = -148.17 \qquad (8.27)$$

The duration is once again similar to the previously computed values providing additional confidence to the PiVe principals about the correct hedge ratio. The convexity, while negative, is smaller than the one computed using PSA projections. The PiVe principals conjectured that one explanation of the difference may be that while the empirical variation reflects an historical average about the relation between prices and swap rates, the PSA projections may include more recent market trends, that may have increased the convexity of GNSF 6 compared to swap rates. Another possibility is that the polynomial regression is rather restrictive in determining the exact shape of GNSF 6 price with respect to swap rates.

8.7.4 The Hedge Ratio

Given an estimate of the duration D of GNSF 6, what is the position in the 5-year swaps that PiVe capital has to take? First, an increase in the interest rate causes the value of GNSF to drop. To counterbalance this change, we need a position N in a swap that increases in value when the interest rate drops. That is, we must enter the swap as a fixed-rate payer. Thus, the change in the portfolio Π that is long the Ginnie Mae I and a fixed rate swap has the following sensitivity to changes in the interest rate

$$\frac{d\Pi}{d\,r} = \frac{d\,P}{d\,r} + N \times \frac{d\,V^{swap}(5)}{d\,r} = -D \times P + N\left(-D^{\$}_{Swap}\right)$$

where $V^{swap}(5)$ is the value of the 5-year swap, N is the notional position in the swap, and $D^{\$}_{Swap}$ is the swap dollar duration. From Chapter 5, a swap is given by a portfolio that is long a floating rate bond (with duration close to zero) and short a fixed rate coupon bond. From the current swap curve, PiVe principals compute the duration of the fixed-rate leg of the swap as $D^{Swap}_{fixed} = 4.3934$, and its dollar duration per \$100 notional as $D^{Swap\ \$}_{fixed} = 439.34$. Given that the dollar duration of the floating rate bond is just $D^{Swap\ \$}_{float} = 25$, the swap dollar duration is $D^{Swap\$} = D^{Swap\ \$}_{float} - D^{Swap\ \$}_{fixed} = 414.34$ for \$100 notional.

The hedging strategy requires the portfolio Π to be insensitive to changes in interest rates. That is, we want to find N such that

$$\frac{d\Pi}{d\,r} = 0$$

This condition implies that the notional is given by:

$$N = -\frac{D \times P}{D^{\$}_{Swap}} = \frac{4.4725 \times \$300\text{ million}}{414.3369} = 3.23\text{ million}$$

where \$300 million is the position in GNSF 6. Because the dollar duration of the swap was on a \$100 notional, we have that the notional in the 5-year swap must be \$323 million.

---

[21] This statement is exactly true if the term structure of interest rates is flat, or if duration is computed with respect to the yield-to-maturity, instead of the spot rate curve.

Figure 8.12   GNSF 6 Price and the 5-Year Swap Rate

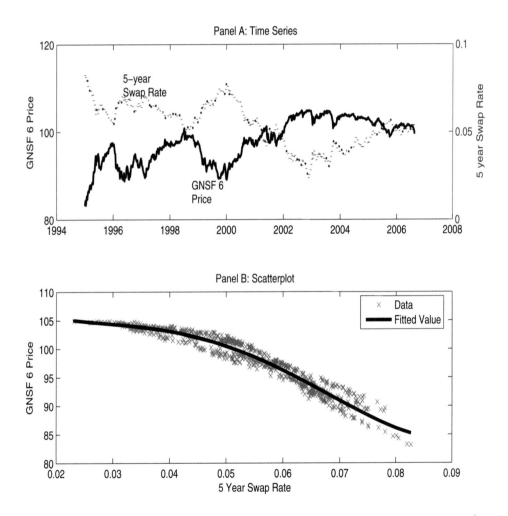

Data Source: Bloomberg.

8.8 APPENDIX: EFFECTIVE CONVEXITY

The approximating formula in Equation 8.19 stems from the definition of second derivative, discussed in Chapter 4. Specifically, the second derivative equals the change in the first derivative, i.e., the slope of the curve at the current interest rate:

$$\frac{d^2 P}{dr^2} = \frac{d \left(dP/dr\right)}{dr}.$$

The slope of the curve at the current interest rate can be approximated by $dP/dr \approx (P - P(-x\ bps))/(x\ bps)$, while the slope of the curve when the interest rate increases by $x\ bps$ can be approximated as $dP/dr \approx (P(+x\ bps) - P)/(x\ bps)$. Taking the difference in slopes, and dividing by $x\ bps$, gives Equation 8.19, that is,

$$
\begin{aligned}
C &\approx \frac{1}{P} \frac{\left(\frac{P(+x\ bps)-P}{x\ bps}\right) - \left(\frac{P-P(-x\ bps)}{x\ bps}\right)}{x\ bps} \\
&= \frac{1}{P} \frac{P(+x\ bps) + P(-x\ bps) - 2P}{(x\ bps)^2}
\end{aligned}
$$

PART II

TERM STRUCTURE MODELS: TREES

In this second part of the book we move one step forward in the understanding of fixed income instruments. In particular, we introduce the notion of no arbitrage, and the basics of term structure *modeling*. To advance the topic, let's consider the following example.

Example

Consider a trader in a prominent investment bank. By using a bootstrap methodology or any of the other methodologies discussed in Chapter 2, the trader has estimated the current discount function $Z(0, T)$. Recall that $Z(0, T)$ gives the value today (0) of one dollar at time T.

If a client asks the trader to quote the price of 10%, 5-year, T-bond, the trader has all the information needed. The price can be computed from

$$P(0, T) = 5 \times \sum_{i=1}^{10} Z(0, T_i) + 100 \times Z(0, T)$$

Suppose now that the client asks the trader to quote the price of a 10%, 5-year, *callable* T-bond, that is, such that the Treasury has the option to buy it back at par at some date in the future.

- How can the trader compute the value of such a bond?

- How can the trader effectively hedge it?

Methodology 1 (*Naive*)

Naively we can follow this reasoning:

1. We have data on interest rates, so we can use past data on interest rates to forecast future interest rates.

2. The Treasury will exercise the options when interest rates are low in the future, as low interest rates imply high bond prices.

3. By forecasting future interest rates, we can forecast the future cash flows of the bond: If interest rates go up, the cash flow remains at 5% per period and 100 in 5 years. If interest rates go down, the cash flow may stop early, as we will receive 100 as soon as the Treasury calls the bond.

So, by using past interest rates, we can compute the *expected* cash flows for each maturity $T_1, .., T_n$

$$E\left[CF_{T_1}\right], \ E\left[CF_{T_2}\right], \ ..., E\left[CF_{T_n}\right]$$

At this point it appears we are done: We just need to compute the present value (PV) of these cash flows

$$P^C\left(0, T\right) = \sum_{i=1}^{n} E\left[PV\left(CF_{T_i}\right)\right]$$

However, here we stumble into a roadblock: How do we compute the present value? Can we use again the discount function $Z\left(0, T\right)$?

No. The discount function $Z\left(0, T\right)$ is the the discount to be applied to future cash flows that are *known* today. Instead, the cash flows from a callable bond are not known today, and in fact, we can only estimate the *expected* cash flows.

One alternative would then be to use some sophisticated asset pricing model, such as the Capital Asset Pricing Model, according to which we should discount cash flows that are uncertain, and therefore possibly risky, by using a rate of return that is adjusted for a risk premium. For instance, the Capital Asset Pricing Model implies computing the yield of risky cash flows as $y(t; T) = r(0; T) + \beta \times$(Market premium). However, even in this case, what is the "beta" of these cash flows?

This methodology is very hard to implement, as it requires we are able to (*a*) forecast future interest rates and thus compute expected cash flows; and (*b*) discount these expected cash flows using a proper risk adjusted discount rate. Both are difficult, and imprecise tasks. Term structure models are models for the interest rates that overcome both problems, by using the notion of no arbitrage.

Methodology 2 (No Arbitrage)

A better methodology is to develop a *model* of the term structure, and use the concept of no arbitrage to obtain the value of the callable bonds from the noncallable bond. More specifically, the methodology that we use is the following:

1. Postulate a model for interest rates.

2. Estimate the model using bond data, so that the model is consistent with current traded bonds.

3. Calculate the price of additional securities, such as the callable bonds, by using the model with same estimated parameters.

Step 3 essentially involves pricing additional securities from more primitive securities, using no arbitrage arguments.

The question then is how we can *develop* a model of the term structure. This has been a very active field of research among academic researchers, traders, and practitioners in investment banks and hedge funds. There are numerous models that have been proposed for the term structure of interest rates, each of which has some good properties and some bad properties. There isn't such a thing as the perfect interest rate model (or the "right" model), but only better and worse models of interest rates for the pricing of interest rate securities. Some models have more realistic features than others, but they may be harder to work with, or take longer to estimate, or to use to price fixed income securities. Some other models may have less realistic features, but imply analytical formulas for many interest rate derivatives, a property that make them particularly useful to value large portfolios of securities. The choice of the proper model to use always depends on the task at hand.

In the coming chapters we discuss many models, and highlights their pros and cons. The important concept across models, though, is the notion of no arbitrage, meaning that each model has to be internally consistent and not leave any arbitrage opportunities on the table. Traders then employ these models to both spot potential arbitrage opportunities, whenever traded securities are not in line with the prediction of their models, or to price additional, exotic securities from more primitive ones.

CHAPTER 9

ONE STEP BINOMIAL TREES

In this chapter we introduce binomial trees. This is a model for interest rates that has three advantages: (1) it is simple, as it does not require high-tech mathematics; (2) when extended to multi-steps, it can be used to price most derivative securities; (3) it is used extensively by practitioners to price real securities. Before we get to this latter part, we must start from basics. We begin the analysis using a specific example, the term structure of interest rates on January 8, 2002.[1]

9.1 A ONE-STEP INTEREST RATE BINOMIAL TREE

Today is January 8, 2002. The term structure of interest rates is depicted in Figure 9.1. The prices and continously compounded yields of zero coupon bonds (STRIPS) up to $T = 1.5$ to maturity are provided in Table 9.1.

An interest rate model starts with the specification of the dynamics of the short-term interest rate. These dynamics reflect our predictions of future interest rates, as discussed in Chapter 7. We take the short-term interest rate as exogenous, in the sense that it is driven by monetary policy choices, and market participants cannot affect it. In principle, this characteristic is really appropriate for the overnight (Federal funds) rate, but for now we keep matters simple, and we take the 6-month rate as the exogenous rate.

---

[1]We often use this date in Part II and III of the book, as the term structure on January 8, 2002 was very steep. This fact generates interesting implications for term structure models.

Figure 9.1 Term Structure of Interest Rates on January 8, 2002

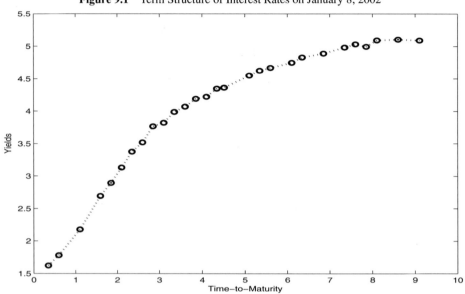

Data Source: *The Wall Street Journal.*

Table 9.1 Interpolated Treasury STRIPS on January 8, 2002

Maturity	Price	Yield
0.5	99.1338	1.74 %
1	97.8925	2.13 %
1.5	96.1531	2.62 %

Data Source: *The Wall Street Journal.*

Table 9.2   A One-Period Binomial Interest Rate Tree

period $\Longrightarrow$	$i = 0$	$i = 1$	
time (in years) $\Longrightarrow$	$t = 0$	$t = 0.5$	

$$r_0 = 1.74\%$$

$$r_{1,u} = 3.39\% \qquad \text{with prob. } p = 1/2$$

$$r_{1,d} = 0.95\% \qquad \text{with prob. } 1 - p = 1/2$$

Given that the 6-month rate is much lower than in the past, we predict that it will rise in the future. Suppose that our prediction of the interest rate in the future is in fact 2.21%. Bear in mind that this is just a prediction, and we do not know for sure. In particular, we believe that in six months there is an equal chance that the 6-month rate will be either 3.39% or 0.95%.[2] We can graphically describe these beliefs in a binomial tree, as in Table 9.2.

In Table 9.2 r_0 denotes the current continuously compounded 6-month interest rate, which is given in the top row in Table 9.1. The notation $r_{1,u}$ indicates the 6-month (c.c.) interest rate in period $i = 1$ after an *up* move (u) in the interest rate, while $r_{1,d}$ indicates the 6-month interest rate at the same time after a *down* move (d). Given that each scenario has a 50-50 chance, the expected (predicted) interest rate in six months is

$$E\left[r_1\right] \quad = \quad \frac{1}{2}r_{1,u} + \frac{1}{2}r_{1,d} = 2.17\% \tag{9.1}$$

This binomial tree for interest rates produces interesting implications for the *relative* pricing of Treasury bonds, as well as other securities whose value depends on interest rates. The logic is the following: When we posit a model for interest rates such as the one in Table 9.2, we are implicitly imposing strong restrictions *across* bonds. In particular, it cannot be the case that the 1-year bond and the 1.5-year bond move independently, for instance, as both prices are going to be affected in a particular direction by the exogenous movement of the short-term interest rate r_1. If r_1 goes up, then both bonds will go down, and vice versa, if r_1 goes down, both the 1-year and the 1.5-year bond will go up in prices. This is because the interest rate tree in Table 9.2 implicitly assumes that only the short term interest rate matters for all of the bonds. As discussed in Chapter 7 this is indeed the hope of the Federal Reserve: By changing only the (overnight) Federal funds rate, the Federal Reserve hopes to be able to also influence long-term bonds. While in model 9.2 this happens, in richer models we will see that the long-term bonds are affected by other factors as well. However, for now, we keep things simple and find the no arbitrage relations that must exist between bond prices.

---

[2]These numbers are consistent with the volatility of interest rates being around 0.0173, as estimated from variation of interest rates. Then, we have $r_{1,u} = 0.0217 + 0.0173 \times \sqrt{0.5}$ and $r_{1,d} = 0.0217 - 0.0173 \times \sqrt{0.5}$. These numbers are obtained from a model introduced in Chapter 10

[handwritten top:] $V_0 = E_0(V_1) Z(0,1) - \lambda(V_{1,u} - V_{1,u})$
C risk premium

Since $E_0(V_1) Z(0,1) - V_0 > 0$

$\lambda = \dfrac{E_0(P(2))(DF_0) - P_0}{P_{1D} - P_{1u}}$

$E(P_i(2)) = P_1, d(2) + p(P_1, u(2) - P_1 d(2))$ *let* $p = .05$

9.1.1 Continuous Compounding

[handwritten:] $\lambda - = MU$, *higher at up than down.*

Note that we chose to model the binomial tree in Table 9.2 using continuously compounded rates. An alternative is to consider semi-annually compounded interest rates on the tree, since we are considering six-month intervals. However, our choice is motivated by the following considerations: First, remember that there is always a one-to-one relation between continuously compounded rates and any other rate, given by the fact that the following relation must always hold

[handwritten:] $\to r \times n$

$$\boxed{e^{r \times \Delta}} = 1 + r_n \times \Delta \tag{9.2}$$

where $\Delta = 1/n$ is the compounding frequency, r is the continuously compounded rate, and r_n is the $n-$times compounded rate. Second, when we apply the model to the pricing of realistic securities, we will consider very high frequency trees, easily with 200 or 300 steps. Continuous compounding allows us to vary only the time interval between nodes, and not also the rate itself as we increase the frequency of movement. Third, many interest rate securities and derivatives have cash flows that depend on different compounding frequency: for instance, simple plain vanilla swaps have floating rates compounded quarterly and fixed payment compounded semi-annually. Using continuous compounding, and then Equation 9.2 allows for a simple method to model the cash flows of these securities. Finally, this assumption allows us to better link the term structure trees developed in this part of the book with the more advanced continuous time models developed in Part III.

9.1.2 The Binomial Tree for a Two-Period Zero Coupon Bond

The first implication of the interest tree in Table 9.2 together with the information in Table 9.1 is that we can obtain the 2-period tree for the bond with one year to maturity. First, though, let's introduce a convenient notation to denote the value of securities *along* the tree:

[handwritten:] $\to$ *up or down.*

$$P_{i,j}(k) = \text{Bond price in period } i, \text{ in node } j, \text{ and with maturity in period } k \tag{9.3}$$

So for example $P_0(2)$ denotes the zero coupon bond price at time 0, and maturing in period $k = 2$ (i.e. time $t = 1$). Similarly, $P_{1u}(2)$ denotes the zero coupon bond price in period $i = 1$, if the interest rate went up – so in node u – and still maturing in period $k = 2$.

Moving now to the example, consider the bond that will mature in period $i = 2$, which from Table 9.1 has a price of $P_0(2) = 97.8925$. If the interest rate goes up, to $r_{1,u} = 3.39\%$, then the bond maturity in period $i = 2$ will have a price $P_{1,u}(2) = e^{-r_{1,u} \times 0.5} \times 100 = 98.3193$. If instead the interest rate moves down, to $r_{1,d} = 0.95\%$, the zero coupon bond is $P_{1,d}(2) = e^{-r_{1,u} \times 0.5} \times 100 = 99.5261$. Since the zero coupon bond pays 100 at maturity $i = 2$ independently of the behavior of the interest rate at that time, we obtain the tree in Table 9.3.

9.2 NO ARBITRAGE ON A BINOMIAL TREE

We now exploit the binomial tree for the one-year zero coupon bond in Table 9.3 to obtain the fair, no-arbitrage price of additional securities whose final payoff depends on the interest rate.

Consider for instance an interest rate option with maturity $i = 1$, such that at time $i = 1$ pays the following amounts:

[handwritten:] *strike k*

$$(\text{Payoff at } i = 1) = 100 \times \max(r_K - r_1, 0) \tag{9.4}$$

[handwritten:] *Put Option* $\to$ *C at i=1*

[handwritten left margin:] $P + 7$ *are entangled in the same forces.* $\to$ *1 doesn't other.*

Assume $\pi = 0$ *risk neutral*

people get p

get p ∗ $p \times (P\,log)^+$

$P(2) = Pswap - expt(P\,log)$
$z(0,1)$

$G = (G + P(C_{1,u} - (1-q))z(0,1))$

[handwritten: V_{1u} = Price shock in P.1 when $r\uparrow(u)$. ...]

[handwritten: discount bucket.]

[handwritten: V_0 = Value at 0]

Table 9.3   The One-Year Zero Coupon Bond Binomial Tree

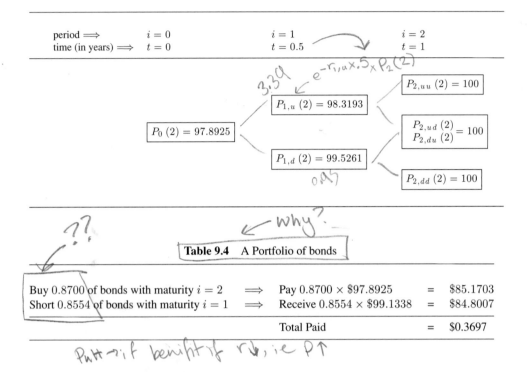

[handwritten: 3.39, $e^{-r_{1,u}\times.5}\times P_2(2)$]

[handwritten: 0.95]

[handwritten: ?? ← why?]

Table 9.4   A Portfolio of bonds

Buy 0.8700 of bonds with maturity $i = 2$	$\Longrightarrow$ Pay 0.8700 × \$97.8925	=	\$85.1703
Short 0.8554 of bonds with maturity $i = 1$	$\Longrightarrow$ Receive 0.8554 × \$99.1338	=	\$84.8007
	Total Paid	=	\$0.3697

[handwritten: Put→?if benifit if $r\downarrow$, ie $P\uparrow$]

where r_K is the strike rate, e.g. $r_K = 2\%$ and r_1 denotes the interest rate at time 1. That is, if the interest rate increases at $i = 1$, this security pays $100 \times \max(2\% - 3.39\%, 0) = \$0$, while if the interest rate decreases at $i = 1$, this security pays $100 \times \max(2\% - 0.95\%, 0) = \$1.05$. That is,

$$(\text{Payoff at } i = 1 \text{ if } r_{1,u}) = \$0$$
$$(\text{Payoff at } i = 1 \text{ if } r_{1,d}) = \$1.05$$

(9.5)

What is the price of this security at time $i = 0$? What is the relation between this security and the zero coupon bond in Table 9.3?

Consider the portfolio of bonds described in Table 9.4. In this portfolio, a trader is long 0.8700 of zero coupon bonds maturing on $i = 2$ and short 0.8554 zero coupon bonds maturing on $i = 1$. These bond prices are in Table 9.1. The transaction implies a payment of \$85.1703 to buy the long-term bonds, and the receipt of \$84.8007 from selling (short) the 6-month bonds. The net payment is of \$0.3697.

What is the value of the portfolio in Table 9.4 at time $i = 1$, in the two scenarios u and d? Using the tree in Table 9.3 we find: *[handwritten: Iteration?]*

Value of Portfolio if $r_{1,u}$	=	$0.8700 \times P_{1,u}(2) - 0.8554 \times \$100 = \$0$
Value of Portfolio if $r_{1,d}$	=	$0.8700 \times P_{1,d}(2) - 0.8554 \times \$100 = \$1.05$

[handwritten: buy, short.]

The values of the portfolio in the two scenarios are identical to the payoffs of the option in Equations 9.5. That is, the portfolio that is long 0.8700 of the $P_0(2)$ bond and short

$N_1 \times P_{1,u}(2) - N_2$

Table 9.5   The Option Value Tree

$i = 0$	$i = 1$

$$V_0 = \$0.3697$$

$$
\begin{aligned}
V_{1,u} &= 100 \times \max\left(2\% - 3.39\%, 0\right) \\
&= \$0
\end{aligned}
$$

→iteration to find long/short.

$$
\begin{aligned}
V_{1,d} &= 100 \times \max\left(2\% - 0.95\%, 0\right) \\
&= \$1.05
\end{aligned}
$$

0.8554 of the $P_0(1)$ bond *replicates* the payoff of the option. This finding implies that the value of the option with payoffs in Equations 9.5 at time $i = 0$ must be exactly \$0.3697, that is, the cost of the portfolio obtained in Table 9.4.

Why must the option have the same value of the portfolio in Table 9.4? Otherwise, an arbitrage opportunity arises: If for instance a trader is able to sell the option for \$1, he or she can then enter into an offsetting position by purchasing the portfolio in Table 9.4 for \$0.3697 and pocket today the difference of \$0.6303. Because at time $i = 1$ the option is perfectly hedged by the portfolio payoff, there is no risk, and today the trader has made a profit. In well-functioning markets, such opportunities cannot be sustained. We therefore obtain the tree for the option in Table 9.5.

This discussion prompts the following definition of a replicating portfolio:

Definition 9.1 *A **replicating portfolio** of a security with payoffs $V_{1,u}$ and $V_{1,d}$ in the two nodes u and d at time $i = 1$ is a portfolio of bonds that exactly replicates the values of the security at time $i = 1$. That is, if $\Pi_{i,j}$ denotes the value of the portfolio at time i in node j, we have $\Pi_{1,u} = V_{1,u}$ and $\Pi_{1,d} = V_{1,d}$. The value of the option at $i = 0$ equals the value of the portfolio $\Pi_0 = V_0$*

9.2.1   The Replicating Portfolio Via No Arbitrage

The interesting fact about the portfolio in Table 9.4 is that it replicates exactly the payoff of the security (option) whose payoffs are given in Equations 9.5. Is this a general property? Can we always find a portfolio that replicates *any* payoff structure at time $i = 1$? We now show that this is indeed a general property of binomial trees, which is the reason of their popularity. Consider the generic tree of a security whose value at time $i = 1$ depends on the interest rate, as given in Table 9.6.

Consider now a portfolio with N_1 units of the bond with maturity $i = 1$ and N_2 units of the bond with maturity $i = 2$. We call this portfolio $\Pi_{i,j}$ at time i and node j. At time $i = 0$, the value of the portfolio is then

$$\Pi_0 = N_1 \times P_0(1) + N_2 \times P_0(2) \tag{9.6}$$

$V_0 =$

Table 9.6   The Tree of an Interest Rate Security

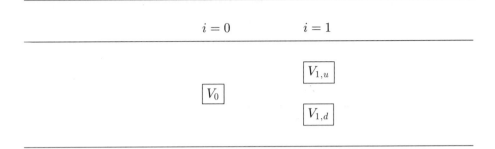

	$i = 0$	$i = 1$
		$\boxed{V_{1,u}}$
	$\boxed{V_0}$	
		$\boxed{V_{1,d}}$

where $P_0(1)$ and $P_0(2)$ are in Table 9.1. At time $i = 1$, the portfolio value will be

Payoff in last example $\left\{\begin{array}{l}\Pi_{1,u} = N_1 \times 100 + N_2 \times P_{1,u}(2)\\ \Pi_{1,d} = N_1 \times 100 + N_2 \times P_{1,d}(2)\end{array}\right.$

where the "100" is the value of $P_1(1)$, and $P_{1,u}(2)$ and $P_{1,d}(2)$ are given in Table 9.3. We want Π to replicate the value of the security V at time $i = 1$. Thus, we impose the following two equations   *at time node up.*

$$\boxed{\Pi_{1,u}} = \boxed{N_1 \times 100 + N_2 \times P_{1,u}(2) = V_{1,u}} \tag{9.7}$$
$$\Pi_{1,d} = N_1 \times 100 + N_2 \times P_{1,d}(2) = V_{1,d} \tag{9.8}$$

This is a system of two equations in two unknowns (N_1 and N_2) which we can solve. In particular, subtract Equation 9.8 from Equation 9.7, and factor N_2 out to obtain

$$N_2 \times (P_{1,u}(2) - P_{1,d}(2)) = (V_{1,u} - V_{1,d})$$

★ what is the diff between V and P.

We can then solve for N_2

$$N_2 = \frac{V_{1,u} - V_{1,d}}{P_{1,u}(2) - P_{1,d}(2)} \tag{9.9}$$

Given N_2 and Equation 9.7, we can solve for N_1 to find

V is option pricing → value of option

$$N_1 = \frac{1}{100} \times [V_{1,u} - N_2 \times P_{1,u}(2)] \tag{9.10}$$

Given N_1 and N_2, the value of the portfolio at time $i = 0$ is given by Equation 9.6.

The next example shows that indeed the portfolio in Table 9.4 satisfies Equations 9.9 and 9.10, explaining why it exactly replicates the option's payoffs in Equation 9.5.

■ **EXAMPLE 9.1**

Consider the option payoff in Equation 9.5, which implies $V_{1,u} = \$0$ and $V_{1,d} = \$1.05$. We can compute the replicating portfolio by using the binomial tree of the 2-period bond in Table 9.3. Applying the formulas in Equations 9.9 and 9.10 we obtain:

→ option vs actual prices

$$N_2 = \frac{V_{1,u} - V_{1,d}}{P_{1,u}(2) - P_{1,d}(2)} = \frac{0 - \$1.05}{\$98.3193 - \$99.5261} = 0.8700$$

↳ hedge ratio !

$$N_1 = \frac{1}{100} \times (V_{1,u} - N_2 \times P_{1,u}(2)) = \frac{1}{100} \times (0 - 0.8700 \times 98.3193) = -0.8554,$$

N

which is the bond portfolio described in Table 9.4. The negative sign on N_1 indicates a short position in the bond with maturity $i = 1$.

The above methodology can be used to price *any* security that depends on the interest rate r_1. The following examples illustrate the methodology.

■ **EXAMPLE 9.2**

Consider a swap that pays at time $i = 1$ the amount $\frac{100}{2} \times (r_1 - c)$, where c is the swap rate. Let $c = 2\%$. Then, the value of the swap from the fixed rate payer perspective is

$$V_{1,u} = \frac{100}{2} \times (3.39\% - 2\%) = \$0.695;$$

$$V_{1,d} = \frac{100}{2} \times (0.95\% - 2\%) = -\$0.525$$

We can obtain the replicating portfolio by choosing N_1 and N_2 according to Equations 9.10 and 9.9:

$$N_2 = \frac{V_{1,u} - V_{1,d}}{P_{1,u}(2) - P_{1,d}(2)} = \frac{\$0.695 - (-\$0.525)}{\$98.3193 - \$99.5261} = -1.011$$

$$N_1 = \frac{1}{100} \times (V_{1,u} - N_2 \times P_{1,u}(2)) = \frac{1}{100} \times (0.695 - (-1.011) \times 98.3193) = 1.001$$

In this case, the replicating portfolio calls for a long position of 1.001 in the short-term bond, and a short position of 1.011 in the long(er)-term bond. We can check that the replicating portfolio in fact replicates:

$$\Pi_{1,u} = N_1 \times 100 + N_2 \times P_{1,u}(2) = 1.001 \times 100 - 1.011 \times 98.3193 = \$0.695$$

$$\Pi_{1,d} = N_1 \times 100 + N_2 \times P_{1,d}(2) = 1.001 \times 100 - 1.011 \times 99.5261 = -\$0.525$$

Because this portfolio indeed replicates the payoff from the swap, the value at $i = 0$ of the swap is

$$\Pi_0 = N_1 \times P_0(1) + N_2 \times P_0(2) = 1.001 \times 99.1338 - 1.011 \times 97.8925 = \$0.259$$

Given to you Prior

The interest rate dependence of a security can also stem from the value of a bond itself. That is, a security that depends on the value of a bond implicitly also depends on the interest rate. In this case, the no arbitrage relation still holds. Consider, for instance, the following option on a bond.

■ **EXAMPLE 9.3**

Consider an option with a payoff at time $i = 1$ that depends on the zero coupon bond that matures at time $i = 2$. In particular, let this option yield the following payoff at time $i = 1$:

$$(\text{Payoff at } i = 1) = \max\left(P_1(2) - K, 0\right)$$

where the strike price $K = \$99.00$. In this case, the payoff at $i = 1$ from the option is

$$V_{1,u} = \max(98.3193 - 99.00, 0) = 0;$$
$$V_{1,d} = \max(99.5261 - 99.00, 0) = \$0.5261$$

Once again, we can obtain the replicating portfolio by choosing N_1 and N_2 according to Equations 9.10 and 9.9, respectively:

$$N_2 = \frac{V_{1,u} - V_{1,d}}{P_{1,u}(2) - P_{1,d}(2)} = \frac{0 - \$0.5261}{\$98.3193 - \$99.5261} = 0.436$$

$$N_1 = \frac{1}{100} \times (V_{1,u} - N_2 \times P_{1,u}(2)) = \frac{1}{100} \times (0 - 0.436 \times 98.3193) = -0.429$$

In this case, the replicating portfolio calls for a short position of 0.429 in the short-term bond, and a long position of 0.436 of the long(er)-term bond. Once again, we can check that the replicating portfolio in fact replicates:

$$\Pi_{1,u} = N_1 \times 100 + N_2 \times P_{1,u}(2) = -0.429 \times 100 + 0.436 \times 98.3193 = \$0$$
$$\Pi_{1,d} = N_1 \times 100 + N_2 \times P_{1,d}(2) = -0.429 \times 100 + 0.436 \times 99.5261 = \$0.5261$$

Because this portfolio indeed replicates the payoff from the option, the value of the option at $i = 0$ is

$$\Pi_0 = N_1 \times P_0(1) + N_2 \times P_0(2) = -0.429 \times 99.1338 + 0.436 \times 97.8925 = \$0.185$$

It is useful to summarize these results as follows:

Fact 9.1 *On a binomial tree, any interest rate security with values $V_{1,u}$ and $V_{1,d}$ at time $i = 1$ can be replicated by a (replicating) portfolio Π whose positions in bonds with maturity $i = 1$ and $i = 2$ are given by N_1 and N_2 in Equations 9.10 and 9.9, respectively. The price of the security at time 0 is then given by*

$$V_0 = N_1 \times P_0(1) + N_2 \times P_0(2) \tag{9.11}$$

We can then summarize the (first) recipe to price derivative securities:

Recipe 1:

1. Compute N_1 and N_2 from Equations 9.10 and 9.9.

2. Compute the price of the derivative security V_0 according to Equation 9.11.

9.2.2 Where Is the Probability p?

The prices of the derivative securities discussed in previous pages were obtained without any reference to the probability p of an *up* movement in interest rates (see Table 9.2). This fact seems puzzling: How is possible that the price of an option that pays when interest rates go down, for instance, is *independent* of the probability that the rate will in fact go down? The logic is the following: From Fact 9.1 the price of the derivative security is computed from a portfolio of other bonds. The prices of these bonds *do* depend on the probability that market participants assign to an increase in future interest rate. Everything else equal, if market participants have a lower expectation of the 6-month rate next period, then the long-term bond would have a higher price, which in turn would increase the price of the option. Yet, for *given* bond prices, the price of the option can be computed only by the replication of its payoff and thus the exact knowledge of the probability p is not necessary.

9.3 DERIVATIVE PRICING AS PRESENT DISCOUNTED VALUES OF FUTURE CASH FLOWS

The methodology developed in the previous section is relatively cumbersome. To obtain the price of an interest rate security, we must first obtain the replicating portfolio, and then obtain the price of the derivative security as the value of the portfolio. In Section 9.4 we will develop a technique that substantially simplifies the computation, especially when we move to longer (and more realistic) trees. However, before we get there, we need to introduce another concept, namely, the pricing of derivatives as risk-adjusted discounted present value of future cash flows. This intermediate step also clarifies much of the (sometimes confusing) terminology adopted in the pricing of interest rate securities.

9.3.1 Risk Premia in Interest Rate Securities

The price of the zero coupon bond maturing at $i = 2$ is $P_0(2) = 97.8925$ (see Table 9.1). Given the tree in Table 9.3, we can compute the present value of the expected bond price at time $i = 1$, $E[P_1(2)]$, using the risk free rate to discount to time $i = 0$. Let $\Delta = 1/2$ be the time interval between steps. Given $p = 1/2$, we have:

$$
\begin{aligned}
\text{Present value of } E[P_1(2)] \quad &= \quad e^{-r_0 \times \Delta} \times E[P_1(2)] & (9.12)\\
&= \quad 0.9913 \times (p \times 98.3193 + (1-p) \times 99.5261)\\
&= \quad 98.0658
\end{aligned}
$$

We find then that the price of the 2-period zero coupon bond is less than the present value of its value at $i = 1$. That is, from Equation 9.12 we have

$$
P_0(2) = 97.8925 < e^{-r_0 \times \Delta} \times E[P_1(2)] = 98.0658 \tag{9.13}
$$

The price is lower because of a risk premium embedded in the price of longer term bonds.

What risk? Clearly, there is no default risk in U.S. Treasury bonds, as the U.S. government is extremely unlikely to default on its obligations. That is, an investment in Treasury securities is safe if held to maturity. However, as discussed in Chapters 3, 4, and 7, an investment in Treasury securities is risky because an investor would suffer capital losses if the bond is sold before maturity after an increase in interest rates.

For later reference, let us define the (dollar) risk premium as follows:

Definition 9.2 *The* **dollar risk premium** *from investing in the long-term bond with maturity* $i = 2$ *is defined as*

$$\text{Dollar risk premium} = e^{-r_0 \times \Delta} \times E\left[P_1(2)\right] - P_0(2) \tag{9.14}$$

[handwritten annotations: Av $(N P_{1u} + N P_{1o})$; price now]

The word "dollar" clarifies that this is a risk premium expressed in dollar units, rather than in percentages. The dollar risk premium defined in Equation 9.14 is useful in binomial trees, as shown below. In the example above we have:

$$\text{Dollar risk premium} = e^{-r_0 \times \Delta} \times E\left[P_1(2)\right] - P_0(2) = 0.1733 \tag{9.15}$$

[handwritten annotation: Amt: in Dollars.]

9.3.2 The Market Price of Interest Rate Risk

We now establish a relation between derivative securities. First, consider again the derivation of N_1 and N_2: recall that given N_2 in Equation 9.9, we computed the value of N_1 by substituting N_2 into Equation 9.7, thereby obtaining Equation 9.10. Equivalently, we could substitute the same value of N_2 into Equation 9.8, in which case we would obtain $N_1 = V_{1,d} - N_2 \times P_{1,d}(2)$. Clearly, the solution of the system of equation N_1 is the same independently of where we substitute. That is, we have

$$N_1 \times 100 = V_{1,u} - N_2 \times P_{1,u}(2) = V_{1,d} - N_2 \times P_{1,d}(2)$$

This implies that we can also write, *equivalently*

$$N_1 = \frac{1}{100} \times \{E[V_1] - N_2 \times E[P_1(2)]\} \tag{9.16}$$

[handwritten annotation: Dep on Prob]

where $E[V_1] = pV_{1,u} + (1-p)V_{1,d}$ and $E[P_1(2)] = pP_{1,u}(2) + (1-p)P_{1,d}(2)$. This expression leads to an interesting relation. In fact, recall from Equation 9.11 that the value of the security at time $i = 0$ is given by $V_0 = N_1 \times P_0(1) + N_2 \times P_0(2)$. Thus, we can substitute N_1 into Equation 9.16 to obtain

[handwritten annotation: Prious!]

$$V_0 = E[V_1] \times \frac{P_0(1)}{100} - N_2 \times E[P_1(2)] \times \frac{P_0(1)}{100} + N_2 \times P_0(2)$$

Factoring out N_2 and rearranging, we obtain

[handwritten annotations: 1yr ; at 1yr ; 2yr ; Dont get...]

$$N_2 \times \left[E[P_1(2)] \times \frac{P_0(1)}{100} - P_0(2)\right] = E[V_1] \times \frac{P_0(1)}{100} - V_0$$

Substitute $N_2 = (V_{1,u} - V_{1,d})/(P_{1,u}(2) - P_{1,d}(2))$ (see Equation 9.9), divide both sides by $(V_{1,u} - V_{1,d})$, and remember that $P_0(1) = 100 \times e^{-r_0 \times \Delta}$, to obtain the following relation:

[handwritten annotations: ZCB's ; What the actual Fuck ; Derives.]

$$\frac{e^{-r_0 \times \Delta} E[P_1(2)] - P_0(2)}{P_{1,u}(2) - P_{1,d}(2)} = \frac{e^{-r_0 \times \Delta} E[V_1] - V_0}{V_{1,u} - V_{1,d}} \tag{9.17}$$

This is a key relation between securities in no arbitrage pricing. In fact, note the following:

1. The left-hand side involves only the zero coupon bond prices, while the right-hand side involves only the derivative security prices.

2. The expression on the left-hand side for the 2-period bond is *identical* to the expression on the right-hand side for the derivative security.

3. The numerators of both expressions are nothing other than the (dollar) *risk premium* investors require from holding bonds (on the left-hand side) or the derivative security (on the right-hand side), as defined in Equation 9.14 for the 2-period bond.

4. The denominators represent instead the risk of an investment in bonds (on the left-hand side) or in the derivative security (on the right-hand side), as it is given by the fluctuations of the security across the two possible states. For instance, the risk from investing in the 2-period zero coupon bond is

$$\text{Dollar Risk} = P_{1,u} - P_{1,d} = -1.2068 \tag{9.18}$$

Note that the negative sign is simply a reflection of the fact that the bond price *decreases* when the interest rate *increases*. It is not wise to use absolute values here, as for hedging purposes we need to know whether a security moves in the same direction as or in the opposite direction as the interest rates. The negative sign shows that it moves in the opposite direction.

Given this terminology, and the definition of a risk premium in Equation 9.14, Equation 9.17 says the following:

Fact 9.2 All *interest rate securities on a binomial tree have the same ratio between risk premium and risk. That is,*

$$\frac{\text{Risk premium}}{\text{Risk}} = \frac{e^{-r_0 \times \Delta} E[V_1] - V_0}{V_{1,u} - V_{1,d}} = \lambda_0 \tag{9.19}$$

where λ_0 *is* common *across all interest rate securities.*

That is, whether we are considering a zero coupon bond with maturity k or a derivative security, the ratio between risk premium and risk is always the same. This ratio has a name:

Definition 9.3 *The ratio between risk premium and risk that is common across all interest rate securities,* λ_0 *in Equation 9.19, is called* **market price of (interest rate) risk**.

9.3.3 An Interest Rate Security Pricing Formula

Fact 9.2 above has an important implication for the pricing of derivative securities. If we *know* λ_0 at time $i = 0$, we can compute the price of any security as

$$V_0 = e^{-r_0 \times \Delta} \times E[V_1] - \lambda_0 \times (V_{1,u} - V_{1,d}) \tag{9.20}$$

How can we compute λ_0? We can use the information about the bond with maturity $i = 2$ to compute it

$$\lambda_0 = \frac{e^{-r_0 \times \Delta} E[P_1(2)] - P_0(2)}{P_{1,u}(2) - P_{1,d}(2)} \tag{9.21}$$

This methodology leads to the second recipe to price derivative securities.

Recipe 2:

1. Compute the market price of risk λ_0 from Equation 9.21;

2. Compute the price of the interest rate security from the pricing formula in Equation 9.20.

For instance, from Table 9.3, we obtain:

$$\lambda_0 = \frac{e^{-r_0 \times \Delta} E[P_1(2)] - P_0(2)}{P_{1,u}(2) - P_{1,d}(2)} = \frac{98.0658 - 97.8925}{98.3193 - 99.5261} = -0.1436 \qquad (9.22)$$

We can then apply this number to compute the price of any interest rate security by using Equation 9.20. As an example, we can compute the value of the interest rate securities in Examples 9.1 through 9.3 as follows:

1. (Option)

    (*a*) Present value of expected payoff $= 0.9913 \times (p \times 0 + (1-p) \times 1.05) = 0.5205$

    (*b*) Risk adjustment $= \lambda_0 \times (0 - 1.05) = 0.1508$

    (*c*) Value $= (a) - (b) = 0.3697$.

2. (Swap)

    (*a*) Present value of expected payoff $= 0.9913 \times [p \times 0.695 + (1-p) \times (-0.525)] = 0.084$

    (*b*) Risk adjustment $= \lambda_0 \times [0.695 - (-0.525)] = -0.175$

    (*c*) Value $= (a) - (b) = 0.259$.

3. (Bond Option)

    (*a*) Present value of expected payoff $= 0.9913 \times [p \times 0 + (1-p) \times 0.5261] = 0.261$

    (*b*) Risk adjustment $= \lambda_0 \times [0 - 0.5261] = 0.076$

    (*c*) Value $= (a) - (b) = 0.185$.

The key is that once we know λ_0 and the probability p, the pricing formula is always identical, and it can be applied to price any interest rate derivative or security.

9.3.4   What If We Do Not Know p?

What if we make a mistake and miscalculate p? Does this imply that all of our calculations go astray because of it? It seems like this methodology is inferior to the previous one based on dynamic replication, as now we need to know p.

In fact, as it turns out, even if we make a mistake in computing p in the original tree, the pricing of the interest rate securities is not affected. The key is to realize that λ_0 also depends on p itself (see Equation 9.19). Thus, if we miscalculate p, we will also miscalculate the risk adjustment. It turns out that one error exactly counterbalances the other. For instance, Table 9.7 shows the value of the market price of risk λ_0, and the value of the option discussed in Example 9.1 for values of the probability p ranging between 10%

Table 9.7 The Value of the Option for Various Probabilities p

Probability	Present Value of Expected Payoff	Market Price of Risk	Risk Adjustment	Value at $i = 0$
p	$e^{-r_0 \times \Delta} E[V_1]$	λ_0	$\lambda_0 \times (V_{1,u} - V_{1,d})$	V_0
0.1	0.9368	-0.5401	0.5671	0.3697
0.2	0.8327	-0.4410	0.4630	0.3697
0.3	0.7286	-0.3419	0.3589	0.3697
0.4	0.6245	-0.2427	0.2549	0.3697
0.5	0.5205	-0.1436	0.1508	0.3697
0.6	0.4164	-0.0445	0.0467	0.3697
0.6448	0.3697	0.0000	0.0000	0.3697
0.7	0.3123	0.0547	-0.0574	0.3697
0.8	0.2082	0.1538	-0.1615	0.3697
0.9	0.1041	0.2529	-0.2656	0.3697

and 90%. The last column contains the key result: The value of the security is always equal to \$0.5385 independently of the probability p (in the first column).

Table 9.7 shows that as the probability p increases, the expected discounted value of the future payoff decreases, as shown in Column 2 (recall that the option pays when the interest rate declines). However, this effect is counterbalanced by another equally powerful effect, and this is that the risk adjustment (Column 4) is also declining. The reason is that an increase in p also changes the market price of risk λ_0, as shown in Column 3. To understand this effect, recall that we compute λ_0 from the price of the bond that expires at time $i = 2$. In particular, an increase in the probability p decreases the expected discounted value of the long-term bond $e^{-r_0 \times \Delta} E[P_1(2)]$, and thus the risk premium in Equation 9.14. Thus, the market price of risk λ_0 becomes less negative as the probability p increases.

9.4 RISK NEUTRAL PRICING

Table 9.7 also shows that for $p = 0.6448$ the risk adjustment λ_0 necessary to evaluate the derivative security is zero. Denote this special probability p^*. In this case, the pricing Equation 9.20 is simply equal to

$$V_0 = e^{-r_0 \times \Delta} \times E^*[V_1] \tag{9.23}$$

where

$$E^*[V_1] = p^* \times V_{1,u} + (1 - p^*) \times V_{1,d} \tag{9.24}$$

The pricing Equation 9.23 is much simpler to remember than Equation 9.20, as it says that the price of the option is simply equal to the discounted value of the future payoff, in which we use the risk free rate to discount the payoff. In particular, the complicated quantity λ_0, the market price of risk, is not there. However, recall, Equation 9.23 is obtained by using a very special probability, $p^* = 0.6448$, which is larger than the true (original) probability $p = 0.5$, which underlies the original tree in Table 9.2. Yet, if we had a methodology to compute that particular probability p^* which makes the pricing Equation 9.23 true, it would be a tremendous simplification for the pricing of interest rate securities.

9.4.1 Risk Neutral Probability

How can we compute this probability p^* that makes Equation 9.23 true? Recall that this probability is the one that makes the market price of risk $\lambda_0 = 0$. Because λ_0 is common across all securities, it follows that the probability p^* is the same for all securities. In particular, the pricing Equation 9.23 must hold for the zero coupon bond

$$
\begin{aligned}
P_0(2) &= e^{-r_0 \times \Delta} \times E^*[P_1] \\
&= e^{-r_0 \times \Delta} \times (p^* \times P_{1,u}(2) + (1 - p^*) \times P_{1,d}(2))
\end{aligned}
$$

From the zero coupon bond tree in Table 9.3, we know $P_{1,u}$ and $P_{1,d}$, while $P_0(2)$ is known from today's bond price. Thus, we can solve for p^* obtaining

$$
p^* = \frac{e^{r_0 \times \Delta} P_0(2) - P_{1,d}(2)}{P_{1,u}(2) - P_{1,d}(2)}
\tag{9.25}
$$

Definition 9.4 *The* **risk neutral probability** *p^* is the particular value of the probability p such that* every *interest rate security is given by the present value of future expected payoff, where the present value is computed using the risk free rate. That is, such that Equations 9.23 and 9.24 hold. The risk neutral probability p^* can be computed out of the current two period bond tree in Table 9.3 from Equation 9.25.*

9.4.2 The Price of Interest Rate Securities

The risk neutral probability p^* and the risk neutral valuation formula allow us to obtain a third (equivalent) methodology to obtain the price of an interest rate security.

Recipe 3:

1. Compute the risk neutral probability p^* from Equation 9.25;

2. Compute the price of the interest rate security from the pricing formula in Equation 9.23.

For instance, the risk neutral probability p^* in Table 9.7 is computed as follows

$$
p^* = \frac{e^{r_0 \times \Delta} P_0(2) - P_{1,d}(2)}{P_{1,u}(2) - P_{1,d}(2)} = \frac{e^{0.0174/2} 97.8925 - 99.5261}{98.3193 - 99.5261} = 0.6448
\tag{9.26}
$$

We can then apply this risk neutral probability to compute the price of any interest rate security by using Equation 9.23. As an example, the value of the interest rate securities in Examples 9.1 through 9.1 can be computed as follows:

1. (Option) $V_0 = 0.9913 \times [\, p^* \times 0 + (1 - p^*) \times 1.05 \,] = 0.3697$

2. (Swap) $V_0 = 0.9913 \times [\, p^* \times 0.695 + (1 - p^*) \times (-0.525) \,] = 0.259$

3. (Bond Option) $V_0 = 0.9913 \times [\, p^* \times 0 + (1 - p^*) \times 0.5261 \,] = 0.185$

It works beautifully.

Table 9.8 The Swap Tree

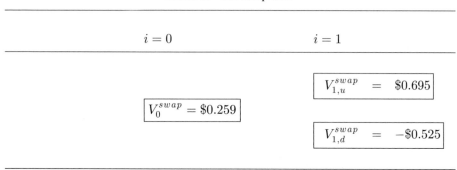

$i = 0$	$i = 1$
	$V_{1,u}^{swap}$ = $0.695
V_0^{swap} = $0.259	
	$V_{1,d}^{swap}$ = −$0.525

9.4.3 Risk Neutral Pricing and Dynamic Replication

The simplicity of the risk neutral methodology is its main virtue. It is important to realize that there is no underlying assumption that market participants are risk neutral. They are not, as in fact under the true probability ($p = 1/2$ in the tree in Table 9.2), market participants would require a risk premium to hold long-term bonds, given in Equation 9.14 in Section 9.3.1. The risk neutral methodology in Recipe 3 is just a convenient way of using the no arbitrage argument to obtain the price of derivative securities. Underlying its logic is the existence of the replicating portfolio in Definition 9.1.

What is key to realize, however, is that the dynamic replication strategy exists among any two interest rate securities. For instance, we saw in Chapter 1 and 5, the swap market has grown tremendously in the last two decades, and it is larger now, for instance, than the U.S. Treasury bond market. In the context of our Example 9.2, we considered the swap as a derivative security, whose price depends on the one of Treasuries. However, in our model, if we happen to know the value of swaps, we can replicate the options, or even the payoff of Treasuries, by using swaps instead. For instance, the next example shows the use of swaps to replicate the option in Example 9.1. Risk neutral pricing here is instrumental to derive the price of the swap. Given that, we can use it to replicate the option.

■ **EXAMPLE 9.4**

We are going to use a portfolio with N_2 swaps (as in Example 9.2), and N_1 of 1-period bonds. The methodology is the same as in Section 9.2.1, namely, Equations 9.9 and 9.10, with the only difference that instead of the value of bonds, we must use the value of the swap along the way. In particular, let V_{ij}^{swap} be the value of the swap in node ij. In Example 9.2 we obtained V_0 = $0.259, and thus the swap binomial tree is as in Table 9.8.

Using the formulas for N_1 and N_2 in Equations 9.10 and 9.9, respectively, we obtain that the portfolio of a swap and short-term bond is given by

$$N_2 = \frac{V_{1,u} - V_{1,d}}{V_{1,u}^{swap} - V_{1,d}^{swap}} = \frac{0 - 1.05}{0.695 - (-0.525)} = -0.861$$

$$N_1 = \frac{1}{100} \times \left[V_{1,u} - N_2 \times V_{1,u}^{swap}\right] = \frac{1}{100} \times [0 - (-0.861) \times 0.695] = 0.006$$

The value of this portfolio is

$$\Pi_0 = N_1 \times P_0(1) + N_2 \times V_0^{swap} = 0.006 \times \$99.1338 - 0.861 \times \$0.259 = \$0.3697$$

The value of the portfolio is identical to the value of the option that was obtained by using the portfolio of bonds, as in Table 9.4. Does this replicating portfolio replicate?

$$\begin{aligned}
\Pi_{1,u} &= N_1 \times P_{1,u}(1) + N_2 \times V_{1,u}^{swap} = 0.006 \times 100 - 0.861 \times \$0.695 = \$0 \\
\Pi_{1,d} &= N_1 \times P_{1,d}(1) + N_2 \times V_{1,d}^{swap} = 0.006 \times 100 - 0.861 \times \$(-0.525) = \$1.05
\end{aligned}$$

It replicates the option in Table 9.5 exactly.

9.4.4 Risk Neutral Expectation of Future Interest Rates

The expected future interest rate under the risk neutral probability is given by

$$E^*[r_1] = p^* \times r_{1,u} + (1-p^*) \times r_{1,d} = 0.6448 \times 3.39\% + 0.3552 \times 0.95 = 2.5234\% \quad (9.27)$$

This number is much higher than the true expected interest rate computed in Equation 9.1, which was equal to $E[r_1] = 2.17\%$. Risk neutral pricing is tantamount to including the risk premium in the probability of an up move (from p to p^*) and thus increasing the predicted future interest rates. However, this does *not* mean that market participants expect the interest rate in six months to be 2.5234%, instead of 2.17%. The higher risk neutral predicted rate is due only to the higher discount that market participants require to hold risky securities.

We are going to see that to some extent, the risk neutral expectation of future interest rates is close to the forward rate. Indeed, from the data in Table 9.1, the continuously compounded forward rate between period $i = 1$ and $i = 2$ is given by

$$f(0, 1, 2) = -\frac{1}{2} \times \ln\left(\frac{P_0(1)}{P_0(2)}\right) = 2.52\%$$

This is indeed very close to the risk neutral expected future interest rate in Equation 9.27. Note, in particular, that the forward rate is quite different from the true expected future interest rate $E[r_1] = 2.17\%$, as discussed in Chapter 7 (see e.g. Example 7.2). This finding has two implications:

1. Forward rates are *not* equal to the market expectation of future interest rates. In this model, the former is 2.52% while the latter is only 2.17%.

2. The forward rate (=2.52%) is not even equal to the risk neutral expected future interest rate (=2.5234%), although they are quite close.

Point 1 implies that we should be careful in interpreting futures rates as expected future interest rates, because although there is a relation, they are not the same. Thus, if today we observe high forward rates we should think about two possibilities: Either market participants expect higher future interest rates; *or* they are strongly averse to risk, and thus the price of long term bonds is low today. From our earlier discussion, high aversion to risk manifests itself in a high (negative) market price of risk λ_0 or, equivalently, on a high risk neutral probability p^*. The evidence presented in Chapter 7 shows that the second interpretation is more consistent with the data.

Point 2 states that the forward rate is close to the risk neutral expected future interest rate. Although the equality is much closer than with true probabilities, the two numbers are not exactly the same. Briefly, the reason is that risk neutral pricing is based on the notion of dynamic replication, as discussed in Section 9.2.1, which involves the trading of securities. Thus, the important quantities are the *prices* at which transactions occur. Interest *rates*, as discussed many times, only represent prices through a convex relation. The fact that there is not a linear relation between prices and interest rates is the source of the difference between expected future interest rates $E^*[r_1]$ and forward rates $f(0, 1, 2)$. This can be seen directly from the risk neutral pricing formula (9.23), which implies that for zero coupon bonds

$$P_0(2) = e^{-r_0 \times \Delta} E^*[P_1(2)]$$

From the definition of forward rate, however, we also have

$$P_0(2) = e^{-r_0 \times \Delta} e^{-f(0,1,2) \times \Delta} \times 100$$

Comparing these two equations, because both must be true, and because we can write $E^*[P_1(2)] = E^*[e^{-r_1 \times \Delta}] \times 100$ it follows that

$$e^{-f(0,1,2) \times \Delta} = E^*[e^{-r_1 \times \Delta}] \tag{9.28}$$

Finally, note that the exponential function $e^{-r_1 \times \Delta}$ is a decreasing convex function of the rate r_1. Thus, Jensen's Inequality implies that[3]

$$E^*[e^{-r_1 \times \Delta}] > e^{-E^*[r_1] \times \Delta} \tag{9.29}$$

Equality 9.28 and Inequality 9.29 imply that

$$e^{-f(0,1,2) \times \Delta} > e^{-E^*[r_1] \times \Delta}$$

which implies

$$f(0, 1, 2) < E^*[r_1] \tag{9.30}$$

Note that this is indeed true in the above example, in which $f(0, 1, 2) = 2.52\%$ and $E^*[r_1] = 2.5234\%$. This discussion also suggests an adjustment to be made to the risk neutral expected future interest rate to make it closer to the forward rate, and we will discuss this adjustment – a popular practice in the industry – in Chapter 21.

9.5   SUMMARY

In this chapter we covered the following topics:

1. One step interest rate binomial tree: This type of binomial tree describes the two possible scenario for the short term-rate next period.

---

[3]Jensen's inequality states that if $f(x)$ is a convex function of a variable x, then $E[f(x)] > f[E(x)]$.

2. Bond price binomial tree: From the two scenarios for one-period interest rates next period, we can compute the two scenarios of the one-period bond next period. Using today's current quoted price of this bond, we obtain the tree for a two-period bond.

3. Replicating portfolio: This is a portfolio made up of a long-term security and short-term bond that replicates the payoffs of another interest rate security in the two possible interest rate scenarios next period. For instance, a long-term bond and a short-term bond in appropriate proportion can replicate the payoff of an interest rate option. The value of the replicating portfolio must equal the value of the derivative security, otherwise an arbitrage opportunity arises.

4. Market price of risk: No arbitrage requires that all long-term securities must have the same ratio of expected return to risk, otherwise an arbitrage opportunity arises.

5. Risk neutral probability: This is a "fake" probability that enables us to obtain a convenient formula for the pricing of derivative securities by no arbitrage. Given this "fake" probability p^*, the value of any interest rate security on the binomial tree equals the expected present value of the future payoff discounted at the risk free rate. p^* differs from the real probability of an upward movement in the interest rate as it contains a component that is due to the risk premium that investors require to hold long-term bonds.

9.6 EXERCISES

1. Consider the interest rate tree in Table 9.9.

    (a) Compute the expected 6-month Treasury rate $E[r_1]$.

    (b) The 1-year Treasury bill is trading at $P_0(2) = 97.4845$. What is the (continuously compounded) forward rate for the periods $i = 1$ to $i = 2$? How does it compare with the expected rate computed in Part (a)? Explain.

    (c) Compute the market price of risk λ. Interpret.

    (d) Compute the risk neutral probability p^*. Interpret.

2. Consider again Exercise 1 and the interest rate tree in Table 9.9.

    (a) Consider an option with payoff

    $$\text{Option payoff at } 1 = 100 \times max(r_1 - 2\%, 0)$$

    Compute the value at time $i = 0$ of the option by using the three methodologies discussed in Sections 9.2.1, 9.3.3 and 9.4.2.

    (b) Use the risk neutral pricing methodology to compute the value of a bond option with payoff

    $$\text{Bond option payoff at } 1 = max(P_1(2) - 98.5, 0)$$

3. Consider the tree in Table 9.10. You estimated the *risk neutral* probability to move up the tree to be $p^* = 1/2$.

Table 9.9   A One-Step Binomial Interest Rate Tree

period $\Longrightarrow$	$i = 0$	$i = 1$
time (in years) $\Longrightarrow$	$t = 0$	$t = 0.5$

$r_0 = 2\%$

$r_{1,u} = 4\%$ with prob. $p = 1/2$

$r_{1,d} = 1\%$ with prob. $1 - p = 1/2$

Table 9.10   A One-Period Risk Neutral Interest Rate Tree

period $\Longrightarrow$	$i = 0$	$i = 1$
time (in years) $\Longrightarrow$	$t = 0$	$t = 0.5$

$r_0 = 4\%$

$r_{1,u} = 6\%$ with risk neutral prob. $p^* = 1/2$

$r_{1,d} = 3\%$ with risk neutral prob. $1 - p^* = 1/2$

(a) Compute the value of the zero coupon bonds maturing at time $i = 1$ and at $i = 2$.

(b) Compute the continuously compounded yields for both bonds.

(c) Compute the value of an option with payoff

$$\text{Option Payoff at } 1 = 100 \times max(r_1 - 4\%, 0)$$

(d) Set up the replicating portfolio that uses the bond prices determined in Part (a), that is able to replicate the option's payoff. Check that this portfolio in fact replicates the option.

(e) Given the tree for the option, set up a replicating portfolio made of the short-term bond and *the option* that is able to replicate the prices of the long-term bond at time 1, that is, $P_{1,u}(2)$ and $P_{1,d}(2)$.

4. In the previous exercise, do you have enough information to compute the market price of risk λ, and therefore the expected return on a bond maturing at time $i = 2$? Explain.

5. The current 6-month and 1-year Treasury bills are trading at $P_{bill}(0, 0.5) = 97.531$ and $P_{bill}(0, 1) = 95.1241$, respectively. Consider now a binomial tree with root r_0, and $r_{1,u}$ and $r_{1,d}$ as two interest rate scenarios after an upward or downward movement in the interest rate, respectively.

(a) What is r_0?

(b) Let $p^* = 0.5$ be the risk neutral probability. Do you have enough information to pin down a unique value of $r_{1,u}$ and $r_{1,d}$? Provide at least three examples of values of the pair $(r_{1,u}, r_{1,d})$ that are consistent with the two bond prices above. What is the difference across the three pairs of values?

(c) An option with payoff

$$\text{Option payoff at } 1 = 100 \times max(r_1 - 5\%, 0)$$

is also trading at $C_0(1) = \$0.97531$. Do you now have sufficient information to pin down the pair $(r_{1,u}, r_{1,d})$? Explain.

(d) Suppose you did not know $p^* = 0.5$. What other information would you need to compute also p^*? Provide an example.

CHAPTER 10

MULTI-STEP BINOMIAL TREES

We now move to multi-step binomial trees. The key is to realize that a multi-step tree is nothing more than a sequence of one-step trees. Therefore, any argument we made for each little tree in Chapter 9 holds here too.

10.1 A TWO-STEP BINOMIAL TREE

Consider extending the binomial tree in Table 9.2 in Chapter 9 to one more period. Recall that the interest rates on the tree are continuously compounded (see discussion in Section 9.1.1 in Chapter 9). The binomial tree in Table 10.1 is recombining, which means that an "up and down" movement in interest rates leads to the same level as a "down and up" movement. This, of course, need not be the case in general. But using recombining trees becomes particularly helpful when we move to very long trees, with hundreds of steps. Non-recombining trees require massive computing power to be solved.

Finally, we assume that the probability p of an up movement is constant and equal to 1/2 along the tree. This assumption is not necessary, and it is made here only for convenience. This interest rate tree was computed on January 8, 2002, in a way that its implied forecasts of future interest rates are reasonable given the information available at that time. In particular, since the top node uu is reached with probability $p \times p = 1/4$, the bottom one dd is reached with probability $(1 - p) \times (1 - p) = 1/4$, and the middle with probability

Table 10.1   A Two Step Interest Rate Tree

period $\Longrightarrow$	$i = 0$	$i = 1$	$i = 2$
time $\Longrightarrow$	$t = 0$	$t = 0.5$	$t = 1$

$$r_{2,uu} = 5.00\%$$

$$r_{1,u} = 3.39\%$$

$$r_0 = 1.74\%$$

$$\begin{aligned} r_{2,ud} \\ r_{2,du} \end{aligned} = 2.56\%$$

$$r_{1,d} = 0.95\%$$

$$r_{2,dd} = 0.11\%$$

probability of "up" movement: $p = 1/2$

Table 10.2   Treasury STRIPS on January 8, 2002

Maturity	Price	Yield
0.5	99.1338	1.74 %
1	97.8925	2.13 %
1.5	96.1462	2.62 %

Source: *The Wall Street Journal.*

$2 \times p \times (1 - p) = 1/2$, we have the predicted rate in six and twelve months

$$
\begin{aligned}
E[r_1] &= \frac{1}{2}r_{1,u} + \frac{1}{2}r_{1,d} = 2.17\% \\
E[r_2] &= \frac{1}{4}r_{2,uu} + \frac{1}{2}r_{2,ud} + \frac{1}{4}r_{2,dd} = 2.6\%
\end{aligned}
$$

Given the current 6-month interest rate of 1.74%, much lower than the post-war average rate of about 5%, it was reasonable to expect a substantial increase in the 6-month interest rate within the following year, all the way up to 2.56%.

The zero coupon term structure of interest rates on January 8, 2002, is in Figure 9.1 in Chapter 9, while the STRIPS up to maturity $T = 1.5$ are reported in Table 10.2.

10.2 RISK NEUTRAL PRICING

The two key results discovered in Chapter 9 were:

$$p^* = \frac{e^{r_0 \Delta} P_0(2) - P_{1,d}(2)}{P_{1,u}(2) - P_{1,d}(2)} \Rightarrow \lambda_0 = 0$$

1. We can obtain the price of any interest rate security at time 0 by using the risk neutral approach, that is

$$V_0 = e^{-r_0 \times \Delta} \times [p^* \times V_{1,u} + (1 - p^*) \times V_{1,d}] \qquad (10.1)$$

2. We can replicate the payoff of any interest rate security by using another interest rate security.

We now apply these concepts to binomial trees with more steps (two, for the moment).

In particular, we found in Chapter 9 that given the interest rate tree in Table 10.1 and the zero coupon bonds in Table 10.2 the *risk neutral* probability of moving up at time $i = 0$ is $p^* = 0.6448$. Assume that like the true probability p in the interest rate tree in Table 10.1, the risk neutral probability p^* is constant as well on the tree. What is the price, say, of a zero coupon bond maturing on $i = 3$ under these conditions? The next section answers these questions.

10.2.1 Risk Neutral Pricing by Backward Induction

We can compute the price of the 3-period bond by starting from the end of the tree, and applying the one-step risk neutral pricing formula repeatedly. Recall the notation first: Let $\Delta = 0.5$ denote the time step and

$$P_{i,j}(k) = \text{Bond price at time } i \text{ in node } j \text{ with maturity } k$$

From the interest rate tree in Table 10.1 the bond prices in the three nodes at time $i = 2$ are given by

$$
\begin{aligned}
P_{2,uu}(3) &= e^{-r_{2,uu} \times \Delta} \times 100 = 97.5310 \\
\left\{ \begin{array}{c} P_{2,ud}(3) \\ P_{2,du}(3) \end{array} \right\} &= e^{-r_{2,du} \times \Delta} \times 100 = 98.7282 \\
P_{2,dd}(3) &= e^{-r_{2,dd} \times \Delta} \times 100 = 99.9450
\end{aligned}
$$

What about the prices at time $i = 1$? Moving backward on the tree, we can apply the formula in Equation 10.1, but rather than time $i = 0$, we use time $i = 1$, in both nodes $(1, u)$ and $(1, d)$. In this case, the formula for bonds in the two nodes becomes

$$
\begin{aligned}
(1, u) \text{ node: } P_{1,u}(3) &= e^{-r_{1,u} \times \Delta} \times [p^* \times P_{2,uu}(3) + (1 - p^*) \times P_{2,ud}(3)] \quad (10.2) \\
&= 0.9831 \times [0.6448 \times 97.5310 + 0.3552 \times 98.7282] \\
&= 96.3098 \\
(1, d) \text{ node: } P_{1,d}(3) &= e^{-r_{1,d} \times \Delta} \times [p^* \times P_{2,du}(3) + (1 - p^*) \times P_{2,dd}(3)] \quad (10.3) \\
&= 0.9951 \times [0.6448 \times 98.7282 + 0.3552 \times 99.9450] \\
&= 98.6904
\end{aligned}
$$

We can now use these two prices to compute the price today

$$
\begin{aligned}
P_0(3) &= e^{-r_0 \times \Delta} \times [p^* \times P_{1,u}(3) + (1 - p^*) \times P_{1,d}(3)] \\
&= 0.9913 \times [0.6448 \times 96.3098 + 0.3552 \times 98.6904] \\
&= 96.3137 \qquad (10.4)
\end{aligned}
$$

Table 10.3 The 3-Period Zero Coupon Bond Tree with Constant $p^* = 0.6448$

$i = 0$ $t = 0$	$i = 1$ $t = 0.5$	$i = 2$ $t = 1$	$i = 3$ $t = 1.5$

$$P_{3,uuu}(3) = 100$$

$$P_{2,uu}(3) = 97.5310$$

$$P_{1,u}(3) = 96.3098$$

$$\left.\begin{array}{l} P_{3,uud}(3) \\ P_{3,udu}(3) \\ P_{3,duu}(3) \end{array}\right\} = 100$$

$$P_0(3) = 96.3137$$

$$\left.\begin{array}{l} P_{2,ud}(3) \\ P_{2,du}(3) \end{array}\right\} = 98.7282$$

$$P_{1,d}(3) = 98.6904$$

$$\left.\begin{array}{l} P_{3,udd}(3) \\ P_{3,dud}(3) \\ P_{3,ddu}(3) \end{array}\right\} = 100$$

$$P_{2,dd}(3) = 99.9450$$

$$P_{3,ddd}(3) = 100$$

The price of the bond expiring at $i = 3$ is $P_0(3) = \$96.3137$. Table 10.3 plots the resulting zero coupon bond tree.

The risk neutral pricing methodology is very convenient, as it provides a simple rule to obtain prices of interest rate securities. However, recall the two key ingredients to use the risk neutral pricing techniques recipe:

1. The interest rate tree (e.g., Table 10.1).

2. The risk neutral probability (e.g. $p^* = 0.6448$)

Given these two quantities, we can compute the price of any interest rate security. Let's do this by looking at the following example.

■ **EXAMPLE 10.1**

Consider a security that pays at $i = 2$, $(t = 1)$, the following amount

$$\text{Payoff at } i = 2 : V_2 = \max\left(P_2(3) - K, 0\right) + \max\left(K - P_2(3), 0\right)$$

where $K = 98.7282$. This payoff is given by a combination of a long call and a long put with the same strike price, an investment strategy called a **Straddle**. A straddle pays little when the bond price at maturity is close to the common strike price K,

Table 10.4 A Straddle

period $\Longrightarrow$	$i = 0$	$i = 1$	$i = 2$
time $\Longrightarrow$	$t = 0$	$t = 0.5$	$t = 1$

$$V_{2,uu} = 1.1972$$

$$V_{1,u} = 0.7590$$

$$V_0 = 0.6366$$

$$\frac{V_{2,ud}}{V_{2,du}} = 0$$

$$V_{1,d} = 0.4301$$

$$V_{2,dd} = 1.2169$$

but it pays handsomely if the price is far away from the strike, independently of whether it is high or low. Because it pays when the price is far away from K, this strategy tends to payoff in an environment with high bond price volatility. The risk neutral pricing methodology can provide the price of this security immediately by using a backward methodology. Namely, we start from the end of the tree ($i = 2$) and compute the payoffs of the security. And then we move backward on the tree by adopting Equation 10.1 in the various nodes. The risk neutral probability p^* to use is the same as above, namely, $p^* = 0.6448$, as this probability applies to *all* interest rate securities. Table 10.4 contains the tree in this case. The price is $V_0 = 0.6366$.

10.2.2 Dynamic Replication

It is important to recall that behind the risk neutral pricing approach there is an underlying *replication strategy* that allows a trader to replicate the final payoff by a portfolio of long-term and short-term bonds. In multistep trees, this portfolio needs to be rebalanced over time, as interest rate change. In this sense, the strategy is called dynamic replication strategy, or dynamic hedging strategy, as the strategy now involves the sale and purchases of bonds over time, as we move along the tree.

More specifically, the dynamic replication strategy involves positions in long-term and short-term bonds that change along the binomial tree. At each node (i, j), we let $N_{i,j}^L$ be the position in the bond expiring at $i = 3$, and $N_{i,j}^S$ be the position in the one-period bond expiring at $i + 1$.

How do we choose $N_{i,j}^L$ and $N_{i,j}^S$? The key is that a long tree tree is a sequence of little one-step binomial trees. Thus, the formulas are the same as (9.9) and (9.10) in Chapter 9, but applied along the longer tree. For instance, if we are at time $i = 1$ after an up movement, i.e., $(i, j) = (1, u)$, then the replicating portfolio calls for the following positions:

$$N_{1,u}^L = \frac{V_{2,uu} - V_{2,ud}}{P_{2,uu}(3) - P_{2,ud}(3)} \tag{10.5}$$

$$N_{1,u}^S = \frac{1}{100} \left[V_{2,uu} - N_{1,u}^L \times P_{2,uu}(3) \right] \tag{10.6}$$

and similarly in the node $(1, d)$.

Consider Example 10.1, for instance. The following trading strategy replicates the Straddle in Table 10.4.

■ **EXAMPLE 10.2**

Time $i = 0$: At time zero, the dynamic replication calls for

$$N_0^L = \frac{V_{1,u} - V_{1,d}}{P_{1,u}(3) - P_{1,d}(3)} = \frac{0.7590 - 0.4301}{96.3098 - 98.6904}$$

$$= -0.1381$$

$$N_0^S = \frac{1}{100} \left[V_{1,u} - N_0^L \times P_{1,u}(3) \right] = \frac{1}{100} \left[0.7590 - (-0.1381) \times 96.3098 \right]$$

$$= 0.1406$$

The value of the replicating portfolio is

$$\Pi_0 = N_0^S \times P_0(1) + N_0^L \times P_0(3) = 0.1406 \times 99.1338 - 0.1381 \times 96.3137 = 0.6366$$

Of course, the value of the portfolio is the same as the one we obtained from risk neutral pricing. Just to check, what happens to the portfolio at time $i = 1$ in the two nodes, u and d?

$$\Pi_{1,u} = N_0^S \times 100 + N_0^L \times P_{1,u}(3) = 0.1406 \times 100 - 0.1381 \times 96.3098$$

$$= 0.7590 = V_{i,u}$$

$$\Pi_{1,d} = N_0^S \times 100 + N_0^L \times P_{1,d}(3) = 0.1406 \times 100 - 0.1381 \times 98.6904$$

$$= 0.4301 = V_{i,d}$$

The portfolio, so far, replicates the straddle in Table 10.4. What happens next?

Time $i = 1$: At time $i = 1$, the new position in long-term bonds depends on whether the interest rate went up or down. Consider the two cases:

Node $(1, u)$: Apply Equations 10.5 and 10.6 again, to obtain

$$N_{1,u}^L = -1; \quad N_{1,u}^S = 0.9873$$

where note that $N_{1,u}^S$ is the position in bond $P_{1,u}(2)$, expiring at time $i = 2$, and whose value is $P_{1,u}(2) = 98.3193$ (see Table 9.3 in Chapter 9). How much does this portfolio cost? Let's denote this portfolio $\Pi_{1,u}^{new}$:

$$\Pi_{1,u}^{new} = N_{1,u}^S \times P_{1,u}(2) + N_{1,u}^L \times P_{1,u}(3)$$

$$= 0.9873 \times 98.3193 - 1 \times 96.3098$$

$$= 0.7590$$

The value of the portfolio equals the value of the security we are replicating. In particular, this portfolio value is also identical to the amount delivered in this node $(1, u)$ by the replicating portfolio formed at time 0. That is, we have

$$\Pi_{1,u} = \Pi_{1,u}^{new}$$

This implies that the old portfolio will deliver exactly enough money to buy the new portfolio. In other words, the trading strategy is *self financing*.

Does portfolio $\Pi_{1,u}^{new}$ replicate the final payoff at time $i = 2$?

$$
\begin{aligned}
\Pi_{2,uu}^{new} &= N_{1,u}^S \times 100 + N_{1,u}^L \times P_{2,uu}(3) = 0.9873 \times 100 - 1 \times 97.5310 \\
&= 1.1972 \\
\Pi_{2,ud}^{new} &= N_{1,u}^S \times 100 + N_{1,u}^L \times P_{2,ud}(3) = 0.9873 \times 100 - 1 \times 98.7282 \\
&= 0
\end{aligned}
$$

Yes, it works.

Node $(1, d)$**:** Apply Equations 10.5 and 10.6 but to the $(1, d)$ node, to obtain:

$$N_{1,u}^L = 1; \quad N_{1,u}^S = -0.9873$$

The cost of the new portfolio is now (recall from Table 9.3 in Chapter 9 that $P_{1,d}(2) = 99.5261$):

$$
\begin{aligned}
\Pi_{1,d}^{new} &= N_{1,d}^S \times P_{1,d}(2) + N_{1,d}^L \times P_{1,d}(3) \\
&= -0.9873 \times 99.5261 + 1 \times 98.6904 \\
&= 0.4301
\end{aligned}
$$

This implies, as before, that $\Pi_{1,d} = \Pi_{1,d}^{new}$, and thus that the old portfolio delivers enough cash to form the new portfolio. At time $i = 2$, then

$$
\begin{aligned}
\Pi_{2,du}^{new} &= N_{1,d}^S \times 100 + N_{1,d}^L \times P_{2,du}(3) = -0.9873 \times 100 + 1 \times 98.7282 \\
&= 0 \\
\Pi_{2,dd}^{new} &= N_{1,d}^S \times 100 + N_{1,d}^L \times P_{2,dd}(3) = -0.9873 \times 100 + 1 \times 99.9450 \\
&= 1.2169
\end{aligned}
$$

It works.

Table 10.5 shows the dynamic portfolio strategy over time. Although this procedure appears cumbersome, computers can be programmed to carry out the replication strategy automatically. Indeed, program trading has become a standard tool for proprietary trading desks and hedge funds. As trading strategies become increasingly complex, more and more powerful computers are employed to help decide the optimal trading strategy in order to achieve some goal, such as the replication of the straddle in Example 10.1.

Table 10.5 Dynamic Replication

$i = 0$	$i = 1$	$i = 2$
$t = 0$	$t = 0.5$	$t = 1$

$$- - - - - - -Rebalance - - - - - - -$$

$$
\begin{array}{l}
N^L_{1,u} = -1 \\
N^S_{1,u} = 0.9873 \\
\Pi^{new}_{2,uu} = 1.1972
\end{array}
$$

$$
\begin{array}{lcl}
N^L_0 = -0.1381 & \longrightarrow & N^L_{1,u} = -1 \\
N^S_0 = 0.1406 & \longrightarrow & N^S_{1,u} = 0.9873 \\
\Pi_{1,u} = 0.7590 & \longrightarrow & \Pi^{new}_{1,u} = 0.7590
\end{array}
\qquad
\begin{array}{l}
N^L_{1,u} = -1 \\
N^S_{1,u} = 0.9873 \\
\Pi^{new}_{2,ud} = 0
\end{array}
$$

$$
\begin{array}{l}
N^L_0 = -0.1381 \\
N^S_0 = 0.1406 \\
\Pi_0 = 0.6366
\end{array}
$$

held stable.

$$
\begin{array}{lcl}
N^L_0 = -0.1381 & \longrightarrow & N^L_{1,u} = 1 \\
N^S_0 = 0.1406 & \longrightarrow & N^S_{1,u} = -0.9873 \\
\Pi_{1,d} = 0.4301 & \longrightarrow & \Pi^{new}_{1,d} = 0.4301
\end{array}
\qquad
\begin{array}{l}
N^L_{1,d} = 1 \\
N^S_{1,d} = -0.9873 \\
\Pi^{new}_{2,du} = 0
\end{array}
$$

$$
\begin{array}{l}
N^L_{1,d} = 1 \\
N^S_{1,d} = -0.9873 \\
\Pi^{new}_{2,dd} = 1.2169
\end{array}
$$

10.3 MATCHING THE TERM STRUCTURE

The binomial tree in Table 10.3 was meant to illustrate the risk neutral methodology in longer trees. To this end, we assumed that the risk neutral probability p^* was the same along the tree. However, there is a problem, namely, that the price of the zero coupon bond that the tree produces, $P_0(3) = 96.3137$, is different from the traded prices on the same day (January 8, 2002). In fact, from Table 10.2, the price of the bond at that time was $P_0(3) = 96.1462$, which is lower. Since the risk neutral probability $p^* = 0.6448$ was computed from the 2-period bond $P_0(2)$, there is no a priori reason why it should be constant along the tree itself.

Assume then that p^* may change over time and denote by p_i^* its value at time i. The risk neutral probability obtained earlier is then denoted by $p_0^* = 0.6448$. The risk neutral probability at time $i = 1$ is denoted p_1^*. In the example above we have then simply assumed $p_1^* = p_0^*$, but this restriction is unnecessary.

How can we then compute p_1^*?

Unfortunately, it is not possible to find a simple formula like the one developed in Chapter 9 (see Equation 9.25). Instead, we must search for the value p_1^* that yields the correct price of the 3-period bond. Table 10.6 shows the zero coupon bond value obtained from the tree for various values of p_1^*, ranging from 0.1 to 0.9. More specifically, for each probability p_1^* in the first column, the computation of the 3-period bond is performed exactly as in Section 10.2.1, but with the only difference that when we compute $P_{1,u}(3)$ and $P_{1,d}(3)$, we use p_1^* in Equations 10.2 and 10.3 instead of p^*. The second column in Table 10.6 shows that the price of the 3-period zero coupon bond decreases as p_1^* increases, ranging from 96.9560 for $p_1^* = .1$ to 96.0129 for $p_1^* = .9$.

Table 10.6 also shows that when $p_1^* = 0.7869$, the model price of the zero coupon bond is 96.1462, which is equal to the current traded price in Table 10.2. The corresponding binomial tree for the 3-period bond is in Table 10.7.

Along with the risk neutral probability p_1^*, the value of derivative securities (and the dynamic replication) also change. For instance, the value of the security described in Example 10.1 is now given in Table 10.8.

10.4 MULTI-STEP TREES

We now extend the model to trees with longer maturity, or with more frequent steps. To build multi-steps trees, we need a methodology. The following procedure is particularly convenient.

1. Define the predicted future interest rate $E[r_i]$ for many future horizons $i = 1, 2, ..., n$.

2. Define some errors of the predictions (e.g., $r_{1,u} = 3.39\%$ and $r_{1,d} = 0.95\%$ are errors around the expected rate $E[r_1] = 2.17\%$).

3. Find the risk neutral probabilities that price bonds.

up + down are errors around expected!

Table 10.6 The 3-Period Zero Coupon Bond Price for Risk Neutral Probabilities p_1^*

RN Probability p_1^*	Model Price $P_0(3)$
0.1	96.9560
0.2	96.8381
0.3	96.7202
0.4	96.6024
0.5	96.4845
0.6	96.3666
0.7	96.2487
0.7869	96.1462
0.8	96.1308
0.9	96.0129

Table 10.7 The 3-Period Zero Coupon Bond Tree that Matches the Bond Data

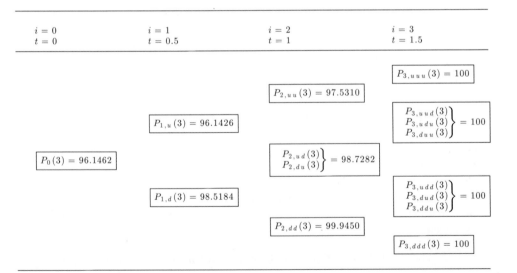

$i = 0$ $t = 0$	$i = 1$ $t = 0.5$	$i = 2$ $t = 1$	$i = 3$ $t = 1.5$

Table 10.8   The Price of the Straddle with $p_1^* = 0.7896$

period $\Longrightarrow$	$i = 0$	$i = 1$	$i = 2$
time $\Longrightarrow$	$t = 0$	$t = 0.5$	$t = 1$

$$V_{2,uu} = 1.1972$$

$$V_{1,u} = 0.9263$$

$$V_0 = 0.6830$$

$$\dfrac{V_{2,ud}}{V_{2,du}} = 0$$

$$V_{1,d} = 0.2580$$

$$V_{2,dd} = 1.2169$$

Step 1 depends on our best predictions of future monetary policy actions, and therefore, our predictions of future inflation, real GDP growth, and so on. These predictions may be based on statistical models, or even simply our forecasts of future rates. As in Chapter 7 we use data on 6-month rates from December 1961 to December 2001 and run a regression on r_{t+1} onto r_t. Given the estimated parameters, and the current interest rate $r_{Jan2002} = 1.74\%$, we can forecast the future interest rate as in Table 10.9. Specifically, the third column of this table reports the forecasts of the 6-month rate from July 2002 to January 2007. The prediction, according to the regression model, is that the interest rate will rise steadily in the next five years. Of course, predictions may be wrong, and they would have been in 2002: the Federal Reserve, concerned with the weakening of the U.S. economy, decreased the Federal funds rate further in 2002 and 2003. As a consequence, the realized (ex post) 6-month rate also decreased, from 1.71% in July 2002 to 0.95% in July 2003. However, rates climbed up quite rapidly after that, shooting up to 4.35% by January 2006, almost matching the model forecast (of 4.22% in the third column). For July, 2006 to January, 2007, the model's forecasts were even lower than the realized rate.

10.4.1   Building a Binomial Tree from Expected Future Rates

We now take these expected rates and build a binomial tree around them. Define the expected change in interest rate in the future as

$$m_i = E[r_{i+1} - r_i] \tag{10.7}$$

We then introduce errors in our predictions as follows:

$$r_{1,u} = r_0 + m_0 \times \Delta + \sigma\sqrt{\Delta} \tag{10.8}$$

$$r_{1,d} = r_0 + m_0 \times \Delta - \sigma\sqrt{\Delta} \tag{10.9}$$

Table 10.9 Interest Rate Prediction as of 8 January 2002

Semester i	Month/Year	Model Prediction	Realized Rate Ex Post
1	Jul 2002	2.17 %	1.71 %
2	Jan 2003	2.56 %	1.20 %
3	Jul 2003	2.91 %	0.95 %
4	Jan 2004	3.22 %	0.97 %
5	Jul 2004	3.51 %	1.67 %
6	Jan 2005	3.77 %	2.62 %
7	Jul 2005	4.00 %	3.45 %
8	Jan 2006	4.22 %	4.35 %
9	Jul 2006	4.41 %	5.12 %
10	Jan 2007	4.58 %	5.01 %

Data Source: Federal Reserve.

for the first period, where the up or down movements occur with probability 1/2. The second period, similarly,

$$
\begin{aligned}
r_{2,uu} &= r_{1,u} + m_1 \times \Delta + \sigma\sqrt{\Delta} \\
r_{2,ud} &= r_{1,u} + m_1 \times \Delta - \sigma\sqrt{\Delta} \\
r_{2,du} &= r_{1,d} + m_1 \times \Delta + \sigma\sqrt{\Delta} \\
r_{2,dd} &= r_{1,d} + m_1 \times \Delta - \sigma\sqrt{\Delta}
\end{aligned}
$$

and so on. This model naturally generates a recombining tree. In fact, note that by substituting $r_{1,u}$ and $r_{1,d}$ from the first equations, we find

$$
r_{2,ud} = r_0 + (m_0 + m_1) \times \Delta = r_{2,du}. \tag{10.10}
$$

That is, an up and down movement leads to the same rate as a down and up movement. From the construction, it also follows that $r_{2,ud} = r_{2,du} = E[r_2]$, i.e. 2.56% from Table 10.9.

Table 10.10 reports the resulting interest rate tree, under the assumption that $\sigma = 0.0173$, as estimated from the same data from 1961 to 2001. To interpret the entries in this table, we need to clarify the convention we are going to denote the points on the tree. That is, the earlier notation u, uu, and so on is fine for small trees. But when we move to long trees, we must use a slightly different notation. The tree in Table 10.10 shows that each point on the tree can be described by a time index i and a node index j. Looking at the tree, an upward movement is described by an increase in the index i, but not in the index j. A downward movement is described by both an increase in the index i and j. That is:

$$
r_{i,j} \longrightarrow \begin{cases} r_{i+1,j} & \text{an upward movement in interest rate} \\ r_{i+1,j+1} & \text{a downward movement in interest rate} \end{cases} \tag{10.11}
$$

In particular, it is important to remember that from any point in the tree, there are only two possibilities: either go across, or go down. For instance, from the interest rate 2.56

Table 10.10   Interest Rate Tree

$i \Rightarrow$	0	1	2	3	4	5	6	7	8
j									
0	1.74	3.39	5.00	6.58	8.12	9.63	11.11	12.57	14.00
1		0.95	2.56	4.13	5.67	7.18	8.66	10.12	11.56
2			0.11	1.68	3.22	4.73	6.22	7.67	9.11
3				−0.76	0.78	2.29	3.77	5.23	6.66
4					−1.67	−0.16	1.32	2.78	4.22
5						−2.60	−1.12	0.34	1.77
6							−3.57	−2.11	−0.68
7								−4.56	−3.12
8	probability of up movement: $p = 1/2$								−5.57

in position $(i, j) = (2, 1)$, we can only go to 4.13 (an up movement) or to 1.68 (a down movement). Although there is also the temptation to go to 6.58, this is not allowed in the binomial tree. This latter interest rate (6.58%) can only be reached from 5.00% in the earlier period. The tree in Table 10.10 shows this fact, as it also reports the arrows linking the rates on the tree. However, these arrows are cumbersome, and so we will not report them in future trees.

The simplicity of the model described in Equations 10.8 and 10.9 comes at a cost, though. The model may generate negative interest rates, as is shown in the tree in Table 10.10. This is economically unreasonable: A negative interest rate means that investors are willing to give $100 to the government today, in return for $90, for instance, in one year. While negative *real* rates are a possibility, as inflation may be higher than nominal rates, as occurred at the end of the 1970s, the interest rates in Table 10.10 are nominal. This is a clear drawback of the model, and we will investigate models that overcome this problem. However, we can anticipate that many interest rate models used daily by practitioners may generate negative interest rates. We discuss this issue further in Chapter 11.

10.4.2 Risk Neutral Pricing

Obtaining the prices of derivative securities on a longer tree is no more difficult than obtaining them on a short tree, such as the ones discussed in Chapter 9 and earlier in this chapter. In particular, if we know the risk neutral probability at time i for an up movement, then the formula of the price at time i in node j is

$$V_{i,j} = e^{-r_{i,j} \times \Delta} \times E^*[V_{i+1}] \tag{10.12}$$
$$= e^{-r_{i,j} \times \Delta} \times [p_i^* \times V_{i+1,j} + (1 - p_i^*) \times V_{i+1,j+1}] \tag{10.13}$$

Therefore, if we know the value of the security at maturity (e.g., a zero coupon bond must deliver $100) then we can move backward on the tree by using Equation 10.13. The procedure is particularly easy to implement on a spreadsheet as the formula in Equation

Table 10.11   Zero Coupon Bond Prices on January 8, 2002

Maturity (years)	Price	Yield
0.5	99.1338	1.74
1.0	97.8925	2.13
1.5	96.1462	2.62
2.0	94.1011	3.04
2.5	91.7136	3.46
3.0	89.2258	3.80
3.5	86.8142	4.04
4.0	84.5016	4.21
4.5	82.1848	4.36
5.0	79.7718	4.52
5.5	77.4339	4.65

Source: *The Wall Street Journal.*

10.13 can be entered into a given cell, and then copied and pasted in the remaining part of the tree. Automatically, the spreadsheet delivers the outcome.

Where do we get the risk neutral probabilities p_i^*? One methodology is the one discussed in the previous pages, namely, we use current zero coupon bond prices to compute p_i^*'s. In particular, we can proceed recursively, meaning that we start from the bond expiring at time $i = 2$ to compute p_0^* (the bond expiring at time $i = 1$ does not depend on risk neutral probabilities, as its value is simply $P_0(1) = e^{-r_0 \times \Delta} \times 100$), the bond expiring at time $i = 3$ to compute p_1^*, and so on.

Table 10.11 provides the zero coupon prices on January 8, 2002, up to maturity $T = 5$ years.

We already know from previous sections that $p_0^* = 0.6448$ and $p_1^* = 0.7869$. We now illustrate the procedure to find p_2^*. The other probabilities can be obtained in a similar fashion. These are the steps:

1. Choose a value for p_2^*, for instance, $p_2^* = 0.5$, and build a four-step tree (the computer does this for us) for the zero coupon bond with maturity $i = 4$. This is accomplished by using the formula in Equation 10.13.

   - The bond price we obtain will be in general different from the one in the data, which is $P_0(4) = 94.1011$ in Table 10.11, because we are using a value of p_i^* chosen ad hoc. This fact is illustrated in Panel A of Table 10.12.

   - Note that this tree, however, uses the correct risk neutral probabilities $p_0^* = 0.6448$ and $p_1^* = 0.7869$, as they were computed in the first two steps.

2. Once we have the tree, we can then search for p_2^* that matches the bond price in the data. For instance, in Microsoft Excel, we can use the *solver* function. In this function, we require the spreadsheet to find p_2^* so that the root of the tree (in the box) equals the value of the bond in the data. The result of this procedure is illustrated in Panel B of Table 10.12. The resulting risk neutral probability $p_2^* = 0.6490$.

Table 10.12   Two Trees for the 2-Year Bond

Panel A: Tree with Exogenously Specified $p_2^* = 0.5$

Price to Match	94.1011				

time i	0	1	2	3	4
RN prob. p_i^*	0.6448	0.7869	0.5		

94.2732	93.8524	94.9560	96.7635	100	
	97.3565	97.3063	97.9562	100	
		99.7173	99.1635	100	
			100.3807	100	
				100	

Panel B: Tree with Optimally Chosen p_2^*

Price to Match	94.1011				

time i	0	1	2	3	4
RN prob. p_i^*	0.6448	0.7869	0.6490		

94.1011	93.6811	94.7827	96.7635	100	
	97.1789	97.1287	97.9562	100	
		99.5360	99.1635	100	
			100.3807	100	
				100	

Table 10.13   The 5-Year Bond Tree

time ⟹	0	0.5	1	1.5	2	2.5	3	3.5	4	4.5	5
period i ⟹	0	1	2	3	4	5	6	7	8	9	10
RN prob. p_i^* (%)	64.48	78.69	64.90	72.30	54.18	40.02	38.93	49.93	60.96	45.15	
j											
0	79.77	77.28	76.91	76.46	77.38	78.33	79.79	82.46	86.74	92.58	100
1		86.27	84.82	83.30	83.28	83.27	83.79	85.55	88.88	93.72	100
2			93.54	90.75	89.62	88.52	87.99	88.75	91.09	94.88	100
3				98.85	96.44	94.10	92.40	92.06	93.34	96.04	100
4					103.79	100.03	97.04	95.50	95.65	97.22	100
5						106.34	101.90	99.07	98.02	98.42	100
6							107.01	102.77	100.45	99.63	100
7								106.62	102.94	100.86	100
8									105.49	102.10	100
9										103.36	100
10											100

Table 10.13 shows the result of this procedure as we go forward to use all of the bonds available in Table 10.11. In particular, it shows the tree for a 5-year zero coupon bond. We are next going to use this tree in a couple of examples.

Given the tree in Table 10.13 and the risk neutral probabilities, we can now obtain the price of any other interest rate security. The next section provides an application.

10.5   PRICING AND RISK ASSESSMENT: THE SPOT RATE DURATION

Numerous structured products contain implicit positions in options which make the security sensitive to changes in interest rates. Risk managers must be able to:

1. Correctly evaluate the value of such embedded option.

2. Correctly evaluate the risk of the investment.

Although the two tasks are clearly related, they differ in an important respect. Pricing (task 1) is performed by using risk *neutral* probabilities, as shown earlier. Risk assessment (task 2) is performed by using risk *natural*, i.e., true, probabilities. Example 10.3 below illustrates the difference. Before discussing the example, however, it is useful to introduce a measure of interest rate risk that is similar to the notion of duration described in Chapter 3, Section 3.2 (see Equation 3.1). Because on a binomial tree the interest risk stems from the variation of the spot rate, we call this risk measure spot rate duration, defined next:

Definition 10.1 *The* **spot rate duration** *measures the percentage sensitivity of an interest rate security price to the interest rate r and it is given by*

$$D = -\frac{1}{V} \times \frac{dV}{dr} \qquad (10.14)$$

How do we compute dV/dr on a binomial tree? We can use the values of the security and the interest rate on the tree to approximate the variation in the price of the security due to a variation in the interest rate (we use here the "u" and "d" notation, which is more intuitive):

$$\frac{dV}{dr} \approx \frac{V_{1,u} - V_{1,d}}{r_{1,u} - r_{1,d}} \tag{10.15}$$

■ **EXAMPLE 10.3**

A fund manager is offered a structured 5-year zero coupon bond, with the specific characteristics that the total amount of principal repaid at time $T = 5$ is related to the level of interest rates. Specifically, the bond pays at least 94% of the total principal when interest rates are below 8.55%. When the interest rate increases above 8.55%, the total principal paid increases proportionally with interest rates. The specific payoff at time $T = 5$ $(i = 10)$ is given by

$$\text{Payoff at } i = 10 : V_{10} = max(11 \times 100 \times r_{10}, 94) \tag{10.16}$$

The payoff at maturity of this bond is in Figure 10.1.

1. What is the fair value of this security?

> The methodology developed in the previous pages provides an answer. We can use the interest rate tree and the risk neutral probabilities that we computed to price also this structured derivative (and many others). The binomial tree that prices this security is contained in Table 10.14. The fair value is $79.88, which is very close to the $79.77, the price of a standard zero coupon bond on the same date (see Table 10.13). That is, the payoff at maturity is structured so that the lower principal amount received when the interest rate is low is compensated by a higher payoff when the interest rate is high.

2. What is the risk implicit in this security?

   (a) First, we use the definition of spot rate duration in Equation 10.14 to compute the sensitivity of the structured bond to changes in interest rates. From the approximation in Equation 10.15 and the data in Tables 10.10 and 10.14, the sensitivity to interest rate in the case of the structured bond is

$$D = -\frac{1}{V_0} \times \frac{V_{1,u} - V_{1,d}}{r_{1,u} - r_{1,d}} = -\frac{1}{79.88} \times \frac{79.14 - 83.19}{3.39\% - 0.95\%} = 2.08 \tag{10.17}$$

   The same quantity computed for the standard five-year zero coupon bond (in Table 10.13) yields $D_5 = 4.62$, a much higher number. From this perspective, therefore, the structured bond is less risky than the straight 5-year zero coupon bond. The intuition is simple: Bond prices decline when interest rate increase. The structured bond provides protection against this scenario, as it increases the final payout when the interest rate increases. A similar protection could be bought by purchasing some type of interest rate derivative. However, such strategy would cost money today. The structured bond "pays" for the protection

Figure 10.1   Payoff of Structured Zero Coupon Bond

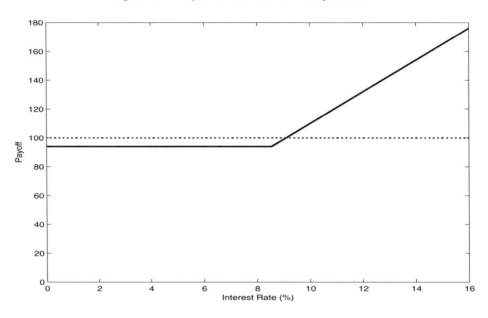

against an increase in the interest rate by reducing the principal repaid if the interest rate instead declines.

(b) Second, we can evaluate the long-term payoff distribution of the security. However, while for pricing we use risk neutral probabilities, for risk analysis we must use the true, or risk *natural*, probabilities. The original tree with the original p probabilities is therefore important in order to perform other types of calculations that have nothing to do with pricing. The result is very different depending on which probability we use. For instance, Table 10.15 shows the bond payoffs at maturity, and both the true probabilities and the risk neutral probabilities to obtain such payoffs. While the risk neutral probabilities assign 69.87% chance of ending up with the sub-par payoff of 94, the true probabilities assign the much larger value of 82.81%. Conversely, while the risk neutral probabilities assign over 30% to having a payoff above par (i.e., larger than 100), the true probabilities assign only around 17%. These results should not be too surprising, as we already noted that risk neutral probabilities make the expectation of future interest rates higher. Because this structured security pays in a high-interest rate environment, it is overly optimistic. But the point here is that any risk analysis, including Value-at-Risk and expected shortfall discussed in Chapter 3, must be performed under the true probabilities. Risk neutral probabilities are adjusted to take into account the market price of risk, and therefore are distorted.

Table 10.14   5-year Structured Bond Tree

i	0	1	2	3	4	5	6	7	8	9	10
j											
0	79.88	79.14	80.01	82.14	85.64	92.27	104.06	120.36	138.44	157.56	184.91
1		83.19	82.27	81.85	82.90	85.55	92.00	103.39	117.94	134.29	158.07
2			88.45	86.06	85.26	84.96	86.47	91.40	99.61	110.38	131.12
3				93.00	90.76	88.65	87.34	87.80	90.34	94.69	104.17
4					97.56	94.03	91.22	89.77	89.91	91.39	94.00
5						99.96	95.79	93.13	92.14	92.52	94.00
6							100.59	96.61	94.42	93.65	94.00
7								100.22	96.76	94.81	94.00
8									99.16	95.97	94.00
9										97.15	94.00
10											94.00

Table 10.15   Payoff at $T = 5$ of Structured Derivative

Payoff at T	True Probability	Risk Neutral Probability
184.91	0.10%	0.28%
158.07	0.98%	2.35%
131.12	4.39%	8.76%
104.17	11.72%	18.74%
94.00	82.81%	69.87%

10.6 SUMMARY

In this chapter we covered the following topics:

1. Two-step binomial tree: This is a one-step extension of the the one-step binomial tree. After a first upward movement in the interest rate, the interest rate can then move again either upward or downward. Similarly, after a downward movement in the interest rate, the interest rate can then move again either upward or downward. There are four possible scenarios at time $i = 2$: (up, up), (up, down), (down, up), (down, down). Most of the time, we choose nodes so that the interest rate after an up/down movement equals the interest rate after a down/up movement. This is called a recombining tree.

2. Risk neutral pricing: Given a risk neutral probability p^*, the value of any security equals the present value of the payoff discounted at the risk free rate. On a binomial tree, this implies moving backward from the end of the tree, and at any node, computing the discounted expected value.

3. Dynamic replication strategy: A portfolio of long-term and short-term bonds can replicate the value of a derivative security along its binomial tree. The trading strategy calls for the rebalancing of the portfolio at any node of the tree. The value of the portfolio at time 0 equals the value of the derivative security.

4. Self financing strategy: The dynamic replicating strategy pays for itself, in the sense that the replication strategy does not require any additional capital along the way.

5. Multi-step trees. Long-term binomial tree: We covered one specific way to construct such a tree. Start from the forecast of future interest rates, and then consider symmetric variations around the expected value, to obtain a simple recombining tree.

6. Risk neutral probabality computation: Use the current term structure of interest rates to compute the risk neutral probability. By moving recursively from the shortest maturity bonds to the longer maturity bonds it is possible to compute the probability for every future period. This probabability can then be used to compute the value of any other interest rate derivative.

7. Spot rate duration: The spot rate duration is the sensitivity of the interest rate security to changes in the spot rate. The key is to approximate the value of the first derivative (dV/dr) by the ratio of the difference in values of the security in the subsequent nodes divided by the difference in spot rates in those nodes. It provides a measure of risk of the security.

10.7 EXERCISES

1. Using the past history of short-term interest rates, you estimated by regression the model

$$r_{t+dt} = \alpha + \beta r_t + u_{t+dt}$$

Suppose that the parameter estimates generated the tree for interest rates in Table 10.16, where there is equal probability to move up or down the tree. Assume also

Table 10.16   An Interest Rate Tree

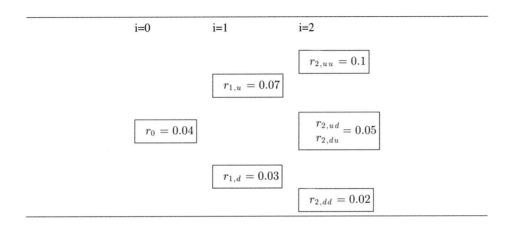

for simplicity that each interval of time represents *1 year*, that is, $\Delta = 1$. Finally, assume that the current zero coupon bond expiring at time $i = 2$ has a price equal to

$$Z_0\left(2\right) = 0.9$$

(a) How does the 2-year bond $Z_0\left(2\right)$ evolve? Compute $Z_{1,u}\left(2\right)$ and $Z_{1,d}\left(2\right)$, and draw the tree for the bond that expires at time $i = 2$ [recall the notation: $Z_{i,j}\left(k\right)$ is the bond at time i in node j with maturity *date k*.]

(b) Use the calculation in Part (a) to compute the market price of risk λ embedded in the current 2-year zero coupon bond $Z_0\left(2\right)$.

(c) Consider an option with maturity $T = 1$ to buy (at $T = 1$) one unit of a 1-year zero coupon bond at the price of $K = 95$.

i. What is the market price of risk of this option? Why?

ii. Use your calculation in part i to compute the value of the option.

iii. Confirm your calculation by using the risk neutral approach.

(d) Assume that the risk neutral probabilities computed above are constant over time. Compute the price of a 2-year European call option on a 1-year zero coupon bond, with strike price $K = .96$.

(e) Compute the replicating portfolio that replicates the option payoff in Part (d). Check that the portfolio indeed replicates the payoff. Discuss the intuition.

2. Consider the interest rate tree in Table 10.17. Assume that each interval of time represents *1 year*. All entries are continuously compounded interest rates. You received mixed up information about the risk neutral and the risk natural (true) probability of moving up the tree. You know it can only be one of the two cases in Table 10.18. That is, in Case 1 the risk neutral probability is 70% and the true probability is 30%. In Case 2, the risk neutral probability is 30% and the true

Table 10.17   An Interest Rate Tree

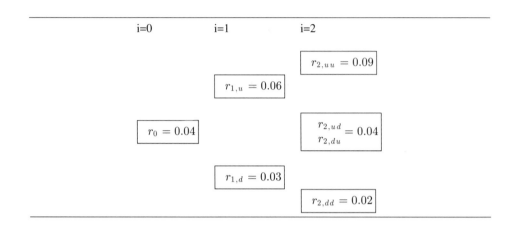

i=0	i=1	i=2

$r_0 = 0.04$

$r_{1,u} = 0.06$

$r_{1,d} = 0.03$

$r_{2,uu} = 0.09$

$r_{2,ud} = 0.04$
$r_{2,du}$

$r_{2,dd} = 0.02$

Table 10.18   Risk Neutral and Risk Natural Probabilities

	Risk Neutral q	Risk Natural (True) p
Case 1	0.7	0.3
Case 2	0.3	0.7

probability is 70%. Only Case 1 or Case 2 is correct, but you do not know which one. However, you know that a 2-year zero coupon bond costs $Z(0,2) = 91.31$.

(a) Use the information provided to find the risk neutral probability of moving up the tree, and compute the tree corresponding to a 3-year zero coupon bond.

(b) An investor buys the 2-year zero coupon bond at time $i = 0$. What is his/her 1-year *expected* return on the investment, as of $i = 0$? What if the trader buys at $i = 0$ the 3-year zero coupon bond? What is his/her 1-year expected return then?

(c) A **range bond** is structured security, which can be described as follows: It is like a standard coupon bond, but it pays the coupon at some given time t if the reference interest rate at time $t - 1$ is within a given interval (the range). Otherwise, it pays no coupon at that time (it may pay it in the future, if the condition is met). In any case, it will pay the principal at maturity T. Consider a 3-year range bond, with a coupon equal to $10 / year. The range bond pays the coupon at time i if the (continuously compounded) interest rate at time $i - 1$ is within the interval $[\underline{r}, \bar{r}] = [0.025, 0.05]$.

   i. Compute the value of the range bond at time $i = 0$.

   ii. You are conducting a long-term risk analysis of this bond. Draw a histogram of the value of the bond at time $i = 2$ and compute the 9%

Value-at-Risk (VaR) at time $i = 2$. For simplicity, in this computation, simply compare the value of the bond at time $i = 2$ with the value of the bond at time $i = 0$ (i.e. forget about the coupons).

iii. You can compute the 9% VaR by using either p or q above. Explain which one you should use and discuss what difference you would get if you used the wrong probability.

iv. What is the advantage of a range bond over a regular bond? Why do you think these bonds became very popular around 1993? Explain.

3. **Building a multi-step tree**. Using quarterly past data on 3-month LIBOR (see Britsh Bankers' Association web site *www.bba.org.uk*), run the regression

$$r_{t+1} = \alpha + \beta r_t + \epsilon_{t+1}$$

where $\epsilon_t \sim \mathcal{N}(0, \sigma^2)$.

(a) Use the fitted values α and β to compute the projected future interest rate $m_{t+i} = E[r_{today+i}]$ (see Chapter 7).

(b) Use the estimated σ to define a binomial tree, as in Section 10.4.

(c) Using the swap rates for the same date, available at the Federal Reserve Web Site (*www.federalreserve.gov/Releases/h15/data.htm*), compute the zero coupon yield curve. Assume for simplicity that both fixed and floating rate payments occur at quarterly frequency.

(d) Compute the risk neutral probabilities. Can you make sure the probabilities are between 0 and 1? If not, try to increase the volatility σ used to fit the tree.

(e) Compute the expected risk neutral interest rate, and compare it with the predicted interest rate in Part (a). Discuss the difference.

CHAPTER 11

RISK NEUTRAL TREES AND DERIVATIVE PRICING

The methodology illustrated in Chapter 10 to build a binomial tree has some drawbacks. For instance, there is no guarantee that the probability p_i^*s that are obtained from matching the term structure of interest rates are always between zero and one, as they should be. To make sure that p_i^*s are between these natural boundaries, we sometimes need to decrease the step size Δ appropriately, a relatively cumbersome procedure.

To overcome this problem, the industry practice has moved to a different strategy, namely, the construction of risk neutral trees without any reference to the true interest rate tree. In this section, we review two popular risk neutral tree constructions, in which the risk neutral probabilities are set equal to $p^* = 1/2$, and the nodes of the tree are chosen in a way consistent with the prices of interest rate securities. In addition, in this chapter we extend the binomial tree methodology to price a wide variety of interest rate securities, from coupon bonds to standard derivatives, such as caps, floors, and swaptions.

11.1 RISK NEUTRAL TREES

In this section we describe two popular interest rate models that are widely used to price and hedge interest rate derivative securities.

11.1.1 The Ho-Lee Model

The Ho-Lee model is one of the simplest models that exactly fits the term structure of interest rates. It is related to the model for interest rates we studied in Section 10.4 in

Chapter 10. The model is specified as follows. First, let's fix a time step, such as $\Delta = 0.5$. Let $r_{i,j}$ be the continuously compounded interest rate in node j between steps i and $i + 1$. Then, for every (i, j) the Ho-Lee model postulates

$$r_{i+1,j} = r_{i,j} + \theta_i \times \Delta + \sigma \times \sqrt{\Delta} \quad \text{with RN probability } p^* = 1/2 \quad (11.1)$$

$$r_{i+1,j+1} = r_{i,j} + \theta_i \times \Delta - \sigma \times \sqrt{\Delta} \quad \text{with RN probability } p^* = 1/2 \quad (11.2)$$

[handwritten: "sigma being volatility of stocks.", "up", "Redown."]

where recall from Chapter 10 that an upward movement in the binomial tree is characterized by the node j remaining constant, and a downward movement by an increase in the node j. As we showed in Chapter 10, this binomial tree is recombining.

What are the "θ_i," for $i = 0, 1, ...$, appearing in expressions (11.1) and (11.2)? These are free parameters that are chosen to fit exactly the current term structure of interest rates. Different levels of θ_i imply different nodes on the tree, while the risk neutral probability p^* remain the same. As we did for risk neutral probabilities in Section 10.4 in Chapter 10, we choose θ_0 to exactly price the bond with maturity $i = 2$ (the bond with maturity $i = 1$ only depends on r_0, and so it is independent of the location of $r_{1,0}$ and $r_{1,1}$); then we choose θ_1 to exactly price the bond with maturity $i = 3$, and so on. An example of the methodology will clarify the procedure. Recall that on multi-step trees we denote

$$P_{i,j}(k) = \text{Bond price at time } i \text{ in node } j \text{ with maturity at (step) } k$$

■ EXAMPLE 11.1

Consider the term structure of interest rates on January 8, 2002. The term structure of interest rates and the zero coupon bonds are given in Table 10.11 in Chapter 10. In the data, the zero coupon bond expiring on date $k = 1$ is $P_0(1) = 99.1338$, implying $r_0 = 1.74\%$, which is the root of the tree.

θ_0: In the data, the zero coupon bond expiring on date $k = 2$ is $P_0(2) = 97.8925$. We now choose θ_0 so that the binomial tree exactly gives $P_0(2) = 97.8925$ as price. From the model in Equations 11.1 and 11.2, we have

$$r_{1,0} = 1.75\% + \theta_0 \times \Delta + \sigma \times \sqrt{\Delta} \quad \text{with RN probability } p^* = 1/2$$

$$r_{1,1} = 1.75\% + \theta_0 \times \Delta - \sigma \times \sqrt{\Delta} \quad \text{with RN probability } p^* = 1/2$$

We first set σ as the volatility of interest rates, given by $\sigma = 0.0173$ according to the data (see Chapter 10). Second, we can now choose θ_0 so that the following equation is satisfied

$$97.8925 = e^{-r_0 \times \Delta} \times \left(\frac{1}{2} \times e^{-r_{1,0} \times \Delta} + \frac{1}{2} \times e^{-r_{1,1} \times \Delta} \right) \times 100$$

Price of zero in the data $=$ Risk neutral price from binomial tree

[handwritten margin note: "Using Set ① Solve"]

Given $r_0 = 1.73\%$ and $\sigma = 0.0173$, $r_{1,0}$ and $r_{1,1}$ both depend only on the level of θ_0. Thus, we have one equation in one unknown. Using a search algorithm (e.g.

Table 11.1 Two Trees for a Zero Coupon Bond Expiring on $k = 3$

Price to Match: 96.1462

$\theta_1 = 0$				Optimal $\theta_1 = 0.021824$			
Interest Rate Tree				Interest Rate Tree			
1.74%	3.75%	4.97%		1.74%	3.75%	6.06%	
	1.30%	2.52%			1.30%	3.61%	
		0.08%				1.17%	
Zero Coupon Bond Price				Zero Coupon Bond Price			
96.6722	96.3241	97.5455	100	96.1462	95.8000	97.0147	100
	98.7098	98.7461	100		98.1727	98.2088	100
		99.9614	100			99.4175	100
			100				100

solver in Microsoft Excel), we find $\theta_0 = 1.5674\%$. Given this value for θ_0, the two interest rates are $r_{1,0} = 3.75\%$ and $r_{1,1} = 1.30\%$.

θ_1: In the data, the zero coupon expiring on date $k = 3$ has price $P_0(3) = 96.1462$. Keeping θ_0 as determined in the previous step, we now look for θ_1 such that the tree exactly yields a price $P_0(3) = 96.1462$. Rather than using an equation to find θ_1, we use a different methodology, namely, the binomial tree itself. More specifically, let us set up a three-step binomial tree for a given θ_1, e.g. $\theta_1 = 0$. This tree will provide a bond value different from the one that we need. However, we can then vary θ_1 until we reach the correct value for the bond. Table 11.1 shows the result: On the left-hand side there is an interest rate tree and bond price for the case in which $\theta_1 = 0$. On the right-hand side of the table, instead, there is the interest rate tree and the bond price for the θ_1 that exactly matches the bond price in the data for maturity $k = 3$. As can be seen comparing the two trees, the one on the right-hand side has nodes $r_{2,0}$,$r_{2,1}$ and $r_{2,2}$ that are higher than the corresponding nodes on the left-hand side. That is, θ_1 had to be chosen greater than 0 to match the term structure of interest rates.

Moving on in this fashion, we obtain the risk neutral tree in Table 11.2 This risk neutral tree exactly matches the term structure of interest rates.

11.1.2 The Simple Black, Derman, and Toy (BDT) Model

The main drawback of the binomial trees introduced earlier, both in Chapter 10 and above in Section 11.1.1 is that it allows for negative interest rates. In this section we go over a model that solves this problem. The model is specified as follows. For every time/node (i, j) define the variable

$$z_{i,j} = \ln (r_{i,j})$$

Table 11.2 The Risk Neutral Ho-Lee Interest Rate Tree

Time T	0	0.5	1	1.5	2	2.5	3	3.5	4	4.5	5
Period i	0	1	2	3	4	5	6	7	8	9	10
$\theta_i(\times 100)$	1.5675	2.1824	1.4374	1.7324	0.7873	0.0423	-0.0628	0.4322	0.9271	0.1202	
j											
0	1.74	3.75	6.06	8.00	10.09	11.71	12.95	14.15	15.59	17.27	18.56
1		1.30	3.61	5.56	7.65	9.26	10.51	11.70	13.14	14.83	16.11
2			1.17	3.11	5.20	6.82	8.06	9.25	10.69	12.38	13.66
3				0.66	2.75	4.37	5.61	6.81	8.25	9.93	11.22
4					0.31	1.92	3.17	4.36	5.80	7.49	8.77
5						-0.52	0.72	1.91	3.35	5.04	6.32
6							-1.73	-0.53	0.91	2.59	3.88
7								-2.98	-1.54	0.15	1.43
8									-3.99	-2.30	-1.02
9										-4.75	-3.46
10											-5.91

The model specifies then that $z_{i,j}$ follows the process

$$z_{i+1,j} = z_{i,j} + \theta_i \times \Delta + \sigma \times \sqrt{\Delta} \quad \text{with RN probability } p^* = 1/2 \quad (11.3)$$

$$z_{i+1,j+1} = z_{i,j} + \theta_i \times \Delta - \sigma \times \sqrt{\Delta} \quad \text{with RN probability } p^* = 1/2 \quad (11.4)$$

This is the same model as Ho-Lee in Equations 11.1 and 11.2, but in logarithms. That is, the model specifies a dynamic for the log of interest rates $z_{i,j}$, which can be negative, but the interest rate is then given instead by

$$r_{i,j} = e^{z_{i,j}}, \quad (11.5)$$

which is always positive.

As for the Ho-Lee model, the constants θ_i, for $i = 1, 2, \dots$ are determined to fit the term structure of interest rates. This model is a special case of a more general model, developed in Section 11.3 and called the Black, Derman and Toy model, in which also σ depends on the time step i. To avoid confusion, we refer to the simpler version as "simple" BDT model.

The next example illustrate the simple BDT model for the same set of bonds as in Example 11.1.

■ **EXAMPLE 11.2**

The strategy to fit the term structure of interest rates is the same as for that of the Ho-Lee model. Namely, we first look for θ_0 that yields exactly the price of a bond maturing on $k = 2$. Then, we move to find θ_1 that fits exactly the price of the bond maturing on $k = 3$. And so on. Without repeating the details of the procedure, as they are the same as in Example 11.1, Table 11.3 shows the risk neutral tree. The important detail to notice is the level of σ that we need to choose for the model. Note that differently from the Ho-Lee model, now σ is the volatility of log-interest rates $z_i = log(r_i)$. As such, it must be estimated from a log interest rate series. Taking log differences in monthly interest rates from 1961/12 to 2001/12, we obtain an (annualized) level of volatility equal to $\sigma = 21.42\%$.

Table 11.3   The Risk Neutral Simple Black, Derman, and Toy Interest Rate Tree

time T	0	0.5	1	1.5	2	2.5	3	3.5	4	4.5	5
period i	0	1	2	3	4	5	6	7	8	9	10
$\theta_i\,(\times 100)$	71.82	69.16	33.48	33.79	11.82	-2.30	-4.38	4.55	12.81	-1.26	
j											
0		1.74	2.90	4.77	6.56	9.03	11.15	12.83	14.60	17.38	21.56	24.93
1			2.14	3.52	4.84	6.67	8.24	9.47	10.78	12.84	15.92	18.41
2				2.60	3.58	4.93	6.08	7.00	7.97	9.48	11.76	13.60
3					2.64	3.64	4.49	5.17	5.88	7.00	8.69	10.05
4						2.69	3.32	3.82	4.35	5.17	6.42	7.42
5							2.45	2.82	3.21	3.82	4.74	5.48
6								2.08	2.37	2.82	3.50	4.05
7									1.75	2.09	2.59	2.99
8										1.54	1.91	2.21
9											1.41	1.63
10												1.21

11.1.3   Comparison of the Two Models

By construction (i.e. choice of θ_i's), the two models discussed in the previous sections are equally able to fit the current term structure of interest rates on January 8, 2002. However, the two models generate important differences in the implied risk neutral probability distribution of interest rates in the future. To illustrate the differences, Figure 11.1 shows the (smoothed) risk neutral distribution of interest rates at $T = 5$ (i.e. $i = 10$) under the two models. The difference is apparent:

1. The Ho-Lee model gives non-zero probability to negative interest rates, and small probability to high interest rates.

2. The Simple Black, Derman, and Toy model gives essentially zero probability to interest rates below 1%, but it assigns a much higher probability to high interest rates.

The type of probability distribution is in fact different: The Ho-Lee model generates a symmetric, bell-shaped distribution of interest rates in the future, that looks like a normal distribution. In contrast, the Simple Black, Derman and Toy model generates an asymmetric, positively skewed distribution of interest rates, that looks like a log-normal distribution. In fact, as the time step Δ approaches zero, the distribution becomes normal in the case of the Ho-Lee model and log-normal in the case of the Simple Black, Derman and Toy model (see Chapter 14).

By construction, these differences are not important for bond prices, as both models exactly match the term structure of interest rates. However, they will generate important differences for other securities that have asymmetric payoff structures, such as options. As a simple example, the structured zero coupon bond discussed in Section 10.5 in Chapter 10 has quite a different price depending on whether we use the Ho-Lee model or the Simple Black, Derman and Toy model. Recall that the structured bond discussed in Section 10.5 has a payoff

$$\text{Payoff of structured bond at } T = \max\left(11 \times 100 \times r_T, 94\right)$$

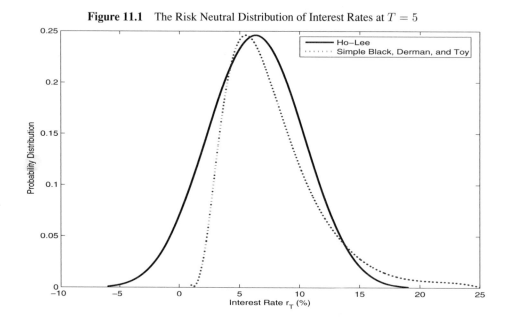

Figure 11.1   The Risk Neutral Distribution of Interest Rates at $T = 5$

Using the same methodology used in Table 10.14, we find

$$\text{Price of structured bond: Ho-Lee} = \$80.0645$$
$$\text{Price of structured bond: Simple Black, Derman, and Toy} = \$78.9135$$

The lower price in the Simple Black, Derman and Toy model highlights the differences of the model: Although the positive skewness of the risk neutral distribution in the BDT model implies a higher risk neutral expected payoff for the Simple BDT model, the higher interest rates implied by the model also imply a higher discount applied to the payoff. The higher discount effect more than compensates for the higher expected return.

11.1.4   Risk Neutral Trees and Future Interest Rates

There is often a temptation to interpret too much from the implied risk neutral interest rate trees. For instance, the Simple Black, Derman, and Toy model fitted in Table 11.3 implies that from the current interest rate $r_0 = 1.74\%$, future interest rates can only go up. In fact, both interest rates $r_{1,u}$ and $r_{1,d}$ are higher than the current interest rate. Although of course this is a rather peculiar property of an interest rate process, we have to remember what a *risk neutral* interest rate tree is. This is a tree whose only purpose is to compute the price of interest rate securities through no arbitrage. The fact that the interest rate can only go up in the model fitted in Table 11.3 has little to do with the real world expectation of future interest rates, as we have to remember that a risk neutral tree embeds the risk aversion of investors, as discussed in Chapter 10. In this model, risk aversion is embedded in the level of θ_i. Lower risk aversion, for instance, would imply a lower level of θ_i and thus a better behaved tree.

Having said so, however, the fitted Simple Black, Derman, and Toy model in Table 11.3 does expose a shortcoming of the model, and this is the fact that it does not allow enough (risk neutral) probability mass to low interest rates. In contrast, the Ho-Lee model in Table 11.2 allows perhaps too much (risk neutral) probability to low interest rates, and in fact even to negative interest rates. Derivative security prices are very sensitive to this distributional differences. The Simple Black, Derman and Toy model, as well as the full BDT model discussed below, does not perform too well in low interest rate environments, such as those in 2003 and, in fact, 2008. The reason is that to fit the term structure of interest rates, it turns out that such models must give essentially zero probability to further declines in interest rates, as in Table 11.3, a property that leads to a serious difficulty in matching the prices of options, as discussed below.

11.2 USING RISK NEUTRAL TREES

In this section we illustrate the use of risk neutral trees to price other interest rate securities, such as caps, floors, swaps and swaptions. First, we must learn how to include intermediate cash flows.

11.2.1 Intermediate Cash Flows

Notice that given a tree, we can insert any type of known cash flow. Specifically, at any time-node (i, j), we just must add the cash flow to the value to discount at time $i + 1$.

$$P_{i,j} = e^{-r_{i,j} \times \Delta} \times \left(\frac{1}{2} P_{i+1,j} + \frac{1}{2} P_{i+1,j+1} + CF(i+1) \right) \qquad (11.6)$$

where $CF(i + 1)$ is the cash flow that will be paid at time $i + 1$.

■ **EXAMPLE 11.3**

Consider the price of a 1.5-year, 3% coupon bond on January 8, 2002. Let us use the Simple Black, Derman, and Toy interest rate model fitted in Section 11.1.2. We can calculate the price of the coupon bond using the tree in Table 11.4. In each step, we add the cash flow $CF(i + 1) = 1.5$ $(= 3\% \times 100/2)$ to the price in the following period, and take the present value according to Equation 11.6. So, for example, the value of the bond if the interest rate goes up twice (to $r_{2,uu} = 4.77\%$) is equal to the present value of the bond value in the next period, equal to $100, plus the coupon to be received next period, equal to $1.5. The present value is then $P_{2,uu} = \$99.1094$. The prices on the tree are ex-coupon prices, that is, the price of the bond right after the coupon has been paid.

11.2.2 Caps and Floors

A *plain vanilla cap* with maturity T, strike rate r_K, and notional N is a security that pays a stream of cash-flows at given dates $T_1, T_2, ..., T_m = T$, according to the formula

$$CF(T_i) = \Delta \times N \times \max(r_n(T_i - \Delta) - r_K, 0) \qquad (11.7)$$

where n is the number of payments per year (e.g. $n = 2$), $\Delta = 1/n = T_i - T_{i-1}$ is the amount of time between payments and $r_n(T)$ is a reference floating rate interest rate with

Table 11.4   A Coupon Bond Tree with Maturity $k = 3$

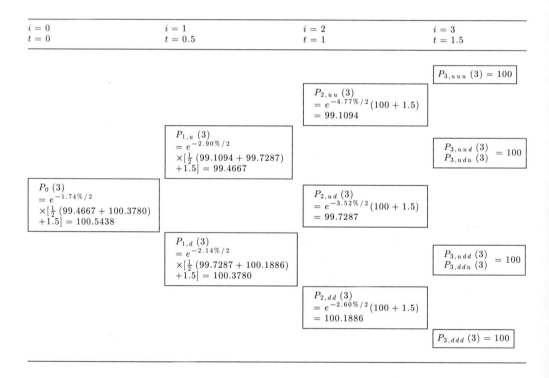

| $i = 0$ | $i = 1$ | $i = 2$ | $i = 3$ |
| $t = 0$ | $t = 0.5$ | $t = 1$ | $t = 1.5$ |

$P_{3,uuu}(3) = 100$

$P_{2,uu}(3)$
$= e^{-4.77\%/2}(100 + 1.5)$
$= 99.1094$

$P_{1,u}(3)$
$= e^{-2.90\%/2}$
$\times [\frac{1}{2}(99.1094 + 99.7287)$
$+ 1.5] = 99.4667$

$\begin{matrix} P_{3,uud}(3) \\ P_{3,udu}(3) \end{matrix} = 100$

$P_0(3)$
$= e^{-1.74\%/2}$
$\times [\frac{1}{2}(99.4667 + 100.3780)$
$+ 1.5] = 100.5438$

$P_{2,ud}(3)$
$= e^{-3.52\%/2}(100 + 1.5)$
$= 99.7287$

$P_{1,d}(3)$
$= e^{-2.14\%/2}$
$\times [\frac{1}{2}(99.7287 + 100.1886)$
$+ 1.5] = 100.3780$

$\begin{matrix} P_{3,udd}(3) \\ P_{3,ddu}(3) \end{matrix} = 100$

$P_{2,dd}(3)$
$= e^{-2.60\%/2}(100 + 1.5)$
$= 100.1886$

$P_{3,ddd}(3) = 100$

compounding frequency n, such as the 6-month T-bill rate or LIBOR.[1] Each individual payment is called *caplet*. Note the temporal difference between the timing of the cash flow payment, time T_i, and the timing of the interest rate that determines this cash flow, time $T_i - \Delta$. In other words, it is the interest rate at time T_{i-1} that determines the cash flow at time T_i.

Caps are very popular interest rate securities that offer insurance against the interest rate increasing above to some level r_K. They are often attached to floating rate bonds, for instance, so as to limit the amount of interest the bond issuers have to pay. Indeed, as a practical example, homeowners who finance the purchase of their homes through adjustable rate mortgages, most likely they also buy a cap, as these floating rate mortgages typically have a provision stating that the mortgage rate will never exceed a given maximum rate.

A *plain vanilla floor* is instead a security that pays the stream of cash flows:

$$CF\left(T_i\right) = \Delta \times N \times \max\left(r_K - r_n\left(T_i - \Delta\right), 0\right) \tag{11.8}$$

In this case, the insurance is against a decrease in interest rates. While borrowers like insurance against interest rate hikes, lenders like insurance against interest rate declines. Some adjusttable rate mortgages, for instance, also define a minimum interest rate, which can be thought of as a floor.

Pricing caps and floors is simple with trees, as cash flows are determined by the interest rate itself. The only difficulty is the time difference between when the cash flow is determined $(T_i - \Delta)$ and when the cash flow is paid (T_i). In particular, it is convenient to denote by $CF_{i,j}(k)$ the cash flow *determined* in node (i,j), that is, by the floating interest rate $r_{i,j}$, but paid at time $k > i$. According to the terms of the contract, if the tree time step is equal to $\Delta = 1/n$, then $k = i + 1$. In other words, while solving for the price of the cap, we have to remember that the cash flow is not paid at time/node (i, j), when it is determined by $r_{i,j}$, but at time $i + 1$, independent of whether at time $i + 1$ the interest rate increased or decreased.

More specifically, assuming that the time step of the tree is in fact $\Delta = 1/n$, the cash flow determined by the interest rate $r_{i,j}$ is

$$CF_{i,j}\left(i + 1\right) \quad = \quad \Delta \times N \times \max\left(r_n(i,j) - r_K, 0\right) \tag{11.9}$$

where

$$r_n\left(i, j\right) = n \times \left(e^{r_{i,j} \times \Delta} - 1\right) \tag{11.10}$$

is the corresponding interest rate with compounding frequency equal to n. Given these cash flows, we use the backward recursive formula to obtain the value of the cap along the tree. That is, we have

$$V_{i,j} \quad = \quad \text{Value at time/node } (i,j) \text{ of all cash flows at times } k > i \tag{11.11}$$

$$= \quad e^{-r_{i,j} \times \Delta} \times \left(\frac{1}{2}V_{i+1,j} + \frac{1}{2}V_{i+1,j+1} + CF_{i,j}\left(i + 1\right)\right) \tag{11.12}$$

The following example illustrates the methodology.

---

[1] For notational simplicity, in this chapter we suppress the maturity of the reference interest rate itself, i.e., we denote $r_n\left(T\right) = r_n\left(T, T + \Delta\right)$.

Table 11.5 The Cash Flow Tree of a 1.5-Year Cap

$i = 0$ $t = 0$	$i = 1$ $t = 0.5$	$i = 2$ $t = 1$	$i = 3$ $t = 1.5$
		$r_{2,uu} = 4.77\%$ $r_2(2, uu) = 4.82\%$ $CF_{2,uu}(3) = 1.162$ $\longrightarrow$ paid here	
	$r_{1,u} = 2.90\%$ $r_2(1, u) = 2.92\%$ $CF_{1,u}(2) = 0.210$ $\longrightarrow$ paid here		
$r_0 = 1.74\%$ $r_2(0) = 1.75\%$ $CF_0(1) = 0$		$r_{2,ud} = 3.52\%$ $r_2(2, ud) = 3.55\%$ $CF_{2,ud}(3) = 0.526$ $\longrightarrow$ paid here	
	$r_{1,d} = 2.14\%$ $r_2(1, d) = 2.15\%$ $CF_{1,d}(2) = 0$		
		$r_{2,dd} = 2.60\%$ $r_2(2, dd) = 2.62\%$ $CF_{2,dd}(3) = 0.059$ $\longrightarrow$ paid here	

■ **EXAMPLE 11.4**

Consider the value on January 8, 2002, of a 1.5-years cap, with semi-annual payment ($n = 2$, $\Delta = 0.5$), and with strike rate $r_K = 3\%$. Let the notional $N = 100$. We apply the same Simple Black, Derman, and Toy risk neutral tree computed above in Table 11.3. We proceed in two steps:

1. **Cash Flow Tree.** The first step to obtain the price of the cap is to build a cash flow tree, that is, a tree that defines the cash flow that is *determined* (not paid) in a given node (i, j). Given Equation 11.9, we obtain the tree in Table 11.5. The cash flow tree in this table also shows not only the time of the formation of the cash flows, but also when they would be paid (i.e., one period later). For instance, if the interest rate increases twice, it ends up in $r_{2,uu} = 4.77\%$. The corresponding semi-annually compounded interest rate, from Equation 11.10, is $r_2(2, uu) = 2 \times \left(e^{4.77\%/2} - 1\right) = 4.82\%$. Thus, the cash flow determined at time/node $(2, uu)$ is $C_{2,uu}(3) = 100/2 \times \max(4.82\% - 2.5\%, 0) = 1.162$. Note, however, this cash flow is not paid at time $(2, uu)$ but at time $i = 3$, as the tree shows.

2. **Cap Value Tree.** Given the cash flow tree, we can compute the value of the cap by using the backward formula in Equation 11.12. The resulting tree is in Table 11.6. We obtain a value of the cap at time $i = 0$ given by $V_0 = \$0.647$.

Table 11.6 The 1.5-Year Cap Value Tree

$i = 0$	$i = 1$	$i = 2$	$i = 3$
$t = 0$	$t = 0.5$	$t = 1$	$t = 1.5$

$$V_{2,uu} = \\ = e^{4.77\%/2} \times 1.162 = 1.135$$

$$CF_{2,uu}(3) = 1.162$$

$$V_{1,u} = e^{-2.90\%/2} \times \\ \times [\tfrac{1}{2}(1.135 + 0.517) + 0.210] \\ = 1.021$$

$$V_{2,ud} = \\ = e^{-3.52\%/2} \times 0.526 = 0.517$$

$$CF_{2,ud}(3) = 0.526$$

$$V_0 = e^{-1.74\%/2} \times \\ \times [\tfrac{1}{2}(1.021 + 0.285) + 0] \\ = 0.647$$

$$V_{1,d} = e^{-2.14\%/2} \times \\ \times [\tfrac{1}{2}(0.517 + 0.058) + 0] \\ = 0.285$$

$$V_{2,dd} = \\ = e^{-2.60\%/2} \times 0.059 = 0.058$$

$$CF_{2,dd}(3) = 0.058$$

Table 11.7   A 5-Year Cap

Panel A: Cash Flow Tree

Period i	0	1	2	3	4	5	6	7	8	9
Node j										
0	0.00	0.21	1.16	2.08	3.37	4.48	5.37	6.32	7.83	10.13
1		0.00	0.53	1.20	2.14	2.95	3.60	4.29	5.38	7.04
2			0.06	0.55	1.25	1.84	2.31	2.81	3.61	4.81
3				0.08	0.59	1.02	1.37	1.74	2.31	3.19
4					0.10	0.42	0.68	0.95	1.37	2.01
5						0.00	0.17	0.37	0.68	1.15
6							0.00	0.00	0.17	0.52
7								0.00	0.00	0.05
8									0.00	0.00
9										0.00

Panel B: Cap Value Tree

Period i	0	1	2	3	4	5	6	7	8	9
Node j										
0	9.44	12.19	15.10	17.35	18.93	19.44	18.89	17.29	14.33	9.10
1		6.86	9.21	11.25	12.76	13.42	13.25	12.25	10.22	6.50
2			4.64	6.45	7.89	8.68	8.82	8.33	7.06	4.53
3				2.84	4.13	5.00	5.40	5.32	4.65	3.05
4					1.46	2.24	2.79	3.03	2.83	1.95
5						0.52	0.92	1.30	1.47	1.12
6							0.12	0.23	0.44	0.51
7								0.01	0.03	0.05
8									0.00	0.00
9										0.00

This approach can be extended without any difference to any maturity, and to higher frequency. Table 11.7 provides a 5-year cap with semi-annual payments and cap rate equal to $r_K = 2.5\%$. Panel A reports the cash flow tree (at time/node of cash flow formation) while Panel B reports the value tree. Note that the table only shows periods until $i = 9$ as the last cash flow, in Period $i = 9$, is in fact paid at time $i = 10$, i.e. in five years.

11.2.3   Swaps

Recall our discussion of interest rate swaps in Section 5.4 in Chapter 5. The valuation of this type of interest rate security can be simply obtained from the discount factors $Z(0, T)$. However, the last two decades have seen the development of a large number of interest rate securities whose payoffs depend on the value of interest rate swaps. Thus, understanding the dynamics of the value of the interest rate swap on an interest rate tree is instrumental to obtaining the price of these other interest rate derivatives. We now apply the risk neutral tree methodology to value interest rate swaps. On top of these interest rate swaps, then, we will cover a popular interest rate derivative, called swaptions.

The cash flow from a plain vanilla swap is

$$CF(T_i) = \Delta \times N \times (r_n(T_i - \Delta) - c) \tag{11.13}$$

where, recall, n is the number of payments per year (e.g. $n = 2$), $\Delta = 1/n$ is the amount of time between payments, c is the swap rate, and $r_n(T)$ is a reference floating rate interest rate, such as the LIBOR, with n compounding frequency. The methodology to value the interest rate swap is identical to the one discussed earlier for caps. Briefly, we follow two steps:

1. Compute a cash flow tree using

$$CF_{i,j}(i+1) = \Delta \times N \times (r_n(i,j) - c) \tag{11.14}$$

where, recall, $r_n(i,j) = n \times \left(e^{r_{i,j} \times \Delta} - 1\right)$

2. Compute the value of the swap on the tree as the present value of the risk neutral expectation of future cash flows by moving backward on the tree:

$$V_{i,j}(k,c) = e^{-r_{i,j} \times \Delta} \times \left(\frac{1}{2}V_{i+1,j}(k,c) + \frac{1}{2}V_{i+1,j+1}(k,c) + CF_{i,j}(i+1)\right)$$

where

$$V_{i,j}(k,c) = \text{Value of the swap in } (i,j) \text{ with maturity } (k), \text{ and swap rate } c \tag{11.15}$$

The next example illustrates the methodology.

■ **EXAMPLE 11.5**

Consider a 5-year fixed-for-floating swap on January 8, 2002, defined on the 6-month T-bill rate and with semi-annual payments.[2] According to Equation 5.43 in Chapter 5, the swap rate is

$$c = \frac{1}{2}\frac{1 - Z(0,10)}{\sum_{i=1}^{10} Z(0,i)} = 4.49\% \tag{11.16}$$

Recall that this swap rate is the one that makes the value of the interest rate swap equal to zero at inception. Given the Simple Black, Derman and Toy tree in Table 11.3, we obtain the cash flow tree and swap value tree in Panels A and B of Table 11.8, respectively. The comforting fact is that the root of the swap value tree, in Panel B, indeed gives $V_0 = 0$, as it should be from the definition of c. This is not surprising, as the tree used to value this swap was calibrated to zero coupon bonds. However, we have confirmation that the tree methodology works, as it correctly values the interest rate swap.

---

[2]As discussed in Chapter 5, the most popular interest rate swaps have floating rates linked to the LIBOR rate. However, as over-the-counter contracts, interest rate swaps are defined on most floating rates, including T-bill rates, commercial paper rate, and others.

Table 11.8 A 5-Year Swap Tree

Panel A: Cash Flow Tree

Period i	0	1	2	3	4	5	6	7	8	9
Node j										
0	-1.37	-0.78	0.17	1.09	2.38	3.49	4.38	5.33	6.83	9.14
1		-1.17	-0.47	0.21	1.15	1.96	2.61	3.30	4.39	6.04
2			-0.93	-0.44	0.25	0.84	1.32	1.82	2.61	3.81
3				-0.91	-0.41	0.03	0.37	0.74	1.32	2.20
4					-0.89	-0.57	-0.32	-0.05	0.38	1.02
5						-1.01	-0.82	-0.63	-0.31	0.15
6							-1.20	-1.05	-0.82	-0.48
7								-1.36	-1.20	-0.94
8									-1.47	-1.28
9										-1.54

Panel B: Swap Value Tree

Period i	0	1	2	3	4	5	6	7	8	9
Node j										
0	0.00	4.27	8.18	11.38	13.86	15.22	15.50	14.72	12.58	8.20
1		-1.53	2.04	5.04	7.48	9.03	9.71	9.58	8.42	5.58
2			-2.79	0.05	2.44	4.14	5.18	5.58	5.21	3.60
3				-3.83	-1.47	0.36	1.67	2.51	2.77	2.10
4					-4.47	-2.54	-1.00	0.18	0.92	0.99
5						-4.74	-3.02	-1.58	-0.46	0.15
6							-4.55	-2.90	-1.50	-0.47
7								-3.89	-2.27	-0.93
8									-2.85	-1.27
9										-1.52

11.2.4 Swaptions

Recall from Chapter 6, Section 6.2, that a **swaption**, or option on a swap, is an interest rate contract between two counterparties in which one counterparty (the option buyer) has the right, but not the obligation, to enter at a prespecified time T into a given interest rate swap with maturity $T^{swap} > T$ and (strike) swap rate r_K. The other counterparty (the option seller) has the obligation to take the other side of the swap contract if the option buyer exercises the option.

Two main types of plain vanilla swaptions are the following:

1. A *receiver swaption* is an option to enter into a swap and receive the fixed rate r_K.

2. A *payer swaption* is an option to enter into a swap and pay the fixed rate r_K.

As with any option, swaptions provide insurance. In the case of swaptions the insurance to the option buyer is against movements in interest rates. For instance, consider a company that has issued a floating rate bond. The potential future liabilities from issuing a floating rate bond is high, because if the floating rate increases, then the company has to make large interest rate payments. A payer swaption at a given strike rate r_K allows the company to insure against increases in the floating interest rate. If the floating rate is high at maturity, the company can exercise its option to enter into a fixed-for-floating swap, in which it pays fixed rate r_K and receives the floating rate. After the company exercises the option, it effectively changes its liability into a fixed rate bond, as the floating rate it receives from the swap can be used to hedge the floating rate payments the company must make to service its debt.

As a second example, swaptions are also very popular hedging instruments for investors in callable securities, such as callable bonds or mortgage backed securities.[3] For instance, an investor in callable bonds is worried about prepayment risk, namely, the risk that if the interest rate declines, the issuer of the bond will call back the bond, and the investor will receive his capital back too early. The investor then not only does not receive any more coupons, but because the current interest rate is low, his investment opportunities probably deteriorated, and so he or she won't be able to invest the capital at the same attractive rates of the original callable bond (being called). To hedge against this possibility the issuer can buy a receiver swaption at a rate r_K close to the original coupon of the callable bond. If the interest rate declines and the bond is called, then, the investor can exercise the option and receive the fixed rate payments instead of floating rates. The investor can also readily meet the floating rate payments of the swap, as he can invest the capital he received back from the issuer of the original callable bond in any instrument that pays a floating rate, such as a money market account. Effectively, the investor can still receive the fixed rate r_K rate on the capital, as if the callable bond hadn't been called.

How do we value the swaption premium today? The interest rate tree methodology discussed earlier provides the answer. It is convenient to provide the methodology through the discussion of an example:

---

[3]In fact, American swaptions are even better as hedging instruments. We cover them in Chapter 12.

■ **EXAMPLE 11.6**

Consider a European payer swaption with two years to maturity ($i = 4$), to enter at $i = 4$ into a 3-year swap and pay the fixed rate $r_K = 4.49\%$. The maturity date of the swap is then five years from now, i.e. $k = 10$.

Let $c_{i,j}(k)$ be the swap rate at time/node (i, j) for a swap maturing at time k.[4] Intuitively, then, the buyer of a payer swaption will exercise the option if and only if the current swap rate at maturity $i = 4$ is higher than the strike swap rate r_K. That is, exercise if and only if $c_{4,j}(10) > r_K$. The reason is that if the current swap rate is high, the holder of the option has the opportunity to exercise the option and pay the lower amount r_K rather than the current swap rate $c_{4,j}(10)$. Vice versa, if the current swap rate is low, i.e. $c_{4,j}(10) < r_K$, then it is more convenient for the option holder to give up the option and enter into the payer swap at the current (lower) swap rate.

All this sounds complicated, as it appears we must first compute the dynamics of the swap rate $c_{i,j}(10)$ before we can solve for the value of the swaption value. Instead, we must only remember how $c_{i,j}(10)$ is defined. In particular, recall that the swap rate $c_{i,j}(10)$ is that rate that makes the swap value at time (i, j) equal to zero. That is, using the notation in (11.15), $c_{i,j}(10)$ is such that

$$V_{i,j}(10, c_{i,j}(10)) = 0. \tag{11.17}$$

As a consequence, if the current market swap rate at time $i = 4$ and node j is above the strike rate, $c_{4,j}(10) > r_K$, then the value of the swap with swap rate r_K must be greater than zero (which from Equation 11.17 is the value of the swap at the current market swap rate). That is,

$$c_{4,j}(10) > r_K \quad \text{if and only if} \quad V_{4,j}(10, r_K) > 0 \tag{11.18}$$

This fact enables us to easily obtain the value of the swaption. In fact, Equation 11.18 implies that the value of the swaption at the option maturity $i = 4$ is

$$\text{Payoff of swaption at time } i = 4 : \max\left(V_{4,j}(10, r_K), 0\right) \tag{11.19}$$

In our example, $r_K = 4.49\%$, which is the same as the swap rate used in the swap tree in Table 11.8. Thus, $V_{4,j}(10, r_K)$, for $j = 0, 1, \ldots 4$ are given by the fifth column in the table. For instance, $V_{4,0}(10, r_K) = 13.86$, $V_{4,1}(10, r_K) = 7.48$ and so on. The payoff from entering into the swap is then given by the swap value in node $j = 0$, $j = 1$ and $j = 2$, and zero otherwise. Given the final payoff of the swaption, we then obtain the value at time $i = 0$ by solving the tree backward, as in the tree in Table 11.9. The price of the swaption is $3.41.

To summarize the methodology, Example 11.6 illustrates the fact that three steps are necessary to price a European swaption on a binomial tree:

1. Compute the tree of the underlying swap value whose swap rate is equal to the swaption's strike rate r_K.

2. Compute the swaption payoff as in Equation 11.19.

3. Use the risk neutral binomial tree to compute the price of the swaption from its payoff.

---

[4]Note that the swap rate moves over time on the tree, as the short-term interest rate does.

Table 11.9   A 2-Year Payer Swaption

i	0	1	2	3	4
j					
0	3.41	5.11	7.41	10.33	13.86
1		1.76	2.97	4.84	7.48
2			0.59	1.20	2.44
3				0.00	0.00
4					0.00

11.3   IMPLIED VOLATILITIES AND THE BLACK, DERMAN, AND TOY MODEL

In our earlier examples on the pricing of interest rate caps, floors, and swaptions, we used the empirical volatility σ as input in the interest rate tree in Table 11.3. That is, σ was computed as the standard deviation of past realized changes in the short term interest rates. Given the value of σ, we computed the tree that fitted exactly the term structure of interest rates. However, it is an empirical regularity that such a value of σ typically underprices caps, floors and swaptions. That is, the binomial trees built using the empirical interest rate volatility give a valuation of standard options that is typically too low.

It has become standard practice in the industry, then, to compute σ not out of the *past* changes in the interest rates r_t, but rather straight from the traded prices of caps, floors, and swaptions. In other words, the value of σ is chosen in a way that prices caps and floors. Once σ is chosen, the term structure of interest rates is also fitted. This volatility level is called implied volatility.

Definition 11.1   *The* **empirical volatility** *of interest rates is the level of interest rate variation σ computed from a time series of past interest rate changes. For instance, in the two models discussed in Section 11.1, the empirical volatility is*

$$\text{Ho-Lee Model}   :   \sigma = st.dev.\ of\,(r_{t+\Delta} - r_t) \qquad (11.20)$$
$$\text{Simple Black, Derman, and Toy Model}   :   \sigma = st.dev.\ of\,(\ln(r_{t+\Delta}) - \ln(r_t)) \quad (11.21)$$

We now define the option's implied volatility. We provide the definition for caps, but an equivalent definition holds for any option's contract.

Definition 11.2   *Consider a given derivative security, such as a cap, with maturity T and strike rate r_K, and let $cap^{Data}\,(T, r_K)$ be the current price level of the cap. The* **implied volatility** *of this cap is the level of interest rate variation σ such that the chosen interest rate model yields a price of the cap identical to the $cap^{Data}\,(T, r_K)$.*

We now illustrate these concepts using an example. The important caveat, though, is that market data on caps, floors, and swaptions are readily available in case the underlying floating rate is the LIBOR interest rate, as opposed to the Treasury bill rate used in the previous sections. Thus, to be consistent between the term structure of interest rates and the value of these derivative securities, we must fit the interest rate tree to the term structure of interest rates implied by the LIBOR rate. Plain vanilla swaps, for instance, are LIBOR-based, and thus we use the discount curve $Z(0, T)$ that is implied by swap rates. (The methodology to extract $Z(0, T)$ from swap rates was illustrated in Section 5.4 in Chapter 5. Section 6.5 in Chapter 6 also discusses the use of Eurodollar futures to construct the LIBOR curve.)

Table 11.10 contains the swap rates $c(0, T)$, the implied discount factors $Z(0, T)$, and the cap prices on November 1, 2004.[5] The swaps and the caps quoted in this table are for quarterly payments. For each cap, the corresponding strike rate r_K is given by the swap rate with the same maturity. A cap with such a strike rate is said to be at-the-money. The last two columns in Table 11.10 contain the prices of the same caps computed from the Simple Black, Derman and Toy and Ho-Lee interest rate tree model when each is fitted to the discount factors $Z(0, T)$ in column four.

Consider, for instance, the 1-year cap, whose value in the data is $V^{data}(0, 1) = 0.1859$ and the strike rate is $r_K = c(0, 1) = 2.555\%$. Using the Simple Black, Derman, and Toy model with the empirical volatility of LIBOR rates, i.e. $\sigma = 15.06\%$, the resulting interest rate tree is shown in Panel A of Table 11.11. Panel B shows the tree for a 1-year zero coupon bond. The price $P^{model}(0, T) = 97.4834$ indeed corresponds to the zero coupon bond price in Table 11.10. Panel C of Table 11.11 contains the cash flow tree for the cap, and Panel D the cap value tree. As can be seen, the value is $V^{model}(0, 1) = \$0.1520$, which is substantially lower than the corresponding value in the data, namely, $V^{data}(0, 1) = \$0.1859$.

The final two columns in Table 11.10 show the results of similar exercises performed for all maturities for both the Simple BDT and Ho-Lee model with constant volatilities ($\sigma = 15.06\%$ for the Simple BDT, and $\sigma = 0.8326177\%$ for Ho-Lee). As can be see, both the Simple BDT and Ho Lee model with constant empirical volatility miss the cap prices for all of the maturities.

One interesting finding in Table 11.10 is that the Ho-Lee model appears to overprice short term caps, and underprice long term caps, while the Simple BDT model in this case always underprices. Note that we used exactly the same data to estimate both models, namely, the realized 3-months LIBOR rates for the 1987 to 2004 period, and the swap rates in the second column of Table 11.10. The different performance of the two models, Simple BDT versus Ho-Lee, stems from the different implied (risk neutral) probability distribution of interest rates, as discussed in Section 11.1.3.

11.3.1   Flat and Forward Implied Volatility

One possible problem with the model is that the volatility σ has been mis-measured. After all, the volatility of interest rates is time varying, and thus we may be using the wrong level of volatility. The biggest problem, however, is that a single value of σ that makes the observed cap price consistent with the model does not exist. Table 11.12 reports the cap prices across maturities for various volatility levels. More specifically, the second column reports the cap prices in the data. The next four columns report the cap prices implied by the Simple Black Derman and Toy model for four levels of volatility $\sigma = 0.188$,

---

[5]As discussed in Chapter 20, caps, floors, and swaptions are in fact quoted in implied volatility units by dealers. The implied volatility is from the Black model of interest rates, which we discuss in Chapters 20 and 21. The dollar prices contained in Table 11.10 are computed out of the original implied volatility quotes using such a model.

Table 11.10   Swap Rates and Cap Prices on November 1, 2004

Maturity T	Swap Rates $c(0,T)(\%)$	Discount $Z(0,T)$	Cap Prices		
			Data	Simple BDT Model	Ho Lee Model
0.25	2.1800	99.4580	–	–	–
0.50	2.3177	98.8510	0.0456	0.0400	0.0689
0.75	2.4420	98.1899	0.1059	0.0948	0.1512
1.00	2.5550	97.4834	0.1859	0.1520	0.2349
1.25	2.6586	96.7385	0.2887	0.2106	0.3366
1.50	2.7546	95.9598	0.4157	0.3038	0.4457
1.75	2.8451	95.1503	0.5662	0.3984	0.5670
2.00	2.9320	94.3109	0.7364	0.4982	0.7050
2.25	3.0167	93.4417	0.9201	0.6062	0.8485
2.50	3.0991	92.5456	1.1129	0.7229	1.0008
2.75	3.1784	91.6268	1.3126	0.8586	1.1579
3.00	3.2540	90.6899	1.5194	0.9961	1.3252
3.25	3.3254	89.7397	1.7352	1.1386	1.4911
3.50	3.3930	88.7778	1.9598	1.2838	1.6643
3.75	3.4577	87.8050	2.1916	1.4344	1.8415
4.00	3.5200	86.8212	2.4288	1.5889	2.0247
4.25	3.5805	85.8263	2.6691	1.7542	2.2129
4.50	3.6393	84.8218	2.9117	1.9208	2.4007
4.75	3.6962	83.8102	3.1562	2.0954	2.5946
5.00	3.7510	82.7938	3.4029	2.2706	2.7889

Original Data Source: Bloomberg.

Table 11.11   LIBOR-Based Interest Rate Tree and the 1-Year Cap Value

Time t	0	0.25	0.5	0.75	1
Period i	0	1	2	3	4

Panel A: Interest Rate Tree

j					
0	2.17%	2.63%	3.10%	3.59%	
1		2.26%	2.67%	3.09%	
2			2.30%	2.66%	
3				2.29%	

Panel B: Zero Coupon Bond

j					
0	97.4834	97.8669	98.4023	99.1064	100
1		98.1623	98.6241	99.2308	100
2			98.8153	99.3380	100
3				99.4303	100
4					100

Panel C: Cap Cash Flow Tree

j					
0	0.0000	0.0216	0.1400	0.2629	
1		0.0000	0.0308	0.1364	
2			0.0000	0.0277	
3				0.0000	

Panel D: Cap Value Tree

j					
0	0.1520	0.2434	0.3353	0.2606	
1		0.0622	0.1114	0.1353	
2			0.0137	0.0275	
3				0.0000	

Table 11.12   Cap Implied Volatilities: The Simple BDT and Ho-Lee Models

		SIMPLE BDT			HO-LEE			
		Implied Volatilities σ for Caps with Maturity T (in Parenthesis)						
		0.188	0.2291	0.30277	0.28504	0.00458	0.00584	0.01006	0.010997
Maturity	Data	$(T = 0.5)$	$(T = 1)$	$(T = 3)$	$(T = 5)$	$(T = 0.5)$	$(T = 1)$	$(T = 3)$	$(T = 5)$
0.50	0.0456	0.0456	0.0518	0.0628	0.0602	0.0456	0.0534	0.0796	0.0854
0.75	0.1059	0.1061	0.1184	0.1398	0.1347	0.1047	0.1204	0.1727	0.1843
1.00	0.1859	0.1674	0.1859	0.2262	0.2166	0.1644	0.1859	0.2723	0.2926
1.25	0.2887	0.2385	0.2715	0.3324	0.3178	0.2224	0.2601	0.3899	0.4187
1.50	0.4157	0.3374	0.3735	0.4542	0.4336	0.3105	0.3510	0.5128	0.5522
1.75	0.5662	0.4428	0.4958	0.5944	0.5710	0.4053	0.4544	0.6594	0.7094
2.00	0.7364	0.5583	0.6258	0.7492	0.7182	0.4988	0.5651	0.8076	0.8668
2.25	0.9201	0.6790	0.7648	0.9274	0.8884	0.5996	0.6811	0.9697	1.0353
2.50	1.1129	0.8154	0.9202	1.1118	1.0640	0.7077	0.8005	1.1441	1.2233
2.75	1.3126	0.9577	1.0819	1.3115	1.2559	0.8256	0.9297	1.3287	1.4213
3.00	1.5194	1.1156	1.2543	1.5194	1.4528	0.9508	1.0625	1.5194	1.6245
3.25	1.7352	1.2751	1.4373	1.7454	1.6709	1.0740	1.2044	1.7071	1.8265
3.50	1.9598	1.4442	1.6291	1.9749	1.8895	1.2010	1.3457	1.9021	2.0375
3.75	2.1916	1.6160	1.8252	2.2170	2.1200	1.3288	1.4905	2.1047	2.2501
4.00	2.4288	1.7959	2.0283	2.4643	2.3560	1.4606	1.6387	2.3170	2.4777
4.25	2.6691	1.9791	2.2418	2.7226	2.6078	1.5976	1.7885	2.5288	2.7025
4.50	2.9117	2.1717	2.4639	2.9931	2.8646	1.7361	1.9432	2.7433	2.9337
4.75	3.1562	2.3696	2.6889	3.2734	3.1329	1.8781	2.0986	2.9592	3.1670
5.00	3.4029	2.5712	2.9181	3.5562	3.4029	2.0193	2.2597	3.1818	3.4029

0.2291, 0.30277, and 0.28504. Each level of volatility σ was chosen in such a way that the Simple BDT model exactly prices one given cap, whose maturity is reported underneath the volatility level. For instance, the first volatility level $\sigma_{6-mo} = 0.2291$ exactly prices the cap maturing in six months, which is emphasized by the presence of a box around the cap price level. The second volatility level σ_{1-yr} exactly prices the cap with one year to maturity. And so on. Note that for each choice of σ, the interest rate tree, and thus θ_i, has to be refitted to the current zero coupon yield curve.

The results in this table clearly show that even if the Simple BDT model with constant volatility σ was able to exactly price one given cap, it would fail to price caps with different maturities. The same comment applies to the Ho-Lee model.

The exercise in Table 11.12 also illustrates the notion of an implied volatility. For instance, $\sigma_{6-mo} = 0.188$ is the implied volatility of a cap with maturity of six months, and strike price $r_K = 2.3177$ (= swap rate from Table 11.10). Similarly, $\sigma_{5-yr} = 0.28504$ is the implied volatility of a 5-year cap, with strike rate $r_K = 3.7510$. And so on. In the industry, these types of implied volatility are referred to as *flat volatility*, because a single number characterizes the price of a given cap. The term flat is temporal in meaning: The same volatility applies for every period in the future *for that particular cap*. However, this notion of implied volatility is merely a quoting convention to characterize a given cap with

Figure 11.2 Implied (Flat) and Forward Volatility on November 1, 2004

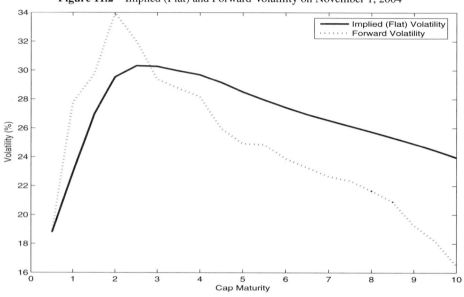

Original Data Source: Bloomberg.

one number. Taken literally, in fact, it leads to a contradiction, as we discuss in the next subsection.

Definition 11.3 *The* **implied flat volatility** *of an interest rate cap with maturity T and strike rate r_K is the level of $\sigma(r_K, T)$ in the interest rate model that exactly prices the cap.*

One interesting fact we can gather from the data in Table 11.12 is that the Simple BDT implied (flat) volatility first increases and then decreases with time to maturity. For instance, $\sigma_{6-mo} = 0.1880$, but it then increases for maturity of 1 year and 3 year ($\sigma_{1-yr} = 0.2291$ and $\sigma_{3-yr} = 0.30277$), and then declines again to $\sigma_{5-yr} = 0.28504$. The solid line in Figure 11.2 shows the implied flat volatility curve on November 1, 2004 for cap maturities up to ten years.

11.3.2 Forward Volatility and the Black, Derman, and Toy Model

The tree that uses the implied volatility of a cap with maturity T (e.g. one year) and strike rate r_K (e.g., 2.4420%) is consistent with the current term structure of interest rates (swap rates) and this particular cap. However, the fact that different maturities / strike prices need different implied volatilities generates a logical inconsistency for the risk neutral pricing methodology. Recall from Chapter 9 that risk neutral pricing stems from the possibility of replicating one given interest rate security with another interest rate security (e.g. the 1-year zero coupon bond with the 2-year zero coupon). Different implied volatilities generate different trees. This suggests that it is not possible to replicate, for instance, the 1-year cap by using the 2-year cap. According to the theory, if it is not possible to replicate, there must be an arbitrage opportunity. All this is not satisfactory. Instead, we would like to have an interest rate model that is able to fit exactly all of the zero coupon bonds *and* all of the caps. The full Black, Derman and Toy model is such a model. The key step is to free up the volatility σ, and let it take different values in the future, i.e. set σ_i for $i = 1, 2, ...$

One difficulty with simply adding a time index i to σ in the Simple BDT model in Equations 11.3 and 11.4 is that the tree is no longer recombining. In fact, the log rate $z_{i,j} = log(r_{i,j})$ after an up and down movement is different from the log rate after a down and up movement. Indeed, it is simple to verify that

$$z_{2,ud} = z_0 + (\theta_0 + \theta_1) \times \Delta + (\sigma_1 - \sigma_2) \times \sqrt{\Delta}$$
$$z_{2,du} = z_0 + (\theta_0 + \theta_1) \times \Delta - (\sigma_1 - \sigma_2) \times \sqrt{\Delta}$$

which differ from each other, unless $\sigma_1 = \sigma_2$.

The Black, Derman and Toy model retains the spirit of the Simple BDT model (which as we have noted is a special case), but resolves the issue by using a different procedure to construct the tree. To introduce this procedure, it is convenient to see it first in the context of the simple model presented in Equations 11.3 and 11.4. In this model, note first that for every i we can write

$$z_{i,j+1} = z_{i,j} - 2 \times \sigma \times \sqrt{\Delta} \quad \text{for} \quad j = 0, 1, ..., i - 1 \tag{11.22}$$

We can see this by simply subtracting Equation 11.4 from Equation 11.3 and rearranging terms. For instance, according to the model, the first step is $z_{1,u} = z_0 + \theta_0 \times \Delta + \sigma\sqrt{\Delta}$ and $z_{1,d} = z_0 + \theta_0 \times \Delta - \sigma \times \sqrt{\Delta}$. Taking the difference of the first from the second, we obtain $z_{1,d} - z_{1,u} = -2 \times \sigma \times \sqrt{\Delta}$ and thus $z_{1,d} = z_{1,u} - 2 \times \sigma \times \sqrt{\Delta}$.

The implication of Equation 11.22 is that instead of searching for θ_i at any step i, we can instead search for $z_{i+1,0}$, that is, the top element in the interest rate tree. In fact, for given value $z_{i+1,0}$, all of the remaining log rates $z_{i+1,j+1}$ can be computed using Equation 11.22. To put it differently, the top interest rate $z_{i+1,0}$ takes the place of θ_i.

The interesting aspect of this alternative but equivalent construction of the Simple BDT model in Equation 11.3 and 11.4 is that we can now extend it to have different step-by-step volatility, σ_i, but the model still generates a recombining tree. This is exactly the Black, Derman, and Toy model. In every step i, then, we look for two values, the top interest rate on the tree $z_{i,0}$, and the volatility level σ_i, in a way that the model contemporaneously fits the zero coupon bond and the cap with maturity (period) $i + 1$. Given that at each stage we have two equations in two unknowns, we are in a good position to be able to obtain a *unique* tree that prices exactly both zero coupon bonds *and* caps. More specifically, for every step i, $i = 1, ...,$ log interest rate $z_{i,j+1}$ is set according to the algorithm

$$z_{i,j+1} = z_{i,j} - 2 \times \sigma_i \times \sqrt{\Delta} \quad \text{for} \quad j = 0, 1, ..., i - 1 \tag{11.23}$$

where the only difference from Equation 11.22 is that now σ_i appears on the right-hand side. Although not necessary, we go one step further and express $z_{i,j+1}$ directly as a function only of top interest rate $z_{i,0}$, instead of $z_{i,j}$. By substituting repeatedly $z_{i,j}, z_{i,j-1}$ on the right-hand side of Equation 11.23 we find

$$z_{i,j+1} = z_{i,0} - 2 \times (j + 1) \times \sigma_i \times \sqrt{\Delta} \tag{11.24}$$

Table 11.13   The Black, Derman and Toy model

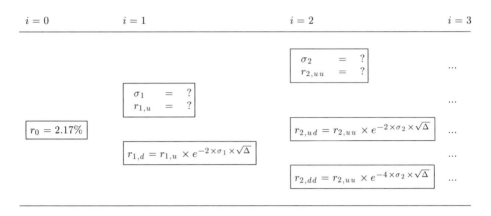

Using directly the actual interest rates $r_{i,j} = e^{z_{i,j}}$, Table 11.13 shows the methodology to construct the tree.

Table 11.14 shows the BDT model that prices both the swap-implied zero coupon bonds and the caps in Table 11.10. The row denoted by σ_i reports the estimated step-i volatility that was necessary to fit the cap prices. The step-i volatility σ_i is called forward volatility, and it is plotted in Figure 11.2 for maturity up to 10 years.[6]

Definition 11.4 *The **forward volatility** σ_i is the level of volatility in step i in the Black, Derman, and Toy model that matches the cap price with maturity $i + 1$.*

From the figure, it appears clear that there is a relation between the forward and the flat volatility. Indeed, it is possible to think of the flat volatility as a sort of weighted average of forward volatility: If the forward volatility of a cap with maturity $i + 1$ is higher than the forward volatility of a cap with maturity i, then the implied volatility of the former cap is also (likely) higher than of the latter.

Once the BDT model is fitted to both the term structure of interest rates and cap prices, it can be used to value other derivative securities that depend on interest rates. Chapters 12 and 13 contain several examples.

11.4 RISK NEUTRAL TREES FOR FUTURES PRICES

In this section we elaborate on the behavior of futures prices on risk neutral trees. Because futures markets, such as the Eurodollar futures or the T-bond futures, are very liquid, traders extract as much information as possible from the behavior of futures prices to build risk neutral trees. Before considering specific contracts, we have to find out what the general behavior of a futures price on an interest rate tree is. Let $F_{i,j}(k)$ denote the futures price

---

[6]In the figure, the forward volatility σ_i has been shifted forward by one period, to match the timing of the implied volatility. That is, σ_i is the forward volatility in step i, which is obtained by pricing a cap that matures at time $i + 1$. For consistency with the implied volatility maturity convention, the figure plots the flat volatility by one quarter forward.

Table 11.14   The Black, Derman and Toy Model on November 1, 2004

Time $\Longrightarrow$	0	0.25	0.5	0.75	1	1.25	1.5	1.75	2	2.25	2.5
Period $i \Longrightarrow$	0	1	2	3	4	5	6	7	8	9	10
$\sigma_i(\%) \Longrightarrow$		18.77	18.66	27.77	30.19	29.76	30.75	33.98	31.77	31.99	30.28
node j											
0	2.17	2.68	3.21	4.26	5.37	6.45	7.97	10.58	12.02	14.63	16.36
1		2.22	2.66	3.23	3.97	4.79	5.86	7.53	8.74	10.62	12.08
2			2.21	2.44	2.94	3.56	4.31	5.36	6.36	7.72	8.93
3				1.85	2.17	2.64	3.17	3.82	4.63	5.60	6.59
4					1.60	1.96	2.33	2.72	3.37	4.07	4.87
5						1.46	1.71	1.94	2.45	2.95	3.60
6							1.26	1.38	1.79	2.15	2.66
7								0.98	1.30	1.56	1.96
8									0.95	1.13	1.45
9										0.82	1.07
10											0.79

of a contract maturing at time k at time/node (i, j). If a trader enters into a futures contract in (i, j), what is the expected one-period profit? The key characteristics of futures, we may recall, is that they are marked-to-market daily, that is, at the end of every trading day, profits / losses accrue to the account of the trader.

Assume that mark-to-market occurs at the same frequency of the time steps on the tree, for simplicity (or assume that the time step is one day). From the mechanics of futures markets, then, the profits per period are given by the change in the futures price between one period to the next. That is, if the interest rate moves up on the tree from $r_{i,j}$ to $r_{i+1,j}$, for instance, then the profit from the futures is $N \times (F_{i+1,j}(k) - F_{i,j}(k))$, where N is the contract size.

Since the interest rate tree is risk neutral, by construction, we find that the risk neutral expected profit from a position in futures is given by

$$\begin{array}{ll} \text{Risk neutral} \\ \text{expected profit / loss} \end{array} = E^*[F_{i+1}(k) - F_{ij}(k)] \qquad (11.25)$$

$$= \frac{1}{2} \times (F_{i+1,j}(k) - F_{i,j}(k)) + \frac{1}{2}(F_{i+1,j+1}(k) - F_{i,j}(k)) \qquad (11.26)$$

The key question is the following: If all market participants *were* risk neutral, what should the expected risk neutral profit be? Because it costs nothing to enter into a futures position, the answer is the expected profit should be zero. In fact, if the risk neutral expected profit was positive, then risk neutral agents, who care only about expected profits and not about risk, would go infinitely long in the contract, pushing up the futures price. Similarly, if the risk neutral expected profits from futures was negative, all risk neutral agents would short the futures.[7]

---

[7]Recall, once again, that the risk neutral pricing methodology is not to assume that agents are risk neutral, but rather that the probabilities along the tree have been changed to incorporate the risk aversion of the market participants. See again Chapter 9.

The key implication of the risk neutral pricing methodology applied to futures is then the following restriction:

$$\text{Risk neutral expected profit / loss } = 0 \Longrightarrow E^*[F_{i+1}(k) - F_{ij}(k)] = 0 \qquad (11.27)$$

Using Equation 11.26, we then obtain a relation between the futures price in node (i, j) and the two subsequent nodes.

$$F_{i,j}(k) = \frac{1}{2} \times F_{i+1,j}(k) + \frac{1}{2}F_{i+1,j+1}(k) \qquad (11.28)$$

Equation 11.28 is going to be our main tool to build a risk neutral tree for futures. This equation allows us to move backward on the tree, exactly as we did for other securities: given the futures prices at nodes at time $i + 1$, we can compute the futures price at node i.

One final step in the construction of the risk neutral tree for futures prices is to find the final value, at maturity, of the futures price. We use the *convergence property* of futures prices: At maturity, the futures price must converge to the value of the security underlying the futures contract. Denote by $V_{i,j}$ the final payoff from the futures contract at maturity i. For instance, in a T-bond futures $V_{i,j}$ is the value of the appropriate Treasury bond scheduled for delivery in node (i, j). The convergence property then requires that at maturity i, the futures price equals the value of the security underlying the futures contract

$$F_{k,j}(k) = N \times V_{k,j} \qquad (11.29)$$

where $k = $ maturity. From the risk neutral interest rate tree, we can obtain the value of $V_{k,j}$ at maturity k of the futures contract, and thus obtain the final condition for the risk neutral futures tree. Equation 11.28 then provides the backward methodology to build the rest of the tree. The next two sections provide two examples, by focusing on the Eurodollar futures and T-bond futures.

11.4.1   Eurodollar Futures

We discussed the details of Eurodollar futures in Section 6.1 of Chapter 6. Recall from Table 6.3 in that chapter that the underlying final cash payment depends on $N \times (\text{3-month LIBOR})$ where $N = \$1,000,000$ is the contract size. From the same table we remember that the Eurodollar futures contract with maturity k in node (i, j) is *quoted* as $F_{i,j}(k) = (100 - f_{i,j}(k))$ where $f_{i,j}(k)$ is the futures rate, in percentage.

Denoting by $r_4(i, j)$ the 3-month LIBOR rate in node (i, j), it follows then that the Eurodollar futures LIBOR rate at maturity must converge to

$$f_{k,j}(k) = N \times r_4(k, j) \qquad (11.30)$$

where $k = $ maturity, and recall the notation $r_n(i, j)$ denotes the rate with n compounding frequency, at time/node (i, j).

Consider again the Black, Derman and Toy model in Table 11.14, which was fitted to the swap rates and cap prices on November 1, 2004. Assume first for simplicity that the futures contract also matures at quarters $i = 1, 2, 3$, and 4 in Table 11.14.[8] Recall also

---

[8]Because Eurodollar futures contract expirations are in the March cycle, these maturities are all off by 1 1/2 months, but it simplifies the discussion to first assume that the futures themselves also mature at the same time of the swaps used in the fitting exercise.

Table 11.15 Eurodollar Futures Trees

	3-Month Futures Rates Tree						3-Month Eurodollar Futures Price				
i	0	1	2	3	4	i	0	1	2	3	4
j						j					
0	2.46	2.69				0	97.54	97.31			
1		2.23				1		97.77			

	6-Month Futures Rates Tree					6-Month Eurodollar Futures Price			
j					j				
0	2.69	2.95	3.22		0	97.31	97.05	96.78	
1		2.44	2.67		1		97.56	97.33	
2			2.21		2			97.79	

	9-Month Futures Rates Tree					9-Month Eurodollar Futures Price				
j						j				
0	2.90	3.30	3.76	4.28		0	97.10	96.70	96.24	95.72
1		2.50	2.85	3.24		1		97.50	97.15	96.76
2			2.15	2.45		2			97.85	97.55
3				1.86		3				98.14

	1-Year Futures Rates Tree						1-Year Eurodollar Futures Price				
j						j					
0	2.18	2.69	3.22	4.28	5.41	0	97.82	97.31	96.78	95.72	94.59
1		2.23	2.67	3.24	3.99	1		97.77	97.33	96.76	96.01
2			2.21	2.45	2.95	2			97.79	97.55	97.05
3				1.86	2.18	3				98.14	97.82
4					1.61	4					98.39

that the Black, Derman, and Toy model generates an interest rate tree in which rates are continously compounded. The 3-month LIBOR rate underlying the Eurodollar futures contract is instead linearly compounded, which implies that the futures rate at a given maturity k must equal

$$f_{k,j}(k) = r_4(k,j) = 4 \times \left(e^{r_{k,j} \times 0.25} - 1\right) \tag{11.31}$$

where we assume the contract size is $N = 1$. Table 11.15 reports the trees for the Eurodollar futures prices with 3-, 6-, 9- and 12-month maturities. Consider first the left-hand side trees in Table 11.15: The first tree at the top represents the tree of the futures rate $f_{i,j}$: The last two entries at $i = 1$ are given by Equation 11.31, where recall that $r_4(1,j)$ is obtained from $r_{1,j}$ in Table 11.14. The root of the tree is obtained from the no arbitrage condition in Equation 11.28. That is, $f_0(1) = f_{1,0}(1)/2 + f_{1,1}(1)/2$. Similarly, the 6-month futures rate tree, right below, starts at the end with Equation 11.31 for $k = 2$, and again $r_{k,j}$ stems from Table 11.14. Given the final condition, we move backward to obtain the whole tree for the futures price, using Equation 11.28.

The right-hand side trees in Table 11.15 simply contain the implied quotes for the Eurodollar futures, as it is convention to quote it as $F_{i,j}(k) = 100 - f_{i,j}(k)$.

The methodology above implies that given an interest rate tree, such as the one in Table 11.14, we can obtain the implied Eurodollar futures prices. As we did for the implied volatilities from cap prices, we can also reverse the methodology and obtain the tree that is consistent with quoted Eurodollar futures prices. Indeed, Eurodollar futures are much more liquid instruments than swaps, the securities used to obtain the tree in Table 11.14.

Thus, instead of using swaps, traders typically use Eurodollar futures with maturities up to 3-years (the most liquid ones) to obtain the tree.

11.4.2   T-Note and T-Bond Futures

We introduced T-note and T-bond futures in Chapter 6. In this section we go over some features of the 10-year Treasury note futures and the 30-year Treasury bond futures, as their characteristics generate some interesting features that deserve study. Table 6.2 in Chapter 6 describes the term of the 10-year T-note futures contract. Upon examination of the terms of the futures contract, we realize that the party who is taking a short position in these futures, and thus commits to deliver the underlying security at maturity, is actually also acquiring implicitly some valuable options. They are as follows:

1. *Quality option:* There are several securities that are eligible for delivery: For the 10-year contract, these are all the Treasury notes that have a maturity between 6 1/2 and 10 years. For the 30-year Treasury Bond futures the deliverable securities must have at least 15 years to maturity (or to call). It follows that the trader who is short the futures contract has the choice of which Treasury note or bond to deliver. Across all the securities that are eligible for delivery, the short trader will choose the one that is least expensive, which is then called *cheapest-to-deliver*. The cheapest-to-deliver note or bond is not always the same over the life of the futures, as we will see below in an example.

2. *Wild card option:* There is a whole month to deliver the note or bond. During this month the futures contract trades until the seventh business day before the last business day. Every trading day in the delivery month, the short may deliver until 8 pm (Chicago time), while the contract stops trading at 2 pm (Chicago time). The trader who is short the futures contract can then participate in any price decline in the note or bond prices between 2 pm to 8 pm every day. Essentially, the trader short the contract has about 15 sequential six-hours put options during each day of the delivery month until the last day of futures trading.

3. *End-of-month option:* Trading stops seven days prior to the last business day of the contract month. However, delivery can occur up to the last trading day. Before the invoice price of the futures has been fixed on the last trading day, but bond prices keep trading, the short has a timing option as it can select any day during the last week to deliver.

The existence of these options has an impact on the futures price itself. Consider for instance the quality option. The short trader will deliver the bond that is least expensive. Clearly, if no correction was made to the futures price, the cheapest bond or note would correspond to the one with the lowest maturity and coupon. To avoid liquidity issues and manipulations, it is desirable to make all of the securities eligible for delivery as similar as possible, i.e. to standardize them. The exchange achieves this result by modifying the (futures) price that the long side of the contract will pay in exchange for the bond or note that it receives. In particular, the invoice price paid by the long side to the short side equals the futures price F_{t^*} at maturity t^* multiplied by a conversion factor C. This conversion factor is defined to make the deliverable bond comparable to a 6% coupon bond or note.

Table 11.16 Conversion Factors for 10-Year Treasury Note Futures

	Coupon	Issue Date	Maturity Date	Cusip Number	Issuance (Billions)	6% Conversion Factors					
						Mar. 2008	Jun. 2008	Sep. 2008	Dec. 2008	Mar. 2009	Jun. 2009
1.) @	3 1/2	02/15/08	02/15/18	912828HR4	$23.0	0.8174	0.8210	0.8244	0.8281	0.8317	0.8354
2.)	4	02/15/05	02/15/15	912828DM9	$23.0	0.8902	0.8937	—	—	—	—
3.)	4 1/8	05/16/05	05/15/15	912828DV9	$22.0	0.8941	0.8971	0.9003	—	—	—
4.)	4 1/4	11/15/04	11/15/14	912828DC1	$23.0	0.9069	—	—	—	—	—
5.)	4 1/4	08/15/05	08/15/15	912828EE6	$21.0	0.8983	0.9012	0.9040	0.9069	—	—
6.)	4 1/4	11/15/07	11/15/17	912828HH6	$21.0	0.8747	0.8771	0.8797	0.8821	0.8848	0.8873
7.)	4 1/2	11/15/05	11/15/15	912828EN6	$21.0	0.9105	0.9128	0.9153	0.9177	0.9202	
8.)	4 1/2	02/15/06	02/15/16	912828EW6	$21.0	0.9080	0.9105	0.9128	0.9153	0.9177	0.9202
9.)	4 1/2	05/15/07	05/15/17	912828GS3	$21.0	0.8968	0.8990	0.9013	0.9034	0.9058	0.9080
10.)	4 5/8	11/15/06	11/15/16	912828FY1	$21.0	0.9095	0.9115	0.9136	0.9157	0.9179	0.9200
11.)	4 5/8	02/15/07	02/15/17	912828GH7	$21.0	0.9074	0.9095	0.9115	0.9136	0.9157	0.9179
12.)	4 3/4	08/15/07	08/15/17	912828HA1	$21.0	0.9122	0.9140	0.9158	0.9177	0.9195	0.9215
13.)	4 7/8	08/15/06	08/15/16	912828FQ8	$21.0	0.9275	0.9293	0.9310	0.9328	0.9346	0.9365
14.)	5 1/8	05/15/06	05/15/16	912828FF2	$21.0	0.9450	0.9463	0.9478	0.9491	0.9506	0.9519

Footnotes: "@" indicates the most recently auctioned U.S. Treasury security eligible for delivery.
The information contained in this publication is taken from sources believed to be reliable, but is not guaranteed by the
CME Group as to its accuracy or completeness, nor any trading result,
and is intended for purposes of information and education only. The Rules and Regulations of the CME Group should be
consulted as the authoritative source on all current contract
specifications and regulations. To obtain updated conversion factors, please visit the Exchange's website at www.cmegroup.com.

Source: CBOT web site: http://www.cbot.com/cbot/pub/cont_detail/0,3206,1391+20356,00.html accessed on June 11, 2008.

The exact formula determining the conversion factor is given by the price of a security that is equivalent to the delivered note, but with a constant yield equal to 6%. That is, setting $y = .06$, the conversion factor of a bond with a coupon equal to c for a futures with expiration date t^* is given by[9]

$$C = P_c(t^*, T) = \sum_{i=1}^{n} \frac{c/2}{(1 + y/2)^{2 \times (T_i - t^*)}} + \frac{1}{(1 + y/2)^{2 \times (T_n - t^*)}} \quad (11.32)$$

For instance, Table 11.16 reports some of the conversion factors to be applied to the various notes eligible for delivery on March 2008 and following months for the 10-year Treasury note futures. In this case, all of the notes that are eligible for delivery have a coupon that is lower than 6%, and thus the futures price will be adjusted downwards ($C < 1$) at maturity of the futures contract in order to determine the invoice price.

How does the short trader determine the best bond to deliver? Denote by $F_{i,j}(k)$ the futures price with maturity k in time/node (i, j). Let there be n notes that are eligible for delivery. For each note h, $h = 1, \ldots, n$, let C^h denote its conversion factor, and let $P^h_{k,j}$ denote its clean price. If the short trader elects to deliver a given bond h, he or she will receive then $F_{k,j}(k) \times C^h$ in exchange of a security with clean price $P^h_{k,j}$. For each note h we can compute the difference in price, called the basis:

$$\text{Basis of Note } h = P^h_{k,j} - F_{k,j}(k) \times C^h \quad (11.33)$$

[9]A convenient formula is the following: Let $a = 1/(1 + y/2)$. Then $\sum_{j=1}^{n} = (a - a^{n+1})/(1 - a)$. It follows that assuming that (a) there are exactly n coupon payments between the futures maturity and the bond maturity, and (b) the futures delivery date is on a coupon date, the conversion factor is given by the simpler formula $C = c/2 * (a - a^{n+1})/(1 - a) + a^n$. If (b) is not satisfied, a small time adjustment needs to be made.

The bond h with the smallest basis is called cheapest-to-deliver. [10] It is important to note that the basis cannot be negative during the delivery month, otherwise a simple arbitrage exists. In fact, if this was the case, a trader could short the futures, buy the bond and immediately deliver it, making an instant profit.

How does the presence of these options affect the futures price? We now build a tree along the lines of the previous sections but to illustrate the impact of these implicit options on futures prices. For simplicity, we only consider the quality option in a simplified environment.

■ **EXAMPLE 11.7**

Consider the interest rate tree obtained in Example 11.1 by fitting the Ho-Lee model to the term structure of interest rates on January 8, 2002. By using a procedure similar to the one illustrated in that example, the resulting interest tree in Table 11.2 can be extended to longer horizons to price longer-term notes and bonds. More specifically, Panel A of Table 11.17 contains the zero coupon bond data on January 8, 2002 up to maturity $T = 8$. Panel B contains the fitted Ho-Lee model (the first part is the same as the one in Table 11.2).

Consider now for instance a 10-year Treasury note futures, with maturity of one year (December, 2003). According to the terms of the contract, described in Table 6.2 in Chapter 6, only Treasury notes with maturities between 6 1/2 and 10 years can be delivered. As explained above, the futures price will be adjusted by the appropriate conversion factor to make each possible deliverable bond comparable to a 6% bond. To illustrate the tree methodology to T-note futures, it is convenient to first consider the case in which the security underlying the future is exactly a 6%, 7-year Treasury note (assuming one exists). Given the risk neutral interest rate tree in Panel B, we can compute the risk neutral tree for the deliverable T-note, which is contained in Panel C of Table 11.17. The T-note priced on this tree is a 8-year, 6% note, rather than 7-year note, the reason being that the T-note must have 7 years to maturity at the maturity of the futures contract, in one year from the present.

If this was the only possible deliverable security, what would be the corresponding futures price at maturity? We know that at maturity the futures price must converge to the value of the underlying security to avoid an arbitrage. In other words, denoting by $k = 2$ the node corresponding to the maturity of the futures contract (one year from now), we must have

$$F_{k,j}(k) = P_{k,j} \tag{11.34}$$

where $P_{k,j}$ is the price of the bond at time k and node j. What about the futures price before maturity? At this point, we proceed backward by using Equation 11.28. Table 11.18 shows the risk neutral futures price tree.

Consider now the case in which in addition to the 6% note described earlier, two addition notes are also available, one with a 3% coupon and one with a 9% coupon. Assume all of these notes have the same maturity. Using the same interest rate tree

---

[10]Note that the accrued interest is not part of the basis, as both the futures price and the T-note price are clean prices. In other words, suppose the short trader has to purchase bond k from the market in order to deliver it. Then, the short trader would pay $P_{k,j}^h$ plus accrued interest, but he/she will receive $F_{k,j} \times C^h$ plus accrued interest. Thus, the basis computed using values instead of clean prices is still given by Equation 11.33.

as in Panel B of Table 11.17 we can obtain the trees of these T-notes as well. They are contained in Panel A and Panel B of Table 11.19. The next step is to compute the conversion factor for each of these notes. We can apply the formula in Equation 11.32 to each of these notes, and obtain

$$\text{Conversion factor 3\% note} = C^1 = 0.830558903 \tag{11.35}$$
$$\text{Conversion factor 6\% note} = C^2 = 1 \tag{11.36}$$
$$\text{Conversion factor 9\% note} = C^3 = 1.169441097 \tag{11.37}$$

Consider now the futures maturity date k. For each node j, we can compute the basis for each bond. We know that at each of these nodes (k, j), the trader who is short the futures will choose to deliver the bond with the smallest basis. Node by node, we therefore compute

$$\text{Node } (k, j): \ \min_h \left(P_{k,j}^h - F_{k,j}(k) \times C^h \right) \tag{11.38}$$

The futures price at time k in node j, $F_{k,j}(k)$, will move to prevent arbitrage, so that for every j the following must occur

$$\text{Node } (k, j): \ \min_h \left(P_{k,j}^h - F_{k,j}(k) \times C^h \right) = 0 \tag{11.39}$$

where the minimization is taken across the bonds $h = 1, ..., n$ that are eligible for delivery. In other words, the futures price moves to make the bond price with the smallest basis in fact equal to the futures price (corrected by the conversion factor). That is, $F_{k,j}(k)$ is given by

$$F_{k,j}(k) = \min_h \frac{P_{k,j}^h}{C^h} \tag{11.40}$$

Once $F_{k,j}$ has been computed, the rest of the risk neutral futures tree follows from Equation 11.28. Table 11.20 illustrate the calculations. The last three columns report the converted bond price, namely, $\frac{P_{k,j}^h}{C^h}$ for each bond h (3%, 6% and 9%) and for each interest rate node $j = 0, 1, 2$. The futures price at each node j will equal the minimum across each row. That is, the futures price in node $(k, j) = (2, 0)$ is given by $F_{2,0}(2) = 87.86$ which corresponds to the converted note price of the 3% note. This is the minimum across the three bonds for that particular interest rate, and thus the cheapest-to-deliver is the 3% T-note. Similarly, $F_{2,2}(2) = 117.28$ corresponds to the converted price of the 9% Treasury note, which in this case is the minimum across all three available notes. The cheapest-to-deliver is the 9% T-note. This finding implies that depending on whether interest rates increase or decrease, the T-note that is the cheapest-to-deliver alternates between T-notes with different coupons. The rest of the tree, as mentioned, stems from the general Equation 11.28.

The futures prices in the tree in Table 11.20 are always lower than the corresponding futures prices for the case when only the 6% Treasury note was available. This lower futures price reflects the option that is implicit in the futures contract. The other two options (wild card option and end-of-the-month option) would also decrease the futures price.

Table 11.17 The 6% Bond Tree

Panel A. Zero Coupon Bond Data

Time T	0	0.5	1	1.5	2	2.5	3	3.5	4	4.5	5	5.5	6	6.5	7	7.5	8
Period i	0	1	2	3	4	5	6	7	8	9	10	11	12	13	14	15	16
Data		99.1338	97.8925	96.1462	94.1011	91.7136	89.2258	86.8142	84.5016	82.1848	79.7718	77.4339	75.292	72.961	70.865	68.677	66.764

Panel B. The Fitted Ho-Lee Interest Rate Tree

$\theta_i\,(\times100)$	1.5675	2.1824	1.4374	1.7324	0.7873	0.0423	-0.0628	0.4322	0.9271	0.1202	-0.5194	1.5300	-0.7335	1.0813	-1.0233	0.7313	-1.7140
node j																	
0	1.74	3.75	6.06	8.00	10.09	11.71	12.95	14.15	15.59	17.27	18.56	19.52	21.51	22.36	24.13	24.84	26.43
1		1.30	3.61	5.56	7.65	9.26	10.51	11.70	13.14	14.83	16.11	17.07	19.06	19.92	21.68	22.39	23.98
2			1.17	3.11	5.20	6.82	8.06	9.25	10.69	12.38	13.66	14.63	16.61	17.47	19.24	19.95	21.54
3				0.66	2.75	4.37	5.61	6.81	8.25	9.93	11.22	12.18	14.17	15.02	16.79	17.50	19.09
4					0.31	1.92	3.17	4.36	5.80	7.49	8.77	9.73	11.72	12.58	14.34	15.05	16.64
5						-0.52	0.72	1.91	3.35	5.04	6.32	7.29	9.27	10.13	11.90	12.61	14.20
6							-1.73	-0.53	0.91	2.59	3.88	4.84	6.83	7.68	9.45	10.16	11.75
7								-2.98	-1.54	0.15	1.43	2.39	4.38	5.24	7.00	7.71	9.30
8									-3.99	-2.30	-1.02	-0.05	1.94	2.79	4.56	5.27	6.86
9										-4.75	-3.46	-2.50	-0.51	0.35	2.11	2.82	4.41
10											-5.91	-4.95	-2.96	-2.10	-0.34	0.37	1.96
11												-7.39	-5.40	-4.55	-2.78	-2.07	-0.48
12													-7.85	-6.99	-5.23	-4.52	-2.93
13														-9.44	-7.68	-6.97	-5.38
14															-10.12	-9.41	-7.82
15																-11.86	-10.27
16																	-12.72

Panel C. The 6%, 8-Year Treasury Note Tree

j																	
0	106.77	96.83	88.93	82.83	78.11	74.65	72.17	70.46	69.49	69.35	70.17	71.88	74.48	78.52	83.79	90.97	100
1		112.57	102.40	94.50	88.31	83.65	80.14	77.54	75.77	74.90	75.05	76.10	78.02	81.36	85.83	92.09	100
2			118.21	108.04	100.01	93.85	89.09	85.39	82.65	80.92	80.28	80.58	81.74	84.30	87.92	93.22	100
3				123.76	113.45	105.44	99.13	94.11	90.21	87.46	85.90	85.33	85.64	87.35	90.06	94.37	100
4					128.89	118.61	110.41	103.80	98.52	94.56	91.93	90.37	89.73	90.51	92.26	95.53	100
5						133.57	123.09	114.56	107.65	102.28	98.41	95.73	94.03	93.79	94.51	96.71	100
6							137.35	126.52	117.67	110.66	105.36	101.41	98.53	97.19	96.82	97.90	100
7								139.82	128.69	119.76	112.84	107.44	103.26	100.72	99.18	99.10	100
8									140.80	129.65	120.86	113.85	108.22	104.37	101.60	100.32	100
9										140.40	129.48	120.65	113.42	108.16	104.08	101.56	100
10											138.74	127.86	118.88	112.09	106.62	102.81	100
11												135.53	124.60	116.17	109.22	104.07	100
12													130.61	120.39	111.89	105.35	100
13														124.78	114.62	106.65	100
14															117.42	107.96	100
15																109.29	100
16																	100

Table 11.18   Futures Price Tree if only a 7-year, 6% Note is Available for Delivery

Period i	0	1	2
Node j			
0	102.98	95.66	88.93
1		110.30	102.40
2			118.21

11.5 IMPLIED TREES: FINAL REMARKS

The methodology developed in this section is rather powerful. The Black, Derman and Toy model, for instance, is able to fit the whole term structure of interest rates and the option prices. This is remarkable. Moreover, it implies that in principle, on the tree, we can replicate caps using zero coupon bonds, or a short-term cap using long-term caps, and so on. However, all this comes with a cost, and the cost is called *overfitting*. The model has a number of degrees of freedom equal to the number of securities we want to price. Therefore, it will lack stability of the parameters (e.g. σ_i's) and won't have any predicting power. Indeed, traders using these models simply refit the model day by day in order to have a single (big) model able to price all of these interest rate securities at once.

The question is, then, what do we do with this model now? By construction, the model exactly prices zeros and caps, so we cannot use this model to price those. There are two answers:

1. The model is useful for computing hedge ratios. If a trader sells a particular cap, he may want to hedge it by taking a position in the underlying swaps. How can the trader hedge the exposure? As we discussed in Chapter 9, a binomial tree offers the answer. The hedge ratio is always given by

$$\text{Hedge ratio} = \frac{c_{1,u} - c_{1,d}}{V_{1,u} - V_{1,d}} \tag{11.41}$$

   where $c_{1,u}$ and $c_{1,d}$ are the values of the interest rate security sold (e.g., a cap) in the two interest rate scenarios $r_{1,u}$ and $r_{1,d}$, and $V_{1,u}$ and $V_{1,d}$ are the values of the interest rate security chosen to hedge the exposure (e.g., a swap) in the same nodes.

2. Once fitted to zeros and caps, the model can be used to obtain the price of other interest rate securities, such as structured notes, swaptions, American swaptions, and so on. The price of these additional derivative securities will be naturally in line with those of caps that have been used to price them. In particular, we could hedge the more complicated security using the basic, and more liquid securities, such as caps.

11.6 SUMMARY

In this chapter we covered the following topics:

Table 11.19 3% and 6% Treasury Note Price Trees

Panel A. The 3%, 8-Year Treasury Note Tree

Period i / Node j	0	1	2	3	4	5	6	7	8	9	10	11	12	13	14	15	16
0	86.77	79.01	72.97	68.47	65.15	62.93	61.57	60.93	60.98	61.82	63.59	66.27	69.86	74.91	81.28	89.65	100
1		93.04	85.04	78.97	74.38	71.11	68.88	67.46	66.81	67.02	68.20	70.29	73.26	77.66	83.27	90.75	100
2			99.26	91.21	85.01	80.44	77.10	74.72	73.23	72.68	73.16	74.56	76.84	80.52	85.32	91.87	100
3				105.47	97.26	91.06	86.35	82.81	80.29	78.83	78.48	79.10	80.59	83.48	87.41	93.00	100
4					111.39	103.16	96.78	91.82	88.06	85.52	84.20	83.92	84.53	86.54	89.56	94.14	100
5						116.96	108.53	101.84	96.62	92.79	90.35	89.04	88.67	89.73	91.76	95.30	100
6							121.77	113.01	106.03	100.71	96.97	94.47	93.01	93.03	94.02	96.47	100
7								125.45	116.39	109.31	104.07	100.25	97.57	96.45	96.33	97.66	100
8									127.80	118.68	111.71	106.39	102.35	100.00	98.70	98.86	100
9										128.87	119.93	112.91	107.37	103.69	101.12	100.08	100
10											128.76	119.83	112.64	107.51	103.61	101.31	100
11												127.19	118.17	111.47	106.16	102.56	100
12													123.98	115.58	108.77	103.82	100
13														119.84	111.44	105.10	100
14															114.18	106.39	100
15																107.70	100
16																	100

Panel B. The 9%, 8-Year Treasury Note Tree

Node j	0	1	2	3	4	5	6	7	8	9	10	11	12	13	14	15	16
0	126.77	114.66	104.88	97.19	91.07	86.38	82.77	80.00	78.01	76.88	76.75	77.50	79.11	82.12	86.30	92.29	100
1		132.10	119.77	110.03	102.24	96.18	91.41	87.62	84.72	82.78	81.89	81.92	82.79	85.05	88.39	93.43	100
2			137.16	124.88	115.02	107.27	101.07	96.06	92.07	89.16	87.40	86.60	86.64	88.08	90.52	94.58	100
3				142.05	129.64	119.83	111.91	105.41	100.14	96.09	93.31	91.56	90.69	91.22	92.72	95.74	100
4					146.39	134.05	124.04	115.78	108.98	103.61	99.66	96.83	94.94	94.48	94.96	96.92	100
5						150.18	137.65	127.27	118.68	111.76	106.46	102.42	99.39	97.85	97.26	98.12	100
6							152.92	140.03	129.32	120.61	113.76	108.35	104.05	101.35	99.62	99.32	100
7								154.18	141.00	130.20	121.60	114.63	108.95	104.98	102.03	100.55	100
8									153.81	140.62	130.00	121.31	114.08	108.74	104.50	101.78	100
9										151.93	139.03	128.38	119.47	112.64	107.04	103.04	100
10											148.71	135.89	125.11	116.68	109.63	104.30	100
11												143.86	131.04	120.87	112.29	105.59	100
12													137.25	125.21	115.01	106.89	100
13														129.72	117.81	108.20	100
14															120.67	109.54	100
15																110.88	100
16																	100

Table 11.20   Treasury Note Futures when 3%, 6% and 8% Notes Are Available

Period i	0	1	2	Converted Note Prices $P_{i*,j}^k/C^k$		
Node j				3% Note	6% Note	9% Note
0	102.48	95.12	87.86	87.86	88.93	89.68
1		109.83	102.38	102.38	102.40	102.42
2			117.28	119.51	118.21	117.28

1. Risk neutral trees: Risk neutral trees are binomial trees that are specifically designed to price interest rate securities, as the probabalities of upward and downward movements are risk neutral. Three examples are:

   (a) Ho-Lee model. The main variable is the level of the short-term interest rates. The risk neutral tree is set up to exactly fit the term structure of interest rates. With sufficient steps, the probabality distribution of interest rates in the future converges to a bell-shaped normal distribution. One drawback is that it allows for negative interest rates.

   (b) Simple Black, Derman, and Toy (BDT). In the simple BDT model the main variable is the natural logarithm of the short-term interest rate. Like the Ho-Lee, the simple BDT model also fits exactly the term structure of interes rates, but it does not allow for negative interest rates. With sufficient steps, the probability distribution of interest rates in the future converges to a log-normal distribution. One drawback is that it gives too little probability to low interest rates.

   (c) Black, Derman, and Toy. Unlike the Ho-Lee and the simple BDT, the full BDT model is also able to fit the term structure of volatility of caps, as it assumes that the volatility of interest rates can be different step after step. The simple BDT model is obtained as a special case by assuming constant volatility.

2. Caps and floors: These are portfolios of options, called caplets or floolets, that pay when the short-term interest rate is above a strike rate (caps) or below a strike rate (floors). They can be priced on a binomial tree, through the construction first of a cash flow tree, which defines the cash flow that is paid by the cap or floor along the tree.

3. Empirical interest rate volatility: This is the volatility of interest rate movements computed from the historic time series of interest rate changes. For the Ho-Lee model, such volatility can be computed as the annualized standard deviation of interest rate changes, while for the simple BDT model such volatility can be computed as the annualized standard deviation of changes in log interest rates.

4. Cap/floor implied volatility. The volatility of the interest rate process that matches exactly a given cap or floor is called the cap/floor implied volatility. It is also called flat volatility.

5. Cap/floor forward volatility. This is the volatility that prices a given caplet/floorlet in a cap/floor. The implied (flat) volatility can be thought of as a weighted average

Table 11.21   An Interest Rate Tree

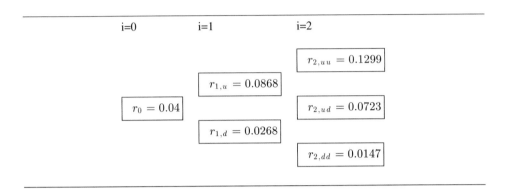

of forward volatilities. The forward volatility can be computed while fitting the full BDT model to bonds and caps.

6. Swaps and swaptions: Swaps are contracts to exchange cash flows in the future, according to a specific formula. Fixed-for-floating swaps, the most common, entail a counterparty to pay a fixed coupon in exchange for a floating rate that depends on a reference rate. Swaptions are options to enter into a given swap at some time in the future. In a receiver swaption, the option holder has the right to enter into a swap as a fixed rate receiver, while in a payer swaption the option holder has the right to enter into a swap as a fixed rate payer.

7. Risk neutral binomial trees for futures: Futures contracts are marked-to-market. The profits and losses within a short period are just given by the change in the futures price. The risk neutral methodology implies that the futures price today is equal to the risk neutral expected futures price tomorrow. Given the convergence property of futures prices, it is possible to construct the futures tree by moving backward from the futures price at maturity, which equals the underlying value.

8. Cheapest-to-deliver: In T-bond and T-note futures, the short side has the option to deliver any note or bond within a class of deliverable Treasury securities. Although an adjustment is made to adjust the futures price to the coupon and maturity of the bond, still there is a bond that is the least expensive to deliver at maturity. This bond is called the cheapest-to-deliver. Which bond has this characteristics depends on the interest rate itself.

11.7 EXERCISES

1. You have estimated the risk neutral model for the continuously compounded interest rate as in Table 11.21. There is equal probability to move up or down the tree and each interval time represents *1 year*, that is, $\Delta = 1$.

    (a) Compute the *current* ($i = 0$) zero coupon spot curve, for all possible maturities;

Table 11.22   An Interest Rate Tree

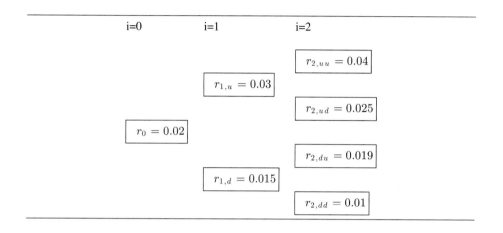

(b) Compute the price of a security that pays $100 at time $i = 2$ if the interest rate at that time is .0723 and zero otherwise. That is,

$$CF(2) = \begin{cases} 100 & \text{if} \quad r(2) = .0723 \\ 0 & \text{otherwise} \end{cases}$$

(c) Compute the price of a 3-year floor with strike rate $r_K = .04$ and notional 100. Recall that a floor pays at time $i + 1$ the cash flows (determined at time i):

$$CF(i+1) = N \times \max(r_K - r_1(i), 0)$$

where $r_1(i)$ is the annually compounded rate at time i.

(d) Compute the spread between the 2-year zero coupon yield and the 1-year zero coupon yield, both at time $i = 0$ and at time $i = 1$. What is the expected change in the spread?

(e) Suppose that you want to hedge against an increase in the spread between $i = 0$ and $i = 1$. What is the price of a European *spread call* option, with 1 year to maturity, strike spread $\overline{sp} = .008$ and notional amount $N = 100$? The spread call option pays

$$CF(1) = N \times \max(Spread(1) - \overline{sp}, 0)$$

where "$Spread(1)$" is the spread between the 2-year and the 1-year continuously compounded zero coupon yields as of time $i = 1$ (that is, 1 year from now).

2. You have estimated the model for continuously compounded interest rates in Table 11.22. There is equal risk neutral probability to move up or down the tree and each interval time represents *1 year*, that is, $\Delta = 1$.

(a) Compute the *current* ($i = 0$) zero-coupon spot curve, for all possible maturities.

Table 11.23   An Interest Rate Tree

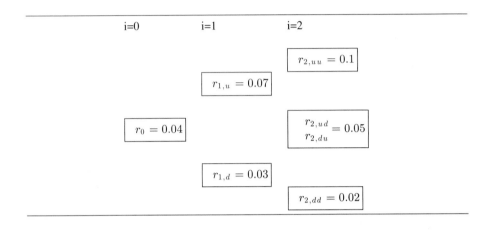

(b) Compute the price of a 3-year, 3% coupon bond.

(c) Compute the price of a standard 3-year floating rate bond, with coupon equal to the risk-free rate (you should remember the timing of cashflows, here). Is the price what you expected?

(d) Compute the value of a swap, from the perspective of a fixed rate payer, with swap rate equal to 3% and notional 100.

(e) Compute the price of a 3-year cap with strike rate 3%, and notional 100. What do you think the price of a floor, with strike rate 3%, should be?

3. Suppose that you estimated the risk neutral tree for interest rates in Table 11.23, where there is equal risk neutral probability to move up or down the tree. Assume also for simplicity that each interval of time represents 1 *year*, that is, $\Delta = 1$.

(a) Compute the price of a 1-, 2-, and 3-year zero coupon bond.

(b) Compute the swap rate $c\,(3)$ for a plain vanilla swap with annual cash flows and maturing on $i = 3$. Recall that cash flows are given by

$$CF_{i,j}\,(i+1) \quad = \quad N \times (r_1(i,j) - c(3)) \tag{11.42}$$

where, $r_1(i,j) = \left(e^{r_{i,j} \times 1} - 1\right)$ is the annually compounded rate that corresponds to $r_{i,j}$.

(c) Consider an option with maturity $i = 1$ with the following payoff

$$s_1 = \max\left(0.98 \times \left(\frac{r_1(1,j)}{.06}\right) - Z_1\,(3), 0\right) \tag{11.43}$$

where $r_1(1,j)$ is the annually compounded rate at time $i = 1$, and $Z_1\,(3)$ is the zero coupon at time $i = 1$ that pays 1 at time $i = 3$.

   i. What is the value of this option?

Table 11.24   An Interest Rate Tree

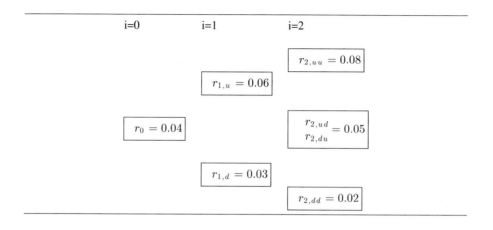

i=0	i=1	i=2
		$r_{2,uu} = 0.08$
	$r_{1,u} = 0.06$	
$r_0 = 0.04$		$r_{2,ud} = 0.05$ $r_{2,du}$
	$r_{1,d} = 0.03$	
		$r_{2,dd} = 0.02$

ii. If you sell this option, how can you hedge it? Write down the hedging strategy and confirm its perfomance at $i = 1$. Be precise in the description of the steps.

(d) **Procter & Gamble Leveraged Swap**: In November 1993, Procter & Gamble (P&G) entered a swap with Bankers Trust (BT) where BT would pay P&G a fixed rate $\bar{r}$, and P&G would pay BT a floating rate plus a spread. The spread was going to be equal to 0 at time of initiation, and would be set at time $i = 1$ equal to the value s_1 in Equation 11.43. The spread remains constant thereafter. To provide an example, suppose that the interest rate increases at $i = 1$ to $r_{1,u}$ and decreases afterwards to $r_{2,ud}$. The spread is set to $s_{1,u}$ at time $i = 1$, implying that P&G has to pay at time $i = 1$ simply $r_0 \times N$, at time $i = 2$ the cash flow $(r_1(1, u) + s_{1,u}) \times N$, and at time $i = 3$ the cash flow $(r_1(2, ud) + s_{1,u}) \times N$, where $N = 100$ is the notional. (Remember that in swaps, the floating rate at time i determines the cash flows at time $i + 1$).

   i. Assume the maturity of the levereged swap is 3 years. What is the value of the swap for P&G if $\bar{r} = c(3)$, where $c(3)$ is the swap rate determined in Part (b)?

   ii. Given your answer to part i, the value of $\bar{r}$ that makes the swap value equal 0 at $i = 0$ is higher or lower than $c(3)$? Provide an brief intuition.

   iii. Using a spreadsheet, compute the value of $\bar{r}$ (this can be done by using solver in Microsoft Excel, or simply by trial and error).

4. Suppose that you estimated the *risk neutral* tree for the continuously compounded interest rates in Table 11.24, where there is equal probability to move up or down the tree. Assume also for simplicity that each interval of time represents *1 year*, that is, $\Delta = 1$.

   (a) Compute the term structure of interest rates at time $i = 0$.

(b) From the term structure, compute the swap rate $c(3)$ for an annual swap maturing at $i = 3$. Use the tree to check that the value of the swap rate is indeed zero. Take the perspective of the fixed rate payer into your calculations.

(c) An **index amortizing swap** is a swap whose notional value decreases over time depending on the interest rate scenario. Consider the index amortizing swap with initial notional $N_0 = 100$ and with the following characteristics:

- Maturity $i = 3$
- Ammortization schedule:

if $r_i = .02$	then	100 % reduction in notional
if $r_i = .03$	then	50 % reduction in notional
if $r_i = .05$	then	20 % reduction in notional
if $r_i > .05$	then	no reduction in notional

- At $i = 0$ no ammortization takes place (lockout period).

For example, if at time $i = 1$ the interest rate declined to $r_{1,d} = 0.03$, then the notional to apply to the next payment (at $i = 2$) is not $N = 100$ but $N = 50$. If instead at $i = 1$ the interest rate was $r_{1,u} = .06$, then no reduction in notional would take place.

  i. Intuitively, is the fixed rate payer better off or worse off compared to the plain vanilla swap in Part (b) if the swap rate of the index ammortizing swap is also $c(3)$ as computed earlier? Explain. (*Hint: Thera are no computations needed here. Only intuition.*)

  ii. Obtain the value of the swap for the fixed rate payer assuming $c(3)$ as in Part (b). (*Hint: Recall that the notional becomes path dependent. How does this fact affect the tree for cash flows?*)

  iii. Use a spreadsheet to obtain the value of the fixed swap rate for the index amortizing swap (you can use either a solver, as in Microsoft Excel, or trial and error). Is this fixed rate higher or lower than $c(3)$ computed in Part (b)? Discuss.

  iv. Suppose you "sold" the swap whose value you found in Part iii. How would you hedge it? Provide the initial hedge ratio at $i = 0$. You can consider any instrument that you like, such as zero coupon bonds or plain vanilla swaps.

5. Let today be November 3, 2008.

  (a) Use the LIBOR rate and the swap data on November 3, 2008 in Table 11.26 and fit the LIBOR curve.

  (b) From the LIBOR discount curve, fit the Ho-Lee model of the interest rates, with quarterly steps. You can use the LIBOR volatility reported in the text, or estimate the LIBOR volatility yourself. Data on LIBOR are available on the British Bankers Association Web site (www.baa.org.uk).

  (c) Compare risk neutral expected future interest rates to the continuously compounded interest rates. How does the difference depend on the assumed volatility of the interest rate? (*Hint: For each assumed volatility of the interest rate,*

Table 11.25   Term Sheet 5-year Corridor Note

Issuer	HAL Corp.
Rating	AAA
Pricing Date	November 3, 2008
Maturity Date	November 3, 2013
Principal	100
Coupon Frequency	Quarterly
Coupon	5.4% if reference rate within corridor bounds; 0% otherwise
Corridor Lower Bound	1%
Corridor Upper Bound	5%
Reference Rate	3 Month LIBOR on previous fixing date

you need to refit the tree to make sure that the tree correctly reflects the forward rates. Do the exercise for 3 values of volatility).

(d) Compute the value of 1-year, 2-year and 3-year cap. Compare your value with the one in the data, in Table 11.26.

(e) Compute the value of a 5-year swap (the swap rate in Table 11.26) with quarterly payments (i.e., assume that both floating and fixed payers pay at quarterly frequency). Is the value of the swap obtained from the tree what you would expect from first principles?

(f) Use the swap tree computed in Part (e) to compute the value of 1-year, at-the-money swaption to enter into a 4-year swap.

6. On November 3, 2008, the AAA rated company HAL issued a 5 year, corridor note with a quarterly coupon, according to the term sheet in Table 11.25. Given the Ho-Lee model fitted in Exercise 5, compute the following:

(a) Obtain the value of the corridor note discussed in Table 11.25.

(b) Compute the value of a straight quarterly coupon bond, and determine the (annualized) coupon rate that generates a price similar to the one of the corridor note. Is this coupon higher or lower than 5%? Comment.

(c) Compute the spot rate duration of the corridor note and of the straight bond obtained in Part (b). Which one is higher? Why?

(d) Consider the future time $t = 2$ (step $i = 8$). Plot the value of the corridor note at $i = 8$ against the interest rate scenarios at the same time. On the same graph also report the values of the straight fixed coupon bond. Comment on the difference between the two securities. Which one appears to have negative convexity? Why?

(e) Consider the simple BDT model. Fit this model to the same data [again, either use the LIBOR volatility in the text, or estimate it using the same data as in Part (b)] and recompute the value of the corridor note. Is this the same value you obtained using the Ho-Lee model? Comment.

Table 11.26   Swap Rates and Cap Prices on November 3, 2008

3 Month LIBOR (%)	2.8588	
Maturity	Swap Rate (%)	Cap Price ($\times 100$)
0.50	2.6486	0.0528
0.75	2.4929	0.1313
1.00	2.4320	0.2401
1.25	2.4491	0.3826
1.50	2.4938	0.5405
1.75	2.5561	0.7106
2.00	2.6260	0.8932
2.25	2.7252	1.1095
2.50	2.8630	1.3729
2.75	3.0108	1.6636
3.00	3.1400	1.9502
3.25	3.2471	2.2235
3.50	3.3474	2.4973
3.75	3.4408	2.7711
4.00	3.5270	3.0451
4.25	3.6076	3.3208
4.50	3.6835	3.5968
4.75	3.7531	3.87
5.00	3.8150	4.137

Original Data Source: Bloomberg.
Reported Data are interpolated from quoted swap rates and flat volatilities, and then computed using Black's model.

7. Today is November 3, 2008, and the 3-month LIBOR, swap rates and cap prices are as in Table 11.26.

   (a) Fit the LIBOR curve (see Exercise 5).

   (b) Compute the implied volatilities from the simple BDT model.

   (c) Compute the forward volatilities from the BDT model.

   (d) On this tree, value the corridor note discussed in Table 11.25 (see Exercise 6).

CHAPTER 12

AMERICAN OPTIONS

Numerous interest rate securities have embedded American options, that is, the right of the option holder to receive a payoff of some kind any time before a predefined maturity. Some of these options are explicitly outlined within the terms of a contract, but others are somewhat hidden and are only embedded within another interest rate security. Let's recall first the definition of an American option (see also Chapter 6).

Definition 12.1 *An **American call option** is a contract between two counterparties in which one party (the option buyer) has the right, but not the obligation, to buy a given security at a predetermined price on or before a maturity time T, and the other party (the option seller) has the obligation to sell such security. An **American put option** is a similar contract in which the option buyer has the right to sell a given security at a predetermined price on or before a maturity time T, and the option seller has the obligation to purchase such security.*

In this chapter we show that the tree methodology developed in Chapters 10 and 11 can be readily adapted to obtain pricing and hedging strategies for this more complicated security. We apply this methodology to classic American option securities, namely, callable bonds, American swaptions and mortgage backed securities.

Table 12.1   U.S. Treasury Callable Bonds on January 8, 2002

Maturity	Coupon	First Call Date	Bid	Ask
20070215	7.625	20020215	100.5625	100.5938
20071115	7.875	20021115	104.7188	104.7500
20080815	8.375	20030815	108.4219	108.4531
20081115	8.750	20031115	110.1406	110.1719
20090515	9.125	20040515	112.3438	112.3750
20091115	10.375	20041115	117.3906	117.4219
20100215	11.750	20050215	122.4688	122.5000
20100515	10.000	20050515	118.0000	118.0313
20101115	12.750	20051115	129.9063	129.9375
20110515	13.875	20060515	137.2500	137.2813
20111115	14.000	20061115	140.8750	140.9063
20121115	10.375	20071115	127.8594	127.9219
20130815	12.000	20080815	139.2344	139.2969
20140515	13.250	20090515	150.1406	150.2031
20140815	12.500	20090815	146.4688	146.5313
20141115	11.750	20091115	142.4844	142.5469

Source: Data excerpted from CRSP (Daily Treasuries) ©2009 Center for Research in
Security Prices (CRSP), The University of Chicago Booth School of Business.

12.1   CALLABLE BONDS

Many bond issuers, including the U.S. government in the late 1970s and early 1980s, may issue callable bonds, that is, standard fixed coupon bonds, but ones in which the issuer retains the option to buy back the bond for its par value during a defined time interval before maturity. For example, Table 12.1 shows the available U.S. Treasury callable bonds on January 8, 2002.[1]

In this table, the November 2012 U.S. Treasury bond is callable at par starting on November 2007. This implies that after November 2007, the U.S. government can purchase this bond for $100 any time it desires to do so. (If the U.S. government calls the bond between coupon days, it has to pay the accrued interest to the bond holder.) Of course, the U.S. government, or the issuer of a callable bond more generally, will exercise its option to purchase back a bond only when it is convenient to do so. For instance, the U.S. government issued numerous callable bonds during the high interest rate period in the early 1980s, with the expectation that inflation and thus interest rates would decline in the future. If interest rates effectively decline in the future, it would be beneficial for the U.S. government to refinance its old bonds bearing a high coupon rate and exchange them for other bonds that reflect the current lower rates.

How can we determine the optimal timing at which the issuers of callable bonds should exercise their option to purchase the bonds? How does this optionality affect the pricing and the hedging of these bonds? The interest rate tree methodology developed in Chapters 10 and 11 provides us a convenient methodology, illustrated in the following example.

---

[1] I will use this date in Example 12.2 to provide a concrete example of the binomial tree methodology. This is the same date of most examples in Chapter 11

■ **EXAMPLE 12.1**

Consider the 1.5-year, 3% coupon bond we discussed in Section 11.2.1 of Chapter 11, Table 11.4, but assume it is callable at par (100) starting on $i = 1$ (that is, it cannot be called at time $i = 0$). To find the price of the callable bond, we think of this security as a portfolio composed by two securities: The first security is a straight non-callable bond, whose value is $P_{i,j}(3)$ in node (i,j) is computed in Table 11.4 in Chapter 11 and reported in Panel A of Table 12.2. The second security is an American call option in which, upon calling the bond, the government receives the payoff

$$\text{Payoff from call option at node } (i,j) = \max(P_{i,j}(3) - 100, 0) \qquad (12.1)$$

That is, by exercising the option, the government has to pay \$100 to the bond holders, but it receives back the bond with value $P_{i,j}(3)$. The question is then *when* it is optimal to exercise this option.

Moving backward on the tree we can resolve this problem. In fact, at any node (i,j) the issuer can decide whether to exercise the option or wait. If it exercises, the payoff (= value of the option) is

$$C_{i,j}^{\text{Ex}} = P_{i,j}(3) - 100$$

If it waits, the value of the option

$$
\begin{aligned}
C_{i,j}^{\text{Wait}} &= e^{-r_{i,j}\Delta} E^* [C_{i+1}] \\
&= e^{-r_{i,j}\Delta} \left(\frac{1}{2} C_{i+1,j} + \frac{1}{2} C_{i+1,j+1} \right)
\end{aligned}
$$

The option holder should act to maximize the value of its option. Therefore, at any node (i,j) the option holder will choose between Wait and Exercise so as to maximize the payoff. It follows that the value of the option at time/node (i,j) is

$$
\begin{aligned}
C_{i,j} &= \max \left(C_{i,j}^{\text{Wait}}, C_{i,j}^{\text{Ex}} \right) \qquad (12.2) \\
&= \max \left(e^{-r_{i,j} \times \Delta} E^* [C_{i+1}], P_{i,j}(3) - 100 \right)
\end{aligned}
$$

Since the option expires worthless at maturity, as the issuer has to redeem the bond at par value, at maturity $I = T/\Delta$ we have

$$C_{I,j} = 0 \text{ for all } j$$

Given this final value of the option, we can start the backward procedure in Equation 12.2. The resulting tree is in Table 12.2, and the current value of the option to call the bond early is $C_0 = 0.1874$.

What then is the price of the callable bond? Because the buyer of a callable bond is really long a non-callable bond and short the American call option (sold to the issuer), the price of the callable bond is

$$
\begin{aligned}
V_0^{cb}(3) &= P_0(3) - C_0 \\
&= 100.5438 - 0.1874 \\
&= 100.3564
\end{aligned}
$$

Table 12.2 The Call Option in a Callable Bond

| $t = 0$ | $t = 0.5$ | $t = 1$ | $t = 1.5$ |
| $i = 0$ | $i = 1$ | $i = 2$ | $i = 3$ |

Panel A: The 3%, 1.5 year non-callable bond

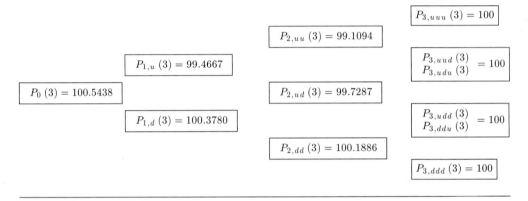

$P_{3,uuu}(3) = 100$

$P_{2,uu}(3) = 99.1094$

$P_{1,u}(3) = 99.4667$

$\dfrac{P_{3,uud}(3)}{P_{3,udu}(3)} = 100$

$P_0(3) = 100.5438$

$P_{2,ud}(3) = 99.7287$

$P_{1,d}(3) = 100.3780$

$\dfrac{P_{3,udd}(3)}{P_{3,ddu}(3)} = 100$

$P_{2,dd}(3) = 100.1886$

$P_{3,ddd}(3) = 100$

Panel B: The Option to Call

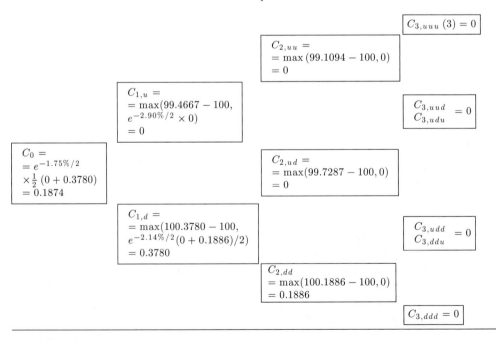

$C_{3,uuu}(3) = 0$

$C_{2,uu} =$
$= \max(99.1094 - 100, 0)$
$= 0$

$C_{1,u} =$
$= \max(99.4667 - 100,$
$e^{-2.90\%/2} \times 0)$
$= 0$

$\dfrac{C_{3,uud}}{C_{3,udu}} = 0$

$C_0 =$
$= e^{-1.75\%/2}$
$\times \frac{1}{2}(0 + 0.3780)$
$= 0.1874$

$C_{2,ud} =$
$= \max(99.7287 - 100, 0)$
$= 0$

$C_{1,d} =$
$= \max(100.3780 - 100,$
$e^{-2.14\%/2}(0 + 0.1886)/2)$
$= 0.3780$

$\dfrac{C_{3,udd}}{C_{3,ddu}} = 0$

$C_{2,dd}$
$= \max(100.1886 - 100, 0)$
$= 0.1886$

$C_{3,ddd} = 0$

In the example above the issuer calls the bond at time $i = 1$ if the interest rate moves to $r_{1,d}$ or $r_{2,dd}$, but not otherwise. The effect is intuitive, as when the interest rate decreases, the price of the bond increases, and it becomes profitable for the government to purchase a highly priced security for only $100. Another way to say this is that the government can refinance its debt at a cheaper rate when interest rates decline.[2]

12.1.1 An Application to U.S. Treasury Bonds

Does this "optimal" exercise model work? Is it producing reasonable prices? To check whether the model described in the previous section is accurate, we can proceed as follows. We can first use the Simple Black, Derman, and Toy (BDT) model in Section 11.1.2 in Chapter 11 and fit it to the *non-callable* bonds. Then, if the methodology described in the previous subsection for the pricing of American call options is accurate, the model should then deliver the correct prices for the callable bonds on the same day. The next example carries out the calculation.[3]

■ **EXAMPLE 12.2**

Table 11.3 in Chapter 11 contains the Simple BDT model fitted to the zero coupon bonds on January 8, 2002. We can use this tree to price callable bonds. Consider for instance the callable bond expiring on August 15, 2014 in Table 12.1. The first call date is August 15, 2009. To price this bond, we need to extend the interest rate tree in Table 11.3 to a longer maturity. The resulting tree for the American call option embedded in the Treasury Bond is provided in Table 12.3. In this table, the shaded areas correspond to the time / node combination in which the exercise of the American call option takes place. Clearly, before time $T = 7.5$, the option cannot be exercised. When $T = 7.5$, the option is exercised when the interest rate is below $r_{15,6} = 8.11\%$.

What is the price of the callable bond then? From Panel A in Table 12.3 the price of the non-callable bond is equal to $169.732, while from Panel B the value of the call option is $22.33. Thus, the value of the callable bond is equal to

$$V_0^{cb}(T) = \$169.732 - \$22.33 = \$147.40$$

This value is close to the traded value in Table 12.1, which equals $146.5 (average bid and ask).

As a final comment, note that in the simple three-period example in Table 12.2 it is always the case that the issuer exercises whenever the option is in the money, that is when $P_{i,j} - 100 > 0$. But this is not always the case, as there is a value to waiting. There are situations in which an immediate exercise would give a positive payoff, while it may be optimal to wait anyway, as the option can get even more profitable. This is apparent in Table 12.3. Consider position $(i, j) = (15, 5)$, in which case the value of the American call

---

[2]In the example, the interest rate does not actually decline, but it moves below the risk neutral expected interest rate, pushing up bond prices.

[3]The next example carries out the exercise in a simple manner, and abstracting from a few institutional details that are bound to affect the price. For instance, the U.S. Treasury must announce four months in advance its intention to call back a bond on the next call date.

Figure 12.1 The Negative Convexity in Callable Bonds

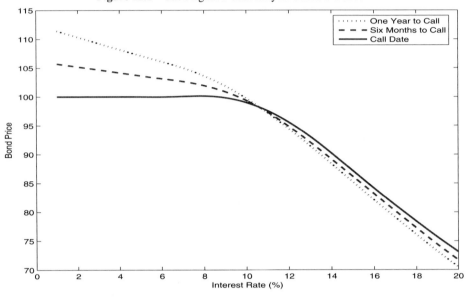

is $C_{i,j} = \$8.37$. The non-callable bond price in such node is $P_{i,j}(3) = \$107.404$. Thus, an immediate exercise would yield $P_{i,j}(3) - 100 = 107.404 - 100 = \$7.404$. Yet, waiting yields a higher (risk neutral) expected profit. In fact, by waiting, there is (risk neutral) 0.5 probability of getting \$4.59 if interest rates move to $r_{i+1,j}$ and 0.5 probability of getting \$13.10, if interest rates move to $r_{i+1,j+1}$. The discounted risk neutral expectation of these payoffs at time $i+1$ is $e^{-10.99\%/2} \times (4.59 + 13.10)/2 = \$8.372$, which is higher than the immediate payoff. Thus, it is beneficial for the issuer (Treasury) to wait in this case.[4]

12.1.2 The Negative Convexity in Callable Bonds

How does the short American option implicit in a callable bond affect the relation between its price and interest rates? As we know from basic principles, and especially Chapter 4, there is a natural positive convex relation between interest rates and the price of the non-callable securities. This is no longer true for callable bonds. Indeed, Figure 12.1 shows the profile of the price of the August 15, 2014 callable Treasury Bond in Example 12.2 around the first call date (August 15, 2009). We see that the bond price convexity is negative for interest rates below 14%. That is, while lower interest rates still increase the price of the bond, they do so at an increasingly lower rate, as opposed to an increasing rate as for any non callable bond. The reason for this behavior is as follows: As interest rates decline to below 14% it becomes increasingly likely that the Treasury will call back the bond whenever possible. As a consequence, the bond price has to converge to the call price (\$100) as interest rates decline.

---

[4]Recall from Chapter 9 that a high risk neutral expected cash flow means that there is a replicating portfolio that yields a higher cash flows than exercising the option does.

Table 12.3 The American Call Tree

Panel A: The non-callable bond

time	0.0	0.5	1.0	1.5	2.0	2.5	3.0	3.5	4.0	4.5	5.0	5.5	6.0	6.5	7.0	7.5	8.0	8.5	9.0	9.5	10.0	10.5	11.0	11.5	12.0	12.5
i	0.0	1.0	2.0	3.0	4.0	5.0	6.0	7.0	8.0	9.0	10.0	11.0	12.0	13.0	14.0	15.0	16.0	17.0	18.0	19.0	20.0	21.0	22.0	23.0	24.0	25.0
0	169.732	155.631	141.906	129.058	116.933	105.887	95.589	85.705	76.203	67.424	59.768	52.782	45.994	40.868	35.854	32.319	28.701	26.430	23.363	21.038	19.598	19.393	21.289	27.610	45.419	100.000
1		174.299	161.400	149.100	137.286	126.284	115.828	105.636	95.689	86.318	77.927	70.122	62.474	56.452	50.554	46.189	41.778	38.823	35.092	32.276	30.580	30.427	32.737	39.657	56.714	100.000
2			178.451	166.933	155.724	145.103	134.859	124.758	114.788	105.246	96.516	88.264	80.115	73.466	66.930	61.883	56.818	53.226	48.915	45.614	43.568	43.215	45.414	51.945	66.826	100.000
3				182.141	171.669	161.615	151.811	142.065	132.368	122.976	114.228	105.853	97.532	90.527	83.614	78.068	72.520	68.371	63.586	59.819	57.321	56.506	58.102	63.486	75.435	100.000
4					184.957	175.531	166.265	157.007	147.747	138.696	130.144	121.873	113.621	106.476	99.403	93.523	87.652	83.037	77.882	73.679	70.664	69.196	69.861	73.673	82.499	100.000
5						186.892	178.172	169.433	160.666	152.041	143.794	135.755	127.713	120.574	113.488	107.404	101.333	96.341	90.904	86.307	82.757	80.552	80.144	82.281	88.138	100.000
6							187.723	179.472	171.184	162.991	155.082	147.325	139.553	132.500	125.487	119.287	113.103	107.811	102.164	97.224	93.168	90.231	88.755	89.256	92.550	100.000
7								187.404	179.542	171.744	164.158	156.683	149.188	142.265	135.351	129.094	122.850	117.325	111.520	106.293	101.785	98.182	95.736	94.811	95.950	100.000
8									186.063	178.604	171.302	164.081	156.840	150.032	143.245	136.962	130.692	124.987	119.066	113.604	108.714	104.537	101.260	99.140	98.541	100.000
9										183.899	176.835	169.829	162.807	156.113	149.435	143.144	136.864	131.022	125.015	119.367	114.164	109.513	105.554	102.467	100.500	100.000
10											181.068	174.238	167.394	160.799	154.214	147.925	141.644	135.699	129.628	123.834	118.381	113.352	108.847	104.997	101.972	100.000
11												177.588	170.886	164.370	157.863	151.579	145.301	139.278	133.160	127.253	121.606	116.280	111.349	106.907	103.073	100.000
12													173.522	167.071	160.625	154.347	148.073	141.992	135.840	129.846	124.049	118.494	113.236	108.341	103.894	100.000
13														169.100	162.702	156.430	150.161	144.036	137.858	131.800	125.889	120.159	114.650	109.413	104.505	100.000
14															164.257	157.990	151.725	145.568	139.371	133.264	127.266	121.404	115.707	110.211	104.958	100.000
15																159.154	152.883	146.711	140.501	134.356	128.294	122.333	116.495	110.805	105.294	100.000
16																	153.762	147.563	141.342	135.170	129.060	123.024	117.080	111.245	105.543	100.000
17																		148.195	141.967	135.775	129.628	123.537	117.514	111.572	105.727	100.000
18																			142.430	136.223	130.050	123.918	117.836	111.814	105.864	100.000
19																				136.556	130.362	124.200	118.074	111.993	105.965	100.000
20																					130.594	124.408	118.250	112.125	106.039	100.000
21																						124.563	118.381	112.223	106.094	100.000
22																							118.477	112.295	106.135	100.000
23																								112.349	106.165	100.000
24																									106.187	100.000
25																										100.000

Panel B: The option to call

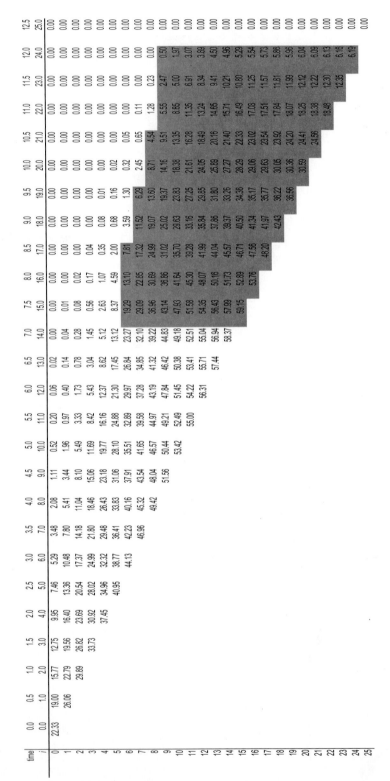

time	0.0	0.5	1.0	1.5	2.0	2.5	3.0	3.5	4.0	4.5	5.0	5.5	6.0	6.5	7.0	7.5	8.0	8.5	9.0	9.5	10.0	10.5	11.0	11.5	12.0	12.5
i	0.0	1.0	2.0	3.0	4.0	5.0	6.0	7.0	8.0	9.0	10.0	11.0	12.0	13.0	14.0	15.0	16.0	17.0	18.0	19.0	20.0	21.0	22.0	23.0	24.0	25.0
0	22.33	19.00	15.77	12.75	9.95	7.46	5.29	3.48	2.08	1.11	0.52	0.20	0.06	0.02	0.00	0.00	0.00	0.00	0.00	0.00	0.00	0.00	0.00	0.00	0.00	0.00
1		26.06	22.79	19.56	16.40	13.36	10.48	7.80	5.41	3.44	1.96	0.97	0.40	0.14	0.04	0.01	0.00	0.00	0.00	0.00	0.00	0.00	0.00	0.00	0.00	0.00
2			29.89	26.82	23.69	20.54	17.37	14.18	11.04	8.10	5.49	3.33	1.73	0.78	0.28	0.08	0.02	0.00	0.00	0.00	0.00	0.00	0.00	0.00	0.00	0.00
3				33.73	30.92	28.02	24.99	21.80	18.46	15.06	11.69	8.42	5.43	3.04	1.45	0.56	0.17	0.04	0.00	0.00	0.00	0.00	0.00	0.00	0.00	0.00
4					37.45	34.96	32.32	29.48	26.43	23.18	19.77	16.16	12.37	8.62	5.12	2.63	1.07	0.35	0.08	0.01	0.00	0.00	0.00	0.00	0.00	0.00
5						40.95	38.77	36.41	33.83	31.06	28.10	24.88	21.30	17.45	13.12	8.37	4.59	2.00	0.68	0.16	0.02	0.00	0.00	0.00	0.00	0.00
6							44.13	42.23	40.16	37.91	35.51	32.89	29.97	26.84	23.27	19.29	13.10	7.81	3.59	1.30	0.32	0.05	0.00	0.00	0.00	0.00
7								46.96	45.32	43.54	41.65	39.58	37.28	34.85	32.10	29.09	22.85	17.32	11.52	6.29	2.45	0.65	0.11	0.00	0.00	0.00
8									49.42	48.04	46.57	44.97	43.19	41.32	39.22	36.96	30.89	24.99	19.07	13.60	8.71	4.54	1.28	0.23	0.00	0.00
9										51.56	50.44	49.21	47.84	46.42	44.83	43.14	36.86	31.02	25.02	19.37	14.16	9.51	5.55	2.47	0.50	0.00
10											53.42	52.49	51.45	50.38	49.18	47.93	41.64	35.70	29.63	23.83	18.38	13.35	8.85	5.00	1.97	0.00
11												55.00	54.22	53.41	52.51	51.58	45.30	39.28	33.16	27.26	21.61	16.28	11.36	6.91	3.07	0.00
12													56.31	55.71	55.04	54.35	48.07	41.99	35.84	29.85	24.05	18.49	13.24	8.34	3.89	0.00
13														57.44	56.94	56.43	50.16	44.04	37.86	31.80	25.89	20.16	14.65	9.41	4.50	0.00
14															58.37	57.99	51.73	45.57	39.37	33.26	27.27	21.40	15.71	10.21	4.96	0.00
15																59.15	52.89	46.71	40.53	34.36	28.29	22.33	16.49	10.80	5.29	0.00
16																	53.76	47.56	41.34	35.17	29.06	23.02	17.08	11.25	5.54	0.00
17																		48.20	41.97	35.77	29.63	23.54	17.51	11.57	5.73	0.00
18																			42.43	36.22	30.05	23.92	17.84	11.81	5.86	0.00
19																				36.56	30.36	24.20	18.07	11.99	5.96	0.00
20																					30.59	24.41	18.25	12.12	6.04	0.00
21																						24.56	18.38	12.22	6.09	0.00
22																							18.48	12.30	6.13	0.00
23																								12.35	6.16	0.00
24																									6.19	0.00
25																										0.00

12.1.3   The Option Adjusted Spread

Securities with embedded American options are often traded on an option-adjusted-spread (OAS) basis. This spread reflects the discrepancy between the value of the security according to the model used to price it, and the traded value. For instance, on January 8, 2002, the August 2014, 7.5% callable bond discussed in Example 12.2 was trading for $V^{Quote}(0, T) = \$146.5$ (average bid and ask in Table 12.1). The term structure model used to price this bond gave the price $V_0^{cb}(T) = \$147.40$, which is higher than the quoted price. According to the model the market is *undervaluing* the callable bond, which suggests a buy strategy. The OAS represents the increase in the spot curve that is necessary for the model price $V_0^{cb}(T)$ to equal the traded price. A positive OAS implies that we had to increase the yields of the model to match the traded price, suggesting that the bond will generate a higher yield compared to the fair one even after accounting for the embedded option.[5] For instance, in Example 12.2 it turns out that if we increase the term structure in a parallel fashion of only 11 basis points, and then redo the computations as in Table 12.3 (including fitting the interest rate tree) we obtain $V_0^{cb}(T) = \$146.55$, which equals the ask price (see Table 12.1). Thus, in this case

$$\text{Option Adjusted Spread} = 11 \text{ basis points}$$

There are numerous reasons why the OAS of a bond may be different from zero. For instance, if a callable bond has low liquidity, it tends to trade at a discount compared to its fair (option adjusted) value, yielding a positive OAS. In this case, the positive OAS may reflect liquidity risk, that is, the risk of not being able to sell the bond for its fair value when needed.

It is also important to realize that the size of the OAS depends on the model used to compute it: It is possible that different term structure models may generate different OAS, in the same way they generate different values of options even when using the same inputs, as discussed in Chapter 11.

12.1.4   Dynamic Replication of Callable Bonds

The higher the option adjusted spread (OAS), the more underpriced is the bond compared to the model, and thus the higher the incentive to purchase the bond should be. Indeed, because of dynamic replication, if a callable bond turns out to be underpriced then one can engage in the strategy "Buy Cheap and Sell Dear," according to which a trader purchases the underpriced callable bond, and sells a portfolio of non-callable bonds chosen in a way it replicates the callable bonds. Dynamic replication was discussed in Chapters 9 and 10. Recall in particular that the replication strategy involves a position $N_{i,j}^L$ in a long-term security, such as a non-callable bond in this case, and a position $N_{i,j}^S$ in the short-term bond, expiring in period $i + 1$. There are two differences compared to the cases discussed in Chapters 9 and 10:

1. The callable bond pays coupons, and therefore the dynamic strategy must take those coupons into account.

---

[5]Note that a parallel shift in the spot curve results in an equal shift in the forward curve, so that the OAS can alternatively be computed from a shift in the forward curve.

2. The issuer should exercise optimally according to the tree, but it may not do so. Therefore, the replicating strategy must take into account the possibility that the issuer does not exercise when it should according to the model.

We use the simple Example 12.1 to illustrate the methodology.

■ **EXAMPLE 12.3**

Consider again Example 12.1. Assume that the market is trading this callable bond at a positive OAS, and let for instance the price be $P^{mkt}(0,3) = 100.1$, while the computations in Table 12.2 imply its price should be $V_0^{cb}(3) = 100.3564$. Let's assume for simplicity that a non-callable, 3% bond with maturity $i = 3$ is also trading, and it is fairly priced according to the model. That is, from Panel A of Table 12.2 the non-callable bond is trading at $P_0(3) = 100.5438$.

Before discussing the arbitrage strategy, consider first the replicating portfolio. Recall from Equations 9.9 and 9.10 in Chapter 9 that at any node (i,j) we must take the following positions:

$$N_{i,j}^L = \frac{V_{i+1,j} - V_{i+1,j+1}}{P_{i+1,j}(3) - P_{i+1,j+1}(3)} \tag{12.3}$$

$$N_{i,j}^S = \frac{1}{100}\left[V_{i+1,j} - N_{i,j}^L \times P_{i+1,j}(3)\right] \tag{12.4}$$

where $V_{i,j}$ is the value of the security we want to replicate (the callable bond), and $P_{i,j}(3)$ is the value of the security we use to replicate (the non-callable bond). Equations 12.3 and 12.4 though do not take into account the fact that both $V_{i,j}$ and $P_{i,j}$ pay coupons at each time i. The same logic discussed in Chapter 9 however shows that with coupons, the only change is in Equation 12.4, which becomes

$$N_{i,j}^S = \frac{1}{100}\left[\left(V_{i+1,j} + CF_{i+1}^V\right) - N_{i,j}^L \times \left(P_{i+1,j}(3) + CF_{i+1}^P\right)\right] \tag{12.5}$$

where CF_{i+1}^V and CF_{i+1}^P denote the cash flow at $i + 1$ paid by securities V and P, respectively. For the case of the callable and non-callable bonds with identical coupon rates, we have $CF_{i+1}^V = CF_{i+1}^P = 1.5$.

As an example, we initially have (we use the notation u, uu to denote nodes, for simplicity):

$$N_0^L = \frac{V_{1,u} - V_{1,d}}{P_{1,u}(3) - P_{1,d}(3)} = \frac{99.4667 - 100}{99.4667 - 100.3780} = 0.5852$$

$$N_0^S = \frac{1}{100}\left[\left(V_{1,u} + CF_1^V\right) - N_0^L \times \left(P_{1,u}(3) + CF_1^P\right)\right]$$

$$= \frac{1}{100}\left[(99.4667 + 1.5) - 0.5852 \times (99.4667 + 1.5)\right] = 0.4188$$

The initial value of this portfolio is

$$\Pi_0 = N_0^L \times V_0 + N_0^S \times (Z_0(1) \times 100) = 0.5852 \times 100.5438 + 0.4188 \times 99.1338$$

$$= 100.3564$$

which is the value of the callable bond according to the model. For convenience, Panel A of Table 12.4 reports the ex-coupon prices of the callable bond $V_{i,j}$ along with the binomial tree. Note that if the interest rate declines, then $V_{1,d} = 100$ and the bond is called back. The tree after that point effectively disappears. The replicating portfolio has to take this fact into account. Panel B of the same table reports the dynamic replicating portfolio on the tree. The positions just computed are at the root of the tree.

Consider now an upward movement in the interest rate, that is $r_0 \rightarrow r_{1,u}$. The portfolio value is

$$
\begin{aligned}
\Pi_{1,u} &= N_0^L \times (P_{1,u}(3) + CF_1^P) + N_0^S \times 100 \\
&= 0.5852 \times (99.4667 + 1.5) + 0.4188 \times 100 \\
&= 100.9667,
\end{aligned}
$$

where we have to take into account that the long position in the non-callable bond pays the 1.5 coupon at time $i = 1$. At first sight, the value of the portfolio $\Pi_{1,u} = 100.9667$ appears higher than $V_{1,u} = 99.4667$ in Panel A. However, we must recall that the latter is an ex-coupon price. The replicating portfolio has to pay the cash flow $\$1.5$ to its holder in order to exactly replicate the callable bond. After this payment is taken into account, we indeed have $\Pi_{1,u} = 99.4667 = V_{1,u}$.

At this point, as in Section 10.2.2 of Chapter 10, we need to rebalance the portfolio. By applying Equations 12.3 and 12.5, we find that the new positions and portfolio value must be:

$$
\begin{aligned}
N_{1,u}^L &= 1 \\
N_{1,u}^S &= 0 \\
\Pi_{1,u} &= 99.4667
\end{aligned}
$$

Note in particular that we simply purchase the non-callable bond. The reason is that if the interest rate goes up to $r_{1,u}$, from our previous calculations it becomes never optimal for the issuer to call back the bond in the future. That is, the callable bond effectively becomes non-callable, and the replication strategy simply requires a long position in the non-callable bond.

What if the interest rate declines at time $i = 1$? In this case the portfolio value is

$$
\Pi_{1,d} = 101.5
$$

After the payment of the coupon, the value of the portfolio is $\Pi_{1,d} = 100$, and it matches the value of the callable bond. The latter's price is exactly $V_{1,d} = 100$ because the issuer is calling it back in this case. Since the callable bond effectively does not exist anymore after node $(1, d)$, the replicating portfolio must also be unwound at this point as well. That is, the rebalancing simply consists of putting $N_{1,d}^L = 0$ and $N_{1,d}^S = 0$.

12.1.4.1 The Arbitrage Strategy

How then can an arbitrageur take advantage of the mispricing in the market? Applying the arbitrageurs' motto "Buy Cheap and Sell Dear," when OAS is positive the following is the arbitrage strategy:

1. Buy Cheap. Purchase the underpriced callable bond for its market value.

2. Sell Dear. Sell (short) the replicating portfolio, whose value at time zero is higher than the security market price.

This strategy generates a positive inflow today. If the replicating portfolio exactly replicates the cash flows and payoffs of the callable bond, then the long/short position is perfectly hedged, in the sense that the long position in the callable bond generates exactly the right cash flows to cover the short positions.

■ EXAMPLE 12.4

Consider again Example 12.3. As discussed, assume that the market price of the callable bond is $P^{mkt}(0,3) = 100.1$. The strategy is then as follows

1. Buy Cheap. Purchase the bond for $P^{mkt}(0,3) = 100.1$.

2. Sell Dear. Sell the replicating portfolio, that is

    (a) Sell short $N_0^L = 0.5852$ units of a 1.5-year, 3% non-callable bond;
    (b) Sell short $N_0^S = 0.4188$ units of a 6-month T-bill.

By construction, this strategy implies today an inflow of money

$$\text{Inflow today} = \Pi_0 - P^{mkt}(0,3) = 100.3564 - 100.1 = 0.2564$$

At time $i = 1$, the callable bond pays its coupon and it is either called back (for 100), or it converges in price to the non-callable bond. If the price discrepancy vanishes, the arbitrage can be in fact closed at time $i = 1$, with the cash flow from the non-callable bond that is exactly sufficient to cover the cash flow for the short position. For instance, if the interest rate declines, the long position in the callable bond generates a cash flow of 115 (principal plus coupon). With this cash flow, the arbitrageur can (a) pay the coupon due on the non-callable bond short position $0.5852 \times 1.5 = 0.8778$; (b) pay the principal due on the short T-bill position $0.4188 \times 100 = 41.88$; (c) pay to close the short position in the non-callable bond, by repurchasing 0.5852 bonds at the current price $P_{1,d}(3) = 100.3780$ for $0.5852 \times 100.3780 = 58.74061$. The total of $(a) + (b) + (c)$ is $0.8778 + 41.88 + 58.74061 = 101.5$, which equals the total cash flow received from the callable bond.[6]

12.1.4.2 *What If the Issuer Does Not Exercise Optimally?*   The key to the dynamic replication is that the issuer behaves as the model prescribes it should. However, exercising an American option optimally is not mandatory, and it is perfectly reasonable that the issuer may exercise sub-optimally. How does a sub-optimal exercise impact the arbitrage strategy discussed earlier? The next example answers this question.

■ EXAMPLE 12.5

Consider again Examples 12.3 and 12.4, but assume that in node $(1,d)$, the issuer of the callable bond forgets to call it back. In this case, the bond is not retired and we have to add some prices in the binomial tree in Panel A of Table 12.4. Table 12.4 reports the sub-tree of the callable bond starting from (time/node) $(1,d)$: In

---

[6]As usual, there are some small rounding errors in these computations, which disappear if we increase the number of decimals.

particular, the new call option price still takes into account the fact that at time $i = 2$ if the interest rate declines again, then the bond will be called back then. Since in this last scenario the value of the option would be $C_{2,dd} = \max(P_{2,dd}(3) - 100, 0) = 100.1886 - 100 = 0.1886$, the risk neutral pricing formula implies the value of the American option in $(1, d)$ is

$$C_{1,d}(3) = e^{-r_{1,d} \times \Delta} \times \frac{(C_{2,du}(3) + C_{2,dd}(3))}{2} = e^{-2.14\% \times 0.5} \times \frac{(0 + .1886)}{2}$$
$$= 0.0932$$

The value of the callable bond is then

$$V_{1,d} = P_{1,d}(3) - C_{1,d}(3) = 100.2848$$

The value of the callable bond if the issuer forgets to call it back is clearly higher than the principal value \$100. Since the optimal exercise did not occur, the value of the callable bond jumps up to a higher value. This is good news for the arbitrageur, because he or she is long the callable bond. At this node the arbitrageur can then simply sell the callable bond for $V_{1,d} = \$100.2848$, use \$100 of this cash to close the short position (see Example 12.4), and pocket the net \$0.2848. This inflow of cash is in addition to the inflow already received at time $i = 0$, which was \$0.2564.

If the issuer of the callable bond does not exercise optimally the option, the arbitrageur stands to receive an inflow of money also at the time when the optimal exercise was supposed to occur but it did not, as the callable bond price increases in value above par. By selling the callable bond and closing the short position the strategy generates even more profits. Intuitively, recall that the callable bond is obtained by considering the best possible exercise strategy for the issuer. This strategy maximizes the value of the American option embedded in the callable bond, which in turn depresses the fair value of the callable bond. If the exercise time is not optimal, then the ex-post value of the call option has to be lower than the one computed earlier under the optimal exercise, which in turn implies the callable bond has to jump up in price, as discussed.

12.2 AMERICAN SWAPTIONS

Section 11.2.4 in Chapter 11 discusses European swaptions, that is, options to enter into a swap, either as a fixed rate payer (payer swaption) or a fixed rate receiver (receiver swaption). We now generalize the approach to American swaptions, which are options to enter into a swap any time before maturity. As discussed in Chapter 11, swaptions are used by market participants to hedge against changes in interest rates, and in many occasions it is advisable to use American swaptions, rather than European swaptions, as American options provide an extra layer of protection. For instance, an investor in the Treasury callable bonds discussed in the previous section may be worried that the Treasury will call back the bonds at the incoming call dates. The option of the U.S. Treasury is American, as it can be exercised any time before maturity, although after the lockout period. An American receiver swaption with strike rate equal to the Treasury coupon would hedge against the prepayment risk. Indeed, if the Treasury calls back the security, the holder of the American swaption can exercise it, receiving the fixed strike rate from the swap in exchange for a

Table 12.4 The Dynamic Replication Strategy

$i = 0$	$i = 1$	$i = 2$	$i = 3$

Panel A: The Theoretical 3%, 1.5-year Callable Bond (Ex-Coupon Prices)

$$V_{3,uuu}(3) = 100$$

$$V_{2,uu}(3) = 99.1094$$

$$V_{1,u}(3) = 99.4667$$

$$\begin{array}{c} V_{3,uud}(3) \\ V_{3,udu}(3) \end{array} = 100$$

$$V_0(3) = 100.3564$$

$$V_{2,ud}(3) = 99.7287$$

$$V_{3,udd}(3) = 100$$

Issuer calls the bond
$$V_{1,d}(3) = 100$$
$\longrightarrow \longrightarrow \longrightarrow \longrightarrow \longrightarrow$ [retired] $\longrightarrow \longrightarrow$ [retired]

Panel B: The Replicating Portfolio

$$\Pi_{3,uuu} = 100 + 1.5$$

$$\begin{aligned} N^L_{2,uu} &= 1 \\ N^S_{2,uu} &= 0 \\ \Pi_{2,uu} &= 100.6094 \\ &\rightarrow \text{Pay 1.5 coupon} \\ &\rightarrow \Pi_{1,u} = 99.1094 \end{aligned}$$

Rebalancing

Old Position		New Position
$N^L_{1,u} = 0.5852$	$\rightarrow$	$N^L_{1,u} = 1$
$N^S_{1,u} = 0.4188$	$\rightarrow$	$N^S_{1,u} = 0$
$\Pi_{1,u} = 100.9667$		
Pay 1.5 coupon		
$\rightarrow \Pi_{1,u} = 99.4667$	$\rightarrow$	$\Pi_{1,u} = 99.4667$

$$\Pi_{3,uud} = 100 + 1.5$$

$$\begin{aligned} N^L_{2,ud} &= 1 \\ N^S_{2,ud} &= 0 \\ \Pi_{1,ud} &= 101.2287 \\ &\rightarrow \text{Pay 1.5 coupon} \\ &\rightarrow \Pi_{1,u} = 99.7287 \end{aligned}$$

$$\begin{aligned} N^L_0 &= 0.5852 \\ N^S_0 &= 0.4188 \\ \Pi_0 &= 100.3564 \end{aligned}$$

Rebalancing

Old Position		New Position
$N^L_{1,d} = 0.5852$	$\rightarrow$	$N^L_{1,d} = 0$
$N^S_{1,d} = 0.4188$	$\rightarrow$	$N^S_{1,d} = 0$
$\Pi_{1,d} = 101.5$		
Pay 1.5 coupon		
$\rightarrow \Pi_{1,d} = 100$	$\rightarrow$	$\Pi_{1,d} = 0$

$$\Pi_{3,udd} = 100 + 1.5$$

[Position closed]

[Position closed]

Table 12.5   The Callable Bond and Replicating Portfolio in Case of Suboptimal Exercise

$$
\begin{aligned}
&P_{3,duu}(3) = 100 \\
&C_{3,duu}(3) = 0 \\
&V_{3,duu}(3) = 100
\end{aligned}
$$

$$
\begin{aligned}
&P_{2,du}(3) = 99.7287 \\
&C_{2,du}(3) = 0 \\
&V_{2,du}(3) = 99.7287
\end{aligned}
$$

$$
\begin{aligned}
&P_{1,d}(3) = 100.3780 \\
&C_{1,d}(3) = 0.0932 \\
&V_{1,d}(3) = 100.2848
\end{aligned}
$$

$$
\begin{aligned}
&P_{3,dud}(3) = 100 \\
&C_{3,dud}(3) = 0 \\
&V_{3,dud}(3) = 100
\end{aligned}
$$

$$
\begin{aligned}
&P_{2,dd}(3) = 100.1886 \\
&C_{2,dd}(3) = 0.1886 \\
&\text{[Issuer calls the bond]} \\
&V_{2,dd}(3) = 100
\end{aligned}
$$

[retired]

floating rate. The floating rate payment the investors must make in the swap is naturally hedged as the investor can invest the capital received back from the U.S. Treasury into floating bearing securities, such as a money market account.

How do we determine the premium of an American swaption? We can extend the binomial tree methodology discussed in Chapter 11, Section 11.2.4, to American swaptions. For convenience, we consider the same example discussed in Chapter 11.

■ EXAMPLE 12.6

Consider Example 11.6 in Chapter 11. In that example we considered a 2-year European payer swaption to enter into a 3-year semi-annual swap at the strike swap rate $r_K = 4.49\%$. Recall that the logic behind the exercise decision at maturity $(i = 4)$ is as follows. If the market swap rate two years from now is higher than the strike rate $r_K = 4.49\%$, e.g. 6%, then the swaption holder will find it profitable to exercise the option and pay $r_K = 4.49\%$ instead of the market rate of 6%. Vice versa, if in two years the market swap rate is below $r_K = 4.49\%$, e.g. 3%, then the option holder will not exercise the option, and rather enter into a swap at current market rates.

Panel A of Table 12.6 reports the interest rate tree used in Chapter 11. The underlying security is a fixed-for-floating swap with maturity $k = 10$ (five years from now) and with fixed swap rate $r_K = 4.49\%$. Panel B of Table 12.6 reports the tree of the swap value, denoted by $V_{i,j}(10, r_K)$, where $k = 10$ is the maturity of the swap, and r_K is the swap rate. The calculations are in Section 11.2.4 of Chapter 11. In a 2-year European swaption, we only have to decide whether to exercise or not at maturity, $i = 4$. Recall that since the market swap rate at any point in time is defined as the particular swap rate that makes the swap value equal to zero, the rule "exercise if the market swap rate is above the strike rate $r_K = 4.49\%$" discussed earlier translates into

$$\text{Exercise if and only if } V_{4,j}(10; r_K) > 0. \tag{12.6}$$

The American counterpart is as follows: The underlying swap is still $V_{i,j}(10, r_K)$ in Panel B of Table 12.6. Differently from the European option, the holder of an American option can exercise the option *any time* before maturity $i = 4$. Thus, as we discussed for the callable bonds, the holder of the American option at any time / node (i, j) must decide whether to exercise the option or to wait. If the option's holder exercises, he or she gets the immediate payoff $V_{i,j}(10, r_K)$ in Panel B. If instead the option's holder waits, he/she retains the option to exercise in the future. This is given by the risk neutral expectation of future cash flow from the option.

More formally, let $C_{i,j}^A$ denote the value of the American option at time/node (i, j). At maturity, we know $C_{4,j}^A = \max(V_{4,j}(10, r_K), 0)$. To compute the value at earlier periods, we need to compute the value of the option if the option's holder waits. This is given by:

$$C_{i,j}^{Wait} = e^{-r_{i,j} \times \Delta} \times \left(\frac{1}{2} \times C_{i+1,j}^A + \frac{1}{2} \times C_{i+1,j+1}^A \right) \tag{12.7}$$

Thus, the backward methodology is completed by choosing step by step the maximum between the immediate payoff and the option value if the investor decides to wait. Namely, we have:

$$C_{i,j}^A = \max \left(C_{i,j}^{Wait}, V_{i,j}(10, r_K) \right) \tag{12.8}$$

Panel C of Table 12.6 reports the results of the American option. In the tree, we can see the times of early exercise by comparing the swaption tree with the underlying swap value. If the swaption tree equals the value of the swap itself, as in for instance $i = 3$ and $j = 0$, then early exercise took place there. Because of this extra flexibility of the American option versus its European counterpart, the price of an American option is always as large as the one of the corresponding European. In this case, the value of the American option is $C_0^A = \$3.65$, which is quite higher than the corresponding value of a European swaption, given by $\$3.41$ (see Table 11.9 in Chapter 11).

12.3 MORTGAGES AND RESIDENTIAL MORTGAGE BACKED SECURITIES

In this section we return to the residential mortgage backed securities discussed in Chapter 8. We first look at the optimal decision of a homeowner who has a fixed rate mortgage, and who can decide to refinance it when interest rates decline. We then study how this optimal decision affects the value of pass-through securities and other mortgage backed securities. The model of optimal refinancing time developed here abstracts from the other reasons why homeowners may refinance their mortgages discussed in Chapter 8 (see Section 8.2.2). We incorporate these other motives for refinancing in an extension of the model in Chapter 13 (Section 13.6), where we introduce a new tool, Monte Carlo simulations, for the pricing of interest rate securities. Still, as dicussed in Chapter 8, the variation of interest rates is the main factor affecting refinancing decisions, and the understanding of the optimal refinancing time is the first step to the understanding of prepayments in MBS.

Table 12.6   A 5-Year Swap Tree

Panel A: The Simple BDT Interest Rate Tree Model

Time T	0	0.5	1	1.5	2	2.5	3	3.5	4	4.5	5
Period i	0	1	2	3	4	5	6	7	8	9	10
$\theta_i(\times 100)$	71.82	69.16	33.48	33.79	11.82	-2.30	-4.38	4.55	12.81	-1.26	

j											
0	1.74	2.90	4.77	6.56	9.03	11.15	12.83	14.60	17.38	21.56	24.93
1		2.14	3.52	4.84	6.67	8.24	9.47	10.78	12.84	15.92	18.41
2			2.60	3.58	4.93	6.08	7.00	7.97	9.48	11.76	13.60
3				2.64	3.64	4.49	5.17	5.88	7.00	8.69	10.05
4					2.69	3.32	3.82	4.35	5.17	6.42	7.42
5						2.45	2.82	3.21	3.82	4.74	5.48
6							2.08	2.37	2.82	3.50	4.05
7								1.75	2.09	2.59	2.99
8									1.54	1.91	2.21
9										1.41	1.63
10											1.21

Panel B: The Swap Value Tree

Node j										
0	0.00	4.27	8.18	11.38	13.86	15.22	15.50	14.72	12.58	8.20
1		-1.53	2.04	5.04	7.48	9.03	9.71	9.58	8.42	5.58
2			-2.79	0.05	2.44	4.14	5.18	5.58	5.21	3.60
3				-3.83	-1.47	0.36	1.67	2.51	2.77	2.10
4					-4.47	-2.54	-1.00	0.18	0.92	0.99
5						-4.74	-3.02	-1.58	-0.46	0.15
6							-4.55	-2.90	-1.50	-0.47
7								-3.89	-2.27	-0.93
8									-2.85	-1.27
9										-1.52

Panel C: The American Swaption Tree

j					
0	3.65	5.54	8.18	11.38	13.86
1		1.81	3.07	5.04	7.48
2			0.59	1.20	2.44
3				0.00	0.00
4					0.00

12.3.1   Mortgages and the Prepayment Option

A homeowner who has a fixed rate mortgage can be thought of as an issuer of a special type of callable bond. In fact, like the issuer of a callable bond, the homeowner is simply borrowing (from a bank) cash at some fixed rate (the coupon), but retains the option to close the mortgage any time he or she wishes to do so. As discussed in Chapter 8 there are many reasons why a homeowner may close (i.e. prepay) a mortgage. In this chapter we focus on the "rational" reason, that is, like the U.S. Treasury with callable bonds, a homeowner closes a mortgage simply to refinance it at a lower mortgage rate. Assuming that interest rate variation is the only reason a homeowner will refinance, it is intuitive that he/she will refinance the mortgage only if the fixed rate of a new mortgage is lower than the fixed rate of the old mortgage (with similar characteristics). As with callable bonds, trees are particularly useful in obtaining the optimal refinancing time, as it may be optimal to wait to refinance even if the new mortgage rate is below the old rate, for the same argument made in previous sections.

Although the tree methodology to compute the value of the option to refinance is similar to the one used for callable bonds, mortgages have some important differences. As usual, let's begin by considering an example.

■ **EXAMPLE 12.7**

Consider a 5-year mortgage with $100,000 principal with semi-annual payments. The unrealistic short maturity and the semiannual payment assumptions allow us to show all of the computations explicitly. Let today be January 31, 2000. The term structure of interest rates is given in Panel A of Table 12.7. Panel B reports the simple BDT model with constant volatility fitted to the term structure of interest rates (see Chapter 11).

Let the semiannually compounded mortgage rate $r_2^m = 7.564\%$, where the subscript "2" denotes semi-annual compounding. The first step in valuing the refinancing option is to find the amount of coupon paid by the homeowner every period. In this example, a period corresponds to a semester. Recall that the coupon satisfies the present value relation

$$\$100,000 = \sum_{i=1}^{10} \frac{C}{\left(1 + \frac{r_2^m}{2}\right)^{2 \times i}}$$

which yields[7]

$$C = \frac{\$100,000}{\sum_{i=1}^{10} \frac{1}{\left(1 + \frac{r_2^m}{2}\right)^{2 \times i}}} = \$12,196$$

Given the coupon payment per period C, we can compute the value of the mortgage *without prepayment option*: This is the benchmark to which we want to compare the outstanding notional. In the same way as for callable bonds, where we first computed the non-callable bond and the option to call, for a mortgage we can apply similar

---

[7]We approximate to the nearest integer.

Table 12.7   Zero Coupon Bonds and the Simple BDT Model on January 31, 2000

Panel A: Term Structure of Interest rates

Maturity	0.5	1	1.5	2	2.5	3	3.5	4	4.5	5
Zero	97.11	94.00	90.86	87.77	84.79	81.94	79.26	76.59	74.14	71.70
Yield	5.86%	6.19%	6.39%	6.52%	6.60%	6.64%	6.64%	6.67%	6.65%	6.65%

Panel B: Simple BDT Model

θ_i	0.187	0.069	0.011	-0.018	-0.031	-0.080	0.055	-0.118	0.057	-0.103	0.059
i	0	1	2	3	4	5	6	7	8	9	10

j											
0	5.86%	7.49%	9.02%	10.55%	12.17%	13.94%	15.58%	18.64%	20.44%	24.47%	27.04%
1		5.53%	6.66%	7.79%	8.99%	10.30%	11.51%	13.77%	15.10%	18.07%	19.97%
2			4.92%	5.76%	6.64%	7.61%	8.50%	10.17%	11.15%	13.35%	14.75%
3				4.25%	4.90%	5.62%	6.28%	7.51%	8.24%	9.86%	10.90%
4					3.62%	4.15%	4.64%	5.55%	6.08%	7.28%	8.05%
5						3.07%	3.43%	4.10%	4.49%	5.38%	5.95%
6							2.53%	3.03%	3.32%	3.97%	4.39%
7								2.24%	2.45%	2.94%	3.24%
8									1.81%	2.17%	2.40%
9										1.60%	1.77%
10											1.31%

reasoning, namely:

Value of mortgage = Value of mortgage without prepayment + Value of option to prepay

$$(12.9)$$

The value of the mortgage without the prepayment option can be computed by using the standard binomial tree valuation method, that is, by moving backward on the tree and applying recursively the formula

$$V_{i,j}^{np}(10) = e^{-r_{i,j} \times \Delta} \left(\frac{1}{2} \times V_{i+1,j}^{np}(10) + \frac{1}{2} \times V_{i+1,j+1}^{np}(10) + C \right)$$

where "10" is the maturity period of the mortgage, and "np" stands for "no prepayment". Note that as opposed to standard bonds, at maturity there is no payment of the principal, as this is paid over time within the coupon C. Panel A of Table 12.8 computes the value of the mortgage without prepayment option. The resulting value is $V_0^{np}(10) = \$102,220$, which is higher than the amount of principal received for the mortgage. The difference is due to the value of the option to prepay, as we now show.

To compute the prepayment option we need to know the outstanding principal balance every period, as the homeowner will compare the value of its liability to the outstanding balance. Recall from Chapter 8 that to comptue the outstanding balance, we first compute the interest paid per period, the principal payment, and thus the remaining principal, as in Equations 8.4 and 8.5. This calculation is performed in Panel B of Table 12.8. For instance, the first interest payment is $r_2^m \times \$100,000/2 = \$3,782$, which is reported in the first row, second column, in Panel B. Given the

Table 12.8   The Mortgage Value without Prepayment Option and the Outstanding Principal

Panel A: The Mortgage Value without Prepayment Option Tree

i	0	1	2	3	4	5	6	7	8	9	10
j											
0	102220	90816	80008	69644	59617	49838	40216	30550	20912	10791	0
1		95314	84165	73363	62826	52484	42263	32007	21764	11142	0
2			87420	76278	65340	54552	43858	33135	22419	11408	0
3				78528	67280	56147	45084	33999	22916	11609	0
4					68760	57362	46017	34654	23292	11760	0
5						58280	46721	35147	23574	11872	0
6							47249	35517	23784	11956	0
7								35793	23941	12018	0
8									24058	12064	0
9										12098	0
10											0

Panel B: Computation of Outstanding Balance

Interest Paid	0	3782	3464	3134	2791	2435	2066	1683	1285	873	0
Principal Paid	0	8414	8732	9062	9405	9761	10130	10513	10910	11323	0
Outstanding Principal	100000	91586	82855	73792	64388	54627	44497	33985	23074	11751	0

Panel C: Prepayment Option Tree

i	0	1	2	3	4	5	6	7	8	9	10
j											
0	2220	845	294	81	12	0	0	0	0	0	0
1		3728	1460	534	159	25	1	0	0	0	0
2			4566	2485	952	307	52	2	0	0	0
3				4735	2892	1519	587	107	4	0	0
4					4372	2735	1519	669	218	8	0
5						3653	2223	1163	500	121	0
6							2752	1532	710	204	0
7								1808	867	267	0
8									984	313	0
9										347	0
10											0

Panel D: The Interest Rate that Triggers Prepayment

i	0	1	2	3	4	5	6	7	8	9	10
Trigger rate		5.53%	4.92%	5.76%	6.64%	5.62%	6.28%	5.55%	6.08%	7.28%	–

semiannual coupon of $C = \$12,196$, the principal paid with the first coupon must be $\$12,196 - \$3,782 = \$8,414$, which appears in the second row, second column. It follows that the remaining principal at the end of the first period is $\$100,000 - \$8414 = \$91,586$, reported in the third row, second column. The entries in the third column are computed in a similar fashion, and so on for all the others.

The level of the outstanding principal remaining at the end of each period corresponds to the strike price of the American option that the homeowner implicitly possesses together with his or her mortgage. Every coupon period i the homeowner will compare the value of the mortgage, given current interest rates, with the value of the remaining principal. He or she will refinance if the current value of the mortgage, which corresponds to a liability for the homeowner, exceeds the principal remaining.

The final step then is to compute the value of the prepayment option. Denoting by L_i the outstanding principal in period i, the prepayment option has the payoff

$$\text{Prepayment option payoff} = C_{i,j}^{Exercise} = \max\left(V_{i,j}^{np}(10) - L_i, 0\right) \qquad (12.10)$$

In fact, by exercising the option, the homeowner has to pay the remaining principal L_i but he or she is released from his loan, whose value is $V_{i,j}^{np}(10)$.

How do we value the prepayment option, then? Since this is an American option, we must use the same backward induction technique discussed earlier in Section 12.1. More precisely, at any node (i,j) the homeowner can decide whether to exercise the refinancing option, obtaining the payoff in Equation 12.10, or to wait. In this latter case, we have

$$C_{i,j}^{Wait} = e^{-r_{i,j} \times \Delta} \times \left(\frac{1}{2} \times C_{i+1,j} + \frac{1}{2} \times C_{i+1,j+1} \right) \qquad (12.11)$$

The homeowner exercises the option whenever $C_{i,j}^{Exercise} > C_{i,j}^{Wait}$. The tree of the option is then determined by the backward procedure

$$C_{i,j} = \max\left(C_{i,j}^{Wait}, C_{i,j}^{Exercise}\right) \qquad (12.12)$$

Panel C of Table 12.8 shows the tree for the value of the prepayment option, which gives $C_0 = \$2,220$. The value of the mortgage in node (i,j) is given by $V_{i,j}(1) = V_{i,j}^{\text{no prepay}}(10) - C_{i,j}$. For instance, at the root of the tree the value of the mortgage is

$$\begin{aligned} V_0(10) &= V_0^{np}(10) - C_0 & (12.13) \\ &= \$102,220 - \$2,220 & (12.14) \\ &= \$100,000 & (12.15) \end{aligned}$$

That is, the value of the mortgage at time 0 is exactly equal to \$100,000, the amount of principal. In fact, we chose the mortgage rate $r_2^m = 7.564\%$ so that at initiation of the mortgage, the amount received by the homeowner is exactly equal to the fair valuation of the mortgage. In other words, the mortgage rate r_2^m contains two different components: One component is the compensation for the time value of money, as the lender is giving the funds to the homeowner instead of investing them in some other security. The second component, though, is a compensation to the lender for the prepayment option that implicitly the bank sold to the homeowner together with the mortgage. Thus, even without any risk of default, the mortgage rate is pushed up by the additional compensation that the bank wants to receive for having sold an option to the homeowner.

As for callable bonds, note that it is not always optimal to exercise as soon as the prepayment option is in-the-money. For instance, if the interest rate increases and then decreases, we end up in node $(i, j) = (2, 1)$, in which $r_{ij} = 6.66\%$. In this case, the value of the mortgage without prepayment option is $V_{2,1}^{np} = \$84,165$ while the outstanding balance is only $L_2 = \$82,855$. Immediate exercise would lead to a payoff $V_{2,1}^{np} - L_2 = \$1,310$. However, waiting has a higher value, as from Panel C of Table 12.8 we find $C_{2,1} = \$1,460 > \$1,310$. That is, exercising the option to refinance would be a mistake in this case, and waiting would be optimal. Indeed, for each period i we can compute a trigger interest rate $\underline{r}_i$ such that, if the short rate $r_{i,j}$ drops below that interest rate, the homeowner will refinance. Panel D of Table 12.8 reports such trigger interest rates.

12.3.2   The Pricing of Residential Mortgage Backed Securities

Once we know the optimal exercise time, we can compute the cash flows that are implicit in the tree. Suppose we have a mortgage pool that is made up by many mortgages identical to the one as discussed in Example 12.7. Then we know also the timing of the cash flows in this example, and thus we can use the tree to compute the price of additional mortgage backed securities. In the simplified setting of Example 12.7, in which homeowners only prepay optimally depending on interest rates, there is not much room to consider CMOs with different tranches (see Chapter 8). The reason is that all of the prepayments would occur at once, when all of the home owners prepay.[8] In Chapter 13 we extend the methodology developed here to take into account other factors that affect the decision to refinance a mortgage. In this section, we only consider the pricing of a simple Pass Through Security.

■ **EXAMPLE 12.8**

Consider a pool of mortgages identical to the one described in Example 12.7, with total principal of $100 million. Consider now a pass-through security with interest rate $r_2^{PT} = 7\%$. How do we compute the value of this security? The key is to realize that the tree in Table 12.8 exactly predicts when prepayment will occur. We can use this information together with the pass-through rate of 7% to determine the cash flows of this security over time. Given the cash flows, we can compute the value of the security.

As usual, we move backward on the tree. Table 12.9 reports the calculations. First, the top row shows the interest rate paid by the pass-through security. This equals the previous period outstanding principal L_{i-1} (the third row in Table 12.9) times the pass-through coupon rate

$$\text{Interest paid}_i = L_{i-1} \times \frac{r_2^{PT}}{2}$$

---

[8] This model, however, can be used by being more specific about the characteristics of the underlying mortgages. For instance, heterogeneity in maturity and coupon rates would generate different timings of the optimal exercise time, resulting in some interesting differences in cash flows across MBS tranches.

The second row in Table 12.9 reports the scheduled principal payment.

The tree uses the conventional methodology, already described in previous chapters, to compute the price at node (i, j) as present value of *future* cash flows, that is, it is an ex-coupon price. In this particular case, we need to consider two possibilities in each node (i, j):

1. Prepayment occurs in node (i, j)

   - $\implies$ the value of the pass-through security equals the outstanding principal:

$$P_{i,j}^{PT}(10) = L_i$$

   .

2. Prepayment does not occur in node (i, j)

   - $\implies$ the value of the pass-through security equals the risk neutral expected discounted value of the security next period $(i + 1)$, *plus* the discounted interest payment next period, *plus* the scheduled principal payment next period. In formulas

$$P_{i,j}^{PT}(10) = e^{-r_{i,j} \times \Delta} \left(\frac{1}{2} \times P_{i+1,j}^{PT}(10) + \frac{1}{2} \times P_{i+1,j+1}^{PT}(10) + CF(i+1) \right) \tag{12.16}$$

   where

$$CF(i+1) = \text{Interest payment} + \text{Scheduled principal at } i + 1 \tag{12.17}$$

For instance, in Table 12.9, consider the column corresponding to $i = 9$ (almost last period). The first entry $(j = 0)$ is equal to the present value of interest and scheduled principal at $i = 10$. That is

$$P_{9,0}^{PT}(10) = e^{-24.47\% \times 0.5} \times (\$411 + \$11,751) = \$10,762$$

where 24.47% is the interest rate in node $(9, 0)$, as shown in Table 12.7. Similarly, in the same columns, nodes $j = 1, 2, 3$ are the present value of cash flow at time $i = 10$. In contrast, the entry $11, 751$ in node $j = 4$ equals the outstanding principal at time $i = 9$. The rationale is that if the interest rate at time $i = 9$ is $r_{9,3} = 9.86\%$, then the homeowners exercise their options, and the investor in the pass through will receive back exactly the notional. We can see from the tree in Table 12.9 the nodes in which optimal exercise takes place. They are the ones in which the value of the security exactly equals the value of the outstanding principal, given in the third row of the table. As we would expect, refinancing occurs when interest rates are low.

Because of their embedded American options, mortgage backed securities display a negative convexity, meaning that their value increases by less and less as interest rates decline. Indeed, Figure 12.2 plots the value of the pass-through security against interest rates one year from initiation.[9] As the interest rate declines, it becomes increasingly more likely that homeowners will prepay the mortgage, and the value of the pass-through security converges to its remaining principal.

---

[9]For this figure, we assume the same characteristics of the pass through in Example 12.8, but we use monthly payments in order to obtain a clearer picture.

Table 12.9   A Pass-Through Security

	0.0	1.0	2.0	3.0	4.0	5.0	6.0	7.0	8.0	9.0	10.0
Interest Paid (Pass Through)		3500	3206	2900	2583	2254	1912	1557	1189	808	411
Scheduled Priincipal Paid (Pool)		8414	8732	9062	9405	9761	10130	10513	10910	11323	11751
Outstdanding Principal (Pool)	100000	91586	82855	73792	64388	54627	44497	33985	23074	11751	0
i	0.0	1.0	2.0	3.0	4.0	5.0	6.0	7.0	8.0	9.0	10.0
j											
0	99323	89141	78947	68867	59054	49435	39942	30384	20827	10762	0
1		91586	82265	72388	62168	52053	41981	31833	21675	11112	0
2			82855	73792	64388	53969	43542	32962	22328	11377	0
3				73792	64388	54627	44497	33762	22835	11577	0
4					64388	54627	44497	33985	23074	11751	0
5						54627	44497	33985	23074	11751	0
6							44497	33985	23074	11751	0
7								33985	23074	11751	0
8									23074	11751	0
9										11751	0
10											0

Figure 12.2   The Negative Convexity in a Pass Through Security

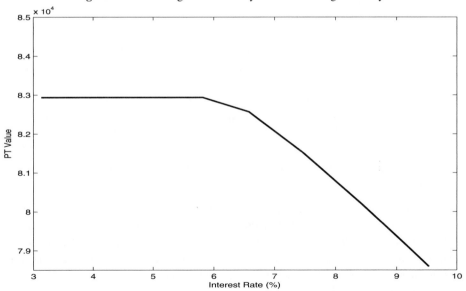

12.3.2.1 Principal Only and Interest Only Strips We can also use the tree methodology to compute the value of individual derivatives of RMBS, such as interest only (IO) and principal only (PO) strips. As discussed in Chapter 8, principal only strips are claims only to the principal payments, whether scheduled or unscheduled. In contrast, interest only strips are claims only on the interest portion of the derivative. Differently from Treasury STRIPS, IO and PO MBS strips have some interesting peculiarities, as shown in the next example.

■ **EXAMPLE 12.9**

Consider again the pass-through security in Example 12.8. We now strip the principal payments from the interest payments, thereby obtaining two securities. More specifically, the principal only security is essentially identical to the pass through discussed above, but in Equation 12.16, the cash flow $CF(i+1)$ is given only by "scheduled principal at $i+1$" instead of "interest payment + scheduled principal at $i+1$" (see Equation 12.17). The calculation is performed in Panel A of Table 12.10.

The interest only security is a claim to interest payments only, and thus two changes must be performed compared to the pass-through security:

1. First, in case of prepayment in node (i,j), the IO cash flow is zero (instead of L_i as in the pass through).

2. Second, the cash flow in Equation 12.16 is $CF(i+1) =$ interest payment at $i+1$.

The price of the principal only and the interest only MBS must add up to the price of the pass through security. Panel B of Table 12.10 contains the calculation of the IO strip security.

The main peculiarity of the IO strip, which is quite apparent on the tree, is the fact that most often its price moves inversely to the interest rate. For instance, at time $i=3$ we see that the price declines from \$9508 in the top node to \$5447 in the middle node, to 0 in the bottom node. The intuition is straightforward: The lower the interest rate, the higher the probability of prepayment. But in the case of prepayment, the cash flow to the IO security stops, as the prepaid principal goes to the PO strip, and not to the IO strip. Figure 12.3 plots the profile of interest only (the solid line) and principal only (the dashed line) against the underlying interest rate. The interest only strip shows that as interest rates decline, its value drops dramatically to zero.

12.3.3 The Spot Rate Duration of MBS

One implication of the behavior of IO strips discussed in the previous section is that the duration of IO strips is typically negative, in contrast to standard Treasury STRIPS. To see this, we apply to IO strips the analog definition of duration, the spot rate duration, as we defined it in Chapter 10, Section 10.5. More specifically, recall that the spot rate duration measures the sensitivity of the security to changes in the spot interest rates and it is given by

$$D = -\frac{1}{P}\frac{dP}{dr} \tag{12.18}$$

Figure 12.3   Interest Only and Principal Only Strips

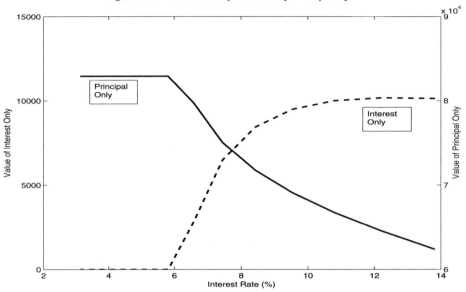

On a tree, recall that this quantity can be approximated as follows (we use the standard upward and downward notation u and d here for clarity):

$$D \approx -\frac{1}{P_0} \times \frac{P_{1,u} - P_{1,d}}{r_{1,u} - r_{1,d}} \tag{12.19}$$

The pass-through security in Table 12.9 and the PO and IO strips in Table 12.10 have spot rate duration given by

$$D^{PT} = -\frac{1}{99,323} \frac{89,141 - 91,586}{7.49\% - 5.53\%} = 1.2574 \tag{12.20}$$

$$D^{PO} = -\frac{1}{90,928} \frac{78,851 - 91,586}{7.49\% - 5.53\%} = 7.1542 \tag{12.21}$$

$$D^{IO} = -\frac{1}{8,396} \frac{10,290 - 0}{7.49\% - 5.53\%} = -62.6083 \tag{12.22}$$

The results show the following: First, the pass-through security has in fact a relatively low duration. The reason for this is that the original mortgage in Table 12.8 was computed for the mortgage rate such that the principal exactly equals the value of the mortgage. In that setting, it is optimal for the homeowner to refinance as soon as the interest rate declines, which is unrealistic. In reality, there are some costs of refinancing, so that homeowners would wait longer than the model in Table 12.8 would recommend. This slightly higher hurdle would increase the duration.

Important, though, is the impact of interest rate changes on PO and IO strips. The PO strips have a much higher sensitivity to interest rates than the original pass-through security. If interest rates decline, the price of the PO increases dramatically and for two reasons: The discount rate is smaller (and so prices go up) and also the cash flow increases (because of prepayments). This double effect pushes up the

Table 12.10 Principal Only and Interest Only Strips

				Panel A: Principal Only MBS							
i	0	1	2	3	4	5	6	7	8	9	10
j											
0	90928	78851	69439	60236	52217	44442	36549	28314	19763	10398	0
1		91586	76818	66925	55973	47021	38491	29681	20574	10736	0
2			82855	73792	64388	50549	40259	30836	21197	10992	0
3				73792	64388	54627	44497	32153	21872	11186	0
4					64388	54627	44497	33985	23074	11751	0
5						54627	44497	33985	23074	11751	0
6							44497	33985	23074	11751	0
7								33985	23074	11751	0
8									23074	11751	0
9										11751	0
10											0

				Panel B: Interest Only MBS							
i	0	1	2	3	4	5	6	7	8	9	10
j											
0	8396	10290	9508	8631	6837	4993	3393	2070	1063	364	0
1		0	5447	5463	6195	5032	3490	2152	1101	376	0
2			0	0	0	3421	3282	2125	1131	385	0
3				0	0	0	0	1609	963	392	0
4					0	0	0	0	0	0	0
5						0	0	0	0	0	0
6							0	0	0	0	0
7								0	0	0	0
8									0	0	0
9										0	0
10											0

duration. In stark contrast, the spot rate duration of IO strip is *negative*, meaning that as interest rates decline, so does the value of the IO strip. The intuition is relatively simple: In a IO strip, a decline in interest rates triggers prepayments, and thus lower future interest payments. Thus, a lower interest rate is accompanied by a lower future cash flow, and the duration is negative. We note that this behavior is quite in contrast with the duration calculation we performed using the PSA methodology in Section 8.3.3. In that section, we found that the IO strip had a positive duration, as the simple methodology applied in that section assumes a speed of prepayments, and then does not vary it as the interest rate changes. For that reason, as with any bond, the duration of IO becomes negative. As already anticipated in Section 8.3.3, a term structure model in which prepayment is taken into due account as the interest rate changes is able to uncover the true sign of the duration of an IO strip, and highlights the possible pitfalls that we can incur if we use only the PSA methodology. In reality, of course, homeowners do not prepay as soon as interest rates drop a little, and they prepay for many other reasons. The next chapter shows how we can use other models – prepayment models – together with Monte Carlo simulations to find the price of mortgage backed securities.

12.4 SUMMARY

In this chapter we covered the following topics:

1. American options: These are options that can be exercised any time before maturity. Their value is always at least as high as their European counterparts.

2. Optimal exercise time. Any time before maturity, the option holder has the choice between exercising the option or waiting (and exercising later). The decision depends on the comparison between the immediate payoff and the risk neutral expected value of the option if the holder does not exercise. The backward procedure employed when working with binomial trees makes it particularly convenient to compute these prices.

3. Callable bonds: Fixed coupon bonds that can be called back by the issuer in exchange for their par value are known as callable bonds. They can be thought of as a portfolio of a non-callable fixed coupon bond minus an American call option on the non-callable bond with strike price equal to par value.

4. Negative convexity: Callable bonds have a strong negative convexity: As interest rates decline it becomes more likely that the issuer will exercise, and thus the bond price converges to par. It follows that the sensitivity of the bond to changes in interest rates declines as the interest rate declines.

5. American swaptions: American swaptions are options to enter into a swap as a fixed rate payer (payer swaptions) or fixed rate receiver (receiver swaptions). As with European swaptions, the pricing consists of two steps: First compute the tree for the underlying swap with a swap rate equal to the option's strike rate. Then compute the value of the option that has a payoff given by the maximum between the value of the swap and zero.

6. Prepayment option in mortgages: Homeowners have the option to repay their debt at any time before the maturity. Therefore, a bank extending a mortgage is implicitly buying a non-callable mortgage and selling an American option to the homeowner. Binomial trees can be used to compute the value of the prepayment option. This is similar to the case of callable bonds, with the only difference that the scheduled outstanding principal declines over time. The homeowner's payoff from exercising the American option is the difference between value of the future coupon payments and the outstanding principal.

7. Pass-through securities: The binomial tree methodology can be employed to price pass-through securities. The binomial tree on the mortgage identifies the optimal times of refinancing, and thus the times in which the pass-through securities would pay back the principal to investors. For other times, investors receive the mortgage rate defined on the remaining principal.

8. Interest Only (IO) and Principal Only (PO) MBS. Mortgage backed securities collateralized by a pass through, according to which all of the interest payments on the principal go to IO investors, while all of the principal payments go to PO investors.

Table 12.11   An Interest Rate Tree

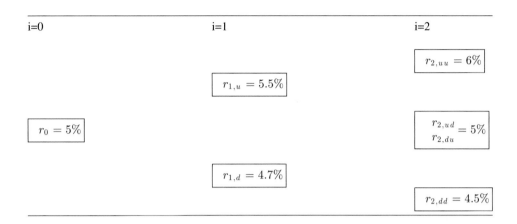

i=0	i=1	i=2
		$r_{2,uu} = 6\%$
	$r_{1,u} = 5.5\%$	
$r_0 = 5\%$		$\begin{array}{l} r_{2,ud} \\ r_{2,du} \end{array} = 5\%$
	$r_{1,d} = 4.7\%$	
		$r_{2,dd} = 4.5\%$

IO securities typically decline in price as the interest rate declines, implying a negative duration. PO securities typically increase substantially when the interest rate declines, implying a high spot rate duration.

12.5 EXERCISES

1. Suppose that you estimated the risk neutral tree for interest rates in Table 12.11, where there is equal risk neutral probability to move up or down the tree. Assume also for simplicity that each interval of time represents *1 year*, that is, $\Delta = 1$.

    (a) Compute the value of a non-callable and callable bonds, with principal = 100, maturity $i = 3$, and annual coupon rate = 5.25%. Which of the two bonds is more expensive for investors? Why?

    (b) Consider a 2-year mortgage with $10,000 face value, and a continously compounded mortgage rate of 5.097%.

        i. If there is no prepayment, what is the annual payment?
        ii. Given the annual payment, compute the principal and interest payment each period ($t = 1$ and $t = 2$). Also, compute the value of the mortgage along the tree.
        iii. Compare the value of the mortgage at each node with the principal outstanding: What is the option value? When is it optimal to exercise the option?
        iv. From your results above, compute the value of the mortgage with prepayment: What is the homeowner really paying?

    (c) How would you calculate the duration of the mortgage in this exercise?

2. Consider again the risk neutral tree for interest rates in Table 12.11, where there is equal risk neutral probability to move up or down the tree.

Table 12.12   Zero Coupon Bond Prices on January 8, 2002

Maturity (Years)	Price	Yield
0.5	99.1338	1.74
1.0	97.8925	2.13
1.5	96.1462	2.62
2.0	94.1011	3.04
2.5	91.7136	3.46
3.0	89.2258	3.80
3.5	86.8142	4.04
4.0	84.5016	4.21
4.5	82.1848	4.36
5.0	79.7718	4.52

Source: *The Wall Street Journal.*

(a) Compute the tree for an American swaption with maturity $i = 3$ and strike rate $c = 5.25\%$.

(b) Consider now a callable bond with maturity $i = 3$, principal = 100, and annual coupon rate = 5.25%.

(c) An investor is long the callable bond priced in the previous exercise, and is worried about prepayment risk. Can you suggest how the investor can employ an American swaption to hedge against prepayment risk? Assume the investor is *not* worried about interest rate risk.

(d) Assume that the investor in the callable bond is instead worried about interest rate risk. Can you suggest a hedging strategy that would cover the investor against changes in the interest rates?

3. **Mortgage backed securities**. In this exercise we look at some features of the optimal time of exercise the prepayment option embedded in mortgage pools. To keep things simple, we consider a short maturity (only 5 years, instead of 30) and semi-annual payments (instead of monthly). More specifically, consider a 5-year to maturity mortgage pool with average semi-annually compounded mortgage rate $r_2^m = 4\%$. Assume semi-annual payments of the coupon C. Let market rates evolve according to a simple BDT model, with volatility $\sigma = 20\%$, and θ_t obtained to fit the zero coupon bonds in Table 12.12.

(a) The mortgage:

i. Compute the value of the coupon C and the stream of scheduled interest payments, principal payments, and the remaining principal over the 10 semesters.

ii. From the estimates of σ and θ_t for the simple BDT model, construct an interest rate tree at semi-annual frequency.

iii. Compute the evolution on the tree of the net present value of future coupon payments without the prepayment option.

Table 12.13 LIBOR and Swap Rates on November 8, 2006

Maturity	Rate
3-month LIBOR	5.37442%
6-month LIBOR	5.38063%
1-year swap	5.3340 %
2-year swap	5.1325 %
3-year swap	5.0740%
4-year swap	5.0665%
5-year swap	5.0765%
7-year swap	5.1155%
10-year swap	5.1690%

Source: Bloomberg.

    iv. Compute the value of the American option implicit in the mortgage.

    v. Compute the option-adjusted value of the mortgage.

        A. When is the prepayment option going to be exercised? Show all the nodes when the exercise of the option would occur (if interest rates reach that far).

        B. Is there a path of interest rates whereby the prepayment option is only exercised in year 3 or later?

        C. Given your estimates and disregarding default, is the mortgage fairly priced?

        D. How would you expect the value of the mortgage to change if the homeowner does not exercise the option optimally (that is, he/she forgets to exercise when he/she should or vice versa, prepay when he/she should not)?

  (b) The mortgage backed securities:

    i. Consider a 3.5% pass-through security that is collateralized by the same mortgages as above (in average). Compute the value of the pass-through security, as well as its spot rate duration.

    ii. Now make two independent trees for the interest rate only (IO) strip and the principal only (PO) strip, and compute their values at time zero.

        A. Is the sum of the values of the IO and PO strips equal to the value of the pass-through security computed earlier?

4. Today is November 8, 2006. You have been retained to suggest an effective hedging strategy to an investor, who invested in callable bonds. In particular, the bond portfolio is long in 5%, 10-year AAA rated corporate coupon bonds (par = 500 million), which will become callable in exactly three years. The investor is worried about prepayment risk, and your job is to set up an effective hedging strategy using American swaptions. The current LIBOR and swap rates are in Table 12.13.

(a) From the LIBOR and swap rates compute the semi-annual discount curve $Z(0, T)$ up to $T = 10$.

(b) Use the discount curve $Z(0, T)$ to fit a simple BDT tree with semi-annual steps up to $T = 10$. The volatility σ can be estimated from the variation of 3-month or 6-month LIBOR (see data at British Bankers Association Web site *www.baa.gov.uk*).

(c) Using the tree, compute the value of the portfolio of bonds (by no arbitrage, this should equal the traded value of the AAA callable bonds; assume it is). Remember that the bonds become callable starting in three years.

(d) Compute the spot rate duration and the spot rate convexity of the portfolio. Recall that the spot rate duration can be computed as

$$D_0 = -\frac{1}{V_0} \frac{V_{1,u} - V_{1,d}}{r_{1,u} - r_{1,d}}$$

In a similar fashion, the spot rate convexity can be computed as

$$C_0 = -\frac{1}{V_0} \frac{D_{1,u} - D_{1,d}}{r_{1,u} - r_{1,d}}$$

where $D_{1,u}$ and $D_{1,d}$ are the spot rate durations computed in time/nodes $(1, u)$ and $(1, d)$.

(e) Plot the callable and non-callable portfolio against interest rates at time $t = $ "Call time $-$ 1 semester." Use the BDT tree and the values of the bonds on the BDT tree to do so: Select the column that corresponds to one semester before call time, and plot the values of the portfolios against the interest rates. Comment.

(f) Repeat Part (a) for another few periods before the bond becomes callable (e.g., one year before, or 1 1/2 year before). What can you say about the convexity of the callable bond?

(g) To execute the hedging strategy you have to select an appropriate American swaption that is able to hedge the investor against prepayment risk. (Note, the investor does not mind interest rate risk per se, but only prepayment risk.)

   i. Value the American swaption that you propose to your counterparty.

   ii. Plot the swaption value against interest rates at time $t = $"Call Time $-$ 1 quarter." Why does this swaption address the issue of the investor?

   iii. If the investor at time $t = 0$ buys the swaption, he/she will be long both the swaption and the callable bond portfolio. Plot the value of this portfolio against interest rates. Comment.

5. Today is June 7, 2007. Freddie Mac is issuing a 10-year Bermudan note on June 15 2007 under the terms described in Table 12.14[10]. A Bermudan security is like a callable security, but with call dates defined ex-ante in the term sheet. Prices of Treasury bills and notes for the same date are in Table 12.15.

---

[10]From Pricing Supplement Dated May 31, 2007. Security CUSIP: 3128X6CD6

Table 12.14   Freddie Mac, June 2017, 6% Fixed Rate Medium-Term Bermudan Note

Issue Date	June 15, 2007
Maturity Date	June 15, 2017
Subject to Redemption	Yes. The Medium-Term Notes are redeemable at our [Freddie Mac] option, upon notice of not less than 5 Business Days, at a price of 100% of the principal amount, plus accrued interest to the Redemption Date
Redemption Date(s)	Semi-annually, on June 15 and December 15, commencing on June 15, 2009.
Interest Rate Per Annum	6%
Frequency of Interest Payments	Semiannually, in arrears, commencing December 15, 2007
Interest Payment Dates	June 15 and December 15
Principal Payment	at maturity, or upon redemption
CUSIP Number	3128X6CD6

(a) From the Treasury data obtain the discount curve $Z(0, T)$ up to June 2017. Plot your results. (You can use bootstrap, or curve fitting, or any other methodology. See Chapter 2.)

(b) From the discount curve $Z(0, T)$, fit a simple semi-annual BDT model, as in Chapter 11. Assume a constant σ. The volatility σ can be estimated from the variation of 6-month T-bills (see data at the Federal Reserve Web site *www.federalreserve.gov/Releases/h15/data.htm*).

(c) i. Use the simple BDT binomial tree to value the Freddie Mac callable medium term note. What price did you obtain? (Recall that the note becomes callable on June 15, 2009.)

  ii. If the price is not equal to the quoted price (100), you can compute the option adjusted spread (OAS) of this security. What OAS did you obtain?

  iii. What volatility σ would you need to make OAS = 0?

(d) Price again the callable bond, but use the Ho-Lee model instead of the simple BDT model. Is the price the same as with the simple BDT model? Comment.

(e) Compute the spot rate duration of the callable bond.

(f) Compute the spot rate convexity of the bond. This convexity can be defined analogously to the spot rate duration, and it is given by

$$\text{Spot rate convexity} = \frac{1}{P}\frac{d^2 P}{d\, r^2} = \frac{1}{P}\frac{d\left(\frac{d\, P}{d\, r}\right)}{d\, r} = -\frac{1}{P}\frac{dD^\$}{d\, r} \qquad (12.23)$$

where $D^\$$ denotes the dollar spot rate duration. On a tree, we can approximate the spot rate convexity in time/node (i, j) as follows

  i. Compute the dollar spot rate duration at nodes $(i+1, j)$ and $(i+1, j+1)$, and denote them $D^\$_{i+1,j}$ and $D^\$_{i+1,j}$, respectively.

Table 12.15   Treasury Bills and Notes on June 7, 2007

Maturity Date	Type	Coupon Rate	Bid	Ask	Time to Maturity	Accrued Interest
20070705	4	0.000	99.635	99.636	0.078	0.000
20070809	4	0.000	99.187	99.189	0.172	0.000
20070815	2	2.750	99.586	99.617	0.189	0.856
20070906	4	0.000	98.821	98.823	0.247	0.000
20071004	4	0.000	98.474	98.477	0.325	0.000
20071011	4	0.000	98.374	98.378	0.344	0.000
20071108	4	0.000	97.992	97.996	0.419	0.000
20071115	4	0.000	97.900	97.905	0.439	0.000
20071206	4	0.000	97.591	97.596	0.497	0.000
20080215	2	3.375	98.852	98.883	0.689	1.050
20080815	2	4.125	98.898	98.930	1.189	1.283
20090215	2	4.500	99.086	99.117	1.689	1.400
20090815	2	4.875	99.617	99.648	2.189	1.517
20100215	2	4.750	99.219	99.250	2.689	1.478
20100815	2	4.125	97.281	97.313	3.189	1.283
20110215	2	5.000	99.875	99.906	3.689	1.556
20110815	2	5.000	99.844	99.875	4.189	1.556
20120215	2	4.875	99.234	99.266	4.689	1.517
20120815	2	4.375	97.031	97.063	5.189	1.361
20130215	2	3.875	94.188	94.219	5.689	1.206
20130815	2	4.250	95.703	95.734	6.189	1.322
20140215	2	4.000	93.813	93.844	6.689	1.244
20140815	2	4.250	94.781	94.813	7.189	1.322
20150215	2	4.000	92.844	92.875	7.689	1.244
20150815	2	4.250	94.141	94.172	8.189	1.322
20160215	2	4.500	95.625	95.656	8.689	1.400
20160815	2	4.875	97.953	97.984	9.189	1.517
20170215	2	4.625	96.016	96.047	9.689	1.439
20170815	1	8.875	128.813	128.875	10.189	2.761
20190215	1	8.875	131.375	131.438	11.689	2.761
20190815	1	8.125	125.500	125.563	12.189	2.528
20200215	1	8.500	129.563	129.625	12.689	2.644
20200815	1	8.750	132.547	132.609	13.189	2.722
20210215	1	7.875	124.781	124.844	13.689	2.450
20220815	1	7.250	119.828	119.891	15.189	2.256
20230215	1	7.125	118.859	118.922	15.689	2.217
20230815	1	6.250	109.844	109.906	16.189	1.944
20250215	1	7.625	126.063	126.125	17.689	2.372
20250815	1	6.875	117.844	117.906	18.189	2.139
20260215	1	6.000	107.875	107.938	18.689	1.867
20260815	1	6.750	116.984	117.047	19.189	2.100
20270215	1	6.625	115.750	115.813	19.689	2.061
20270815	1	6.375	112.922	112.984	20.189	1.983
20280815	1	5.500	102.375	102.438	21.189	1.711
20290215	1	5.250	99.313	99.375	21.689	1.633
20290815	1	6.125	110.688	110.750	22.189	1.906
20310215	1	5.375	101.234	101.297	23.689	1.672
20360215	1	4.500	89.016	89.078	28.689	1.400
20370215	1	4.750	92.766	92.797	29.689	1.478

Source: Data excerpted from CRSP (insert database name) ©2009 Center for Research in Security Prices (CRSP), The University of Chicago Booth School of Business.
Type Legend: 1= T-bond; 2 = T-note; 4 = T-bill.

Table 12.16   Freddie Mac, June, 2028 Zero Coupon Medium-Term Bermudan Note

Issue Date	June 7, 2007
Maturity Date	June 7, 2028
Subject to Redemption	Yes. The Medium-Term Notes are redeemable at our [Freddie Mac] option, upon notice of not less than 5 Business Days. See "Redemption" below. We [Freddie Mac] will redeem all of the Medium Term Notes if we exercise our option.
Redemption Date(s)	June 7, 2010, June 7, 2013, June 7, 2016, June 7, 2019,June 7, 2022, June 7, 2025, and June 7, 2028
Interest Rate Per Annum	None
Principal Payment	at maturity, or upon redemption
CUSIP Number	3128X6BZ8

Redemption	
Redemption Date	Call Price Percentage
June 7, 2010	32.316531
June 7, 2013	39.011018
June 7, 2016	47.092292
June 7, 2019	56.847631
June 7, 2022	68.623824
June 7, 2025	82.839498
June 7, 2028	100.00000

ii. Compute

$$\text{Spot rate convexity} \approx \frac{1}{P_{i,j}} \times \frac{D^{\$}_{i+1,j} - D^{\$}_{i+1,j+1}}{r_{i+1,j} - r_{i+1,j+1}}$$

(g) How does your result depend on the lockout period? Recompute the convexity assuming that the note is callable starting June, 2008. Is it the same?

6. Today is June 7, 2007. The Treasury data are in Table 12.15. On this date, Freddie Mac issued a medium/long term Bermudan, zero coupon bond. The terms are in Table 12.16.[11] In particular, because the zero coupon is always below par and its price increases over time, the call prices have to be adjusted to reflect the pure time value of money. The term sheet indicates that Freddie Mac can only call the zero coupon on specific dates, and at call prices as indicated in the term sheet. For instance, if Freddie Mac calls the zero back on June 7, 2010, Freddie Mac would pay investors 32.316531% of the principal. This security was issued on June 7, 2007 at the price of 26.770852% of principal.

(a) Use the Treasuries in Table 12.15 to obtain the discount curve $Z(0, T)$ at semi-annual (or annual) intervals. Note that the bootstrap methodology would not

---

[11] From the pricing supplement dated May 30, 2007.

work after 10 years, and so fitting a Nelson Siegel model (see Chapter 2) may be necessary.

(b) Fit the simple Black, Derman, and Toy model to the Treasury curve. The volatility σ can be obtained from the standard deviation of the 6-month T-bill rate, whose time series can be obtained from the Federal Reserve Web site (*www.federalreserve.gov/Releases/h15/data.htm*).

(c) Compute the price of the zero coupon Bermudan note. Is this the same as the issue price?

(d) What is the spot rate duration?

(e) You can use the tree in this exercise and price the June 2017, 6% Fixed-Rate Medium-Term Bermudan Note in Table 12.14. Compute the volatility that makes the price of one of these two securities (the 6% note or the zero coupon note) exactly right, and then check that the other security is fairly priced. If not, can you suggest an arbitrage strategy?

7. On June 7 2007, the Ginnie Mae pass through GNSF 6 was quoted at [ASK, BID]=[99.40625, 99.375].[12] This pass-through security was collateralized by a pool of mortgages with a weighted average coupon (WAC) = 6.5%, and a weighted average maturity (WAM) = 320 (months). The Treasury data for this day is shown in Table 12.15.

(a) Extract the discount curve $Z(0, T)$ from the Treasuries. Note that you need a long maturity (up to 320 months), and thus bootstrap may not be sufficient. You may have to use the Nelson Siegel model (see Chapter 2). Ideally, you should obtain the discount curve at monthly frequency, but quarterly frequency may also be used.

(b) Fit the simple BDT or the Ho-Lee model to the discount curve $Z(0, T)$. The volatility σ can be obtained from the standard deviation of the appropriate T-bill rate, whose time series can be obtained from the Federal Reserve Web site (*www.federalreserve.gov/Releases/h15/data.htm*)

(c) Use the binomial tree to obtain the price of the the pass-through security GNSF 6. To obtain this value, recall you must:

i. Compute the dollar coupon and the scheduled interest and principal payments. These calculations allow you to compute the scheduled outstanding principal balance.

ii. Compute the value of the non-callable mortgage on the tree (i.e., present value of future coupons).

iii. Compute the optimal time of prepayment.

iv. Use the GNSF coupon rate (6%) and the optimal prepayment time to compute the cash flows of the pass-through security

(d) Is the price that you obtained close to the quoted one? If not, explain why not. What is the OAS?

[12]Source: Bloomberg.

CHAPTER 13

MONTE CARLO SIMULATIONS ON TREES

In this chapter we introduce an important methodology for pricing interest rate securities and their derivatives: Monte Carlo Simulations. In Monte Carlo simulations, we use computers to simulate several interest rate scenarios in the future, and then obtain the value of the security by averaging an appropriate discounted value of the payoff. In this chapter, we develop the Monte Carlo simulation methodology on binomial trees, and show that we can value quite complex path-dependent interest rate derivatives. In Chapter 17 the Monte Carlo simulation methodology is extended to a more general framework.

13.1 MONTE CARLO SIMULATIONS ON A ONE-STEP BINOMIAL TREE

Consider a one-step risk neutral binomial tree in which the interest rate has an equal chance to move up or down the tree. We want to price an interest rate option that pays at time $T = 0.5$ (i.e. $i = 1$) if the interest rate increases. That is, the payoff of the option is $c_1 = 100 \times \max(r_1 - r_K, 0)$, where r_K is the strike rate and r_1 is the rate at time $i = 1$. Using risk neutral pricing, the value of the option is:

$$c_0 = E^* \left[e^{-r_0 \times T} \times c_1 \right] = e^{-r_0 \times T} \left[\frac{1}{2} \times c_{1,u} + \frac{1}{2} \times c_{1,d} \right] \tag{13.1}$$

Table 13.1 computes the value of the option for a given binomial tree.

An alternative way of computing the expected future payoff is to *simulate* upward and downward movements in the tree using a computer. For instance, in Excel the function

Table 13.1 Interest Rate Option

	$i = 0$	$i = 1$
		$r_{1,u} = 3.75\%$ $c_{1,u} = 1.747$
	$r_0 = 1.74\%$ $c_0 = e^{-1.74\%/2} \times \frac{1}{2} \times 1.747$ $= 0.8660$	
		$r_{1,d} = 1.30\%$ $c_{1,d} = 0$

$RAND()$ simulates a realization from a uniform distribution between $[0, 1]$. Thus, if we let the computer compute $RAND()$, it will provide a number with 50% chance of being between 0 and 0.5 and a 50% chance of being between 0.5 and 1. As a consequence, we can simulate $RAND()$ a large number N of times, and then impose the following:

(a) Whenever the realization $RAND() < 0.5$ we say that the interest rate moved *up* the tree.

(b) Whenever the realization $RAND() \geq 0.5$, we say the interest rate moved *down* the tree.

For each of these realizations of $RAND()$, we can then compute the value of the interest rate at time $i = 1$, $r_{1,u}$ or $r_{1,d}$, and compute the corresponding payoff. For convenience, let $s = 1, 2, ..., N$ denote the simulation number, so that we can denote by r_1^s the realized interest rate at time 1 in simulation number s. For each simulation s, we can also compute the value of the option at time 1, $c_1^s = 100 \times \max(r_1^s - r_K, 0)$.

The expected discounted payoff in Equation 13.1 can then be approximated by the average of the discounted payoff across all simulations. That is:

$$
\begin{aligned}
\widehat{c}_0 &= \text{average of } \left\{ e^{-r_0 \times T} \times c_1^1, e^{-r_0 \times T} \times c_1^2, e^{-r_0 \times T} \times c_1^3, ..., e^{-r_0 \times T} \times c_1^3 \right\} \\
&= \frac{1}{N} \sum_{s=1}^{N} e^{-r_0 \times T} c_1^s
\end{aligned}
\tag{13.2}
$$

Table 13.2 illustrates the procedure. This table shows the result from ten simulations. The first column reports the simulation number. The second column displays the actual realization of the $RAND()$ function in Excel. The third column tells us the movement in the tree implied by the $RAND()$ realization. The fourth column reports the payoff at maturity, i.e. $c_1^s = 100 \times \max(r_1^s - r_K, 0)$. The last column computes the discounted payoff, $e^{-r_0 \times T} \times c_1^s$. For instance, in the first row (Simulation number 1), the realization of $RAND()$ was $RAND() = 0.67901$. Because this number is above 0.5, we consider this realization as a downward movement in the tree. Thus, in this simulation, the interest

Table 13.2   Ten Simulations on the Binomial Tree

Simulation Number	Realization of $RAND()$	Move on the Tree	Interest Rate Realization	Payoff at Maturity T	Discounted Payoff
1	0.67901	down	1.30%	0.000	0.000
2	0.222179	up	3.75%	1.747	1.732
3	0.684549	down	1.30%	0.000	0.000
4	0.761836	down	1.30%	0.000	0.000
5	0.140407	up	3.75%	1.747	1.732
6	0.092252	up	3.75%	1.747	1.732
7	0.999465	down	1.30%	0.000	0.000
8	0.472856	up	3.75%	1.747	1.732
9	0.521622	down	1.30%	0.000	0.000
10	0.575471	down	1.30%	0.000	0.000
				Average	0.693

rate is $r_1^1 = r_{1,d} = 1.30\%$. The payoff corresponding to this realization is zero, and so is its discounted value. Consider now the second simulation $s = 2$. In this case, $RAND() = 0.222179 < 0.5$ and hence we consider this an upward movement in the tree. The realized interest rate in this simulation is then $r_1^2 = r_{1,u} = 3.75\%$ and the payoff is $c_1^2 = 1.7470$. The discounted payoff to today is then 1.732. And so on for all 10 realizations.

The value of the security is, approximately, the average of the discounted payoffs, that is, the average of the numbers in the final column. In this case, $\widehat{c}_0 = 0.693$. With only $N = 10$ simulation, it is no surprise that the value of the security $\widehat{c}_0 = 0.693$ comes in rather different than the value from the tree ($c_0 = 0.8660$ in Table 13.1). However, as the number of simulations N increases, the value from the simulations becomes more and more accurate. For instance, with 500 simulations we get $\widehat{c}_0 = 0.897$, and with 1,000 simulations $\widehat{c}_0 = 0.888$.

13.2   MONTE CARLO SIMULATIONS ON A TWO-STEP BINOMIAL TREE

The methodology on a two-step tree is similar. Consider once again the same option, but now with one year to maturity, $T = 1$ (i.e. $i = 2$). Table 13.3 shows the two step binomial tree and the value of the option.

To understand Monte Carlo simulations on the two-step binomial tree, however, it is important to recall that the binomial tree backward computation methodology is equivalent to the outright calculation of the value of the security as the risk neutral present discounted value of the payoff at maturity, discounted at the risk free rate. That is, the value of the security is equal to

$$c_0 = E^* \left[\underbrace{\left(e^{-r_0 \times 0.5} \right)}_{(\text{Discount } 1 \to 0)} \times \underbrace{\left(e^{-r_1 \times 0.5} \right)}_{(\text{Discount } 2 \to 1))} \times \underbrace{c_2}_{\text{Payoff at } 2} \right] \tag{13.3}$$

$$= E^* \left[e^{-(r_0 + r_1) \times 0.5} \times c_2 \right] \tag{13.4}$$

Table 13.3   The 1-year Option

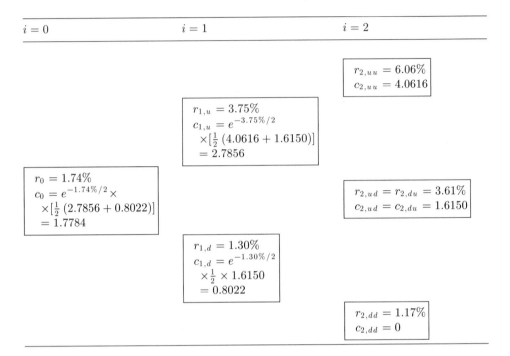

$i = 0$	$i = 1$	$i = 2$

Indeed, note that each of the four interest rates $r_{2,uu}$, $r_{2,ud}$, $r_{2,du}$ and $r_{2,dd}$ will occur with a 25% chance (it is useful at this point to keep the events $r_{2,ud}$, $r_{2,du}$ distinct from one another). Thus, the value of the option is also equal to

$$
\begin{aligned}
c_0 &= 0.25 \times e^{-(r_0 + r_{1,u}) \times 0.5} \times c_{2,uu} + 0.25 \times e^{-(r_0 + r_{1,u}) \times 0.5} \times c_{2,ud} \qquad (13.5) \\
&\quad + 0.25 \times e^{-(r_0 + r_{1,d}) \times 0.5} \times c_{2,du} + 0.25 \times e^{-(r_0 + r_{1,d}) \times 0.5} \times c_{2,dd} \qquad (13.6) \\
&= 0.25 \times e^{-(1.75\% + 3.75\%) \times 0.5} \times 4.0616 + 0.25 \times e^{-(1.75\% + 3.75\%) \times 0.5} \times 1.6150 \\
&\quad + 0.25 \times e^{-(1.75\% + 1.30) \times 0.5} \times 1.6150 + 0.25 \times e^{-(1.75\% + 1.30\%) \times 0.5} \times 0 \\
&= 1.7784,
\end{aligned}
$$

the same price we saw before in Table 13.3.

We now perform exactly the same simulation exercise as in the previous section, with the only difference that for each simulation we must obtain two random realizations of $RAND()$, the first for the first movement on the tree, and the second for the second movement on the tree. Table 13.4 shows the methodology with ten simulations. Consider the first row, $s = 1$. The first $RAND() = 0.468691837 < 0.5$, which implies an upward movement in the interest rate to $r_1^1 = 3.75\%$. The second realization, $RAND() = 0.51301168 > 0.5$ implies instead a downward movement at $i = 1$, resulting in the final interest rate $r_2^1 = r_{2,ud} = 3.61\%$. The payoff at time $i = 2$ from the first simulation is then 1.615. The only caveat compared to the one-period case in the previous section is to figure out how we should discount this cash flow. The expression in (13.4), and its explicit development in Equations 13.5 and 13.6 provide the answer: We must discount this cash flow by using the *realized* interest rate path in that simulation. In particular, in this simulation, the time 0 interest rate is $r_0 = 1.74\%$ (this is always true for all simulations) and the time $i = 1$ simulated interest rate is $r_1^1 = 3.75\%$. Thus, we must discount the payoff at time $i = 2$ in simulation $s = 1$ as

$$\text{Discounted payoff in simulation 1} = e^{-(1.74\% + 3.75\%) \times 0.5} \times 1.615 \quad (13.7)$$
$$= 1.571 \quad (13.8)$$

The final column in Table 13.4 reports this number. The second simulation $s = 2$ implies first an upward movement and then again an upward movement, resulting in the final interest rate equal to $r_2^2 = r_{2,uu} = 6.06\%$. The final payoff, 4.062, is now discounted using the discount factor $e^{-(r_0 + r_1^1) \times 0.5} = e^{-(1.74\% + 3.75\%) \times 0.5}$, obtaining a discounted value of 3.952, shown in the final column again. And so on for all of the ten simulations. The value of the security is (approximately) given by the average of the numbers in the last column, which is $\hat{c}_0 = 1.975$. Given the low number of simulations, the average is not too close to the true value, $c_0 = 1.7784$, but, once again, a larger number of simulations results in a more accurate price. For instance, repeating the above procedure for $N = 1,000$ simulations, we obtain a value $\hat{c} = 1.839$, close to the true value.

13.2.1 Example: Non-Recombining Trees in Asian Interest Rate Options

The question at this point is: Why should we use Monte Carlo simulations to compute the value of an option when the binomial tree approach appears so much simpler? The answer relies on the fact that while for plain vanilla securities a tree may be better, for more "exotic" securities a tree may prove very hard to use. We cover some more detailed examples below, but here we can consider a simple case, namely, an Asian interest rate option.

Definition 13.1 *An **Asian interest rate option** is an option whose payoff at maturity is given by*

$$Payoff\ at\ T = \begin{cases} \max\left(average\ rate\ from\ 0\ to\ T - r_K, 0\right) & (Asian\ Call) \\ \max\left(r_K - average\ rate\ from\ 0\ to\ T, 0\right) & (Asian\ Put) \end{cases} \quad (13.9)$$

The payoff of this option then depends not only on the interest rate in the final node of the tree, but on the whole history of past interest rates. The reason is that the average interest rate between time 0 and maturity T depends on the values the interest rate took during this period. Mathematically, the average interest rate is given by

$$Average\ rate\ from\ 0\ to\ T = \bar{r} = \frac{1}{n} \sum_{i=0}^{n} r_i \quad (13.10)$$

where n is the number of steps between 0 and T. The notation $\bar{r}$ denotes "average".

Consider then an Asian interest rate call option with strike rate $r_K = 2\%$. What is the problem with using a binomial tree approach to value the option? Table 13.5 shows the two-step binomial interest rate tree discussed earlier, together with the value of the average interest rate from $i = 0$ to $i = 2$. The problem is with the middle part of the tree, namely,

Table 13.4 Ten Simulations on the Two-Step Binomial Tree

Simulation Number	First Realization of $RAND()$	First Move on the Tree	Interest Rate Realization at Time $i = 1$	Second Realization of $RAND()$	Second Move on the Tree	Interest Rate Realization at Time $i = 2$	Payoff at Maturity	Discounted Payoff
1	0.468692	up	3.75%	0.513012	down	3.61%	1.615	1.571
2	0.103819	up	3.75%	0.164345	up	6.06%	4.062	3.952
3	0.848307	down	1.30%	0.340712	up	3.61%	1.615	1.591
4	0.702089	down	1.30%	0.254097	up	3.61%	1.615	1.591
5	0.001839	up	3.75%	0.118779	up	6.06%	4.062	3.952
6	0.444781	up	3.75%	0.241821	up	6.06%	4.062	3.952
7	0.066274	up	3.75%	0.55081	down	3.61%	1.615	1.571
8	0.386942	up	3.75%	0.765509	down	3.61%	1.615	1.571
9	0.769553	down	1.30%	0.627444	down	1.17%	0.000	0.000
10	0.888142	down	1.30%	0.97949	down	1.17%	0.000	0.000
						Average		1.975

Table 13.5   An Asian Interest Rate Option on a Binomial Tree

$i = 0$	$i = 1$	$i = 2$

$$r_0 = 1.74\%$$

$$r_{1,u} = 3.75\%$$
$$\bar{r}_{1,u} = 2.7\%$$

$$r_{1,d} = 1.30\%$$
$$\bar{r}_{1,d} = 1.52\%$$

$$r_{2,uu} = 6.06\% \atop \bar{r}_{2,uu} = 3.85\%$$ $\Longrightarrow$ $c_{2,uu} = 1.8495$

$$r_{2,ud} = 3.61\% \atop \bar{r}_{2,ud} = 3.03\%$$ $\Longrightarrow$ $c_{2,ud} = 1.0340$

$$r_{2,du} = 3.61\% \atop \bar{r}_{2,ud} = 2.22\%$$ $\Longrightarrow$ $c_{2,du} = 0.2185$

$$r_{2,dd} = 1.17\% \atop \bar{r}_{2,ud} = 1.40\%$$ $\Longrightarrow$ $c_{2,dd} = 0$

the interest rate path "up and down" leads to a different average interest rate than the path "down and up." That is

$$(r_0 = 1.74\% \rightarrow r_{1,u} = 3.75\% \rightarrow r_{2,ud} = 3.61\%) \quad \Longrightarrow \quad \bar{r}_{2,ud} = 3.03\%$$
$$(r_0 = 1.74\% \rightarrow r_{1,d} = 1.30\% \rightarrow r_{2,du} = 3.61\%) \quad \Longrightarrow \quad \bar{r}_{2,du} = 2.22\%$$

The tree for the average interest rate *does not* recombine. While for the two-period model it is still simple to compute the value of the security, for longer trees the lack of the recombining property may generate some difficulties in computing the value of the option. Moreover, the type of path dependency may be very complex – as we are going to see for amortizing index swaps or mortgage backed securities – in which case the binomial tree approach becomes impractical.

What is the value of the Asian interest rate option? Even if the tree is not recombining we can still use the backward methodology and find the value of the Asian option. This calculation is performed in Table 13.6.

13.2.2   Monte Carlo Simulations for Asian Interest Rate Options

Monte Carlo Simulations are especially useful to compute the value of path dependent securities, that is, securities whose value at maturity does not depend only on the interest rate at maturity, but on the *whole history* of interest rates. An example is the Asian interest rate option discussed above. Indeed, compared to the pricing of a standard option (as in

Table 13.6   The Valuation of the Asian Interest Rate Option on a Binomial Tree

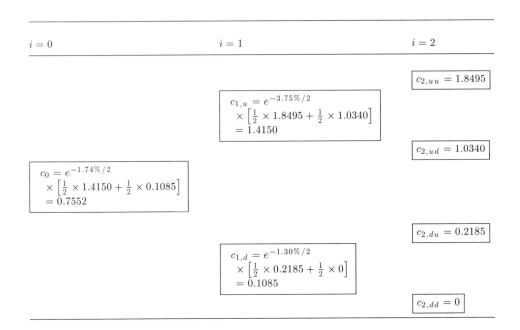

$i = 0$	$i = 1$	$i = 2$

$$c_{2,uu} = 1.8495$$

$$
\begin{aligned}
c_{1,u} &= e^{-3.75\%/2} \\
&\times \left[\tfrac{1}{2} \times 1.8495 + \tfrac{1}{2} \times 1.0340 \right] \\
&= 1.4150
\end{aligned}
$$

$$c_{2,ud} = 1.0340$$

$$
\begin{aligned}
c_0 &= e^{-1.74\%/2} \\
&\times \left[\tfrac{1}{2} \times 1.4150 + \tfrac{1}{2} \times 0.1085 \right] \\
&= 0.7552
\end{aligned}
$$

$$c_{2,du} = 0.2185$$

$$
\begin{aligned}
c_{1,d} &= e^{-1.30\%/2} \\
&\times \left[\tfrac{1}{2} \times 0.2185 + \tfrac{1}{2} \times 0 \right] \\
&= 0.1085
\end{aligned}
$$

$$c_{2,dd} = 0$$

Table 13.4) we only have to change the payoff at maturity to make it equal to the average of the simulated interest rate, path by path. In essence, we only modify Column 8 in Table 13.4 to reflect the new payoff. Everything else is performed exactly as before, including the discounting (Column 9) and the average across simulations to calculate the price of the derivative. Table 13.7 is the analog of Table 13.4 but for the Asian option. Note that the only difference between the two tables is in fact in the last two columns. The Monte Carlo simulation price with $N = 10$ gives a value of $\widehat{c}_0 = 0.6097$. With 1,000 simulations, this number is $\widehat{c}_0 = 0.786$, closer to the value obtained from the binomial tree.

13.3   MONTE CARLO SIMULATIONS ON MULTI-STEP BINOMIAL TREES

The approach can readily be extended to multi-period binomial trees, which is an important extension as it allows us to evaluate relatively complex securities. In this case, it is convenient to recall our original (risk neutral) interest rate model. Consider, for instance, the Ho-Lee model, discussed in Chapter 11, Section 11.1.1. The model postulates that interest rates move according to the following dynamics:

$$r_{i+1,j} = r_{i,j} + \theta_i \times \Delta + \sigma \times \sqrt{\Delta} \quad \text{with RN probability } p^* = 1/2 \quad (13.11)$$
$$r_{i+1,j+1} = r_{i,j} + \theta_i \times \Delta - \sigma \times \sqrt{\Delta} \quad \text{with RN probability } p^* = 1/2 \quad (13.12)$$

Because the interest rate process goes up or down with equal probabilities, it is relatively straightforward to simulate the paths on the tree. Once again, we can use the Excel function $RAND()$ to determine whether the interest rate movement is positive (i.e., $+\sigma \times \sqrt{\Delta}$) or negative (i.e., $-\sigma \times \sqrt{\Delta}$). We can then record each path, and price securities accordingly.

Table 13.7 Ten Simulations for the Asian Options

Simulation Number	First Realization of $RAND()$	First Move on the Tree	Interest Rate Realization at Time $i = 1$	Second Realization of $RAND()$	Second Move on the Tree	Interest Rate Realization at Time $i = 2$	Payoff at Maturity	Discounted Payoff
1	0.468692	up	3.75%	0.513012	down	3.61%	1.034	1.006
2	0.103819	up	3.75%	0.164345	up	6.06%	1.84953	1.799
3	0.848307	down	1.30%	0.340712	up	3.61%	0.21847	0.215
4	0.702089	down	1.30%	0.254097	up	3.61%	0.21847	0.215
5	0.001839	up	3.75%	0.118779	up	6.06%	1.84953	1.799
6	0.444781	up	3.75%	0.241821	up	6.06%	1.84953	1.799
7	0.066274	up	3.75%	0.55081	down	3.61%	1.034	1.006
8	0.386942	up	3.75%	0.765509	down	3.61%	1.034	1.006
9	0.769553	down	1.30%	0.627444	down	1.17%	0	0.000
10	0.888142	down	1.30%	0.97949	down	1.17%	0	0.000
						Average :		0.885

As an example of this methodology, Panel A of Table 13.8 shows the Ho-Lee model obtained in Chapter 11 from zero coupon bond prices. That is, this binomial tree is such that the prices of zero coupon bonds computed from it exactly match the data. Panel B reports ten simulated paths of interest rates, performed as above. For each step, we use the $RAND()$ function to decide whether the movement on the tree is upward or downward. Depending on the outcome, the next interest rate is determined by either Equation 13.11, if upward, or Equation 13.12, if downward.

Panel C of Table 13.8 reports the simulated discount $Z^s(0, T_i)$ for each simulation path s, and for each maturity $T_i = 0.5, ..., 5.5$. Recall that a discount factor $Z(0, T_i)$ equals the risk neutral expected discounted value of \$1 at time T_i. That is, from risk neutral pricing, we have

$$
\begin{aligned}
Z(0, T_i) &= E^* \left[\text{Present Value of \$1 at maturity } T_i \right] \\
&= E^* \left[e^{-(r_0 + r_1 + r_2 + ... + r_{i-1}) \times \Delta} \times \$1 \right]
\end{aligned}
$$

Note that the last interest rate used to discount a payoff at time T_i (i.e., period i) is the one corresponding to the previous period, $i - 1$, as there is a lag of one period between the cash flow and the interest rate needed to discount it. For instance, the first interest rate r_0 is used to discount a cash flow at $i = 1$.

For each simulated interest rate path $r_0, r_1^s, r_2^s, ..., r_{n-1}^s$, for $s = 1, .., N$, we can then compute the discount corresponding to that path. For given maturity T_i, where i is the time period in which the payoff is paid, we can compute

$$
Z^s(0, T_i) = e^{-\left(r_0 + r_1^s + r_2^s + ... + r_{i-1}^s \right) \times \Delta} \tag{13.13}
$$

The first ten simulated path-by-path discounts are reported in Panel C of Table 13.8. For instance, the first term in the first row is simply $Z^1(0, 0.5) = e^{-r_0 \times \Delta} = e^{-1.74\%/2} = 0.9913$. The second term in the first row is $Z^1(0, 1) = e^{-(r_0 + r_1^1) \times \Delta} = e^{-(1.74\% + 1.30\%)/2} = 0.9849$, where $r_1^1 = 1.30\%$ comes from the corresponding element in Panel B. The third element in the first row is $Z^1(0, 1.5) = e^{-(r_0 + r_1^1 + r_2^1) \times \Delta} = e^{-(1.74\% + 1.30\% + 3.61\%)/2} = 0.9673$. And so on. Given all of the simulation paths, for each maturity T_i we can compute the average discount *across simulations*. That is, we can compute

$$
\widehat{Z}(0, T_i) = \frac{1}{N} \sum_{s=1}^{N} Z^s(0, T_i) \tag{13.14}
$$

Again, we insert a hat "^" on top of the "Z" to denote the fact that this is not really the true discount (given by Equation 13.13) but rather an approximation obtained by Monte Carlo simulations.

13.3.1 Does This Procedure Work?

One way to check whether the Monte Carlo simulations methodology provides the correct value of derivative securities is to use the same simulations to also compute the values of zero coupon bonds. In fact, we may recall from Chapter 11 that the Ho-Lee interest rate tree, now reported in Panel A of Table 13.8, was computed so that the tree would price *exactly* the zero coupon bond prices. Since Monte Carlo simulations are designed to provide the same answers as any security computed on the tree, with an approximation that depends on the number of simulations, it follows that the zero coupon bond prices obtained from the application of Equation 13.14 should match the zero coupon bonds we used to estimate the model. Table 13.9 reports the initial data used to estimate the model (see Table 10.2 in Chapter 10) together with the ones obtained from Monte Carlo simulations, with 1,000 simulations. The prices are indeed quite close to each other, and the discrepancy is mainly due to the low number of simulations used.

13.3.2 Illustrative Example: Long-Term Interest Rate Options

As an additional example of the methodology, consider the same interest rate option we started out with, that is, an option that pays at maturity T_i the amount

$$\text{Payoff at } T_i = 100 \times \max\left(r_i - r_K, 0\right) \tag{13.15}$$

where r_K is a strike rate, and r_i is the interest rate at time i.[1] Risk neutral pricing implies that the price of this option is given by

$$
\begin{aligned}
c_0(T_i) &= E^* \left[\text{Present value of payoff at } T_i\right] \tag{13.16} \\
&= E^* \left[e^{-(r_0 + r_1 + \dots + r_{i-1}) \times \Delta} \times 100 \times \max\left(r_i - r_K, 0\right)\right] \tag{13.17}
\end{aligned}
$$

Note that this is the same equation as Equation 13.13, with the only difference that the payoff now also depends on the interest rate. However, by the same logic, for each simulation path s, $r_0,, r_1^s, r_2^s, \dots, r_n^s$, $s = 1, \dots, N$, we must compute the discounted payoff

$$
\begin{aligned}
c_0^s(T_i) &= e^{-\left(r_0 + r_1^s + r_2^s + \dots + r_{i-1}^s\right) \times \Delta} \times 100 \times \max\left(r_i^s - r_K, 0\right) \\
&= Z^s(0, T_i) \times \times 100 \times \max\left(r_i^s - r_K, 0\right) \tag{13.18}
\end{aligned}
$$

where we used the fact that, from Equation 13.13, $Z^s(0, T_i) = e^{-\left(r_0 + r_1^s + r_2^s + \dots + r_{i-1}^s\right) \times \Delta}$. This fact, incidentally, will make our computations simpler, as from the original paths $s = 1, \dots, N$ we have already computed $Z^s(0, T_i)$ for every maturity (e.g. they are in Panel C of Table 13.8).

Today's value of the option with maturity T_i is then given by the average of $c_0^s(T_i)$

$$\widehat{c}_0(T_i) = \frac{1}{N} \sum_{s=1}^{N} c_0^s(T_i) \tag{13.19}$$

Panel A of Table 13.10 reports the value of interest rate options with maturity from $T_i = 0.5$ to $T_i = 5$ and for a strike rate $r_K = 1.74\%$. Panel B shows the results of the first ten simulated discounted payoffs (Equation 13.18). For instance, the first element of the first row is given by

$$c_0^1(0.5) = Z^1(0, 0.5) \times 100 \times \max(r_1^1 - r_K, 0) = 0.9913 \times 100 \times \max(1.30\% - 1.74\%, 0) = 0,$$

---

[1]Note a difference from a caplet of a plain vanilla cap (see Chapter 11), as in a caplet the payoff at time T_i depends on the interest rate at time T_{i-1}.

Table 13.8   Ten Monte Carlo Simulations of Ho-Lee Interest Rate Tree

Time T	0	0.5	1	1.5	2	2.5	3	3.5	4	4.5	5
Period i	0	1	2	3	4	5	6	7	8	9	10
$\theta_i (\times 100)$	1.5675	2.1824	1.4374	1.7324	0.7873	0.0423	-0.0628	0.4322	0.9271	0.1202	

Panel A: The Ho-Lee Interest Rate Tree

j											
0	1.74	3.75	6.06	8.00	10.09	11.71	12.95	14.15	15.59	17.27	18.56
1		1.30	3.61	5.56	7.65	9.26	10.51	11.70	13.14	14.83	16.11
2			1.17	3.11	5.20	6.82	8.06	9.25	10.69	12.38	13.66
3				0.66	2.75	4.37	5.61	6.81	8.25	9.93	11.22
4					0.31	1.92	3.17	4.36	5.80	7.49	8.77
5						-0.52	0.72	1.91	3.35	5.04	6.32
6							-1.73	-0.53	0.91	2.59	3.88
7								-2.98	-1.54	0.15	1.43
8									-3.99	-2.30	-1.02
9										-4.75	-3.46
10											-5.91

Panel B: Ten Simulated Paths of Ho-Lee Tree

	──────── Period i ────────										
Simulation	0	1	2	3	4	5	6	7	8	9	10
1	1.74	1.30	3.61	5.56	5.20	6.82	8.06	6.81	8.25	7.49	6.32
2	1.74	3.75	3.61	3.11	2.75	4.37	5.61	6.81	5.80	5.04	3.88
3	1.74	3.75	3.61	3.11	5.20	6.82	8.06	9.25	8.25	9.93	8.77
4	1.74	3.75	6.06	5.56	7.65	9.26	8.06	6.81	8.25	7.49	8.77
5	1.74	1.30	3.61	3.11	5.20	6.82	5.61	6.81	5.80	7.49	6.32
6	1.74	1.30	3.61	3.11	5.20	4.37	5.61	6.81	5.80	7.49	6.32
7	1.74	1.30	3.61	5.56	5.20	4.37	3.17	4.36	3.35	2.59	1.43
8	1.74	1.30	1.17	0.66	2.75	1.92	0.72	1.91	3.35	5.04	3.88
9	1.74	3.75	3.61	3.11	5.20	6.82	8.06	6.81	5.80	7.49	8.77
10	1.74	3.75	6.06	8.00	10.09	9.26	8.06	9.25	10.69	12.38	11.22

Panel C: Ten Simulated Discounts $Z^s (0, T_i)$

	──────── Maturity T_i ────────										
Simulation	0.5	1	1.5	2	2.5	3	3.5	4	4.5	5	5.5
1	0.9913	0.9849	0.9673	0.9408	0.9166	0.8859	0.8509	0.8224	0.7892	0.7602	0.7366
2	0.9913	0.9729	0.9555	0.9408	0.9279	0.9078	0.8827	0.8532	0.8288	0.8082	0.7927
3	0.9913	0.9729	0.9555	0.9408	0.9166	0.8859	0.8509	0.8124	0.7796	0.7418	0.7100
4	0.9913	0.9729	0.9439	0.9180	0.8836	0.8436	0.8103	0.7832	0.7515	0.7239	0.6929
5	0.9913	0.9849	0.9673	0.9523	0.9279	0.8968	0.8720	0.8428	0.8187	0.7886	0.7641
6	0.9913	0.9849	0.9673	0.9523	0.9279	0.9078	0.8827	0.8532	0.8288	0.7983	0.7735
7	0.9913	0.9849	0.9673	0.9408	0.9166	0.8968	0.8827	0.8637	0.8493	0.8384	0.8324
8	0.9913	0.9849	0.9792	0.9759	0.9626	0.9534	0.9499	0.9409	0.9253	0.9022	0.8849
9	0.9913	0.9729	0.9555	0.9408	0.9166	0.8859	0.8509	0.8224	0.7989	0.7696	0.7366
10	0.9913	0.9729	0.9439	0.9069	0.8622	0.8232	0.7907	0.7549	0.7156	0.6727	0.6360

Table 13.9 Simulated Zero Coupon Bonds versus Data (January 8, 2002)

Maturity	Data	Simulated Zeros
0.5	99.1338	99.1338
1.0	97.8925	97.9140
1.5	96.1462	96.2376
2.0	94.1011	94.3031
2.5	91.7136	92.0217
3.0	89.2258	89.6090
3.5	86.8142	87.2894
4.0	84.5016	85.0911
4.5	82.1848	82.8855
5.0	79.7718	80.5609
5.5	77.4339	78.3302

Table 13.10 Monte Carlo Simulations for Long-Term Interest Rate Options

Panel A: Simulated Interest Rate Call Options									
				Maturity T_i					
0.5	1	1.5	2	2.5	3	3.5	4	4.5	5
0.9650	1.8857	2.4959	3.1892	3.4691	3.4134	3.2866	3.4007	3.6378	3.5060

Panel B: Ten Simulated Discounted Payoffs										
					Maturity T_i					
Simulation	0.5	1	1.5	2	2.5	3	3.5	4	4.5	5
1	0.00	1.85	3.69	3.25	4.65	5.60	4.31	5.35	4.53	3.48
2	1.99	1.82	1.31	0.95	2.44	3.52	4.47	3.46	2.73	1.73
3	1.99	1.82	1.31	3.25	4.65	5.60	6.39	5.29	6.39	5.21
4	1.99	4.20	3.60	5.42	6.65	5.33	4.11	5.10	4.32	5.09
5	0.00	1.85	1.33	3.29	4.71	3.47	4.42	3.42	4.70	3.61
6	0.00	1.85	1.33	3.29	2.44	3.52	4.47	3.46	4.76	3.66
7	0.00	1.85	3.69	3.25	2.41	1.28	2.31	1.39	0.72	0.00
8	0.00	0.00	0.00	0.99	0.18	0.00	0.16	1.52	3.05	1.93
9	1.99	1.82	1.31	3.25	4.65	5.60	4.31	3.34	4.59	5.41
10	1.99	4.20	5.91	7.58	6.49	5.20	5.94	6.76	7.61	6.37

where the sequence of the simulated interest rate and discounts are given in Panels B and C of Table 13.8. Similarly, the second entry in the first row is given by

$$c_0^1(1) = Z^1(0,1) \times 100 \times \max(r_2^1 - r_K, 0) = 0.9849 \times 100 \times \max(3.61\% - 1.74\%, 0) = 1.85.$$

The option values in Panel A are then computed as the average of values in the corresponding column in Panel B (although the average is taken over all the 1,000 simulated paths, rather than only the ten paths reported in Panel B).

13.3.3 How Many Simulations are Enough?

We can think of a price of an interest rate security computed by Monte Carlo Simulations as an estimate of the true price. Indeed, using simulations we are essentially generating a *sample* of observations of the price of the security, under various scenarios for (risk neutral) future interest rates. As with any statistical estimate, we can compute a measure that calculates how confident we are in the number we estimated. That is, if we simulate 500 paths, our estimate will be less accurate than if we simulate 1,000 paths, which in turn must be less accurate than if we simulate 10,000 paths. Since we cannot simulate an infinite amount, how many paths are sufficient to obtain a good estimate?

The number of paths N should be large enough to obtain a reasonable standard error, that is, standard deviation of the estimated average itself. This is computed as the standard deviation of the discounted payoff, i.e., c_0^s in Equation 13.18, divided by $\sqrt{N}$:

$$\text{Standard error} = \frac{\text{Standard deviation of } \{c_0^1, c_0^2, c_0^3, ..., c_0^N\}}{\sqrt{N}}$$

For instance, the first two rows in Table 13.11 report the prices (again) and standard errors of the long-term interest call options discussed in Table 13.10.

How small should a standard error be to make a trader confident on the price of the option? The related concept of confidence interval answers this question:

$$\text{Confidence interval} = [\widehat{c}_0 - 2 \times \text{St. Err.}, \widehat{c}_0 + 2 \times \text{St. Err.}]$$

A confidence interval can be interpreted as follows: Given the number of simulations N, there is 95% probability that the true value of the security is between the upper and lower boundary of the confidence interval. For instance, in Table 13.11 the upper and lower boundaries of the confidence interval are reported in the third and fourth rows, respectively. Consider the 6-month option (first column) for instance. From the values of the confidence interval we can gauge that with 95% probability, the true value of the option lies between 0.9021 and 1.0279. Similarly, for the 1-year option (second column), the true value lies between 1.7930 and 1.9784. And so on.

Indeed, the very last row in the table reports the value of the option from the Binomial Tree itself. This can be computed from the (by now, familiar to us) backward computation on the binomial tree as in Chapter 11. As it can be seen, in all but one case, the true price is within the confidence interval. The only exception is for the option with maturity $T = 1.5$. In this case, the true value from the Binomial Tree $c_0(2.5) = 2.612$ is above the upper level of the confidence interval, given by 2.6083. Is this surprising? No, because as mentioned earlier, there is only 95% probability that the true value lies within the confidence interval. This means that for 5% of the time, the true value will *not* be within the confidence interval.[2]

The confidence intervals in Table 13.11 are quite wide, and so no trader would use them, as one should quote more precise prices. This is due to the fact that we are only using 1,000 simulations for this exercise. Raising the number of simulations reduces the spread in the confidence interval.

---

[2]We may ask: Why don't we compute confidence intervals such that the true value is *always* within the confidence intervals? The reason is that the confidence interval becomes very wide (in fact infinitely wide), and thus it has no meaning anymore.

Table 13.11 Standard Errors and Confidence Intervals

	0.5	1	1.5	2	2.5	3	3.5	4	4.5	5
					Maturity T_i					
Price	0.9650	1.8857	2.4959	3.1892	3.4691	3.4134	3.2866	3.4007	3.6378	3.5060
Standard Errors	0.0315	0.0464	0.0562	0.0639	0.0708	0.0715	0.0751	0.0737	0.0758	0.0745
Upper C.I.	1.0279	1.9784	2.6083	3.3170	3.6107	3.5563	3.4368	3.5482	3.7893	3.6550
Lower C.I.	0.9021	1.7930	2.3835	3.0613	3.3274	3.2705	3.1363	3.2532	3.4862	3.3569
True Price (Tree)	1.000	1.976	2.612	3.309	3.542	3.507	3.361	3.463	3.687	3.596

13.4 PRICING PATH DEPENDENT OPTIONS

So far we have looked at the application of Monte Carlo simulations to compute prices of securities that could also be computed using the original binomial tree. This exercise was useful to verify that Monte Carlo simulations work well as a pricing tool. In this section we illustrate the methodology in order to price securities for which binomial trees are not convenient.

13.4.1 Illustrative Example: Long-Term Asian Options

Let's start out with the long-term Asian options already discussed in Section 13.2.2. We can now use exactly the same simulated paths that we used to compute the long-term interest rate options in Table 13.10 to compute the value of Asian options. The convenient feature of Monte Carlo simulations is that we need to change only the payoff at maturity to obtain the price of the new security, but the simulated paths can be the same. Table 13.12 reports the simulation results (in Panel A), along with the first ten paths of discounted payoffs. Panel A now also reports the options' standard errors as well as the confidence intervals. Asian options, as it can be seen, are cheaper than standard options, as the underlying (the average of interest rates) is less volatile than interest rates themselves.

13.4.2 Illustrative Example: Index Amortizing Swaps

In 1993 Banc One invented a new security to increase the yield on its investments, the amortizing interest rate swap (AIRS).[3] The idea was to synthetically replicate an investment in mortgage backed securities (see Chapter 8). Indeed, Banc One invested a large portion of its assets in MBS, as they had high yield compared to other more standard investments (e.g., Treasuries). As discussed in Chapter 8, the higher yield of MBS is a compensation to *prepayment risk*, i.e. the risk of receiving the principal back when the interest rate r_t is low, that is, when investment opportunities are not excellent.

Using swaps to replicate such investments is an attractive way of increasing the liquidity of the investment (see Chapter 5 for a discussion about swaps). For instance, instead of investing $500 million in MBS, Banc One could invest those funds in short-term floating

---

[3]Discussion material in this section partly draws on Esty, Tufano and Headley, (1994).

Table 13.12   Monte Carlo Simulations for Asian Interest Rate Options

| | Panel A: Simulated Interest Rate Asian Call Options | | | | | | | | | |
| | | | | Maturity T_i | | | | | | |
	0.5	1	1.5	2	2.5	3	3.5	4	4.5	5
price	0.4825	0.9079	1.2579	1.6022	1.8616	2.0189	2.1100	2.1750	2.2386	2.2647
standard errors	0.0157	0.0243	0.0308	0.0351	0.0382	0.0401	0.0416	0.0424	0.0428	0.0426
Upper C.I.	0.5140	0.9566	1.3194	1.6723	1.9380	2.0991	2.1932	2.2598	2.3242	2.3500
Lower C.I.	0.4510	0.8592	1.1964	1.5320	1.7851	1.9386	2.0269	2.0902	2.1529	2.1794

| | Panel B: Ten Simulated Discounted Payoffs | | | | | | | | | |
| | | | | Maturity T_i | | | | | | |
simulation #	0.5	1	1.5	2	2.5	3	3.5	4	4.5	5
1	0.00	0.47	1.27	1.64	2.11	2.55	2.68	2.90	2.95	2.90
2	0.99	1.26	1.25	1.18	1.38	1.66	1.97	2.08	2.09	2.01
3	0.99	1.26	1.25	1.64	2.11	2.55	2.94	3.08	3.30	3.33
4	0.99	2.05	2.39	2.95	3.47	3.60	3.54	3.61	3.55	3.57
5	0.00	0.47	0.68	1.19	1.75	1.95	2.21	2.28	2.46	2.49
6	0.00	0.47	0.68	1.19	1.38	1.66	1.97	2.08	2.29	2.34
7	0.00	0.47	1.27	1.64	1.73	1.64	1.70	1.63	1.52	1.34
8	0.00	0.00	0.00	0.00	0.00	0.00	0.00	0.00	0.29	0.44
9	0.99	1.26	1.25	1.64	2.11	2.55	2.68	2.67	2.79	2.94
10	0.99	2.05	2.97	3.80	4.09	4.09	4.18	4.30	4.43	4.36

rate bonds, and enter into a fixed-for-floating swap in which it receives fixed and pays floating. In fact, an investment in a floating rate bond plus a fixed-for-floating swap is equivalent to an investment in a fixed-rate bond with a coupon equal to the swap rate. To see this, note that the floating part of the swap is naturally hedged by the cash inflows from the investment in floating rate bonds: If short-term interest rates increase, for instance, Banc One would be able to meet the larger outflows needed in the swap position by using the larger inflows from the floating rate bond. It follows that the higher Banc One could push the swap rate, through some creative structuring of the swap, and the higher would be the return on the investment.

After consultation with many investment banks, AIRS were born. An **(index) amortizing interest rate wap** is a swap in which the notional decreases as the interest rate decreases. The rate of change in the notional is determined by specific contract rules, as discussed below.

How could such an investment help a bank increase the yield on its investment? To understand the logic, consider a plain vanilla swap. Recall that the market swap rate, call it $c(0, T)$, is determined at time 0 such that the value of the swap with maturity T is equal to zero at initiation. If we use the plain vanilla swap rate $c(0, T)$ in an AIRS, then the fixed rate receiver is worse off. This is because when interest rates go up, the notional is constant, and thus the fixed rate receiver must make high payments. When interest rates go down, in contrast, the fixed rate receiver would receive a positive net payment $(c(0, T) - r_4(t))$, but this amount is now multiplied by a *lower* notional, because the latter decreases when interest rates decline. To make the value of the swap equal to zero at time 0, we must increase the swap rate *above* the market rate of plain vanilla swaps.

Table 13.13   Representative Term Sheet of an Index Amortizing Interest Rate Swap

Trade Date	May 9, 2005
Notional Amount	$500 million, subject to amortization schedule
Maximum Maturity Date	3 years
Early Maturity Date (Cleanup Provision)	On any fixing date leading to a notional amount less than or equal to 10% of original notional
Bank ABC Pays	in USD, 3m LIBOR, paid quarterly (current LIBOR =3.25%)
Bank ABC Receives	Fixed rate $r_{\text{Fxd}} = 4.55\%$

Amortization Schedule

USD 3m LIBOR	Notional Reduction
$\leq 3.25\%$	Total Amortization
4.25%	Reduced by 30%
5.25%	Reduced by 10%
$\geq 6.25\ \%$	No Amortization

(If the spot rate falls between two entries, the amortization amount is interpolated.)

Lockout period	1 year (included)

Source: Ben Esty, Peter Tufano, and Johnathan Headley, BancOne Corporation: Asset Liability Management, Case no. 9-294-079. Boston
Harvard Business School, 1994.

The difficulty in pricing AIRS is that the payoffs over time are highly path dependent. Table 13.13 produces a representative term sheet describing an AIRS.[4] The important distinction from plain vanilla swaps comes from the amortization schedule, which calls for substantial reductions in notional whenever the LIBOR is below 6.25%.

Indeed, the amortization schedule implies that every three months (time t) Bank ABC receives the net flow

$$CF(t) = \frac{1}{4} \times \left(r_{\text{Fxd}} - r_4^L(t - 0.25) \right) \times \textbf{Notional}_{t-0.25}$$

---

[4]While representative, the exact trading details in this term sheet are fictituous.

Table 13.14   A Hypothetical Path of the 3-Months LIBOR

Time	LIBOR
0.75	3.5%
1.00	4%
1.25	4.25%
1.50	5.25%

where the "1/4" denotes the quarterly payment, and $r_4^L(t)$ denotes the three month LIBOR at time t. The important difference from a plain vanilla swap is that the notional also depends on time, as its level depends on the past history of interest rates. For example, suppose the LIBOR follows the sequence in Table 13.14. Then, the following cash flows are generated:

1. At time $t = 1.25$, Bank ABC receives:

$$\frac{1}{4}\left(r_{\text{Fxd}} - 4\%\right) \times 500 \text{ million}$$

   Note that no reduction occurred at time $t = 1$ because of the one-year lockout period.

2. At time $t = 1.5$, Bank ABC instead receives:

$$\frac{1}{4}\left(r_{\text{Fxd}} - 4.25\%\right) \times .70 \times 500 \text{ million}$$

   That is, the notional has been reduced by 30%, to 70% percent of its initial value.

The notional level is path dependent: Not only does the level of the interest rate at time $t - 1$ matter, but also the whole history (path) of interest rates does. For instance, consider time $t = 1.75$ in the previous example. Because at time $t = 1.5$, the LIBOR was 5.25%, the notional to apply at time $t = 1.75$ is:

$$\text{Notional}_{1.75} = (.70 \times 500) \times .90 = 315 \text{ million}$$

If instead at an earlier time, say time $t = 1.25$, the LIBOR was 5.25% instead of the 4.25% assumed in Table 13.14, then the notional would be

$$\text{Notional}_{1.75} = (.90 \times 100) \times .90 = 405 \text{ million}$$

In other words, even if the last value of the LIBOR is the same (5.25%) the fact that interest rates in the past had a different sequence matters for today's cash flows. In short, cash flows are path dependent.

How can we value this complicated security? We can use Monte Carlo simulations on a binomial tree fitted to the LIBOR yield curve. More specifically, we just have to make the cash flows received over time contingent on interest rates. In particular, we can simulate

Table 13.15 A Schematic Representation of Simulated Interest Rates and Cash Flows

Simulation number	0	period			
		1	2	...	n
Simulation 1	r_0	r_1^1	r_2^1	...	r_n^1
		CF_1^1	CF_2^1	...	CF_n^1
Simulation 2	r_0	r_1^2	r_2^2	...	r_n^2
		CF_1^2	CF_2^2	...	CF_n^2
$\vdots$		$\vdots$	$\vdots$	$\ddots$	$\vdots$
Simulation N	r_0	r_1^N	r_2^N	...	r_n^N
		CF_1^N	CF_2^N	...	CF_n^N

interest rates at a quarterly frequency, and for every interest rate path s, $r_0,, r_1^s, r_2^s, ... r_n^s$, we define the cash flow in period i as:

$$CF_i^s = \text{Notional}_{i-1}^s \times \frac{1}{4} \times (r_{\text{Fxd}} - r_4^s(i-1)) \tag{13.20}$$

where $r_4^s(i-1) = 4 \times (e^{r_{i-1}^2 \times 0.25} - 1)$ is the quarterly compounded rate corresponding to r_{i-1}^s. In addition, we can compute the notional to be applied in the next period $i+1$. This cash flow will depend on the Notional_i^s, which is computed as

$$\text{Notional}_i^s = \text{Notional}_{i-1}^s \times Adj\left(r_i^s\right)$$

We compute the adjustment $Adj\left(r_i^s\right)$ according to the amortization schedule in the term sheet in Table 13.13.

For each simulated interest rate path, then, we obtain both a sequence of interest rates and a sequence of cash flows, as schematically shown in Table 13.15.

For every simulation s, we obtain the time-0 value of future cash-flows as

$$P^s = e^{-\frac{1}{4}r_0} \times CF_1^s + e^{-\frac{1}{4}(r_0+r_1^s)} \times CF_2^s + ... + e^{-\frac{1}{4}(r_0+r_1^s+...+r_{n-1})} \times CF_n^s$$

As before, the simulated value of the future cash flows is

$$P = \frac{1}{N}\sum_{j=1}^{N} P^j$$

13.4.2.1 *AIRS Pricing by Monte Carlo Simulations*   Table 13.16 illustrates the pricing methodology for AIRS. We go in steps:

1. **What Data?** First, we must choose the type of data to use to compute the interest rate tree. Because we are pricing a LIBOR-linked asset, we should use LIBOR-based plain vanilla swaps. Panel A of Table 13.16 shows the swap data on May 9, 2005. Note in particular that the 3-year swap rate on a plain vanilla swap is 4.2655%, which is lower than the fixed rate promised in the AIRS of 4.55% (see term sheet in Table 13.13). The intuition, again, is that for a given swap rate, the fixed rate receiver is

worse off, as when he receives positive net cash flows, interest rates are low and the notional shrinks.

From swap data, we can compute the discount $Z(0, T_i)$ for every maturity up to the maturity of the AIRS (3 years). The methodology is discussed in Section 5.4, Chapter 5, and the result is in Panel A.[5]

2. **What Model?** Next, we must choose the model to use, such as Black, Derman, and Toy or Ho-Lee. Let's use Ho-Lee model for this exercise, as interest rates were already very low in 2005, and we want to give them a chance to get even lower. As we know from Chapter 11, the log-normal assumption of Black, Derman, and Toy model, although reasonable to keep interest rates positive, may give too low a probability to low interest rates. The volatility σ of interest rates is set to its historical value (as of 2005) of $\sigma = 0.9504\%$, computed using monthly LIBOR data from January 1987 to April 2005. Panel B of Table 13.16 reports the (risk neutral) Ho-Lee interest rate tree implied by the data in Panel A.

3. **Simulate Interest Rates.** We use the tree as in previous sections to simulate interest rate paths. Panel C of Table 13.16 reports ten such simulated paths. The important caveat is that cash flow computations and amortization trigger rates are expressed with quarterly compounding. Thus, after simulating the Ho-Lee interest rate, which is continuously compounded, we must then convert the interest rates into quarterly compounding, by using the formula $r_4^s(i) = \left(e^{r_i^s/4} - 1\right) \times 4$. The first simulated rate is the same across simulations, and it corresponds to the 3-month LIBOR (=3.25% on May 9, 2005).

4. **Simulate Notional.** For an AIRS, it is key to simulate the dynamics of the notional, as it changes over time as interest rates change. Panel D of Table 13.16 plots the dynamics of the notional over the ten simulated paths. The first column is the initial notional, on which the first payment is based. The next four columns show the same notional. The reason is that the term sheet allows for a lockout period (1 year included), which entails that no changes to notional should take place for the first year. Then, as can be seen, the notional decreases, possibly reaching zero. A comparison between Panels C and D shows that indeed, when interest rates decline, the notional declines as well. Simulation 4 shows the most dramatic decline: In particular, in period $i = 5$ the interest rate was 3.79%. (In fact, with no rounding, 3.790218%. This number will be important below.) From the term sheet in Table 13.13, this interest rate is between the thresholds 3.25% and 4.25%, which entail full (100%) amortization and 30% amortization, respectively. To find out the level of amortization, we must interpolate. That is, we have the following rule: Let $r_4^s(i)$ be the simulated interest rate, $\underline{r}$ and $\overline{r}$ be the two thresholds surrounding it (3.25% and 4.25%, in this case), and let $\underline{A}$ and $\overline{A}$ be their corresponding amortization levels (100% and 30%). Then:

$$\text{Amortization} = (1 - w_i^s) \times \underline{A} + w_i^s \times \overline{A}$$

[5]For simplicity, we assume here that also plain vanilla swaps pay quarterly cash flows.

where
$$w_i = \frac{r_4^s(i) - \underline{r}}{\overline{r} - \underline{r}}.$$

We obtain approximately $w_5 = 54.0218\%$ and thus the amortization is 62.18%. This implies that the new notional is $N_5^4 = N_4^5 \times (1 - 62.18\%) = 500 \times 37.8152\% = 189.08$.

5. **Simulate Discounted Cash Flows.** Given the paths of notionals and interest rates, we can compute the discounted cash flows. As in the previous section, we calculate first the discounts $Z^s(0, T_i)$ path-by-path (not reported in the table) and use them to discount each of the cash flows. Panel E of Table 13.16 reports the discounted cash flows for the ten simulations.

What is the value of the AIRS? Different from the long-term options computed in the earlier section, the AIRS provides some cash flows over time, as long as the notional is non-zero. Thus, risk neutral pricing implies

$$
\begin{aligned}
P_0 &= E^* \left[\text{Sum of present values of cash flows at } T_i \text{ for } i = 1, 2, ..., n \right] \quad (13.21) \\
&= E^* \left[\sum_{i=0}^{n-1} e^{-(r_0 + ... + r_i) \times \Delta} \times CF(i+1) \right] \quad (13.22)
\end{aligned}
$$

where $CF(i+1)$ denotes the net payment to Bank ABC. This tells us that in order to obtain the value of the AIRS, we must sum all of the rows in Panel E of Table 13.16, and then take the average of the resulting sums to obtain the average (i.e., expected) discounted value of future cash flows. That is,

$$
\widehat{P}_0 = \frac{1}{N} \sum_{s=1}^{N} \left[\sum_{i=0}^{n-1} e^{-(r_0 + ... + r_i^s) \times \Delta} \times CF^s(i+1) \right] \quad (13.23)
$$

Using 1,000 simulations, as in the earlier examples, we find

$$
\begin{aligned}
\text{AIRS price} &= 0.0059; \\
\text{Standard error} &= 0.3101; \\
\text{Confidence interval} &= [-0.6143, 0.6260];
\end{aligned}
$$

That is, the price is reasonably close to zero, as it should be because this is a swap. The confidence interval is rather wide, though, demonstrating that more simulations are necessary to obtain accurate pricing.

Notice, however, that if we were to use the 3-year swap rate of plain vanilla swaps, 4.2655% from Panel A of Table 13.16, the value of AIRS according to our simulations would be strongly negative. In fact:

$$
\begin{aligned}
\text{AIRS price with } r_{\text{fxd}} = 4.2655\% &= -2.5614; \\
\text{Standard error} &= 0.3319; \\
\text{Confidence interval} &= [-3.2252, -1.8976];
\end{aligned}
$$

Indeed, note that in this case the confidence interval is all negative, indicating that a plain vanilla swap rate does make the fixed rate receiver in an AIRS quite worse off.

Table 13.16   Pricing the Index Amortizing Interest Rate Swap by Monte Carlo Simulations

<table>
<tr><td colspan="13" align="center">Panel A: Data on May 9, 2005</td></tr>
<tr><td>Maturity</td><td>0.25</td><td>0.5</td><td>0.75</td><td>1</td><td>1.25</td><td>1.5</td><td>1.75</td><td>2</td><td>2.25</td><td>2.5</td><td>2.75</td><td>3</td></tr>
<tr><td>Swap Rate</td><td>3.2500</td><td>3.4390</td><td>3.6280</td><td>3.8170</td><td>3.8927</td><td>3.9685</td><td>4.0442</td><td>4.1200</td><td>4.1564</td><td>4.1927</td><td>4.2291</td><td>4.2655</td></tr>
<tr><td>Discount</td><td>99.1940</td><td>98.3020</td><td>97.3260</td><td>96.2680</td><td>95.2668</td><td>94.2398</td><td>93.1876</td><td>92.1113</td><td>91.0951</td><td>90.0730</td><td>89.0454</td><td>88.0126</td></tr>
</table>

Panel B: The Fitted Interest Rate Tree

i	0	1	2	3	4	5	6	7	8	9	10	11
j												
0	3.24	4.19	5.14	6.10	6.48	7.21	7.95	8.68	9.05	9.71	10.37	11.03
1		3.04	3.99	4.95	5.34	6.07	6.80	7.54	7.91	8.56	9.22	9.88
2			2.85	3.80	4.19	4.92	5.65	6.39	6.76	7.42	8.07	8.73
3				2.65	3.04	3.77	4.51	5.24	5.61	6.27	6.93	7.59
4					1.89	2.62	3.36	4.09	4.46	5.12	5.78	6.44
5						1.48	2.21	2.95	3.32	3.97	4.63	5.29
6							1.06	1.80	2.17	2.83	3.48	4.14
7								0.65	1.02	1.68	2.34	2.99
8									-0.13	0.53	1.19	1.85
9										-0.62	0.04	0.70
10											-1.11	-0.45
11												-1.60

Panel C: Ten Simulated Paths of the Quarterly Interest Rate

						Period						
Simulation	0	1	2	3	4	5	6	7	8	9	10	11
1	3.25	3.05	2.86	3.82	4.21	4.95	4.53	5.28	4.49	3.99	3.50	4.16
2	3.25	3.05	4.01	4.98	5.37	4.95	5.69	5.28	5.65	5.15	4.66	5.33
3	3.25	3.05	4.01	4.98	5.37	4.95	5.69	6.44	6.82	7.48	6.99	6.49
4	3.25	3.05	2.86	3.82	4.21	3.79	3.37	2.96	3.33	2.84	3.50	3.01
5	3.25	4.21	5.17	4.98	5.37	6.11	6.86	7.61	7.99	7.48	6.99	7.66
6	3.25	4.21	5.17	4.98	5.37	6.11	6.86	6.44	5.65	5.15	4.66	4.16
7	3.25	3.05	4.01	3.82	3.05	3.79	4.53	4.11	3.33	2.84	3.50	3.01
8	3.25	3.05	2.86	3.82	4.21	3.79	4.53	5.28	5.65	5.15	5.82	5.33
9	3.25	4.21	5.17	6.14	5.37	4.95	4.53	5.28	4.49	5.15	5.82	5.33
10	3.25	3.05	4.01	4.98	4.21	3.79	3.37	4.11	4.49	5.15	4.66	4.16

Panel D: The Simulated Notional

Simulation												
1	500.00	500.00	500.00	500.00	500.00	420.03	317.64	286.68	214.37	111.44	19.38	12.40
2	500.00	500.00	500.00	500.00	500.00	420.03	396.65	357.99	336.54	269.38	231.63	210.21
3	500.00	500.00	500.00	500.00	500.00	420.03	396.65	396.65	396.65	396.65	396.65	396.65
4	500.00	500.00	500.00	500.00	500.00	189.08	16.19	0.00	0.00	0.00	0.00	0.00
5	500.00	500.00	500.00	500.00	500.00	493.18	493.18	493.18	493.18	493.18	493.18	493.18
6	500.00	500.00	500.00	500.00	500.00	493.18	493.18	493.18	463.64	408.31	319.10	204.15
7	500.00	500.00	500.00	500.00	500.00	189.08	142.99	86.52	4.85	0.00	0.00	0.00
8	500.00	500.00	500.00	500.00	500.00	189.08	142.99	129.05	121.32	106.84	102.25	92.79
9	500.00	500.00	500.00	500.00	500.00	420.03	317.64	286.68	214.37	188.79	180.67	163.96
10	500.00	500.00	500.00	500.00	500.00	189.08	16.19	9.80	7.33	6.45	5.04	3.23

Panel E: The Simulated Discounted Cash Flow

						Time of Cash Flow						
Simulation	0.25	0.5	0.75	1	1.25	1.5	1.75	2	2.25	2.5	2.75	3
1	1.61	1.84	2.07	0.88	0.41	-0.40	0.01	-0.48	0.03	0.14	0.00	0.00
2	1.61	1.84	0.65	-0.52	-0.98	-0.39	-1.05	-0.59	-0.83	-0.04	-0.05	-0.35
3	1.61	1.84	0.65	-0.52	-0.98	-0.39	-1.05	-1.71	-2.01	-2.56	-2.09	-1.63
4	1.61	1.84	2.07	0.88	0.41	0.34	0.00	0.00	0.00	0.00	0.00	0.00
5	1.61	0.42	-0.76	-0.51	-0.97	-1.79	-2.60	-3.38	-3.73	-3.13	-2.55	-3.19
6	1.61	0.42	-0.76	-0.51	-0.97	-1.79	-2.60	-2.10	-1.13	-0.54	-0.07	0.17
7	1.61	1.84	0.65	0.88	1.79	0.34	0.01	0.09	0.00	0.00	0.00	0.00
8	1.61	1.84	2.07	0.88	0.41	0.34	0.01	-0.22	-0.30	-0.15	-0.29	-0.16
9	1.61	0.42	-0.76	-1.90	-0.97	-0.39	0.01	-0.47	0.03	-0.25	-0.50	-0.27
10	1.61	1.84	0.65	-0.52	0.40	0.34	0.00	0.00	0.00	0.00	0.00	0.00

Data source: Bloomberg.

Figure 13.1   AIRS Value versus LIBOR and Lockout Period

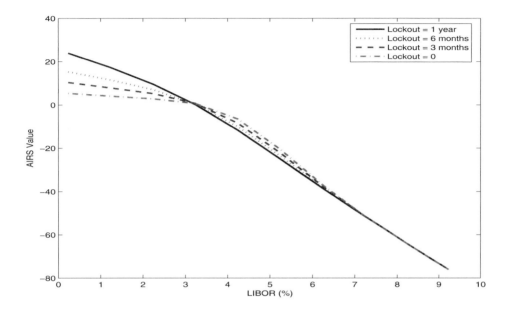

13.4.2.2 *The Negative Convexity of AIRS*   After the calculation of the AIRS, we can perform some additional analysis to understand in what sense this security is supposed to mimic the behavior of mortgage backed securities. Figure 13.1 shows the relation between the value of AIRS and the starting 3-months LIBOR for different lockout periods. First, we observe that an investment in AIRS is in fact an investment in a security with negative convexity, in the sense that as the interest rate drops, the increase in value of the security is much smaller than the drop in value in case of an interest rate hike. We may recall from Chapter 12 that negative convexity indeed characterizes securities that are short some type of option, such as callable bonds (see Figure 12.1 in Chapter 12) or mortgage backed pass-through securities (see Figure 12.2 in the same chapter). Second, the negative convexity becomes stronger the shorter the lockout period is. In other words, as time goes by, the negative convexity becomes more and more important. This characteristic belongs to callable bonds as well, as we have recognized a similar pattern as the call date was getting nearer over time. Such temporal behavior is hard to see in mortgage backed securities, instead.

13.5 SPOT RATE DURATION BY MONTE CARLO SIMULATIONS

The last point to make concerns risk analysis. How can we compute some measures of risk of a security, such as its duration, if we use Monte Carlo simulations to compute its value? We can use Monte Carlo simulations to compute the spot rate duration, introduced in Section 10.5 of Chapter 10. Recall that this risk measure is given by

$$\text{Spot rate duration} = -\frac{1}{P}\frac{dP}{dr} \qquad (13.24)$$

We proceed as follows. We perform two Monte Carlo simulations: The first starts at r_0, our root of the tree. The second Monte Carlo simulation starts instead slightly higher, at $r_0 + dr$, where dr is a small number, such as one basis point. We can then compute the value of the security under these two different starting values $\widehat{P}(r_0)$ and $\widehat{P}(r_0 + dr)$. The spot rate duration can then be approximated by

$$\text{Spot rate duration} \approx -\frac{1}{\widehat{P}(r_0)} \frac{\widehat{P}(r_0 + dr) - \widehat{P}(r_0)}{dr} \qquad (13.25)$$

To avoid introducing some simulation errors in this approximation, it is important to use the *same* realizations of the RAND() function for the computation of the two prices.

Does it work? In Table 13.9 we computed the values of zero coupon bonds obtained by Monte Carlo simulations. These values are close to the data, as we fit the Ho-Lee model to match the term structure of interest rates. Panel A of Table 13.17 contains the spot rate duration from the approximation in Equation 13.25. Specifically, the second and the third rows contain the simulated zero coupon bond prices $\widehat{Z}(r_0, T_i)$ and $\widehat{Z}(r_0 + dr, T_i)$ for the two starting values of the interest rate, $r_0 = 1.74\%$ and $r_0 + dr = 1.75\%$. The simulated spot rate duration is in the fourth row (we left the decimal points to show the precision of the approximation): The values are essentially identical to the durations of the zero coupon bonds, which equal their time to maturity (see Chapter 3). It may be surprising to see that the spot rate duration in the Ho-Lee model equals the standard duration defined in terms of small parallel shifts, as seen in Chapter 3. The reason for the equality stems from the properties of this particular model, but it is not true in general (it is not true, for instance, for the Black, Derman, and Toy model). For the Ho-Lee model, in fact, it turns out that an increase in the interest rate at the root of the binomial tree (i.e., r_0) implies a parallel upward shift of the same amount of the overall term structure of interest rates. As such, the spot rate duration as approximated by Equation 13.25 is close to the standard definition of duration.

By way of example, we can also compute the spot rate duration of the long-term options and Asian options obtained earlier. The results are in Panels B and C. First of all, note that the spot rate duration of the interest rate call option is negative: An increase in interest rates makes the option more valuable, as it is now more likely it will yield a positive payoff, and thus its price increases. Second, even if Asian options are defined on an underlying that is less volatile than the interest rate itself, namely, the average of the interest rate, the duration is not smaller than the one in Panel B for regular, plain vanilla options. The reason is that although indeed the price of the Asian option is less affected by fluctuations in interest rates, its price is also much smaller. Thus, in percentage, the sensitivity of the Asian option to changes in interest rates is higher.

13.6 PRICING RESIDENTIAL MORTGAGE BACKED SECURITIES

In this final section we apply the Monte Carlo simulation methodology to price residential mortgage backed securities. In particular, Chapter 8 discusses the market, the type of securities that are backed by mortgages, such as pass through and collateralized mortgage obligations, as well as some industry conventions to describe them, including the PSA measure of prepayment speed. In Chapter 12 we saw how the American option that is implicit in mortgages can be valued on risk neutral binomial trees: We can start from the

Table 13.17   Spot Rate Duration by Monte Carlo Simulations

Maturity	0.5	1	1.5	2	2.5	3	3.5	4	4.5	5
	Panel A: Simulated Spot Rate Duration of Zero Coupon Bonds									
$\widehat{Z}(r_0, T_i)$	99.1338	97.9105	96.2084	94.2228	91.8927	89.4423	87.0761	84.8009	82.5165	80.1298
$\widehat{Z}(r_0 + dr, T_i)$	99.1288	97.9007	96.1940	94.2039	91.8698	89.4155	87.0456	84.7670	82.4794	80.0897
Spot Rate Duration	0.5000	1.0000	1.4999	1.9998	2.4997	2.9996	3.4994	3.9992	4.4990	4.9988
	Panel B: Simulated Spot Rate Duration of Long-Term Call Options									
$\widehat{c}(r_0)$	0.9650	1.8857	2.4959	3.1892	3.4691	3.4134	3.2866	3.4007	3.6378	3.5060
$\widehat{c}(r_0 + dr)$	0.9697	1.8927	2.5038	3.1973	3.4770	3.4202	3.2935	3.4064	3.6434	3.5107
Spot Rate Duration	-49.3222	-37.1823	-31.5883	-25.4278	-22.9155	-19.8689	-21.0933	-16.8563	-15.5984	-13.4163
	Panel C: Simulated Spot Rate Duration of Asian Call Options									
$\widehat{c}^A(r_0)$	0.4825	0.9079	1.2579	1.6022	1.8616	2.0189	2.1100	2.1750	2.2386	2.2647
$\widehat{c}(r_0 + dr)$	0.4873	0.9150	1.2659	1.6099	1.8693	2.0264	2.1171	2.1816	2.2450	2.2708
Spot Rate Duration	-99.1445	-78.3049	-64.1551	-48.3325	-41.7412	-37.4040	-33.7344	-30.3088	-28.5699	-26.9281

end of the tree and move backward, while deciding step by step whether it is optimal to exercise the option or it is better to wait. However, as discussed in these two earlier chapters, many other factors influence the decision to prepay a mortgage that may not be related to interest rates. In this chapter we illustrate how to combine Monte Carlo simulations with binomial trees to take these other factors into account.

For convenience, we begin with Example 12.7 from Chapter 12 to illustrate the methodology. The first question is: How can we simulate the homeowner's prepayment decision on a tree?

13.6.1   Simulating the Prepayment Decision

Before looking into realistic models of prepayment behavior, we first show how Monte Carlo simulations can be used on a tree to mimic the optimal decision obtained in Example 12.7. This discussion will serve as benchmark to which we can compare other results. In particular, we found in Example 12.7 that for each period i there is a trigger interest rate $\underline{r}_i$ such that if the interest rate drops below the trigger rate at i, the homeowner prepays the mortgage (see Panel D in Table 12.8). This fact suggests a way to use Monte Carlo simulations on the tree and incorporate the optimal decision of the homeowner: We can simulate the interest rates on the tree, and whenever the simulated interest rate drops below the trigger rate, the whole remaining principal is paid back. Before the trigger rate is hit the mortgage owner only pays interest plus scheduled principal.

Table 13.18 illustrates the procedure. Panel A reports the scheduled interest and principal payments as well as the outstanding principal that were computed in Chapter 12. Panel B displays the trigger interest rate, from Panel D in Table 12.8, as well as ten simulated interest rates on the simple Black, Derman, and Toy model.[6] For each simulated path, the table indicates with a box the time at which the simulated rate hits the trigger rate, and

---

[6]The simulation procedure is the same as for the Ho-Lee model in Chapter 13, except that we simulated log rates.

thus prepayment occurs. For instance, in the first simulation, prepayment occurs at the first payment date $T_1 = 0.5$. In the second path, prepayment occurs in the third period, $T_3 = 1.5$, and so on. In the last row, the trigger rate is never hit, and thus no prepayment occurs.

Given the prepayment times uncovered in Panel B, Panel C reports the discounted cash flow that results from the decision of prepayments.[7] For instance, in Simulation 1, prepayment occurs on the first payment period. Thus, the cash flow generated on the day equals the scheduled interest plus the total principal. This amounts to $3782 + \$100000$ which, discounted at the rate $r_0 = 5.85\%$, gives $\$100,784$. Similarly, in Simulation 2, prepayment occurs in period $T_3 = 1.5$. Thus, in the first two periods the mortgage owner pays only the scheduled interest and principal, that is, the constant coupon of $\$12,195.71$. The first two entries in Simulation 2 show the discounted value of this amount. At time $T_3 = 1.5$, though, prepayment occurs and the total payment is the scheduled interest, $\$2791$, plus any outstanding principal given by $\$9062 + \$73792$. This yields a total of $\$85,988$, which, given the interest rates $r_0 = 5.86\%$, $r_1^1 = 7.49\%$ and $r_2^1 = 6.66\%$ (see Panel B), results in a discounted value of $e^{-(r_0 + r_1^1 + r_2^1) \times \Delta} \times$ cash flow $= \$77,799$.

What is the value of the mortgage from the Monte Carlo simulations? Given the discounted cash flows in Panel C, we can apply the same rule as in the AIRS example (see the Case Study in Section 13.4.2). In particular, by summing up all the entries in each row we find the present value of all the cash flows for each simulated path s. The average of all of these cash flows gives us the value of the mortgage. That is, the formula to apply is given by

$$\widehat{V}_0(10) = \frac{1}{N} \sum_{s=1}^{N} \left[\sum_{i=0}^{n-1} e^{-(r_0 + \ldots + r_i^s) \times \Delta} \times CF^s(i+1) \right] \qquad (13.26)$$

where $\widehat{V}_0(10)$ is the simulated value of the mortgage at time $i = 0$ with ten periods to maturity, and $CF^s(i+1)$ is the total cash flow in simulation s in period $i+1$.

The value of the mortgage that we obtain using 1,000 simulations is $\widehat{V}_0(10) = 100,096$, with confidence interval $C.I. = [99,998; 100,195]$. We may recall from Chapter 12, Equations 12.13 through 12.15, that the mortgage rate r^m was set in order for the mortgage value to be par, i.e. $V_0(10) = 100,000$. The fact that Monte Carlo simulations yield almost the same number provides some reassurance that we did not make any mistake in coding the simulations.

In the same fashion, we could use Monte Carlo simulations to obtain the value of the other mortgage backed securities discussed in Section 12.3.2. Instead of doing so, however, let's explore how we can now add some more factors that can affect the homeowner's decision to prepay the mortgage. These additional factors induce path dependencies that cannot be modeled using the optimal refinancing decision approach discussed in Chapter 12.

13.6.2 Additional Factors Affecting the Prepayment Decision

We now add additional factors and insert them into our Monte Carlo simulation methodology.

---

[7]Path-by-path discounts are computed as in Panel C of Table 13.8, although for the BDT model. Because the procedure is the same, we do not report it.

Table 13.18 The Prepayment Decision in Simulations

Panel A: Mortgage Payments and Outstanding Principal

	0	1	2	3	4	5	6	7	8	9	10
					Period i						
Interest Payment		3782	3464	3134	2791	2435	2066	1683	1285	873	444
Scheduled Principal		8414	8732	9062	9405	9761	10130	10513	10910	11323	11751
Outstanding Principal	100000	91586	82855	73792	64388	54627	44497	33985	23074	11751	0

Panel B: Trigger Rate and Ten Simulated Paths

Trigger rate $\underline{r}_i \Longrightarrow$		5.53	4.92	5.76	6.64	5.62	6.28	5.55	6.08	7.28	–
Simulation											
1	5.86	5.53	6.66	7.79	6.64	7.61	8.50	7.51	8.24	7.28	5.95
2	5.86	7.49	6.66	5.76	4.90	5.62	6.28	7.51	6.08	5.38	4.39
3	5.86	7.49	6.66	5.76	6.64	7.61	8.50	10.17	8.24	9.86	8.05
4	5.86	7.49	9.02	7.79	8.99	10.30	8.50	7.51	8.24	7.28	8.05
5	5.86	5.53	6.66	5.76	6.64	7.61	6.28	7.51	6.08	7.28	5.95
6	5.86	5.53	6.66	5.76	6.64	5.62	6.28	7.51	6.08	7.28	5.95
7	5.86	5.53	6.66	7.79	6.64	5.62	4.64	5.55	4.49	3.97	3.24
8	5.86	5.53	4.92	4.25	4.90	4.15	3.43	4.10	4.49	5.38	4.39
9	5.86	7.49	6.66	5.76	6.64	7.61	8.50	7.51	6.08	7.28	8.05
10	5.86	7.49	9.02	10.55	12.17	10.30	8.50	10.17	11.15	13.35	10.90

Panel C: Discounted Cash Flows

Simulation	0.5	1	1.5	2	2.5	3	3.5	4	4.5	5
					Maturity T_i					
1	100784	0	0	0	0	0	0	0	0	0
2	11843	11408	77799	0	0	0	0	0	0	0
3	11843	11408	77799	0	0	0	0	0	0	0
4	11843	11408	10905	10488	10027	9524	9128	8791	16566	0
5	100784	0	0	0	0	0	0	0	0	0
6	100784	0	0	0	0	0	0	0	0	0
7	100784	0	0	0	0	0	0	0	0	0
8	100784	0	0	0	0	0	0	0	0	0
9	11843	11408	77799	0	0	0	0	0	0	0
10	11843	11408	10905	10344	9734	9245	8861	8421	7965	7450

1. **Random Event.** Homeowners may prepay their mortgages for reasons completely independent of interest rates. The most important of these is the house sale. This may be due to numerous reasons, including simply the fact that a homeowner may change job location. Similarly, homeowners' defaults trigger prepayments in agency MBS, as the agencies, which insured investors against homeowners' defaults, have to step in and pay the principal back to investors. To capture these random events of prepayment, we insert in our Monte Carlo simulations a probability p_i that prepayment occurs independently of the level of the interest rate. To have some guidance on the size of this probability, let us assume that p_i is related to the PSA measure of prepayment speed, discussed in Section 8.3.1 of Chapter 8. To simulate a prepayment event that is unrelated to interest rates, we can make use of the uniform distribution, $RAND()$ function again. Given a probability p_i of prepayment, we can simulate the prepayment event by requiring that prepayment occurs when $RAND() < p_i$.

2. **Seasonality.** Homeowners tend to move much more frequently in summer than in any other season in the year, so prepayments have a strong seasonal component, with a peak in summer months. The reason is related to the school year, as parents change location during summer and move their children from one school to another. We can capture this seasonality in our simulations by requiring the probability p_i above to be higher during summers.

3. **Not Optimal Exercise.** When interest rates decline many homeowners do not take advantage of the refinancing opportunity, and wait too long to benefit. This behavior is related to the interest rate level. For instance, in the example in Table 13.18, it is optimal to refinance whenever the rate hits the trigger rate. Homeowners, however, may not do this, either because they do not pay attention to current rates, or because there are some additional costs to refinancing that make them hesitate. However, it is reasonable to assume that the lower the rate, the greater the probability that homeowners will in fact pay attention to rates and decide to refinance. We can capture this behavior by assuming that even if it is optimal to refinance, i.e. the simulated rate is below the trigger rate $r_i^s < \underline{r}_i$, homeowners do so only with a probability $q(r_i^s)$ that depends on the level of interest rates. In the simulations, we assume the simple form

$$q_i^s = a \times e^{-b \times r_i^s} \qquad \text{if} \quad r_i^s < \underline{r}_i \qquad (13.27)$$

where a and b are two constants that we choose to model the behavior of homeowners. For instance, if $a = 1$ and $b = 0$, the $q_s^i = 1$, which implies that homeowners always refinance when it is optimal to do so, as in Table 13.18. If $a = 0.5$ and $b = 0$, then homeowners refinance only with 50% probability when it is optimal to do so. Finally, if $b > 0$, then lower interest rates make it more likely that homeowners will refinance when it is optimal. In the simulations below we consider the parameters $a = 0.8$ and $b = 20$, which implies that the probability of refinancing (when optimal) is anywhere between 18% (for high rates) and 80% (for low rates). In each simulation s, then, given q_i^s at time i, we assume that prepayment occurs if $RAND() < 1 - q_i^s$.

Let's now think about the effect of the above additional factors on the valuation of the mortgage in the example in Table 13.18. Panel A of Table 13.19 shows the assumptions we make in this exercise: In particular, the 100% PSA shows the probabilities according to the PSA experience, as discussed in Chapter 8. In the simulation, we use 50% PSA as probability driving the additional factors that may trigger a prepayment independent of interest rates. This number is lower than is typically used, but it reflects the fact that the simulations will take into account other factors as well. The row entitled "season" reports the assumption about seasonality. Since we are simulating at the semi-annual horizon, we assume that summer is six months away, and that the 50% PSA probability doubles during summer. Hence, the 1, 2, 1, 2, ... sequence. Finally, because the PSA defines the Conditional Prepaymnet Rate (CPR) over time, and the CPR is an annualized prepayment probability, we must translate this annual probability into a semi-annual one. We do so using the same methodology employed in Chapter 8:

$$p_i = \text{season index} \times (1 - (1 - CPR)^{1/2})$$

where the "season index" is either 1 or 2.

Panel A also reports the parameters $a = 0.8$ and b of the probability to prepay given that it is optimal to do so (Equation 13.27).

A comparison of Panel B of Table 13.19 with Panel C of Table 13.18 illustrates the differences. In both panels, the simulated rates are the same (see Panel B of Table 13.18), yet the timing of prepayments is quite different. For instance, with optimal refinancing, in Simulation 1 it is best to refinance immediately at time $i = 1$, while in the current model refinancing only occurs at time $i = 4$, as now there is a lower probability of refinancing even if it is optimal. In Simulation 4, on the other hand, it is optimal to never prepay according to the optimal rule, but instead prepayment occurs in period $i = 6$.

The value of the mortgage using the same 1,000 simulated interest rate paths in this case is $\widehat{V}_0(10) = 101,006$, with confidence interval $C.I. = [100,864 - 101,149]$, which is higher than in the case of optimal refinancing. This should not be surprising: The mortgage backed security with optimal refinancing time maximizes the value of the option for the homeowner, and thus decreases the value of the mortgage for the investor. If the homeowner does not act optimally, intuitively the value of his or her option is lower, and this is good news for the investor. That is, the value of the mortgages (and mortgage backed securities) are higher when homeowners do not exercise their option optimally.

13.6.3   Residential Mortgage Backed Securities

Given the simulated cash flows, and especially prepayment times, we can finally divide these cash flows across the various types of securities, as described in Chapter 8. As we did in Chapter 12 we now assume that the mortgage discussed in the previous section is in fact a mortgage pool, with principal equal to 100 million (instead of $100,000).

13.6.3.1 Pass-Through, IO and PO Strips   Table 13.20 contains the simulated discounted cash flows of the 7% pass-through and its principal only and interest only strips, discussed in Section 12.3.2. Using the usual 1,000 simulations, we obtain the following prices:

$$
\begin{aligned}
\text{Pass-through price} \ &= \ \$99,996; \ \ \text{Confidence interval} = [\$99,848, \$100,144]; \\
\text{IO strip price} \ &= \ \$12,540; \ \ \text{Confidence interval} = [\$12,211, \$12,868]; \\
\text{PO strip price} \ &= \ \$87,456; \ \ \text{Confidence interval} = [\$87,057, \$87,855];
\end{aligned}
$$

Table 13.19   Pricing MBS by Monte Carlo Simulations with Additional Factors

---

Panel A: Assumptions about Additional Factors

100%PSA	1.20%	2.40%	3.60%	4.80%	6.00%	6.00%	6.00%	6.00%	6.00%	6.00%
PSA% Used in Simulations	50									
Season	1	2	1	2	1	2	1	2	1	2
Monthly Probability	0.30%	1.20%	0.90%	2.41%	1.51%	3.02%	1.51%	3.02%	1.51%	3.02%

Parameters for Prepayment Probability when Optimal to Exercise $q = a \times e^{-b \times r_i^s}$:

a	0.8	b	20

Panel B: Discounted Cash Flows

Simulation	— Maturity T_i									
	0.5	1	1.5	2	2.5	3	3.5	4	4.5	5
1	11843	11520	11143	67297	0	0	0	0	0	0
2	11843	11408	11034	10721	57320	0	0	0	0	0
3	11843	11408	11034	10721	10371	9984	9569	9094	8727	8307
4	11843	11408	10905	10488	10027	44274	0	0	0	0
5	11843	11520	11143	10827	10473	10082	9771	27215	0	0
6	11843	11520	78564	0	0	0	0	0	0	0
7	100784	0	0	0	0	0	0	0	0	0
8	11843	89786	0	0	0	0	0	0	0	0
9	11843	11408	11034	67323	0	0	0	0	0	0
10	11843	11408	10905	10344	9734	9245	8861	8421	7965	7450

Table 13.20   Pass-Through MBS and IO and PO Strips

Panel A: Pass-Through Interest, Scheduled Principal, and Outstanding Principal

	─────────── Maturity T_i ───────────									
	0.5	1	1.5	2	2.5	3	3.5	4	4.5	5
Interest (PT)	3500	3206	2900	2583	2254	1912	1557	1189	808	411
Principal	8414	8732	9062	9405	9761	10130	10513	10910	11323	11751
Outstanding Principal	91586	82855	73792	64388	54627	44497	33985	23074	11751	0

Panel B: Pass-Through MSB – Ten Simulated Discounted Cash Flows
─────────── Maturity T_i ───────────

Simulation	0.5	1	1.5	2	2.5	3	3.5	4	4.5	5
1	11569	11276	10929	67114	0	0	0	0	0	0
2	11569	11166	10823	10538	57164	0	0	0	0	0
3	11569	11166	10823	10538	10217	9858	9470	9023	8681	8285
4	11569	11166	10696	10309	9878	44153	0	0	0	0
5	11569	11276	10929	10642	10317	9955	9670	27141	0	0
6	11569	11276	78350	0	0	0	0	0	0	0
7	100510	0	0	0	0	0	0	0	0	0
8	11569	89542	0	0	0	0	0	0	0	0
9	11569	11166	10823	67140	0	0	0	0	0	0
10	11569	11166	10696	10168	9589	9129	8769	8355	7922	7430

Panel C: IO Strip – Ten Simulated Discounted Cash Flows
─────────── Maturity T_i ───────────

Simulation	0.5	1	1.5	2	2.5	3	3.5	4	4.5	5
1	3399	3028	2650	2270	0	0	0	0	0	0
2	3399	2998	2624	2270	1933	0	0	0	0	0
3	3399	2998	2624	2270	1916	1565	1222	887	578	280
4	3399	2998	2593	2221	1853	1493	0	0	0	0
5	3399	3028	2650	2293	1935	1581	1248	918	0	0
6	3399	3028	2650	0	0	0	0	0	0	0
7	3399	0	0	0	0	0	0	0	0	0
8	3399	3028	0	0	0	0	0	0	0	0
9	3399	2998	2624	2270	0	0	0	0	0	0
10	3399	2998	2593	2191	1799	1449	1132	821	527	251

Panel D: PO Strip – Ten Simulated Discounted Cash Flows
─────────── Maturity T_i ───────────

Simulation	0.5	1	1.5	2	2.5	3	3.5	4	4.5	5
1	8171	8248	8280	64844	0	0	0	0	0	0
2	8171	8168	8199	8268	55231	0	0	0	0	0
3	8171	8168	8199	8268	8300	8293	8248	8136	8103	8005
4	8171	8168	8103	8088	8025	42660	0	0	0	0
5	8171	8248	8280	8349	8382	8374	8422	26223	0	0
6	8171	8248	75701	0	0	0	0	0	0	0
7	97111	0	0	0	0	0	0	0	0	0
8	8171	86514	0	0	0	0	0	0	0	0
9	8171	8168	8199	64870	0	0	0	0	0	0
10	8171	8168	8103	7977	7790	7679	7638	7534	7395	7179

13.6.3.2   Collateralized Mortgage Obligations   As a final example of the Monte Carlo simulation approach to pricing, we can obtain the price of collateralized mortgage obligations, discussed in Chapter 8. Let us concentrate on the sequential structure (see Section 8.4.1). Recall that in such a structure, we have to assign individual principal payments, whether scheduled or unscheduled, sequentially to various tranches. Assume there are only three Tranches, A, B, and C, with principals of $50,000, $30,000 and $20,000, respectively. Tranche A is the first to receive all of the principal payments, up to the point where its principal ($50,000) is fully retired. At that point, Tranche B receives all of the principal, until its principal is paid back. Finally, Tranche C receives the principal back. Monte Carlo simulations prove their usefulness here: As the interest rate moves in each simulation and principal prepayment occurs, whether scheduled or unscheduled, we simply assign the principal payments to the various tranches, in the order above. Table 13.21 shows the usual ten simulated paths for the three tranches.

13.6.4   Prepayment Models

The approach above is still rather stylized. In particular, for each mortgage pool we still assume that if prepayment occurs, the whole principal is paid back. This approach, albeit sufficiently simple to understand how to use Monte Carlo simulations to price MBS, is unsatisfactory. Why? Because we would like to know not only whether prepayments occur, but also how much of the prepayment will occur. More complicated models of prepayment can be set up to take this additional quantity (amount of prepayment) into account. Indeed, a widespread methodology used by investment banks and hedge funds to price mortgage backed securities is to estimate a prepayment model, that is, a model that helps predict the amount of prepayment that will be realized, depending on market conditions. For instance, we mentioned that besides the interest rate, other factors such as seasonality, pool age, housing prices, and general economic conditions have an impact on the amount of prepayments. A prepayment model combines historical data on these external factors together with historical prepayments, often within a regression framework, to obtain a forecast of the amount of prepayment for each possible future scenario. This methodology is then made operational by using Monte Carlo simulations on these factors, and computing the price of mortgage backed securities quite in the same way as discussed in the previous sections.

13.7   SUMMARY

In this chapter we covered the following topics:

1. Monte Carlo simulations: Monte Carlo simulations is the name given to the procedure of simulating interest rates according to a specific model, such as a binomial tree model. The methodology calls for the simulation of a random variable that has a uniform distribution, and considering upward and downward movements depending on the outcome of this random variable (e.g., above or below 0.5).

2. Pricing by MC simulations: The simulation of interest rates determines a sequence of cash flows. For each path of interest rates we can discount future cash flows to today. The value of a security is approximately equal to the average simulated price.

Table 13.21 Collateralized Mortgage Obligation

Panel A: Tranche A – Ten Simulated Discounted Cash Flows

	0	0.5	1	1.5	Maturity T_i 2	2.5	3	3.5	4	4.5	5
Interest		1750	1456	1150	833	504	162	0	0	0	0
Scheduled Principal		8414	8732	9062	9405	9761	4627	0	0	0	0
Outstanding Principal	50,000	41586	32855	23792	14388	4627	0	0	0	0	0

Simulation											
1		9870	9623	9330	21639	0	0	0	0	0	0
2		9870	9529	9239	9000	12774	0	0	0	0	0
3		9870	9529	9239	9000	8728	3921	0	0	0	0
4		9870	9529	9131	8804	8439	3740	0	0	0	0
5		9870	9623	9330	9088	8814	3959	0	0	0	0
6		9870	9623	31068	0	0	0	0	0	0	0
7		50255	0	0	0	0	0	0	0	0	0
8		9870	40658	0	0	0	0	0	0	0	0
9		9870	9529	9239	21648	0	0	0	0	0	0
10		9870	9529	9131	8684	8192	3631	0	0	0	0

Panel B: Tranche B – Ten Simulated Discounted Cash Flows

	0	0.5	1	1.5	2	2.5	3	3.5	4	4.5	5
Interest		1050	1050	1050	1050	1050	1050	857	489	108	0
Scheduled Principal		0	0	0	0	0	5503	10513	10910	3074	0
Outstanding Principal	30000	30000	30000	30000	30000	30000	24497	13985	3074	0	0

Simulation											
1		1020	992	959	27285	0	0	0	0	0	0
2		1020	982	950	923	26634	0	0	0	0	0
3		1020	982	950	923	893	5364	8921	8501	2277	0
4		1020	982	939	903	863	24248	0	0	0	0
5		1020	992	959	932	902	5417	9109	11169	0	0
6		1020	992	28369	0	0	0	0	0	0	0
7		30153	0	0	0	0	0	0	0	0	0
8		1020	29330	0	0	0	0	0	0	0	0
9		1020	982	950	27296	0	0	0	0	0	0
10		1020	982	939	891	838	4967	8261	7872	2078	0

Panel C: Tranche C – Ten Simulated Discounted Cash Flows

	0	0.5	1	1.5	2	2.5	3	3.5	4	4.5	5
Interest		700	700	700	700	700	700	700	700	700	411
Scheduled Principal		0	0	0	0	0	0	0	0	8249	11751
Outstanding Principal	20000	20000	20000	20000	20000	20000	20000	20000	20000	11751	0

Simulation											
1		680	661	640	18190	0	0	0	0	0	0
2		680	655	633	615	17756	0	0	0	0	0
3		680	655	633	615	595	573	549	522	6404	8285
4		680	655	626	602	576	16165	0	0	0	0
5		680	661	640	621	601	579	561	15973	0	0
6		680	661	18913	0	0	0	0	0	0	0
7		20102	0	0	0	0	0	0	0	0	0
8		680	19554	0	0	0	0	0	0	0	0
9		680	655	633	18197	0	0	0	0	0	0
10		680	655	626	594	559	531	509	483	5844	7430

3. Path dependent interest rate securities: These are securities whose payoffs depend on the entire path of interest rates during the life of the security, not only the final interest rate level. Asian options are such an example, as the payoff at maturity depends on the average interest rate over the life of the option. Index ammortizing interest rate swaps, whose notional amount declines as the interest rate declines, are another example.

4. Application to residential mortgage backed securities: Since homeowners may repay their mortgage any time during the life of the mortgage, and for reasons that are not strictly related to interest rates, MC simulations are a good methodology to price RMBS. It is possible to combine the optimal interest-rate related decision to repay a mortgage, obtained on a binomial tree, with a probability that the homeowner may not repay at this time. Similarly, it is possible to include external factors to prepayment as well as seasonalities.

13.8 EXERCISES

1. Consider Exercise 1 in Chapter 11. Solve to answer the same questions using the Monte Carlo Simulations approach. Make sure to compute both the price and the standard error, as well as the confidence interval. Compare your results with those obtained in Chapter 11.

2. **Interest rate barrier options.** An interest rate barrier option is a regular option whose payoff at maturity depends on whether or not a certain level of interest rate has been touched during the life of the option. For instance, a down-and-out option is an interest rate option that expires if before maturity the interest rate hits a given barrier. Let the current term structure of interest rates be flat at the continuously compounded 5% rate. Consider an at-the-money, down-and-out call option with $100 million notional and one year to maturity. The barrier is set at $\underline{r} = 3\%$. You also know that a 6-month regular call option on the 1-month interest rate trades at $C(1/12) = 2.6505$ (for 100 of notional).

   (a) Fit the Ho-Lee interest rate tree with monthly steps to the term structure of interest rates. Make sure that the tree can price (approximately) the simple 6-month option described above.

   (b) Use Monte Carlo simulations to compute the value of the down-and-out option. What goes wrong if you try to compute the value of the down-and-out call option by using the backward methodology?

   (c) Fit a simple BDT interest rate model and do the same exercise. Is the price the same? Discuss.

3. This exercise is related to Exercise 3 in Chapter 12. Consider the binomial tree and the mortgage backed securities obtained in that exercise.

   (a) On the tree, obtain the trigger rates $\underline{r}_i$ such that prepayment occurs when $r_i < \underline{r}_i$.

   (b) Use Monte Carlo simulations and compute the value of the mortgage. Do you obtain the same value as from the tree (see Exercise 3 in Chapter 12)?

(c) Use Monte Carlo simulations to obtain the price of the 3.5% pass-through security.

(d) Add some prepayment probability to the model, such as:

    i. A PSA related probability of prepayment even when $r_i > \underline{r}_i$. How is the price of the pass through affected by this additional probability? Discuss.

    ii. A probability of no prepayment even if $r_i < \underline{r}_i$. How is the price of the pass through affected by this additional probability? Discuss.

(e) Suppose that the price of the mortgage is given by the optimal prepayment policy (i.e., only from the tree), but that homeowners act non-optimally with respect to interest rates, and therefore prepay when they shouldn't and vice versa, as discussed above. Is this good news or bad news for the bank issuing the mortgage? Discuss. (*Hint: what is the effect of irrational prepayment on the value of the mortgage?*)

(f) What is the price of interest only (IO) and principal only (PO) strips? Compute their spot rate duration and compare them with the spot rate duration of the pass-through security.

4. Today is November 3, 2008, and the 3-month LIBOR, swap rates, and cap prices are as in Table 13.22.

(a) Fit the LIBOR curve to these data (e.g., see Exercise 5 in Chapter 11).

(b) Fit a binomial tree that exactly matches the term structure of interest rates (e.g., the Ho-Lee model or the simple BDT model). There is no need to match cap prices.

(c) Use the Monte Carlo simulations method on the tree to recompute the value of zero coupon bonds. Are these the same as in the data? How many simulations do you need in order to do a "good job" in the pricing? How does the number of simulations depend on the level of the assumed volatility?

(d) Choose a volatility level on the tree that matches the value of the cap price (on the tree) for a given maturity T (e.g., $T = 1$). Then use the Monte Carlo simulations approach to price the same cap. Is the price you obtain by Monte Carlo simulations the same as in the data?

(e) On this tree, use the Monte Carlo simulation approach to price an at-the-money Asian cap with maturity $T = 2$. The Asian cap has quarterly cash flows (caplets) given by

$$CF_t = N \times \Delta \times \max\left(\text{average } r(t - \Delta) - r_K, 0\right)$$

where N is the notional, $\Delta = 1/4$ is the payment frequency, and "average $r(t - \Delta)$" is the average rate at quarterly frequency from time 0 to $t - \Delta$.

(f) Compute the spot rate duration of the Asian cap calculated in Part (e).

5. **Corridor Note**. On October 26, 2004, PiVe International Bank, a AAA company, issued 10-year corridor note. This note has several features that makes it rather difficult to price: First, it accrues a coupon only so long as a reference rate is within

Table 13.22   Swap Rates and Cap Prices on November 3, 2008

3-Month LIBOR (%)	2.8588	
Maturity	Swap Rate (%)	Cap Price ($\times 100$)
0.50	2.6486	0.0528
0.75	2.4929	0.1313
1.00	2.4320	0.2401
1.25	2.4491	0.3826
1.50	2.4938	0.5405
1.75	2.5561	0.7106
2.00	2.6260	0.8932
2.25	2.7252	1.1095
2.50	2.8630	1.3729
2.75	3.0108	1.6636
3.00	3.1400	1.9502
3.25	3.2471	2.2235
3.50	3.3474	2.4973
3.75	3.4408	2.7711
4.00	3.5270	3.0451
4.25	3.6076	3.3208
4.50	3.6835	3.5968
4.75	3.7531	3.8700
5.00	3.8150	4.1370

Original Data Source: Bloomberg.
Reported Data are interpolated from quoted swap rates and flat volatilities,
and then computed using Black model.

Table 13.23 Term Sheet Corridor Note*

Trade Date	26 October 2004
Start Date	09 November 2004
Maturity Date	09 November 2014
Redemption Price : 100.00%	
Coupon :	Years 1-5: 9.00% x b/B x Day Count Fraction
	Years 6-10: (3-Month LIBOR + 2.50%) x b/B x Day Count Fraction
	where:
	"b" is the number of calendar days in the relevant Interest Period on which the Reference Rate as observed on such calendar day fixes on or within the Corridor Range for that Interest Period.
	"B" is the total number of calendar days in the corresponding Interest Period to "b" above.
	Interest Rate Period: Time between coupon payments.
Reference Rate	6-Month LIBOR
Corridor Range	Year 1: 0% to 4%
for relevant Interest	Year 2: 0% to 4.5%
Period	Year 3-5: 0% to 5%
	Year 6-7: 0% to 6%
	Year 8-10: 0% to 6.5%
Day Count Fraction	90/360
Interest Payment Dates	Quarterly

*: This term sheet is a stripped down version of a an actual term sheet for a callable, 10-year corridor note.

Table 13.24 Swap Rates on October 26, 2004

years	1	2	3	4	5	7	10
rates	2.46	2.85	3.16	3.42	3.64	4.01	4.39

Source: Federal Reserve Web Site.

some bounds. The bounds themselves, however, change over time according to a given schedule. In addition, the coupon moves from fixed to floating at some point in the future. The term sheet is in Table 13.23. On October 26, the 3-month LIBOR was 2.11%, and the 6-month LIBOR was 2.24%. The swap rates for maturities up to 10 years are in Table 13.24.

(a) Obtain the discount factors $Z(T)$ for the relevant maturities as of October 26, 2004. Make sure to plot your results in a figure and comment on them.

(b) Fit a binomial tree of your choise to the discount factors obtained in Part (a). Use monthly steps to avoid too long a tree.

(c) Employ a Monte Carlo simulations method to obtain the price of the security.

- Note that there are two LIBOR rates to simulate, the 3-month and 6-month. To ensure no arbitrage is preserved, the 3-month and 6-month LIBOR must be simulated together. One methodology is to simulate the short-term rate r_i on the tree, and from it (and the tree) compute both the 3-month and 6-month LIBOR rates.

(d) What are the benefits of these notes for an investor, compared to other available instruments? Why would you think that corridor notes are popular?

(e) Compute the spot rate duration of these notes. Is it high? Plot the value of the corridor note for many values of the starting short-term interest rate. Comment on your results, and link them to your answer to Part (d).

6. This Exercise is related Exercise 7 in Chapter 12. Treasury data for the estimation are in Table 12.15 of that chapter. Recall that on June 7, 2007, the Ginnie Mae pass-through GNSF 6 was quoted at [ASK, BID]=[99.40625, 99.375].[8] This pass-through security was collateralized by a pool of mortgages with a weighted average coupon (WAC) = 6.5%, and a weighted average maturity (WAM) = 320 (months). From the tree estimated in Exercise 7 in Chapter 12, do the following:

(a) Compute the trigger interest rates $\underline{r}_i$ under which prepayment occurs on the tree. Use Monte Carlo simulations on the tree assuming that prepayment occurs exactly when the rate $r_i < \underline{r}_i$. Is the price of the GNSF 7 the same as the one obtained by solving the binomial tree backward (see Exercise 7 in Chapter 12)?

(b) Add some irrational prepayment features to the model, such as:

i. A constant probability that prepayment occurs even if the simulated $r_i > \underline{r}_i$.

ii. A constant probability that prepayment does not occur even if the simulated $r_i < \underline{r}_i$.

How do these prepayment probabilities affect the price of GNSF 6? Is it higher or lower than in the case when they are zero? Choose "implied" probabilities to match exactly the price of GNSF 6.

(c) Use Monte Carlo simulations to compute the spot rate duration. How does it compare with the spot rate duration computed using the rational prepayment model?

(d) What is the price of interest only (IO) and principal only (PO) strips? What is their spot rate duration?

---

[8]Source: Bloomberg.

TERM STRUCTURE MODELS: CONTINUOUS TIME

In this third part of the book we discuss one of the most applied tools used to price and hedge fixed income instruments, namely, continuous time methodologies. In a nutshell, we consider the case in which underlying variables, such as interest rates or yields, move at a high frequency, such as daily and even intra-daily. Why do we want to do that? For at least three reasons:

1. **Realism:** Market variables *do* move at a high frequency. That is, if a bank sells a derivative product and it has to hedge its variation by using some underlying security, the bank will need to mark-to-market and rehedge the position very frequently, typically daily. While trees are excellent devices, a model that takes into account the high frequency nature of trading is welcome, as it offers immediacy to the trading necessities.

2. **Simplicity:** A number of analytical tools are available to analyze fixed income instruments and their derivatives when the trading interval time is small (when, in fact, it converges to zero).

3. **Analytical Formulas**: For many fixed income instruments and derivatives, we will obtain analytical formulas for their prices or hedge ratios. These analytical formulas

enourmously influence the speed at which trades can be implemented. The ability to react swiftly to market changes is an important tool in modern markets.

CHAPTER 14

INTEREST RATE MODELS IN CONTINUOUS TIME

In this chapter we move to continuous time. This methodology is by far the most applied in term structure models, and it can be best explained by referring to the Ho-Lee model discussed in Chapter 11. Recall that the Ho-Lee model postulates that from an interest rate $r_{i,j}$ in time/node (i, j), the next interest rate on the tree is either of the following, depending on whether there is an upward movement or a downward movement, respectively:

$$r_{i+1,j} = r_{i,j} + \theta_i \Delta + \sigma \sqrt{\Delta} \quad \text{with RN probability } p^* = 1/2 \quad (14.1)$$

$$r_{i+1,j+1} = r_{i,j} + \theta_i \Delta - \sigma \sqrt{\Delta} \quad \text{with RN probability } p^* = 1/2 \quad (14.2)$$

where Δ is the time step, θ_i is a sequence of constants that depends on time (period) i, σ is a parameter determining the volatility of interest rates, and "RN" stands for "risk neutral." Consider the simple case in which θ_i is constant over periods $i = 0, 1, 2...$, and, for simplicity, assume it is equal to 0, $\theta_i = 0$. Finally, assume that the interest rate volatility is $\sigma = 0.02$. Consider now a time interval $[0, 1]$, and let's divide it into n subintervals. $\Delta = 1/n$ is then the size of each individual interval. Figure 14.1 plots three paths of interest rates for $n = 10, 100, 1000$, that is, with step sizes $\Delta = 1/10$, $\Delta = 1/100$, and $\Delta = 1/1000$. All of these paths start at the same initial interest rate $r_0 = 0.06$. As can be observed, the interest rate process becomes more and more jagged as Δ gets smaller and the number n of intervals increases.

It is noteworthy that as we decrease Δ, the number of possible outcomes at $T = 1$ increases, as should be clear from glancing over the Ho Lee interest rate tree in Chapter 11. Recall, in particular, that if there are n steps between 0 and T, then the number of possible

Figure 14.1 Three Simulated Interest Rate Paths from the Ho-Lee Model

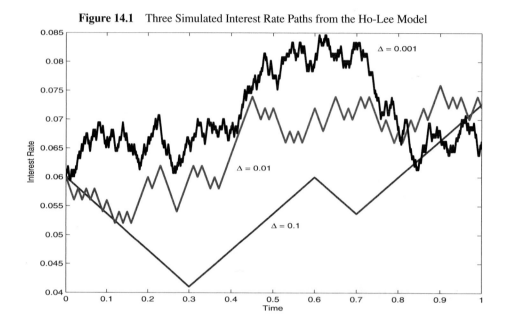

outcomes at T is $n + 1$. How does the distribution of outcomes depend on n and thus on the time step $\Delta = T/n$? Figure 14.2 simulates 1000 paths for the cases in which the number of time steps are $n = 10$, $n = 50$, $n = 75$, and $n = 100$, and plot the histogram of interest rates at $T = 1$. Given the number of steps, the sizes of the time steps are $\Delta = 1/10 = 0.1$, $\Delta = 1/50 = 0.02$, $\Delta = 1/75 = 0.0133$, and $\Delta = 1/100 = 0.01$. As can be seen, as n increases (Δ decreases) the distribution of interest rates at time $T = 1$ resembles more and more a bell-shaped distribution. Indeed, as we decrease Δ toward zero, interest rates under the Ho-Lee model become exactly normally distributed. This is evident for the cases $n = 75$ and $n = 100$, as alongside the histograms we also plot the normal distribution with the same mean and variance of the simulated interest rates. In particular, note that in all four cases, the mean of the distribution is at the initial value for the interest rate, namely, $r_0 = 0.06$.

The above exercise was undertaken by assuming $T = 1$ and for the Ho-Lee model with $\theta_i = 0$. However, even if we fix T at any other number, possibly even a very small one, it is still the case that as we decrease Δ sufficiently toward zero, the distribution of interest rates at T can be made normal. This is a consequence of the central limit theorem, according to which the average of independent random variables, independently of their distribution, always converges to a normal distribution. Figure 14.3 shows the simulated distribution of interest rates for four maturities $T = 0.1, 0.25, 0.5$, and 1. For each panel, the number of steps used to simulate interest rates has been kept constant, and equal to $n = 100$. This implies that for shorter maturities, the time step $\Delta = T/n$ is smaller. This is exactly the point: The histogram of simulated interest rates at the various maturities looks normal, as can be seen by the solid line that is plotted alongside the histogram. A longer time T simply increases the dispersion of the distribution, but it is still normal. Indeed, in all four cases the distribution is centered around the initial interest rate, $r_0 = 0.06$, while the standard

Figure 14.2   The Statistical Distribution of Ho-Lee Interest Rates at $T = 1$ as n Increases

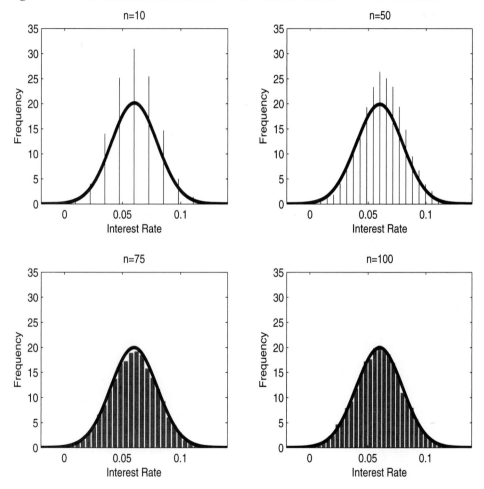

Figure 14.3 The Statistical Distribution of Ho-Lee Interest Rates at Various Horizons

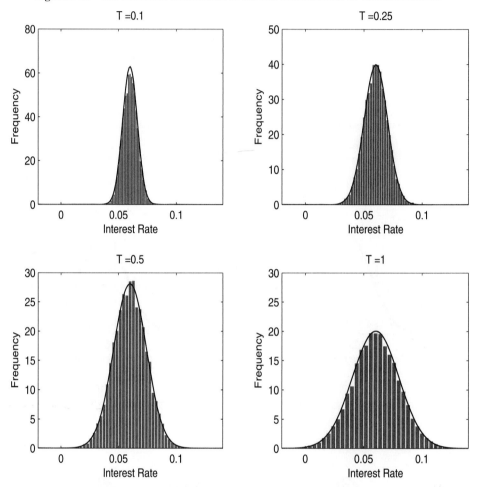

deviation is given by $\sigma\sqrt{T} = 0.0063, .01, .0141,, .02$, respectively. The reason for this behavior is the subject of the next section.

A similar construction leads to the definition of a Brownian motion, which is the main tool we use to analyze the pricing and hedging of interest rate securities.

14.1 BROWNIAN MOTIONS

Following up on the exercise in the previous section, we can introduce the concept of a Brownian motion as follows. Fix a given time interval $[0, t]$ (for instance, one year, i.e., $t = 1$) and let us divide it into n intervals, each of them with length

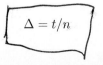

$$\Delta = t/n$$

For $i = 1, ..., n$ let Z_i be a random variable that has a 50% chance of being equal to $\sqrt{\Delta}$ and a 50% chance of being equal to $-\sqrt{\Delta}$:

$$Z_i = \begin{cases} \sqrt{\Delta} & \text{with probability } \frac{1}{2} \\ -\sqrt{\Delta} & \text{with probability } \frac{1}{2} \end{cases} \tag{14.3}$$

Two properties of Z_i are important:

1. Mean zero: $E[Z_i] = \frac{1}{2}(\sqrt{\Delta}) + \frac{1}{2}(-\sqrt{\Delta}) = 0$

2. Variance Δ: $Variance(Z_i) = E[Z_i^2] = \frac{1}{2}(\sqrt{\Delta})^2 + \frac{1}{2}(-\sqrt{\Delta})^2 = \Delta$

In item 2 above we used the fact from statistics that the variance of a mean zero variable, like Z_i, is equal to the second moment $E[Z_i^2]$.

Consider now the following quantity, namely, a summation of the random variables Z_i:

$$X_t = \sum_{i=1}^{n} Z_i \tag{14.4}$$

For given n, what are the properties of X_t? We have the following fact:

Fact 14.1 *Consider two times t_1 and t_2, with $t_2 > t_1$, and let m be the number of intervals between t_1 and t_2. Consider the value of X_t at these two times, X_{t_1} and X_{t_2}, and consider their difference. From its definition in Equation 14.4, and given that there are m intervals between t_1 and t_2, we have*

$$X_{t_2} - X_{t_1} = \sum_{i=1}^{m} Z_i \tag{14.5}$$

where Z_i is defined as in Equation 14.3 with $\Delta = (t_2 - t_1)/m$. The following properties follow:

1. **Mean Zero:** *The mean value of $(X_{t_2} - X_{t_1})$ is zero:*

$$E[(X_{t_2} - X_{t_1})] = 0 \tag{14.6}$$

2. **Variance Proportional to Time**: *The variance of $(X_{t_2} - X_{t_1})$ is equal to $t_2 - t_1$*

$$Variance[(X_{t_2} - X_{t_1})] = t_2 - t_1 \tag{14.7}$$

3. **Symmetric Distribution:** *The distribution of $(X_{t_2} - X_{t_1})$ is symmetric around zero.*

These properties can be derived from the definition of X_t and the properties of expectations. For instance, from statistics the expectation of a sum is the sum of expectations. Therefore, from Equation 14.5, we obtain

$$E[(X_{t_2} - X_{t_1})] = E\left[\sum_{i=1}^{m} Z_i\right] = \sum_{i=1}^{m} E[Z_i] = 0 \tag{14.8}$$

Similarly, from statistics we know that if some random variables are identically and independently distributed, then the variance of the sum is equal to the sum of variances. Therefore

$$Variance\left[(X_{t_2} - X_{t_1})\right] = Variance\left[\sum_{i=1}^{m} Z_i\right] = \sum_{i=1}^{m} Variance[Z_i] \quad (14.9)$$

$$= \sum_{i=1}^{m} \Delta = m\left(\frac{t_2 - t_1}{m}\right) = t_2 - t_1 \quad (14.10)$$

Finally, the last property stems from the symmetry of the distribution of Z_is, as there is equal chance of going up or down (symmetrically) by the same amount.

A Brownian motion is essentially given by X_t as we consider intervals Δ of smaller and smaller magnitudes. That is, we have the following definition:[1]

Definition 14.1 *A **Brownian motion** is given by the stochastic variable X_t in Equation 14.4 as n increases to infinity, and thus $\Delta = t/n$ converges to zero.*

14.1.1   Properties of the Brownian Motion

What are the properties of the Brownian motion? The properties discussed in Fact 14.1 do not depend on n, and thus they must hold also for the limit as n diverges to infinity and Δ becomes smaller and smaller.

The main property that is achieved by taking the limit is that if we take any two times, t_1 and t_2, with $t_2 > t_1$, then the difference $(X_{t_2} - X_{t_1})$ is normally distributed.

Fact 14.2 Normal Distribution. *As in Fact 14.1, consider two times t_1 and t_2, with $t_2 > t_1$, and let m be the number of intervals between t_1 and t_2. As m increases to infinity, the distribution of $(X_{t_2} - X_{t_1})$ converges to a normal with mean zero and variance $t_2 - t_1$, that is*

$$(X_{t_2} - X_{t_1}) \sim \mathcal{N}(0, t_2 - t_1) \quad (14.11)$$

This last property can be understood from observing again Figure 14.2, because the only difference between the Ho-Lee interest rate movements in that example and the Brownian motion is the dispersion σ, which is set equal to one in the case of a Brownian motion. Figure 14.4 plots the Brownian motion distribution over time, for $t = 0.1, 0.5, 1$, and 1.5. In all cases it is a normal distribution, and in all cases it has mean zero. However, the variance is equal to t, and thus, as time evolves, the distribution becomes wider and wider. The "floor" of the figure also shows the two standard deviation bounds (the curved lines) of the normal distribution over time, and the three more erratic lines are three simulated paths of the Brownian motion.

One additional property is important:

---

[1]This is an informal definition. The proper definition of Brownian motion relies on relatively more complicated mathematics, and is not covered in this book

Figure 14.4 The Distribution of a Brownian Motion X_t over Time

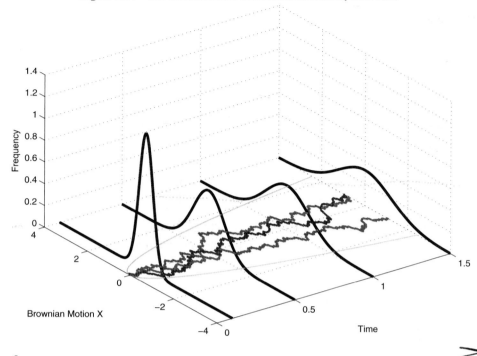

Fact 14.3 Martingale Property. *The best forecast of the value of a Brownian motion in the future is its value today. That is, if we know that at $t = 0$ the value of the Brownian motion X_0, then for every $t > 0$*

$$E\left[X_t | X_0\right] = X_0 \tag{14.12}$$

14.1.2 Notation

Fact 14.2 shows that between any two points t_1 and t_2, with $t_2 > t_1$, the change in the Brownian motion $X_{t_2} - X_{t_1}$ is normally distributed. This applies even if the two times t_1 and t_2 are extremely close to each other. The logic is that even if these two points in time are extremely close to each other, we can still divide the interval in n subintervals and take the limit as n increases to infinity. It turns out that it is convenient to work with small time intervals, denoted $dt = t_2 - t_1$. During this small time interval, the Brownian motion changes by $dX = X_{t_2} - X_{t_1}$. In general, we denote the change in the Brownian motion between a time t and its subsequent (small) time $t + dt$ by dX_t, that is, $dX_t = X_{t+dt} - X_t$. From the properties above, namely Fact 14.2, we then have

$$dX_t \sim \mathcal{N}(0, dt) \tag{14.13}$$

■ **EXAMPLE 14.1**

Driftless Ho-Lee model

To illustrate the use of Brownian motions, let us return to the Ho-Lee model described earlier. As shown there, for the case in which $\theta_i = 0$, the statistical distribution of the interest rates at any horizon T converges to a normal distribution, with mean r_0, the initial interest rate, and variance $\sigma^2 T$. For this special case, then, we can represent the Ho-Lee interest rate model using a Brownian motion by postulating

$$r_t = r_0 + \sigma X_t \qquad (14.14)$$

Because σ is constant, we can also represent it in its differential form

$$dr_t = \sigma dX_t \qquad (14.15)$$

where $dr_t = r_{t+dt} - r_t$ is the change in interest rates between t and $t + dt$. Because from Equation 14.13 dX_t is normally distributed, so is the change in interest rate dr_t. That is

$$dr_t \sim \mathcal{N}(0, \sigma^2 dt) \qquad (14.16)$$

Before applying the concept of Brownian motion to the pricing of interest rate securities, we must develop another important concept, the one of differential equations.

14.2   DIFFERENTIAL EQUATIONS

We now consider a second building block of continuous time models, namely, the concept of differential equations. To introduce the concept, it is convenient to rely on a couple of simple examples.

■ **EXAMPLE 14.2**

Bank Account Balance

Suppose at $t = 0$ Ms. Stanton deposits \$100 in a bank. The bank account yields a constant annualized interest rate r. At a later time $t > 0$ the amount grew to $B(t)$. As we know from Chapter 2, if interest is compounded annually, the amount deposited at time $t + 1$ is

$$B(t+1) = (1+r) B(t)$$

If interest instead accrues every $\Delta = 1/n$ periods, we have

$$B(t + \Delta) = (1 + r\Delta) B(t)$$

We can rewrite this as

$$\frac{B(t + \Delta) - B(t)}{\Delta} = rB(t) \qquad (14.17)$$

This equation says that the change in $B(t)$ over a small period of time Δ is proportional to the current amount in the bank account $B(t)$ itself. Taking the limit as $\Delta \to 0$ we find that the right-hand side of Equation 14.17 converges to the first derivative of $B(t)$ with respect to time t. That is, we obtain:

$$\frac{dB(t)}{dt} = r B(t) \qquad (14.18)$$

This equation establishes then a relation between the *rate of change* of $B(t)$ and its value at time t, $B(t)$. This is a **differential equation**. A solution is a *function of time $B(t)$* that satisfies Equation 14.18, and in addition is such that $B(0) = \$100$, the initial deposit made.

As we know from the formula for continuously compounded interest rates (see Chapter 2), the exponential function is the (only) solution to Equation 14.18:

$$B(t) = \$100\, e^{rt} \tag{14.19}$$

How do we know this is a solution? First, it must satisfy the initial condition, that is, that at time $t = 0$ the bank account equals $\$100$, $B(0) = \$100$. This is easy to see, as the exponential function is one when its exponent is zero. Second, the proposed solution in Equation 14.19 has to satisfy the differential equation (Equation 14.18), which means that if we take the first derivative of Equation 14.19 with respect to time – the left-hand side of Equation 14.18 – we should get exactly "$rB(t)$" – the right-hand side of Equation 14.18. Taking then the first derivative of Equation 14.19 we find

$$\frac{dB(t)}{dt} = \$100\, r\, e^{rt} \tag{14.20}$$

Now, use again the proposed solution in Equation 14.19 and substitute $B(t)$ for $\$100\, e^{rt}$ in Equation 14.20, obtaining

$$\frac{dB(t)}{dt} = \$100\, r\, e^{rt} = r\, B(t) \tag{14.21}$$

The right-hand side of Equation 14.21 indeed coincides with the right-hand side of Equation 14.18 and thus $B(t) = \$100\, e^{rt}$ satisfies the differential equation (Equation 14.18).

■ EXAMPLE 14.3

Interest Rate Policy

Suppose that the short-term interest rate at time $t = 0$ is $r(0) = 2\%$. Assume that because of fear of inflation, the U.S. Federal Reserve announces that it will increase the interest rates going forward. As we know from Chapter 7 the Federal Reserve sets the Federal funds rate and the discount rate, and movements typically take place around the eight Federal Open Market Committee meetings during the year. However, abstracting a little from the actual rules, we can imagine that the Federal Reserve may announce that it intends to increase the interest rate to 5.4% (the U.S. average in the past 50 years). However, as usual, the Fed will not do so in one big step (from 2% to 5.4%) but rather in small steps over time. Assume that there is no uncertainty whatsoever on this policy.

How can we represent such a monetary policy choice?

One methodology is the following: Let $\bar{r} = 5.4\%$ be the interest rate to which the Federal Reserve wants eventually to converge. Every period Δ the Fed may increase the interest rate *proportionally* to the current distance between the long-term targe rate $\bar{r} = 5.4\%$ and the current rate $r(t)$. That is, a possible rule is the following

$$r(t + \Delta) - r(t) = \gamma\,(\bar{r} - r(t))\,\Delta \tag{14.22}$$

where γ measures the speed at which the Federal Reserve wants to move the interest rate from its current level to the target level $\bar{r}$. For instance, since there are eight meetings per year, a plausible "Δ" is $\Delta = 1/8 = 0.125$. Given the current rate $r(0) = 2\%$, at time $t = 0$ we have $(\bar{r} - r(0)) = 3.4\%$. Thus, if $\gamma = 1$, we obtain the first change in interest rate equal to $0.425\% = 1 \times 3.4\% \times 0.125$. Since now the interest rate is $r(\Delta) = 2.425\%$, the next movement at the next meeting will depend on $(\bar{r} - r(\Delta)) = 2.975\%$, that is, it is equal to $0.3719\% = 1 \times 2.975\% \times 0.125$, setting the interest rate equal to $r(2 \times \Delta) = 2.8\%$. And so on. If γ is lower, the changes in interest rates will not be as aggressive, and it will take longer to reach the target rate $\bar{r}$.[2]

How can we describe the movement of this interest rate through time? Divide both sides of Equation 14.22 by Δ and take the limit as Δ goes to zero, obtaining

$$\frac{dr(t)}{dt} = \gamma(\bar{r} - r(t)) \tag{14.23}$$

Once again, Equation 14.23 is a differential equation, as it describes a relation between the *rate of change* of the interest rate and the level of the interest rate. A solution to the differential equation is a *function of time* $r(t)$ that satisfies Equation 14.23, as well as the initial condition $r(0) = 2\%$.

The solution of Equation 14.23 is:

$$r(t) = \bar{r} + (2\% - \bar{r})e^{-\gamma t} \tag{14.24}$$

How can we verify this is a solution? First, it must satisfy the initial condition, that is, that the interest rate at time $t = 0$ is indeed equal to 2%. Setting $t = 0$ in Equation 14.24 we find that indeed $r(0) = 2\%$. Second, the solution must satisfy the differential equation (Equation 14.23), that is, if we take the first derivative with respect to t of $r(t)$ in Equation 14.24 – the left-hand side of Equation 14.23 – we should obtain "$\gamma(\bar{r} - r(t))$" – the right-hand side of Equation 14.23. We now verify this is the case. Take the first derivative of the proposed solution in Equation 14.24, then,

$$\frac{dr}{dt} = -\gamma(2\% - \bar{r})e^{-\gamma t} \tag{14.25}$$

As in the previous example, we now need to use again the proposed solution (Equation 14.24). In particular, we can rewrite Equation 14.24 as $r(t) - \bar{r} = (2\% - \bar{r})e^{-\gamma t}$. Thus, we can substitute $(2\% - \bar{r})e^{-\gamma t}$ on the right-hand side of Equation 14.25 for $(r(t) - \bar{r})$, obtaining

$$\begin{aligned} \frac{dr}{dt} &= -\gamma(2\% - \bar{r})e^{-\gamma t} \\ &= \gamma(\bar{r} - r(t)), \end{aligned}$$

which is the right-hand side of the original differential equation in Equation 14.24.

Panel A of Figure 14.5 plots three paths of interest rates, starting at $r(0) = 2\%$, $r(0) = 5.4\%$, and $r(0) = 8\%$, for the case in which $\gamma = 1$. As expected from the example, if the interest rate is low ($r(0) = 2\%$), then the path of interest rates is

---

[2] Strictly speaking, the interest rate $r(t)$ never reaches $\bar{r}$, but it gets closer and closer to it.

Figure 14.5   Interest Rate Paths

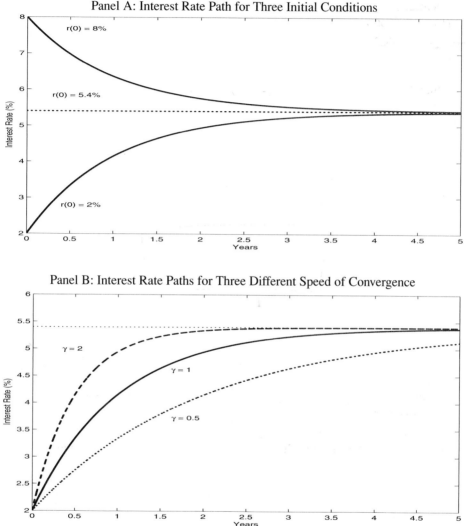

Panel A: Interest Rate Path for Three Initial Conditions

Panel B: Interest Rate Paths for Three Different Speed of Convergence

increasing. In contrast, if the initial interest rate is high, then the path of interest rates is decreasing, as it also tends toward the average $\bar{r} = 5.4\%$. Panel B of Figure 14.5 plots three paths of interest rates, all of them starting at $r(0) = 2\%$, but for three values of the parameter γ, namely, $\gamma = 0.5$ (the dotted line), $\gamma = 1$ (the solid line) and $\gamma = 2$ (the dashed line). As can be seen, the level of γ regulates the speed at which $r(t)$ converges to $\bar{r}$: A higher level of γ makes $r(t)$ converge faster. Within the monetary policy example, a higher γ implies a more aggressive monetary policy rule, in which interest rates are increased more quickly to prevent higher inflation, for instance.

The previous two examples provide instances of differential equations. In this book there is no need to learn how to solve differential equations. However, it is important to understand what a differential equation is and, in particular, what a *solution* to a differential equation is. Consider, therefore, this heuristic definition of a differential equation and its solution:

Definition 14.2 *Let $f(t)$ be a function of a variable t, and let $G(\cdot)$ be a function that relates $f(t)$ to the rate of change of $f(t)$:*

$$\frac{df}{dt} = G\left(\, f(t)\,\right) \tag{14.26}$$

Given an initial condition $f(0) = k$, $f(t)$ is the solution (or satisfies) the **ordinary differential equation** *in Equation 14.26 if for every t, its derivative df/dt equals $G(f(t))$ and if indeed $f(0) = k$.*

In Example 14.2, $f(t) = B(t)$ and $G(f) = rf$, while in Example 14.3 we have $f(t) = r(t)$ and $G(f) = \gamma\,(\bar{r} - f)$. More examples follow in the next sections in the context of bond and derivative pricing.

14.3   CONTINUOUS TIME STOCHASTIC PROCESSES

We talked about Brownian motions (Section 14.1) and differential equations (Section 14.2). A Brownian motion is a process that is completely erratic, fully unpredictable. The best guess of what the value of a Brownian motion will be at some point in the future is its value today. That is, if we know that $X_0 = 10$, then $E[X_t] = X_0 = 10$. The process resulting from a differential equation is exactly the opposite: It is perfectly predictable. For instance, in Example 14.3, given the interest rate $r(0) = 2\%$ and the (ordinary) differential equation in Equation 14.23, it is possible to predict *exactly* the value of interest rates in the future. In fact, from Figure 14.5, we can predict exactly that after one year the interest rate will be $r(1) = 4.94\%$, after two years it will be $r(2) = 5.34\%$, and so on. Indeed, to some extent Example 14.3 is the exact opposite of Example 14.1, in which the interest rate is simply proportional to a Brownian motion. In the latter example, like the Brownian motion, the interest rate would be fully unpredictable, and the best forecast of the interest rate in the future equals the interest rate today. More important, as time gets large, this model (the Ho-Lee model) may imply that interest rates become extremely large or extremely negative.

A more natural case is one that combines both Examples 14.3 and 14.1, that is, one in which the short-term interest rate is not perfectly forecastable but also not perfectly "unforecastable." The following example highlights this case.

■ **EXAMPLE 14.4**

Vasicek Model

Consider the discrete time interest rate process described in Equation 14.22. Taking the limit as Δ becomes smaller and smaller, it is intuitive that we can rewrite it as

$$dr_t = \gamma\,(\bar{r} - r_t)\,dt \tag{14.27}$$

where we use the notation r_t instead of $r(t)$ to denote the interest rate at time t, as it is more convenient. As in Equation 14.23, the solution to Equation 14.27 is the perfectly predictable interest rate in Equation 14.24. We can now add some randomness to this process by adding a random component in the form of a Brownian motion, such as the one in Equation 14.15. That is,

$$dr_t = \gamma \left(\bar{r} - r_t \right) dt + \sigma dX_t \tag{14.28}$$

In other words, the change in interest rate $dr_t = r_{t+dt} - r_t$ between t and $t + dt$ has two components: The first component "$\gamma \left(\bar{r} - r_t \right) dt$" is a predictable term, while the second component "σdX_t" is an unpredictable shock to interest rates. In the terminology of continuous time finance, the first predictable component is called the **drift rate** of the process, while the second random component is called the **diffusion term**.

The constant "σ" regulates how much randomness we want to put in the model for interest rates. For instance, $\sigma = 0$ makes Equation 14.28 equal to Equation 14.27. Similarly, γ regulates how fast the interest rate r_t converges back to the long run value $\bar{r}$ on average. Note that $\gamma = 0$ implies that the interest rate r_t never converges back, and in fact in this case we return to the driftless Ho-Lee model in Example 14.1.

Figure 14.6 illustrates the effect of σ on the path of interest rates. Panel A plots a simulated interest rate path starting from $r_0 = 2\%$ for $\sigma = 0.5\%$ and $\gamma = 1$. The solid curve line represents the path under $\sigma = 0$, i.e. the interest rate in Equation 14.24, that solves Equation 14.27. Recall this same line is also represented in Figure 14.5. Once we add randomness, the dotted line represents a possible path of interest rates according to the process in Equation 14.28.

Two features are noteworthy: First, initially, the dotted line follows the solid curved line relatively closely. Second, as soon as the solid line is close to the long-term mean $\bar{r} = 5.4\%$, the dotted line moves more erratically, but it keeps around the long-term mean of 5.4%. To understand this behavior, we need to examine the two terms in Equation 14.28. When the interest rate r_t is relatively far from the mean $\bar{r}$, the drift term (the "dt" term) is relatively large, and tends to influence the movement in interest rates dr_t. That is, if r_t is very small, then dr_t will tend to be positive unless the realized normally distributed Brownian shock $dX_t \sim \mathcal{N}(0, dt)$ is unusually negative. This explains why initially, when $r_t \approx 2\%$, the interest rate is close to the case in which $\sigma = 0$. However, as soon as r_t gets closer to the long term mean $\bar{r}$, then the drift term in Equation 14.28 becomes closer to zero and thus loses in relative importance and the second random term – the Brownian motion dX_t – tends to dominate the variation in interest rates. However, as soon as these random shocks dX_t move interest rates sufficiently far from $\bar{r}$, the first term becomes increasingly important, pulling the interest rate back toward $\bar{r}$.

The bottom panel of Figure 14.6 shows that indeed if we increase σ, then the random component becomes important from the very beginning. Even if r_t is close to 2%, the Brownian random shocks dX_t have enough of an impact to move interest rates around. However, as before, interest rates tend to move around the long run mean $\bar{r}$. For this reason, processes like the one described in Equation 14.28 are called **mean reverting processes**. The specific interest rate model in Equation 14.28 is called the **Vasicek** model of interest rates.[3]

---

[3] Processes of the form in Equation 14.28 are generically called Ornstein-Uhlenbeck processes.

Vasecheck
Simple!

$dr_t = \gamma(\bar{r} - r_t)dt + \sigma dX$

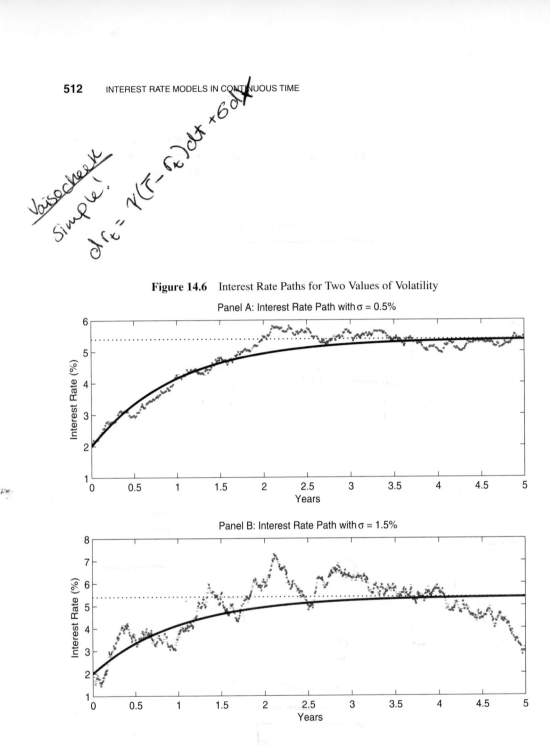

Figure 14.6   Interest Rate Paths for Two Values of Volatility

The Vasicek model in Equation 14.28 is just one of the many continuous time models of interest rates that have been used by practitioners and by academics alike. The key features of the Vasicek model are that it is simple, it is reasonable, and it can deliver analytical solutions for the prices of Treasury securities and many derivatives. For this reason, we use it extensively in this book. Note, though, it is definitely *not* the most frequently used in the industry. The reason will be clear as we go along. Indeed, as in Chapter 11, we will see that different models have different properties and deliver different prices for the same securities. Practitioners choose the model that in their view is better able to capture reasonable features of the particular interest rate market they are dealing with. Different models may be necessary in different markets. For instance, a very widely used model is the Ho-Lee model, which we can now express in its continuous time form.

■ **EXAMPLE 14.5**

The Ho-Lee model.

In Chapter 11 we introduced the Ho-Lee model to price derivative securities. This model is also described in Equations 14.1 and 14.2. The continuous time version in Equation 14.15, assumes that $\theta_i = 0$ for all i. What is the continuous time version of the Ho-Lee model without the simplifying assumption that interest rates are driftless? A good guess from observing Equations 14.1 and 14.2 is to assume

$$dr_t = \theta_t dt + \sigma dX_t \qquad (14.29)$$

where, recall, dt is a small interval of time. In Equation 14.29, the drift rate is "$\theta_t dt$" while the diffusion is "σdX_t." As in Chapter 11, the drift rates θ_t will be chosen to match the current term structure of interest rates, but we will return to this procedure in Chapter 19.

In general, when it is not convenient to be too specific on the type of model of interest rate we are considering, we denote the process as follows:

$$dr_t = m(r_t, t)dt + s(r_t, t)dX_t \qquad (14.30)$$

← norm b

where $m(r_t, t)$ and $s(r_t, t)$ are two functions of the interest rate and possibly time. For instance, in the Vasicek model, we have $m(r_t, t) = \gamma(\bar{r} - r_t)$ and $s(r_t, t) = \sigma$, while in the Ho-Lee model we have $m(r_t, t) = \theta_t$ and, again, $s(r_t, t) = \sigma$.

Definition 14.3 *The* **drift** *term of the stochastic process in Equation 14.30 is*

$$Drift = m(r_t, t)dt \qquad (14.31)$$

← Predictable

The drift term represents the predictable component of the stochastic process, in the sense that, given the knowledge of the current interest rate r_t, we determine that the expected change in interest rate r_t between t and $t + dt$ is

$$E[dr_t] = m(r_t, t)dt \qquad (14.32)$$

The **diffusion** *term of the stochastic process in Equation 14.30 is*

$$Diffusion = s(r_t, t)dX_t \qquad (14.33)$$

← un predict

The diffusion term is the unpredictable component of the stochastic process, due to the lack of predictability of the Brownian motion dX_t.

We proceed with our example about the Vasicek model, to study the properties of interest rates that are implied by this model.

■ **EXAMPLE 14.6**

Vasicek Model (cont.)

Let the interest rate at time $t = 0$ be given by r_0 (for instance, 2%). Consider a future time $t > 0$. What is the statistical distribution of the interest rate at t according to the Vasicek model? It turns out that r_t is normally distributed:

$$r_t \sim \mathcal{N}\left(\mu\left(r_0, t\right), \sigma^2\left(t\right)\right) \tag{14.34}$$

where

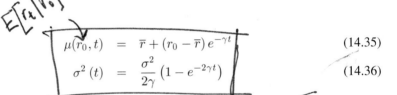

$$\mu(r_0, t) = \bar{r} + (r_0 - \bar{r}) e^{-\gamma t} \tag{14.35}$$

$$\sigma^2(t) = \frac{\sigma^2}{2\gamma}\left(1 - e^{-2\gamma t}\right) \tag{14.36}$$

Two properties are noteworthy: First, the expected future interest rate $E[r_t|r_0] = \mu(r_0, t)$ given in Equation 14.35 is indeed identical to the solution (Equation 14.24) to the differential equation in Equation 14.23. In this sense, the drift term $m(r_t, t) = \gamma(\bar{r} - r_t)$ represents the predictable component to interest rates. Second, the variance $\sigma^2(t)$ in Equation 14.36 does not diverge to infinity as t increases to infinity. The reason is that even if we let time go to infinity, interest rates are moving around the long-term mean $\bar{r}$ and thus the dispersion of the possible interest rates never goes to infinity.

To gauge the properties of this model, it is convenient to consider the **stationary distribution** of interest rates, that is, the statistical distribution of interest rates as t becomes larger and larger. Heuristically, this distribution corresponds to the histogram of interest rates in a simulation which lasts for a very long time (such as thousands of years). The stationary distribution is obtained from Equation 14.34 by simply taking the limit as t diverges to infinity. In this case, the distribution remains normal, with mean $\bar{r}$ and variance $\sigma^2/(2\gamma)$. The stationary distribution of interest rates estimated from data from 1954 to 2008 is represented in Figure 14.7.

One important point to notice from the figure is that it gives positive probability to negative nominal interest rates. This feature may seem puzzling at first, because we estimated this distribution from data, and in the history of the U.S. we never had negative nominal interest rates. How come then that the estimated distribution gives positive probability to negative rates? The answer lies in the symmetry of the normal distribution. In fact, there are only two quantities that characterize a normal distribution: Its mean and its variance. The mean is fixed by the average interest rates (5.4%). What about the variance? Although it is true that the U.S. never experienced negative nominal rates, it did experience extremely high, double-digit interest rates in the late 1970s and early 1980s. These observations push up the variance of the distribution, so that the tail of the normal distribution gives positive weight to them.

Figure 14.7   Estimated Stationary Distribution for Vasicek model

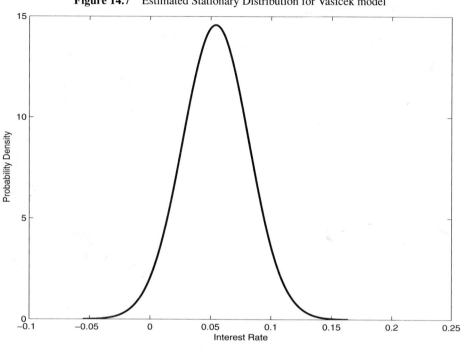

The drawback is that the symmetry of the distribution then forces the model to provide positive weight to negative nominal rates, that never happened.

Indeed, this is one of the reasons why the Vasicek model lost its favor as a model of interest rates in the past. It provides positive probability to an event that is extremely unlikely.[4] Note that the Ho-Lee model in Example 14.5 also yields negative interest rates. A number of other models have been proposed to correct this shortcoming, as we will see.

14.4 ITO'S LEMMA

Ito's lemma provides the "rules" of calculus to link the variation of an underlying stochastic variable, such as the interest rate r_t, to the price of securities that depend on it. For instance, if the interest rate is moving randomly through time, so must be the value of the securities that depend on interest rates, such as Treasury bonds or options. Knowing the exact relation between interest rates and security prices is of fundamental importance, as it allows us to compute the return processes for such securities, their volatility, their sensitivity to movements in the underlying interest rate, and so on. In turn, the knowledge of volatility and expected return allows us to successfully engage in risk management and,

---

[4]A negative nominal interest rate means that investors would like to purchase a zero coupon Treasury bond for $100 with the agreement to receive, for instance, $90 in the future. Keeping the $100 under the mattress yields a higher return, unless there is a good chance this money may be stolen.

as we shall see, even to apply the rules of no arbitrage and therefore obtain the value of interest rate securities themselves.

Consider the driftless Ho-Lee model in Example 14.1. In the case in which $\sigma = 1$, we indeed have that, according to this model, the interest rate $r_t = X_t$, as shown in Equation 14.14. Consider now a bond price, denoted by P_t. As we know from the basics, when the interest rate increases, the bond price decreases and vice versa. Therefore, we could expect that the bond price at time t may be a function of the interest rate $P_t = F(r_t)$. Variation in r_t yields variations in P_t, and the question is how much variation. Ito's lemma provides the answer. We study three versions of Ito's lemma, in increasing order of generality. The first version considers the case in which the underlying variable is just the Brownian motion itself X_t. An economic argument is the case in which $r_t = X_t$, as in the driftless Ho-Lee model just discussed.

Fact 14.4 *Ito's Lemma: Let $P_t = F(X_t)$ be a function of the Brownian motion X_t, then*

$$dP_t = \frac{1}{2}\left(\frac{d^2F}{dX^2}\right)dt + \left(\frac{dF}{dX}\right)dX_t \qquad (14.37)$$

where $\frac{dF}{dX}$ and $\frac{d^2F}{dX^2}$ denote the first and second derivative of F with respect to X.

Heuristically, if P_t denotes the price of a bond, then dP_t is the change in the price of the bond between t and $t + dt$, that is, $dP_t = P_{t+dt} - P_t$ is the *capital gain* dollar return on the bond. Then, interpreting X_t as an interest rate, Ito's lemma (Equation 14.37) says that the capital gain dollar return of a bond has two components: The first component is a predictable dt component that depends on the curvature of the function $F(X)$. The second component is a random term given by the sensitivity of the bond price to changes in the underlying variable (the first derivative (dF/dX)) multiplied by the random component itself dX_t.

To get an intuition why Equation 14.37 is true (and to remember the formula), recall Equation 4.2 in Chapter 4, in which we provide an approximation of the change in price of a bond in terms of duration and convexity. Identifying here r_t with X_t we find

$$dP_t = F(X_{t+dt}) - F(X_t) \approx \left(\frac{dF}{dX}\right)dX_t + \frac{1}{2}\left(\frac{d^2F}{dX^2}\right)dX_t^2 \qquad (14.38)$$

Because from the properties of a Brownian motion we also know

$$E\left(dX_t^2\right) = dt,$$

substituting (approximately) $dX^2 = dt$, Equation 14.37 follows.[5]

The most interesting, and important, point to ponder ragarding Ito's lemma is the following: Why do we have the additional dt term in Equation 14.37? That is, the function F depends only on the Brownian motion X_t, which is erratic and fully unpredictable. Why does $P_t = F(X_t)$ also contain a drift component, which is predictable?

To obtain an intuition, consider the following example: Let $r_t = X_t$, as in the driftless Ho-Lee model with $\sigma = 1$, and let $F(r)$ be a *nonlinear* function of r, such as the one in

---

[5]This not a proof of Ito's lemma, but just a heuristic derivation of it.

Figure 14.8 Explaining Ito's Lemma

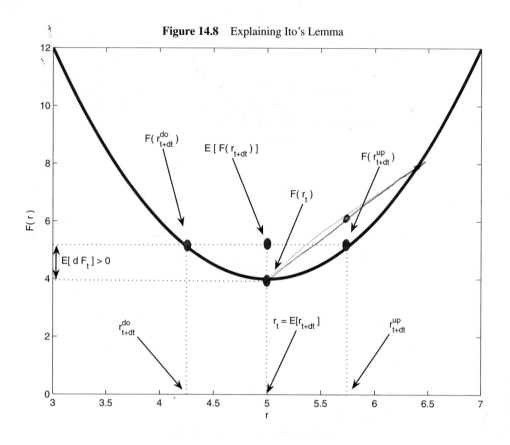

Figure 14.8[6] Suppose that at t we have $r_t = 5\%$, so that $F(r_t) = 4$. Consider a small time interval dt. From the properties of a Brownian motion we know that $E(r_{t+dt}|r_t) = r_t = 5\%$. Since $r_t = X_t$ is a Brownian motion, we now have to ask ourselves: What is the only thing that we can predict about r_{t+dt}?

We do not know whether r_{t+dt} will go up or down, but we can definitely predict that at time $t + dt$ the interest rate (Brownian motion) will have moved away from its current value and thus it will *not* be equal to 5%. That is, we can be certain that $r_{t+dt} \neq r_t$. It follows that since at t we are at the *minimum* of $F(r)$, $F(5) = 4$, we can predict that at $t + dt$ the price of the security $P_{t+dt} = F(r_{t+dt})$ will be *higher*, as it cannot get any lower. It is natural then to find that

$$E[F(r_{t+dt})] > F(r_t),$$

which implies

$$E[dP_t] = E[F(r_{t+dt}) - F(r_t)] > 0$$

That is, there is *predictability* in the price movement and, hence, there must exist a positive drift in the process for the price $P_t = F(r_t)$. Figure 14.8 illustrates this point by considering the case in which r_{t+dt} can take only two possible values, as in the tree-based Ho-Lee model (see the process in Equations 14.1 and 14.2 with $\theta_i = 0$ and $\sigma = 1$). Because there is 1/2

---

[6]A simple security whose price "looks like" $F(r)$ in Figure 14.8 is a long straddle, namely a portfolio that is long call and long a put on the interest rate with the same strike price.

Entirely dependent on curvature

Figure 14.9 Ito's Lemma and Convexity

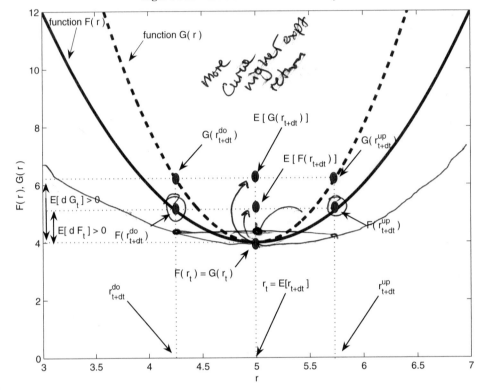

not period v is higher than r_t's regardless of expectations.

more curve higher expected return

probability to either go up to $r_{t+dt}^{up} = 5.75\%$ or down to $r_{t+dt}^{do} = 4.25\%$, we determine that the expected interest rate for the next period is $E[r_{t+dt}] = 0.5 \times 5.75\% + 0.5 \times 4.25\% = 5\% = r_t$. However, the figure shows that *independent* of whether the interest rate moves up or down, the value of $F(r)$ in the next period is equal to the same number, that is $F(r_{t+dt}^{up}) = F(r_{t+dt}^{do}) = 5.125 > 4 = F(r_t)$. That is, we expect to make a capital gain between now and the next period, even if we do not know in which direction the interest rate will be moving. Thus, the process for capital gains dP_t is predictable, and it should have a "dt" term.

Ito's lemma *quantifies* this predictable drift component to be equal to the curvature of the function, given by its second derivative:

$$E\left(dP_t\right) = \frac{1}{2}\frac{d^2 F}{dX^2}dt$$

more curve more drift

Indeed, Figure 14.9 shows the same situation as in Figure 14.8 but in which a function $G(r)$, which is more convex than $F(r)$, is also plotted. It is immediately apparent that the expected return implied by the function $G(r)$ is higher than the one implied by the function $F(r)$ because of the higher convexity of $G(r)$ with respect to $F(r)$.

Notice also that because the function $F(r)$ must go up in the next dt period, we have basically no stochastic shock. This is also apparent from Ito's lemma, because the stochastic shock dX_t is premultiplied by (dF/dX), which is *zero* in the case illustrated in Figure 14.8.

Don't understand

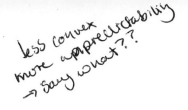

less convex
more appreciability
→ say what??

Figure 14.10   Ito's Lemma Again

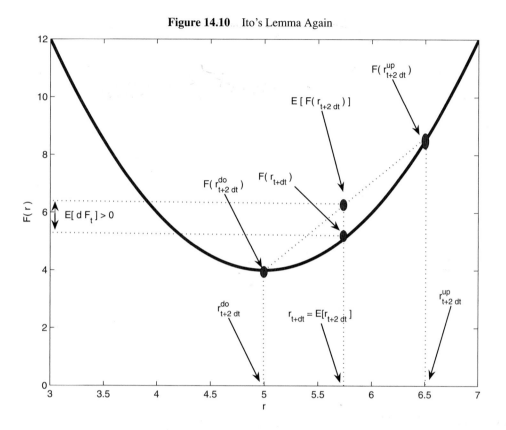

The argument about predictability of dP_t when $F(r)$ is convex does not hinge on the fact that $F(r)$ in Figure 14.8 is at its minimum for the current interest rate r_t, although this case makes the argument transparent. Even if $F(r)$ was not at its minimum, a similar argument follows. In fact, consider again the example illustrated in Figure 14.8 and suppose that at time $t + dt$ indeed the interest rate increased to $r_{t+dt} = 5.75\%$. Consider now the next step, between $t + dt$ to $t + 2dt$, and assume that the interest rate can still move up or down by 1.25% with equal probability. The next possible interest rate scenarios can only be $r_{t+2dt}^{do} = 5\%$ or $r_{t+2dt}^{up} = 6.5\%$. It follows, again, that $E[r_{t+2dt}] = 5.75\% = r_{t+dt}$, that is, the expected change in interest rates is zero. What about the expected profit $E[dP_{t+dt}] = E[P_{t+2dt} - P_{t+dt}]$? Figure 14.10 illustrates this case. With 50% probability, the price will be $F(r_{t+2dt}^{up}) = F(6.5) = 8.5$, while with 50% the price is $F(r_{t+2dt}^{do}) = F(5) = 4$. The expected price is then $E[F(r_{t+2dt})] = 0.5 \times 8.5 + 0.5 \times 4 = 6.25$. This is larger than the current price at $t + dt$, $F(r_{t+dt}) = 5.125$. Thus, we expect again a capital gain, even if we do not know the direction of the movement of interest rates.

There are two more versions of Ito's lemma to look at. The first one includes a time dimension to it. This is important, as the value of most interest rate securities changes over time even if the interest rate does not move. For instance, a zero coupon bond increases in value over time as it approaches its maturity, even if the short-term interest rate is not moving at all. Similarly, interest rate option prices move even without changes in the underlying interest rate because of changes in time to maturity.

Fact 14.5 Ito's Lemma 2 *(Adding time): Let $P_t = F(t, X_t)$, then*[7]

[handwritten: Brueter]

[handwritten: pass of ti... convexity]

$$dP_t = \left\{ \left(\frac{\partial F}{\partial t} \right) + \frac{1}{2} \left(\frac{\partial^2 F}{\partial X^2} \right) \right\} dt + \left(\frac{\partial F}{\partial X} \right) dX_t \qquad (14.39)$$

[handwritten: passage of time creates difference]

The passage of time is predictable. Therefore, the drift ("dt") term now includes one more term in addition to the convexity term also present in Equation 14.37. This additional term captures the variation in price due to the passage of time. It is described by the sensitivity of the pricing function $F(t, X)$ with respect to time $\partial F/\partial t$. For instance, a zero coupon Treasury bond increases in value through time as it approaches maturity even if the short-term interest rate is constant. Thus, the expected capital gain of a bond $dP_t = P_{t+dt} - P_t$ during this period, the drift term, has the additional positive component $\partial F/\partial t > 0$.

A final version of Ito's lemma concerns the case in which F is a function of an interest rate process, such as the one in Equation 14.23, and not only of the Brownian motion X_t. This is the most relevant case, as our strategy going forward will be to postulate a reasonable interest rate model, such as the Vasicek model in Equation 14.28, and then obtain the prices of bonds and derivative securities as well as the hedging trading strategies from the properties of the interest rate process. To carry out our computations, we need to know what is the capital gain process dP_t of a security that depends on the short term interest rate r_t according to the function $P_t = F(t, r_t)$.

Fact 14.6 Ito's Lemma 3 *(General version): Let r_t follow the generic interest rate process*

[handwritten: Classic dep d on rand time]

$$dr_t = m(r_t, t)dt + s(r_t, t)dX_t \qquad (14.40)$$

where $m(r, t)$ and $s(r, t)$ may be functions of the interest rate r and time t and let the price of a security be given by $P_t = F(t, r_t)$. Then, the capital gain process is

$$dP_t = \left\{ \left(\frac{\partial F}{\partial t} \right) + \left(\frac{\partial F}{\partial r} \right) m(r_t, t) + \frac{1}{2} \left(\frac{\partial^2 F}{\partial r^2} \right) s(r_t, t)^2 \right\} dt + \left(\frac{\partial F}{\partial r} \right) s(r_t, t)dX_t \qquad (14.41)$$

[handwritten: Cap gain due to time. variates   Convexity   moves further up higher gains cut   higher vol of states higher gains from convexity]

The drift term of the capital gain process has three components. The first is the capital gain (or loss if it's negative) due to the passage of time. The second is the capital gain due to expected variation in interest rates: If for instance we expect the Federal Reserve to decrease interest rates, $m(r, t) < 0$, then we expect the value of bond prices to increase (as for bonds $\left(\frac{\partial F}{\partial r} \right) < 0$), generating an expected capital gain $\left(\frac{\partial F}{\partial r} \right) \times m(r_t, t)$. The final component is the expected capital gain due to a convexity effect, as discussed earlier: We know that the short-term interest rate moves over time, and thus a positive convexity of the bond or the derivative security with respect to interest rate generates an expected capital gain. The only noteworthy point on convexity is that now the second derivative term $\left(\frac{\partial^2 F}{\partial r^2} \right)$

---

[7]The symbol $\partial F/\partial X$, called "partial derivative," denotes the derivative of $F(X, t)$ with respect to X while keeping t fixed. Similarly, $\partial F/\partial t$ denotes the derivative of $F(X, t)$ with respect to t while keeping X fixed. Finally, $\partial^2 F/\partial X^2$ denotes the second order partial derivative.

Figure 14.11 Ito's Lemma and Volatility

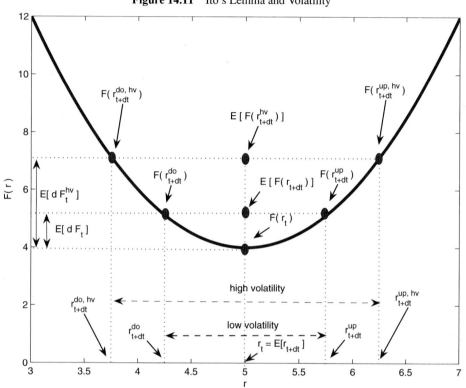

is multiplied by the variance of the interest rate process itself $s(r_t, t)^2$. This is intuitive: The higher the volatility of the interest rate, the higher are the gains from convexity, as the interest rate will move further away (up or down) from its current level. For instance, if the interest rate does not have a stochastic variation, i.e., $s(r_t, t)^2 = 0$, then there is no convexity effect.[8] Figure 14.11 illustrates this point. In addition to the interest rate movements already discussed in Figure 14.8, note the interest rate realizations further away from the initial rate $r_t = 5\%$, namely $r_{t+dt}^{up,hv} = 6.25\%$ and $r_{t+dt}^{do,hv} = 3.75\%$, where the superscript "hv" stands for "high volatility." It is logical to conclude from the figure that the expected change in the function $F(r)$ under the high volatility scenario is larger than in the case with low volatility. It follows that the expected capital gain return should be higher the higher the volatility. This explains why the second partial derivative in Equation 14.41 is multiplied by the variance of interest rates $s(r_t, t)^2$.

14.5 ILLUSTRATIVE EXAMPLES

In this section we look at some examples of the application of Ito's lemma and its usefulness for risk management.

---

[8]Note that even if there is no stochastic variation, the interest rate may be moving deterministically, as shown in Example 14.3. This variation does not generate a convexity effect, but it does generate expected gains / losses from the expected changes in interest rate, i.e., through the term $\left(\frac{\partial F}{\partial r}\right) m(r_t, t)$.

■ **EXAMPLE 14.7**

Bond Prices in the Driftless Ho-Lee Model

Consider the driftless Ho-Lee interest rate model in Example 14.1. As we will see in Chapter 19, if the current interest rate is r_t, the price at time t of a zero coupon bond with maturity time T is given by[9]

$$P_t = e^{\frac{\sigma^2}{6}(T-t)^3 - (T-t)r_t} \tag{14.42}$$

We will return to the source of this equation in Chapter 19. For now, let's believe the bond pricing formula in Equation 14.42, and let's ask the following question: How does the variation in interest rates affect bond prices? This question is important as investors buying long-term bonds want to know what type of market risk they are exposed to. Ito's lemma provides the answer to this question. In this case, the function of time t and interest rate r is given by

$$F(t,r) = e^{\frac{\sigma^2}{6}(T-t)^3 - (T-t)r_t}$$

The first derivative with respect to time t is

$$\frac{\partial F}{\partial t} = \left(-\frac{\sigma^2}{2}(T-t)^2 + r_t\right) F(t,r)$$

The first derivative with respect to r is

$$\frac{\partial F}{\partial r} = -(T-t)F(t,r)$$

The second derivative with respect to r is

$$\frac{\partial^2 F}{\partial r^2} = (T-t)^2 F(t,r)$$

We now find the capital gain process for the bond by substituting these expressions in Ito's lemma (Equation 14.41). Note that in this case, we have $m(r,t) = 0$ and $s(r,t) = \sigma$ (compare Equation 14.15 to Equation 14.40). Substituting yields the following expression for the capital gain process:

$$dP_t = \left\{\left(\frac{\partial F}{\partial t}\right) + \left(\frac{\partial F}{\partial r}\right)m(r_t,t) + \frac{1}{2}\left(\frac{\partial^2 F}{\partial r^2}\right)s(r_t,t)^2\right\}dt + \left(\frac{\partial F}{\partial r}\right)s(r_t,t)dX_t$$

$$= \left\{\left(-\frac{\sigma^2}{2}(T-t)^2 + r_t\right)F(t,r) + \frac{1}{2}(T-t)^2 F(t,r)\sigma^2\right\}dt - (T-t)F(t,r)\sigma dX_t$$

This expression is not nice. We can simplify it, though, by recalling that $P_t = F(t,r_t)$. Substituting again in the last expression, we see that the process for the bonds' capital gain return is given by:

$$dP_t = r_t P_t dt - (T-t)P_t \sigma dX_t \tag{14.43}$$

[9]The formula in Equation 14.42 follows under the assumption that the Ho-Lee process in Equation 14.15 is the risk neutral interest rate process, as discussed in Chapter 17.

That is, if the interest rate follows the driftless Ho-Lee process in Equation 14.15 and the bond pricing formula is given by Equation 14.42, then the capital gain return process is given by (14.43). In particular, by dividing both sides by P_t, we obtain the process for bond returns expressed in percentage returns:

$$\frac{dP_t}{P_t} = r_t dt - (T - t)\sigma dX_t \tag{14.44}$$

We obtain the following facts:

1. The expected return on the long-term bond is equal to the instantaneous risk free rate:

$$\text{Expected return} = E\left[\frac{dP_t}{P_t}\right] = r_t\, dt \tag{14.45}$$

2. The volatility of the bond is proportional to the time to maturity of the bond:

$$\text{Volatility} = \sqrt{E\left[\left(\frac{dP_t}{P_t}\right)^2\right]} = (T - t)\,\sigma \tag{14.46}$$

3. The covariance between changes in interest rates and bond returns is negative:

$$\text{Covariance} = E\left[\frac{dP_t}{P_t} \times dr_t\right] = -(T - t)\,\sigma^2 dt \tag{14.47}$$

The first property says that under the assumptions of this model, long-term bonds should yield the same rate of return as an investment in the short-term bonds. Indeed, the right-hand side of Equation 14.45 does not depend on time to maturity $T - t$. The second property shows that the volatility of bond returns depends instead on maturity, as longer-term bonds have a higher volatility than short-term bonds. This volatility also depends on the volatility of interest rates σ. If σ is small, i.e., the short-term interest rate r_t is not very volatile, it follows that long-term bonds should not be volatile. Finally, the last property shows that the covariance between interest rates and bond prices is negative. This is intuitive, as an increase in the short-term interest rate tend to decrease bond prices, from first principles.

The knowledge of the sensitivity of bond prices to variation in interest rates is important for numerous reasons, such as risk analysis and risk management. For instance, consider a bond portfolio manager with a large position in 10-year zero coupon bonds. Let the volatility of interest rate be $\sigma = 2\%$. Under the model for interest rates in Equation 14.15 and thus the bond pricing formula in Equation 14.42, the volatility of the bond position is $(T - t)\sigma = 10 \times 2\% = 20\%$.

■ **EXAMPLE 14.8**

Term Structure Movement in the Driftless Ho-Lee Model

How does the term structure of interest rates move over time according to the Ho-Lee model in Example 14.1? Denote the long-term continuously compounded interest rate with *time to maturity* $\tau = T - t$ as $r_t(\tau)$. Then, from Equation 14.42 and the definition of continuously compounded interest rate we have

$$r_t(\tau) = -\frac{\ln(P_t(T))}{T-t} = -\frac{\sigma^2}{6}\tau^2 + r_t \tag{14.48}$$

How does this long-term interest rate move over time? For instance, if $\tau = 10$, how does the 10-year yield change over time according to the model? Because in this case we want to keep the time to maturity τ fixed, we can answer this question by an application of Ito's lemma. In fact, we have in this case that

$$F(r) = -\frac{\sigma^2}{6}\tau^2 + r_t$$

Thus,

$$\frac{\partial F}{\partial t} = 0; \quad \frac{\partial F}{\partial r} = 1; \quad \frac{\partial^2 F}{\partial r^2} = 0$$

Applying the formula in Equation 14.41, we obtain

$$dr_t(\tau) = \sigma dX_t \tag{14.49}$$

That is, the changes in long-term yields are identical to the changes in short-term yields, as the right-hand side of Equation 14.49 also equals dr_t. In other words, the model produces parallel shifts in the term structure of interest rates, providing substance to the duration approach to risk management discussed in Chapter 3. However, this property also demonstrates the shortcoming of the driftless Ho-Lee model, as we know from Chapter 4 that the term structure of interest rates does not move only in a parallel fashion. We will consider more elaborate models in subsequent chapters.

■ **EXAMPLE 14.9**

Hedging with Futures

Consider the risk manager in Example 14.7. Consider a futures contract on the 3-month rate $r_t(\tau)$, where $\tau = 0.25 = 3$ months. Let T be the maturity of the futures contract, and denote by f_t the futures rate. Given the process in Equation 14.49 for the 3-month interest rate, it is intuitive that the process for the futures is also given by

$$df_t = \sigma dX_t \tag{14.50}$$

The manager with a position in 10-year bonds can then hedge its interest rate risk by taking an appropriate position in futures. Consider a position N in futures, and let Π_t define the portfolio that is long the bonds and with N futures. The change in value between t and $t + dt$ in the portfolio will equal the change in value in the long term bonds dP_t plus N times the change in value of the futures df_t. That is

$$d\Pi_t = dP_t + N \times df_t$$

Using the expressions for dP_t in Equation 14.43 and df_t in Equation 14.50 we obtain

$$d\Pi_t = r_t P_t dt - (T - t) P_t \sigma dX_t + N \times \sigma dX_t$$

It follows that to eliminate any stochastic variation dX_t from the portfolio, we must choose

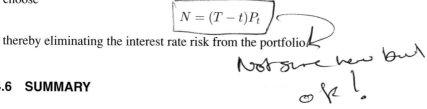

$$N = (T - t)P_t$$

thereby eliminating the interest rate risk from the portfolio.

14.6 SUMMARY

In this chapter we covered the following topics:

1. Brownian motion: This is a stochastic variable that evolves over time in a very erratic manner. The best prediction of its value at any time in the future is its value today. The statistical distribution of its difference between any two points in time t_1 and $t_2 > t_1$ is normal, with mean zero and variance equal to $t_2 - t_1$. Within any two points in times, no matter how close to each other, there are an infinite number (in the limit) of realizations of a binomially distributed variable.

2. Differential equation: A differential equation relates the rate of change of a variable to its current value. The solution is a function of time that satisfies both an initial condition as well as the equation itself. A differential equation can be considered a special process, in which the future value of the variable is perfectly predictable, as it is a function of time.

3. Stochastic processes: While on the one hand Brownian motions are erratic and their change over time unpredictable, and on the other hand differential equations imply perfectly predictable process, the reality is in the middle of these two extremes. Continuous time stochastic processes have an element of predictability (the "dt" component, called drift) and an element of randomness (the "dX" component, called diffusion).

4. The Vasicek model of interest rates: This is a widely known model for the variation of interest rate. It postulates that interest rates are mean reverting, which means that if they diverge too much from a central value they tend to revert back to it. The speed at which the interest rate reverts back to the mean depends on the model's parameters. Random (Brownian) shocks make the interest rate move away from the central value, but the drift pulls the interest rate back. The model implies that the statistical distribution of interest rates in the future is normal. This implies that there is always a (possibly small) chance of negative interest rates, a drawback of the model.

5. The Ho-Lee model: It is the continuous time version of the model studied in Chapter 11. It is similar to the Vasicek model, except for its drift term, which depends only on time. As with the Vasicek model, the statistical distribution of the interest rate in the future is normal, which implies a positive probability of negative interest rates. Unlike the Vasicek model, the dispersion of this statistical distribution diverges to infinity as we consider the far future.

6. Ito's lemma: Ito's lemma provides an equation that relates the change in the value of a function $F(X)$ of a Brownian motion X_t to its changes dX_t. The key result is

that the variation of a function of a Brownian motion has two components: First, an *unpredictable* component that depends on the sensitivity of the function to changes in X_t, i.e., its first derivative (dF/dX). Second, a *predictable* component that depends on the convexity of the function $F(X)$ with respect to X. Ito's lemma is useful in finance as it provides the rules to compute:

(a) The expected change in value of interest rate securities (e.g., the expected capital gain $E[dP_t]$);

(b) The volatility of interest rate security prices induced by variation in interest rates;

(c) The hedge ratios needed for interest rate risk management;

(d) The expected gains from convexity that occurs due to the random variation of interest rates.

In addition to the basic case, we saw two additional versions of Ito's lemma:

(a) Time dependence: The function $F(t, X)$ may depend on time. For instance, most interest rate securities have a time-to-maturity that affects the value of the security even if nothing changes in the random variable X.

(b) Interest rate processes: The function $F(t, r)$ is a function of the underlying interest rate process r instead of the Brownian motion X. In this case, the amount of convexity return depends on the volatility of interest rates (term $(\partial^2 F/\partial r^2)\, s(r, t)^2$ in Ito's lemma). For instance, high volatility tends to generate high capital gains from convexity. In addition, the expected capital gain depends also on the expected change in interest rates (term $(\partial F/\partial r)\, m(r, t)$ in Ito's lemma). For instance, an expected increase in Fed funds rate implies an expected capital loss in a bond portfolio.

14.7 EXERCISES

1. Use a spreadsheet program, such as Microsoft Excel, to replicate Figures 14.1, 14.2 and 14.3.

2. Consider the Ho Lee model on trees in equations (14.1) and (14.2), and the Ho–Lee model in continuous time in equation (14.29). Assume $\theta_t = 0$ in both. In the previous exercise, you simulated the Ho Lee model on the tree and obtained the equivalent of Figure 14.3. In this exercise, you have to simulate the Continuous Time Ho Lee model and replicate the same Figure. In particular, for each time step dt, you have to simulate the realization of the Brownian motion $dX_t \sim \mathcal{N}(0, dt)$ (see (14.13)), and then use the approximation

$$r_{t+dt} = r_t + \sigma dX_t$$

How can you simulate a Normal distribution? One of four methods:

(a) Most spreadsheet programs have the normal distribution random variable generator. Just use it.

(b) Use the definition of X_t in (14.4). That is, $X_t = \sum_{i=1}^{m} Z_i$ where $Z_i = \sqrt{dt}$ or $Z_i = -\sqrt{dt}$ with equal probabilities. See Chapter 13 to see how to simulate a variable that can take only two values.

(c) Invert the normal distribution. Most spreadsheet program can simulate a uniform (e.g. RAND() in Microsoft Excel). From a uniformly simulated variable u_i one can obtain a normally distributed variable ϵ_i from

$$\epsilon_i = N^{-1}(u_i)$$

where $N^{-1}(u)$ is the inverse of the cumulative normal distribution, also available in most program (e.g. NORMINV() in Microsoft Excel).

(d) Use the central limit theorem. Simulate n uniform variables u_i, $i = 1, ..., n$. Each uniform has mean 1/2 and variance 1/12. Thus, the normalized variable $\widehat{u}_i = (u_i - 1/2)\sqrt{12}$ has mean 0 and variance 1 (why?). It follows that for large n (but $n = 12$ is already enough), approximately:

$$\epsilon = \frac{1}{n}\sum_{i=1}^{n} \widehat{u}_i \sim \mathcal{N}(0, 1)$$

This computation tends to be faster than inverting the normal distribution.

Use any of these methodologies (or all of them) and replicate Figure 14.3. Compare your results with those in the previous exercise.

3. Use a spreadsheet program to verify that Equation 14.24 is indeed the solution to (14.23). In order to do so, solve "numerically" (14.23) as follows:

(a) Choose a small time interval dt, two parameters γ and $\bar{r}$, and a starting value $r(0)$ (e.g. 2%).

(b) Compute recursively $r(t + dt) \approx r(t) + \gamma(\bar{r} - r(t))dt$.

(c) Verify that for every time t, the computed value from the recursion is similar to the value you would obtain from the solution (14.24).

(d) How does your answer to the previous point depend on the interval size dt? Discuss

4. Consider the Vasicek model of interest rate

$$dr_t = \gamma(\bar{r} - r_t)dt + \sigma dX_t$$

Let $\bar{r} = 5\%$. Do the following:

(a) Let r_0 be the short term interest rate today (you can find this value on any financial newspaper, or on the Federal Reserve Web site *http://www.federalreserve.gov/releases/h15/data.htm*). Choose a small "dt" (e.g. $dt = 1/252 = 1$ day) and simulate the process over a 5 year period for various choices of γ and σ. Plot the results. How does the process depend on these two parameters? (See exercise 2 on how to simulate $dX_t \sim \mathcal{N}(0, dt)$.)

(b) Fix γ and σ, and simulate the process over a 5 year period for various choices of the initial condition r_0. How does the process depend on the initial condition?

5. Consider the Vasicek model of interest rates. Download daily data on the one-month T-bill rate from the Federal Reserve web site (*http://www.federalreserve.gov/releases/ h15/data.htm*) and use these data to estimate γ, $\bar{r}$ and σ. This estimation can be accomplished through a linear regression. Take literally $dt = 1/252 = 1$ day and "discretize" the process into

$$(r_{t+dt} - r_t) = \gamma(\bar{r} - r_t)dt + \epsilon_{t+dt}$$

where $\epsilon_{t+dt} \sim \mathcal{N}(0, \sigma^2 dt)$. This looks similar to a regression

$$(r_{t+dt} - r_t) = \alpha + \beta r_t + \epsilon_{t+dt}$$

(a) What are α and β in terms of the original parameters γ and $\bar{r}$? How can you estimate σ? Be careful with the "annualization" (your data are daily, but we need to be "annualized"). Also, recall that r_t in the Vasicek model is a continuosly compounded rate.

(b) Given your parameter estimates, and the current rate today, perform a forecast of the future interest rate as of today. Extend your forecast up to 5 years in the future.

(c) Use simulations to perform a scenario analysis about the future possible interest rates. Compute the histogram of the interest rates in 1, 3, and 5 years from now and compare it to your forecasted value.

6. Use Ito's Lemma to compute the law of motion of $P = F(X)$, where X is a Brownian motion, and $F(X)$ given by

(a) $F(X) = A + BX$ where A, B are two constants.

(b) $F(X) = e^{A+BX}$ where A, B are two constants.

7. Let r follows the process

$$dr_t = \gamma(\bar{r} - r_t)dt + \sigma dX_t$$

Use Ito's Lemma to compute the law of motion of $P = F(r)$, for $F(X)$ given by

(a) $F(r) = A + B\,r$ where A, B are two constants.

(b) $F(r) = e^{A - B\,r}$ where A, B are two constants, and $B > 0$.

8. In the previous exercise,

(a) Compute the expected capital gain return $E[dP]$ and decompose it into its components.

(b) Compute the "diffusion" of the security σ. Is this parameter positive or negative? How does it relate to the volatility (i.e. the standard deviation) of the security P?

14.8 APPENDIX: RULES OF STOCHASTIC CALCULUS

When computing the prices of securities and applying Ito's Lemma, some "rules" of calculus are useful. In particular, the following are important:

$$E[dX] = 0 \tag{14.51}$$

$$E[dX^2] = dt \tag{14.52}$$

$$Var[dX] = E[dX^2] - \{E[dX]\}^2 = dt \tag{14.53}$$

$$E[dX \times dt] = E[dX]\,dt = 0 \tag{14.54}$$

$$Var\left[(dX)^2\right] = E\left[(dX)^4\right] - E\left[(dX)^2\right]^2 = 3dt^2 - dt^2 = 0 \tag{14.55}$$

$$E\left[(dXdt)^2\right] = E\left[(dX)^2\right]dt^2 = 0 \tag{14.56}$$

$$Var\,(dXdt) = E\left[(dXdt)^2\right] - E\,[dXdt]^2 = 0 \tag{14.57}$$

The important insight is that any computation that leads to a term that is proportional to $(dt)^a$ where $a > 1$ implies that this term is zero. The reason, recall, is that the Brownian motion is obtained in the limit as $\Delta = t/n$ decreases to zero. In our notation, $\Delta \longrightarrow dt$, where dt denotes an infinitesimal interval of time. Clearly, Δ^2, for instance, would converge to zero much faster than Δ, yielding the property that $dt^2 = 0$ in Equation 14.55, for instance. The same is true for any case in which a term in $(dt)^a$ appears, with $a > 1$.

CHAPTER 15

NO ARBITRAGE AND THE PRICING OF INTEREST RATE SECURITIES

In this chapter we illustrate the key steps in the derivation of prices of interest rate securities, including Treasury bonds and derivative instruments. The key is to impose the understanding that financial markets do not leave arbitrage opportunities available for arbitrageurs. Why is this approach useful? It provides constraints that have to be satisfied if there are no arbitrage opportunities left on the table. Sometimes frictions prevent market prices from moving in a way to eliminate arbitrage opportunities, and thus an arbitrageur can step in, set up a trade, and make arbitrage profits. The way an arbitrageur can detect the presence of an arbitrage opportunity is by checking the difference between market prices and the ones dictated by no arbitrage rules. If the discrepancy is large, it means that an arbitrage is potentially feasible. Of course, this procedure is based on the arbitrageur's faith in his or her own model used to detect the presence of the arbitrage opportunity. That is to say, what could be deemed an arbitrage opportunity in one model may not be an arbitrage opportunity according to another model. Because reality is much more complex than what a model can describe, models provide guidance in setting up arbitrage strategies, but some error margin may still exist.

Even so, using a model to decide the feasibility of an arbitrage trade is a key step. A model determines the feasibility of a trade opportunity, defines the trading strategy that is required to exploit it, and yields a prediction on profits. Models are as important also for risk management: A model determines the sensitivities of interest rate securities to variation in interest rates and other factors that affect bond prices.

In this chapter we mainly focus on the Vasicek model to illustrate the methodology. The same methodology, however, can be applied to other models, and we will review the more general case at the end of the chapter. The methodology we use is the same that we applied in Chapter 11 when we considered interest rate trees. On a tree, recall, as the interest rate moves from one step to another, it induces changes in all of the interest rate securities prices. By studying the sensitivity of such securities to interest rate changes, we can impose a no arbitrage relation by determining a long-short portfolio. We use the same methodology here.

We begin with a simple case to illustrate the no arbitrage methodology.

15.1   BOND PRICING WITH DETERMINISTIC INTEREST RATE

Consider again Example 14.3 in Chapter 14. In that example, we assume that the short-term interest rate r_t moves according to the following process

$$dr_t = \gamma(\bar{r} - r_t)dt \tag{15.1}$$

Recall that r_t is the rate at which one arbitrageur can borrow or lend cash for the period between t and $t + dt$. Given that most of these transactions are made through the repo market, we can heuristically identify r_t in fact with the overnight repo rate (see Chapter 1). Note that Equation 15.1 is the special case of the Vasicek model in Equation 14.28 with $\sigma = 0$. Consider now a zero coupon bond that yields \$1 at maturity T. The price of this security must depend on the current short-term interest rate r_t and time to maturity T, and nothing else, because our model, so far, considers only the interest rate r_t as unique determinant of the price of securities. In later chapters we will consider additional factors that move long-term bonds. But for now, we assume that r_t is the only factor influencing the dynamics of prices. Let us denote the price of this security by $Z(r_t, t; T)$. Given that the short-term interest rate r_t moves according to Equation 15.1, what is the price of this zero coupon bond?

First of all, we should ask the following question: Is this zero coupon bond risky at all? Because $Z(r_t, t; T)$ only depends on the interest rate r_t and time t and both are fully forecastable variables (with no random variation and thus no risk), this zero coupon bond also must be risk free. The meaning "risk free" here indicates the fact that from our perfect forecast of interest rates we can perfectly forecast the change in value of $Z(r_t, t; T)$ between t and $t + dt$. If this security is risk free, then *no arbitrage* implies that its rate of return between t and $t + dt$ must be just the risk free rate r_t itself. Recalling that the notation dZ_t indicates the capital gain dollar return between t and $t + dt$, i.e., $dZ_t = Z_{t+dt} - Z_t$, the *rate* of return between t and $t + dt$ of a long position in this security is given by dZ_t/Z_t. Thus, we have the following:

$$\text{No arbitrage} \Longrightarrow \frac{dZ_t}{Z_t} = r_t dt \tag{15.2}$$

In fact, if the equality in Equation 15.2 were not true, then an arbitrage opportunity would obtain. For instance, consider the two other possibilities:

1. $dZ_t/Z_t > r_t dt$. Then, an arbitrageur at t can

    (a) borrow Z_t dollars at the risk free rate r_t (e.g., in the repo market);

    (b) buy one unit of the security for Z_t dollars.

    At t there is no cash outlay, but at $t + dt$ the arbitrageur would make $dZ_t/Z_t - r_t dt > 0$ without risk whatsoever.

2. $dZ/Z < r_t dt$. Then, an arbitrageur at t can

    (a) borrow the security (e.g., in the repo market) and short it in the market, receiving Z_t dollars;

    (b) invest the proceeds from the short sale (Z_t dollars) at the risk free rate r_t.

    At t there is no cash outlay, but at $t + dt$, the arbitrageur would make $r_t dt - dZ_t/Z_t > 0$.

The no arbitrage restriction in Equation 15.2 provides us with the price of the bond. In fact, the condition $dZ_t/Z_t = r_t dt$ can be rewritten as

$$dZ_t = r Z_t dt, \tag{15.3}$$

which defines a particular equation for $Z(t; T)$, an equation that we can solve. We provide further details on the equation and the solution below. For now, we note that the solution to Equation 15.3 is given by the following:

Fact 15.1 *Let $\sigma = 0$ in the Vasicek model. Then, no arbitrage implies that the price of a zero coupon bond with \$1 principal at time t with maturity date T when the short-term interest rate is r_t, is given by*

$$Z(r_t, t; T) = e^{A(t;T) - B(t;T) r_t} \tag{15.4}$$

[handwritten: points I don't understand.]

where

$$B(t; T) = \frac{1}{\gamma}\left(1 - e^{-\gamma(T-t)}\right)$$

$$A(t; T) = \bar{r}\left(B(t; T) - (T - t)\right)$$

[handwritten: less of an impact if $r_t \ne \bar{r}$ as $\gamma \to 0$]

Note that $A(t; T)$ and $B(t; T)$ are only functions of time t and they converge to zero at t approaches maturity T. That is, $A(T; T) = 0$ and $B(T; T) = 0$. This implies that indeed at maturity, the value of the zero coupon bond is exactly equal to \$1 independently of the interest rate r_T:

[handwritten: as $T-t$ approaches 0]

$$Z(r_T, T; T) = e^{0 - 0 \times r_T} = 1. \tag{15.5}$$

[handwritten: $\ge 1 \ldots e^0 = 1$]

Moreover, the formula in Equation 15.4 is intuitive: First, because $B(t; T) > 0$, a higher interest rate r_t implies a lower bond price. Second, if $r_t = \bar{r}$, i.e., the interest rate already converged to $\bar{r}$, then the price of the bond reverts back to the standard formula $Z(r_t, t; T) = e^{-\bar{r}(T-t)}$. Finally, as discussed further below, the longer it takes the interest rate r_t to converge to the long-term mean $\bar{r}$, the higher is the impact of the difference $\bar{r} - r_t$ on the bond prices: If $r_t > \bar{r}$, the price is lower the lower γ is, while the opposite is true if $r_t < \bar{r}$.

The key question at this point is how do we know that Equation 15.4 is the solution to Equation 15.3? As we did in Chapter 14, Section 14.2, we have to check that the solution in Equation 15.4 *satisfies* the differential equation in Equation 15.3. That is, if we compute dZ_t on the left-hand side we should get the right-hand side. We can compute dZ_t using Ito's Lemma 3 in Fact 14.6, with $m(r_t, t) = \gamma(\bar{r} - r_t)$ and $s(r, t) = 0$. In this case, Ito's Lemma reduces to

$$dZ_t = \left(\frac{\partial Z}{\partial t} + \frac{\partial Z}{\partial r}\gamma(\bar{r} - r_t) \right) dt$$

Substituting on the left-hand side, Equation 15.3 becomes[1]

$$\frac{\partial Z}{\partial t} + \frac{\partial Z}{\partial r}\gamma\left(\bar{r} - r\right) = rZ \tag{15.6}$$

This is a **partial differential equation** (PDE), that is, a differential equation on many variables (r and t). As any differential equation, a *solution* to the differential equation (Equation 15.6) is a function of r and t such that: (i) If we take the derivatives on the left-hand side we get the right-hand side (i.e. $r \times Z$); (ii) It satisfies some boundary condition, such as $Z(r, T; T) = 1$.

We therefore need to check that indeed the proposed solution in Equation 15.4 satisfies Equation 15.6. This exercise is carried out in the appendix at the end of the chapter.

The main message of this section, however, is the following: Imposing the no arbitrage condition (Equation 15.2) we obtain an (differential) equation for the interest rate security (Equation 15.6) whose solution yields the value of the interest rate security itself. That is, schematically:

1. No arbitrage $\Longrightarrow$ partial differential equation

2. Solution to partial differential equation $\Longrightarrow$ Price of interest rate security

We will see that the same principle applies for more complicated models.

In addition to the price of the interest rate security, the model's solution yields a measure of the sensitivity of the interest rate security to changes in the interest rate, a quantity we call spot rate duration in Chapter 10. This is given by

$$D_Z = -\frac{1}{Z}\frac{\partial Z}{\partial r} \tag{15.7}$$

In this case, we obtain $\frac{\partial Z}{\partial r} = -B(t; T)Z$, which implies that the spot rate duration is

$$D_Z = B(t; T) = \frac{1}{\gamma}\left(1 - e^{-\gamma(T-t)}\right) \tag{15.8}$$

That is, the sensitivity of the zero coupon bond with respect to the interest rate is increasing in time to maturity $T - t$ and decreasing in the speed of mean reversion γ. Interpreting γ as the speed of adjustment of interest rates toward the long-run mean $\bar{r}$, the faster the adjustment takes place, the lower is the sensitivity of bond prices to changes in interest rates. Although in this section the short-term interest rate moves over time deterministically, and so the spot rate duration is not really a measure of risk (there is no risk), it turns out that the same spot rate duration holds also for the case in which interest rates are stochastic, to which we now turn.

---

[1]Because this equation has to hold for every interest rate r_t and every time t, there is no need to keep the time notation on the interest rate r_t.

15.2 INTEREST RATE SECURITY PRICING IN THE VASICEK MODEL

The Vasicek model of interest rates is

$$dr_t = \gamma(\bar{r} - r_t)dt + \sigma dX_t \tag{15.9}$$

Consider an interest rate security, whose price we denote again as $Z(r, t; T)$. Because r is moving stochastically over time, then also $Z(r, t; T)$ will move stochastically. That is, the interest rate security is risky. Therefore, it is no longer true that its rate of return has to equal the risk free rate $r_t dt$ during a short interval $[t, t + dt]$. Risk averse investors now want to be compensated to bear the risk of holding the security. Note that the term "risk" here means "capital gain risk" and not "default risk": If $Z(r, t; T)$ is a zero coupon Treasury security, for instance, then holding it until maturity will provide the investor with the riskless amount equal to \$1. However, while the investor waits until maturity T, a sudden increase in the short-term interest rate may generate capital losses on the bond. Because of this, the investment in a Treasury security is risky.

How can we determine the riskiness of the security? Ito's lemma in Equation 14.41 in Chapter 14 gives us a formula for it. We now have

$$dZ_t = \left\{ \left(\frac{\partial Z}{\partial t}\right) + \left(\frac{\partial Z}{\partial r}\right)\gamma(\bar{r} - r_t) + \frac{1}{2}\left(\frac{\partial^2 Z}{\partial r^2}\right)\sigma^2 \right\} dt + \left(\frac{\partial Z}{\partial r}\right)\sigma dX_t \tag{15.10}$$

Unfortunately, until we impose additional conditions – such as the no arbitrage condition – we cannot say more than this about the price of the interest rate security $Z(r, t; T)$. In fact, because Z_t is now a risky security, we have no way to pin down its value, without additional information. However, if we consider more than one security at a time, in fact two securities in this case, then we may be able to construct a portfolio that is immune to stochastic changes in interest rates. This portfolio would then be risk free and thus we can apply the no arbitrage argument used in Section 15.1.

15.2.1 The Long / Short Portfolio

Consider a portfolio with two zero-coupon bonds. For instance, long one unit of a short-term bond with maturity *date* T_1 and short Δ units of a long-term bond with maturity *date* $T_2 > T_1$. Let $Z_1(r, t)$ and $Z_2(r, t)$ be the two prices for the T_1 and T_2 maturity dates, at time t when the current interest rate is r. Let's denote the value of this portfolio by Π. The value of the portfolio Π at time t is then

$$\Pi(r, t) = Z_1(r, t) - \Delta Z_2(r, t) \tag{15.11}$$

We now choose Δ to make this portfolio insensitive to changes in interest rates, that is, riskless. In particular, we want to choose Δ so that the sensitivity of portfolio Π to changes in interest rate r_t is equal to zero:

$$\frac{\partial \Pi(r, t)}{\partial r} = 0 \tag{15.12}$$

From the definition of the portfolio (Equation 15.11), the equality in Equation 15.12 implies

$$\frac{\partial Z_1(r, t)}{\partial r} - \Delta \frac{\partial Z_2(r, t)}{\partial r} = 0 \tag{15.13}$$

This equation yields the hedging strategy:

$$\Delta = \frac{\partial Z_1/\partial r}{\partial Z_2/\partial r} \tag{15.14}$$

The hedging strategy is intuitive: If we are long the bond with maturity T_1, then we must short the bond with maturity T_2 according to the relative sensitivity of each bond to changes in interest rates.

What is the process for the "hedged" portfolio between t and $t + dt$? Ito's lemma in Equation 14.41 in Chapter 14 gives the answer:

$$d\Pi_t = \left\{ \left(\frac{\partial \Pi}{\partial t}\right) + \left(\frac{\partial \Pi}{\partial r}\right) \gamma(\bar{r} - r_t) + \frac{1}{2}\left(\frac{\partial^2 \Pi}{\partial r^2}\right)\sigma^2 \right\} dt + \left(\frac{\partial \Pi}{\partial r}\right)\sigma dX_t \tag{15.15}$$

Because of the hedging strategy in Equation 15.14, though, we have from Equation 15.12 that $\partial \Pi/\partial r = 0$. This term enters both in the drift and in the diffusion term of Equation 15.15, which then becomes

$$d\Pi_t = \left\{ \left(\frac{\partial \Pi}{\partial t}\right) + \frac{1}{2}\left(\frac{\partial^2 \Pi}{\partial r^2}\right)\sigma^2 \right\} dt \tag{15.16}$$

The portfolio Π is now riskless, in the sense that between t and $t + dt$ there is no random shock that affects the value of this portfolio, as we hedged it away. As in Section 15.1, the no arbitrage principle implies that the portfolio Π must now earn the risk free rate r_t between t and $t + dt$. As before, we now have

$$\text{No arbitrage} \implies \frac{d\Pi_t}{\Pi_t} = r_t dt \tag{15.17}$$

This no arbitrage condition provides us with an equation whose solution is the solution of the bond. In fact, multiplying both sides on Equation 15.17 by Π and substituting the right-hand side of Equation 15.16 for $d\Pi$, we obtain

$$\frac{\partial \Pi}{\partial t} + \frac{1}{2}\frac{\partial^2 \Pi}{\partial r^2}\sigma^2 = r_t \Pi_t \tag{15.18}$$

From the definition of $\Pi_t = Z_{1,t} - \Delta Z_{2,t}$ we have

$$\frac{\partial \Pi}{\partial t} = \frac{\partial Z_1}{\partial t} - \Delta\frac{\partial Z_2}{\partial t} \tag{15.19}$$

$$\frac{\partial^2 \Pi}{\partial r^2} = \frac{\partial^2 Z_1}{\partial r^2} - \Delta\frac{\partial^2 Z_2}{\partial r^2} \tag{15.20}$$

Substitute on the left-hand side and on the right-hand side of (15.18), and move all the "1" terms to the left-hand side and the "2" terms to the right-hand side, to find

$$\left(\frac{\partial Z_1}{\partial t} + \frac{1}{2}\frac{\partial^2 Z_1}{\partial r^2}\sigma^2 - r_t Z_1\right) = \Delta\left(\frac{\partial Z_2}{\partial t} + \frac{1}{2}\frac{\partial^2 Z_2}{\partial r^2}\sigma^2 - r_t Z_2\right) \tag{15.21}$$

Use finally

$$\Delta = \frac{\partial Z_1/\partial r}{\partial Z_2/\partial r}$$

for all rates

and rearrange to find

$$\frac{\left(\frac{\partial Z_1}{\partial t} + \frac{1}{2}\frac{\partial^2 Z_1}{\partial r^2}\sigma^2 - r_t Z_1\right)}{\partial Z_1/\partial r} = \frac{\left(\frac{\partial Z_2}{\partial t} + \frac{1}{2}\frac{\partial^2 Z_2}{\partial r^2}\sigma^2 - r_t Z_2\right)}{\partial Z_2/\partial r} \tag{15.22}$$

This is the key relation across interest rate securities that stems from the no arbitrage condition (Equation 15.17). In particular, we see that the formulas on the left-hand side and on the right-hand side of the equality are identical, but applied to two different bonds. To interpret the ratio that appears on each side of the equality, recall the following facts:

1. $(\partial Z_i/\partial t)$ = Annualized dollar capital gain (or loss) due to the passage of time.

2. $\frac{1}{2}\left(\partial^2 Z_i/\partial r^2\right)\sigma^2$ = Annualized dollar capital gain (or loss) due to convexity and the stochastic nature of interest rates.

3. $r_t Z_i$ = Annualized dollar interest payment in order to borrow the value Z_i to purchase the bond.

4. $(\partial Z_i/\partial r)$ = Annualized sensitivity of the bond price to change in the interest rate.

The numerator of each of the expressions in Equation 15.22 gives the annualized capital gain return due to the passage of time or convexity of a leveraged position in the security. The denominator provides the "risk" of the long position in the security, expressed in terms of its sensitivity to changes in interest rates.

15.2.1.1 An Important Missing Term
One important term that *does not* appear on either side of Equation 15.22 is the *drift rate* of the interest rate process. That is, the term $E[dr_t] = \gamma\left(\bar{r} - r_t\right)dt$ does not enter at all in the no arbitrage restriction: Whether we predict the interest rate to rise or decline, the restriction remains identical. Where did we lose this term? Comparing Equations 15.15 and 15.16, the drift rate of the interest rate process disappeared because of the hedging strategy $\partial\Pi/\partial r = 0$. Intuitively, if we are hedging a long position in $Z_1(t, r)$ with a short position in $Z_2(t, r)$, our prediction of the interest rate movement has an impact on $Z_1(t, r)$ that is exactly counterbalanced by its impact on $Z_2(t, r)$. In other words, the hedging strategy not only hedges the unpredictable changes in the interest rate (i.e., σdX_t) but also its predictable part (i.e., $E[dr_t] = \gamma(\bar{r} - r)dt$).

hedging gets rid of all risk

15.2.1.2 Other Interest Rate Securities
Note that up to now, nothing in the derivations really hinged on the fact that $Z(r, t; T)$ was a zero coupon bond. In fact, we can do all of the steps above thinking of Z_1 as a zero coupon bond and Z_2 as an interest rate option, for instance. All of the results would go through. In particular, such an interest rate option would also satisfy Equation 15.22. That is, *all* interest rate securities must satisfy Equation 15.22.

15.2.2 The Fundamental Pricing Equation

Because all interest rate securities must satisfy Equation 15.22, we can give a name to this common value. That is, for every interest rate security with generic price $Z(r, t; T)$, we must have:

$$\frac{\left(\frac{\partial Z}{\partial t} + \frac{1}{2}\frac{\partial^2 Z}{\partial r^2}\sigma^2 - r_t Z\right)}{\partial Z/\partial r} = -m^*(r, t) \tag{15.23}$$

where $m^*(r, t)$ is some function of the interest rate and possibly time, which is common across *all* the interest rate securities. The negative sign in front of $m^*(r, t)$ is for convenience only, so that we can rewrite this equation as:

$$\frac{\partial Z}{\partial t} + \frac{\partial Z}{\partial r} m^*(r, t) + \frac{1}{2} \frac{\partial^2 Z}{\partial r^2} \sigma^2 = rZ \tag{15.24}$$

As in the simpler case in Section 15.1 we obtain a partial differential equation (PDE). The bond price $Z(r, t; T)$ is then the solution to this PDE. That is, it is a function of time t and interest rate r such that: (i) if we take its (partial) derivatives and substitute them into the left-hand side of Equation 15.24, we obtain the right-hand side; and (ii) it satisfies the boundary condition

$$Z(r, T; T) = 1 \tag{15.25}$$

We solve for $Z(T, r)$ in the next subsection.

As mentioned in Subsection 15.2.1.2 above, nothing in the derivations hinges on $Z(r, t; T)$ being a zero coupon bond. In particular, $Z(r, t; T)$ could be the price of an option, a structured note, or a portfolio of securities. Any of these interest rate securities must satisfy Equation 15.23, and thus the PDE in Equation 15.24. But then, what distinguishes one interest rate security from another? It is the final condition at maturity T. For instance, if $Z(r, t; T)$ is a zero coupon bond, the final condition is in Equation 15.25, as above. But if $Z(r, t; T)$ is the value at time t of an interest rate option with maturity T and strike rate r_K, for instance, then its price must also satisfy Equation 15.24 but the final condition is not the one in Equation 15.25, but rather

$$Z(r, T; T) = N \times \max(r - r_K, 0) \tag{15.26}$$

We can summarize all of the above findings in the following:

Fact 15.2 *Assume that the short-term interest rate r_t follows the Vasicek model (Equation 15.9). Then the price $Z(r, t; T)$ of any interest rate security with maturity T and payoff $g(r_T, T)$ satisfies the partial differential equation in Equation 15.24, with the final condition $Z(r_T, T; T) = g(r_T, T)$.*

Because all of the interest rate securities must satisfy the same equation (Equation 15.24), this equation is called **fundamental pricing equation**. It is important to recognize that this fundamental pricing equation depends on the choice of the model, in our case the Vasicek model. A different model will yield a slightly different equation. As we shall see in Section 15.4, the fundamental pricing equation has the same form as Equation 15.24, but the coefficients of the first and second partial derivatives will depend on the specific assumptions about the interest rate model.

15.2.3 The Vasicek Bond Pricing Formula

We now derive the bond pricing formula for the Vasicek model. Before doing so, we need to specify the form of $m^*(r, t)$ appearing in the fundamental pricing equation (Equation 15.24). The Vasicek model assumes that $m^*(r, t)$ has the same form as the drift rate of the original interest rate process in Equation 15.9, although possibly with different parameters. In particular, let

$$m^*(r, t) = \gamma^* (\bar{r}^* - r) \tag{15.27}$$

where γ^* and $\bar{r}^*$ are two constants. The appendix shows the following:

Fact 15.3 *The solution to Equation 15.24 when $m^*(r,t)$ is in Equation 15.27 and the final condition $Z(r,T;T) = 1$ is given by*

$$Z(r,t;T) = e^{A(t;T)-B(t;T)\times r} \qquad (15.28)$$

where $A(t;T)$ and $B(t;T)$ are given by

$$B(t;T) = \frac{1}{\gamma^*}\left(1 - e^{-\gamma^*(T-t)}\right) \qquad (15.29)$$

$$A(t;T) = (B(t;T) - (T-t))\left(\bar{r}^* - \frac{\sigma^2}{2(\gamma^*)^2}\right) - \frac{\sigma^2 B(t;T)^2}{4\gamma^*} \qquad (15.30)$$

It follows that the price of a coupon bond with maturity T and coupon rate c is given by

$$P_c(r,t;T) = \frac{100 \times c}{2} \sum_{i=1}^{n} Z(r,t;T_i) + 100 \times Z(r,t;T_n) \qquad (15.31)$$

Given a discount factor function $Z(r,t;T)$, as a function of T, we can compute the zero coupon spot rate, i.e., the term structure of interest rates. Before we do this, it is important to recall the distinction between maturity date and time to maturity and to discuss the notation for the two concepts.

15.2.3.1 Notation: Maturity Date versus Time to Maturity
We must pause to clarify the notation going forward. The bond pricing formula in Equation 15.28 is written as a function of interest rate r, the current time t, and the maturity *date* T. This notation helps in the adoption of Ito's lemma when necessary. However, it hides the fact that the value of the zero coupon bond at time t depends only on *time to maturity* $\tau = T - t$. This appears clear from the formulas $A(t;T)$ and $B(t;T)$ in Equations 15.30 and 15.29. In fact, note that

$$B(t;T) = B(0;T-t) \qquad (15.32)$$
$$A(t;T) = A(0;T-t) \qquad (15.33)$$

Note that when we want to emphasize the time to maturity aspect of a bond, we will use the notation $\tau = T - t$ as well as the following notation

$$Z(r_t,\tau) = Z(r_t,t;T) \qquad (15.34)$$
$$A(\tau) = A(0;T-t) \qquad (15.35)$$
$$B(\tau) = B(0;T-t). \qquad (15.36)$$

It is only a question of notation and nothing substantial changes.

15.2.3.2 The Term Structure of Interest Rates in the Vasicek Model
We can denote the term structure of interest rates as a function of the current interest rate r_t and time to maturity τ. This is given by

$$r_t(\tau) = -\frac{\ln(Z(r_t,\tau))}{\tau} = -\frac{A(\tau)}{\tau} + \frac{B(\tau)}{\tau}r_t \qquad (15.37)$$

Figure 15.1   Three Spot Curves Implied by the Vasicek Model

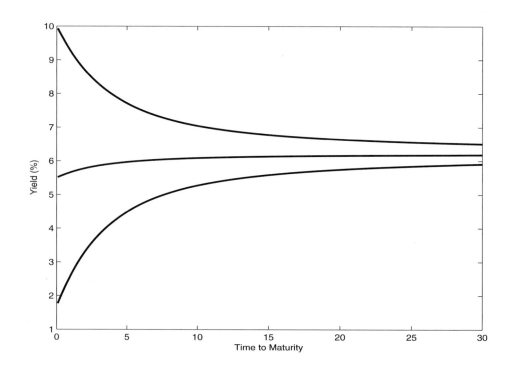

That is, each point on the term structure is a linear function of the current short-term interest rate r_t. As r_t moves over time according to the Vasicek model, so does the whole term structure of interest rates. Figure 15.1 plots three spot curves for estimated parameters. The figure shows that if the current short-term interest rate r_t is low, the Vasicek model implies a rising term structure of interest rates. If instead the current short-term interest rate is high, the Vasicek model implies a decreasing term structure. Note that as the interest rate moves up and down, the term structure moves too. In particular, the level, slope and curvature change over time. One important drawback, however, is that all of these movements are perfectly correlated. A multifactor model of interest rates, derived in the same fashion as the Vasicek model, will take care of that problem (see Chapter 22).

15.2.3.3 The Dynamics of Long Term Yields in the Vasicek Model   The

movement over time of long-term yields, with time to maturity τ, can be analyzed by applying Ito's lemma to $r_t(\tau)$ in Equation 15.37. Note that we keep τ fixed in this exercise, thus there is no time derivative to take:

$$dr_t(\tau) = \left(\frac{B(\tau)}{\tau} \gamma(\bar{r} - r_t) \right) dt + \frac{B(\tau)}{\tau} \sigma dX_t \qquad (15.38)$$

Because the quantity $B(\tau)/\tau < 1$, it follows that shocks to short-term interest rates, such as changes in monetary policy, have a softer effect on longer-term bonds. Moreover, the quantity $B(\tau)/\tau$ decreases with maturity, implying that longer-term rates move more slowly then the short-term rate. This behavior is evident in Figure 15.1: The vertical distance between the three lines is smaller the longer the time to maturity, implying that the variation of long-term interest rates is lower than the variation of short-term interest rates.

The key determinant of the speed of variation of long term bonds is γ^*, as it is the only parameter that enters the function $B(\tau)$ (see Equation 15.29). Since for given time to maturity τ, $B(\tau)$ is decreasing in γ^*, it follows that the variation of long-term interest rates is higher the lower is γ^*.

15.2.3.4 *Spot Rate Duration in the Vasicek Model*

In the previous section we discussed the variation of long-term yields in response to changes in the short-term rate r_t. The main finding is that the volatility of long-term spot rates is smaller than the volatility of short-term yields. It is important to realize that this does *not* imply that the volatility of long-term bond prices is smaller than the volatility of short-term bonds. As we remember from the basic concept of duration discussed in Chapter 3, the variation of yields translates to variation in bond prices through the duration of the bond. Thus, long-term bond prices have a higher volatility because their duration is higher.

Instead of using the concept of duration, which is defined in terms of small parallel shifts in the term structure, we have to rely on the notion of spot rate duration, $D_Z = -\frac{1}{Z}\frac{\partial Z}{\partial r}$, introduced in Chapter 10. The notion of parallel shifts is not well defined within an interest rate model such as the Vasicek model, because the term structure does *not* move in a parallel fashion, as it is apparent from Figure 15.1. The whole term structure depends on the short-term interest rate r_t (see Equation 15.37), and thus characterizing risk in terms of the spot rate duration is more appropriate.

Fact 15.4 *In the Vasicek model, the* **spot rate duration** *of a zero coupon bond with time to maturity τ is*

$$D_Z(\tau) = -\frac{1}{Z}\frac{\partial Z}{\partial r} = B(\tau) = \frac{1}{\gamma^*}\left(1 - e^{-\gamma^* \times \tau}\right) \tag{15.39}$$

It follows that the spot rate duration of a coupon bond is given by

$$D_P = \sum_{i=1}^{n} w_i D_Z(\tau_i) \tag{15.40}$$

where $w_i = 100 \times c/2 \times Z(r, \tau_i)/P(r, \tau)$ for $i = 1, ..., n-1$ and $w_n = 100 \times (1 + c/2) \times Z(r, \tau_n)/P(r, \tau)$.

The parameter γ^* controls the sensitivity of long(er) term bond prices to variation in the short-term interest rate. For given maturity T, the lower is γ^* and the higher is the spot-rate duration. We see below how to estimate γ^*.

15.2.4 Parameter Estimation

To make the Vasicek model operational for interest rate security pricing, as well as for risk management, we need to estimate its parameters. The Vasicek process for r_t in Equation 15.9 has three parameters: γ, $\bar{r}$ and σ. However, the bond pricing equation (Equation 15.28) has two more γ^* and $\bar{r}^*$. Overall we have then five parameters. An important fact, though, is that the parameters γ and $\bar{r}$ do not appear in the bond pricing equation (Equation 15.28), and, vice versa, their "star" counterparts γ^* and $\bar{r}^*$ do not enter in the original process for interest rates (Equation 15.9).[2] The only parameter that enters both the original interest rate process and the bond pricing formula is the volatility parameter σ. This implies that if our aim is only to obtain accurate pricing parameters, we do not need to know γ and $\bar{r}$, but only σ. The next example illustrates the methodology.

■ EXAMPLE 15.1

Assume that today is January 8, 2002.[3] Table 15.1 reports the STRIPS prices on that day, with maturity ranging from May 15, 2002 to February 15, 2011. The third column reports time to maturity T, and the last column depicts the continuously compounded yields.

To estimate the model, we proceed as follows. First, we note from the formula in Equation 15.28 that the bond pricing formula depends on three parameters, $\bar{r}^*$, γ^*, and σ. According to the Vasicek interest rate model (Equation 15.9), the volatility σ can be estimated directly from the time series of interest rates r_t. In principle we should use data on overnight government bonds. Here we use monthly data on the 1-months T-bill rate to estimate σ. Taking the standard deviation of the first difference in interest rates, we obtain an estimate of $\sigma = 2.21\%$. It is important to note, however, that from a time series of interest rate data it is **not** possible to recover the other two parameters, $\bar{r}^*$, γ^*. In fact, from the time series of short-term interest rates we can at most get $\bar{r}$ and γ. Indeed, we can compute $\bar{r}$ as the average short-term rate over the sample period. For instance, using data from 1952 to 2001, we obtain $\bar{r} = 5.09\%$, while we can obtain γ (as an approximation) by regressing the changes in interest rate $(r_{t+\delta} - r_t)$ on $r_t \times \delta$, where δ is the time between observations, in this case $\delta = 1/12$. By running this regression, we find that $\gamma = 0.3261$. To make the model operational for derivative pricing, however, $\bar{r}$ and γ are not relevant, as for pricing we need instead $\bar{r}^*$ and γ^*.

How can we estimate γ^* and $\bar{r}^*$? We proceed as follows: First, we note that for any choice of these two parameters, we can compute the prices of zero coupon bonds according to the Vasicek formula $Z^{Vasicek}(0, r_0; T)$ in Equation 15.28 for every maturity.[4] We can then compare the Vasicek zero coupon bonds to the Treasury STRIPS data in Table 15.1, for various maturities.

We can then search for the parameters for which the Vasicek prices are close, in some sense, to the data. For instance, we can search γ^* and $\bar{r}^*$ such that the following quantity is minimized:

$$J(\gamma^*, \bar{r}^*) = \sum_{i=1}^{n} \left(Z^{Vasicek}(r_0, 0; T_i) - Z^{Data}(0, T_i) \right)^2. \tag{15.41}$$

---

[2]The reason, we may recall, is that the hedging condition $\partial\Pi/\partial r = 0$ eliminates expected changes in interest rates from the arbitrage argument.

[3]We use this date for this exercise in this and later chapters, as the yield curve was particularly steep, which in turn highlights some issues that arise when using the Vasicek model.

[4]We emphasize the name "Vasicek" as a superscript in the zero coupon bond formula $Z^{Vasicek}(0, r_0; T_i)$ to reiterate that it is a price obtained from the Vasicek model, and to better differentiate it from the data prices, denoted by $Z^{Data}(0, T_i)$.

Table 15.1   STRIPS on January 8, 2002

Maturity Date	STRIPS $Z(0,T)$	Time to Maturity T	Yield (%) $r(0,T)$
15-May-2002	99.4375	0.3479	1.6212
15-Aug-2002	98.9375	0.6000	1.7803
15-Feb-2003	97.6250	1.1041	2.177
15-Aug-2003	95.7813	1.6000	2.694
15-Nov-2003	94.7813	1.8521	2.894
15-Feb-2004	93.6250	2.1038	3.1311
15-May-2004	92.3750	2.3497	3.3754
15-Aug-2004	91.2500	2.6011	3.5203
15-Nov-2004	89.8125	2.8525	3.7668
15-Feb-2005	88.8125	3.1041	3.8221
15-May-2005	87.5000	3.3479	3.9885
15-Aug-2005	86.3750	3.6000	4.0687
15-Nov-2005	85.0938	3.8521	4.1904
15-Feb-2006	84.0938	4.1041	4.2211
15-May-2006	82.7813	4.3479	4.3462
15-Jul-2006	82.1250	4.5151	4.3616
15-Feb-2007	79.2813	5.1041	4.5487
15-May-2007	78.0938	5.3479	4.6235
15-Aug-2007	77.0000	5.6000	4.6672
15-Feb-2008	74.8438	6.1038	4.7473
15-May-2008	73.5938	6.3497	4.8287
15-Nov-2008	71.5313	6.8525	4.8893
15-May-2009	69.3438	7.3479	4.9823
15-Aug-2009	68.2188	7.6000	5.0322
15-Nov-2009	67.5625	7.8521	4.9938
15-Feb-2010	66.1875	8.1041	5.0922
15-Aug-2010	64.4688	8.6000	5.1045
15-Feb-2011	62.9063	9.1041	5.0914

Source: *The Wall Street Journal*

Figure 15.2   Fitted Zero Coupon Yield Curves from STRIPS: January 8, 2002

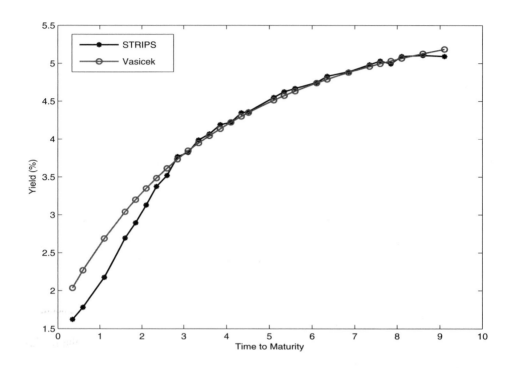

Data Source: *The Wall Street Journal*

Each term in the parenthesis is the model's pricing error for each maturity T_i, that is, the distance between the model price and the data. If the model works well, each pricing error should be small, and thus also the sum of the pricing errors squared.

The minimization procedure in Equation 15.41, called **nonlinear least squares**, yields estimates of the two parameters of interest using information from the cross-section of bonds at time 0. In particular, in this case the minimization procedure yields $\bar{r}^* = 0.0634$ and $\gamma^* = 0.4653$. Figure 15.2 plots the zero coupon yields for both the STRIPS in Table 15.1 and those implied by the Vasicek model.

As can be seen, the Vasicek model is not able to exactly match the term structure of interest rates on January 8, 2002, especially failing at the short-end of the yield curve. This deficiency of the Vasicek model is in part due to the fact that the Vasicek model is a "simple" model, with only three parameters and one driving factor. However, it is also true that on January 8, 2002, the term structure was very steep, in part due to the action of the Federal Reserve to lower the target Fed funds rate to boost the U.S. economy, and many more complicated models had indeed a hard time matching the term structure of interest rates on that day. In the next chapter we exploit this deficiency of the Vasicek model in order to illustrate the notion of relative value strategies on the yield curve, a relatively popular trading strategy in proprietary trading desks and hedge funds.

15.3 DERIVATIVE SECURITY PRICING

Under the assumptions of the Vasicek model, Fact 15.2 says that *any* interest rate derivative security must satisfy the fundamental pricing equation (Equation 15.24), subject to a boundary condition determined by the security's final payoff. In the case of the Vasicek model, it is possible to obtain analytical formulas for a number of derivative securities. One of the most important results is the pricing of options on zero coupon bonds.[5]

15.3.1 Zero Coupon Bond Options

Consider an option with maturity T_O and with payoff

$$\text{Payoff at } T_O = \max\left(Z(T_O; T_B) - K, 0\right) \tag{15.42}$$

where K is a strike price, and $Z(T_O; T_B)$ is the value at time T_O of a zero coupon bond with maturity date T_B (and thus, time to maturity $T_B - T_O$). Under the Vasicek model, the formula in Equation 15.28 shows that the zero coupon bond at time T_O will depend on the interest rate r_{T_O} according to the formula $Z(T_O, r_{T_O}; T_B) = e^{A(T_O; T_B) - B(T_O; T_B) r_{T_O}}$, where $A(T_0; T_B)$ and $B(T_0; T_B)$ are in Equations 15.30 and 15.29, respectively. It follows that the payoff in Equation 15.42 depends on the interest rate r_{T_O}. Thus, the value of the option with the payoff in Equation 15.42 is going to be an interest rate security that depends on the current interest rate r_t and time t. We can denote the value of this security by $V(r_t, t)$.

As any interest rate security, the zero coupon bond option must also satisfy the fundamental pricing equation (Equation 15.24), with final condition

$$V(r_{T_O}, T_O) = \max\left(Z(r_{T_O}, T_O; T_B) - K, 0\right) \tag{15.43}$$

It turns out that under the assumptions of the Vasicek model, the option pricing formula $V(r_t, t)$ is known in closed form.

Fact 15.5 *Under the Vasicek model, a* **European call option** *with strike price K and maturity T_O on a zero coupon bond maturing on $T_B > T_O$ is given by*

$$V(r_0, 0) = Z(0, r_0; T_B)\mathcal{N}(d_1) - KZ(0, r_0; T_O)\mathcal{N}(d_2) \tag{15.44}$$

where $\mathcal{N}(x)$ is the cumulative standard normal distribution, and

$$
\begin{cases}
d_1 & = & \dfrac{1}{\mathcal{S}_Z(T_O)} \log\left(\dfrac{Z(0, r_0; T_B)}{KZ(0, r_0; T_O)}\right) + \dfrac{\mathcal{S}_Z(T_O)}{2} & (15.45) \\[2ex]
d_2 & = & d_1 - \mathcal{S}_Z(T_O) & (15.46)
\end{cases}
$$

$$\mathcal{S}_Z(T_O) = B(T_O; T_B) \times \sqrt{\frac{\sigma^2}{2\gamma^*}\left(1 - e^{-2\gamma^* T_O}\right)} \tag{15.47}$$

Similarly, a **European put option** *is given by*

$$V(r_0, 0) = KZ(0, r_0; T_O)\mathcal{N}(-d_2) - Z(0, r_0; T_B)\mathcal{N}(-d_1) \tag{15.48}$$

---

[5]Chapter 19 shows how this formula can be applied to pricing standard derivatives, such as caps, floors and swaptions, which are among the most popular interest rate derivatives traded over-the-counter.

Note that $\mathcal{S}_Z(T_O)^2$ is the variance of the log return between 0 and T_O of the underlying zero coupon bond. In fact, because $\log(Z(t_O, r_{T_O}; T_B)) = A(T_O; T_B) - B(T_O; T_B) \times r_{T_O}$, we have:

$$
\begin{aligned}
Variance\left[\log\left(\frac{Z(r_{T_O}, T_O; T_B)}{Z(r_0, 0; T_B)}\right)\right] &= Variance\left[\log\left(Z(r_{T_O}, T_O; T_B)\right)\right] \\
&= Variance\left[A(T_O; T_B) - B(T_O; T_B) \times r_{T_O}\right] \\
&= B(T_O; T_B)^2 \times Variance\left[r_{T_O}\right]
\end{aligned}
$$

which leads to Equation 15.47 once we also use the result about $Variance[r_{T_O}]$ contained in Equation 14.36 in Chapter 14.[6] Indeed, the option pricing formula in Equation 15.44 is identical to the celebrated Black and Scholes option pricing formula – originally developed for stock options – applied to the zero coupon bond.[7]

■ EXAMPLE 15.2

Suppose that on January 8, 2002 a client asks for a quote on a 1-year call option on a 4-year zero coupon bond, with strike $K = \$80$ out of a $\$100$ principal. Let $T_0 = 1$ be the maturity of the option. Because the security underlying the option is a zero coupon bond that will have 4 years to maturity at the option's expiration, the maturity of the underlying zero coupon bond as of now is $T_B = 5$. The payoff of the option is given by

$$\text{Payoff at time } 1 = \max\left(Z(T_0; T_B) \times 100 - 80, 0\right) \tag{15.49}$$

How can we price this option? In order to use the formula in Equation 15.44, we need to estimate the model's parameters first. We have performed this estimation in Example 15.1. Given the parameter estimates, we insert their values into Equation 15.44 and obtain that the value of the call option on January 8, 2002, is

$$
\begin{aligned}
Z(r_0, 0; T_O) &= 0.9743; \\
Z(r_0, 0; T_B) &= 0.7991; \\
\mathcal{S}_Z(T_O) &= 3.23\% \\
d_1 &= 0.7891 \\
\text{Call}(\times 100) = V(r_0, 0) &= \$2.2921
\end{aligned}
$$

---

[6]An important distinction is that we use the "risk neutral" interest rate process $dr_t = \gamma^* (\bar{r}^* - r_t) + \sigma dX_t$ for the calculations. We will discuss these concepts in Chapter 17

[7]To better see the similarity to the Black and Scholes formula, note that besides the assumption of no frictions and no arbitrage, the main assumption of the Black and Scholes formula is that the stock price S_T is *lognormally* distributed. It then follows that the price of a call option is $C = S_0 \mathcal{N}(d_1) - Ke^{-rT}\mathcal{N}(d_2)$ where T is maturity, K is the strike price, S_0 is the current stock price, $\sigma\sqrt{T}$ is the volatility of S_T, and r is the current (constant) interest rate. In addition, $d_1 = \ln\left(S_0/(Ke^{-rT})\right)/\sqrt{\sigma^2 \times T} + \frac{\sigma\sqrt{T}}{2}$ and $d_2 = d_1 - \sigma\sqrt{T}$. This formula is indeed identical to Equation 15.44, as it can be verified by matching terms. The reason is that under the Vasicek model, the security underlying the options, the zero coupon bond $Z(r_{T_O}, T_O; T_B)$, is indeed log-normally distributed, as in the original Black and Scholes formula, because $Z(r_{T_O}, T_O; T_B)$ is an exponential function of r_{T_O} which is itself normally distributed according to the Vasicek model. The only difficulty is that in this case the discount rate r_t is time-varying while it is constant in Black and Scholes model. Chapter 21 resolves this issue.

Note that this value considers a par value of $100 of the underlying zero coupon bond, rather than unity, which was assumed in the formula in Equation 15.44. The level of the underlying notional value proportionally increases the price of the option.

15.3.2   Options on Coupon Bonds

Fact 15.5 shows a formula for an option on zero coupon bonds. Many options though are written on coupon bearing bonds. Fortunately, in the case of the Vasicek model, it is possible to extend the formula to this case as well.

Fact 15.6 *Let $P_c(r_t, t; T_B)$ be the price at time t of a coupon bond with coupon rate c and maturity date T_B. Let Δ be the time interval between coupons. Consider a call option with maturity T_O and strike rate K written on the above coupon bond, that is, whose payoff is*

$$\text{Payoff of call option at } T_O = \max(P_c(r_{T_O}, T_O; T_B) - K, 0) \tag{15.50}$$

The value at time 0 of the call option can be computed as follows. Let r_K^* be the interest rate, such that $P_c(r_K^*, T_O, T_B) = K$, and define $K_i = Z(r_K^*, T_O; T_i)$ for each coupon date T_i. The value of the call option is

$$Call = \sum_{i=1}^{n} c(i) \times (Z(r_0, 0; T_i) \times \mathcal{N}(d_1(i)) - K_i \times Z(r_0, 0; T_O) \times \mathcal{N}(d_2(i))) \tag{15.51}$$

where $c(i)$ is the cash flow paid by the coupon bond at time T_i, that is, $c(i) = c/2$ for $i = 1, .., n - 1$ and $c(n) = 1 + c/2$, and

$$d_1(i) = \frac{1}{\mathcal{S}_Z(T_O; T_i)} \log\left(\frac{Z(0, r_0; T_i)}{K_i Z(0, r_0; T_O)}\right) + \frac{\mathcal{S}_Z(T_O; T_i)}{2} \tag{15.52}$$

$$d_2(i) = d_1(i) - \mathcal{S}_Z(T_O; T_i) \tag{15.53}$$

and where $\mathcal{S}_Z(T_O; T_i)$ is in (15.47).
  Similarly, the value of a put option with payoff

$$\text{Payoff of put option at } T_O = \max(K - P_c(r_{T_O}, T_O; T_B), 0) \tag{15.54}$$

is

$$Put = \sum_{i=1}^{n} c(i) \times (K_i \times Z(r_0, 0; T_O) \times \mathcal{N}(-d_2(i)) - Z(r_0, 0; T_i) \times \mathcal{N}(-d_1(i)))$$
$$\tag{15.55}$$

The next example illustrates the methodology.

■ **EXAMPLE 15.3**

Suppose that on January 8, 2002 a client asks for a quote on a 1-year call option on a 4-year, 5% coupon bond, with strike $K = \$100$ out of a $100 principal. The first step is to obtain the parameters of the model: Recall that this estimation was performed in Example 15.1. In particular, $\bar{r}^* = 0.0634$, $\gamma^* = 0.4653$ and $\sigma = 2.21\%$.

Table 15.2 Coupon Bond Option Pricing

T_i	$A(T_O;T_i)$	$B(T_O;T_i)$	K_i	$Z(0;T_i)$	$S_Z(T_O;T_i)$	$d_1(i)$	$Call_i (\times 100)$
1.50	-0.0034	0.4461	0.9815	0.9564	0.0079	0.0178	0.3082
2.00	-0.0127	0.7996	0.9608	0.9363	0.0142	0.0241	0.5430
2.50	-0.0265	1.0797	0.9386	0.9148	0.0192	0.0291	0.7185
3.00	-0.0440	1.3017	0.9154	0.8923	0.0232	0.0330	0.8469
3.50	-0.0643	1.4775	0.8916	0.8692	0.0263	0.0362	0.9382
4.00	-0.0869	1.6169	0.8675	0.8458	0.0288	0.0387	1.0006
4.50	-0.1112	1.7274	0.8435	0.8224	0.0307	0.0406	1.0406
5.00	-0.1370	1.8149	0.8195	0.7991	0.0323	0.0422	1.0634

Given the model parameters, we next compute the $A(T_0;T_i)$ and $B(T_0;T_i)$ for every coupon date T_i *after* the maturity of the option. These quantities can be computed from the formulas in Equations 15.30 and 15.29, respectively. The results are in the second and third column in Table 15.2. Given these quantities, we can look for r_K^* that indeed makes the price of coupon bond price at T_O equal to the strike price. That is, we solve for the equation

$$\frac{c \times 100}{2} \times \sum_{i=1}^{n} Z(r,T_O;T_i) + 100 \times Z(r,T_O;T_n) = K$$

where the unknown is r. In this case, we find the solution is $r_K^* = 3.42\%$.

Next, we must compute $K_i = Z(r_K^*,T_O;T_i) \times 100$. These are contained in the fourth column of Table 15.2. Finally, given the discounts, and the other parameters, we can compute $S_Z(T_O;T_i)$ and thus $d_1(i)$ and $d_2(i)$ for every maturity. The final column in Table 15.2 reports each individual zero coupon bond option for each of the maturities. The value of the option on the coupon bonds is then given by

$$
\begin{aligned}
\text{Call Price} &= \frac{c}{2} \sum_{i=1}^{n} Call_i + Call_n \\
&= \$2.4536
\end{aligned}
$$

15.3.3 The Three Steps to Derivative Pricing

The previous two examples stress the standard procedure financial institutions use to price derivative securities by no arbitrage. This procedure can be summarized as follows:

1. *Select* an interest rate model, such as the Vasicek model.

2. *Estimate* the parameters of the model, using available data, such as zero coupon bonds.

3. *Price* the derivative security using the model.

To these three steps we must add a fourth one, though, which is discussed in Chapter 16. After selling the option to a client, we need to:

4. *Hedge* the option exposure through a position in the underlying security.

The model provides the hedge ratios necessary to carry out the hedging strategy.

15.4   NO ARBITRAGE PRICING IN A GENERAL INTEREST RATE MODEL

In Section 15.2 we consider the case in which interest rate moves over time according to the Vasicek model given in Equation 15.9. In this section we consider the more general case, in which the short-term interest rate r_t moves over time according to the general model

$$d\, r_t = m(r_t, t)dt + s(r_t, t)dX_t \tag{15.56}$$

where $m(r_t, t)$ and $s(r_t, t)$ are two functions of the interest rate and time.[8] For instance, in the Vasicek model, we have $m(r_t, t) = \gamma(\bar{r} - r_t)$ and $s(r_t, t) = \sigma$. In general, time could also enter the dynamics of interest rates or its volatility. As an example, the Ho-Lee model discussed in Chapter 11 and again in Chapter 14 has a drift rate equal to $m(r, t) = \theta_t$, which depends only on time.

As in Section 15.2 we want to find the price of interest rate securities when the interest rate model is given by Equation 15.56. Exactly the same procedure leads to an equation whose solution is the pricing formula we are looking for. Compared to the derivations in Section 15.2.1, the only thing that changes is that wherever $\gamma(\bar{r} - r_t)$ appears, we have to substitute the more general term $m(r_t, t)$, and wherever σ appears, we have to substitute $s(r_t, t)$. For instance, if $Z(t, t; T)$ denotes the value of an interest rate security, Ito's lemma implies that the capital gain process for Z is

$$dZ_t = \left(\frac{\partial Z}{\partial t} + \frac{\partial Z}{\partial r} m(r, t) + \frac{1}{2} \frac{\partial^2 Z}{\partial r^2} s(r, t)^2 \right) dt + \frac{\partial Z}{\partial r} s(r, t) dX_t \tag{15.57}$$

The steps are otherwise the same, namely:

1. Set up the portfolio with two interest rate securities

$$\Pi(r, t) = Z_1(r, t) - \Delta Z_2(r, t) \tag{15.58}$$

2. Hedge away interest rate risk

$$\frac{\partial \Pi(r, t)}{\partial r} = 0 \Longrightarrow \Delta = \frac{\partial Z_1 / \partial r}{\partial Z_2 / \partial r} \tag{15.59}$$

3. Find the dynamics of $\Pi(r, t)$:

$$d\Pi_t = \left\{ \left(\frac{\partial \Pi}{\partial t} \right) + \frac{1}{2} \left(\frac{\partial^2 \Pi}{\partial r^2} \right) s(r, t)^2 \right\} dt \tag{15.60}$$

---

[8]Not all of the functions are viable, and more restrictions may be needed to make the process in Equation 15.56 well defined.

4. Impose no arbitrage. Because $d\Pi_t$ is perfectly riskless between t and $t + dt$, it must yield the risk free rate

$$d\Pi_t = r_t \, \Pi \, dt \tag{15.61}$$

5. Substitute all of the formulas for $d\Pi_t$ and Π_t into Equation 15.61, reshuffle the equations and obtain the no arbitrage condition

$$\frac{\left(\frac{\partial Z_1}{\partial t} + \frac{1}{2}\frac{\partial^2 Z_1}{\partial r^2}s(r,t)^2 - rZ_1\right)}{\partial Z_1/\partial r} = \frac{\left(\frac{\partial Z_2}{\partial t} + \frac{1}{2}\frac{\partial^2 Z_2}{\partial r^2}s(r,t)^2 - rZ_2\right)}{\partial Z_2/\partial r} \tag{15.62}$$

6. Define by $-m^*(r,t)$ the common ratio across securities in Equation 15.62:

$$\frac{\left(\frac{\partial Z}{\partial t} + \frac{1}{2}\frac{\partial^2 Z}{\partial r^2}s(r,t)^2\right) - rZ}{\partial Z/\partial r} = -m^*(r,t) \tag{15.63}$$

7. Rearrange and obtain the fundamental pricing equation

$$\frac{\partial Z}{\partial t} + \frac{\partial Z}{\partial r}m^*(r,t) + \frac{1}{2}\frac{\partial^2 Z}{\partial r^2}s(r,t)^2 = r\,Z \tag{15.64}$$

We can then summarize the finding in the following:

Fact 15.7 *Under the assumption that the interest rate model is given in Equation 15.56, the no arbitrage value of* any *interest rate security with payoff at T given by a function $g(r_T, T)$ is the solution to the fundamental pricing equation (Equation 15.64) under the boundary condition*

$$Z(r_T, T; T) = g(r_T, T) \tag{15.65}$$

The important issue is then how to solve for the fundamental pricing equation (Equation 15.64) under specific assumptions about the volatility of interest rates $s(r,t)$, the quantity $m^*(r,t)$, and the final (payoff) condition $g(r_t, T)$. Sometimes we are able to find analytical solutions for many interest rate securities, such as bonds and options in the Vasicek model. Other times, we have to resort on numerical solutions of the equation, as we will in Chapter 17.

15.4.1 The Cox, Ingersoll, and Ross Model

One of the main drawbacks of the Vasicek model is that is allows for negative interest rates. Cox, Ingersoll and Ross (1985) proposed a model for the short-term interest rate that is similar to the Vasicek model, but that ensures that interest rates are always positive. In particular, the CIR model is given by

$$dr_t = \gamma\left(\bar{r} - r_t\right)dt + \sqrt{\alpha r_t}dX_t \tag{15.66}$$

This model, which also goes under the name of the **square root model** of interest rates, is slightly less tractable than the Vasicek model, in the sense that analytical formulas for some securities are not available. However, since interest rates are always positive in this model, this has been considered an important step forward in term structure modeling. The reason why interest rates are always positive in this model can be seen from observing the diffusion term $\sqrt{\alpha r_t}$ in Equation 15.66. When the interest rate r_t is moving toward zero, the diffusion part $\sqrt{\alpha r_t}$ declines, and it becomes in fact zero when r_t hits zero. When $r_t = 0$, the only term left in Equation 15.66 is $dr_t = \gamma \bar{r} > 0$. Thus, the next step will be for sure that r_t increases (because the change $dr > 0$). One important caveat is that to ensure the interest rate process is always positive (and well defined), we must have the following technical condition satisfied:

$$\gamma \times \bar{r} > \frac{1}{2}\alpha$$

That is, the term that "pulls up" the interest rate when r_t hits zero, "$\gamma \bar{r}$," must be large enough: Otherwise, even in continuous time, there is a chance that right before hitting zero the realized Brownian motion dX_t is large enough to drive the interest rate negative.

What are the properties of the distribution of interest rates at a future date t, given a current interest rate r_0? It turns out that the distribution of r_t is as noncentral chi-square with first and second moments given by

$$E[r_t|r_0] = \bar{r} + (r_0 - \bar{r})e^{-\gamma t} \tag{15.67}$$

$$Var[r_t|r_0] = r_0\frac{\alpha}{\gamma}\left(e^{-\gamma t} - e^{-2\gamma t}\right) + \frac{\bar{r}\alpha}{2\gamma}\left(1 - e^{-\gamma t}\right)^2 \tag{15.68}$$

Figure 15.3 plots the stationary distribution of the CIR model for the same data used to obtain the stationary distribution in the Vasicek model in Figure 14.7 in Chapter 14.[9] As can be seen, while the Vasicek model gives positive probability to negative interest rates, the CIR model cuts out the negative part of the distribution. The noncentral chi-square distribution is positively skewed, giving some positive probability to high interest rates, such as the ones realized in the 1970s and beginning of the 1980s.

15.4.2 Bond Prices under the Cox, Ingersoll, and Ross Model

The CIR model also has closed form solutions for zero coupon bonds. The same steps we follow with the Vasicek model show that any interest rate security must satisfy the following fundamental pricing equation

$$\frac{\partial Z}{\partial t} + \frac{\partial Z}{\partial r}m^*(r,t) + \frac{1}{2}\frac{\partial^2 Z}{\partial r^2}r\alpha = rZ \tag{15.69}$$

In particular, a bond price must satisfy this partial differential equation under the boundary condition $Z(T,r) = 1$.

Fact 15.8 *Let*

$$m^*(r,t) = \gamma^*\left(\bar{r}^* - r\right).$$

with $\gamma^* \times \bar{r}^* > \frac{1}{2}\alpha$. Then the solution to Equation 15.69 is given by

$$Z(r,t;T) = e^{A(t;T) - B(t;T) \times r} \tag{15.70}$$

---

[9]Recall that a stationary distribution corresponds to the distribution of interest rates in the long-run. For instance, taking the limit as $t \to \infty$, Equations 15.67 and 15.68 imply that the mean and variance of the stationary distribution are $E[r] = \bar{r}$ and $Var[r] = \bar{r}\alpha/(2\gamma)$. Heuristically, we can think of simulating the interest rates according to the CIR model for a very long time, and then plot the histogram.

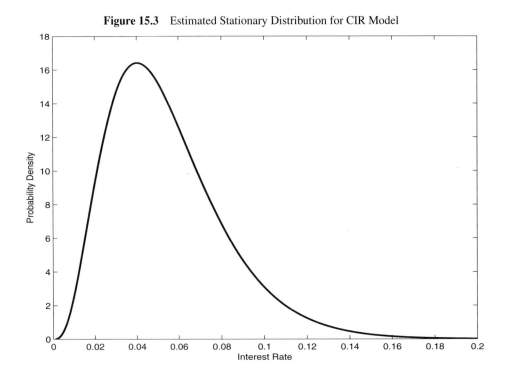

Figure 15.3   Estimated Stationary Distribution for CIR Model

where

$$B(t;T) = \frac{2\left(e^{\psi_1(T-t)} - 1\right)}{(\gamma^* + \psi_1)\left(e^{\psi_1(T-t)} - 1\right) + 2\psi_1} \tag{15.71}$$

$$A(t;T) = 2\frac{\bar{r}^*\gamma^*}{\alpha}\log\left(\frac{2\psi_1 e^{(\psi_1+\gamma^*)\frac{(T-t)}{2}}}{(\gamma^* + \psi_1)\left(e^{\psi_1(T-t)} - 1\right) + 2\psi_1}\right) \tag{15.72}$$

and

$$\psi_1 = \sqrt{(\gamma^*)^2 + 2\alpha};$$

Figure 15.4 shows the types of yield of curves that are possible under the CIR model.[10] As with the Vasicek model (see Figure 15.1), if the current short-term rate r_0 is low, then the model implies a rising term structure of interest rates. If instead r_0 is high, the model implies a declining term structure. As with the Vasicek model, the whole term structure is perfectly correlated with the short-term interest rate.

15.5   SUMMARY

In this chapter we covered the following topics:

---

[10]The parameter estimates are obtained by fitting the CIR model to the term structure of interest rates as of January 8, 2002, as in Example 15.1. The parameters are $\gamma^* = 0.3807$, $\bar{r}^* = 7.2\%$, and $\alpha = 0.0548$. The fit of the CIR model on January 8, 2002 is identical to that of the Vasicek model obtaining a figure identical to Figure 15.2.

Figure 15.4   Three Spot Curves Implied by the CIR Model

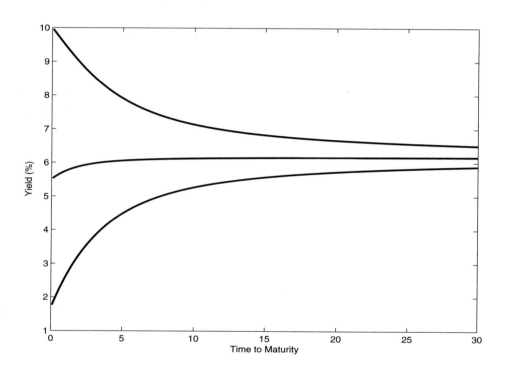

1. No arbitrage: A portfolio of traded securities that is immune to random shocks during the time interval $[t, t + dt]$ must have a rate of return equal to the risk free rate. Otherwise, an arbitrage strategy is available.

2. The fundamental pricing equation: A long-short portfolio of bonds in appropriate proportion is immune to changes in the short-term interest rate during a small interval of time. By no arbitrage, this portfolio must yield a rate of return equal to the risk free rate. This restriction yields a partial differential equation that all of the interest rate securities must satisfy.

3. The Vasicek bond pricing formula: The solution to the fundamental pricing equation under the Vasicek model is known in closed form, and it has an exponential form. The statistical distribution of a future zero coupon bond is log-normal.

4. The spot rate duration in the Vasicek model: The model provides a measure of interest rate risk. The spot rate duration is analogous to the duration definition, but for the short-term (spot) rate of interest. Long-term bonds have a higher spot rate duration than short-term bonds. The estimated parameters of the Vasicek model defines the spot rate duration.

5. Nonlinear least squares: The parameters of the Vasicek model can be estimated from the term structure of interest rates. The methodology consists of computing the difference between the model prices and the data, and minimizing the sum of squares of these "pricing errors". Such minimization has to be performed numerically.

6. The Vasicek option pricing formula: The Vasicek model provides closed form formulas for the prices of call and put options defined on zero coupon bonds. The formula looks similar to the Black and Scholes formula for pricing options on stocks.

7. No arbitrage for general interest rate models: The long/short portfolio and no arbitrage argument can be carried out for any interest rate model. The fundamental pricing equation has the same form, independently of the model for interest rate used.

8. The Cox, Ingersoll, and Ross (CIR) model for bond prices: The CIR model for interest rates modifies the Vasicek model to ensure its interest rate is always positive. The bond pricing formula has the same exponential form as that of the Vasicek model, but for different parameters.

15.6 EXERCISES

1. You have estimated the parameters for the Vasicek model, and the results are in Table 15.3, where the notation is the same as that used in this chapter. The current overnight rate is 2%.

    (a) Compute the value of zero coupon bonds (with $1 principal) up to 10 years to maturity. What parameters did you use?

    (b) Compute the spot rate of each zero coupon bond up to 10 years, and plot the results on a graph.

    (c) Compute the spot rate duration for each zero coupon bond.

Table 15.3 Estimates for the Vasicek model

γ	$\bar{r}$	σ	γ^*	$\bar{r}^*$
0.3262	5.09%	2.21 %	0.4653	6.34%

2. The zero coupon bond pricing formula under the Vasicek model depends on three parameters: γ^*, $\bar{r}^*$, and σ, and the current short-term interest rates, r_0. How does the spot rate $r(\tau) = -\ln(Z(r,\tau))/\tau$ depend on each of these parameters? Assume the current short-term rate $r_0 = 2\%$. Using the parameter values in Table 15.3 as a baseline case:

   (a) Plot on a graph the term structure of interest rates for three choices of γ^*, keeping the remaining parameters costant.

   (b) Do the same as in Part (a), but vary $\bar{r}^*$.

   (c) Do the same as in Part (a), but vary σ;

   Comment on your results.

3. Rework the previous exercise, but using the Cox, Ingersoll, and Ross model, whose bond pricing formula is in Equation 15.70. Use the following parameters as a baseline case: $\gamma^* = 0.3807$, $\bar{r}^* = 7.2\%$, and $\alpha = 0.0548$. For each plot, vary γ^*, $\bar{r}^*$ and α.

4. Consider the estimated parameters for the Vasicek model in Table 15.3 Simulate 1000 paths of interest rates under each set of parameters, i.e., $(\gamma, \bar{r}, \sigma)$ and $(\gamma^*, \bar{r}^*, \sigma)$. Plot the histogram of the distribution for $T = 10$ for each set of parameters, and comment on the differences.

5. Consider the spot rate duration for a zero coupon bond, in Equation 15.39. Plot the spot rate duration across time to maturity τ up to $\tau = 10$ for various values of $\gamma^* > 0$.

   (a) How does the spot rate duration depend on time to maturity τ?

   (b) How does the spot rate duration depend on γ^*?

   (c) What happens to the spot rate duration if $\gamma^* < 0$?

6. Equation 15.38 reports the dynamics of the yield with time to maturity τ. Its volatility is given by $\sigma(\tau) = \frac{B(\tau)}{\tau}\sigma$, where $B(\tau) = (1-e^{-\gamma^* \tau})/(\gamma^*)$. Plot the volatility with respect to time to maturity τ. Which bonds have a higher yield volatility? Long-term bonds or short-term bonds? What is the relation between yield volatility and *return* volatility? Are these the same?

7. Equation 15.28 reports the pricing formula for the Vasicek zero coupon bond (with $1 principal). Check that it satisfies the fundamental pricing equation (Equation 15.24). That is, take the partial derivatives on the left-hand-side of Equation 15.24, substitute, and check that the left-hand side is equal to the right-hand side.

8. Consider the parameter estimated in Table 15.3. Today's short-term interest rate is $r_0 = 2\%$. Equation 15.28 reports the pricing formula for the Vasicek zero coupon bond (with $1 principal).

   (a) Use Ito's lemma to compute the expected return $E[dZ/Z]$ on zero coupon bonds with 1 year and 10 years to maturity. Which one has the highest expected return?

   (b) Use Ito's lemma to compute the volatility of returns. Which bond has the highest volatility?

   (c) Consider the *risk premium* for each bond, namely, $E[dZ/Z] - r_0 dt$. How is this related to the volatility just computed? That is, for each bond, compute the ratio $\frac{risk\ premium}{volatility}$. How does it differ across the two bonds? How does it depend on the level of the short-term rate r_0?

   (d) Rework the previous point but with $\gamma^* = 0.3262 = \gamma$. How do your results change?

9. **Orange County Bankruptcy.** In Chapters 2 (Section 2.8) and 3 (Section 3.7) we analyzed the risk and return of the Orange County portfolio, using the building blocks of zero coupon bonds and duration. In this exercise, we analyze the same case using the Vasicek model. In particular, let today be December 31, 1993. Then:

   (a) Parameter Estimation:

       i. Using the data in Table 2.6 in Chapter 2, estimate the parameters γ^* and $\bar{r}^*$ of the Vasicek model by nonlinear least squares, as in Equation 15.41.

       ii. Download daily data on the 1-month T-bill rate from the Federal Reserve Web site (*http://www.federalreserve.gov/releases/h15/data.htm*) up to December 31, 1993, and use these data to estimate γ, $\bar{r}$, and σ in the Vasicek model. This estimation can be accomplished through a linear regression (see Exercises in Chapter 14). Take literally $dt = 1/252 = 1$ day and discretize the process into

   $$(r_{t+dt} - r_t) = \gamma(\bar{r} - r_t)dt + \epsilon_{t+dt}$$

   where $\epsilon_{t+dt} \sim \mathcal{N}(0, \sigma^2 dt)$. This looks similar to a regression

   $$(r_{t+dt} - r_t) = \alpha + \beta r_t + \epsilon_{t+dt}$$

   What are α and β in terms of the original parameters γ and $\bar{r}$? How can you estimate σ? [*Hint: Be careful with the annualization (your data are daily, but we need to be annualized). Also, recall that r_t in the Vasicek model is a continuosly compounded rate.*]

       iii. Compare $(\bar{r}, \gamma)$ with $(\bar{r}^*, \gamma^*)$. Interpret the differences and discuss.

   (b) Consider now a portfolio with a fraction $x = 0.1366$ in 1-year T-bills and the remainder $(1 - x)$ in 3-year inverse floaters (see Section 3.7.5 in Chapter 3). We take this portfolio as given. Let r be the continuously compounded interest rate on January 3, 1994.

       i. If $P^{IF}(r, t; T)$ denotes the price of the inverse floater discussed in Section 2.8 in Chapter 2, compute its sensitivity to changes in the interest rate $\partial P^{IF}/\partial r$. (You may maintain the assumption that $r < 15\%$ with certainty.)

   ii. Compute the dollar convexity of the inverse floater, that is, the second derivative $\partial^2 P^{IF}/\partial r^2$.

   iii. If $\Pi(r, t; T)$ denotes the value of the entire portfolio, compute its sensitivity to changes in the interest rate r, $\partial \Pi(r, t; T)/\partial r$, as well as its dollar convexity $\partial^2 \Pi(r, t; T)/\partial r^2$.

(c) The portfolio $\Pi(r, t; T)$, as any other security, must satisfy a fundamental pricing equation (Equation 15.24):

   i. Write down the equation that $\Pi(r, t; T)$ must satisfy.

   ii. Given your answers above, can you compute the change in value of the portfolio due to the passage of time? That is, what is $d\Pi/dt$?

   iii. For each day, what then is the capital gain or loss that can be imputed only to the passage of time? What is the intuition behind it? How does this relate to the level of Gamma?

(d) Value-at-Risk: We can use simulations and the Vasicek model to compute a 1-year Value-at-Risk, that is, the maximum loss that the portfolio may incur with $\alpha\%$ probability due to the movement in interest rates. Proceed as follows:

   i. Given the parameter estimates of the model, simulate M interest rate paths (M large) over a one-year horizon.

   ii. For each simulated scenario about the interest rate at time $t = 1$, r_t, apply the Vasicek formula and compute the distribution of the Orange County portfolio. Plot the histogram of the portfolio distribution at $t = 1$.

   iii. Compute the 1% and 5% worst cases of the portfolio distribution, and thus obtain the 1% VaR and 5% VaR. Are the ex-post losses suffered by Orange County's portfolio completely unexpected?

10. Equation 15.44 reports the value of a call option on a zero coupon bond. Use the parameters in Table 15.3 and let the short-term rate be $r_0 = 2\%$.

(a) What is the value of a call option with one year to maturity ($T_O = 1$), strike price $K = 90$, written on a zero coupon bond with 5 years to maturity ($T_B - T_O = 5$)?

(b) How does the value of the option depend on the current interest rate r_0? Compute the value also for $r_0 = 5.09\%$ and $r_0 = 10\%$.

(c) How does the value of the option depend on maturity? Compute the value also for $T_O = 0.5$ and $T_O = 2$.

(d) How does the value of the option depend on the maturity of the underlying? Compute the value also for $T_B - T_O = 1$ and $T_B - T_O = 10$.

11. Rework the previous exercise, but for a put option. In addition

(a) Consider a call option and a put option with the same strike price $K = 90$ and the same maturity $T_O = 1$ written on the same bond with $T_B - T_O = 5$. What is the value of this portfolio of two options? How does it relate to a forward contract to deliver the underlying bond with delivery price K? (See Chapter 5 for a discussion of forward contracts.)

Table 15.4   Treasury STRIPS on September 25, 2008

Year	Month	Day	Bid	Ask	Chg	Asked Yield	Time to Maturity
2008	11	15	99.898	99.918	0.001	0.6	0.139
2009	2	15	99.478	99.498	-0.068	1.31	0.389
2009	5	15	98.979	98.999	-0.056	1.59	0.639
2009	8	15	98.473	98.493	-0.146	1.72	0.889
2009	11	15	97.982	98.002	-0.194	1.78	1.139
2010	2	15	97.487	97.507	-0.236	1.83	1.389
2010	5	15	96.879	96.899	-0.277	1.93	1.639
2010	8	15	96.294	96.314	-0.318	2	1.889
2010	11	15	95.722	95.742	-0.359	2.05	2.139
2011	2	15	94.83	94.85	-0.413	2.23	2.389
2011	5	15	94.304	94.324	-0.442	2.23	2.639
2011	8	15	93.274	93.294	-0.539	2.42	2.889
2011	11	15	92.957	92.977	-0.481	2.34	3.139
2012	2	15	91.072	91.092	-0.48	2.78	3.389
2012	5	15	90.705	90.725	-0.515	2.69	3.639
2012	8	15	89.274	89.294	-0.566	2.94	3.889
2012	11	15	88.498	88.518	-0.589	2.97	4.139
2013	2	15	87.478	87.498	-0.607	3.07	4.389
2013	5	15	86.684	86.704	-0.647	3.1	4.639
2013	8	15	85.988	86.008	-0.666	3.11	4.889
2013	11	15	85.014	85.034	-0.725	3.18	5.139
2014	2	15	83.999	84.019	-0.763	3.26	5.389
2014	5	15	83.172	83.192	-0.814	3.29	5.639
2014	8	15	82.185	82.205	-0.828	3.36	5.889
2014	11	15	81.257	81.277	-0.903	3.41	6.139
2015	2	15	79.706	79.726	-0.462	3.58	6.389
2015	5	15	78.898	78.918	-0.489	3.6	6.639
2015	8	15	77.972	77.992	-0.502	3.64	6.889
2015	11	15	76.772	76.792	-0.525	3.73	7.139
2016	2	15	75.885	75.905	-0.538	3.77	7.389
2016	5	15	74.437	74.457	-0.573	3.9	7.639
2016	8	15	73.593	73.613	-0.599	3.92	7.889
2016	11	15	72.086	72.106	-0.707	4.06	8.139

Source: *The Wall Street Journal.*

12. Equation 15.51 reports the value of a call option on a coupon bond. Use the parameters in Table 15.3 and let the short-term rate be $r_0 = 2\%$.

   (a) What is the value of call option with one year to maturity ($T_0 = 1$), strike price $K = 100$, written on a coupon bond with 5 years to maturity ($T_B - T_O = 5$) and a coupon rate of 3%?

13. **Freddie Mac Callable Bonds.** Today is September 25, 2008. As a trader at PiVe Asset Management, you are considering the fair valuation of a callable note, issued by Freddie Mac a couple of years earlier. In particular, this is a 5.5% coupon bond,

with maturity March 28, 2016, and with call date March 28, 2011 only. The exercise time is European.[11] Treasury STRIPS as of today are in Table 15.4.

    (a) Use the data in Table 15.4 to estimate the Vasicek model as of September 25, 2008. Use the nonlinear least square methodology illustrated in Equation 15.41. To compute the volatility σ of the short-term rate, you can download data from the Federal Reserve Web site (*http://www.federalreserve.gov/releases/h15/ data.htm*) up to September 25, 2008. Alternatively, you can use the non-linear least square methodology illustrated in Equation 15.41 *also* to compute the volatility σ (it is a useful exercise to use both methodologies and compare results).

    (b) A callable bond can be considered as a portfolio of a non-callable bond and a call option. Use the results in the previous step to compute the value of the non-callable, 5.5% coupon bond with maturity T_B = March 28, 2011. As an approximation, assume today is a coupon date.

    (c) Compute the call option embedded in the callable bond. The bond can be called on T_O = March 28, 2016, for par. What is the value of the callable bond?

    (d) How does your answer to Part (c) change if the bond was callable in 1 year instead? Discuss.

15.7 APPENDIX: DERIVATIONS

15.7.1 Derivation of the Pricing Formula in Equation 15.4

We now check here that the solution in Equation 15.4 satisfies Equation 15.6. We proceed in two steps. First, compute the first derivatives on the left of Equation 15.6. To do this, note first that

$$\frac{\partial B(t;T)}{\partial t} = -e^{-\gamma(T-t)} \tag{15.73}$$

$$
\begin{aligned}
\frac{\partial Z}{\partial t} &= \left(\frac{\partial A(t;T)}{\partial t} - \frac{\partial B(t;T)}{\partial t}r\right) Z \\
&= \left(\bar{r}\left(\frac{\partial B(t;T)}{\partial t} - \frac{\partial (T-t)}{\partial t}\right) - \frac{\partial B(t;T)}{\partial t}r\right) Z \\
&= \left(\bar{r}\left(-e^{-\gamma(T-t)} + 1\right) + e^{-\gamma(T-t)}r\right) Z \\
&= \left(\bar{r}\gamma B(t;T) + (1 - \gamma B(t;T))r\right) Z \\
&= \left((\bar{r} - r)\gamma B(t;T) + r\right) Z
\end{aligned}
$$

where we used the fact that $e^{-\gamma(t-t)} = 1 - \gamma B(t;T)$. Similarly

$$\frac{\partial Z}{\partial r} = -B(t;T)Z$$

Thus, the left-hand side of Equation 15.6 is

$$\text{Left-hand side of Equation 15.6} \quad = \quad \frac{\partial Z}{\partial t} + \frac{\partial Z}{\partial r}\gamma\left(\bar{r} - r\right)$$

---

[11] See Pricing Supplemente Prospectus Dated on April 21, 2006. This security ID is CUSIP: 3128X4W72.

$$
\begin{aligned}
&= \left((\bar{r} - r)\gamma B(t;T) + r\right)Z - B(t;T)Z\gamma\left(\bar{r} - r\right) \\
&= rZ = \text{Right-hand side of Equation 15.6}
\end{aligned}
$$

15.7.2   The Derivation of the Vasicek Pricing Formula

From the assumption $m^*(r,t) = \gamma^* \times (\bar{r}^* - r)$, Equation 15.24 can be rewritten as

$$
rZ = \frac{\partial Z}{\partial t} + \frac{\partial Z}{\partial r}\gamma^*\left(\bar{r}^* - r\right) + \frac{1}{2}\frac{\partial^2 Z}{\partial r^2}\sigma^2 \tag{15.74}
$$

The methodology used to obtain the pricing formula is as follows. We first guess that the solution takes the form

$$
Z(r,t;T) = e^{A(t;T) - B(t;T)\times r}
$$

for some functions of time $A(t;T)$ and $B(t;T)$ yet to be found. We now use the general partial differential equation (PDE) in Equation 15.74 to find the two functions $A(t;T)$ and $B(t;T)$. Denote by $A'(t;T)$ and $B'(t;T)$ the first derivatives of $A(t;T)$ and $B(t;T)$ with respect to t. Compute first the partial derivatives:

$$
\begin{aligned}
\frac{\partial Z}{\partial t} &= \left(A'(t;T) - rB'(t;T)\right)e^{A(t;T) - rB(t;T)} = \left(A'(t;T) - rB'(t;T)\right)Z(r,t;T) \\
\frac{\partial Z}{\partial r} &= -B(t;T)e^{A(t;T) - rB(t;T)} = -B(t;T)Z(r,t;T) \\
\frac{\partial^2 Z}{\partial r^2} &= B(t;T)^2 e^{A(t;T) - rB(t;T)} = B(t;T)^2 Z(r,t;T)
\end{aligned}
$$

Substitute everything into Equation 15.74 to find

$$
\begin{aligned}
rZ(r,t;T) &= \left(A'(t;T) - rB'(t;T)\right)Z(r,t;T) + \frac{1}{2}B(t;T)^2 Z(r,t;T)\sigma^2 \\
&\quad - B(t;T)Z(r,t;T)\gamma^* \times (\bar{r}^* - r)
\end{aligned}
$$

Delete $Z(r,t;T)$ from both sides and collect terms containing r to find

$$
\left(1 + B'(t;T) - B(t;T)\gamma^*\right)r = A'(t;T) + \frac{1}{2}B(t;T)^2\sigma^2 - B(t;T)\bar{r}^*\gamma^* \tag{15.75}
$$

The left-hand side depends on r while the right-hand side does not. Hence, the equality in Equation 15.75 can hold only if the coefficient of r is equal to zero. This observation yields

$$
\begin{aligned}
B'(t;T) &= B(t;T)\gamma^* - 1 \tag{15.76} \\
A'(t;T) &= B(t;T)\bar{r}^*\gamma^* - \frac{1}{2}B(t;T)^2\sigma^2 \tag{15.77}
\end{aligned}
$$

These two ordinary differential equations (ODEs) can be solved sequentially: We first solve Equation 15.76 and then plug the result into Equation 15.77 and find the second function. From the boundary condition

$$
Z(r,T;T) = e^{A(T;T) - rB(T;T)} = 1
$$

we find the final condition

$$
A(T;T) = 0 \; ; \; B(T;T) = 0 \tag{15.78}
$$

The solution of $B(t;T)$ in Equation 15.76 is given in Equation 15.29.[12] Plugging this solution into Equation 15.77 we easily find the second solution is Equation 15.30.

15.7.3 The CIR Model

Conditional on $r(0) = r_0$

$$r(t)|_{r(0)=r_0} \sim \text{non-central chi-square}$$

Specifically, the density is given by[13]

$$f(r|r_0) = c_t \, \chi^2(c_t r, v, \lambda_t)$$

where $\chi^2(., v, \lambda_t)$ is a non-central chi squared distribution with v degrees of freedom, and non centrality parameter λ_t, with

$$
\begin{aligned}
c_t &= \frac{4\gamma}{\alpha(1 - e^{-\gamma t})} \\
v &= \frac{4\gamma}{\alpha} \times \bar{r} \\
\lambda_t &= c_t r_0 e^{-\gamma t}
\end{aligned}
$$

We can obtain the stationary distribution by taking the limit as $t \to \infty$.

---

[12] In fact, we have that $B(T) = 0$ and $B'(t;T) = -e^{-\gamma(T-t)} = \gamma B(t;T) - 1$.
[13] See e.g. Brigo and Mercurio (2007).

CHAPTER 16

DYNAMIC HEDGING AND RELATIVE VALUE TRADES

The no-arbitrage pricing methodology we discussed in Chapter 15, Section 15.2.1, is also at the basis of dynamic hedging strategies and relative value trades. In the next section we examine the concept of dynamic replication in continuous time. Recall that we looked at the concept of dynamic replication in no arbitrage models in Chapter 10, Section 10.2.2, in the context of binomial trees. The discussion in the next section extends those concepts to the more general continuous time framework.

16.1 THE REPLICATING PORTFOLIO

Consider again the portfolio $\Pi(r, t)$ in Equation 15.11 in Chapter 15, given by a long position in bond $Z_1(r, t)$ and short Δ units of bond $Z_2(r, t)$:

$$\Pi(r, t) = Z_1(r, t) - \Delta Z_2(r, t) \tag{16.1}$$

Recall that according to the hedging rule in Equation 15.14, we choose Δ equal to the ratio of the sensitivities of the two bonds to the interest rate:

$$\Delta = \frac{\partial Z_1 / \partial r}{\partial Z_2 / \partial r} \tag{16.2}$$

The process for Π_t, according to Ito's lemma, is

$$d\Pi_t = dZ_{1,t} - \Delta dZ_{2,t} \tag{16.3}$$

Let us now rewrite this equation as

$$dZ_{1,t} = \Delta dZ_{2,t} + d\Pi_t \tag{16.4}$$

Notice an interesting fact. If we know (a) the value of "Δ"; (b) the change in the price of bond 2 between t and $t + dt$, "$dZ_{2,t}$"; and (c) the change in value of the portfolio "$d\Pi_t$", then we can compute the change in value of bond 1, "$dZ_{1,t}$."

We now realize that if we choose Δ according to the hedging rule in Equation 15.14, then the no arbitrage condition stated in Equation 15.17 implies

$$d\Pi_t = r_t \Pi_t dt \tag{16.5}$$

This in turn implies that indeed we do know the change of the total portfolio between t and $t + dt$: It is the same as the return on an investment made at the risk-free rate r_t. In fact, if we invest an amount C_t at the risk-free rate r_t, between t and $t + dt$ the change in the investment value is exactly

$$dC_t = r_t C_t dt. \tag{16.6}$$

It follows that if $C_t = \Pi_t$ at t, then we can rewrite the return process of bond 1 in Equation 16.4 between t and $t + dt$ as

$$dZ_{1,t} = \Delta dZ_{2,t} + dC_t \tag{16.7}$$

This equation says that under no arbitrage, the dollar return on bond 1 can also be obtained by a position Δ in bond 2 plus a position C_t in cash invested (or borrowed, if $C_t < 0$) at the risk-free rate. That is, we can *replicate* the return process of bond 1 by using a position in bond 2 and in cash. This finding leads to the following:

Fact 16.1 *Consider two interest rate securities $Z_1(r,t)$ and $Z_2(r,t)$. Let Δ be given by Equation 16.2, and let C_t be a position in cash (yielding r_t) given by*

$$C_t = Z_1(r_t, t) - \Delta Z_2(r_t, t) \tag{16.8}$$

The portfolio P_t with Δ units in security Z_2 and a C_t in cash (if $C_t < 0$ this position entails borrowing),

$$P_t = \Delta Z_{2,t} + C_t \tag{16.9}$$

replicates the return on security Z_1 between t and $t + dt$, namely

$$dP_t = dZ_{1,t} \tag{16.10}$$

Definition 16.1 *he portfolio P_t described in Equation 16.9 is called a **replicating portfolio**.*

Example 16.1 illustrates the dynamic replication methodology.

Table 16.1 Two Zero Coupon Bond Prices Implied by the Vasicek Model

	$T = 1.1041$	$T = 3.3479$
$B(0, T)$	0.8634	1.6964
$A(0, T)$	-0.0152	-0.1037
$Z(r_0, 0; T)$ $(\times 100)$	97.0756	87.6233
$y(r_0, 0; T)$	2.6882	3.9464

■ **EXAMPLE 16.1**

In Section 15.2.4 in Chapter 15 we estimated the following parameters for the Vasicek model: $\bar{r} = 5.09\%$, $\gamma = 0.3261$, $\sigma = 2.21\%$, $\gamma^* = 0.4653$, and $\bar{r}^* = 6.34\%$. Let the current short-term interest rate be $r_0 = 1.68\%$. Consider two zero coupon bonds with maturities $T_1 = 1.1041$ and $T_2 = 3.3479$. Applying the pricing formula in Equation 15.28, Table 16.1 shows that we obtain $Z(r_0, 0; T_1) = 97.0756$ and $Z(r_0, 0; T_2) = 87.6233$ (for \$100 principal). In addition, because $\partial Z / \partial r = -B(0, T)Z(r, 0; T)$, we find that in this case the hedge ratio is:

$$\Delta = \frac{B(0, T_1)Z(r_0, 0; T_1)}{B(0, T_2)Z(r_0, 0; T_2)} = \frac{0.8634 \times 97.0756}{1.6964 \times 87.6233} = 0.5638 \qquad (16.11)$$

That is, the replicating portfolio must have a long position in the T_2−bond of 0.5638. The initial position in cash, C_0, from Equation 16.8 is then given by

$$C_0 = Z(r_0, 0; T_1) - \Delta_0 Z(r_0, 0; T_2) = 97.0756 - 0.5638 \times 87.6233 = 47.6696 \quad (16.12)$$

From Equation 16.9, the replicating portfolio is then

$$P_0 = \Delta_0 Z(r_0, 0; T_2) + C_0 = 0.5638 \times 87.6233 + 47.6696 = 97.0756 = Z(r_0, 0; T_1)$$

By construction, the value of the replicating portfolio at time 0 equals the value of the security that we want to replicate, namely, the T_1 bond. Does this portfolio replicate the T_1−bond price between 0 and dt? To answer this question, let's compute the values at dt of both the T_1−bond and the portfolio P under various interest rate scenarios. This exercise is performed in Table 16.2 for two levels of rebalancing period dt, daily ($dt = 1/252$) and weekly ($dt = 1/52$). The current rate is $r_0 = 1.68\%$. As can be seen, whether the interest rate moves up or down, the value P_t of the replicating portfolio is close to the T_1-bond price $Z(r_{dt}, dt; T_1)$. This is especially true in the case of daily rebalancing.

16.2 REBALANCING

The strategy underlying Fact 16.1 calls for a position at time t of $\Delta = \frac{\partial Z_1 / \partial r}{\partial Z_2 / \partial r}$ in security $Z_{2,t}$ and a position in cash C_t. This portfolio yields a return equal to the one of security

Table 16.2 Performance of Replicating Portfolio between $[0, dt]$

	$dt = 1/252 = 0.004$		$dt = 1/52 = 0.0192$	
r_{dt} (%)	$Z(r_{dt}, dt; T_1)$	P_{dt}	$Z(r_{dt}, dt; T_1)$	P_{dt}
0.50	98.0814	98.0928	98.1427	98.1415
1.00	97.6603	97.6673	97.7279	97.7164
1.50	97.2411	97.2454	97.3149	97.2949
1.68	97.0924	97.0962	97.1684	97.1459
2.00	96.8236	96.8270	96.9036	96.877
2.50	96.4079	96.4122	96.4941	96.4626
3.00	95.9940	96.0009	96.0863	96.0517

1 at time $t + dt$. By construction, at time t we choose C_t so that $P_t = Z_{1,t}$. If the dollar returns between t and $t + dt$ of the portfolio and the bond are the same, it follows that at time $t + dt$ we will also have $P_{t+dt} = Z_{1,t+dt}$.

To carry out the trade in the next period, however, we need to *rebalance* the portfolio. Indeed, at this point $(t + dt)$ the hedge ratio Δ must have changed, as the spot rate r_t has changed to r_{t+dt}, and so have the prices $Z_{1,t+dt}$ and $Z_{2,t+dt}$. Rebalancing the portfolio means to take action so that the portfolio position in security 2 is equal to the new Δ_{t+dt}. The latter is still given by Equation 16.2, but for the new prices and time to maturity. For instance, if Δ_{t+dt} increases with respect to Δ_t, we need to increase our position in $Z_{2,t+dt}$. This stronger position can be obtained by decreasing the amount of cash balances C_{t+dt} (or by borrowing more if $C_t < 0$). In particular, we compute

$$\text{Cash needed for rebalancing} = (\Delta_{t+dt} - \Delta_t) Z_{2,t+dt} \qquad (16.13)$$

The new position in cash is therefore

$$C_{t+dt} = C_t + C_t r_t dt - \text{Cash needed for rebalancing} \qquad (16.14)$$

That is, the amount in cash position at time $t + dt$ equals the amount at time t plus interest minus any withdrawal needed for rebalancing. After rebalancing, the value of the portfolio is $P_{t+dt} = \Delta_{t+dt} Z_{2,t+dt} + C_{t+dt}$. According to Fact 16.1 the portfolio will replicate the next movement in interest rates.

■ **EXAMPLE 16.2**

Consider again Example 16.1. After the first period, whose outcome is illustrated in Table 16.2 for various interest rate scenarios, the portfolio must be rebalanced according to Equation 16.14 to ensure that at time dt the replicating portfolio has a position in the T_2 bond equal to the new Δ. More explicitly, Table 16.3 shows the computations for the rebalancing at time dt in the various interest rate scenarios at $dt = 1/252$. For instance, assume that at dt the interest rate increases to $r_{dt} = 2.50\%$ from $r_0 = 1.68\%$. In this case, the second column shows that the position in T_2 bond has to increase to $\Delta_{dt} = 0.5662$ from $\Delta_0 = 0.5638$ (see Equation 16.11). Increasing the position from Δ_0 to Δ_{dt} at the current price of the T_2 bond, namely

Table 16.3 Portfolio Rebalancing at dt

r_{dt} (%)	Δ_{dt}	$Z(r_{dt}, dt; T_2)$	Cash Needed	Interest	C_{dt}
0.50	0.5568	89.4218	-0.6306	0.0032	48.3034
1.00	0.5591	88.6671	-0.4189	0.0032	48.0916
1.50	0.5615	87.9188	-0.2098	0.0032	47.8825
1.68	0.5623	87.6543	-0.1361	0.0032	47.8088
2.00	0.5638	87.1769	-0.0033	0.0032	47.6761
2.50	0.5662	86.4411	0.2005	0.0032	47.4723
3.00	0.5685	85.7116	0.4017	0.0032	47.2710

$Z(r_{dt}, dt; T_2) = 86.4411$ in the third column, generates a cash need equal to $0.2005. This amount can be obtained from liquidating some of the initial cash position $C_0 = 47.6696$ (see Equation 16.12). In particular, after accounting for the interest of $.0032 received over one day (in Column 5 in Table 16.3), the cash position after rebalancing is

$$C_d t = C_0 + C_0 r_0 dt - \text{Cash needed} = \$47.6696 + \$0.0032 - \$0.2005 = \$47.4723$$

This procedure can be reiterated every day (in fact, in theory, every instant dt) until maturity T_1. At this time, the replicating portfolio $P_t = \Delta_t Z(r_t, t; T_2) + C_t$ should be worth exactly $P_{T_1} = \$100 = Z(r_{T_1}, T_1; T_1)$, independent of what the interest rates does along the way.

Does it work?

Figures 16.1 and 16.2 plot the performance of the replication strategy on a simulated interest rate path for two rebalancing frequencies: daily ($dt = 1/252$) and weekly ($dt = 1/52$). In both figures, the top panel represents a simulated interest rate path.[1] The middle panels report the position in the T_2 bond, Δ_t (in percentage) and cash balance C_t. As can be seen, the replication strategy calls for a progressive decrease in the T_2 bond and an increase in cash balances, to reach exactly $100 by T_1. The bottom panel plots the replicating portfolio (the solid line) and the T_1 zero coupon bond (the dotted line). Figure 16.1 speaks for itself: One line is exactly on top of the other, and therefore it is not even possible to see any difference between the replicating portfolio and the bond to be replicated. The weekly rebalancing in Figure 16.2 also shows that replication works, but less perfectly so. In this case, a little occasional discrepancy between the zero coupon bond and the replicating portfolio is visible.

The bottom line of this example is to show the principle according to which in the Vasicek model – and in fact any one factor model – the price and the payoff of any bond can be replicated by a position in another bond. In fact, *any* interest rate security can be replicated

---

[1] The simulation is carried out using the Vasicek model with parameters $\bar{r} = 5.09\%, \gamma = 0.3261$ and $\sigma = 2.21\%$.

Figure 16.1   Replicating a $T_1 = 1.1$ STRIP on a Simulated Interest Rate Path – Daily Rebalancing

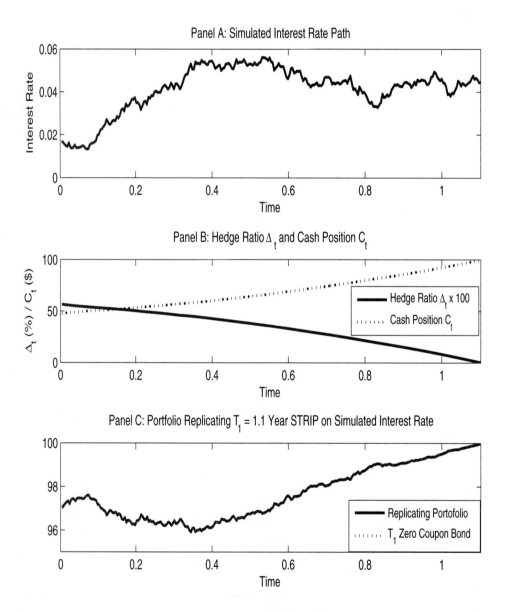

Figure 16.2   Replicating a $T_1 = 1.1$ STRIP on a Simulated Interest Rate Path – Weekly Rebalancing

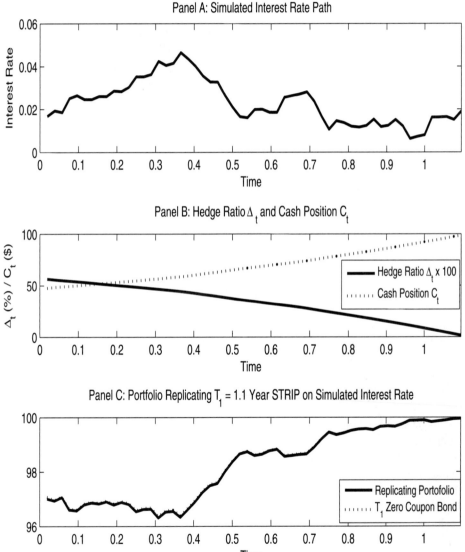

by another interest rate security. This fact is at the basis of relative value trades, and the next few sections illustrate the methodology.

16.3   APPLICATION 1: RELATIVE VALUE TRADES ON THE YIELD CURVE

In this section we explore an application of the Vasicek model for arbitrage trading. This application is only illustrative, using a simple model, of a more general methodology that employs a term structure model to set up arbitrage trades.

Consider again Example 15.1 in Chapter 15. Assume that today is January 8, 2002. Table 15.1 in Chapter 15 reports the prices of STRIPS prices on January 8, 2002. The question an arbitrageur would ask is simple: Can these STRIPS prices be reconciled with the Vasicek model? If not, is it possible to find a trading strategy to profit from the price discrepancy? The answer to these questions stand at the basis of relative value trades, in which we use a model – the Vasicek model in this case – to find out whether the value of one security *relative* to another security is correct. We proceed as follows:

1. **Parameter Estimation**: We estimate the parameters of the Vasicek model so as to best match the prices in Table 15.1.

2. **Relative Pricing Error Discovery**: We confront the Vasicek prices with the data, and find out whether they are in line with each other.

3. **Set Up a Trading Strategy**: If the model does not agree with the data, according to the model there is an arbitrage opportunity. We set up a trading strategy to profit from the discrepancy.

We already carried out the first step, "parameter estimation," in Example 15.1 in Chapter 15. In particular, recall, we searched for the parameters $\bar{r}^*$ and γ^* that best fit the data available on January 8, 2002.[2] We found $\bar{r}^* = 0.0634$ and $\gamma^* = .4653$. Figure 16.3 reports both the yield curve obtained from the STRIPS data on the same day, as well as the model yields from the fitted model.

16.3.1   Relative Pricing Errors Discovery

As can be seen from Figure 16.3, the model is not able to correctly price short-term bonds, compared to long-term bonds. Because this is the "best" the model could do, there isn't any other set of parameters of the model that can fit the yield curve any better. According to the model, then, there is an arbitrage opportunity. In particular, the model reveals that short-term bonds are too expensive (interest rate too low) compared to long-term bonds. Therefore, a *relative value trade* ("buy cheap / sell dear") in this case calls for a long position in medium/long-term bonds, and short position in short-term bonds.

16.3.2   Setting Up the Arbitrage Trade

More specifically, an arbitrageur can:

---

[2]We fixed the parameters σ equal to the standard deviation of short-term T-bill rate changes, as the model would imply. Fitting σ as well to best match the term structure of interest rates does not change the fit of the model.

Figure 16.3 Fitted Zero Coupon Yield Curves from STRIPS: January 8, 2002

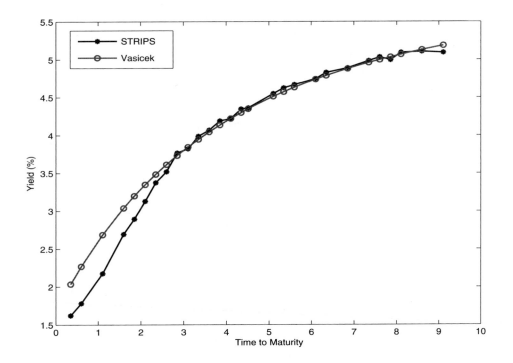

Data Source: *The Wall Street Journal*

1. Sell short the STRIP with $T_1 = 1.1$ years to maturity, for $\widehat{Z}(T_1) = \$97.625$.

2. Go long Δ STRIP with maturity $T_2 = 3.34$ years (which are fairly priced, according to the model).

3. Choose Δ according to the theory so as to *replicate* the T_1 year STRIP with the T_2 year STRIP.

4. Use the dynamic replication strategy to replicate the short position.

This example is the same one that we utilized in Examples 16.1 and 16.2 to illustrate the replication strategy of short-term bonds using long-term bonds. To summarize, we already know from that example that the position in the T_2 bond has to be $\Delta_0 = 0.5638$ and the position in cash has to be $C_0 = \$47.6696$. The value of this portfolio at 0 is the same as the "Vasicek" price of the T_1 bond $P_0 = \$97.0756$. This value is lower than the value of the traded security $Z^{data}(r_0, 0; T_1) = \$97.625$. So, overall, we sell short one T_1-STRIPS for $\$97.6250$ mm, we buy 0.5638 T_2-STRIPS for $\$49.3365$ mm, realizing a $\$48.2885$ mm inflow of cash. However, to start the dynamic hedging strategy, we need to invest $\$47.6696$ mm in an overnight deposit yielding $r_0 = 1.68\%$. For each T_1 strip sold, we are left with $\$0.6189$ mm inflow of profit, if the replication strategy works. Figures 16.1 and 16.2 show that the strategy *should* work according to the Vasicek model.

16.4 APPLICATION 2: HEDGING DERIVATIVE EXPOSURE

In this section we show that an interest rate model such as the Vasicek model also informs traders of the optimal hedging strategy to employ when they take positions in derivatives. The first subsection describes the dynamic hedging strategy to cover against a short position in a call option, while the second subsection illustrates a relative value trade on derivatives, of the same sort as the one featured in Section 16.3.

16.4.1 Hedging and Dynamic Replication

Consider again Example 15.2 in Chapter 15. In particular, recall, today is January 8, 2002, and a client asks for a quote on a 1-year European call option on a 4-year zero coupon bond, with strike price $K = \$80$. Given the parameter estimates of the Vasicek model computed at that time, Equation 15.44 yields a call option price equal to $\$2.2921$.

Suppose we sold a call option to the client. We do not want to keep the naked short position on our books, and thus an effective risk management strategy requires us to hedge it. Intuitively, we can effectively hedge the short position in the call option by taking a position in the underlying security itself, in this case $Z(t, r; T_B)$. The question is: What position should we take? The methodology used in the earlier section works here too.

Consider the portfolio

$$\Pi(r, t) = -V(r, t) + \Delta \times 100 \times Z(t, r; T_B) \tag{16.15}$$

where Δ is the number of zero coupon bonds to buy (if positive) and we keep the assumption that par value equals $\$100$, as in Example 15.2. We want to make Π insensitive to unexpected changes in the interest rate, and thus choose Δ such that

$$\frac{\partial \Pi}{\partial r} = 0$$

#Chut through Δ
and cash position concept
↳ whatsw/the graphs?

APPLICATION 2: HEDGING DERIVATIVE EXPOSURE   **573**

This equation implies

$$\Delta = \frac{\partial V / \partial r}{100 \, \partial Z / \partial r}$$

From the bonds formula in Equation 15.28 in Chapter 15, we have that at $t = 0$

$$\frac{\partial Z}{\partial r} = -B\left(0; T_B\right) Z\left(0, r_0; T_B\right) = -1.5496$$

The formula for $\partial V / \partial r$ is more involved, and we provide it in Equation 16.31 in the Appendix. We obtain

$$\frac{\partial V}{\partial r} = -73.3186$$

The position in $Z(0, r; t_B)$ is then

$$\Delta_0 = \frac{1}{100} \frac{\partial V / \partial r}{\partial Z / \partial r} = 0.4731 \tag{16.16}$$

That is, if we sell one option on a zero coupon bond, we need a long offsetting position in the zero coupon equal to $\Delta_0 \times 100 \times Z\left(0, r_0; T_B\right) = 0.4731 \times 100 \times 0.7991 = 37.8091$.
    The value of the position is

$$\Pi_0 \quad = \quad -V\left(r_0, 0\right) + \Delta_0 \times 100 \times Z\left(0, r_0; T_B\right) = 35.5170$$

Because this value is positive, it implies that we must borrow this amount of money to set up the replicating portfolio at time 0. As before, let $C_0 = -35.5170$ be the amount borrowed at time 0. The replicating portfolio at time 0 is then given by the long position in long-term bond plus a position in cash equal to C_0, that is

$$P_0 = \Delta_0 \times 100 \times Z\left(0, r_0; T_B\right) + C_0$$

By construction

$$P_0 = V\left(r_0, T_O\right) = 2.2921$$

After $t = 0$ we must dynamically adjust the position in long-term bonds to keep Δ as given by the expression in Equation 16.16: If Δ increases, we need to borrow more, while if it decreases we must borrow less.
    As we did in Example 16.2 we can simulate some sample interest rate paths and see whether the replication strategy works. Figure 16.4 plots the performance of the replication strategy on such a simulated interest rate path, as shown in Panel A. Panel B reports the position Δ_t in the underlying $Z(r_t, t; T_B)$, in percent, as well as the amount borrowed $|C_t|$ (we report the absolute value to show its dynamics next to the Δ_t).
    From Figure 16.4 we see that when the interest rate declines, the position Δ increases. The reason is that a decline in interest rate implies an increase in the underlying bond price, and thus the need of a more extreme position in the underlying to hedge it. When Δ increases, so does the borrowed amount. Panel C plots both the value of the option, according to the formula in Equation 15.44 in Chapter 15, and the value of the replicating portfolio $P_t = \Delta_t Z(r_t, t; T_B) + C_t$. As it can be seen, in this simulation, the replicating portfolio tracks very closely the value of the option itself. In particular, the seller of the option is able to fully hedge its short position.

Figure 16.4 Replicating a Call Option on a Zero Coupon Bond

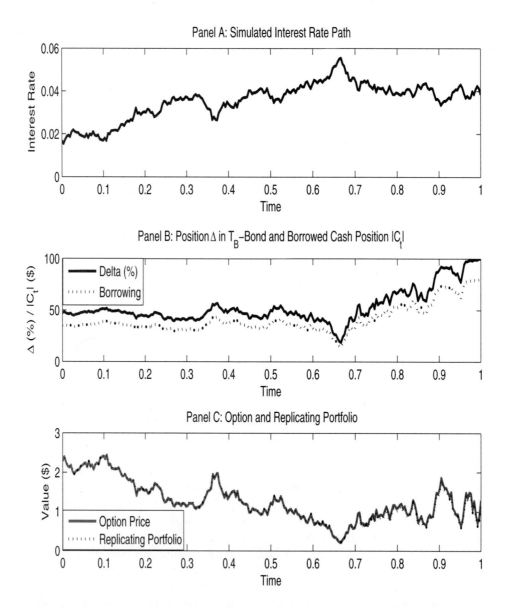

16.4.2   Trading on Mispricing and Relative Value Trades

The term structure model also provides guidance to find mispriced securities. For instance, in the previous example, suppose that we find that a call option is trading at $3.00, while the Vasicek model says its value should be $V(0, r_0) = \$2.2921$. Taking full faith in the model, we can set up a strategy to profit from the mispricing (compared to the model). In particular, we want to:

1. Sell the traded option at its traded price of $3.00.

2. Borrow $39.4519 at the risk free rate r_0.

3. Purchase $\Delta_0 100 Z(0, r_0; T_B) = 0.4731 \times 100 \times 0.7991 = \$37.8091$ of zero coupon bonds.

4. After $t = 0$, rebalance the portfolio according to the rule discussed in the previous section, and illustrated in Figure 16.4.

If the model is correct, then at maturity T_O the replicating portfolio will deliver exactly the payoff of the option we sold today. That is, we are hedged for time T_O. However, the trading strategy allows us to make a profit today, equal to the difference between the sale price of the traded option ($3.00) and the cost of setting up the replicating portfolio. According to the model, the cost of setting up the replicating portfolio exactly equals the value of the option we get from the Vasicek model, that is, by construction, $P_0 = V(0, r_0) = \$2.2921$. Thus, today, the trading strategy allows us to reap a profit of $0.7079=$3-$2.2921.

16.5   THE THETA - GAMMA RELATION

In this final section of the chapter we discuss an important concept, known as the Theta–Gamma relation. To introduce this concept, it is convenient to go back to the informal discussion of Ito's lemma in Chapter 14. In particular, in Figure 14.8 we show heuristically why although a Brownian motion X_t is unpredictable, a non-linear function $F(X)$ of the Brownian motion becomes predictable, that is, it has a drift component (see Ito's lemma in Equation 14.37). In that figure we showed that if for instance $F(X)$ has a minimum, then although we do not know whether $X_{t+\delta}$ will be higher or smaller than X_t, we also give zero probability that $X_{t+\delta} = X_t$. That is, the nature of stochastic processes is that the random variable X_t *will* move in the next δ period. Because $F(X_t)$ is at the minimum, the function $F(X)$ cannot but increase in the next instant, that is, we know for sure that $F(X_{t+\delta}) > F(X_t)$. If X represents the interest rate, for instance, and $P_t = F(X_t)$ represents a security, such as a straddle, that is, a long call and a long put on X_t, then this discussion seems to imply that by increasing the convexity of the position, a trader can make large profits. This conclusion is not warranted, however, because no arbitrage implies that a large convexity (Gamma) is always counterbalanced by a large, and opposite, portfolio sensitivity to time, Theta. That is, we now see that if a Delta-hedged security has a large convexity, it must decline in price because of the simple passage of time. Otherwise, an arbitrage opportunity would occur.

Let's illustrate this fact within an example. Suppose we sold, for instance, a call option on a zero coupon bond and, as discussed in the previous section, we put on a position Δ in the underlying zero coupon bond to hedge the interest rate risk. The portfolio Π is riskless and earns the risk free rate, that is,

$$d\Pi = r\Pi dt$$

This portfolio, short a call option and long the underlying zero coupon bond, must, as any other security, also satisfy the Fundamental Pricing Equation (see Equation 15.24 in Chapter 15), that is

$$\frac{\partial \Pi}{\partial t} + \frac{\partial \Pi}{\partial r} m^*(r,t) + \frac{1}{2} \frac{\partial^2 \Pi}{\partial r^2} \sigma^2 = r\Pi \tag{16.17}$$

However, since this portfolio is Delta hedged, $(\partial \Pi / \partial r) = 0$, the relation is in fact

$$\left(\frac{1}{\Pi} \frac{\partial \Pi}{\partial t} \right) + \frac{1}{2} \left(\frac{1}{\Pi} \frac{\partial^2 \Pi}{\partial r^2} \right) \sigma^2 = r \tag{16.18}$$

where we divided by Π (assumed not to be zero). Equation 16.18 has a strong implication, then, namely:

High Theta $\left(\dfrac{1}{\Pi} \dfrac{\partial \Pi}{\partial t} \right) \Longleftrightarrow$ Low (or even negative) covexity Gamma $\left(\dfrac{1}{\Pi} \dfrac{\partial^2 \Pi}{\partial r^2} \right)$

The intuition stems from a simple no arbitrage argument: A positive-value portfolio with a high Theta is expected to make money because of the pure passage of time. If it was to make more money than the risk-free rate, it would be a pure arbitrage, because a trader could borrow at the risk-free rate, set up the portfolio, and wait. The negative convexity rebalances the pure arbitrage: The movement (i.e., volatility) in the interest rates tends on average to depress the portfolio value.

■ **EXAMPLE 16.3**

Consider again the portfolio discussed in Subsection 16.4.1. The portfolio Π is short a call option, and long Δ of the underlying bond. Figure 16.5 plots the surface of the value of the hedged portfolio as a function of time t and interest rate r. As can be seen, the surface shows a negative convexity when viewed across the interest rate axis. At the same time, the portfolio would increase in value as time t passes. In other words, if this portfolio did not have negative convexity, it would represent a pure arbitrage, as its value would grow at a higher rate than interest rate. An arbitrageur could then borrow (at the risk-free rate), set up the portfolio, and wait. In well-functioning markets, this situation cannot persist, and the negative convexity illustrates the risk of setting up the portfolio. In economic terms, options are instruments with strong positive convexity. Thus, because the portfolio is short an option, it entails a negative convexity and therefore a natural tendency to lose money simply because the interest rate is stochastic (even though we do not know in which direction the interest rate will move). The positive theta is a compensation for the risk stemming from variation in interest rates.

16.6 SUMMARY

In this chapter we covered the following topics:

Figure 16.5   The Hedged Portfolio

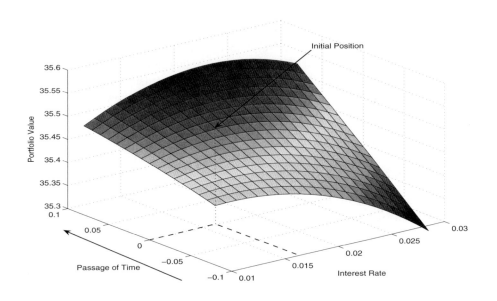

1. Replicating portfolio: A portfolio composed of an interest rate security and cash chosen in a way to mimic the variation in prices of another interest rate security. Theoretically, the dynamic rebalancing of this portfolio, according to an appropriate hedge ratio, allows the replicating portfolio to replicate all of the cash flows of the interest rate security it aims to replicate.

2. Hedge ratio: This is the key input in the replicating portfolio: It is the ratio of the sensitivities of the two interest rate securities, the one to replicate (numerator) and the one used to replicate (denominator). The hedge ratio changes over time as the time to maturity and the level of interest rate change. For this reason, the replicating portfolio must be dynamically adjusted over time.

3. Relative value trades: At times, the yield curve of interest rates or a given interest rate security, such as an option, does not conform with the prediction of an interest rate model, such as the Vasicek model. In these instances, according to the model, there is a mispricing of interest rate securities. Relative value trades consist of taking positions in order to profit from mispricing. The replicating portfolio is instrumental in determining the exact quantities of securities to be bought or sold within the trade, and the rebalancing strategy to follow after the initiation of the trade.

4. Theta-Gamma relation: In any hedged portfolio – such as the ones that we obtain out of the relative value strategies – there is a tight relation between Theta (sensitivity of the portfolio to time) and Gamma (convexity of the portfolio). A security with a high Theta stands to make profits from the simple passage of time. To avoid arbitrage

opportunities, such profits must be counterbalanced by a low or negative Gamma, so that the portfolio stands to lose money only because of the variation in interest rates.

16.7 EXERCISES

1. Today is September 25, 2008. Table 15.4 in Chapter 15 contains the STRIPS data today (see Exercise 12 in Chapter 15). According to the Vasicek model, is there any trading opportunity? Fit the Vasicek model to the data, find pricing errors and discuss the available trading opportunities. Be explicit on how you would exploit these trading opportunities, that is, the long/short positions.

2. Refer to Exercise 1 and set up the trading strategy, as shown in Example 16.1. Check that the one-step replication strategy works, according to the model, by replicating Table 16.2 for this exercise.

3. Use simulations to check the performance of the replicating strategy, as in Figures 16.1 and 16.2. Does the replicating portfolio "replicate" ?

4. On September 25, 2008 a client asks you the price of a call option with maturity November 15, 2010, written on the STRIP maturing on November 15, 2015, and with strike price 82.

   (a) What is the price of the option?

   (b) You sold the option, but you do not want to keep the position naked. So, you want to hedge using the STRIPS maturing on November 15, 2015 itself. Use the Vasicek model to determine the appropriate hedge ratio. (*Hint: Computing the sensitivity of a call price to the interest rate may be difficult. Either you use the formula in Equation 16.31 or compute the hedge ratio numerically, by applying the call option pricing formula in Equation 15.44 in Chapter 15 to two interest rates $r_0 - \delta$ and $r_0 + \delta$, and compute $\partial V / \partial r \approx [V(r_0 + \delta) - V(r_0 - \delta)] / (2 \times \delta)$).*

   (c) Set up the replicating portfolio. Use simulations to check that the replicating portfolio replicates (see Subsection 16.4.1). Obtain a figure similar to 16.4

5. Consider the previous exercise, but for a put option with the same strike price. Derive first the hedge ratio by following the same steps as in the appendix at the end of this chapter. Then, rework the exercise.

6. Consider the Freddie Mac callable bond in Exercise 13 in Chapter 15.

   (a) What is the sensitivity of this callable bonds with respect to interest rates? That is, denoting by $P^C(r, t; T)$ the callable bond, what is $\partial P^C / \partial r$? (*Hint: The callable bond is a portfolio of securities, namely, the non-callable bond minus the option to call. The latter is computed as a portfolio of options on zero coupon bonds. The sensitivity of the callable bond then can be computed from the sensitivity of the securities making up the portfolio.*)

   (b) How would you hedge a long position in the callable bond against variation in the interest rate?

(c) Suppose that the bond becomes callable in one year, instead of 3 years. How would your answer to the previous question change? Discuss.

7. Consider the relative value strategy discussed in the case study in Section 16.8. Instead of the Vasicek model, set up the arbitrage strategy using the Cox, Ingersoll, and Ross model introduced in Section 15.4.1 of Chapter 15. How does the long/short strategy differ? Use a simulated path of interest rates to check the performance of the model.

16.8 CASE STUDY: RELATIVE VALUE TRADES ON THE YIELD CURVE

In this case study we illustrate the concept of relative value trades and dynamic replication on the yield curve by using actual coupon bonds, and following the performance of the relative value trade over time. Let today be February 17, 2004. The first five columns of Table 16.4 contain coupons, maturities, and price quotes of the most recently issued Treasury notes and bonds, in the February - August coupon cycle, with times to maturity less than 20 years. We use the Vasicek model to implement the relative value trade.[3]

The first step to set up a relative value trade is to obtain the parameters $\bar{r}^*$, γ^* and σ of the Vasicek model that best fit the term structure of interest rates. Because realistically the long/short strategy of the trade will involve repurchase agreements, the rate of interest to be used as the short-term rate should be the overnight repo rate. Figure 16.6 shows the time series of the repo rate.

As discussed in Section 15.2.4 in Chapter 15, the parameter σ is given by the volatility of the short-term interest rate. The volatility of the overnight repo rate is substantial, and indeed we get $\sigma = 3.17\%$. Instead, $\bar{r}^*$ and γ^* are estimated by using a nonlinear least square technique. Unlike in Section 16.3 we do not have the zero coupon bond curve $Z(0, t)$ available, but only the T-notes and bonds in Table 16.4. Still the methodology applies, as for each given pair of parameters $(\bar{r}^*, \gamma^*)$, we can compute the discount function from the Vasicek model $Z(0, T) = e^{A(0,T)-B(0,T)\times r_0}$. Using this discount function, we can then compute the T-bond prices implied by the model. In particular, let c_i be the coupon rate of bond i, n_i the number of coupon dates remaining, and $T_{i,j}, j = 1, ..., n_i$ the coupon dates for bond i. The value of the bond according to the Vasicek model is then

$$P_i^{Vasicek} = \frac{c_i \times 100}{2} \times \sum_{j=1}^{n_i} Z(0, T_{i,j}) + 100 \times Z(0, T_{i,n_i}) \qquad (16.19)$$

Columns 4 and 5 of Table 16.4 contain bid and ask quotes on February 17, 2004. To perform the estimation, we should first convert the quoted prices into invoice prices, as discussed in Chapter 2, because the Vasicek bond pricing formula in Equation 16.19 corresponds to an invoice price and not a quoted price.[4] Fortunately, in our case we do not have to do any computation, because February 17, 2004 is a coupon date for all of the

---

[3]Exercise 7 in this chapter asks to do the computations using the Cox, Ingersoll, and Ross model.
[4]To see the logic, consider for instance the sale of a Treasury bond that occurs one day before the coupon is paid by the Treasury. The buyer of the bond will receive the coupon payment the next day. However, since this coupon really belongs to the seller, the buyer has to compensate the seller for the coupon. And indeed $P_i^{Vasicek}$ reflects this payment to the seller, as in this case the discount for the first coupon $Z(0, T_1) \approx 1$, and the Vasicek price is essentially equal to the next coupon payment plus the present value of all future coupons.

Table 16.4 Prices of Treasury Notes on February 17, 2004

Coupon Rate (%)	Maturity Date	Time to Maturity	Bid Price	Ask Price	Mid Invoice Price	Fitted Vasicek	Vasicek Discount
6.000	20040815	0.5	102.4297	102.4609	102.4453	102.3353	99.3547
7.500	20050215	1.0	106.2422	106.2734	106.2578	105.8935	98.4749
6.500	20050815	1.5	107.5313	107.5625	107.5469	106.9791	97.3847
5.625	20060215	2.0	107.7344	107.7656	107.7500	107.1136	96.1077
2.375	20060815	2.5	101.1094	101.1406	101.1250	100.4379	94.6668
2.250	20070215	3.0	100.1719	100.1875	100.1797	99.5983	93.0837
3.250	20070815	3.5	102.8125	102.8438	102.8281	102.2741	91.3793
3.000	20080215	4.0	101.4531	101.4844	101.4688	100.9732	89.5729
3.250	20080815	4.5	101.7734	101.8047	101.7891	101.4577	87.6825
3.000	20090215	5.0	99.9844	100.0000	99.9922	99.7263	85.7248
6.000	20090815	5.5	114.4844	114.5156	114.5000	114.2296	83.7152
6.500	20100215	6.0	117.5469	117.5781	117.5625	117.3790	81.6675
5.750	20100815	6.5	113.5938	113.6250	113.6094	113.4736	79.5943
5.000	20110215	7.0	109.0000	109.0313	109.0156	108.9047	77.5068
5.000	20110815	7.5	108.7188	108.7500	108.7344	108.6984	75.4151
4.875	20120215	8.0	107.6563	107.6875	107.6719	107.5666	73.3281
4.375	20120815	8.5	103.8594	103.8906	103.8750	103.5391	71.2535
3.875	20130215	9.0	99.7500	99.7813	99.7656	99.1346	69.1981
4.250	20130815	9.5	102.0156	102.0469	102.0313	101.4287	67.1678
4.000	20140215	10.0	99.6563	99.6875	99.6719	98.7164	65.1675
—	20140815	10.5	—	—	—	—	63.2015
11.250	20150215	11.0	162.4375	162.5000	162.4688	161.1129	61.2733
10.625	20150815	11.5	158.0938	158.1563	158.1250	157.0004	59.3858
9.250	20160215	12.0	146.0156	146.0781	146.0469	145.4712	57.5412
—	20160815	12.5	—	—	—	—	55.7414
—	20170215	13.0	—	—	—	—	53.9877
8.875	20170815	13.5	144.3281	144.3906	144.3594	142.6901	52.2811
—	20180215	14.0	—	—	—	—	50.6221
—	20180815	14.5	—	—	—	—	49.0110
8.875	20190215	15.0	145.9531	146.0156	145.9844	143.3638	47.4479
8.125	20190815	15.5	138.0313	138.0938	138.0625	136.3987	45.9325
8.500	20200215	16.0	142.6719	142.7344	142.7031	140.7175	44.4645
8.750	20200815	16.5	146.0625	146.1250	146.0938	143.8743	43.0433
7.875	20210215	17.0	136.0625	136.1250	136.0938	134.8678	41.6682
8.125	20210815	17.5	139.3906	139.4531	139.4219	137.9579	40.3383
—	20220215	18.0	—	—	—	—	39.0527
7.250	20220815	18.5	129.1563	129.2188	129.1875	128.3604	37.8105
7.125	20230215	19.0	127.7969	127.8594	127.8281	127.0553	36.6105
6.250	20230815	19.5	116.8125	116.8750	116.8438	116.8364	35.4518

Source: Data excerpted from CRSP (Daily Treasuries) ©2009 Center for Research in Security Prices (CRSP), The University of Chicago Booth School of Business.

Figure 16.6   The Overnight Repo Rate: May 21, 1991 - February 17, 2004

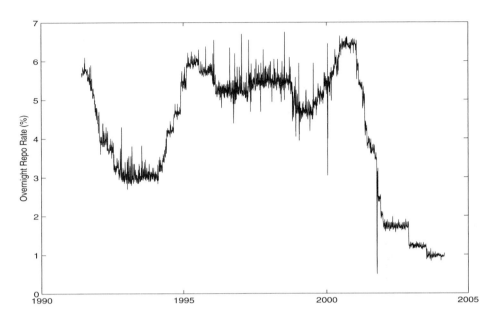

Data Source: Bloomberg.

Treasury notes and bonds that we use in the estimation, and therefore the accrued interest is zero. Column 7 then shows the mid invoice price, that is, in this case, simply the average bid and ask price. We call these invoice prices P_i^{Data} below.

Once we set up the data set, we can search for $(\gamma^*, \overline{r}^*)$ that minimize the sum of squared pricing errors, that is,

$$J(\gamma^*, \overline{r}^*) = \sum_{i=1}^{n} \left(P_i^{Data} - P_i^{Vasicek} \right)^2 . \qquad (16.20)$$

The minimization procedure yields $\overline{r}^* = 18.99\%$ and $\gamma^* = 0.0583$. Figure 16.7 plots the fitted model: Panel A compares the traded prices P_i^{Data} to fitted Vasicek prices $P_i^{Vasicek}$, while Panel B displays the spot curve implied by the Vasicek model.

16.8.1   Finding the Relative Value Trade

Panel A of Figure 16.7 seems to show that the Vasicek model actually fares pretty well in fitting the traded Treasury notes' and bonds' prices, as the two lines "Data" and "Model" seem on top of each other. This impression, though, is deceiving, and it is mainly due to the scale used in the figure, from a minimum of $80 to a maximum of $180. Panel C reports the pricing errors, that is, the difference between the prices in the data and the model:

$$\text{Pricing Error of Treasury Security } i = P_i^{Data} - P_i^{Vasicek}$$

As can be seen, most securities are not priced correctly, and some of them display large differences. For instance, the 10-year T-note appears grossly overpriced by the market,

Figure 16.7 The Fit of the Vasicek Model to Bond Prices

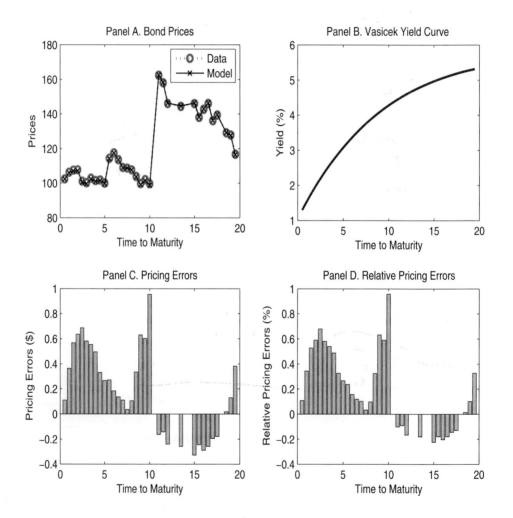

Data Source: CRSP.

as its traded price is almost $1 higher than the Vasicek model's prediction. Indeed, Panel D shows the pricing errors in percentage of the traded prices P_i^{Data}, and the price of the 10-year note is almost 1% higher than the model's prediction.

While the 10-year T-note would be a good candidate to set up an arbitrage trading strategy, we consider here a different trade, which uses short-term T-notes instead. The reason is that we can then follow the performance of the trading strategy up until the maturity of the T-note, and gauge the peformance of the trade. In addition, trading strategies involving long-term bonds need to be designed using multifactor models, such as those discussed in Chapter 22, as their prices tend to be affected by factors other than the short-term rate.

Panels C and D of Figure 16.7 show that short-term bonds are also mispriced. For our exercise, we focus on the T-note maturing on $T = 1.5$, which is overpriced by about 57 basis points compared to the model, as we can also see from Columns 6 and 7 of Table 16.4. Our relative value trade then calls for the following strategy:

Sell high / Buy low $\Longrightarrow$ Sell 1.5-yr T-note / Buy Vasicek 1.5-yr note   (16.21)

That is, we want to sell the overpriced 1.5-year note, and purchase the 1.5-year note implied by the Vasicek model. While performing the first part of the trade is simple, how do we purchase the 1.5-year note that is "implied by the Vasicek model"? Of course, this fair value is just a mathematical formula, so we cannot purchase it per se. The key to the trade is to recall that we can purchase, however, the *replicating portfolio* that according to the Vasicek model exactly replicates the 1.5-year note. So, the proper strategy is

Sell 1.5-yr T-note / Buy portfolio that *replicates* the Vasicek 1.5-yr note   (16.22)

The key insight of no arbitrage and relative value trading is that such a (replicating) portfolio costs exactly the Vasicek value of the 1.5-year note. Because this value is less than the traded price, by selling the 1.5-year T-note and purchasing the replicating portfolio, we will make a gain today. Under the Vasicek model, the replicating portfolio replicates the payoff of the 1.5-year note, and thus will deliver exactly all of the coupons that are needed to cover the short position.

We now illustrate the methodology. First, to set up the replicating portfolio we need to find a security that is fairly priced according to the model, and we therefore use the 7.5-year T-note, which has a pricing error of only 3 basis points. Second, recall that when we derived the no arbitrage condition, we considered the following portfolio, now specialized for the securities at hand:

$$\Pi(r_t, t) = -P_{1.5-yr}^{Vasicek}(r_t, t) + \Delta_t \times P_{7.5-yr}^{Vasicek}(r_t, t) \qquad (16.23)$$

where $P_{1.5-yr}^{Vasicek}(r_t, t)$ and $P_{7.5-yr}^{Vasicek}(r_t, t)$ denote the 1.5-year and the 7.5-year coupon notes, at t, respectively. As in the derivations in Section 16.4.1, the hedging strategy calls for selecting Δ_t in order to make the portfolio insensitive to changes in the interest rate. That is

$$\frac{\partial \Pi}{\partial r} = 0 \Longrightarrow \Delta_t = \frac{\partial P_{1.5-yr}^{Vasicek}(r, t)/\partial r}{\partial P_{7.5-yr}^{Vasicek}(r, t)/\partial r} \qquad (16.24)$$

According to the model, no arbitrage then implies that

$$d\Pi_t = r_t \Pi_t \, dt \qquad (16.25)$$

Where $C_0 = \Pi_0$

that is, Π_t behaves as the return from a safe investment. To figure out the replicating portfolio, we must invert Equation 16.23, and rewrite

$$P_{1.5-yr}^{Vasicek}(r_t, t) = \Delta_t \times P_{7.5-yr}^{Vasicek}(r_t, t) - \Pi(r_t, t) \tag{16.26}$$

According to the model, we can replicate the Vasicek 1.5-year note by using a position in the 7.5-year note, and by borrowing Π_t at the risk free rate r_t. Since Π_t is a borrowed cash position, let us denote it by C_t and let us substitute it into the right-hand side of Equation 16.26. With no arbitrage, the replicating portfolio is then given by

$$P_{1.5-yr}^{Vasicek}(r_t, t) = \Delta_t \times P_{7.5-yr}^{Vasicek}(r_t, t) - C_t \tag{16.27}$$

← Borrowed

Recall that C_t is the amount borrowed for the replication strategy. If $C_t < 0$, then we are net lenders in our position. It follows that once we know C_t and Δ_t, we can follow a rebalancing strategy in which we keep our position Δ_t in the 7.5-year T-note, and borrow or lend cash C_t at the rate r_t, so that indeed $dC_t = r_t C_t dt$. If the Vasicek model is correct, this portfolio will replicate the 1.5-year note payoffs, including all of the coupons that it pays over time.[5] The initial amount borrowed C_0 must be given by the theoretical portfolio value at time 0:

$$C_0 = -P_{1.5-yr}^{Vasicek}(r_0, 0) + \Delta_0 \times P_{7.5-yr}^{Vasicek}(r_0, 0) \tag{16.28}$$

We now turn to the actual computations.

16.8.2 Setting Up the Trade

The Vasicek model provides the formulas to compute the first derivatives needed to determine the position Δ_t in Equation 16.24. Indeed, recalling that a coupon bond is a portfolio of zero coupon bonds, for a generic coupon bond with n remaining coupon dates $T_1,...,T_n$, and coupon rate c, we have

Semi Ann'l bond

$$\frac{\partial P_c(r, 0)}{\partial r} = \frac{c \times 100}{2} \sum_{i=1}^{n} \frac{\partial Z(r, 0; T_i)}{\partial r} + 100 \times \frac{\partial Z(r, 0; T_n)}{\partial r}$$

$R = \frac{1}{2}r$

$$= -\frac{c \times 100}{2} \sum_{i=1}^{n} B(0; T_i) Z(r, 0; T_i) - 100 \times B(0; T_n) Z(r, 0; T_n)$$

where recall $B(0, T_i) = \left(1 - e^{-\gamma^* \times T_i}\right)/\gamma^*$. Because we know γ^*, as it was estimated to fit the term structure, we are also able to compute $B(0, T_i)$ for every maturity. Moreover, since we fit the term structure of interest rates, we also have available the discounts $Z(r, 0; T_i)$, which we report in the final column of Table 16.4. That is, we have available all of the information needed to compute the initial position in the 7.5-year note, Δ_0, in Equation 16.24. In particular, we obtain

$$\Delta_0 = \frac{\partial P_{1.5-yr}(r, 0)/\partial r}{\partial P_{7.5-yr}(r, 0)/\partial r} = \frac{1.4912}{5.6854} = 0.2623 \tag{16.29}$$

---

[5]Indeed, the Partial Differential Equation (PDE) we obtained in Equation 15.24 in Chapter 15 really applies to securities that do not pay any intermediate coupons. However, a coupon bond is a portfolio of individual zero coupon bonds, each of which does satisfy exactly the same PDE. Thus, the PDE does apply to coupon bearing securities, with the additional restriction that the value of the security must equal the coupon plus an ex-coupon bond value at any payment date.

Therefore, for each 1.5-year note sold, we must purchase 0.2623 of the 7.5-year note. Given Δ_0, we can compute the value of C_0

$$C_0 = -106.9791 + 0.2623 \times 108.7344 = -78.4581$$

This is the initial starting value of cash in the replicating portfolio. Note that because the portfolio will be made up of cash C_0 and the 7.5-year *traded* T-note, we need to use the traded value $P^{data}_{7.5-yr}(0) = 108.7344$ in the replicating portfolio.[6] To conclude, the replicating portfolio is then

$$P_0 = \Delta_0 \times P_{7.5-yr}(0) - C_0 = 0.2623 \times 108.7344 + 78.4581 = 106.9791 = P^{Vasicek}_{1.5-yr}(r_0, 0)$$
(16.30)

By selling $P^{data}_{1.5-yr} = 107.5469$ and buying the replicating portfolio, which costs 106.9791, the initial lock in profit is

$$\text{Initial profit} = \$107.5469 - \$106.9791 = \$0.5678$$

It is worth mentioning that the short/long position implicit in this trade is carried out through the repo market. In particular, to short the 1.5-year note, we borrow the note from a repo dealer, sell it in the market, and post cash collateral with the repo dealer, earning the repo rate on the deposit. Similarly, to purchase 0.263 of the 7.5-year note, we borrow cash possibly from a different repo dealer, and use it to purchase the note, and then post the note as collateral with the repo dealer. In this case, we have to pay the repo rate to the dealer. The net position of the effective trade is then equal to $-C_0 + \text{Initial profit} = 79.0259$. The dynamic replicating strategy requires only an interest rate computation on C_t over time. However, the initial profit also will earn interest over time, and we will consider that too in the computation of the final profit.

To conclude this subsection, under the assumptions of the Vasicek model, the replicating portfolio Equation 16.30 will provide exactly the coupons and the final principal to cover the short position. Thus, today, the trader makes \$0.5678 for each \$100 of 1.5-year notes sold. Because the trader performs the strategy through the repo market, the effective return on capital is not \$0.5678/\$100=57 basis points, though, but the profit \$0.5678 divided by the effective equity capital we put into the trade, namely, the haircut (see Chapter 1) on the long position. For instance, in normal times the haircut for Treasury securities is around 2% of the value of the Treasury note, so that we only put into the trade about $\$0.5704 = 2\% \times 0.2623 \times \$108.7344$ for each short-term bond sold, which implies a return on capital of about 100%(= \$0.5678/\$0.5704).[7]

16.8.3 Does It Work? Simulations

It is worth checking that the dynamic replication works in simulations. We begin by simulating one path of the interest rate process

$$dr_t = \gamma(\bar{r} - r_t)dt + \sigma dX_t$$

---

[6]We assume for simplicity that all transaction are performed at the mid invoice price. The main point of this section is to discuss the performance of the dynamic replication strategy with real data. Bid and ask considerations increase the transaction costs, but do not change the point of the discussion.

[7]We are ignoring the fact that we would receive a haircut from the reverse repurchase agreement as well, as we would be a lender in that case.

Note that we must simulate the *true* process for interest rates, which has γ and $\bar{r}$ in it, and not the risk neutral one, which has γ^* and $\bar{r}^*$ in it. The replication strategy has to work in the real world, under the original interest rate dynamics. In this case, r_t represents the repo rate. Using the same data as in Figure 16.6, we obtain $\gamma = 1.7627$ and $\bar{r} = 4.2073\%$, while $\sigma = 3.1655\%$, which is the same value used in the Vasicek model.

The dynamic rebalancing, recall, works as follows:

1. For each new r_t, recompute the optimal hedge ratio Δ_t using Equation 16.24.

2. Compute the new cash requirement $= (\Delta_t - \Delta_{t-dt}) \times P^{data}_{7.5-yr}(t)$.

3. Adjust the amount of cash borrowed $C_t = C_{t-dt} + C_{t-dt} \times r_{t-dt} \times dt + \text{Cash needed}$.[8]

4. At every coupon period T_i, borrow more to pay the coupons due in the short position, and use the coupons received to decrease the amount borrowed.

   Points 1 to 3 are the same as those discussed in Section 16.1. Point 4 instead reflects the fact that the securities used pay coupons, and thus we have to adjust the cash holdings to take into account these cash flows. Overall, we obtain the cash balances are given by:

$$
\begin{aligned}
C_{T_i} = {} & C_{T_i-dt} + C_{T_i-dt} \times r_{T_i-dt} \times dt + \text{ Cash needed } + \left(100 \times \frac{c^{1.5-yr}}{2} \right) \\
& -\Delta_{T_i-dt} \left(\frac{100 \times c^{7.5-yr}}{2} \right)
\end{aligned}
$$

Figure 16.8 shows the performance of the replication strategy on a simulated path of interest rate, reported in Panel A. Panel B shows two lines: The dotted line represents the Vasicek price for the 2-year bond $P^{Vasicek}_{1.5-yr}(r_t, t)$, while the solid line represents the value of the replicating portfolio

$$
P_t = \Delta_t \times P^{Vasicek}_{7.5-yr}(r_t, t) - C_t
$$

It is clear that the two lines overlap exactly, reflecting the fact that theoretically the model works. The jumps in prices that are visible at semi-annual frequency represent the coupon payments, as the figure plots the invoice prices: At coupon dates, the price drops exactly by the amount of the paid coupon. The replicating portfolio does the same.

16.8.4   Does It Work? Data

How does this model perform when we have to trade with real securities? Figure 16.9 provides the answer for this specific trade. In particular, Panel A shows the realized overnight repo rate during the 1.5 years between February 17, 2004 and August 15, 2005, which shows a substantial increase for most of its sample. This sudden increase in the short rate was due to the U.S. monetary policy in that period. Panel B shows two lines: The dotted line depicts the observed 1.5-year note over time; the solid line shows the value of

---

[8]In this specific application, $C_t < 0$, which means that we are net lenders. But this need not be the case in general. It helps to keep the intuition in terms of borrowing, rather than switching all of the signs.

Figure 16.8   The Replicating Portfolio: Simulations

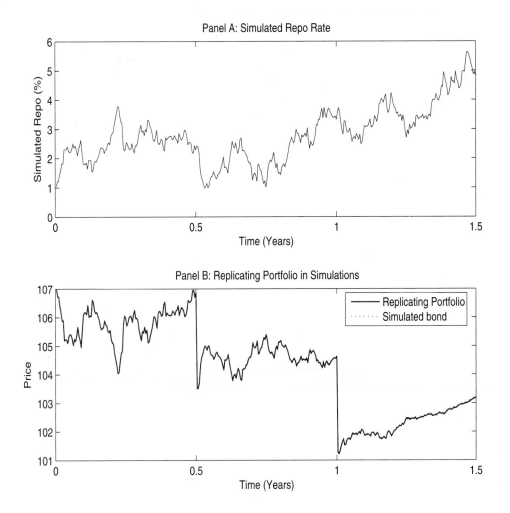

the Vasicek price for the same security.[9] We observe two facts: First, the model price is relatively close to the observed price, and they both converge to their final payout of 100+ 6.50/2=103.25. Second, the volatility of the Vasicek price is not nearly as large as the one of the actual traded price, especially during the initial period, in which the overnight repo rate did not display much fluctuation (see Panel A). This is indeed one of the shortcomings of the Vasicek model, as it does not generate a sufficient volatility of longer-term bond prices, a deficiency that we resolve by moving to more general models in later chapters.

Panel C reports the 7.5-year note in the data (the dotted line) and the one implied by the Vasicek model (the solid line). Different from the 1.5-year note case, the true price and the model price move much less in sync, if at all. Recall that according to the Vasicek model, all bonds of all maturities are perfectly correlated with each other, while in reality long-term bonds are likely affected by other shocks (see Chapter 4). The finding in Panel C seems quite damaging in terms of yielding a good performance of the replicating portfolio, as the latter has to use the traded 7.5-year bond for its implementation.

Panel D shows that, surprisingly, on this occasion the replicating strategy actually worked relatively well, especially when compared with the performance of the Vasicek model in Panel C. In fact, the dotted line in Panel D represents the traded 1.5-year bond, while the solid line represents the value of the replicating portfolio, which only uses traded assets and the true repo rate for its implementation. The initial discrepancy between the two lines represents the arbitrage opportunity that the trader is trying to capture from the trade: Essentially the trader is short the dotted line and long the solid line. As can be seen clearly in the figure, the two lines tend to converge over time, although they did not match exactly by maturity $T = 1.5$, as was the case instead for the simulation in Figure 16.8. In this case, however, the replication error is in our favor, as the value of the replicating portfolio is above the value of the 1.5-year bond, which we are shorting. Therefore, at $T = 1.5$ we can liquidate our position in the replicating portfolio, for $P_T = \$103.4695$ and pay the final coupon and principal on the short position, $P_{1.5-yr}^{data} = \$103.25$. The replication error is then:

$$\text{Final replication error} = P_T - P_{1.5-yr}^{data} = \$103.4695 - \$103.25 = \$0.2195$$

The total profit for this trade is then the sum of the profit at time 0, $0.5678, plus the interest accrued on this profit over 1.5 years, plus the replication error:

$$\text{Total Profit} = \$0.5678/Z(0, 1.5) + \$0.2195 = \$0.5790 + \$0.2195 = \$0.7985$$

where $Z(0, 1.5) = 0.9792$ is the 1.5-year discount factor on February 17, 2004, obtained from a bootstrap procedure of the T-notes in Table 16.4.

16.8.5   Conclusion

Relative value trades are standard trades on Wall Street, and term structure models form the basis of these trades. The key point is that, according to theory, it is possible to replicate one given bond or derivative security by using another bond. Sometimes some bonds trade

---

[9]In this exercise, we keep the parameters γ^* and $\bar{r}^*$ constant to their values estimated earlier. Traders typically re-estimate these parameters on a daily frequency, and thus, by construction, the model price will be closer to the actual traded price.

Figure 16.9   The Replicating Portfolio: Data

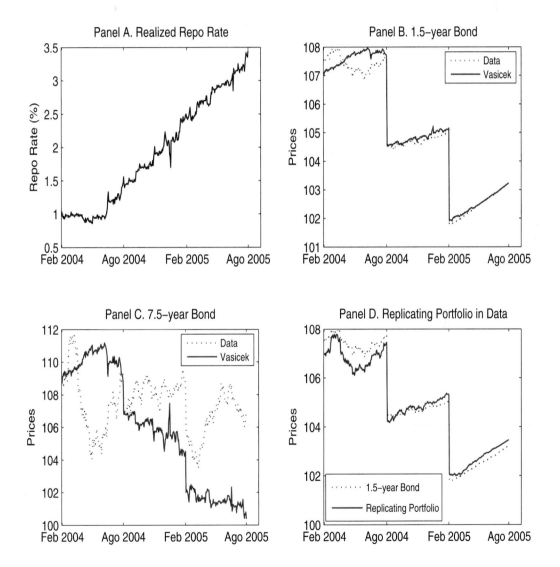

Data Source: Bloomberg and CRSP.

at higher prices than those the model implies, because of imbalances on the demand and supply of the bond. For instance, an on-the-run bond, i.e., the newly issued bond, typically trades at a higher price, because it is perceived as being more liquid. A relative value trade would call for the sale of such a bond, and the replication of its cash flows by using another bond. The important warning, however, is that the model is always imperfect, and therefore the replication strategy may not work as expected. For instance, Panel C of Figure 16.9 shows that the Vasicek model fails to correctly price the 7.5-year bond over time. This discrepancy could possibly result in large replication errors. Therefore, traders undertake relative value arbitrage strategies only when the apparent arbitrage opportunity is large enough to compensate for the potential losses in the replication strategy.

16.9 APPENDIX: DERIVATION OF DELTA FOR CALL OPTIONS

We can write the formula for the option is

$$V = 100 \times Z\left(t, r; T_B\right) \mathcal{N}\left(d_1\right) - K Z\left(t, r; T_O\right) \mathcal{N}\left(d_1 - \mathcal{S}_Z\right)$$

where $\mathcal{N}(x)$ is the cumulative normal distribution and

$$\mathcal{S}_Z = \frac{\sigma}{\gamma}\left(1 - e^{-\gamma(T_B - T_O)}\right)\sqrt{\frac{1 - e^{-2\gamma(T_B - t)}}{2\gamma}}$$

$$d_1 = \frac{1}{\mathcal{S}_Z}\log\left(\frac{100 Z\left(t, r; T_B\right)}{K Z\left(t, r; T_O\right)}\right) + \frac{\mathcal{S}_Z}{2}$$

We want to compute

$$
\begin{aligned}
\frac{\partial V}{\partial r} = {}& 100\frac{\partial Z\left(t, r; T_B\right)}{\partial r}\mathcal{N}\left(d_1\right) + 100 Z\left(t, r; T_B\right)\frac{\partial \mathcal{N}\left(d_1\right)}{\partial r} \\
& -K\frac{\partial Z\left(t, r; T_O\right)}{\partial r}\mathcal{N}\left(d_1 - \mathcal{S}_Z\right) - K Z\left(t, r; T_O\right)\frac{\partial \mathcal{N}\left(d_1 - \mathcal{S}_Z\right)}{\partial r}
\end{aligned}
$$

Notice first that

$$\frac{\partial Z\left(t, r; T_B\right)}{\partial r} = -B\left(t; T_B\right) Z\left(t, r; T_B\right)$$

Also, since

$$\mathcal{N}\left(d_1\right) = \int_{-\infty}^{d_1} \frac{1}{\sqrt{2\pi}} e^{-\frac{x^2}{2}}\, dx$$

the chain rule for integrals shows

$$\frac{\partial \mathcal{N}\left(d_1\right)}{\partial r} = \frac{\partial \mathcal{N}}{\partial d_1}\frac{\partial d_1}{\partial r} = \phi\left(d_1\right)\frac{\partial d_1}{\partial r}$$

where $\phi\left(d_1\right)$ is the normal density. Because we can write

$$
\begin{aligned}
d_1 = {}& \frac{1}{\mathcal{S}_Z}\log\left(\frac{100}{K}\right) + \frac{1}{\mathcal{S}_Z}\left(A\left(t; T_B\right) - A\left(t; T_O\right)\right) \\
& -\frac{1}{\mathcal{S}_Z}\left(B\left(t; T_B\right) - B\left(t; T_O\right)\right) r + \frac{\mathcal{S}_Z}{2}
\end{aligned}
$$

we have

$$\frac{\partial d_1}{\partial r} = \frac{\partial \left(d_1 - \mathcal{S}_Z\right)}{\partial r} = -\frac{B\left(t; T_B\right) - B\left(t; T_O\right)}{\mathcal{S}_Z}$$

Putting everything together, we find

$$
\begin{aligned}
\frac{\partial V}{\partial r} =\ & -100 B\left(t; T_B\right) Z\left(t, r; T_B\right) \mathcal{N}\left(d_1\right) + K B\left(t; T_O\right) Z\left(t, r; T_O\right) \mathcal{N}\left(d_1 - \mathcal{S}_Z\right) \\
& -100 Z\left(t, r; T_B\right) \phi\left(d_1\right) \frac{B\left(t; T_B\right) - B\left(t; T_O\right)}{\mathcal{S}_Z} \\
& + K Z\left(t, r; T_O\right) \phi\left(d_1 - \mathcal{S}_Z\right) \frac{B\left(t; T_B\right) - B\left(t; T_O\right)}{\mathcal{S}_Z}
\end{aligned}
\tag{16.31}
$$

CHAPTER 17

RISK NEUTRAL PRICING AND MONTE CARLO SIMULATIONS

Risk neutral pricing is by far the most utilized methodology to price derivative securities. In this chapter, we review its foundation – no arbitrage and the Feynman-Kac theorem – and apply it to obtain prices and hedge ratios of relatively complex interest rate securities. One important implication of risk neutral pricing is that it provides the theoretical foundation for using Monte Carlo simulations as a tool for pricing.

17.1 RISK NEUTRAL PRICING

Consider the general process

$$dr_t = m(r_t, t)dt + s(r_t, t)dX_t \tag{17.1}$$

where $m(r, t)$ and $s(r, t)$ are functions of r and time t. For instance, in the case of the Vasicek model, we had $m(r, t) = \gamma(\bar{r} - r)$ and $s(r, t) = \sigma$. In Chapter 15 we obtained the Fundamental Pricing Equation by following these steps:

1. Consider a portfolio of two interest rate securities;

2. Choose the number of units in the portfolio in order to make it *riskless*;

3. Use Ito's lemma to find the dynamics of the portfolio capital gains;

4. Impose no arbitrage, and thus, the portfolio return must equal the risk-free rate;

5. Obtain a Partial Differential Equation that needs to be satisfied by every security.

The result was the following: Let $V(r, t)$ be the value of any security that depends on the interest rate r. Let T be the maturity of the interest rate security and $g(r_T, T)$ be the payoff that this security yields at maturity T. Then, $V(r, t)$ must satisfy the Fundamental Pricing Equation:

$$rV = \frac{\partial V}{\partial t} + \frac{\partial V}{\partial r} m^*(r, t) + \frac{1}{2} \frac{\partial^2 V}{\partial r^2} s(r, t)^2 \tag{17.2}$$

subject to the boundary condition

$$V(r_T, T) = g(r_T, T), \tag{17.3}$$

where $m^*(r, t)$ is another function of r and t whose functional form depends on the model. For instance, in the Vasicek model we had $m^*(r, t) = \gamma^*(\bar{r}^* - r)$.

How can we solve this complicated equation? In a few occasions, under some assumptions about $m^*(r, t)$ and $s(r, t)$, and for some specific securities, we are able to solve Equation 17.2 in an analytical form. For instance, in Chapter 15 we obtained an analytical formula for the price of zero coupon bonds under the Vasicek model and the Cox, Ingersoll, and Ross model. Similarly, we obtained analytical formulas for the price of an option on a zero coupon bond. In several other cases, however, we are not able to obtain a solution to Equation 17.2. In these cases, we must resort to numerical methods to compute the price. In the next subsection we introduce the fundamental tool used to solve Equation 17.2.

17.2 FEYNMAN-KAC THEOREM

The Feynman-Kac theorem provides a general solution to the Partial Differential Equation 17.2. In fact, it provides a formula for a case more general than the one in Equation 17.2 which we will be using in later chapters. In light of what is coming next, it is convenient to provide the more general formula first:

Fact 17.1 *Let $V(r, t)$ be the price of a security, with final payoff $V(r_T, T) = g(r_T, T)$, satisfying the partial differential equation*

$$R(r)V = \frac{\partial V}{\partial t} + \frac{\partial V}{\partial r} m^*(r, t) + \frac{1}{2} \frac{\partial^2 V}{\partial r^2} s(r, t)^2 \tag{17.4}$$

Value at payoff?

where $R(r)$ is some function of r. Then $V(r, t)$ is given by

$$V(r_t, t) = E^* \left[e^{-\int_t^T R(r_u) du} g(r_T, T) \,|\, r_t \right] \tag{17.5}$$

where the expectation $E^*[.]$ is taken with respect to the probability distribution induced by the process

$$dr_t = m^*(r_t, t) dt + s(r_t, t) dX_t \tag{17.6}$$

$\gamma^*, \bar{r}^*$

This result is central for the no arbitrage pricing of interest rate securities. Indeed, the fundamental pricing equation (Equation 17.4) has $R(r) = r$, and thus its solution is

$$V(r_t, t) = E^* \left[e^{-\int_t^T r_u du} g(r_T, T) \,|\, r_t \right] \tag{17.7}$$

& How do you get this?

This equation says something deceptively simple: The price of an interest rate security equals the expected discounted value of its payoff $g(r_T, T)$, where the discount is computed using the risk-free rate $\int_t^T r_u\, du$. The key, however, is that the *expectation* $E^*[\cdot]$ is taken with respect to the interest rate process in Equation 17.6 and *not* the original interest rate process in Equation 17.1.

Definition 17.1 *The* **risk neutral** *or* **risk adjusted** *interest rate process is obtained from the original interest rate process (Equation 17.1) by substituting its drift rate $m(r, t)$ with the coefficient that multiplies the term "$\partial V/\partial r$" in the Fundamental Pricing Equation (Equation 17.2), that is*

$$\left[\text{Risk neutral drift} = m^*(r_t, t). \right] \Rightarrow \text{discount} \tag{17.8}$$

The original interest rate process (Equation 17.1) is often referred to as the **risk natural**, *or* **physical**, *or, simply,* **true** *process for interest rates.*

Why is the interest rate process in Equation 17.6 called *risk neutral* process? The following fact explains it:

Fact 17.2 *If the process for interest rates was the one in Equation 17.6, then the expected return of any interest rate security would simply be the risk-free rate. That is, denoting V_t the value at time t of an interest-rate security, then*

$$E^* \left[\frac{dV_t}{V_t} \right] = r_t dt \tag{17.9}$$

where the expectation $E^*[\cdot]$ is taken under the assumption that the interest rate process is in Equation 17.6.

To see why Equation 17.9 holds, we have only to go back to Ito's lemma, but applying it under the assumption that the true interest rate process was as in Equation 17.6. Let $V(r_t, t)$ be the value at time t of any interest rate security. Then, Ito's lemma shows

$$dV_t = \left\{ \frac{\partial V}{\partial t} + \frac{\partial V}{\partial r} m^*(r_t, t) + \frac{1}{2} \frac{\partial^2 V}{\partial r^2} s(r_t, t)^2 \right\} dt + \frac{\partial V}{\partial r} s(r_t, t) dX_t \tag{17.10}$$

It follows that the expected return between t and $t + dt$ is given by $\leftarrow R(r)\cancel{V}$ $R(r)$

$$E^*[dV_t] = \left\{ \frac{\partial V}{\partial t} + \frac{\partial V}{\partial r} m^*(r_t, t) + \frac{1}{2} \frac{\partial^2 V}{\partial r^2} s(r_t, t)^2 \right\} dt \tag{17.11}$$

We now recognize that the right-hand side of this expression is identical to the right hand side of the Fundamental Pricing Equation (Equation 17.2). Using the equality there, we obtain Equation 17.9.

Note that the risk neutral pricing methodology does not require anywhere that market participants are really neutral toward risk. They could in fact be very risk averse, and therefore price down risky securities by requiring a large risk premium. This risk premium is embedded in the drift rate $m^*(r, t)$ of the risk neutral process. The terminology is slightly confusing, however: The risk neutral interest rate process is the interest rate process in which the drift rate $m(r, t)$ has been changed to $m^*(r, t)$ to account for the risk premium that market participants require to hold interest rate securities. For this reason, Definition

17.1 also uses the equivalent terminology "risk adjusted process," which highlights that the change to the interest rate process is performed to reflect the risk premium. We return to this distinction in Chapter 18. See also the discussion in Chapters 9 and 10 in the context of binomial trees.

The next few examples highlight some useful features of the risk neutral methodology.

■ **EXAMPLE 17.1**

Consider a security $V(r_0, 0)$ whose payoff at time T is just equal to $g(r_T, T) = 1$. Then, from Equation 17.7 we obtain

$$
\begin{aligned}
V(r_0, 0) &= E^* \left[e^{-\int_t^T r_u \, du} \, g(r_T, T) \, | r_0 \right] \\
&= E^* \left[e^{-\int_t^T r_u \, du} \, 1 | r_0 \right] \\
&= Z(r_0, 0; T)
\end{aligned}
$$

that is, the zero coupon bond itself. Indeed, if this was not the case, the law of one price would be violated and an arbitrageur could make infinite profits.

■ **EXAMPLE 17.2**

Consider a security $V(r_0, 0)$ whose payoff at time T is just equal to a zero coupon bond with maturity T^*. That is, $g(r_T, T) = Z(r_T, T; T^*)$. What is the value of such security? From Equation 17.7 we obtain

$$
\begin{aligned}
V(r_0, 0) &= E^* \left[e^{-\int_0^T r_u \, du} \, g(r_T, T) \, | r_0 \right] \\
&= E^* \left[e^{-\int_0^T r_u \, du} \, Z(r_T, T) \, | r_0 \right]
\end{aligned}
\tag{17.12}
$$

We know that by no arbitrage, also $Z(r_T, T; T^*)$ itself must satisfy Equation 17.7 although the expectation is taken at time T conditional on r_T, whatever the interest rate will be at that time. That is, $Z(r_T, T; T^*) = E^* \left[e^{-\int_T^{T^*} r_u \, du} 1 | r_T \right]$. Substitute, to find

$$
\begin{aligned}
V(r_0, 0) &= E^* \left[e^{-\int_0^T r_u \, du} \times E^* \left[e^{-\int_T^{T^*} r_u \, du} 1 | r_T \right] | r_0 \right] \tag{17.13} \\
&= E^* \left[e^{-\int_0^T r_u \, du} \times e^{-\int_T^{T^*} r_u \, du} 1 | r_0 \right] \\
&= E^* \left[e^{-\int_0^{T^*} r_u \, du} 1 | r_0 \right] \\
&= Z(r_0, 0; T^*) \tag{17.14}
\end{aligned}
$$

where the second equality stems from the law of iterated expectations, which basically states that the knowledge today that we will receive more information in the future (i.e., we will know r_T at T) about a random variable $g_T = e^{-\int_T^{T^*} r_u \, du}$ cannot change the value of the expectation today (which only is conditional on r_0).[1] That is, a security whose only payoff at T is a zero coupon bond with a longer maturity T^* must have a price equal to the current zero coupon with the maturity T^*. Otherwise, the law of one price would be violated and there would be an arbitrage opportunity.

The next two examples show that the risk neutral pricing methodology easily recover the results we obtained in Chapter 5.

■ **EXAMPLE 17.3**

Consider a forward contract with maturity T written on a zero coupon bond with maturity T^*. Let K be the delivery price at which the counterparties agreed at time 0. The payoff of the forward contract is then

$$\text{Payoff forward contract} = Z(r_T, T; T^*) - K$$

Using the risk neutral pricing methodology (Equation 17.7), the value at time 0 of this payoff is

$$V(r_0, 0) = E^* \left[e^{-\int_0^T r_u \, du} \times [Z(r_T, T; T^*) - K] \right]$$

Since K is not a random variable (we know the delivery price at time 0), we can rewrite this equation as

$$
\begin{aligned}
V(r_0, 0) &= E^* \left[e^{-\int_0^T r_u \, du} Z(r_T, T; T^*) \right] - K \times E^* \left[e^{-\int_0^T r_u \, du} \right] \\
&= Z(r_0, 0; T^*) - K Z(r_0, 0; T)
\end{aligned}
$$

Finally, at initiation of the contract K is the delivery price that makes the value of the forward contract equal to zero. Thus, if 0 is the contract inception time, we have that K must be given by

$$K = \frac{Z(r_0, 0; T^*)}{Z(r_0, 0; T)}$$

which is equal to the forward discount factor $F(0, T, T^*)$, as discussed in Section 5.3 of Chapter 5.

■ **EXAMPLE 17.4**

Consider a forward swap contract, in which two counterparties agree at time 0 to enter into a swap contract at T with maturity $T^* > T$ and at a swap rate c agreed upon today. What is the value of a forward swap contract at time 0?

First, what is the payoff of the swap contract at time T for the fixed rate receiver? For given swap rate c, from Section 5.4.1 in Chapter 5 the value of the swap contract at T is

$$\text{Value swap at } T = N \times \left[\Delta \times c \left(\sum_{j=1}^{n} Z(r_T, T; T_i) \right) + Z(r_T, T; T^*) - 1 \right]$$

---

[1]More formally, given a random variable x and a conditioning events A, then $E[E[x|A]] = E[x]$.

where T_i are the reset dates and $T_n = T$. From Equation 17.7, the risk neutral pricing methodology implies

$$
\begin{aligned}
\text{Value of swap at } 0 \; &= \; E^* \left[e^{-\int_0^{T_O} r_u \, du} \left[\text{Value swap at } T \right] \right] \\
&= \; N E^* \left[e^{-\int_0^T r_u \, du} \left[\Delta c \left(\sum_{j=1}^n Z(r_T, T; T_i) + Z(r_T, T; T^*) - 1 \right) \right] \right] \\
&= \; N \left[\Delta c \left(\sum_{j=1}^n Z(r_0, 0; T_i) \right) + Z(r_0, 0; T^*) - Z(r_0, 0; T) \right] \quad (17.15)
\end{aligned}
$$

where we used the result in Equations 17.13 to 17.14.

The forward swap rate $f_n^s(0, T, T^*)$ is that level of the swap rate c that makes the value of the forward swap contract in Equation 17.15 equal to zero:

$$
f_n^s(0, T, T^*) \; = \; \frac{Z(r_0, 0; T) - Z(r_0, 0; T^*)}{\Delta \sum_{j=1}^n Z(r_0, 0; T_j)} \quad (17.16)
$$

Dividing through by $Z(r_0, 0; T)$, we can also rewrite the forward swap rate $f_n^s(0, T, T^*)$ in terms of the forward discount factor (see Chapter 5)

$$
f_n^s(0, T, T^*) \; = \; \frac{1 - F(0, T, T^*)}{\Delta \sum_{j=1}^n F(0, T, T_j)} \quad (17.17)
$$

which is the same as Equation 5.51 in Chapter 5.

17.3 APPLICATION OF RISK NEUTRAL PRICING: MONTE CARLO SIMULATIONS

One of the most useful implications of risk neutral pricing is that it provides a general methodology for pricing any interest rate security. Indeed, since the solution to the Fundamental Pricing Equation (Equation 17.2) is given by the Equation 17.7, it follows that if we can compute the expecation in Equation 17.7 we obtain the price of the security. Computing this expectation can be effectively performed by using Monte Carlo Simulations, exactly as we did in Chapter 13. The only difference from that chapter is that we are not restricted to simulating the interest rate process on the tree itself. Instead, we can simulate the interest rate using the *risk neutral* process in Equation 17.6. Moreover, as we shall see in Chapter 22, the risk neutral methodology easily extends to multiple factors. Similarly, risk neutral binomial trees, discussed in Chapter 11, can be considered a numerical methodology to implement the risk neutral pricing formula in Equation 17.6.

In this section we illustrate the Monte Carlo simulation for the case of the Vasicek model. We perform two exercises: The first is to price simple coupon bonds using Monte Carlo simulations. This exercise shows that the methodology works as we shall obtain (almost) the same value with both the Vasicek formula and Monte Carlo simulations. The second is to price a more complicated security, such as range notes.

17.3.1 Simulating a Diffusion Process

According to the Feynman-Kac theorem, to price a security with payoff $g(r_T, T)$, we must compute the expectation in Equation 17.7 according to the process in Equation 17.6. First of all, we must see how to simulate the interest rate process in Equation 17.6. The methodology is similar to the one explained in Chapter 13, reviewed next.

We must simulate the interest rate process in Equation 17.6, that is

$$dr_t = m^* (r_t, t) \, dt + s (r_t, t) \, dX_t$$

Discretize first the time interval $[0, T]$ in $N = T/\delta$ intervals of size δ. Let the initial condition be the current interest rate r_0. We approximate :

$$
\begin{aligned}
dr_t &\approx r_{t+\delta} - r_t \\
dt &\approx \delta \\
dX_t &\approx \sqrt{\delta} \times \varepsilon_{t+\delta} \quad \text{where} \quad \varepsilon_{t+\delta} \sim \mathcal{N}(0, 1)
\end{aligned}
$$

The following is called the "Euler discretization scheme":

$$r_{t+\delta} = r_t + m^* (r_t, t) \, \delta + s (r_t, t) \, \sqrt{\delta} \varepsilon_{t+\delta}$$

For example, consider the Vasicek model $m^* (r, t) = \gamma^* (\overline{r}^* - r_t)$ and $s (r, t) = \sigma$. Taking a slight liberty with the notation, let us denote by r_i the interest rate in time step i (i.e., at time $i \times dt$). Starting from r_0, we have

$$
\begin{aligned}
r_1 &= r_0 + \gamma^* (\overline{r}^* - r_0) \, \delta + \sigma \sqrt{\delta} \, \varepsilon_1 \\
r_2 &= r_1 + \gamma^* (\overline{r}^* - r_1) \, \delta + \sigma \sqrt{\delta} \, \varepsilon_2 \\
&\vdots \qquad \vdots \\
r_i &= r_{i-1} + \gamma^* (\overline{r}^* - r_{i-1}) \, \delta + \sigma \sqrt{\delta} \, \varepsilon_i \\
&\vdots \qquad \vdots \\
r_N &= r_{N-1} + \gamma^* (\overline{r}^* - r_{N-1}) \, \delta + \sigma \sqrt{\delta} \, \varepsilon_N
\end{aligned}
$$

17.3.2 Simulating the Payoff

Consider a security with maturity T and payoff $g(r_T)$. We need to compute the expected discounted value of this payoff, where the expectation is obtained from the risk neutral process, and the discount is computed using the risk-free rate. In particular, we want to compute

$$
\begin{aligned}
V(r, t) &= E^* \left[e^{- \int_t^T r_u \, du} \times g(r_T) \right] \\
&\approx E^* \left[e^{- \sum_{i=0}^{N-1} r_i \delta} g(r_N) \right]
\end{aligned}
$$

where again, we switched the subscript notation of the interest rate from time t to step i. The Monte Carlo methodology shows that we can approximate the expectation by:

(a) repeating the simulation of interest rates J times, say $J = 1,000$, and thus obtaining J paths of interest rates $r_0^j, r_1^j, ..., r_{N-1}^j, r_N^j$, for $j = 1, 2, ..., J$;

(b) using each interest rate path j, $j = 1, ..., J$, to compute the present value of the payoff, and thus obtain J values of the present value of the security at T, that is

$$
\begin{aligned}
V^1(r_0, 0) &= e^{-\sum_{i=0}^{N-1} r_i^1 \delta} g\left(r_N^1\right) \\
V^2(r_0, 0) &= e^{-\sum_{i=0}^{N-1} r_i^2 \delta} g\left(r_N^2\right) \\
&\;\;\vdots \qquad \vdots \\
V^j(r_0, 0) &= e^{-\sum_{i=0}^{N-1} r_i^j \delta} g\left(r_N^j\right) \qquad (17.18) \\
&\;\;\vdots \qquad \vdots \\
V^J(r_0, 0) &= e^{-\sum_{i=0}^{N-1} r_i^J \delta} g\left(r_N^J\right) \; ; \text{and}
\end{aligned}
$$

(c) taking the average of the present values $V^1(r_0, 0), V^2(r_0, 0), ..., V^N(r_0, 0)$:

$$
\widehat{V}(r_0, 0) \approx \frac{1}{J} \sum_{j=1}^{J} V^j(r_0, 0) \qquad (17.19)
$$

where the hat "$\;\widehat{}\;$" indicates that this value is an approximation of the true price of the asset obtained by Monte Carlo simulations.

■ **EXAMPLE 17.5**

Coupon Bonds Using the Vasicek Model

Consider the simulation of zero coupon bond prices in the Vasicek model. In this case, $m^*(r, t) = \gamma^*(\bar{r}^* - r)$ and $s(r, t) = \sigma$, and the payoff is simply $g(r_T) = 1$. The value of a zero coupon bond obtained from the simulations is

$$
\widehat{Z}(r_0, 0; T) \approx \frac{1}{J} \sum_{j=1}^{J} \left(e^{-\sum_{i=0}^{N-1} r_i^j \delta} \right)
$$

Given the zero coupon bond price for each maturity, we can then compute the value of coupon bond prices. Let T_k be the coupon dates. We obtain

$$
\widehat{P}_c(r_0, T) = \sum_{k=1}^{K} \frac{c \times 100}{2} \widehat{Z}(r_0, 0; T_k) + 100 \, \widehat{Z}(r_0, 0; T_K)
$$

Figure 17.1 plots the value of coupon bonds on January 8, 2002 obtained from using the Vasicek formula in Equation 15.28 in Chapter 15 and Monte Carlo simulations. In particular, the time-step is $\delta = 1/252$, and the parameter estimates are $\gamma^* = 0.0702$, $\bar{r}^* = 0.2322$, and $\sigma = 0.0464$.[2] Figure 17.1 reveals several facts about simulations.

---

[2]Unlike the exercise in Chapter 15, Section 15.2.4, where we only estimated γ and $\bar{r}^*$ from STRIPS, but restricted $\sigma = 0.0221$ as obtained from changes in the short-term interest rate, in this case we also estimated σ using coupon bond prices. The fit of the term structure is more accurate in this case. Although theoretically, σ should be restricted to equal the time variation of yields, many practitioners prefer to estimate it from bonds in order to obtain a more accurate fit of the term structure.

Figure 17.1   Vasicek Bond Prices: Exact Formula and Simulations

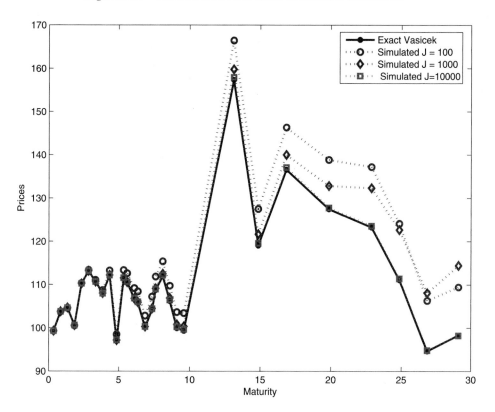

First, a small number of simulations, such as $J = 100$ or $J = 1000$, is too few to price bonds. In fact, the simulated price is relatively far from the target. This is due to the relatively large value of interest rate volatility $\sigma = 0.0464$. $J = 10,000$ approaches the true value quite closely, although probably 100,000 simulations would do a much better job for long-term bonds.

The main point of Figure 17.1 is that whether we use a complicated analytical formula to compute the value of bonds or we simulate many interest rate paths and take averages of discounted values, we obtain (approximately) the same results. It is important to realize that the reason this happens is that both procedures (analytical solution or Monte Carlo simulations) provide a solution to the same partial differential equation (Equation 17.2). In this sense, Feynman-Kac theorem is the key step to risk neutral pricing: It defines a general methodology for solving the Fundamental Pricing Equation 17.2, and thus obtaining prices of interest rate securities. For bond prices, in this case, we also could use the Vasicek formula itself. However, for more complicated securities there is no formula that can be used, and Monte Carlo simulations may be the only way to compute the solution to the Fundamental Pricing Equation 17.2. Section 17.4 and the case study in Section 17.9 illustrate two specific examples.

17.3.3 Standard Errors

How can we decide the appropriate number of simulations? In the case of Figure 17.1 we compare the true value (using the actual Vasicek formula) to the simulated value, and we can see whether the number of simulations J is sufficient. However, the whole point is that we do not have the true value, and that's why we are using Monte Carlo simulations to obtain the price of the security. One methodology is to compute the standard errors of the estimate. That is, given the simulated values $V^j(r_0, 0)$, $j = 1, ..., J$, in Equation 17.18 we can compute the standard deviation of the values $V^1(r_0, 0), ... , V^J(r_0, 0)$, and thus the standard error of the estimated value $\widehat{V}(r_0, 0)$.

Definition 17.2 *The **standard error** of the simulated value* $\widehat{V}(r_0, 0) = \frac{1}{J}\sum_{j=1}^{J} V^j(r_0, 0)$ *is given by*

$$\text{Standard error} = \frac{\text{Standard deviation}}{\sqrt{J}} \tag{17.20}$$

where the standard deviation is computed as

$$\text{Standard deviation} = \sqrt{\frac{1}{J}\sum_{j=1}^{J}\left(V^j(r_0, 0) - \widehat{V}(r_0, 0)\right)^2} \tag{17.21}$$

Roughly speaking, the value of the standard error provides guidance to the accuracy of the simulated price of the security. If the standard error is high, it means that the computed value is not very good, and additional simulations are needed. Roughly, we can say that with 95% probability, the true value of the security is within two standard errors of the simulated value. That is, with 95% chance, the true solution to the Fundamental Pricing Equation (Equation 15.24) is contained in the interval

$$\text{Confidence interval} = \left[\widehat{V}(r_0, 0) - 2 \times \text{st. err.}, \widehat{V}(r_0, 0) + 2 \times \text{st. err.}\right] \tag{17.22}$$

■ **EXAMPLE 17.6**

Table 17.1 illustrates the point concerning standard errors. In particular, the second column reports three bond prices at three different maturities, $T = 5.35$, $T = 14.86$ and $T = 26.87$, reported in the first column. The next three columns report the price obtained by Monte Carlo simulations, for three different numbers of simulations $J = 100$, $J = 1,000$ and $J = 10,000$. The last three columns show the standard errors. For instance, consider the first bond, whose actual price is $P(5.35) = \$111.49$. The Monte Carlo price with $J = 100$ is $\widehat{V}(r_0, 0) = \$114.50$, quite different from the true one. However, suppose we did not know the true price (if we did, there would be no need of Monte Carlo simulations) and we have to decide whether the price $\widehat{V}(r_0, 0) = \$114.50$ is accurate or not. The respective standard error provides the answer. In this case the standard error is $st.err = 3.28$. This means that the confidence interval is $[107.9400, 121.0600]$. That is, we can give 95% probability that the true price is between \$107.94 and \$121.06. This is clearly a very large difference, and it cannot enable a trader to quote a price with confidence. By

Table 17.1   Vasicek Bond Prices and Standard Errors with Monte Carlo Simulations

Maturity	Actual Price	Monte Carlo Price			Standard Errors		
		$J = 100$	$J = 1000$	$J = 10000$	$J = 100$	$J = 1000$	$J = 10000$
5.35 years	111.49	114.50	110.74	111.32	3.28	0.85	0.27
14.86 years	119.03	130.76	120.71	119.96	9.91	3.63	0.93
26.87 years	94.66	94.04	95.33	93.85	9.51	5.43	1.57

Data source: *The Wall Street Journal.*

increasing the number of simulations we obtain a tighter interval. For instance, for the case in which $J = 10,000$ we obtain a Monte Carlo price $\widehat{V}(r_0, 0) = 111.32$, which is indeed closer to the true price. But once again, if we did not know the true price, how confident are we in this simulated price? In this case the standard error is much smaller, only $st.err. = 0.27$. This implies that the confidence interval is $[110.7800, 111.86]$, which is relatively small. A trader would be confident enough to quote prices in this interval, as there is not much difference between the true extremes.

What about long term bonds? Consider now the bond with $T = 26.87$ years. In this case, the true price was $P(26.87) = 94.66$. The Monte Carlo price obtained using $J = 10,000$ is $\widehat{V}(r_0, 0) = 93.85$. How confident are we of the accuracy of this price? The standard error is relatively large, $st.err. = 1.57$, which leads to a relatively wide confidence interval equal to $[90.7100, 96.9900]$. That is, even 10,000 simulations are not enough to obtain accurate prices of long-term bonds. For long-term bonds we need to substantially increase the number of simulations to obtain good prices. The exact number of simulations needed for accurate pricing depend on the estimated parameters of the underlying interest rate process.

17.4   EXAMPLE: PRICING A RANGE FLOATER

So far we obtained by Monte Carlo simulations the prices of securities for which we also had an analytical solution to the price. We now explore the case in which such an analytical solution does not exist. A range floater is such a security. More explicitly, a range floater is a floating rate coupon bond that pays coupons that (a) are higher than those of standard floating rate notes; and (b) are only paid so long as the reference floating rate is within a given range.

Range floaters appeared originally in the market in 1993, in an environment of low short-term interest rates and steep yield curves. Investors found them attractive because of the higher coupons that these notes were bearing compared to the market floating rate notes. In addition, these notes allowed investors to speculate on a view that interest rates would remain within a certain range until maturity of the bond. Similarly, the issuer would be insured against high payments when the interest rate increased.

How can we price a range floater? Given its nonstandard structure, Monte Carlo simulations appear to be a viable methodology. By simulating future interest rates *under the risk neutral dynamics*, we obtain the scenarios under which the interest rate is within the desired range, and thus the amount of coupon that is paid to the investor. That is, we can simulate simultaneously the interest rate and the coupons (that depend on the interest rates). For each simulated path of interest rates, and given the implied sequence of cash flows, we can compute the discounted value of future cash flows. By finally averaging across many interest rate paths, we can compute the value of the range floater. We carry out such an exercise in the next example.

■ **EXAMPLE 17.7**

Let the range floater be described by the following terms:

- **Today**: November 1, 2004
- **Maturity**: November 1, 2007
- **Frequency**: Quarterly
- **Notional**: 100
- **Coupon**: Floating rate equal to [3-month LIBOR + Spread]×Accrual factor/Number of days. That is

$$CF\left(t\right) = \text{Notional} \times (LIBOR_{t-1} + \text{Spread}) \times \frac{\text{Accrual factor (between } t-1 \text{ and } t)}{\text{Number of days}} \tag{17.23}$$

- **Spread over floating**: 1%
- **Number of days**: 360
- **Accrual factor**: The number of days during the relevant interest rate period that the 3-month LIBOR is within the range [1.18%, 4.18%]
- **Current 3-Month LIBOR** = 2.18%;

We proceed as follows. First, we extract the LIBOR yield curve from the current LIBOR and swap data, and fit the Vasicek model to the curve. In particular, from the swap rates on November 1, 2004 and the current LIBOR we can apply the procedure illustrated in Section 5.4.3 in Chapter 5 to obtain the LIBOR discount factor $Z(0, T)$ for every maturity T (see Equation 5.45).

Given $Z(0, T)$ for every T, we can then estimate the parameters of the Vasicek model $\bar{r}^*$, γ^*, and σ that best fit the discount curve by nonlinear least squares, as in Section 15.2.4 in Chapter 15. In fact, according to the Vasicek model, the volatility σ should be estimated from the time series variation of interest rates, and we will do so here.[3] The other two parameters can be obtained from minimizing the quantity

$$J(\bar{r}^*, \gamma^*) = \sum_T \left(Z(0, T) - Z^{Vasicek}(r_0, 0; T)\right)^2$$

where $Z^{Vasicek}(r_0, 0; T) = e^{A(T)-B(T)r_0}$ denotes the Vasicek model price. What r_0 should we insert in this formula? We will use $r_0 = 2.17\%$, which is the continuously compounded 3-month rate corresponding to the 3-month LIBOR, which was 2.18% on November 1, 2004.[4]

---

[3]However, practitioners typically also estimate σ from bond prices, or from option prices.
[4]That is, $2.17\% = 1/.25 \times \log(1 + 90/360 \times 2.18\%)$

We estimate the Vasicek parameters to be $\bar{r}^* = 6.41\%$, $\gamma^* = 0.21$, and the volatility $\sigma = .82\%$. Figure 17.2 shows the fitted bond prices and the yield curve obtained from the estimate.

Next, given the estimated parameters $\bar{r}^* = 6.41\%$, $\gamma^* 0.21$, and $\sigma = .82\%$, we carry out a Monte Carlo simulation of interest rates to compute the price of the range floater. In particular, we need to simulate both the interest rates r_t and the cash flow, as the latter depends on the path of interest rates as well, according to Equation 17.23. More specifically, we proceed as follows:

1. Simulate one path of interest rates r_t^j from time 0 to maturity. If we use daily steps and assume for simplicity that a year has 360 days, then we set the time-step $\delta = 1/360$. We then simulate J paths of interest rates as described earlier. That is, each path j starts from $r_0 = 2.17\%$ (the continuously compounded rate that corresponds to the LIBOR) and it is then simulated according to

$$r_{i+1}^j = r_i^j + \gamma^*(\bar{r}^* - r_i^j)\delta + \sigma \times \sqrt{\delta}\epsilon_{i+1}^j$$

where i denotes the step. For simplicity, we are going to interpret this simulated interest rate r_i^j as the 3-month continuously compounded rate.[5]

2. For *each* path j, we compute the sequence of quarterly cash flows by applying the formula in Equation 17.23. Because the cash flow depends on the LIBOR, while we are simulating a continuously compounded (short-term) interest rate, we need to transform it into a LIBOR, according to the formula

$$LIBOR_i^j = \frac{360}{90}(e^{r_i^j \times 0.25} - 1).$$

3. Given the daily sequence of $LIBOR_i^j$, we can compute the number of days the simulated $LIBOR_i^j$ is within the range, and thus use Equation 17.23 to compute the cash flows. Let i^* be a coupon date in the simulation, and assume 360 days in one year, so that a coupon date is every 90 days. Denote the coupon date sequentially, for simplicity, i.e. $i^* = 1, 2, 3, ..., 12$ although each occurs every 90 days. We then have

$$CF_{i^*}^j = \text{Notional} \times \left(LIBOR_{i^*-1}^j + \text{Spread}\right) \times I_{i^*}^j$$

where $I_{i^*}^j$ is the fraction of days $LIBOR_i^j$ has been in the range in simulation j

$$I_{i^*}^j = \frac{\text{Number of days LIBOR}_i^j \text{ is in range between coupon dates } (i^* - 1) \text{ and } i^*}{360}$$

4. For each simulation j compute the present value of the sequence of cash flows for each simulation

$$V_0^j = \sum_{i^*=1}^{12} \frac{CF_{i^*}}{\left(1 + \frac{LIBOR_0^j}{4}\right) \times \left(1 + \frac{LIBOR_2^j}{4}\right) \times ... \times \left(1 + \frac{LIBOR_{i^*-1}^j}{4}\right)}$$

---

[5] According to the Vasicek model, the 3-month rate $r_t(0.25)$ depends on the instantaneous rate according to $r_t(0.25) = -\frac{A(0.25)}{0.25} + \frac{B(0.25)}{0.25} \times r_t$. It follows that $r_t(0.25)$ follows the same mean reverting process, with a small adjustment to $\bar{r}^*$ and σ. However, since σ is estimated from the 3-month LIBOR, and the risk neutral parameters γ^* and $\bar{r}^*$ are obtained by using the 3-month LIBOR as the short-term interest rate in the Vasicek formula, the approximation error is small.

Table 17.2 Value of Range Note with 5000 Simulations for Three Starting Values

LIBOR$_0$	2.18%	2.08%	2.28%
Value $\widehat{V}$	99.8385	100.0651	99.5966
Standard Error	0.0505	0.0485	0.0526

5. Take the average of simulated present values

$$\widehat{V} = \frac{1}{J} \sum_{j=1}^{J} V_0^j$$

The first column in Table 17.2 shows the result of the Monte Carlo simulations, when the pricing is performed with $J = 5000$ simulations. The range note is priced (essentially) at par, as its price is \$99.8385, and the standard error came out to be $st.err. = 0.0505$. Recall that this floating rate note carries a spread of 1% over a standard floating rate note, whose price would be exactly 100. In other words, an investor may choose to pay 100 and obtain a regular floating rate note, or pay (almost) the same price, and obtain a higher coupon, so long as the reference floating rate is within the range $[1.18\%, 4.18\%]$.

What are the tradeoffs of this security? A range floater is quite a risky investment. Indeed, if interest rates go up, a range floater sharply decreases in value compared even to a fixed rate note. The reason is that not only the discount increases, but cash flow decreases (to zero) when the interest rate increases, generating a precipitous decline in price if the interest rate increases. To illustrate this fact, Figure 17.3 plots the value of the range floater for various starting LIBOR. As can be seen quite clearly, an increase in the interest rate generates a very sharp decline in the price, which passes from \$99.83 for $LIBOR_0 = 2.18\%$ to \$96.5 for $LIBOR_0 = 3.18$, to \$90.4 at the range boundary $LIBOR_0 = 4.18\%$. For comparison, consider a 3-year, semi-annual fixed coupon note with coupon rate $c = 3.27\%$. According to the same discount function obtained earlier, this note would be priced at par when $LIBOR_0 = 2.18\%$. If LIBOR were to increase to 3.18% or 4.18%, the 3-year, fixed coupon note would be priced at \$97.88 and \$95.80, respectively. That is, the loss in value would be much smaller than the one realized by the range floater.[6]

17.5 HEDGING WITH MONTE CARLO SIMULATIONS

As emphasized in previous chapters, pricing a derivative security, or a structured note, is only one side of the coin. As soon as we sell the security, we need to implement an effective hedging strategy to ensure that we have the cash needed to make the payments (see Chapter 16). For instance, in the case of the range floater in the example in Section 17.4, if we

---

[6] As we know from Chapter 2, a pure floating rate note would not change price at all as we increase the LIBOR on ex-coupon dates.

Figure 17.2   Vasicek Fitted Yields and the LIBOR Curve on November 1, 2004

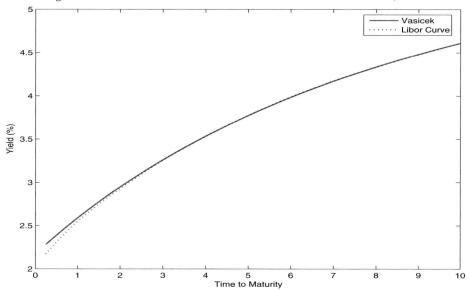

Data source: The Federal Reserve and Bloomberg.

Figure 17.3   Value of Range Floater versus Interest Rate

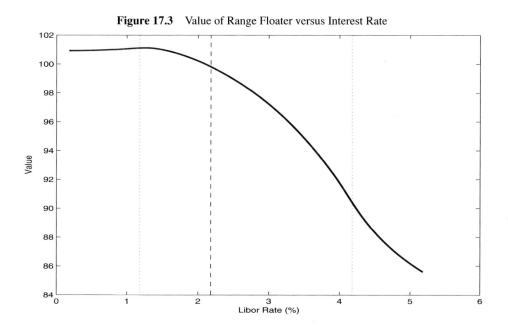

sell such a security, we must come up with 1% spread over LIBOR every quarter so long as the rate is in the range. How can we ensure this outcome? As discussed in Chapter 16, we must apply the portfolio replication argument. The key quantity in the dynamic replication strategy is the sensitivity of the security to interest rates variation $\partial V/\partial r$. In the two examples in Chapter 16, we computed this quantity analytically. However, once we must rely on Monte Carlo simulations to obtain the price of a security, we need to compute this quantity numerically. Fortunately, the methodology is relatively straightforward.

In particular, we are going to use the approximation

$$\frac{\partial V}{\partial r} \approx \frac{\widehat{V}(r_0 + \delta) - \widehat{V}(r_0 - \delta)}{2\delta} \tag{17.24}$$

where δ is a small number, such as one basis point. This approximation to the first derivative of V to the interest rate is called the central approximation. It is more accurate than the more common approximation to the first derivative

$$\frac{\partial V}{\partial r} \approx \frac{\widehat{V}(r_0 + \delta) - \widehat{V}(r_0)}{\delta} \tag{17.25}$$

which is instead called forward approximation. Figure 17.4 illustrates why. The first derivative of a function at a given point r_0 is the slope of the line that is tangent to a curve at r_0. Consider now a small interval δ.[7] Figure 17.4 plots both the forward approximation to the first derivative, as well as the central approximation. As can be seen from the graph, the central approximation does a relatively good job in approximating the slope even for a relatively large δ.

The methodology of obtaining the sensitivity of the security to changes in interest rates by Monte Carlo simulations simply involves the computation of $V(r_0 + \delta)$ and $V(r_0 - \delta)$ by Monte Carlo simulation, a calculation that we can perform along with the calculation of the price of the security.[8] Indeed, when we perform the simulation of interest rates, we have to simply change the starting value of the interest rate (by moving it up and down by δ) and compute the prices. No other change to the simulation code is necessary.

■ **EXAMPLE 17.8**

Consider again Example 17.7. The third and fourth columns in Table 17.2 report the values of the range floater also for the case in which $LIBOR_0$ is moved from its original value of 2.18% by ten basis points. Given the values of the range floater to these two interest rates, we can compute

$$\frac{\partial V}{\partial r} \approx \frac{\$99.5966 - \$100.0651}{2 \times 0.001} = -234.25$$

Figure 17.5 plots this first derivative for many starting interest rates $LIBOR_0$. The figure shows that the sensitivity of V to interest rates becomes very negative very rapidly, as already noted in Figure 17.3.

---

[7]The graph considers a large δ to visually appreciate the difference between the central and the forward approximation.

[8]Indeed, to avoid contaminating the value of the first derivative $\partial V/\partial r$ from random simulation errors, it is important to use the *same* set of random shocks ϵ_i^j across the calculations of V for various starting value. Otherwise, the computation of the sensitivity will be affected by random noise, which is amplified by the choice of a small δ in Equation 17.24.

Figure 17.4   The Central Approximation

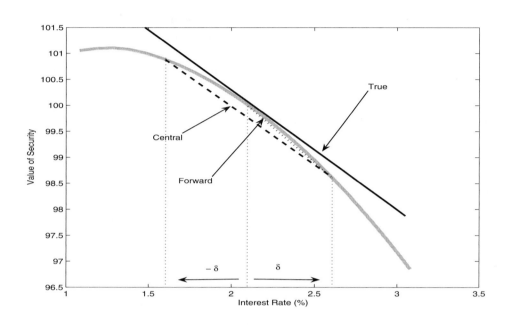

Figure 17.5   Interest Rate Sensitivity of a Range Floater

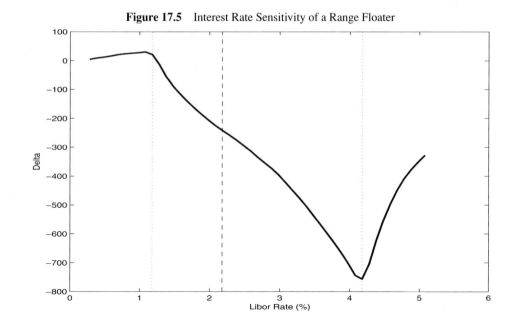

17.6 CONVEXITY BY MONTE CARLO SIMULATIONS

The convexity of an interest rate security with respect to interest rates is a key quantity in gauging the return expectation from investing in the security. Because interest rates are stochastic, everything else equal we should expect a positive capital gain return if the interest rate security has a positive convexity and a negative capital gain return if the interest rate security has a negative convexity. However, as we noted in Chapter 15, "everything is not equal" across securities. No arbitrage arguments push up the Theta of the security whenever the Gamma is low, as discussed in Section 16.5.

How can we compute Gamma $\partial^2 V/\partial r^2$ using Monte Carlo simulations? We can approximate the second derivative as follows

$$\frac{\partial^2 V}{\partial r^2} \approx \frac{\widehat{V}(r_0 + \delta) + \widehat{V}(r_0 - \delta) - 2 \times \widehat{V}(r_0)}{\delta^2} \tag{17.26}$$

Note that all of the necessary quantities to compute the Gamma have already been determined to compute the sensitivity of the security to the interest rate, as shown in Equation 17.24.

■ **EXAMPLE 17.9**

Consider once again the range floater discussed in Examples 17.7 and 17.8. Given the values in Table 17.2, we can compute the Gamma as follows

$$\frac{\partial^2 V}{\partial r^2} \approx \frac{\$99.5966 + \$100.0651 - 2 \times \$99.8385}{.001^2} = -15,300$$

which is negative, as we would expect from glancing at Figure 17.3.

Figure 17.6 plots the convexity of the range floater for many starting interest rates $LIBOR_0$. The figure shows that convexity of the range floater is very sensitive to the current interest rate, as it can be seen also in Figure 17.3. Note in particular how the convexity changes dramatically around the boundaries of the range: When the LIBOR is above the upper boundary of the range, so that it becomes unlikely that any coupon will be paid in the future, then the range floater becomes essentially a zero coupon bond, which has positive convexity.

To conclude, we should remember that no arbitrage implies a strong relation between the convexity of a security and its changes due to the simple passage of time (maturity effect). In particular, in general, the Fundamental Pricing Equation has

$$rV = \frac{\partial V}{\partial t} + \frac{\partial V}{\partial r}m^*(r_t, t) + \frac{1}{2}\frac{\partial^2 V}{\partial r^2}s^2(r, t) \tag{17.27}$$

If we are interested in also computing Theta, i.e., $\frac{\partial V}{\partial t}$, we can do so in two different ways:

1. Use Monte Carlo simulations to compute $\widehat{V}(r_0, t)$ and $\widehat{V}(r_0, t + \delta)$ and approximate

$$\frac{\partial V}{\partial t} \approx \frac{\widehat{V}(r_0, t + \delta) - \widehat{V}(r_0, t)}{\delta} \tag{17.28}$$

2. Use the Fundamental Pricing Equation, and obtain

$$\frac{\partial V}{\partial t} = rV - \frac{\partial V}{\partial r}m^*(r_t, t) - \frac{1}{2}\frac{\partial^2 V}{\partial r^2}s^2(r, t) \tag{17.29}$$

Figure 17.6   Convexity of a Range Floater

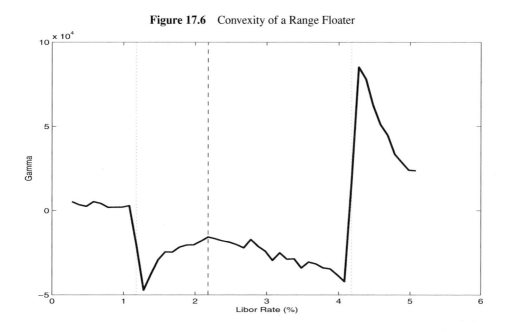

Once we have computed the value of the security V, its sensitivity to interest rate $\partial V/\partial r$ and finally the convexity $\partial^2 V/\partial r^2$, the calculation of Theta from Equation 17.29 becomes immediate.

■ **EXAMPLE 17.10**

The Theta of the range floater in Example 17.7 can be computed from the above quantities by using Equation 17.29. In particular, since $m^*(r_t, t) = \gamma^*(\bar{r}^* - r_0) = 0.0089$ and $s(r, t) = \sigma = 0.0082$, we obtain

$$
\begin{aligned}
\frac{\partial V}{\partial t} &= r_0 V - \frac{\partial V}{\partial r} \times \gamma^*(\bar{r}^* - r_0) - \frac{1}{2}\frac{\partial^2 V}{\partial r^2} \times \sigma^2 \\
&= 0.0217 \times 99.8385 - (-234.25) \times 0.0089 - \frac{1}{2}(-15,300) \times (.0082)^2 \\
&= 3.7403
\end{aligned}
$$

which is positive, consistent with the fact that the security is strongly negatively convex at r_0. Figure 17.7 plots the Theta of the range floater for many starting interest rates $LIBOR_0$. We can see, the Theta is always positive, although it drops in magnitude when the convexity increases (to positive) around the boundaries. This behavior shows that indeed it is not the case that the Theta is positive whenever the convexity is negative and vice versa, as they can be both positive. The values of rV and $\partial V/\partial r$ make part of the difference.

17.7   SUMMARY

In this chapter we covered the following topics:

Figure 17.7   Theta of a Range Floater

1. The concept of risk neutral pricing: The solution to the Fundamental Pricing Equation can be obtained as an expectation of the future cash flow discounted at the risk-free rate, *provided* that such expectation is computed with a modified process for interest rates, whose drift equals the coefficient $\partial V/\partial r$ in the fundamental equation. Because the Fundamental Pricing Equation is obtained from a no arbitrage argument, risk neutral pricing is a consequence of no arbitrage, and *not* that market participants are really neutral to risk.

2. Feynman-Kac Theorem: It provides the solution to the Fundamental Pricing Equation as an expectation.

3. Monte Carlo Simulations: Since we know that the solution of the Fundamental Pricing Equation is an expectation, we can approximate the latter as follows: (a) compute numerous paths of the underlying interest rates; (b) compute the cash flows; (c) discount them to today using the simulated path; (d) take the average. Monte Carlo simulations can be used to price relatively complex securities, and compute hedge ratios and the convexity.

4. Standard Errors: when we uses Monte Carlo Simulations to approximate the price of a security, a question arises as to how close the computed value is to the true value (i.e., the true solution to the Fundamental Pricing Equation). Since effectively we are estimating the value of the security from a sample of simulated values, we can compute the standard error of estimated value and confidence intervals to gauge how close the estimated value is to the true value.

17.8 EXERCISES

1. Use Monte Carlo simulations to replicate Figure 17.1. Use the parameters obtained in this chapter. How does the figure change as you change the parameters γ and σ? Provide several figures for various parameter choices. Comment on your findings. In particular, explain *why* the Monte Carlo simulations method *should* yield (approximately) the same price as the analytical formula.

2. Refer to the previous exercise. Use Monte Carlo simulations to compute the Delta, $\partial V/\partial r$, and Gamma, $\partial^2 V/\partial r^2$. Compare the values from simulations with the actual values from the Vasicek model. Are the simulated values close to the true values? How does the approximation depend on the number of simulations?

3. In this chapter we only considered the Vasicek model. Replicate Figure 17.1 also for the Cox, Ingersoll, and Ross model of interest rates, discussed in Section 15.4.1 in Chapter 15. Use the parameter values in that chapter. How does the figure change as you change the parameters γ and σ? Provide several figures for various parameter choices.

4. **The option embedded in Inverse Floaters.** In Chapter 2, Section 2.8, we considered the pricing of inverse floaters and leveraged inverse floaters. Recall these are securities whose coupons move inversely with the interest rate, according to $c(t) = \bar{c} - k \times r_n(t - \Delta)$, where $\Delta = 1/n$ is the period between payments, n is the number of payments per year, and $r_n(t)$ is the $n-$times compounded rate. In that chapter, to simplify, we assumed that $c(t)$ is always positive. However, it may happen that $r_n(t)$ increases so much as to push $c(t)$ negative. Therefore, the true coupon is $c(t) = \max(\bar{c} - k \times r_n(t - \Delta), 0)$. How does this restriction affect the value of the inverse and leveraged inverse floaters?

   (a) Today is June 30, 2008. Table 17.4 contais the prices of bills and notes. Fit the Vasicek model to these bond prices.

   (b) Consider an inverse floater with the terms in Table 17.3. Obtain a price using a simple portfolio of zero coupon bonds (see Chapter 2).

   (c) Use Monte Carlo simulations to compute the value of the inverse floater, ignoring the restriction that $c(t) > 0$. Is the price obtained from Monte Carlo simulations close to the one just obtained in the previous point? Discuss.

   (d) Now impose the restriction $c(t) > 0$. What is the price of the inverse floater?

   (e) Suppose you sold this inverse floater to a client. How would you hedge your exposure to variation in interest rates? Obtain the hedge ratios and explain.

5. **Puttable Leveraged Inverse Floater.** The investor who purchases the leveraged inverse floater in the previous exercise is worried about an excess decline in price, and therefore decides to purchase the option to sell it back to the issuer at a certain date T_P at 97% of par value. This option is European, that is, it can only be exercised at T_P. Let $T_P = 1$ year. Use Monte Carlo simulations to compute the value of this option.

   (a) What is the payoff of the option at maturity T_P?

Table 17.3 Leveraged Inverse Floater Term Sheet

Date	June 30, 2008
Maturity	June 30, 2013 (5-year)
Payment Frequency	Semi-annual
Interest Payment	Base interest rate $- 2 \times$ Reference interest rate
Base Interest Rate	10%
Reference Interest Rate	6 month T-bill rate with standard 6-month lag

(b) The payoff can be written, generically, as a function of the interest rate at T_P, that is, as $g(r_{T_P})$ [the form of $g(\ )$ is the answer to the previous point]. Given this, how can you use Monte Carlo simulations to price the option? Describe the methodology, and obtain the price of this option.

   i. As a first approximation, compute the value of this option without the restriction $c(t) > 0$.

   ii. (Optional) Impose the restriction $c(t) > 0$. How much does the value of the option change? Why? (This part is computationally more challenging.)

(c) What is then the value of the puttable leveraged inverse floater?

6. **Corridor Note**. On October 26, 2004, PiVe International Bank, a AAA company, issued a 10-year corridor note. This note has several features that makes it rather hard to price: First, it accrues a coupon only so long as a reference rate is within some bounds. The bounds themselves, however, change over time according to a given schedule. In addition, the coupon moves from fixed to floating at some point in the future. The term sheet is in Table 17.5. On October 26, the 3-month LIBOR was 2.11%, and the 6-month LIBOR was 2.24%. The swap rates for maturities up to 10 years are in Table 17.6.

(a) Obtain the discount curve $Z(T)$ for the relevant maturities as of October 26, 2004. Make sure to plot your results in a figure and comment on them.

(b) Fit the Vasicek model or the Cox, Ingersoll, and Ross model to the discount curve obtained in Part (a).

(c) Employ a Monte Carlo simulation method to obtain the price of the security.

   • Note that there are two LIBOR rates to simulate, the 3-month and 6-month rate. To ensure no arbitrage is preserved, the 3-month and 6-month LIBOR must be simulated together. One methodology is to simulate the short term rate r_i and then use the Vasicek or Cox, Ingersoll, Ross pricing formula to compute both the 3-month and 6-month LIBOR rates.

(d) What is the benefit for an investor from investing in these notes, compared to other available instruments? Why would you think that corridor notes are popular?

(e) Use Monte Carlo simulations to compute the sensitivity of the note to changes in interest rates (i.e. its Delta) as well as its convexity (i.e. its Gamma). Plot

Table 17.4   Treasury Bills and Notes on June 30, 2008

CRSPID	CUSIP	Bid	Ask	Accrued Interest	Maturity	Coupon	Time to Maturity
20080731.4	912795F7	99.8558	99.8566	0.0000	20080731	0.000	0.0849
20080828.4	912795G3	99.7189	99.7206	0.0000	20080828	0.000	0.1616
20081002.4	912795G8	99.5183	99.5209	0.0000	20081002	0.000	0.2575
20081030.4	912795H4	99.3714	99.3748	0.0000	20081030	0.000	0.3343
20081128.4	912795H8	99.1380	99.1422	0.0000	20081128	0.000	0.4137
20090102.4	912795J5	98.9047	98.9150	0.0000	20090102	0.000	0.5096
20090228.2	912828GJ	101.6406	101.6719	1.5747	20090228	4.750	0.6658
20090430.2	912828GP	101.7578	101.7891	0.7459	20090430	4.500	0.8329
20090531.2	912828GT	102.2266	102.2578	0.3996	20090531	4.875	0.9178
20090630.2	912828GV	102.4375	102.4688	0.0000	20090630	4.875	1.0000
20090731.2	912828GY	102.3672	102.3984	1.9186	20090731	4.625	1.0849
20090831.2	912828HB	101.8672	101.8984	1.3261	20090831	4.000	1.1699
20090930.2	912828HD	102.0313	102.0625	0.9945	20090930	4.000	1.2521
20091031.2	912828HF	101.6875	101.7188	0.6009	20091031	3.625	1.3370
20091130.2	912828HJ	101.0313	101.0625	0.2562	20091130	3.125	1.4192
20091231.2	912828HL	101.2344	101.2656	0.0000	20091231	3.250	1.5041
20100131.2	912828HP	99.5000	99.5313	0.8815	20100131	2.125	1.5890
20100228.2	912828HS	99.2813	99.3125	0.6630	20100228	2.000	1.6658
20100331.2	912828HU	98.7266	98.7578	0.4351	20100331	1.750	1.7507
20100430.2	912828HX	99.2734	99.3047	0.3522	20100430	2.125	1.8329
20100531.2	912828JA	100.0781	100.1094	0.2008	20100531	2.625	1.9178
20100630.2	912828JC	100.4922	100.5078	0.0000	20100630	2.875	2.0000
20100715.2	912828DZ	102.5234	102.5547	1.7778	20100715	3.875	2.0411
20100815.2	912828ED	103.0469	103.0781	1.5412	20100815	4.125	2.1260
20100915.2	912828EG	102.5938	102.6250	1.1267	20100915	3.875	2.2110
20101015.2	912828EJ	103.5547	103.5859	0.8825	20101015	4.250	2.2932
20101115.2	912828EM	104.1172	104.1484	0.5625	20101115	4.500	2.3781
20101215.2	912828EQ	103.8984	103.9297	0.1793	20101215	4.375	2.4603
20110115.2	912828ES	103.7891	103.8203	1.9499	20110115	4.250	2.5452
20110215.2	9128276T	105.6250	105.6563	1.8681	20110215	5.000	2.6301
20110228.2	912828EX	104.2734	104.3047	1.4919	20110228	4.500	2.6658
20110331.2	912828FA	104.9531	104.9844	1.1810	20110331	4.750	2.7507
20110430.2	912828FD	105.4453	105.4766	0.8081	20110430	4.875	2.8329
20110531.2	912828FH	105.5625	105.5938	0.3996	20110531	4.875	2.9178
20110630.2	912828FK	106.3125	106.3438	0.0000	20110630	5.125	3.0000
20110731.2	912828FN	105.7031	105.7344	2.0223	20110731	4.875	3.0847
20110831.2	912828FS	104.8906	104.9219	1.5333	20110831	4.625	3.1694
20110930.2	912828FU	104.5547	104.5859	1.1189	20110930	4.500	3.2514
20111031.2	912828FW	105.0156	105.0469	0.7666	20111031	4.625	3.3361
20111130.2	912828GA	104.6719	104.7031	0.3689	20111130	4.500	3.4180
20111231.2	912828GC	105.1016	105.1328	0.0000	20111231	4.625	3.5027
20120131.2	912828GF	105.5938	105.6250	1.9705	20120131	4.750	3.5874
20120229.2	912828GK	105.2344	105.2656	1.5333	20120229	4.625	3.6667
20120331.2	912828GM	104.7969	104.8281	1.1189	20120331	4.500	3.7514
20120430.2	912828GQ	104.8828	104.9141	0.7459	20120430	4.500	3.8333
20120531.2	912828GU	105.7891	105.8203	0.3893	20120531	4.750	3.9180
20120630.2	912828GW	106.3047	106.3359	0.0000	20120630	4.875	4.0000
20120731.2	912828GZ	105.4609	105.4922	1.9186	20120731	4.625	4.0849
20120831.2	912828HC	103.5234	103.5547	1.3675	20120831	4.125	4.1699
20120930.2	912828HE	104.1328	104.1641	1.0567	20120930	4.250	4.2521
20121031.2	912828HG	102.5781	102.6094	0.6423	20121031	3.875	4.3370
20121130.2	912828HK	100.5000	100.5313	0.2766	20121130	3.375	4.4192
20121231.2	912828HM	101.5547	101.5859	0.0000	20121231	3.625	4.5041
20130131.2	912828HQ	98.3125	98.3438	1.1927	20130131	2.875	4.5890
20130228.2	912828HT	97.6719	97.7031	0.9117	20130228	2.750	4.6658
20130331.2	912828HV	96.5313	96.5625	0.6216	20130331	2.500	4.7507
20130430.2	912828HY	99.2031	99.2344	0.5180	20130430	3.125	4.8329
20130531.2	912828JB	100.7734	100.8047	0.2678	20130531	3.500	4.9178
20130630.2	912828JD	100.2031	100.2188	0.0000	20130630	3.375	5.0000
20130815.2	912828BH	104.3750	104.4063	1.5879	20130815	4.250	5.1260
20131115.2	912828BR	104.4375	104.4688	0.5313	20131115	4.250	5.3781
20140215.2	912828CA	103.2188	103.2500	1.4945	20140215	4.000	5.6301
20140515.2	912828CJ	107.2656	107.2969	0.5938	20140515	4.750	5.8740

Source: Data excerpted from CRSP (Daily Treasuries) ©2009 Center for Research in Security Prices (CRSP),
The University of Chicago Booth School of Business.
Note: The CRSPID identifies the type of bond. In particular, its form is YYYYMMDD.T, where
YYYY = maturity year, MM = maturity month, DD = maturity day, T = Type of bond:
1 - noncallable bond, 2 - noncallable note, 4 - Treasury bill

Table 17.5   10-year, 9% Corridor Note: Term Sheet*

Trade Date	26 October 2004
Start Date	09 November 2004
Maturity Date	09 November 2014
Redemption Price	100.00%
Coupon	Years 1-5: 9.00% x b/B x Day Count Fraction
	Years 6-10: (3-Month LIBOR + 2.50%) x b/B x Day Count Fraction

where:
"b" is the number of calendar days in the relevant Interest
Period on which the Reference Rate as observed on such calendar day
fixes on or within the Corridor Range for that Interest Period.

"B" is the total number of calendar days in the corresponding
Interest Period to "b" above.

Interest Rate Period: Time between coupon payments.

Reference Rate	6-Month LIBOR
Corridor Range	Year 1: 0% to 4%
for relevant Interest	Year 2: 0% to 4.5%
Period	Year 3-5: 0% to 5%
	Year 6-7: 0% to 6%
	Year 8-10: 0% to 6.5%
Day Count Fraction	90/360
Interest Payment Dates	Quarterly

*: This term sheet is a stripped down version of a an actual term sheet for a callable, 10-year corridor note.

Table 17.6   Swap Rates on October 26, 2004

Maturity (Year)	1	2	3	4	5	7	10
Rates	2.46	2.85	3.16	3.42	3.64	4.01	4.39

Source: Federal Reserve Web site.

Table 17.7   Estimated Relation Between CPR and 5 year Swap Rate

	β_0	β_1	β_2	R^2
coeff	6.93	-246.36	1468.2	82%
t-stat	4.99	-4.28	2.59	

Standard errors use Newey West correction for autocorrelation and heteroskedasticity with 24 lags.

the value of the corridor note for many values of the starting short-term interest rate. Comment on your results, and link them to your answer to Part (d).

7. Pricing a **Mortgage Backed Security** (MBS) by Monte Carlo Simulations. The use of prepayment models has become relatively common in the pricing of MBS and various structures. In this exercise, which relies on the concepts developed in Chapter 8, you have to use Monte Carlo simulations and a simple prepayment model to compute the price of MBS.[9] In particular, assume that when using data on the Conditional Prepayment Rate (CPR) and the 5-year swap rate, you obtained the following relation between CPR and the swap rate $c^{swap}(t)$

$$ CPR(t+1) = \frac{e^{\beta_0 + \beta_1 c^{swap}(t) + \beta_2 c^{swap}(t)^2}}{1 + e^{\beta_0 + \beta_1 c^{swap}(t) + \beta_2 c^{swap}(t)^2}} \qquad (17.30) $$

where Table 17.7 contains the estimates of the parameters β_0, β_1 and β_2. The transformation $CPR(x) = e^x/(1 + e^x)$, called a logit transformation, ensures that CPR is between 0 and 1 for any possible value of x. It is a convenient transformation when we need to compute probabilities. The top panel of Figure 17.8 contains the fit of the model: The stars are actual data points (ex-post CPR level and swap rate) while the solid line is the fitted value from the regression. The bottom panel shows that the model does an accurate job in predicting actual refinancing: The solid line is once again the fitted value, while the dotted line shows the refinancing index, already discussed in Chapter 8.

(a) Today is June 8, 2007. Table 17.8 contain LIBOR and swap rates on this date. Fit the Vasicek or CIR model to these data.

(b) Use the parameters of your interest rate model, as well as the relation in Equation 17.30 to simulate the cash flows of a 6% GNMA pass-through security. On June 8, 2007, the GNMA 6 underlying pool had a WAC = 6.5% and WAM = 320. The quoted prices in the TBA market were [Bid Ask] = [99.4063 99.4375].

   i. Is your price obtained by Monte Carlo simulations close to the traded prices?

   ii. If not, can you explain why? In particular, can Equation 17.30 be used under risk neutral pricing? Or perhaps should an adjustment be made to

---

[9]The data for this exercise are obtained from Bloomberg.

Figure 17.8 Predicting Refinancing from Swap Rates

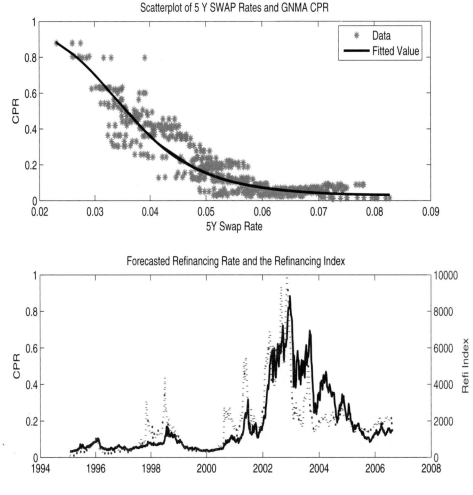

Data Source: Bloomberg.

Table 17.8 LIBOR and Swap Rates on June 8, 2007

LIBOR 1 M	LIBOR 3 M	LIBOR 6 M	LIBOR 1 Y				
5.32	5.36	5.40	5.48				

SWAP 1 Y	SWAP 2 Y	SWAP 3 Y	SWAP 4 Y	SWAP 5 Y	SWAP 7 Y	SWAP 10 Y	SWAP 30 Y
5.4800	5.4700	5.5100	5.5600	5.6100	5.6800	5.7600	5.9300

Source: Bloomberg

take into account the fact that the relation between CPR and r_t is only a statistical relation, and therefore a "market price of risk" should be taken into account? Discuss.

(c) Compute the duration and convexity of the GNMA 6. Comment.

17.9 CASE STUDY: PROCTER & GAMBLE / BANKERS TRUST LEVERAGED SWAP

The 1994 suit of Procter & Gamble (P&G) against Bankers Trust on P&G losses out of a complex swap position has become a standard case study. The case describes both the risk of entering into complex transactions to obtain higher-than-market returns, as well as the fiduciary relation that exists between investment banks and clients. The next page reports excerpts from a 1994 *New York Times* article covering the case. In particular, in 1994 P&G had a fixed-for-floating swap that was about to expire. Under the term of the old swap, P&G was paying a below-market floating rate, and sought to replace the maturing swap with a new one that would replicate the terms of the old one. The problem was that current interest rates were lower than ever, and thus achieving such a low floating rate would be difficult. As described by the article, on November 2 1994, P&G agreed to enter into a complex fixed-for-floating swap, under the condition that if interest rates were to increase, a new spread would be applied to the floating rate paid by P&G. This spread was going to be set six months after the initiation of the contract, according to a complicated formula.

More specifically, the terms of the swap contract were as follows:[10]

- Notional: $200 million

- Contract Date: November 4, 1993

- Maturity Date: November 4, 1998

- Bankers Trust pays: 5.30%

- Procter & Gamble pays: Commercial Paper Rate $-$ 0.75% + "Spread" where the "spread " is determined as follows:

$$
\begin{aligned}
\text{Spread} \;&=\; 0 \quad \text{until November 4, 1994} \\
\text{Spread} \;&=\; \left(\frac{\text{5-Year T-note yield} \times 98.5}{5.78} \right) - \text{Price of 6.25\% 30-year T-bond}
\end{aligned}
$$

$$(17.31)$$

- The "spread" cannot be negative.

The formula determining the spread is the key to understanding this security. In particular, according to the data, the value of the spread was zero at initiation. That is, if interest rates didn't move, indeed Procter & Gamble would be able to lock in a submarket floating rate (CP $-$ 75 basis points).

[10]See Appendix 5 of the case study "Procter & Gamble versus Bankers Trust: Caveat Emptor" prepared by Prof. Robert H. Moffet and Barbara S. Petitt, Case number A06-05-0001, Thunderbird.

P.& G. Sues Bankers Trust Over Swap Deal

By SAUL HANSELL

The Procter & Gamble Company yesterday sued the Bankers Trust Company over a complex financial transaction that caused P.& G., the Cincinnati consumer products company, to take a $102 million loss in April.

[...]

In the suit filed in United States District Court in Cincinnati, P.& G. asserts that Bankers Trust wrongly offered assurances that Procter's losses could be limited if it wanted to get out of the deal, as it ultimately did. The company's central contention is that Bankers Trust did not properly explain the potential cost of getting out.

Bankers Trust, in response, called its dealings with Procter "legal, proper and appropriate" and it denied that the bank ever promised that it could limit Procter's losses.

"We did not and could not represent in advance the cost to end these transactions prematurely," said Douglas Kidd, a spokesman for Bankers Trust. That, he said, "necessarily would have to be based on the market when such a request is made."

The suit seeks $130 million in compensatory damages and unspecified punitive damages.

Derivatives are contracts with terms that are derived from some underlying asset or index. Swaps typically involve cash payments between a corporation and a derivatives dealer, often a bank. They vary with the movements of interest rates and are most often used by companies to change borrowing from fixed interest rates to floating terms, or vice versa.

Last October, Procter was looking to replace a swap transaction relating to $200 million in debt that was scheduled to expire under which it paid a below-market interest rate. With interest rates then at the lowest level in two decades, Procter faced the prospect of accepting less attractive terms to extend the arrangement. Bankers Trust proposed a complex alternative, the suit said, which Procter agreed to on Nov. 2.

But the transaction held a risk. After six months, the rate that Procter would pay would be raised by a "spread" derived by a complex formula based on the yield of a five-year Treasury bond and the price of the 30-year bond.

The company acknowledged that it understood it was selling an option on bonds -- in effect, receiving a payment up front, known as a premium, in return for promising to buy back the bond at a fixed price. That could represent a substantial loss if rates were to rise and bond prices to fall.

Procter said that it was willing to take this risk because of assurances offered by Bankers Trust that it could protect P.& G. against any further losses at any point during the deal. Like all dealers in financial products that are not readily traded on public exchanges, Bankers Trust will generally buy back its derivatives from clients, at whatever it feels the current market price is.

The crux of Procter's complaint is its assertion that the bank, after Procter repeatedly asked it to describe what would happen to the cost of ending the deal if interest rates became much more volatile, insisted that any changes "would not have a significant effect on P.& G.'s position."

When the Federal Reserve began to raise interest rates in February, Procter found the cost of locking in rates had soared, requiring it to pay a staggering 14.12 percent above the normal borrowing costs -- or commercial paper rate -- for established companies. In the next four and a half years, P.& G. says, that will cost the company an extra $130 million.

The company also lost money an another swap with Bankers Trust that involved German marks that was not involved in the suit.

However, what would make the spread increase? From its formula, there are two quantities that are key: the 5-year T-note yield and the price of a given 30-year bond. In particular, if either the 5-year yield increased and/or the price of the 30-year bond declined, then the spread would increase. Note in particular that if the 5-year yield increases it would be likely that the 30-year bond yield would also increase – yields tend to move together, as discussed in Chapter 4– and thus the two events are not uncorrelated. In general, the spread would increase if interest rates increased.

17.9.1 Parameter Estimates

The first task is to estimate the parameters of the Vasicek model. We proceed in two steps. First, using historical data of the short-term interest rate r_t we can compute the value of the volatility σ. Second, we can use the cross-section of bond prices at the beginning of November 1993 to estimate the risk neutral parameters γ^* and $\bar{r}^*$.

What sample size should we use to estimate the volatility of interest rates? A short sample period has the advantage of capturing more recent behavior of rates, insulating the estimates from events in the old past. On the other hand, events in the less recent past can also contain important information that may be useful in forecasting future rates. Here we consider two sample sizes, to make the point: A 3-year sample and a 10-year sample. Approximating the spot rate r_t with the 3-month T-bill rate, Table 17.9 contains the estimates for the 3-year sample (Panel A) and the 10-year sample (Panel B). In particular, the volatility in the shorter sample is only $\sigma = 0.0063$, while in the longer sample it is almost twice that value, $\sigma = .010776$.

Given the volatility level, we can then estimate the remaining two risk neutral parameters γ^* and $\bar{r}^*$ by nonlinear least squares, as discussed in Section 15.2.4 in Chapter 15, and already applied in Example 17.7 in this chapter. In a nutshell, we minimize over γ^* and $\bar{r}^*$ the quantity:

$$J(\gamma^*, \bar{r}^*) = \sum_{i=1}^{N} \left(P_{c^i}^{Vasicek}(0; T^i) - P_{c^i}^{Data}(0; T^i) \right)^2 \tag{17.32}$$

where

$$P_{c^i}^{Vasicek}(0; T^i) = \sum_{j=1}^{n^i} \frac{c^i}{2} Z(0, \tau^i) + Z(0, T^i).$$

Panel A of Table 17.9 reports the estimates for the short sample. In particular, $\bar{r}^* = 7.32\%$ and $\gamma^* = 0.2904$. Figure 17.9 reports the term structure of interest rates estimated from the Vasicek model on November 29, 1993.[11] The top panel shows the performance of the Vasicek model to fit the data on November 29, 1993. The model performs well at the short end and very long end, although it fails to exactly price the bonds with 15 - 20 years to maturity. Panel B plots the implied term structure of interest rates on that day. A similar picture arises if we use the 10-year sample to estimate the volatility of interest rates. The corresponding estimates of the risk neutral parameters are reported in Panel B of Table 17.9. As can be seen, the risk neutral long-term rate $\bar{r}^*$ and mean reversion parameter γ^* are very similar to the previous ones, as the difference in volatility estimates across the two

---

[11]The data for this estimation are obtained from CRSP of the University of Chicago.

Figure 17.9 The Term Structure of Interest Rates on October 29, 1993

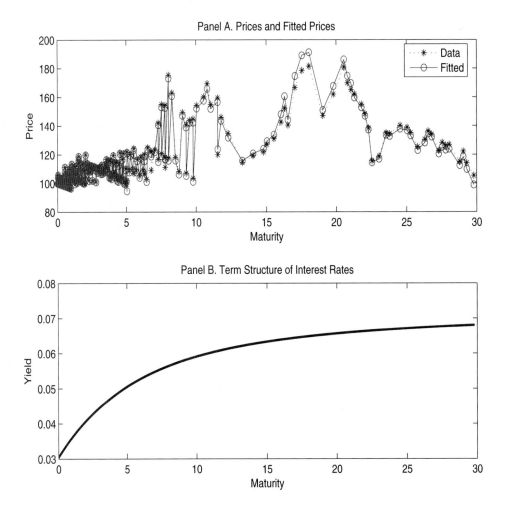

Data Source: CRSP.

panels is not too substantial. The impact of the difference in volatility estimates, however, will be clear in the price of the swap, as well as its risk analysis.

17.9.2 Pricing by Monte Carlo Simulations

We now move to evaluating the swap. One complication that immediately arises when evaluating the swap is that the floating rate is defined on the commercial paper rate, rather than Treasury bill rate or the LIBOR. Figure 17.10 shows that the spread between the two rates moves quite substantially over time, fluctuating between zero and 2.2%. Yet, the correlation between the levels of these two rates is about 98%. To satisfactorily price the swap, we should consider a multi factor model (see Chapter 22). However, given that the aim of this section is to illustrate the Monte Carlo simulation methodology for pricing purposes, we are going to make the simplifying assumption that the spread between commercial paper and treasury rate is constant and equal to the value on valuation date, that is,

$$spread_{cp} = 0.2488 \, bp \qquad (17.33)$$

In addition, we will ignore default risk, and will discount future cash flows using the Treasury curve obtained in the previous section. Although this is once again an approximation, it simplifies the analysis.

Having settled the issues above, let's move to evaluate the swap by Monte Carlo simulations. The Monte Carlo simulation methodology calls for the contemporaneous simulations of cash flows and discounts. We proceed as follows:

1. Simulate the instantaneous interest rate according to the risk neutral parameters up to maturity

$$r_i^j = r_{i-1}^j + \gamma^* \left(\overline{r}^* - r_{i-1}^j \right) \delta + \sigma \sqrt{\delta} \, \varepsilon_i^j \qquad (17.34)$$

where the subscript i denotes the time-step, and the superscript j denotes the simulation number.

2. Compute the semi-annually compounded rates, denoted by $y_i^j(0.5)$, which will be used both to compute the floating part of cash flows, as well as the discounting. These semi-annually compounded rates can be obtained from the Vasicek formula itself. In fact, out of the instantaneous rate r_i^j that is simulated according to Equation 17.34 we can compute the Vasicek zero coupon bond curve $Z(r_i^j, t_i; T) = e^{A(t_i;T)-B(t_i;T)\times r_i^j}$ where $t_i = i/dt$ is the calendar time corresponding to time step i. Given the zero coupon bond curve, the semi-annually compounded interest rate is then given by $y_i^j(0.5) = 2 \times \left(Z(r_i^j, t_i; t_i + 0.5)^{-1/2} - 1 \right)$.

3. At time $t^* = 6$ months, compute the value of the spread in the formula in Equation 17.31. In particular, we need to compute the simulated price of a 30-year coupon bond and the yield to maturity of a 5-year coupon note. These simulated quantities can be computed by appealing again to the Vasicek formula. In fact, let i^* denote the time-step corresponding to six months, $i^* = 0.5/dt$. From the Vasicek formula $Z(r_{t^*}^j, t^*, T) = e^{A(t^*;T)-B(t^*;T)\times r_{t^*}^j}$ we can compute both the value of the 30-year, 6.25% T-bond as well as the yield to maturity of the 5-year bond. From the data we find that the 5-year T-note coupon rate was 9.1%. For each simulation path j, the values of the 30-year coupon Treasury bond and the 5-year coupon Treasury note are then:

$$P^{30}(t^*, 30)^j = \sum_{k=1}^{60} \frac{6.25\%}{2} Z(r_{t^*}^j, t^*, T_k) + Z(r_{t^*}^i, t^*, T_{60}) \qquad (17.35)$$

$$P^5(t^*, 5)^j = \sum_{k=1}^{10} \frac{9.1\%}{2} Z(r_{t^*}^j, t^*, T_k) + Z(r_{t^*}^j, t^*, T_{10}) \qquad (17.36)$$

where T_k, $k = 1, .., 60$ represents the coupon dates of the bonds in semi-annual increments. The yield to maturity of the 5-year zero coupon bond can then be obtained by finding the constant yield Y^j such that (see Section 2.4.3 in Chapter 2):

$$P^5(t^*, 5)^j = \sum_{k=1}^{1} 0\frac{9.1\%/2}{(1 + Y^j/2)^k} + \frac{1}{(1 + Y^j/2)^{10}}$$

Thus, for each simulation j, we can compute the spread

$$spread^j = \max\left(\left(\frac{Y^j \times 98.5}{5.78}\right) - P^{30}(t^*, 30)^j, 0\right) \qquad (17.37)$$

4. Compute the sequence of cash flows. In particular, the net cash flow at payment time $t + 0.5$ in simulation j is given by

$$CF_{t+0.5}^j = \frac{1}{2}\left(5.3\% - (y_t^j(.5) + spread_{cp} - 0.75/100 + spread^j\right)$$

where t's are selected at semi-annual frequency from the simulated rates.

5. Given finally the simulated sequence of semi-annual cash flows, for simulation j, we can discount them directly using the semi-annual rates

$$V^j = \sum_{t=0.5}^{5} e^{-\sum_{i=1}^{t/\delta} r_i^j \delta} CF_{t+0.5}^j \qquad (17.38)$$

6. Take the average of the discount values across all simulated values J

$$\text{Value of swap} = \widehat{V} = \frac{1}{J}\sum_{j=1}^{J} V^j \qquad (17.39)$$

7. Compute the standard error to assess the reliability of the pricing methodology.

$$\text{Standard error on value of swap} = \sqrt{\frac{1}{J}\sum_{j=1}^{J}\left(V^j - \widehat{V}\right)^2} \qquad (17.40)$$

Panel A of Table 17.9 reports the value of the leveraged swap from the perspective of Procter & Gamble for the case in which the volatility of the spot rate is computed out of three years of data. To speed up the computations we chose $\delta = 1/52$, corresponding to weekly interest rates simulations, and a number of simulations $J = 5000$. In this case, we see that the value of swap computed from the above procedure is about $ 1.57 million, with a standard error $0.193 million. Since this value is positive, it means that P&G stood to gain from the swap in this case. That is, they paid zero (there is no exchange of money at initiation of a swap) for something valued by the model at $1.57 million. Panel B of the same table, however, reports the value of the swap under the assumption that we use ten years of data to compute the volatility in the swap computation. In this case, the volatility of the short-term interest rate is much larger, at $\sigma = 1.0776\%$. The value of the swap then turns out to be $-\$9.52$ million. That is, because this number is negative, P&G would stand to lose on average in this swap, as they paid zero for something with a negative value. To

Table 17.9   leveraged Swap Value

Panel A. 3-Year Sample				
$\bar{r}^*$	γ^*	σ ($\times 100$)	Value	st.err
7.32	0.2904	0.6352	1.5716	0.193
Panel B. 10-Year Sample				
$\bar{r}^*$	γ^*	σ ($\times 100$)	Value	st.err
7.37	0.2883	1.0776	-9.5208	0.4563

Figure 17.10   Commercial Paper Rate and the 3-Month Treasury Bill Rate

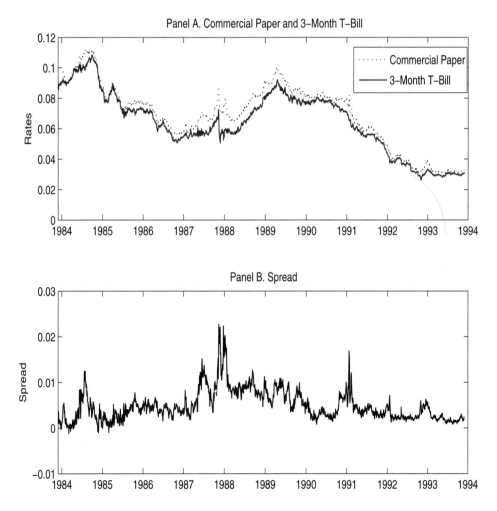

Data Source: Federal Reserve.

Figure 17.11   Value of Leveraged Swap for Various Initial Interest Rates

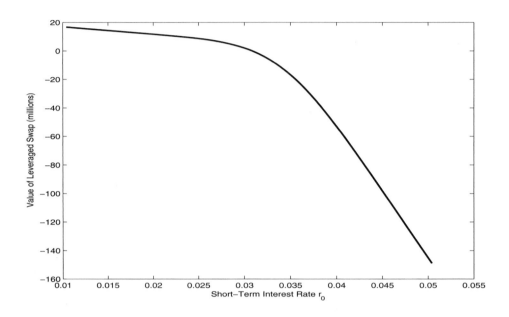

put it differently, according to the higher volatility case, P&G was supposed to pay an even lower floating rate than CP - 0.75% in order to make the value of the swap equal to zero.

The results in Table 17.9 demonstrate the extreme sensitivity of results to assumptions. The reason for this behavior stems from the fact that P&G was effectively selling an option to Bankers Trust, and options increase in value when volatility increases. Since P&G was selling one option, higher volatility implies a lower value of the security for them. This fact can also be seen from a plot of the value of the security against the short-term interest rate at time $t = 0$. Figure 17.11 plots the value of the leveraged swap for various starting short term rates r_0 for the case in which $\sigma = 0.6352\%$, as in Panel A of Table 17.9. Recall that the initial interest rate was $r_0 = 3\%$, which corresponds to a mildly positive value of the leveraged swap. As the figure clearly shows, a higher interest rate would imply a fast drop of the value of the swap, from the $1.57 million for $r_0 = 3\%$ to less than -$100 million for $r_0 = 4.5\%$. Moreover, this drop in value if the interest rate increases does not correspond to a symmetric increase in value if the interest rate decreases. In other words, the leveraged swap has a strong negative convexity: The stochastic variation in interest rates will tend to yield negative capital gain returns, on average. In the terms of the swap this negative convexity is counterbalanced by the below-market floating rates that P&G would have to pay.

CHAPTER 18

THE RISK AND RETURN OF INTEREST RATE SECURITIES

What is the expected return from investing in long-term bonds? What is the premium of holding long-term bonds compared to short-term bonds? The model developed in Chapter 15 also provides a methodology by which to gauge the risk premium that investors require in order to hold the more volatile long-term bonds compared to short-term bonds, or cash. In this chapter we introduce the notion of market price of risk, first in the Vasicek model and then in the general setting, and then show how to employ Monte Carlo simulations to study the risk embedded in interest rate securities. We conclude the chapter with the illustration of a simple macroeconomic model in which the size of the risk, the risk premium, and the market price of risk of nominal bonds is determined by key economic quantities, such as inflation risk, the business cycle, and the risk aversion of market participants.

18.1 EXPECTED RETURN AND THE MARKET PRICE RISK

Consider once again the Vasicek model of interest rates, developed in Chapter 15. The interest rate process is given by

$$dr_t = \gamma(\bar{r} - r_t)dt + \sigma dX_t \tag{18.1}$$

In that chapter we show that no arbitrage implies that any interest rate security must satisfy the following fundamental pricing equation:

$$\frac{\partial Z}{\partial t} + \frac{\partial Z}{\partial r} m^*(r, t) + \frac{1}{2} \frac{\partial^2 Z}{\partial r^2} \sigma^2 = rZ \tag{18.2}$$

where, under the Vasicek assumption,

$$m^*(r,t) = \gamma^*(\bar{r}^* - r) \tag{18.3}$$

Consider now a zero coupon bond (or any interest rate security, in fact) with price $Z(r,t)$. Under the Vasicek interest rate model in Equation 18.1 Ito's lemma implies

$$dZ = \left\{ \frac{\partial Z}{\partial t} + \frac{\partial Z}{\partial r}\gamma(\bar{r} - r) + \frac{1}{2}\frac{\partial^2 Z}{\partial r^2}\sigma^2 \right\} dt + \frac{\partial Z}{\partial r}\sigma dX_t \tag{18.4}$$

Thus, the expected capital gain return during the period t to $t + dt$ is given by

$$E[dZ] = \left\{ \frac{\partial Z}{\partial t} + \frac{\partial Z}{\partial r}\gamma(\bar{r} - r) + \frac{1}{2}\frac{\partial^2 Z}{\partial r^2}\sigma^2 \right\} dt \tag{18.5}$$

as $E[dX_t] = 0$. Rearranging Equation 18.2, we find

$$\frac{\partial Z}{\partial t} + \frac{1}{2}\frac{\partial^2 Z}{\partial r^2}\sigma^2 = rZ - \frac{\partial Z}{\partial r}m^*(r,t)$$

We can then substitute these first two terms on the right-hand side of Equation 18.5, while also recalling that under the Vasicek bond pricing formula $Z(r,t;t) = e^{A(t;T)-B(t;T)r}$, we have $\partial Z/\partial r = -B(r,T)Z$. These substitutions lead to:

$$E[dZ] = rZdt - B(t;T)Z\left(\gamma(\bar{r} - r) - \gamma^* \times (\bar{r}^* - r)\right)dt \tag{18.6}$$

Rearranging, we then obtain the following:

Fact 18.1 *Under the Vasicek interest rate model, the (annualized) risk premium is given by*

$$\textit{Risk premium} = E\left[\frac{dZ}{Z}\right]/dt - r = -B(t;T)\left(\gamma(\bar{r} - r) - \gamma^*(\bar{r}^* - r)\right) \tag{18.7}$$

The risk premium is then proportional to the quantity $B(t;T) = 1/\gamma^*\left(1 - e^{-\gamma^*(T-t)}\right)$ (see Equation 15.29 in Chapter 15), and it varies with the interest rate r in a linear fashion. In particular, the term in parenthesis on the right-hand side of Equation 18.7 is given by the difference between the drift rate of the interest rate process in Equation 18.1 and $m^*(r,t)$, defined in Equation 18.3. Recall that this latter quantity, mechanically the term that multiplies in coefficient $\partial Z/\partial r$ in the Fundamental Pricing Equation (Equation 15.24), is called the *risk neutral drift* of the interest rate process (see Chapter 17). The difference between the drift rate of the interest rate process and its risk neutral counterpart $m^*(r,t)$, scaled by the volatility of interest rate, is called market price of interest rate risk.

Definition 18.1 *In the Vasicek model, the **market price of interest rate risk** is given by quantity*

$$\lambda(r,t) = \frac{1}{\sigma}\left(\gamma(\bar{r} - r) - \gamma^*(\bar{r}^* - r)\right) \tag{18.8}$$

Defining the two constants $\lambda_0 = \frac{1}{\sigma}\left(\gamma\bar{r} - \gamma^*\bar{r}^*\right)$ and $\lambda_1 = \frac{1}{\sigma}\left(\gamma^* - \gamma\right)$, we obtain

$$\lambda(r,t) = \lambda_0 + \lambda_1 r \tag{18.9}$$

The terminology about the market price of risk can be understood as follows. Note first that we can rewrite Equation 18.4 as follows:

$$\frac{dZ}{Z} = \mu_Z dt + \sigma_Z dX \tag{18.10}$$

where

$$\mu_Z = \frac{1}{Z}\left\{\frac{\partial Z}{\partial t} + \frac{\partial Z}{\partial r}\gamma(\bar{r}-r) + \frac{1}{2}\frac{\partial^2 Z}{\partial r^2}\sigma^2\right\} \tag{18.11}$$

$$\sigma_Z = \frac{1}{Z}\frac{\partial Z}{\partial r}\sigma = -B(t;T)\sigma \tag{18.12}$$

Thus, we can express the risk premium in Equation 18.7 as

$$\text{Risk premium} = E\left[\frac{dZ}{Z}\right]/dt - r = \sigma_Z \times \lambda(r,t) \tag{18.13}$$

That is, the risk premium is equal to the market price of risk, $\lambda(r,t)$, times the amount of risk, σ_Z.

An important caveat to understand the relation in Equation 18.13, though, is that since $\sigma_Z = -B(t;T)\sigma < 0$, the risk premium is positive only if $\lambda(r,t) < 0$. This is the standard convention when discussing interest rate risk, as for bond prices the risk is that the interest rate increases. In fact, if r increases, bond prices decline and the investor would suffer a capital loss. The fact that σ_Z is negative captures this risk, and $\lambda(r,t) < 0$ would imply the higher risk premium that investors require in order to hold long term bonds. Section 18.3 below offers a macroeconomic model of the term structure, in which the market price of risk λ follows from macroeconomic risk, such as the risk of high inflation during bad times, as well as the risk aversion of economic agents. The next example, instead, illustrates the estimated market price of risk from the parameter estimates obtained in Section 16.3 in Chapter 16.

■ **EXAMPLE 18.1**

In Section 16.3 in Chapter 16 we estimate the following parameters for the Vasicek model $\bar{r} = 5.09\%$, $\gamma = 0.3261$, $\sigma = 2.21\%$, $\gamma^* = 0.4653$ and $\bar{r}^* = 6.34\%$. It follows that $\lambda_0 = 0.5892$ and $\lambda_1 = -6.3541$. A negative λ_1 implies that a higher interest rate r_t is associated with a more negative $\lambda(r,t)$ and therefore a higher risk premium, as $\sigma_Z = -B(t,T)\sigma < 0$ (see Equation 18.13). Using these values, we can compute the risk premium in Equation 18.13 for zero coupon bonds of various maturities. Figure 18.1 plots the annualized expected excess return for bonds across various maturities, from 0 to 29, for three current interest rates r_0. There are two noteworthy patterns:

1. The return premium from holding long-term bonds is higher than from holding short-term bonds, although this is really true for maturities up to $T = 10$.

2. For given maturity, a lower spot rate r_0 is associated with higher risk premium.

Figure 18.1 Expected Excess Return Implied by the Vasicek Model

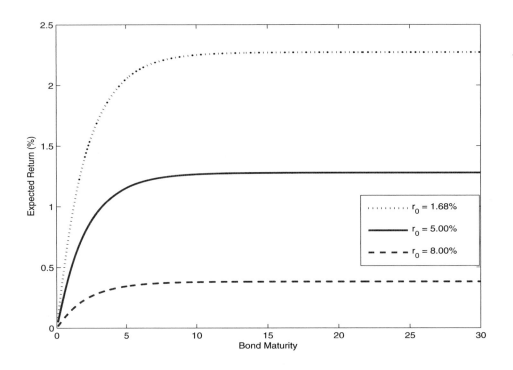

It is useful to link the behavior of expected return and the short-term interest rate in Point 2 with the empirical results discussed in Chapter 7, Section 7.3 (see Table 7.4). In that section we show that empirically, a high forward spread (i.e. difference between the forward rate and the short-term rate) predicts a higher future excess return of long-term bonds. That is, when the term structure is positively sloped, future bond returns tend to yield a premium over short-term bonds. Since in the Vasicek model, a low spot rate is associated with a high forward premium, Point 2 above also reads

3. For given maturity, a higher term premium is associated with a higher risk premium.

That is, if the term structure is sloping upwards, it implies a high risk premium from holding long-term bonds, which then trade cheap, which explains why ex-post we see high realized returns compared to the short-term bond.

Of course, Point 2 also implies that the current short term interest rate should predict future returns, and the latter result is much less strong in the data than the term premium result.

18.1.1   The Market Price of Risk in a General Interest Rate Model

We can extend the above example to a more general model. Consider the general interest rate model

$$dr_t = m(r_t, t)dt + s(r_t, t)dX_t \tag{18.14}$$

The drift rate $m(r_t, t)$ is the "true" interest rate drift. In Chapter 15 we show that the Fundamental Pricing Equation (Equation 15.64) depends instead on $m^*(r_t, t)$, which corresponds to the coefficient that multiplies $\partial V/\partial r$. In particular,

$$rZ = \frac{\partial Z}{\partial t} + \frac{\partial Z}{\partial r}m^*(r, t) + \frac{1}{2}\frac{\partial^2 Z}{\partial r^2}s(r, t)^2 \tag{18.15}$$

By applying the same logic as in the case of the Vasicek model, we obtain the following:

Fact 18.2 *The risk premium from holding long-term bonds is given by*

$$Risk\ premium = E\left[\frac{dZ}{Z}\right]/dt - r = \sigma_Z \lambda(r, t) \tag{18.16}$$

where

$$\sigma_Z = \frac{1}{Z}\frac{\partial Z}{\partial r}s(r, t) \tag{18.17}$$

$$\lambda(r, t) = \frac{1}{s(r, t)}\left(m(r, t) - m^*(r, t)\right) \tag{18.18}$$

The quantity $\lambda(r, t)$ is called the "market price of risk."

18.2   RISK ANALYSIS: RISK *NATURAL* MONTE CARLO SIMULATIONS

We can employ interest rate models and Monte Carlo simulations to carry out an effective analysis of the risk implicit in a given interest rate security. It is paramount to realize, however, that when we simulate interest rates to carry out a risk analysis of the security, we must do so under the risk natural dynamics of interest rates, and *not* the risk neutral dynamics. Recall that in general

$$\text{Risk Natural Dynamics} \quad dr_t = m(r_t, t)dt + s(r_t, t)dX_t \tag{18.19}$$

$$\text{Risk Neutral Dynamics} \quad dr_t = m^*(r_t, t)dt + s(r_t, t)dX_t \tag{18.20}$$

where $m(r, t)$ is the posited drift rate of interest rates, Equation 18.14, while $m^*(r, t)$ is the coefficient of $\partial V/\partial r$ from the Fundamental Pricing Equation (Equation 18.15). We must recall what led us to use Monte Carlo simulations to price securities: It is a combination of a mathematical result, the Feynman-Kac theorem, and statistics. In particular, from Chapter 17, the Feynman-Kac theorem tells us that the solution to the Fundamental Pricing Equation (Equation 17.2) is given by an expectation (Equation 17.7). Statistics, namely the law of large numbers, tells us that the expectation in Equation 17.7 can be approximated by an average of simulated payoffs. These two elements are at the basis of the risk neutral pricing methodology, and thus lead us to simulate the interest rates according to the risk neutral process in Equation 18.20.

In contrast, when we perform the risk analysis, such as the Value-at-Risk or the expected shortfall of a security (see Sections 3.2.8 and 3.2.9 in Chapter 3), we must take into account the true variation of interest rates, that is, the risk natural process in Equation 18.19. The reason is that we want to simulate plausible interest rate scenarios and obtain the value of the security under these various scenarios. The next example presents the risk analysis for the range floater discussed in Section 17.4 in Chapter 17. The case study in Section 18.4 presents the risk analysis for the leveraged swap discussed in the case study in Section 17.9.

■ **EXAMPLE 18.2**

Consider the range floater discussed in Section 17.4 in Chapter 17. We are interested in computing the Profit and Loss distribution one quarter ahead. To perform this exercise, we need to simulate the interest rate r_t over one quarter, and for each realization, compute the value of the range floater. We realize that there are two Monte Carlo simulations nested within each other: The first Monte Carlo simulation simulates interest rate scenarios one quarter from now, and the second Monte Carlo simulation computes the value of the range floater for each interest rate scenario. The former Monte Carlo simulations must be performed under the risk *natural* dynamics, i.e. Equation 18.19, while the latter Monte Carlo simulations must be performed under the risk *neutral* dynamics, that is, Equation 18.20.

Recall that in the specific case of this example, the current interest rate is $r_0 = 2.17\%$, and the risk neutral parameter estimates are $\bar{r}^* = 6.41\%$, $\gamma^* = 0.21$, and $\sigma = .82\%$. The risk natural parameters can be estimated through a regression of the interest rate $r_{t+\delta}$ on itself one period earlier r_t. Since the underlying model is the Vasicek model, in fact, we have that the true interest rate model,

$$dr_t = \gamma(\bar{r} - r_t)dt + \sigma dX_t,$$

can be approximated by

$$r_{t+\delta} = \alpha + \beta r_t + \varepsilon_{t+\delta} \tag{18.21}$$

where $\varepsilon_{t+\delta} \sim N(0, \sigma^2 \delta)$. Using daily data on the 3-month LIBOR, we then estimate the regression coefficient $\beta = 0.9999$, which implies $\gamma = (1 - \beta)/dt = .0212$. Instead, we set $\bar{r} = 5.2\%$ which is the average interest rate in the sample. Finally, $\sigma = .82\%$ which is the same value used in the risk neutral case. Given these parameters, we proceed as follows:

1. Simulate one interest rate scenario using the risk natural parameters $\bar{r} = 5.2\%$, $\gamma = 0.0212$, and $\sigma = 0.88\%$. Let $r_{0.25}^j$ be the interest rate realization for simulation j.

2. For each simulated $r_{0.25}^j$, use Monte Carlo simulations with risk neutral parameters $\bar{r}^* = 6.41\%$, $\gamma^* = 0.21$ and $\sigma = .82\%$ to compute the value of the range note when $r_{0.25}^j$ is the initial value $V^{\text{Range Note}}(r_{0.25}^j)$. Note that the range note now has a maturity of only $T = 2.75$.

Given that there are two simulations nested in each other, this methodology is relatively time consuming. A faster methodology consists of computing the value of the range note for many interest rates $r_{0.25}$ within a given interval which has high probability of being reached, and then compute the value of the range note at any other simulated interest rate by using interpolation.

Figure 18.2 plots the distribution of the profits and losses (P&L) of the range note at one quarter horizon. As can be seen, the distribution is heavily negatively skewed, meaning that the probability of large losses is higher than the probability of symmetrically large gains. Because of the yield enhancement, the range note stands to yield a higher average return than an otherwise identical floating rate note. However, because of the implicit sale of an option to the issuers of the range note, namely the option not to pay the coupon if the interest rate increases, the potential of large losses is also apparent from the figure. We can compute the 1% and 5% Value-at-Risk, which are the worst outcomes with 99% or 95% probability (see Chapter 3). This can easily be performed by Monte Carlo simulations: Simply rank the simulated P/L numbers, and then select the 1% or 5% worst outcomes. From the simulations, we obtain

$$99\% \text{ Value-at-Risk} \quad = \quad \$2.6224 \text{ mil} \qquad (18.22)$$

$$95\% \text{ Value-at-Risk} \quad = \quad \$1.5464 \text{ mil} \qquad (18.23)$$

As discussed in Section 3.2.8 in Chapter 3, the Value-at-Risk measure of financial risk has several drawbacks. One important drawback is that it does not account for fat-tails or extreme events. That is, the 1% or 5% cutoffs do not provide any information about the size of the losses in case a tail event occurs. Figure 18.2, for instance, shows that the P&L distribution of a range note is heavily negatively skewed, meaning that it is possible that with small probability the range note would suffer large losses. In this case, the expected shortfall measure of risk, discussed in Section 3.2.9 in Chapter 3, provides a better sense of the risk of an investment in range notes. Recall that the expected shortfall is given by the expected losses *given* that they are higher than the VaR measure. That is, what do we expect to lose from an investment in the occurrence of a rare event? Monte Carlo simulations allow us to compute the expected shortfall in a rather straightforward manner: Rather than looking only at the 1% of 5% worst outcome, as in the VaR calculation above, we must take the average of all of the P&L below the 1% or 5% cutoffs, obtaining

$$99\% \text{ Expected Shortfall} \quad = \quad \$3.2716 \text{ mil} \qquad (18.24)$$

$$95\% \text{ Expected Shortfall} \quad = \quad \$2.2171 \text{ mil} \qquad (18.25)$$

18.2.1 Delta Approximation Errors

It is often common to approximate the risk of a security through a first order linear approximation. That is, the value of an interest rate security at an interest rate level $r_{t+\delta}$, $V(r_{t+\delta})$, is often approximated through a linear Taylor expansion

$$V(r_{t+\delta}) \approx V(r_t) + \frac{\partial V}{\partial r}(r_{t+\delta} - r_t) \qquad (18.26)$$

The convenience is that we can simply compute the quantity $\frac{\partial V}{\partial r}$, and then from the variation in interest rates $(r_{t+\delta} - r_t)$ obtain an approximation of the variation in the value of the

Figure 18.2   P&L Distribution of Range Note

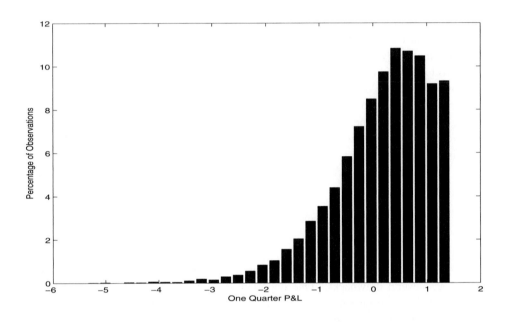

security $V(r_{t+\delta}) \approx V(r_t)$. In fact, it can be seen from the above equation that

$$\text{Standard deviation of } (V(r_{t+\delta}) - V(r_t)) \approx \frac{\partial V}{\partial r} \times \text{Standard deviation of } (r_{t+\delta} - r_t)$$

If the convexity of the security is particularly strong, however, this approximation may yield quite different results. The next example illustrates this fact within the Value-at-Risk of the range floater discussed above in Example 18.2.

■ **EXAMPLE 18.3**

In Example 17.8 in Chapter 17 we computed the sensitivity of the Range Floater to changes in interest rates as

$$\frac{\partial V}{\partial r} = -234 \tag{18.27}$$

Consider still one quarter horizon, as in Example 18.2, that is, $\delta = 1/4$. This is undoubtedly too coarse an approximation to use Equation 18.26, but it allows us to compare this value to what we obtained in Example 18.2.[1] According to the Vasicek model,

$$r_\delta - r_0 \sim N(\mu(r_0, \delta), \sigma^2(\delta)) \tag{18.28}$$

---

[1]Because δ is large, we should take into account also the change in V due to the change in t. This is given by $\partial V/\partial t$.

where

$$\mu(r_0, \delta) = (r_0 - \bar{r}) \times \left(e^{-\gamma\delta} - 1 \right); \quad \sigma(\delta) = \sqrt{\frac{\sigma^2}{2\gamma} \left(1 - e^{-2\gamma\delta} \right)} \qquad (18.29)$$

Given the normality of the interest rate, the 1% and 5% worst case outcomes are obtained for an interest rate realization that is 2.326 and 1.645 standard deviations $[\sigma(\delta)]$ above the mean $[\mu(r_0, \delta)]$, respectively. The formulas in 18.29 imply $\sigma(\delta) = 0.41\%$ and $\mu(r_0, \delta) = 0.0160\%$ yielding the approximations

$$\begin{aligned} 1\% \text{ Value-at-Risk} &= \$2.2584 \text{ mil} \\ 5\% \text{ Value-at-Risk} &= \$1.6081 \text{ mil} \end{aligned}$$

The 1% VaR computed by the first order approximation is smaller than the one computed by Monte Carlo simulations. The 1% VaR is the one corresponding to large positive realizations of the interest rate. In this case, the linear approximation misses the fact that range floater's negative convexity induces an additional negative return when the realized interest rate is high. The issue with convexity is illustrated in Figure 18.3. The solid curved line is the value of the range floater for several initial LIBOR rates, as shown in Figure 17.3 in Chapter 17. The dashed-dotted straight line which is tangent to the value of the range floater represents the linear approximation. As the figure shows, the linear approximation underestimates the true Value-at-Risk, because it does not consider the convexity. The error is larger for more extreme values of the interest rates, such as the 1% highest interest rate depicted in the figure as the second vertical dashed line.[2]

18.3 A MACROECONOMIC MODEL OF THE TERM STRUCTURE

To illustrate the concept of the market price of risk and risk premium of long-term bonds over short-term bonds, it is useful to consider a simple macroeconomic model of the term structure of interest rates. This model allows us to better understand what the shape of the term structure really tells us. The following is a simplified version of more general models that macroeconomists use to understand the forces that move bond yields.

The macroeconomic model has two basic ingredients:

(a) a model for GDP growth, inflation, and expected inflation;

(b) market participants who make decisions to maximize their well-being.

In particular, assume that real log GDP $y_t = \log(Y_t)$ grows according to the stochastic model

$$dy_t = g\,dt + \sigma_y\,dX_{y,t}$$

where the drift rate, g, is constant. The assumption that the drift rate of GDP is constant is clearly unrealistic, but it allows us to focus only on expected inflation as the main driver

---

[2]One additional benefit of the Monte Carlo simulation approach is that it also includes in the VaR the variation in the value of the security due to the passage of time, $\partial V/\partial t$, which is not included in the representation in Figure 18.3

Figure 18.3   The Value-at-Risk of a Range Floater

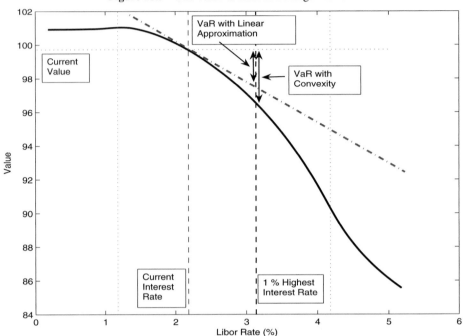

of the term structure of interest rates. Allowing a business cycle variation in GDP growth would generate a two-factor model of the term structure, which is definitely more realistic, but beyond the point we want to make here.

Moving to inflation, the log CPI, $q_t = \log Q_t$, grows according to the stochastic model

$$dq_t \;=\; i_t dt + \sigma_q dX_{q,t}$$

The drift rate of CPI growth, i.e., expected inflation, $i_t = E[dq_t]/dt$ changes over time, and we assume it follows the process

$$di_t \;=\; \gamma\left(\bar{i} - i_t\right) dt + \sigma_i dX_{i,t}$$

That is, expected inflation i_t is mean reverting, with speed of mean reversion γ, and long-term average inflation given by $\bar{i}$.

To illustrate the relation between inflation and expected inflation, Panel A of Figure 18.4 plots both time series. Expected inflation is related to the short-term interest rates, as we see in Panel B, although the relation becomes weaker in the second half of the sample. Finally, Panel C of Figure 18.4 shows the relation between expected inflation and GDP growth. The plots are almost the mirror image of each other, in that higher expected inflation is correlated with lower GDP growth.

18.3.1   Market Participants

Economists assume that market participants take actions, namely, consume and save, so as to maximize their current and future well-being. If today you are awarded a cash bonus

Figure 18.4   Inflation, Expected Inflation, Interest Rates and GDP Growth

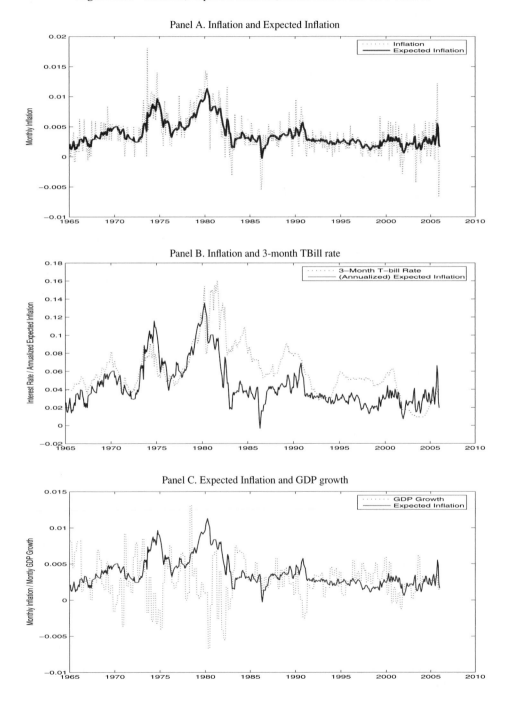

Data Source: U.S. Bureau of Labor Statistics, U.S. Bureau of Economic Analysis, and the Federal Reserve.

of $10,000, you must decide whether to spend it all immediately, or save part of it to spend later on, perhaps to cushion against possible adverse economic conditions. The way economists capture this intertemporal decision between consuming now or consuming tomorrow is through the notion of a "utility function," that is, a function that describe a market participant's level of happiness as a function of the physical amounts of good that he or she consumes. To keep the analysis simple, assume that market participants consume the consumption basket that underlies the CPI index. We denote by C_t the amount of these goods that are consumed by market participants at time t, and denote by

$$U\left(C_t, t\right) = e^{-\rho t} \frac{C_t^{1-h}}{1-h} \tag{18.30}$$

this utility function at time t. The higher the amount of consumption goods that are consumed at time t the happier market participants are. The parameter ρ appearing in the formula in Equation 18.30 describes the fact that market participants tend to prefer early consumption to later consumption, everything else equal.

The key parameter, instead, is h which describes market participants' level of *risk aversion*. This parameter is positive and, in fact, quite large: $h > 1$. A higher h implies that market participants are less inclined to take risk, that is, they would prefer a safer investment to a riskier one. When $h = 0$ we say that market participants are risk neutral, in the sense that risk does not matter to them, but only the expected return on an investment is important. We show below that the market price of risk of interest rate securities crucially depends on the level of risk aversion h, as well as on the amount of risk in the economy.

Consider now a market participant (or agent) who has to decide how to spend an additional dollar of his or her wealth. In particular, this agent has a choice between:

1. Spend $1 today ($t$) and buy $\frac{1}{Q_t}$ amount of the consumption good.

2. Save the dollar today, and buy $\frac{1}{Z(t,T)}$ zero coupon bonds with maturity T. At that time, the agent can buy $\frac{1}{Z(t,T)} \frac{1}{Q_T}$ of the consumption good.

Assume that the agent is currently consuming C_t and thus his or her current utility is $U(C_t, t)$. An additional dollar spent on consumption today would increase his or her happiness, approximately, by

$$\frac{\partial U\left(C_t, t\right)}{\partial C} \frac{1}{Q_t}$$

The second choice would instead leave the current utility unchanged, but would change the market participant's happiness in the future. In particular, if C_T is the level of consumption at time T, the agent would then obtain an amount of additional utility in the future equal to

$$\frac{1}{Z\left(t, T\right)} \frac{1}{Q_T} \frac{\partial U\left(C_T, T\right)}{\partial C_T}$$

Market participants should be indifferent between the first and the second choice, as if they would not consume more or save more until they reach the level of indifference. One problem with the above strategy, though, is that market participants do not know at time t what their exact consumption level at the future time T will be, as this will depend itself on the health of the economy, on the level of inflation, and so on. Therefore, market participants can only compare "consumption today" versus "*expected* consumption in the future" (instead of actual consumption). That is, market participants would save enough cash to make sure that the following condition is satisfied for every future time T:

$$\frac{\partial U\left(C_t, t\right)}{\partial C_t} \frac{1}{Q_t} = E_t\left[\frac{1}{Z\left(t, T\right)} \frac{1}{Q_T} \frac{\partial U\left(C_T, T\right)}{\partial C_T}\right] \tag{18.31}$$

If all market participants make consumption and saving decisions to ensure that Equation 18.31 is satisfied, then the current bond prices $Z(t, T)$ must reflect such decisions, and Equation 18.31 becomes an equilibrium condition. In fact, if financial markets did not adjust to make Equation 18.31 true, then some market participants would shift consumption from today to the future or vice versa, thereby changing the total demand for bonds, and thus bond prices. The market is in equilibrium if no market participant has incentive to change their consumption and saving allocation, and thus only if Equation 18.31 is satisfied. The next section exploits this insight to obtain the equilibrium bond prices.

18.3.2 Equilibrium Nominal Bond Prices

To derive the equilibrium bond prices, we now use the equilibrium condition in Equation 18.31. We need two more simplifying assumptions: First, we assume that all economic agents in the economy are identical to each other, that is, that the agent with utility in Equation 18.30 is representative of the average agent in the economy. Second, that a constant fraction k of total GDP is consumed each year. That is, in aggregate $C_t = kY_t$. In the data, k is approximately 70% of GDP.

We are now in a position to obtain nominal bond prices. In particular, we can rearrange Equation 18.31, to find that the value of a (nominal) zero coupon bond is given by

$$Z\left(t, T\right) = E_t\left[\frac{Q_t}{Q_T} \frac{\partial U\left(C_T, T\right) / \partial C_T}{\partial U\left(C_t, t\right) / \partial C_t}\right]$$

Given Equation 18.30, we have

$$\partial U\left(C_t, t\right) / \partial C_t = C_t^{-h} e^{-\rho t} \quad \text{and} \quad \partial U\left(C_T, T\right) / \partial C_T = C_T^{-h} e^{-\rho T}$$

Substituting this formula and the fact that $C_t = kY_t$, we obtain

$$Z\left(t, T\right) = E_t\left[e^{-\rho(T-t)} \frac{Q_t Y_t^h}{Q_T Y_T^h}\right] \tag{18.32}$$

$$= E_t\left[e^{-\rho(T-t)-(q_T-q_t)-h(y_T-y_t)}\right] \tag{18.33}$$

This expectation can be computed explicitly, and we obtain the following:

Fact 18.3 *The solution to the pricing formula in Equation 18.32 is*

$$Z\left(i, t, T\right) = e^{A(t;T)-B(t;T)(i+c)} \tag{18.34}$$

where $A(t;T)$ and $B(t;T)$ are given by

$$B\left(t; T\right) = \frac{1}{\gamma}\left(1 - e^{-\gamma(T-t)}\right) \tag{18.35}$$

$$A(t;T) = \left(B(t;T) - (T-t)\right)\left(\bar{r}^* - \frac{\sigma^2}{2\gamma^2}\right) - \frac{\sigma^2 B(t;T)^2}{4\gamma} \tag{18.36}$$

with

$$c = \left(\rho + hg - \frac{1}{2}h^2\sigma_y^2\right) - h\sigma_y\sigma_q\rho_{qy} - \frac{1}{2}\sigma_q^2 \tag{18.37}$$

$$\bar{r}^* = \bar{r} - \frac{1}{\gamma}\left(h\sigma_i\sigma_y\rho_{yi} + \sigma_i\sigma_y\rho_{iq}\right) \tag{18.38}$$

$$\bar{r} = \bar{i} + c \tag{18.39}$$

In addition, the spot nominal rate is given by

$$r_t = i_t + c \tag{18.40}$$

and its dynamics are as follows:

$$\text{Risk natural (true) dynamics:} \quad dr_t = \gamma(\bar{r} - r_t)dt + \sigma_i dX_i \tag{18.41}$$

$$\text{Risk neutral dynamics:} \quad dr_t = \gamma(\bar{r}^* - r_t)dt + \sigma_i dX_i \tag{18.42}$$

It is easy to see that $A(t;T)$ and $B(t;T)$ are identical to the same quantities under the Vasicek model of interest rates, namely, the expressions found in Equations 15.30 and 15.29 in Chapter 15, for $\gamma = \gamma^*$. We can now interpret the parameters of the Vasicek pricing formula in light of the parameters of the macroeconomic model.

First of all, from Equation 18.40 the nominal spot rate r_t is given by the expected inflation $i_t = E[dq]$ plus a constant c. The difference c between nominal rate and expected inflation is made explicit in Equation 18.37 and it is given by three components (see also Equation 7.33 in Chapter 7), namely:

1. The real rate of interest, given by the first parenthesis in Equation 18.37. The first term, ρ, measures agents' impatience to consume: Higher impatience implies they want to borrow to consume more and the equilibrium real rate of interest goes up. The second term, hg, depends on the growth rate of the economy. If g is high, then future GDP, and thus consumption, is expected to be high, and thus agents would like to bring some of this consumption to today, by borrowing, which pushes up the rate of interest. Finally, the last term in parenthesis is a precautionary savings term: The higher the volatility of GDP growth, the higher the risk there will be little consumption in the future, and the more agents want to save, which in turn pushes down the borrowing rate.

2. The inflation risk premium, given by the first term after the parenthesis in Equation 18.37. A short-term nominal investment at the rate r_t is now risky for an investor, if the covariance between GDP growth dy and inflation dq is negative. Indeed, if on average when dq is positive we have dy is negative, then the investment in the nominal rate r_t provides devalued cash (because dq is positive) when most investors would need it, i.e. when there is a negative shock to GDP growth. Thus, the nominal rate increases.

3. A convexity term given by the last term in Equation 18.37.

Second, we now can interpret the risk neutral process for interest rates (Equation 18.42). In particular, the central tendency of the risk neutral process, $\bar{r}^*$, is now explicitly given in Equation 18.38, and it has two terms. The first term is the long-run unconditional average nominal rate $\bar{r}$: The higher the average long-term inflation rate, the higher is the central tendency of the risk neutral process. The second term is given by an adjustment for risk "$-h\sigma_i\sigma_y\rho_{iy}/\gamma$" plus another convexity term. The adjustment for risk depends on risk aversion h, the covariance between expected inflation and GDP growth $cov(dy, di) = \sigma_i\sigma_y\rho_{iy}$, and the speed of mean reversion γ. Note first from Figure 18.4 that the correlation between expected inflation and GDP growth is typically negative, $\rho_{iy} < 0$, which implies that the adjustment for risk is positive: $-h\sigma_i\sigma_y\rho_{iy}/\gamma > 0$. Thus, the central tendency $\bar{r}^*$ increases with risk aversion h, with more negative covariance $cov(dr, di)$, or slower mean reversion γ.

What is the economic intuition? The magnitude of the central tendency $\bar{r}^*$ is negatively related to bond prices and thus positively related with the spot rate of long-term bonds, which is given by[3]

$$r_t(\tau) = -\frac{A(\tau)}{\tau} + \frac{B(\tau)}{\tau}(i_t + c)$$

where $\tau = T - t$ is time to maturity, and recall the notation $A(\tau) = A(0; \tau)$, $B(\tau) = B(0; \tau)$.

Thus, higher risk aversion h, lower covariance $cov(dy, di)$, and lower speed of mean reversion γ translate into higher long term yield, that is, an increase in the slope of the term structure of interest rates. Intuitively, holding long-term bonds is risky whenever the covariance between changes in expected inflation di and GDP growth dy is negative. The reason is that from Equation 18.34 an increase in expected inflation i_t decreases the bond price $Z(i, t; T)$. Because of $cov(di, dy) < 0$, we then have that bond prices are low when GDP growth is low, i.e. in bad times. This is bad for investors, as it is exactly during bad times that they would like to liquidate some of their savings to weather temporary economic hardships. Because these bonds' value is low in bad times, agents require a higher yield to hold such bonds, which explains why $r(t, \tau)$ is higher, the lower is $cov(dy, di)$. This effect is magnified the higher the aversion to risk of market participants is, and the lower the mean reversion γ is. Indeed, the lower the mean reversion, the larger is the impact of variations of expected inflation i on the bond price, as $B(t; T) = (1 - e^{-\gamma(T-t)})/\gamma$ is decreasing in γ.

Finally, the market price of risk in Equation 18.8 in this case is given by

$$\lambda = \frac{\gamma}{\sigma_i}(\bar{r} - \bar{r}^*) = h\sigma_y\rho_{yi} + \sigma_y\rho_{iq} \qquad (18.43)$$

Notice first that because $\gamma = \gamma^*$ in this model, the market price of risk is constant. Second, since the correlation between expected inflation and GDP growth is typically negative, $\rho_{yi} < 0$, we expect a negative market price of risk $\lambda < 0$. As discussed in Section 18.1, when $\lambda < 0$, the expected excess return on a long-term bond is positive

$$E\left[\frac{dZ}{Z}\right] - r = \lambda\sigma_Z > 0$$

as $\sigma_Z = -B(t; T)\sigma_i < 0$. The economic model presented in this section then shows that the market price of risk (and thus the risk premium) depend on the level of risk aversion h, the volatility of GDP growth σ_y, and the correlation between GDP growth and expected inflation ρ_{yi}.

---

[3] See Equation 15.37 in Chapter 15.

Table 18.1   GDP Growth and Inflation

$\bar{i}$	γ	g	σ_y	σ_q	σ_i	ρ_{yq}	ρ_{yi}	ρ_{iq}
4.20%	0.3805	0.02*	0.02*	0.0106	0.0073	-.1409	-.2894	0.8360

Data Source: U.S. Bureau of Labor Statistics, U.S. Bureau of Economic Analysis, and the Federal Reserve.
* The estimates of GDP growth were $g = .0321$ and $\sigma_y = 0.0098$, which made it hard to generate sensible yield functions. The parameters assumed are closer to consumption growth

Indeed, using data on inflation, GDP growth and consumption, we obtain the parameters in Table 18.1 By assuming that the parameters for the utility function are $\rho = .1$ and $h = 104$, we obtain a real rate $c = .02$. Panel A of Figure 18.5 plots three yield curves, assuming current expected inflation is $i_0 = 0.01, 0.0420, 0.0720$. The corresponding nominal spot interest rates are $r_0 = 0.0299, 0.0619$, and 0.0919. Panel B instead plots the term spread, $sp(\tau) = r_t(\tau) - r_t$ for three values of the risk aversion $h = 70,104$ and 140, but for average expected inflation $i_t = \bar{i}$. As can be seen, higher risk aversion implies a higher term spread, as it pushes down the price.

18.3.3   Conclusion

The model presented in this section is simple, but it does provide some economic intuition to the term structure models that we have seen in previous chapters, and that we will see in future chapters as well. This model has numerous drawbacks, including the fact that it does not fit the yield curves very well. For instance, while Panel B of Figure 18.5 shows the term spread for various levels of risk aversions, and the spread appears reasonable, the yield curves corresponding to this panel are not reasonables: For $h = 70$ we obtain too low (in fact negative) interest rates, while for $h = 140$ we obtain way too high yields. A smaller variation in h produces reasonable yield curves, but not enough variation in term spreads, and thus on the market price of risk.

The problem with this model is its simplicity, in fact, and indeed this model can be generalized in multiple ways to provide both more reasonable yield curves as well as more interesting dynamics for bond prices and the market price of risk. For instance, we assumed that the expected GDP growth g is constant, which it isn't in the data. Similarly, the level of risk aversion h may be assumed time varying, which induces additional interest dynamics: For instance, we know that a high h implies a higher term spread and a higher market price of risk. This implies that a time variation in h may lead to the empirical observation that a higher slope of the term structure implies a higher expected return, as documented in Section 7.3 in Chapter 7.

But the model can be useful to *interpret* the yield curve. For instance, according to the model, if we observe a yield curve that is relatively steep, this can be due to any of the following three reasons:

1. Market participants expected high future inflation, and thus high future spot rates.

Figure 18.5   Yield Curves in the Macro Economic Model

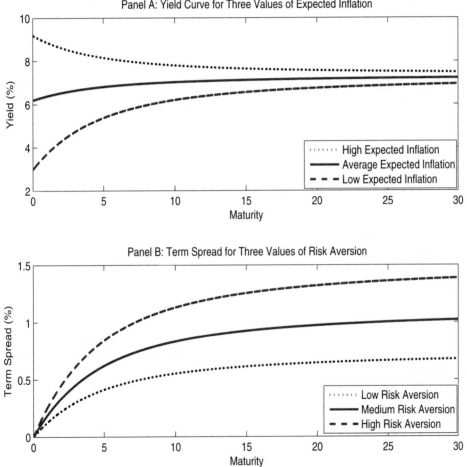

Panel A: Yield Curve for Three Values of Expected Inflation

Panel B: Term Spread for Three Values of Risk Aversion

2. Market participants have a high aversion to risk, and therefore require a higher yield for longer term bonds.

3. The amount of risk is high, and therefore again market participants require a higher yield for longer term bonds.

Only the first point implies that a positively sloped term structure predicts higher future spot rates, while points 2 and 3 do not.

18.4   CASE ANALYSIS: THE RISK IN THE P&G LEVERAGED SWAP

In Section 17.9 of Chapter 17 we investigated the valuation of a complicated interest rate swap, whose cash flows would depend on the setting of a spread six months after the initiation of the contract according to a complicated formula. In this section, we show how we can use Monte Carlo simulations to gauge the riskiness of such an investment.

To perform the risk analysis, we first need to estimate the risk *natural* parameters of the Vasicek model of interest rates. These parameters can be estimated by using the history of interest rates. In Section 17.9, we approximated the short-term interest rate r_t with the 3-month continuously compounded T-bill rate[4] and considered two samples: A 3-year sample and a 10-year sample. The parameter γ is estimated from daily data by using the discretized regression

$$(r_{t+\delta} - r_t) = \alpha + \beta r_t + \varepsilon$$

where $\alpha = \gamma \bar{r}$ and $\beta = \gamma \times \delta$. From the regression coefficient and $\delta = 1/252$, we obtained $\gamma = 0.9098$ and $\gamma = 0.0654$ for the short and long samples, respectively. The average interest rate $\bar{r}$ was obtained from the average rate during the sample, and it turned out to be $\bar{r} = 4.18\%$ and $\bar{r} = 6.43\%$ in the two samples, respectively. We obtained the volatility from the annualized standard deviation of residuals. Given α and β, we can compute

$$\varepsilon = (r_{t+\delta} - r_t) - (\alpha + \beta r_t)$$

and we obtain $\sigma = 1/\sqrt{\delta} \times$ standard deviation of ε. Panels A and B of Table 18.2 report the parameter estimates. It is important to note the difference between risk neutral and risk natural parameters for each sample. In particular, in both panels the risk *neutral* average rate $\bar{r}^*$ is always higher than the average realized rate $\bar{r}$. According to the model, the reason for the difference is not necessarily that market participants expect a higher interest rate in the future, which implies a higher slope of the term structure and thus a higher $\bar{r}^*$. Rather, we must recall that $\bar{r}^*$ also contains a market-price of risk component: The price of a bond may be low (and thus the yield high) simply because it is riskier than holding cash. Using the same arguments as in Section 18.1 we find that the market price of risk

$$\lambda(r) = \lambda_0 + \lambda_1 r$$

---

[4]Note that according to the Vasicek model, the continuously compounded 3-month rate $r_t(0.25)$ and the instantaneous rate r_t are related by $r_t(0.25) = -A(0.25)/0.25 + B(0.25)/0.25 \times r_t$. It follows that the regression coefficient γ is still estimated correctly even using the 3-month rate instead of the instantaneous rate. Instead the average interest rate $\bar{r}$ and the volatility σ should be adjusted by $B(0.25)/0.25$, although, for practical purposes, the difference is small.

has parameters $\lambda_0 = 2.6349$ and $\lambda_1 = -97.5073$. Recall that a negative λ_1 implies that a higher interest rate r_t is correlated with a more negative market price of risk $\lambda(r)$ and thus a higher (more positive) risk premium on long-term bonds

$$E\left[\frac{dZ}{Z}\right] = \lambda(r)\sigma_Z$$

where $\sigma_Z = -B(\tau)\sigma < 0$ and τ is the maturity of the bond.

How do we perform a risk analysis of the leveraged swap, then? Since the key issue is what the value of the spread $spread_{t^*}$ at time $t^* = 0.5$ is, given by

$$spread_{t^*} = \left(\frac{\text{5-year T-note yield} \times 98.5}{5.78}\right) - \text{Price of 6.25\% 30-year T-Bond} ,$$

it is convenient to focus on the value of the swap at that time. We therefore simulate 5000 paths of the Vasicek interest rate process r_i^j according to the risk natural dynamics

$$dr_t = \gamma(\bar{r} - r_t)dt + \sigma dX.$$

We perform the simulation exactly as in Equation 17.34 in Chapter 17 but with γ and $\bar{r}$ instead of the risk neutral counterparts γ^* and $\bar{r}^*$. For each path j we then compute the simulated value of the spread, by applying Equation 17.37 in Chapter 17. In particular, note that the price of the simulated 30-year bond $P^{30}(t^*, 30)^j$ and of the 5-year note $P^5(t^*, 5)^j$ are still given by Equations 17.35 and 17.36, respectively. In particular, these prices still use the risk *neutral* parameters γ^* and $\bar{r}^*$ to compute the zero coupon bond curve $Z(r_{t^*}, t^*, T)^j$. That is, the simulated value of the interest rate $r_{t^*}^j$ to insert in the zero coupon bond pricing formula is simulated using the risk natural model, but the price of these interest rate securities must be computed using risk neutral parameters, as always.

Given the spread at time $t^* = 0.5$, we can compute the value of the swap for Procter & Gamble. In fact, once the spread is set, the value of the swap can be obtained as usual as a long position in fixed rate bond and a short position in a floating rate bond. For convenience, let's bunch up all of the fixed payments in the fixed rate bond, so that the floating rate bond in the swap pays exactly the floating rate, and thus its value is equal to the notional value. That is, for each simulation j resulting in the short rate $r_{t^*}^j$ and the spread $spread_{t^*}^j$, we can compute

$$V_{t^*}^{swap\ j} = \$200\ m. \times \left(\sum_{k=1}^{14} \frac{C^j}{2} Z(r_{t^*}^j, t^*, T_k) + Z(r_{t^*}^j, t^*, T_{14})\right) - \$200\ m \quad (18.44)$$

where

$$C^j = 5.30\% - spread_{cp} + 0.75/100 + spread_{t^*}^j$$

is the total net fixed payment made by Bankers Trust to Procter & Gamble. That is, the first term on the right-hand side of Equation 18.44 is the value of the fixed rate bond with the fixed rate given by the net fixed payments underlying the swap, and the second part is the value of a floating rate bond with \$200 million notional at reset dates.

Figure 18.6 plot the histogram of the simulated values of the swap at time $t^* = 0.5$. Panel A uses the parameters obtained in Panel A of Table 18.2 (the short sample), while Panel B uses the parameters estimated in Panel B of Table 18.2 (the long sample). As can be seen from Panels A and B, then, the distribution of the value of the swap at $t^* = 0.5$ is

Table 18.2   The Risk in Leveraged Swap

Panel A. 3-Year Sample

Valuation: Risk Neutral Monte Carlo Simulations

$\bar{r}^*$	γ^*	$\sigma\,(\times 100)$	Value	st.err
7.32	0.2904	0.6352	1.5716	0.193

Risk Analysis: Risk Natural Monte Carlo Simulations

$\bar{r}$	γ	$\sigma\,(\times 100)$	95% VaR	99% VaR	95% ES	99% ES
4.18	0.9098	0.6352	7.2947	30.4942	21.8151	42.3396

Panel B. 10-Year Sample

Valuation: Risk Neutral Monte Carlo Simulations

$\bar{r}^*$	γ^*	$\sigma\,(\times 100)$	Value	st.err
7.37	0.2883	1.0776	-9.5208	0.4563

Risk Analysis: Risk Natural Monte Carlo Simulations

$\bar{r}$	γ	$\sigma\,(\times 100)$	95% VaR	99% VaR	95% ES	99% ES
6.43	0.0654	1.0776	39.5592	91.4143	71.3696	116.6650

---

strongly negatively skewed: There is a good chance that the swap will end up in the positive area, but with small probability the value would become strongly negative. Indeed, note that by using the parameters in Panel B of 18.2, which feature a higher volatility of interest rates, the left-hand tail of the simulated distribution becomes very negative, giving positive probability to negative values as low as −$200 million, although this quantity has quite a low probability.

Indeed, we can compute the 99% and 95% Value-at-Risk, simply as the 1% and 5% worst possible outcomes across simulations. These are reported in Table 18.2. In particular, in Panel A we find that the 95% and 99% Value-at-Risk are $7.2947 and $30.4942, respectively. Under these assumptions, the more than $100 million losses suffered by P&G have to be deemed very unlikely. Yet, if we consider a longer sample, which induces a higher volatility of interest rates, we find much higher VaR values. As shown in Panel B of Table 18.2 we find these two values given by $39.5592 and $91.4143 million, respectively.

As discussed in Section 3.2.9 in Chapter 3, the VaR measure does not reflect the risk of tail events. Expected shortfall, given by the expected losses *conditional* on a tail event, is a better gauge of the riskiness of an investment. Table 18.2 reports the 95% and 99% expected shortfall for the leverage swap, and it indeed shows that these numbers are substantially higher than the VaR measures, an indication that the left tail of the P&L distribution of the leveraged swap is very long. For instance, Panel A shows that even with low interest rates, the 99% expected shortfall is $42 million, over $10 million higher than the Value-at-Risk figure. When we consider a high interest rate volatility we obtain an expected shortfall of $116 million, higher than the ex-post losses actually suffered by Procter & Gamble.

Figure 18.6   Histogram of Leveraged Swap Value

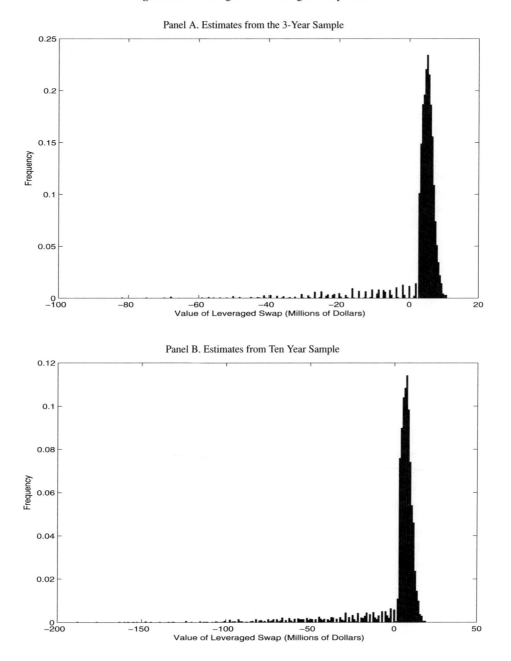

Panel A. Estimates from the 3-Year Sample

Panel B. Estimates from Ten Year Sample

18.5 SUMMARY

In this chapter we covered the following topics:

1. Expected excess return on interest rate securities: This is proportional to the volatility of the security, times a market price of risk.

2. The market price of risk: This is the key quantity determining the expected return on bonds. It is obtained by comparing the risk neutral and the risk natural (true) drift rates of interest rates, divided by the volatility of the interest rate.

3. Risk Natural Monte Carlo Simulations for Risk Analysis: Simulations of interest rate paths under the true probabilities, used to compute loss distributions and Value-at-Risk.

4. Market participants' risk aversion: Market participants require a return premium to hold risky securities, such as long-term bonds versus short-term bonds. The risk aversion determines the size of the return premium: The higher the risk aversion, the lower the price of long-term bonds and therefore the higher the yield. The level of the risk aversion determines the term spread of long-term bonds.

18.6 EXERCISES

1. Consider the inverse floater discussed in Exercise 4 of Chapter 17. Perform a risk analysis using Monte Carlo simulations at the 1-month, 3-month and 6-month horizon. For simplicity, assume in this exercise that the coupon rate $c(t) = \bar{c} - 2 \times r_n(t - \Delta)$ and thus that it can be negative. Discuss the methodology, and make sure to plot the histogram of the P&L at the three horizons.

2. Do the previous exercise, but impose that the inverse floaters cannot have negative coupons, that is, $c(t) = \max(\bar{c} - 2 \times r_n(t - \Delta), 0)$. How harder does it become to perform a risk analysis? Discuss.

3. Consider the corridor note discussed in Exercise 6 of Chapter 17. Perform a risk analysis using Monte Carlo simulations at the 6-month horizon. Discuss the difficulties in computing the VaR for this security. Plot the histogram of the P&L and compute the Value-at-Risk and expected shortfall.

4. You have estimated the parameters for the Vasicek model, and the results are in Table 18.3, where the notation is the same as that used in this chapter. The current overnight rate is 2%.

   (a) Compute the market price of risk. Is it positive or negative? Interpret.

   (b) How does the market price of risk depend on the interest rate?

   (c) Compute the expected excess return on zero coupon bonds with maturity $T = 1, 3, 5$, and 10 years. How does the expected excess return depend on the interest rate?

   (d) Discuss the relation between the spot rate of a zero coupon bond and its expected excess return.

Table 18.3 Estimates for the Vasicek model

γ	$\bar{r}$	σ	γ^*	$\bar{r}^*$
0.3262	5.09%	2.21 %	0.4653	6.34%

(e) Consider now an option on the interest rate, with payoff at $T = 5$ given by $N \times \max(r - r_K, 0)$. Without performing any computation, can you say what the market price of risk of this option is? Discuss.

5. Consider the economic model in Section 18.3. The term structure of interest rates plotted in Figure 18.5 assumes agents' risk aversion is $h = 104$ and temporal discount is $\rho = .1$.

(a) Consider variations of risk aversion h and the discount ρ, and compute the spot rate, the term spread, as well as the market price of risk. Discuss.

(b) How do the term structure of interest rates and market price of risk change with variations in the correlation between GDP growth and expected inflation and the volatility of GDP growth? Discuss.

18.7 APPENDIX: PROOF OF PRICING FORMULA IN MACROECONOMIC MODEL

We now derive Equation 18.34. Define $m_t = \rho t + \log\left(Q_t Y_t^h\right) = \rho t + \log\left(Q_t\right) + h \log\left(Y_t\right) = \rho t + q_t + h y_t$. We can express the value of the nominal zero coupon as

$$Z\left(t, T\right) = E_t\left[e^{m_t - m_T}\right]$$

Ito's lemma implies

$$
\begin{aligned}
dm_t &= \rho dt + dq_t + h dy_t \\
&= \left(\rho + i_t + hg\right) dt + h\sigma_y dX_{1,t} + \sigma_q dX_{3,t}
\end{aligned}
$$

The Feynman-Kac theorem states that the following expectation

$$V\left(i, m, t; T\right) = E_t\left[e^{-m_T} | i, m\right]$$

must satisfy the Partial Differetial Equation (PDE)[5]

$$
\begin{aligned}
0 &= \frac{\partial V}{\partial t} + \frac{\partial V}{\partial i} E\left[di\right] + \frac{\partial V}{\partial m} E\left[dm_t\right] + \frac{1}{2}\frac{\partial^2 V}{\partial i^2} E\left[di^2\right] + \frac{1}{2}\frac{\partial^2 V}{\partial m^2} E\left[dm^2\right] \\
&\quad + \frac{\partial^2 V}{\partial i \partial m} E\left[didm\right]
\end{aligned}
$$

with boundary condition

$$V\left(i, m, T; T\right) = e^{-m}$$

---

[5]We cover the multifactor Feynman-Kac formula in Chapter 22.

We first guess the form of the solution, and verify that it satisfies the PDE above. Consider the following guess solution:

$$V(i_t, m, t; T) = e^{-m_t + A(t;T) - B(t;T)(i_t + c)} \qquad (18.45)$$

where c is a constant to be determined, and with boundary conditions $A(T;T) = 0$ and $B(T;T) = 0$. Then

$$\frac{\partial V}{\partial t} = \left(\frac{\partial A(t;T)}{\partial t} - \frac{\partial B(t;T)}{\partial t}(i_t + c) \right) V$$

$$\frac{\partial V}{\partial i} = -B(t;T) V; \frac{\partial V}{\partial m} = -V;$$

$$\frac{\partial^2 V}{\partial i^2} = B(t;T)^2 V; \frac{\partial^2 V}{\partial m^2} = V; \frac{\partial^2 V}{\partial i \partial m} = B(t;T) V.$$

Substitute in the PDE to find

$$0 = \left(\frac{\partial A(t;T)}{\partial t} - \frac{\partial B(t;T)}{\partial t}(i_t + c) \right) - B(t;T) \gamma \left(\bar{i} - i \right) - (\rho + i + hg)$$

$$+ \frac{1}{2} B(t;T)^2 \sigma_i^2 + \frac{1}{2} \left(h^2 \sigma_y^2 + \sigma_q^2 + 2h\sigma_y \sigma_q \rho_{qy} \right) + B(t;T) \left(h\sigma_i \sigma_y \rho_{yi} + \sigma_i \sigma_y \rho_{iq} \right)$$

Define the following quantities

$$c = \rho + hg - \frac{1}{2} \left(h^2 \sigma_y^2 + \sigma_q^2 + 2h\sigma_y \sigma_q \rho_{qy} \right)$$

$$r = i + c;$$

$$\bar{r} = \bar{i} + c$$

$$\bar{r}^* = \bar{r} - \frac{1}{\gamma} \left(h\sigma_i \sigma_y \rho_{yi} + \sigma_i \sigma_y \rho_{iq} \right)$$

Substitute in the above equation and rearrange to find

$$0 = \left(\frac{\partial A(t;T)}{\partial t} - \frac{\partial B(t;T)}{\partial t} r \right) - B(t;T) \left[\gamma \left(\bar{r}^* - r \right) \right] - r + \frac{1}{2} B(t;T)^2 \sigma_i^2$$

This equation is identical to the equation obtained under the Vasicek model of interest rates (see Equation 15.75 in Chapter 15). Because the boundary conditions are also the same, we obtain $A(t;T)$ and $B(t;T)$ are given by the same solutions as in Vasicek formula, that is, Equations 15.30 and 15.29 in Chapter 15.

The zero coupon bond pricing formula can be obtained from $V(i, m, t; T)$ as

$$Z(i, t; T) = E\left[e^{m_t - m_T} \right] = e^{m_t} E[e^{-m_T}] = e^{m_t} V(i, m, t; T) = e^{A(t:T) - B(t;T)(i_t + c)}$$

CHAPTER 19

NO ARBITRAGE MODELS AND STANDARD DERIVATIVES

When a model is not able to fit exactly the term structure of interest rate, such as the Vasicek model in the relative value trade example in Chapter 16, Section 16.3, then it may imply two possibilities: (a) There is an arbitrage opportunity to be played on the term structure of interest rates; or (b) The model is flawed. Indeed, extensions to the Vasicek or the Cox, Ingersoll, and Ross models with multiple factors have been designed to indeed spot misalignment in the yields across maturities and therefore imply some type of (near) arbitrage strategy across yields. The model in this case is used to determined both the type of strategy to implement, as well as the hedge ratios and trading strategies. We discussed an example of these strategies in Section 16.3 of Chapter 16.

For many market participants, however, term structure models are designed to "simply" compute the fair value of many derivative securities, such as options, caps, floors, and swaptions. For these market participants it is important to fit the term structure of interest rates correctly, as we have done in Chapter 11 with trees. In this chapter, we review the most famous, and in fact most used models, of the term structure of interest rates, and their application to pricing standard derivatives, that is, plain vanilla options that are routinely used by financial institutions and end users to hedge interest rate risk.

19.1 NO ARBITRAGE MODELS

Why is it important to match the current term structure of interest rates? An example, which we will return to later, may help understand why.

■ **EXAMPLE 19.1**

As in example 15.2 in Chapter 15, suppose that on January 8, 2002 we want to sell a 1-year call option on a 4-year zero coupon bond, with strike price of 80 out of a 100 principal. Fact 15.5 in Chapter 15 shows that under the assumptions of the Vasicek model, the value of this call option per unit principal is given by

$$V(r_0, 0) = Z(0, r_0; T_B) \mathcal{N}(d_1) - KZ(0, r_0; T_O) \mathcal{N}(d_2) \tag{19.1}$$

where $\mathcal{N}(x)$ is the cumulative standard normal distribution, and

$$d_1 = \frac{1}{\mathcal{S}_Z(T_O)} \log \left(\frac{Z(0, r_0; T_B)}{KZ(0, r_0; T_O)} \right) + \frac{\mathcal{S}_Z(T_O)}{2} \tag{19.2}$$

$$d_2 = d_1 - \mathcal{S}_Z(T_O) \tag{19.3}$$

$$\mathcal{S}_Z(T_O)^2 = B(T_O; T_B)^2 \frac{\sigma^2}{2\gamma} \left(1 - e^{-2\gamma T_O} \right) \tag{19.4}$$

where T_O is the maturity of the option, and T_B is the maturity of the underlying zero coupon bond.

Figure 15.2 in Chapter 15, however, shows that the Vasicek model is unable to fit the term structure of interest rates on that day. In Section 16.3 of Chapter 16 we indeed exploited this fact to design an arbitrage strategy on the yield curve. However, our goal is not different: We now want to price an option. Note that the Vasicek model performs particularly poorly at the one-year horizon, exactly the maturity of the option we want to sell. Indeed, the Vasicek discount factors for $T_O = 1$ and $T_B = 5$ are $Z^{Vasicek}(0, T_O) = 0.9742$ and $Z^{Vasicek}(0, T_B) = 0.7965$, while the same values according to Treasury STRIPS on that day were $Z(0, T_O) = 0.9790$ and $Z(0, T_B) = 0.7978$.

This situation generates a conundrum: What bond prices $Z(0, r_0; T)$ should we insert in the option pricing formula in Formula 19.1? The model prices, that is, the ones that are true according to the Vasicek model, or the real prices? The difference in the value of the option is in fact quite substantial. Given the parameter estimates $\gamma^* = 0.4653$, $\bar{r}^* = 6.34\%$, and $\sigma = 0.0221$, we obtain $\mathcal{S}_Z(T_O) = 0.0323$ and thus

$$\text{Price of option with Vasicek discount } Z(0, T) = \$2.2921 \tag{19.5}$$
$$\text{Price of option with market discount } Z(0, T) = \$1.9159 \tag{19.6}$$

The almost 20% difference in price is substantial. Intuition would have it to use the market prices in the formula, but then we are inconsistent with the model. In particular, the dynamic trading strategy may provide the wrong hedge ratios. Of course, traders know that all financial models are at best rough approximations of a very complex real world. However, a model that is able to exactly match the term structure of interest rates would provide perhaps a better guidance for the exact hedging strategy. For instance, suppose we sold the option to a client, and now we want to hedge against the short position by going long the underlying zero coupon bond with maturity T_B. What position in the underlying bond do we want to take? The Vasicek model once again generates a conundrum here, as the position may be different depending on whether we insert market prices for $Z(0, T)$ or the Vasicek prices. For instance, in the case above we have

$$
\text{Delta of option with Vasicek discount } Z(T) \;\; = \;\; 0.4561
$$
$$
\text{Delta of option with true discount } Z(T) \;\; = \;\; 0.4366
$$

In this case the difference is not large, but for other strike prices, the percentage difference becomes substantial.

From our discussion in Chapter 11 we know that there are models that exactly fit the term structure of interest rates, such as the Ho-Lee model and the Black, Derman, and Toy model. We are going to revisit these models in their continuous time framework, and add to them additional models that have been proposed.

19.2   THE HO-LEE MODEL REVISITED

Recall that we introduced the Ho-Lee model in Chapter 11, and we then discussed its continuous time limit in Example 14.5 in Chapter 14. Adopting now the terminology of Chapter 17, we specify that the Ho-Lee model assumes that the *risk neutral* process for interest rates is given by

$$
dr_t = \theta_t dt + \sigma dX_t \tag{19.7}
$$

where θ_t is chosen to match the term structure of interest rates. The methodology employed in Chapter 11 of matching one bond at the time recursively, is rather time consuming. It turns out that for the Ho-Lee model, we can obtain an estimate of θ_t directly from the forward curve. In order to see this, we first report some important results about the pricing of these securities.

Fact 19.1 *The zero coupon bond price at time 0 is given by*

$$
Z(r,0;T) = e^{A(0;T)-T\times r} \tag{19.8}
$$

where $A(0;T)$ is given by

$$
A(0,T) = -\int_0^T (T-t)\theta_t dt + \frac{T^3}{6}\sigma^2 \tag{19.9}
$$

Unlike with the Vasicek model, the bond pricing formula here is not fully analytical, because we need to solve the integral in Equation 19.9. However, it turns out that we typically do not need to actually solve this equation to use the Ho-Lee model. In fact, because we choose θ_t to match exactly the bond prices $Z(r,0;T)$ to the data, by construction we will not need to compute the bond prices themselves.

How do we choose θ_t to match the term structure of interest rates? The forward curve contains (almost) all the information we need to obtain θ_t. In fact, recall that the continuously compounded forward rate at time 0 for an investment between time t and $t+\delta$ is given by (see Equations 5.2 and 5.4 in Chapter 5)

$$
f(0,t,t+\delta) = -\frac{\ln\left(Z(0,t+\delta)\right) - \ln\left(Z(0,t)\right)}{\delta} \tag{19.10}
$$

As δ becomes small, we obtain the continuously compounded, *instantaneous forward rate*, given by

$$f(0,t) = -\frac{\partial \ln(Z(0,t))}{\partial t} \tag{19.11}$$

Recalling the notation $r(0,t)$ for the continuously compounded yield between 0 and t, defined by the equation $Z(0,t) = e^{-r(0,t) \times t}$, we obtain the equivalent expression for the instantaneous forward rate

$$f(0,t) = r(0,t) + t \times \frac{\partial r(0,t)}{\partial t} \tag{19.12}$$

That is, the instantaneous forward rate equals the current spot rate plus a term that depends on the slope of the spot rate curve: If the spot rate curve is increasing, the forward rate is above the spot rate, and vice versa (see Chapter 5 for details). The appendix shows that θ_t is related to the slope of the instantaneous forward curve (see Section 19.9.2):

Fact 19.2 *The drift rate θ_t that matches the current term structure of interest rates at time 0 is given by*

$$\theta_t = \frac{\partial f(0,t)}{\partial t} + \sigma^2 \times t \tag{19.13}$$

■ **EXAMPLE 19.2**

Consider again the case of January 8, 2002 featured in Example 19.1. The Vasicek model failed to obtain the correct prices of the zero coupon bonds, which was at the source of the problem. We now show how the Ho-Lee model can resolve the issue. We will work directly with the STRIPS rates also plotted in Figure 15.2 in Chapter 15. From that figure, we immediately see a problem: The yield curve obtained from STRIPS is not smooth. This is a problem as it implies a forward curve that is very erratic, and thus we won't be able to use Equation 19.13 to compute θ_t. The first step, then, is to interpolate the spot curve in order to obtain a twice differentiable curve. Panel A of Figure 19.1 shows the result.[1]

The second step is to obtain the instantaneous forward curve. Because we interpolated the spot rate curve on a fine grid, we can compute the instantaneous forward curve numerically as $f(0,t) \approx r(0,t) + t \times \frac{r(0,t+\delta) - r(0,t)}{\delta}$ where δ is small. Panel A of Figure 19.1 also plots the instantaneous forward curve for every t along with the interpolated spot curve. As we know from Chapter 5, the forward curve looks more unstable than the spot curve, as it depends on the slope of the spot curve. Finally, we compute the function θ_t approximately as

$$\theta_t \approx \frac{f(0,t+\delta) - f(0,t)}{\delta} + \sigma^2 \times t$$

Recalling that the parameter σ is simply the diffusion of the interest rate model under the risk neutral dynamics of interest rates, we can estimate this quantity from past realized changes in the short term interest rates, or from options. For this example,

---

[1]The interpolation is performed by fitting the yields to a 10-th order polynomial of time t.

Figure 19.1   Ho-Lee model: January 8, 2002

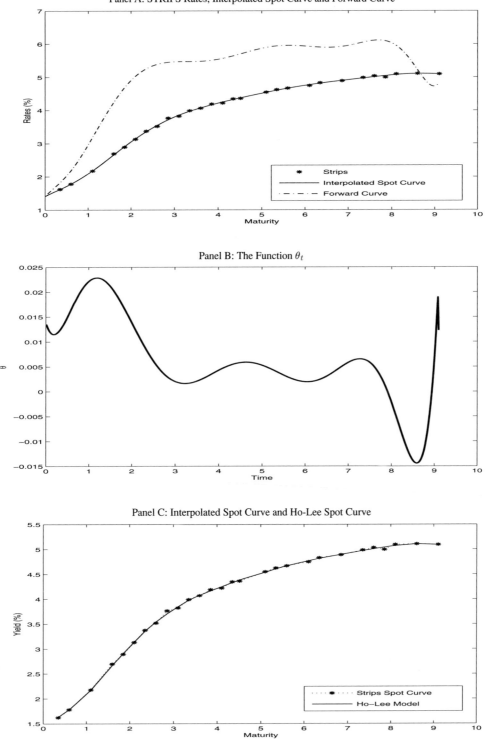

Panel A: STRIPS Rates, Interpolated Spot Curve and Forward Curve

Panel B: The Function θ_t

Panel C: Interpolated Spot Curve and Ho-Lee Spot Curve

Data Source: *The Wall Street Journal.*

we compute σ as the historical standard deviation of changes in short-term rates, which turns out to be $\sigma = .0221$.

Panel B of Figure 19.1 reports the estimated θ_t. Note that since σ^2 is very small, θ_t essentially gives just the slope of the forward curve. Because the latter tends to flatten out, we would expect θ_t to become closer and closer to zero for longer time t.

Given θ_t, we can now proceed to use this model to price other derivative securities, such as options. Before we do so, however, it is a good idea to check that the methodology works. To determine this, we can use the estimated θ_t and check that by inserting it into the zero coupon bond pricing formula in Equation 19.8 we obtain model yields that are identical to the ones used as input in this estimation procedure. To do so, we must compute the function $A(0;T)$ in Equation 19.9. We can approximate the integral in the formula with a summation, as we know from a similar approximation applied to Monte Carlo simulations. That is, approximate

$$\int_0^T \theta_t \, (T - t) \, dt \approx \sum_{j=1}^n \theta_{j \times \delta} \times (T - j\delta) \times \delta$$

Panel C of Figure 19.1 plots the spot curve and the Ho-Lee curve obtained by

$$r_0^{Ho-Lee}(T) = -\frac{\log(Z(r, 0, T))}{T}$$

Clearly, the Ho-Lee model matches the spot curve exactly, thereby verifying the procedure works.

19.2.1 Consistent Derivative Pricing

The model is set up to match exactly the current term structure of interest rates. Hence, we cannot price bonds with this model, because they are the input to the model. So, what is the point of getting a term structure model that cannot be used to price bonds? The simple answer is that once we estimate θ_t from the current term structure of interest rates, we can now move to obtain prices of other securities which depend on interest rates, such as bond options, caps and floors, swaps, swaptions, mortgage backed securities, and in fact, any structured derivative we can think of, such as the P&G / Bankers Trust leveraged swap discussed in Section 17.9 in Chapter 17. If the model does well in capturing the current features of the term structure, we can obtain prices for these other securities that are consistent with the current term structure of interest rates.

Like the Vasicek model, the Ho-Lee model also has a closed form formula for the price of a call option. This is given by the following:

Fact 19.3 *A* **call option** *with maturity T_O written on a zero coupon bond with unit principal maturing on $T_B > T_O$ has a payoff at maturity*

$$Payoff \text{ at } T_O = \max(Z(T_O; T_B) - K, 0) \tag{19.14}$$

where K is the strike price. Under the Ho-Lee model, the value at 0 of this call option is given by

$$V(r_0, 0) = Z(0, r_0; T_B)\mathcal{N}(d_1) - KZ(0, r_0; T_O)\mathcal{N}(d_2) \tag{19.15}$$

where $\mathcal{N}(x)$ is the cumulative standard normal distribution, and

$$d_1 = \frac{1}{\mathcal{S}_Z(T_O;T_B)} \log\left(\frac{Z(0,r_0;T_B)}{KZ(0,r_0;T_O)}\right) + \frac{\mathcal{S}_Z(T_O;T_B)}{2} \quad (19.16)$$

$$d_2 = d_1 - \mathcal{S}_Z(T_O;T_B) \quad (19.17)$$

$$\mathcal{S}_Z(T_O;T_B)^2 = \sigma^2 T_O (T_B - T_O)^2 \quad (19.18)$$

Similarly, a **put option** *with maturity T_O written on a zero coupon bond with unit principal maturing on $T_B > T_O$ has a payoff at maturity*

$$\textit{Payoff at } T_O = \max(K - Z(T_O;T_B),0) \quad (19.19)$$

Under the Ho-Lee model, the value at 0 of this put option is given by

$$V(r_0,0) = KZ(0,r_0;T_O)\mathcal{N}(-d_2) - Z(0,r_0;T_B)\mathcal{N}(-d_1) \quad (19.20)$$

The formula for a call option in the case of the Ho-Lee model (Equation 19.15) is very similar to its counterpart under the Vasicek model (Equation 15.44). Indeed, in both cases, the interest rate r_{T_O} is normally distributed, making the bond price $Z(T_O, r_{T_O}; T_B)$ log-normally distributed. In this case, however, it is no longer unclear about what bond prices to insert in the option pricing formula (Equation 19.15), market prices or model prices. Indeed, because the model exactly matches the term structure of interest rate, model prices equal market prices, and there is no issue.

■ EXAMPLE 19.3

Returning to Example 19.1, let's apply the Ho-Lee formula. An important point to note is that since we know that the Ho-Lee model will price perfectly the zero coupon bonds $Z(0,T)$, there is no need to actually extract the function θ_t in order to use the option pricing formula in Equation 19.15. As can be seen from the formula, θ_t itself does not enter anywhere but in the zero coupon bond prices $Z(r_0,0;T)$. The key simplification is that we can now use the data prices $Z(0,T)$ in lieu of the model prices $Z(r_0,0;T)$, as they are the same by construction. It follows that the only parameter that we need then is σ. Using again the historic standard deviation of 1-month T-bill rates, we obtain $\sigma = .0221$. Given $T_O = 1$ and $T_B = 5$, we obtain $\mathcal{S}_Z(T_O;T_B) = 0.0886$. Substituting into d_1 and thus into Equation 19.15 we find

$$\textit{Price using the Ho-Lee formula} = \$3.5758 \quad (19.21)$$

This value is much larger than any of the two obtained under the Vasicek model, in Equations 19.5 and 19.6. Given in particular that the discount rate $Z(0,T)$ is the same as the one used in Equation 19.6, this result may appear puzzling. However, the difference stems from the different volatility of long-term bonds that is implied by the Ho-Lee model compared to the Vasicek model. Under the Vasicek model, in fact, recall that we computed $\mathcal{S}_Z(T_O;T_B) = 0.0335$ while under the Ho-Lee model the same quantity comes out as $\mathcal{S}_Z(T_O;t_B) = 0.0886$.

Because in both cases we used the same volatility of the interest rate, $\sigma = .0221$, it is informative to understand the source of the difference. In the Vasicek model, the interest rate model is mean reverting. When we consider the relatively large estimated risk neutral speed of mean reversion $\gamma^* = 0.4475$, we find that long-term bonds are not all that volatile. Indeed, recall that the bond volatility depends on the spot rate duration $D_Z = -\frac{1}{Z}\partial Z/\partial r = B(0,T) = (1 - e^{-\gamma^* \times T})/\gamma^* = 1.8615$ for $T = 4$. In the case of the Ho-Lee model, the spot rate duration is instead given by $D_Z = -\frac{1}{Z}\partial Z/\partial r = T = 4$, which is much larger. If we add to this the fact that under the Ho-Lee model the interest rate follows a random walk, whose distribution at time T_O has a variance that increases with $\sigma^2 T_O$, we obtain the much higher volatility of $\mathcal{S}_Z(T_O; T_B)$ to insert in the otherwise identical option pricing formula.

Pragmatically, traders often use option-implied volatilities, which then yield the same value of $\mathcal{S}_Z(T_O; T_B)$ whether we use Ho-Lee or Vasicek.

The Ho-Lee model is simple, and that's its virtue. However, it has some drawbacks that make some traders and market participants uneasy to employ it, and these are:

1. Nonstationarity: The process follows essentially a random walk, and thus for T very large interest rates could grow to plus or minus infinity.

2. A flat the term structure of volatility.

19.2.2   The Term Structure of Volatility in the Ho-Lee Model

Recall that the term structure of volatility is given by the volatility of bond yields as a function of bond maturity. To see the predicted long-term bond yield volatility in the case of the Ho-Lee model, consider first the process for the yield $r_t(\tau)$ on a zero coupon bond with time to maturity τ:

$$r_t(\tau) = -\log(Z(r, t; t + \tau))/\tau \tag{19.22}$$

Given the formula for the zero coupon bond in the case of the Ho-Lee model, Equation 19.8, we can rewrite it as

$$r_t(\tau) = -A(t; t + \tau)/\tau + r_t \tag{19.23}$$

Because the first term on the right-hand side is a nonstochastic term (it only depends on time t in a deterministic fashion), we obtain the following fact:

Fact 19.4   *The volatility of the changes in long-term interest rates $dr_t(\tau)$ equals the volatility of the changes in the short-term interest rate dr_t. That is, for every τ*

$$Variance\,(dr_t(\tau)) = Variance\,(dr_t) = \sigma^2 dt \tag{19.24}$$

This fact stands in contrast with the data. Indeed, Figure 19.2 plots the average standard deviation of changes in zero coupon bond yields for maturities between one month and five years using historical monthly data. As can be seen, the volatility of zero coupon bond yields is much higher at the short-horizon than at the long horizon. The Ho-Lee model, in contrast, would imply that the volatility of these yields is the same, i.e., the model-implied volatility from the Ho-Lee model would be represented by a straight line.

Figure 19.2   Average Term-Structure of Spot Rate Volatility

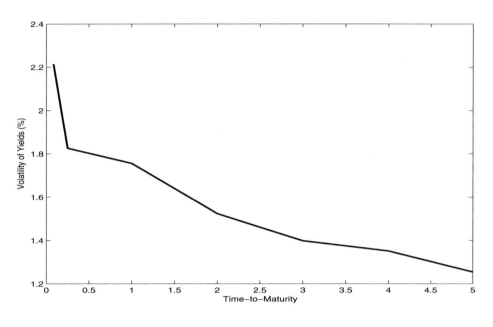

Data Source: The Federal Reserve and CRSP.

19.3   THE HULL-WHITE MODEL

The Hull-White model is similar to the Ho-Lee model, but it has a central tendency:

$$dr_t = \left(\theta_t - \gamma^* r_t \right) dt + \sigma dX_t$$

This is similar to the Vasicek model, as we can see from defining $\bar{r}_t^* = \frac{1}{\gamma^*} \times \theta_t$: Indeed, in the Hull-White model, the central tendency is time dependent, although with a deterministic variation. As in the Ho-Lee model, also in the Hull-White model the function of time θ_t is chosen to match exactly the term structure of interest rates. Given that we have θ_t which will take care of fitting the term structure of interest rates, unlike the Vasicek model, we are now free to choose the parameters σ and γ^* to fit as well as possible the term structure of spot rate volatilities.

More specifically, the following is true:

Fact 19.5 *The bond pricing formula in the Hull-White model is given by*

$$Z\left(r, 0; T \right) = e^{A(0;T) - B(0;T) \times r} \tag{19.25}$$

where

$$B\left(0; T \right) = \frac{1}{\gamma^*} \left(1 - e^{-\gamma^* T} \right) \tag{19.26}$$

and

$$A\left(0; T \right) = - \int_0^T B(t;T) \theta_t \, dt + \frac{\sigma^2}{2(\gamma^*)^2} \left(T + \frac{1 - e^{-2\gamma^* T}}{2\gamma^*} - 2B(0;T) \right) \tag{19.27}$$

By following the same steps as in the Ho-Lee model and assuming that today is $t = 0$, we find that θ_t is as follows:

Fact 19.6 *The function of time θ_t that exactly matches the term structure of interest rates at time 0 is given by*

$$\theta_t = \frac{\partial f(0,t)}{\partial t} + \gamma^* f(0,t) + \frac{\sigma^2}{2\gamma^*} \times \left(1 - e^{-2\gamma^* t}\right) \tag{19.28}$$

In addition, the term structure of volatility is better behaved: Indeed, by following the same steps as in the case of the Ho-Lee model, we see that the yield of a zero coupon bond with maturity τ is

$$r_t(\tau) = -\frac{A(t; t+\tau)}{\tau} + \left(\frac{1}{\gamma^*}\right)\left(\frac{1 - e^{-\gamma^* \tau}}{\tau}\right) r_t$$

Hence, we find the following:

Fact 19.7 *The (annualized) volatility of the changes in long-term interest rates $dr_t(\tau)$, call it $\sigma_t^2(\tau) = variance(dr_t(\tau))/dt$, is given by*

$$\sigma_t(\tau) = \frac{B(\tau)}{\tau}\sigma \tag{19.29}$$

where recall that we use the notation $B(\tau) = B(0; \tau)$.

Panel A of Figure 19.3 plots the term structure of volatility in the Hull-White model for the case in which the parameters σ and γ^* are estimated to minimize the difference between the volatility in the data, and the volatility formula in Equation 19.29. In this case, we obtain $\sigma = .0196$ and $\gamma^* = 0.19$.

Given γ^* and σ, we can finally compute the function θ_t from Equation 19.28 by also using the forward curve. Panel B of Figure 19.3 plots the resulting term structure of interest rates. Clearly, the Hull-White model does as well as the Ho-Lee model in fitting the term structure of interest rates.

19.3.1   The Option Price

What is the value of the option under the Hull-White model? Because θ_t is only a function of time, the value of an option in the case of the Hull-White model is the same as in the case of Vasicek. That is, we have:

Fact 19.8 *Under the Hull-White model, a call option with strike price K and maturity T_O on a zero coupon bond with unit principal maturing on $T_B > T_O$ is given by*

$$V(r_0, 0) = Z(0, r_0; T_B)\mathcal{N}(d_1) - KZ(0, r_0; T_O)\mathcal{N}(d_2) \tag{19.30}$$

where $\mathcal{N}(x)$ is the cumulative standard normal distribution, and

$$d_1 = \frac{1}{\mathcal{S}_Z(T_O; T_B)}\log\left(\frac{Z(0, r_0; T_B)}{KZ(0, r_0; T_O)}\right) + \frac{\mathcal{S}_Z(T_O; T_B)}{2} \tag{19.31}$$

Figure 19.3   The Hull-White Model: January 8, 2002

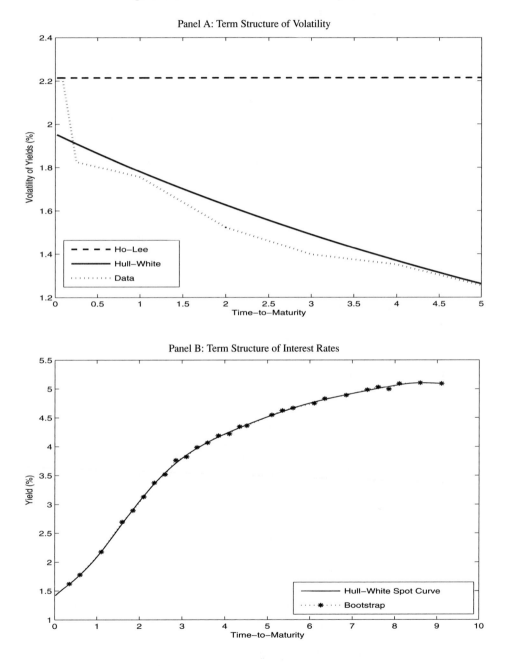

Panel A: Term Structure of Volatility

Panel B: Term Structure of Interest Rates

Data Source: The Federal Reserve, CRSP, and *The Wall Street Journal*.

$$d_2 = d_1 - \mathcal{S}_Z(T_O;T_B) \tag{19.32}$$

$$\mathcal{S}_Z(T_O;T_B)^2 = B(T_O;T_B)^2 \frac{\sigma^2}{2\gamma^*}\left(1 - e^{-2\gamma^*T_O}\right) \tag{19.33}$$

Similarly, a put option with strike price K and maturity T_O on a zero coupon bond with unit principal maturing on $T_B > T_O$ is given by

$$V(r_0,0) = KZ(0,r_0;T_O)\mathcal{N}(-d_2) - Z(0,r_0;T_B)\mathcal{N}(-d_1) \tag{19.34}$$

The call option pricing formula is identical to the one we obtained under the Vasicek model (see Fact 15.5 in Chapter 15). There are two important differences from the case of the Vasicek model, however:

1. There is no difference between model prices and market prices. That is, we resolved the conundrum discussed at the beginning of Section 19.1.

2. The parameters γ^* and σ have been estimated to best fit the term structure of volatility, and thus the option price will likely be more accurate. In contrast, in the Vasicek model, the parameter γ^* was estimated to fit the term structure of interest rates.

■ **EXAMPLE 19.4**

Turning again to Example 19.1, using the same data as before, but also the term structure of volatility in Figure 19.3 (i.e. the parameter estimates $\sigma = .0196$ and $\gamma^* = 0.19$), we obtain a value of the call option under the Hull-White model of Call = \$2.4040. This value is substantially smaller than the one obtained under the Ho-Lee model, whose price was \$3.5758. The reason is twofold: First, the volatility estimate of yields at the 1-year horizon in the case of the Hull-White model is much smaller than in the case of the Ho-Lee, as can be seen from Figure 19.3. Indeed, the Ho-Lee model has a volatility of $\sigma_t(1) = .0221$ while the Hull-White model has $\sigma_t(1) = 0.018$. Second, the mean reversion in interest rates implies that the sensitivity of a 4-year bond to interest rates is smaller in the case of the Hull-White model compared to the Ho-Lee model. In fact, the spot rate durations are $D_Z = -\frac{1}{Z}\frac{\partial Z}{\partial r} = (T_B - T_O) = 4$ for the Ho-Lee model, and $D_Z = -\frac{1}{Z}\frac{\partial Z}{\partial r} = B(T_O;T_B) = 2.8018$ for the Hull-White model.

These two factors, i.e., lower dispersion of the interest rate and lower spot rate duration in the Hull-White model, imply that the volatility $\mathcal{S}_Z(T_O;T_B)$ to insert in the otherwise identical option pricing formula is much smaller in the Hull-White case than in the Ho-Lee case. That is,

$$\mathcal{S}_Z(T_O;T_B)^{\text{Ho-Lee}} = 8.86\%$$
$$\mathcal{S}_Z(T_O;T_B)^{\text{Hull-White}} = 5.00\%$$

The value obtained under the Hull-White model is also quite higher than the value obtained under the Vasicek model, even for the case in which we used market data $Z(0,T_O)$ and $Z(0,T_B)$. Recall that the value of the option was $Call^{Vasicek} = \$1.9482$. Once again the difference in valuation stems from the volatility estimate. In the Vasicek model, γ^* was estimated to fit the term structure of interest rates, resulting therefore in $\gamma^* = 0.4475$ which is substantially higher than the value obtained when this parameter is fitted to match the term structure of volatility, as in the Hull-White model. A high (risk neutral) speed of mean reversion γ^* reduces both $B(T_O, T_B)$, and thus the volatility of long-term bonds (see Equation 19.29) as well as the dispersion of interest rates at T_O. Indeed, under the Vasicek model, we obtained in Example 19.1 a volatility given by

$$\mathcal{S}_Z(T_O; T_B)^{\text{Vasicek}} = 3.35\% \tag{19.35}$$

which is indeed smaller than the one obtained under the Hull-White model.

19.4 STANDARD DERIVATIVES UNDER THE "NORMAL" MODEL

The discussion in the previous sections makes clear that the Vasicek, Ho-Lee, and Hull-White models have in common three important properties:

1. The zero coupon bond price has the form $Z(r, 0; T) = e^{A(0;T) - B(0;T)r_0}$.

2. The distribution of a future interest rate is normally distributed.

3. The option pricing formula is essentially identical, with the only difference stemming from the option volatility $\mathcal{S}_Z(T_O; T_B)$.

The normality of the interest rate r_T gives the name to this class of models, called the "normal" models of interest rates, as opposed to the log-normal models, discussed next. Given that the option pricing formula is the same in all of these cases, and in both the Hull-White and Ho-Lee models, the model prices for bonds are identical to market prices, we can use this common formula to study the pricing of some standard interest rate derivatives, such as options on coupon bonds, caps, floors, and swaptions.

19.4.1 Options on Coupon Bonds

The option pricing formula developed above only holds for zero coupon bonds. Treasury bond options are instead written on coupon bonds. Luckily, as seen in Chapter 15, in this class of "normal" model, it is possible to extend the option pricing formula to the case of options on bonds. In particular, we have the following pricing formula:

Fact 19.9 *Let $P_c(r_t, t; T_B)$ be the price at time t of a coupon bond with coupon rate c and maturity date T_B. Let Δ be the time interval between coupons. Consider a call option with maturity T_O and strike rate K written on the above coupon bond, that is, whose payoff is*

$$\text{Payoff of call option at } T_O = \max(P_c(r_{T_O}, T_O; T_B) - K, 0) \tag{19.36}$$

The value at time 0 of the call option in the "normal" model can be computed as follows. Let r^* be the interest rate, such that $P_c(r^*, T_O, T_B) = K$, and define $K_i = Z(r^*, T_O; T_i)$ for each coupon date T_i. We then have that the value of the call option is

$$\text{Call} = \sum_{i=1}^{n} c(i) \ (Z(r_0, 0; T_i) \mathcal{N}(d_1(i)) - K_i \ Z(r_0, 0; T_O) \mathcal{N}(d_2(i))) \tag{19.37}$$

where $c(i)$ is the cash flow paid by the coupon bond at time T_i, that is, $c(i) = c/2$ for $i = 1, \ldots, n - 1$ and $c(n) = 1 + c/2$, and

$$d_1(i) = \frac{1}{\mathcal{S}_Z(T_O; T_i)} \log\left(\frac{Z(0, r_0; T_i)}{K_i Z(0, r_0; T_O)}\right) + \frac{\mathcal{S}_Z(T_O; T_i)}{2} \quad (19.38)$$

$$d_2(i) = d_1(i) - \mathcal{S}_Z(T_O; T_i) \quad (19.39)$$

and where $\mathcal{S}_Z(T_O; T_i)$ is the option volatility, defined by either Equation 19.18 for the Ho-Lee model, or Equation 19.33 for the Hull-White model.

To explain the procedure, consider the Hull-White model. To apply the option pricing formula above, we first must compute the value of the zero coupon bond at time T_O for various interest rates r_{T_O}, until we find the level r^* such that $P_c(r^*, T_O, T_B) = K$. The formula for the zero coupon at any time $t > 0$ is the same as in Equation 19.25, that is

$$Z(r_t, t; T) = e^{A(t;T) - B(t;T)r_t}$$

and where $A(t; T)$ and $B(t; T)$ are given by Equations 19.27 and 19.26, respectively. In particular, the formula for $A(t; T)$ involves an integral

$$A(t; T) = -\int_t^T B(u; T)\theta_u \, du + \frac{\sigma^2}{2(\gamma^*)^2}\left((T - u) + \frac{1 - e^{-2\gamma^*(T-u)}}{2\gamma^*} - 2B(t; T)\right) \quad (19.40)$$

We can compute this integral numerically in a relatively easy manner, by chopping off the time interval $[t; T]$. However, it turns out that there is an easier formula, that depends only on today (time 0) zero coupon bonds and the instantaneous forward rate $f(0, t)$:

Fact 19.10 *In the Hull-White model, the $A(t; T)$ is alternatively given by*

$$A(t; T) = \log\left(\frac{Z(r_0, 0; T)}{Z(r_0, 0; t)}\right) + B(t; T) f(0, t) - \frac{\sigma^2}{4\gamma^*} B(t; T)^2 \left(1 - e^{-2\gamma^* t}\right) \quad (19.41)$$

Similarly, in the Ho-Lee model, the $A(t; T)$ is alternatively given by

$$A(t; T) = \log\left(\frac{Z(r_0, 0; T)}{Z(r_0, 0; t)}\right) + (T - t)f(0, t) - \frac{\sigma^2}{2}(T - t)^2 t \quad (19.42)$$

This finding greatly simplifies the computation of coupon bond prices. The next example illustrates the methodology.

■ **EXAMPLE 19.5**

Consider the earlier example, in which the parameter estimates to fit the term structure of volatility under the Hull-White model are $\sigma = .0196$ and $\gamma^* = 0.19$. Panel B of Figure 19.3 shows the term structure of interest rates on January 8, 2002. Assume that instead of a call option on a zero coupon bond, investigated in Equation 19.4, we wish to price a call option, written on a coupon bond. In particular, let the underlying coupon bond have a coupon rate $c = 5\%$ and a maturity $T_B = 5$. Let the maturity of the option be $T_O = 1$ and the strike price $K = \$1$ (for $\$1$ of notional). Also, for

Table 19.1   Coupon Bond Option Pricing

T_i	$A(T_O;T_i)$	$B(T_O;T_i)$	K_i	$Z(0;T_i)$	$\mathcal{S}_Z(T_O;T_i)$	$d_1(i)$	$Call_i(\times 100)$
1.5	-0.0035	0.4770	0.9837	0.9623	0.0085	-0.1314	0.2742
2.0	-0.0133	0.9107	0.9627	0.9408	0.0162	-0.1237	0.5148
2.5	-0.0275	1.3052	0.9390	0.9169	0.0233	-0.1166	0.7226
3.0	-0.0441	1.6639	0.9146	0.8923	0.0297	-0.1102	0.9007
3.5	-0.0620	1.9901	0.8905	0.8683	0.0355	-0.1044	1.0526
4.0	-0.0809	2.2867	0.8668	0.8447	0.0408	-0.0991	1.1811
4.5	-0.1012	2.5565	0.8432	0.8214	0.0456	-0.0943	1.2882
5.0	-0.1230	2.8018	0.8195	0.7979	0.0500	-0.0899	1.3758

convenience, let today be an ex-coupon date. The first step is then to compute the $A(T_0;T_i)$ and $B(T_0;T_i)$ for every coupon date T_i *after* the maturity of the option. $B(T_0;T_i) = (1 - e^{-\gamma^*(T_i-T_0)})/\gamma^*$ is relatively simple to compute. To compute $A(T_0;T_i)$ we can use either of the formulas in Equations 19.40 or 19.41. The results are in the second and third columns of Table 19.1. Given these quantities, we can look for r^* that indeed makes the coupon bond price at T_O equal to the strike price. That is, we solve for the equation

$$\frac{c}{2} \times \sum_{i=1}^{n} Z(r,T_O;T_i) + Z(r,T_O;T_n) = K$$

where the unknown is "r." In this case, we find the solution is $r^* = 2.715\%$.

Next, we must compute $K_i = Z(r^*,T_O;T_i)$. These are contained in the second column of Table 19.1. Finally, given the discounts, and the other parameters, we can compute $\mathcal{S}_Z(T_O;T_i)$ and thus $d_1(i)$ and $d_2(i)$ for every maturity. The last column in Table 19.1 reports each individual zero coupon bond option for each of the maturities. The value of the option on the coupon bond is then given by

$$
\begin{aligned}
\text{Call price } (\times 100) &= \frac{c}{2} \sum_{i=1}^{n} Call_i + Call_n \\
&= \$1.5586
\end{aligned}
$$

19.4.2   Caps and Floors

Recall from Chapter 11, Section 11.2.2 that a cap with maturity T, strike rate r_K, and annual payment frequency n, is a security that pays at time $T_1, T_2,...,T_m = T$ with $T_{i+1} = T_i + \Delta$ and $\Delta = 1/n$, the cash flows

$$\text{Cash flow at } T_i = CF(T_i) = \Delta \times N \times \max{(r_n(T_{i-1};T_i) - r_K, 0)} \qquad (19.43)$$

where $r_n(T_{i-1};T_i)$ is $n-$times compounded reference floating rate at time T_{i-1} and maturity T_i. The typical reference interest rate is the LIBOR. The important institutional fact of this contract is that the cash flow at time T_i depends on the floating rate $r_n(T_{i-1}; T_i)$, that is, the rate determined one period earlier $T_{i-1} = T_i - \Delta$. Each individual cash flow described in Equation 19.43 is called a caplet.

How can we use the option pricing formula to price a cap? We now will see that we can transform the cash flow in the formula in Equation 19.43 into one that resembles a put option on a zero coupon bond price. Because we are going to deal with only one cash flow at a time, we drop the subscript i from the payment time T_i, for simplicity.

First, note that the amount to be paid at time T is already known at time $T - \Delta$, because it depends on the interest rate $r_n(T - \Delta; T)$. Therefore, we can compute the present value of the cash flow in Equation 19.43 as of time $T - \Delta$:

$$
\begin{aligned}
PV_{T-\Delta}(CF(T)) &= Z(T - \Delta; T) \times \Delta \times N \times \max(r_n(T - \Delta; T) - r_K, 0) \\
&= Z(T - \Delta; T) \times N \times \max((1 + r_n(T - \Delta; T)\Delta) - (1 + r_K\Delta), 0)
\end{aligned}
$$

Because by definition of a discount, we have $Z(T - \Delta; T) = 1/(1 + r_n(T - \Delta; T)\Delta)$, we can multiply $Z(T - \Delta; T)$ by each term in the maximum, to obtain

$$
\begin{aligned}
PV_{T-\Delta}(CF(T)) &= N \times \max(1 - (1 + r_K\Delta)Z(T - \Delta, T), 0) \\
&= N(1 + r_K\Delta) \times \max\left(\frac{1}{(1 + r_K\Delta)} - Z(T - \Delta, T), 0\right)
\end{aligned}
$$

We now note that $PV_{T-\Delta}(CF(T))$ is equal to the payoff of a put option on a zero coupon $Z(T - \Delta, T)$, strike price $1/(1 + r_K\Delta)$, and notional $N(1 + r_K\Delta)$.

Fact 19.11 *Under the "normal" model, the value of a caplet with maturity T, notional N, strike rate r_K, and payment frequency of the underlying cap n, is given by a put option with maturity $T - \Delta$ and strike price $K = \frac{1}{(1+r_K\Delta)}$, defined on a zero coupon with maturity Δ, and principal amount $M = N(1 + r_K\Delta)$. The value of the caplet is then:*

$$
V(r_0, 0) = M \times (KZ(0, r_0; T - \Delta)\mathcal{N}(-d_2) - Z(0, r_0; T)\mathcal{N}(-d_1)) \qquad (19.44)
$$

where $\mathcal{N}(x)$ is the cumulative standard normal distribution,

$$
\begin{aligned}
d_1 &= \frac{1}{\mathcal{S}_Z(T - \Delta; T)} \log\left(\frac{Z(0, r_0; T)}{KZ(0, r_0; T - \Delta)}\right) + \frac{\mathcal{S}_Z(T - \Delta; T)}{2} \qquad (19.45) \\
d_2 &= d_1 - \mathcal{S}(T - \Delta; T) \qquad (19.46)
\end{aligned}
$$

and where $\mathcal{S}_Z(T - \Delta; T)$ is the option volatility, defined by either Equation 19.18 for the Ho-Lee model, or Equation 19.33 for the Hull-White model.

For later reference, the following summarizes the cap pricing:

Fact 19.12 *Consider a cap with maturity T, annual number of payments n, notional N, and strike rate r_K. Define by T_j the payment times, with $T_j = T_{j-1} + \Delta$, so that the cash flow at time T_j is given by*

$$
CF(T_j) = \Delta \times N \times \max(r_n(T_{j-1}, T_j) - r_K, 0) \qquad (19.47)
$$

where $r_n(T_{j-1}, T_j)$ denotes the $n-$times compounded rate at time T_{j-1}. Then, the cap value at 0 is given by

$$
Cap = \sum_{j=2}^{n} M \times (KZ(0, r_0; T_{j-1})\mathcal{N}(-d_2(j)) - Z(0, r_0; T_j)\mathcal{N}(-d_1(j))) \qquad (19.48)
$$

where

$$d_1(j) = \frac{1}{\mathcal{S}_Z(T_{j-1};T_j)} \log\left(\frac{Z(0,r_0;T_j)}{KZ(0,r_0;T_{j-1})}\right) + \frac{\mathcal{S}_Z(T_{j-1};T_j)}{2} \quad (19.49)$$

$$d_2(j) = d_1(j) - \mathcal{S}_Z(T_{j-1};T_j) \quad (19.50)$$

and $\mathcal{S}_Z(T_{j-1};T_j)$ is given by either Equation 19.18 for the Ho-Lee model, or Equation 19.33 for the Hull-White model.

The valuation of floors is similar.

■ **EXAMPLE 19.6**

Let today be January 8, 2002, and consider a quarterly cap with strike rate $r_K = 5\%$ and maturity $T = 5$, where the underlying floating rate is the 3-months T-bill rate.[2] The Treasury discount curve is the one shown in Figure 19.1 (or, equivalently, Figure 19.3 under the Hull-White model). We can compute the value of the cap using either the Ho-Lee model, with the formula in Equation 19.18 and the estimated $\sigma = .0221$, or the Hull-White model, with the formula in Equation 19.33 and the parameters' estimates $\sigma = .0196$ and $\gamma^* = 0.19$.

Now we can obtain the value of the cap as follows. First, let $K = 1/(1 + r_K \times \Delta) = 0.9877$ and $M = (1 + r_K \times \Delta) = 1.0125$, where $\Delta = 0.25$. Then, let $T_1 = \Delta$ and define $T_j = T_{j-1} + \Delta$ for $j = 2, ..., n$ where $n = T/\Delta = 20$ is the number of periods. We can compute $\mathcal{S}_Z(T_{j-1};T_j)$ using either the Ho-Lee model (Equation 19.18) or the Hull-White formula (Equation 19.33). In either case, we then compute the quantity d_1 in Equation 19.49 for every consecutive period T_j. Each caplet price with maturity T_j, $j = 2, ..., m$, then follows from Equation 19.49, applied to every $j = 2, ..., m$.

Table 19.2 contains the results of the computation. The first column reports each caplet maturity T_j. Columns 2 to 4 contain the results using the Ho-Lee model. In particular, column 2 reports $\mathcal{S}_Z(T_{j-1};T_j)$, column 3 $d_1(j)$ and column 4 the value of the caplet (multiplied by 100 for convenience). Columns 5 to 7 report the same quantities for the Hull-White model. The value of the cap is obtained by summing the caplets. So, we obtain

$$\text{Cap value under Ho-Lee model } (\times 100) = \$5.8319$$

$$\text{Cap value under Hull-White model } (\times 100) = \$3.9752$$

As we noted earlier, the value under the Hull-White model is smaller in this case, as the volatility of long-term yields are closer to their empirical counterparts (see Figure 19.3): In particular, recall that under the Ho-Lee model the volatility of long-term yields is simply equal to the volatility of the short-term yields ($\sigma = 0.0221$, which is higher than their empirical counterparts. The higher volatility of long-term yields combined with the lack of mean reversion in the Ho-Lee model results in a value of $\mathcal{S}_Z(T_{j-1};T_j)$ which is substantially higher than in the Hull-White model, as can be seen by comparing columns 2 and 5 in Table 19.2.

---

[2]Standard plain vanilla caps have the LIBOR as the reference floating rate. However, using the 3-months T-bill rate in this example allows us to put into play the empirical results in the earlier sections. See Section 19.4.3 for the application to LIBOR rates.

Table 19.2   Cap Price: The Ho-Lee model versus the Hull-White model

	Ho-Lee Model			Hull-White Model		
(1)	(2)	(3)	(4)	(5)	(6)	(7)
T_i	$\mathcal{S}_Z(T_{j-1};T_j)$	$d_1(j)$	$Caplet_i\ (\times 100)$	$\mathcal{S}_Z(T_{j-1};T_j)$	$d_1(j)$	$Caplet_i\ (\times 100)$
0.50	0.0039	1.9858	0.0035	0.0032	2.4121	0.0008
0.75	0.0048	1.4293	0.0165	0.0039	1.7757	0.0058
1.00	0.0055	1.0266	0.0436	0.0044	1.3038	0.0195
1.25	0.0062	0.7019	0.0870	0.0048	0.9107	0.0462
1.50	0.0068	0.4385	0.1442	0.0051	0.5805	0.0868
1.75	0.0073	0.2328	0.2079	0.0054	0.3136	0.1365
2.00	0.0078	0.0820	0.2692	0.0057	0.1110	0.1868
2.25	0.0083	-0.0197	0.3210	0.0059	-0.0307	0.2298
2.50	0.0088	-0.0805	0.3599	0.0061	-0.1194	0.2608
2.75	0.0092	-0.1106	0.3863	0.0062	-0.1664	0.2797
3.00	0.0096	-0.1205	0.4028	0.0064	-0.1848	0.2887
3.25	0.0100	-0.1196	0.4133	0.0065	-0.1874	0.2917
3.50	0.0104	-0.1158	0.4212	0.0066	-0.1853	0.2923
3.75	0.0107	-0.1141	0.4293	0.0067	-0.1864	0.2934
4.00	0.0111	-0.1175	0.4392	0.0068	-0.1955	0.2966
4.25	0.0114	-0.1263	0.4512	0.0069	-0.2138	0.3025
4.50	0.0117	-0.1392	0.4649	0.0070	-0.2395	0.3105
4.75	0.0121	-0.1537	0.4790	0.0071	-0.2687	0.3193
5.00	0.0124	-0.1670	0.4920	0.0071	-0.2965	0.3274

19.4.3 Caps and Floors Implied Volatility

Traders rarely use the realized volatility of the interest rate to price standard derivatives, because these historical volatilities generate option prices that are different from the traded ones. The reason for this difference is the subject of heated research in the academic literature, but it essentially boils down to the fact that (i) the volatility of interest rate securities (and interest rates) is not constant, but changes stochastically over time, adding a source of risk for fixed income investors and thus additional motives to hedge; and (ii) the interest rate sometimes jumps discretely, or too fast to be effectively hedged, which again generates additional risks for investors. These added sources of risk are then reflected in option prices. The simple models described earlier do not take into account these effects, and thus generate a substantial mispricing. Traders then use the volatility σ that is implied from options to price additional interest rate securities, knowing that it is an "easy" fix to use simple one-factor models rather than more complex multifactor models.

Consider again the Ho-Lee model. In this case, the volatility entering the option pricing formula, $\mathcal{S}_Z(T_{j-1}; T_j)$, depends on only one parameter, σ, as we see from Equation 19.18. Thus, we can search for this one parameter σ that best fits the cap prices. Consider the cap prices on November 1, 2004, which are reported as the "stars" in Panel A in Figure 19.4. The same panel reports the cap prices for the various maturities from the pricing function in Equation 19.48 for three values of σ, $\sigma = 0.006$ (arbitrarily set), $\sigma = .0084$, which corresponds to the historical volatility of the 3-month LIBOR, and $\sigma = .0107$, which is implied by options. That is, the latter value is the one that minimizes

$$J(\sigma) = \sum_{j=1}^{n} \left(Cap_j^{Data} - Cap_j^{Ho-Lee} \right)^2$$

As can be seen, in fact, the latter $\sigma = 0.0107$ yields cap prices that are in line with the data (the stars are on top of the squares in the figure), although only for a cap maturity above $T = 4$. The bottom panel of Figure 19.4 shows the relative pricing errors, that is,

$$\text{Pricing error of cap } j = \frac{\left(Cap_j^{Data} - Cap_j^{Ho-Lee} \right)}{Cap_j^{Data}} \tag{19.51}$$

This figure shows that indeed at the long end, the model does well, but it misses quite substantially the prices of caps for the low horizon. In particular, it appears that we would need different volatilities σ for different types of caps. For instance, from the figure, we see that $\sigma = 0.006$ would price exactly a cap with a maturity around $T = 1.25$, while $\sigma = .0084$ would price exactly a cap with maturity around $T = 2.25$. Of course, having different volatilities σ for different caps would imply an arbitrage opportunity, as already discussed in Chapter 11.

The Hull-White model has two parameters, γ^* and σ, that we can use now to better fit the term structure of volatility of caps, and perhaps obtain better pricing. The formula for a cap is the same as before, as the only change is in $\mathcal{S}_Z(T_{j-1}, T_j)$, which now depends on these two parameters. We therefore look for both γ^* and σ that minimize the pricing errors

$$J(\gamma^*, \sigma) = \sum_{j=1}^{n} \left(Cap_j^{Data} - Cap_j^{Hull-White} \right)^2$$

Figure 19.5 shows the result of the minimization, comparing the pricing errors (as in Equation 19.51) from the Hull-White model to those from the simpler Ho-Lee model. As

Figure 19.4   Cap Prices in the Ho-Lee Model on November 1, 2004

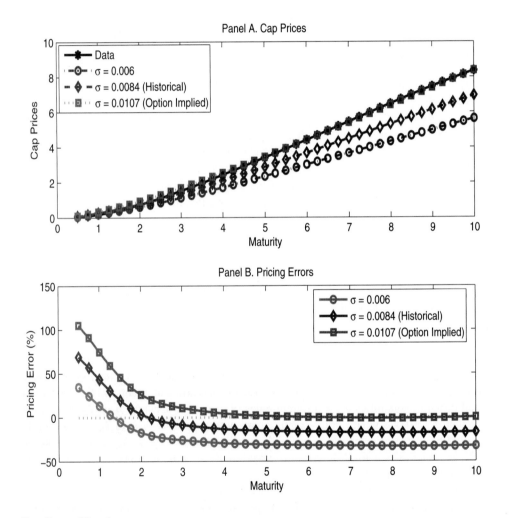

Figure 19.5   Cap Pricing Errors on November 1, 2004

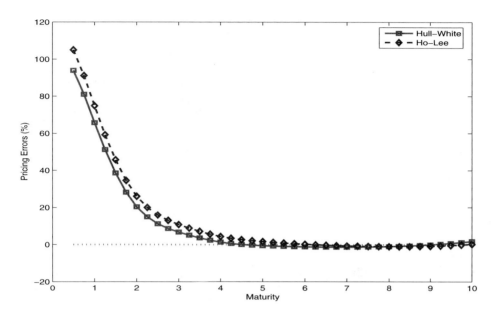

Data Source: Bloomberg.

it can be seen, the Hull-White model does do better, although the difference is not gigantic. In particular, even the Hull-White model has problems fitting the cap prices at the short horizon.

A little troubling, also, is the parameter estimates that we obtain to fit the cap prices. These are

$$\sigma = 0.0099; \quad \gamma^* = -0.0313$$

In particular, the negative value of γ^* implies that the risk neutral interest rate model generates an exploding behavior of interest rates. Indeed, recall from the Hull-White model that

$$dr_t = (\theta_t - \gamma^* r_t)dt + \sigma dX_t$$

Thus, a negative γ^* will tend to imply that when the rate r_t is high, then the expected change in the rate is positive, which in turn will push the rate even higher, on average, and vice versa. Note also that $\gamma^* = -0.0313$ is not too different from zero, which would instead correspond to the Ho-Lee model. This explains why the cap prices under the two models are relatively similar. Indeed, to see the difference between the two models, it is informative to plot the volatility $\mathcal{S}_Z(T_{j-1}, T_j)$ implied by each. We do this in Figure 19.6, in which the dotted line corresponds to the Hull-White model, and the dashed line corresponds to the Ho-Lee model. As is clear from the figure, on this particular day (November 1, 2004) the fitted volatilities of the two models are almost identical.

It is also instructive to perform the following exercise. For each cap, we can compute the volatility $\mathcal{S}_Z(T_{j-1}, T_j)$ in the cap formula (Equation 19.48) that makes the value of the

Figure 19.6 Implied Volatility $\mathcal{S}_Z(T_{j-1}, T_j)$ on November 1, 2004

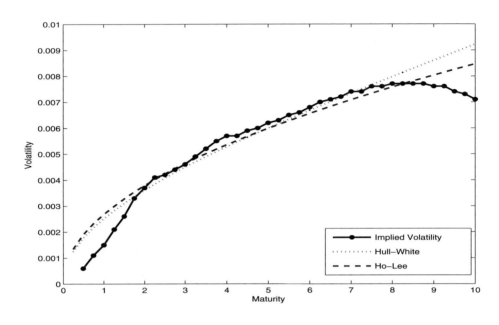

Data Source: Bloomberg.

cap in the data equal to the formula. That is, for each j:

$$\text{Choose } \mathcal{S}_Z(T_{j-1}, T_j) \text{ so that } Cap_j^{Data} = Cap_j^{Model}$$

The implied volatility is plotted in Figure 19.6 as the starred-solid line. As it can be seen, compared to both the Ho-Lee model and the Hull-White model, the data suggest a lower volatility $\mathcal{S}_Z(T_{j-1}, T_j)$ for short horizons, and a much higher volatility for longer maturities.

One way to obtain a better fit, indeed, would be to free up some other parameter in the Ho-Lee or the Hull-White models. For instance, θ_t in both models is chosen so that the model bond prices are in line with the data. A similar exercise can be carried out for volatility. Indeed, we may recall that the Black, Derman, and Toy model discussed in Chapter 11 accomplished exactly this task. Recalling that discussion, however, it is important to note that we must obtain an implied volatility of individual *caplets* that is consistent with Figure 19.6, which instead illustrates the implied volatility of *caps*. That is, we must ensure that the same caplet that appears in different caps has the same price. For instance, consider two caps with maturity $T = 1$ and $T = 1.25$, with the same strike rate. Then, the first three caplets in the two caps are the same, and thus they should have the same price. While this fact is ensured when we use the Hull-White or Ho-Lee model, this restriction is not enforced if we look at the different implied volatilities in Figure 19.6. The reason is that the two implied volatilities obtained in this figure may imply that the same caplets would be priced differently, which would generate an arbitrage.

19.4.4   European Swaptions

As already discussed in Chapter 11, a swaption is an option to enter into a swap. In particular, a receiver swaption is the option to enter into a swap and receive a fixed rate equal to the swaption strike rate r_K. Similarly, a payer swaption is an option to enter into a swap and pay a fixed rate equal to the swaption strike rate r_K. A swaption, like any option, is termed European if the decision to exercise the option can only be taken at a precise time, the maturity of the swaption T.

We saw in Chapter 11 how to price European (and American) swaptions on binomial trees. We now show that we can employ the option pricing formulas in Equations 19.15 and 19.30 to price European swaptions. Indeed, consider a receiver swaption with strike rate r_K, maturity T_O, defined on an underlying swap that matures at $T_S > T_O$. The security underlying the option, then, is a swap with a swap rate r_K and maturity T_S. From basics we learned on swaps (see Chapter 5), the value of this swap at any time t is given by the difference between a fixed rate bond and a floating rate bond with the same maturity. That is,

$$V_t^{swap} = P_c(r_t, t; T_S) - P_{FR}(r_t, t; T_S) \tag{19.52}$$

where $P_{FR}(r_t, t; T_S)$ is the value at time t of a floating rate bond with maturity T_S, and $P_c(r_t, t; T_S)$ is the value of a coupon bond at time t with maturity T_S. Recall from Chapter 2 that both bond values can be computed once we know that discount factors $Z(t, T)$ for every T.

Consider now the maturity of the swaption, T_O. Assume that T_O coincides with a reset date of the underlying swap. In this case, we know from Chapter 2 that $P_{FR}(T_O, T_S) = 100$. Therefore, if we exercise the swaption, it is as if we get a portfolio that is long the fixed coupon bond and short the floating rate bond, while if we do not exercise, we get zero. It follows that the payoff at maturity T_O is given by

$$
\begin{aligned}
\text{Payoff receiver swaption} \quad &= \quad \max\left(P_c(r_{T_O}, T_O; T_S) - P_{FR}(T_O; T_S), 0\right) &(19.53) \\
&= \quad \max\left(P_c(r_{T_O}, T_O; T_S) - 100, 0\right) &(19.54)
\end{aligned}
$$

Comparing this payoff with Equation 19.36, we see that the payoff from the European receiver swaption is identical to a call option on a coupon bearing bond, whose coupon is r_K, the strike rate of the swaption, and strike price equal to $K = 100$. As shown in Section 19.4.1, under the normal model, there is a closed form formula for the value of this option.

■ EXAMPLE 19.7

Let today be November 1, 2004, and consider the volatility estimates obtained in Section 19.4.3 under the Hull-White model (the computations under the Ho-Lee model are the same), namely, $\sigma = 0.0099$ and $\gamma^* = -0.0313$. We can use these estimates, then, to compute the value of a swaption. In particular, consider a 1-year Receiver Swaption on a 5-year swap with quarterly resets.[3] Let this swaption be at-the-money, meaning that the strike rate r_K equals the current swap rate for the

---

[3]In plain-vanilla swaps, the floating leg typically pays quarterly and the fixed leg typically pays semi-annually. For simplicity, we consider the same frequency on both legs.

Table 19.3   A 1-Year Swaption on a 5-Year Quarterly Swap

(1) T_i	(2) K_i	(3) $Z(0;T_i)$	(4) $S_Z(T_O;T_i)$	(5) $d_1(i)$	(6) $Call_i(\times 100)$
1.25	0.9936	0.9674	0.0025	-0.4950	0.0484
1.50	0.9868	0.9596	0.0051	-0.4924	0.0967
1.75	0.9797	0.9515	0.0076	-0.4899	0.1448
2.00	0.9723	0.9431	0.0102	-0.4873	0.1926
2.25	0.9645	0.9344	0.0128	-0.4847	0.2402
2.50	0.9565	0.9254	0.0154	-0.4821	0.2873
2.75	0.9483	0.9163	0.0180	-0.4794	0.3341
3.00	0.9398	0.9069	0.0207	-0.4768	0.3805
3.25	0.9311	0.8974	0.0234	-0.4741	0.4264
3.50	0.9223	0.8878	0.0261	-0.4714	0.4718
3.75	0.9133	0.8780	0.0288	-0.4687	0.5167
4.00	0.9042	0.8682	0.0315	-0.4659	0.5611
4.25	0.8950	0.8582	0.0343	-0.4632	0.6050
4.50	0.8857	0.8482	0.0371	-0.4604	0.6483
4.75	0.8763	0.8381	0.0399	-0.4576	0.6910
5.00	0.8668	0.8280	0.0427	-0.4548	0.7331
5.25	0.8572	0.8178	0.0456	-0.4519	0.7746
5.50	0.8476	0.8076	0.0484	-0.4490	0.8155
5.75	0.8380	0.7974	0.0513	-0.4461	0.8558
6.00	0.8283	0.7872	0.0542	-0.4432	0.8955

same type of swap, i.e., a 5-year swap rate.[4] We now use the same methodology explained in Fact 19.9, and detailed in Example 19.5. More specifically,

1. Compute the value of r^* such that $P_c(r^*, T_O; T_S) = 100$. In this case, we obtain $r^* = 2.478\%$.

2. Compute the strike rates $K_i = Z(r^*, T_O; T_i)$, for $i = 1, \ldots, n$, where T_i are the payment dates of the underlying swap. The first and second columns in Table 19.3 contain T_i and K_i, respectively.

3. Use Equation 19.37 to compute the value of the swaption, in which $c(i) = r_X \times \Delta$ for $i = 1, \ldots, n-1$ and $c(n) = 1 + r_X \times \Delta$. Columns 3 to 6 of Table 19.3 contain the details of this last step, with each $Call_i$ the individual call option implicit in Equation 19.37. The final value of the swaption is then

$$Swaption(\times 100) = \sum_{i=1}^{n} r_K \times \Delta \times Call_i + Call_n = \$0.9866$$

---

[4]The term "at-the-money" may also mean "forward at-the-money" in the sense that the strike rate is equal to the forward swap rate, a concept discussed in Chapter 21.

19.4.5 Swaptions' Implied Volatility

As we did for the case of caps, we can use traded swaption prices to compute the parameters of the Ho-Lee model (σ) or the Hull-White model (σ and γ^*) by minimizing the distance between model prices and traded prices. For instance, in the case of the Hull-White model, we can search for the parameters such that the following is minimized

$$J(\gamma^*, \sigma) = \sum_{j=1}^{n} \left(Swaption_j^{Data} - Swaption_j^{Hull-White}\right)^2$$

A computation of the parameters yields in this case

$$\sigma = 0.0102; \quad \gamma^* = -0.0151$$

Once again, we find that γ^* is negative, which means that the interest rate process is mean averting, or an explosive process. Figure 19.7 plots the percentage pricing errors. Panel A reports the pricing errors for the 3 month maturity of the option, Panel B for the 6 month maturity, and Panel C for the 1 year maturity. In all cases, we consider a swaption's tenor (T_S) that ranges between one year to seven years. Each panel reports two lines: The solid line represents the pricing errors, in percentage of the market price, obtained from the swaption implied volatility. The dashed line reports the pricing errors obtained from fitting the Hull-White model to cap prices, instead of swaption prices. Two comments are important: First, the prices obtained from fitting swaption are close to those obtained from fitting caps. That is, it appears that the two sets of derivative prices, caps and swaptions, are in line with each other. Second, as was true in the case of caps, in percentage the model does not perform well at the short horizon, although it matches the prices quite accurately at the long horizon.

19.5 THE "LOGNORMAL" MODEL

One drawback of the Ho-Lee and the Hull-White models is that the interest rate can become negative. Because this is a nominal rate, a negative interest rate implies an arbitrage opportunity if storing cash at home is feasible. A negative nominal rate implies, for instance, that we are willing to buy a government bond at $100 with the understanding that the government will return $95, for instance, at maturity. Keeping the $100 at home yields a higher return.[5]

One methodology for ensuring that the nominal rate of interest is always positive is to model $\log(r_t)$ instead of r_t, as a mean reverting process with deterministic volatility and drift rate, as shown in Chapter 11. Since $\log(r_t)$ is then normally distributed, the rate r_t is log-normally distributed. This class of models is then called the "lognormal" model.

19.5.1 The Black, Derman, and Toy Model

Chapter 11 introduced the Black, Derman, and Toy model, or BDT model, for short. In this section we review its continuous time counterpart. Let $y_t = log(r_t)$. Then, it can be

---

[5]This argument only works so long there is zero probability that somebody breaks into our home and steals the $100. In fact, holding money in a bank for safekeeping implies, implicitly, a negative interest rate. For instance, checking accounts in U.S. typically do not pay any interest, but there are fixed costs to be paid to keep an account open. If the average balance on the account is small, this agreement with the bank entails implicitly a large negative nominal rate.

Figure 19.7   Swaption Pricing Errors on November 1, 2004

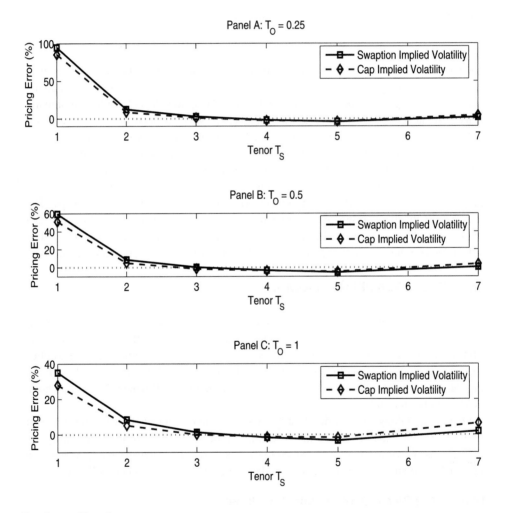

Data Source: Bloomberg.

shown that the BDT model described in that chapter has a continuous time representation given by

$$dy_t = \left(\theta_t + \frac{\partial \sigma_t / \partial t}{\sigma_t} y_t \right) dt + \sigma_t dX_t \qquad (19.55)$$

where θ_t and σ_t are deterministic functions of time. As a special case, if $\sigma_t = \sigma$ is a constant, then $\partial \sigma_t / \partial t = 0$ and the model reduces to

$$dy_t = \theta_t dt + \sigma dX_t \qquad (19.56)$$

that is, it is the same as the Ho-Lee model, but in logarithm.

The main drawback of this model is that it does not allow for a closed form formula for bond prices. The main methodology to price securities through the BDT model is in fact to use binomial trees. Thus, the methodology described in Chapter 11 is the standard methodology. For the case in which σ_t is chosen to match the prices of standard derivatives, however, such as caps and floors, or swaptions, it turns out that the BDT model provides a link between the market model, discussed in the next chapter, Chapter 21, and the binomial trees already discussed in Chapter 11.

19.5.2   The Black and Karasinski Model

The Black and Karasinski model is a generalization to the BDT model, in which $y_t = log(r_t)$ follows

$$dy_t = \left(\theta_t - \gamma_t y_t \right) dt + \sigma_t dX_t \qquad (19.57)$$

where now we have one more parameter, γ_t, to choose. If $\gamma_t = -\frac{\partial \sigma_t / \partial t}{\sigma_t}$, this model reduces to the Black, Derman, and Toy model. Unfortunately, once again, this model does yield closed form representation of bond prices, and so we need numerical methods to solve for interest rate security prices.

19.6   GENERALIZED AFFINE TERM STRUCTURE MODELS

The number of interest rate models that are available is large. The ones we discussed earlier are perhaps the most used in the industry, as they are arguably the simplest and the fastest to implement. But many more are available. A large part of them belongs to the class of the generalized affine model, which has the general form

$$dr_t = (\theta_t - \gamma_t r_t)dt + \sqrt{\sigma_t^2 + \alpha_t r_t} dX_t \qquad (19.58)$$

where θ_t, γ_t, σ_t and α_t are all deterministic functions of time t.[6] For instance, the case in which $\gamma_t = 0$, $\alpha_t = 0$ and $\sigma_t = \sigma$ is constant corresponds to the Ho-Lee model, discussed earlier. The case in which in addition $\gamma_t = \gamma$, a constant, corresponds to the Hull-White model. If instead $\sigma_t = 0$ and $\alpha_t = \alpha$ is a constant, we obtain the generalized

---

[6]Restrictions must be applied to ensure that this model is well defined, that is, that the term $(\sigma_t^2 + \alpha_t r_t)$ has zero probability of becoming negative. These restrictions make this model less flexible than it may appear at first.

Cox, Ingersoll, and Ross model, already discussed in Section 15.4.1 in Chapter 15. The interesting fact about the model in Equation 19.58 is that it allows for a closed form formula for bond prices.

Fact 19.13 *Under the interest rate model in Equation 19.58, the value of a zero coupon bond $Z(r_0, 0; T)$ is given by*

$$Z(r_t, t; T) = e^{A(t;T) - B(t;T)r_t} \qquad (19.59)$$

where $A(t; T)$ and $B(t; T)$ satisfy the two differential equations

$$\frac{\partial B(t;T)}{\partial t} = B(t;T)\gamma_t + \frac{1}{2}B(t;T)^2\alpha_t - 1 \qquad (19.60)$$

$$\frac{\partial A(t;T)}{\partial t} = B(t;T)\theta_t - \frac{1}{2}B(t;T)^2\sigma_t^2 \qquad (19.61)$$

with final condition $A(T; T) = 0$ and $B(T; T) = 0$.

The solution to the differential Equations 19.61 and 19.61 can be obtained numerically in a relatively straightforward manner. In fact, although the bond pricing formula in Equation 19.59 still implies a part that is numerically solved, it is customary to speak of it as an analytical solution to bond prices, as the two terms $A(t; T)$ and $B(t; T)$ are easy to compute. Indeed, given the parameters θ_t, γ_t σ_t and α_t, note that we can compute the values of $A(t; T)$ and $B(t; T)$ by moving backward from the end, $t = T$, in which case we know $A(T; T) = 0$ and $B(T; T) = 0$. For $t < T$ we obtain $A(t; T)$ and $B(t; T)$ from Equations 19.61 and 19.61 by discretizing the differential equation, obtaining

$$B(t - \delta; T) = B(t;T) + \left(B(t;T)\gamma_t + \frac{1}{2}B(t;T)^2\alpha_t - 1\right)\delta \qquad (19.62)$$

$$A(t - \delta; T) = A(t;T) + \left(B(t;T)\theta_t - \frac{1}{2}B(t;T)^2\sigma_t^2\right)\delta \qquad (19.63)$$

where δ is a small number.

19.7   SUMMARY

In this chapter we covered the following topics:

1. No Arbitrage Models: These are models designed to fit exactly the term structure of interest rates and, possibly, the term structure of volatility. The trick is to over-parametrize the models using non-stochastic quantities to match bond prices and possibly options.

2. The Ho-Lee Model: This model assumes that interest rates follow a random walk with deterministic drift. Future interest rates have a normal distribution with variance that increases with horizon, and in fact diverges to infinity. Although the model matches the term structure of interest rates perfectly, it implies counterfactually that yields of various maturities have the same volatility. Its simplicity is its virtue, as this model has closed form expressions for options on zero coupon bonds, as well as other plain

vanilla derivatives. Moreover, it easily generates a recombining tree (as discussed in Chapter 11).

3. The Hull-White Model: A combination of the Vasicek and Ho-Lee models. Like Ho-Lee, the Hull-White model is able to exactly fit the term structure of interest rates. However, like Vasicek, the model contains a mean reverting component which keeps the variance of the statistical distribution of future interest rates bounded. The Hull-White model implies the yields of long-term bonds have lower volatility than short-term bonds, consistently with the data. Like the Vasicek and Ho-Lee model, the Hull-White model has closed form expressions for the pricing of options on zero coupon and coupon bonds.

4. Normal models and standard derivative pricing: The class of normal models (such as Vasicek, Ho-Lee, and Hull-White) has analytical formulas for call and put options on zero coupon bonds and coupon bonds. The payoffs of standard derivatives, such as caps, floors and swaptions, can be rewritten as payoffs involving call and put options on zero coupon bonds (caplets and floolets) or coupon bonds (swaptions). Thus, this class of models yields analytical formulas for plain vanilla standard derivatives.

5. The Black, Derman and Toy model: This model was discussed in Chapter 11. Unlike the Ho-Lee and Hull-White model, it assumes that the logarithm of interest rates is normally distributed, implying that interest rates are always positive. Moreover, it has enough degrees of freedom to match both the term structure of interest rates and the term structure of volatility. The main drawback is that it does not have closed form expressions for bond prices. The standard methodology to price securities is through trees or Monte Carlo simulations.

19.8 EXERCISES

1. Today is November 3, 2008, and the 3-month LIBOR and (interpolated) swap rates are as in Table 19.4.

    (a) Obtain the LIBOR yield curve from the swap rates.[7]

    (b) Let σ be the historical volatility of 3-month LIBOR rates (historical data are available on the Web site of the British Bankers Association at www.BBA.org.uk). Fit the Ho-Lee model to the LIBOR yield curve.

    (c) Plot the resulting θ_t and discuss its relation with the forward curve.

    (d) How does the value of σ affect the ability of the Ho-Lee model to match the LIBOR yield curve? Assume σ is ten times the estimate in Part (b). How does θ_t change?

2. Today is November 3, 2008, and the 3-month LIBOR, swap rates, and cap prices are as in Table 19.4.

    (a) Fit the Ho-Lee model to the current LIBOR yield curve (see previous exercise).

---

[7] Assume for simplicity that both fixed and floating legs of the swap pays at the quarterly frequency.

Table 19.4 Swap Rates and Cap Prices on November 3, 2008

3-Month LIBOR (%)	2.8588	
Maturity	Swap Rate (%)	Cap Price ($\times 100$)
0.50	2.6486	0.0528
0.75	2.4929	0.1313
1.00	2.4320	0.2401
1.25	2.4491	0.3826
1.50	2.4938	0.5405
1.75	2.5561	0.7106
2.00	2.6260	0.8932
2.25	2.7252	1.1095
2.50	2.8630	1.3729
2.75	3.0108	1.6636
3.00	3.1400	1.9502
3.25	3.2471	2.2235
3.50	3.3474	2.4973
3.75	3.4408	2.7711
4.00	3.5270	3.0451
4.25	3.6076	3.3208
4.50	3.6835	3.5968
4.75	3.7531	3.8700
5.00	3.8150	4.1370

Original Data Source: Bloomberg.
Reported Data are interpolated from quoted swap rates and flat volatilities,
and then computed using Black's model.

(b) Obtain the price of the cap with $T = .5$. What is the volatility σ in the Ho-Lee model that matches this value?

(c) Obtain the price of the cap with $T = .75$. What is the volatility σ in the Ho-Lee model that matches this value? Is this the same as the one obtained for $T = .5$ in Part (b)? Comment.

(d) For each maturity $T = 0.5$ to $T = 5$ compute the volatility σ that matches the price of the cap. Plot this volatility against the cap maturity T. What does it look like? Discuss.

(e) Find the value of σ that best matches all of the cap data. Given this σ, plot the pricing errors for the various maturities, that is, the difference (in percentage) between the Ho-Lee cap prices and the traded prices. Comment.

3. Perform the previous exercise, but this time for the Hull-White model. In particular, find both σ and γ that best fit the cap prices. Report the pricing errors on a figure. Discuss.

4. Today is November 3, 2008 and you have available only the cap data in Table 19.4. Consider a European, 1-year at-the-money swaption on a 3-year swap.

   (a) Use the Ho-Lee model to compute the price of the swaption.

   (b) Use the Hull-White model to compute the price of the swaption. Is this the same price you obtain using the Ho-Lee model?

5. Today is November 3, 2008 and you have available only the cap data in Table 19.4. Consider an *American* 1-year at-the-money swaption on a 3-year swap. Select a model and price the American swaption (Hint: See Chapter 12).

19.9   APPENDIX: PROOFS

19.9.1   Proof of the Ho-Lee Pricing Formula

The Fundamental Pricing Equation is

$$rZ = \frac{\partial Z}{\partial t} + \frac{\partial Z}{\partial r}\theta_t + \frac{1}{2}\frac{\partial^2 Z}{\partial r^2}\sigma^2$$

with final condition $Z(r, T; T) = 1$. We now show that Equation 19.8 indeed satisfies the fundamental pricing equation as well as the final condition. First, compute the partial derivatives

$$\frac{\partial Z}{\partial t} = \left(\frac{\partial A(t; T)}{\partial t} + r\right)Z; \quad \frac{\partial Z}{\partial r} = -(T - t)Z; \quad \frac{\partial^2 Z}{\partial r^2} = (T - t)^2 Z$$

Substitute these into the partial differential equation, and divide through by Z to find

$$r = \left(\frac{\partial A(t; T)}{\partial t} + r\right) - (T - t)\theta_t + \frac{1}{2}(T - t)^2 \sigma^2$$

Simplify, and rewrite

$$-\frac{\partial A\left(t;T\right)}{\partial t} = -\left(T-t\right)\theta_t + \frac{1}{2}\left(T-t\right)^2\sigma^2$$

Integrate on both sides, and use $A(T,T) = 0$

$$A(0;T) = -\int_0^T \left(T-t\right)\theta_t dt + \frac{1}{2}\int_0^T \left(T-t\right)^2\sigma^2 dt \qquad (19.64)$$

which equals Equation 19.9.

19.9.2 Proof of the Expression in Equation 19.13

From Equation 19.64, note that

$$\frac{\partial A(0;T)}{\partial T} = -\int_0^T \theta_t dt + \int_0^T \left(T-t\right)\sigma^2 dt \qquad (19.65)$$

$$\frac{\partial^2 A(0;T)}{\partial T^2} = -\theta_T + \sigma^2 T \qquad (19.66)$$

The forward rate at time 0 for an investment between T and $T+\delta$ is given by

$$f(0,T,T+\delta) = -\frac{log(Z(r_0,0,T+\delta)) - log(Z(r_0,0,T))}{\delta}$$

Taking the limit as $\delta \longrightarrow 0$, we obtain that the instantaneous forward rate is

$$f(0,T) = -\frac{\partial log(Z(r_0,0;T))}{\partial T}$$

In the Ho-Lee case, we have $log(Z(r_0,0;T)) = A(0;T) - T \times r_0$ which implies

$$f(0,T) = -\frac{\partial A(0,T)}{\partial T} + r_0$$

It follows that

$$\frac{\partial f(0,T)}{\partial T} = -\frac{\partial^2 A(0,T)}{\partial T^2}$$

Substitute from Equation 19.66 to obtain

$$\frac{\partial f(0,T)}{\partial T} = \theta_T - \sigma^2 T$$

which yields the result upon rearranging.

19.9.3 Proof of the Hull-White Pricing Formula

The Fundamental Pricing Equation is

$$rZ = \frac{\partial Z}{\partial t} + \frac{\partial Z}{\partial r}\left(\theta_t - \gamma^* r\right) + \frac{1}{2}\frac{\partial^2 Z}{\partial r^2}\sigma^2$$

with boundary condition $Z(r, T; T) = 1$. We need to show that $Z(r, t; T) = e^{A(t;T) - B(t;T)r}$ satisfies the partial differential equation (PDE). Taking the partial derivatives and substituting, we obtain

$$0 = \frac{\partial A(t;T)}{\partial t} - B(t;T)\theta_t + \frac{1}{2}B(t;T)^2 \sigma^2 + \left(-\frac{\partial B(t;T)}{\partial t} - 1 + B(t;T)\gamma^*\right)r$$

Note that $B(t;T) = (1 - e^{-\gamma^*(T-t)}/\gamma^*$ implies the last term in parenthesis is zero. Thus, we have that $A(t;T)$ must satisfy

$$-\frac{\partial A(t;T)}{\partial t} = -B(t;T)\theta_t + \frac{1}{2}B(t;T)^2 \sigma^2$$

Integrating on both sides from 0 to T and using $A(T;T) = 0$ gives

$$A(0;T) = -\int_0^T B(t;T)\theta_t dt + \frac{\sigma^2}{2}\int_0^T B(t;T)^2 dt$$

providing the final result.

19.9.4 Proof of the Expression in Equation 19.28

The steps are identical to the ones used in Section 19.9.2, although more cumbersome. In particular, we have

$$\frac{\partial A(0;T)}{\partial T} = -\int_0^T e^{-\gamma^*(T-t)}\theta_t + \sigma^2 \int_0^T B(t;T)e^{-\gamma^*(T-t)}dt$$

$$\frac{\partial^2 A(0;T)}{\partial T^2} = -\theta_T - \gamma^*\frac{\partial A(0;T)}{\partial T} + \frac{\sigma^2}{2\gamma^*}\left(1 - e^{-2\gamma^*T}\right)$$

Moreover, we can write the instantanous forward rate as

$$f(0,T) = -\frac{\partial A(0;T)}{\partial T} + e^{-\gamma^*T}r_0 \tag{19.67}$$

Taking the first derivative with respect to T, and tedious substitutions, yields

$$\frac{\partial f(0,T)}{\partial T} = \theta_T + \gamma^*\frac{\partial A(0;T)}{\partial T} - \frac{\sigma^2}{2\gamma^*}\left(1 - e^{-2\gamma^*T}\right) - \gamma^* e^{-\gamma^*T}r$$

$$= \theta_T + \gamma^*\left(e^{-\gamma^*T}r_0 - f(0,T)\right) - \frac{\sigma^2}{2\gamma^*}\left(1 - e^{-2\gamma^*T}\right) - \gamma^* e^{-\gamma^*T}r$$

$$= \theta_T - \gamma^* f(0;T) - \frac{\sigma^2}{2\gamma^*}\left(1 - e^{-2\gamma^*T}\right)$$

where the second equality stems from substituting $\partial A(0;T)/\partial T$ from Equation 19.67 and the last from canceling common terms. Solving for θ_T yield Equation 19.28.

19.9.5 Proof of the Expressions in Equations 19.41 and 19.42

There are multiple ways of obtaining these expressions. Here we sketch the derivation from the definition of $A(0, T)$ itself. In fact, from the properties of integrals we have

$$A(t;T) = -\int_t^T B(\tau;T)\theta_\tau d\tau + \frac{\sigma^2}{2}\int_t^T B(\tau;T)^2 d\tau$$

$$= A(0;T) - \left[-\int_0^t B(\tau;T)\,\theta_\tau\,d\tau + \frac{\sigma^2}{2}\int_0^t B(\tau;T)^2\,d\tau \right]$$

Since we can also write $B(\tau;T) = B(\tau;t) + B(t;T)\,e^{-\gamma^*(t-\tau)}$, substituting and taking the integrals on the right-hand side, we obtain

$$
\begin{aligned}
A(t;T) &= A(0;T) - A(0;t) + B(t;T)\int_0^t e^{-\gamma^*(t-\tau)}\theta_\tau\,d\tau \\
&\quad -\frac{\sigma^2}{2}\left(B(t;T)^2\int_0^t e^{-2\gamma^*(t-\tau)}\,d\tau + 2B(t;T)\int_0^t B(\tau;t)\,e^{-\gamma^*(t-\tau)}\,d\tau \right)
\end{aligned}
$$

Finally, because

$$f(0,t) = -\frac{\partial A(0;t)}{\partial t} + e^{-\gamma^* t} r_0 = \int_0^t e^{-\gamma^*(t-\tau)}\theta_\tau\,d\tau - \sigma^2\int_0^t B(\tau;t)\,e^{-\gamma^*(t-\tau)}\,d\tau + e^{-\gamma^* t} r_0$$

we can substitute for $\int_0^t e^{-\gamma^*(t-\tau)}\theta_\tau\,d\tau$ in the above expression, and finally obtain (after some algebra)

$$
\begin{aligned}
A(t;T) &= (A(0;T) + B(0;T)\,r_0) - (A(0;t) + B(0;t)\,r_0) \\
&\quad + B(t;T)\,f(0,t) - \frac{\sigma^2}{4\gamma^*}B(t;T)^2\left(1 - e^{-2\gamma^* t}\right)
\end{aligned}
$$

The first two terms are indeed equal $\log\left(Z(0;T)/Z(0;t)\right)$, which proves the formula in Equation 19.41.

Finally, the Ho-Lee model is obtained in the limit as $\gamma^* \to 0$. It is easy to see that in this case $B(t;T) = (1 - e^{-\gamma^*(T-t)})/\gamma^* \to (T - t)$ and similarly $\left(1 - e^{-2\gamma^* t}\right)/(2\gamma^*) \to t$, we obtain Equation 19.42.

CHAPTER 20

THE MARKET MODEL FOR STANDARD DERIVATIVES AND OPTIONS' VOLATILITY DYNAMICS

In earlier chapters we covered standard derivatives, namely caps, floors, and swaptions, which make up a large fraction of the over-the-counter derivative securities market. In this chapter we review the quoting conventions used by market dealers to trade such securities. These quoting conventions rely on the use of a particular option pricing formula, the Black formula, which was originally designed by Fischer Black to price options on commodity futures. Although historically this formula was initially adopted by traders mainly for its simplicity, and with the understanding that the formula has to be used as a simple way to quote the prices of caps, floors, and swaptions, more recently it has been established that this formula follows from a no arbitrage argument under some assumptions about the dynamics of stochastic variables.

We leave the derivation of this formula (and many others) to Chapter 21. In this chapter, instead, we take a more practical view and cover the market convention to quote caps, floors, and swaptions. For instance, Table 20.1 reports quotes for swaptions, caps and floors on November 1, 2004 obtained from Bloomberg. Besides the swap rates in Column 2, all of the quantities appearing in the table are expressed in volatility units. For instance, a 1-year cap was trading on November 1, 2004 at a 23.5% volatility, while a 2-year cap was trading at the much higher 29.89% volatility. Similarly, a European swaption with 3 months to maturity written on a 1-year swap was trading at 27.115% volatility.

What do these quotes mean? How do we translate volatility units into dollar prices? The conversion from quoted volatilities to prices is made through the Black model, discussed

Table 20.1 Swaptions, Caps and Floors Quotes on November 1, 2004

Maturity	Swap Rates	Swaption Vols			Volatilities	
		3M	6M	1Y	Caps	Floors
1 Y	2.555	27.115	30.234	31.750	23.50	23.50
2 Y	2.932	32.210	32.327	31.258	29.89	29.89
3 Y	3.254	31.011	30.937	29.801	30.55	30.55
4 Y	3.520	29.901	29.622	28.491	29.86	29.86
5 Y	3.751	28.719	28.513	27.404	28.62	28.62
7 Y	4.118	25.337	25.332	24.711	26.48	26.48
10 Y	4.505	21.889	21.833	21.570	23.68	23.68

Source: Bloomberg.

next. In addition, the next section also examines the important distinction between flat volatility and forward volatility.

20.1 THE BLACK FORMULA FOR CAPS AND FLOORS PRICING

Recall that a plain vanilla cap with maturity T, strike rate r_K, and annual frequency of payments n, is a security that pays the stream of cash flows at time $T_1, T_2,...,T_m = T$, where $T_{i+1} = T_i + \Delta$ and $\Delta = 1/n$:

$$CF(T_{i+1}) = N \times \Delta \times \max\left(r_n(T_i; T_{i+1}) - r_K, 0\right) \qquad (20.1)$$

where $r_n(T_i; T_{i+1})$ is the $n-$times compounded reference floating rate, such as the LIBOR. It is important to note the lag between the time the interest rate is fixed, T_i, and the timing of the cash flow, which is one period later $T_{i+1} = T_i + \Delta$. Each cash flow in Equation 20.1 is called a caplet.

Similarly, a floor is a security with cash flows at T_{i+1} given by

$$CF(T_{i+1}) = N \times \Delta \times \max\left(r_K - r_n(T_i; T_{i+1}), 0\right) \qquad (20.2)$$

Each individual cash flow is called a floorlet.

In earlier chapters, we showed that the value of any derivative security, and thus of the caplet, can be computed by no arbitrage using the risk neutral approach as

$$Caplet(0; T_{i+1}) = E^* \left[e^{-\int_0^{T_{i+1}} r_s \, ds} CF(T_{i+1})\right]$$

Under the Ho-Lee model and Hull-White model, Fact 19.11 contains pricing formulas for the value of the caplet. However, as mentioned, the industry standard is to *quote* caps and floors by using the Black formula for option pricing.

Fact 20.1 *The Black formula to value a caplet with maturity T_{i+1} and strike rate r_K is given by:*

$$Caplet(0; T_{i+1}) = N \times \Delta \times Z(0, T_{i+1}) \times [f_n(0, T_i, T_{i+1})\mathcal{N}(d_1) - r_K\mathcal{N}(d_2)] \quad (20.3)$$

where $f_n(0, T_i, T_{i+1})$ is the $n-$times compounded forward rate at time 0 for an investment at T_i and maturity T_{i+1}, and

$$d_1 = \frac{1}{\sigma_f \sqrt{T_i}} \log\left(\frac{f_n(0, T_i, T_{i+1})}{r_K}\right) + \frac{1}{2}\sigma_f \sqrt{T_i} \tag{20.4}$$

$$d_2 = d_1 - \sigma_f \sqrt{T_i} \tag{20.5}$$

In Equations 20.4 and 20.5, σ_f is a volatility parameter that is related to the volatility of forward rates, and it is further discussed in Chapter 21.

Similarly, the Black formula to value a floorlet with maturity T_{i+1} and strike rate r_K is given by

$$Floorlet(0; T_{i+1}) = N \times \Delta \times Z(0, T_{i+1}) \times [r_K \mathcal{N}(-d_2) - f_n(0, T_i, T_{i+1})\mathcal{N}(-d_1)] \tag{20.6}$$

Equation 20.3 provides the formula for a caplet, that is, the present value of one of the many cash flows of the cap. The value of the cap itself, then, is given by the sum of its caplets. That is, let T_1, T_2, ..., $T_n = T$ be the cash flow times of the cap, with $T_{i+1} = T_i + \Delta$, then

$$Cap(0; T) = \sum_{i=1}^{n} Caplets(0; T_i) \tag{20.7}$$

The next example illustrates how to convert the *quoted* volatilities for caps, such as those in Table 20.1, into dollar prices.

■ **EXAMPLE 20.1**

Let today be November 1, 2004. Consider a 1-year quarterly cap with strike rate $r_K = 2.555\%$ and let the volatility be $\sigma_f = 23.5\%$ (see Table 20.1). To compute the price of the cap, we need to compute the price of the three caplets that make up the cap, that is, those that expire at $T_2 = 0.5$, $T_3 = 0.75$, and $T_4 = 1$. Note that we do not need to price the first caplet (expiring at $T_1 = 0.25$), as the cash flow would depend on the current interest rate $r_n(0)$ and its payment can be subtracted from the cost of the cap. In other words, payments (if any) will start at $T = 0.5$. To apply the formula in Equation 20.3 for the three maturities, we need to know the forward rates $f_n(0, T_{i-1}, T_i)$, for $i = 1, \ldots, 4$. We can extract those from the LIBOR discount factors. Let the LIBOR discount factors be as in the second column of Table 20.2. We then obtain the quarterly compounded forward rates as follows.

Define the forward discount factor:

$$F(0, T_{i-1}, T_i) = \frac{Z(0, T_i)}{Z(0, T_{i-1})}$$

and then compute:[1]

$$f_4(0, T_{i-1}, T_i) = 4 \times \left(\frac{1}{F(0, T_{i-1}, T_i)} - 1\right)$$

---

[1]Recall from Equation (5.3) in Chapter 5 that $f_n(0, T_{i-1}, T_i) = n\left(\frac{1}{(F(0, T_{i-1}, T_i))^{n \times (T_i - T_{i-1})}} - 1\right)$.
Because $T_i - T_{i-1} = \Delta = 1/n$, we obtain the formula for $f_n(0, T_{i-1}, T_i)$.

Table 20.2 One Year Cap on November 1, 2004

T_i	$Z(0;T_i)(\times100)$	$f(0,T_{i-1};T_i)$	$\sigma_f \times \sqrt{T_{i-1}}$	d_1	d_2	$Caplet(T_i)(\times100)$
0.25	99.4580	-				
0.50	98.8510	2.4562	0.1175	-0.2770	-0.3945	0.0184
0.75	98.1899	2.6932	0.1662	0.4000	0.2338	0.0617
1.00	97.4834	2.8987	0.2035	0.7218	0.5183	0.1057

Data Source: Bloomberg.

The third column of Table 20.2 contains the forward rates. We now have all the inputs to apply the formula in Equation 20.3 three times, to compute the value of the cap. In particular, Column 4 reports the quantity $\sigma_f \times \sqrt{T_{i-1}}$, where recall that $\sigma_f = 23.5\%$. Note, in particular, that when we price the caplet with maturity T_i we need to compute the volatility at time $T_{i-1} = T_i - \Delta$. Indeed, the formulas in Equations 20.3, 20.4 and 20.5 show that the price of a caplet expiring at T_{i+1} depends on volatilities $\sigma_f \sqrt{T_i}$. The next two columns report d_1 and d_2 from Equations 20.4 and 20.5. The last column reports the value of each caplet, as from Equation 20.3. The value of the cap is then

$$Cap(1Y) = \$0.0184 + \$0.0617 + \$0.1057 = \$0.1859$$

20.1.1 Flat and Forward Volatilities

In Example 20.1 we assume that the volatility $\sigma_f = 23.5\%$ is given to us and it applies to all of the caplets making up the cap. Indeed, this is the market convention to quote caps and floors. For instance, Table 20.1 contains quotes on November 1, 2004 for at-the-money instruments, meaning that the strike rate r_K for each cap equals the corresponding swap rate. Given each volatility quote, a trader would translate the volatility into a price by using the Black formula, as we did in Example 20.1. The quoted volatility is called flat volatility, which we may define as follows:

Definition 20.1 *The* **flat volatility** *of a cap with maturity T is the quoted volatility $\sigma_f(T)$ that must be inserted in the Black formula for* each *and* every *caplet that makes up the cap, in order to obtain a dollar price for the cap.*

It is important to note that *the same* volatility is used for each caplet in the cap, even if different caplets have different maturities.

The only missing information then in order to obtain the dollar value of a cap from the flat volatility is really the proper discounts to use, but we can retrieve these from the LIBOR yield curve as well. For instance, in Example 20.1 We exploited the fact that the 3-month LIBOR was $r_4(0) = 2.18\%$, which yields the first discount $Z(0, 0.25) = 1/(1 + r_4(0) \times \Delta) = 0.994580$. The other discounts in Table 20.2 are obtained through interpolation of the swap rates and the LIBOR rate, and then bootstrapped as discussed in Chapter 5.[2]

Table 20.3 translates the quotes in Table 20.1 into dollar prices for every maturity at quarterly intervals. As mentioned, the swap rates are interpolated, and then the discount factors are obtained through a bootstrap procedure. The volatility for maturities shorter than one year is extrapolated from the subsequent volatilities. Figure 20.1 plots the data in Table 20.1 as well as the interpolated volatility in Table 20.3, depicted as the dotted line. It is interesting to note the hump shape in the flat volatility: The implied volatility of interest rates is higher at the one- or two-year horizon, and lower for short-term and long-term caps.

The discussion so far has focused on the quoted volatility, or flat volatility. However, now an issue arises: Consider Table 20.3 and compare the cap maturing on $T = 0.5$ and on $T = 0.75$. The first cap has only one caplet, so that the volatility $\sigma_f(0.5) = 21.1564\%$ has to be applied only to one term. In contrast, the cap with maturity $T = 0.75$ has two caplets, one also maturing on $T = 0.5$ and one more maturing on $T = 0.75$. Note that for *both* caplets the volatility to insert in the Black formula is $\sigma_f(0.75) = 22.0662\%$. This implies that (almost) the same caplet,[3] the one with maturity $T = 0.5$, has a volatility of 21.1564% when it is part of the 6-month cap, but a higher volatility (22.0662%) when it is part of a 9-month cap. Similarly, by looking down Column 5 in Table 20.3, the same 6-month caplet would have a volatility of 23.5% when it is part of the 1-year cap, a volatility of 25.2286% when it is part of the 1.25-year cap, and so on. A similar argument of course holds for the 9-months caplet, the 1-year caplet and so forth.

The fact that the same caplet has different volatilities depending on which cap it is part of may suggest at first that there is a large inconsistency in the traders' quotes of caps, but this is in fact not correct. The trick is to realize that there are two meanings to volatility: One is the quoted volatility, which is a convention that traders in the market place adopt to exchange caps and floors, and a second one is the no arbitrage volatility, which instead would call for the same caplet to have the same volatility independent of which cap it is part of. The latter volatility is called forward volatility, which is defined as follows:

Definition 20.2 *The* **forward volatility** *of a caplet with maturity T and strike rate r_K is the volatility $\sigma_f^{Fwd}(T)$ that characterizes that particular caplet, independent of which cap the caplet belongs to.*

A comparison of Definition 20.2 of forward volatility with Definition 20.1 of flat volatility shows that the forward volatility is applied to caplets while the flat volatility is applied to caps. Table 20.4 diagrams the issue. Each row in the table corresponds to a cap with an increasingly longer maturity, ranging from 0.5 to 10 years, all of them with the same strike rate r_K. The flat volatility $\sigma_f(T)$ pertains to each row, in the sense that the same (flat) volatility has to be entered in each caplet across rows, as shown in Example 20.1. The forward volatility instead applies to each column, as each caplet for each row is exactly the same: It has the same maturity and (we are assuming now) the same strike rate. In other

---

[2]Traders have more information available than the 3-month LIBOR and the swap rates in Table 20.1. In particular, the discount curve is often obtained using three sources of information: LIBOR rates, Eurodollar futures (maturity up to 3 years) and swap rates. Traders prefer Eurodollar futures as they are more liquid than swap contracts, and so better represent the market discount rates. See the discussion in Section 6.5 in Chapter 6 for details.

[3]The 6-month caplet changes for two reason as we go down the columns, the volatility used and the strike price used. But the point remains, as we discuss below.

words, by the principle of no arbitrage the caplets across columns cannot have different values from each other.

The logic then runs as follows: For given forward volatility $\sigma_f^{Fwd}(T)$ for every maturity, we can compute the value of each caplet in Table 20.4, and thus the dollar value of each cap for each maturity. For *quoting* purposes, however, traders like to re-express the dollar value of the cap in terms of a single implied volatility. To do so, they find the constant volatility $\sigma_f(T)$ that can be applied to all of the caplets in each row, and use that to quote and trade caps. The flat volatility stems then from simply a *quoting* convention, and it is not a reflection of no arbitrage or an inefficiency. In a sense, the flat volatility of a cap with maturity T is an average of forward volatilities for the caplets with maturities up to T.

To strike a similarity with perhaps a more familiar security, the flat volatility is the cap-market equivalent of the yield to maturity concept in the bond market (see Section 2.4.3 in Chapter 2). As discussed in Chapter 2, given a discount curve $Z(0,T) = \left(\frac{1}{1+r_2(0,T)/2}\right)^{2\times T}$ we can compute the dollar price of a coupon bond $P_c(0,T^*)$. Given this price, we can compute the yield to maturity of that bond as the constant rate Y such that the dollar price of the bond equals the present value of future coupons when we use $\left(\frac{1}{1+Y/2}\right)^{2\times T}$ as discount factors. The yield to maturity can then be considered an average of the interest rates $r_2(0,T)$ for $T < T^*$, which is bond specific. Traders prefer to trade coupon bonds in terms of yield to maturity rather than dollar prices, although there is one-to-one relation. This allows them to better spot any misalignment of one bond versus another, as the unit (percent yield) is the same across bonds, even if the bonds may differ by maturity.

Similarly, in the cap market, traders prefer to trade in terms of (flat) volatilities instead of the dollar price of caps, because such volatilities have the same unit (annual standard deviation) independent of the number of caplets. For instance, consider the 1-year cap and a 10-year cap in Table 20.1. Notice that their quoted volatility is very similar, reflecting perhaps the fact that the current expected volatility in the short term is equal to about the average volatility for the longer term. This similar level of volatilities does not mean that these two caps have the same price, as one pays many more cash flows that the other. In fact, the 10-year cap price is $cap(10Y) = \$16.95$, against only $cap(1Y) = \$0.1879$ for the 1-year cap. If there is a sudden movement in volatility or expected volatility, however, it is much simpler to adjust the volatility of both short- and long-term caps, rather than their prices, as expected volatility is the first order element in the pricing of options.

The fact is that the expected volatility of interest rates *does* fluctuate quite substantially over time. Figure 20.2 shows the quoted (flat) volatility quotes of 1-year, 3-year and 10-year caps from February 1997 to July 2008. Consider the volatility quotes of 1-year caps, for instance: This volatility ranged from about 6% in 1999 and 2007, to over 60% in 2002 and in 2008. It is much easier for traders to gauge quickly the relative prices of caps with different maturities or strike prices by looking at their volatilities rather than their actual dollar prices, as the latter reflect other information about the options such as their maturities and their strike prices.

20.1.2   Extracting Forward Volatilities from Flat Volatilities

Because traders trade in terms of flat volatilities, the implicit forward volatilities are not typically readily available. In the same way that we do not directly observe the discount

Table 20.3 Cap Prices on November 1, 2004

Maturity	Swap Rate (%)	Cont. Comp. Yield (%)	Discount (×100)	Interp. Cap Vol (%)	Cap Prices (×100)	Fwd Vol (%)
0.25	2.180	2.174	99.4580	–	–	–
0.50	2.318	2.311	98.8510	21.156	0.046	21.156
0.75	2.442	2.436	98.1899	22.066	0.106	22.810
1.00	2.555	2.549	97.4834	23.500	0.186	25.540
1.25	2.659	2.653	96.7385	25.229	0.289	28.560
1.50	2.755	2.749	95.9598	27.023	0.416	31.360
1.75	2.845	2.841	95.1503	28.653	0.566	33.420
2.00	2.932	2.929	94.3109	29.890	0.736	34.040
2.25	3.017	3.015	93.4417	30.571	0.920	32.910
2.50	3.099	3.099	92.5456	30.796	1.113	31.210
2.75	3.178	3.180	91.6268	30.734	1.313	29.660
3.00	3.254	3.258	90.6899	30.550	1.519	28.760
3.25	3.325	3.331	89.7397	30.380	1.735	28.690
3.50	3.393	3.401	88.7778	30.227	1.960	28.670
3.75	3.458	3.468	87.8050	30.063	2.192	28.390
4.00	3.520	3.533	86.8212	29.860	2.429	27.770
4.25	3.581	3.596	85.8263	29.597	2.669	26.820
4.50	3.639	3.658	84.8218	29.288	2.912	25.890
4.75	3.696	3.718	83.8102	28.955	3.156	25.120
5.00	3.751	3.776	82.7938	28.620	3.403	24.570
5.25	3.804	3.832	81.7747	28.301	3.652	24.270
5.50	3.854	3.887	80.7545	28.000	3.904	24.030
5.75	3.903	3.939	79.7343	27.716	4.159	23.800
6.00	3.949	3.989	78.7153	27.447	4.414	23.570
6.25	3.994	4.037	77.6985	27.190	4.671	23.330
6.50	4.037	4.084	76.6846	26.945	4.929	23.100
6.75	4.078	4.129	75.6744	26.709	5.188	22.850
7.00	4.118	4.173	74.6687	26.480	5.446	22.580
7.25	4.156	4.215	73.6679	26.257	5.704	22.290
7.50	4.193	4.256	72.6725	26.039	5.961	21.980
7.75	4.229	4.296	71.6829	25.822	6.216	21.630
8.00	4.263	4.334	70.6994	25.606	6.469	21.250
8.25	4.296	4.372	69.7222	25.389	6.720	20.820
8.50	4.329	4.408	68.7513	25.168	6.968	20.340
8.75	4.360	4.443	67.7869	24.943	7.213	19.810
9.00	4.390	4.478	66.8288	24.711	7.453	19.200
9.25	4.420	4.512	65.8769	24.470	7.688	18.530
9.50	4.449	4.546	64.9311	24.219	7.917	17.780
9.75	4.477	4.579	63.9911	23.957	8.140	16.940
10.00	4.505	4.611	63.0566	23.680	8.356	16.000

Data Source: Bloomberg.

Figure 20.1 The Flat and Forward Volatility on November 1st, 2004

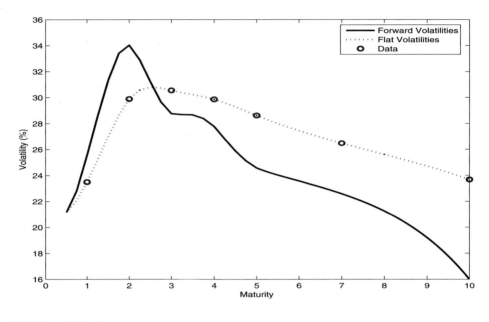

Data Source: Bloomberg.

Figure 20.2 Cap Volatility Over Time

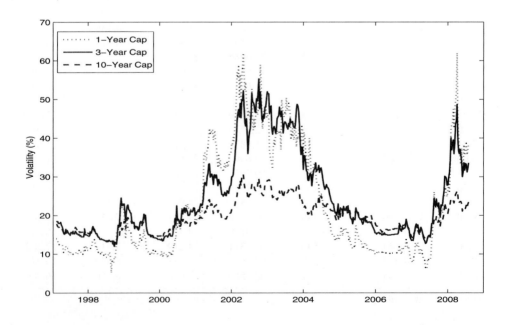

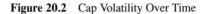

Data Source: Bloomberg.

Table 20.4 The Flat and Forward Volatility of Caps

Flat Volatility		Forward Volatility				
		$\sigma_f^{Fwd}(0.50)$ ⇓	$\sigma_f^{Fwd}(0.75)$ ⇓	$\sigma_f^{Fwd}(1.00)$ ⇓	$\cdots$ $\cdots$	$\sigma_f^{Fwd}(10.0)$ ⇓
$\sigma_f(0.50) \Longrightarrow$	Cap(0.50) =	caplet(0.50)	-	-	$\cdots$	-
$\sigma_f(0.75) \Longrightarrow$	Cap(0.75) =	caplet(0.50) +	caplet(0.75)	-	$\cdots$	-
$\sigma_f(1.00) \Longrightarrow$	Cap(1.00) =	caplet(0.50) +	caplet(0.75) +	caplet(1.00)	-	-
$\vdots$	$\vdots$	$\vdots$	$\vdots$	$\vdots$	$\ddots$	-
$\sigma_f(10.0) \Longrightarrow$	Cap(10.0) =	caplet(0.50) +	caplet(0.75) +	caplet(1.00) +	$\cdots$	caplet(10.0)

curve $Z(0,T)$ that is implicit in coupon bonds or in swaps, but we need to extract it from bond quotes or swap rate quotes (see Chapters 2 and 5), so for caps and floors we need to extract the forward volatilities from (quoted) flat volatilities. The forward volatilities are going to be the no arbitrage ingredients for the pricing of other more complex securities.

How do we extract the forward volatilities from flat volatilities?

Exactly as we did for the discount factors $Z(0,T)$, we can employ a bootstrap methodology to obtain the sequence of forward volatilities. In particular, we exploit the fact that for every T_i, $i = 1, ..., n$ (where $T_1 = 0.5$) the following holds:

$$Cap(T_i) = \sum_{j=1}^{i} Caplet\left(T_j, r_{K,i}, \sigma_f(T_i)\right) \quad \text{(Using Flat Volatility)} \quad (20.8)$$

$$= \sum_{j=1}^{i} Caplet\left(T_j, r_{K,i}, \sigma_f^{Fwd}(T_j)\right) \quad \text{(Using Forward Volatility)} \quad (20.9)$$

where we now emphasize the inputs in the caplets, such as maturity T_j, strike rate $r_{K,i}$ and volatility. Again, for quoting purposes, we use the flat volatility $\sigma_f(T_i)$, which is the *same* across the indices j of the caplets, while from no arbitrage, we use the forward volatility $\sigma_f^{Fwd}(T_j)$, which is indeed different across the caplets. We now illustrate the methodology in more detail:

Step 1 Use the quoted flat volatilities to obtain cap prices for all maturities from Equation 20.8, as it was done in Table 20.3

Step 2 The shortest ($T_1 = 0.5$) cap is made up of only one caplet, which implies

$$\sigma_f^{Fwd}(0.5) = \sigma_f(0.5) \quad (20.10)$$

Step 3 For every $i = 2, \ldots, n$ use the following three-step procedure:

(a) Use the previously extracted forward volatilities $\sigma_f^{Fwd}(T_j)$ for $j = 1, \ldots, i-1$ to compute the caplets up to T_j, $Caplet\left(T_j, r_{K,i}, \sigma_f^{Fwd}(T_j)\right)$

(b) Obtain the dollar value of the remaining caplet T_i as the difference between the cap price for T_i (obtained in Step 1) and the sum of caplets up to T_{i-1}

$$\text{Dollar value of } T_i \text{ caplet} = Cap(T_i) - \sum_{j=1}^{i-1} Caplet\left(T_j, r_{K,i}, \sigma_f^{Fwd}(T_j)\right)$$

(c) Find the (forward) volatility $\sigma_f^{Fwd}(T_i)$ such that

$$Caplet\left(T_i, r_{K,i}, \sigma_f^{Fwd}(T_i)\right) = \text{Dollar value of } T_i \text{ caplet}$$

In general, then, from Equation 20.9 the value of the last caplet T_i of the cap with maturity T_i is given by the formula

$$Caplet\left(T_i, r_{K,i}, \sigma_f^{Fwd}(T_i)\right) = Cap(T_i) - \sum_{j=1}^{i-1} Caplet\left(T_j, r_{K,i}, \sigma_f^{Fwd}(T_j)\right) \quad (20.11)$$

The forward volatility in step c is the volatility $\sigma_f^{Fwd}(T_i)$ that has to be inserted into the Black formula to make Equation 20.11 true.

It is worth providing a detailed example, to clarify the procedure.

■ **EXAMPLE 20.2**

Consider the data in Table 20.3. These are obtained from the quotes on November 1, 2004, after an interpolation of the LIBOR yield curve at the quarterly horizon and of the quoted volatility [the original quotes are in Table 20.1, and the 3-month LIBOR was $r_4(0; 0.25) = 2.1800\%$]. As mentioned, the volatility for maturity less than one year was extrapolated. Because these quotes are for at-the-money instruments, the strike rate used for each cap is given by the swap rate in the second column. We now proceed to extract the forward volatility.

1. The first cap ($T_1 = 0.5$) has only one caplet, which implies that

$$\sigma_f^{Fwd}(T_1) = \sigma_f(T_1) = 21.1564\%$$

2. The second cap ($T_2 = 0.75$) has a dollar price of $Cap(T_2) = \$0.1059$, as can be seen from the last column in Table 20.3. We now use the three-step procedure in Step 3 above:

   (a) Compute the T_1 caplet using the forward volatility $\sigma_f^{Fwd}(T_1) = 21.1564\%$ just computed. Note that the value of this caplet is not equal to the one computed in the previous step, because the strike rate has changed from $r_{K,1} = 2.3177\%$ to the current one $r_{K,2} = 2.4420\%$. Using the Black formula, we obtain

   $$Caplet(T_1, r_{K,2}, \sigma_f^{Fwd}(T_1)) = \$0.0273$$

   (b) The dollar value of the T_2 caplet is then

   $$\begin{aligned} \text{Dollar value of } T_2 \text{ caplet} &= Cap(T_2) - Caplet\left(T_1, r_{K,2}, \sigma_f^{Fwd}(T_1)\right) \\ &= \$0.1059 - \$0.0273 = \$0.0786 \end{aligned}$$

   (c) Use the Black formula again to find the (forward) volatility $\sigma_f^{Fwd}(T_2)$ such that

   $$Caplet\left(T_2, r_{K,2}, \sigma_f^{Fwd}(T_2)\right) = \$0.0786 \implies \sigma_f^{Fwd}(T_2) = 22.81\%$$

3. And so on. For instance, the T_3 forward volatility is obtained as follows

(a) Compute the T_1 and T_2 caplet using the forward volatilities $\sigma_f^{Fwd}(T_1) = 21.1564\%$ and $\sigma_f^{Fwd}(T_2) = 22.81\%$ just computed. Using the Black formula with the new strike rate $r_{K,3} = 2.4420\%$, we obtain

$$Caplet(T_1, r_{K,3}, \sigma_f^{Fwd}(T_1)) = \$0.0157$$
$$Caplet(T_2, r_{K,3}, \sigma_f^{Fwd}(T_2)) = \$0.0605$$

(b) The dollar value of the T_3 caplet is then

$$\text{Dollar value of } T_3 \text{ caplet} = Cap(T_3) - \sum_{j=1}^{2} Caplet\left(T_j, r_{K,3}, \sigma_f^{Fwd}(T_j)\right)$$
$$= \$0.1859 - (\$0.0157 + \$0.0605) = \$0.1096$$

(c) Use the Black formula again to find the (forward) volatility $\sigma_f^{Fwd}(T_3)$ such that

$$Caplet\left(T_3, r_{K,3}, \sigma_f^{Fwd}(T_3)\right) = \$0.1096 \implies \sigma_f^{Fwd}(T_3) = 25.54\%$$

The solid line in Figure 20.1 plots the forward volatility on November 1, 2004 obtained from the above procedure. The numerical values are contained in the last column of Table 20.3. We can see that the forward volatility increases more sharply than the flat volatility (the dotted line) as the latter is increasing, and then it also declines more sharply. Because the flat volatility can be considered a (nonlinear) average of forward volatilities, this behavior is not surprising.

20.1.3   The Behavior of the Implied Forward Volatility

The hump shape of the forward volatility in Figure 20.1 is relatively common in the data. Indeed, Figure 20.3 plots the average forward volatility in the sample 1997 - 2008. However, the shape of the forward volatility curve *does* change over time, exactly as the term structure of interest rates changes. Figure 20.4 plots some of the other shapes that the forward volatility curve took in the past. In Panel A we observe that on October 22, 2003, for instance, the forward volatility curve was mainly declining, with a small hump around the usual maturity $T = 2$. In contrast, on February 2, 2006, the forward volatility curve was mainly increasing, as it was one year later, on February 2, 2007. Finally, on January 25, 2008, the forward volatility curve was strongly decreasing.

The level of the volatility varies dramatically over time: From Figure 20.4, for instance, in Panel A (October 22, 2003) and Panel D (January 25, 2008) the forward volatility was quite high, over 40% at the short end, while in Panel B (February 2, 2006) and Panel C (February 2, 2007), the volatility was much lower, below 10% at the short end, and never above 20%. Panel A of Figure 20.5 plots the average forward volatility across maturities from 1997 to 2008. The variation in average forward volatility is in fact quite large as it ranges from just above 10% to over 35%.

Panel B reports the slope of the forward volatility curve, simply defined here as the difference between the 10-year and 1-year forward volatility. As can be seen, the difference between the long and the short end of the forward curve is not always negative, as we could surmise from the average forward volatility curve in Figure 20.3. Instead, it is often positive,

Figure 20.3   The Average Forward Volatility 1997 - 2008

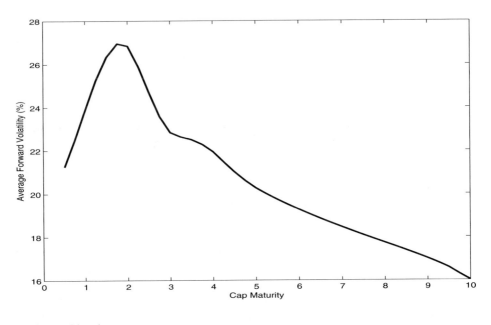

Data Source: Bloomberg.

albeit not very much so. Finally, Panel C plots the curvature of the forward volatility curve, defined as

$$\text{Curvature} = 2 \times \sigma_f^{Fwd}(2) - \sigma_f^{Fwd}(1) - \sigma_f^{Fwd}(10)$$

When the volatility of the 2-year caplet is higher than the short and the long end, we say that the forward volatility curve has a strong curvature. Panel C of Figure 20.5 shows that the curvature shows a good deal of variation as well, and that it is always very low.

What determines the variation of the forward volatility and the shape of the forward volatility curve? Recall that the forward volatility embedded in caps reflects an insurance premium, namely, the amount of money that an investor is willing to pay to be covered against a run up in interest rates. Such insurance is more valuable the higher the uncertainty about future interest rates: If for instance there is a large uncertainty about the action of the Federal Reserve at an upcoming Federal Open Market Committee meeting, we could expect that the forward volatility of short-term options would be higher than in other times. The average hump in the term structure of volatility may be due to uncertainty about medium-term interest rates generated by uncertainty about business cycle variation or inflation. The average low forward volatility at the long end, instead, is due to the mean reversion of interest rates: Interest rates are unlikely to be very high or very low for very long periods of time, and thus there is relatively less uncertainty about the average interest rates over a ten-year span rather than over a two-year span.

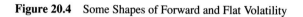

Figure 20.4   Some Shapes of Forward and Flat Volatility

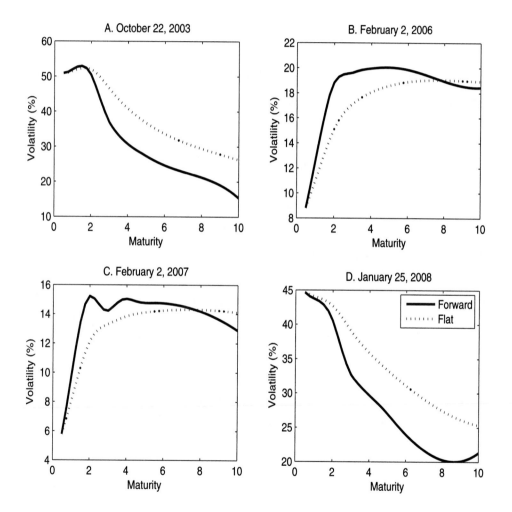

Data Source: Bloomberg.

Figure 20.5 Level, Slope and Curvature of Forward Volatility

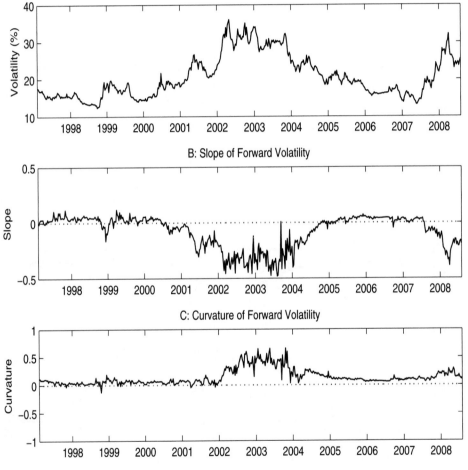

Data Source: Bloomberg.

20.1.4 Forward Volatilities and the Black, Derman, and Toy Model

There is a relation between the forward volatilities obtained from the Black model and the forward volatility from the Black, Derman, and Toy (BDT) model. In particular, recall from Chapter 11 that the BDT model indeed implies that the future spot rates are (approximately) log-normally distributed. It turns out that we can use the forward volatility obtained according to the bootstrap procedure in Section 20.1.2 directly as input in the BDT tree. We can see this, as an example, by comparing the forward volatility in Figure 20.1 with the implied forward volatility that was computed from the BDT tree in Figure 11.2 in Chapter 11. The similarity of the curves is striking, and in fact, they should be exactly identical. We see instead a little difference in levels, which is due to the fact that in Chapter 11 we use a relatively coarse time grid for cap prices (the time-step there is one quarter, $dt = 0.25$). As we decrease the time step dt in the BDT tree, the implied volatility from the tree and from the Black model converge. Indeed, a standard practice to obtain a BDT tree is to use the Black formula to compute $\sigma_f^{Fwd}(T)$ for every maturity, and then, *given* the forward volatility for every maturity, we can fit the BDT tree to match the current term structure of interest rates. This second methodology is much faster than the one illustrated in Chapter 11, especially for the case in which the tree time-step dt is small.

20.2 THE BLACK FORMULA FOR SWAPTION PRICING

Swaptions are options to enter into a swap, as either fixed rate payers (payer swaption) or fixed rate receiver (receiver swaption). We have already discussed some features of these options in Chapter 11 and Chapter 19 in the context of special interest rate models, such as the Ho-Lee and Hull-White model. In this section we review the use of the Black formula to *quote* swaptions in terms of volatility (see e.g. quotes in Table 20.1). Chapter 21 obtains the Black formula from a no arbitrage argument under special assumptions about the behavior of interest rates.

To introduce the Black model to quote swaptions, consider first the payoff of a receiver swaption: As discussed in Section 19.4.4 in Chapter 19, the payoff of a receiver swaption with strike swap rate r_K can be expressed as a call option on a coupon bond, with coupon rate r_K. That is,

$$\text{Payoff receiver swaption} \quad = \quad \max\left(P_c(T_O;T_S) - N, 0\right) \qquad (20.12)$$

where N is the notional, T_O is the maturity of the swaption, and T_S is the maturity of the underlying swap. In Equation 20.12 we have $P_c(T_O;T_S)$ is the value of a coupon bond with coupon rate r_K:

$$P_c(T_O;T_S) = N \times r_K \times \Delta \times \sum_{i=1}^{n} Z(T_O;T_i) + N \times Z(T_0;T_n) \qquad (20.13)$$

where T_i are the swap fixing dates, and $T_n = T_S$. It is convenient to rewrite this payoff in terms of the future swap rate at time T_O (swaption maturity). We denote this future swap rate by $c(T_O;T_S)$, where T_S is the maturity date of the swap underlying the option. By definition, the swap rate at time T_O for a swap with maturity T_S is that rate that makes the value of the swap equal to zero. That is, $c(T_O;T_S)$ satisfies

$$N = N \times c(T_O;T_S) \times \Delta \times \sum_{i=1}^{n} Z(T_O;T_i) + N \times Z(T_0;T_n) \qquad (20.14)$$

Substitute $P_c(T_O; T_S)$ from Equation 20.13 and N from Equation 20.14 into the swaption payoff (Equation 20.12) and rearrange, to obtain the alternative, but *equivalent*, expression for the receiver swaption payoff:

$$\text{Payoff receiver swaption} \quad = \quad N \times \Delta \times \left[\sum_{i=1}^{n} Z(T_O; T_i) \right] \times \max\left(r_K - c(T_O; T_S), 0\right)$$

(20.15)

This payoff structure has a simple interpretation: Suppose that the swap rate at maturity of the receiver swaption $c(T_O; T_S)$ is below r_K. Then, the holder of the swaption can exercise the option, and receive the higher (strike) rate r_K instead of the market swap rate $c(T_O; T_S)$. At every payment date of the swap underlying the option, the option holder (who exercised the option at T_O) gains the constant spread $r_K - c(T_O; T_S)$. Thus, the total payoff from exercising the swaption is given by the present value of these gains, each implicitly paid at a different maturity T_i. The next example illustrates the logic of this payoff structure.

■ EXAMPLE 20.3

Today is November 1, 2004, and the Treasurer of a large corporation forecasts that in one year the corporation will need to enter into a quarterly fixed-for-floating 2-year swap in which it will receive fixed coupons and pay floating coupons. The Treasurer is worried that the 2-year swap rate will decline in the next year from its current value of 2.93% (see Table 20.1). To hedge against the possible decline in the 2-year swap rate, she considers purchasing a receiver swaption defined on a 2-year swap, with strike rate $r_K = 2.931\%$ and maturity $T_O = 1$.

What is the payoff from the swaption? If at maturity $T_O = 1$ the 2-year swap rate is above the strike rate $r_K = 2.931\%$, for instance $c(T_O, T_S) = 4\%$ where $T_S = T_O + 2 = 3$, then the corporation is better off entering into a 2-year swap at the current market rate $c(T_O, T_S) = 4\%$. In fact, by letting the option expire worthless, the corporation will receive the fixed rate 4% per year in exchange of the 3-month LIBOR. If at maturity $T_O = 1$ the 2-year swap rate is below the strike rate $r_K = 2.931\%$, for instance $c(T_O, T_S) = 1.58\%$, then the Treasurer can exercise the option and have the corporation receive the strike rate $r_K = 2.931\%$ every quarter for the next two years in exchange of the 3-month LIBOR.[4] The corporation then gains the difference between the strike rate r_K and the current market rate $c(T_O, T_S)$ every quarter from $T_O + 0.25$ until the maturity of the underlying swap $T_S = T_O + 2$.

Figure 20.6 illustrates the payoff for this swaption under an hypothetical path of the 2-year swap rate $c(t, t + \tau)$, where $\tau = 2$ is the tenor of the underlying swap. In the figure, at maturity of the swaption, $T_O = 1$, the 2-year swap rate is $c(T_O, T_S) = 1.58\%$. By exercising the receiver swaption, then, the Treasurer would receive $r_K = 3\%$ up to the maturity of the swap, instead of the market swap rate $c(T_O, T_S) = 1.58\%$. Therefore, its gain *per period* is $N \times \Delta \times (r_K - c(T_O, T_S)) = 100 \times 0.25 \times 0.0142 = .35$ for $N = 100$.

---

[4] As discussed in Section 5.4.6 in Chapter 5, in a plain vanilla swap, the floating rate payer pays at a quarterly frequency while the fixed rate payer pays at a semi-annual frequency. For simplicity, we assume that both parties pay at a quarterly frequency.

Figure 20.6   The Payoff of a Receiver Swaption

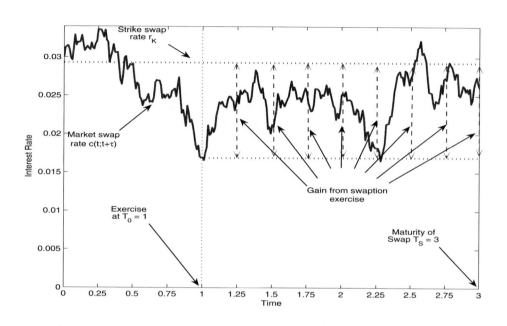

In a similar fashion, we obtain that the payoff of a payer swaption can be written as:

$$\text{Payoff payer swaption} \quad = \quad N \times \Delta \times \left[\sum_{i=1}^{n} Z(T_O, T_i)\right] \times \max\left(c(T_O, T_S) - r_K, 0\right) \tag{20.16}$$

Fact 20.2 *The Black formula to value a* **European receiver swaption** *with strike rate r_K and maturity T_O on a swap with maturity T_S is given by*

$$V(0, T_O; T_S) = N \times \Delta \times \left[\sum_{i=1}^{n} Z(0; T_i)\right] \times \left[r_K \mathcal{N}(-d_2) - f_n^s(0, T_O, T_S)\mathcal{N}(-d_1)\right] \tag{20.17}$$

where $f_n^s(0, T_O, T_S)$ is the $n-$ times compounded forward swap rate at time 0 to enter at T_O into a swap with maturity T_S (see Section 5.4.5, Chapter 5),

$$d_1 = \frac{1}{\sigma_f^s \sqrt{T_O}} \ln\left(\frac{f_n^s(0, T_O; T_S)}{r_K}\right) + \frac{1}{2}\sigma_f^s \sqrt{T_O}; \quad d_2 = d_1 - \sigma_f^s(T_O; T_S)\sqrt{T_O} \tag{20.18}$$

In Equation 20.18, σ_f^s is a volatility parameter that is related to the volatility of forward rates, and it is further discussed in Chapter 21.

Similarly, the Black formula to value a **European payer swaption** *with maturity T_O and strike swap rate r_K on a swap with maturity T_S, is given by*

$$V(0, T_O; T_S) = N \times \Delta \times \left[\sum_{i=1}^{n} Z(0; T_i)\right] \times \left[f_n^s(0, T_O, T_S)\mathcal{N}(d_1) - r_K \mathcal{N}(d_2)\right] \tag{20.19}$$

The next example offers an illustration of the Black swaption pricing formula.

■ **EXAMPLE 20.4**

Let today be November 1, 2004. The LIBOR zero coupon curve, interpolated at quarterly frequency, is contained in Table 20.3. Consider a 1-year receiver swaption defined on a 5-year swap, thus $T_O = 1$ and $T_S = 6$. Let the swaption strike rate $r_K = 3.751\%$, and the volatility $\sigma_f^s = 27.404\%$. If exercised, the swap underlying the swaption will generate cash flows at quarterly intervals starting at $T_1 = 1.25$. The discounts at these times are given in Column 2 in Table 20.5. It follows that $\Delta \times \sum_{i=1}^{n} Z(0, T_i) = 4.4046$. To apply the Black formula in Equation 20.17 to compute the value of the receiver swaption, we must compute the forward swap rate $f_4^s(0, T_O, T_S)$. First, the forward discount factor for each maturity T_i is given by the formula $F(0, T_O, T_i) = Z(0, T_i)/Z(0, T_O)$, and is reported in Column 5 of Table 20.5. The forward swap rate is then given by Equation 5.51 in Chapter 5 and it yields $f_4^s(0, T_O, T_S) = 4.26\%$. Inserting this quantity into d_1 and d_2 in Equation 20.18, we obtain $d_1 = 0.6023$ and $d_2 = 0.3282$. The Black formula in Equation 20.17 for $N = 100$ yields

$$V(0, 1; 6) = \$1.0026$$

As for caps and floors, swaption dealers trade swaptions in terms of implied volatilities, that is, the volatility σ_f^s to insert in the Black formula to obtain the dollar value of the swaption. For instance, quotes on November 1, 2004, are given Table 20.1. Visually, they are shown in Figure 20.7. As for caps and floors, we note a hump in the implied volatility of the swaption for given option's maturity. While the swaption's implied volatility for short-term swaps is low, it increases for longer-term swaps, and then it declines again, resembling the forward volatility obtained for caps.

20.3   SUMMARY

In this chapter we covered the following topics:

1. The Black formula for the valuation of caps, floors, and swaptions: The Black formula is the option pricing formula used by practitioners to quote plain vanilla derivatives, such as caps, floors and swaptions. Quotes are in terms of volatility, the key quantity that has to be inserted in the Black formula to price caps, floors, and swaptions.

2. Flat volatility: This is the quoted volatility for a cap or floor. This same number has to be inserted in the Black formula to price each individual caplet. Because the notion of flat volatility is the product of a quoting convention and not a no arbitrage argument, the same caplet belonging to two caps that differ only by maturity may have different volatility, which is a violation of a no arbitrage condition.

3. Forward volatility: This is the no arbitrage consistent volatility of caplets of various maturities. It can be bootstrapped out of the caps themeselves. This volatility is

Table 20.5 LIBOR Discount and Forward Discount on November 1, 2004

Maturity	Discount (×100)	Forward Discount (×100)
1.2500	96.7402	99.2367
1.5000	95.9608	98.4372
1.7500	95.1491	97.6045
2.0000	94.3075	96.7412
2.2500	93.4385	95.8498
2.5000	92.5449	94.9331
2.7500	91.6294	93.9940
3.0000	90.6949	93.0354
3.2500	89.7441	92.0600
3.5000	88.7793	91.0703
3.7500	87.8027	90.0686
4.0000	86.8162	89.0566
4.2500	85.8211	88.0358
4.5000	84.8186	87.0075
4.7500	83.8100	85.9728
5.0000	82.7963	84.9329
5.2500	81.7786	83.8890
5.5000	80.7584	82.8424
5.7500	79.7370	81.7947
6.0000	78.7161	80.7474

Original Swap Data Source: Bloomberg.

Figure 20.7 Swaption Quoted Volatility. November 1, 2004

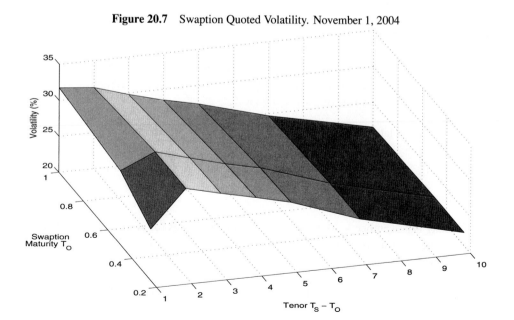

Data Source: Bloomberg.

Table 20.6   Swaptions, Caps, and Floors Quotes on November 3, 2008

| Maturity | Swap Rates | Swaption Vols | | | Volatilities | |
		3M	6M	1Y	Caps	Floors
1 Y	2.412/452	67.8	60.6	49.3	60.59/61.59	60.59/61.59
2 Y	2.619/633	59.7	52.8	41.6	52.26/53.26	52.26/53.26
3 Y	3.120/160	52.8	46.5	37.7	42.32/43.32	42.32/43.32
4 Y	3.507/547	48.7	42.5	35.3	35.99/36.99	35.99/36.99
5 Y	3.808/822	46.6	40.3	34.1	32.24/33.24	32.24/33.24
7 Y	4.171/197	41.3	36.3	31.4	27.82/28.82	27.82/28.82
10 Y	4.422/462	36.8	33.1	29.0	24.21/25.21	24.21/25.21

Source: Bloomberg.

related to the volatility of forward rates, and it can be used as input in the Black, Derman, and Toy model.

4. The term structure of forward volatilities: The term structure of forward volatilities is the relation between forward volatility and maturity. Like the term structure of interest rates, the term structure of forward volatilities also may have an increasing, decreasing, or a hump shape. The volatility changes substantially over time, most likely reflecting uncertainty surrounding the interest rate policy as well as future inflation and future economic growth. As for the term structure of interest rates, we can decompose the term structure of volatility in level, slope, and curvature.

20.4   EXERCISES

1. Table 20.6 contains quotes for swaps, caps, floors, and European swaptions on November 3, 2008. The 3-month LIBOR was $r_4(0, 0.25) = 2.8588\%$ while the 6-month LIBOR was $r_2(0, 0.5) = 3.0856\%$.

   (a) Interpolate the swap curve at the quarterly frequency, and obtain the LIBOR curve.

   (b) Use the Black formula to compute the dollar value of 1- and 2-year caps (recall that the strike rate equals the swap rate).

2. Today is November 3, 2008. Table 20.6 contains quotes for swaps, caps, floors, and European swaptions. The 3-month LIBOR was $r_4(0, 0.25) = 2.8588\%$ while the 6-month LIBOR was $r_2(0, 0.5) = 3.0856\%$.

   (a) Interpolate the swap curve at the quarterly frequency, and obtain the LIBOR curve (see the previous exercise).

   (b) Use the Black formula to compute the dollar value of caps up to 10 years to maturity (recall that the strike rate equals the swap rate).

Table 20.7 Swap Rates and Cap dollar Prices

Maturity	Swap Rate (%)	Cap Price ($\times 100$)
3M (LIBOR)	4.3000	-
1Y	4.8000	0.1905
2Y	4.9040	0.5734
3Y	4.9580	1.122
4Y	4.9890	1.7414
5Y	5.0325	2.4307
7Y	5.0895	3.8679
10Y	5.1720	6.0648

Source: Bloomberg.

    (c) Use the result in Part(b) , and the bootstrap procedure in Section 20.1.2 to obtain the forward volatility $\sigma_f^{Fwd}(T)$. Plot the forward volatility and the flat volatility against the maturity of caps.

    (d) Comment on the shape of the forward volatility. Does it have the usual shape? Can you link the shape of the foward volatility curve to the events of 2008 (see Section 7.7 in Chapter 7)?

3. From the data in Table 20.6, use the Black formula to compute the dollar value of a 1-year European swaption written on a 5-year swap. Recall that the table reports quotes for at-the-money instruments, meaning that the strike rate is equal to the current 5-year swap rate.

4. You are trading caps, and your no arbitrage model provides the dollar prices for caps in Table 20.7. Convert the dollar prices into quoted flat volatilities.

5. In Chapter 11 we covered the Black, Derman, and Toy (BDT) model. In particular, in Section 11.3.2 we covered the notion of forward volatility implicit in caps and floors. To build the BDT tree, at each step i we had to match both a zero coupon bond with maturity $i + 1$ and the cap with maturity $i + 1$ by searching for two quantities, the interest rate $r_{i,1}$ and the volatility σ_i. A more widespread practice is to use directly the forward volatilities σ_i, computed from caps and floors from the Black formula, as in Exercise 2. Using this methodology, the BDT tree results are simpler to build, as at each step i it is necessary to search only for one variable, $r_{i,1}$, that matches the term structure of interest rates.

    (a) Using the data in Table 20.6 compare the two methodologies.

    (b) Does the tree obtained using the methodology illustrated here (i.e. first σ_i from the Black formula) price the caps correctly? Comment.

6. Are the caps volatility quotes consistent with the swaptions volatility quotes? Use the BDT tree built in the previous exercise and price an at-the-money, 1-year swaption on the 5-year swap. Is the value the same as the one obtained directly from the European swaption volatility quotes?

CHAPTER 21

FORWARD RISK NEUTRAL PRICING AND THE LIBOR MARKET MODEL

Chapter 20 introduced the Black formula to price caps, floors, and swaptions. In this chapter we review a recent methodology that provides a no arbitrage underpinning of this formula. In addition, this pricing methodology is particularly convenient for the analysis of other fixed income securities as well. The methodology is called forward risk neutral Pricing, and it is at the basis of the LIBOR market model, or BGM model, from Brace, Gatarek, and Musiela (1997), the article that set out the framework. In this chapter, we also review the Heath, Jarrow, and Morton (HJM) framework, whose pathbreaking result in a famous 1990 article led the way to the current approach to fixed income security pricing.

21.1   ONE DIFFICULTY WITH RISK NEUTRAL PRICING

To motivate the logic behind this methodology, it is convenient to review the risk neutral pricing methodology, discussed in Chapter 17. Consider an interest rate model

$$dr_t = m(r_t, t)dt + s(r_t, t)dX_t$$

By no arbitrage, the price $V(r, t; T)$ of a fixed income security with payoff $g_T = G(r_T, T)$ at T must satisfy the Fundamental Pricing Equation

$$rV = \frac{\partial V}{\partial t} + \frac{\partial V}{\partial r}m^*(r, t) + \frac{1}{2}\frac{\partial^2 V}{\partial r^2}s(r, t)^2 \qquad (21.1)$$

subject to the boundary condition $V(r, T) = g_T = G(r_T, T)$. The Feynman-Kac theorem says that the price of this security is given by

$$V(r, t; T) = E^* \left[e^{-\int_t^T r_u \, du} g_T \right] \tag{21.2}$$

where the expectation $E^*[.]$ is taken with respect to the probability distribution implied by the risk neutral process

$$dr_t = m^*(r_t, t)dt + s(r_t, t)dX_t \tag{21.3}$$

The major difficulty in computing the expectation in Equation 21.2 stems from the fact that the interest rate r_t enters twice in the formula: First, in the discount term $e^{-\int_t^T r_u \, dt}$ and, second, in the final payoff $g_T = G(r_T, T)$. For instance, if we are pricing a put option with maturity T_O and strike K written on a zero coupon bond with maturity $T_B > T_O$, then $g_{T_O} = \max(K - Z(r_{T_O}, T_O; T_B), 0)$. Computing this expectation is then hard as we need to take into account the natural correlation that exists between the discount and the payoff. Indeed, the covariance formula $cov(Z, Y) = E[ZY] - E[Z]E[Y]$, where Z and Y are any two random variables, implies that we can write

$$V(r, t; T) = E^* \left[e^{-\int_t^T r_u \, du} g_T \right] = E^* \left[e^{-\int_t^T r_u \, du} \right] \times E^*[g_T] + cov \left(e^{-\int_t^T r_u \, du}, g_T \right)$$

If we could eliminate the covariance term in this expression, computing the expected value of each individual term $E^* \left[e^{-\int_t^T r_u \, du} \right]$ and $E^*[g_T]$ appears much easier. Indeed, we already know the first term, as it is equal to a zero coupon bond, $Z(0, T) = E^* \left[e^{-\int_t^T r_u \, du} \right]$. So, effectively we would be left to value the second term. The "change of numeraire" technique accomplishes exactly this separation. This methodology leads to the definition of the "forward risk neutral dynamics."

21.2   CHANGE OF NUMERAIRE AND THE FORWARD RISK NEUTRAL DYNAMICS

The numeraire is the unit of account used to express the value of goods and financial securities. For instance, in the U.S. the numeraire is the dollar, while in Europe it is the euro. However, we can decide collectively to change the unit of account into something else, such as U.S. Treasury bills, for instance. For example, if a financial security costs $112.5 and a 1-year Treasury bill is trading at $90, we may equivalently express the value of the financial security as 1.25 units of T-bills. In fact, $112.5/$90 = 1.25. Such changes of numeraire take place daily in the foreign exchange market, for instance, as the value of the same good is expressed in different currencies.

We now see why choosing a particular numeraire leads to a simplification of derivative pricing formulas. Let $V(r, t; T)$ be the dollar value of the derivative security, and consider the following renormalization:

$$\tilde{V}(r, t; T) = \frac{V(r, t; T)}{Z(r, t; T)} \tag{21.4}$$

where $Z(r, t; T)$ is a zero coupon bond with maturity T. $\widetilde{V}(r, t; T)$ is the value of the interest rate security in multiples of a zero coupon bond maturing on the same date as the derivative security itself. That is, rather than expressing the value of the security in dollars, we express it in terms of the zero coupon bond.

The appendix at the end of this chapter shows that $\widetilde{V}(r, t; T)$ satisfies a partial differential equation that is similar to the Fundamental Pricing Equation, namely

$$0 = \frac{\partial \widetilde{V}}{\partial t} + \frac{\partial \widetilde{V}}{\partial r} \left(m^*(r, t) + \sigma_Z(r, t) s(r, t) \right) + \frac{1}{2} \frac{\partial^2 \widetilde{V}}{\partial r^2} s(r, t)^2 \tag{21.5}$$

In this equation,

$$\sigma_Z(r, t) = \frac{1}{Z} \frac{\partial Z}{\partial r} s(r, t) \tag{21.6}$$

denotes the diffusion term of the bond price process[1]

$$\frac{dZ}{Z} = \mu_Z(r, t) dt + \sigma_Z(r, t) dX_t \tag{21.7}$$

Equation 21.5 differs from the Fundamental Pricing Equation 21.1 in two important respects:

1. The term "rV" disappeared from the left-hand side of the partial differential equation;

2. The coefficient of $\partial \widetilde{V} / \partial r$ has now one more term, namely $\sigma_Z(r, t) s(r, t)$.

We can now apply the Feynman-Kac theorem to this new equation. In particular, consider the results in Section 17.2 of Chapter 17. Comparing Equation 21.5 above with Equation 17.4 in Chapter 17, we see that we now have $R(r) = 0$. Thus, the application of the Feynman-Kac formula in Equation 17.5 of Chapter 17 to this case yields the following:

Fact 21.1 *The solution to the partial differential equation (Equation 21.5) subject to the final condition $\widetilde{V}(r, T) = g_T$ is given by*

$$\widetilde{V}(r, t; T) = E_f^*[g_T] \tag{21.8}$$

where $E_f^*[.]$ is the expectation operator obtained using the process

$$dr_t = \left(m^*(r, t) + \sigma_Z(r, t) s(r, t) \right) dt + s(r, t) dX_t \tag{21.9}$$

The process in Equation 21.9 is called **forward risk neutral** or, sometimes, $T-$ forward risk neutral, to emphasize that the bond used to normalize the value of the derivative security has maturity T.

What is the price of the derivative security? Using again the definition of $\widetilde{V}(r, t)$ in Equation 21.4 we obtain:

Fact 21.2 *The interest rate security price is given by*

$$V(r, t; T) = Z(r, t; T) E_f^*[g_T] \tag{21.10}$$

---

[1] We do not need to recall what μ_Z is in Equation 21.7, as we do not need it for pricing.

Comparing the pricing formula in Equation 21.10 with the earlier Equation 21.2, it looks like we took the discount, $E^* \left[e^{-\int_t^T r_u \, du} \right]$, outside the expectation operator in the Feynman-Kac formula. In many cases, it is simpler to obtain the price of a derivative security under the forward risk neutral dynamics.

21.2.1   Two Important Results

Two results are particularly important in the forward risk neutral methodology. The first one has to do with the behavior of forward prices. In particular, consider a forward contract at time t to deliver at time T a given interest rate security (or, in fact, any security) whose value will be g_T at time T. The forward price, recall, is that value of the delivery price determined at initiation, time t, that makes the value of the forward contract today equal to zero. Let $F(t, T)$ be the forward price at t for delivery at T. The payoff at maturity is then

$$\text{Payoff at } T = N \times (F(t, T) - g_T)$$

According to the result in Equation 21.10 in the previous section, the value of this security at t is given by

$$V_t = Z(t, T) E_f^* \left[N \times (F(t, T) - g_T) \right]$$

The forward price $F(t, T)$ is determined at time t to make this value zero, which implies that is must satisfy the equation

$$E_f^* \left[F(t, T) - g_T \right] = 0$$

Given the convergence property of forward prices, namely, $F(T, T) = g_T$, we then obtain the following important result:

Fact 21.3 *Under the* T*-forward risk neutral dynamics, the forward price for delivery at* T *is a martingale, that is:*

$$F(t, T) = E_f^* \left[F(T, T) \right] = E_f^* \left[g_T \right]$$

This is a generic result, that implies that under the forward risk neutral dynamics, the process for a forward price is driftless

$$dF(t, T) = \sigma_{F,t} F(t, T) dX_t$$

where $\sigma_{F,t}$ is the diffusion term of the forward price. We do not need to specify it at the moment, but it can be derived, for instance, from any of the interest rate models that we have discussed in earlier chapters.

The second important result is related to options, and it states the following (see the appendix at the end of this chapter for a proof):

Fact 21.4 *Let* g_T *be lognormally distributed under the* T*-forward risk neutral dynamics. In particular,* $\log(g_T) \sim N(\mu_T, \sigma_T^2)$. *Then*

$$E_f^* \left[\max(g_T - K, 0) \right] = F(0, T) \mathcal{N}(d_1) - K \mathcal{N}(d_2) \tag{21.11}$$

where $\mathcal{N}(\cdot)$ *denotes the standard normal cumulative distribution, and*

$$d_1 = \frac{1}{\sigma_T} \log\left(\frac{F(0,T)}{K}\right) + \frac{1}{2}\sigma_T \tag{21.12}$$

$$d_2 = d_1 - \sigma_T \tag{21.13}$$

*The value of a **call option** with payoff* g_T *and strike* K *is then*

$$Call = Z(0,T) \times [F(0,T)\mathcal{N}(d_1) - K\mathcal{N}(d_2)] \tag{21.14}$$

*Similarly, the value of a **put option** on* V_T *with strike price* K *is*

$$Put = Z(0,T) \times [K\mathcal{N}(-d_2) - F(0,T)\mathcal{N}(-d_1)] \tag{21.15}$$

21.2.2 Generalizations

We conclude this section by emphasizing that the results obtained above can be greatly generalized. In particular, the only requirement is that the security used as a new numeraire is a traded security. In particular, it does not need to have the same maturity as the derivative that we are in fact evaluating. The following summarizes the results:

Fact 21.5 *Let* $V(r,t;T)$ *be the price of a security at time* t *with payoff at* T *given by* g_T. *Let* $P(r,t)$ *be the price at* t *of another interest rate security. By no arbitrage, both securities satisfy Equation 21.1. Consider the normalized security*

$$\widetilde{V}(r,t;T) = \frac{V(r,t;T)}{P(r,t)}$$

Then:

1. $\widetilde{V}(r,t;T)$ *satisfies*

$$0 = \frac{\partial \widetilde{V}}{\partial t} + \frac{\partial \widetilde{V}}{\partial r}\left(m^*(r,t) + \sigma_P(r,t)s(r,t)\right) + \frac{1}{2}\frac{\partial^2 \widetilde{V}}{\partial r^2}s(r,t)^2 \tag{21.16}$$

where $\sigma_P(r,t) = \frac{1}{P}\frac{\partial P}{\partial r}s(r,t)$, *with final condition*

$$\widetilde{V}(r,T;T) = \frac{g_T}{P(r,T)} \tag{21.17}$$

2. The Feynman-Kac theorem then implies that the value $\widetilde{V}(r,t;T)$ *is given by*

$$\widetilde{V}(r,t;T) = E_f^*\left[\frac{g_T}{P(r,T)}\right] \tag{21.18}$$

where the expectation is taken with respect to the interest rate process

$$dr_t = \left(m^*(r,t) + \sigma_P(r,t)s(r,t)\right)dt + s(r,t)dX \tag{21.19}$$

3. *In terms of dollars, we then have that for any earlier time $t < T$:*

$$V(r, t; T) = P(r, t) E_f^* \left[\frac{g_T}{P(r, T)} \right] \tag{21.20}$$

4. *The process for $V(r, t; T)$ under the forward risk neutral dynamics induced by $P(r, t)$ is*

$$dV = (r + \sigma_P \sigma_V) V dt + \sigma_V V dX_t \tag{21.21}$$

where $\sigma_V = \frac{1}{V} \frac{\partial V}{\partial r} s(r, t)$ is the volatility of dV/V.

The discussion so far focuses on the case in which the underlying variable driving the value of derivative securities is an interest rate process r_t. In particular, Fact 21.5 shows that the process for r under the dynamics induced by the numeraire $P(r, t)$ is given by Equation 21.19 and the dynamics of the traded security V are given by Equation 21.21. It turns out that these latter two results hold much more generally, so long as a no arbitrage condition is satisfied. We have the following:

Fact 21.6 *Consider two traded securities P and V, and let their risk neutral processes be given by*

$$
\begin{aligned}
dP &= rP dt + \sigma_{P,t} P dX_t \\
dV &= rV dt + \sigma_{V,t} V dX_t
\end{aligned}
$$

where $\sigma_{P,t}$ and $\sigma_{V,t}$ are two volatility functions. Let P now be chosen as the numeraire. Then, the process of V under the forward risk neutral dynamics induced by P is

$$dV = V(r + \sigma_{P,t} \sigma_{V,t}) dt + \sigma_V V dX_t \tag{21.22}$$

Similarly, let Y be a process with risk neutral dynamics

$$dY = m^*(Y, t) dt + s(Y, t) dX$$

Then, the process for Y under the forward risk neutral dynamics induced by P is

$$dY_t = (m^*(Y, t) + \sigma_{P,t} s(Y, t)) \, dt + s(Y, t) dX_t \tag{21.23}$$

21.3 THE OPTION PRICING FORMULA IN "NORMAL" MODELS

It is illustrative to see one important application of this methodology. Consider again the case in which we need to price an option on a zero coupon bond (see Chapter 19). Assume that the interest rate follows a "normal" model, such as Vasicek, Ho-Lee or Hull-White. According to the risk neutral pricing methodology we must compute

$$V(r_0, 0) = E^* \left[e^{-\int_0^{T_O} r_t dt} \max \left(Z(r_{T_O}, T_O; T_B) - K, 0 \right) \right] \tag{21.24}$$

where T_O is the maturity of the option, K its strike price and T_B is the maturity of the underlying bond. In Chapter 19 we gave the pricing formula for the "normal" class of interest rate models, but without much justification, besides saying that it looks like the Black-Scholes formula for stocks (see e.g. Equation 19.15 for the Ho-Lee model, or Equation 19.30 for the Hull-White model). This result is intuitive because under the normal class of models, the zero coupon $Z(r_{T_O}, T_O; T_B) = e^{A(T_O;T_B)-B(T_O;T_B)r_{T_O}}$ is lognormally distributed, which is the same assumption of the Black-Scholes model. However, one difficulty with the argument is that in Equation 21.24 the discount "$\left(e^{-\int_0^{T_O} r_t dt}\right)$" is correlated with the bond prices "$Z(r_{T_O}, T_O; T_B)$" and the risk neutral pricing argument used in the computation of the Black-Scholes formula cannot be applied exactly, as Black and Scholes assumed constant interest rate. The forward risk neutral methodology solves this problem. We proceed as follows:

1. Choose as a new numeraire the zero coupon bond that matures at time T_O, the maturity of the option that we want to price.

2. Compute the forward risk neutral dynamics of the interest rate. Assume for instance that we are using the Ho-Lee model.[2] We then have $Z(r_t, t; T_O) = e^{A(t;T_O)-(T_O-t)r_t}$, which implies that the volatility of the bond price is

$$\sigma_Z(r,t) = \frac{1}{Z}\frac{\partial Z}{\partial r}\sigma = -(T_O - t)\sigma$$

Thus, from Equation 21.9 the T_O−forward risk neutral dynamics of the interest rate are given by

$$dr_t = (\theta_t - (T_O - t)\sigma^2)dt + \sigma dX_t$$

If we define by $\theta_t^* = \theta_t - (T_O - t)\sigma^2$, the interest rate process under the T_O-forward risk neutral dynamics has the same form as the original Ho-Lee model

$$dr_t = \theta_t^* dt + \sigma dX_t$$

Thus, the interest rate r_{T_O} has a normal distribution $r_{T_O} \sim N(\mu(r_0, T_O), \sigma^2 \times T_O)$ where

$$\mu(r_O, T_O) = \int_0^{T_O} \theta_t^* dt.$$

3. It follows that the underlying bond at maturity T_O, $Z(r_{T_O}, T_O; T_B) = e^{A(T_O;T_B)-(T_B-T_O)r_{T_O}}$ is lognormally distributed under the T_O−forward risk neutral dynamics, with mean equal to the bond's forward price[3]

$$E_f^* [Z(r_{T_O}, T_O; T_B)] = F(0, T_O; T_B) = \frac{Z(0, T_B)}{Z(0, T_O)}$$

and variance

$$\mathcal{S}_Z(T_O; T_B)^2 = (T_B - T_O)^2 \times T_O \times \sigma^2$$

4. Now apply Equation 21.11 to find

$$\widetilde{V}(r_0, 0) = E_f^* [\max(Z(r_{T_O}, T_O; T_B) - K, 0)] = F(0, T_O; T_B)\mathcal{N}(d_1) - K\mathcal{N}(d_2)$$

---

[2] Similar computations can be made under the Vasicek model or the Hull-White model.
[3] The forward price $F(0, T_O; T_B)$ can be computed from first principles, as in Equation 5.2 in Chapter 5.

with

$$
d_1 = \frac{1}{\mathcal{S}_Z(T_O, T_B)} \log\left(\frac{F(0, T_O; T_B)}{K}\right) + \frac{1}{2} \mathcal{S}_Z(T_O, T_B); \quad (21.25)
$$

$$
d_2 = d_1 - \mathcal{S}_Z(T_O; T_B) \quad (21.26)
$$

5. Because by definition $\widetilde{V} = Call/Z(0; T_O)$, the price of the option is then

$$
Call = Z(0, T_O)\widetilde{V}(r_0, 0) = Z(0, T_B)\mathcal{N}(d_1) - Z(0, T_O)K\mathcal{N}(d_2)
$$

which is the pricing formula discussed in Chapter 19.

21.4   THE LIBOR MARKET MODEL

In this section we apply the forward risk neutral methodology to discuss more in detail the LIBOR market model, or BGM model from Brace, Gatarek, and Musiela (1997).[4] We first show that the Black formula of valuing caps and floors introduced in Chapter 20 can be derived as an application of the forward risk neutral pricing model. We then use this result to show how to price additional fixed income securities by using the caplets' forward volatilities as the only input, as obtained in Chapter 20.

At the heart of the LIBOR market model is the specification of the dynamics of LIBOR-based forward rates under specific dynamics. In particular, consider again the result in Fact 21.3, but applied to a forward contract on the LIBOR. Specifically, consider a forward contract with maturity T and payoff

Payoff of forward contract with maturity $T = N \, \Delta \, (r_n(\tau, T) - K)$

where K is the delivery rate and $\tau = T - \Delta$ is the last reset date that determines the payoff amount. Recall also that $r_n(\tau, T)$ denotes the n−times compounded LIBOR at τ with maturity T, where $n = 1/\Delta$.

The forward risk neutral pricing formula in Equation 21.20, with $P(r, t) = Z(t, T)$, implies that the value of this forward contract at $t = 0$ is

$$
V^{fwd}(0; T) = Z(0, T) \, N \, \Delta \, E_f^*[r_n(\tau, T) - K] \quad (21.27)
$$

where the expectation is taken with respect to the dynamics induced by the new numeraire $Z(0, T)$, also called $T-$ **forward risk neutral dynamics**.[5]

The forward rate today $f_n(0, \tau, T)$ is that delivery rate K that makes the value of this contract equal to zero today (time 0), that is, such that $E_f^*[r_n(\tau, T) - f_n(0, \tau, T)] = 0$. This implies

$$
f_n(0, \tau, T) = E_f^*[r_n(\tau, T)]
$$

---

[4]We will refer to this model as the LIBOR market model. Sometimes, market participants refer to this model as the BGM model, or as the HJM model, the latter terminology stemming from the pathbreaking paper by Heath, Jarrow, and Morton (1992), whose framework is reviewed in Section 21.6, which effectively laid the foundations to the LIBOR market model. Additional important contributions were provided by Jamshidian (1997), and Miltersen, Sandmann, and Sonderman (1997).

[5]The argument is slightly more subtle than this, because the payoff at T depends on the interest rate at τ, and therefore the version of the Feynman-Kac formula in Equation 21.8 does not exactly apply. However, the result holds nontheless, as shown in the Appendix.

Moreover, because the forward rate must converge to the spot rate at maturity, we have $f_n(\tau, \tau, T) = r_n(\tau, T)$, the forward rate is a martingale under the T−forward risk neutral dynamics.

The LIBOR market model assumes that the forward rate $f_n(t, \tau, T)$ follows a log-normal diffusion process under the T−forward risk neutral dynamics. Since $f_n(t, \tau, T)$ is a martingale, its process can be described as a driftless diffusion process:

$$\frac{df_n(t, \tau, T)}{f_n(t, \tau, T)} = \sigma_f(t)dX_t \qquad (21.28)$$

where the volatility (diffusion) term $\sigma_f(t)$ is a deterministic function of time.

Because of the convergence property of forward rates, according to which at τ we have $r_n(\tau, T) = f_n(\tau, \tau, T)$, it follows that under the T−forward risk neutral dynamics, the LIBOR spot rate $r_n(\tau, T)$ has a log-normal distribution with mean $f_n(0, \tau, T)$ and variance $\int_0^\tau \sigma_f(t)^2 dt$:

$$r_n(\tau, T) \sim LogN\left(f_n(0, \tau, T), \int_0^\tau \sigma_f(t)^2 dt\right) \qquad (21.29)$$

For instance, if $\sigma_f(t) = \sigma_f$ is a constant, then the variance of $r_n(\tau, T)$ is simply $\sigma_f^2 \times \tau$.

We now show how the key assumption of the LIBOR market model, namely Equation 21.28, translates into a simple formula to price caps and floors, the Black formula, discussed in Fact 20.1 in Chapter 20.

21.4.1   The Black Formula for Caps and Floors

Fact 20.1 in Chapter 20 describes the Black formula for the pricing of caps and floors. We now see how the LIBOR market model and the forward risk neutral dynamics methodology enable us to recover this formula from no arbitrage principles. Recall that a cap is a fixed income security with a stream of payments at T_i, for $i = 1, \ldots, n$, with $T_{i+1} = T_i + \Delta$, given by

$$CF(T_{i+1}) = N \, \Delta \, \max(r_n(T_i, T_{i+1}) - r_K, 0) \qquad (21.30)$$

where $r_n(T_i, T_{i+1})$ describes the n−times compounded reference floating rate (e.g., LIBOR) at time T_i and maturity T_{i+1}, with $n = 1/\Delta$. Each of these individual payoffs is called a caplet.

From the forward risk neutral pricing formula in Equation 21.20, with $P(r, t) = Z(t, T_{i+1})$, the value of the caplet maturing at T_{i+1} is

$$Caplet(0; T_{i+1}) = Z(0, T_{i+1}) \, N \, \Delta \, E_f^*\left[\max(r_n(T_i, T_{i+1}) - r_K, 0)\right] \qquad (21.31)$$

where the expectation is taken with respect to the T_{i+1}−forward risk neutral dynamics, that is, the dynamics of stochastic variables induced by the new numeraire choice $Z(t, T_{i+1})$.[6]

The previous section shows that under these dynamics, the LIBOR $r_n(T_i, T_{i+1}) = f_n(T_i, T_i, T_{i+1})$ has a log-normal distribution with mean $f_n(0, T_i, T_{i+1})$ and variance $\sigma_f^2 T_i$, where we are assuming the diffusion volatility in Equation 21.28 is constant. Thus, Fact 21.4 implies that the value of the caplet is

$$Caplet(0; T_{i+1}) = N \, \Delta \, Z(0, T_{i+1}) \, [f_n(0, T_i, T_{i+1})\mathcal{N}(d_1) - r_K\mathcal{N}(d_2)] \qquad (21.32)$$

---

[6]As in footnote 5, the result is slightly more subtle. See the Appendix.

where

$$d_1 = \frac{1}{\sigma_f \sqrt{T_i}} \log \left(\frac{f_n(0, T_i, T_{i+1})}{r_K} \right) + \frac{1}{2} \sigma_f \sqrt{T_i} \qquad (21.33)$$

$$d_2 = d_1 - \sigma_f \sqrt{T_i} \qquad (21.34)$$

as reported in Fact 20.1 in Chapter 20.

21.4.2   Valuing Fixed Income Securities that Depend on a Single LIBOR rate

Why is it important to provide a no arbitrage framework for the Black formula? The answer is the usual: We can use quotes from caps and floors, relatively liquid instruments, to then calibrate the model for forward rates and obtain the prices of additional securities. This is the key point of the LIBOR market model.

For instance, in Chapter 20, Example 20.2, we obtained the caplet forward volatilities, that is, the values of volatilities $\sigma_f^{Fwd}(T_i)$ that would price correctly the caplets implicit in cap quotes. As an example, we found that the 1-year caplet has a forward volatility $\sigma_f^{Fwd}(T) = 25.54\%$. How can we use this information together with the current term structure of interest rates to price additional securities?

Let's consider a fixed income security whose payoff at time $T = 1$ depends on the LIBOR at time $\tau = T - \Delta = 0.75$:

$$g_T = G(r_n(\tau, T))$$

for some function $G(\cdot)$. The forward risk neutral pricing methodology and information about caplet volatilities provide a straightforward way to value this payoff, independent of the form of the function $G()$. In fact, first, we know that from Equation 21.20 with $P(r,t) = Z(t,T)$, the value of the security can be written as

$$V = Z(0,T) \, E_f^* \left[G(r_n(\tau, T)) \right]$$

where the expectation is taken with respect to the $T-$forward risk neutral dynamics.

Second, the LIBOR market model assumes that under the $T-$forward risk neutral dynamics the forward rates $f_n(t, \tau, T)$ follows the log-normal process in Equation 21.28. What volatility σ_f should we use in this process? We know that if we choose $\sigma_f = \sigma_f^{Fwd}(T) = 25.54\%$, this *same* process prices exactly a caplet with maturity T. Therefore, the caplet forward volatility extracted from caps allows us to fully characterize the process of $f_n(t, \tau, T)$. Because at maturity the forward rate converges to the LIBOR, $f_n(\tau, \tau, T) = r_n(\tau, T)$, the LIBOR market model provides the probability density of the LIBOR at maturity, again under the $T-$forward risk neutral dynamics. Indeed, as discussed earlier, we have that $r_n(\tau, T)$ is log-normally distributed with mean $f_n(0, \tau, T)$ and variance $\sigma_f^2 \times \tau$, that is

$$\log(r_n(\tau, T)) \sim N \left(\log(f_n(0, \tau, T)) - \frac{1}{2} \sigma_f^2 \, \tau, \sigma_f^2 \, \tau \right)$$

Even if the function $G(r_n(\tau, T)$ were complicated, a relatively simple Monte Carlo simulation or numerical integration would yield the price quickly, as we can simulate directly the final rate $r_n(\tau, T)$ out of the log-normal distribution.

The next two examples illustrate this methodology.

■ **EXAMPLE 21.1**

Today is November 1, 2004. A speculator is interested in purchasing a call option on the "square" of the 3-month LIBOR, that is, with payoff

$$g_T = N \, \max(r_n(\tau, T)^2 - K, 0)$$

where $\tau = 0.75$, $T = 1$ year, $K = (0.0256)^2$ and $N = \$100$ million.

This is called a **power option**. Using the forward risk neutral dynamics approach, it turns out we can value this security using Black formula. Let the current forward rate be $f_n(0, .75, 1) = 2.8987\%$ and the current caplet forward volatility $\sigma_f^{Fwd}(1) = 25.54\%$.

The convenient property of power options stems from the properties of log-normal distributions: In particular, if a variable x has a lognormal distribution with mean $\overline{x} = E[x]$ and variance $var\,[\log(x)] = \sigma_x^2$, then for any constant α, x^α has also a log-normal distribution with mean $E\,[x^\alpha] = \overline{x}^\alpha \, e^{\frac{(\alpha-1)\alpha}{2} \sigma_x^2}$ and variance $var\,[\log(x^\alpha)] = \alpha^2 \sigma_x^2$.[7] It follows that we can use Fact 21.4 to obtain an analytical formula for a power option with any α. Specifically, denote the $(T-$forward risk neutral$)$ expected 3-month LIBOR raised to the α power, and its variance, respectively, by

$$g(0, \tau, T) = E_f^*\,[r_n(\tau, T)^\alpha] = f_n(0, \tau, T)^\alpha e^{\frac{(\alpha-1)\alpha}{2} \sigma_f^{Fwd}(T)^2 \, \tau}$$

$$\sigma_T^2 = V\,[r_n(\tau, T)^\alpha] = \alpha^2 \sigma_f^{Fwd}(T)^2 \, \tau.$$

From Fact 21.4 we obtain:

$$\text{Power call} = N \, Z(0, T) \, [g(0, \tau, T)\mathcal{N}(d_1) - K\mathcal{N}(d_2)]$$

$$d_1 = \frac{1}{\sigma_T} \log\left(\frac{g(0, \tau, T)}{K}\right) + \frac{1}{2}\sigma_T$$

$$d_2 = d_1 - \sigma_T$$

Given $f_n(0, .75, 1) = 2.8987\%$, $\sigma_f^{Fwd}(T) = 25.54\%$, $Z(0, 1) = 0.9748$, and $\alpha = 2$, we find that the price of the squared option on the LIBOR is

$$\text{Power call } (\alpha = 2) = \$0.0271 \text{ million}$$

If instead the investor wanted a power call with $\alpha = 1/2$, the same calculations would immediately yield

$$\text{Power call } (\alpha = 1/2) = \$1.2558 \text{ million}$$

These values of power options are in line with the current caplet forward volatility, as the latter is used as input in the formula.

Even in the case in which we cannot use an analytical formula, if the payoff depends only on $r_n(\tau, T)$, we can obtain the value by using a Monte Carlo simulation.

---

[7]To see this result, note that $\log(x) \sim N\left(\log(\overline{x}) - \frac{1}{2}\sigma_x^2, \sigma_x^2\right)$, thus $\log(x^\alpha) = \alpha \log(x) \sim N\left(\alpha(\log(\overline{x}) - \frac{1}{2}\sigma_x^2), \alpha^2\sigma_x^2\right)$. Hence, $E\,[x^\alpha] = E\left[e^{\alpha \log(x)}\right] = e^{\alpha\left(\log(\overline{x}) - \frac{1}{2}\sigma_x^2\right) + \frac{1}{2}\alpha^2\sigma_x^2}$, which yields the result.

■ EXAMPLE 21.2

Today is November 1, 2004. A speculator is interested in purchasing a LIBOR based security with the following payoff at T:

$$g_T = N \, \exp(-\lambda \, |r_n(\tau, T) - K|)$$

where $|\,|$ denotes absolute value, K is a strike price, λ is a parameter. For instance, Figure 21.1 plots the payoff for $\lambda = 300$, $K = .0256$ and $N = \$1$ million. This security payoff allows the speculator to bet that the 3-month LIBOR is within some bounds.[8] Since we know that under the $T-$forward risk neutral dyanmics the 3 month LIBOR $r_n(\tau, T)$ has a log-normal distribution, with mean $f_n(0, \tau, T)$ and variance $\sigma_f^{Fwd}(T)^2 \times \tau$, we can proceed as follows:

1. From the log-normal distribution, obtain S simulated values of $r_n(\tau, T)$. We can do this by simulating

$$r_n^s = e^{\log(f(0, \tau, T)) - \frac{1}{2}\sigma_f^{Fwd}(T)^2 \times \tau + \sigma_f^{Fwd}(T) \times \sqrt{\tau} \times \varepsilon^s}$$

where $\varepsilon^s \sim N(0, 1)$.

2. Compute the discounted final payoffs

$$V^s = Z(0, T) \, N \, \exp(-\lambda \, |r_n^s - K|)$$

3. Compute the value of the security as the average

$$\widehat{V} = \frac{1}{S} \sum_{s=1}^{S} V^s$$

In the case of the option above, using 100,000 simulations we obtain

$$\widehat{V} = \$0.3354 \text{ million}$$

Note that unlike with the methodology discussed in Chapter 17, we do not need to simulate the whole path of forward rates betwee 0 and τ, but we can simulate directly the LIBOR at time τ, which greatly simplifies the calculations.

21.4.3 The LIBOR Market Model for More Complex Securities

More work is needed however to price other securities that depend on many forward rates, even for the case in which the forward rates depend on a single factor and thus are perfectly correlated.[9] For instance, consider a relatively simple security that at time $\overline{T}$ has a payoff that depends on the 3-year zero coupon bond (with unit principal)

$$g_{\overline{T}} = G\left(Z(\overline{T}, \overline{T} + 3)\right)$$

---

[8] The payoff structure of this instrument is similar to a butterfly spread on the 3-month LIBOR, which has payoff $\max(r_n(\tau, T) - K_1, 0) - 2 * \max(r_n(\tau, T) - K_2, 0) + \max(r_n(\tau, T) - K_2, 0)$, with $K_{i+1} = K_i + h$. A butterfly spread can easily be evaluated using the Black formula. This example shows an instance in which the Black formula cannot be used.

[9] See Chapter 22 for a generalization of the BGM model to the multifactor case.

Figure 21.1   A Smoothed Butterfly Spread

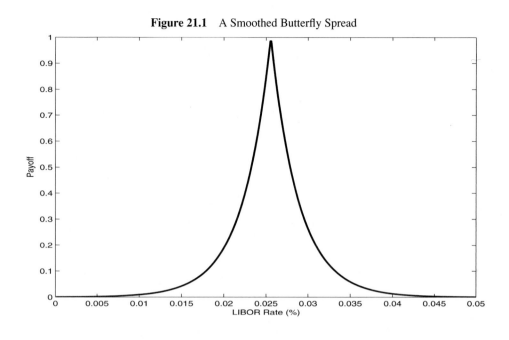

where $G(\cdot)$ is a function. The problem in evaluating such a security is that in the LIBOR market model we are modeling forward rate dynamics and not zero coupon bonds. Indeed, let us try to apply the same logic used to price securities that depend on one individual LIBOR only, as in the previous section. The first step is to note that under the $\overline{T}-$forward risk neutral dynamics, the value of the security is

$$V = Z(0,\overline{T})E_f^* \left[G\left(Z(\overline{T},\overline{T}+3) \right) \right] \qquad (21.35)$$

The second step is to use the statistical distribution of $Z(\overline{T},\overline{T}+3)$ under the $\overline{T}-$forward risk neutral dynamics to compute the expectation. So, what is the statistical distribution of $Z(\overline{T},\overline{T}+3)$? It turns out that this is not obvious.

From first principles, we can map bond prices into forward rates (and vice versa). In fact, assuming that n is the compounding frequency, with $\Delta = 1/n$, let $\bar{i}$ be the step index corresponding to $\overline{T}$, that is, $\overline{T} = T_{\bar{i}}$ and let $\overline{T} + 3 = T_{\bar{i}+m}$. Then, we can always write:[10]

$$Z(T_{\bar{i}}, T_{\bar{i}+m}) = \frac{1}{1 + r_n(T_{\bar{i}}, T_{\bar{i}+1})\Delta} \times \frac{1}{1 + f_n(T_{\bar{i}}, T_{\bar{i}+1}, T_{\bar{i}+2})\Delta} \times \cdots$$
$$\cdots \times \frac{1}{1 + f_n(T_{\bar{i}}, T_{\bar{i}+m-1}, T_{\bar{i}+m})\Delta}$$

Thus, from the joint statistical distribution of forward rates $f_n(T_{\bar{i}+j}, T_{\bar{i}+j+1}), j = 1, .., m-1$, under the $\overline{T}-$forward risk neutral dynamics we can recover the distribution of $Z(\overline{T}, \overline{T}+3)$.

The problem, however, is that the LIBOR market model assumes that each $f_n(t, T_i, T_{i+1})$ is log-normally distributed under the $T_{i+1}-$forward risk neutral dynamics induced by the

---

[10]This is an analog to Equation 5.19 in Chapter 5.

normalization $Z(t, T_{i+1})$. That is, each forward rate follows the process

$$\frac{df_n(t, T_i, T_{i+1})}{f_n(t, T_i, T_{i+1})} = \sigma_f^{i+1}(t)dX_t, \tag{21.36}$$

but each process is defined in terms of a different numeraire, namely, $Z(t, T_{i+1})$ for the forward rate maturing at T_{i+1}. Recall that this assumption is required for the LIBOR market model to price exactly the caplets quotes in the market through Black formula, the reason why we also allow for different volatilities $\sigma_f^{i+1}(t)$ across forward rates. The problem is that the dynamics of the forward rates under the common $\overline{T}$–forward dynamics needed to evaluate Equation 21.35 are not log-normal. Indeed, we have the following:

Fact 21.7 *The dynamics of the forward rate $f_n(t, T_i, T_{i+1})$ under the $\overline{T}$–forward risk neutral dynamics for $\overline{T} < T_{i+1}$ are given by*

$$\frac{df_n(t, T_i, T_{i+1})}{f_n(t, T_i, T_{i+1})} = \left(\sum_{j=\overline{i}}^{i} \frac{\Delta f_n(t, T_j, T_{j+1}) \sigma_f^{i+1}(t) \sigma_f^{j+1}(t)}{1 + \Delta f_n(t, T_j, T_{j+1})} \right) dt + \sigma_f^{i+1}(t)dX_t \tag{21.37}$$

where $\overline{i}$ is the index such that $T_{\overline{i}} = \overline{T}$.
   If instead, $\overline{T} > T_{i+1}$, then

$$\frac{df_n(t, T_i, T_{i+1})}{f_n(t, T_i, T_{i+1})} = - \left(\sum_{j=i}^{\overline{i}-1} \frac{\Delta f_n(t, T_j, T_{j+1}) \sigma_f^{i+1}(t) \sigma_f^{j+1}(t)}{1 + \Delta f_n(t, T_j, T_{j+1})} \right) dt + \sigma_f^{i+1}(t)dX_t \tag{21.38}$$

Clearly, the processes in Equations 21.37 and 21.38 are much more complicated than the one in Equation 21.36. Still, these two expressions show that the only inputs necessary to price a derivative security are the volatility $\sigma_f^{i+1}(t)$. The next section shows how to recover these volatilities from cap quotes.

21.4.4 Extracting the Volatility of Forward Rates from Caplets' Forward Volatilities

The key input in forward dynamics (Equations 21.37 and 21.38) is the volatility $\sigma_f^{i+1}(t)$. For instance, in Subsection 21.4.2 we considered σ_f^{i+1} constant for each forward rate, but this is not a good assumption. Indeed, it would imply that if at time 0, the 3-year forward rate had 30% volatility, then in one year the 2-year forward rate would have 30% volatility, and then in two years the 1-year forward rate would have 30% volatility. The data just do not show such behavior. Indeed, recalling the discussion in Section 20.1.1 in Chapter 20, typically caplet volatility shows a hump at around two years to maturity, and this is relatively stable over time, although there are substantial variations as well, as discussed then.
   Relatively standard alternate assumptions about $\sigma_f^{i+1}(t)$ are the following:

1. The volatility of forward rates depends only on time to maturity, $\sigma_f^{i+1}(t) = S(T_{i+1} - t)$ for some function $S(\cdot)$.

2. The function $S(\cdot)$ is constant on each expiry period of the cap, i.e., periods (t, T_1), $(T_1, T_2),....,(T_{i-1}, T_i)$.

Consider a cap with maturity T, and let T_i, $i = 1, \ldots, M$ be the caplet maturities, with $T_M = T$. In this case, we have to keep track of M forward rates. Table 21.1 illustrates the volatility structure on each forward rate according to assumptions 1 and 2.[11]

These assumptions imply that the distribution of the floating (LIBOR) rate at T_i, $r_n(T_i, T_{i+1}) = f_n(T_i, T_i, T_{i+1})$, is log-normally distributed under the T_{i+1}−forward risk neutral dynamics, but with variance

$$\text{Variance of } r_n(T_i, T_{i+1}) = S_i^2 \times (T_1 - t) + S_{i-1}^2 \times \Delta + \cdots + S_1^2 \times \Delta$$

where recall that $\Delta = 1/n = T_{i+1} - T_i$.

Given the caplets' forward volatility $\sigma_f^{Fwd}(T_i)$ obtained from the Black model, we can extract the volatility structure of forward rates by matching terms. That is, by imposing that for each caplet T_i we have

$$\left\{ \begin{array}{c} \text{Variance of } r_n(T_i, T_{i+1}) \\ \text{from the Black formula} \end{array} \right\} = \left\{ \begin{array}{c} \text{Variance of } r_n(T_i, T_{i+1}) \\ \text{implied by } f_n(t, T_i, T_{i+1}) \end{array} \right\}$$

That is, we have the formula

$$\sigma_f^{Fwd}(T_{i+1})^2 \times (T_i - t) = S_i^2 \times (T_1 - t) + S_{i-1}^2 \times \Delta + \cdots + S_1^2 \times \Delta \qquad (21.39)$$

where, recall from Chapter 20, that $\sigma_f^{Fwd}(T_{i+1})$ denotes the implied volatility of a caplet maturing at T_{i+1}. It is important to remember that because of the natural lag between payment (T_{i+1}) and determination of the payoff (T_i), the caplet's implied volatility must be multiplied by $(T_i - t)$ and not $(T_{i+1}$-t). For instance, let $t = 0$ and consider the first caplet maturing in $T_2 = 0.5$ years. The payoff of this caplet depends on the LIBOR determined one quarter from now, i.e., $T_1 = 0.25$, and thus the implied caplet volatility has to be multiplied $T_1 = 0.25$. This caplet volatility indeed corresponds to the volatility of the forward rate $f_n(0, T_1, T_2)$, which implies a variance of $r_n(T_1, T_2)$ given by $S_1^2 \times T_1$. That is, we indeed have the special case of the formula in Equation 21.39 for the first element:

$$\sigma_f^{Fwd}(0.5)^2 \times 0.25 = S_1^2 \times 0.25$$

This condition provides the first element of the variance structure of forward rates $S_1 = \sigma_f^{Fwd}(0.5)$. The next example shows the bootstrap procedure that can be applied to obtain volatility of forward rates $S_1, S_2, \ldots, S_{M-1}$.

■ **EXAMPLE 21.3**

Let today be November 1, 2004. The caplet forward volatilities from the Black's formula are contained in Column 3 in Table 21.2. These forward volatilities were obtained in Example 20.2 in Chapter 20, and are plotted also in Figure 20.1. Note that the second column contains the time T_i, which corresponds to the time of the caplet's cash flow determination and not the maturity of the caplet (one quarter later).

---

[11] See e.g. Brigo and Mercurio (2006) for a discussion of several alternative volatility structures.

Table 21.1   Forward Rate Volatilities

	Volatility					
	$t < T_1$	$T_1 \leq t < T_2$	$T_2 \leq t < T_3$	$\cdots \quad T_{i-1} \leq t < T_i$	$\cdots$	$T_{M-2} \leq t < T_{M-1}$
$f_n(t, T_1, T_2)$	S_1					
$f_n(t, T_2, T_3)$	S_2	S_1				
$f_n(t, T_3, T_4)$	S_3	S_2	S_1			
$\vdots$	$\vdots$	$\vdots$	$\vdots$			
$f_n(t, T_i, T_{i+1})$	S_i	S_{i-1}	S_{i-2}	$\cdots \quad S_1$		
$\vdots$	$\vdots$	$\vdots$	$\vdots$	$\vdots \qquad \vdots$		
$f_n(t, T_{M-1}, T_M)$	S_{M-1}	S_{M-2}	S_{M-3}	$\cdots \qquad \cdots$	$\cdots$	S_1

Table 21.2   Caplets' Forward Volatilities and Forward Rates Volatilities

i	T_i	$\sigma^{Fwd}(T_{i+1})$ (%)	S_i (%)
1	0.25	21.16	21.16
2	0.50	22.81	24.35
3	0.75	25.54	30.27
4	1.00	28.56	36.14
5	1.25	31.36	40.68
6	1.50	33.42	42.24
7	1.75	34.04	37.55
8	2.00	32.91	23.53
9	2.25	31.21	10.10
10	2.50	29.66	5.53
11	2.75	28.76	17.36
12	3.00	28.69	27.91

Notes: Calculations based on caps and swaps data from Bloomberg.

Starting with the intial condition

$$S_1 = \sigma_f^{Fwd}(0.25)$$

the other elements of forward rate volatilities can be obtained by the recursive formula

$$S_i = \sqrt{\frac{1}{\Delta} \times \left(\sigma_f^{Fwd}(T_{i+1}) \times T_i - \sum_{j=1}^{i-1} S_j^2 \times \Delta \right)}$$

where we assumed that today is $t = 0$. Table 21.2 reports the resulting S_i for up to three years to maturity.

One difficulty with the assumption that the volatility of forward rates only depends on the time to maturity is that we cannot always fit the term structure of forward volatilities. We can see why from examining Equation 21.39. In particular, consider a situation in which the forward volatility not only is declining, a standard behavior as discussed in Chapter 20, but it declines very rapidly with maturity. In particular, let $t = 0$ for simplicity and assume that

$$\sigma_f^{Fwd}(T_{i+1})^2 \times T_i < \sigma_f^{Fwd}(T_i)^2 \times T_{i-1} \qquad (21.40)$$

In this case, using Equation 21.39 and substituting both on the left- and right-hand sides of Equation 21.40 we find (recall that $T_1 = \Delta$):

$$\left(S_i^2 + S_{i-1}^2 + \cdots + S_1^2\right) \times \Delta < \left(S_{i-1}^2 + \cdots + S_1^2\right) \times \Delta \qquad (21.41)$$

That is,

$$S_i^2 < 0$$

which is not possible, as this is a variance element. Indeed, Example 21.3 and Table 21.2 already hint at this problem, at least partly. If we consider the volatility element S_i in the last column of Table 21.2 corresponding to $T_i = 2.50$, we see that $S_{10} = 5.53\%$, which is much smaller than the preceding and following volatility elements $S_9 = 10.10\%$ and $S_{11} = 17.36\%$. The reason is that the forward volatility in Column 3 of Table 21.2 has a steep drop between $T_9 = 2.25$ and $T_{10} = 2.5$, from 31.21% to 29.66%. To accommodate this large drop, the additional S_{10} has to be very small. The next example illustrates the severity of the problem.

■ **EXAMPLE 21.4**

Consider again Example 21.3. We now extract the volatility of forward rates S_i for additional maturities. The result is in Figure 21.2. This figure reports three lines: the dotted line is the (flat) quoted volatility of caps. The dashed line is the forward volatility of caplets. These two lines also appear in Figure 20.1 in Chapter 20. The solid line is the step function representing the S_i extracted from the caplet forward volatility, as illustrated above. As can be seen, beside being very erratic, this function also drops to zero in areas in which the forward volatility declines sufficiently fast. In those areas in which the step function equals zero we indeed find that $\sigma_f^{Fwd}(T_{i+1})^2 \times T_i$ is declining, as discussed above.

21.4.5 Pricing Fixed Income Securities by Monte Carlo Simulations

Given the volatility specification $\sigma^{i+1}(t)$ obtained in the previous section, we can finally use the forward dynamics in Equation 21.37 to price a security with maturity $\overline{T} = T_{\overline{i}}$. We can perform this last step with Monte Carlo simulations. In particular, as in Chapter 17 we can discretize the process with a time-step δ, simulate random normal shocks $\varepsilon_t^s \sim N(0, 1)$, multiply them by $\sqrt{\delta}$, and use them in lieu of the Brownian motion dX_t. It is convenient to simulate the logarithm of the $f_n(t, T_i, T_i + 1)$, that is, use the scheme

$$f_n^s(t + \delta, T_i, T_{i+1}) = f_n^s(t, T_i, T_{i+1}) e^{m_{i+1}^s(t)\delta + S(T_{i+1} - t)\sqrt{\delta}\,\varepsilon_t^s} \qquad (21.42)$$

where s is the simulation number, $s = 1, ..., \mathcal{S}$,

$$m_{i+1}^s(t) = \sum_{j=\overline{i}}^{i} \frac{\Delta f_n^s(t, T_j, T_{j+1}) S(T_{i+1} - t) S(T_{j+1} - t)}{1 + \Delta f_n^s(t, T_j, T_{j+1})} - \frac{1}{2} S(T_{i+1} - t)^2$$

Figure 21.2   Forward Volatility and Volatility of Forwards

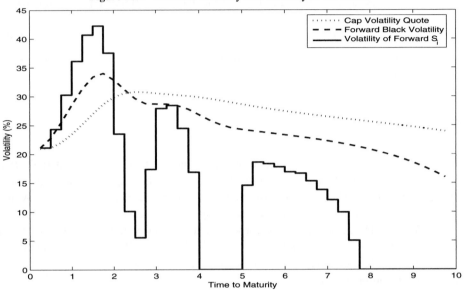

Original Data Source: Bloomberg.

and $S(T_{i+1} - t)$ is the volatility of the forward rates extracted from options, discussed in the previous section (see Figure 21.2). Note that we have to simulate all of the forward rates at the same time, as forward rate $f_n^s(t, T_j, T_{j+1})$ enters the process of $f_n^s(t, T_i, T_{i+1})$ and vice versa. Notice that the same simulated shocks $\varepsilon_{t+\delta}^s$ affect all of the forward rates.

■ **EXAMPLE 21.5**

Today is November 1, 2004. A speculator wants to purchase a 1-year call option on the 3-year LIBOR discount factor $Z(T_O, T_M)$, where $T_O = 1$ and $T_M = T_O + 3 = 4$ with strike price $K = 0.9$. That is, the payoff of the option is

$$\text{Payoff} = \max(Z(T_O, T_M) - K, 0)$$

Under the T_O-forward risk neutral dynamics, we know we can compute the value of the option as

$$V = Z(0, T_O) E_f^* [\max(Z(T_O, T_M) - K, 0)]$$

The value of the option crucially depends on the volatility of $Z(T_O, T_M)$. We can use cap prices to infer the market expected volatility of $Z(T_O, T_M)$. In fact, as discussed earlier, denoting $\bar{i}$ the quarterly index for which $T_O = T_{\bar{i}}$ and $\bar{i} + m$ the index for which $T_M = T_{\bar{i}+m}$ we have

$$
\begin{aligned}
Z(T_O, T_M) &= \frac{1}{1 + r_n(T_{\bar{i}}, T_{\bar{i}+1})\Delta} \times \frac{1}{1 + f_n(T_{\bar{i}}, T_{\bar{i}+1}, T_{\bar{i}+2})\Delta} \times \dots \\
&\quad \dots \times \frac{1}{1 + f_n(T_{\bar{i}}, T_{\bar{i}+m-1}, T_{\bar{i}+m})\Delta}
\end{aligned}
\tag{21.43}
$$

We then proceed as follows:

1. Use cap prices today to calibrate the volatilities $\sigma_f^{i+1}(t)$. This is done in Example 21.3 under the assumption $\sigma_f^{i+1}(t) = S(T_{i+1} - t)$, that is, the volatility of a caplet depends only on its time to maturity.

2. Express the dynamics of forward rates under the T_O−dynamics, by using Equation 21.37.

3. Simulate the forward rates using the algorithm in Equation 21.42.

To illustrate the simulation approach, Figure 21.3 reports one simulation run of forward rates according to the procedure above. The top panel shows the simulated paths for the 12 forward rates, which are necessary to compute the simulated value of the 3-year bond at T_O. The bottom panel plots the simulated forward curve at maturity of the option, $T_O = 1$, together with the resulting semi-annually compounded spot rate curve. We can easily compute the latter, as from the forward rates, we can use Equation 21.43 above to determine the discount curve $Z(T_O, T_M)$ for any maturity T_M. Note that the short term of the simulated forward curve corresponds to the 3-months LIBOR, implicitly simulated here as well.

Repeating this simulation 10,000 times, and given the current 1-year discount $Z(0, 1) = 0.9748$, we obtain

$$\widehat{V} \approx Z(0,1) \frac{1}{10000} \sum_{s=1}^{10000} \max(Z^s(T_O, T_M) - K, 0) = \$0.5889 \ \ (\text{per } \$100 \text{ principal})$$

Clearly, once we have learned how to simulate the model, we can become more ambitious, and use this simulation method to price other securities.

■ **EXAMPLE 21.6**

Consider a European receiver swaption with maturity $T_O = 1$ to enter into a 3-year swap at the strike swap rate $r_K = .035$. For each simulation run s, from the simulated LIBOR discount $Z^s(T_O, T)$ we can compute the value of a receiver swap with swap rate r_K as:[12]

$$V^{Swap,s}(T_O; T_M) = 100 \times \left(\sum_{i=1}^{n} \Delta r_K Z^s(T_O, T_i) + Z^s(T_O, T_n) - 1 \right)$$

We can then compute the expected value of the swaption payoff at T_O under the T_O−forward risk neutral dynamics as

$$E_f^* \left[\max(V^{Swap}(T_O; T_M), 0) \right] \approx \frac{1}{10000} \sum_{s=1}^{10000} \max(V^{Swap,s}(T_O; T_M), 0)$$

The simulated value of the swaption is

$$\widehat{V} \approx Z(0,1) \frac{1}{10000} \sum_{s=1}^{10000} \max(V^{Swap,s}(T_O; T_M), 0) = \$0.6107$$

---

[12] We retain the usual simplifying assumption that both fixed and floating legs reset at quarterly frequency.

Figure 21.3   One Simulation Run of Forward Rates

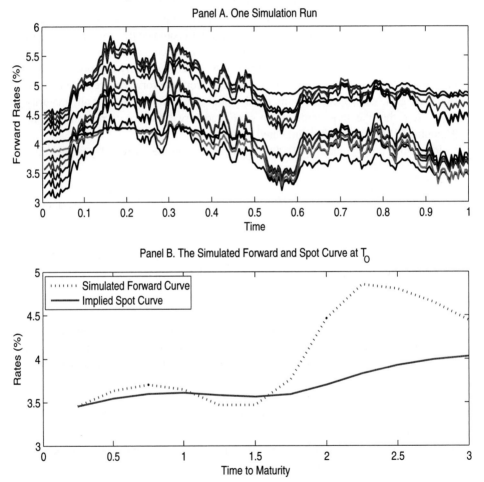

We can also consider path dependent securities, as shown in the next example.

■ **EXAMPLE 21.7**

Consider a 1-year, European Asian option on the 3-year swap rate, that is, a security with payoff

$$g_T = N \, \max(\text{Ave}(c(t, t+3)) - r_K, 0)$$

where

$$\text{Ave}(c(t, t+3)) = \text{Average of the 3-year swap rate } c(t, t+3) \text{ from 0 to } T_O = 1$$

We can compute this average in the simulations from the forward rates. Indeed, for every day t before maturity T_O and each simulation run s, we can compute the LIBOR discount curve $Z^s(t, T)$ and, from it, the 3-year swap rate from the usual formula:

$$c^s(t, t+3) = \frac{1 - Z^s(t, t+3)}{\Delta \sum_{j=1}^{12} Z^s(t, t + \Delta j)}$$

Finally, for $r_K = 3.25\%$ and $N = 100$ we find

$$
\begin{aligned}
V &= Z(0, T_O) \, N \, E_f^* \left[\max(\text{Ave}(c(t, t+3))^s - r_K, 0) \right] & (21.44) \\
&\approx Z(0, T_O) \, 100 \, \frac{1}{10000} \sum_{s=1}^{10000} \left[\max(\text{Ave}(c(t, t+3))^s - r_K, 0) \right] & (21.45) \\
&= \$3.805 & (21.46)
\end{aligned}
$$

To conclude, the LIBOR market model provides a powerful methodology by which to price derivative securities, whose only input is the volatility structure of forward rates and the current term structure of interest rates. Moreover, its consistency with the pricing of caps and floors makes the estimation of this volatility structure relatively simple. We now look at the application of a similar model to price European swaptions, another large and liquid market that can be used for the calibration of fixed income derivative models.

21.5 FORWARD RISK NEUTRAL PRICING AND THE BLACK FORMULA FOR SWAPTIONS

Fact 20.2 in Chapter 20 discusses the Black formula to price swaptions. In this section we obtain the Black formula as a result of the forward risk neutral pricing methodology. The model we discuss now is sometimes called the log-normal swap market model.[13]

From the previous chapter recall that we can express the payoff of a receiver swaption as follows (see Equation 20.15)

$$\text{Payoff receiver swaption} = N \Delta \sum_{i=1}^{n} Z(T_O; T_i) \, \max(r_K - c(T_O; T_S), 0)$$

$$(21.47)$$

---

[13] See e.g. Brigo and Mercurio (2006, Chapter 6).

We proceed as follows.

Step 1 **Select a convenient numeraire**. Given Equation 21.47 for the payoff of the swaption, it is convenient to select as numeraire $P(t) = \sum_{i=1}^{n} Z(t; T_i)$. This choice yields a normalized payoff at maturity T_O given by

$$
\begin{aligned}
\text{Swaption normalized} \atop \text{payoff at } T_O &= \frac{N \Delta \sum_{i=1}^{n} Z(T_O, T_i) \max(r_K - c(T_O, T_S), 0)}{P(T_O)} \\
&= N \Delta \max(r_K - c(T_O, T_S), 0)
\end{aligned}
$$

Step 2 **Obtain the proper forward rate**. Consider a forward swap contract with maturity T_O to enter into a swap with maturity T_S at the delivery rate K. The same logic behind Equation 21.47 implies that the payoff at T_O is given by

$$
N \Delta \sum_{i=1}^{n} Z(T_O, T_i) \; (K - c(T_O, T_S)) \tag{21.48}
$$

Denote by $f_n^s(t; T_0; T_S)$ the forward swap rate at time t that underlies this forward swap contract, that is, the delivery rate K that makes the value of the forward swap contract equal to zero at t. The subscript n denotes that this is a $n-$times compounded rate. Using the same argument as in Section 21.4 for the LIBOR market model, we obtain

$$
f_n^s(t, T_0; T_S) = E_f^*[c(T_0, T_S)]
$$

where the expectation is taken with respect to the dynamics implied by $P(t) = \sum_{i=1}^{n} Z(t; T_i)$. The forward rate $f_n^s(t, T_O, T_S)$ is called the *forward swap rate* (see Section 5.4.5 in Chapter 5).

The convergence property also implies that at maturity $f_n^s(T_O, T_O, T_S) = c(T_O, T_S)$, and thus the forward swap rate is a martingale.

Step 3 **Assume the forward swap rate has log-normal dynamics under the $P(t)$ forward risk neutral dynamics.** We can assume

$$
\frac{df_n^s(t, T_O, T_S)}{f_n^s(t, T_O, T_S)} = \sigma_f^s dX_t \tag{21.49}
$$

where the diffusion term σ_f^s is constant.

Step 4 **Use Fact 21.4 to obtain the option pricing formula.** Because from Equation 21.49 the future swap rate $c(T_0, T_S) = f_n^s(T_0, T_O, T_S)$ has a log-normal distribution with mean $f_n^s(0, T_O; T_S)$ and variance $(\sigma_f^s)^2 \times T_O$, it then follows that the normalized value of the **receiver swaption** is given by

$$
\begin{aligned}
\widetilde{V}(0; T_O; T_S) &= N \Delta E_f^*[\max(r_K - c(T_O; T_S), 0)] \\
&= N \Delta [r_K \mathcal{N}(-d_2) - f_n^s(0, T_O; T_S)(-d_1)]
\end{aligned}
$$

where

$$
d_1 = \frac{1}{\sigma_f^s \sqrt{T_O}} \ln\left(\frac{f_n^s(0, T_O; T_S)}{r_K}\right) + \frac{1}{2} \sigma_f^s \sqrt{T_O}; \quad d_2 = d_1 - \sigma_f^s \sqrt{T_O} \tag{21.50}
$$

Using then $V(0, T_O; T_S) = P(0) \, V(0, \widetilde{T_O}; T_S)$, the Black formula for the value of a European receiver swaption is then

$$V(0, T_O; T_S) = N \, \Delta \, \left(\sum_{i=1}^{n} Z(0; T_i) \right) \, [r_K \mathcal{N}(-d_2) - f_n^s(0, T_O; T_S)(-d_1)]$$

(21.51)

This works similarly for a payer swaption. The results are contained in Fact 20.2 in Chapter 20.

21.5.1   Remarks: Forward Risk Neutral Pricing and No Arbitrage

The forward neutral pricing methodology is a powerful method of pricing securities. In particular, combined with special assumptions on the behavior of some forward rates (under the appropriate forward risk neutral dynamics), it allows us to use relatively standard results on the pricing of options to quickly compute the prices of plain vanilla options, through the Black option pricing formula.

However, we should not forget that the forward risk neutral pricing strategy, as any pricing methodology, stems from the same no arbitrage methodology discussed in Chapter 14. Indeed, this setting can be greatly generalized to consider multiple factors and multiple securities. But the fact that we are using a risk neutral approach to compute the value of the security presumes a no arbitrage argument. In particular, the key step of this no arbitrage argument is that there is a sufficient number of traded securities to allow us to create a riskless portfolio. This in turn implies the partial differential equation of the type shown in Equation 21.1 and thus the use of Feynman-Kac formula.

One implication of the approach is that it is always possible to dynamically replicate the payoff of any traded interest rate security using a portfolio of *other* traded securities. In particular, we should be able to hedge, for instance, a swaption by using a position in zero coupons and/or caps. However, this fact implies that there should be some type of consistency between the pricing of caps and swaptions, which is not obvious from the assumptions we made earlier. In particular, note that for caps we had to assume that forward rates follow a log-normal process under the T_{i+1} forward risk neutral dynamics [induced by $Z(t, T_{i+1})$], while for swaptions we had to assume that forward swap rates follow a log-normal process under the dynamics induced by $P(t) = \sum_{i=1}^{n} Z(t, T_i)$. An important question is whether these two assumptions are consistent with each other, that is, whether there is a model in which after the proper adjustments, both the forward rates and the forward swap rates are log-normally distributed under their respective dynamics. The answer is, unfortunately, no. That is, there is not a unifying model that makes these two assumptions consistent with each other. See Brigo and Mercurio (2006).

21.6   THE HEATH, JARROW, AND MORTON FRAMEWORK

The main point of the LIBOR market model, and partly the reason for its success, is that in order to price *any* derivative security we only need to know the current term structure of interest rates and the volatility of forward rates. We can see this for instance from the formulas in Equations 21.37 and 21.38, which show the processes of forward rates under the same forward dynamics. This key insight was in fact the key result of an earlier pathbreaking research article by Heath, Jarrow, and Morton (1992), an article that led the way to the LIBOR market model itself.[14]   We now review the argument of the Heath, Jarrow, and Morton (HJM) framework, and link it to the results in previous sections.

Consider a zero coupon bond with maturity T and let the following be its *risk neutral* process

$$\frac{dZ(t,T)}{Z(t,T)} = r_t dt + \sigma_Z(t,T) dX_t$$

where r_t is the current instantaneous interest rate, and $\sigma_Z(t,T)$ is some volatility function. Notice that the above T is fixed, so that t is moving toward T. It follows that at maturity we must have zero volatility, as bond prices become in fact riskless. That is, the only restriction that HJM impose is that

$$\sigma_Z(t,T) \to 0 \text{ as } t \to T$$

Recall that the continuously compounded forward rate at time t for an investment between T and $T + \tau$ is defined as that interest rate $f(t,T,T+\tau)$ such that

$$e^{r(t,T)(T-t)} e^{f(t,T,T+\tau)\tau} = e^{r(t,T+\tau)(T+\tau-t)}$$

This implies

$$f(t,T,T+\tau) = \frac{\ln(Z(t,T)) - \ln(Z(t,T+\tau))}{\tau}$$

Using Ito's lemma, we find

$$df(t,T,T+\tau) = \frac{\sigma_Z(t,T+\tau)^2 - \sigma_Z(t,T)^2}{2\tau} dt + \frac{\sigma_Z(t,T) - \sigma_Z(t,T+\tau)}{\tau} dX_t$$

$$\tag{21.52}$$

The key result of HJM is to now notice that *only* the volatility terms enter into this formula. That is, given the volatility function $\sigma_Z(t,T)$, we have determined the *risk neutral* process for *all* of the forward rates. Because in pricing securities we need only a risk neutral process, this is an important result, as it says that the only input that we really must have is the volatility of either bonds or forward rates. The latter are "easy" to estimate from either the historical data on forward rates, or from options' implied volatilities, as we discussed in Chapter 20.

Moving one step further, consider now the case in which $\tau \to 0$. We then obtain the instantaneous forward rate $f(t,T) = f(t,T,T)$ (we drop the second "T" from the arguments of the function for simplicity). This follows the process

$$df(t,T) = \left(\sigma_Z(t,T) \frac{\partial \sigma_Z(t,T)}{\partial T} \right) dt - \frac{\partial \sigma_Z(t,T)}{\partial T} dX_t \tag{21.53}$$

Equation 21.53 shows that there is a tight link between the drift and the volatility of the risk-neutral process of the instantaneous forward rate. Indeed, by inverting the integral with the derivative, we obtain the following:

Fact 21.8 *Let the risk neutral process of the instantaneous forward rate $f(t,T)$ be given by*

$$df(t,T) = m(t,T)dt + \sigma_f(t,T)dX_t \tag{21.54}$$

---

[14]Indeed, in the industry some refer to the LIBOR market model as the HJM model.

then the risk neutral drift $m(t, T)$ is given by

$$m(t, T) = \sigma_f(t, T) \int_t^T \sigma_f(t, \tau) d\tau \qquad (21.55)$$

The HJM result applies to a very large class of models, and it only requires that no arbitrage opportunities exist. In particular, the no arbitrage models such as Ho-Lee, Hull-White, and so on are all special cases of the framework, in which special assumptions about the volatility of $\sigma_Z(t, T)$ have to be made. For instance:

1. In the Ho-Lee model, the bond price is $Z(t, T) = e^{A(t,T)-(T-t)r_t}$, and thus its volatility is

$$\sigma_Z(t, T) = -(T - t)\sigma$$

Therefore, the volatility of the instantaneous forward rate is

$$\sigma_f(t, T) = \sigma$$

and the risk neutral drift of a forward rates is

$$m(t, T) = (T - t)\sigma^2$$

2. In the Hull-White model the bond is $Z(t, T) = e^{A(t,T)-B(t,T)r_t}$, and thus its volatility is

$$\sigma_Z(t; T) = -B(t, T)\sigma = -\frac{1 - e^{-\gamma^*(T-t)}}{\gamma^*}\sigma$$

Then, the volatility of the instantaneous forward rate is

$$\sigma_f(t, T) = \sigma \, e^{-\gamma^*(T-t)}$$

and the risk neutral drift of the instantaneous forward rate process is then

$$m(t, T) = \frac{1 - e^{-\gamma^*(T-t)}}{\gamma^*}\sigma^2 \, e^{-\gamma^*(T-t)}$$

It follows that all of the results already derived for the Ho-Lee and the Hull-White models are special cases of the HJM framework, which can instead accommodate much richer dynamics of volatility. Unfortunately, as soon as we move away from simple special cases, most analytical formulas for options are no longer available, and we must resort to Monte Carlo simulations, as we did in Section 21.4.5 for the LIBOR market model. One additional difficulty with the HJM model, and partly the reason for its extention to the LIBOR market model, is that its focus is on continuously compounded forward rates, which practitioners tend to dislike as they require some additional calculations.

21.6.1 Futures and Forwards

We know that the HJM framework is for continuously compounded forward rates. However, in a number of markets, such as the Eurodollar futures market, we have readily available futures contracts, which are often preferable to forward contracts or swaps to calibrate interest rate models as futures are more liquid. The HJM framework provides a readily available mapping between (continuously compounded) futures and forward rates.

Consider first a futures contract with maturity τ defined on the floating rate $r(\tau, T)$ and let its futures rate at t be denoted by $f^{fut}(t, \tau, T)$. Assume that the true process for the futures can be described by the diffusion

$$df^{fut}(t, \tau, T) = \mu_{fut}(t, T)dt + \sigma_{fut}(t, T)dX_t$$

What is the risk neutral process for the futures contract? The instantaneous profit or loss from a position in the futures contract is $N \times df^{fut}(t, \tau, T)$, where N is the contract size. Because it does not cost anything to enter into the futures position, the risk neutral process must be driftless. That is, we must have

$$E^*[df^{fut}(t, \tau, T)] = 0 \qquad (21.56)$$

In fact, if $E^*[df^{fut}(t, \tau, T)] > 0$, then in a world neutral to risk we would have investors who massively go long the futures. If instead, $E^*[df^{fut}(t, \tau, T)] < 0$, risk neutral investors would take short positions. It follows from Equation 21.56 that the futures price is a martingale under the risk neutral dynamics, that is:

$$f^{fut}(0, \tau, T) = E^*[f^{fut}(t, \tau, T)]$$

Finally, because at maturity the futures must converge to the underlying rate $r(\tau, T)$, we also have the condition

$$f^{fut}(0, \tau, T) = E^*[r(\tau, T)] \qquad (21.57)$$

Consider now the risk neutral process for the continuously compounded forward rate $f(t, \tau, T)$ obtained by the HJM model in Equation 21.52. Let $\sigma_Z(t, T)$ be a deterministic function of time, as for instance in Ho-Lee or Hull-White models. What is the risk neutral expectation of the future continuously compounded interest rate $r(\tau, T)$? Because the forward rate has to converge to it, $r(\tau, T) = f(\tau, \tau, T)$, we can obtain the latter first from the risk neutral process in Equation 21.52. In fact, we can write:

$$\begin{aligned}
f(\tau, \tau, T) - f(0, \tau, T) &= \int_0^\tau df(t, \tau, T)dt \\
&= \int_0^\tau \frac{\sigma_Z(t, T+\tau)^2 - \sigma_Z(t, T)^2}{2\tau} dt \\
&\quad + \int_0^\tau \frac{\sigma_Z(t, T) - \sigma_Z(t, T+\tau)}{\tau} dX_t
\end{aligned}$$

Thus, taking the risk neutral expectation on both sides of the equality, and knowing $E^*[dX_t] = 0$, the risk neutral expectaion of the future spot rate $r(\tau, T)$ is

$$E^*[r(\tau, T)] = f(0, \tau, T) + \int_0^\tau \frac{\sigma_Z(t, T+\tau)^2 - \sigma_Z(t, T)^2}{2\tau} dt \qquad (21.58)$$

Matching this result with Equation 21.57 we obtain the following:

Fact 21.9 *The continuously compounded forward rate and futures rate are related to each other by*

$$f(0, \tau, T) = f^{fut}(0, \tau, T) - \int_0^\tau \frac{\sigma_Z(t, T + \tau)^2 - \sigma_Z(t, T)^2}{2\tau} dt \qquad (21.59)$$

For example, under the Ho-Lee model, we have $\sigma_Z(t, T + \tau)^2 = (T - t)^2 \sigma^2$ and computing explicitly the integral yields

$$f(0, \tau, T) = f^{fut}(0, \tau, T) - \frac{1}{2}\sigma^2 \tau T \qquad (21.60)$$

An application of these results is contained in Section 6.5 of Chapter 6, where we discussed the fact that market traders calibrate the LIBOR curve – the key input in most term structure models – to futures rates rather than swap rates, at least for maturities up to a few years.

21.7 UNNATURAL LAG AND CONVEXITY ADJUSTMENT

The LIBOR market model assumes a relatively straightforwad dynamics of forward rates $f_n(t, \tau, T)$ under their "natural" numeraire $Z(t, T)$. In particular, consider again the security with payoff at time T given by

$$g_T = G(r_n(\tau, T))$$

where $\tau = T - \Delta$ and $n = 1/\Delta$ is the compounding frequency. As in caps, floors and swaps, there is a lag between the time the payoff is generated, τ, and the time it is paid, T. *Because of this lag* we were able to use the forward risk neutral dynamics implied by the LIBOR market model and obtain nice formulas, e.g., for a power option. The basic idea is that under the $T-$forward risk neutral dynamics, $f_n(t, \tau, T)$ follows a log-normal model with mean $f_n(0, \tau, T)$ and variance $\sigma_f(T) \times \tau$, and thus the no arbitrage valuation is

$$V = Z(0, T)E_f^*[G(r_n(\tau, T))]$$

What happens if the security pays at τ instead of T? Such a situation occurs very often for numerous securities, called in arrears securities. For instance, an in-arrears swap is like a plain vanilla swap, but in which the cash flow at time T_i is

$$CF_{T_i} = N \Delta (r_n(T_i, T_{i+1}) - c)$$

where c is the swap rate. Note that in this case, the cash flow at time T_i depends on the LIBOR at time T_i (and not T_{i-1}). Similarly, in arrears caps are like plain vanilla caps but pay

$$CF_{T_i} = N \Delta \max(r_n(T_i, T_{i+1}) - r_K, 0)$$

where r_K is the strike rate.

Consider then a security with payoff at τ given by

$$g_\tau = G(r_n(\tau, T))$$

In the LIBOR market model, the LIBOR rate $r_n(\tau, T)$ has nice properties under the natural numeraire $Z(t, T)$, namely, the fact that it has a log-normal distribution with mean $E_f^*[r_n(\tau, T)] = f_n(0, \tau, T)$ and variance $\sigma_f^2 \times \tau$. Thus, using this numeraire we find from the formula in Equation 21.18 that the no arbitrage value of the security is

$$V = Z(0, T) E_f^* \left[\frac{G(r_n(\tau, T))}{Z(\tau, T)} \right]$$

where the expectation is computed under the T−forward risk neutral dynamics. The next example, however, illustrates a difficulty.

■ **EXAMPLE 21.8**

Consider the simple case in which the payoff is linear in 3-month LIBOR

$$G(r_n(\tau, T)) = N \, \Delta \, (r_n(\tau, T) - r_K). \tag{21.61}$$

Let $N = \$100$ million, $r_K = 1.5\%$, $\tau = 0.75$, $T = 1$. As of November 1, 2004, we also had a forward rate of $f_n(0, .75, 1) = 2.8987\%$, its implied (caplet) volatility $\sigma_f^{Fwd}(T) = 25.54\%$, and the discount rates were $Z(0, .75) = 0.9819$ and $Z(0, 1) = 0.9748$.

If the payoff in Equation 21.61 is paid at time $T = 1$, then the forward risk neutral methodology implies that its value is

$$\begin{aligned} V &= Z(0, T) \, E_f^*[G(r_n(\tau, T))] = Z(0, T) E_f^*[N \, \Delta \, (r_n(\tau, T) - r_K)] \\ &= Z(0, T) \, N \, \Delta(f_n(0, \tau, T) - r_K) = \$0.6817 \text{ million} \end{aligned}$$

where the last step stems from the fact that under the T−forward risk neutral dynamics, $E_f^*[r_n(\tau, T)] = f_n(0, \tau, T)$.

Consider now the case in which the same payoff in Equation 21.61 is paid at τ. Then:

$$\begin{aligned} V &= Z(0, T) \, E_f^* \left[\frac{G(r_n(\tau, T))}{Z(\tau, T)} \right] \\ &= Z(0, T) \, N \, \Delta \, E_f^* \left[(r_n(\tau, T) - r_K) \, (1 + r_n(\tau, T)\Delta) \right] \\ &= Z(0, T) \, N \, \Delta \, \left\{ f_n(0, \tau, T) - r_K - f_n(0, \tau, T) r_K \Delta + E_f^*[r_n(\tau, T)^2]\Delta \right\} \end{aligned}$$

Above, the second equality stems from the definition $Z(\tau, T) = 1/(1 + r_n(\tau, T)\Delta)$, while the last equality stems from developing the multiplication inside the square parenthesis and using again $E_f^*[r_n(\tau, T)] = f_n(0, \tau, T)$ whenever possible.

The latter formula is clearly more complicated then the earlier one. However, luckily, under the LIBOR market model we have a closed form expression for $E_f^*[r_n(\tau, T)^2]$ under the T−forward risk neutral dynamics. Indeed, recall that in Example 21.1 we obtained the distribution $r_n(\tau, T)^2$ when we computed the value of power options. Given those results, we know

$$E_f^*[r_n(\tau, T)^2] = f_n(0, \tau, T)^2 \; e^{\sigma_f(T)^2 \times \tau} = 8.8235E - 004$$

The final value is then

$$V = \$0.6926 \text{ million}$$

This value is higher than in the case in which the payoff occurred at T. Note in particular that the volatility of interest rates enters into the pricing formula.

21.7.1   Unnatural Lag and Convexity

The result in the previous example leaves us with a puzzle: Why does the volatility of the underlying LIBOR rate enter into the pricing formula when the payoff is linear? Is this a problem with the LIBOR market model or a more general phenomenon? To see the issue, it is useful to return to the pricing methodology of this simple security and the role of the lag between the timing of cash flow formation and its payment.[15] Let $N = 1$ for simplicity. In the case when the payment occurs at T, we have

$$G(r_n(\tau, T)) = \Delta \left(r_n(\tau, T) - r_K \right) = (1 + r_n(\tau, T)\Delta) - (1 + r_K \Delta)$$

The second term is a fixed payment and its value today is simply $Z(0, T)(1 + r_K \Delta)$, so there is no uncertainty here. The first term appears hard to compute, as we have to predict $r_n(\tau, T)$. However, here enters the fact that although this payment occurs at T it is formed at τ, when $r_n(\tau, T)$ is realized. So, at time τ we will be able to value this cash flow exactly as a simple present value. Indeed, we have

$$\text{Present value as of } \tau \text{ of } (1 + r_n(\tau, T)\Delta) = \frac{(1 + r_n(\tau, T)\Delta)}{(1 + r_n(\tau, T)\Delta)} = 1$$

It follows that the value *today* of the first term is simply the discount factor $Z(0, \tau)$, and there is no uncertainty here either. Therefore, the value of the security today, from first principles, is simply

$$V = Z(0, \tau) - (1 + r_K \Delta) Z(0, T)$$

This valuation is model free: It does not depend on whether we use LIBOR market model, or any other model. Finally, note that by factoring out $Z(0, T)$, we obtain

$$V = Z(0, T) \left[\frac{Z(0, \tau)}{Z(0, T)} - (1 + r_K \Delta) \right] = Z(0, T) \left[f_n(0, \tau, T) - r_K \right] \Delta$$

which results in the valuation formula we used earlier.

Note that the lag between cash flow formation (τ) and its payment ($T = \tau + \Delta$) was key in eliminating the uncertainty about the future value of $r_n(\tau, T)$. No volatility of $r_n(\tau, T)$ should enter the formula with the natural lag. If instead there is no lag, then we still have to deal with the uncertainty about $r_n(\tau, T)$: Intuitively, then, the expected future value of $r_n(\tau, T)$ appears through its expected value $E_f^*[r_n(\tau, T)] = f_n(0, \tau, T)$. Why does the volatility also enter, though? In particular, why does it increase the value of the security?

To understand this last point, compare the floating leg of the security that pays at τ with the one that pays at T. In both cases, the cash flow is $r_n(\tau, T)\Delta$. Because the τ−security pays earlier than T−security, this cash flow is more valuable in the former case than in the latter. How much more valuable? By the capitalization of the payment $r_n(\tau, T)$ from τ to T, that is $r_n(\tau, T) \times (1 + r_n(\tau, T)\Delta)$. This implies a convexity effect: A high interest rate not only produces a high cash flow but also a greater return from compounding this cash flow from τ to T. Similarly, a low interest rate produces a low cash flow, but also a low compounding to T. Because of this convexity, higher volatility of the interest rate increases the value of the τ−security compared to the T−security.

---

[15]The logic of what follows is the same as discussed in Chapter 2, Section 2.5.

21.7.2   A Convexity Adjustment

Consider again Example 21.8. In that example we priced the payoff at τ by using the $T-$forward risk neutral dynamics. Why not using the $\tau-$forward risk neutral dynamics? This approach leads to a popular convexity adjustment, often employed by practitioners to price securities with unnatural lag.

To see the argument, consider again the payoff

$$g_\tau = \Delta \left(r_n \left(\tau, T \right) - r_K \right)$$

Let us try to value this payoff under the $\tau-$forward risk neutral dynamics, that is, those corresponding to the payment time τ. In this case, the numeraire is $Z(t, \tau)$ and according to the forward risk neutral methodology, the value of the security is

$$V = Z(0, \tau) \Delta E_f^{*\tau} \left[r_n \left(\tau, T \right) - r_k \right] \tag{21.62}$$

where we now insert a superscript "τ" to clarify that the expectation is taken with respect to $\tau-$forward dynamics. The key question is: What is $E_f^{*\tau} \left[r_n \left(\tau, T \right) \right]$? It is not $f_n \left(0, \tau, T \right)$, as this equality is only true under $T-$forward dynamics.

We can obtain an accurate approximation of $E_f^{*\tau} \left[r_n \left(\tau, T \right) \right]$ as follows.[16] Consider first the value of a forward contract on a zero coupon bond $Z(\tau, T)$, that is, with payoff at τ given by $\left(Z \left(\tau, T \right) - K \right)$, where K is the delivery price. Using $Z \left(t, \tau \right)$ as numeraire, we know the value of such a security is

$$V = Z \left(0, \tau \right) E_f^{*\tau} \left[Z \left(\tau, T \right) - K \right]$$

The forward price is the delivery price K that makes $V = 0$, that is $F \left(0, \tau, T \right) = E_f^{*\tau} \left[Z \left(\tau, T \right) \right]$. Let now $G(x)$ be the function $G(x) = 1/(1 + x\Delta)$. By definition of spot rate and forward rate, we have

$$Z(\tau, T) = G(r_n(\tau, T)) \quad \text{and} \quad F(0, \tau, T) = G(f_n(0, \tau, T))$$

Consider now a Taylor expansion of $G(r_n(\tau, T))$ around $f_n(0, \tau, T)$,

$$
\begin{aligned}
G \left(r_n \left(\tau, T \right) \right) &\approx G \left(f_n \left(0, \tau, T \right) \right) + G' \left(f_n \left(0, \tau, T \right) \right) \left(r_n \left(\tau, T \right) - f_n \left(0, \tau, T \right) \right) \\
&+ \frac{1}{2} G'' \left(f_n \left(0, \tau, T \right) \right) \left(r_n \left(\tau, T \right) - f_n \left(0, \tau, T \right) \right)^2
\end{aligned}
$$

Taking expectations $E_f^{*\tau} \left[\cdot \right]$ on both sides of the equality

$$
\begin{aligned}
E_f^{*\tau} \left[G \left(r_n \left(\tau, T \right) \right) \right] &\approx G \left(f_n \left(0, \tau, T \right) \right) + G' \left(f_n \left(0, \tau, T \right) \right) \left(E_f^{*\tau} \left[r_n \left(\tau, T \right) \right] - f_n \left(0, \tau, T \right) \right) \\
&+ \frac{1}{2} G'' \left(f_n \left(0, \tau, T \right) \right) E_f^{*\tau} \left[\left(r_n \left(\tau, T \right) - f_n \left(0, \tau, T \right) \right)^2 \right]
\end{aligned}
$$

Using the fact that $G \left(f_n \left(0, \tau, T \right) \right) = F \left(0, \tau, T \right) = E_f^{*\tau} \left[Z(\tau, T) \right] = E_f^{*\tau} \left[G(r_n(\tau, T)) \right]$ we finally obtain

$$
\begin{aligned}
E_f^{*\tau} \left[r_n \left(\tau, T \right) \right] &\approx f_n \left(0, \tau, T \right) - \frac{1}{2} \frac{G'' \left(f_n \left(0, \tau, T \right) \right)}{G' \left(f_n \left(0, \tau, T \right) \right)} E_f^{*\tau} \left[\left(r_n \left(\tau, T \right) - f_n \left(0, \tau, T \right) \right)^2 \right] \\
&\approx f_n \left(0, \tau, T \right) + \frac{f_n \left(0, \tau, T \right)^2 \Delta}{1 + f_n \left(0, \tau, T \right) \Delta} \sigma_f^2 \tau
\end{aligned} \tag{21.63}
$$

---

[16]See e.g. John Hull, 2009, Options, Futures, and Other Derivatives, Seventh Edition, Prentice Hall

where the last step stems from computing $G'(x)$ and $G''(x)$, and also by noticing that

$$E_f^{*\tau}\left[\left(\frac{r_n\left(\tau,T\right)-f_n\left(0,\tau,T\right)}{f_n\left(0,\tau,T\right)}\right)^2\right]\approx\sigma_f^2\tau$$

Equation 21.63 shows that the expected spot rate $r_n\left(\tau,T\right)$ under the $\tau-$forward risk neutral dynamics equals the forward rate $f_n\left(0,\tau,T\right)$ plus a convexity adjustment term that depends on the interest rate volatility. This adjustment stems from the convex relation that naturally links bond prices – the key quantity for forward risk neutral pricing – and interest rates.

■ **EXAMPLE 21.9**

Consider again Example 21.8. The expected payoff under the $\tau-$forward risk neutral dynamics is

$$E_f^{*\tau}\left[g_\tau\right]=N\Delta\left[E_f^{*\tau}\left(r_n\left(\tau,T\right)\right)-r_K\right]$$

Recalling $f_n\left(0,.75,1\right)=2.8987\%$ and $\sigma_f=25.54\%$, we can use (21.63) and approximate the expectation by

$$\begin{aligned}E_f^{*\tau}\left(r_n\left(\tau,T\right)\right)&\approx f_n\left(0,\tau,T\right)+\frac{f_n\left(0,\tau,T\right)^2\Delta}{1+f_n\left(0,\tau,T\right)\Delta}\sigma_f^2\tau\\&\approx 2.8987\%+\frac{\left(2.8987\%\right)^2\Delta}{1+2.8987\%\Delta}\times\left(25.54\%\right)^2\times 0.75\\&\approx 2.9007\%\end{aligned}$$

This calculation, leads to an approximate value of the security of

$$V\approx\$0.6877\text{ million}$$

This is lower than the exact value obtained under the LIBOR market model ($0.6926 million), but higher than the value obtained under the natural lag, i.e. when the payoff occurs at T ($0.6817 million).

Convexity adjustments can be made on numerous securities, and they often significanlty speed up computations compared to the alternative of using Monte Carlo simulations.

21.8 SUMMARY

In this chapter we covered the following topics:

1. Change of numeraire: This is the procedure to express the value of securities in terms of the price of another security, akin to expressing the value of a good in different currencies (e.g., dollars or Euros). Redefining the numeraire in which we express the value of securities helps in simplifying the Fundamental Pricing Equation.

2. Forward Risk Neutral Pricing: The risk neutral pricing methodology that obtains when we define the value of securities in terms of the price of another (conveniently chosen) security is known as the forward risk neutral pricing. The word "forward"

stems from the fact that the forward price of the security used as numeraire follows a martingale.

3. LIBOR market model (or BGM model). This is a model for the LIBOR-based forward rates, according to which each forward rate with maturity T follows a log-normal diffusion process under the dynamics implied by the zero coupon bond with maturity T. This model has several properties:

   (a) It provides a no arbitrage derivation of the Black formula to price caps and floors.

   (b) It provides a framework for pricing derivative securities with the only input of caplet implied volatilities and the current term structure of interest rates. By its very nature, the model is able to fit caps' and floors' volatility very accurately.

   (c) For complicated securities, the model provides the methodology to use Monte Carlo simulations for pricing.

4. Swap Market Model: The swap market model is a model for the LIBOR-based swap rate processes, according to which the forward swap rate follows a log-normal model. It provides a no arbitrage derivation of the Black formula used by practitioners to quote European swaptions. Unfortunately, the assumptions necessary to obtain this result are incompatible with the assumptions underlying the LIBOR market model.

5. Heath, Jarrow, and Morton (HJM) framework: This framework studies the properties of continuously compounded forward rates, and shows that the risk neutral dynamics of forward rates are fully characterized by the volatility of forward rates. Given a volatility structure of forward rates and the initial term structure of interest rates, nothing else is necessary to price derivative securities by no arbitrage. The HJM model provides a general framework, and, in particular, the models for the spot rate interest rate, such as Ho-Lee or Hull-White models, can be considered special cases under particular assumptions about the volatility structure.

6. Convexity adjustments: The forward risk neutral methodology implies that the expected future price of the bond used as numeraire equals its current forward price. If a derivative security's payoff depends on the yield of the bond instead of its price, then the forward risk neutral expected future yield is approximated well by the forward rate plus a convexity adjustment. The latter takes into account the natural convexity that exists between the value of a bond and its yield. The convexity adjustment is zero when there is a "natural" lag between cash flow formation and payment date.

21.9   EXERCISES

1. Today is November 1, 2004. The current LIBOR discount curve and caplet forward volatility are in Table 20.3 in Chapter 20. Consider the power option discussed in Example 21.1. Let maturity be $T = 2$ and the strike rate be $r_K = .03^\alpha$, where α is the parameter of the power option.

   (a) Plot the payoff of the power option for various levels of the power α. When is the payoff larger?

(b) Obtain the price of the power option for at least two levels of α.

(c) Use Monte Carlo simulations to compute the price of the power option. Do you obtain the same value you obtained in the Part (b)?

2. Table 21.2 contains the estimated volatility function $S(T_i - t)$ of forward rates (see also Table 21.1 for their interpretation). The current LIBOR zero coupon curve is in Table 20.3 in Chapter 20.

(a) Use the LIBOR market model to obtain the value of a 3-year swap in-arrears, that is, with cash flows given by

$$CF_{T_i} = N\Delta(r_n(T_i, T_{i+1}) - c(0,3))$$

for a swap rate $c(0,3) = 3.254\%$.

(b) Compute the value of the swap with its natural lag and compare it with the value obtained in Part (a). Comment on the difference.

3. Table 21.2 contains the estimated volatility function $S(T_i - t)$ of forward rates (see also Table 21.1 for their interpretation). The current LIBOR zero coupon curve is in Table 20.3 in Chapter 20.

(a) Use the LIBOR market model to obtain the value of a 3-year cap in-arrears, that is, with cash flows given by

$$CF_{T_i} = N\Delta \max(r_n(T_i, T_{i+1}) - r_K, 0)$$

for a cap rate $r_K = 3.254\%$.

(b) Compute the value of the cap with its natural lag and compare it with the value obtained in Part (a). Comment on the difference.

4. Today is November 1, 2004. The current LIBOR discount curve and caplet forward volatility are in Table 20.3 in Chapter 20. Use this information to estimate the volatility of forward rates $\sigma_f^{i+1}(t)$. In particular, compare the two cases in which the volatility only depends on t (i.e., all the forward rates have the same volatility at time t independently of their maturity) with the case in which volatility only depends on maturity, as discussed in the chapter.

5. Use the estimates of the volatility of forward rates $\sigma_f^{i+1}(t)$ obtained in the previous exercise and Monte Carlo simulations to compute the values of some of the European Swaptions in Table 20.1 in Chapter 20 [some of the estimates of $\sigma_f^{i+1}(t) = S(T_{i+1} - 1)$ are also in Table 21.2 in this chapter]. Compare the value of the swaptions obtained using cap volatilities to the value of the quoted swaptions. Are they close to each other?

6. A **constant maturity swap** (CMS) is a swap with cash flow at time T_i is given by

$$CF_{T_i} = N\Delta(c(T_i, T_{i+m}) - K)$$

where $c(T_i, T_{i+m})$ is the swap rate for a given maturity $T_{i+m} - T_i$, and K is the CMS swap rate. Let the constant maturity be $T_{i+m} - T_i = 3$ years and $K = 3\%$.

Use the estimates of volatility of forward rates obtained in the previous exercise to obtain the value of the constant maturity swap.

(a) Consider each payment T_i independently. For each payment, select an appropriate forward risk neutral dynamics and use Monte Carlo simulations to simulate several LIBOR curves $Z^s(T_i, T)$. For each simulation run s you can compute the swap rate $c^s(T_i, T_{i+m})$ and thus value the payoff as usual.

(b) Repeat the procedure above for each payment date T_i. Are the forward risk neutral dynamics used to obtain the value of payment T_i the same as those used to compute the value of payment T_j, for $j \neq i$? Comment.

7. Today is November 3, 2008. Exercise 2 in Chapter 20 provides the caps and swap rates quotes on that date, and asks you to compute the caplet forward volatilities.

(a) Using the caplet forward volatilities, compute the volatility of forward rates $\sigma_f^{i+1}(t)$. In particular, for the case in which the volatility only depends on time to maturity $\sigma_f^{i+1}(t) = S(T_{i+1} - 1)$, how well does the procedure work? Comment on your findings.

(b) Use the estimated volatility of forward rates to compute the value of a 1-year receiver swaption to enter into a 3-year swap. Compare the value obtained here from cap volatilities with the quoted value available in Table 20.6 in Chapter 20.

8. Section 21.6.1 contains the convexity adjustment needed to convert Eurodollar futures quotes into forward rates according to the Ho-Lee model. Follow the same steps to obtain the convexity adjustment for the Hull-White model.

9. Table 6.14 in Chapter 6 contain Eurodollar futures quotes. Extract the forward rates from futures using both the Ho-Lee model and the Hull-White model. Work the exercise for various parameters of the two models and comment on the difference. Intuitively, why should futures and forward rates be different?

21.10 APPENDIX: DERIVATIONS

21.10.1 Derivation of the Partial Differential Equation in the Forward Risk Neutral Dynamics

Consider

$$\widetilde{V} = \frac{V}{Z}$$

where Z is a zero coupon bond with maturity T. Clearly, Z also depends on r, and thus

$$\frac{\partial V}{\partial t} = \frac{\partial \widetilde{V}}{\partial t} Z + \frac{\partial Z}{\partial t} \widetilde{V}; \quad \frac{\partial V}{\partial r} = \frac{\partial \widetilde{V}}{\partial r} Z + \frac{\partial Z}{\partial r} \widetilde{V}$$

$$\frac{\partial^2 V}{\partial r^2} = \frac{\partial^2 \widetilde{V}}{\partial r^2} Z + 2 \frac{\partial \widetilde{V}}{\partial r} \frac{\partial Z}{\partial r} + \frac{\partial^2 Z}{\partial r^2} \widetilde{V}$$

Substitute

$$
r\widetilde{V}Z = \frac{\partial \widetilde{V}}{\partial t}Z + \frac{\partial Z}{\partial t}\widetilde{V} + \frac{\partial \widetilde{V}}{\partial r}Zm^*(r,t) + \frac{\partial Z}{\partial r}\widetilde{V}m^*(r,t) + \frac{1}{2}\frac{\partial^2 \widetilde{V}}{\partial r^2}Zs(r,t)^2
$$
$$
+ \frac{\partial \widetilde{V}}{\partial r}\frac{\partial Z}{\partial r}s(r,t)^2 + \frac{1}{2}\frac{\partial^2 Z}{\partial r^2}\widetilde{V}s(r,t)^2
$$

Pull together the terms in $\widetilde{V}$

$$
0 = \frac{\partial \widetilde{V}}{\partial t}Z + \left(\frac{\partial Z}{\partial t} + \frac{\partial Z}{\partial r}m^*(r,t) + \frac{1}{2}\frac{\partial^2 Z}{\partial r^2}s(r,t)^2 - rZ\right)\widetilde{V} + \frac{\partial \widetilde{V}}{\partial r}Zm^*(r,t)
$$
$$
+ \frac{1}{2}\frac{\partial^2 \widetilde{V}}{\partial r^2}Zs(r,t)^2 + \frac{\partial \widetilde{V}}{\partial r}\frac{\partial Z}{\partial r}s(r,t)^2
$$

Because the Fundamental Pricing Equation implies

$$
\frac{\partial Z}{\partial t} + \frac{\partial Z}{\partial r}m^*(r,t) + \frac{1}{2}\frac{\partial^2 Z}{\partial r^2}s(r,t)^2 = rZ
$$

we can rewrite as

$$
0 = \frac{\partial \widetilde{V}}{\partial t}Z + \frac{\partial \widetilde{V}}{\partial r}Zm^*(r,t) + \frac{1}{2}\frac{\partial^2 \widetilde{V}}{\partial r^2}Zs(r,t)^2 + \frac{\partial \widetilde{V}}{\partial r}\frac{\partial Z}{\partial r}s(r,t)^2
$$

or

$$
0 = \frac{\partial \widetilde{V}}{\partial t}Z + \frac{\partial \widetilde{V}}{\partial r}\left(Zm^*(r,t) + \frac{\partial Z}{\partial r}s(r,t)^2\right) + \frac{1}{2}\frac{\partial^2 \widetilde{V}}{\partial r^2}Zs(r,t)^2
$$

Dividing through by Z, we obtain

$$
0 = \frac{\partial \widetilde{V}}{\partial t} + \frac{\partial \widetilde{V}}{\partial r}\left(m^*(r,t) + \frac{\partial Z}{\partial r}\frac{1}{Z}s(r,t)^2\right) + \frac{1}{2}\frac{\partial^2 \widetilde{V}}{\partial r^2}s(r,t)^2
$$

Define

$$
\sigma_Z(r,t) = \frac{\partial Z}{\partial r}\frac{1}{Z}s(r,t)
$$

so that we can rewrite the PDE as

$$
0 = \frac{\partial \widetilde{V}}{\partial t} + \frac{\partial \widetilde{V}}{\partial r}\left(m^*(r,t) + \sigma_Z(r,t)s(r,t)\right) + \frac{1}{2}\frac{\partial^2 \widetilde{V}}{\partial r^2}s(r,t)^2
$$

21.10.2 Derivation of the Call Option Pricing Formula (Equations 21.11)

Under the T-forward risk neutral dynamics, the assumption is

$$
V_T \sim \log N\left(F_0(T),\sigma_T^2\right)
$$

We must compute

$$
E_f^* \max(V_T - K,0) = \int_K^\infty V_T p_f^*(V_T)\,dV_T - K\int_K^\infty p_f^*(V_T)\,dV_T
$$
$$
= \int_{\log(K)}^\infty e^{v_T} p_f^*(v_T)\,dv_T - K\int_{\log(K)}^\infty p_f^*(v_T)\,dv_T
$$

where $p_f^*(v_T)$ denotes the normal density function

$$v_T = \log(V_T) \sim N\left(\log(F_0(T)) - \frac{1}{2}\sigma_T^2, \sigma_T^2\right).$$

That is,

$$p_f^*(v_T) = \frac{1}{\sqrt{2\pi\sigma_V^2}} e^{-\frac{1}{2\sigma_V^2}\left(\log(F_0(T)) - \frac{1}{2}\sigma_T^2 - v_T\right)^2}$$

The following two integration rules are useful:

$$\int_a^\infty \frac{1}{\sqrt{2\pi}s} e^{-\frac{(x-b)^2}{2s^2}}\,dx = \int_{\frac{a-b}{s}}^\infty \frac{1}{\sqrt{2\pi}} e^{-x^2}\,dx = N\left(\frac{b-a}{s}\right)$$

and

$$\int_a^\infty \frac{1}{\sqrt{2\pi}s} e^{-\frac{(x-b)^2}{2s^2}} e^x\,dx = e^{\frac{1}{2}s^2+b}\int_{\frac{a-b}{s}-s}^\infty \frac{1}{\sqrt{2\pi}} e^{-x^2}\,dx = e^{\frac{1}{2}s^2+b} N\left(\frac{b-a}{s}+s\right)$$

Applying these two rules of integration, we obtain

$$
\begin{aligned}
K\int_{\log(K)}^\infty p_f^*(v_T)\,dv_T &= K\int_{\left(\frac{\log(K)-\left(\log(F_0(T))-\frac{1}{2}\sigma_T^2\right)}{\sigma_T}\right)}^\infty \frac{e^{-\frac{1}{2}v_T^2}}{\sqrt{2\pi}}\,dv_T \\
&= KN\left(\frac{1}{\sigma_T}\log\left(\frac{F_0(T)}{K}\right) - \frac{1}{2}\sigma_T\right) \\
&= KN(d_2)
\end{aligned}
$$

and

$$
\begin{aligned}
\int_{\log(K)}^\infty e^{v_T} p_f^*(v_T)\,dv_T &= e^{\frac{1}{2}\sigma_T^2+\left(\log(F_0(T))-\frac{1}{2}\sigma_T^2\right)}\int_{\frac{\log(K)-\left(\log(F_0(T))-\frac{1}{2}\sigma_T^2\right)}{\sigma_T}-\sigma_T}^\infty \frac{e^{-\frac{1}{2}v_T^2}}{\sqrt{2\pi}}\,dv_T \\
&= F_0(T) N\left(\frac{1}{\sigma_T}\log\left(\frac{F_0(T)}{K}\right) + \frac{1}{2}\sigma_T\right) \\
&= F_0 N(d_1)
\end{aligned}
$$

where d_1 and d_2 are given in Equations 21.12 and 21.13, respectively.

21.10.3   Derivation of the Formula in Equations 21.27 and 21.31

The argument leading to both Equations 21.27 and 21.31 is slightly imprecise. Here, we make the argument precise. One issue with the argument is that in both cases, the payoff at time T, g_T, actually depends on the value of the interest rate at an earlier time τ and not T. The version of the Feynman-Kac formula used in this book requires that the payoff at T depend on the interest rate at T. However, Equations 21.12 can be obtained from the following argument:

Because the payoff of the forward contract is actually known at τ, it is convenient to compute its present value to τ, and express the payoff, equivalently, as:

Payoff at τ of forward with maturity $T = Z(\tau, T)\,N\,\Delta\,(r_n(\tau, T) - K)$

Consider the bond maturing at T, $Z(t,T)$, as the new numeraire. The payoff at τ expressed in units of the new numeraire is

$$
\text{Normalized payoff of forward at } \tau = \frac{Z(\tau,T) \ N \ \Delta \ (r_n(\tau,T) - K)}{Z(\tau,T)}
$$

$$
= N \ \Delta \ (r_n(\tau,T) - K)
$$

The result in Equation 21.20, with $P(r,t) = Z(t,T)$, then implies

$$
V^{fwd}(0;T) = Z(0,T) \ N \ \Delta \ E_f^* [r_n(\tau,T) - K]
$$

which is the formula in Equation 21.27.

The argument proving Equation 21.31 is identical.

21.10.4   Derivation of the Formula in Equation 21.21

These dynamics follow from an application of Ito's lemma. In fact, under the condition that the dynamics of the interest rate are as in Equation 21.19, from Ito's lemma we have

$$
\begin{aligned}
dV &= \left[\left(\frac{\partial V}{\partial t} \right) + \left(\frac{\partial V}{\partial r} \right) (m^*(r,t) + \sigma_P s(r,t)) + \frac{1}{2} \frac{\partial^2 V}{\partial r^2} s(r,t)^2 \right] dt + \frac{\partial V}{\partial r} s(r,t) \, dX_t \\
&= \left[\left(\frac{\partial V}{\partial t} \right) + \left(\frac{\partial V}{\partial r} \right) m^*(r,t) + \frac{1}{2} \frac{\partial^2 V}{\partial r^2} s(r,t)^2 + \left(\frac{\partial V}{\partial r} \right) \sigma_P s(r,t) \right] dt + \frac{\partial V}{\partial r} s(r,t) \, dX
\end{aligned}
$$

From the Fundamental Pricing Equation (Equation 21.1) we can substitute the first three terms in the square parenthesis simply for rV, obtaining

$$
dV = \left[rV + \left(\frac{\partial V}{\partial r} \right) \sigma_P s(r,t) \right] dt + \frac{\partial V}{\partial r} s(r,t) \, dX
$$

Defining $\sigma_V = \frac{1}{V} \left(\frac{\partial V}{\partial r} \right) s(r,t)$ gives the result.

21.10.5   Derivation of the Formula in Equation 21.37

Fact 21.6 implies that the processes for any variable Y under the forward risk neutral dynamics induced by two different securities $Z(0, T_{i+1})$ and $Z(0, T_{\bar{i}})$ are

$$
dY_t = \left(m^*(Y,t) + \sigma_{Z,T_{i+1}}(t) s(Y,t) \right) dt + s(Y,t) dX_t \tag{21.64}
$$

$$
dY_t = \left(m^*(Y,t) + \sigma_{Z,T_{\bar{i}}}(t) s(Y,t) \right) dt + s(Y,t) dX_t \tag{21.65}
$$

where $\sigma_{Z,T}$ is the diffusion of $Z(t,T)$, whose risk neutral process is

$$
\frac{dZ(t,T)}{Z(t,T)} = r dt + \sigma_{Z,T}(t) dX_t
$$

Equations 21.64 and 21.65 imply that when we move from the dynamics implied by $Z(0, T_{i+1})$ to those implied by $Z(0, T_{\bar{i}})$ we must increase the drift rate of the process dY_t by

$$
\text{Change in drift in } dY_t = \left(\sigma_{Z,T_{\bar{i}}} - \sigma_{Z,T_{i+1}} \right) s(Y,t) \tag{21.66}
$$

In our case, let the variable Y_t be the forward rate $f_n(t, T_i, T_{i+1})$. Since its dynamics implied by the numeraire $Z(t, T_{i+1})$ are

$$df_n(t, T_i, T_{i+1}) = \sigma_f^{i+1}(t) f_n(t, T_i, T_{i+1}) dX_t$$

it follows that the last term in Equation 21.66 is $s(Y, t) = \sigma_f^{i+1}(t) f_n(t, T_i, T_{i+1})$. We must then derive the factor $\left(\sigma_{Z, T_{\bar{i}}} - \sigma_{Z, T_{i+1}} \right)$. Note that we can write

$$\frac{Z(t, T_{i+1})}{Z(t, T_{\bar{i}})} = \frac{1}{1 + \Delta f_n(t, T_{\bar{i}}, T_{\bar{i}+1})} \times \frac{1}{1 + \Delta f_n(t, T_{\bar{i}+1}, T_{\bar{i}+2})} \times \ldots \times \frac{1}{1 + \Delta f_n(t, T_i, T_{i+1})}$$

which implies

$$\log \left(\frac{Z(t, T_{i+1})}{Z(t, T_{\bar{i}})} \right) = - \sum_{j=\bar{i}}^{i} \log(1 + \Delta f(t, T_j, T_{j+1}))$$

If we define $J_t = \log \left(\frac{Z(t, T_{i+1})}{Z(t, T_{\bar{i}})} \right)$, note that Ito's Lemma implies

$$dJ_t = (\text{Drift}) \, dt - \left(\sigma_{Z, T_{\bar{i}}} - \sigma_{Z, T_{i+1}} \right) dX_t$$

where we do not have to specify its drift as we are only interested in the diffusion term. Similarly, defining $\tilde{J}_t = - \sum_{j=\bar{i}}^{i} \log(1 + \Delta f(t, T_j, T_{j+1}))$, we find that Ito's lemma implies

$$d\tilde{J}_t = (\text{Drift}) \, dt - \sum_{j=\bar{i}}^{i} \frac{1}{1 + \Delta f(t, T_j, T_{j+1})} \Delta \sigma^{j+1}(t) f(t, T_j, T_{j+1}) dX_t$$

Because by definition $J_t = \tilde{J}$, the two diffusion terms must be the same, which implies

$$\left(\sigma_{Z, T_{\bar{i}}} - \sigma_{Z, T_{i+1}} \right) = \sum_{j=\bar{i}}^{i} \frac{1}{1 + \Delta f(t, T_j, T_{j+1})} \Delta \sigma^{j+1}(t) f(t, T_j, T_{j+1})$$

In conclusion, the change in drift when the dynamics of $f_n(t, T_i, T_{i+1})$ move from $Z(t, T_{i+1})$ to $Z(t, T_{\bar{i}})$ is

$$\text{Change in drift in } dY_t = \left(\sigma_{Z, T_{\bar{i}}} - \sigma_{Z, T_{i+1}} \right) s(Y, t)$$

$$= \left(\sum_{j=\bar{i}}^{i} \frac{1}{1 + \Delta f(t, T_j, T_{j+1})} \Delta \sigma^{j+1}(t) f(t, T_j, T_{j+1}) \right) \sigma_f^{i+1}(t) f_n(t, T_i, T$$

as in Equation 21.37.

The proof of Equation 21.38 is analogous, with the only change that if $\overline{T} = T_{\bar{i}} > T_{i+1}$, then

$$\log \left(\frac{Z(t, T_{i+1})}{Z(t, T_{\bar{i}})} \right) = \sum_{j=i}^{\bar{i}-1} \log(1 + \Delta f(t, T_j, T_{j+1}))$$

The rest of the derivation is identical.

CHAPTER 22

MULTIFACTOR MODELS

In this chapter we introduce multifactor models. This is an important extension of the no arbitrage model discussed so far, as from Chapter 4 we saw that we need at least three factors to "explain" the variation in yields. In other words, the yield curve not only moves up and down, but it also changes slope as well as curvature. The models developed so far did not allow for independent variation of these quantities: For instance, in the Vasicek model, the level, slope, and curvature of the yield curve are all tied to the short-term interest rate r_t, and thus they are perfectly correlated.

The good news is that the methodology extensively covered in the previous chapters readily extends to many factors, including the risk neutral pricing methodology. This implies that (almost) all of the pricing technique learned in previous chapters can be applied to the multifactor case. We now illustrate the changes to be made.

22.1 MULTIFACTOR ITO'S LEMMA WITH INDEPENDENT FACTORS

As in the single factor case, the most important tool is the extension of Ito's Lemma, discussed in Chapter 14, to the multifactor case. We start with the simple case in which there are only two independent factors affecting the term structure of interest rates. The general multifactor model is dealt with below.

Consider two independent factors, generically denoted by $\phi_{1,t}$ and $\phi_{2,t}$, and assume they move according to the processes

$$d\phi_{1,t} = m_1\left(\phi_{1,t}, t\right) dt + s_1\left(\phi_{1,t}, t\right) dX_{1,t} \tag{22.1}$$

$$d\phi_{2,t} = m_2\left(\phi_{2,t}, t\right) dt + s_2\left(\phi_{2,t}, t\right) dX_{2,t} \tag{22.2}$$

where $X_{1,t}$ and $X_{2,t}$ are two independent Brownian motions.

We now state the version of Ito's lemma that holds with multiple independent factors. For notational convenience, and to keep formulas short, whenever there is no confusion we drop the explicit dependence of the functions $m_i(\phi_{i,t}, t)$ and $s_i(\phi_{i,t}, t)$, for $i = 1, 2$, from their arguments. In particular, we will denote $m_{i,t} = m_i(\phi_i, t)$ and $s_{i,t} = s_i(\phi_i, t)$.

Fact 22.1 *Multivariate Ito's Lemma with Independent Factors. Let $\phi_{1,t}$ and $\phi_{2,t}$ follow the processes in Equations 22.1 and 22.2. Let the price of a security be given by $P_t = F(t, \phi_{1,t}, \phi_{2,t})$. Then, the capital gain process is*

$$\begin{aligned}
dP_t &= \left\{\left(\frac{\partial F}{\partial t}\right) + \left(\frac{\partial F}{\partial \phi_1}\right) m_{1,t} + \left(\frac{\partial F}{\partial \phi_2}\right) m_{2,t} + \frac{1}{2}\left(\frac{\partial^2 F}{\partial \phi_1^2}\right) s_{1,t}^2 + \frac{1}{2}\left(\frac{\partial^2 F}{\partial \phi_2^2}\right) s_{2,t}^2\right\} dt \\
&\quad + \left(\frac{\partial F}{\partial \phi_1}\right) s_{1,t} dX_{1,t} + \left(\frac{\partial F}{\partial \phi_2}\right) s_{2,t} dX_{2,t}
\end{aligned} \tag{22.3}$$

The expression in Equation 22.3 should be compared with the analog expression in Equation 14.41 in Chapter 14 for the single factor case. It is immediately apparent that the multivariate Ito's lemma with independent factors is simply a replica with multiple identical terms of the single factor one, except for the first term $\partial F/\partial t$. More specifically, Equation 22.3 contains several familiar terms:

1. $\left(\frac{\partial F}{\partial t}\right)$ is the predictable capital gain due to the passage of time (called "Theta", Θ). For instance, we know that a zero coupon bond increases in value over time even if factors do not move, just because the maturity of the bond is getting closer.

2. $\left(\frac{\partial F}{\partial \phi_i}\right) m_{i,t}$, for $i = 1, 2$, is the expected capital gain due to the sensitivity of the security to changes in the factor ϕ_i times the expected change in the factor $m_{i,t} = E[d\phi_{i,t}]$. For instance, if ϕ_1 is the "level" factor, then we expect to lose money on a bond if we anticipate an increase in the average level of interest rates.

3. $\frac{1}{2}\left(\frac{\partial^2 F}{\partial \phi_i^2}\right) s_{i,t}^2$, for $i = 1, 2$, is the predictable expected return of the security due to the (Ito) convexity term. This latter effect, recall, stems from the stochastic nature of factor i, as discussed in Section 14.4 in Chapter 14. The higher the variance of factor i, $s_{i,t}^2$, the higher is the convexity effect.

4. $\left(\frac{\partial F}{\partial \phi^i}\right) s_i dX_{i,t}$ for $i = 1, 2$ is the stochastic component of the dollar return on the portfolio, which is due to the shocks to factor i, i.e. the realization of the Brownian motion $dX_{i,t}$.

22.2   NO ARBITRAGE WITH INDEPENDENT FACTORS

We now go over the no arbitrage argument to determine a pricing relation for the case of multifactor models. First, we must specify the relation between the short-term interest rate r_t and the factors. One possibility is that r_t is simply in fact one of the two factors, and this will be a special case. However, for generality, let's just assume that the short-term instantaneous interest rate r_t depends on the two factors according to $r_t = R(\phi_{1,t}, \phi_{2,t})$, where $R(\cdot, \cdot)$ is a given function.

As in Chapter 15, consider now a portfolio composed of one zero coupon bond with maturity T_1, denoted by $Z_1(\phi_{1,t}, \phi_{2,t}, t)$, and Δ_2 and Δ_3 units of T_2 and T_3 zero coupon bonds, denoted by $Z_2(\phi_{1,t}, \phi_{2,t}, t)$ and $Z_3(\phi_{1,t}, \phi_{2,t}, t)$, respectively. Note that the zero coupon bonds depend on the factors $\phi_{1,t}$ and $\phi_{2,t}$. We then have that the portfolio value at time t is given by

$$\Pi(\phi_{1,t}, \phi_{2,t}, t) = Z_1(\phi_{1,t}, \phi_{2,t}, t) + \Delta_2 \times Z_2(\phi_{1,t}, \phi_{2,t}, t) + \Delta_3 \times Z_3(\phi_{1,t}, \phi_{2,t}, t) \quad (22.4)$$

We now proceed exactly as in Section 15.2.1 in Chapter 15. In particular, we first choose Δ_2 and Δ_3 in order to eliminate any risk from the two factors $\phi_{1,t}$ and $\phi_{2,t}$. That is, such that

$$\frac{\partial \Pi}{\partial \phi_1} = 0 \quad \text{and} \quad \frac{\partial \Pi}{\partial \phi_2} = 0 \quad (22.5)$$

Substituting the expression for the portfolio, we obtain two equations that pin down the two Δ's

$$\frac{\partial Z_1}{\partial \phi_1} + \Delta_2 \times \frac{\partial Z_2}{\partial \phi_1} + \Delta_3 \times \frac{\partial Z_3}{\partial \phi_1} = 0 \quad (22.6)$$

$$\frac{\partial Z_1}{\partial \phi_2} + \Delta_2 \times \frac{\partial Z_2}{\partial \phi_2} + \Delta_3 \times \frac{\partial Z_3}{\partial \phi_2} = 0 \quad (22.7)$$

This is a system of two equations in two unknowns (Δ_2 and Δ_3) that can be solved to obtain the optimal hedge ratios.

The second step is to consider the dynamics of the portfolio $\Pi_t = \Pi(\phi_{1,t}, \phi_{2,t}, t)$ over time. We can use Ito's lemma in Equation 22.3 to determine its variation over time. It is important to realize that given Equation 22.5, many terms drop out from Ito's formula. Indeed, applying Equation 22.3 to this case we have

$$d\Pi_t = \left\{ \left(\frac{\partial \Pi}{\partial t}\right) + \frac{1}{2}\left(\frac{\partial^2 \Pi}{\partial \phi_1^2}\right)s_{1,t}^2 + \frac{1}{2}\left(\frac{\partial^2 \Pi}{\partial \phi_2^2}\right)s_{2,t}^2 \right\} dt \quad (22.8)$$

The capital gain $d\Pi_t$ is riskless between t and $t + dt$, as the risk factors have been hedged away. Therefore, the portfolio must yield the risk free rate $r_t = R(\phi_{1,t}, \phi_{2,t})$. That is,

$$\text{No Arbitrage} \implies d\Pi_t = r_t \Pi_t dt \quad (22.9)$$

The no arbitrage restriction is the same one discussed in Chapter 15 (see Equation 15.17). As then, we now substitute Π_t from Equation 22.4 on the right-hand side of Equation 22.9 and "$d\Pi_t$" in Equation 22.8 on its left-hand side. Given that the resulting expressions are rather long, for convenience we denote

$$G_i(\phi_1, \phi_2, t) = R(\phi_1, \phi_2) \times Z_i(\phi_1, \phi_2, t) - \quad (22.10)$$
$$\left\{ \left(\frac{\partial Z_i}{\partial t}\right) + \frac{1}{2}\left(\frac{\partial^2 Z_i}{\partial \phi_1^2}\right)s_{1,t}^2 + \frac{1}{2}\left(\frac{\partial^2 Z_i}{\partial \phi_2^2}\right)s_{2,t}^2 \right\}$$

From Equation 22.9 we then obtain

$$G_1(\phi_1, \phi_2, t) + \Delta_2 \times G_2(\phi_1, \phi_2, t) + \Delta_3 \times G_3(\phi_1, \phi_2, t) = 0 \qquad (22.11)$$

Note that Δ_2 and Δ_3 have already been selected as solutions to Equations 22.6 and 22.7. Therefore, for Equation 22.11 to also be satisfied, the only possibility is that this equation is a linear combination of Equations 22.6 and 22.7. That is, there must be two quantities $m_{1,t}^*$ and $m_{2,t}^*$ such that, heuristically

$$\text{[Equation 22.11]} = m_{1,t}^* \times \text{[Equation 22.6]} + m_{2,t}^* \times \text{[Equation 22.7]}$$

Indeed, under this condition, because the right-hand sides of Equations 22.6 and 22.7 are zero, so will be the right-hand side of Equation 22.11. This leads to the following condition: For every $i = 1, 2, 3$, we must have

$$G_i(\phi_1, \phi_2, t) = m_{1,t}^* \times \left(\frac{\partial Z_i}{\partial \phi_1}\right) + m_{2,t}^* \times \left(\frac{\partial Z_i}{\partial \phi_2}\right) \qquad (22.12)$$

Substituting the expression for G_i from Equation 22.10 into this last equation we obtain a partial differential equation that each bond $Z_i(\phi_{1,t}, \phi_{2,t}, t)$ has to satisfy. Indeed, as explained in Chapter 15, since the above derivation does not hinge on the particular characteristics of the interest rate security Z_i, which could be an option or any other interest rate security, we state the pricing result in terms of a generic security with price $V(\phi_1, \phi_2, t)$.

Fact 22.2 *Let $V(\phi_1, \phi_2, t)$ be the price of a security that depends on time t and the two factors ϕ_1 and ϕ_2 whose dynamics are described in Equations 22.1 and 22.2, and with final payoff g_T. Then, the value of this security is given by the solution to the* **Fundamental Pricing Equation** *given by*

$$R(\phi_1, \phi_2)V = \frac{\partial V}{\partial t} + \frac{\partial V}{\partial \phi_1}m_{1,t}^* + \frac{\partial V}{\partial \phi_2}m_{2,t}^* + \frac{1}{2}\frac{\partial^2 V}{\partial \phi_1^2}s_{1,t}^2 + \frac{1}{2}\frac{\partial^2 V}{\partial \phi_2^2}s_{2,t}^2 \qquad (22.13)$$

with the final condition that

$$V(\phi_1, \phi_2, T) = g_T$$

As in previous chapters, we call *risk neutral processes* the factor processes with drift rates equal to $m_{i,t}^*$ instead of the original $m_{i,t}$. That is, the risk neutral processes are given by

$$d\phi_{1,t} = m_1^*\left(\phi_{1,t}, t\right)dt + s_1\left(\phi_{1,t}, t\right)dX_{1,t} \qquad (22.14)$$
$$d\phi_{2,t} = m_2^*\left(\phi_{2,t}, t\right)dt + s_2\left(\phi_{2,t}, t\right)dX_{2,t} \qquad (22.15)$$

22.2.1 A Two-Factor Vasicek Model

Let us illustrate immediately the implications of the multifactor Fundamental Pricing Equation (Equation 22.13). Assume that the short-term interest rate is given by

$$r_t = \phi_{1,t} + \phi_{2,t} \qquad (22.16)$$

and make the following assumptions about $m_{i,t}^*$ and $s_{i,t}$, for $i = 1, 2$:

$$m_i^* (\phi_{i,t}, t) = \gamma_i^* \left(\overline{\phi}_i^* - \phi_{i,t} \right); \quad \text{and} \quad s_i (\phi_{i,t}, t) = \sigma_i.$$

In other words, under the risk neutral dynamics, each process follows a Vasicek type of model:

$$d\phi_{1,t} = \gamma_1^* \left(\overline{\phi}_1^* - \phi_{1,t} \right) dt + \sigma_1 dX_{1,t} \tag{22.17}$$

$$d\phi_{2,t} = \gamma_2^* \left(\overline{\phi}_2^* - \phi_{2,t} \right) dt + \sigma_2 dX_{2,t} \tag{22.18}$$

The same calculations as in Chapter 15 show the following:

Fact 22.3 *Let the risk neutral factor dynamics be given by the Vasicek model in Equations 22.17 and 22.18, and the interest rate be linear in the factors, as in Equation 22.16. Then the zero coupon bond price is given by*

$$Z \left(\phi_{1,t}, \phi_{2,t}, t; T \right) = e^{A(t;T) - B_1(t;T)\phi_{1,t} - B_2(t;T)\phi_{2,t}} \tag{22.19}$$

where, for $i = 1, 2$

$$B_i(t; T) = \frac{1}{\gamma_i^*} \left(1 - e^{-\gamma_i^*(T-t)} \right); \tag{22.20}$$

$$A(t; T) = (B_1(t; T) - (T - t)) \left(\overline{\phi}_1^* - \frac{\sigma_1^2}{2(\gamma_1^*)^2} \right) - \frac{\sigma_1^2}{4\gamma_1^*} B_1(t; T)^2$$

$$+ (B_2(t; T) - (T - t)) \left(\overline{\phi}_2^* - \frac{\sigma_2^2}{2(\gamma_2^*)^2} \right) - \frac{\sigma_2^2}{4\gamma_2^*} B_2(t; T)^2 \tag{22.21}$$

To understand this pricing formula, note that if parameters are such that $\phi_{2,t} = 0$ for every t, and this happens when $\phi_{2,0} = 0$, $\overline{\phi}_2^* = 0$ and $\sigma_2 = 0$, then the first factor $\phi_{1,t}$ is identical to the short-term rate, $r_t = \phi_{1,t}$, and the formula reverts back to the standard Vasicek formula obtained in Chapter 15 (see Equation 15.28).

What happens then when the second factor $\phi_{2,t}$ is non zero but it moves over time?

To see the impact of the second factor, it is convenient to rewrite the processes in Equations 22.17 and 22.18 with $r_t = \phi_{1,t} + \phi_{2,t}$ as a process for the short-term rate. Using Ito's lemma on $r_t = \phi_{1,t} + \phi_{2,t}$, we obtain $dr_t = d\phi_{1,t} + d\phi_{2,t}$. Substituting $d\phi_{1,t}$ and $d\phi_{2,t}$ from Equations 22.17 and 22.18, respectively, and after rearranging, we can write the process for the short term rate r_t as follows:

$$dr_t = \left[\gamma_1^* \left(\overline{\phi}_1^* - r_t \right) + \gamma_2^* \overline{\phi}_2^* + (\gamma_1^* - \gamma_2^*) \phi_{2,t} \right] dt + \sigma_1 dX_1 + \sigma_2 dX_2 \tag{22.22}$$

$$d\phi_{2,t} = \gamma_2^* \left(\overline{\phi}_2^* - \phi_{2,t} \right) dt + \sigma_2 dX_{2,t} \tag{22.23}$$

That is, the short-term rate follows a mean reverting process, as in the standard Vasicek model, but now its risk neutral drift depends on the second factor $\phi_{2,t}$. Assuming $\gamma_1^* - \gamma_2^* > 0$, for instance, then for given current rate r_t, when the second factor $\phi_{2,t}$ increases, the risk neutral expectation of future short-term rate increases, which in turn implies a steepening of the term structure of interest rates. In other words, the factor $\phi_{2,t}$ affects the slope of the term structure, in addition to its movement implied by r_t.

Indeed, consider a long-term yield, with time to maturity $\tau = T - t$. By definition, this is given as

$$r_t(\tau) = -\frac{\log\left(Z\left(\phi_{1,t}, \phi_{2,t}, t; T\right)\right)}{\tau} = -\frac{A(\tau)}{\tau} + \frac{B_1(\tau)}{\tau}\phi_{1,t} + \frac{B_2(\tau)}{\tau}\phi_{2,t} \quad (22.24)$$

where we use the notation as in Chapter 15, namely $A(\tau) = A(0;\tau)$, $B_i(\tau) = B_i(0,\tau)$. By our definition of r_t in Equation 22.16 we can rewrite $\phi_{1,t} = r_t - \phi_{2,t}$. We can substitute this into the equation above, to obtain the long-term yield as a function of the short-term rate r_t plus another factor $\phi_{2,t}$.

$$r_t(\tau) = -\frac{A(\tau)}{\tau} + \frac{B_1(\tau)}{\tau}r_t + \frac{C(\tau)}{\tau}\phi_{2,t} \quad (22.25)$$

where $C(\tau) = B_2(\tau) - B_1(\tau)$. We may now recall that one important issue with the Vasicek model was that all the yields were perfectly correlated with each other. The two-factor model presented here, instead, partly decouples the long-term yield $r_t(\tau)$ from the short-term rate r_t. Indeed, for given r_t we now may have different long term yields $r_t(\tau)$, which depend on $\phi_{2,t}$.

22.2.2 A Dynamic Model for the Short and Long Yield

In fact, we can go one step further and express all of the yields in terms of only the short-term rate r_t and the long-term yield $r_t(\tau_\ell)$ for a given *maturity* τ_ℓ, such as $\tau_\ell = 10$ for instance. For notational convenience, denote this particular long-term zero coupon spot rate by

$$r_{\ell,t} = r_t(\tau_\ell) \quad (22.26)$$

From Equation 22.25 we can write

$$\phi_{2,t} = \frac{\tau_\ell}{C(\tau_\ell)}\left(r_{\ell,t} + \frac{A(\tau_\ell)}{\tau_\ell} - \frac{B_1(\tau_\ell)}{\tau_\ell}r_t\right)$$

We can finally substitute this "factor" back into Equation 22.25, so that for *any* other yield, we obtain the following

Fact 22.4 *The price of any zero coupon bond at t with maturity T can be written as*

$$Z(r_t, r_{\ell,t}, t; T) = e^{A_{\tau_\ell}(\tau) - B_{\tau_\ell,1}(\tau)\, r_t - C_{\tau_\ell}(\tau)\, r_{\ell,t}} \quad (22.27)$$

where $\tau = T - t$ and

$$A_{\tau_\ell}(\tau) = A(\tau) - C(\tau) \times \frac{A(\tau_\ell)}{C(\tau_\ell)} \quad (22.28)$$

$$B_{\tau_\ell,1}(\tau) = B_1(\tau) - C(\tau) \times \frac{B_1(\tau_\ell)}{C(\tau_\ell)} \quad (22.29)$$

$$C_{\tau_\ell}(\tau) = C(\tau) \times \frac{\tau_\ell}{C(\tau_\ell)} \quad (22.30)$$

The zero coupon spot rate with maturity τ is then given by

$$r_t(\tau) = -\frac{A_{\tau_\ell}(\tau)}{\tau} + \frac{B_{\tau_\ell,1}(\tau)}{\tau}r_t + \frac{C_{\tau_\ell}(\tau)}{\tau}r_{\ell,t} \quad (22.31)$$

Note that $r_t(\tau) = r_{\ell,t}$ for $\tau = \tau_\ell$, as a $A_{\tau_\ell}(\tau_\ell) = B_{\tau_\ell,1}(\tau_\ell) = 0$ and $C_{\tau_\ell}(\tau_\ell) = \tau_\ell$. That is, the model reprices itself correctly, as this is a tautology.

What are the risk neutral processes for r_t and $r_{\ell,t}$? We can derive them from the properties of $\phi_{1,t}$ and $\phi_{2,t}$. In particular, we obtain

$$dr_t = (A_r + B_r\ r_t + C_r\ r_{\ell,t})\,dt + \sigma_1\,dX_1 + \sigma_2\,dX_2 \qquad (22.32)$$

$$dr_{\ell,t} = (A_{r,\ell} + B_{r,\ell}\,r_t + C_{r,\ell}\,r_{\ell,t})\,dt + \sigma_{\ell,1}dX_1 + \sigma_{\ell,2}dX_2 \qquad (22.33)$$

where the coefficients A_r, B_r, C_r, $A_{r,\ell}$, $B_{r,\ell}$, $C_{r,\ell}$ are given in Equations 22.112 through 22.117 in the appendix at the end of this chapter, and $\sigma_{\ell,1}$, and $\sigma_{\ell,2}$ are below in Equation 22.34.

The two-factor model in Equations 22.16, 22.17, and 22.18, can then be thought of as a joint process for the short end (r_t) and the long end of the yield curve $(r_{\ell,t})$, in which all the other yields are obtained from these two extremes from Equation 22.31. The joint dynamics of the short and long interest rate, (Equations 22.32 and 22.33), imply that the short-term rate feeds into the long-term yield, and vice versa, the short-term rate is affected by the long-term rate.

It is important to emphasize that the alternative procedure of starting off directly from a dynamic model of the short and long yield as generic processes does not necessarily generate a model that is consistent with no arbitrage. Indeed, it is important to note that there are restrictions that have to hold across the coefficients A_r, B_r, C_r, $A_{r,\ell}$, $B_{r,\ell}$, $C_{r,\ell}$, $\sigma_{\ell,1}$, and $\sigma_{\ell,2}$. For instance, we have a very strict relation between the volatility of the long-term yield and the short-term yield, which is given by

$$\sigma_{\ell,1} = \sigma_1 \frac{1 - e^{-\gamma_1^* \tau_\ell}}{\tau_\ell}; \quad \sigma_{\ell,2} = \sigma_2 \frac{1 - e^{-\gamma_2^* \tau_\ell}}{\tau_\ell} \qquad (22.34)$$

It follows that we cannot simply assume any numbers for the quantities entering in Equations 22.32 and 22.33, as we would likely end up with a model that violates no arbitrage. Starting instead from a factor model, and deriving the yields from the solution to the no arbitrage Fundamental Pricing Equation (Equation 22.13) guarantee that all of the no arbitrage restrictions across yields are satisfied.

■ **EXAMPLE 22.1**

This example takes after Section 16.3 in Chapter 16. Let today be January 8, 2002. We now use the two-factor model to fit coupon bonds that were traded on that day, and estimate the parameters using the nonlinear least square methodology discussed in Chapter 16. As discussed above, in addition to the current short-term risk free rate r_0 we have to select a long term yield to insert in the pricing function in Equation 22.27. We select the 5-year yield as the long-term zero coupon yield, $\tau_\ell = 5$, and the 1-month T-bill rate for the short term. One immediate difficulty is that while the 1-month T-bill rate can be observed daily, the 5-year zero coupon yield cannot, as it must be estimated from fitting the discount curve $Z(0, T)$ to the bond prices.[1]

---

[1]If we were doing this exercise for the LIBOR curve, we would have no problems, as we can obtain the longer term yields directly from the observation of swap rates.

For simplicity, we use STRIPS prices around $\tau_\ell = 5$ to interpolate the yield of the 5-year zero coupon bond. We then obtain $r_0 = 1.68\%$ for the short-term yield, and $r_{\ell,0} = r(0,5) = 4.52\%$ for the 5-year yield.

As we did in Section 16.3, we are also fixing the volatility of the 1-month rate and the 5-year yield to their empirical values. In particular, these two volatility levels are given by $\sigma_{r,1m} = 0.0221$ and $\sigma_{r,5y} = 0.0125$, respectively. It is not immediately clear how we can use this information, though. However, from Equations 22.32 and 22.33 we obtain the following restrictions

$$\text{Volatility of short-term rate } dr_t = 0.0221 = \sqrt{\sigma_1^2 + \sigma_2^2} \tag{22.35}$$

$$\text{Volatility of long-term rate } dr_{\ell,t} = 0.0125 = \sqrt{\sigma_{\ell,1}^2 + \sigma_{\ell,2}^2} \tag{22.36}$$

One additional issue in the estimation concerns the two terms $\overline{\phi}_1^*$ and $\overline{\phi}_2^*$. Unfortunately, the cross-section of bonds does not contain enough information for us to estimate both parameters independently, because their only effect on the interest rate r_t is to determine its average level, which is equal to $\overline{\phi}_1^* + \overline{\phi}_2^*$. To solve this identification problem, we can simply set one of them equal to zero, that is, we impose the restriction $\overline{\phi}_2^* = 0$.

We can perform the estimation by the usual nonlinear least square methodology, that is, we can search for the parameters $(\gamma_1^*, \overline{\phi}_1^*, \sigma_1, \gamma_2^*, \sigma_2)$ that satisfy Equations 22.35 and 22.36, and also minimize the pricing errors, that is, the quantity:

$$J(\gamma_1^*, \overline{\phi}_1^*, \sigma_1, \gamma_2^*, \sigma_2) = \sum_{j=1}^{n} \left(P_i^{model} - P_i^{data} \right)^2 \tag{22.37}$$

The minimization yields the following parameter estimates:[2]

$$\gamma_1^* = 0.6615; \qquad \overline{\phi}_1^* = 0.0068; \quad \sigma_1 = 0.0197$$
$$\gamma_2^* = -0.0450; \qquad \overline{\phi}_2^* = 0; \quad \sigma_2 = 0.0099$$

Before commenting these estimates, let us look at Panel A in Figure 22.1, which plots the performance of the model in fitting bond prices. For comparison's sake, the figure also reports the fitted values of the Vasicek model. As can be seen, the two factor model performs much better than the one factor model in matching the term structure of bonds.

The performance of the two-factor model stems from its ability to add curvature to the yield curve, as we can see in Panel B of Figure 22.1. While the one-factor Vasicek model implies a modest amount of curvature, and it finds a hump shape hard to obtain, the two-factor model has a sufficient number of additional parameters that allow for this flexibility. In particular, the different frequency of mean reversion, and in fact, the mean aversion of the second factor, generates the curvature in the two-factor model. The estimated parameters show that indeed the second factor has a negative γ_2, that is, in order to fit the term structure of interest rates, the risk neutral process for the second factor needs to be mean-averting, or explosive.

---

[2]Given these estimates, and the zero coupon spot curve, we can also compute the value of the factor $\phi_{2,0}$, which is given by $\phi_{2,0} = 0.0436$. However, since we are using the expression in Equation 22.27 to price zero coupons, this is not really necessary.

Figure 22.1   Fitted Bond Prices on January 8, 2002

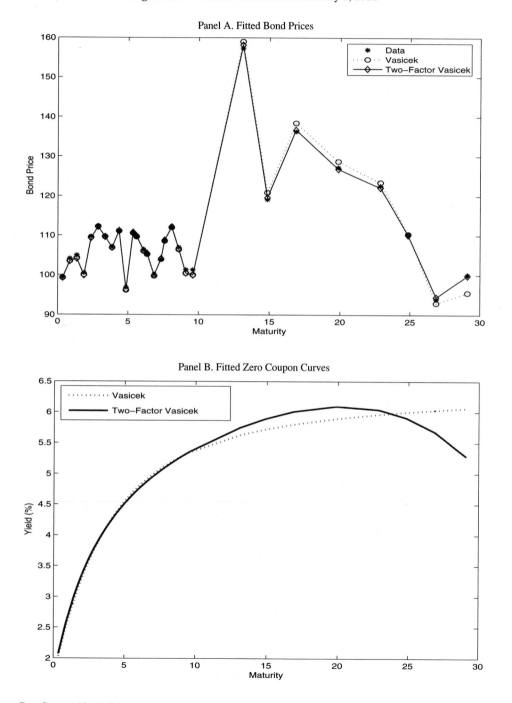

Panel A. Fitted Bond Prices

Panel B. Fitted Zero Coupon Curves

Data Source: *The Wall Street Journal.*

Figure 22.2   Fitted Zero Coupon Curves from STRIPS: January 8, 2002

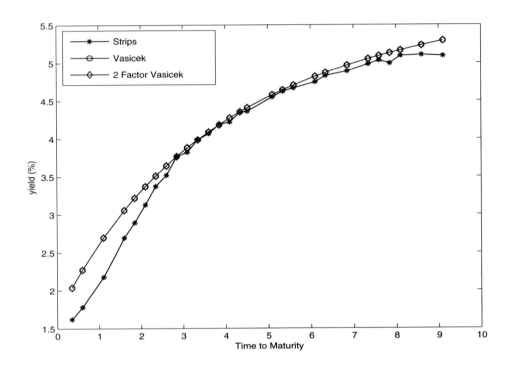

Data Source: *The Wall Street Journal.*

In Section 16.3 in Chapter 16, we also illustrated the use of the Vasicek model to provide a guidance on setting up arbitrage strategies on the yield curve. The two-factor model can be used with the same purpose. In fact, it is interesting to note from Figure 22.2 that at the short end, the two-factor model does not seem to fit the STRIPS any better than the one-factor model, as the two yield curves are exactly on top of each other. As discussed then, and also in this case, the yield curve on January 8, 2002 was too steep and too "curved" to be consistent with no arbitrage within a two-factor model, at least under the assumptions of this model. It is then possible to set up a long-short strategy to gain from the mispricing, along the lines discussed in Section 16.3 (see also Section 16.8).

22.2.3   Long-Term Spot Rate Volatility

Two factor models also provide more flexibility to match the volatility of spot rates at many horizons. For instance, recall from Chapter 19 that the Vasicek model implies that the volatility of the spot rate with maturity τ is given by

$$\text{Vasicek volatility of } dr_t(\tau) = \sigma_t(\tau) = \frac{\sigma}{\gamma^*}\frac{1 - e^{-\gamma^*\tau}}{\tau} \qquad (22.38)$$

where γ^* is the risk neutral mean reversion coefficient in the Vasicek model. This formula implies that the volatility can only decrease with maturity: Long-term spot rates have a lower volatility than short-term spot rates. While this description fits the realized historical volatility of yields, as we have seen in Chapter 19, the volatility that is implied from options typically shows a hump shape. This hump shape makes it then hard for the Vasicek model to fit the implied volatility of options. A two-factor model helps from this perspective as well.

We can use the formula for the long-term spot rate $r_t(\tau)$ in Equation 22.24 and Ito's lemma to find:

$$\text{Volatility of } dr_t(\tau) = \sigma_t(\tau) = \sqrt{\sigma_1^2 \left(\frac{B_1(\tau)}{\tau} \right)^2 + \sigma_2^2 \left(\frac{B_2(\tau)}{\tau} \right)^2} \tag{22.39}$$

We illustrate the gain in flexibility of the two-factor model over the one-factor model in the next example.

■ **EXAMPLE 22.2**

In the two-factor Vasicek model fitted in the Example 22.1 we used both the 1-month volatility and 5-year volatility as inputs in the estimation. This means that the model automatically will fit exactly those two data points. All of the other volatilities depend on the parameters according to Equation 22.39. Figure 22.3 plots the yield volatility computed as the standard deviation of historical changes in yields, $\sigma^{data}(\tau) = st.\ dev.(r_{t+dt}(\tau) - r_t(\tau)) \times 1/dt$, where $dt = 1/12 = 1$ month is the data frequency in the estimation, and $1/dt$ is thus the annualization factor. The figure also reports the volatility obtained from the Vasicek model, namely Equation 22.38. The figure shows that the two factor model does in fact fit the two extremes of the volatility, while the one-factor model only matches the shortest volatility level. Indeed, in the one-factor model, we use only one parameter (σ) to fit the volatility, and the other two (γ^* and $\bar{r}^*$) to fit the term structure. In contrast, in the two-factor model, we effectively use two parameters to exactly match the two extremes of the term structure of volatility, and the remaining four to fit the term structure of interest rates.

22.2.4 Options on Zero Coupon Bonds

One of the advantages of the Vasicek model, as well as the "normal" models discussed in Chapter 19, is that they allow for a closed form formula for options on zero coupon bonds. This result can then be extended to obtain analytical formulas for caps and floors. The two-factor Vasicek model shares this nice property, and the reason is as follows. Consider an option with maturity T_O on a zero coupon bond that matures at T_B. The future value of the zero coupon bond per unit principal equals the discount factor, and thus is:

$$Z \left(\phi_{1,T_O}, \phi_{2,T_O}, T_O; T_B \right) = e^{A(T_O;T_B) - B_1(T_O;T_B)\, \phi_{1,T_O} - B_2(T_O;T_B)\, \phi_{2,T_O}}$$

Figure 22.3 The Volatility of Long-Term Yields: January 8, 2002

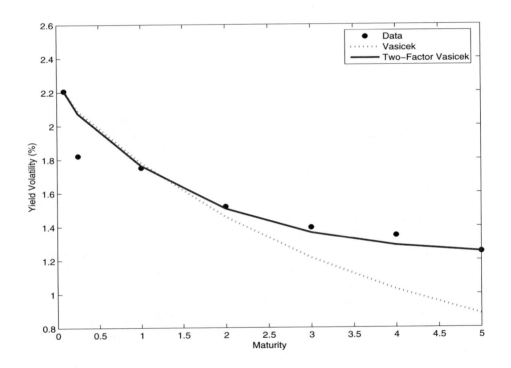

Data Source: The Federal Reserve and CRSP.

Because each of the two factors follows a Vasicek model, it follows that ϕ_{1,T_O} and ϕ_{2,T_O} are jointly normally distributed,[3] and so is the composite variable $B_1(T_O;T_B)\,\phi_{1,T_O} + B_2(T_O;T_B)\,\phi_{2,T_O}$. That is, $Z\left(\phi_{1,T_O},\phi_{2,T_O},T_O;T_B\right)$ is log-normally distributed. It is intuitive then that the same arguments in Chapter 15 apply, and that an option pricing formula results. The key entry is the volatility of $\log\left(Z\left(\phi_{1,T_O},\phi_{2,T_O},T_O;T_B\right)\right)$, which is given by

$$\mathcal{S}_Z(T_O)^2 = B_1^2(T_O;T_B)\frac{\sigma_1^2}{2\gamma_1^*}(1-e^{-2\gamma_1^*T_O}) + B_2^2(T_O;T_B)\frac{\sigma_2^2}{2\gamma_2^*}(1-e^{-2\gamma_2^*T_O}) \quad (22.40)$$

We then obtain:

Fact 22.5 *The price of a call option with maturity T_O and strike price K written on a zero coupon bond with maturity T_B is given by*

$$V(\phi_{1,0},\phi_{2,0},0) = Z\left(\phi_{1,0},\phi_{2,0},0;T_B\right)\mathcal{N}(d_1) - KZ\left(\phi_{1,0},\phi_{2,0},0;T_O\right)\mathcal{N}(d_2) \quad (22.41)$$

where $\mathcal{N}(x)$ is the cumulative standard normal distribution, $\mathcal{S}_Z(T_O)$ is given in Equation 22.40 and

$$d_1 = \frac{1}{\mathcal{S}_Z(T_O)}\log\left(\frac{Z\left(\phi_{1,0},\phi_{2,0},0;T_B\right)}{KZ\left(\phi_{1,0},\phi_{2,0},0;T_O\right)}\right) + \frac{\mathcal{S}_Z(T_O)}{2} \quad (22.42)$$

$$d_2 = d_2 - \mathcal{S}_Z(T_O) \quad (22.43)$$

The price of a put option is

$$V(\phi_{1,0},\phi_{2,0},0) = -Z\left(\phi_{1,0},\phi_{2,0},0;T_B\right)\mathcal{N}(-d_1) + KZ\left(\phi_{1,0},\phi_{2,0},0;T_O\right)\mathcal{N}(-d_2) \quad (22.44)$$

22.3 CORRELATED FACTORS

We now illustrate Ito's lemma and the fundamental pricing equation in the case in which the factors $\phi_{1,t}$ and $\phi_{2,t}$ are correlated. That is, we assume that the correlation between the two Brownian motions dX_1 and dX_2 is given by

$$E[dX_{1,t}dX_{2,t}] = \rho\,dt \quad (22.45)$$

In essence, the correlation between the Brownian motions defines the extent to which they are moving up and down together. To illustrate, recall that within a small interval of time dt, each Brownian motion increment $dX_{1,t}$ and $dX_{2,t}$ is normally distributed with mean zero and variance dt, that is $dX_{1,t} \sim \mathcal{N}(0,dt)$ and $dX_{2,t} \sim \mathcal{N}(0,dt)$, approximately. The correlation ρ captures the joint movement. Figure 22.4 illustrates the point: Let $X_{1,t} = X_{2,t} = 0$. What is the joint distribution of the pair $(X_{1,t+dt}, X_{2,t+dt})$? Panel A

---

[3]In particular,$\phi_{i,T_O} \sim \mathcal{N}(\mu_i(\phi_{i,0},T_O),\sigma_i^2(T_O))$ where $\mu_i(\phi_{i,0},T_O) = \overline{\phi}_i^* + \left(\phi_{i,0} - \overline{\phi}_i^*\right)e^{-\gamma_i^*T_O}$ and $\sigma_i^2(T_O) = \sigma_i^2/(2\gamma_i^*(1-e^{-2\gamma_i^*T_O}))$.

shows that the joint distribution for the case in which $\rho = 0$, that is, the two Brownian motions are uncorrelated.[4] In this case, it is apparent the joint distribution is exactly symmetric, assigning essentially equal probability to joint movement up, joint movement down, or up-and-down. We should contrast this joint density with the ones in Panel B and Panel C. In Panel B we assume $\rho = -0.9$, that is, when X_1 is going up it is also likely that X_2 goes down, and vice versa. Indeed, now the joint density on the space (X_1, X_2) is mainly concentrated on the negative diagonal. That is, when for instance $X_1 = -2$ it is more likely that X_2 is around $+2$ than -2. Similarly, when $X_1 = +2$, it is also more likely that X_2 is around -2 rather than $+2$. The two variables X_1 and X_2 move opposite to each other. Similarly, Panel C shows the case in which $\rho = 0.9$, that is, the two Brownian motions are likely to move up and down together. In this case, the joint distribution gives substantial probability to the positive diagonal. That is, if $X_1 = 2$, for instance, then it is more likely that X_2 is also around $+2$ rather than -2.

Consider now a security that depends on both $\phi_{1,t}$ and $\phi_{2,t}$ and assume that the factors move according to the general processes

$$d\phi_{1,t} = m_1\left(\phi_{1,t}, \phi_{2,t}, t\right) dt + s_1\left(\phi_{1,t}, \phi_{2,t}, t\right) dX_{1,t} \tag{22.46}$$

$$d\phi_{2,t} = m_2\left(\phi_{1,t}, \phi_{2,t}, t\right) dt + s_2\left(\phi_{1,t}, \phi_{2,t}, t\right) dX_{2,t} \tag{22.47}$$

where we now also allow the drift rates $m_1(.)$ and $m_2(.)$ and volatilities s_1 and s_2 to depend on both factors. Ito's Lemma is given by the following:

Fact 22.6 *Multivariate Ito's Lemma.* *Let $\phi_{1,t}$ and $\phi_{2,t}$ follow the processes in Equations 22.1 and 22.2. Let the price of a security be given by $P_t = F(t, \phi_{1,t}, \phi_{2,t})$. Then, the capital gain process is*

$$
\begin{aligned}
dP_t &= \left\{ \left(\frac{\partial F}{\partial t}\right) + \left(\frac{\partial F}{\partial \phi_1}\right) m_{1,t} + \left(\frac{\partial F}{\partial \phi_2}\right) m_{2,t} + \frac{1}{2}\left(\frac{\partial^2 F}{\partial \phi_1^2}\right) s_{1,t}^2 + \frac{1}{2}\left(\frac{\partial^2 F}{\partial \phi_2^2}\right) s_{2,t}^2 \right. \\
&\quad \left. + \left(\frac{\partial^2 F}{\partial \phi_1 \partial \phi_2}\right) s_{1,t}\, s_{2,t}\, \rho \right\} dt \\
&\quad + \left(\frac{\partial F}{\partial \phi^1}\right) s_{1,t}\, dX_{1,t} + \left(\frac{\partial F}{\partial \phi_2}\right) s_{2,t}\, dX_{2,t}
\end{aligned}
\tag{22.48}
$$

where recall the notation $m_{i,t} = m_i\left(\phi_{1,t}, \phi_{2,t}, t\right)$ and $s_{i,t} = s_i\left(\phi_{1,t}, \phi_{2,t}, t\right)$, for $i = 1, 2$.

Comparing this expression for dP_t with the case of independent factors in Equation 22.3, we see that the only difference is given by the additional term in the drift rate in Equation 22.48, namely

$$\left(\frac{\partial^2 F}{\partial \phi_1 \partial \phi_2}\right) s_{1,t}\, s_{2,t}\, \rho$$

This term reflects the component of the expected capital gain return $E[dP_t]$ that is stemming from the joint movement in the two factors between today t and tomorrow $t + dt$. Indeed, the second derivative term $\left(\frac{\partial^2 F}{\partial \phi_1 \partial \phi_2}\right)$ defines the convexity of the interest rate security along the diagonal on the space (X_1, X_2) and this convexity is multiplied by the covariance

---

[4]The figure is plotted in the (X_1, X_2) space in "dt" units, that is, for unit variance.

Figure 22.4   Bivariate Normal Distribution

Panel A: $\rho = 0$

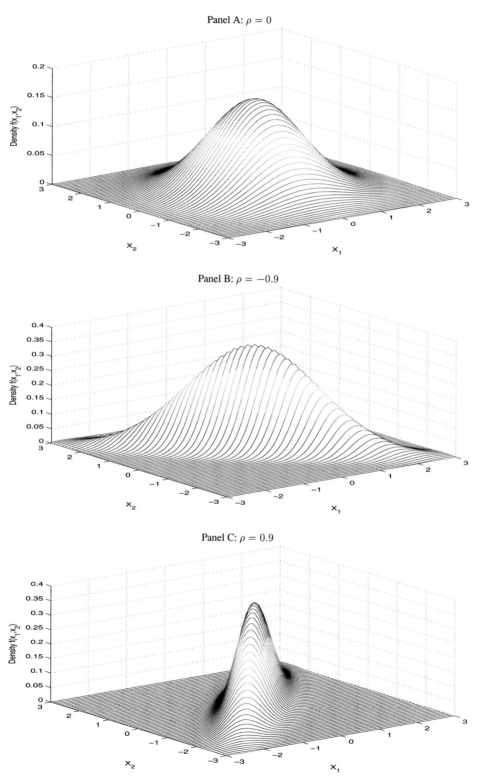

Panel B: $\rho = -0.9$

Panel C: $\rho = 0.9$

between the two factors, that is, the likely joint movement along the direction defined by the second joint derivative.

What is the fundamental pricing equation? Exactly the same steps carried out in Section 22.2 yield the following:

Fact 22.7 *Let $V(\phi_1, \phi_2, t)$ be the price of a security that depends on time t and the two factors ϕ_1 and ϕ_2 described in Equations 22.46 and 22.47 and with final payoff g_T. Then, the value of this security is given by the solution to the* **Fundamental Pricing Equation** *given by*

$$R(\phi_1, \phi_2)V = \frac{\partial V}{\partial t} + \frac{\partial V}{\partial \phi_1} m_{1,t}^* + \frac{\partial V}{\partial \phi_2} m_{2,t}^* + \frac{1}{2}\frac{\partial^2 V}{\partial \phi_1^2} s_{1,t}^2 + \frac{1}{2}\frac{\partial^2 V}{\partial \phi_2^2} s_{2,t}^2$$
$$+ \frac{\partial^2 V}{\partial \phi_1 \partial \phi_2} s_{1,t}\, s_{2,t}\, \rho \tag{22.49}$$

with the final condition

$$V(\phi_1, \phi_2, T) = g_T$$

The only difference between the Fundamental Pricing Equation in Equation 22.49 and the one in Equation 22.13 obtained with independent factor is the presence of an additional term (the last), capturing the correlation across factors. If this correlation $\rho = 0$ we obtain the previous equation. The next subsections illustrate the use of the general Fundamental Pricing Equation.

22.3.1   The Two-Factor Vasicek Model with Correlated Factors

Consider again the same factor model in Equations 22.17 and 22.18 in Section 22.2.1, but in which the two Brownian motions $dX_{1,t}$ and $dX_{2,t}$ are now correlated, with correlation ρ. Without going through all of the details, we obtain the following result:

Fact 22.8 *Let the factors follow the risk neutral processes as in Equations 22.17 and 22.18, but with correlated Brownian motions $E[dX_{1,t}dX_{2,t}] = \rho dt$, and let $r_t = \phi_{1,t} + \phi_{2,t}$. Then the value of a zero coupon bond for unit principal at time t with maturity T is given by*

$$Z(\phi_{1,t}, \phi_{2,t}, t; T) = e^{A(t;T) - B_1(t;T)\,\phi_{1,t} - B_2(t;T)\,\phi_{2,t}} \tag{22.50}$$

where $B_i(t;T) = \frac{1}{\gamma_i^*}\left(1 - e^{-\gamma_i^*(T-t)}\right)$, and

$$\begin{aligned}
A(t;T) &= [B_1(t;T) - (T-t)]\left(\bar{\phi}_1^* - \frac{\sigma_1^2}{2(\gamma_1^*)^2} - \frac{\sigma_1\sigma_2\rho}{\gamma_1^*\gamma_2^*}\right) - \frac{\sigma_1^2}{4\gamma_1^*}B_1(t;T)^2 \\
&+ [B_2(t;T) - (T-t)]\left(\bar{\phi}_2^* - \frac{\sigma_2^2}{2(\gamma_2^*)^2} - \frac{\sigma_1\sigma_2\rho}{\gamma_1^*\gamma_2^*}\right) - \frac{\sigma_2^2}{4\gamma_2^*}B_2(t;T)^2 \\
&+ [B_3(t;T) - (T-t)]\frac{\sigma_1\sigma_2\rho}{\gamma_1^*\gamma_2^*}
\end{aligned}$$

and

$$B_3(t;T) = \frac{1 - e^{-(\gamma_1^* + \gamma_2^*)(T-t)}}{\gamma_1^* + \gamma_2^*}$$

The only difference between the zero coupon bond formula in Equation 22.50 and the one with independent factors in Equation 22.19 is in the term $A(t; T)$. Indeed, it is only in this term that the correlation ρ appears. The intuition is that the different levels of correlation ρ affect the dynamics of r_t, such as its volatility and autocorrelation. The volatility of the interest rate process, for instance, positively affects the level of the zero coupon bond price, as a zero coupon bond is positively convex with respect to the interest rate.

While the bond pricing formula remains similar to before, the volatility of yields and correlation among yields present the major differences from the case in which the factors are independent. In fact, the volatility of the short-term rate and the long-term rates are now given by

$$
\begin{array}{ll}
\text{Volatility} \\
\text{of } dr_t
\end{array}
\quad = \quad \sigma_r = \sqrt{\sigma_1^2 + \sigma_2^2 + 2\sigma_1\sigma_2\rho}
\tag{22.51}
$$

$$
\begin{array}{ll}
\text{Volatility} \\
\text{of } dr_t(\tau)
\end{array}
\quad = \quad \sigma(\tau)
$$

$$
= \quad \sqrt{\sigma_1^2 \left(\frac{B_1(\tau)}{\tau}\right)^2 + \sigma_2^2 \left(\frac{B_2(\tau)}{\tau}\right)^2 + 2\left(\frac{B_1(\tau)}{\tau}\right)\left(\frac{B_2(\tau)}{\tau}\right)\sigma_1\sigma_2\rho}
\tag{22.52}
$$

In addition, the correlation between the short-term rate and any long-term rate with maturity τ is

$$
\begin{array}{ll}
\text{Correlation} \\
\text{between } (dr_t, dr_t(\tau))
\end{array}
\quad = \quad \rho(0, \tau)
$$

$$
= \quad \frac{\sigma_1^2 \left(\frac{B_1(\tau)}{\tau}\right) + \sigma_2^2 \left(\frac{B_2(\tau)}{\tau}\right) + \left(\frac{B_1(\tau)}{\tau} + \frac{B_2(\tau)}{\tau}\right)\sigma_1\sigma_2\rho}{\sigma_r \sigma(\tau)}
\tag{22.53}
$$

The case in which the factors are independent is recovered from these formulas by setting $\rho = 0$.

■ EXAMPLE 22.3

Consider again Example 22.2. From Figure 22.3 the two-factor model with independent factors does quite well in matching the term structure of volatility of yield changes. As mentioned already, the main point of introducing multiple factors is to decouple the perfect correlation among yields that is implied by one-factor models, such as the Vasicek model. The question is whether the model fitted in Example 22.2 achieves this goal. Figure 22.5 shows that this is not the case. This figure plots the correlation of each yield with maturity τ (on the x-axis) versus the short-term yield r_t, both in the data (stars) and according to various models. For instance, the dotted line corresponds to the Vasicek model, in which case the correlation between the change in yield of maturity τ and the short-term interest rate is equal to 100%. The solid line plots the correlation implied by the model with independent factors. Note that such correlation can be computed as in Equation 22.53 with $\rho = 0$. As can be seen, although the model with independent factors does imply a lower correlation between long-term yields and the short-term rate, the difference with the data is quite substantial. For instance, the 5-year yield has a correlation of only 50% with the short-term yield, but the model implies a correlation of over 80%.

The two-factor model with correlated factors does slightly better. In particular, we now have enough degrees of freedom to also target the correlation among factors while searching for the risk neutral parameters γ_1^*, $\overline{\phi}_1^*$, γ_2^*, and $\overline{\phi}_2^*$. For instance, we know from the data that the corelation between the 5-year yield and the short-term rate is only 47.13%. We can then set the three restrictions[5]

$$\text{Volatility of short-term rate } dr_t \;=\; 0.0221 = \sigma_r \qquad (22.54)$$

$$\text{Volatility of long-term rate } dr_{\ell,t} \;=\; 0.0125 = \sigma(\tau_\ell) \qquad (22.55)$$

$$\text{Correlation between } (dr_t, dr_{\ell,t}) \;=\; 0.4713 = \rho(0, \tau_\ell) \qquad (22.56)$$

Setting again $\overline{\phi}_2^* = 0$ as it cannot be identified, we then search for the parameters γ_1^*, $\overline{\phi}_1^*$, σ_1, γ_2^*, σ_2, and ρ that satisfy these three equations, and in addition minimize the squared pricing errors, as in Equation 22.37. In this case, we obtain

$$\gamma_1^* = 0.8269; \qquad \overline{\phi}_1^* = -0.0413; \qquad \sigma_1 = 0.0250$$
$$\gamma_2^* = -0.0288; \qquad \overline{\phi}_2^* = 0; \qquad \sigma_2 = 0.0132$$
$$\rho = -0.4755$$

The risk neutral value of $\overline{\phi}_1^*$ is negative while factor 2 is mean averting. The dashed line in Panel A of Figure 22.5 shows that indeed, the model is able to also match the low correlation of the 5-year yield. However, this more general model performs as poorly as the Vasicek model and the two-factor Vasicek with independent factors in terms of matching the correlation of rates of shorter maturity with the 1-month T-bill rate. Indeed, it is interesting to note that the correlation between the one-month rate and the three-month rate is in fact very low. Two factors are not enough to capture the difference.

One question that may arise is what we lose from matching the correlation of the 5-year yield in terms of matching the volatility of yields and the bond prices. The model does slightly worse on bond prices, although the difference is negligible (the picture looks essentially like Figure 22.1 and it is omitted for brevity). The volatility is instead plotted in Panel B of Figure 22.5. By construction, the model exactly matches the short-term and long-term volatility, but it does not do so well for intermediate maturities.

22.3.2 Zero Coupon Bond Options

How do correlated factors affect the price of a call option? Once again, we just have to remember that the zero coupon bond pricing formula is still the same as with uncorrelated

---

[5]In the implementation, we target the covariance between dr_t and $dr_{\ell,t}$ instead of the correlation, as correlations are typically more difficult to estimate. The covariance is given by the numerator of the expression in Equation 22.53.

Figure 22.5   The Correlation and Volatility of Long Term Yields: January 8, 2002

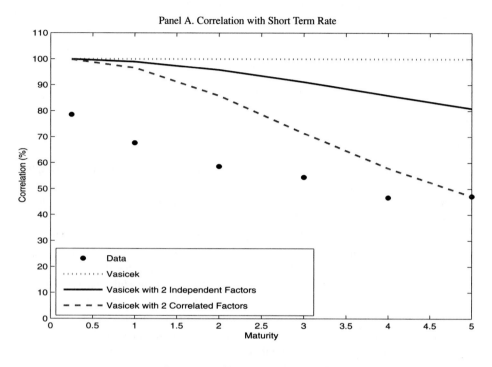

Panel A. Correlation with Short Term Rate

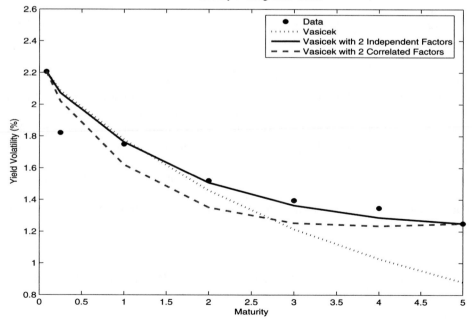

Panel B. Volatility of Long Term Yields

Data Source: The Federal Reserve and CRSP.

factors, and thus the same argument in Section 22.2.4 holds true here as well. In particular, the values of calls and puts are still given as in Fact 22.5, but with a slightly different volatility of $\log \left(Z(\phi_{1,T_O}, \phi_{2,T_O}, T_O; T_B) \right)$, now given by

$$
\begin{aligned}
\mathcal{S}_Z(T_O)^2 &= B_1^2(T_O; T_B) \frac{\sigma_1^2}{2\gamma_1^*}(1 - e^{-2\gamma_1^* T_O}) + B_2^2(T_O; T_B) \frac{\sigma_i^2}{2\gamma_2^*}(1 - e^{-2\gamma_2^* T_O}) \\
&\quad + B_1(T_O; T_B) B_2(T_O; T_B) \sigma_1 \sigma_2 \rho \frac{(1 - e^{-(\gamma_1^* + \gamma_2^*)T_O})}{\gamma_1^* + \gamma_2^*}
\end{aligned}
\tag{22.57}
$$

22.3.3 The Two-Factor Hull–White Model

The two-factor Vasicek model is the simple extension of the one-factor model to capture the fact that yields do not move in sync. However, as with the Vasicek model, the two factor Vasicek model is not able to fit the term structure of interest rates exactly. While this fact could be desirable if we want to design no arbitrage trades on the yield curve, it is not a good property if we want instead to price complicated derivative securities. In this case, we need a no arbitrage model, such as those studied in Chapter 19. Indeed, in that chapter we illustrated the Hull-White model, which is a generalization of the one-factor Vasicek model to match the term structure of interest rates. The two-factor Hull-White model also builds on the two-factor Vasicek model to fit the term structure of interest rates, and obtain a better fit for the term structure of volatility and some correlations across volatilities.

Consider again the two-factor Vasicek model as expressed in Equations 22.22 and 22.23, and as in the Hull-White model, assume that $\theta_t = \gamma_1^* \overline{\phi}^*$ is a function of time. In addition, assume that $\overline{\phi}_2^* = 0$. We obtain

$$
\begin{aligned}
dr_t &= \left[\theta_t - \gamma_1^* r_t + (\gamma_1^* - \gamma_2^*)\, \phi_{2,t} \right] dt + \sigma_1 dX_1 + \sigma_2 dX_2 \tag{22.58} \\
d\phi_{2,t} &= -\gamma_2^*\, \phi_{2,t}\, dt + \sigma_2 dX_{2,t} \tag{22.59}
\end{aligned}
$$

The generalization of this model over the two-factor Vasicek model is only in θ_t, which is now a deterministic function of time that has to be defined to match exactly the term structure of zero coupon bonds.[6] On the other hand, there is no difference between this model compared to the two factor Vasicek model in terms of volatility and correlation, implying that the formulas in Equations 22.51, 22.52, and 22.53 still hold for the two-factor Hull-White model.

In contrast, the zero coupon bond pricing formula slightly changes, as shown next.

Fact 22.9 *The value of a zero coupon bond under the two factor Hull-White model is given by*

$$
Z(r_t, \phi_{2,t}, t; T) = e^{A(t;T) - B_1(t;T)r_t - C(t;T)\phi_{2,t}}
\tag{22.60}
$$

where $B_i(t; T)$ is as in (22.20), $C(t; T) = B_2(t; T) - B_1(t; T)$ and $A(t; T)$ is in the appendix at the end of this chapter.

---

[6]The second factor entering the drift rate in Equation 22.58 can be renormalized, which is what Hull and White in fact do. Let $u_t = \left(\gamma_1^* - \gamma_2^* \right) \phi_{2,t}$. Then, it follows $du_t = -\gamma_2^* u_t dt + \sigma_u dX_{1,t}$, which is Hull and White's assumption. We retain our notation so that we can use the previously developed formulas.

The benefit from introducing a deterministic θ_t that allows the model to exactly match the term structure of interest rates is that the volatility structure of bonds can now be chosen to better match the properties of the data.

■ **EXAMPLE 22.4**

Consider again Example 22.3. The benefit of the Hull-White model compared to the two-factor Vasicek model is that we have the θ_t function available now to match the term structure of interest rates. Thus, we are free to choose the other model parameters, namely γ_1^*, γ_2^*, σ_1, σ_2 and ρ to match the volatility and the correlation structure of yields. Because in the Hull-White model the volatility and correlations are still given by Equations 22.51, 22.52, and 22.53, we can search for the volatility parameters in order to minimize

$$ J(\gamma_1^*, \gamma_2^*, \sigma_1, \sigma_2, \rho) = \sum_{i=1}^{n} \left(\sigma_t(\tau_i) - \sigma(\tau_i)^{data} \right)^2 + \left(\rho(0, \tau_i) - \rho(0, \tau_i)^{data} \right)^2 $$

Figure 22.6 shows the results of this exercise. Panel A reports the fitted volatility for the Hull-White model, as well as the Vasicek model, and the data. As can be seen, the two-factor Hull-White model succeeds at matching the volatility structure of yields quite closely. Panel B shows the correlation structure between yields of various maturities (on the $x-$axis) and the short-term spot rate. Again, the model performs quite well. In addition, although not plotted, by computing θ_t as in Equation 22.122 in the appendix, we are guaranteed to match exactly the term structure of interest rates.

As a second example, we now illustrate the performance of the Hull-White two-factor model to match cap prices. As illustrated in Chapter 19, we can price caps by using the zero coupon option pricing formula in Fact 22.5, which holds under the Hull-White two-factor model with volatility $S_Z(T_O)$ given in Equation 22.57. The trick, recall, is to consider a caplet as a put option on a short term zero coupon bond.

■ **EXAMPLE 22.5**

In this example we use the same data as in Chapter 19, Section 19.4.3, in which we compared the Hull–White model to the Ho–Lee model and examined their performance to match cap prices on November 1, 2004. We can now search for all of the five parameters $(\gamma_1^*, \sigma_1, \gamma_2^*, \sigma_2, \rho)$ appearing in the volatility function $S_Z(T)$ in Equation 22.57 to match as closely as possible cap prices. Panel A of Figure 22.7 demonstrates the performance of the two-factor Hull-White model on November 1, 2004. As can be seen, the added flexibility in the volatility function in Equation 22.57 unfortunately does not help match the term structure of volatilities of cap prices in this instance. Indeed, Panel B of Figure 22.7 compares the fitted volatility in the case of the two-factor Hull-White model, with the one-factor Hull-White model, the Ho-Lee model, as well as the implied volatility from caps themselves. The extreme curvature of the implied cap volatility curve is hard to match.

Figure 22.6 The Yield Volatilities and Correlations in the Two-Factor Hull-White Model: January 8, 2002

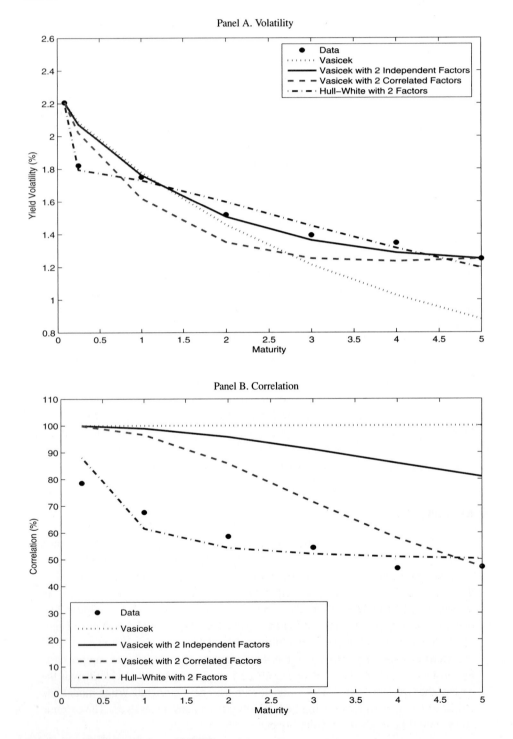

Data Source: The Federal Reserve and CRSP.

Figure 22.7   Cap Pricing Errors and Implied Volatilities on November 1, 2004

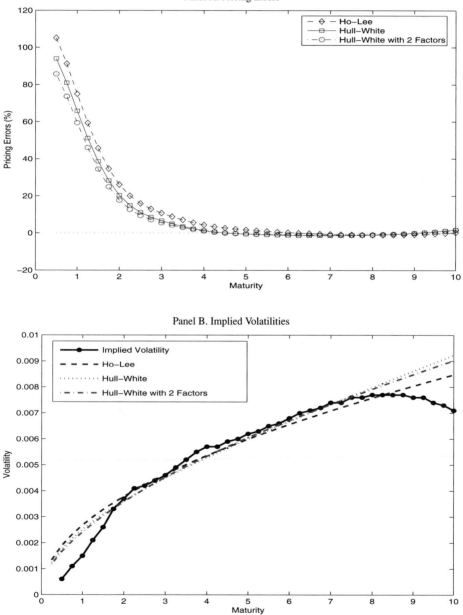

Data Source: Bloomberg.

22.4 THE FEYNMAN-KAC THEOREM

The Feynman-Kac formula we introduced in Chapter 17 can also be applied to the multi-factor case. Indeed, we have the following:

Fact 22.10 *Let* $V\left(\phi_{1,t},\phi_{2,t},t\right)$ *be the price of a security, with final payoff* $V\left(\phi_{1,T},\phi_{2,T},T\right) = g_T$, *satisfying the partial differential equation in Equation 22.49. Then* $V\left(\phi_{1,t},\phi_{2,t},t\right)$ *is given by*

$$V\left(\phi_{1,t},\phi_{2,t},t\right) = E^*\left[e^{-\int_t^T R(\phi_{1,u},\phi_{2,u})du}\,g_T\,|\phi_{1,t},\phi_{2,t}\right] \tag{22.61}$$

where the expectation $E^*\left[.\right]$ *is taken with respect to the probability distribution induced by the risk neutral processes*

$$d\phi_{1,t} = m_{1,t}^*dt + s_{1,t}dX_{1,t} \tag{22.63}$$

$$d\phi_{2,t} = m_{2,t}^*dt + s_{2,t}dX_{2,t} \tag{22.62}$$

The formula in Equation 22.61 allows us to obtain the solution of the fundamental pricing equation (Equation 22.49), and thus the value of the interest rate security we want to price, as an expectation of the future payoff, discounted at the risk-less rate. It follows that whenever the model is too complicated to solve, we can always rely on Monte Carlo simulations, exactly as discussed in Chapter 17. Indeed, note that while closed form solutions for options and other securities are available for some special cases, in general multivariate fixed income models do not yield analytical formulas, and Monte Carlo simulations are the only viable alternative.

22.4.1 Application: Yield Curve Steepener

Multifactor models are especially useful to price securities that depend on either different yield curves, or to make bets on different points on the curve. As an example, a curve steepener is an interest rate security whose cash flows depend on the relative value of different points on the term structure of interest rates. Table 22.1 shows an excerpt from a prospectus from Morgan Stanley describing a yield curve steepener that it was offering in March 2006.

This yield curve steepener makes only one payment at time T = March 3, 2008, and this is given by

$$CF_T = 1000 + 1000 \times 15 \times \max\left(r_{cmt}(T;10) - r_{LIBOR}(T;0.25),0\right) \tag{22.64}$$

Notice that these notes do not pay any interest, and therefore, normally, they would be priced at a discount to par value, like any zero coupon bond. Instead, they are sold exactly at par value. The reason is that the option component in Equation 22.64 is very valuable, and makes up for the discount.

Note that the steepener in Table 22.1 involves two different curves, the LIBOR curve and the Treasury curve. As discussed in Chapter 5, because the LIBOR rate is the (offer) rate in the interbanking lending market, the difference between the LIBOR and the Treasury is essentially due to the credit risk implicit in banks loans. Because the purpose of this section is to illustrate the multivariate Monte Carlo simulation methodology, we will consider two simplifying assumptions for the calculations: First, the short-term rate is in fact the 3-month

Table 22.1 Excerpt from Morgan Stanley Steepener Prospectus

Yield Curve Steepener Capital-Protected Notes due March 3, 2008
Based on the Difference Between 10-Year Constant Maturity Treasury and 3-Month LIBOR Rates

Issue Date	March 3, 2006
Maturity Date	March 3, 2008
Offering Price	$1,000 per note
Maturity Redemption Amount	$1,000 + Supplemental Redemption Amount
Supplemental Redemption Amount	$1,000 multiplied by the Rate Spread multiplied by the Leverage Factor; provided that the Supplemental Redemption Amount will not be less than zero.
Rate Spread	10 Year Constant Maturity Rate minus 3 month LIBOR on the 5th business day before maturity date.
Leverage Factor	15.

Source: SEC Filing, Morgan Stanley Pricing Sheet date February 28, 2006.

Treasury bill. Second, the long-term rate is in fact the yield of a zero coupon bond with the same maturity. That is, we assume that the cash flow at time T is given by

$$CF_T = g(\phi_{1,T}, \phi_{2,T}) = 1000 + 1000 \times 15 \times \max\left(r(T;10) - r(T;0.25), 0\right) \quad (22.65)$$

We then proceed as follows:

1. **Estimate the two-factor Vasicek model.** We first apply the same methodology illustrated in Section 22.3.1 to estimate the two-factor Vasicek model. Using all of the traded Treasury bills, Treasury notes, and bonds on March 3, 2006, we obtain the following estimates:

$$\gamma_1^* = 1.7227; \qquad \overline{\phi}_1^* = 0.2993; \quad \sigma_1 = 0.0222$$
$$\gamma_2^* = 0.0434; \qquad \overline{\phi}_2^* = 0; \quad \sigma_2 = 0.0147$$
$$\rho = -0.3969$$

where we also use the current short-term rate $r_0 = 4.37\%$, the 5-year zero coupon yield $r_0(5) = 4.54\%$, and match the volatility of the short-term rate, $\sigma(dr_t(0.25)) = 0.0213$, the volatility of the 5-year yield $\sigma(dr_t(5)) = 0.0124$, and their correlation $Corr(dr_t(0.25), dr_t(5)) = 0.4554$.

2. **Simulate the factor processes**. As in Chapter 17, we can discretize the processes for $\phi_{1,t}$ and $\phi_{2,t}$. In particular, we set $\delta = 1/252$ (one day), start the simulation at $\phi_{1,0}$ and $\phi_{2,0}$ obtained from the estimation part, and simulate

$$\phi_{1,i+1}^j = \phi_{1,i}^j + \gamma_1^* \left(\overline{\phi}_1^* - \phi_{1,i}^j\right)\delta + \sigma_1\sqrt{\delta}\,\epsilon_{1,i+1}^j \quad (22.66)$$

$$\phi^j_{2,i+1} = \phi^j_{2,i} + \gamma^*_2 \left(\bar{\phi}^*_2 - \phi^j_{2,i} \right) \delta + \sigma_2 \sqrt{\delta} \, \epsilon^j_{2,i+1} \qquad (22.67)$$

where i is the time-step, and j is the simulation number. In addition, the simulated random variables $\epsilon^j_{1,i+1}$ and $\epsilon^j_{2,i+1}$ are obtained from a correlated standard normal distribution

$$\begin{pmatrix} \epsilon^j_{1,i+1} \\ \epsilon^j_{2,i+1} \end{pmatrix} \sim N \left(\begin{pmatrix} 0 \\ 0 \end{pmatrix}, \begin{pmatrix} 1 & \rho \\ \rho & 1 \end{pmatrix} \right) \qquad (22.68)$$

3. **Compute the discounted payoff.** For each simulation j, we can compute the discounted payoff as follows: First, given the last two simulated factor values, $\phi^j_{1,n}$ and $\phi^j_{2,n}$, where n is the number of time-steps, we can use the two-factor Vasicek formula to compute the yields. In particular, we have

$$g^j_T = 1000 + 1000 \times 15 \times \max \left(r^j_n(10) - r^j_n(0.25), 0 \right)$$

where $r^j_n(\tau)$ is the model-implied continuously compounded yield with maturity τ, $r^j_n(\tau) = -\frac{A_0(\tau)}{\tau} + \frac{B_1(\tau)}{\tau} \phi^j_{1,n} + \frac{B_2(\tau)}{\tau} \phi^j_{2,n}$. Second, recalling that the short-term interest rate is given by $r^j_i = \phi^j_{1,i} + \phi^j_{2,i}$, we can use the simulated factors to compute the corresponding discount as

$$Z^j(0,T) = e^{-\sum_{i=0}^{n-1} r^j_i \times \delta}$$

The discounted payoff in simulation j is then

$$V^j = Z^j(0,T) \times g^j_T$$

4. **Compute the steepener's value and standard errors.** Finally, the value of the security is given by

$$\widehat{V} = \frac{1}{J} \sum_{j=1}^{J} V^j = 995.1379$$

and its standard error is

$$St.Err = \sqrt{\frac{\frac{1}{J} \sum_{j=1}^{J} (V^j - \widehat{V})^2}{J}} = 1.0552$$

where $J = 10,000$ is the number of simulations. The value of the security is relatively close to the asking price in Table 22.1, although we should keep in mind that the security considered here is not exactly the same (and in fact it is simpler) than the one described in Table 22.1.

22.4.2 Simulating Correlated Brownian Motions

One last practical point is the following: How do we simulate two *correlated* normally distributed variables? If the computer software is only able to simulate independent random variables, as in Chapter 17, it is possible to apply a transformation to induce any correlation ρ. In particular, let ε_1 and ε_2 be uncorrelated standard normals:

$$\begin{pmatrix} \varepsilon_1 \\ \varepsilon_2 \end{pmatrix} \sim N \left(\begin{pmatrix} 0 \\ 0 \end{pmatrix}, \begin{pmatrix} 1 & 0 \\ 0 & 1 \end{pmatrix} \right) \qquad (22.69)$$

Define now

$$\epsilon_2 = \rho \times \varepsilon_1 + \sqrt{1 - \rho^2} \times \varepsilon_2$$

We then have that $(\varepsilon_1, \epsilon_2)$ have a joint standard normal distribution, with correlation ρ. To see this, note that ϵ_2 is a sum of normals, so it is normal. Moreover,

$$
\begin{align}
E[\epsilon_2] &= \rho \times E[\varepsilon_1] + \sqrt{1 - \rho^2} \times E[\varepsilon_2] = 0 & (22.70) \\
Var[\epsilon_2] &= \rho^2 \times Var[\varepsilon_1] + (1 - \rho^2) \times Var[\varepsilon_2] = 1 & (22.71) \\
Cov(\varepsilon_1, \epsilon_2) &= \rho \times Cov(\varepsilon_1, \varepsilon_1) + \sqrt{1 - \rho^2} \times Cov(\varepsilon_1, \varepsilon_2) = \rho & (22.72)
\end{align}
$$

as $Cov(\varepsilon_1, \varepsilon_1) = Var[\epsilon_1] = 1$ and $Cov(\varepsilon_1, \varepsilon_2) = 0$. In other words, if we can only simulate uncorrelated random variables $(\varepsilon_{1,i+1}^j, \varepsilon_{2,i+1}^j)$, we can still simulate correlated factors as

$$
\begin{align}
\phi_{1,i+1}^j &= \phi_{1,i}^j + \gamma_1^* \left(\overline{\phi}_1^* - \phi_{1,i}^j \right) \delta + \sigma_1 \sqrt{\delta}\, \varepsilon_{1,i+1}^j \\
\phi_{2,i+1}^j &= \phi_{2,i}^j + \gamma_2^* \left(\overline{\phi}_2^* - \phi_{2,i}^j \right) \delta + \sigma_2 \sqrt{\delta} \left(\rho \times \varepsilon_{1,i+1}^j + \sqrt{1 - \rho^2} \times \varepsilon_{2,i+1}^j \right)
\end{align}
$$

22.5   FORWARD RISK NEUTRAL PRICING

Recall that the Feynman-Kac theorem also provides the basis of the forward risk neutral pricing methodology, discussed in Chapter 21. In what follows we consider only the simple case in which the two factors are uncorrelated. The case with correlated factors can be analyzed in a similar manner.

Consider for instance the normalized security

$$\widetilde{V}(\phi_1, \phi_2, t; T) = \frac{V(\phi_1, \phi_2, t; T)}{Z(\phi_1, \phi_2, t; T_B)}$$

In the case in which factors are uncorrelated, the price of the normalized security must satisfy

$$0 = \frac{\partial \widetilde{V}}{\partial t} + \frac{\partial \widetilde{V}}{\partial \phi_1} \left(m_{1,t}^* + \sigma_{Z,1} s_{1,t} \right) + \frac{\partial \widetilde{V}}{\partial \phi_2} \left(m_{2,t}^* + \sigma_{Z,2} s_{2,t} \right) + \frac{1}{2} \frac{\partial^2 \widetilde{V}}{\partial \phi_1^2} s_{1,t}^2 + \frac{1}{2} \frac{\partial^2 \widetilde{V}}{\partial \phi_2^2} s_{2,t}^2$$

$$(22.73)$$

with the final condition

$$\widetilde{V}(\phi_1, \phi_2, T) = \tilde{g}_T = \frac{g_T}{Z(\phi_{1,T}, \phi_{2,T}, T; T_B)}$$

Above, for $i = 1, 2$,

$$\sigma_{Z,i} = \frac{1}{Z} \frac{\partial Z}{\partial \phi_i} s_{i,t}$$

An application of the Feynman-Kac formula the yields the following result:

Fact 22.11 *The value of the normalized security is*

$$\widetilde{V}(\phi_1, \phi_2, t; T) = E_f^* \left[\frac{g_T}{Z(\phi_{1,T}, \phi_{2,T}, T; T_B)} \right]$$

and therefore, the value of the interest rate security is

$$V(\phi_1, \phi_2, t; T) = Z(\phi_1, \phi_2, t; T_B) E_f^* \left[\frac{g_T}{Z(\phi_{1,T}, \phi_{2,T}, T; T_B)} \right]$$

where the expectation is taken with respect to the forward risk neutral processes

$$d\phi_{i,t} = (m_{i,t}^* + \sigma_{Z,i} s_{i,t}) dt + s_{i,t} dX_{i,t} \tag{22.74}$$

for $i = 1, 2$. Moreover, the process for $V(\phi_1, \phi_2, t; T)$ under the forward risk neutral dynamics induced by $Z(\phi_1, \phi_2, t; T_B)$ is

$$dV = V(r + \sigma_{Z,1} \sigma_{V,1} + \sigma_{Z,2} \sigma_{V,2}) dt + \sigma_{V,1} V dX_{1,t} + \sigma_{V,2} V dX_{2,t} \tag{22.75}$$

where $\sigma_{V,i} = \frac{1}{V} \frac{\partial V}{\partial \phi_i} s_{i,t}$ is the loading of dV/V on factor $dX_{i,t}$

As in Chapter 21, this result can be generalized to the following:

Fact 22.12 *Consider two traded securities P and V, and let their risk neutral processes be given by*

$$\begin{aligned} \frac{dP_t}{P_t} &= r_t dt + \sigma_{P,1,t} dX_{1,t} + \sigma_{P,2,t} dX_{2,t} \\ \frac{dV_t}{V_t} &= r_t dt + \sigma_{V,1,t} dX_{1,t} + \sigma_{V,2,t} dX_{2,t} \end{aligned}$$

where $\sigma_{P,i,t}$ and $\sigma_{V,i,t}$, $i = 1, 2$ are the loadings on the two shocks $dX_{1,t}$ and $dX_{2,t}$. Let P now be chosen as numeraire. Then, the process of V under the forward risk neutral dynamics induced by P is

$$\frac{dV_t}{V_t} = (r_t + \sigma_{P,1,t} \sigma_{V,1,t} + \sigma_{P,2,t} \sigma_{V,2,t}) dt + \sigma_{V,1,t} dX_{1,t} + \sigma_{V,2,t} dX_{2,t} \tag{22.76}$$

Similarly, let Y be a process with risk neutral dynamics

$$dY_t = m_t^* dt + s_{1,t} dX_{1,t} + s_{2,t} dX_{2,t}$$

Then, the process for Y under the forward risk neutral dynamics induced by P is

$$dY_t = (m_t^* + \sigma_{P,1,t} s_{1,t} + \sigma_{P,2,t} s_{2,t}) dt + s_{1,t} dX_{1,t} + s_{2,t} dX_{2,t} \tag{22.77}$$

This last result shows that when we change the numeraire, the processes of both traded securities (such as V in Equation 22.76) and stochastic variables (such as Y in Equation 22.77) change in their drift rates only. In particular, the new drift rate equals the old drift rate plus a term capturing the covariance between the traded security used as new numeraire and the variable we are considering. In other words, we have

$$\text{Covariance} \left(\frac{dP}{P}, \frac{dV}{V} \right) / dt = \sigma_{P,1,t} \sigma_{V,1,t} + \sigma_{P,2,t} \sigma_{V,2,t} \tag{22.78}$$

$$\text{Covariance} \left(\frac{dP}{P}, dY \right) / dt = \sigma_{P,1,t} s_{1,t} + \sigma_{P,2,t} s_{2,t} \tag{22.79}$$

22.5.1   Application: Options on Coupon Bonds

In the previous section we demonstrated that under the multivariate normal model, it is still possible to obtain the value of options on zero coupon bonds (see Fact 22.5). Unlike in the one-factor case discussed in Chapter 19, however, the pricing formula for coupon bonds does not follow from the one of zero coupon bonds. That is, the methodology illustrated in Section 19.4.1 in Chapter 19 does not carry over to the case of multiple factors. This fact is particularly problematic, as European swaptions can also be valued using a formula for options on coupon bonds.

However, we now illustrate how to use the forward risk neutral dynamics and the Feynman-Kac formula to compute the price of coupon bonds for the two factor Vasicek model in a semi-analytical format. We consider for simplicity the case in which the two factors $\phi_{1,t}$ and $\phi_{2,t}$ are independent, although a similar argument can be made in the more general case. In particular, because in the two factor Vasicek model we have

$$\sigma_{Z,i} = \frac{1}{Z}\frac{\partial Z}{\partial \phi_i}\sigma_i = -B_i(t;T)\sigma_i$$

where $B_i(t;T) = \left(1 - e^{-\gamma_i^*(T-t)}\right)/\gamma_i^*$, the forward risk neutral dynamics of $\phi_{i,t}$, for $i = 1, 2$ are given by

$$d\phi_{i,t} = (\gamma_i^*(\overline{\phi}_i^* - \phi_{i,t}) - B_i(t;T)\sigma_i^2)dt + \sigma_i dX_{i,t} \tag{22.80}$$

Let now T_O be the maturity of the option. We consider the forward risk neutral dynamics with respect to $Z(0, T_O)$, the zero coupon bond maturing at T_O. In this case, the factors ϕ_{i,T_O} are still jointly normally distributed. Indeed, in the case of independence we have that at T_O

$$\phi_{i,T_O} \sim N\left(\mu_i, \Sigma_i^2\right) \tag{22.81}$$

where

$$\mu_i = \overline{\phi}_i + e^{-\gamma_i T_O}(\phi_{i,0} - \overline{\phi}_i) - B(0;T_O)^2\frac{\sigma_i^2}{2} \tag{22.82}$$

$$\Sigma_i^2 = \frac{\sigma_i^2}{2\gamma_i^*}\left(1 - e^{-2\gamma_i^*T_O}\right) \tag{22.83}$$

Consider now the payoff of the coupon bond option at maturity T_O:

$$\text{Payoff at } T_O = g\left(\phi_{1,T_O}, \phi_{2,T_O}\right) = \max\left(P(\phi_{1,T_O}, \phi_{2,T_O}, T_O; T_B) - K, 0\right)$$

where $P(\phi_{1,T_O}, \phi_{2,T_O}, T_O; T_B)$ is the price at time T_O of the coupon bond, with coupon rate c and maturity T_B, that is,

$$P(\phi_{1,T_O}, \phi_{2,T_O}, T_O; T_B) = \frac{c}{2}\sum_{i=1}^{n} Z(\phi_{1,T_O}, \phi_{2,T_O}, T_O; T_i) + Z(\phi_{1,T_O}, \phi_{2,T_O}, T_O; T_i)$$

From the forward risk neutral dynamics, the price today of the coupon bond option is given by

$$V = Z(0,T)\, E_f^*\left[g\left(\phi_{1,T_O}, \phi_{2,T_O}\right)\right]$$

Recall that an expectation is an integral over all the possible values of $(\phi_{1,T_O}, \phi_{2,T_O})$ weighted by the probability (density) of each pair. Given Equation 22.81 and factor independence, we then have that the joint density is

$$f(\phi_{1,T_O}, \phi_{2,T_O}) = f_1(\phi_{1,T_O}) \times f_2(\phi_{2,T_O})$$

where $f_i(\phi_{1,T_O})$ is the normal distribution density with mean given in Equation 22.82 and variance given in Equation 22.83. Explicitly,

$$f_i(\phi_{i,T_O}) = \frac{1}{\sqrt{2\pi\Sigma_i^2}} e^{-\frac{(\phi_{i,T_O} - \mu_i)^2}{2\Sigma_i^2}}$$

It follows that the formula of the coupon bond option can be obtained by evaluating the (double) integral implicit in the forward risk neutral expectation

$$V = Z(0, T_O) \int_{-\infty}^{\infty} \int_{-\infty}^{\infty} g\left(\phi_{1,T_O}, \phi_{2,T_O}\right) f\left(\phi_{1,T_O}, \phi_{2,T_O}\right) d\phi_{1,T_O} \, d\phi_{2,T_O} \quad (22.84)$$

Numerical routines can be applied to compute the integral efficiently and accurately. However, roughly, it boils down to a double sum, which we can compute with any package

$$V \approx Z(0, T_O) \sum_{i=1}^{n_1} \sum_{j=1}^{n_2} g(\phi_{1,i}, \phi_{2,j},) f\left(\phi_{1,i}, \phi_{2,j}\right) d\phi_{1,i} d\phi_{2,j} \quad (22.85)$$

where the sums are carried over the range of ϕ_1 and ϕ_2 over which $f\left(\phi_{1,i}, \phi_{2,j}\right) > \varepsilon$, where ε is a small number.

■ **EXAMPLE 22.6**

Consider again Example 22.1, and suppose that on January 8, 2002 we want to evaluate an option with strike price $K = 100$ and maturity $T_O = $ February 15, 2003, written on the coupon bond that will have five years to maturity at T_O. Such a coupon bond will then expire on $T_B = $ February 15, 2007. This bond has a coupon of 5.5% and it is currently trading at $P(0, T_B) = \$106.4008$. Using the parameters in Example 22.1, we can use the formulas in Equations 22.20 and 22.21 and compute $A(T_O; T_i)$, $B_1(T_O; T_i)$ and $B_2(T_O; T_i)$ for each coupon date T_i after the option expiration T_O.

Given these quantities, we are equipped to compute the value of the payoff $g_T = \max(P(T_O; T_B) - K, 0)$ for a wide range of possible values of (ϕ_1, ϕ_2). The value of this payoff is in Panel A of Figure 22.8. As it can be seen, the payoff is zero for high values of ϕ_2 and ϕ_1. In addition, the value of the bond seems more sensitive to ϕ_2 than to ϕ_1. The reason is that in order to fit the term structure, we obtained $\gamma_2^* = -0.0450$, that is, an explosive process for ϕ_2. Thus, little variation of this factor implies a large impact on the price of the fixed income security.

Given the parameters in Example 22.1, we can next compute the forward risk neutral distribution of ϕ_{1,T_O} and ϕ_{2,T_O} from Equations 22.82 and 22.83. In particular, we obtain $\mu_1 = -0.0095$, $\mu_2 = 0.0458$, $\Sigma_1 = 0.0150$ and $\Sigma_2 = 0.0107$. The joint (normal) density is plotted in Panel B of Figure 22.8.[7] This probability density gives

---

[7]From the estimation in Example 22.1, the current levels of the two factors are $\phi_{2,0} = 0.0436$ and $\phi_{1,0} = r_0 - 0.0268$, which center the distribution, and determine $\mu_1 = -0.0095$, $\mu_2 = 0.0458$.

zero probability to large payoff realizations. Finally, we can use approximation in Equation 22.85 to compute the price of the option, which in this case is given by

Value of the option $= \$2.8032$

How can be certain that this procedure is correct? In case we did not trust the formulas, or are worried about a typo in the numerical computation of the option, it is always a good habit to compute the price of another security for which we have a closed form formula. For instance, we can also compute the value of a zero coupon bond option to check the accuracy of our approximation. Indeed, in this case, the solution in Equation 22.84, approximated by Equation 22.85, should give the same answer as the formula for a zero coupon bond option, already developed in Fact 22.5 in Equation (22.41. In this case, assuming a strike price $K = 80$, and the same maturity T_B as in the previous case, we find

Value of option using Equation 22.85= $\$0.8248955$.
Value of option using Equation 22.41= $\$0.8249188$.

The two methodologies give (almost) the same value, where the discrepancy at the fifth decimal place is due to the approximation error introduced in Equation 22.84.

22.6   THE MULTIFACTOR LIBOR MARKET MODEL

The LIBOR market model discussed in Chapter 21 assumes that all of the forward rates are driven by a single Brownian motion. For this reason, it is a single-factor model, as all forward rates are perfectly correlated. However, for numerous securities it is important to explicitly model the correlation across forward rates. This is achieved by simply assuming that forward rates are driven by multiple Brownian motions. Again, for simplicity, we consider here only a two-factor model, but the model can be greatly generalized. The two factor LIBOR market model assumes that under the $T_{i+1}-$forward risk neutral dynamics, the forward rate $f_n(t, T_i, T_{i+1})$ follows the log-normal model

$$\frac{df(t, T_i, T_{i+1})}{f(t, T_i, T_{i+1})} = \sigma_{f,1}^{i+1}(t)dX_{1,t} + \sigma_{f,2}^{i+1}(t)dX_{2,t} \qquad (22.86)$$

where $X_{1,t}$ and $X_{2,t}$ are independent Brownian motions.

If we are interested in pricing securities whose payoffs depend only on one LIBOR rate $r_n(T_i, T_{i+1})$, then the multivariate model is as good as the single-factor model, because we can redefine a new Brownian motion $\tilde{X}_t$ such that

$$\sigma_f^{i+1}(t)d\tilde{X}_t = \sigma_{f,1}^{i+1}(t)dX_{1,t} + \sigma_{f,2}^{i+1}(t)dX_{2,t}$$

thereby obtaining back the main assumption of the single-factor LIBOR market model. In particular, $r_n(T_i, T_{i+1})$ is log-normally distributed with mean $f_n(0, T_i, T_{i+1})$ and variance $\int_0^{T_i} \left(\sigma_f^{i+1}(t)\right)^2 dt$, and all of the conclusions in Chapter 21 follow.

The gain from a multifactor model stems from securities whose payoffs at maturity depend on many forward rates, as discussed in Section 21.4.3. For instance, a security whose payoff is tied to the value of a LIBOR-based bond $Z(T_O, T_M)$ or a swap rate

Figure 22.8 Payoff and Density of Coupon Bond Option

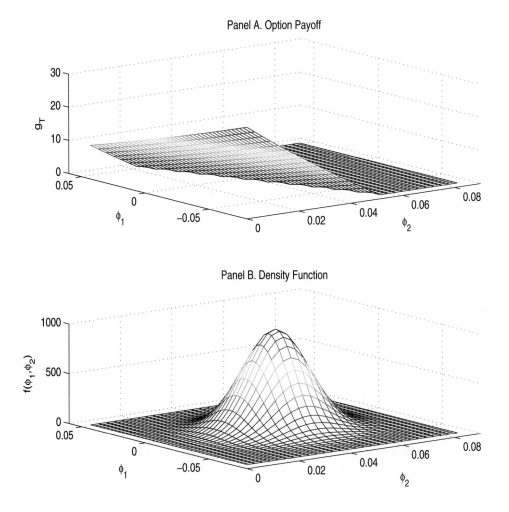

$c(T_O, T_M)$ depends on the whole structure of forward rates at T_O. This implies that the joint distribution of forward rates at maturity, and thus in particular whether they are highly correlated or not, will have an impact on the price of the security. In these cases, the correlation across forward rates then makes a difference. In particular, denote the covariance between the forward rates by $\rho_{i+1,j+1}(t)$. We then have

$$\rho_{i+1,j+1}(t) = Cov\left(\frac{df(t, T_i, T_{i+1})}{f(t, T_i, T_{i+1})}, \frac{df(t, T_j, T_{j+1})}{f(t, T_j, T_{j+1})}\right)/dt \tag{22.87}$$

$$= \sigma_{f,1}^{i+1}(t)\sigma_{f,1}^{j+1}(t) + \sigma_{f,2}^{i+1}(t)\sigma_{f,2}^{j+1}(t) \tag{22.88}$$

we have the following:

Fact 22.13 *The dynamics of the forward rate $f_n(t, T_i, T_{i+1})$ under the $\overline{T}$-forward risk neutral dynamics for $\overline{T} < T_{i+1}$ are given by*

$$\frac{df_n(t, T_i, T_{i+1})}{f_n(t, T_i, T_{i+1})} = \left(\sum_{j=\overline{i}}^{i} \frac{\Delta f_n(t, T_j, T_{j+1})\rho_{i+1,j+1}(t)}{1 + \Delta f_n(t, T_j, T_{j+1})}\right) dt + \sigma_{f,1}^{i+1}(t)dX_{1,t} + \sigma_{f,2}^{i+1}(t)dX_{2,t}$$

$$\tag{22.89}$$

where $\overline{i}$ is the index such that $T_{\overline{i}} = \overline{T}$.
If instead, $\overline{T} > T_{i+1}$, then

$$\frac{df_n(t, T_i, T_{i+1})}{f_n(t, T_i, T_{i+1})} = -\left(\sum_{j=i}^{\overline{i}-1} \frac{\Delta f_n(t, T_j, T_{j+1})\rho_{i+1,j+1}(t)}{1 + \Delta f_n(t, T_j, T_{j+1})}\right) dt + \sigma_{f,1}^{i+1}(t)dX_{1,t} + \sigma_{f,2}^{i+1}(t)dX_{2,t}$$

$$\tag{22.90}$$

Once we are given the covariance structure across forward rates $\rho_{i+1,j+1}(t)$, or equivalently, the volatility functions $\sigma_{f,k}^{i+1}(t)$, the pricing methodology is identical to the one discussed in Section 21.4.3 of Chapter 21. It is, however, not obvious immediately how to calibrate the volatility functions $\sigma_{f,k}^{i+1}(t)$. For instance, caplets' forward volatilities do not contain sufficient information to calibrate both $\sigma_{f,1}^{i+1}(t)$ and $\sigma_{f,2}^{i+1}(t)$, because their value only depends on their (squared) sum $(\sigma_{f,1}^{i+1}(t))^2 + (\sigma_{f,2}^{i+1}(t))^2$. One possibility is to use European swaptions quotes: Because swaptions' payoffs at T_O depend on the whole term structure $Z(T_O, T)$, their quotes implicitly contain information about the correlation across forward rates. The procedure, though, requires a fast computation of a European swaption from the LIBOR market model. Recall that under the assumptions of the LIBOR market model the European swaption does not have an analytical formula, although it can be computed by Monte Carlo simulations. Unfortunately, the latter methodology is quite slow, and it makes it hard to use European swaptions efficiently for calibration purposes. Yet, numerous approximating analytical formulas have been proposed in the literature. In what follows, we show an alternative empirical methodology, for the sake of illustration.

22.6.1 Level, Slope, and Curvature Factors for Forward Rates

One possibility is to extract factor loadings from the time series of forward rates. Principal component analysis, reviewed in Section 4.6 in Chapter 4 provides a methodology to compute loadings for forward rates that depend on factors. More specifically, assume that log forward rates follow the process

$$d\log(f_n(t, T_i, T_{i+1})) = \mu_f^{i+1} dt + S_1(T_{i+1} - t)dX_{1,t} + S_2(T_{i+1} - t)dX_{2,t} + S_3(T_{i+1} - t)dX_{3,t}$$
$$(22.91)$$

where we assume three factors. Principal component analysis provides the time series estimate of the $S_k(T - t)$ functions, which are reported in Figure 22.9 for swap data ranging from Janaury 1997 to April 2008. The first factor loading $S_1(T - t)$ appears hump shaped, as the implied volatility from cap quotes discussed in Chapter 20. This component of volatility is always positive, implying that when the first factor $dX_{1,t}$ increases, all of the forward rates increase, although the short-term forward rates increase by more (in percentage). The second factor is negative at the short end and positive at the long end, implying that an increase in the second factor decreases the forward rates with low maturity and increases the ones with high maturity. For this reason, one may call this factor a "slope" factor. Note that by construction, this variation in slope is independent of the variation of the first factor (see Chapter 4). The third factor is positive at the short and long end of the maturity structure, but negative for medium maturities. For this reason, this factor may be called a "curvature" factor.

The key point is that we can use these volatility estimates to price derivative securities by no arbitrage. Because the only necessary input to price derivatives by no arbitrage are the functions $\sigma_{f,k}^{i+1}(t)$ in Equations 22.89 and 22.90, the result follows by defining covariances out of the estimated $S_k(T - t)$ plotted in Figure 22.9.

■ **EXAMPLE 22.7**

Today is April 1, 2008. The current LIBOR-based discount factors $Z(0, T)$ are in the second column of Table 22.2. Column 3 reports the total volatility of forward rates, as estimated simply by taking the standard deviation of the change in log forward rates. Columns 4 to 6 report the results of a principal component analysis on the change in log forward rates, also plotted in Figure 22.9.[8] Given these data, we compute the value of a European receiver swaption with one year to maturity to enter into a 5-year swap. We do so in two cases: In the first case we only consider the total volatility of the (log) forward rate, in Column 3. In the second case we also consider the three factors, and therefore, the empirical correlation between forward rates. The pricing methodology is identical to the one discussed in Example 21.6 in Chapter 21. In particular, we discretize the process for forward rates in Equation 22.89 according to the log-normal recursion

$$f_n^s(t + \delta, T_i, T_{i+1}) = f_n^s(t, T_i, T_{i+1})e^{m_{i+1}^s(t)\delta + \sum_{k=1}^{3} S_k(T_{i+1} - t)\sqrt{\delta}\,\varepsilon_{k,t}^s} \quad (22.92)$$

where s is the simulation number, $s = 1, ..., \mathcal{S}$,

$$m_{i+1}^s(t) = \sum_{j=\bar{i}}^{i} \frac{\Delta f_n^s(t, T_j, T_{j+1})\left(\sum_{k=1}^{3} S_k(T_{i+1} - t)S_k(T_{j+1} - t)\right)}{1 + \Delta f_n^s(t, T_j, T_{j+1})}$$

---

[8]The loadings have been adjusted for the volatility of the resulting factors, so that these can be interpreted as annualized factor loadings on independent factors with unit variance.

Table 22.2 Principal Components of Volatility of Forward Rates

Maturity T_i	Discount $Z(0,T_i)$	Volatility Forward Rate (%) $S(T_i)$	Volatility Factor 1 (%) $S_1(T_i)$	Volatility Factor 2 (%) $S_2(T_i)$	Volatility Factor 3 (%) $S_3(T_i)$
0.25	99.3335	41.729	27.915	-27.035	14.192
0.50	98.7306	42.793	35.810	-21.802	8.038
0.75	98.1650	44.158	40.363	-16.928	1.738
1.00	97.5928	44.205	41.638	-12.766	-3.830
1.25	96.9817	40.384	38.296	-7.409	-6.078
1.50	96.3332	34.341	33.337	-1.992	-6.473
1.75	95.6477	30.275	29.143	1.657	-6.240
2.00	94.9351	28.316	26.747	2.830	-6.681
2.25	94.1756	26.115	24.807	3.036	-6.613
2.50	93.3460	22.869	21.772	4.467	-4.839
2.75	92.4668	21.001	19.755	5.826	-3.082
3.00	91.5700	20.513	18.950	6.923	-2.008
3.25	90.6647	20.287	18.459	7.644	-1.474
3.50	89.7365	19.642	17.450	8.216	-0.564
3.75	88.7915	18.801	16.479	8.369	-0.040
4.00	87.8366	17.645	15.402	8.103	-0.196
4.25	86.8735	16.519	14.183	7.860	-0.440
4.50	85.9017	15.788	13.163	7.842	-0.149
4.75	84.9257	15.369	12.579	8.078	0.576
5.00	83.9505	15.182	12.462	8.280	1.162
5.25	82.9731	15.042	12.260	8.414	1.421
5.50	81.9888	14.859	11.741	8.713	1.848
5.75	81.0003	14.707	11.274	8.941	2.245
6.00	80.0106	14.557	10.858	9.092	2.604
6.25	79.0226	14.381	10.493	9.159	2.920
6.50	78.0396	14.162	10.179	9.137	3.183
6.75	77.0650	13.897	9.919	9.018	3.387
7.00	76.1024	13.690	9.856	8.828	3.343

Original Data Source: LIBOR and Swap Rates from Bloomberg.

Figure 22.9   Forward Factor Loadings from Principal Component Analysis

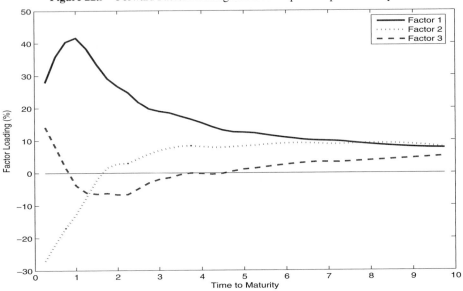

$$-\frac{1}{2}\left(\sum_{k=1}^{3} S_k\,(T_{i+1}-t)^2\right)$$

Above, $\varepsilon_{k,t}^s$ are independently normally distributed shocks. Using $r_K = 3.5\%$ as the European swaption strike rate, we obtain the following result:

$$1 \text{ Factor} \quad : \quad \widehat{V} = 0.60; \tag{22.93}$$

$$3 \text{ Factors} \quad : \quad \widehat{V} = 0.52. \tag{22.94}$$

The multifactor model generates a lower value of the European swaption. Intuitively, recall that the zero coupon bond price at T_O with maturity T_M is given by

$$Z(T_O, T_M) = \frac{1}{1+r_n\,(T_{\bar{i}}, T_{\bar{i}+1})\Delta} \times \frac{1}{1+f_n\,(T_{\bar{i}}, T_{\bar{i}+1}, T_{\bar{i}+2})\Delta} \times \dots$$
$$\dots \times \frac{1}{1+f_n\,(T_{\bar{i}}, T_{\bar{i}+m-1}, T_{\bar{i}+m})\Delta} \tag{22.95}$$

Thus, although the volatility of the forward rates is the same in the two cases above, when there is perfect correlation across forward rates all the terms in the sum in Equation 22.95 move up and down together. This implies a higher volatility of the bond price $Z(T_O, T_M)$ compared to the case in which forward rates are not perfectly correlated across maturities. Therefore, lower correlation across forward rates of various maturities decreases the total volatility of the variable underlying the option, and so the price of the option itself.

22.7 AFFINE AND QUADRATIC TERM STRUCTURE MODELS

We conclude this chapter with a brief overview of two classes of models widely used by macroeconomists to study the properties of the term structure of interest rates, the affine class and quadratic class of the term structure. These classes of models generalize the Vasicek model and the Cox, Ingersoll, and Ross model discussed in earlier chapters to take into account the fact that several factors affect the time variation of interest rates. The following description is only cursory and it is only meant to provide some hints on the types of models that are available to study the interest rate dynamics.

22.7.1 Affine Models

The generic affine model of the term structure has the following elements:

1. A set of n factors $\phi_t = [\phi_{1,t}, \phi_{2,t}, ..., \phi_{n,t}]'$, evolving over time according to a risk neutral model:

$$d\phi_t = \mathbf{\Gamma}^* \left(\overline{\phi}^* - \phi_t \right) dt + \mathbf{\Sigma}\sqrt{\mathbf{S}_t}d\mathbf{X}_t \qquad (22.96)$$

where $\mathbf{\Gamma}^*$ is a $(n \times n)$ matrix, $\overline{\phi}^*$ is a $(n \times 1)$ vector, $\mathbf{\Sigma}$ is also a $(n \times n)$ matrix, and finally, $\mathbf{S}_t$ is a diagonal matrix with $ii-$the element given by:

$$\mathbf{S}_{ii,t} = \alpha_i + \beta_i'\phi_t$$

2. The risk free rate is

$$r_t = \delta_0 + \delta_1'\phi_t \qquad (22.97)$$

where δ_1 is a $(n \times 1)$ vector of constants.

It should be emphasized that not all of the parameter combinations work for this model. For instance, we need to make sure that $\mathbf{S}_{ii,t} > 0$ for possible times t, otherwise the processes do not exist. Moreover, many parameter combinations are equivalent in the sense that they lead to the same processes. The Fundamental Pricing Equation for any interest rate security whose price depends on the set of factors ϕ_t is

$$rV = \frac{\partial V}{\partial t} + \frac{\partial V}{\partial \phi}\mathbf{\Gamma}^* \left(\overline{\phi}^* - \phi_t \right) + \frac{1}{2}trace\left(\frac{\partial^2 V}{\partial \phi \partial \phi'}\mathbf{\Sigma S_t \Sigma} \right) \qquad (22.98)$$

where all of the partial derivatives are vector derivatives.[9] It turns out that zero coupon bonds have an analytical formula.

Fact 22.14 *Let $Z(\phi, t; T)$ denote the price of a discount bond with maturity T with final payoff $Z(\phi, T; T) = 1$. Then, the value of the bond before maturity is given by*

$$Z(\phi, t; T) = e^{A(t;T) + \mathbf{B}(t;T)'\phi_t} \qquad (22.99)$$

where $A(t; T)$ and $\mathbf{B}(t; T)$ satisfy the Ordinary Differential Equations

$$0 = \frac{\partial \mathbf{B}(t;T)'}{\partial t} + \delta_1' - \mathbf{B}(t;T)'\mathbf{\Gamma}^* - \frac{1}{2}\sum_{i=1}^{n}[\mathbf{\Sigma}'\mathbf{B}(t;T)]_{ii}\beta_i' \qquad (22.100)$$

$$0 = \frac{\partial A(t;T)}{\partial t} - \delta_0 - \mathbf{B}(t;T)'\mathbf{\Gamma}^*\overline{\phi}^* + \frac{1}{2}\sum_{i=1}^{n}[\mathbf{\Sigma}'\mathbf{B}(t;T)]_{ii}\alpha_i \qquad (22.101)$$

[9]The trace of a matrix $\mathbf{H}$ is the sum of the elements on its diagonal.

with $A(T;T) = 0$ and $\mathbf{B}(T;T) = \mathbf{0}$.

It should be emphasized that solving numerically the system of ordinary differential equations in Equations 22.100 and 22.101 is infinitely easier than solving the partial differential equation in Equation 22.98. The reason is that since we have the final condition, we can start from the end T, and unravel backward the values of $A(t;T)$ and $\mathbf{B}(t;T)$. Indeed, approximate $\partial \mathbf{B}(t;T)/\partial t \approx (\mathbf{B}(t;T) - \mathbf{B}(t-\delta;T))/\delta$ and $\partial A(t;T)/\partial t \approx (A(t;T) - A(t-\delta;T))/\delta$, where δ is a small positive number, substitute in Equations 22.100 and 22.101, and rearrange to obtain the backward recursion:

$$\mathbf{B}(t-\delta;T)' = \mathbf{B}(t;T)' + \left\{ \boldsymbol{\delta}_1' - \mathbf{B}(t;T)'\boldsymbol{\Gamma}^* - \frac{1}{2}\sum_{i=1}^{n}[\boldsymbol{\Sigma}'\mathbf{B}(t;T)]_{ii}\boldsymbol{\beta}_i' \right\} \delta \qquad (22.102)$$

$$A(t-\delta;T) = \partial A(t;T) + \left\{ -\delta_0 - \mathbf{B}(t;T)'\boldsymbol{\Gamma}^*\overline{\phi}^* + \frac{1}{2}\sum_{i=1}^{n}[\boldsymbol{\Sigma}'\mathbf{B}(t;T)]_{ii}\alpha_i \right\} \delta \quad (22.103)$$

Using the final condition $\mathbf{B}(T;T) = \mathbf{0}$ and $A(T;T) = 0$, we can start the procedure and obtain $\mathbf{B}(t;T)$ and $A(t;T)$ for every t and T. The class of affine term structure model is very large, and it encompasses several intuitive models of the term structure, depending on the specification of the factors. For instance:

1. **The Stochastic Volatility Model**. The following specification, due to Fong and Vasicek, generalizes the simple Vasicek model to the case of stochastic volatility:

$$\begin{align} dr_t &= \gamma_r^*(\overline{r}^* - r_t)dt + \sqrt{v_t}dX_{1,t} & (22.104) \\ dv_t &= \gamma_v^*(\overline{v}^* - v_t)dt + \sigma_v\sqrt{v_t}dX_{2,t} & (22.105) \end{align}$$

Clearly, the value of the zero coupon bond is still given by Equation 22.99, which then specializes to

$$Z(r,v,t;T) = e^{A(t;T) - B_1(t;T)r_t + B_2(t;T)v_t}$$

Variation in the interest rate volatility affects the price of long term bonds.

2. **The Canonical $A_2(3)$ Model**. This is a largely used model with three factors, two of which affect volatility:

$$\begin{align} dr_t &= \gamma_r^*(\phi_{2,t} - r_t)dt + \sqrt{v_t}dX_{1,t} & (22.106) \\ dv_t &= \gamma_v^*(\overline{v}^* - v_t)dt + \sigma_v\sqrt{v_t}dX_{2,t} & (22.107) \\ d\phi_{2,t} &= \gamma_\phi^*(\overline{\phi}_2^* - \phi_{2,t})dt + \sigma_2\sqrt{\phi_{2,t}}dX_{3,t} & (22.108) \end{align}$$

This model also generalizes the two-factor Vasicek model to the case of stochastic volatility.

There is a large body of research on the performance of these models to match both the time series and the cross-section of bond prices and options. One key step in this study is to decide how to move from the risk neutral factor dynamics to their true (physical) dynamics, which are the relevant dynamics to study the time series properties of bond yields. As discussed in Chapter 18 the link between risk neutral and risk natural (true) dynamics is provided by the specification of the market price of risk. There are two popular specifications:

1. **Affine**: The market price of risk takes the form:

$$\lambda_t = \sqrt{\mathbf{S}_t}\lambda_1$$

where λ_1 is a $(n \times 1)$ vector. This specification implies that the risk natural (true) drift of the factors is also affine:

$$E[d\phi_t]/dt = \mathbf{\Gamma}^* \left(\overline{\phi}^* - \phi_t\right) + \left(\mathbf{\Sigma}\sqrt{\mathbf{S}_t}\right)\left(\sqrt{\mathbf{S}_t}\lambda_1\right) = \mathbf{\Gamma}\left(\overline{\phi} - \phi_t\right)$$

where $\mathbf{\Gamma}$ and $\overline{\phi}$ are defined by the equation itself.

2. **Essentially Affine**: The market price of risk takes the form:

$$\lambda_t = \sqrt{\mathbf{S}_t}\lambda_1 + \widehat{\mathbf{S}}_t^{-1/2}\lambda_2\phi_t$$

where λ_2 is a $(n \times n)$ matrix, and $\widehat{\mathbf{S}}_t$ is a diagonal matrix such that

$$[\widehat{\mathbf{S}}_t]_{ii} = \begin{cases} \alpha_i + \beta_i\phi_t & \text{if} \quad \min(\alpha_i + \beta_i\phi_t) > 0 \\ 0 & \text{if} \quad \min(\alpha_i + \beta_i\phi_t) = 0 \end{cases}$$

Also in this case, the true drift rate of the factors is still affine

$$\begin{aligned} E[d\phi_t]/dt &= \mathbf{\Gamma}^* \left(\overline{\phi}^* - \phi_t\right) + \mathbf{\Sigma}\mathbf{S}_t^{\frac{1}{2}}\left(\mathbf{S}_t^{\frac{1}{2}}\lambda_1 + \widehat{\mathbf{S}}_t^{-\frac{1}{2}}\lambda_2\mathbf{X}_t\right) \\ &= \mathbf{\Gamma}\left(\overline{\phi} - \phi_t\right) \end{aligned}$$

where again $\mathbf{\Gamma}$ and $\overline{\phi}$ are defined by the equation itself.

The definition of the affine market price of risk (Case 1) generates some inconsistencies with the time series data of yields. In particular, it has been observed that it is hard for such a model to recover the predictability results discussed in Chapter 7. The main issue is that in such models, the main predictor of future expected excess return should be the volatility of interest rates, which instead does not have much power in the data. The essentially affine specification (Case 2), due to Duffee (2002), is instead better able to capture both the cross-section and the time series properties of bond returns. Singleton (2006) contains a review of the performance of these models.

22.7.2 Quadratic Models

A relatively recent development in term structure models is provided by the class of quadratic term structure models. These models get their name from a quadratic specification of the short term interest rate in terms of factors. More specifically, a quadratic term structure model has the following elements:

1. A set of n factors $\phi_t = [\phi_{1,t}, \phi_{2,t}, ..., \phi_{n,t}]'$, evolving over time according to a linear risk neutral model:

$$d\phi_t = \mathbf{\Gamma}^* \left(\overline{\phi}^* - \phi_t\right)dt + \mathbf{\Sigma}d\mathbf{X}_t \tag{22.109}$$

where $\mathbf{\Gamma}^*$ is a $(n \times n)$ matrix, $\overline{\phi}^*$ is a $(n \times 1)$ vector, $\mathbf{\Sigma}$ is also a $(n \times n)$ matrix;

2. The risk free rate is quadratic in the factors:

$$r_t = \delta_0 + \boldsymbol{\delta}_1' \boldsymbol{\phi}_t + \boldsymbol{\phi}_t' \boldsymbol{\delta}_2 \boldsymbol{\phi}_t \tag{22.110}$$

where $\boldsymbol{\delta}_2$ is a $(n \times n)$ matrix.

3. The market price of risk is given by

$$\boldsymbol{\lambda}_t = \boldsymbol{\lambda}_0 + \boldsymbol{\lambda}_1 \boldsymbol{\phi}_t$$

which is similar to the one discussed in Chapter 18 for the Vasicek model.

Unlike in the affine model, the factors $\boldsymbol{\phi}_t$ do not display any stochastic volatility per se. This property makes it easier to work with this class of models, because we do not need to worry to select parametrizations that ensure some positivity constraint. However, the quadratic specification of the interest rate in Equation 22.110 implies that the process of the interest rate itself has in fact stochastic volatility. For instance, if there is only one factor, Equation 22.110 can be written as

$$r_t = \delta_0 + \delta_1 \phi_t + \delta_2 \phi_t^2$$

It follows from Ito's lemma that the diffusion process for r_t is

$$dr_t = \left[(\delta_1 + 2\delta_2 \phi_t)\gamma^*(\overline{\phi}^* - \phi_t) + \delta_2 \sigma^2 \right] dt + (\delta_1 + 2\delta_2 \phi_t)\sigma dX_t$$

When ϕ_t changes over time, so does the volatility of the interest rate. Note that if $\delta_2 = 0$, then the model is the same as the simple Vasicek model.

The fundamental pricing equation is the same as before:

$$rV = \frac{\partial V}{\partial t} + \frac{\partial V}{\partial \boldsymbol{\phi}} \boldsymbol{\Gamma}^* \left(\overline{\boldsymbol{\phi}}^* - \boldsymbol{\phi}_t \right) + \frac{1}{2} trace \left(\frac{\partial^2 V}{\partial \boldsymbol{\phi} \partial \boldsymbol{\phi}} \boldsymbol{\Sigma} \boldsymbol{\Sigma} \right) \tag{22.111}$$

Also this class of models allows for an analytical formula for bond prices, summarized in the following:

Fact 22.15 *Let $Z(\phi, t; T)$ denote the price of a discount bond with maturity T with final payoff $Z(\phi, T; T) = 1$. Then, the value of the bond before maturity is given by*

$$Z\left(\mathbf{X}_t, t; T \right) = e^{A(t;T) + \mathbf{B}(t;T)' \boldsymbol{\phi}_t + \boldsymbol{\phi}_t' \mathbf{C}(t;T) \boldsymbol{\phi}_t}$$

where $A(t; T)$, $\mathbf{B}(t; T)$, and $\mathbf{C}(t; T)$ satisfy a set of ordinary differential equations.

$$0 = \frac{\partial \mathbf{C}(t; T)}{\partial t} - \boldsymbol{\delta}_2 + 2\mathbf{C}(t; T) \boldsymbol{\Sigma} \boldsymbol{\Sigma}' \mathbf{C}(t; T)' - 2\mathbf{C}(t; T) \boldsymbol{\Gamma}^*$$

$$0 = \frac{\partial \mathbf{B}(t; T)}{\partial t} - \boldsymbol{\delta}_1 - (\boldsymbol{\Gamma}^*)' \mathbf{B}(t; T) + 2\mathbf{C}(t; T) \boldsymbol{\Gamma}^* \overline{\boldsymbol{\phi}}^* + 2\mathbf{C}(t; T) \boldsymbol{\Sigma} \boldsymbol{\Sigma}' \mathbf{B}(t; T)$$

$$0 = \frac{\partial A(t; T)}{\partial t} - \delta_0 + \mathbf{B}(t; T)' \boldsymbol{\Gamma}^* \overline{\boldsymbol{\phi}}^* + \frac{1}{2} trace \left(\mathbf{B}(t; T) \mathbf{B}(t; T)' \boldsymbol{\Sigma} \boldsymbol{\Sigma}' + 2\mathbf{C}(t; T) \boldsymbol{\Sigma} \boldsymbol{\Sigma}' \right)$$

Recent research seems to suggest that the quadratic class of models tends to perform better than the affine class, in the sense that its dynamic properties better match the empirical properties of bond yields discussed in Chapter 7. Singleton (2006) contains a detailed discussion of the empirical performance of this class of models.

22.8 SUMMARY

In this chapter we covered the following topics:

1. Multivariate Ito's lemma: This is an extension of Ito's lemma to the case in which a security price, or a stochastic variable, depends on many factors. The form of the multivariate Ito's lemma is similar to the case with one factor, but with more convexity terms in the drift rate to reflect the stochastic variation of the various factors as well as their correlation.

2. Two-Factor Vasicek Model: A model for interest rates, in the two-factor Vasicek model each factor follows a mean reverting process. The bond pricing formula and option pricing formula are in closed form. Moreover, the model can be expressed as a model of the short-term interest rate and long-term yield. The model helps fitting the term structure of volatility, and also, a little, the term structure of correlation across yields.

3. Two-Factor Hull-White Model: This model is similar to two-factor Vasicek model, but with drift rate specified to fit exactly the term structure of interest rates. The additional flexibility increases the ability of the model to match the correlations across yields.

4. Yield Curve Steepener: This is a fixed income note whose final payoff is linked to the slope of the term structure. Multifactor models are particulary useful for these types of securities, as single-factor models instead imply that the level of interest rates is perfectly correlated with the slope. Thus, it may over- or under-estimate the true value of the security, whose price should only depend on the characteristics of the slope factor itself, and not the level.

5. Multifactor LIBOR Market Model: This model is a relatively simple generalization of the single-factor LIBOR market model. Using a multifactor model only helps for those securities whose prices depend on multiple forward rates. Relaxing perfect correlation tends to decrease the volatility of securities that depend on the full term structure of forward rates. Options on these fixed income instruments tend to have lower prices, as a consequence.

6. Multifactor Affine and Quadratic Term Structure Models: These are classes of models with many factors that lead to closed form expressions for bond prices. In many of the specifications, the dynamics of interest rates display stochastic volatility, in line with the data.

22.9 EXERCISES

1. Today is November 3, 2008. Table 22.3 provides the caps and swap rates quotes on this date. Fit the two-factor Vasicek model to these data. Discuss the performance of the model in fitting both the term structure of interest rates and cap prices.

2. Today is November 3, 2008. Table 22.3 provides the caps and swap rates quotes on this date.

Table 22.3 Swaptions, Caps and Floors Quotes on November 3, 2008

| Maturity | Swap Rates | Swaption Vols | | | Volatilities | |
		3M	6M	1Y	Caps	Floors
1 Y	2.412/452	67.8	60.6	49.3	60.59/61.59	60.59/61.59
2 Y	2.619/633	59.7	52.8	41.6	52.26/53.26	52.26/53.26
3 Y	3.120/160	52.8	46.5	37.7	42.32/43.32	42.32/43.32
4 Y	3.507/547	48.7	42.5	35.3	35.99/36.99	35.99/36.99
5 Y	3.808/822	46.6	40.3	34.1	32.24/33.24	32.24/33.24
7 Y	4.171/197	41.3	36.3	31.4	27.82/28.82	27.82/28.82
10 Y	4.422/462	36.8	33.1	29.0	24.21/25.21	24.21/25.21

Source: Bloomberg.

(a) Fit the two-factor Hull-White model to the cap prices. Is there any gain compared to the one-factor Hull-White model (discussed in Chapter 19)?

(b) Given the volatility estimates, fit the model to the LIBOR curve.

(c) Use the model to price a European swaption, whose quotes are available in Table 20.6 in Chapter 20. How well does the model do?

3. Consider the two-factor Hull-White model estimated in the previous exercise. Now price a one-year caplet "in arrears," that is, such that its cash flow at time T_i is

$$CF(T_i) = N \, \Delta \, \max(r_n(T_i, T_{i+1}) - r_K, 0)$$

with strike rate $r_K = 2\%$. Describe the procedure to obtain the price of this derivative security and compute its price.

4. Today is November 3, 2008. Table 22.3 provides the European Swaptions and swap rates quotes on this date.

(a) Fit the two-factor Hull-White model to the European swaptions.

(b) Is there any gain over the one-factor Hull-White model?

5. Table 22.2 contains the LIBOR discount factors $Z(0, T)$, the estimated volatility function $S(T_i - t)$ of forward rates, as well as its decomposition in three factor loadings $S_k(T_i - t)$.

(a) Use the multivariate LIBOR market model to obtain the value of a 3-year swap in arrears, that is, with cash flows given by

$$CF(T_i) = N\Delta(r_n(T_i, T_{i+1}) - c(0, 3))$$

for a swap rate $c(0, 3) = 3\%$.

(b) Is there any difference between the multivariate LIBOR market model and the single-factor LIBOR market model introduced in Chapter 21? Discuss.

6. A **constant maturity swap** (CMS) is a swap with cash flow at time T_i given by

$$CF(T_i) = N\Delta(c(T_i, T_{i+m}) - K)$$

where $c(T_i, T_{i+m})$ is the swap rate for a given maturity $T_{i+m} - T_i$, and K is the CMS swap rate. Let the constant maturity be $T_{i+m} - T_i = 3$ years and $K = 3\%$ (see Exercise 6 in Chapter 21). Use the LIBOR discount factors and volatility estimates in Table 22.2 to value the constant maturity swap for both the single-factor and the multi-factor LIBOR market model. In particular, do the following:

(a) Consider each payment T_i independently. For each payment, select appropriate forward risk neutral dynamics and use Monte Carlo Simulations to simulate several LIBOR curves $Z^s(T_i, T)$. For each simulation run s you can compute the swap rate $c^s(T_i, T_{i+m})$ and thus value the payoff as usual.

(b) Is the value of the CMS the same under the single-factor and the multi-factor LIBOR market model? Comment.

22.10   APPENDIX

22.10.1   The Coefficients of the Joint Process for Short- and Long-Term Rates

$$A_r = \left(\gamma_1^* \overline{\phi}_1^* + \gamma_2^* \overline{\phi}_2^* + \frac{(\gamma_1^* - \gamma_2^*)}{B_2(\tau_\ell) - B_1(\tau_\ell)} A(\tau_\ell) \right) \tag{22.112}$$

$$B_r = -\left(\frac{\gamma_1^* B_2(\tau_\ell) - \gamma_2^* B_1(\tau_\ell)}{B_2(\tau_\ell) - B_1(\tau_\ell)} \right) \tag{22.113}$$

$$C_r = \tau_\ell \left(\frac{\gamma_1^* - \gamma_2^*}{B_2(\tau_\ell) - B_1(\tau_\ell)} \right) \tag{22.114}$$

$$A_{r,\ell} = \frac{1}{\tau_\ell} \left(B_1(\tau_\ell) \gamma_1^* \overline{\phi}_1^* + B_2(\tau_\ell) \gamma_2^* \overline{\phi}_2^* + \frac{(B_1(\tau_\ell) \gamma_1^* - B_2(\tau_\ell) \gamma_2^*)}{B_2(\tau_\ell) - B_1(\tau_\ell)} A(\tau_\ell) \right) \tag{22.115}$$

$$B_{r,\ell} = -\frac{1}{\tau_\ell} \left(\frac{B_1(\tau_\ell) B_2(\tau_\ell) (\gamma_1^* - \gamma_2^*)}{B_2(\tau_\ell) - B_1(\tau_\ell)} \right) \tag{22.116}$$

$$C_{r,\ell} = \frac{(B_1(\tau_\ell) \gamma_1^* - B_2(\tau_\ell) \gamma_2^*)}{B_2(\tau_\ell) - B_1(\tau_\ell)} \tag{22.117}$$

22.10.2   The Two-Factor Hull-White Model

The function $A(t; T)$ is given by

$$A(0; T) = -\int_0^T B_1(t; T) \theta_t dt \tag{22.118}$$

$$+ [B_1(0; T) - T] \left(-\frac{\sigma_1^2}{2(\gamma_1^*)^2} - \frac{\sigma_1 \sigma_2 \rho}{\gamma_1^* \gamma_2^*} \right) - \frac{\sigma_1^2}{4\gamma_1^*} B_1(0; T)^2 \tag{22.119}$$

$$+ [B_2(0; T) - T] \left(-\frac{\sigma_2^2}{2(\gamma_2^*)^2} - \frac{\sigma_1 \sigma_2 \rho}{\gamma_1^* \gamma_2^*} \right) - \frac{\sigma_2^2}{4\gamma_2^*} B_2(0; T)^2 \tag{22.120}$$

$$+ \left[B_3\left(0; T\right) - T\right] \frac{\sigma_1 \sigma_2 \rho}{\gamma_1^* \gamma_2^*} \tag{22.121}$$

where for $i = 1, 2$, $B_i(t; T) = (1 - e^{-\gamma_i^*(T-t)})/\gamma_i^*$ and $B_3(t; T) = (1 - e^{-(\gamma_1^* + \gamma_2^*)(T-t)})/(\gamma_1^* + \gamma_2^*)$.

The θ_t function that exactly matches the term structure of interest rates when $\phi_{2,0} = 0$ (as in the assumptions of Hull-White model), is given by

$$\theta_t \ = \ \frac{\partial f\left(0, t\right)}{\partial t} + \gamma_1^* f\left(0, t\right) + \gamma_1^* \Phi(0; t) + \frac{\Phi(0; t)}{\partial t} \tag{22.122}$$

where

$$\Phi(0; t) = \frac{\sigma_1^2}{2} B_1(0; t)^2 + \frac{\sigma_2^2}{2} B_2(0; t)^2 + \sigma_1 \sigma_2 \rho B_1(0, t) B_2(0; t)$$

and therefore, explicitly,

$$\frac{\partial \Phi(0; t)}{\partial t} = \sigma_1^2 B_1(0; t) e^{-\gamma_1^* t} + \sigma_2^2 B_2(0; t) e^{-\gamma_2^* t} + \sigma_1 \sigma_2 \rho \left(B_1(0, t) e^{-\gamma_2^* t} + B_2(0; t) e^{-\gamma_1^* t} \right)$$

REFERENCES

Further Readings for Chapter 1

1. Buraschi, Andrea and Davide Menini. 2001. "Liquidity Risk and Specialness: How Well Do Forward Repo Spreads Price Future Specialness?" *Journal of Financial Economics.*

2. Duffie, Darrell. 1996. "Special Repo Rates," *The Journal of Finance*, 60, 2, 493 - 526.

3. Fabozzi, Frank. 2001. *Fixed Income Securities*. Second Edition, John Wiley & Sons.

4. Grinblatt, Mark, and Francis A. Longstaff. 2000. "Financial Innovation and the Role of Derivative Securities: An Empirical Analysis of the U.S. TreasuryŠs STRIPS Program." *The Journal of Finance*, 55, 141536.

5. Fleming, Michael J., and Kenneth D. Garbade. 2004. "When the Back Office Moved to the Front Burner: Settlement Fails in the Treasury Market after 9/11," Federal Reserve Bank of New York Economic Policy Review.

6. Jordan, Bradford, and Susan Jordan. 1997. "Special Repo Rates: An Empirical Analysis." *The Journal of Finance,* 52, 205172.

7. Longstaff, Francis. 2004. "The Flight to Liquidity Premium in U.S. Treasury Bond Prices," *The Journal of Business* 77, 511-526.

8. Martellini, Lionell, Philippe Priaulet and Stephanie Priaulet. 2003. *Fixed-Income Securities: Valuation, Risk Management and Portfolio Strategies*. John Wiley & Sons.

9. Sundaresan, Suresh. 2009. *Fixed Income Markets and Their Derivatives*. Third Edition, Elsevier.

10. Tuckman, Bruce. 2002. *Fixed Income Securities*. Second Edition, John Wiley & Sons.

Further Readings for Chapter 2

11. Anderson, Nicola. 1996. *Estimating and Interpreting the Yield Curve.* John Wiley & Sons

12. Bliss, Robert. 1997. "Testing Term Structure Estimation Methods," *Advances in Futures and Options Research* 9, 197-231.

13. Bliss, Robert. 1999, "Fitting Term Structures to Bond Prices." Working paper, Chicago Fed.

14. Campbell, John Y.. 1995. "Some Lessons from the Yield Curve," *Journal of Economic Perspectives* 9, 3, 129152.

15. Carleton, Willard, and Ian Cooper. 1976. "Estimation and uses of the term structure of interest rates." *The Journal of Finance,* 31, 1067 - 1083.

16. Nelson, Charles R., and Andrew F. Siegel. 1987. "Parsimonious Modeling of Yield Curves," *Journal of Business*, 60, 4, 473 - 489.

17. Schaefer, Stephen. 1977. "The problem with Redemption Yields," *Financial Analyst Journal,* 33, 3 -11.

18. Svensson, Lars. 1994. "Estimating and Interpreting Forward Rates, Sweden 1992 - 94," CEPR Discussion Paper 1051.

Further Readings for Chapters 3 and 4

19. Barber, Joel R ., and Mark L . Copper. 1996. "Immunization Using Principal Component Analysis," *The Journal of Portfolio Management,* 23, 1.

20. Barber, Joel R ., and Mark L . Copper. 1997. "Is Bond Convexity a Free Lunch?," *The Journal of Portfolio Management*, 24, 1, 113-119.

21. Chambers, Donald R., Willard T. Carleton, Richard W. McEnally. 1988. "Immunizing Default-Free Bond Portfolios with a Duration Vector," *The Journal of Financial and Quantitative Analysis*, 23, 1, pp. 89-104.

22. Christensen, Peter Ove, and Bjarne G . Slrensen. 1994. "Duration, Convexity, and Time Value," *The Journal of Portfolio Management*, 20, 2.

23. Fabozzi, Frank J.. 1999. *Duration, Convexity, and Other Bond Risk Measures.* John Wiley & Sons.

24. Hodges, Stewart, and Naru Parekh. 2006. "Term Structure Slope Risk Convexity Revisited," *The Journal of Fixed Income,* 16, 3.

25. Ilmanen, Antti. 1996. "Does Duration Extension Enhance Long-Term Expected Return?" *Journal of Fixed Income*, 6, 2, 23-36.

26. Ingersoll, Johnathan E., Jeffrey Skelton, and Roman K. Weil. 1978. "Duration Forty Years After," *Journal of Financial and Quantitative Analysis,* 34, 627 - 648.

27. Jorion, Philippe. 2006. *Value at Risk: The New Benchmark for Managing Financial Risk*, 3rd edition, McGraw-Hill.

28. Jorion, Philippe. 1995. *Big Bets Gone Bad: Derivatives and Bankruptcy in Orange County*, Academic Press.

29. Jorion, Philippe. 1997. "Lessons from the Orange County Bankruptcy," *Journal of Derivatives.*

30. Litterman, Robert, and Jose Scheinkman. 1991. "Common Factors Affecting Bond Returns," *The Journal of Fixed Income*, 1, 5461.

31. Nawalkha, Sanjay K., and Donald R. Chambers. 1996. "An Improved Immunization Strategy: M-Absolute," *Financial Analysts Journal*, 52, 5, 69-76.

32. Schaefer, Stephen. 1984. "Immunisation and Duration: A Review of Theory, Performance and Applications," *Midland Corporate Finance Journal,* 41-58.

33. Stulz, Rene M. 2003. *Risk Management & Derivatives* South-Western, Ohio.

34. Willner, Ram. 1996. "A New Tool for Portfolio Managers: Level, Slope, and Curvature Durations," *The Journal of Fixed Income,* 6, 1, 48-59.

Further Readings for Chapters 5 and 6

35. Bicksler, James, and Andrew H. Chen. 1985. "An Economic Analysis of Interest Rate Swaps," *The Journal of Finance,* 41, 3, 645-655.

36. Cecchetti, Stephen G., Robert E. Cumby and Stephen Figlewski. 1988. "Estimation of the Optimal Futures Hedge," *The Review of Economics and Statistics,* 70, 4, 623-630.

37. Duffie, Darrell, and Ming Huang. 1996. "Swap Rates and Credit Quality." *The Journal of Finance*, 51, 921-49.

38. Duffie, Darrell and Kenneth Singleton. 1997. "An Econometric Model of the Term Structure of Interest Rate Swap Yields," *The Journal of Finance*, 52, 1287-1323.

39. Gorton, Gary, and Richard Rosen. 1995. "Banks and Derivatives," *NBER Macroeconomics Annual*, 10, 299-339

40. Grinblatt, Mark, and Narasimhan Jegadeesh. 1996. "Relative Pricing of Eurodollar Futures and Forward Contracts," *The Journal of Finance,* 51, 4, 1499-1522.

41. Feldhütter, Peter, and David Lando. 2008. "Decomposing swap spreads," *Journal of Financial Economics,* 88, 2, 375-405.

42. Litzenberger, Robert H., 1992, "Swaps: Plain and Fanciful," *The Journal of Finance,* 47, 3, 831-850.

43. Rendleman, Richard J.. 1999, "Duration Based Hedging with Treasury Bond Futures," *The Journal of Fixed Income,* 9, 1, 84 - 91.

44. Titman, Sheridan. 1992. "Interest Rate Swaps and Corporate Financing Choices," *The Journal of Finance,* 47, 4, 1503-1516 .

45. , Turnbull, Stuart. 1987. "Swaps: A Zero Sum Game?" *Financial Analyst Journal,* 16, 1, 15-21.

Further Readings for Chapter 7

46. Ang, Andrew, Sen Dong, and Monika Piazzesi. 2004. "No-Arbitrage Taylor Rules." Working Paper, University of Chicago.

47. Bekaert, Geert and Robert Hodrick. 2001. "Expectations Hypothesis Tests," *The Journal of Finance*, 56, 115-38.

48. Bekaert, Geert, Robert Hodrick, and David Marshall. 1997. "On Biases in Tests of the Expectations Hypothesis of the Term Structure of Interest Rates." *Journal of Financial Economics*, 44, 309-48.

49. Brown, Roger H., and Stephen M. Schaefer. 1994. "The Term Structure of Real Interest Rates and the Cox, Ingersoll, and Ross Model," *Journal of Financial Economics*, 35, 342.

50. Campbell, John Y. 1995. "Some Lessons from the Yield Curve," *Journal of Economic Perspectives*, 9, 3, 129152.

51. Campbell, John Y., Andrew W. Lo, and A. Craig MacKinlay. 1997. *The Econometrics of Financial Markets,* Princeton University Press.

52. Campbell, John Y., and Robert Shiller. 1991. "Yield Spreads and Interest Rates: A Bird's Eye View." *Review of Economic Studies*, 58, 495-514.

53. Cochrane, John. 2001. *Asset Pricing,* Princeton University Press.

54. Cochrane, John, and Monika Piazzesi. 2002. "The Fed and Interest Rates a High Frequency Identification," *American Economic Review*, 92, 90-95.

55. Cochrane, John, and Monika Piazzesi, 2005, "Bond Risk Premia," *American Economic Review*, 95, 1, 138-160.

56. Cochrane, John, and Monika Piazzesi, 2008, "Decomposing the Yield Curve," Working Paper, NBER.

57. Diebold, Francis X., and Calin Li. 2006. "Forecasting the Term Structure of Government Bond Yields," *Journal of Econometrics.*

58. Fama, Eugene F.. 1990. "Term-Structure Forecasts of Interest Rates, Inflation, and Real Returns," *Journal of Monetary Economics*, 25, 59-76.

59. Fama, Eugene F., and Robert R. Bliss. 1987. "The Information in Long-Maturity Forward Rates," *American Economic Review*, 77, 680-92.

60. Longstaff, Francis. 1990. "Time Varying Term Premia and Traditional Hypotheses about the Term Structure," *The Journal of Finance*, 45, 1307-1314.

61. Longstaff, Francis. 2000. "The Term Structure of Very Short Term Rates: New Evidence for the Expectations Hypothesis," *Journal of Financial Economics*, 58, 397-415.

62. Piazzesi, Monika, and Eric Swanson. 2008. "Futures Prices as Risk-Adjusted Forecasts of Monetary Policy," *Journal of Monetary Economics*, 55, 677-691.

63. Singleton, Kenneth J. 2006. *Empirical Dynamic Asset Pricing,* Princeton University Press.

64. Stambaugh, Robert F. 1988. "The Information in Forward Rates," *Journal of Financial Economics*, 21, 4170.

Further Readings for Chapter 8

65. Boudoukh, Jacob, Matthew Richardson, Richard Stanton, and Robert Whitelaw, 1995, "A New Strategy for Dynamically Hedging Mortgage-Backed Securities," *Journal of Derivatives*, 2, 60-77.

66. Boudoukh, Jacob, Matthew Richardson, Richard Stanton, and Robert Whitelaw, 1997, "Pricing Mortgage-Backed Securities in a Multifactor Interest Rate Environment: A Multivariate Density Estimation Approach," *Review of Financial Studies*, 10, 405-446.

67. Duarte, Jefferson. 2009. "The Causal Effect of Mortgage Refinancing on Interest-Rate Volatility: Empirical Evidence and Theoretical Implications," *Review of Financial Studies,* 21, 1689-1731

68. Duarte, Jefferson, Francis Longstaff, and Fan Yu. 2007. "Risk and Return in Fixed Income Arbitrage: Nickels in Front of a Steamroller?" *Review of Financial Studies,* 20, 3, 769-811

69. Fabozzi, Frank. 2000. *The Handbook of Fixed Income Securities,* Sixth Edition, McGraw-Hill.

70. Stanton, Richard, 1995, "Rational Prepayment and the Valuation of Mortgage-Backed Securities," *Review of Financial Studies,* 8, 677-708.

Further Readings for Chapters 9 to 12

71. Black, Fischer, Emmanuel Derman, and William Toy. 1990. "A One-Factor Model of Interest Rates and Its Application to Treasury Bond Options" *Financial Analysts Journal*, 33-39.

72. Ho, Thomas S.Y., and Sang-Bin Lee. 1986. "Term Structure Movements and the Pricing of Interest Rate Contingent Claims," *The Journal of Finance*, 41, 1011-1029.

73. Hull, John. 2009. *Options, Futures, and Other Derivatives*, Seventh Edition, Pearson - Prentice Hall.

74. Hull, John, and Alan White. 1994. "Numerical Procedures for Implementing Term Structure Models I," *Journal of Derivatives*, Fall 1994, 7-16.

75. Hull, John, and Alan White. 1994. "Numerical Procedures for Implementing Term Structure Models II," *Journal of Derivatives*, Winter 1994, 37-48.

76. Hull, John, and Alan White. 1996. "Using Hull-White Interest Rate Trees," *Journal of Derivatives*, 3, 3, 2636 .

77. Li, A., P. Ritchken, and L. Sankarasubramanian. 1995. "Lattice Models for Pricing American Interest Rate Claims," *The Journal of Finance*, 50, 2, 719-737.

78. Longstaff, Francis. 1992. "Are Negative Option Prices Possible? The Callable U.S. Treasury-Bond Puzzle," *Journal of Business*, 65, 571-592.

79. McDonald, Robert L. 2006. *Derivatives Markets*, Second Edition, Pearson - Addison Wesley.

Further Readings for Chapter 13

80. Boyle, Phelim P. 1977. "Options: A Monte Carlo Approach." *Journal of Financial Economics*, 4, 323-338.

81. Boyle, Phelim P., Mark Broadie, and Paul Glasserman. 1997. "Monte Carlo Methods for Security Pricing," *Journal of Economic Dynamics and Control*, 21, 8-9, 1267 - 1321.

82. Duffie, Darrell. and Peter Glynn. 1995. "Efficient Monte Carlo Simulations for Security Prices," *The Annals of Applied Probability*, 5, 4, 897-965.

83. Esty, Ben, Peter Tufano, and Jonathan Headley. 1994. "Banc One Corporation: Asset Liability Management." *Journal of Applied Corporate Finance*, 7, 3, 33 - 52.

84. Glasserman, Paul. 2003. *Monte Carlo Methods in Financial Engineering.* Springer-Verlag.

Further Readings for Chapter 14

85. Baxter, Martin, and Andrew Rennie. 1996. *Financial Calculus.* Cambridge University Press.

86. Birkhoff G., and G. C. Rota. 1989. *Ordinary Differential Equations.* Fourth edition, John Wiley & Sons Inc.

87. Cvitanic, Jaksa, and Fernando Zapatero, 2004, *Introduction to the Economics and Mathematics of Financial Markets,* MIT Press.

88. Harrison, J. Michael. 1985. *Brownian Motion and Stochastic Flow Systems.* John Wiley & Sons.

89. Vasicek, Oldrich A.. 1977. "An Equilibrium Characterization of the Term Structure," *Journal of Financial Economics*, 5, 2, 177-188.

Further Readings for Chapters 15, 16, and 17

90. Chan, K.C., G. Andrew Karolyi, Francis A. Longstaff, and Anthony B. Sanders. 1992. "An Empirical Comparison of Alternative Models of the Short-Term Interest Rate," *The Journal of Finance*, 47, 1209-1227.

91. Cox, John C., Jonathan E. Ingersoll, and Stephen A. Ross. 1985. "A Theory of the Term Structure of Interest Rates," *Econometrica*, 53, 385–407.

92. Gibbons, Michael R., and Krishna Ramaswamy. 1993. "A Test of the Cox, Ingersoll, and Ross Model of the Term Structure," *Review of Financial Studies*, 6, 619–658.

93. Jamshidian, Farshid. 1989. "An Exact Bond Option Formula," *The Journal of Finance*, 44, 205-209.

94. Longstaff, Francis. 1993. "The Valuation of Options on Coupon Bonds," *Journal of Banking & Finance*, 17, 27-42.

95. Longstaff, Francis. 1990. "The Valuation of Options on Yields," *Journal of Financial Economics*, 26, 97-121.

96. Pearson, Neil, and T.-S. Sun. 1994. "An Empirical Examination of the Cox, Ingersoll, and Ross Model of the Term Structure of Interest Rates using the Method of Maximum Likelihood," *Journal of Finance*, 54, 929-959.

97. Vasicek, Oldrich A. 1977. "An Equilibrium Characterization of the Term Structure," *Journal of Financial Economics*, 5, 2, 177-188.

Further Readings for Chapter 18

98. Ang, Andrew, and Monika Piazzesi. 2003. "A No-Arbitrage Vector Autoregression of Term Structure Dynamics with Macroeconomic and Latent Variables," *Journal of Monetary Economics,* 50, 4, 745-787.

99. Ang, Andrew, Monika Piazzesi, and Min Wei, 2006. "What does the Yield Curve Tell us about GDP Growth?" *Journal of Econometrics*, 131, 359-403.

100. Diebold, Francis X., Monika Piazzesi, and Glenn Rudebush. 2005. "Modeling Bond Yields in Finance and Macroeconomics," *American Economic Review P&P,* 415-420

101. Goldstein, Robert, and Fernando Zapatero. 1996. "General Equilibrium with Constant Relative Risk Aversion and Vasicek Interest Rates," *Mathematical Finance*, 6, 331-340.

102. Piazzesi, Monika. 2005. "Bond Yields and the Federal Reserve." *Journal of Political Economy,* 113, 311-344.

103. Rudebusch, Glenn, and Tau Wu. 2005. "A Macro-Finance Model of the Term Strucutre, Monetary Policy, and the Economy," *Economic Journal*, 118, July 2008, 906-926.

Further Readings for Chapter 19

104. Black, Fisher, and Piotr Karasinksi. 1991. "Bond and Option Pricing when Short Rates are Lognormal" *Financial Analyst Journal,* 52-59.

105. Carverhill, A.. 1988. "The Ho and Lee Term Structure Theory: A Continuous Time Version," Technical report, Financial Options Research Centre, University of Warwick.

106. Hull, John C., and Alan White. 1990. "Pricing Interest-Rate-Derivative Securities," *Review of Financial Studies*, 3, 573–592.

107. Hull, John C., and Alan White. 1993. "One-Factor Interest Rate Models and the Valuation of Interest Rate Derivative Securities," *Journal of Financial and Quantitative Analysis*, 28, 235–254.

108. Jamshidian, Farshid. 1991. "Bond and Option Evaluation in the Gaussian Interest Rate Model," in A. Chen, eds., *Research in Finance,* Volume 9, 131-170, JAI Press.

Further Readings for Chapters 20 and 21

109. Amin, K. and A. Morton. 1994. "Implied Volatility Functions in Arbitrage-Free Term Structure Models," *Journal of Financial Economics,* 35, 141–180.

110. Black, Fischer. 1976. "The Pricing of Commodity Contracts," *Journal of Financial Economics*, 3, 167–179.

111. Black, Fisher, and Myron Scholes. 1973. "The Pricing of Options and Corporate Liabilities," *Journal of Political Economy,* 81, 637–654.

112. Buhler, W., M. Ulrig-Homberg, U. Walter, and T. Weber. 1999. "An Empirical Comparison of Forward ans Spot-Rate Models for Valuing Interest Rate Options," *Journal of Finance,* 54, 1, 269 – 305.

113. Brace, Alan, Darius Gatarek, and Marek Musiela. 1997. "The Market Model of Interest Rate Dynamics," *Mathematical Finance*, 7, 127–155.

114. Brigo, Damiano and Fabio Mercurio. 2007. *Interest Rate Models - Theory and Practice,* Second Edition, Springer-Verlag.

115. Duffie, Darrell. 2001. *Dynamic Asset Pricing Theory,* Third Edition, Princeton University Press.

116. Heath, David, Robert Jarrow, and Andrew Morton. 1992. "Bond Pricing and the Term Structure of Interest Rates," *Econometrica*, 60, 77–106.

117. Hull, John. 2009. *Options, Futures, and Other Derivatives,* Seventh Edition, Pearson - Prentice Hall.

118. Hull, John and Alan White. 2000. "Forward Rate Volatilities, Swap Rate Volatilities, and the Implementation of the LIBOR Market Model" *Journal of Fixed Income,* 10, 2, 46-62.

119. Jamshidian, Farshid. 1997. "Libor and Swap Market Models and Measures," *Finance and Stochastics*, 1, 290–330.

120. Jarrow, Robert A.. 2002. *Modeling Fixed Income Securities and Interest Rate Options,* Second Edition, Stanford University Press.

121. Jeffrey, A.. 1995. "Single Factor Heath-Jarrow-Morton Term Structure Models based on Markov Spot Interest Rate Dynamics," *Journal of Financial and Quantitative Analysis,* 30, 619–642.

122. Miltersen, K., K. Sandman, and D. Sondermann. 1997. "Closed Form Solutions for Term Structure Derivatives with Lognormal Interest Rate," *The Journal of Finance,* 52, 1, 409 – 430.

123. Rebonato, Riccardo. 2002. *Modern Pricing of Interest Rate Derivatives,* Princeton University Press.

Further Readings for Chapter 22

124. Ahn, Dong-Hyun, Robert F. Dittmar, and A. Ronald Gallant. 2002. "Quadratic Term Structure Models: Theory and Evidence," *Review of Financial Studies,* 15, 243-288.

125. Backus, David, Saverio Foresi, and Chris Telmer, 2001, "Affine Term Structure Models and the Forward Premium Anomaly," *The Journal of Finance*, 56, 279-304.

126. Balduzzi, Pierluigi, S. R. Das, S. Foresi, and R. Sundaram. 1996. "A Simple Approach to Three Factor Affine Term Structure Models," *Journal of Fixed Income,* 6, December, 43-53.

127. Brace, Alan, Darius Gatarek, and Marek Musiela. 1997. "The Market Model of Interest Rate Dynamics," *Mathematical Finance*, 7, 127–155.

128. Chen R. and L. Scott. 1995. "Interest Rate Options in Multifactor Cox-Ingersoll-Ross Models of the Term Structure," *Journal of Derivatives,* 3, 53-72.

129. Collin-Dufresne, Pierre, and Robert Goldstein. 2001. "Efficient Pricing of Swaptions in the Affine Framework," *The Journal of Derivatives.*

130. Constantinides, George. 1992. "A Theory of the Nominal Term Structure of Interest Rates," *Review of Financial Studies*, 5, 531-52.

131. Dai, Qiang, and Kenneth J. Singleton. 2000. "Specification Analysis of Affine Term Structure Models," *The Journal of Finance*, 55, 1943–1978.

132. Dai, Qiang and Kenneth Singleton. 2002. "Expectation Puzzles, Time-Varying Risk Premia, and Affine Models of the Term Structure," *Journal of Financial Economics*, 63, 415-441.

133. Dai, Qiang and Kenneth Singleton. 2003. "Term Structure Modeling in Theory and Reality," *Review of Financial Studies.*

134. Duarte, Jefferson. 2004. "Evaluating an Alternative Risk Preference in Affine Term Structure Models" *Review of Financial Studies.*

135. Duffee, Gregory. 2002. "Term Premia and Interest Rate Forecasts in Affine Models," *The Journal of Finance.* 57, 405-443.

136. Duffie, Darrell and Rui Kan. 1996. "A Yield-Factor Model of Interest Rates." *Mathematical Finance*, 6, 379-406.

137. Duffie, Darrell, and Kenneth Singleton. 1997. "An Econometric Model of the Term Structure of Interest Rate Swap Yields," *The Journal of Finance*, 52, 1287-1323.

138. Longstaff, Francis A. and Eduardo S. Schwartz. 1992. "Interest Rate Volatility and the Term Structure: A Two-Factor General Equilibrium Model," *The Journal of Finance*, 47, 1259–1282.

139. Longstaff, Francis A. and Eduardo S. Schwartz. 1992. "A Two-Factor Interest-Rate Model and Contingent Claims Valuation," *The Journal of Fixed Income*, 2, 16-23.

140. Longstaff, Francis A. and Eduardo S. Schwartz. 1993. "Implementation of the Longstaff-Schwartz Interest Rate Model," *The Journal of Fixed Income*, 3, 7-14.

141. Longstaff, Francis, Pedro Santa-Clara, and Eduardo Schwartz. 2001. "The Relative Valuation of Caps and Swaptions: Theory and Empirical Evidence," *The Journal of Finance*, 56, 2067-2109.

142. Singleton, Kenneth J. 2006. *Empirical Dynamic Asset Pricing,* Princeton University Press.

INDEX

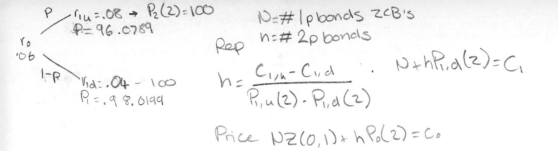

r_0
$.06$

P ⟶ $r_{1,u} = .08$ → $P_2(2) = 100$
$P = 96.0789$

$1-P$ ⟶ $r_{1,d} = .04$ — 100
$P_1 = .98.0199$

$N = \#$ $1p$ bonds $ZCB's$
$h = \#$ $2p$ bonds

Rep

$$h = \frac{C_{1,u} - C_{1,d}}{P_{1,u}(2) - P_{1,d}(2)} \qquad N + h P_{1,d}(2) = C_1$$

Price $N Z(0,1) + h P_0(2) = C_0$

int rates → one period, discount for 1 pd
⤷ Four drales   obsolete.
                         ↙
DF = e^{-r×Δt} $P_2(2) = FV$